Contemporary Business

Boone and Kurtz, 16th Edition

Authors

David L. Kurtz • Louis E. Boone

ISBN 9781119247388

Printed in the United States of America 10 9 8 7 6 5 4 3 2 1

List of Titles

Contemporary Business, 16th edition
by Louis E. Boone and David L. Kurtz
Copyright © 2015, ISBN: 978-1-118-77239-3

Table of Contents

Frontmatter 9
  Originally from *Contemporary Business, 16th edition*

About the Author 13
  Originally from *Contemporary Business, 16th edition*

Preface 14
  Originally from *Contemporary Business, 16th edition*

What Are Learning Styles? 16
  Originally from *Contemporary Business, 16th edition*

Acknowledgments 19
  Originally from *Contemporary Business, 16th edition*

Contemporary Business 21
  Originally from *Contemporary Business, 16th edition*

Chapter 1. The Changing Face of Business 22
  Originally Chapter 1 of *Contemporary Business, 16th edition*

Chapter 2. Business Ethics and Social Responsibility 50
  Originally Chapter 2 of *Contemporary Business, 16th edition*

Chapter 3. Economic Challenges Facing Contemporary Business 82
  Originally Chapter 3 of *Contemporary Business, 16th edition*

Chapter 4. Competing in World Markets 112
  Originally Chapter 4 of *Contemporary Business, 16th edition*

Chapter 5. Forms of Business Ownership and Organization 146
  Originally Chapter 5 of *Contemporary Business, 16th edition*

Chapter 6. Starting Your Own Business: The Entrepreneurship Alternative ... 180
  Originally Chapter 6 of *Contemporary Business, 16th edition*

Chapter 7. Management, Leadership, and the Internal Organization 208
  Originally Chapter 7 of *Contemporary Business, 16th edition*

Chapter 8. Human Resource Management: From Recruitment to Labor Relations ... 238
  Originally Chapter 8 of *Contemporary Business, 16th edition*

Chapter 9. Top Performance through Empowerment, Teamwork, and Communication 266

Originally Chapter 9 of *Contemporary Business, 16th edition*

Chapter 10. Production and Operations Management 292

Originally Chapter 10 of *Contemporary Business, 16th edition*

Chapter 11. Customer-Driven Marketing 324

Originally Chapter 11 of *Contemporary Business, 16th edition*

Chapter 12. Product and Distribution Strategies 354

Originally Chapter 12 of *Contemporary Business, 16th edition*

Chapter 13. Promotion and Pricing Strategies 388

Originally Chapter 13 of *Contemporary Business, 16th edition*

Chapter 14. Using Technology to Manage Information 424

Originally Chapter 14 of *Contemporary Business, 16th edition*

Chapter 15. Understanding Accounting and Financial Statements 450

Originally Chapter 15 of *Contemporary Business, 16th edition*

Chapter 16. The Financial System 480

Originally Chapter 16 of *Contemporary Business, 16th edition*

Chapter 17. Financial Management 510

Originally Chapter 17 of *Contemporary Business, 16th edition*

Appendix A: Business Law 539

Originally from *Contemporary Business, 16th edition*

Appendix B: Insurance and Risk Management 555

Originally from *Contemporary Business, 16th edition*

Appendix C: Personal Financial Planning 565

Originally from *Contemporary Business, 16th edition*

Appendix D: Developing a Business Plan 576

Originally from *Contemporary Business, 16th edition*

Appendix E: Careers in Contemporary Business 585

Originally from *Contemporary Business, 16th edition*

Glossary 603

Originally from *Contemporary Business, 16th edition*

Notes 615

Originally from *Contemporary Business, 16th edition*

Name Index   637

     Originally from *Contemporary Business, 16th edition*

Subject Index   647

     Originally from *Contemporary Business, 16th edition*

International Index   663

     Originally from *Contemporary Business, 16th edition*

Weekly Updates

Jupiter Interactive

Wiley's WEEKLY UPDATES news site sparks classroom debate around current events that apply to your business course topics. We save you time by emailing you—every Monday—the most relevant news articles and videos tagged to your textbook and complemented by discussion questions.

The ZOOM BUSINESS SIMULATION™ GAME allows your students to sit in the driver's seat of a new automobile company as they make all the relevant sales, marketing, operational, and financial decisions necessary for the company to succeed. Student teams compete against each other as they learn core business principles and how to make good business decisions.

BOONE & KURTZ

BOONE & KURTZ CASE VIDEOS

Accompanying each chapter, documentary-style video clips of successful companies like Zipcar, Timberland, and Comet Skateboards reinforce key concepts while exposing students to innovative business practices.

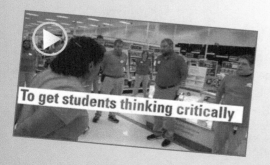

To get students thinking critically

BOONE & KURTZ STUDENT CASE VIDEOS

The Student Case Videos feature six recent business graduates in the workplace as they share their experiences and career goals. Each video illustrates the central theme of the six parts of Boone & Kurtz *Contemporary Business.*

Available in *WileyPLUS* and on the *Contemporary Business* Book Companion Site

9

WileyPLUS Learning Space

An easy way to help your students learn, collaborate, and grow.

Personalized Experience

Students create their own study guide while they interact with course content and work on learning activities.

Flexible Course Design

Educators can quickly organize learning activities, manage student collaboration, and customize their course—giving them full control over content as well as the amount of interactivity between students.

Clear Path to Action

With visual reports, it's easy for both students and educators to gauge problem areas and act on what's most important.

Instructor Benefits

- Assign activities and add your own materials
- Guide students through what's important in the interactive e-textbook by easily assigning specific content
- Set up and monitor collaborative learning groups
- Assess learner engagement
- Gain immediate insights to help inform teaching

Student Benefits

- Instantly know what you need to work on
- Create a personal study plan
- Assess progress along the way
- Participate in class discussions
- Remember what you have learned because you have made deeper connections to the content

We are dedicated to supporting you from idea to outcome.

 WILEY

WILEY

John Wiley & Sons, Inc.

David L. Kurtz
University of Arkansas

Boone & Kurtz's
Contemporary
BUSINESS

16TH EDITION

The 16th edition of *Contemporary Business* is dedicated to my wife, Diane.
She is the best thing that ever happened to me.
—Dave Kurtz

To my loving parents, who took me to the library and talked
a lot about the importance of education.
—Susan Berston

Vice President & Executive Publisher	George Hoffman
Executive Editor	Lisé Johnson
Project Editor	Jennifer Manias
Development Editor	Cate Rzasa
Assistant Editor	Katherine Bull
Editorial Assistant	Amanda Dallas
Content Manager	Dorothy Sinclair
Senior Production Editor	Valerie A. Vargas
Director of Marketing	Amy Scholz
Senior Marketing Manager	Kelly Simmons
Marketing Assistant	Elisa Wong
Creative Director	Harry Nolan
Senior Designer	Wendy Lai
Senior Photo Editor	Mary Ann Price
Senior Product Designer	Allison Morris
Media Specialist	Elena Santa Maria

This book was set in Janson Text LT Std-Roman 10/12 by MPS Limited, India and printed and bound by Quad/Graphics-Versailles. The cover was printed by Quad/Graphics-Versailles.

This book is printed on acid free paper. ∞

Founded in 1807, John Wiley & Sons, Inc. has been a valued source of knowledge and understanding for more than 200 years, helping people around the world meet their needs and fulfill their aspirations. Our company is built on a foundation of principles that include responsibility to the communities we serve and where we live and work. In 2008, we launched a Corporate Citizenship Initiative, a global effort to address the environmental, social, economic, and ethical challenges we face in our business. Among the issues we are addressing are carbon impact, paper specifications and procurement, ethical conduct within our business and among our vendors, and community and charitable support. For more information, please visit our website: www.wiley.com/go/citizenship.

ISBN-13   978-1-118-77239-3 (Binder Ready Version)

Printed in the United States of America

10 9 8 7 6 5 4 3 2 1

| About the Author |

During Dave Kurtz's high school days, no one in Salisbury, Maryland, would have mistaken him for a scholar. In fact, he was a mediocre student, so bad that his father steered him toward higher education by finding him a succession of backbreaking summer jobs. Thankfully, most of them have been erased from his memory, but a few linger, including picking peaches, loading watermelons on trucks headed for market, and working as a pipefitter's helper. Unfortunately, these jobs had zero impact on his academic standing. Worse yet for Dave's ego, he was no better than average as a high school athlete in football and track.

But four years at Davis & Elkins College in Elkins, West Virginia, turned him around. Excellent instructors helped get Dave on sound academic footing. His grade point average soared—enough to get him accepted by the graduate business school at the University of Arkansas, where he met Gene Boone. Gene and Dave became longtime co-authors; together they produced more than 50 books. In addition to writing, Dave and Gene were involved in various entrepreneurial ventures.

This long-term partnership ended with Gene's death a few years ago. But, this book will always be Boone & Kurtz's *Contemporary Business*.

If you have any questions or comments about the new 16th edition, Dave can be reached at ProfKurtz@gmail.com.

About the Contributor

During Susan Berston's four years as a campus tour guide while a student at the University of California, Berkeley, she endured hundreds of elevator rides crammed with visitors eager to reach the Campanile's observation deck 200 feet above. It was during these years that her excitement for teaching and learning became deeply engrained.

After completing an MBA at the University of San Francisco, Susan worked in the corporate banking division of a Japanese bank. However, after a few years, Susan found herself bit by the sales bug. She joined the sales force of printer RR Donnelley & Sons Company, which is where her passion for satisfying customers, outsmarting competitors, providing solutions, and building relationships was realized.

She returned to academia and campus life to eventually become a full-time instructor at City College of San Francisco—where her father, also a textbook author, taught business for close to six decades. Here Susan feels incredibly lucky rooting for her students, whether as a faculty advisor to the Kiva Microfinance Club, as an engaged guide and mentor, or as a member of the school's Senate Executive Council. But it's the storytelling that keeps Susan going, bringing ideas to life in both the classroom and on the pages of this very textbook. And watching students learn, evolve, and succeed is simply the icing on the cake.

Preface

A part of every business is change; now more than ever, business moves at a pace that is unparalleled. Containing the most important introductory business topics, *Contemporary Business* includes the most current information available and the best supplementary package on the market. You'll find that this new edition gets your students excited about the world of business, helps them improve their critical-thinking skills, and offers you and your students solutions at the speed of business.

For Instructors Consistent with recent editions of *Contemporary Business*, the instructor resources are designed to propel the instructor into the classroom with all the materials needed to engage students and help them understand text concepts. As always, all the major teaching materials are contained within the Instructor's Manual. The PowerPoint Presentations and Test Bank have also been updated and improved. Greensburg, KS—our continuing case—is highlighted in part videos, plus we've added two other videos: "One Year Later" and "Future Plans." Our Wiley Business End-of-Chapter Video Series showcases companies such as Zipcar, Necco, Timberland, New Harvest Coffee Roasters, and Comet Skateboards.

For Students With contemporary being the operative word, we've added two videos to update our Greensburg, Kansas video series. As always, every chapter is loaded with up-to-the-minute business issues and examples to enliven classroom discussion and debate, such as how "social entrepreneurs" are making their mark on emerging businesses. Processes, strategies, and procedures are brought to life through videos highlighting real companies and employees, an inventive business model, and collaborative learning exercises. And to further enhance the student learning process, with *WileyPLUS Learning Space*, instructors and students receive 24/7 access to resources that promote positive learning outcomes. Throughout each study session, students can assess their progress and gain immediate feedback on their strengths and weaknesses so they can be confident they are spending their time effectively.

How Boone & Kurtz Became the Leading Brand in the Market For more than three decades, *Contemporary Business* has provided the latest in content and pedagogy. Our current editions have long been the model for our competitors' *next* editions. Consider Boone & Kurtz's proven record of providing instructors and students with pedagogical firsts:

- *Contemporary Business* was the first introductory business text written specifically for the student—rather than the instructor—featuring a motivational style students readily understood and enjoyed.

- *Contemporary Business* has always been based on marketing research, written the way instructors actually teach the course.

- *Contemporary Business* was the first text to integrate computer applications—and later, Internet assignments—into each chapter.

- *Contemporary Business* was the first business text to offer end-of-chapter video cases as well as end-of-part cases filmed by professional producers.

- *Contemporary Business* was the first to use multimedia technology to integrate all components of the Introduction to Business ancillary program, videos, and PowerPoints for both instructors and students—enabling instructors to custom-create lively lecture presentations.

Wiley is proud to be publishing a book that has represented the needs of students and instructors so effectively and for so many years. The 16th edition will continue this excellent tradition and will continue to offer students and instructors solutions at the speed of business.

Continuing to Build the Boone & Kurtz Brand: What's New Trends, strategies, and practices are evolving, and students must understand business in today's fast-paced world. Keeping this in mind, here are just a few of the important business trends and practices we've focused on for this new edition to help move students forward into a great business career.

Throughout the textbook, several global updates have been made, including new chapter opening vignettes, features, and cases; new web assignments; and new end-of-chapter exercises. Business statistics have been updated and cover such topics as the price of gasoline; U.S. and global GDP data; updates on populations, languages, and wealth; information on the world's leading companies based on sales, market value, and profits; top U.S. trading partners; top U.S. merchandise exports and imports; and the best industries for starting a new business.

Companies and topics highlighted in chapter-opening vignettes include Microsoft's new CEO embracing business opportunities; Toyota regaining the top spot in the global auto industry; Anytime Fitness leading the U.S. franchise list; how the new sharing economy generates business start-ups; why Quicken Loans is a great place to work; and how Glassdoor, the online job site, helps both job seekers and employers.

"Career Kickstart" provides students with timely tips on how to succeed in the business world. Specific topics include mastering social networking; using Twitter to find a job or new employees; becoming a pro at electronic business communications; and preparing for a performance review.

"Going Green" continues to highlight what contemporary companies are doing to be socially responsible and to help protect the environment. Companies and topics featured include a company that buys used boxes and resells them to consumers as part of moving-day kits; a new form of corporate ownership called B Corporations, in which businesses state their social and environmental goals in company bylaws; eBay and its push for green commerce; and ice cream company Häagen-Dazs' commitment to honey bee research.

"Hit & Miss" shines a spotlight on companies, business leaders, and entrepreneurs. Success stories include AT&T's commitment to hiring military vets; Chipotle's niche in the fast-casual dining sector; Tory Burch and her foundation's support of women entrepreneurs; Apple's move to reshore manufacturing work back to the United States; and the entrepreneur's story behind the highly successful Rainbow Loom.

What Are Learning Styles?

Have you ever repeated something to yourself over and over to help remember it? Or does your best friend ask you to draw a map to someplace where the two of you are planning to meet, rather than just tell her the directions? If so, then you already have an intuitive sense that people learn in different ways, Researchers in learning theory have developed various categories of learning styles. Some people, for example, learn best by reading or writing. Others learn best by using various senses—seeing, hearing, feeling, tasting, or even smelling. When you understand how you learn best, you can make use of learning strategies that will optimize the time you spend studying. To find out what your particular learning style is, www.wiley.com/college/boone and take the learning styles quiz you find there. The quiz will help you determine your primary learning style:

Visual Learner	Print Learner	Auditory Learner
Haptic Learner	Kinesthetic Learner	Interactive Learner

Then, consult the information below and on the following pages for study tips for each learning style. This information will help you better understand your learning style and how to apply it to the study of business.

Study Tips for Visual Learners

If you are a Visual Learner, you prefer to work with images and diagrams. It is important that you see information.

Visual Learning
- Draw charts/diagrams during lecture.
- Examine textbook figures and graphs.
- Look at images and videos on *WileyPLUS* and other websites.
- Pay close attention to charts, drawings, and handouts your instructor uses.
- Underline; use different colors.
- Use symbols, flowcharts, graphs, different arrangements on the page, white spaces.

Visual Reinforcement
- Make flashcards by drawing tables/charts on one side and definition or description on the other side.
- Use art-based worksheets; cover labels on images in text and then rewrite the labels.
- Use colored pencils/markers and colored paper to organize information into types.
- Convert your lecture notes into "page pictures." To do this:
  - Use the outlined visual learning strategies.

- Reconstruct images in different ways.
- Redraw pages from memory.
- Replace words with symbols and initials.
- Draw diagrams where appropriate.
- Practice turning your visuals back into words.

If visual learning is your weakness: If you are not a Visual Learner but want to improve your visual learning, try re-keying tables/charts from the textbook.

Study Tips for Print Learners

If you are a Print Learner, reading will be important but writing will be much more important.

Print Learning
- Write text lecture notes during lecture.
- Read relevant topics in textbook, especially textbook tables.
- Look at text descriptions in animations and websites.
- Use lists and headings.
- Use dictionaries, glossaries, and definitions.
- Read handouts, textbooks, and supplementary library readings.
- Use lecture notes.

Print Reinforcement
- Rewrite your notes from class, and copy classroom handouts in your own handwriting.
- Make your own flashcards.
- Write out essays summarizing lecture notes or textbook topics.
- Develop mnemonics.
- Identify word relationships.
- Create tables with information extracted from textbook or lecture notes.
- Use text based worksheets or crossword puzzles.
- Write out words again and again.
- Reread notes silently.

- Rewrite ideas and principles into other words.
- Turn charts, diagrams, and other illustrations into statements.
- Practice writing exam answers.
- Practice with multiple choice questions.
- Write paragraphs, especially beginnings and endings.
- Write your lists in outline form.
- Arrange your words into hierarchies and points.

If print learning is your weakness: If you are not a Print Learner but want to improve your print learning, try covering labels of figures from the textbook and writing in the labels.

Study Tips for Auditory Learners

If you are an Auditory Learner, then you prefer listening as a way to learn information. Hearing will be very important, and sound helps you focus.

Auditory Learning
- Make audio recordings during lecture.
- Do not skip class; hearing the lecture is essential to understanding.

- Play audio files provided by instructor and textbook.
- Listen to narration of animations.
- Attend lecture and tutorials.
- Discuss topics with students and instructors.

- Explain new ideas to other people.
- Leave spaces in your lecture notes for later recall.
- Describe overheads, pictures, and visuals to somebody who was not in class.

Auditory Reinforcement
- Record yourself reading the notes and listen to the recording
- Write out transcripts of the audio files.
- Summarize information that you have read, speaking out loud.
- Use a recorder to create self-tests.

- Compose "songs" about information.
- Play music during studying to help focus.
- Expand your notes by talking with other and with information from your textbook.
- Read summarized notes out loud.
- Explain your notes to another auditory learner.

- Talk with the instructor.
- Spend time in quiet places recalling the ideas.
- Say your answers out loud.

If auditory teaming is your weakness: If you are not an Auditory Learner but want to improve your auditory learning, try writing out the scripts from pre-recorded lectures.

Study Tips for Interactive Learners

If you are an Interactive Learner, you will want to share your information. A study group will be important.

Interactive Learning
- Ask a lot of questions during lecture or review sessions.
- Contact other students, via e-mail or discussion forums, and ask them to explain what they learned.

Interactive Reinforcement
- "Teach" the content to a group of other students.
- Talking to an empty room may seem odd, but it will be effective for you.
- Discuss information with others, making sure that you both ask and answer questions.

- Work in small group discussions, making a verbal and written discussion of what others say.

If interactive learning is your weakness: If you are not an Interactive Learner but want to improve prove your interactive learning, try asking your study partner questions and then repeating them to the instructor.

Study Tips for Haptic Learners

If you are a Haptic Learner, you prefer to work with your hands. It is important to physically manipulate material.

Haptic Learning
- Take blank paper to lecture to draw charts/tables/diagrams.
- Using the textbook, run your fingers along the figures and graphs to get a "feel" for shapes and relationships.

Haptic Reinforcement
- Trace words and pictures on flashcards.
- Perform electronic exercises that involve drag-and-drop activities.
- Alternate between speaking and writing information.
- Observe someone performing a task that you would like to learn.

- Make sure you have freedom of movement while studying.

If haptic learning is your weakness: If you are not a Haptic Learner but want to improve your haptic learning, try spending more time in class working with graphs and tables while speaking or writing down information.

Study Tips for Kinesthetic Learners

If you are a Kinesthetic Learner, it will be important that you involve your body during studying.

Kinesthetic Learning
- Ask permission to get up and move during lecture.
- Participate in role-playing activities in the classroom.
- Use all your senses.
- Go to labs; take field trips.
- Listen to real-life examples.
- Pay attention to applications.
- Use trial-and-error methods.
- Use hands-on approaches.

Kinesthetic Reinforcement
- Make flashcards; place them on the floor, and move your body around them.
- Move while you are teaching the material to others.
- Put examples in your summaries.
- Use case studies and applications to help with principles and abstract concepts.
- Talk about your notes with another kinesthetic person.

- Use pictures and photographs that illustrate an idea.
- Write practice answers.
- Role-play the exam situation.

If kinesthetic learning is your weakness: If you are not a Kinesthetic Learner but want to improve your kinesthetic learning, try moving flash cards to reconstruct graphs and tables, etc.

LEARNING STYLES SURVEY CHART

Resources	Visual	Print	Auditory	Interactive	Haptic	Kinesthetic
Hit & Miss	✔	✔		✔		
Launching Your Career	✔	✔		✔		
Learning Goals	✔	✔		✔		
Going Green	✔	✔				
Career Kickstart	✔	✔		✔		
Solving an Ethical Controversy	✔	✔				
Assessment Checks	✔	✔		✔		
Review Questions	✔	✔		✔		
Cases	✔	✔		✔		
Project/Teamwork Applications	✔	✔		✔		
Flashcards	✔	✔		✔	✔	✔
Business Terms	✔	✔		✔		
Interactive Quizzes	✔	✔		✔		
Student PowerPoints	✔	✔		✔	✔	
Audio Summary (English/Spanish)	✔	✔	✔	✔	✔	
Animated Figures	✔	✔	✔	✔	✔	
Case Study Animations	✔	✔	✔	✔	✔	✔
E-lectures	✔	✔	✔	✔	✔	
Greensburg, KS Continuing Case	✔	✔	✔	✔	✔	✔
End-of-Chapter Videos	✔	✔	✔	✔	✔	✔
Final Exam Questions	✔	✔		✔		
Quiz Questions	✔	✔		✔		
Pre-lecture Questions	✔	✔		✔		
Post-lecture Questions	✔	✔		✔		
Video Questions	✔	✔	✔	✔		✔
Drop-box Questions	✔	✔		✔		

Acknowledgments

Contemporary Business has long benefited from the instructors who have offered their time as reviewers. Recent editions have been enhanced based on the timely and thoughtful feedback provided by our Advisory Board:

Contemporary Business Advisory Board

Frank Barber – *Cuyahoga Community College*
Cathleen Behan – *Northern Virginia Community College*
Thomas Byrnes – *Wake Tech Community College*
Nathaniel Calloway – *University of Maryland University College*
Diana Carmel – *Golden West College*
Gary Cohen – *University of Maryland*
Tom Darling – *Central New Mexico Community College*
Kellie Emrich – *Cuyahoga Community College*
Gil Feiertag – *Columbus State Community College*
Janice Feldbauer – *Schoolcraft College*
Kelly Gold – *Fayetteville Tech Community College*
Mary Gorman – *University of Cincinnati*
Kim Goudy – *Central Ohio Technical College*
Karen Halpern – *South Puget Sound Community College*
Frank Harber – *Indian River State College*
Annette Haugen – *Merced Community College*
Linda Hefferin – *Elgin Community College*
John Hilston – *Eastern Florida State College*
Lynda Hodge – *Guilford Tech Community College*
Eileen Kearney – *Montgomery County Community College*
Robin Kelly – *Cuyahoga Community College*
Susan Kendall – *Arapahoe Community College*
Chuck Kitzmiller – *Indian River State College*
Marian Matthews – *Central New Mexico Community College*

John McCoy – *Suffolk University*
Cynthia Miree-Coppin – *Oakland University*
Thomas Mobley – *Miami University*
David Oliver – *Edison State College – Lee Campus*
Laura Portolese-Dias – *Central Washington University*
Sally Proffitt – *Tarrant County Community College – Northeast*
Jayre Reaves – *Rutgers University*
David Robinson – *University of California – Berkeley*
Joseph Schubert – *Delaware Technical and Community College*
Douglas Scott – *State College of Florida*
Janet Seggern – *Lehigh Carbon Community College*
Patricia Setlik – *William Rainey Harper College*
Phyllis Shafer – *Brookdale Community College*
Christy Shell – *Houston Community College*
Rudy Soliz – *Houston Community College*
John Striebich – *Monroe Community College*
Ted Tedmon – *North Idaho College*
Rodney Thirion – *Pikes Peak Community College*
Sal Veas – *Santa Monica College*
Donna Waldron – *Manchester Community College*
Richard Warner – *Lehigh Carbon Community College*
Colette Wolfson – *Ivy Tech Community College – South Bend*
Lisa Zingaro – *Oakton Community College – Des Plaines Campus*

In Conclusion

I would like to thank Susan Berston and John Fritschen for their contributions to this edition. I would also like to thank Cate Rzasa for her editorial and production efforts on behalf of *Contemporary Business*.

Let me conclude by noting that this new edition would never have become a reality without the outstanding efforts of the Wiley editorial, production, and marketing teams. Special thanks to George Hoffman, Lisé Johnson, Jennifer Manias, Kelly Simmons, Katherine Bull, Amanda Dallas, Allison Morris, Wendy Lai, and Valerie Vargas.

Dave Kurtz

Contemporary BUSINESS

Learning Objectives

1. Define *business*.
2. Identify and describe the factors of production.
3. Describe the private enterprise system.
4. Identify the seven eras in the history of business.
5. Explain how today's business workforce and the nature of work itself is changing.
6. Identify the skills and attributes needed for the 21st-century manager.
7. Outline the characteristics that make a company admired.

Chapter 1

The Changing Face of Business

© Chris Schmidt/iStockphoto

Energy Production Comes Home

Have you heard of Southwestern Energy? Pioneer Natural Resources? Range Resources? These companies and others are all part of a recent U.S. news story that is very important to American business. For the first time in 25 years, the United States is now producing more oil domestically than we are importing. Oil production increased due in large part to the widespread adoption of two drilling technologies: horizontal drilling and fracking.

Horizontal drilling allows oil companies to get more oil from a single well as the drill bit first goes down vertically through the overlying rock and then is turned horizontally to drill along and through the oil-rich layers. Multiple horizontal holes can be drilled from a single site, greatly increasing the amount of oil reserves available in a single well. Once the holes are drilled in the oil-producing layers, high-pressure water mixed with fine sand is pumped into the well to fracture the rock and extract oil.

Fracking has also been widely used to drill into shale formations and extract natural gas, such as the Marcellus formation in Pennsylvania, the Fayetteville formation in Arkansas, and the Bakken formation in North Dakota. The result of these efforts has been a significant increase in the availability and reserves of domestic oil and gas.

Why is this significant to U.S. consumers and business? First, for the past several decades one of the largest imports into the United States has been crude oil. As we will see in later chapters, when the overall value of imports is reduced compared to the value of exports, the U.S. balance of trade becomes more favorable, which is generally a benefit to U.S. consumers.

Second, industries such as steel, glass, and cement, which are heavy consumers of energy, will be more competitive as their cost of production decreases. Many of these industries have had a hard time competing with foreign sources due to their lower cost basis. Lower energy costs will help these industries.

Third, because of the increased supply and reduced price of natural gas, utility companies are switching away from burning coal to produce electricity. As a fuel, natural gas contains less carbon than coal and consequently produces less carbon dioxide as a combustion product. This plus other conservation efforts have allowed the United States to achieve the emission targets of the Kyoto protocol—reducing greenhouse gasses by more than 5 percent—a goal that many experts thought impossible just a decade ago.

Increased domestic oil and gas production creates a more favorable balance of trade, more competitive domestic industries, and reduced greenhouse gas emissions. Any one of these stories would be newsworthy by itself, but together they represent significant and positive changes for U.S. consumers and businesses.[1]

Overview

Business is the nation's engine for growth. A growing economy—one that produces more goods and services with fewer resources over time—yields income for business owners, their employees, and stockholders. So a country depends on the wealth its businesses generate, from large enterprises such as the Walt Disney Company to tiny online start-ups, and from venerable firms such as 160-year-old jeans maker Levi Strauss & Company to powerhouses such as Google. What all these companies and many others share is a creative approach to meeting society's needs and wants.

Businesses solve our transportation problems by marketing cars, tires, gasoline, and airline tickets. They bring food to our tables by growing, harvesting, processing, packaging, and shipping everything from spring water to cake mix and frozen shrimp. Restaurants buy, prepare, and serve food, and some even deliver. Construction companies build our schools, homes, and hospitals, while real estate firms bring property buyers and sellers together. Clothing manufacturers design, create, import, and deliver our jeans, sports shoes, work uniforms, and party wear. Entertainment for our leisure hours comes from hundreds of firms that create, produce, and distribute films, television shows, video games, books, and music downloads.

To succeed, business firms must know what their customers want so that they can supply it quickly and efficiently. That means they often reflect changes in consumer tastes, such as the growing preference for sports drinks and vitamin-fortified water. But firms can also *lead* in advancing technology and other changes. They have the resources, the know-how, and the financial incentive to bring about new innovations as well as the competition that inevitably follows, as in the case of Apple's iPhone and Google's Android operating system.

You'll see throughout this book that businesses require physical inputs such as auto parts, chemicals, sugar, thread, and electricity, as well as the accumulated knowledge and experience of their managers and employees. Yet they also rely heavily on their own ability to change with the times and with the marketplace. Flexibility is a key to long-term success—and to growth.

In short, business is at the forefront of our economy—and *Contemporary Business* is right there with it. This book explores the strategies that allow companies to grow and compete in today's interactive and hyper-competitive marketplace, along with the skills that you will need to turn ideas into action for your own success in business. This chapter sets the stage for the entire text by defining business and revealing its role in society. The chapter's discussion illustrates how the private enterprise system encourages competition and innovation while preserving business ethics.

⌐1⌐ What Is Business?

What comes to mind when you hear the word *business*? Do you think of big corporations like ExxonMobil or The Coca-Cola Company? Or does the local deli or shoe store pop into your mind? Maybe you recall your first summer job. The term *business* is a broad, all-inclusive term that can be applied to many kinds of enterprises. Businesses provide the bulk of employment opportunities, as well as the products that people enjoy.

Business consists of all profit-seeking activities and enterprises that provide goods and services necessary to an economic system. Some businesses produce tangible goods, such as automobiles, breakfast cereals, and smart phones; others provide services such as insurance, hair styling, and entertainment ranging from Six Flags theme parks and NFL games to concerts.

Business drives the economic pulse of a nation. It provides the means through which its citizens' standard of living improves. At the heart of every business endeavor is an exchange between a buyer and a seller. A buyer recognizes a need for a good or service and trades money with a seller to obtain that product. The seller participates in the process in hopes of gaining profits—a main ingredient in accomplishing the goals necessary for continuous improvement in the standard of living.

Profits represent rewards earned by businesspeople who take the risks involved in blending people, technology, and information to create and market want-satisfying goods and services. In contrast, accountants think of profits as the difference between a firm's revenues and the expenses it incurs in generating those revenues. More generally, however, profits serve as incentives for people to start companies, expand them, and provide consistently high-quality competitive goods and services.

The quest for profits is a central focus of business because without profits, a company could not survive. But businesspeople also recognize their social and ethical responsibilities. To succeed in the long run, companies must deal responsibly with employees, customers, suppliers, competitors, government, and the general public.

business all profit-seeking activities and enterprises that provide goods and services necessary to an economic system.

profits rewards earned by businesspeople who take the risks involved in blending people, technology, and information to create and market want-satisfying goods and services.

Antoine Antoniol/Bloomberg/Getty Images, Inc.

A business, such as this cell phone store, survives through the exchange between a buyer and a seller.

Not-for-Profit Organizations

What do Purdue's athletic department, the U.S. Postal Service, the American Lung Association, and your local library have in common? They all are classified as **not-for-profit organizations**, businesslike establishments that have primary objectives other than returning profits to their owners. These organizations play important roles in society by placing public service above profits, although it is important to understand that these organizations need to raise money so that they can operate and achieve their social goals. Not-for-profit organizations operate in both the private and public sectors. Private-sector not-for-profits include museums, libraries, trade associations, and charitable and religious organizations. Government agencies, political parties, and labor unions, all of which are part of the public sector, are also classified as not-for-profit organizations.

Not-for-profit organizations are a substantial part of the U.S. economy. Currently, more than 1.5 million nonprofit organizations are registered with the Internal Revenue Service in the United States, in categories ranging from arts and culture to science and technology.[2] These organizations control more than $2.9 trillion in assets and employ close to 11 million people—more people than the federal government and all 50 state governments combined.[3] In addition, millions of volunteers work for them in unpaid positions. Not-for-profits secure funding from private sources, including donations, and from government sources. They are commonly exempt from federal, state, and local taxes.

Although they focus on goals other than generating profits, managers of not-for-profit organizations face many of the same challenges as executives of profit-seeking businesses. Without funding, they cannot do research, obtain raw materials, or provide services. St. Jude Children's Research Hospital's pediatric treatment and research facility in Memphis treats nearly 7,800 children a year for catastrophic diseases, mainly cancer, immune system problems, and infectious and genetic disorders. Patients come from all 50 states and all over the world and are accepted without regard to the family's ability to pay. To provide top-quality care and to support its research in gene therapy, chemotherapy, bone marrow transplantation, and the psychological effects of illness, among many other critical areas, St. Jude relies on contributions, with some assistance from federal grants.[4]

Other not-for-profits mobilize their resources to respond to emergencies. Superstorm Sandy was one of the biggest U.S. disasters that the American Red Cross has had to respond to in recent years. To date, Sandy is the second costliest hurricane in U.S. history, with damages topping $68 billion.[5]

Some not-for-profits sell merchandise or set up profit-generating arms to provide goods and services for which people are willing and able to pay. College bookstores sell everything from sweatshirts to coffee mugs with school logos imprinted on them, while the Sierra Club and the Appalachian Mountain Club both have full-fledged publishing programs. Founded in 1912, The Girl Scouts of the USA are known for their mouth-watering cookies. The organization has created a cookie empire valued at more than $700 million through sales by local scout troops.[6] Handling merchandising programs like these, as well as launching other fund-raising campaigns, requires managers of not-for-profit organizations to develop effective business skills and experience. Consequently, many of the concepts discussed in this book apply to not-for-profit organizations as well as to profit-oriented firms.

not-for-profit organizations businesslike establishments that have primary objectives other than returning profits to their owners.

Assessment Check ☑

1. What activity lies at the center of every business endeavor?

2. What is the primary objective of a not-for-profit organization?

The Red Cross mobilized its efforts to respond to disaster on the East Coast after Superstorm Sandy struck.

Paul J Richards/AFP/Getty Images

Chapter 1 *The Changing Face of Business*   **5**

[2] Factors of Production

An economic system requires certain inputs for successful operation. Economists use the term **factors of production** to refer to the four basic inputs: natural resources, capital, human resources, and entrepreneurship. Table 1.1 identifies each of these inputs and the type of payment received by firms and individuals who supply them.

Natural resources include all production inputs that are useful in their natural states, including agricultural land, building sites, forests, and mineral deposits. One of the largest wind farms in the world, the Roscoe Wind Complex near Roscoe, Texas, generates enough power to support more than a quarter-million homes. Natural resources are the basic inputs required in any economic system.

Capital, another key resource, includes technology, tools, information, and physical facilities. *Technology* is a broad term that refers to such machinery and equipment as computers and software, telecommunications, and inventions designed to improve production. Information, frequently improved by technological innovations, is another critical factor because both managers and operating employees require accurate, timely information for effective performance of their assigned tasks. Technology plays an important role in the success of many businesses. Sometimes technology results in a new product, such as hybrid autos that run on a combination of gasoline and electricity, or electric cars that use energy stored in batteries.

Technology often helps a company improve its own products. Netflix, once famous for its subscription-based DVD-by-mail service, offers on-demand Internet streaming media and original content streaming TV service. Netflix has exclusive rights to streaming movies and original TV shows, like "Orange Is the New Black."[7]

And sometimes firms rely on technology to help move and track their products more efficiently. UPS has partnered with the Red Cross to launch emergency logistics teams in several U.S. cities. UPS emergency coordinators in each city gather expert volunteers, ensure that supplies reach disaster areas, and provide storage space.[8]

To remain competitive, a firm needs to continually acquire, maintain, and upgrade its capital, and businesses need money for that purpose. A company's funds may come from owner-investments, profits plowed back into the business, or loans extended by others. Money then goes to work building factories; purchasing raw materials and component parts; and hiring, training, and compensating workers. People and firms that supply capital receive factor payments in the form of interest.

Human resources represent another critical input in every economic system. Human resources include anyone who works, from the chief executive officer (CEO) of a huge corporation to a self-employed writer or editor. This category encompasses both the physical labor and the intellectual inputs contributed by workers. Companies rely on their employees as a valued source of ideas and innovation, as well as physical effort. Some companies solicit employee ideas through traditional means, such as an online "suggestion box" or in staff

TABLE 1.1 Factors of Production and Their Factor Payments

FACTOR OF PRODUCTION	CORRESPONDING FACTOR PAYMENT
Natural resources	Rent
Capital	Interest
Human resources	Wages
Entrepreneurship	Profit

factors of production four basic inputs: natural resources, capital, human resources, and entrepreneurship.

natural resources all production inputs that are useful in their natural states, including agricultural land, building sites, forests, and mineral deposits.

capital includes technology, tools, information, and physical facilities.

human resources include anyone who works, including both the physical labor and the intellectual inputs contributed by workers.

Competent, effective human resources can be a company's best asset. Providing benefits to those employees to retain them is in a company's best interest.

meetings. Others encourage creative thinking during company-sponsored hiking or rafting trips or during social gatherings. Effective, well-trained human resources provide a significant competitive edge because competitors cannot easily match another company's talented, motivated employees in the way they can buy the same computer system or purchase the same grade of natural resources.

Hiring and keeping the right people matters, as we'll see later in the case at the end of this chapter. Employees at Mars, Inc. feel they have a great place to work, partly because of the opportunities for advancement and generous pay the company provides.[9]

Entrepreneurship is the willingness to take risks to create and operate a business. An entrepreneur is someone who sees a potentially profitable opportunity and then devises a plan to achieve success in the marketplace and earn those profits. By age 20, Jessica Mah was co-founder and CEO of inDinero, a San Francisco-based company that created an app designed to help small businesses keep track of their money. Mah had "noticed that anything that touches money is much harder for entrepreneurs than it should be," so she took a risk and started a firm designed to help them.[10]

U.S. businesses operate within an economic system called the *private enterprise system*. The next section looks at the private enterprise system, including competition, private property, and the entrepreneurship alternative.

3 The Private Enterprise System

No business operates in a vacuum. All operate within a larger economic system that determines how goods and services are produced, distributed, and consumed in a society. The type of economic system employed in a society also determines patterns of resource use. Some economic systems, such as communism, feature strict controls on business ownership, profits, and resources to accomplish government goals.

entrepreneurship
willingness to take risks to create and operate a business.

Assessment Check ☑

1. Identify the four basic inputs to an economic system.
2. List four types of capital.

Hit&Miss

Live Nation Connects Superstar Artists and Fans

Chances are, the last concert you attended may have been produced by Beverly Hills–based powerhouse, Live Nation Entertainment. The largest producer of live music concerts worldwide, Live Nation sells millions of tickets each year for events that range from folk to electronic dance music and that feature entertainers from new artists to music legends. A few years ago, Live Nation merged with ticket-selling giant Ticketmaster Entertainment to create Live Nation Entertainment.

Over 250 million fans access various entertainment platforms each year, attending more than 180,000 events in 47 countries. While more than 65 percent of the company's revenues come from its concert segment, other distinct business units include venue operations, ticketing services, and artist management and services.

If you've ever thought about a career as a concert promoter, consider the "accidental trajectory" of then college student Jodi Goodman. After urging a failing jazz club owner in Boston to allow her to book a few rock music events, Goodman not only turned the club around, but word soon got out about her knack for managing both artists and fans. It was not long before other venues sought her talent, and her career took her to San Francisco. Jodi Goodman is now president of Live Nation Entertainment for Northern California. With skill and market expertise, Goodman continues to bring artists and fans together in one of the top music markets in the country.

Concert revenues continue to rise and the future looks bright. Some of this success can be attributed to the Boston college kid who read the local music market by bringing some good old rock 'n' roll to a jazz club on the brink of closure.

Questions for Critical Thinking

1. Ticketmaster, now part of Live Nation Entertainment, responded to the threat of the secondary ticket resale market (by firms like Craigslist and StubHub) by launching its own ticket marketplace. How will Ticketmaster's marketplace impact secondary market competitors?
2. Live Nation anticipates double-digit growth in the number of concertgoers worldwide over the next several years. What factors could contribute to such a healthy increase in attendance?

Sources: Company website, "2013 Annual Report," http://livenation.com, accessed January 9, 2014; "Live Nation's New Groove: Electronic Dance Music and Scalped Tickets," *Bloomberg Businessweek*, accessed January 9, 2014, www.businessweek.com; Glenn Peoples, "Live Nation Revenue Hits a Record $2.26 Billion in Third Quarter," *Billboard Biz*, accessed January 9, 2014, www.billboard.com; Christine Ryan, "Hot 20: The Music Woman, Jodi Goodman," *7x7 Magazine*, accessed January 9, 2014, www.7x7.com; Ina Fried, "Live Nation Aims to Unify Ticketmaster, Ticket Resale Businesses," *All Things Digital*, accessed January 9, 2014, http://allthingsd.com.

---

private enterprise system economic system that rewards firms for their ability to identify and serve the needs and demands of customers.

capitalism economic system that rewards firms for their ability to perceive and serve the needs and demands of consumers; also called the private enterprise system.

competition battle among businesses for consumer acceptance.

competitive differentiation unique combination of organizational abilities, products, and approaches that sets a company apart from competitors in the minds of customers.

In the United States, businesses function within the **private enterprise system**, an economic system that rewards firms for their ability to identify and serve the needs and demands of customers. The private enterprise system minimizes government interference in economic activity. Businesses that are adept at satisfying customers gain access to necessary factors of production and earn profits.

Another name for the private enterprise system is **capitalism**. Adam Smith, often identified as the father of capitalism, first described the concept in his book, *The Wealth of Nations*, published in 1776. Smith believed that an economy is best regulated by the "invisible hand" of **competition**, the battle among businesses for consumer acceptance. Smith thought that competition among firms would lead to consumers' receiving the best possible products and prices because less efficient producers would gradually be driven from the marketplace.

The invisible hand concept is a basic premise of the private enterprise system. In the United States, competition regulates much of economic life. To compete successfully, each firm must find a basis for **competitive differentiation**, the unique combination of organizational abilities, products, and approaches that sets a company apart from competitors in the minds of customers. Businesses operating in a private enterprise system face a critical task of keeping up with changing marketplace conditions. Firms that fail to adjust to shifts in consumer preferences or ignore the actions of competitors leave themselves open to failure. Live Nation Entertainment connects millions of concertgoers with their favorite artists at venues worldwide; see the Hit & Miss feature for keys to the company's success.

Throughout this book, our discussion focuses on the tools and methods that 21st-century businesses apply to compete and differentiate their goods and services. We also discuss many of the ways in which market changes will affect business and the private enterprise system in the years ahead.

Part 1 *Business in a Global Environment*

Basic Rights in the Private Enterprise System

For capitalism to operate effectively, people living in a private enterprise economy must have certain rights. As shown in Figure 1.1, these include the rights to private property, profits, freedom of choice, and competition.

The right to **private property** is the most basic freedom under the private enterprise system. Every participant has the right to own, use, buy, sell, and bequeath most forms of property, including land, buildings, machinery, equipment, patents on inventions, individual possessions, and intangible properties.

The private enterprise system also guarantees business owners the right to all profits—after taxes—they earn through their activities. Although a business is not assured of earning a profit, its owner is legally and ethically entitled to any income it generates in excess of costs.

Freedom of choice means that a private enterprise system relies on the potential for citizens to choose their own employment, purchases, and investments. They can change jobs, negotiate wages, join labor unions, and choose among many different brands of goods and services. A private enterprise economy maximizes individual prosperity by providing alternatives. Other economic systems sometimes limit freedom of choice to accomplish government goals, such as increasing industrial production of certain items or military strength.

The private enterprise system also permits fair competition by allowing the public to set rules for competitive activity. For this reason, the U.S. government has passed laws to prohibit "cutthroat" competition—excessively aggressive competitive practices designed to eliminate competition. It also has established ground rules that outlaw price discrimination, fraud in financial markets, and deceptive advertising and packaging.[11]

The Entrepreneurship Alternative

The entrepreneurial spirit beats at the heart of private enterprise. An **entrepreneur** is a risk taker in the private enterprise system. You hear about entrepreneurs all the time—two college students starting a software business in their dorm room or a mom who invents a better baby carrier. Many times their success is modest but, once in a while, the risk pays off in huge profits. Individuals who recognize marketplace opportunities are free to use their capital, time, and talents to pursue those opportunities for profit. The willingness of individuals to start new ventures drives economic growth and keeps pressure on existing companies to continue to satisfy customers. If no one were willing to take economic risks, the private enterprise system wouldn't exist.

By almost any measure, the entrepreneurial spirit fuels growth in the U.S. economy. Of all the businesses operating in the United States, about one in seven firms started operations during the past year. These newly formed businesses are also the source of many of the nation's new jobs. Every year, they create more than one of every five new jobs in the economy. These companies are a significant source of employment or self-employment. Of the 27.5 million U.S. small businesses currently in operation, more than 21 million consist of self-employed people without any employees. Almost 8.5 million U.S. employees currently work for a business with fewer than 20 employees.[12] Does starting a business require higher education? Not necessarily, although it can help. Figure 1.2 presents the results of a survey of small-business owners, which shows that about 24 percent of all respondents had graduated from college, and 19 percent had postgraduate degrees.

Besides creating jobs and selling products, entrepreneurship provides the benefits of innovation. In contrast to more established firms, start-up companies tend to innovate most in fields of technology, making new products available to businesses and consumers. Because small

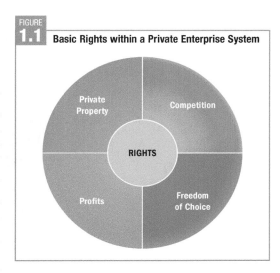

FIGURE 1.1 Basic Rights within a Private Enterprise System

private property most basic freedom under the private enterprise system; the right to own, use, buy, sell, and bequeath land, buildings, machinery, equipment, patents, individual possessions, and various intangible kinds of property.

entrepreneur person who seeks a profitable opportunity and takes the necessary risks to set up and operate a business.

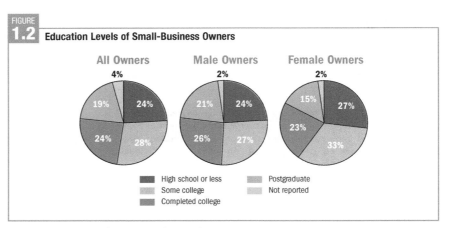

FIGURE 1.2 Education Levels of Small-Business Owners

All Owners / Male Owners / Female Owners

Legend:
- High school or less
- Some college
- Completed college
- Postgraduate
- Not reported

Note: Numbers may not total to 100 percent due to rounding.

Source: Data from "Survey of Business Owners (SBO): Owner's Education Levels at Start-Up, Purchase, or Acquisition of the Business," U.S. Census Bureau, http://www.census.gov, accessed January 9, 2014.

companies are more flexible, they can make changes to products and processes more quickly than larger corporations. Entrepreneurs often find new ways to use natural resources, technology, and other factors of production. Often, they do this because they have to—they may not have enough money to build an expensive prototype or launch a wide-scale promotional campaign.

Sometimes an entrepreneur may innovate by simply tweaking an existing idea. When Carrie Ferrence and Jacqueline Gjurgevich were attending Bainbridge Graduate Institute on Bainbridge Island in Washington State, they noticed that many of the surrounding neighborhoods were "food deserts," lacking stores that sold fresh, locally grown produce and other basic necessities. They founded Stockbox Grocers, which converts old shipping containers into little food stores. The company won a small grant and raised additional funds through Kickstarter. The first StockBox grocery store soon opened in Seattle. Carrie Ferrence says, "It's a tough job market, and you have really few instances in your life to do something that you really love. It's not that this is the alternative. It's the new Plan A."[13]

Entrepreneurship is also important to existing companies in a private enterprise system. More and more, large firms are recognizing the value of entrepreneurial thinking among their employees, hoping to benefit from enhanced flexibility, improved innovation, and new market opportunities. eBay has used mobile technology to reinvent itself and its business customers—many of whom are entrepreneurs. Using augmented reality—which allows such activities as virtually "trying on" clothes via smart phone—eBay sellers have extended their reach to consumers' hands even when they aren't thinking about a purchase. Mobile commerce will allow eBay to do business everywhere—without brick-and-mortar outlets.[14]

As the next section explains, entrepreneurs have played a vital role in the history of U.S. business. They have helped create new industries, developed successful new business methods, and improved U.S. standing in global competition.

Assessment Check ✅

1. What is an alternative term for *private enterprise system*?

2. What is the most basic freedom under the private enterprise system?

3. What is an entrepreneur?

[4] Seven Eras in the History of Business

In the roughly 400 years since the first European settlements appeared on the North American continent, amazing changes have occurred in the size, focus, and goals of U.S. businesses. As Figure 1.3 indicates, U.S. business history is divided into seven distinct time periods: (1) the Colonial period, (2) the Industrial Revolution, (3) the age of industrial entrepreneurs, (4) the production era, (5) the marketing era, (6) the relationship era, and (7) the

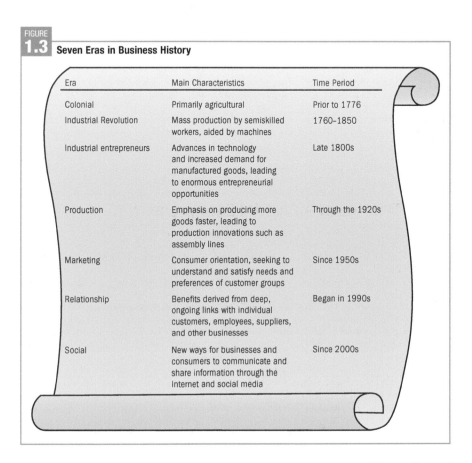

FIGURE
1.3 **Seven Eras in Business History**

Era	Main Characteristics	Time Period
Colonial	Primarily agricultural	Prior to 1776
Industrial Revolution	Mass production by semiskilled workers, aided by machines	1760–1850
Industrial entrepreneurs	Advances in technology and increased demand for manufactured goods, leading to enormous entrepreneurial opportunities	Late 1800s
Production	Emphasis on producing more goods faster, leading to production innovations such as assembly lines	Through the 1920s
Marketing	Consumer orientation, seeking to understand and satisfy needs and preferences of customer groups	Since 1950s
Relationship	Benefits derived from deep, ongoing links with individual customers, employees, suppliers, and other businesses	Began in 1990s
Social	New ways for businesses and consumers to communicate and share information through the Internet and social media	Since 2000s

social era. The next sections describe how events in each of these time periods have influenced U.S. business practices.

The Colonial Period

Colonial society emphasized rural and agricultural production. Colonial towns were small compared to European cities, and they functioned as marketplaces for farmers and craftspeople. The economic focus of the nation centered on rural areas, because prosperity depended on the output of farms, orchards, and the like. The success or failure of crops influenced every aspect of the economy.

Colonists depended on England for manufactured items as well as financial backing for their infant industries. Even after the Revolutionary War (1776–1783), the United States maintained close economic ties with England. British investors continued to provide much of the financing for developing the U.S. business system, and this financial influence continued well into the 19th century.

The Industrial Revolution

The Industrial Revolution began in England around 1750. It moved business operations from an emphasis on independent, skilled workers who specialized in building products one by one

Steinway has built pianos for home use and for artists from John Lennon to Billy Joel.

to a factory system that mass-produced items by bringing together large numbers of semiskilled workers. The factories profited from the savings created by large-scale production, bolstered by increasing support from machines over time. As businesses grew, they could often purchase raw materials more cheaply in larger lots than before. Specialization of labor, limiting each worker to a few specific tasks in the production process, also improved production efficiency.

Influenced by these events in England, business in the United States began a time of rapid industrialization. Agriculture became mechanized, and factories sprang up in cities. During the mid-1800s, the pace of the revolution was increased as newly built railroad systems provided fast, economical transportation. In California, for example, the combination of railroad construction and the gold rush fueled a tremendous demand for construction.

The Age of Industrial Entrepreneurs

Building on the opportunities created by the Industrial Revolution, entrepreneurship increased in the United States. Henry Engelhard Steinway of Seesen, Germany, built his first piano by hand in his kitchen in 1825 as a wedding present for his bride. In 1850, the family emigrated to New York, where Henry and his sons opened their first factory in Manhattan in 1853. Over the next 30 years, they made innovations that led to the modern piano. Through an apprenticeship system, the Steinways transmitted their skills to the following generations. Steinway pianos have long been world famous for their beautiful tone, top-quality materials and workmanship, and durability. Now known as Steinway Musical Instruments, the company still builds its pianos by hand in its factory in Astoria, New York, under the same master-apprentice system that Henry and his sons began. Building each piano takes nearly a year from start to finish. In response to 21st-century demands, the company has launched Etude, an app for the iPad that displays sheet music the user can play on an on-screen piano keyboard.[15]

Inventors created a virtually endless array of commercially useful products and new production methods. Many of them are famous today:

- Eli Whitney introduced the concept of interchangeable parts, an idea that would later facilitate mass production on a previously impossible scale.

- Robert McCormick designed a horse-drawn reaper that reduced the labor involved in harvesting wheat. His son, Cyrus McCormick, saw the commercial potential of the reaper and launched a business to build and sell the machine. By 1902, the company was producing 35 percent of the nation's farm machinery.

- Cornelius Vanderbilt (railroads), J. P. Morgan (banking), and Andrew Carnegie (steel), among others, took advantage of the enormous opportunities waiting for anyone willing to take the risk of starting a new business.

The entrepreneurial spirit of this golden age in business did much to advance the U.S. business system and raise the country's overall standard of living. That market transformation, in turn, created new demand for manufactured goods.

The Production Era

As demand for manufactured goods continued to increase through the 1920s, businesses focused even greater attention on the activities involved in producing those goods. Work became increasingly specialized, and huge, labor-intensive factories dominated U.S. business. Assembly lines, introduced by Henry Ford, became commonplace in major industries. Business owners turned over their responsibilities to a new class of managers trained in operating established companies. Their activities emphasized efforts to produce even more goods through quicker methods.

During the production era, business focused attention on internal processes rather than external influences. Marketing was almost an afterthought, designed solely to distribute items generated by production activities. Little attention was paid to consumer wants or needs. Instead, businesses tended to make decisions about what the market would get. If you wanted to buy a Ford Model T automobile, your color choice was black—the only color produced by the company.

The Marketing Era

The Great Depression of the early 1930s changed the shape of U.S. business yet again. As incomes nosedived, businesses could no longer automatically count on selling everything they produced. Managers began to pay more attention to the markets for their goods and services, and sales and advertising took on new importance. During this period, selling was often synonymous with marketing.

Demand for all kinds of consumer goods exploded after World War II. After nearly five years of doing without new automobiles, appliances, and other items, consumers were buying again. At the same time, however, competition also heated up. Soon businesses began to think of marketing as more than just selling; they envisioned a process of determining what consumers wanted and needed and then designing products to satisfy those needs. In short, they developed a **consumer orientation**.

Businesses began to analyze consumer desires before beginning actual production. Consumer choices skyrocketed. Automobiles came in a wide variety of colors and styles, and car buyers could choose among them. Companies also discovered the need to distinguish their goods and services from those of competitors. **Branding**—the process of creating an identity in consumers' minds for a good, service, or company—is an important marketing tool. A **brand** can be a name, term, sign, symbol, design, or some combination that identifies the products of one firm and differentiates them from competitors' offerings.

Branding can go a long way toward creating value for a firm by providing recognition and a positive association between a company and its products. Some of the world's most famous—and enduring—brands include Apple, Google, Coca-Cola, IBM, Microsoft, GE, McDonald's, Samsung, and Intel.[16]

The marketing era has had a tremendous effect on the way business is conducted today. Even the smallest business owners recognize the importance of understanding what customers want and the reasons they buy.

The Relationship Era

As business continues in the 21st century, a significant change is taking place in the ways companies interact with customers. Since the Industrial Revolution, most businesses have concentrated on building and promoting products in the hope that enough customers will buy them to cover costs and earn acceptable profits, an approach called **transaction management**.

In contrast, in the **relationship era**, businesses are taking a different, longer-term approach to their interactions with customers. Firms now seek ways to actively nurture customer loyalty by carefully managing every interaction. They earn enormous paybacks for their efforts. A company that retains customers over the long haul reduces its advertising and sales costs. Because customer spending tends to accelerate over time, revenues also grow. Companies with long-term customers often can avoid costly reliance on price discounts to attract new business, and they find that many new buyers come from loyal customer referrals.

consumer orientation business philosophy that focuses first on determining unmet consumer wants and needs and then designing products to satisfy those needs.

branding process of creating an identity in consumers' minds for a good, service, or company; a major marketing tool in contemporary business.

brand name, term, sign, symbol, design, or some combination that identifies the products of one firm and differentiates them from competitors' offerings.

transaction management building and promoting products in the hope that enough customers will buy them to cover costs and earn profits.

relationship era business era in which firms seek ways to actively nurture customer loyalty by carefully managing every interaction.

Tips for Social Networking

Building a network of personal contacts in your chosen field is a good career move. Online social networks make this especially easy—but the Internet's informality can also make it tricky to network in a professional way. Here are suggestions for presenting yourself well on sites such as Facebook, LinkedIn, and others.

1 Know the purpose of the networking site you choose. Most people consider Facebook to be social, whereas LinkedIn purposely maintains a more professional look and feel.

2 Potential employers, mentors, and other professionals will check your Facebook page, despite the site's mostly fun-oriented profile. Look objectively at what they'll see there.

3 Keep in mind the image you intend to present. Avoid posting photos that are too personal or that compromise someone else's image.

4 Keep your posts brief and neither overly detailed nor overly personal. Also, strictly limit information about family members.

5 To network with someone you haven't met, find someone you both know and ask that person to make an online introduction.

6 Posting interesting information about your area of professional expertise is one way to build relationships.

7 Avoid posting anything about current or past employers. One survey reveals that 63 percent of businesses fear that social networking may endanger their corporate security.

8 Everything you post is as public as a newspaper's front page. Edit yourself, and check your privacy settings.

Sources: Lauren Simonds, "Business, Etiquette and Social Media," *Time*, accessed January 9, 2014, http://business.time.com; C. G. Lynch, "Facebook Etiquette: Five Dos and Don'ts," *PC World*, accessed January 9, 2014, http://www.pcworld.com; Susan M. Heathfield, "10 Reasons Social Media Should Rock Your World," *About.com*, accessed January 9, 2014, http://humanresources.about.com.

Business owners gain several advantages by developing ongoing relationships with customers. Because it is much less expensive to serve existing customers than to find new ones, businesses that develop long-term customer relationships can reduce their overall costs. Long-term relationships with customers enable businesses to improve their understanding of what customers want and prefer from the company. As a result, businesses enhance their chances of sustaining real advantages through competitive differentiation.

The relationship era is an age of connections—between businesses and customers, employers and employees, technology and manufacturing, and even separate companies. The world economy is increasingly interconnected, as businesses expand beyond their national boundaries. In this new environment, techniques for managing networks of people, businesses, information, and technology are critically important to contemporary business success. As you begin your own career, you will soon see how important relationships are, including your online presence; see the "Career Kickstart" feature for suggestions on presenting yourself in a positive way through social networking.

The Social Era

The <u>social era</u> of business can be described as a new approach to the way businesses and individuals interact, connect, communicate, share, and exchange information with each other in virtual communities and networks around the world.

The social era, based on the premise that organizations create value through connections with groups or networks of people with similar goals and interests, offers businesses immense opportunities, particularly through the use of technology and <u>relationship management</u>—the collection of activities that build and maintain ongoing, mutually beneficial ties with customers and other parties.

Social media tools and technologies come in various shapes and sizes. They include weblogs, blogs, podcasts, and microblogs (such as Twitter); social and professional networks (such as Facebook and LinkedIn); picture-sharing platforms (such as Instagram and Tumblr); and content communities (such as YouTube), to name a few.[17]

As consumers continue to log fewer hours on computers and more time on mobile devices, companies have implemented mobile strategies using real-time data and location-based technology. Businesses use mobile social media applications to engage in marketing research, communications, sales promotions, loyalty programs, and other processes. In the social era, businesses tailor specific promotions to specific users in specific locations at specific times to build customer loyalty and long-term relationships. For example, Facebook offers free wi-fi to users in exchange for checking in at selected retailers, hotels, and restaurants.[18]

social era business era in which firms seek ways to connect and interact with customers using technology.

relationship management collection of activities that build and maintain ongoing, mutually beneficial ties with customers and other parties.

Strategic Alliances

Businesses are also finding that they must form partnerships with other organizations to take full advantage of available opportunities. One form of partnership between organizations is a strategic alliance, a partnership formed to create a competitive advantage for the businesses involved.

E-business has created a whole new type of strategic alliance. A firm whose entire business is conducted online, such as Amazon or Wayfair.com, may team up with traditional retailers that contribute their expertise in buying the right amount of the right merchandise, as well as their knowledge of distribution. Through its Amazon Services branch, Amazon.com, the world's largest e-commerce firm, has formed strategic alliances with retailers to facilitate technology services, merchandising, customer service, and order fulfillment. Name-brand retailers offer their products via Amazon's retail site, backed by over 80 million square feet in its fulfillment sites located around the world. In a recent Customers Choice survey, Amazon has the best customer service among U.S. firms.[19]

The Green Advantage

Another way of building relationships is to incorporate issues that your customers care about into your business. As environmental concerns continue to influence consumers' choices of everything from yogurt to clothing to cars, many observers say the question about "going green" is no longer whether, but how. The need to develop environmentally friendly products and processes is becoming a major new force in business today.

Companies in every industry are researching ways to save energy, cut emissions and pollution, reduce waste, and, not incidentally, save money and increase profits as well. King & King Architects of Syracuse, New York, a member of the Green Building Council, recently relocated to a 48,000-square-foot warehouse. A grant from the New York State Energy Research and Development Authority (NYSERDA) enabled King & King to install energy-improved, high-efficiency windows, heating and cooling, ventilation, and insulation. These and many other improvements will save the company the equivalent amount of electricity consumed by

Many companies have begun to address the energy issue. SolarCity provides clean solar energy by installing rooftop solar cells on houses.

© Josef Becker/iStockphoto

24 single-family homes per year—and won the company a High Performance Building Plaque from NYSERDA.[20]

Energy is among the biggest costs for most firms, and carbon-based fuels such as coal are responsible for most of the additional carbon dioxide in the atmosphere. Many companies have begun to address this issue, none perhaps with more flair than Greensulate, a small business in New York city that insulates rooftops with beautiful meadows of lavender, native grasses, and a hardy plant called sedum. The firm's efforts to date have eliminated more than 3,000 pounds of carbon from the atmosphere.[21] Clean solar energy is coming into its own and may soon be more viable and more widely available. SolarCity, a California installer of rooftop solar cells, has become a leader in clean energy services for businesses, schools, and not-for-profit organizations.[22]

Each new era in U.S. business history has forced managers to reexamine the tools and techniques they formerly used to compete. Tomorrow's managers will need creativity and vision to stay on top of rapidly changing technology and to manage complex relationships in the global business world of the fast-paced 21st century. As green operations become more cost-effective, and consumers and shareholders demand more transparency from management, few firms will choose to be left behind.

Assessment Check ✔

1. What was the Industrial Revolution?
2. During which era was the idea of branding developed?
3. What is the difference between transaction management and management in the relationship era?

[5] Today's Business Workforce

A skilled and knowledgeable workforce is an essential resource for keeping pace with the accelerating rate of change in today's business world. Employers need reliable workers who are dedicated to fostering strong ties with customers and partners. They must build workforces capable of efficient, high-quality production needed to compete in global markets. Savvy business leaders also realize that the brainpower of employees plays a vital role in a firm's ability to stay on top of new technologies and innovations. In short, a first-class workforce can be the foundation of a firm's competitive differentiation, providing important advantages over competing businesses. See how one entrepreneur-turned billionaire is using his wealth to help China breathe easier in the "Going Green" feature.

Changes in the Workforce

Companies now face several trends that challenge their skills for managing and developing human resources. Those challenges include aging of the population and a shrinking labor pool, growing diversity of the workforce, the changing nature of work, the need for flexibility and mobility, and the use of collaboration to innovate.

Aging of the Population and Shrinking Labor Pool By 2030, the number of U.S. workers 65 or older will reach 72 million—double what it is today—and many of them will soon retire from the workforce, taking their experience and expertise with them. As Table 1.2 shows, the U.S. population as a whole is trending older. Yet today, many members of the Baby Boom generation, the huge number of people born between 1946 and 1964, are still hitting the peaks of their careers. At the same time, members of so-called Generation X (born from 1965 to 1981) and Generation Y (born from 1982 to 2005) are building their careers, so employers are finding more generations in the workforce simultaneously than ever before. This broad age diversity brings management challenges with it, such as accommodating a variety of work lifestyles, changing expectations of work, and varying levels of technological expertise. Still, despite the widening age spectrum of the workforce, some economists predict the U.S. labor pool could soon fall short by as many as 10 million people as the Baby Boomers retire.

More sophisticated technology has intensified the hiring challenge by requiring workers to have ever more advanced skills. Although the number of college-educated workers has

GoingGreen

doubled in the past 20 years, the demand is still greater than the supply. Because of these changes, companies are increasingly seeking—and finding—talent at the extreme ends of the working-age spectrum. Teenagers are entering the workforce sooner, and some seniors are staying longer—or seeking new careers after retiring from their primary careers. Many older workers work part-time or flexible hours. Meanwhile, for those older employees who do retire, employers must administer a variety of retirement planning and disability programs and insurance benefits.

Increasingly Diverse Workforce The U.S. workforce is growing more diverse, in age and in every other way as well. The two fastest-growing ethnic populations in the United States are Hispanics and people of Asian origin. By the year 2050, the number of Hispanics in the U.S. will grow from a current 35 million to 102 million, or 24 percent of the total

TABLE

⌐1.2¬ Aging of the U.S. Population

AGE	2010	2020	2025
16–64	203 million	214 million	218 million
	66% of total	63% of total	61% of total
65 and older	40 million	55 million	64 million
	13% of total	16% of total	18% of total
Median	37 years	38 years	38.5 years

Source: U.S. Census Bureau, "Resident Population Projections by Sex and Age: 2010 to 2050," *Statistical Abstract of the United States*, http://www.census.gov, accessed January 9, 2014.

Chapter 1 *The Changing Face of Business* **17**

population. The Asian population will increase from 10 million to 33 million, or 8 percent of the total U.S. population.[23] Considering that minority groups will make up half the total U.S. population by the year 2050, managers must learn to work effectively with diverse ethnic groups, cultures, and lifestyles to develop and retain a superior workforce for their company.

Diversity, blending individuals of different genders, ethnic backgrounds, cultures, religions, ages, and physical and mental abilities, can enhance a firm's chances of success. Some of the firms that made the top 10 in a recent list of "Top 50 Companies for Diversity" were also leaders and innovators in their industries, including Sodexo, PricewaterhouseCoopers, Kaiser Permanente, Ernst & Young, MasterCard Worldwide, Novartis Pharmaceuticals, Procter & Gamble, Prudential Financial, Accenture, and Johnson & Johnson.[24] Several studies have shown that diverse employee teams and workforces tend to perform tasks more effectively and develop better solutions to business problems than homogeneous employee groups. This result is due in part to the varied perspectives and experiences that foster innovation and creativity in multicultural teams. Practical managers also know that attention to diversity issues can help them avoid costly and damaging legal battles.

Outsourcing and the Changing Nature of Work Not only is the U.S. workforce changing, but so is the very nature of work. Manufacturing used to account for most of U.S. annual output, but the balance has now shifted to services such as financial management and communications. This means firms must rely heavily on well-trained service workers with knowledge, technical skills, the ability to communicate and deal with people, and a talent for creative thinking. The Internet has made possible another business tool for staffing flexibility—**outsourcing**, using outside vendors to produce goods or fulfill services and functions that previously were handled in house. In the best situation, outsourcing allows a firm to reduce costs and concentrate its resources on the things it does best while gaining access to expertise it may not have. But outsourcing also creates its own challenges, such as differences in language or culture.

Offshoring is the relocation of business processes to lower-cost locations overseas. This can include both production and services. In recent years, China has emerged as a dominant location for production offshoring for many firms, while India, the Philippines, and Ireland are key players in offshoring services.[25] Some U.S. companies are now structured so that entire divisions or functions are developed and staffed overseas—the jobs were never in the United States to start with. Another trend in some industries is **nearshoring**, outsourcing production or services to locations near a firm's home base.

Flexibility and Mobility Younger workers in particular are looking for something other than the work-comes-first lifestyle exemplified by the Baby Boomer generation. But workers of all ages are exploring different work arrangements, such as telecommuting from remote locations and sharing jobs with two or more employees. Employers are also hiring growing numbers of temporary and part-time employees, some of whom are more interested in using and developing their skills than climbing the career ladder. While the cubicle-filled office will likely never become entirely obsolete, technology makes productive networking and virtual team efforts possible by allowing people to work where they choose and easily share knowledge, a sense of purpose or mission, and a free flow of ideas across any geographical distance or time zone.

Managers of global workforces need to build and earn their trust, in order to retain valued employees and to ensure that all members are acting ethically and contributing their share without the day-to-day supervision of a more traditional work environment. These managers, and their employees, need to be flexible and responsive to change while work, technology, and the relationships between them continue to evolve.

Innovation through Collaboration Some observers also see a trend toward more collaborative work in the future, as opposed to individuals working alone. Businesses using

diversity blending individuals of different genders, ethnic backgrounds, cultures, religions, ages, and physical and mental abilities.

outsourcing using outside vendors to produce goods or fulfill services and functions that were previously handled in-house or in-country.

offshoring relocation of business processes to lower-cost locations overseas.

nearshoring outsourcing production or services to locations near a firm's home base.

teamwork hope to build a creative environment where all members contribute their knowledge and skills to solve problems or seize opportunities.

The old relationship between employers and employees was pretty simple: workers arrived at a certain hour, did their jobs, and went home every day at the same time. Companies rarely laid off workers, and employees rarely left for a job at another firm. But all that—and so much more—has changed. Employees are no longer likely to remain with a single company throughout their entire careers and do not necessarily expect lifetime loyalty from the companies they work for. They do not expect to give that loyalty either. Instead, they build their own careers however and wherever they can. These changes mean that many firms now recognize the value of a partnership with employees that encourages creative thinking and problem solving and that rewards risk taking and innovation.

6

The 21st-Century Manager

Today's companies look for managers who are intelligent, highly motivated people with the ability to create and sustain a vision of how an organization can succeed. The 21st-century manager must also apply critical-thinking skills and creativity to business challenges and lead change within the organization.

Importance of Vision

To thrive in the 21st century, businesspeople need <u>vision</u>, the ability to perceive marketplace needs and what an organization must do to satisfy them. Marc Benioff, CEO of Salesforce.com, and co-founder Parker Harris, a pioneer of cloud computing, are visionary leaders. Benioff and Harris founded Salesforce.com to replace traditional enterprise software—computer programs with business applications—with an on-demand information management service. Because of social and mobile cloud technologies, businesses now have the opportunity to connect with

Marc Benioff, CEO of Salesforce.com, is considered a visionary leader because of his approach to technology and cloud computing.

Bloomberg/Getty Images

Assessment Check ☑

1. Define *outsourcing, offshoring,* and *nearshoring.*
2. Describe the importance of collaboration and employee partnership.

vision the ability to perceive marketplace needs and what an organization must do to satisfy them.

Chapter 1 *The Changing Face of Business*   **19**

Hit&Miss

Twitter's Dorsey: 140 Characters at a Time

At age 13, Jack Dorsey was fascinated with dispatch routing. While a student in college, he began to create software related to dispatch logistics, which is still used by taxi companies today.

Dorsey has always been interested in business. In San Francisco, he started Odeo, a podcasting company, which quickly became extinct when iTunes surfaced. This setback didn't stop Dorsey from trying again. Twitter began as an interoffice microblogging platform created by Odeo programmers. When a small earthquake shook San Francisco, word of the quake spread quickly via Twitter—and a new company was born.

Square, Dorsey's most recent business venture, allows credit card payments to be made to individuals and businesses by attaching a small device to a smart phone or tablet.

Dorsey is guided by three principles—simplicity, constraint, and craftsmanship—still very much part of Twitter's culture today. Dorsey serves as Twitter's executive chairman, Square's CEO, and recently joined Disney's board of directors.

Questions for Critical Thinking

1. How can businesses apply Dorsey's three guiding principles to create a strategic vision?
2. What lessons can be learned from Jack Dorsey about perseverance, technology, and starting a business?

Sources: Anthony Ha, "Dorsey Joins Disney's Board of Directors," *TechCrunch*, accessed January 12, 2014, http://techcrunch.com; Kit Eaton, "Twitter IPO Player's Club," *Fast Company*, accessed January 12, 2014, www.fastcompany.com; Nicholas Carlson, "The Real History of Twitter," *Business Insider*, accessed January 12, 2014, www.businessinsider.com; Brandon Griggs, "Twitter's Jack Dorsey Eyes New York Mayor's Job," *CNN.com*, accessed January 12, 2014, http://cnn.com; Noah Robischon, "Square Brings Credit Card Swiping to Mobile Masses, *Fast Company*, accessed January 12, 2014, www.fastcompany.com; Mitch Wagner, "Twitter CEO Jack Dorsey Talks About Its Business Model," *Information Week*, accessed January 12, 2014, www.informationweek.com.

---

customers, employees, partners, and others in more strategic and effective ways. At a recent conference, Benioff was quoted as saying, "Salesforce.com needs to be for enterprise customers what Steve Jobs has always been to me—to be visionary and paint the future as much as possible."[26] Another leader with a definite vision is Twitter's Jack Dorsey. See the "Hit & Miss" feature for his story.

Importance of Critical Thinking and Creativity

Critical thinking and creativity are essential characteristics of the 21st-century workforce. Today's businesspeople need to look at a wide variety of situations, draw connections among disparate information, and develop future-oriented solutions. This need applies not only to top executives, but to mid-level managers and entry-level workers as well.

critical thinking ability to analyze and assess information to pinpoint problems or opportunities.

Critical thinking is the ability to analyze and assess information to pinpoint problems or opportunities. The critical-thinking process includes activities such as determining the authenticity, accuracy, and worth of information, knowledge, and arguments. It involves looking beneath the surface for deeper meaning and connections that can help identify critical issues and solutions. Without critical thinking, a firm may encounter serious problems.

creativity capacity to develop novel solutions to perceived organizational problems.

Creativity is the capacity to develop novel solutions to perceived organizational problems. Although most people think of it in relation to writers, artists, musicians, and inventors, that is a very limited definition. In business, creativity refers to the ability to see better and different ways of doing business. A computer engineer who solves a glitch in a software program is executing a creative act.

Sometimes a crisis calls for creative leadership. In less than a decade, the U.S. automobile industry has made an amazing comeback. Falling deep into financial crisis, General Motors (GM), one of the industry's big three automakers, was forced to seek help from the federal government. Almost out of cash, GM was forced to file bankruptcy, and its CEO resigned.

Today, General Motors is a smaller, restructured version of its former self, and it repaid its government loans ahead of time. The company's revised strategy includes fewer brands, a focus on improved quality, and more competitive pricing for its products. General Motors' new CEO, Mary Barra, began her career at GM as an intern on the factory floor. Barra, the first woman to run a U.S. automobile company, previously held posts in product development, engineering, communications, and human resources.[27]

With some practice and mental exercise, you can cultivate your own ability to think creatively. Here are some exercises and guidelines:

- In a group, brainstorm by listing ideas as they come to mind. Build on other people's ideas, but don't criticize them. Wait until later to evaluate and organize the ideas.

- Think about how to make familiar concepts unfamiliar. A glue that doesn't stick very well? That's the basis for 3M's popular Post-it® notes.

- Plan ways to rearrange your thinking with simple questions such as, "What features can we leave out?" or by imagining what it feels like to be the customer.

- Cultivate curiosity, openness, risk, and energy as you meet people and encounter new situations. View these encounters as opportunities to learn.

- Treat failures as additional learning experiences.

- Get regular physical exercise. When you work out, your brain releases endorphins, and these chemicals stimulate creative thinking.

- Pay attention to your dreams and daydreams. You might find that you already know the answer to a problem.

Creativity and critical thinking must go beyond generating new ideas, however. They must lead to action. In addition to creating an environment in which employees can nurture ideas, managers must give them opportunities to take risks and try new solutions.

Ability to Lead Change

Today's business leaders must guide their employees and organizations through the changes brought about by technology, marketplace demands, and global competition. Managers must be skilled at recognizing employee strengths and motivating people to move toward common goals as members of a team. Throughout this book, real-world examples demonstrate how companies have initiated sweeping change initiatives. Most, if not all, have been led by managers comfortable with the tough decisions that today's fluctuating conditions require.

Factors that require organizational change can come from both external and internal sources; successful managers must be aware of both. External forces might include feedback from customers, developments in the international marketplace, economic trends, and new technologies. Internal factors might arise from new company goals, emerging employee needs, labor union demands, or production problems.

⌜7⌟ What Makes a Company Admired?

Who is your hero? Is it someone who has achieved great feats in sports, government, entertainment, or business? Why do you admire the person? Does he or she run a company, earn a lot of money, or give back to the community and society? Every year, business magazines and organizations publish lists of companies that they consider to be "most admired." Companies, like individuals, may be admired for many reasons. Most people

Solving an Ethical Controversy

Can Fair Trade Be Ethical and Flexible?

Fair Trade USA (FTUSA), the U.S. national fair trade organization, recently rocked the $6 billion fair trade world by splitting from the parent organization, the Fairtrade Labeling Organization (FLO). FTUSA will now set its own ethical standards, certifying coffee, cocoa, and fruit from large plantations employing seasonal workers, as well as from the small, FLO-approved cooperative farms practicing democratic management and ethical treatment of employees. Some fear the split will undermine the fair trade movement.

Can fair trade practices extend to larger producers that don't fit the model of small-farm, participative management?

PRO

1. Paul Rice, head of Fair Trade USA, says his decision to include larger farms will double sales of fair trade goods, benefiting more producers and raising consumer awareness.

2. FTUSA promises to model its plantation standards after FLO's. "We are after results," says Rice. "We want to get things done."

CON

1. Some opponents of Rice's decision have vowed to boycott FTUSA participants such as Green Mountain Coffee, saying the new standards will be lower and will undermine fair trade values.

2. Under the new standards, chocolate bars can carry the FTUSA label if the cocoa is approved even if the sugar is not. Critics call that compromise "unacceptable."

Summary

The success of fair trade ultimately lies with consumers. Will they be confused by two different labeling systems and different standards?

Sources: Organization website, http://fairtradeusa.org, accessed January 27, 2014; Paul Rice, "Fair Trade USA: Why We Parted Ways with Fair Trade International," *Triple Pundit*, accessed January 27, 2014, www.triplepundit.com; Twilight Greenaway, "Fair Trade Lite: Fair Trade USA Moves Away from Worker Co-Ops," *Grist*, accessed January 27, 2014, http://grist.org; Simon Clark, "U.S. Rebel's Split Riles $6 Billion World of Ethical Commerce," *Bloomberg News*, accessed January 27, 2014, www.bloomberg.com; "Fractures in Fair Trade: Fair Trade USA Leaves Fairtrade Labeling Organization," *Fair Trade Vancouver*, accessed January 27, 2014, www.fairtradevancouver.ca.

---

would mention solid profits, stable growth, a safe and challenging work environment, high-quality goods and services, and business ethics and social responsibility. *Business ethics* refers to the standards of conduct and moral values involving decisions made in the work environment. *Social responsibility* is a management philosophy that includes contributing resources to the community, preserving the natural environment, and developing or participating in nonprofit programs designed to promote the well-being of the general public. You'll find business ethics and social responsibility examples throughout this book, as well as a deeper exploration of these topics in Chapter 2. For businesses to behave ethically and responsibly, their employees need to have strong moral compasses that guide them. The "Solving an Ethical Controversy" feature demonstrates some of the challenges of defining what is ethical.

As you read this text, you'll be able to make up your mind about why companies should—or should not—be admired. *Fortune* publishes two lists of most-admired companies each year, one for U.S.–based firms and one for the world. The list is compiled from surveys and other research conducted by the Hay Group, a global human resources and organizational consulting firm. Criteria for making the list include innovation, people management, use of corporate assets, social responsibility, quality of management, and quality of products and services.[28] Table 1.3 lists the top 10 "Most Admired Companies" for a recent year.

Assessment Check ✅

1. Identify three criteria used to judge whether a company might be considered admirable.

2. Define *business ethics* and *social responsibility*

Part 1 *Business in a Global Environment*

⌐1.3⌐ *FORTUNE's*® Top Ten Most Admired Companies

1 Apple	**5** Starbucks	**9** Southwest Airlines
2 Amazon.com	**6** The Coca-Cola Company	**10** General Electric
3 Google	**7** Walt Disney	
4 Berkshire Hathaway	**8** FedEx	

Source: "World's Most Admired Companies 2014," *Fortune*, accessed April 11, 2014, http://fortune.com. Copyright 2014 by Time, Inc. Used by permission and protected by the copyright laws of the United States. The printing, copying, redistribution, or retransmission of the material without express permission is prohibited. Fortune and Time Inc. are not affiliated with, and do not endorse products or services of Wiley.

What's Ahead

As business speeds along in the 21st century, new technologies, population shifts, and shrinking global barriers are altering the world at a frantic pace. Businesspeople are catalysts for many of these changes, creating new opportunities for individuals who are prepared to take action. Studying contemporary business will help you prepare for the future.

Throughout this book, you'll be exposed to the real-life stories of many businesspeople. You'll learn about the range of business careers available and the daily decisions, tasks, and challenges that they face. By the end of the course, you'll understand how marketing, production, accounting, finance, and management work together to provide competitive advantages for firms. This knowledge can help you become a more capable employee and enhance your career potential.

Now that this chapter has introduced some basic terms and issues in the business world of the 21st century, Chapter 2 takes a detailed look at the ethical and social responsibility issues facing contemporary business. Chapter 3 deals with economic challenges, and Chapter 4 focuses on the difficulties and opportunities faced by firms competing in world markets.

Chapter in Review

■ Summary of Learning Objectives

⌐1⌐ Define *business*.

Business consists of all profit-seeking activities that provide goods and services necessary to an economic system. Not-for-profit organizations are business-like establishments whose primary objective is public service over profits.

Assessment Check Answers ✓

1.1 What activity lies at the center of every business endeavor? At the heart of every business endeavor is an exchange between a buyer and a seller.

1.2 What is the primary objective of a not-for-profit organization? Not-for-profit organizations place public service above profits, although they need to raise money in order to operate and achieve their social goals.

⌐2⌐ Identify and describe the factors of production.

The factors of production consist of four basic inputs: natural resources, capital, human resources, and entrepreneurship. Natural resources include all productive inputs that are useful in their natural states. Capital includes technology, tools, information, and physical facilities.

Human resources include anyone who works for the firm. Entrepreneurship is the willingness to take risks to create and operate a business.

Assessment Check Answers ✔️

2.1 Identify the four basic inputs to an economic system. The four basic inputs are natural resources, capital, human resources, and entrepreneurship.

2.2 List four types of capital. Four types of capital are technology, tools, information, and physical facilities.

⌐3⌐ Describe the private enterprise system.

The private enterprise system is an economic system that rewards firms for their ability to perceive and serve the needs and demands of consumers. Competition in the private enterprise system ensures success for firms that satisfy consumer demands. Citizens in a private enterprise economy enjoy the rights to private property, profits, freedom of choice, and competition. Entrepreneurship drives economic growth.

Assessment Check Answers ✔️

3.1 What is an alternative term for *private enterprise system*? Capitalism is an alternative word for private enterprise system.

3.2 What is the most basic freedom under the private enterprise system? The most basic freedom is the right to private property.

3.3 What is an entrepreneur? An entrepreneur is a risk taker who is willing to start, own, and operate a business.

⌐4⌐ Identify the seven eras in the history of business.

The seven historical eras are the Colonial period, the Industrial Revolution, the age of industrial entrepreneurs, the production era, the marketing era, the relationship era, and the social era. In the Colonial period, businesses were small and rural, emphasizing agricultural production. The Industrial Revolution brought factories and mass production to business. The age of industrial entrepreneurs built on the Industrial Revolution through an expansion in the number and size of firms. The production era focused on the growth of factory operations through assembly lines and other efficient internal processes. During and following the Great Depression, businesses concentrated on finding markets for their products through advertising and selling, giving rise to the marketing era. In the relationship era, businesspeople focused on developing and sustaining long-term relationships with customers and other businesses. In the social era, businesses use technology and relationship management to connect and communicate with consumers and promote innovation. Strategic alliances create a competitive advantage through partnerships. Concern for

the environment also helps build strong relationships with customers.

Assessment Check Answers ✔️

4.1 What was the Industrial Revolution? The Industrial Revolution began around 1750 in England and moved business operations from an emphasis on independent, skilled workers to a factory system that mass-produced items.

4.2 During which era was the idea of branding developed? The idea of branding began in the marketing era.

4.3 What is the difference between transaction management and management in the relationship era? Transaction management is an approach that focuses on building, promoting, and selling enough products to cover costs and earn profits. In the relationship era, businesses seek ways to actively nurture customer loyalty by carefully managing every interaction.

⌐5⌐ Explain how today's business workforce and the nature of work itself is changing.

The workforce is changing in several significant ways: (1) it is aging and the labor pool is shrinking, and (2) it is becoming increasingly diverse. The nature of work has shifted toward services and a focus on information. More firms now rely on outsourcing, offshoring, and nearshoring to produce goods or fulfill services and functions that were previously handled in-house or in-country. In addition, today's workplaces are becoming increasingly flexible, allowing employees to work from different locations. And companies are fostering innovation through teamwork and collaboration.

Assessment Check Answers ✔️

5.1 Define *outsourcing, offshoring,* and *nearshoring*. Outsourcing involves using outside vendors to produce goods or fulfill services and functions that were once handled in house. Offshoring is the relocation of business processes to lower-cost locations overseas. Nearshoring is the outsourcing of production or services to locations near a firm's home base.

5.2 Describe the importance of collaboration and employee partnership. Businesses are increasingly focusing on collaboration rather than on individuals working alone. No longer do employees just put in their time at a job they hold their entire career. The new employer–employee partnership encourages teamwork, creative thinking, and problem solving.

⌐6⌐ Identify the skills and attributes needed for the 21st-century manager.

Today's managers need vision, the ability to perceive marketplace needs, and the way their firm can satisfy them.

Critical-thinking skills and creativity allow managers to pinpoint problems and opportunities and plan novel solutions. Finally, managers are dealing with rapid change, and they need skills to help lead their organizations through shifts in external and internal conditions.

Assessment Check Answers ✔️

6.1 Why is vision an important managerial quality? To thrive in the 21st century, managers need vision, the ability to perceive marketplace needs and to determine what an organization must do to satisfy those needs.

6.2 What is the difference between creativity and critical thinking? Critical thinking is the ability to analyze and assess information to pinpoint problems or opportunities. Creativity is the capacity to develop novel solutions to perceived organizational problems.

⌈7⌉ Outline the characteristics that make a company admired. A company is usually admired for its solid profits, stable growth, a safe and challenging work environment, high-quality goods and services, and business ethics and social responsibility.

Assessment Check Answers ✔️

7.1 Identify three criteria used to judge whether a company might be considered admirable. Criteria in judging whether companies are admirable include three of the following: solid profits, stable growth, a safe and challenging work environment, high-quality goods and services, and business ethics and social responsibility.

7.2 Define *business ethics* and *social responsibility*. Business ethics refers to the standards of conduct and moral values involving decisions made in the work environment. Social responsibility is a management philosophy that includes contributing resources to the community, preserving the natural environment, and developing or participating in nonprofit programs designed to promote the well-being of the general public.

◼ Business Terms You Need to Know

business 4
profits 4
not-for-profit organizations 5
factors of production 6
natural resources 6
capital 6
human resources 6
entrepreneurship 7
private enterprise system 8
capitalism 8

competition 8
competitive differentiation 8
private property 9
entrepreneur 9
consumer orientation 13
branding 13
brand 13
transaction management 13
relationship era 13
social era 14

relationship management 14
strategic alliance 15
diversity 18
outsourcing 18
offshoring 18
nearshoring 18
vision 19
critical thinking 20
creativity 20

◼ Review Questions

1. Why is business so important to a country's economy?

2. In what ways are not-for-profit organizations a substantial part of the U.S. economy? What unique challenges do not-for-profits face?

3. Identify and describe the four basic inputs that make up factors of production. Give an example of each factor of production that an auto manufacturer might use.

4. What is a private enterprise system? What four rights are critical to the operation of capitalism? Why would capitalism function poorly in a society that does not ensure these rights for its citizens?

5. In what ways is entrepreneurship vital to the private enterprise system?

6. Identify the seven eras of business in the United States. How did business change during each era?

7. Describe the focus of the most recent era of U.S. business. How is this different from previous eras?

8. Define partnership and strategic alliance. How might a motorcycle dealer and a local radio station benefit from an alliance?

9. Identify the major changes in the workforce that will affect the way managers build a world-class workforce in the 21st century. Why is brainpower so important?

10. Identify four qualities that managers of the 21st century must have. Why are these qualities important in a competitive business environment?

Projects and Teamwork Applications

1. The entrepreneurial spirit fuels growth in the U.S. economy. Choose a company that interests you—one you have worked for or dealt with as a customer—and read about the company in the library or visit its website. Learn what you can about the company's early history: Who founded it and why? Is the founder still with the organization? Do you think the founder's original vision is still embraced by the company? If not, how has the vision changed?

2. Brands distinguish one company's goods or services from those of its competitors. Each company you purchase from hopes that you will become loyal to its brand. Some well-known brands are Taco Bell, Pepsi, Marriott, and Gap. Choose a type of good or service you use regularly and identify the major brands associated with it. Are you loyal to a particular brand? Why or why not?

3. More and more businesses are forming strategic alliances to become more competitive. Sometimes, businesses pair up with not-for-profit organizations in a relationship that is beneficial to both. Choose a company whose goods or services interest you, such as REI, FedEx, Kashi, or Sam's Club. On your own or with a classmate, research the firm on the Internet to learn about its alliances with not-for-profit organizations. Then describe one of the alliances, including goals and benefits to both parties. Create a presentation for your class.

4. This chapter describes how the nature of the workforce is changing: the population is aging, the labor pool is shrinking, the workforce is becoming more diverse, the nature of work is changing, the workplace is becoming more flexible and mobile, and employers are fostering innovation and collaboration among their employees. Form teams of two to three students. Select a company and research how that company is responding to changes in the workforce. When you have completed your research, be prepared to present it to your class. Choose one of the following companies or select your own: Allstate, Cargill, Staples, or Microsoft.

5. Many successful companies today use technology to help them improve their relationship management. Suppose a major supermarket chain's management team has asked you to assess its use of technology for this purpose. On your own or with a classmate, visit one or two local supermarkets and also explore their corporate websites. Note the ways in which firms in this industry already use technology to connect with their customers, and list at least three ideas for new ways or improvements to existing ones. Present your findings to the class as if they were the management team.

Web Assignments

1. **Using search engines.** Gathering information is one of the most popular applications of the web. Using two of the major search engines, such as Google and Bing, search the web for information pertaining to brand and relationship management. Sort through your results—you're likely to gets thousands of hits—and identify the three most useful. What did you learn from this experience regarding the use of a search engine?

   www.google.com

   www.bing.com

2. **Companies and not-for-profits.** In addition to companies, virtually all not-for-profit organizations have websites. Four websites are listed below, two for companies (Alcoa and Sony) and two for not-for-profits (Mayo Clinic and National Audubon Society). What is the purpose of each website? What type of information is available? How are the sites similar? How are they different?

   www.alcoa.com

   www.sony.com

   www.mayoclinic.org

   www.audubon.org

3. **Characteristics of U.S. workforce.** Visit the website listed below. It is the home page for the U.S. Bureau of Labor Statistics—a good source of basic demographic and economic data. Click on "Subjects." Use the relevant sections listed to prepare a brief profile of the U.S. workforce (gender, age, occupation, and so forth). How is this profile expected to change over the next 10 years?

   www.bls.gov

Note: Internet web addresses change frequently. If you don't find the exact sites listed, you may need to access the organization's home page and search from there or use a search engine such as Google or Bing.

Mars, Inc.: A Sweet Place to Work

Stricken with childhood polio, Frank C. Mars learned the art of hand-dipping chocolate in his mother's kitchen, and he went on to start Mars back in the early 1900s. A privately held business in its fourth generation of family ownership, Mars has more than 70,000 employees around the globe. Some of the company's sweet brands include Snickers, Starburst, M&Ms, LifeSavers, Skittles, and Juicy Fruit and Orbit chewing gum. The company also owns Uncle Ben's Rice and several animal care and dry pet food brands.

As America's third-largest private company with over $30 billion in sales, Mars, which is based in McLean, Virginia, rarely grants interviews to the media, even preferring to keep information like how the little "m" gets stamped on the outer shell of an M&M private. Internally, however, there remain few, if any, secrets—flat screens throughout its facilities display up-to-date financial information about the company. This reflects the company's philosophy of closely tying employee compensation to financial results. Employees can earn bonuses of 10 percent to 100 percent of their salaries for team performance.

For the second time, Mars recently made it on to *Fortune*'s roster of 100 Best Companies to Work For. Even without many of the perks offered by other companies, some families are into their third generation of employment at Mars. Turnover is less than 5 percent among its U.S. employees, known as "Martians," who still use an antiquated time card system. If you're late, your pay is docked 10 percent, but be on time and a 10 percent annual bonus is yours.

Perhaps the most significant feature of this "Best Company" is its internal advancement and reward opportunities. The company develops and encourages cross-division talent and expects its employees to follow its five guiding principles of quality, responsibility, mutuality, efficiency, and freedom. "The consumer is our boss, quality of our work and value for money is our goal," reads the Mars quality principle.

Questions for Critical Thinking

1. Explain how tying employee compensation to company financial results helps keep Mars's employee turnover rate low.
2. Known for its secrecy to the outside world, how can Mars leverage its "Best Company" award to attract new employees and customers?

Sources: Company website, "History of Mars," and "The Five Principles," www.mars.com, accessed January 27, 2014; "100 Best Companies to Work For: 2014," *Fortune*, accessed January 27, 2014, http://money.cnn.com; David A. Kaplan, "Mars: A Pretty Sweet Place to Work," *Fortune*, accessed January 10, 2014, http://management.fortune .cnn.com; Vandana Sinha, "Read Our First-Ever Conversation with Mars," *Biz Beat*, accessed January 10, 2014, www.bizjournals.com.

Nordstrom Rides High

Nordstrom, the high-end clothing retailer headquartered in Seattle, continues to be on a roll as annual sales almost reached $12 billion and market share grew despite the company's aversion to price markdowns. Competitors such as Saks, Macy's, and Gap struggled during the same period, stumped by slowed consumer spending during the recent economic slump.

Nordstrom, founded in 1901 and still family-run, boasts 117 full-line stores and more than 141 Nordstrom Racks outlets. It has high expectations for its burgeoning online operations and has begun expanding overseas, but cautiously, to nearby Canada. A few key elements have always differentiated the chain. Perhaps the best known is its commitment to outstanding customer service, which some say the company practically invented. Regularly ranked near the top in customer satisfaction surveys, the company rewards its sales associates for their attention to customers with generous pay and a tradition of promoting from within. It also provides superior sales tools, such as an unrivaled new inventory system that allows salespeople to quickly find what customers want. The system changed the way the store's buyers worked, but the results were worth it.

"We're not trying to make a buck and move on to the next thing," says Peter Nordstrom, in charge of merchandise. "This is our life. We do not want to be the generation who screws it up."

Questions for Critical Thinking

1. How does Nordstrom differentiate itself from other clothing retailers?

2. What makes Nordstrom salespeople stay with the company?

Sources: Company website, www.nordstrom.com, accessed January 10, 2014; Dan Moskowitz, "Nordstrom Has Reinvented Itself," *Motley Fool,* accessed January 10, 2014, www.fool.com; Walter Loeb, "Nordstrom: How to Remain Relevant in a Tech Savvy World," *Forbes,* accessed January 10, 2014, www.forbes.com; Cotton Timberlake, "How Nordstrom Bests Its Retail Rivals," *Bloomberg Businessweek,* accessed January 10, 2014, www.businessweek.com.

CASE 1.3 New Harvest Coffee Roasters Brews Up Fresh Business

If you're one of those people for whom the scent of freshly roasted coffee is irresistible, you have something in common with Rik Kleinfeldt. Kleinfeldt, the co-founder and president of New Harvest Coffee Roasters, is a self-proclaimed coffee fanatic. He dwells on the aroma and flavor of coffee. He measures the freshness of roasted coffee in hours and days, instead of weeks and months. Kleinfeldt started New Harvest Coffee Roasters 10 years ago as a way to pay homage to fresh coffee and build a business around it.

Kleinfeldt observes Starbucks's tremendous success at creating gathering places for people to enjoy coffee and tea—as well as baked goods—in a relaxed social atmosphere. But he also notes with humor that, although cafes and coffee bars were thriving a decade ago, these popular hang-outs "weren't really about coffee. They were about smoothies and cookies. I thought, maybe it's time to get back to basics and roast some coffee." Kleinfeldt recalls that friends and colleagues—fellow coffee fans—felt the same way. He believed that he had a basis to start a business. "We're coffee people," he explains. "There is a like-minded group of people."

Kleinfeldt also points out that the movement toward locally grown or produced foods has been a big help in establishing and building support for his business. "The idea of local coffee starts with the local roaster," he explains. Although the coffee beans themselves are grown elsewhere—mostly on farms in Costa Rica—they are roasted at New Harvest's facility in Rhode Island, where the company is based. "Freshness is a huge factor" in a good cup of coffee, says Kleinfeldt. "Once it's roasted, it's good for about two to twelve days, which is a good incentive to buy local."

Buying local is exactly what retailers and coffee shops such as Blue State Coffee do, creating a collaborative relationship with New Harvest. Alex Payson, COO of Blue State Coffee—a thriving shop in Rhode Island—observes that most of his customers live within a 5- or 10-minute walk from his business. Blue State customers are educated about the coffee they drink. "They want to *know*," says Payson smiling. "We connect with our coffee farmers. Our customers ask about the story *behind* our coffee," including farming practices and working conditions. Payson and his colleagues from New Harvest have traveled together to some of the coffee farms in Costa Rica that grow the beans they purchase. In fact, loyal customers can view the progress of such trips on New Harvest's Facebook page.

Relationships with companies like Blue State Coffee as well as with consumers are the basis for New Harvest's growth as a business. "We need strategic alliances," says Rik Kleinfeldt. "Blue State is a great example of that. They buy into what we're doing and we support what they are doing. They collaborate with us—what's good for Blue State is also good for New Harvest." Blue State educates its customers and employees about the benefits of buying from a local firm like New Harvest, which in turn works with certified organic, free trade growers. When Blue State's workers are able to discuss their products knowledgeably with customers—including where and how they are grown, harvested and roasted—a relationship is developed.

Sharing activities, comments, news, and anecdotes with customers, retailers, and coffee shops through social media such as Facebook and Twitter allows New Harvest to broaden its base without spending more on marketing and advertising. These connections also put a personal face on the company and allow New Harvest to gain important knowledge about the views and preferences of its customers. In addition, they provide valuable opportunities to showcase some of the company's work in the community as well as its support for organizations such as the Rainforest Alliance and New England GreenStart.

"Our mission is to be the leader in our region in developing the palate and expectations of coffee drinkers, in order to create a permanent market for the coffee produced by passionate and skilled growers," states the New Harvest website. For Rik Kleinfeldt's company and customers, coffee is much more than a hot cup of joe in the morning. Coffee—organically grown, freshly roasted, and served locally—represents a sustainable way to do business.

Questions for Critical Thinking

1. Give examples of each of the four factors of production that New Harvest must rely on to be a successful operation. How does each contribute to the firm's success?

2. Visit New Harvest's Facebook page. Note specific examples of the ways in which the firm is using social media to manage its relationships.

3. Rik Kleinfeldt notes the importance of strategic alliances with firms like Blue State Coffee. Describe how you think New Harvest benefits from alliances with not-for-profit organizations such as Rainforest Alliance, New England GreenStart, and Rhode Island PBS.

4. New Harvest builds much of its reputation on its efforts toward environmental sustainability. How does this reputation affect its relationship with consumers?

Sources: New Harvest website, http://www.newharvestcoffee.com, accessed January 27, 2014; Blue State Coffee website, http://www.bluestatecoffee.com, accessed January 27, 2014.

Learning Objectives

[1] Explain the concern for ethical and societal issues.

[2] Describe the contemporary ethical environment.

[3] Discuss how organizations shape ethical conduct.

[4] Describe how businesses can act responsibly to satisfy society.

[5] Explain the ethical responsibilities of businesses to investors and the financial community.

Chapter 2

Business Ethics and Social Responsibility

© loops7/iStockphoto

Ⓟanera Cares®: A Cafe on a Mission

To be socially responsible means more than donating a few dollars to worthy causes, using recyclable packaging, or planting trees. It is about aligning an entire organization's culture with the values of its community. Panera Bread takes corporate social responsibility seriously. Although the $4 billion company donates more than $150 million in food products each year, it wasn't enough. CEO and founder Ron Shaich made it personal by setting up several Panera Care restaurants as "pay what you can" community cafes. These Panera cafes don't have list prices or use cash registers to charge customers. Instead, there is a donation box on the counter with a sign stating, "take what you need; leave your fair share."

The company recently opened its fifth Panera Cares restaurant in Boston. The four restaurants already in operation in other states are covering almost all of their costs, and they run a program to train disadvantaged young men and women who are learning life skills. The company then hires some of those young people to work at Panera. Together, the five restaurants serve more than half a million people.

With Panera Cares and its food donation program, "Panera Bread Foundation," the company is setting a powerful example of corporate social responsibility—building a business based on living its core values. Or as the company's advertising campaign states, "live consciously, eat deliciously." Shaich knows that five pay-what-you-want cafés aren't going to change the world, but he wants the Panera experiment to challenge other companies to demonstrate social responsibility.

Firms like Panera take their corporate social responsibility to a higher level. These firms provide consumers, employees, and society in general with good, wholesome products that respect the environment and embrace the communities they serve. And for Panera, incorporating core values into its organization is a lot like the yeast in its bread dough—it raises the entire organization.[1]

Overview

Panera Bread's work with local communities in the form of Panera Cares® cafes demonstrates how collaboration between business and other groups can bring about change and make a difference in society. Many companies—large and small—are concerned with such issues as poverty and hunger. Seeking answers to such problems sometimes requires a company to forgo short-term profits in favor of longer-term gains. It may also involve creating mutually beneficial solutions, as Panera has done.

Although most organizations strive to combine ethical behavior with profitable operation, some have struggled to overcome major ethical lapses in recent years. Ethical failures in a number of large or well-known firms led to lawsuits against firms. The image of the CEO—and of business in general—suffered as the evening news carried reports of executives pocketing millions of dollars in compensation while their companies floundered.

But sometimes bad news is a prelude to good news. In the wake of such stories, companies have renewed their efforts to conduct themselves in an ethical manner and one that reflects a responsibility to society, to consumers, and to the environment. Recently, the U. S. Sentencing Commission expanded and strengthened its guidelines for ethics compliance programs, and more and more firms began to pay attention to formulating more explicit standards and procedures for ethical behavior. Companies also began to recognize the enormous impact of setting a good rather than a bad example. Today you are likely to hear about the goodwill that companies such as Google, The Walt Disney Company, and Microsoft generate when they give back to their communities by tutoring school kids, reducing their environmental impact, and donating software to not-for-profit groups worldwide.[2]

As we discussed in Chapter 1, the underlying aim of business is to serve customers at a profit. But most companies today try to do more than that, looking for ways to give back to customers, society, and the environment. Sometimes they face difficult questions in the process. When does a company's self-interest conflict with society's and customers' well-being? And must the goal of seeking profits conflict with upholding ethical standards? In response to the second question, a growing number of businesses of all sizes are answering no.

[1]

Concern for Ethical and Societal Issues

business ethics
standards of conduct and moral values regarding right and wrong actions in the work environment.

An organization that wants to prosper over the long term is well advised to consider **business ethics**, the standards of conduct and moral values governing actions and decisions in the work environment. Businesses also must take into account a wide range of social issues, including how a decision will affect the environment, employees, and customers. These issues are at the heart of *social responsibility*, whose primary objective is the enhancement of society's welfare through philosophies, policies, procedures, and actions. In short, businesses must find the proper balance between doing what is right and doing what is profitable. L'Oreal purchases 850 tons of palm oil annually to produce its skin and hair care products. The palm oil is sourced from sustainable plantations certified by the Roundtable on Sustainable Palm Oil, a not-for-profit association of international stakeholders across the palm oil industry. The purchase of palm oil does not threaten forests, biodiversity, or wildlife.[3]

In business, as in life, deciding what is right or wrong in a given situation does not always involve a clear-cut choice. Firms have many responsibilities—to customers, to employees, to investors, and to society as a whole. Sometimes conflicts arise in trying to serve the different needs of these separate constituencies. The ethical values of executives and individual employees at all levels can influence the decisions and actions a business takes. Throughout your own career, you will encounter many situations in which you will need to weigh right and wrong before making a decision or taking action. So we begin our discussion of business ethics by focusing on individual ethics.

Business ethics are also shaped by the ethical climate within an organization. Codes of conduct and ethical standards play increasingly significant roles in businesses in which doing the right thing is both supported and applauded. This chapter demonstrates how a firm can create a framework to encourage—and even demand—high standards of ethical behavior and social responsibility from its employees. The chapter also considers the complex question of what business owes to society and how societal forces mold the actions of businesses. Finally, it examines the influence of business ethics and social responsibility on global business.

Assessment Check ✓

1. To whom do businesses have responsibilities?
2. If a firm is meeting all its responsibilities to others, why do ethical conflicts arise?

[2]

The Contemporary Ethical Environment

Business ethics are now in the spotlight as never before. Companies realize that they have to work harder to earn the trust of the general public, and many have taken on the challenge as if their very survival depends on it. This movement toward *corporate social responsibility* should benefit all—consumers, investors, the environment, and the companies themselves.

Most business owners and managers have built and maintained enduring companies without breaking the rules. One example of a firm with a long-standing commitment to ethical practice is Johnson & Johnson, the giant multinational manufacturer of health care products. The most admired pharmaceutical maker and the ninth most-admired company in the world, according to *Fortune*, Johnson & Johnson has abided by the same basic code of ethics, its well-known credo, for more than 70 years. The credo, reproduced in Figure 2.1, remains the

32   **Part 1** *Business in a Global Environment*

ethical standard against which the company's employees periodically evaluate how well their firm is performing. Management is pledged to address any lapses that are reported. This pledge was recently put to the test when the company recalled 200,000 bottles of infant formula Motrin when it learned the bottles might be contaminated with plastic particles.[4]

Many companies are conscious of how ethical standards can translate into concern for the environment. Recently, The Coca-Cola Company released its global sustainability report, highlighting goals related to women, water, and well-being:

1. to economically empower 5 million women entrepreneurs across its value chain by 2020,

2. to meet 2020 water use and efficiency reduction and replenishment goals, and

3. to offer more than 800 low- and no-calorie options worldwide or 25 percent of its global product portfolio.

The company's commitment to reduce its environmental impact by 25 percent by 2020 is an ambitious new goal that is part of its climate protection program.[5]

In its latest National Business Ethics Survey, the Ethics Resource Center found that workplace misconduct appears to be at an all-time low, with more employees willing to report such behavior when they witness it. However, workers also said that although ethical cultures were stronger, some felt more pressure to cut corners to save money and get the job done, particularly in a challenging economy.[6]

The **Sarbanes-Oxley Act of 2002** established new rules and regulations for securities trading and accounting practices. Companies are now required to publish their code of ethics, if they have one, and inform the public of any changes made to it. The law may actually motivate even more firms to develop written codes and guidelines for ethical business behavior. The federal government also created the U.S. Sentencing Commission to institutionalize ethics compliance programs that would establish high ethical standards and end corporate misconduct. The requirements for such programs are shown in Table 2.1.

The current ethical environment of business also includes the appointment of new corporate officers specifically charged with deterring wrongdoing and ensuring that ethical standards are met. Ethics compliance officers, whose numbers are rapidly rising, are responsible for conducting employee training programs that help spot potential fraud and abuse within the firm, investigating sexual harassment and discrimination charges, and monitoring any potential conflicts of interest. But practicing corporate social responsibility is more than just monitoring behavior. Many companies now adopt a three-pronged approach to ethics and social responsibility:

1. engaging in traditional corporate philanthropy, which involves giving to worthy causes

2. anticipating and managing risks

3. identifying opportunities to create value by doing the right thing.[7]

FIGURE **2.1**

Johnson & Johnson Credo

Our Credo

We believe our first responsibility is to the doctors, nurses and patients, to mothers and fathers and all others who use our products and services. In meeting their needs everything we do must be of high quality. We must constantly strive to reduce our costs in order to maintain reasonable prices. Customers' orders must be serviced promptly and accurately. Our suppliers and distributors must have an opportunity to make a fair profit.

We are responsible to our employees, the men and women who work with us throughout the world. Everyone must be considered as an individual. We must respect their dignity and recognize their merit. They must have a sense of security in their jobs. Compensation must be fair and adequate, and working conditions clean, orderly and safe. We must be mindful of ways to help our employees fulfill their family responsibilities. Employees must feel free to make suggestions and complaints. There must be equal opportunity for employment, development and advancement for those qualified. We must provide competent management, and their actions must be just and ethical.

We are responsible to the communities in which we live and work and to the world community as well. We must be good citizens—support good works and charities and bear our fair share of taxes. We must encourage civic improvements and better health and education. We must maintain in good order the property we are privileged to use, protecting the environment and natural resources.

Our final responsibility is to our stockholders. Business must make a sound profit. We must experiment with new ideas. Research must be carried on, innovative programs developed and mistakes paid for. New equipment must be purchased, new facilities provided and new products launched. Reserves must be created to provide for adverse times. When we operate according to these principles, the stockholders should realize a fair return.

Source: "Our Company Credo," Johnson & Johnson website, http://www.jnj.com, accessed January 17, 2014, © Johnson & Johnson.

Sarbanes-Oxley Act of 2002 federal legislation designed to deter and punish corporate and accounting fraud and corruption and to protect the interests of workers and shareholders through enhanced financial disclosures, criminal penalties on CEOs and CFOs who defraud investors, safeguards for whistle-blowers, and establishment of a new regulatory body for public accounting firms.

Chapter 2 *Business Ethics and Social Responsibility* **33**

TABLE 2.1

Minimum Requirements for Ethics Compliance Programs

Compliance standards and procedures. Establish standards and procedures, such as codes of ethics and identification of areas of risk, capable of reducing misconduct or criminal activities.
High-level personnel responsibility. Assign high-level personnel, such as boards of directors and top executives, the overall responsibility to actively lead and oversee ethics compliance programs.
Due care in assignments. Avoid delegating authority to individuals with a propensity for misconduct or illegal activities.
Communication of standards and procedures. Communicate ethical requirements to high-level officials and other employees through ethics training programs or publications that explain in practical terms what is required.
Establishment of monitoring and auditing systems and reporting system. Monitor and review ethical compliance systems, and establish a reporting system employees can use to notify the organization of misconduct without fear of retribution.
Enforcement of standards through appropriate mechanisms. Consistently enforce ethical codes, including employee discipline.
Appropriate responses to the offense. Take reasonable steps to respond to the offense and to prevent and detect further violations.
Self-reporting. Report misconduct to the appropriate government agency.
Applicable industry practice or standards. Follow government regulations and industry standards.

Sources: "An Overview of the United States Sentencing Commission and the Federal Sentencing Guidelines," Ethics and Policy Integration Centre, accessed January 17, 2014, http://www.epic-online.net; "The Relationship between Law and Ethics, and the Significance of the Federal Sentencing Guidelines for Organizations," Ethics and Policy Integration Centre, accessed January 17, 2014, http://www.ethicaledge.com; U.S. Sentencing Commission, "Sentencing Commission Toughens Requirements for Corporate Compliance and Ethics Programs," USSC news release, http://www.ussc.gov, accessed January 17, 2014.

Individuals Make a Difference

In today's business environment, individuals can make the difference in ethical expectations and behavior. As executives, managers, and employees demonstrate their personal ethical principles—or lack of ethical principles—the expectations and actions of those who work for and with them can change.

What is the current status of individual business ethics in the United States? Although ethical behavior can be difficult to track or define in all circumstances, evidence suggests that some individuals do act unethically or illegally on the job. The National Business Ethics Survey identifies such behaviors as putting one's own interests ahead of the organization, abuse of company resources, misreporting hours worked, Internet abuse, and safety violations, among others.[8]

Technology seems to have expanded the range and impact of unethical behavior. For example, anyone with computer access to data has the potential to steal or manipulate the data or to shut down the system, even from a remote location. Banks, insurance companies, and other financial institutions are often targeted for such attacks. Customers swiping debit and credit cards at Target retail stores became vulnerable when some 110 million accounts were hacked and information made available for sale through a black market website. While some might shrug these occurrences away, in fact they have an impact on how investors, customers, and the general public view a firm. In response to the incident, Target offered customers a 10 percent discount on purchases for a brief time and access to free credit monitoring services for one year.[9]

Nearly every employee, at every level, wrestles with ethical questions at some point or another. Some rationalize questionable behavior by saying, "Everybody's doing it." Others act unethically because they feel pressured in their jobs or have to meet performance quotas. Yet some avoid unethical acts that don't mesh with their personal values and morals. To help you understand the differences in the ways individuals arrive at ethical choices, the next section focuses on how personal ethics and morals develop.

Development of Individual Ethics

Individuals typically develop ethical standards in the three stages shown in Figure 2.2: the preconventional, conventional, and postconventional stages. In stage 1, the preconventional stage, individuals primarily consider their own needs and desires in making decisions. They obey external rules only because they are afraid of punishment or hope to receive rewards if they comply.

In stage 2, the conventional stage, individuals are aware of and act in response to their duty to others, including their obligations to their family members, co-workers, and organizations. The expectations of these groups influence how they choose between what is acceptable and unacceptable in certain situations. Self-interest, however, continues to play a role in decisions.

Stage 3, the postconventional stage, represents the highest level of ethical and moral behavior. The individual is able to move beyond mere self-interest and duty and take the larger needs of society into account as well. He or she has developed personal ethical principles for determining what is right and can apply those principles in a wide variety of situations. One issue that you may face at work is an ethically compromised situation; the "Career Kickstart" feature lists some tips for relying on basic etiquette to help you steer clear.

An individual's stage in moral and ethical development is determined by a large number of factors. Experiences help shape responses to different situations. A person's family, educational, cultural, and religious backgrounds can also play a role, as can the environment within the firm. Individuals can also have different styles of deciding ethical dilemmas, no matter what their stage of moral development.

To help you understand and prepare for the ethical dilemmas you may confront in your career, let's take a closer look at some of the factors involved in solving ethical questions on the job.

On-the-Job Ethical Dilemmas

In the fast-paced world of business, you will sometimes be called on to weigh the ethics of decisions that can affect not just your own future but possibly the future of your fellow workers, your company, and its customers. As already noted, it's not always easy to distinguish between what is right and wrong in many business situations, especially when the needs and concerns of various parties conflict. In the recent past, some CEOs (or their companies) who were accused of wrongdoing simply claimed that they had no idea crimes were being committed, but today's top executives are making a greater effort to be informed of all activities taking place in their firms.

Some clothing retailers donate unworn, unsold garments to charities such as clothing banks. Others, like Sweden-based H&M, destroy and dispose of unsold merchandise.

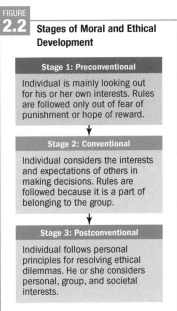

FIGURE 2.2 Stages of Moral and Ethical Development

Stage 1: Preconventional

Individual is mainly looking out for his or her own interests. Rules are followed only out of fear of punishment or hope of reward.

Stage 2: Conventional

Individual considers the interests and expectations of others in making decisions. Rules are followed because it is a part of belonging to the group.

Stage 3: Postconventional

Individual follows personal principles for resolving ethical dilemmas. He or she considers personal, group, and societal interests.

How to Avoid Ethical Issues at Work

You might be surprised to discover how easy it is to make an ethical slip at work. If you've mastered the fundamentals of business etiquette, however, you'll have a good ethical foundation for making good decisions in tough situations. Here are some guidelines:

- *Stay focused on your business purpose.* If you develop a close personal relationship with a client or supplier, you may risk a conflict of interest.
- *Don't abuse privileges.* It's tempting to use sick days or personal days for mini-vacations, but if your company distinguishes between these breaks, you should too.
- *Live your values.* Few people are brought up to be untrustworthy. Even if no one knows about it, an unethical choice that betrays your personal values weakens your self-respect and reduces your contribution to the workplace.
- *Don't depend on excuses.* If you're constantly making excuses for your behavior, what does that say about your behavior?
- *Monitor your digital reputation.* Never post anything online you wouldn't want to see on the news tomorrow.
- *Don't steal.* Using your work computer for personal tasks like shopping and social networking is just as much theft of company resources as is taking home office supplies.
- *Treat others as you would be treated.* This rule never fails to point the way to ethical behavior and decisions you can be proud of.

Sources: Pamela Eyring, "Modern Etiquette: Minding Your Manners in the Workplace," *Reuters*, accessed January 17, 2014, www.reuters.com; Susan M. Healthfield, "Did You Bring Your Ethics to Work Today?" *About.com*, accessed January 17, 2014, http://humanresources.about.com; Lydia Ramsey, "The Top Twelve Business Etiquette Tips for Social Media," *Business Know How*, accessed January 17, 2014, www.businessknowhow.com.

H&M's practice came to the attention of a student in New York City. When her offer to help put H&M in contact with aid organizations went unanswered, the student contacted *The New York Times*, which published a story detailing how H&M—among other retailers—routinely mutilated unsold garments before discarding them to render them unsalable by street vendors or other black-market sellers. The story prompted H&M management to stop destroying unsold clothing. H&M recently introduced a new initiative in its stores: collecting used garments, which would otherwise end up in landfills, to reduce textile waste and convert into new yarn. In addition, H&M's Conscious Collection consists of sustainable fashion garments made from organic cotton, recycled linen, and hemp.[10]

Businesses may sometimes refuse to purchase goods or services from a particular country because of rights abuses by the government of that country. The United States currently prohibits the importation of rubies, jade, and articles of jewelry that contain these gems from Myanmar. The ban is the result of human rights abuses in the profitable gem sector controlled by Myanmar's military.[11]

Solving ethical dilemmas is not easy. In many cases, each possible decision can have both unpleasant consequences and positive benefits that must be evaluated. The ethical issues that confront manufacturers with unsold merchandise are just one example of many different types of ethical questions encountered in the workplace. Figure 2.3 identifies four of the most common ethical challenges that businesspeople face: conflict of interest, honesty and integrity, loyalty versus truth, and whistle-blowing.

conflict of interest situation in which an employee must choose between a business's welfare and personal gain.

Conflict of Interest A conflict of interest occurs when a businessperson is faced with a situation in which an action benefiting one person or group has the potential to harm another. Conflicts of interest may pose ethical challenges when they involve the businessperson's own interests and those of someone to whom he or she has a duty or when they involve two parties to whom the businessperson has a duty. Lawyers, business consultants, or advertising agencies would face a conflict of interest if they represented two competing companies: a strategy that would most benefit one of the client companies might harm the other client. Handling the situation responsibly would be possible, but it would also be difficult. A conflict may also exist between someone's personal interests and those of an organization or its customers. An offer of gifts or bribes for special treatment creates a situation in which the buyer, but not necessarily the company, may benefit personally.

A conflict of interest may also occur when one person holds two or more similar jobs in two different workplaces. Ethical ways to handle conflicts of interest include (1) avoiding them and (2) disclosing them. Some companies have policies against taking on clients who are competitors of existing clients. Most businesses and government agencies have written policies prohibiting employees from accepting gifts or specifying a maximum gift value. Or a member of a board of directors or committee might abstain from voting on a decision in which he or she has a personal interest. In other situations, people state their potential conflict of interest so that the people affected can decide whether to get information or help they need from another source instead.

Honesty and Integrity Employers highly value honesty and integrity. An employee who is honest can be counted on to tell the truth. An employee with <u>integrity</u> goes beyond truthfulness. Having integrity means adhering to deeply felt ethical principles in business situations. It includes doing what you say you will do and accepting responsibility for mistakes. Behaving with honesty and integrity inspires trust, and as a result, it can help build long-term relationships with customers, employers, suppliers, and the public. Employees, in turn, want their managers and the company as a whole to treat them honestly and with integrity.

Unfortunately, violations of honesty and integrity are all too common. Some people misrepresent their academic credentials and previous work experience on their résumés or job applications. Although it may seem tempting to embellish a résumé in a competitive job market, the act shows a lack of honesty and integrity—and eventually it will catch up with you. A technology CEO resigned after it was discovered that a degree he allegedly "earned" was not offered by the university cited on his résumé.[12]

Others steal from their employers by taking home supplies or products without permission or by carrying out personal business during the time they are being paid to work. For example, Internet misuse during the work day is increasing. Employees use the Internet for personal shopping, e-mail, gaming, and social networking. This misuse costs U.S. companies an estimated $85 billion annually in lost productivity.[13] While the occurrence of such activity varies widely—and employers may feel more strongly about cracking down on some activities than others—most agree that Internet misuse is a problem. Some have resorted to electronic monitoring and surveillance. Compliance with laws regarding the privacy and security of client information is another major reason given for the continuing increase in such monitoring.

Loyalty versus Truth Businesspeople expect their employees to be loyal and to act in the best interests of the company. But when the truth about a company is not favorable, an ethical conflict can arise. Individuals may have to decide between loyalty to the company and truthfulness in business relationships. People resolve such dilemmas in various ways. Some place the highest value on loyalty, even at the expense of truth. Others avoid volunteering negative information but answer truthfully if someone asks them a specific question. People may emphasize truthfulness and actively disclose negative information, especially if the cost of silence is high, as in the case of operating a malfunctioning aircraft or selling tainted food items.

Whistle-Blowing When an individual encounters unethical or illegal actions at work, that person must decide what action to take. Sometimes it is possible to resolve the problem by working through channels within the organization. If that fails, the person should weigh the potential damages to the greater public good. If the damage is significant, a person may conclude that the only solution is to blow the whistle. <u>Whistle-blowing</u> is an employee's disclosure to company officials, government authorities, or the media of illegal, immoral, or unethical practices.

A whistle-blower must weigh a number of issues in deciding whether to come forward. Resolving an ethical problem within the organization can be more effective, assuming higher-level managers cooperate. A company that values ethics will try to correct a problem; staying at a company that does not value ethics may not be worthwhile. In some cases, however,

FIGURE 2.3 Common Business Ethical Challenges

- Conflict of Interest
- Honesty and Integrity
- Whistle-Blowing
- Loyalty versus Truth

Ethical Challenges

integrity adhering to deeply felt ethical principles in business situations.

whistle-blowing employee's disclosure to company officials, government authorities, or the media of illegal, immoral, or unethical practices committed by an organization.

Chapter 2 *Business Ethics and Social Responsibility* **37**

Employers and employees value honesty and integrity, but what should happen when employees misuse Internet privileges for personal purposes?

people resort to whistle-blowing because they believe the unethical behavior is causing significant damage that outweighs the risk that the company will retaliate against the whistle-blower. Those risks have been real in some cases.

State and federal laws protect whistle-blowers in certain situations, such as reports of discrimination, and the Sarbanes-Oxley Act of 2002 now requires that firms in the private sector provide procedures for anonymous reporting of accusations of fraud. Under the act, anyone who retaliates against an employee for taking concerns of unlawful conduct to a public official can be prosecuted. In addition, whistle-blowers can seek protection under the False Claims Act, under which they can file a lawsuit on behalf of the government if they believe that a company has somehow defrauded the government. Charges against health care companies for fraudulent billing for Medicare or Medicaid are examples of this type of lawsuit.

Despite these protections, whistle-blowing has its risks. When employee Hector Aldana reported safety concerns to his supervisor and the human resources director at Virgin America Airlines, his worries fell on deaf ears. After making numerous attempts to alert management officials, Aldana warned that he would have to contact the FAA. Aldana was immediately fired. Within a short time, he was not only jobless but also bankrupt and homeless. When later asked if the current whistle-blowing laws protected him, Aldana replied with an emphatic "no."[14]

Obviously, whistle-blowing and other ethical issues arise relatively infrequently in firms with strong organizational climates of ethical behavior. The next section examines how a business can develop an environment that discourages unethical behavior among individuals.

Assessment Check ✅

1. What role can an ethics compliance officer play in a firm?

2. What are the three components of a typical company's approach to ethics and social responsibility?

⌐3⌐ How Organizations Shape Ethical Conduct

No individual makes decisions in a vacuum. Choices are strongly influenced by the standards of conduct established within the organizations where people work. Most ethical lapses in business reflect the values of the firms' corporate cultures.

As shown in Figure 2.4, development of a corporate culture to support business ethics happens on four levels:

1. ethical awareness,

2. ethical education,

3. ethical action, and

4. ethical leadership.

If any of these four factors is missing, the ethical climate in an organization will weaken.

Ethical Awareness

The foundation of an ethical climate is ethical awareness. As we have already seen, ethical dilemmas occur frequently in the workplace. So employees need help in identifying ethical problems when they occur. Workers also need guidance about how the firm expects them to respond.

One way for a firm to provide this support is to develop a code of conduct, a formal statement that defines how the organization expects employees to resolve ethical questions. According to its code of business conduct and ethics, LinkedIn expects its employees to "act and perform their duties ethically, honestly, and with integrity—doing the right thing even when no one is looking."[15] Johnson & Johnson's credo, presented earlier, is such a code. At the most basic level, a code of conduct may simply specify ground rules for acceptable behavior, such as identifying the laws and regulations that employees must obey. Other companies use their codes of conduct to identify key corporate values and provide frameworks that guide employees as they resolve moral and ethical dilemmas. Some companies use these to guide employees' online behavior, as the "Solving an Ethical Controversy" box suggests.

The aerospace giant Lockheed Martin, headquartered in Bethesda, Maryland, and with branch offices around the world, has issued a code of conduct to define its values and help employees put them into practice. The code of conduct emphasizes "maintaining a culture of integrity" and defines three basic core values: "Do what's right; respect others; perform with excellence." All employees at every level are expected to treat fellow employees, suppliers, and customers with dignity and respect and to comply with environmental, health, and safety regulations. The code reminds leaders that their language and behavior must not put or even seem to put pressure on subordinates that might induce them to perform in a way that is contrary to the standards set forth in the code. The code also outlines procedures for reporting violations to a local company ethics officer, promising confidentiality and nonretaliation for problems reported in good faith. Lockheed Martin issues a copy of this code of conduct to each employee and also posts it (in 17 languages) on its website.[16] Other firms incorporate similar codes in their policy manuals or mission statements; some issue a code of conduct or statement of values in the form of a small card that employees and managers can carry with them.

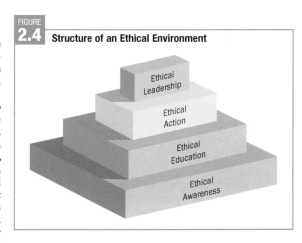

FIGURE 2.4 Structure of an Ethical Environment

- Ethical Leadership
- Ethical Action
- Ethical Education
- Ethical Awareness

code of conduct formal statement that defines how an organization expects its employees to resolve ethical issues.

Ethical Education

Although a code of conduct can provide an overall framework, it cannot detail a solution for every ethical situation. Some ethical questions have black-and-white answers, but others do not. Businesses must provide the tools employees need to evaluate the options and arrive at suitable decisions.

Many firms have either instituted their own ethics training programs or hired organizations such as SAI Global, which provides outsourced ethics and compliance programs to businesses. Among other services, SAI Global hosts employee reporting services with an anonymous hotline and an ethics case management system. It also helps companies develop appropriate ethics codes with training customized to each company's needs, including specialized online, interactive training systems.[17]

Many authorities debate whether ethics can be taught, but training can give employees the chance to practice applying ethical values to hypothetical situations before they face real-world situations. Similar strategies are being used in many business school ethics programs, where case studies and practical scenarios work best. Convicted white-collar criminal Walter Pavlo, a former employee at telecommunications firm MCI, speaks at colleges and universities about

Solving an Ethical Controversy

The Need for Social Networking Policies

A recent survey of 120 multinational firms found that while 76 percent use social networking for business, nearly half lack social networking policies. It's probably not surprising, then, that 43 percent have experienced employee misuse of these sites, and nearly one in three has been forced to take disciplinary action. About a quarter of the firms block employee access to social networks, and another quarter permit access at work but monitor it. Should firms also restrict what employees do online in their off-hours?

Should firms control employees' off-duty use of social networks?

PRO

1. An Ethics Resource Center survey shows nearly half of U.S. employees observed a legal or ethical lapse at work, to which the use of social media "appears to be contributing."

2. Employees increasingly believe employees must be expected to properly represent the organization at all times, including at home and online.

CON

1. Some states have laws that protect employees engaged in legal recreational activities when they're not working, which may be construed to include accessing social networks.

2. Companies should hire people they can trust to govern their own behavior.

Summary

This question will continue to be debated. Meanwhile, regardless of the path they choose, companies should hire people they trust; discourage employees from developing personal relationships with clients, bosses, or subordinates; issue clear guidelines for posting company information; and act promptly on any inappropriate employee posts.

Sources: Jeanne Meister, "To Do: Update Company's Social Media Policy ASAP," *Forbes*, accessed January 20, 2014, www.forbes.com; Chad Brooks, "Social Media Contributes to Ethical Lapses at Work," *Business News Daily*, accessed January 20, 2014, www.businessnewsdaily.com; "Charting the Industry: When Social Networking Gets Personal," *PR News*, accessed January 20, 2014, www.prnewsonline.com.

---

his experiences in the firm and prison. Pavlo, who along with other MCI associates stashed money in offshore accounts, speaks about his actions in an effort to warn students of the consequences of cheating.

Ethical Action

Codes of conduct and ethics training help employees recognize and reason through ethical problems. In addition, firms must provide structures and approaches that allow decisions to be turned into ethical actions. Texas Instruments gives its employees a reference card to help them make ethical decisions on the job. The size of a standard business card, it lists the following guidelines:

- Is the action legal?
- Does it comply with our values?
- If you do it, will you feel bad?
- How will it look in the newspaper?
- If you know it's wrong, don't do it!

- If you're not sure, ask.

- Keep asking until you get an answer.

Goals set for the business as a whole and for individual departments and employees can affect ethical behavior. A firm whose managers set unrealistic goals for employee performance may find an increase in cheating, lying, and other misdeeds, as employees attempt to protect themselves. In today's Internet economy, the high value placed on speed can create a climate in which ethical behavior is sometimes challenged. Ethical decisions often require careful and quiet thought, a challenging task in today's fast-paced business world.

Some companies encourage ethical action by providing support for employees faced with dilemmas. One common tool is an employee hotline, a telephone number that employees can call, often anonymously, for advice or to report unethical behavior they have witnessed. Ethics compliance officers, as mentioned previously, can guide employees through ethical minefields.

Ethical Leadership

Executives must not only talk about ethical behavior but also demonstrate it in their actions. This requires employees to be personally committed to the company's core values and be willing to base their actions on them. The recent recession exposed executive-level misdeeds that damaged or even destroyed entire organizations and wiped out people's life savings. In the aftermath, some organizations and business leaders have made a commitment to demonstrate ethical leadership and increased social responsibility.

The owner of several juice bars paid her employees to take work shifts where their only job was to perform random acts of kindness—acts that would brighten someone else's day. The "22 Days of Kindness" program was a huge success not only among the company employees but also among members of the community. After the kindness campaign was featured in the local media, the business owner was flooded with applications from people who wanted to work for her company.[18]

Unfortunately, not all organizations are able to build a solid framework of business ethics. Because the damage from ethical misconduct can powerfully affect a firm's **stakeholders** — customers, investors, employees, and the public—pressure is exerted on businesses to act in acceptable ways. But when businesses fail, the law must step in to enforce good business practices. Many of the laws that affect specific industries or individuals are described in other chapters in this book. For example, legislation affecting international business operations is discussed in Chapter 4. Laws designed to assist small businesses are examined in Chapter 5.

Laws related to labor unions are described in Chapter 8. Legislation related to banking and the securities markets is discussed in Chapters 16 and 17. Finally, for an examination of the legal and governmental forces designed to safeguard society's interests when businesses fail at self-regulation, see Appendix A, "Business Law."

stakeholders
customers, investors, employees, and public affected by or with an interest in a company.

Assessment Check ☑

1. Identify the four levels of a company's ethical environment.

2. How does ethical leadership contribute to ethical standards throughout a company?

[4] ## Acting Responsibly to Satisfy Society

A second major issue affecting business is the question of social responsibility. In a general sense, **social responsibility** is management's acceptance of the obligation to consider profit, consumer satisfaction, and societal well-being of equal value in evaluating the firm's performance. It is the recognition that business must be concerned with the qualitative dimensions of consumer, employee, and societal benefits, as well as the quantitative measures of sales and

social responsibility
business's consideration of society's well-being and consumer satisfaction, in addition to profits.

Going Green

Thinking Outside the Box

Packing and moving involves many decisions: Where to get boxes to pack possessions? How to get rid of the boxes once the move has taken place? Marty Metro has a solution.

Metro is the founder of UsedCardboardBoxes.com (UCB), a multi-million dollar Los Angeles–based company. He has built a business around buying and reselling used cardboard boxes—not just for moves, but for packing, shipping, and storage.

The idea for UCB came to Metro when he saw people throwing out perfectly good cardboard boxes after a move. Manufacturing and recycling cardboard boxes uses energy and produces emissions, which negatively impacts the environment. A zero-waste company, UCB purchases truck-loads of quality used boxes from large companies for a little more money than the company would pay to have them taken away and recycled.

UCB packs the used boxes with other accessories into low-cost kits for consumers, which consist of boxes in shapes and sizes typically used by do-it-yourself movers and professional moving companies. Metro assures his customers that each rescued box must undergo three quality inspections before being sold to them. If a box fails inspection, it is recycled by UCB.

Questions for Critical Thinking

1. Metro has created a successful company with an innovative strategy of buying and using cardboard boxes multiple times before they are recycled. How does this approach help both businesses and consumers?

2. In addition to being successful, Metro's company website states that more than 600,000 trees have been saved by UCB's business model. How can Metro use that information to attract new business and residential customers?

Sources: Company website, "About Us," www.usedcardboardboxes.com, accessed January 20, 2014; Michael Cyger, "UsedCardboardBoxes.com: From Storefront Failure to Dot Com Success—With Marty Metro," *Domain Sherpa*, accessed January 20, 2014, www.domainsherpa.com; Deborah Sweeney, "Entrepreneur Spotlight on UsedCardboardBoxes.com Founder Marty Metro," *Forbes*, accessed January 20, 2014, www.forbes.com; Lisa Girard, "From Business Failure to Multimillion-Dollar 'Green' Niche," *Entrepreneur*, accessed January 20, 2014, www.entrepreneur.com.

---

profits, by which business performance is traditionally measured. Businesses may exercise social responsibility because such behavior is required by law, because it enhances the company's image, or because management believes it is the ethical course of action. The "Going Green" feature tells the story of how a business owner saw a way to reuse cardboard boxes instead of throwing them away.

Historically, a company's social performance has been measured by its contribution to the overall economy and the employment opportunities it provides. Variables such as total wages paid often indicate social performance. Although profits and employment remain important, today many factors contribute to an assessment of a firm's social performance, including providing equal employment opportunities; respecting the cultural diversity of employees; responding to environmental concerns; providing a safe, healthy workplace; and producing high-quality products that are safe to use.

A business is also judged by its interactions with the community. To demonstrate their social responsibility, many corporations highlight charitable contributions and community service in their annual reports and on their websites. Cisco Systems most recent corporate social responsibility report focuses on improving lives, building communities, and preserving the environment. The company is also committed to improving access to health care in rural parts of the world, developing technologies that can help reduce greenhouse gas emissions, and fostering diversity and ethical standards throughout its business and supply chain.[19]

© Steve Debenport/iStockphoto

Businesses are judged by their interactions with the surrounding community, including employees volunteering at charitable events.

42   **Part 1** *Business in a Global Environment*

Cambridge, Massachusetts–based Bidding for Good is an e-commerce or "charitable commerce" website with a unique online platform that helps schools and not-for-profit organizations raise funds. In the company's "Bidder" community, there are more than 8,000 customers and over 400,000 like-minded shoppers. Taking the place of live auctions, the website auctions donations of everything from hot air balloon rides to overseas vacations.[20]

Some firms measure social performance by conducting **social audits**, formal procedures that identify and evaluate all company activities that relate to social issues such as conservation, employment practices, environmental protection, and philanthropy. The social audit informs management about how well the company is performing in these areas. Based on this information, management may revise current programs or develop new ones.

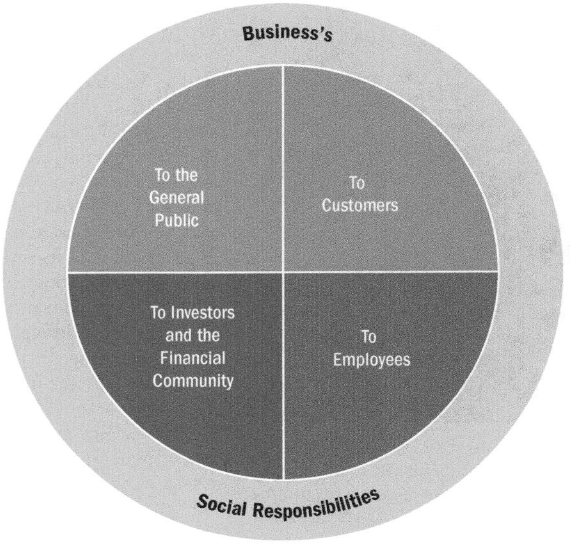

Outside groups may conduct their own evaluations of businesses. Various environmental, religious, and public-interest groups have created standards of corporate performance. Reports on many of these evaluations are available to the general public. The Consumer Financial Protection Bureau (CFPB), for example, is tasked with monitoring banks, credit unions, securities firms, and payday lenders by promoting fairness for consumer mortgages, credit cards, and student loans. CFPB recently ordered a well-known credit card company to refund consumers $75 million for illegal credit card billing and for misleading them about other add-on products like identity theft protection.[21]

As Figure 2.5 shows, the social responsibilities of business can be classified according to its relationships to the general public, customers, employees, and investors and other members of the financial community. Many of these relationships extend beyond national borders.

FIGURE 2.5 Business's Social Responsibilities

social audits
formal procedures that identify and evaluate all company activities that relate to social issues such as conservation, employment practices, environmental protection, and philanthropy.

Responsibilities to the General Public

The responsibilities of business to the general public include dealing with public health issues, protecting the environment, and developing the quality of the workforce. Many would argue that businesses also have responsibilities to support charitable and social causes and organizations that work toward the greater public good. In other words, they should support the communities in which they earn profits. Such efforts are called *corporate philanthropy*.

Public-Health Issues One of the most complex issues facing business as it addresses its ethical and social responsibilities to the general public is public health. Central to the public-health debate is the question of what businesses should do about dangerous products such as tobacco and alcohol. Tobacco products represent a major health risk, contributing to heart disease, stroke, and cancer among smokers. Families and co-workers of smokers share this danger as well, as their exposure to secondhand smoke increases their risks for cancer, asthma, and respiratory infections. Many cities have not only banned smoking in public places, but also in commercial businesses such as restaurants. Several states, including Arkansas, California, Louisiana, and Maine, have bans on smoking in cars when children under the age of 18 are present.[22]

To do their part to aid the general public, some businesses collaborate with urban neighborhoods to set up community gardens as a way of showing kids how to eat healthy.

Heart disease, diabetes, and obesity have become major public health issues as the rates of these three conditions have been rising. According to the Centers for Disease Control and Prevention, the obesity rate for children between the ages of 6 and 11 in the United States has tripled over the last four decades. Three-quarters of obese teenagers will become obese adults at risk for diabetes and heart disease. Jared Fogle became famous for losing 245 pounds over a two-year period through exercise and a diet that included low-fat SUBWAY sandwiches. He has since set up the Jared Foundation with the goal of fighting childhood obesity by encouraging children to develop healthy diet and exercise habits. Spreading his message through speaking tours, grants to schools, and programs for children and their families, Fogle says, "My goal is to help children avoid the physical and emotional hardships I went through living with obesity." SUBWAY's website lists the nutritional values of its menu items and sources of diet and nutrition advice. The website also features a linked page supporting the Jared Foundation and its mission.[23]

Substance abuse is another serious public health problem worldwide. Revelations of the use of illegal steroids by many athletes, particularly in professional baseball, highlight the difficulty of devising accurate tests for performance-enhancing and muscle-building drugs and fairly evaluating the results. Many of the drugs in question are so similar to compounds naturally present in the body that identification is extremely difficult. A scandal linked to professional baseball includes three-time American League MVP Alex Rodriguez, who was recently suspended for an entire baseball season for his use of performance-enhancing drugs. With regard to drug testing, athletes' individual rights to privacy have been questioned, particularly due to their widespread influence on youthful fans. Steroid use is on the rise among high school athletes, despite the publicity about the dangers of such drugs. Tougher penalties for professional players who fail drug tests are being implemented.[24]

Protecting the Environment Businesses impact the environment in a variety of ways—through the energy they consume, the waste they produce, the natural resources they use, and more. Today, many businesses have built goals into their corporate philosophy for taking steps toward protecting the environment. Some have even launched sustainability initiatives—operating in such a way that the firm not only minimizes its impact on the environment, but actually regenerates or replaces used resources. Procter & Gamble and Kaiser Permanente maintain sustainability assessments of their suppliers, rating them on energy and water use, recycling, waste production, greenhouse gases produced, and other factors. Both organizations expect suppliers to meet green standards—or risk losing them as customers.[25]

For many managers, finding ways to minimize pollution and other environmental damage caused by their products or operating processes has become an important economic and legal issue as well as a social one. When Tesla Motors unveiled the Model S, its first new premium, five-door hatchback electric sedan, the car generated a lot of buzz. Running on a lithium battery pack, the Model S has a range of 265 miles.[26]

Despite the efforts of companies like Procter & Gamble, Kaiser Permanente, Tesla Motors, and thousands of others, production and manufacturing methods still leave behind large quantities of waste materials that can further pollute the air, water, and soil. Some products themselves, such as electronics that contain lead and mercury, are difficult to recycle or reuse—although scientists and engineers are finding ways to do this. In other instances, the action (or lack of action) on the part of a firm results in an environmental disaster, as in the case of the 2010 explosion and large-scale spill from BP's offshore drilling rig in the Gulf of Mexico. The months-long spill not only affected the ocean and coastal environments, but also the lives of residents and local economies.[27] Despite the difficulty, however, companies are finding that they can be environmentally friendly and profitable, too. Another solution to the problems of pollutants is **recycling**—reprocessing used materials for reuse. Recycling can sometimes provide much of the raw material that manufacturers need, thereby conserving the world's natural resources and reducing the need for landfills. The "Hit & Miss" feature describes a new take on shopping—"shwopping"—a creative twist on recycling.

recycling reprocessing of used materials for reuse.

44   **Part 1** *Business in a Global Environment*

Hit&Miss

"Shwopping" to Help Others

British multinational retailer Marks & Spencer (M&S) encourages its customers to "shwop" when visiting its more than 700 stores in the UK. "Shwopping"—swapping gently used clothing for a rewards voucher for future retail purchases—has been quite the hit with M&S customers and has helped the retailer become one of the world's most sustainable retailers.

More than 1 billion clothing items are sent to landfills annually, and about 30 percent of clothing in an average wardrobe has not been worn in over a year. M&S created "shwopping" to encourage customers to bring in their gently used clothing to stores for donations to Oxfam, a global charitable organization. Oxfam then resells, reuses, and recycles shwop donations through enterprises in countries around the world to help people living in poverty. Some of the apparel is sold in bulk to companies that reprocess the items as mattresses or car seat filling; other garments are repurposed into fibers for new garments.

M&S's corporate philosophy that old clothes should have a future has been met with overwhelming success. More than 11 million items worth over $13 million have been passed along to Oxfam to be used in third-world regions.

Questions for Critical Thinking

1. Does donating gently used clothes encourage shoppers to purchase new ones? Why or why not?

2. Discuss the benefits of Marks & Spencer's "buy one, give one" culture and how it enhances the retailer's social responsibility initiatives.

Sources: Company website, "Oxfam Change the World Shwop," www.marksandspencers .com, accessed January 20, 2014; organization website, "Oxfam and Marks & Spencer Shwopping Partnership," www.sofii.org, accessed January 20, 2014; organization website, www.oxfam.org, accessed January 20, 2014; Sally Williams, "The Other Rag Trade: Joanna Lumley Goes 'Shwopping' with Marks & Spencer's in Senegal," *Telegraph*, accessed January 20, 2014, http://fashion.telegraph.co.uk.

According to the Environmental Protection Agency, discarded electronic items now make up as much as 40 percent of the lead in landfills in the United States. The Institute of Scrap Recycling Industries estimates that about 8.8 billion pounds of used and end-of-life electronic equipment were recycled in a recent year.[28] Firms such as Best Buy are trying to make it easier for consumers to recycle their unwanted electronics, no matter where they bought them. Free of charge, consumers can drop off ink and toner cartridges, rechargeable batteries, and cables, wires, cords, and other small items in kiosks at store entrances. Best Buy also accepts larger items for recycling, such as PCs, VCRs, DVD players, TVs, and computer monitors, and offers Best Buy gift cards for gently used consumer electronics. Other retailers such as Target and Apple offer recycling and trade-in programs, while service providers such as AT&T and Verizon provide drop-off locations for phones and other equipment. At over 3,600 U.S. Walmart stores and Sam's Club locations, a trade-in program for smart phones is under way in an effort to keep them out of landfills.[29]

Many consumers have favorable impressions of environmentally conscious businesses. To target these customers, companies often use **green marketing**, a marketing strategy that promotes environmentally safe products and production methods. A business cannot simply claim that its goods or services are environmentally friendly, however. The Federal Trade Commission (FTC) has issued guidelines for businesses to follow in making environmental claims. A firm must be able to prove that any environmental claim made about a product has been substantiated with reliable scientific evidence. In addition, as shown in Figure 2.6, the FTC has given specific directions about how various environmental terms may be used in advertising and marketing.

Other environmental issues—such as finding renewable sources of clean energy and developing **sustainable** agriculture—are the focus of many firms' efforts. Sun Microsystems founder Vinod Khosla works with a group of entrepreneurs and investors in Silicon Valley to develop a new generation of energy, known as clean tech.[30] Solar energy, geothermal energy, biodiesel, and wind power are just a few of the renewable sources of energy being developed by entrepreneurs, large energy firms, and small engineering companies.

Mars Incorporated, the maker of Dove Chocolate and other candies, has committed to using only sustainably grown cocoa in all of its chocolate products by 2020. Its Dove dark chocolate line represents the first of its products to be made with the cocoa.[31]

green marketing a marketing strategy that promotes environmentally safe products and production methods.

sustainable the capacity to endure in ecology.

Chapter 2 *Business Ethics and Social Responsibility*   **45**

FIGURE 2.6 FTC Guidelines for Environmental Claims in Green Marketing

If a business says a product is ...	The product or package must ...
Biodegradable	break down and return to nature in a reasonably short period of time.
Recyclable	be entirely reusable as new materials in the manufacture or assembly of a new product or package.
Refillable	be included in a system for the collection and return of the package for refill. If consumers have to find a way to refill it themselves, it is not **refillable**.
Ozone Safe/Ozone Friendly	must not contain any ozone-depleting ingredient.

Developing the Quality of the Workforce In the past, a nation's wealth has often been based on its money, production equipment, and natural resources. A country's true wealth, however, lies in its people. An educated, skilled workforce provides the intellectual know-how required to develop new technology, improve productivity, and compete in the global market-place. It is becoming increasingly clear that to remain competitive, U.S. business must assume more responsibility for enhancing the quality of its workforce, including encouraging diversity of all kinds.

In developed economies like that of the United States, many new jobs require college-educated workers. With an increased demand for workers with advanced skills, the difference between the highest-paid and lowest-paid workers has been increasing. Education plays an important role in earnings, despite success stories of those who dropped out of college or high school to start businesses. Workers with a college degree earn an average of $1,174 a week, whereas those with some high school but no diploma earn less than $500.[32] Businesses must encourage students to stay in school, continue their education, and sharpen their skills. Amazon sponsors a career choice program for full-time hourly employees working at its many fulfillment centers around the country. The company will pay up to 95 percent of tuition, textbooks, and associated fees up to $3,000 a year for four years. The company says it will pay for study in areas that are well paying and in high demand, such as aircraft mechanics, machine tool technology, and medical laboratory science—funding education in those areas regardless of whether those skills are relevant to a career at Amazon.[33]

Organizations also face enormous responsibilities for helping women, members of various cultural groups, returning military veterans, and those who are physically challenged to contribute fully to the economy. Failure to do so is not only a waste of more than half the nation's workforce but also devastating to a firm's public image. Some socially responsible firms also encourage diversity in their business suppliers. A recent list of DiversityInc's top companies for supplier diversity include AT&T, Marriott International, Health Care Service Corporation, Hilton Worldwide, Windham Worldwide, KeyCorp, Accenture, Abbott, WellPoint, and Union Bank.[34]

Corporate Philanthropy As Chapter 1 pointed out, not-for-profit organizations play an important role in society by serving the public good. They provide the

Recycling can help companies do their part to protect the environment. Best Buy stores will take your old TVs, DVD players, computers, cell phones, and other electronic devices to avoid having them end up in landfills.

human resources that enhance the quality of life in communities around the world. To fulfill this mission, many not-for-profit organizations rely on financial contributions from the business community. Firms respond by donating billions of dollars each year to not-for-profit organizations. This **corporate philanthropy** includes cash contributions, donations of equipment and products, and supporting the volunteer efforts of company employees. Recipients include cultural organizations, adopt-a-school programs, neighborhood sports programs, and housing and job training programs.

Corporate philanthropy can have many positive benefits beyond the purely "feel-good" rewards of giving, such as higher employee morale, enhanced company image, and improved customer relationships. General Mills, for instance, is a major contributor to Susan G. Komen, a foundation dedicated to curing breast cancer, through its line of yogurt products marketed under the Yoplait brand name. Yoplait's target market is health-conscious women, the same group most likely to know of or become involved with the foundation's fund-raising efforts. Through its other brands, General Mills sponsors other nationwide initiatives that support education, families, and community improvement projects.[35]

Corporate philanthropy can enhance a company's customer relationships. Through sales of its Yoplait yogurt line, General Mills contributes to Susan G. Komen, a charity that supports breast cancer research.

Companies often seek to align their marketing efforts with their charitable giving. Many contribute to the Olympics and create advertising that features the company's sponsorship. This is known as *cause-related marketing*. In a recent survey, nearly nine out of ten young people said they believed companies had a duty to support social causes, and nearly seven in eight said they would switch brands in order to reward a company that did so. Consumers are often willing to pay even more for a product, such as Newman's Own salad dressings and salsa, because they know the proceeds are going to a good cause.

Another form of corporate philanthropy is volunteerism. In their roles as corporate citizens, thousands of businesses encourage their employees to contribute their efforts to projects as diverse as Habitat for Humanity, the Red Cross, and the Humane Society. In addition to making tangible contributions to the well-being of fellow citizens, such programs generate considerable public support and goodwill for the companies and their employees. In some cases, the volunteer efforts occur mostly during off-hours for employees. In other instances, firms permit their workforces to volunteer during regular working hours. Sometimes volunteers with special skills are indispensable. In response to the recent super typhoon in the Philippines, corporate philanthropy included generous support from Bank of America, Travelers Insurance, and PepsiCo, among others.[36]

Responsibilities to Customers

Businesspeople share a social and ethical responsibility to treat their customers fairly and act in a manner that is not harmful to them. **Consumerism**—the public demand that a business consider the wants and needs of its customers in making decisions—has gained widespread acceptance. Consumerism is based on the belief that consumers have certain rights. A frequently quoted statement of consumer rights was made by President John F. Kennedy in 1962. Figure 2.7 summarizes those consumer rights. Numerous state and federal laws have been implemented since then to protect the rights.

The Right to Be Safe Contemporary businesspeople must recognize obligations, both moral and legal, to ensure the safe operation of their products. Consumers should feel assured

corporate philanthropy effort of an organization to make a contribution to the communities in which it earns profits.

consumerism public demand that a business consider the wants and needs of its customers in making decisions.

FIGURE
2.7

Consumer Rights as Proposed by President Kennedy

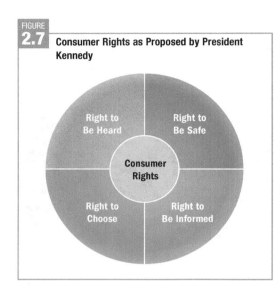

product liability
the responsibility of manufacturers for injuries and damages caused by their products.

that the products they purchase will not cause injuries in normal use. **Product liability** refers to the responsibility of manufacturers for injuries and damages caused by their products. Items that lead to injuries, either directly or indirectly, can have disastrous consequences for their makers.

Many companies put their products through rigorous testing to avoid safety problems. Still, testing alone cannot foresee every eventuality. Companies must try to consider all possibilities and provide adequate warning of potential dangers. When a product does pose a threat to customer safety, a responsible manufacturer responds quickly to either correct the problem or recall the dangerous product. Although we take for granted that our food—and our pets' food—is safe, sometimes contamination leaks in, which can cause illness or even death. Recently a concern about salmonella, a microorganism that produces dangerous infections, caused Procter & Gamble to issue a voluntary recall of dry pet food under the IAMS and Eukanuba brands. No illnesses or deaths were reported, but the company wanted to be certain the products were safe for pets to consume.[37]

The Right to Be Informed Consumers should have access to enough education and product information to make responsible buying decisions. In their efforts to promote and sell their goods and services, companies can easily neglect consumers' right to be fully informed. False or misleading advertising is a violation of the Wheeler-Lea Act, a federal law enacted in 1938. The FTC and other federal and state agencies have established rules and regulations that govern advertising truthfulness. These rules prohibit businesses from making unsubstantiated claims about the performance or superiority of their merchandise. They also require businesses to avoid misleading consumers. Businesses that fail to comply face scrutiny from the FTC and consumer protection organizations. The FTC recently required General Mills to eliminate pictures of strawberries from the packaging for its Strawberry Naturally Flavored Fruit Roll-Ups—because the product is made with pear concentrate, not strawberries. The company must also identify the amount of fruit juice it uses in the product if it continues to use the words "Made with Real Fruit" on the wrapper. These actions are the result of a consumer lawsuit.[38]

The Food and Drug Administration (FDA), which sets standards for advertising conducted by drug manufacturers, eased restrictions for prescription drug advertising on television. In print ads, drug makers are required to spell out potential side effects and the proper uses of prescription drugs. Because of the requirement to disclose this information, prescription drug television advertising was limited. Now, however, the FDA says drug ads on radio and television can directly promote a prescription drug's benefits if they provide a quick way for consumers to learn about side effects, such as displaying a toll-free number or Internet address.

The responsibility of business to preserve consumers' right to be informed extends beyond avoiding misleading advertising. All communications with customers—from salespeople's comments to warranties and invoices—must be controlled to clearly and accurately inform customers. Most packaged-goods firms, personal-computer makers, and other makers of products bought for personal use by consumers include toll-free customer service numbers on their product labels so that consumers can get answers to questions about a product.

To protect their customers and avoid claims of insufficient disclosure, businesses often include warnings on products. As Figure 2.8 shows, sometimes these warnings go far beyond what a reasonable consumer would expect. Others are downright funny.

The Right to Choose Consumers should have the right to choose which goods and services they need and want to purchase. Socially responsible firms attempt to preserve this right, even if they reduce their own sales and profits in the process. Brand-name drug makers have recently gone on the defensive in a battle being waged by state governments, insurance

FIGURE
2.8 **Actual Wacky Warning Labels**

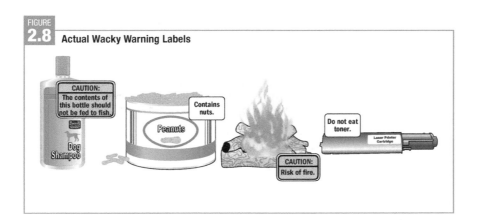

companies, consumer groups, unions, and major employers such as General Motors and Verizon. These groups want to force down the rising price of prescription drugs by ensuring that consumers have the right and the opportunity to select cheaper generic brands.

The Right to Be Heard Consumers should be able to express legitimate complaints to appropriate parties. Many companies expend considerable effort to ensure full hearings for consumer complaints. The auction website eBay assists buyers and sellers who believe they were victimized in transactions conducted through the site, deploying employees to work with users and law enforcement agencies to combat fraud. The company has strict guidelines for buyers and sellers and rules for leaving feedback about a buyer or seller. For example, buyers must operate within a list of acceptable goods for sale and may not offer such items as alcohol, pornography, drugs, counterfeit currency, or artifacts from cave formations, graves, or Native American sites. The protection of copyrights is also an important part of eBay's policy.[39]

Responsibilities to Employees

Companies that can attract skilled and knowledgeable employees are better able to meet the challenges of competing globally. In return, businesses have wide-ranging responsibilities to their employees, both here and abroad. These include workplace safety, quality-of-life issues, ensuring equal opportunity on the job, avoiding age discrimination, and preventing sexual harassment and sexism.

Workplace Safety A century ago, few businesses paid much attention to the safety of their workers. In fact, most business owners viewed employees as mere cogs in the production process. Workers—many of whom were young children—toiled in frequently dangerous conditions. In 1911, a fire at the Triangle Shirtwaist Factory in New York City killed 146 people, mostly young girls. Contributing to the massive loss of life were the sweatshop working conditions at the factory, including overcrowding, blocked exits, and a lack of fire escapes.

Workplace safety is an important business responsibility. In potentially dangerous areas, workers are required to wear safety equipment, including hard hats and protective eyewear.

Chapter 2 *Business Ethics and Social Responsibility*   **49**

This horrifying tragedy forced businesses to begin to recognize their responsibility for their workers' safety.

The safety and health of workers on the job is now an important business responsibility. The Occupational Safety and Health Administration (OSHA) is the main federal regulatory force in setting workplace safety and health standards. These mandates range from broad guidelines on storing hazardous materials to specific standards for worker safety in industries such as construction, manufacturing, and mining. OSHA tracks and investigates workplace accidents and has the authority to fine employers who are found liable for injuries and deaths that occur on the job.

One unsettling fact is that as many as 90 teens die every year in the United States as a result of work injuries. Most of these fatalities occur because of unsafe equipment, inadequate safety training, and dangerous work that is illegal or inappropriate for youth. OSHA is taking steps to educate employers and teen workers about safety, health, and a positive work environment. The OSHA website has a special section for teens with the answers to most frequently asked questions about such issues as wages, labor standards, harassment issues, and safety at work. In addition, the U.S. Department of Labor's YouthRules! initiative is designed to further educate and empower young workers. The YouthRules! web page offers information and activities for teens, parents, educators, and employers.[40]

Quality-of-Life Issues Balancing work and family is becoming harder for many employees. They find themselves squeezed between working long hours and handling child-care problems, caring for elderly parents, and solving other family crises. A *sandwich generation* of households, those caring for two generations—their children and their aging parents—has arisen. As the population ages, the share of American households providing some type of care to a relative or friend age 50 or older has grown dramatically in the early years of the 21st century.

As women spend more time working outside the home, they have fewer hours per week to spend on family. However, working mothers aren't the only employees juggling work with life's other demands. Childless couples, single people, and men all express frustration at the pressures of balancing work with family and personal needs. To help with the work–life balance, some employers are offering flexible work schedules so that parents can meet the needs of their children (or aging parents) as well as their jobs. *Working Mother* magazine offers up its list of 100 best companies to work for offering work–life balance. Criteria for selection include the option to telecommute, flexible scheduling, job sharing, and access to childcare. Some of the magazine's top choices are Bank of America, DuPont, Procter & Gamble, General Mills, and IBM.[41] Increasingly, women are starting their own businesses so they can set their own hours and goals.

Some companies have come up with truly innovative ways to deal with work schedules, including paid time off for vacation or illness. At some of its locations, IBM has done away with prescribed vacation time altogether—the focus is on results. Employees have an informal agreement with their supervisors about when they will be out of the office, based on their ability to complete their work on schedule. The number of days they take off is not tracked; instead vacation time is considered open ended. But the catch is, the work has to be done. Perhaps surprisingly, the firm found that employees put in just as many hours, if not more, under the new program.[42]

Another solution has been to offer **family leave** to employees who need to deal with family matters. Under the Family and Medical Leave Act of 1993, employers with 50 or more employees must provide unpaid leave annually for any employee who wants time off for the birth or adoption of a child; to become a foster parent; or to care for a seriously ill relative, spouse, or self if he or she has a serious health condition or injury. The law requires employers to grant up to 12 weeks of leave each year, and leave may be taken intermittently as medical conditions make necessary. This unpaid leave also applies to an employee who has a serious illness. Workers must meet certain eligibility requirements. Employers must continue to provide health benefits during the leave and guarantee that employees will return to equivalent jobs. The issue of who is entitled to health benefits can also create a dilemma as companies struggle to balance the needs of their employees against the staggering costs of health care.

family leave the Family and Medical Leave Act of 1993 states that employers with 50 or more employees must provide unpaid leave up to 12 weeks annually for any employee who wants time off for the birth or adoption of a child, to become a foster parent, or to care for a seriously ill relative, spouse, or self.

Hit&Miss

AT&T's Commitment to Hiring Military Vets

A group of corporate leaders, with AT&T at the forefront, has made a commitment to change the job status of military veterans seeking to transition into the civilian workforce. Consistent with equal employment opportunities, AT&T has stepped up its nationwide recruitment of veterans with its Military Talent Attraction Team, whose dual focus is to promote jobs to veterans while continuing to educate company managers of the benefits these former servicemen and women can provide to the organization. Over the next five years, AT&T, known for its excellent wages, benefits, and training and development programs, will hire 10,000 military veterans and their family members.

According to the Bureau of Labor Statistics, nearly 10 percent of the veterans who served in Iraq or Afghanistan are unemployed, nearly 3 percent more than the general population. One of the challenges veterans face is a lack of understanding by civilians about the breadth of occupations and jobs that people hold in the military. Civilian managers are challenged to understand the actual leadership, self-discipline, teamwork, project management, logistics, and technical skills that veterans possess. Such important job skills may not necessarily be reflected in an official military title. For example, a civilian manager may be unable to understand what an ordnance specialist or petty officer can bring to the corporate environment.

In Ohio alone, where AT&T invested more than $1.5 billion over the last five years in its broadband and wireless networks, the company will hire 200 employees in customer service, retail, and technical positions—some of which could be filled by veterans. Nationwide, over the past year, AT&T has hired 3,600 veterans into positions such as IT professionals,

retail and call center representatives, project managers, financial analysts, and supply chain managers. Junior officers and college-educated veterans are being recruited into AT&T's leadership development programs. The strategic and creative-thinking skills demonstrated by U.S. military veterans and AT&T's commitment to hiring the best appear to be a winning combination.

Questions for Critical Thinking

1. What advantages might military veterans bring to private businesses?

2. As a communications company, discuss some of the ways AT&T can continue to promote its hiring message to veterans as the company expands its wireless and broadband networks across the country.

Sources: Bureau of Labor Statistics, "Table 2A. Employment Status of Persons 18 Years and Over by Veteran Status, Age, and Period of Service, 2012 Annual Averages," accessed January 20, 2014, www.bls.gov; "AT&T Continues Hiring Drive in Ohio; About 300 Jobs Currently Available; Military Veterans Sought," *Market Watch*, accessed January 20, 2014, www.marketwatch.com; Julian E. Barnes, "Companies Double Hiring Goal for Veterans," *The Wall Street Journal*, accessed January 20, 2014, http://blogs.wsj.com; Shasha Dai, "PE Firms Make Progress with Veteran-Hiring Programs," *The Wall Street Journal*, accessed January 20, 2014, http://blogs.wsj.com; Sophie Quinton, "Why Are Companies Reluctant to Hire Military Veterans?" *National Journal*, accessed January 20, 2014, www.nationaljournal.com.

Ensuring Equal Opportunity on the Job Businesspeople face many challenges managing an increasingly diverse workforce in the 21st century. Technological advances are expanding the ways people with physical disabilities can contribute in the workplace. Businesses also need to find ways to responsibly recruit and manage older workers and workers with varying lifestyles. More than 60 percent of *Fortune* 500 companies currently offer domestic-partner benefits to their employees.[43]

To a great extent, efforts at managing diversity are regulated by law. The Civil Rights Act (1964) outlawed many kinds of discriminatory practices, and Title VII of the act specifically prohibits **discrimination**—biased treatment of a job candidate or employee—in the workplace. As shown in Table 2.2, other nondiscrimination laws include the Equal Pay Act (1963), the Age Discrimination in Employment Act (1967), the Equal Employment Opportunity Act (1972), the Pregnancy Discrimination Act (1978), the Civil Rights Act of 1991, and numerous executive orders. The Americans with Disabilities Act (1990) protects the rights of physically challenged people. The Vietnam Era Veterans Readjustment Act (1974) protects the employment of veterans of the Vietnam War. The Genetic Information Nondiscrimination Act (2008) prohibits discrimination on the basis of genetic tests or the medical history of an individual or that individual's family. To learn what AT&T is doing to ensure equal opportunity for U.S. military vets, see the "Hit & Miss" feature.

discrimination biased treatment of a job candidate or employee.

⌐2.2⌐ Laws Designed to Ensure Equal Opportunity

LAW	KEY PROVISIONS
Title VII of the Civil Rights Act of 1964 (as amended by the Equal Employment Opportunity Act of 1972)	Prohibits discrimination in hiring, promotion, compensation, training, or dismissal on the basis of race, color, religion, sex, or national origin.
Age Discrimination in Employment Act of 1967 (as amended)	Prohibits discrimination in employment against anyone age 40 or older in hiring, promotion, compensation, training, or dismissal.
Equal Pay Act of 1963	Requires equal pay for men and women working for the same firm in jobs that require equal skill, effort, and responsibility.
Vocational Rehabilitation Act of 1973	Requires government contractors and subcontractors to take affirmative action to employ and promote qualified disabled workers. Coverage now extends to all federal employees. Coverage has been broadened by the passage of similar laws in more than 20 states and, through court rulings, to include people with communicable diseases, including AIDS.
Vietnam Era Veterans Readjustment Act of 1974	Requires government contractors and subcontractors to take affirmative action to employ and retain disabled veterans. Coverage now extends to all federal employees and has been broadened by the passage of similar laws in more than 20 states.
Pregnancy Discrimination Act of 1978	Requires employers to treat pregnant women and new mothers the same as other employees for all employment-related purposes, including receipt of benefits under company benefit programs.
Americans with Disabilities Act of 1990	Makes discrimination against the disabled illegal in public accommodations, transportation, and telecommunications; stiffens employer penalties for intentional discrimination on the basis of an employee's disability.
Civil Rights Act of 1991	Makes it easier for workers to sue their employers for alleged discrimination. Enables victims of sexual discrimination to collect punitive damages; includes employment decisions and on-the-job issues such as sexual harassment, unfair promotions, and unfair dismissal. The employer must prove that it did not engage in discrimination.
Family and Medical Leave Act of 1993	Requires all businesses with 50 or more employees to provide up to 12 weeks of unpaid leave annually to employees who have had a child or are adopting a child, are becoming foster parents, are caring for a seriously ill relative or spouse, or are themselves seriously ill. Workers must meet certain eligibility requirements.
Uniformed Services Employment and Reemployment Rights Act of 1994	Prohibits employers from denying employment benefits on the basis of employees' membership in or obligation to serve in the uniformed services and protects the rights of veterans, reservists, and National Guard members to reclaim their jobs after being absent due to military service or training.
Genetic Information Nondiscrimination Act of 2008	Prohibits employers from discriminating against employees or applicants on the basis of genetic information, including genetic tests of an individual or family member or an individual's personal or family medical history.

Equal Employment Opportunity Commission (EEOC) this commission was created to increase job opportunities for women and minorities and to help end discrimination based on race, color, religion, disability, gender, or national origin in any personnel action.

The **Equal Employment Opportunity Commission (EEOC)** was created to increase job opportunities for women and minorities and to help end discrimination based on race, color, religion, disability, gender, or national origin in any personnel action. To enforce fair-employment laws, it investigates charges of discrimination and harassment and files suit against violators. The EEOC can also help employers set up programs to increase job opportunities for women, minorities, people with disabilities, and people in other protected categories.

Fair treatment of employees is more than a matter of complying with EEOC regulations, however. All employees want to be treated with respect. A minority employee who misses out on a plum assignment may miss out on the big raise that goes with it. As the employee's salary grows more slowly, managers may eventually begin to use the size of the salary as an indicator that the employee contributes less to the organization. While in the past the EEOC has focused on this type of individual situation, currently it is addressing what it terms *systemic discrimination*, which it defines as "a pattern or practice, policy and/or class cases where the alleged discrimination has a broad impact on an industry, profession, company, or geographic location." A systemic discrimination charge usually becomes a class-action suit, which costs considerably more to defend than an individual lawsuit. So firms are examining their employment practices carefully to make sure they are not open to discrimination charges.[44] Chapter 9 takes a closer look at diversity and employment discrimination issues as part of a discussion of human resource management.

Age Discrimination With the average age of U.S. workers steadily rising, more than half the workforce is projected to be age 40 or older in a few years. Yet some employers find it less expensive to hire and retain younger workers, who generally have lower medical bills as well as lower salary and benefits packages. At the same time, many older workers have training and skills that younger workers have yet to acquire. The Age Discrimination in Employment Act of 1967 (ADEA) protects individuals who are age 40 or older, prohibiting discrimination on the basis of age and denial of benefits to older employees.

Ruling in a lawsuit brought under the ADEA, the Supreme Court determined that employers can be held liable for age discrimination against older workers even if they intended no harm. At the same time, the court allowed employers to use "reasonable" factors, such as cost cutting, to defend business practices that might have more severe impacts on older than on younger workers. However, a recent Court ruling shifted the burden of proof onto employees seeking to prove that age discrimination was a factor in their demotion or dismissal.[45]

Legal issues aside, employers might do well to consider not only the experience that older workers bring to the workplace but also their enthusiasm. Many surveys report that older workers who remain on the job by choice—not because they are forced to do so for economic reasons—are often happy with their employment. But other studies show that aging Baby Boomers are increasingly dissatisfied with the workplace due to the falling value of their retirement investments and diminishing options such as relocation. Still, employees with decades of work experience can be a valuable asset to any firm.[46]

In all cases, employers need to plan ahead for the aging of the workforce, finding ways to retain accumulated business wisdom, prepare for the demand for health services, and be ready for growth in the industries that serve seniors. The 55-and-older age group is projected to comprise nearly 37 percent of the population by the end of this decade, whereas the 35-to-44 age group will decrease to about 16 percent. These numbers signify a coming shift in the workforce, as well as in the goods and services needed.[47]

Sexual Harassment and Sexism Every employer has a responsibility to ensure that all workers are treated fairly and are safe from sexual harassment. <u>Sexual harassment</u> refers to unwelcome and inappropriate actions of a sexual nature in the workplace. It is a form of sex discrimination that violates the Civil Rights Act of 1964, which gives both men and women the right to file lawsuits for intentional sexual harassment. About 8,000 sexual harassment complaints are filed with the EEOC each year, of which about 18 percent are filed by men.[48] Thousands of other cases are either handled internally by companies or never reported.

Two types of sexual harassment exist. The first type occurs when an employee is pressured to comply with unwelcome advances and requests for sexual favors in

sexual harassment
unwelcome and inappropriate actions of a sexual nature in the workplace.

Gregg Matthews/The New York Times/Redux Pictures

Employers are responsible for avoiding age discrimination in the workplace. As the average age of workers rises, employers will benefit from the older generation's knowledge.

return for job security, promotions, and raises. The second type results from a hostile work environment in which an employee feels hassled or degraded because of unwelcome flirting, lewd comments, or obscene jokes. The courts have ruled that allowing sexually oriented materials in the workplace can create a hostile atmosphere that interferes with an employee's ability to do the job. Employers are also legally responsible to protect employees from sexual harassment by customers and clients. The EEOC's website informs employers and employees of criteria for identifying sexual harassment and how it should be handled in the workplace.

Preventing sexual harassment can be difficult because it involves regulating the conduct of individual employees. Sometimes victims, especially young employees, are intimidated or unaware of their rights, but the EEOC has set up a Youth@Work program (http://www.eeoc.gov/youth) to ensure that young workers can learn about the various types of discrimination and ways to avoid them.

The cost in settlements or fines can be enormous. So, in addition to ethical and legal reasons, it makes good business sense for firms to prevent this kind of behavior from happening. To avoid sexual harassment problems, many firms have established policies and employee education programs aimed at preventing such violations. An effective harassment prevention program should include the following measures:

- Issue a specific policy statement prohibiting sexual harassment.

- Develop a complaint procedure for employees to follow.

- Create a work atmosphere that encourages sexually harassed staffers to come forward.

- Investigate and resolve complaints quickly and take disciplinary action against harassers.

Unless all these components are supported by top management, sexual harassment is difficult to eliminate.

Sexual harassment is often part of the broader problem of **sexism**—discrimination against members of either sex, but primarily affecting women. One important sexism issue is equal pay for equal work.

Lilly Ledbetter was near retirement when she found out that for a considerable length of time, men at her management level had been getting paid more than she had been. But the Supreme Court threw out her case because she did not sue within the statute of limitations—that is, within 180 days of the first instance of a lower paycheck. Recently the statute of limitations was extended in these types of cases.[49]

U.S. Census statistics show that overall, women still earn 77 cents for every $1 earned by men. The number drops to 68 cents for African American women and 58 cents for Hispanic women. Education, occupation, work hours, and other factors don't seem to affect the gap, which remains unexplained other than the penalty of gender.[50] In some extreme cases, differences in pay and advancement can become the basis for sex discrimination suits, which, like sexual harassment suits, can be costly and time consuming to settle. As in all business practices, it is better to act legally and ethically in the first place.

sexism discrimination against members of either sex, but primarily affecting women.

Assessment Check ✔

1. What is meant by social responsibility, and why do firms exercise it?

2. What is green marketing?

3. What are the four main consumer rights?

---

[5] # Responsibilities to Investors and the Financial Community

Although a fundamental goal of any business is to make a profit for its shareholders, investors and the financial community demand that businesses behave ethically and legally. When firms fail in this responsibility, thousands of investors and consumers can suffer.

State and federal government agencies are responsible for protecting investors from financial misdeeds. At the federal level, the Securities and Exchange Commission (SEC)

investigates suspicions of unethical or illegal behavior by publicly traded firms. It investigates accusations that a business is using faulty accounting practices to inaccurately portray its financial resources and profits to investors. Regulation FD (Fair Disclosure) is an SEC rule that requires publicly traded companies to announce major information to the general public, rather than first disclosing the information to selected major investors. The agency also operates an Office of Internet Enforcement to target fraud in online trading and online sales of stock by unlicensed sellers. Recall that the Sarbanes-Oxley Act of 2002 also protects investors from unethical accounting practices. Chapter 17 discusses securities trading practices further.

Assessment Check ☑

1. Why do firms need to do more than just earn a profit?
2. What is the role of the Securities and Exchange Commission?

What's Ahead

The decisions and actions of businesspeople are often influenced by outside forces such as the legal environment and society's expectations about business responsibility. Firms also are affected by the economic environments in which they operate. The next chapter discusses the broad economic issues that influence businesses around the world. Our discussion will focus on how factors such as supply and demand, unemployment, inflation, and government monetary policies pose both challenges and opportunities for firms seeking to compete in the global marketplace.

Chapter in Review

▌ Summary of Learning Objectives

⌐1⌐ Explain the concern for ethical and societal issues.

Business ethics refers to the standards of conduct and moral values that businesspeople rely on to guide their actions and decisions in the workplace. Businesspeople must take a wide range of social issues into account when making decisions. Social responsibility refers to management's acceptance of the obligation to place a significant value on profit, consumer satisfaction, and societal well-being in evaluating the firm's performance.

Assessment Check Answers ☑

1.1 To whom do businesses have responsibilities? Businesses are responsible to customers, employees, investors, and society.

1.2 If a firm is meeting all its responsibilities to others, why do ethical conflicts arise? Ethical conflicts arise when business is trying to serve the different needs of its constituents.

⌐2⌐ Describe the contemporary ethical environment.

Among the many factors shaping individual ethics are personal experience, peer pressure, and organizational culture.

Individual ethics are also influenced by family, cultural, and religious standards. Additionally, the culture of the organization where a person works can be a factor.

Assessment Check Answers ☑

2.1 What role can an ethics compliance officer play in a firm? Ethics compliance officers are charged with deterring wrongdoing and ensuring that ethical standards are met.

2.2 What are the three components of a typical company's approach to ethics and social responsibility? The three components are (1) engaging in typical corporate philanthropy; (2) anticipating and managing risks; and (3) identifying opportunities to create value by doing the right thing.

⌐3⌐ Discuss how organizations shape ethical conduct.

Choices are strongly influenced by the standards of conduct established within any organization. Most ethical lapses in business reflect the values of the firms' corporate cultures. Development of a corporate culture to support business ethics happens on four levels: ethical awareness; ethical education; ethical action; and ethical leadership. Ethical awareness involves providing help to employees in identifying ethical problems when they occur and giving them guidance about how the firm expects them to respond. One way to provide this support is to develop a code of conduct for the organization. Ethical education involves implementing an ethics training program for employees or hiring an outside firm to develop ethics and compliance programs for the organization. Ethical action involves companies providing structures and approaches for employees that allow decisions to be turned into appropriate business actions. Ethical leadership involves commitment to the company's core values at all levels of the organization.

Assessment Check Answers ✔

3.1 Identify the four levels of a company's ethical environment. Development of a corporate culture to support business ethics happens on four levels: ethical awareness; ethical education; ethical action; and ethical leadership.

3.2 How does ethical leadership contribute to ethical standards throughout a company? Employees more readily commit to the company's core values when they see that executives and managers behave ethically.

⌐4⌐ Describe how businesses can act responsibly to satisfy society.

Today's businesses are expected to weigh their qualitative impact on consumers and society, in addition to their quantitative economic contributions such as sales, employment levels, and profits. One measure is their compliance with labor and consumer protection laws and their charitable contributions. Another measure some businesses take is to conduct social audits. Public-interest groups also create standards and measure companies' performance relative to those standards. The responsibilities of business to the general public include protecting the public health and the environment and developing the quality of the workforce. Additionally, many would argue that businesses have a social responsibility to support charitable and social causes in the communities in which they earn profits. Business also must treat customers fairly and protect consumers, upholding their rights to be safe, to be informed, to choose, and to be heard. Businesses have wide-ranging responsibilities to their workers. They should make sure that the workplace is safe, address quality-of-life issues, ensure equal opportunity, and prevent sexual harassment and other forms of discrimination.

Assessment Check Answers ✔

4.1 What is meant by social responsibility, and why do firms exercise it? Social responsibility is management's acceptance of its obligation to consider profit, consumer satisfaction, and societal well-being to be of significant value when evaluating the firm's performance. Businesses demonstrate social responsibility because such behavior is required by law, because it enhances the company's image, or because management believes it is the right thing to do.

4.2 What is green marketing? Green marketing is a marketing strategy that promotes environmentally safe products and production methods.

4.3 What are the four main consumer rights? The four main consumer rights are the right to be safe, to be informed, to choose, and to be heard.

⌐5⌐ Explain the ethical responsibilities of businesses to investors and the financial community.

Investors and the financial community demand that businesses behave ethically as well as legally in handling their financial transactions. Businesses must be honest in reporting their profits and financial performance to avoid misleading investors. The Securities and Exchange Commission is the federal agency responsible for investigating suspicions that publicly traded firms have engaged in unethical or illegal financial behavior.

Assessment Check Answers ✔

5.1 Why do firms need to do more than just earn a profit? Although a fundamental goal of any business is to make a profit for its shareholders, investors and the financial community demand that businesses behave ethically and legally.

5.2 What is the role of the Securities and Exchange Commission? Among other functions, the Securities and Exchange Commission investigates suspicions of unethical or illegal behavior by publicly traded firms.

▦ Business Terms You Need to Know

business ethics 32	social responsibility 41	product liability 48
Sarbanes-Oxley Act of 2002 33	social audits 43	family leave 50
conflict of interest 36	recycling 44	discrimination 51
integrity 37	green marketing 45	Equal Employment Opportunity
whistle-blowing 37	sustainable 45	Commission (EEOC) 52
code of conduct 39	corporate philanthropy 47	sexual harassment 53
stakeholders 41	consumerism 47	sexism 54

56   **Part 1** *Business in a Global Environment*

Review Questions

1. What do the terms *business ethics* and *social responsibility* mean? Why are they important components of a firm's overall philosophy in conducting business?

2. In what ways do individuals make a difference in a firm's commitment to ethics? Describe the three stages in which an individual develops ethical standards.

3. What type of ethical dilemma does each of the following illustrate? (A situation might involve more than one dilemma.)

   a. Due to the breakup with a client, an advertising agency suddenly finds itself representing rival companies.

   b. A newly hired employee learns that the office manager plays computer games on company time.

   c. An employee is asked to destroy documents that implicate his or her firm in widespread pollution.

   d. A company spokesperson agrees to give a press conference that puts a positive spin on his or her firm's use of sweatshop labor.

4. Describe how ethical leadership contributes to the development of each of the other levels of ethical standards in a corporation.

5. In what ways do firms demonstrate their social responsibility?

6. What are the four major areas in which businesses have responsibilities to the general public? In what ways can meeting these responsibilities give a firm a competitive edge?

7. Identify and describe the four basic rights that consumerism tries to protect. How has consumerism improved the contemporary business environment? What challenges has it created for businesses?

8. What are the five major areas in which companies have responsibilities to their employees? What types of changes in society are now affecting these responsibilities?

9. Identify which equal opportunity law (or laws) protects workers in the following categories:

   a. an employee who must care for an elderly parent

   b. a National Guard member who is returning from deployment overseas

   c. a job applicant who is HIV positive

   d. a person who is over 40 years old

   e. a woman who has been sexually harassed on the job

   f. a woman with a family history of breast cancer

10. How does a company demonstrate its responsibility to investors and the financial community?

Projects and Teamwork Applications

1. Write your own personal code of ethics. Create standards for your behavior at school, in personal relationships, and on the job. Then assess how well you meet your own standards and revise them if necessary.

2. On your own or with a classmate, visit the website of one of the following firms, or choose another that interests you. On the basis of what you can learn about the company from the site, construct a chart or figure that illustrates examples of the firm's ethical awareness, ethical education, ethical actions, and ethical leadership. Present your findings to class.

   a. Nike

   b. NFL, NHL, NBA, MLB, MLS (or any other major professional sports league)

   c. eBay

   d. Aetna

   e. Walmart

   f. Costco

   g. IKEA

3. Take the company you chose for question 2 (or choose another), and search for information about the company's social and environmental responsibility practices—some companies publish annual social and environmental reports. Present to the class the company's successes and challenges for the most recent year.

4. On your own or with a classmate, go online or flip through a magazine to identify a firm that is engaged in green marketing. Next, go to the firm's website to learn more about the product or process advertised. Does the firm make claims that comply with the FTC guidelines? Present your findings in class.

5. As technology becomes more pervasive, new and complex ethical issues have arisen in the workplace, which have contributed to ethical and sometimes legal challenges for employers and employees. Consider the action of transmitting confidential or proprietary company data, for example. With a classmate or alone, come up with a list of ways technology has affected or compromised ethics at work, school, or home.

Web Assignments

1. **Ethical standards.** Go to the Boeing website and review its supplier page listed below. With more than 23,000 different suppliers listed, review and list the criteria Boeing uses when choosing suppliers.

   www.boeingsuppliers.com

2. **Starting a career.** Each year *Fortune* magazine publishes its "Best Companies to Work For" list of the top 100 employers. Using the most recent list, choose three of the companies listed and find specific examples of how each has demonstrated corporate social responsibility. How do these compare with the criteria *Fortune* used to compile the list?

   http://money.cnn.com/magazines/fortune/best-companies/

3. **Social responsibility.** Athletic footwear manufacturer New Balance is one of the few companies in its industry that still manufactures products in the United States. Go to the website listed below and learn more about the firm's commitment to U.S. manufacturing. What other companies are committed to U.S.–only production? Discuss what these companies have in common with New Balance, and how they relate to the firm's core values.

   http://www.newbalance.com/company/

Note: Internet web addresses change frequently. If you don't find the exact sites listed, you may need to access the organization's home page and search from there or use a search engine such as Google or Bing.

CASE 2.1

Hilton Joins the Global Soap Project

"When living as a refugee in Kenya, I realized soap was hard to come by, even completely nonexistent sometimes. . . . People were suffering from illness simply because they couldn't wash their hands." This experience motivated Derreck Kayongo to found the Global Soap Project, an initiative to provide bars of soap for developing countries, where even schools, hospitals, and health clinics can lack such basic supplies.

A highly effective and inexpensive way to prevent diarrheal diseases, infections, and pneumonia, hand washing can save millions of lives every year. In North America alone, nearly 3 million bars of hotel soap are discarded every day after minimal use. Kayongo's idea was to recycle them into new bars and distribute them to those in need. In its first three years, the Global Soap Project sent more than 25 tons of soap to 20 vulnerable countries, relying on volunteers, non-profit organizations, and non-governmental organizations (NGOs) to get things off the ground.

Now the project has been joined by Hilton Worldwide. The hotel company promises to donate more than 1 million new bars of soap and will invest $1.3 million in the project, along with its own operational expertise to help it expand.

Questions for Critical Thinking

1. One observer notes that the Global Soap Project appears to be a good fit with Hilton's existing sustainability efforts. Why might that be true of a hotel chain?

2. Which organization will benefit more from their partnership, the Global Soap Project or Hilton? Why?

Sources: Organization website, www.globalsoap.org, accessed January 20, 2014, Raz Godelnik, "A Soap Opera at Hilton Hotels," Triple Pundit. com, accessed January 20, 2014, www.triplepundit.com; organization press release, "Hilton Worldwide Announces Partnership with the Global Soap Project," accessed January 20, 2014, www.globalsoap.org; "Hilton Worldwide Collaborates with the Global Soap Project to Recycle Used Soap," Hotel Interactive.com, accessed January 20, 2014, www.hotelinteractive.com.

In the world of supply chain management—the complex network of activities used to transport raw materials and finished goods—a pallet is a portable square platform used to move materials and goods stacked several rows high. A wooden pallet, the most common type, can easily be transported by a forklift, and most pallets can be stacked on top of each other to conserve space during warehousing or shipping.

Around the world, more than 90 percent of all goods are moved on pallets. Companies are looking for ways to keep the transport of such items as cost-efficient as possible and to reduce the environmental impact of using wooden pallets.

Delivering pallets of products to end users involves transportation, and most modes of transportation cause some level of pollution. In an effort to reduce pollution and increase sustainability, companies are examining alterative ways to transport goods along their supply chain, and the wooden pallet seems to be one part of the process that may be eliminated in an effort to save transportation and environmental costs.

The average weight of a wooden pallet is 80 pounds, a plastic pallet 50 pounds, and an aluminum pallet 40 pounds. In terms of lifespan, the wooden pallet typically lasts the shortest of the three types—with aluminum pallets lasting the longest (10 years on average). Perhaps the most interesting fact is the load rating of the three pallet types. The average moving load of a wooden pallet is 2,500 pounds; the plastic version is up to 6,000 pounds, and the aluminum pallet carries nearly six times the load of a wooden pallet—up to 14,000 pounds.

It is estimated that 500 billion pallets are manufactured worldwide each year, and at any given point in time, there are 2 billion pallets in circulation in the United States. Although wooden pallets won't become obsolete any time soon, many global companies are considering a shift to plastic and aluminum pallets as they continue to focus on reducing costs and making their supply chains greener.

Questions for Critical Thinking

1. One of the goals of green supply chain management is to eliminate or minimize any type of waste along a company's supply chain. What would be the advantage of using aluminum pallets?

2. Discuss why the use of wooden pallets is criticized by environmentalists.

Sources: "U.S. Pallets Market," *Market Watch,* accessed January 20, 2014, www.marketwatch.com; company website, www.alpallet.com, accessed January 20, 2014; company website, "The Eco Aluminum Difference," http://ecoaluminumpallets.com, accessed January 20, 2014; company website, "Making the Switch to Aluminum Pallets," www.freshplaza.com, accessed January 20, 2014; Bill Roth, "Green Innovation: Recycled Aluminum Pallets," *Earth 2017 Sustainable Strategies,* accessed January 20 2014, www.earth2017.com.

Timberland got its name from the iconic yellow work boot introduced more than four decades ago. Nathan Swartz founded the company in South Boston as the Abington Shoe Company, and he set out to create the most premium, durable waterproof leather boots on the market to help workers withstand the harsh New England winters. Today, the New Hampshire-based footwear manufacturer, retailer, and global lifestyle company has found a place in the fashion world with celebrities and non-celebrities alike. As importantly, Timberland has also found its place as a model for best practices in corporate social responsibility (CSR). The company's passion for the outdoors, along with its responsibility to stakeholders, plays a major part in Timberland's overall business culture.

At its core, the company is committed to a culture of protecting the very essence of what keeps it in business—the outdoors and the environment. Each of Timberland's strategies demonstrates a synergy between commerce and social responsibility. The company's CSR activities are not limited to a separate department but integrated into all of its business strategies. Timberland focuses its CSR efforts on the three areas of responsible products, community engagement, and resource efficiency.

Maintaining transparency in product manufacturing is integral to Timberland's culture of taking steps to preserve the environment. Apparel and footwear manufacturing can have a variety of environmental consequences, which include the amount of water used to grow cotton, toxic chemicals used in tanning leather, and large amounts of crude oil and volatile compounds released during the production of synthetic fibers and fabrics. Timberland chooses to use leather tanneries that have wastewater purifying systems as part of their manufacturing process. Timberland collaborates with manufacturers of leather goods in various industries ranging from automobile to apparel to footwear. Together, the companies influence leather tanners to create a standard to monitor their processes in how leather goods are made and sourced.

Protecting the environment is one of Timberland's responsibilities to the general public. The company labels its products with respect to their environmental impact in much the same way that food products contain nutritional information. Through the Sustainable Apparel Coalition and the Outdoor Industry Association, Timberland, along with other footwear and apparel makers, has worked diligently to create awareness through an industry-wide standard of measurement and transparency of the environmental impact of products found in retail outlets. To reduce a product's environmental impact, better raw material choices at

the beginning of product design are essential. At the front end, Timberland collaborates with designers and developers by making sure that they choose less environmentally harmful product materials.

Timberland is engaged in a variety of activities to protect the environment. The company is most proud of the advancements made in the use of recycled, renewable, and organic materials such as plastic water bottles and coffee grounds to make its apparel and shoes. A few years ago, the company invested in the planting of five million trees in Haiti to create a sustainable business model that provides jobs for their partners there. The result, the Smallholder Farmers Alliance, is a network of community nurseries where planted trees are maintained by 2,000 volunteer farmers in exchange for non-genetically modified seeds and agricultural training to plant and grow crops of their own. Timberland's investment in Haiti has provided a better life for the country's people and a sustainable model that can be replicated and scaled in other farming applications around the world.

To create greater transparency about where products are made, Timberland was one of the first companies to go public with its list of suppliers. Historically, the names of suppliers and their whereabouts have been closely guarded in the ready-made garment industry. With hundreds of thousands of workers involved in the production of its products, Timberland is committed to improving the quality of life for those workers through "responsible product," which translates to making sure that supplier engagement goes beyond compliance with rules and regulations. In the communities in which it operates, Timberland has provided transportation and housing, along with access to clean drinking water. In addition, the company has opened up daycare centers and provided educational and financial literacy programs for workers. Timberland has found that investing in workers and giving back to the communities in which they live and work translates to better business and higher morale.

Timberland takes community engagement seriously. For over two decades, through its Path of Service™ program, the company's employees have logged over a million hours—or a total of 114 years of service—to communities where its global employees live and work. Each employee is granted, on an annual basis, the opportunity to engage in up to 40 paid hours of community service. Working side-by-side outside the organizational structure with others throughout the company has proven to be not only an exercise in teambuilding and leadership but also a way to increase morale within the organization.

Resource efficiency targets include reducing greenhouse gas emissions, increasing the use of renewable energy, and reducing waste. Timberland was recognized as the Corporate Citizen of the Year at the New England Clean Energy Council's Annual Green Tie Gala.

Timberland's president, Patrik Frisk, believes that corporate responsibility should not be treated as an add-on to a business's agenda; rather it should provide the company a powerful competitive advantage. Frisk demonstrates ethical leadership and takes a wide range of issues into account when making business decisions. Consumer satisfaction and social well-being are of significant value and part of Timberland's performance assessment.

The next time you consider making a fashion statement with the purchase of a new pair of the iconic yellow boots, or see your favorite celebrities sporting theirs, you might also consider the trend-setting example Timberland has demonstrated in the realm of corporate social responsibility.

Questions for Critical Thinking

1. Compare and contrast the CSR efforts of three of Timberland's competitors. How do they compare to and/or differ from Timberland's efforts?
2. Discuss Patrik Frisk's comment that CSR does not have to be an add-on but instead can work as a competitive advantage. Provide three examples of how Timberland's commitment to corporate social responsibility has created a competitive advantage for the company.

3. The Timberland Responsibility website is a wealth of information about the company's approach to corporate social responsibility. Evaluate Timberland's most recent CSR report, and expand on some of the company's most recent initiatives. Discuss the company's progress against its targets set around its three areas of corporate social responsibility.
4. Download Timberland's Service Toolkit handout about how to develop and manage powerful community service events. Go to http://responsibility.timberland.com, click on "Service," and download the "Service Tool Kit." Discuss how you would define project parameters (1.0), research community needs and assets (2.0), and select service partners (3).

Sources: Company website, www.vfc.com, accessed June 25, 2014; company website, "About Us," www.timberland.com, accessed June 25, 2014; company website, http://responsibility.timberland.com, accessed June 25, 2014; company website, www.timberland.com/en/yellow-boot, accessed June 25, 2014; Fawnia Soo Hoo, "Will the Return of Timberland's Classic Boot Help Sell Its Other Styles?" *Fashionista*, accessed June 25, 2014, http://fashionista.com; Natalie Burg, "Timberland and Its Corporate Transparency," *Business Insider*, accessed June 25, 2014, www.businessinsider.com; Karizza Sanchez, "Trend Watch: Celebrities Wearing Timberlands This Winter," *Complex Style*, accessed June 25, 2014, www.complex.com; Nick Wingfield and Charles Duhigg, "Apple Lists Its Suppliers for First Time," *The New York Times*, accessed June 25, 2014, www.nytimes.com; Christina Binkley, "How Green Is My Sneaker?" *The Wall Street Journal*, accessed June 24, 2014, http://online.wsj.com; Melissa Korn and Audria Cheng, "VF to Buy Timberland, Build Up Outdoor Lines," *The Wall Street Journal*, accessed June 24, 2014, http://online.wsj.com.

Chapter 3

Learning Objectives

1. Discuss microeconomics and explain the forces of demand and supply.
2. Describe macroeconomics and the issues for the entire economy.
3. Identify how to evaluate economic performance.
4. Discuss managing the economy's performance.
5. Describe the global economic challenges of the 21st century.

Economic Challenges Facing Contemporary Business

© Aquir/iStockphoto

New Microsoft CEO Embraces Business Opportunities

Software giant Microsoft recently named only its third CEO since the company began almost 40 years ago. Satya Nadella, the new CEO, has worked at Microsoft for more than two decades, most recently as head of the company's successful cloud-computing business.

The business landscape has changed dramatically for Microsoft over the last ten years, as many consumers have switched from PCs to tablets and smartphones, and the company has been slow to embrace mobile technology. Recent reports estimate that 90 percent of PCs run Microsoft Windows, but only about 4 percent of smartphones use the software. The company's lack of involvement in mobile has put Microsoft at an economic disadvantage, as Apple and Google have become leaders in this fast-changing business.

Some observers believe Microsoft needs to shift its focus from producing hardware to making software available for every type of mobile device. Nadella has wasted little time in shaking things up at Microsoft. He recently announced that Windows would be free for all devices with nine-inch or smaller screens—a strategy to compete with Google's Android operating system. He also announced that Microsoft Office would be available for Apple's iPad, news well received by consumers and businesses alike. And Nadella recently announced a partnership with cloud-computing rival Salesforce.com, a move seen as a business opportunity that would benefit both companies.

In addition to taking the reins as CEO, Nadella will become the tenth member of the company's board of directors, which includes former CEO Steve Ballmer and co-founder Bill Gates. In announcing Nadella's new role, the company also said Gates will step aside as company chairman and devote more time to product development as a company director—a change applauded by industry observers who believe the company can benefit from Gates' involvement in developing new products.

Nadella realizes that Microsoft needs to fine-tune its business strategies and embrace new opportunities quickly in order to remain relevant in the technology sector. His next big challenge might be the integration of Nokia's handset business into Microsoft, a $7 billion deal made recently while Ballmer was CEO. Nadella seems to welcome the opportunity to lead Microsoft into the company's next phase of innovation. "The opportunity ahead for Microsoft is vast," he says, "but to seize it, we must focus clearly, move faster, and continue to transform."[1]

Overview

When we examine the exchanges that companies and societies make as a whole, we are focusing on the *economic systems* operating in different nations. These systems reflect the combination of policies and choices a nation makes to allocate resources among its citizens. Countries vary in the ways they allocate scarce resources.

Economics, which analyzes the choices people and governments make in allocating scarce resources, affects each of us, because everyone is involved in producing, distributing, or simply consuming goods and services. In fact, your life is affected by economics every day. Whether you buy tickets to a NASCAR race or decide to stay home and watch TV instead, you are making an economic choice. Understanding how the activities of one industry affect those of other industries, and how they relate in the overall economic status of a country, is an important part of understanding economics.

The choices you make actually may be international in scope. If you are in the market for a new car, you might visit several dealers in a row on the same street—Ford, Chrysler, Honda, Hyundai, and General Motors. You might decide on Hyundai—a Korean firm—but your car might very well be manufactured in the United States, using parts from all over the world. Although firms sometimes emphasize the American origin of their products in order to appeal to consumers' desire to support the U.S. economy, many items are made of components from a variety of nations.

Businesses and not-for-profit organizations also make economic decisions when they choose how to use human and natural resources; invest in equipment, machinery, and buildings; and form partnerships with

economics social science that analyzes the choices people and governments make in allocating scarce resources.

other firms. Economists refer to the study of small economic units, such as individual consumers, families, and businesses, as microeconomics.

The study of a country's overall economic issues is called macroeconomics (macro means "large"). Macroeconomics addresses such issues as how an economy uses its resources and how government policies affect people's standards of living. The substitution of ethanol for gasoline or biodiesel for diesel fuel has macroeconomic consequences—affecting many parts of the U.S. economy and suppliers around the world. Macroeconomics examines not just the economic policies of individual nations, but the ways in which those individual policies affect the overall world economy. Because so much business is conducted around the world, a law enacted in one country can easily affect a transaction that takes place in another country. Although macroeconomic issues have a broad scope, they help shape the decisions that individuals, families, and businesses make every day.

This chapter introduces economic theory and the economic challenges facing individuals, businesses, and governments in the global marketplace. We begin with the microeconomic concepts of supply and demand and their effect on the prices people pay for goods and services. Next we explain the various types of economic systems, along with tools for comparing and evaluating their performance. Then we examine the ways in which governments seek to manage economies to create stable business environments in their countries. The final section in the chapter looks at some of the driving economic forces currently affecting people's lives.

[1] ## Microeconomics: The Forces of Demand and Supply

microeconomics study of small economic units, such as individual consumers, families, and businesses.

Think about your own economic activities. You shop for groceries, subscribe to a cell phone service, pay college tuition, fill your car's tank with gas. Now think about your family's economic activities. When you were growing up, your parents might have owned a home or rented an apartment. You might have taken a family vacation. Your parents may have shopped at discount clubs or at local stores. Each of these choices relates to the study of **microeconomics**. They also help determine both the prices of goods and services and the amounts sold. Information about these activities is vital to companies because their survival and ability to grow depends on selling enough products priced high enough to cover costs and earn profits. The same information is important to consumers who must make purchase decisions based on prices and the availability of the goods and services they need.

demand willingness and ability of buyers to purchase goods and services.

supply willingness and ability of sellers to provide goods and services.

At the heart of every business endeavor is an exchange between a buyer and a seller. The buyer recognizes that he or she needs or wants a particular good or service—whether it's a hamburger or a haircut—and is willing to pay a seller for it. The seller requires the exchange in order to earn a profit and stay in business. So the exchange process involves both demand and supply. **Demand** refers to the willingness and ability of buyers to purchase goods and services at different prices. The other side of the exchange process is **supply**, the amount of goods and services for sale at different prices. Understanding the factors that determine demand and supply, as well as how the two interact, can help you understand many actions and decisions of individuals, businesses, and government. This section takes a closer look at these concepts.

Factors Driving Demand

For most of us, economics amounts to a balance between what we want and what we can afford. Because of this dilemma, each person must choose how much money to save and how much to spend. We must also decide among all the goods and services competing for our attention. Suppose you wanted to purchase a smart phone. You'd have to choose from a variety of brands and models. You'd also have to decide where you wanted to go to buy one. After shopping around, you might decide you didn't want a smart phone at all. Instead, you might purchase something else, or save your money.

Demand is driven by a number of factors that influence how people decide to spend their money, including price and consumer preferences. It may also be driven by outside circumstances or larger economic events. During the previous decade, the restaurant industry experienced uninterrupted growth. However, during the economic downturn, dinnertime business at restaurants fell by more than 3 percent, or 650 million visits. Analysts predict it might take several years for restaurants to regain dinnertime visits to pre-recession levels.[2]

Demand can also increase the availability of certain types of websites and services. In addition to public messaging, an Instagram app, Instagram Direct, allows users to send private messages to one or two followers at a time. This app has intensified the competition between Instagram and another well-known social network, Twitter. Both Instagram and Twitter allow messages to be sent to individuals or small groups, or a blast message to a broader public following. If Twitter and Instagram begin to resemble one another too closely, many wonder which service the upcoming generation of social media users will choose.[3]

In general, as the price of a good or service goes up, people buy smaller amounts. In other words, as price rises, the quantity demanded declines. At lower prices, consumers are generally willing to buy more of a good. A **demand curve** is a graph of the amount of a product that buyers will purchase at different prices. Demand curves typically slope downward, meaning that buyers will purchase greater quantities of a good or service as its price falls.

Gasoline provides a classic example of how demand curves work. The left side of Figure 3.1 shows a possible demand curve for the total amount of gasoline that people will purchase at different prices. For discussion purposes, the prices shown reflect a recent national average for gas, though they may not reflect the actual price in your location at this particular time. When gasoline is priced at $3.56 a gallon, drivers may fill up their tanks once or twice a week. At $3.86 a gallon, many of them start economizing. They may combine errands or carpool to work. So the quantity of gasoline demanded at $3.86 a gallon is lower than the amount demanded at $3.56 a gallon. The opposite happens at $3.26 a gallon. More gasoline is sold at $3.26 a gallon than at $3.56 a gallon, as people opt to run more errands

You shop for groceries, subscribe to a cell phone service, pay college tuition, fill your car's tank with gas. Each of these choices relates to the study of microeconomics. They also help determine the prices of goods and the amounts sold.

demand curve graph of the amount of a product that buyers will purchase at different prices.

FIGURE 3.1 Demand Curves for Gasoline

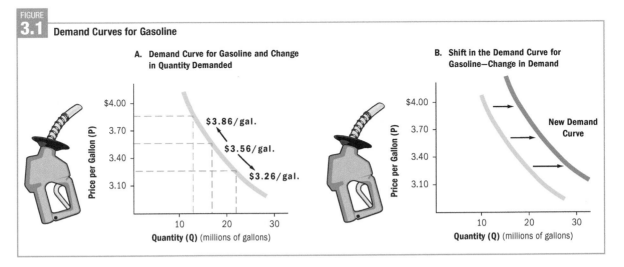

A. Demand Curve for Gasoline and Change in Quantity Demanded

B. Shift in the Demand Curve for Gasoline—Change in Demand

---

or take a weekend trip. However, as mentioned earlier, other factors may cause consumers to accept higher prices anyway. They may have made vacation plans in advance and do not want to cancel them. Or they may be required to drive to work every day.

Economists clearly distinguish between changes in the quantity demanded at various prices and changes in overall demand. A change in quantity demanded, such as the change that occurs at different gasoline prices, is simply movement along the demand curve. A change in overall demand, on the other hand, results in an entirely new demand curve. Businesses are constantly trying to make predictions about both kinds of demand, and a miscalculation can cause problems. In the case of gasoline, which is derived from crude oil, many factors come into play. For the foreseeable future, we will still depend on fossil fuels until we develop alternative fuel sources. In the long run, many people hope that the investment in and development of alternative or renewable energy sources such as shale oil, biodiesel, wind, and solar power may level off the demand for oil. When a downturn in the U.S. economy occurs, so does the demand for oil and other goods. But disruptions in energy sources have the opposite effect; international tensions in oil-rich nations or extreme weather that takes refineries offline increase the demand for the oil that is available.[4]

We can illustrate how the increased demand for gasoline worldwide has created a new demand curve, as shown in Figure 3.1. The new demand curve shifts to the right of the old demand curve, indicating that overall demand has increased at every price. A demand curve can also shift to the left when the demand for a good or service drops. However, the demand curve still has the same shape.

Although price is the underlying cause of movement along a demand curve, many factors can combine to determine the overall demand for a product—that is, the shape and position of the demand curve. These influences include customer preferences and incomes, the prices of substitute and complementary items, the number of buyers in a market, and the strength of their optimism regarding the future. Changes in any of these factors produce a new demand curve.

Changes in household income also change demand. As consumers have more money to spend, firms can sell more products at every price. This means the demand curve has shifted to the right. When income shrinks, fewer product purchases are made, and the demand curve shifts to the left. When housing construction declines, retailers like Lowes and Home Depot also experience a drop in demand. As housing rebounds, other industries like lumber, steel, and appliance manufacturers benefit.[5] Meanwhile, retailers such as Walmart and Costco experience an increase in sales, so their curve shifts to the right.[6] Table 3.1 describes how a demand curve is likely to respond to each of these changes.

TABLE

⌐3.1⌐ Expected Shifts in Demand Curves

FACTOR	DEMAND CURVE SHIFTS	
	TO THE RIGHT *IF:*	TO THE LEFT *IF:*
Customer preferences	Increase	Decrease
Number of buyers	Increase	Decrease
Buyers' incomes	Increase	Decrease
Prices of substitute goods	Increase	Decrease
Prices of complementary goods	Decrease	Increase
Future expectations become more	Optimistic	Pessimistic

For a business to succeed, management must carefully monitor the factors that may affect demand for the goods and services it hopes to sell. Costco has free sampling stations throughout its stores where customers can try small portions of various foods prepared on site. This practice encourages customers to buy something in the department where they are sampling.

Factors Driving Supply

Important economic factors also affect supply, the willingness and ability of firms to provide goods and services at different prices. Just as consumers must decide about how to spend their money, businesses must decide what products to sell, and how.

Sellers would prefer to charge higher prices for their products. A **supply curve** shows the relationship between different prices and the quantities that sellers will offer for sale, regardless of demand. Movement along the supply curve is the opposite of movement along the demand curve. So as price rises, the quantity that sellers are willing to supply also rises. At progressively lower prices, the quantity supplied decreases. In Figure 3.2, a possible supply curve for gasoline shows that increasing prices for gasoline should bring increasing supplies to market.

Businesses need certain inputs to operate effectively in producing their output. As discussed in Chapter 1, these *factors of production* include natural resources, capital, human resources, and entrepreneurship. Natural resources include land, building sites, forests, and mineral deposits. Capital refers to resources such as technology, tools, information, physical facilities, and financial capabilities. Human resources include the physical labor and intellectual inputs contributed by employees. Entrepreneurship is the willingness to take risks to create and operate a business. Factors of production play a central role in determining the overall supply of goods and services.

A change in the cost or availability of any of these inputs can shift the entire supply curve, either increasing or decreasing the amount available at every price. If the cost of land increases, a firm might not be able to purchase a site for a more efficient manufacturing plant, which would lower production levels, shifting the supply curve to the left. But if the company finds a way to speed up the production process, allowing it to turn out more products with less labor, the change reduces the overall cost of the finished products, which shifts the supply curve to the right.

Table 3.2 summarizes how changes in various factors can affect the supply curve. Sometimes forces of nature can affect the supply curve. Sometimes a drought or reduced rain can affect the supply curve. In Oklahoma, where many of the nation's pecans are grown, several years of drought have taken a major toll on the production of this popular nut. The result has been a dramatic drop in supply, or 15 million fewer pounds.[7]

The pharmaceutical industry recently experienced supply curve shifts due to drug shortages. In an effort to avert a drug shortage for cancer patients, the Food and Drug Administration now requires pharmaceutical makers to notify it of any potential shortages or production stoppages for drugs known to be in short supply. A recent drug shortage, the result of poor quality control of glass sterilization during manufacturing, was considered dangerous.[8]

How Demand and Supply Interact

Separate shifts in demand and supply have obvious effects on prices and the availability of products. In the real world, changes do not alternatively affect demand and supply. Several

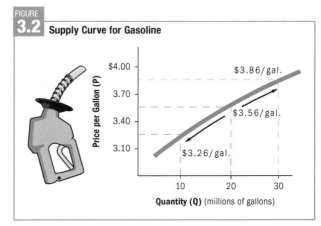

FIGURE 3.2 Supply Curve for Gasoline

supply curve graph that shows the relationship between different prices and the quantities that sellers will offer for sale, regardless of demand.

3.2 Expected Shifts in Supply Curves

FACTOR	SUPPLY CURVE SHIFTS	
	TO THE RIGHT *IF:*	TO THE LEFT *IF:*
Costs of inputs	Decrease	Increase
Costs of technologies	Decrease	Increase
Taxes	Decrease	Increase
Number of suppliers	Increase	Decrease

factors often change at the same time—and they keep changing. Sometimes such changes in multiple factors cause contradictory pressures on prices and quantities. In other cases, the final direction of prices and quantities reflects the factor that has changed the most. Demand and supply can affect employment as well as products.

Figure 3.3 shows the interaction of both supply and demand curves for gasoline on a single graph. Notice that the two curves intersect at *P*. The law of supply and demand states that prices (*P*) are set by the intersection of the supply and demand curves. The point where the two curves meet identifies the **equilibrium price**, the prevailing market price at which you can buy an item.

If the actual market price differs from the equilibrium price, buyers and sellers tend to make economic choices that restore the equilibrium level. A bumper corn crop can mean lower market prices. The government's proposal to reduce the amount of biofuel (made with corn) to be mixed with gasoline would be another pressure on corn prices. On the other hand, a drought might potentially cause a decrease in the corn crop, triggering a price increase. Lower demand for corn could potentially lead to government subsidies for farmers.[9]

For a number of years, fast-food chains like McDonald's and Wendy's reacted to market forces by reducing prices and offering everyday value menus and coupons. During the recent economic downturn and accompanying high unemployment rate, consumers were more likely to eat at home or purchase fast-food value meals rather than choose to dine at a more expensive, sit-down eatery.

As the economy rebounds, the fast-casual dining segment has become popular. A fusion of fast food and casual dining, fast-casual dining restaurants are places where customers are willing to pay more for food that is a cut above fast food. Chipotle Mexican Grill represents the "fast-casual" dining segment, and the chain's growth trajectory proves its customers don't mind paying a premium for quality food ingredients.[10] See the "Hit & Miss" feature for more about Chipotle.

As pointed out earlier, the forces of demand and supply can be affected by a variety of factors. One important variable is the larger economic environment. The next section explains how macroeconomics and economic systems influence market forces and, ultimately, demand, supply, and prices.

equilibrium price prevailing market price at which you can buy an item.

Assessment Check ☑

1. Define microeconomics and macroeconomics.

2. Explain demand and supply curves.

3. How do factors of production influence the overall supply of goods and services?

FIGURE

3.3 Law of Supply and Demand

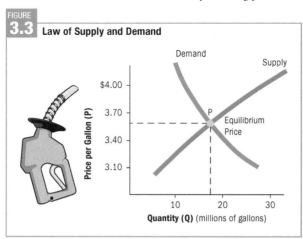

Part 1 *Business in a Global Environment*

Hit&Miss

Chipotle's Fast-Casual Dining Scores with Customers

A little over two decades ago, chef Steve Ells, classically trained in French cooking, became the force behind Chipotle Mexican Grill. With a loan of $85,000 from his father, and inspiration from authentic Mexican *taquerias* found in San Francisco's Mission District, he opened his first restaurant in a Colorado college town. Ells projected he would need to sell at least 107 burritos a day to cover his expenses. After a month in business, Ells was selling more than a thousand of his high-quality burritos.

Ells envisioned his concept as a hybrid between fast and casual—and food served fast didn't have to mean a fast-food experience. Chipotle is classified as "fast-casual," an emerging market for high-quality food and service that coincides with that of a "casual" dining experience rather than a "fast" one.

Ells has teamed up with meat producers, many of whom operate family farms, to create a market for farmers raising livestock in a more humane way. In addition, Chipotle's choice of selective, organic, hormone-free, and locally sourced ingredients will, at some point, include no genetically modified food items. When you bite into a delicious burrito at one of Chipotle's more than 1,500 restaurants, rest assured that you're enjoying top-quality, sustainable, natural, organic, non–genetically

modified food, and naturally raised ingredients. That makes delicious business sense from a company whose mission is "food with integrity."

Questions for Critical Thinking

1. In its most recent annual report, Chipotle Mexican Grill's vision and mission statement states: "to change the way people think about and eat fast food." Discuss the company's vision and mission statement and whether it sets the company apart from the competition. If so, how?
2. Chipotle targets a slightly different crowd than fast-food eaters. Explain why Chipotle customers are willing to pay more for the company's fast-casual dining experience.

Sources: Company website, www.chipotle.com, accessed January 24, 2014; Tom Gara, "Coming Up in 2014: An Organically Grown Price Rise at Chipotle," *The Wall Street Journal*, January 24, 2014, http://blogs.wsj.com; "Investor Relations," http://ir.chipotle.com, accessed January 24, 2014; Brian Shaw, "Chipotle's Strengths Will Drive Further Gains in 2014," *Motley Fool*, January 3, 2014, www.fool.com.

---

[2] Macroeconomics: Issues for the Entire Economy

Macroeconomics is the study of a country's overall economic issues. Each nation's policies and choices help determine its economic system. But the political, social, and legal environments differ in every country. In general, however, these systems can be classified into three categories: private enterprise systems; planned economies; or combinations of the two, referred to as mixed economies. As business becomes an increasingly global undertaking, it is important to understand the primary features of the various economic systems operating around the world.

Capitalism: The Private Enterprise System and Competition

Most industrialized nations operate economies based on the *private enterprise system*, also known as *capitalism* or a *market economy*. A private enterprise system rewards businesses for meeting the needs and demands of consumers. Government tends to favor a hands-off attitude toward controlling business ownership, profits, and resource allocations. Instead, competition regulates economic life, creating opportunities and challenges that businesspeople must handle to succeed.

The relative competitiveness of a particular industry is an important consideration for every firm because it determines the ease and cost of doing business within that industry. Four basic types of competition take shape in a private enterprise system: pure competition, monopolistic competition, oligopoly, and monopoly. Table 3.3 highlights the main differences among these types of competition.

Pure competition is a market structure, like that of small-scale agriculture or fishing, in which large numbers of buyers and sellers exchange homogeneous products like sugar, rice, and wheat, and no single participant has a significant influence on price. Instead, prices are set

macroeconomics study of a nation's overall economic issues, such as how an economy maintains and allocates resources and how a government's policies affect the standards of living of its citizens.

pure competition market structure in which large numbers of buyers and sellers exchange homogeneous products and no single participant has a significant influence on price.

Chapter 3 *Economic Challenges Facing Contemporary Business*

69

⌐3.3⌐ Types of Competition

CHARACTERISTICS	TYPES OF COMPETITION			
	PURE COMPETITION	**MONOPOLISTIC COMPETITION**	**OLIGOPOLY**	**MONOPOLY**
Number of competitors	Many	Few to many	Few	No direct competition
Ease of entry into industry by new firms	Easy	Somewhat difficult	Difficult	Regulated by government
Similarity of goods or services offered by competing firms	Similar	Different	Similar or different	No directly competing products
Control over price by individual firms	None	Some	Some	Considerable in a pure monopoly; little in a regulated monopoly
Examples	Small-scale farmer in Indiana	Local fitness center	Boeing aircraft	Rawlings Sporting Goods, exclusive supplier of major-league baseballs

monopolistic competition market structure in which large numbers of buyers and sellers exchange heterogeneous products so each participant has some control over price.

Fishing is a good example of pure competition. Because seafood caught by one boat is virtually identical to that landed by others, the price rises and falls with changes in supply and demand. For example, whenever a harmful "red tide" of algae infests the fishing areas, the supply of fresh seafood plummets and the price skyrockets.

by the market as the forces of supply and demand interact. Firms can easily enter or leave a purely competitive market because no single company dominates. Also, in pure competition, buyers see little difference between the goods and services offered by competitors.

The fishing industry is a good example of pure competition. As weather and ocean conditions affect seafood supplies, the prices for this commodity rise or fall according to the laws of supply and demand. The clams and mussels that one fishing boat gathers off the coast of New England are virtually identical to those gathered by others. The region's notorious "red tide" of algae sometimes contaminates part of the season's supply of shellfish just when summer tourists want them the most—and prices skyrocket.

Monopolistic competition is a market structure, like that for retailing, in which large numbers of buyers and sellers exchange differentiated (heterogeneous) products, so each participant has some control over price. Sellers can differentiate their products from competing offerings on the basis of price, quality, or other features. In an industry that features monopolistic competition, it is relatively easy for a firm to begin or stop selling a good or service. The success of one seller often attracts new competitors to such a market. Individual firms also have some control over how their goods and services are priced.

One example of monopolistic competition is the market for pet food. Consumers can choose from private-label (store brands such as Walmart's Ol'Roy) and brand-name products such as Purina in bags, boxes, and cans. Producers of pet food and the stores that sell it have wide latitude in setting prices. Consumers can choose the store or brand with the lowest prices, or sellers can convince them that a more expensive offering, for example the Fromm brand, is worth more because it offers better nutrition, more convenience, or other benefits.

An **oligopoly** is a market situation in which relatively few sellers compete and high start-up costs form barriers to keep out new competitors. In some oligopolistic industries, such as paper and steel, competitors offer similar products. In others, such as aircraft and automobiles, they sell different models and features. The huge investment required to enter an oligopoly market tends to discourage new competitors. The limited number of sellers also enhances the control these firms exercise over price. Competing products in an oligopoly usually sell for very similar prices because substantial price competition would reduce profits for all firms in the industry. So a price cut by one firm in an oligopoly will typically be met by its competitors. However, prices can vary from one market to another, as from one country to another.

Google Play has disrupted the monopoly Apple's iTunes once enjoyed due to the increasing popularity of the Android operating system on mobile devices.

AFP/Getty Images

The final type of market structure is a **monopoly**, in which a single seller dominates trade in a good or service for which buyers can find no close substitutes. A pure monopoly occurs when a firm possesses unique characteristics so important to competition in its industry that they form barriers to prevent entry by would-be competitors. There are a number of companies once thought to dominate their respective markets, but disruptive technology, a new technology that unexpectedly replaces an existing one, has changed that. PayPal's e-commerce payment system, Google's search engine, Facebook's social networking platform, and Apple's iTunes no longer dominate their respective markets as they once did.[11]

Many firms create short-term monopolies when research breakthroughs permit them to receive exclusive patents on new products. In the pharmaceuticals industry, drug giants such as Merck and Pfizer invest billions in research and development programs. When the research leads to successful new drugs, the companies can enjoy the benefits of their patents: the ability to set prices without fear of competitors undercutting them. Once the patent expires, generic substitutes enter the market, driving down prices.

Because a monopoly market lacks the benefits of competition, many governments regulate monopolies. Besides issuing patents and limiting their life, the U.S. government prohibits most pure monopolies through antitrust legislation such as the Sherman Act and the Clayton Act. The U.S. government has applied these laws against monopoly behavior by Microsoft and by disallowing proposed mergers of large companies in some industries. In other cases, the government permits certain monopolies in exchange for regulating their activities.

With **regulated monopolies**, a local, state, or federal government grants exclusive rights in a certain market to a single firm. Pricing decisions—particularly rate-increase requests—are subject to control by regulatory authorities such as state public service commissions. An example is the delivery of first-class mail, a monopoly held by the U.S. Postal Service. The USPS is a self-supporting corporation wholly owned by the federal government. Its postal rates are set by a postal commission and approved by a board of governors.

During the 1980s and 1990s, the U.S. government trended away from regulated monopolies and toward deregulation. Regulated monopolies that have been deregulated include transportation, energy, and communications. The idea is to improve customer service and reduce prices for customers through increased competition. The FCC has yet to regulate broadband Internet services in the same way it has telecommunications services. The result is that the Internet is not subject to the same set of rules as landline phone services. There is

oligopoly market situation in which relatively few sellers compete and high start-up costs form barriers to keep out new competitors.

monopoly market situation in which a single seller dominates trade in a good or service for which buyers can find no close substitutes.

regulated monopolies market situation in which a local, state, or federal government grants exclusive rights in a certain market to a single firm.

talk of converting the old, analog phone system used nationwide into a new Internet-based network. This has resulted in a conflict between old and new technology regulations.[12]

Planned Economies: Socialism and Communism

In a **planned economy**, government controls determine business ownership, profits, and resource allocation to accomplish government goals rather than those set by individual firms. Two forms of planned economies are communism and socialism.

Socialism is characterized by government ownership and operation of major industries such as communications. Socialists argue that major industries are too important to a society to be left in private hands and that government-owned businesses can serve the public's interest better than private firms. However, socialism allows private ownership in industries considered less crucial to social welfare, such as retail shops, restaurants, and certain types of manufacturing facilities. Scandinavian countries such as Denmark, Sweden, and Finland have many socialist features in their societies, as do some African nations and India.

The writings of Karl Marx in the mid-1800s formed the basis of communist theory. Marx believed that private enterprise economies created unfair conditions and led to worker exploitation because business owners controlled most of society's resources and reaped most of the economy's rewards. Instead, he suggested an economic system called **communism**, in which all property would be shared equally by the people of a community under the direction of a strong central government. Marx believed that elimination of private ownership of property and businesses would ensure the emergence of a classless society that would benefit all. Each individual would contribute to the nation's overall economic success, and resources would be distributed according to each person's needs. Under communism, the central government owns the means of production, and the people work for state-owned enterprises. The government determines what people can buy because it dictates what is produced in the nation's factories and farms.

Several nations adopted communist-like economic systems during the early 20th century in an effort to correct abuses they believed occurred in their existing systems. In practice, however, the new governments typically gave less freedom of choice in regard to jobs and purchases and might be best described as totalitarian socialism. These nations often made mistakes in allocating resources to compete in the growing global marketplace. Government-owned monopolies often suffer from inefficiency.

Consider the former Soviet Union, where large government bureaucracies controlled nearly every aspect of daily life. Shortages became chronic because producers had little or no incentive to satisfy customers. The quality of goods and services also suffered for the same reason. When Mikhail Gorbachev became the last president of the dying Soviet Union, he tried to improve the quality of Soviet-made products. Effectively shut out of trading in the global marketplace and caught up in a treasury-depleting arms race with the United States, the Soviet Union faced severe financial problems. Eventually, these events led to the collapse of Soviet communism and the breakup of the Soviet Union itself.

Today, communist-like systems exist in just a few countries, such as North Korea. By contrast, the People's Republic of China has shifted toward a more market-oriented economy. The national government has given local government and individual plant managers more say in business decisions and has permitted some private businesses. Households now have more control over agriculture, in contrast to the collectivized farms introduced during an earlier era. In addition, Western products such as McDonald's restaurants and Coca-Cola soft drinks are now part of Chinese consumers' lives.

Mixed Market Economies

Private enterprise systems and planned economies adopt basically opposite approaches to operating economies. In reality, though, many countries operate **mixed market economies**, economic systems that draw from both types of economies, to different degrees. In nations generally considered to have a private enterprise economy, government-owned firms

planned economy economic system in which government controls determine business ownership, profits, and resource allocation to accomplish government goals rather than those set by individual firms.

socialism economic system characterized by government ownership and operation of major industries such as communications.

communism economic system in which all property would be shared equally by the people of a community under the direction of a strong central government.

mixed market economies economic system that draws from both types of economies, to different degrees.

frequently operate alongside private enterprises. In the United States, programs such as Medicare are government run.

France has blended socialist and free enterprise policies for hundreds of years. The nation's energy production, public transportation, and defense industries are run as nationalized industries, controlled by the government. Meanwhile, a market economy operates in other industries. Over the past two decades, the French government has loosened its reins on state-owned companies, inviting both competition and private investment into industries previously operated as government monopolies.

The proportions of private and public enterprise can vary widely in mixed economies, and the mix frequently changes. Dozens of countries have converted government-owned and operated companies into privately held businesses in a trend known as **privatization**. Even the United States has seen proposals to privatize everything from the postal service to Social Security.

Governments may privatize state-owned enterprises in an effort to raise funds and improve their economies. The objective is to cut costs and run the operation more efficiently. One example is the Student Loan Marketing Association (SLMA). Originally a government-sponsored enterprise, it is the largest originator of federally insured student loans in the country. After going through a successful privatization process, SLMA originates, services, and collects payments on student loans.[13] Table 3.4 compares the alternative economic systems on the basis of ownership and management of enterprises, rights to profits, employee rights, and worker incentives.

privatization conversion of government-owned and operated companies into privately held businesses.

Assessment Check ✅

1. What is the difference between pure competition and monopolistic competition?

2. On which economic system is the U.S. economy based?

3. What is privatization?

TABLE

⌐3.4⌐ Comparison of Alternative Economic Systems

SYSTEM FEATURES	CAPITALISM (PRIVATE ENTERPRISE)	PLANNED ECONOMIES		
		COMMUNISM	SOCIALISM	MIXED ECONOMY
Ownership of enterprises	Businesses are owned privately, often by large numbers of people. Minimal government ownership leaves production in private hands.	Government owns the means of production with few exceptions, such as small plots of land.	Government owns basic industries, but private owners operate some small enterprises.	A strong private sector blends with public enterprises.
Management of enterprises	Enterprises are managed by owners or their representatives, with minimal government interference.	Centralized management controls all state enterprises in line with three- to five-year plans. Planning now is being decentralized.	Significant government planning pervades socialist nations. State enterprises are managed directly by government bureaucrats.	Management of the private sector resembles that under capitalism. Professionals may also manage state enterprises.
Rights to profits	Entrepreneurs and investors are entitled to all profits (minus taxes) that their firms earn.	Profits are not allowed under communism.	Only the private sector of a socialist economy generates profits.	Entrepreneurs and investors are entitled to private-sector profits, although they often must pay high taxes. State enterprises are also expected to produce returns.
Rights of employees	The rights to choose one's occupation and to join a labor union have long been recognized.	Employee rights are limited in exchange for promised protection against unemployment.	Workers may choose their occupations and join labor unions, but the government influences career decisions for many people.	Workers may choose jobs and labor union membership. Unions often become quite strong.
Worker incentives	Considerable incentives motivate people to perform at their highest levels.	Incentives are emerging in communist countries.	Incentives usually are limited in state enterprises but do motivate workers in the private sector.	Capitalist-style incentives operate in the private sector. More limited incentives influence public-sector activities.

Ideally, an economic system should provide two important benefits for its citizens: a stable business environment and sustained growth. In a stable business environment, the overall supply of needed goods and services is aligned with the overall demand for these items. No wild fluctuations in price or availability make economic decisions complicated. Consumers and businesses not only have access to ample supplies of desired products at affordable prices but also have money to buy the items they demand.

Growth is another important economic goal. An ideal economy incorporates steady change directed toward continually expanding the amount of goods and services produced from the nation's resources. Growth leads to expanded job opportunities, improved wages, and a rising standard of living.

Flattening the Business Cycle

A nation's economy tends to flow through various stages of a business cycle: prosperity, recession, depression, and recovery. No "true" economic depressions have occurred in the United States since the 1930s, and some economists believe that society is capable of preventing future depressions through effective economic policies. Consequently, they expect recessions to give way to periods of economic recovery. The "Going Green" feature discusses how one U.S. community is exploring the development of alternative sources of energy that will create new jobs to stimulate the economy.

Both business decisions and consumer buying patterns differ at each stage of the business cycle. In periods of economic prosperity, unemployment remains low, consumer confidence about the future leads to more purchases, and businesses expand—by hiring more employees, investing in new technology, and making similar purchases—to take advantage of new opportunities.

recession cyclical economic contraction that lasts for six months or longer.

As recent events show, during a **recession**—a cyclical economic contraction that lasts for six months or longer—consumers frequently postpone major purchases and shift buying patterns toward basic, functional products carrying low prices. Businesses mirror these changes in the marketplace by slowing production, postponing expansion plans, reducing inventories, and often cutting the size of their workforces. During recessions, people facing layoffs and depletions of household savings become much more conservative in their spending, postponing luxury purchases and vacations. They often turn to generic brands and lower-priced retailers such as Dollar Tree and Dollar General for the goods they need.[14] And they have sold cars, jewelry, and securities to make ends meet. They have also sold everything from old books to artwork to kitchenware on eBay.

If an economic slowdown continues in a downward spiral over an extended period of time, the economy falls into depression. Many Americans have grown up hearing stories about their great-grandparents who lived through the Great Depression of the 1930s, when food and other basic necessities were scarce and jobs were rare.

In the recovery stage of the business cycle, the economy emerges from recession and consumer spending picks up steam. Even though businesses often continue to rely on part-time and other temporary workers during the early stages of a recovery, unemployment begins to decline as business activity accelerates and firms seek additional workers to meet

© Jim Jurica/iStockphoto

During a recession, consumers may shift buying patterns toward basic, functional products carrying low prices. People facing layoffs and depletions of household savings become much more conservative in their spending and often sell cars, jewelry, and securities to make ends meet.

GoingGreen

Raleigh Takes the Lead in Smart Grid Technology

Smart-grid technology involves digitally enabled electrical grids that gather, distribute, and act on information about electrical usage in a specific area. It not only holds out the promise of cleaner, cheaper, and more efficient electronic delivery of power for U.S. homes, cars, and businesses; someday it could even allow consumers to generate their own energy and sell surplus capacity to utility companies. Imagine making money from your energy use instead of paying for it.

Raleigh, North Carolina, is the country's major smart-grid development hub. North Carolina State University (NCSU) hosts the multi-university FREEDM Center (for Future Renewable Electric Energy, Delivery, and Management), funded by the National Science Foundation, which is helping develop a digital "smart transformer" that MIT's *Technology Review* calls one of the world's 10 most important emerging technologies.

About 41 technology firms are in partnership with FREEDM, including ABB, Siemens, Eaton, Tantalus Solutions, and Intel, and the project employs about 3,000 people in the area. The U.S. government has provided billions of dollars to fund FREEDM and similar projects around the country, to develop the new technology and make it operational on a large scale. New hardware, software, meters, and controls will be required, and utility companies will need to sign on in numbers.

But the Raleigh team is optimistic. According to FREEDM's director, NCSU professor Alex Huang, smart-grid technology is about five years ahead of its time with the Raleigh experience: "We are pushing electronics into the power grid."

Questions for Critical Thinking

1. Do you think the government's investment in clean energy through initiatives such as FREEDM will pay off? Why or why not?
2. What are some of the benefits the FREEDM Center brings to the local Raleigh economy?

Sources: "The Smarts of the Smart Grid," FREEDM Systems Center, http://freedm.ncsu .edu, accessed January 24, 2014; Venessa Wong, "Raleigh's Smart Grid Bid," *Bloomberg Businessweek*, accessed January 24, 2014, www.businessweek.com; "New Report Shows Smart Grid Dominance in the Triangle," Research Triangle Cleantech Cluster, accessed January 24, 2014, www.researchtrianglecleantech.org; "Why Was NC State Chosen to Lead the New Research Consortium?" *Smart Grid Technologies*, January 15, 2014, www.raleigh-wake.org.

---

growing production demands. Gradually, the concerns of recession begin to disappear, and consumers start eating out at restaurants, booking vacations, and purchasing new cars again.

Productivity and the Nation's Gross Domestic Product

An important concern for every economy is **productivity**, the relationship between the goods and services produced in a nation each year and the inputs needed to produce them. In general, as productivity rises, so does an economy's growth and the wealth of its citizens. In a recession, productivity stalls or even declines.

Productivity describes the relationship between the number of units produced and the number of human and other production inputs necessary to produce them. Productivity is a ratio of output to input. When a constant amount of inputs generates increased outputs, an increase in productivity occurs.

Total productivity considers all inputs necessary to produce a specific amount of outputs. Stated in equation form, it can be written as follows:

$$\text{Total Productivity} = \frac{\text{Output (goods or services produced)}}{\text{Input (human/natural resources, capital)}}$$

Many productivity ratios focus on only one of the inputs in the equation: labor productivity or output per labor-hour. An increase in labor productivity means that the same amount of work produces more goods and services than before. Many of the gains in U.S. productivity can be attributed to technology.

Productivity is a widely recognized measure of a company's efficiency. In turn, the total productivity of a nation's businesses has become a measure of its economic strength and standard of living. Economists refer to this measure as a country's **gross domestic product (GDP)**—the sum of all goods and services produced within its boundaries. The GDP is based on the per-capita output of a country—in other words, total national output divided by

productivity relationship between the number of units produced and the number of human and other production inputs necessary to produce them.

gross domestic product (GDP) sum of all goods and services produced within a country's boundaries during a specific time period, such as a year.

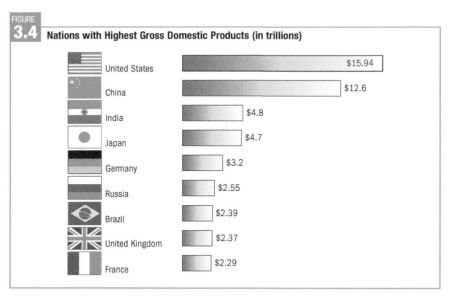

FIGURE 3.4 Nations with Highest Gross Domestic Products (in trillions)

United States	$15.94
China	$12.6
India	$4.8
Japan	$4.7
Germany	$3.2
Russia	$2.55
Brazil	$2.39
United Kingdom	$2.37
France	$2.29

Source: *World Factbook*, Central Intelligence Agency, https://www.cia.gov, accessed January 24, 2014.

the number of citizens. As Figure 3.4 shows, the United States has an estimated GDP of $15.94 trillion. Only the European Union, with its 28 member nations and estimated GDP of $15.98 trillion, has a GDP higher than the United States.[15] In the United States, GDP is tracked by the Bureau of Economic Analysis (BEA), a division of the U.S. Department of Commerce. Current updates and historical data on the GDP are available at the BEA's website (http://www.bea.gov). A new economic aggregate, gross output (GO), has been introduced recently by the BEA. It will measure total sales volume at all production stages rather than just final output.[16]

Price-Level Changes

Another important indicator of an economy's stability is the general level of prices. For the past 100 years, economic decision makers concerned themselves with **inflation**, rising prices caused by a combination of excess consumer demand and increases in the costs of raw materials, component parts, human resources, and other factors of production. The **core inflation rate** is the inflation rate of an economy after energy and food prices are removed. This measure is often an accurate prediction of the inflation rate that consumers, businesses, and other organizations can expect to experience during the near future.

Excess consumer demand generates what is known as demand-pull inflation while increases in the costs of factors of production generates cost-push inflation. America's most severe inflationary period during the last half of the 20th century peaked in 1980 at over 14 percent. In extreme cases, an economy may experience **hyperinflation**—an economic situation characterized by soaring prices. The most recent severe case of hyperinflation occurred in Zimbabwe, with prices doubling almost every 24 hours.[17]

Inflation devalues money as persistent price increases reduce the amount of goods and services people can purchase with a given amount of money. This is bad news for people whose

inflation economic situation characterized by rising prices caused by a combination of excess consumer demand and increases in the costs of raw materials, component parts, human resources, and other factors of production.

core inflation rate inflation rate of an economy after energy and food prices are removed.

hyperinflation economic situation characterized by soaring prices.

earnings do not keep up with inflation, who live on fixed incomes, or who have most of their wealth in investments paying a fixed rate of interest. Inflation can be good news for people whose income is rising or those with debts at a fixed rate of interest. A homeowner with a fixed-rate mortgage during inflationary times is paying off that debt with money that is worth less and less each year. However, despite the changes in the stock and housing markets, the number of U.S. households with a net worth of at least $1 million is still growing, though much slower than pre-recession levels.[18]

When increased productivity results in stabilized prices, it can have a major positive impact on an economy. In a low-inflation environment, businesses can make long-range plans without the constant worry of sudden inflationary shocks. Low interest rates encourage firms to invest in research and development and capital improvements, both of which are likely to produce productivity gains. Consumers can purchase growing stocks of goods and services with the same amount of money, and low interest rates encourage major acquisitions such as new homes and autos. But there are concerns. The fluctuating cost of oil—which is used to produce many goods—remains an issue. Businesses need to raise prices to cover their costs. Also, smaller firms have gone out of business or have been merged with larger companies, reducing overall competition and increasing the purchasing power of the larger corporations. Business owners continue to keep a watchful eye on signs of inflation.

The opposite situation—**deflation**—occurs when prices continue to fall. In Japan, where deflation has been a reality for several years, shoppers pay less for a variety of products ranging from groceries to homes. While this situation may sound ideal to consumers, it can weaken the economy. For instance, industries such as housing and auto manufacturing need to maintain strong prices in order to support all the related businesses that depend on them.

deflation opposite of inflation, occurs when prices continue to fall.

Consumer Price Index (CPI) measurement of the monthly average change in prices of goods and services.

Measuring Price Level Changes In the United States, the government tracks changes in price levels with the **Consumer Price Index (CPI)**, which measures the monthly average change in prices of goods and services. The federal Bureau of Labor Statistics (BLS) calculates the CPI monthly based on prices of a "market basket," a compilation of the goods and services most commonly purchased by urban consumers. Figure 3.5 shows the categories included in the CPI market basket. Each month, BLS representatives visit thousands of stores, service establishments, rental units, and doctors' offices all over the United States to price the multitude of items in the CPI market basket. They compile the data to create the CPI. Thus, the CPI provides a running measurement of changes in consumer prices.

Employment Levels People need money to buy the goods and services produced in an economy. Because most consumers earn that money by working, the number of people in a nation who currently have jobs is an important indicator of how well the economy is doing. In general, employment has dropped during the recent U.S. recession, although it recently began to rebound. Areas that have seen gains include professional and technical services, as well as education, health

© Lya Cattel/iStockphoto

When increased productivity keeps prices steady, it can have a major positive impact on an economy. Low interest rates encourage firms to invest in capital improvements—such as building a new company headquarters or expanding existing space—which are likely to produce productivity gains.

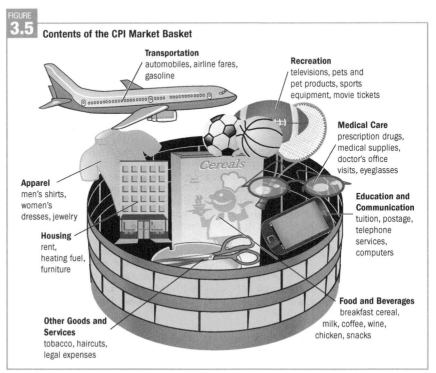

FIGURE 3.5 Contents of the CPI Market Basket

Transportation
automobiles, airline fares, gasoline

Recreation
televisions, pets and pet products, sports equipment, movie tickets

Medical Care
prescription drugs, medical supplies, doctor's office visits, eyeglasses

Apparel
men's shirts, women's dresses, jewelry

Education and Communication
tuition, postage, telephone services, computers

Housing
rent, heating fuel, furniture

Food and Beverages
breakfast cereal, milk, coffee, wine, chicken, snacks

Other Goods and Services
tobacco, haircuts, legal expenses

Source: Information from Bureau of Labor Statistics, "Consumer Price Indexes: Frequently Asked Questions," http://www.bls.gov/cpi, accessed January 24, 2014.

care, and social assistance.[19] The "Hit & Miss" feature discusses a foundation that helps working women and their families.

Economists refer to a nation's **unemployment rate** as an indicator of its economic health. The unemployment rate is usually expressed as a percentage of the total workforce actively seeking work but currently unemployed. The total labor force includes all people who are willing and available to work at the going market wage, whether they currently have jobs or are seeking work. The U.S. Department of Labor, which tracks unemployment rates, also measures so-called discouraged workers and underemployed workers. Discouraged workers are individuals who want to work but have given up looking for jobs. Underemployed workers are individuals who have taken lower-paying positions than their qualifications would suggest. Unemployment can be grouped into the four categories shown in Figure 3.6: frictional, seasonal, cyclical, and structural.

Frictional unemployment is experienced by members of the workforce who are temporarily not working but are looking for jobs. This pool of potential workers includes new graduates, people who have left jobs for any reason and are looking for other employment, and former workers who have decided to return to the labor force. **Seasonal unemployment** is the joblessness of people in a seasonal industry. Construction workers, farm laborers, fishing boat operators, and landscape employees may contend with bouts of seasonal unemployment when conditions make work unavailable.

Cyclical unemployment includes people who are out of work because of a cyclical contraction in the economy. During periods of economic expansion, overall employment is likely to rise, but as growth slows and a recession begins, unemployment levels commonly rise. At such times, even workers with good job skills may face temporary unemployment. Workers

unemployment rate percentage of the total workforce actively seeking work but currently unemployed.

frictional unemployment applies to members of the workforce who are temporarily not working but are looking for jobs.

seasonal unemployment joblessness of workers in a seasonal industry.

cyclical unemployment people who are out of work because of a cyclical contraction in the economy.

Hit&Miss

Tory Burch Foundation Aids Women's Businesses

Tory Burch is an American icon—fashion designer, businesswoman, and philanthropist. Burch, a working mother, launched a successful fashion design company and later established the Tory Burch Foundation. Her research revealed some grim statistics: The majority of poor people in the United States are women.

Having a child is one of the leading reasons a woman's income falls below the cost of living—making single mothers the group most likely to sink into poverty. In response to the demands of childcare and earning a living, many women have started their own businesses.

Inspired by microlenders in the developing world, Burch formed a partnership with ACCION USA, an American microlender. At $500 to $50,000, ACCION USA's loans are somewhat larger than those in developing nations, but many have the same purpose: "to economically empower women." Their clients are more likely to be rejected by traditional banks, so these microloans are essential to their success. Forty percent are women, and more than 80 percent are members of minority groups. ACCION USA reports that more than 90 percent of these microloans have been repaid.

Burch remarks that financing women's companies is more than social responsibility, it's good business and good for the economy. "Women are the hardest hit by the economy," says Burch. "And they repay their loans more often than not."

Questions for Critical Thinking

1. Research and discuss the types of businesses women have started. Are some in response to the dual demands of childcare and earning a living?

2. Why do you think that women repay their loans more often than not? Why is the payback rate so high?

Sources: Tory Burch Foundation, www.toryburchfoundation.org, accessed January 24, 2014; "Tory Burch Foundation, National Women's Business Week, and a Free CD," *The Clothes Whisperer*, accessed January 24, 2014, www.theclotheswhisperer.co.uk; Marshall Heyman, "Fashion Designer Shares the Wealth," *The Wall Street Journal*, accessed January 24, 2014, http://online.wsj.com.

---

in high-tech industries, air travel, and manufacturing have all faced unemployment during economic contraction.

Structural unemployment applies to people who remain unemployed for long periods of time, often with little hope of finding new jobs like their old ones. This situation may arise because these workers lack the necessary skills for available jobs or because the skills they

> **structural unemployment** people who remain unemployed for long periods of time, often with little hope of finding new jobs like their old ones.

Assessment Check ✔

1. Describe the four stages of the business cycle.

2. What are some measures that economists use to determine the health of an economy?

FIGURE 3.6 Four Types of Unemployment

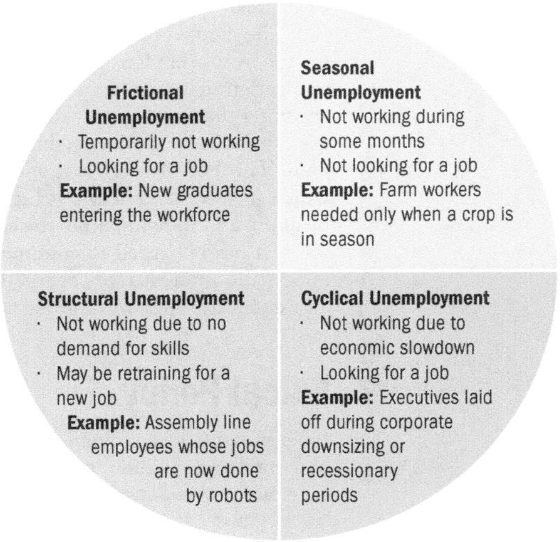

Frictional Unemployment
· Temporarily not working
· Looking for a job
Example: New graduates entering the workforce

Seasonal Unemployment
· Not working during some months
· Not looking for a job
Example: Farm workers needed only when a crop is in season

Structural Unemployment
· Not working due to no demand for skills
· May be retraining for a new job
Example: Assembly line employees whose jobs are now done by robots

Cyclical Unemployment
· Not working due to economic slowdown
· Looking for a job
Example: Executives laid off during corporate downsizing or recessionary periods

monetary policy government actions to increase or decrease the money supply and change banking requirements and interest rates to influence bankers' willingness to make loans.

expansionary monetary policy government actions to increase the money supply in an effort to cut the cost of borrowing, which encourages business decision makers to make new investments, in turn stimulating employment and economic growth.

restrictive monetary policy government actions to reduce the money supply to curb rising prices, overexpansion, and concerns about overly rapid economic growth.

fiscal policy government spending and taxation decisions designed to control inflation, reduce unemployment, improve the general welfare of citizens, and encourage economic growth.

have are no longer in demand. For instance, technological developments have increased the demand for people with computer-related skills but have created structural unemployment among many types of manual laborers or workers who may have been injured and unable to return to work.

[4] Managing the Economy's Performance

Government can use both monetary policy and fiscal policy in its efforts to fight unemployment, increase business and consumer spending, and reduce the length and severity of economic recessions. For instance, the Federal Reserve System can increase or reduce interest rates, and the federal government can enact tax cuts and rebates, or propose other reforms.

Monetary Policy

A common method of influencing economic activity is **monetary policy**, government actions to increase or decrease the money supply and change banking requirements and interest rates to influence spending by altering bankers' willingness to make loans. An **expansionary monetary policy** increases the money supply in an effort to cut the cost of borrowing, which encourages business decision makers to make new investments, in turn stimulating employment and economic growth. By contrast, a **restrictive monetary policy** reduces the money supply to curb rising prices, overexpansion, and concerns about overly rapid economic growth.

In the United States, the Federal Reserve System ("the Fed") is responsible for formulating and implementing the nation's monetary policy. It is headed by a chair and board of governors, all of whom are nominated by the president. The current chair is Janet Yellen, the first woman to head the central bank in its 100-year history. All national banks must be members of this system and keep some percentage of their checking and savings funds on deposit at the Fed. The Federal Open Market Committee (FOMC) oversees the nation's open market operations, which consist of buying and selling treasury securities.

The Fed's board of governors uses a number of tools to regulate the economy. By changing the required percentage of checking and savings accounts that banks must deposit with the Fed, the governors can expand or shrink funds available to lend. The Fed also lends money to member banks, which in turn make loans at higher interest rates to business and individual borrowers. By changing the interest rates charged to commercial banks, the Fed affects the interest rates charged to borrowers and, consequently, their willingness to borrow.

Janet Yellen is the first woman to chair the Federal Reserve in the central bank's 100-year history.

Bloomberg/Getty Images

Fiscal Policy

Governments also influence economic activities by making decisions about taxes and spending. Through revenues and expenses, the government implements **fiscal policy**. This is the second technique that officials use to control inflation, reduce unemployment, improve the general standard of living, and encourage economic growth. Increased taxes may restrict economic activities, while lower taxes and increased government spending usually boost spending and profits, cut unemployment rates, and fuel economic expansion. To create jobs and increase GDP, an ongoing discussion of reducing corporate taxes—a way to stimulate investment and spending—remains.

International Fiscal Policy Nations in the industrial world, including the United States, are currently struggling to find ways to help developing nations modernize their economies. One proposal is to forgive the debts of some of these countries, particularly those in Africa, to stimulate their economies to grow. But not all fiscal experts agree with this idea. They suggest that any debt forgiveness should come with certain conditions so that these countries can build their own fiscal policies. Countries should encourage and allow citizens to own property, lower their tax rates, avoid devaluing their currencies, lay a path for new businesses to start, and reduce trade barriers. In addition, they must improve agriculture, education, and health care so their citizens can begin to set and reach financial goals. The World Bank is an organization that offers such programs as low-interest loans and interest-free credit and grants to developing countries. To date, the World Bank Group has provided nearly $1 billion in financial assistance to aid recovery efforts in the Philippines after Typhoon Haiyan.[20] Another way to assist developing countries is to ship them outdated electronics to recycle or to restore for people to use. This practice is not without criticism, however. See the "Solving an Ethical Controversy" feature for more.

The Federal Budget Each year, the president proposes a **budget** for the federal government, a plan for how it will raise and spend money during the coming year, and presents it to Congress for approval. A typical federal budget proposal undergoes months of deliberation and many modifications before receiving approval. The federal budget includes a number of different spending categories, ranging from defense and Social Security to interest payments on the national debt. The decisions about what to include in the budget have a direct effect on various sectors of the economy. During a recession, the federal government may approve increased spending on interstate highway repairs to improve transportation and increase employment in the construction industry. During prosperity, the government may allocate more money for scientific research toward medical breakthroughs.

The primary sources of government funds to cover the costs of the annual budget are taxes, fees, and borrowing. Both the overall amount of these funds and their specific combination have major effects on the economic well-being of the nation. One way governments raise money is to impose taxes on sales, income, and other sources. But increasing taxes leaves people and businesses with less money to spend. This might reduce inflation, but overly high taxes can also slow economic growth. Governments then try to balance taxes to give people necessary services without slowing economic growth.

Taxes don't always generate enough funds to cover every spending project the government hopes to undertake. When the government spends more than the amount of money it raises through taxes, it creates a **budget deficit**. To cover the deficit, the U.S. government borrows money by selling Treasury bills, Treasury notes, and Treasury bonds to investors. All of this borrowing makes up the **national debt**. If the government takes in more money than it spends, it is said to have a **budget surplus**. A **balanced budget** means total revenues raised by taxes equal the total proposed spending for the year.

Achieving a balanced budget—or even a budget surplus—does not erase the national debt. Congress continually debates how to use revenues to reduce its debt. Most families want to wipe out debt—from credit cards, automobile purchases, and college, to name a few sources. To put the national debt into personal perspective, with roughly 317 million U.S. citizens, each one owes about $54,418 as his or her share.[21]

But for the federal government, the decision is more complex. When the government raises money by selling Treasury bills, it makes safe investments available to investors worldwide. If

budget organization's plan for how it will raise and spend money during a given period of time.

budget deficit situation in which the government spends more than the amount of money it raises through taxes.

national debt money owed by government to individuals, businesses, and government agencies who purchase Treasury bills, Treasury notes, and Treasury bonds sold to cover expenditures.

budget surplus excess funding that occurs when government spends less than the amount of funds raised through taxes and fees.

balanced budget situation in which total revenues raised by taxes equal the total proposed spending for the year.

Solving an Ethical Controversy

Recycling Outdated Electronics

As companies roll out new versions of electronics and other gadgets in an effort to get consumers to buy the latest products, U.S. consumers, corporations, and government agencies are recycling surplus, broken, and old items. Some e-waste goes to U.S. landfills, and some is shipped overseas by businesses to recycle and sell components. The growing concern is that computer monitors and older TVs contain toxic components. If not handled properly, this e-waste might cause harm to people and communities engaged in the recycling process.

Is it responsible behavior to recycle e-waste?

PRO

1. Recycling e-waste is environmentally more responsible than placing electronic waste in landfills.

2. Recycling used electronics may help a developing nation sustain employment rates, sell affordable products to consumers, and provide Internet access to its citizens.

CON

1. Used electronics sent overseas typically end up in a landfill, where toxic substances can pollute groundwater.

2. In an effort to appear green, some companies say they recycle electronics but are not forthcoming about where the e-waste is sent.

Summary

To establish appropriate recycling practices, the Environmental Protection Agency legitimately sends e-waste overseas for recycling. However, people remain concerned about the health and environmental hazards to inhabitants of less-developed countries, where the e-waste is dismantled and components extracted for precious metals.

Sources: "The Politics of e-Waste: A Cadmium Lining," *The Economist*, accessed January 18, 2014, www.economist.com; government website, "e-cycling," www.epa.gov, accessed January 18, 2014; "The Great e-Waste Recycling Debate," Grid Adrenal website, accessed January 18, 2014, www.grida.com; "Electronic Waste: EPA Needs to Better Control Harmful U.S. Exports through Stronger Enforcement and More Comprehensive Regulation," *GAO Highlights*, accessed January 18, 2014, www.gao.gov.

Assessment Check ☑

1. What is the difference between an expansionary monetary policy and a restrictive monetary policy?

2. What are the three primary sources of government funds?

3. Does a balanced budget erase the national debt?

foreign investors cannot buy Treasury notes, they might turn to other countries, reducing the amount of money flowing into the United States. U.S. government debt has also been used as a basis for pricing riskier investments. If the government issues less debt, the interest rates it commands are higher, raising the overall cost of debt to private borrowers. In addition, the government uses the funds from borrowing, at least in part, to invest in such public services as education and scientific research.

⌐5⌐ Global Economic Challenges of the 21st Century

Businesses face a number of important economic challenges in the 21st century. As the economies of countries around the globe become increasingly interconnected, governments and businesses must compete throughout the world. To maintain global competitiveness, government and business will need to address several challenges. The annual World Economic Forum meeting identifies global risks in the following five categories: economic, environmental,

3.5 Global Economic Challenges

CHALLENGE	TYPE OF RISK	FACTS AND EXAMPLES
Chronic Fiscal Imbalances	Economic	Failure to redress excessive government debt obligations
Rising Greenhouse Gas Emissions	Environmental	Governments, businesses, and consumers fail to reduce greenhouse gas emissions and expand carbon sinks.
Water Supply Crisis	Societal	Decline in the quality and quantity of fresh water combine with increased competition among resource-intensive systems, such as food and energy production.
Mismanagement of Population Aging	Societal	Failure to address both the rising costs and social challenges associated with population aging.

Source: Organization website, "World Economic Forum 2013 Global Risks Report," http://www3.weforum.org, accessed January 24, 2014.

geopolitical, societal, and technological.[22] Table 3.5 outlines the World Economic Forum's *Global Risks Report* developed from an annual survey of more than 1,000 experts from industry, government, academia, and the general public. The top risks by likelihood include (1) chronic fiscal imbalances; (2) rising greenhouse gas emissions; (3) water supply crises; and (4) mismanagement of population aging.[23]

No country is an economic island in today's global economy. Not only is an ever-increasing stream of goods and services crossing national borders, but a growing number of businesses have become true multinational firms, operating manufacturing plants and other facilities around the world. Even small firms can take advantage of the global workforce, if they are savvy about applying technology and understanding cultural differences. See the "Career Kickstart" feature for some tips.

As global trade and investments grow, events in one nation can reverberate around the globe. But despite the risks of world trade, global expansion can offer huge opportunities to U.S. firms. With U.S. residents accounting for just over 1 in every 22 of the world's more than 7 billion people, growth-oriented American companies cannot afford to ignore the world market.[24] U.S. businesses also benefit from the lower labor costs in other parts of the world, and some are finding successful niches importing goods and services provided by foreign firms. Still, it is extremely important for U.S. firms to keep close track of the foreign firms that supply their products. A number of U.S. companies have tried having their goods manufactured in China because production costs are significantly lower than they would be in the United States. But there have been so many product recalls of Chinese-made goods during the past several years—ranging from toys and pet food to construction drywall and drinking glasses—that the U.S. Consumer Products Safety Commission (CPSC) has opened an office in Beijing. The goal is to provide the CPSC with closer observation and better communication between U.S. and Chinese firms.[25]

U.S. firms must also develop strategies for competing with each other and with foreign firms to meet the needs and wants of consumers overseas. In the huge and fragmented beverage industry, experts predict that the Japanese and Chinese markets for healthy soft drinks, including juice-based and tea-based drinks, will grow significantly over the next few years.[26]

Assessment Check ☑

1. Why is virtually no country an economic island these days?

2. Describe two ways in which global expansion can benefit a U.S. firm.

Chapter 3 *Economic Challenges Facing Contemporary Business*

83

Dealing with the Global Workforce

The new global workforce, or "Work 3.0," offers 24/7 access to "the best people no matter where they are in the world," says Gary Swart, CEO of oDesk, a freelancers' website. Key to success is being able to "work with those people as if they're in the room with you."

Here are some tips for finding and working with global employees:

1 Judge language skills wisely. If you need someone to interact with customers, superb command of written and verbal English is a must. If you need a tech worker, don't be put off by slightly less fluency.

2 Set up formal rules for keeping touch with employees you can't see, and make sure everyone adheres to them.

3 Make your expectations clear, and communicate them to all, as often as necessary.

4 Connect time zones to your needs. If you depend on meetings and real-time collaboration, choose remote workers with whom your workday overlaps.

5 To simplify compensation, identify your top candidates and weigh what they can offer *you* and focus less on what their competitors halfway across the world might earn.

6 If you need to train employees, customize your program to their culture. Find out what motivates them and how they can best learn.

Sources: Craig E. Bentley, "How to Communicate with Your Global Workforce: Strategies for Success," *Bates Communications*, accessed January 24, 2014, www.bates-communications.com; Constance Ward, "12 Tips for Effectively Managing Remote Employees and Teams," *Thought Leader Zone*, accessed January 24, 2014, http://thoughtleaderzone.com; Darrell Etherington, "Work 3.0 Is Just Getting Underway, Says oDesk's Gary Swart," Gigaom.com, accessed January 24, 2014, http://gigaom.com; Alison Green, "How to Manage Remote Employees," The Quick Base Blog, accessed January 24, 2014, http://quickbase.intuit.com; "How to Leverage the Global Workforce: 5 Quick Tips," oDeskblog, accessed January 24, 2014, www.odesk.com.

What's Ahead

Global competition is a key factor in today's economy. In Chapter 4, we focus on the global dimensions of business. We cover basic concepts of doing business internationally and examine how nations can position themselves to benefit from the global economy. Then we describe the specific methods used by individual businesses to expand beyond their national borders and compete successfully in the global marketplace.

Chapter in Review

■ Summary of Learning Objectives

⌐1⌐ Discuss microeconomics and explain the forces of demand and supply.

Microeconomics is the study of economic behavior among individual consumers, families, and businesses whose collective behavior in the marketplace determines the quantity of goods and services demanded and supplied at different prices. Macroeconomics is the study of the broader economic picture and how an economic system maintains and allocates its resources; it focuses on how a government's monetary and fiscal policies affect the overall operation of an economic system.

Demand is the willingness and ability of buyers to purchase goods and services at different prices. Factors that drive demand for a good or service include customer preferences, the number of buyers and their incomes, the prices of substitute goods, the prices of complementary goods, and consumer expectations about the future. Supply is the willingness and ability of businesses to offer products for sale at different prices. Supply is determined by the cost of inputs and technology resources, taxes, and the number of suppliers operating in the market.

Assessment Check Answers ✔

1.1 Define microeconomics and macroeconomics. *Microeconomics* is the study of economic behavior among individual consumers, families, and businesses. *Macroeconomics* is the study of a nation's overall economic issues and how an economic system maintains and allocates its resources.

1.2 Explain demand and supply curves. A demand curve is a graph of the amount of a product that buyers will purchase at different prices. A supply curve shows the relationship between different prices and the quantities that sellers will offer for sale, regardless of demand.

1.3 How do factors of production influence the overall supply of goods and services? A change in the cost or availability of any of the inputs considered to be factors of production can shift the entire supply curve, either increasing or decreasing the amount available at every price.

⌐2⌐ Describe macroeconomics and the issues for the entire economy.

Four basic models characterize competition in a private enterprise system: pure competition, monopolistic competition, oligopoly, and monopoly. Pure competition is a market structure, like that in small-scale agriculture, in which large numbers of buyers and sellers exchange homogeneous products and no single participant has a significant influence on price. Monopolistic competition is a market structure, like that of retailing, in which large numbers of buyers and sellers exchange differentiated products, so each participant has some control over price. Oligopolies are market situations, like those in the steel and airline industries, in which relatively few sellers compete and high start-up costs form barriers to keep out new competitors. In a monopoly, one seller dominates trade in a good or service, for which buyers can find no close substitutes.

The major economic systems are private enterprise economy, planned economy (such as communism or socialism), and mixed market economy. In a private enterprise system, individuals and private businesses pursue their own interests—including investment decisions and profits—without undue governmental restriction. In a planned economy, the government exerts stronger control over business ownership, profits, and resources to accomplish governmental and societal—rather than individual—goals. Socialism, one type of planned economic system, is characterized by government ownership and operation of all major industries. Communism is an economic system with limited private property; goods are owned in common, and factors of production and production decisions are controlled by the state. A mixed market economy blends government ownership and private enterprise, combining characteristics of both planned and private enterprise economies.

Assessment Check Answers ✔

2.1 What is the difference between pure competition and monopolistic competition? Pure competition is a market structure in which large numbers of buyers and sellers exchange homogeneous products, and no single participant has a significant impact on price. Monopolistic competition is a market structure in which large numbers of buyers and sellers exchange differentiated (heterogenous) products, so each participant has some control over price.

2.2 On which economic system is the U.S. economy based? The U.S. economy is based on the private enterprise system.

2.3 What is privatization? Privatization is the conversion of government-owned and operated companies into privately held businesses.

⌐3⌐ Identify how to evaluate economic performance.

The four stages of the business cycle are prosperity, recession, depression, and recovery. Prosperity is characterized by low unemployment and strong consumer confidence. In a recession, consumers often postpone major purchases, layoffs occur, and household savings may be depleted. A depression occurs when an economic slowdown continues in a downward spiral over a long period of time. During recovery, consumer spending begins to increase and business activity accelerates, leading to an increased number of jobs.

As productivity rises, so do an economy's growth and the wealth of its citizens. In a recession, productivity stalls or possibly declines. Changes in general price levels—inflation or deflation—are important indicators of an economy's general stability. The U.S. government measures price-level changes by the Consumer Price Index. A nation's unemployment rate is an indicator of both overall stability and growth. The unemployment rate shows, as a percentage of the total labor force, the number of people actively seeking employment who are unable to find jobs.

Assessment Check Answers ☑

3.1 Describe the four stages of the business cycle. The four stages are prosperity, recession, depression, and recovery. Prosperity is characterized by low unemployment and strong consumer confidence. Recession may include consumers postponing major purchases, layoffs, and decreased household savings. A depression occurs when an economic slowdown continues in a downward spiral over a long period of time. In recovery, consumer spending increases and business activity accelerates.

3.2 What are some measures that economists use to determine the health of an economy? Gross domestic product (GDP), general level of prices, core inflation rate, the Consumer Price Index, and the unemployment rate are all measures used to determine the health of an economy.

⌐4⌐ Discuss managing the economy's performance.
Monetary policy encompasses a government's efforts to control the size of the nation's money supply. Various methods of increasing or decreasing the overall money supply affect interest rates and therefore affect borrowing and investment decisions. By changing the size of the money supply, government can encourage growth or control inflation. Fiscal policy involves decisions regarding government revenues and expenditures. Changes in government spending affect economic growth and employment levels in the private sector. However, a government must also raise money, through taxes or borrowing, to finance its expenditures. Because tax payments are funds that might otherwise have been spent by individuals and businesses, any taxation changes also affect the overall economy.

Assessment Check Answers ☑

4.1 What is the difference between an expansionary monetary policy and a restrictive monetary policy? An expansionary monetary policy increases the money supply in an effort to cut the cost of borrowing. A restrictive monetary policy reduces the money supply to curb rising prices, overexpansion, and concerns about overly rapid economic growth.

4.2 What are the three primary sources of government funds? The U.S. government acquires funds through taxes, fees, and borrowing.

4.3 Does a balanced budget erase the national debt? No, a balanced budget does not erase the national debt; it just doesn't increase it.

⌐5⌐ Describe the global economic challenges of the 21st century.
Businesses face four key global challenges in the 21st century: (1) chronic fiscal imbalances; (2) rising greenhouse gas emissions; (3) water supply crises; and (4) mismanagement of population aging.

Assessment Check Answers ☑

5.1 Why is virtually no country an economic island these days? No business or country is an economic island because many goods and services travel across national borders. Companies now are becoming multinational firms.

5.2 Describe two ways in which global expansion can benefit a U.S. firm. A firm can benefit from global expansion by attracting more customers and using less expensive labor and production in other parts of the world to produce goods and services.

▩ Business Terms You Need to Know

economics 63
microeconomics 64
demand 64
supply 64
demand curve 65
supply curve 67
equilibrium price 68
macroeconomics 69
pure competition 69
monopolistic competition 70
oligopoly 71
monopoly 71
regulated monopolies 71
planned economy 72

socialism 72
communism 72
mixed market economies 72
privatization 73
recession 74
productivity 75
gross domestic product (GDP) 75
inflation 76
core inflation rate 76
hyperinflation 76
deflation 77
Consumer Price Index (CPI) 77
unemployment rate 78
frictional unemployment 78

seasonal unemployment 78
cyclical unemployment 78
structural unemployment 79
monetary policy 80
expansionary monetary policy 80
restrictive monetary policy 80
fiscal policy 80
budget 81
budget deficit 81
national debt 81
budget surplus 81
balanced budget 81

Review Questions

1. How does microeconomics affect business? How does macroeconomics affect business? Why is it important for businesspeople to understand the fundamentals of each?

2. Draw supply and demand graphs that estimate what will happen to demand, supply, and the equilibrium price of coffee if these events occur:

   a. Widely reported medical studies suggest that coffee drinkers are less likely to develop certain diseases.

   b. The cost of manufacturing paper cups increases.

   c. The state imposes a new tax on takeout beverages.

   d. The biggest coffee chain leaves the area.

3. Describe the four different types of competition in the private enterprise system. In which type of competition would each of the following businesses be likely to engage?

   a. large drug stores chain

   b. small yoga studio

   c. steel mill

   d. large farm whose major crop is corn

   e. Facebook

4. Distinguish between the two types of planned economies. What factors do you think keep them from flourishing in today's economic environment?

5. What are the four stages of the business cycle? In which stage do you believe the U.S. economy is now? Why?

6. What is the gross domestic product? What is its relationship to productivity?

7. What are the effects of inflation on an economy? What are the effects of deflation? How does the Consumer Price Index work?

8. What does a nation's unemployment rate indicate? Describe what type of unemployment you think each of the following illustrates:

   a. discharged armed forces veteran

   b. bus driver who has been laid off due to cuts in his or her city's transit budget

   c. worker who was injured on the job and must start a new career

   d. lifeguard

   e. dental hygienist who has quit one job and is looking for another

9. Explain the difference between monetary policy and fiscal policy. How does the government raise funds to cover the costs of its annual budget?

10. What is the difference between the budget deficit and the national debt? What are the benefits of paying down the national debt? What might be the negative effects?

Projects and Teamwork Applications

1. Describe a situation in which you have had to make an economic choice in an attempt to balance your wants with limited means. What factors influenced your decision?

2. Choose one of the following products and describe the different factors that you think might affect its supply and demand.

   a. Nike running shoes

   b. e-Reader

   c. Miles by Discover credit card

   d. newly created name-brand drug

   e. Detroit Lions football tickets

3. Go online to research one of the following government agencies—its responsibilities, its budget, and the like. Then make the case for privatizing it:

   a. Veterans Administration

   b. Bureau of the Census

   c. Smithsonian Institution

   d. Transportation Security Administration

   e. Social Security

4. Some businesses automatically experience seasonal unemployment. More and more, however, owners of these businesses are making efforts to increase demand—and employment—during the off season. Choose a classmate to be your business partner, and together select one of the following businesses. Create a plan for developing business and keeping employees for a season during which your business does not customarily operate:

   a. children's summer camp

   b. ski lodge

   c. inn located near a beach resort

   d. house painting service

   e. greenhouse

5. On your own or with a classmate, go online to research the economy of one of the following countries. You may use the

World Factbook website (www.cia.gov) to learn about the type of economy the country has, its major industries, and its competitive issues. (Note which industries or services are privatized and which are government owned.) Take notes on unemployment rates, monetary policies, and fiscal policies. Present your findings to the class.

a. China

b. New Zealand

c. India

d. Denmark

e. Mexico

f. Canada

g. Chile

h. Brazil

▨ Web Assignments

1. **What did things cost the year you were born?** Go to the Federal Reserve Bank of Minneapolis website (www .minneapolisfed.org) to see the calculator called "What is a dollar worth?" The calculator allows you to see what an item purchased in the past costs today. Insert the year you were born, a dollar amount, and the current year. What are your results? Discuss the implications in economic terms.

2. **Unemployment.** In the United States, the Bureau of Labor Statistics (BLS) compiles and publishes data on unemployment. Go to the BLS website (http://www.bls.gov) and click on "Unemployment" (under "Subject Areas"). Read through the most recent report and answer the following questions:

   a. What is the current unemployment rate in the United States? How does it compare with those of other developed countries?

   b. Which state has the highest unemployment rate? Which state has the lowest unemployment rate?

   c. What is the underemployment rate?

3. **Financial debt.** Go to the U.S. Debt Clock website (www .usdebtclock.org) to see the dizzying array of real-time estimates of debt. This website was created by an individual who wanted to alert people to the amount of debt in the United States. On the upper right-hand side you will see an icon that reads "Debt Clock Time Machine." Click on the icon and go back in time to the year 2000. Compare the figures from 2000 to those of today's date for the following:

   • U.S. GDP

   • Credit card debt

   • Personal debt per citizen

   • U.S. population

   • U.S. national debt

   • Debt per citizen

   • Unemployment figures

Discuss the differences. Which number revealed the greatest difference? Why?

Note: Internet web addresses change frequently. If you don't find the exact sites listed, you may need to access the organization's home page and search from there or use a search engine such as Google or Bing.

CASE 3.1 **The State of Nuclear Energy**

There are 430 nuclear power plants in operation in 31 countries, and of those, more than 100 are in the United States. Operating nuclear plants continue to generate almost 20 percent of America's electricity. Wind and solar energy together generate less than 5 percent.

An alloy of enriched uranium powers nuclear reactors. Uranium, a metal, can be found in rocks and even seawater as well as in ore deposits in the earth. With 24 percent, Australia has the largest supply overall, but Kazakhstan recently declared that it had surpassed Australia's output. Canada has less than 10 percent of the world's supply but has the highest concentration of top-quality ore. Worldwide, about 75,000 tons of uranium are used each year. At current demand, that supply is expected to last about 70 years.

The World Nuclear Association (WNA) predicts that nuclear reactor capacity will increase by about 27 percent in the next decade and that the demand for uranium will grow by 33 percent.

Eventually the demand for uranium will be greater than the supply that can be mined economically. Some analysts believe that the world will run out of uranium sooner rather than later.

Environmentalists object to destructive mining techniques and fear the exploitation of indigenous Australians. A lack of infrastructure and a shortage of experienced workers drive up uranium-processing costs. A still-unsolved and crucial problem is how to manage safe, long-term storage of spent nuclear rods, which continue to emit radioactivity.

The World Nuclear Association disagrees. First, not all uranium deposits have been discovered. Since 1975, the number of known deposits has tripled. The WNA predicts that at *current* rates of usage, known supplies will last 200 years rather than 70 or 80.

Second, the end of the Cold War also meant the end of the nuclear arms race between the United States and the USSR (now Russia). Nuclear warheads contain high-quality enriched uranium. Utility companies and governments also have uranium stockpiles.

Third, researchers are working to make enrichment facilities and reactors more energy efficient.

Fourth, uranium can be recycled from spent nuclear fuel rods and from tailings (uranium left over from the enrichment process). Other sources, such as phosphates and seawater, could become economically viable in the future.

Occurring in a 1960-designed reactor several years ago, Japan's Fukushima Daiichi nuclear accident continues to spur debate and controversy about worldwide nuclear safety and nuclear energy policies. In response to the horrific accident, Germany has agreed to shut its reactors by 2022 and will no longer extend the operations of existing nuclear plants. Italy has banned nuclear power altogether. As a result, the International Atomic Energy Agency has reduced its nuclear-generating capacity estimates for the next several years. Despite the bans on nuclear energy in some countries, others, like China and India, continue to look to nuclear energy as a reliable energy source. Currently there are more than 70 nuclear power reactors under construction in 13 countries worldwide.

Questions for Critical Thinking

1. **What factors do you think will affect the supply and demand curve for nuclear energy?**
2. **Describe what type of competition you predict will arise in the nuclear energy industry.**

Sources: Mycle Schneider, "World Nuclear Industry Status [Updated]," *World Nuclear Industry Status Report,* accessed January 24, 2014, www.worldnuclearreport.org; Oliver Joy, "After Fukushima: Could Germany's Nuclear Gamble Backfire?" *CNN,* accessed January 24, 2014, http://edition.cnn.com; World Nuclear Association, "Nuclear Power in the USA," accessed January 24, 2014, www.world-nuclear.org; "The Nuclear Reactor—How They Are Constructed," Virtual Nuclear Tourist, accessed January 24, 2014, www.nucleartourist.com; "Power Reactor Information Systems," International Atomic Energy Agency, accessed January 24, 2014, www.iaea.org; Matthew Philips, "The U.S. Nuclear Power Industry's Dim Future," *Bloomberg Businessweek,* accessed January 24, 2014, www.businessweek.com.

Pawnshops Go Mainstream

People facing layoffs and depleted savings become increasingly conservative in their spending and often resort to selling valuable items for cash or using them as collateral for a loan. As a result, the pawnshop, once considered a lender of last resort, has gone mainstream.

The recent recession and credit crunch have created a short-term loan alternative for small businesses and individuals. Without a rigorous credit check or bank approval, and very little paperwork, people bring an item of value to the pawnshop where it is held as collateral against a loan. If the loan is repaid, and most are, the item is retrieved. If not, the pawnshop sells the item to the public.

A new breed of high-end pawnshops like Borro can be found in places such as New York City and Beverly Hills. Borro, the largest upscale pawnshop, has loaned nearly $100 million.

Technology plays a part in pawnshops going mainstream. Many high-end collateral lenders have added online services where borrowers can get items appraised and then ship them to the lender. Online players like iPawn and Pawngo have made it easy for consumers and small businesses to access short-term loans without feeling embarrassed or losing their privacy. Collectively, iPawn and Pawngo have loaned tens of millions of dollars to customers.

The industry has been glamorized by reality TV shows like *Pawn Stars,* which profiles the colorful world of the pawn business in Las Vegas. Americans in all economic groups, along with small-business owners, are utilizing pawnshops in place of traditional credit lenders. As the economy recovers and consumer confidence grows, it remains to be seen whether pawnshops will continue to be popular.

Questions for Critical Thinking

1. **What is your perception of pawnshops, and do you have personal experience or know anyone who has bought something there? Are pawnshops a substitute for banks?**

2. The dark side of the pawn industry is its lack of regulation and exorbitant loan rates. Do some additional research to discuss the pros and cons of this trend.

Sources: Greg Avery, "Online Pawn Is Taking the Industry Upscale, Says Pawngo CEO," *Denver Business Journal*, accessed January 24, 2014, www.bizjournals.com; Ianthe Jeanne Dugan, "High-Class Pawnshops Fill a Lending Void," *The Wall Street Journal*, accessed January 24, 2014, http://online.wsj.com; Geoff Williams, "Pawn Shops Go Mainstream," *U.S. News and World Report,* accessed January 24, 2014, http://money .msn.com; Ashlea Ebeling, "Short on Cash? Luxury Pawn Shop Borro Loans $10,000 to $1 Million," *Forbes,* accessed January 24, 2014, www.forbes.com; association website, "Industry Overview," www.nation-alpawnbrokers.org, accessed January 24, 2014.

CASE 3.3 ▶ Secret Acres: Selling Comics Is Serious Business

Just about everyone remembers a favorite comic book from childhood—whether it was *Spiderman, Tin Tin,* or even *Garfield.* Leon Avelino and Barry Matthews readily acknowledge that they are kids in grown-up bodies with real day jobs (Avelino works for *Sports Illustrated* and Matthews is an accountant for an e-commerce firm) who happen to love comic books and their latest incarnation, graphic novels. Their love for comics in all forms—along with the desire to start their own business—led them to found Secret Acres, a comic book and graphic novel publisher based in New York City. In addition to publishing several works from up-and-coming authors (they have eight books on their list so far), the Secret Acres duo sells books from independent distributors.

Acknowledging that Secret Acres faces many economic challenges if it's going to hang on and eventually succeed, Matthews observes, "Every decision we make, we know what the outcome is going to be because it's all small and it's very close to us." Right now, Secret Acres can use its small size to build relationships with its customers. "We are able, because we're small, to produce a very specific kind of comic book, a specific kind of graphic novel, that appeals to a specific audience," explains Matthews. "I love that. We have a lot of control over what we do and we're not doing anything specifically to turn a buck." That said, the accountant in Matthews knows that in order to stay in business, Secret Acres must sell enough books to push unit costs down, keeping production expenses and prices as low as possible.

Matthews also refers to relationships with book stores, which are personal because he and Avelino do all the communicating themselves. "When you have a small group of stores you are selling from, you have to collect from them on a one-to-one basis," says Matthews. Sometimes the relationship becomes awkward when Matthews or Avelino has to remind a book store owner personally of an unpaid balance.

Another challenge facing the duo is the uncertain future of the print publishing market. The introduction of e-readers such as Amazon's Kindle and Barnes & Noble's Nook creates a new delivery system for printed work. While the e-reader hasn't created the sensation among consumers that its manufacturers had hoped (some competing models have already disappeared from the marketplace), online delivery of printed matter is alive and well—and it's likely that some form of e-reader will eventually catch on. "Publishers are nervous because no one knows how popular e-readers will be in the long run," says Matthews.

Another phenomenon that has taken hold over the last decade is the graphic novel, the fiction genre that combines comic book techniques with the longer, more complex structure of a novel. Graphic novels are particularly popular among teens and college students, but they have received serious attention from the literary world. Some college courses are now taught around the graphic novel, and the American Library Association publishes a list of recommended graphic novels for teens each year. A firm like Secret Acres could capitalize on a literary trend that continues to gain ground.

Matthews and Avelino haven't quit their day jobs yet. They know it will be awhile before they can call themselves full-time publishers. But they love the comic book business and they are willing to wait for the good times they believe are ahead. "We have faith in the fact that if these books find the right audience, they'll do fine," says Avelino. "I'm OK with being patient. We need to keep going long enough to build a back list that is self-supporting." And Secret Acres already has a following among comic fans—their secret is out.

Questions for Critical Thinking

1. What steps might Matthews and Avelino take to create demand for their books? How must a small business like Secret Acres balance supply with demand?
2. How might Secret Acres make the most of an economy that is recovering slowly? What advantages and disadvantages might the firm have over a large publishing company?
3. How would you categorize the competition that Secret Acres faces?
4. Do you think Secret Acres should pursue online distribution through e-readers and other delivery systems? Why or why not?

Sources: Company website, http://secretacres.com, accessed January 24, 2014; "Great Graphic Novels for Teens," *Young Adult Library Services Association,* accessed January 24, 2014, www.ala.org/yalsa; "What Tablet Device Should You Buy for Your Digital Comic Books?" *Comic Book Herald,* accessed January 24, 2014, www.comicbookherald.com; Harry McCracken, "E-Readers May Be Dead, But They're Not Going Away Yet," *Tech Hive,* accessed January 24, 2014, www.techhive.com.

Chapter 4

Learning Objectives

[1] Explain why nations trade.

[2] Describe how trade is measured between nations.

[3] Identify the barriers to international trade.

[4] Discuss reducing barriers to international trade.

[5] Explain the decisions to go global.

[6] Discuss developing a strategy for international business.

Competing in World Markets

omohiro Ohsumi/Bloomberg/Getty Images

Toyota Back on Top of Global Auto Industry

It's good to be king, and Toyota is—when it comes to auto sales. Toyota is very close to producing more than 10 million vehicles annually worldwide, which would be an all-time record for any automaker. GM and Volkswagen currently are tied for second place. In the United States, Toyota Motor Sales sold more light vehicles than the Ford Motor Company, despite having fewer dealers and selling fewer models. So, what is driving Toyota's sales?

Toyota is reaping the rewards of a technological and financial risk it took 20 years ago—developing a gas-electric power train and installing it in the Prius. This strategy began the adoption of the gas-electric hybrid as the preferred alternative to the internal combustion engine. Once considered marginal and on the fringe, hybrids have been purchased by more than 300,000 consumers over the past few years. There were plenty of doubters when the first Prius arrived in the United States in 1999. In fact, a GM executive once dismissed hybrids as "an interesting curiosity." More than a decade ago, with gas selling at $1.50 per gallon, it may have been just a curiosity, but now that gas has been averaging $3.50 per gallon over the past several years, Toyota's gamble has paid off.

In the U.S., Toyota's hybrid sales are accelerating. According to the company, 25 percent of the Toyota Avalon's sales volume is its hybrid model. And for the Lexus brand, most models are available as hybrids, and some, like the CT 200h, are only available as hybrids. Beyond the hybrid, Toyota is co-producing the RAV 4EV with Tesla Motors, the upstart electric car company. Tesla now uses Toyota's New United Motors facility in Fremont, California, to produce its cars, which is where Toyota produced small, fuel-efficient vehicles by the tens of thousands. Should the partnership blossom, Toyota could bring huge benefits to the relationship.

Will Toyota be able to keep its number 1 status and the bragging rights that go along with that ranking? For now, it appears so. However, in the hypercompetitive world of vehicle manufacturers, Toyota would do well to keep an eye on its competitors, as both GM and Volkswagen want to make Toyota's reign as the top brand a short one.[1]

Overview

Consider for a moment how many products you used today that came from outside the United States. Maybe you drank Brazilian coffee with your breakfast, wore clothes manufactured in Honduras or Malaysia, drove to class in a German or Japanese car fueled by gasoline refined from Canadian crude oil, and watched a movie on a new curved 4K Ultra HDTV assembled in Mexico for a Japanese company such as Sony. A fellow student in Germany may be wearing Zara jeans, using a Samsung cell phone, and drinking Pepsi.

U.S. and foreign companies alike recognize the importance of international trade to their future success. Economic interdependence is increasing throughout the world as companies seek additional markets for their goods and services and the most cost-effective locations for production facilities. No longer can businesses rely only on domestic sales. Today, foreign sales are essential to U.S. manufacturing, agricultural, and service firms as sources of new markets and profit opportunities. Foreign companies also frequently look to the United States when they seek new markets.

Thousands of products cross national borders every day. Together, U.S. exports and imports make up about a quarter of the U.S. gross domestic product (GDP). The United States ranks third in the world among exporting nations, with exports exceeding $1.5 trillion and second in the world with annual imports of more than $2.3 trillion. That total amount is more than double the nation's imports and exports of just a decade ago.[2]

Transactions that cross national boundaries may expose a company to an additional set of factors such as new social and cultural practices, economic and political environments, and legal restrictions.

This chapter travels through the world of international business to see how both large and small companies approach globalization. First, we consider the reasons nations trade, the importance and characteristics of the global marketplace, and the ways nations measure international trade. Then we examine barriers to international trade that arise from cultural and environmental differences. To reduce these barriers, countries turn to organizations that promote global business. Finally, we look at the strategies firms implement for entering foreign markets and the way they develop international business strategies.

[1] Why Nations Trade

exports domestically produced goods and services sold in other countries.

imports foreign-made products purchased by domestic consumers.

As domestic markets mature and sales growth slows, companies in every industry recognize the increasing importance of efforts to develop business in other countries. **Exports** are domestically produced goods and services sold in other countries. **Imports** are foreign-made products purchased by domestic consumers. Walmart now operates over 2,000 stores in Mexico, Boeing sells jetliners in Asia, and currently 6 of the 20 elite English soccer clubs are owned by U.S. billionaires.[3] These are only a few examples of the many U.S. companies taking advantage of large populations, substantial resources, and rising standards of living abroad that boost foreign interest in their goods and services. Likewise, the U.S. market, with the world's greatest purchasing power, attracts thousands of foreign companies to its shores.

International trade is vital to a nation and its businesses because it boosts economic growth by providing a market for its products and access to needed resources. Companies can expand their markets, seek growth opportunities in other nations, and make their production and distribution systems more efficient. They also reduce their dependence on the economies of their home nations.

International Sources of Factors of Production

Business decisions to operate abroad depend on the availability, price, and quality of labor, natural resources, capital, and entrepreneurship—the basic factors of production—in the foreign country. Colleges and universities in India and China produce thousands of highly qualified computer scientists and engineers each year. To take advantage of this talent, many U.S. computer software and hardware firms have set up operations overseas, and many others are outsourcing information technology and customer service jobs there.

Trading with other countries also allows a company to spread risk, because different nations may be at different stages of the business cycle or in different phases of development. If demand falls off in one country, the company may still enjoy strong demand in other nations. Companies such as The Hain Celestial Group, a New York–based natural and organic food company, tripled its sales by aggressively expanding overseas.[4]

Size of the International Marketplace

In addition to human and natural resources, entrepreneurship, and capital, companies are attracted to international business by the sheer size of the global marketplace. Only one in six of the world's more than 7.2 billion people lives in a relatively well-developed country. The share of the world's population in the less-developed countries will increase over the coming years because more-developed nations have lower birthrates. But the U.S. Census Bureau says the global birthrate is slowing overall, and the average woman in today's world bears half as many children as her counterpart did 35 years ago.[5]

As developing nations expand their involvement in global business, the potential for reaching new groups of customers dramatically increases. Firms looking for new revenue are inevitably attracted to giant markets such as China and India, with respective populations of about 1.3 billion and 1.2 billion. However, people alone are not enough to create a market. Consumer demand also requires purchasing power. As Table 4.1 shows, population size is no guarantee of economic prosperity. Of the 10 most populous countries, only the United States appears on the list of those with the highest per-capita GDPs.

Although people in developing nations have lower per-capita incomes than those in the highly developed economies of North America and Western Europe, their huge populations do represent lucrative markets. Even when the higher-income segments are only a small percentage of the entire country's population, their sheer numbers may still represent significant and growing markets.

Also, many developing countries have typically posted high growth rates of annual GDP. The U.S. GDP generally averages between 2 and 4 percent growth per year. By contrast, GDP growth in less-developed countries is much greater—China's GDP growth rate, recently slowing, had exceeded double digits for most of the last decade, and India's averaged 7.6 percent over the last decade.[6] These markets represent opportunities for global businesses, even though their per-capita incomes lag behind those in more-developed countries. Many firms are establishing operations in these and other developing countries to position themselves to benefit from local sales driven by expanding economies and rising standards of living. Walmart is one of those companies. As the largest retail firm in the world, Walmart employs 2.2 million workers (called "associates") in 11,000 stores worldwide. Walmart International is growing fast, with more than 6,400 stores and 900,000 employees in 27 countries as far-ranging as Lesotho and Swaziland in Africa. More than 90 percent of Walmart's overseas stores operate under a local banner.[7]

TABLE 4.1 The World's Top 10 Nations Based on Population and Wealth

COUNTRY	POPULATION (IN MILLIONS)	COUNTRY	PER-CAPITA GDP (IN U.S. DOLLARS)
China	1,349	Qatar	$100,900
India	1,221	Luxembourg	$78,000
United States	317	Singapore	$60,800
Indonesia	251	Norway	$54,400
Brazil	201	Brunei	$54,100
Pakistan	193	Hong Kong	$50,900
Nigeria	175	United States	$51,700
Bangladesh	164	Switzerland	$44,900
Russia	142	Netherlands	$41,500
Japan	127	United Arab Emirates	$29,200

Source: *World Factbook*, https://www.cia.gov, accessed January 6, 2014.

FIGURE 4.1 Top 10 Trading Partners with the United States

Country	Total U.S. Imports and Exports
Canada	$154.7 billion
China	$131.2
Mexico	$126.5
Japan	$50.3
Germany	$41.4
South Korea	$26.8
United Kingdom	$24.7
France	$19.0
Saudi Arabia	$18.5
Brazil	$17.2

Source: Data from U.S. Census Bureau, "Top Ten Countries with Which the U.S. Trades: March 2014," accessed May 22, 2014, www.census.gov.

The United States trades with many other nations. As Figure 4.1 shows, the top five are Canada, China, Mexico, Japan, and Germany. With South Korea, the United Kingdom, France, Saudi Arabia, and Brazil, they represent nearly two-thirds of U.S. imports and exports every year. Over half of the world's wheat, corn, soybean, and cotton exports comes from the United States. Individual states like Texas export more than $264 billion of goods annually, and California exports more than $162 billion. Other big exporting states include Florida, Illinois, New York, and Washington.[8]

Absolute and Comparative Advantage

Few countries can produce all the goods and services their people need. For centuries, trading has been the way that countries can meet the demand. If a country focuses on producing what it does best, it can export surplus domestic output and buy foreign products that it lacks or cannot efficiently produce. The potential for foreign sales of a particular item depends largely on whether the country has an absolute advantage or a comparative advantage.

A country has an *absolute advantage* in making a product for which it can maintain a monopoly or that it can produce at a lower cost than any competitor. For centuries, China enjoyed an absolute advantage in silk production. The fabric was woven from fibers recovered from silkworm cocoons, making it a prized raw material in high-quality clothing. Demand among Europeans for silk led to establishment of the famous Silk Road, a 5,000-mile link between Rome and the ancient Chinese capital city of Xi'an.

Absolute advantages are rare these days. But some countries manage to approximate absolute advantages in some products. Climate differences can give some nations or regions an advantage in growing certain plants. With an annual harvest in Japan of less than 1,000 tons, a highly coveted and highly priced mushroom is the maitake, or matsutake, mushroom. Known for its spicy, aromatic odor, it hides under fallen leaves on the forest floor, which makes it even more difficult to find. A basket of five mushrooms can cost hundreds of dollars.[9]

A nation can develop a *comparative advantage* if it can supply its products more efficiently and at a lower price than it can supply other goods, compared with the outputs of other countries. China is profiting from its comparative advantage in producing textiles. On the other hand, ensuring that its people are well educated is another way a nation can develop a comparative advantage in skilled human resources. India offers the services of its educated, English-speaking tech workers at a lower wage. But sometimes these strategies backfire. Recently, some U.S. firms

A country can develop a comparative advantage if it supplies its products more efficiently and at a lower price than it supplies other goods. China enjoys a comparative advantage in producing textiles.

have pulled back from manufacturing or locating customer service operations overseas because of consumer complaints about quality.

To boost its longstanding advantage in research and innovation as global competition increases, pharmaceutical giant Merck & Co., an example of the globalization of research and development, recently established research and development hubs in Boston, San Francisco, London, and Shanghai to rely less on outside R&D efforts and to identify other opportunities.[10]

Measuring Trade between Nations

Clearly, engaging in international trade provides tremendous competitive advantages to both the countries and individual companies involved. But how do we measure global business activity? To understand what the trade inflows and outflows mean for a country, we need to examine the concepts of balance of trade and balance of payments. Another important factor is currency exchange rates for each country.

A nation's **balance of trade** is the difference between its exports and imports. If a country exports more than it imports, it achieves a positive balance of trade, called a *trade surplus*. If it imports more than it exports, it produces a negative balance of trade, called a *trade deficit*. The United States has run a trade deficit every year since 1976. Despite being one of the world's top exporters, the United States has an even greater appetite for foreign-made goods, which creates a trade deficit.

A nation's balance of trade plays a central role in determining its **balance of payments**— the overall flow of money into or out of a country. Other factors also affect the balance of payments, including overseas loans and borrowing, international investments, profits from such investments, and foreign aid payments. To calculate a nation's balance of payments, subtract the monetary outflows from the monetary inflows. A positive balance of payments, or a *balance-of-payments surplus*, means more money has moved into a country than out of it. A negative balance of payments, or *balance-of-payments deficit*, means more money has gone out of the country than entered it.

Major U.S. Exports and Imports

The United States, with combined exports and imports of about $4.9 trillion, leads the world in the international trade of goods and services. As listed in Table 4.2, the leading categories of goods exchanged by U.S. exporters and importers range from machinery and vehicles to crude oil and chemicals. Strong U.S. demand for imported goods is partly a reflection of the nation's prosperity and diversity.

Although the United States imports more goods than it exports, the opposite is true for services. U.S. exporters sell more than $600 billion in services annually. Much of that money comes from travel and tourism—money spent by foreign nationals visiting the United States.[11] The increase in that figure is especially significant because the dollar has declined and continues to fluctuate in terms of foreign currencies in recent years. U.S. service exports also include business and technical services such as engineering, financial services, computing, legal services, and entertainment, as well as royalties and licensing fees. Major service exporters include Citibank, the Walt Disney Company, Allstate Insurance, and Federal Express, as well as retailers such as McDonald's and Starbucks.

Businesses in many foreign countries want the expertise of U.S. financial and business professionals. Accountants are in high demand in Russia, China, the Netherlands, and Australia— Sydney has become one of Asia's biggest financial centers. Entertainment is another major growth area for U.S. service exports. The Walt Disney Company already has theme parks in Europe and Asia and is now building its second resort in China—Shanghai Disney Resort, a multi-billion-dollar theme park.[12]

With annual imports of more than $2.7 trillion, the United States is by far the world's leading importer. American tastes for foreign-made goods for everything from clothing to

Assessment Check ✅

1. Why do nations trade?

2. Cite some measures of the size of the international marketplace.

3. How does a nation acquire a comparative advantage?

balance of trade difference between a nation's exports and imports.

balance of payments overall flow of money into or out of a country.

4.2 Top 10 U.S. Merchandise Exports and Imports

EXPORTS	AMOUNT (IN BILLIONS)	IMPORTS	AMOUNT (IN BILLIONS)
Agricultural commodities	$115.82	Crude oil	$260.1
Vehicles	88.1	Vehicles	178.9
Mineral fuel	80.5	Televisions, VCRs	137.3
Electrical machinery	77.0	Electrical machinery	119.6
Petroleum preparations	53.5	Automated data processing equipment	113.5
General industrial machinery	51.8	Agricultural commodities	82.0
Specialized industrial machinery	46.8	Clothing	78.5
Scientific instruments	44.3	Petroleum preparations	67.4
Chemicals—plastics	42.0	Chemicals—medicinal	65.2
Chemicals—medicinal	41.9	General industrial machinery	60.4

Source: U.S. Census Bureau, "U.S. Exports and General Imports by Selected SITC Commodity Groups," *Statistical Abstract of the United States,* www.census.gov, accessed January 6, 2014.

consumer electronics show up as huge trade deficits with the consumer-goods-exporting nations of China and Japan.

Exchange Rates

A nation's exchange rate is the value of one nation's currency relative to the currencies of other countries. **Exchange rate** is the rate at which its currency can be exchanged for the currencies of other nations. It is important to learn how foreign exchange works because we live in a global community, and the value of currency is an important economic thermometer for every country. Each currency's exchange rate is usually quoted in terms of another currency, such as the number of Mexican pesos needed to purchase one U.S. dollar. Roughly 13 pesos are needed to exchange for a U.S. dollar. A Canadian dollar can be exchanged for close to $1 in the United States. The euro, the currency used in most of the European Union (EU) member countries, has fluctuated in exchange value. European consumers and businesses use the euro to pay bills online, by credit card, or bank transfer. Euro coins and notes are also used in many EU-member countries.

Foreign exchange rates are influenced by a number of factors, including domestic economic and political conditions, central bank intervention, balance-of-payments position, and speculation over future currency values. Currency values fluctuate, depending on the supply and demand for each currency in the international market. In this system of *floating exchange rates*, currency traders create a market for the world's currencies based on each country's relative trade and investment prospects. In theory, this market permits exchange rates to vary

exchange rate the rate at which a nation's currency can be exchanged for the currencies of other nations.

freely according to supply and demand. In practice, exchange rates do not float in total freedom. National governments often intervene in currency markets to adjust their exchange rates.

Nations influence exchange rates in other ways as well. They may form currency blocs by linking their exchange rates to each other. Many governments practice protectionist policies that seek to guard their economies against trade imbalances. For instance, nations sometimes take deliberate action to devalue their currencies as a way to increase exports and stimulate foreign investment. **Devaluation** describes a drop in a currency's value relative to other currencies or to a fixed standard. Venezuela, an oil-exporting country, has devalued its currency periodically in an effort to address its economic imbalances.

For an individual business, the impact of currency devaluation depends on where that business buys its materials and where it sells its products. Business transactions are usually conducted in the currency of the particular region in which they take place. When business is conducted in Japan, transactions are likely to be in yen. In the United Kingdom, transactions are in pounds. With the adoption of the euro in the EU, the number of currencies in that region has been reduced. At present, there are 18 EU-member countries using the euro, including Austria, Belgium, Cyprus, Estonia, Finland, France, Germany, Greece, Ireland, Italy, Latvia, Luxembourg, Malta, the Netherlands, Portugal, Slovakia, Slovenia, and Spain. Examples of other countries' currencies include the British pound, Australian dollar, the Indian rupee, the Brazilian real, the Mexican peso, the Taiwanese dollar, and the South African rand.

Exchange rate changes can quickly create opportunity—or eliminate—a competitive advantage, so they are crucial factors in foreign investment decisions. In Europe, a declining dollar means that a price of 10 euros is worth more, so companies may lower prices. At the same time, if the dollar falls, it makes European vacations less affordable for U.S. tourists because their dollars are worth less relative to the euro. There are numerous online currency converters to calculate conversions and help you understand the spending power of a U.S. dollar in other countries.

Currencies that owners can easily convert into other currencies are called *hard currencies*. Examples include the euro, the U.S. dollar, and the Japanese yen. The Russian ruble and many central European currencies are considered soft currencies because they cannot be readily converted. Exporters trading with these countries sometimes prefer to barter, accepting payment in oil, timber, or other commodities that they can resell for hard-currency payments.

The foreign currency market is the largest, most liquid and efficient financial market in the world, with a daily volume of about $ 5.3 trillion in U.S. dollars.[13]

Venezuela, an oil producer and exporter, has devalued its currency periodically in an effort to address fiscal imbalances in the country's economy.

Yuri Cortez/AFP/Getty Images

devaluation drop in a currency's value relative to other currencies or to a fixed standard.

Assessment Check ✅

1. Compare balance of trade and balance of payments.
2. Explain the function of an exchange rate.
3. What happens when a currency is devalued?

[3] Barriers to International Trade

All businesses encounter barriers in their operations, whether they sell only to local customers or trade in international markets. Italy's shopkeepers, whose hours of operation were once regulated, are now able to keep their stores open longer. In addition to complying with a variety

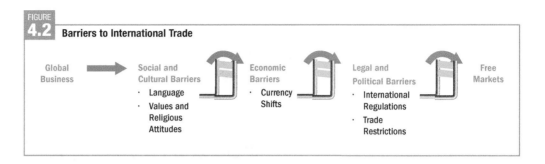

FIGURE 4.2 Barriers to International Trade

Global Business → Social and Cultural Barriers
· Language
· Values and Religious Attitudes

Economic Barriers
· Currency Shifts

Legal and Political Barriers
· International Regulations
· Trade Restrictions

Free Markets

of laws and different currencies, international companies may also have to reformulate their products to accommodate different buying preferences by location. McDonald's has benefitted from stronger sales in Europe to offset its slumping U.S. sales. The company will continue to expand its franchise business model in key markets of Russia and China.[14]

In addition to social and cultural differences, companies engaged in international business face economic barriers as well as legal and political ones. Some of the hurdles shown in Figure 4.2 are easily breached, but others require major changes in a company's business strategy. To successfully compete in global markets, companies and their managers must understand not only how these barriers affect international trade but also how to overcome them.

Social and Cultural Differences

The social and cultural differences among nations range from language and customs to educational background and religious holidays. Understanding and respecting these differences are critical to pave the way for international business success. Businesspeople with knowledge of host countries' cultures, languages, social values, religious beliefs, lifestyles, and practices are well equipped for the marketplace and the negotiating table. Sensitivity to such elements as local attitudes, forms of address, and expectations regarding dress, body language, and punctuality also helps them win customers and achieve their business objectives. The "Career Kickstart" feature offers some insight into majoring in international business.

Language Mandarin Chinese is the most widely spoken language in the world, followed by English, Spanish, Hindi, Arabic, and Bengali. Understanding a business colleague's primary language may prove to be the difference between closing an international business transaction and losing the sale to someone else. Company representatives operating in foreign markets must not only choose correct and appropriate words but also must translate words correctly to convey the intended meanings. Firms may also need to rename products or rewrite slogans for foreign markets.

Potential communication barriers include more than translation errors. Companies may present messages through inappropriate media, overlook local customs and regulations, or ignore differences in taste. One U.S. executive recently lost a deal in China by giving the prospective client a set of four antique clocks wrapped in white paper. Unfortunately, the number four and the Chinese word for clock are similar to the word "death," while white is the traditional color for funerals.[15] Cultural sensitivity is especially critical in cyberspace. Website developers must be aware that visitors to a site may come from anywhere in the world. Some icons that seem friendly to U.S. Internet users may shock people from other countries. A person making a high-five hand gesture would be insulting people in Greece; the same is true of making a circle with the thumb and index finger in Brazil, a thumbs-up sign in Egypt, and a two-fingered peace sign with the back of the hand facing out in Great Britain.

Gift-giving traditions employ the language of symbolism. For example, in Latin America, knives and scissors should not be given as gifts because they represent the severing of friendship. Flowers are generally acceptable but are used in Day of the Dead festivities in Mexico, and yellow flowers can be associated with death.

Values and Religious Attitudes Even though today's world is shrinking in many ways, people in different countries do not necessarily share the same values or religious attitudes. Marked differences remain in workers' attitudes from country to country, for instance.

U.S. society places a higher value on business efficiency and low unemployment than does European society, where employee benefits are more valued. The U.S. government does not legally mandate vacation time or paid leave, and employees typically receive no paid vacation during their first year of employment, then two weeks' vacation, and eventually up to three or four weeks if they stay with the same employer for many years. In contrast, the EU mandates a minimum paid vacation of four weeks per year, and most Europeans get five or six weeks. In these countries, a U.S. company that opens a manufacturing plant may not be able to hire any local employees without offering vacations in line with a nation's business practices.

U.S. culture values national unity, with tolerance of regional differences. The United States is viewed as a national market with a single economy. European countries that are part of the 28-member EU are trying to create a similar marketplace. However, many resist the idea of being European citizens first and British, Danish, or Dutch citizens second. British consumers differ from Italians in important ways, and U.S. companies that fail to recognize this variation will run into problems with brand acceptance.

Religion plays an important role in every society, so businesspeople must also cultivate sensitivity to the dominant religions in countries where they operate. Understanding religious cycles and the timing of major holidays can help prevent embarrassing moments when scheduling meetings, trade shows, conferences, or events such as the opening of a new manufacturing plant. People doing business in Saudi Arabia must take into account Islam's month-long observance of Ramadan, when work ends at noon. Friday is the Muslim formal day of worship, so the Saudi workweek runs from Saturday through Thursday. Also, many Muslims abstain from alcohol and pork products, so gifts of this kind would be considered offensive.

Economic Differences

Business opportunities are flourishing in densely populated countries such as China and India, as local consumers eagerly buy Western products. Although such prospects might tempt American firms, managers must first consider the economic factors involved in doing business

Hit&Miss

Ford Motor Company: Engineered and Made in Mexico

Three of Ford Motor Company's 77 worldwide factories are located in Mexico, a country once viewed by carmakers as an assembly-only manufacturing destination. Ford's Mexico unit has tripled its engineering staff and produced 40 patents in less than three years, which may be one reason why the number of engineering students enrolled in Mexican universities has doubled.

Mexico's appeal to U.S. and foreign carmakers alike has to do with its proximity to the largest auto market in the world, lower wages, and the growing demand for cars in other parts of Latin and South America. In addition, labor costs for engineers in Mexico are 40 percent of what they are for their U.S. counterparts.

As Mexico continues to transform into a world-class manufacturing destination, foreign carmakers have also taken notice and poured over $12 billion of investments into the country over the last few years. With less than a decade of experience, as Ford's engineers gain momentum, look for quality Ford cars not only to be made but also designed by engineers in Mexico.

Questions for Critical Thinking

1. Considering Mexico's history of drug violence, what challenges do you see for the auto industry in Mexico?
2. How can foreign auto companies ensure there are skilled job candidates available to work in Mexican manufacturing facilities?

Sources: Company website, "List of Operations Worldwide," http://corporate.ford.com, accessed January 6, 2014; Brendan Case, "Mexico's Surprising Engineering Strength," *Bloomberg Businessweek*, accessed January 6, 2014, www.businessweek.com; "Steaming Hot," *The Economist*, accessed January 6, 2014, www.economist.com; Andres Martinez, "Mexico: The Stranger Next Door," *Bloomberg Businessweek*, accessed January 6, 2014, www.businessweek.com.

---

in these markets. A country's size, per-capita income, and stage of economic development are among the economic factors to consider when evaluating it as a candidate for an international business venture. Ford Motor Company, along with other automobile companies, has invested heavily in Mexico, which is no longer seen as an assembly-only destination. See the "Hit & Miss" feature for more details.

Infrastructure Along with other economic measures, businesses should understand a country's infrastructure. **Infrastructure** refers to basic systems of communications, transportation, and energy facilities. The Internet and technology use can also be considered part of a country's infrastructure.

> **infrastructure** basic systems of communication, transportation, and energy facilities in a country.

Financial systems provide a type of infrastructure for businesses. In the United States, buyers have widespread access to many forms of payment processing, including online, electronic, and credit and debit cards. In many African countries, such as Ethiopia, local businesses do not accept credit cards, so travelers to the capital city of Addis Ababa are warned to bring plenty of cash and traveler's checks.

Currency Conversion and Shifts Despite growing similarities in infrastructure, businesses crossing national borders may still encounter basic economic differences, including national currencies. Foreign currency fluctuations may present challenges to global businesses. As explained earlier in the chapter, the values of the world's major currencies fluctuate—sometimes drastically—in relation to each other. Rapid and unexpected currency shifts can make pricing in local currencies difficult. Shifts in exchange rates can also influence the attractiveness of various business decisions. A devalued currency may make a nation less desirable as an export destination because of reduced demand in that market. However, devaluation can make the nation desirable as an investment opportunity because investments there will be a bargain in terms of the investor's currency.

Political and Legal Differences

Like social, cultural, and economic differences, legal and political differences in host countries can pose barriers to international trade. To compete in today's world marketplace, international business executives must be well versed in laws that affect their industries. Some countries impose general trade restrictions. Others have established detailed rules that regulate how foreign companies can operate.

Political Climate An important factor in any international business investment is the stability of the political climate. The political structures of many nations promote stability similar to that in the United States. Other nations, such as Indonesia, Thailand, and Congo, feature quite different—and frequently changing—structures.[16] Host nations often pass laws designed to protect their own interests, sometimes at the expense of foreign businesses.

Legal Environment When conducting business internationally, managers must be familiar with three dimensions of the legal environment: U.S. law, international regulations, and the laws of the countries in which they plan to operate. Some laws protect the rights of foreign companies to compete in the United States. Others dictate actions allowed for U.S. companies doing business in foreign countries.

The *Foreign Corrupt Practices Act* forbids U.S. companies from bribing foreign officials, political candidates, or government representatives. Although the law has been in effect since 1977, in the past few years the U.S. government has increased its enforcement, including major proceedings in the pharmaceutical, medical device, and financial industries. The United States, United Kingdom, France, Germany, and 36 other countries have signed the Organization for Economic Cooperation and Development Anti-Bribery Convention.

Still, corruption continues to be an international problem. Its pervasiveness, combined with U.S. prohibitions, creates a difficult obstacle for U.S. businesspeople who want to do business in many foreign countries. Chinese pay *huilu*; Russians rely on *vzyatka*. In the Middle East, palms are greased with *baksheesh*. Figure 4.3 compares 179 countries based on surveys

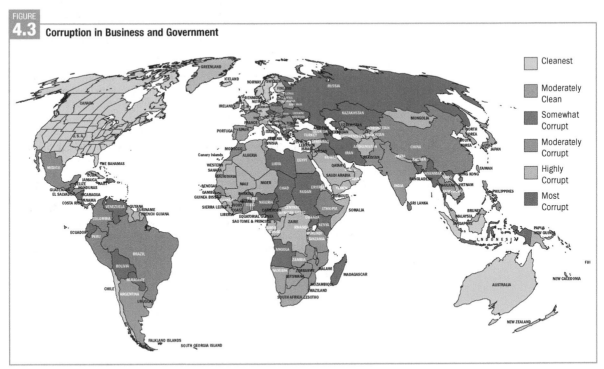

FIGURE 4.3 Corruption in Business and Government

Legend:
- Cleanest
- Moderately Clean
- Somewhat Corrupt
- Moderately Corrupt
- Highly Corrupt
- Most Corrupt

Source: Data from Transparency International, "Annual Corruption Perceptions Index," http://www.transparency.org, accessed January 6, 2014.

Chapter 4 *Competing in World Markets*   **103**

GoingGreen

Canon Helps with Global Reforestation

Forests are home to some 300 million people around the globe, about 1.6 billion of whom depend almost entirely on forest habitats for their survival. Nearly 2 million people worldwide make their living from forests in some way, and those numbers don't begin to describe the plant and animal species that flourish in forest habitats.

Canon, the $40 billion global digital imaging company, is stepping in to help reforesting efforts around the world. Its Canon Forestry Program has planted more than 200,000 trees so far, not only in U.S. locations such as Wisconsin and South Carolina in partnership with the Arbor Day Foundation, but also in Vietnam, where reforestation can help reduce the deadly impact of floods as well as help remove harmful carbon dioxide from the air.

An Arbor Day Foundation manager said, "These trees will provide cleaner air and water, habitat for wildlife, and beauty for everyone to enjoy for years to come. By planting trees, Canon USA is demonstrating their commitment to helping the environment for this and future generations."

Questions for Critical Thinking

1. Where else in the world do you think Canon could take an active role in reforestation?

2. Canon USA also plants trees when consumers purchase its environmentally friendly "Generation Green" brand products. Do you think this strategy would work globally? Why or why not?

Sources: Company website, "Canon U.S.A. Honors Arbor Day 2013 with Environmental and Sustainability Initiatives," "2012/2013 Canon Social & Cultural Support Activities," and "Canon Vietnam Continues Reforestation Project," www.canon.com, accessed January 6, 2014; organization website, "What Does FAO Do? Forestry," www.fao.org, accessed January 6, 2014.

---

of perceived corruption. The Corruption Perceptions Index is computed by Transparency International, a Berlin-based organization that rates the degree of corruption observed around the world.

The growth of e-commerce has introduced new challenges to the legal climate of international business. Patents, brand names, trademarks, copyrights, privacy, and other intellectual property are difficult to enforce, given the availability of information on the Internet. However, some countries are adopting laws to protect information obtained by electronic contacts. Recently, 10 men in the Zhejiang province of China were sentenced to up to two years in prison for hijacking World of Warcraft gaming accounts. State regulations in China ban invasive access of "ordinary computer information systems."[17]

International Regulations To regulate international commerce, the United States and many other countries have ratified treaties and signed agreements that dictate the conduct of international business and protect some of its activities. The United States has entered into many *friendship, commerce, and navigation* (FCN) *treaties* with other nations. Such treaties address many aspects of international business relations, including the right to conduct business in the treaty partner's domestic market. Other international business agreements involve product standards, patents, trademarks, reciprocal tax policies, export controls, international air travel, and international communications. Some international efforts to protect the environment are voluntary, such as Canon's reforestation project. See the "Going Green" feature for the story.

Many types of regulations affect the actions of managers doing business in international markets. Not only must worldwide producers and marketers maintain required minimum quality levels for all the countries in which they operate, but they must comply with numerous specific local regulations. Britain prevents advertisers from encouraging children to engage in such unhealthy behavior as overeating or replacing regular meals with candy and snack foods. Malaysia's Censorship Board prohibits nudity and profanity on TV. Germany and France allow publishers to set prices that retailers charge for their books.

Italian clothing manufacturers have long enjoyed high status for their fabrics and workmanship. However, they believed they were being victimized by a lax labeling system when international clothing designers bought less-expensive fabric in China or Bulgaria, had the garments cut in countries with lower labor costs, then sent them to Italy for final sewing. There, they tacked on the prestigious "Made in Italy" label and charged a high price for the goods. The Italian manufacturers pushed for a law requiring that two of the four stages of clothing production must take place in Italy in order to earn the "Made in Italy" label.[18]

Types of Trade Restrictions

Trade restrictions such as taxes on imports and complicated administrative procedures create additional barriers to international business. They may limit consumer choices while increasing the costs of foreign-made products. Trade restrictions are also imposed to protect citizens' security, health, and jobs. Other restrictions are imposed to promote trade with certain countries. Still others protect countries from unfair competition. Regardless of the political reasons for trade restrictions, most take the form of tariffs. In addition to tariffs, governments impose a number of non-tariff—or administrative—barriers. These include quotas, embargoes, and exchange controls.

Tariffs Taxes, surcharges, or duties on foreign products are referred to as <u>tariffs</u>. Governments may assess two types of tariffs—revenue and protective tariffs—both of which make imports more expensive for domestic buyers. Revenue tariffs generate income for the government. Cars and trucks imported into the United States carry a tax that goes directly to the U.S. Treasury. The sole purpose of a protective tariff is to raise the retail price of imported products to match or exceed the prices of similar products manufactured in the home country. In other words, protective tariffs seek to limit imports and level the playing field for local competitors.

Of course, tariffs create a disadvantage to companies that want to export to the countries imposing the tariffs. In addition, governments do not always agree on the reasons behind protective tariffs, so they do not always have the desired effect. The United States imposes a tariff on foreign competitors accused of selling products at lower prices in the United States than U.S. manufacturers charge. Congress passed a bill giving the money from these tariffs directly to U.S. plaintiff companies, instead of to the Treasury as in the past. In a move to prompt other countries to remove tariffs on sake, a Japanese alcoholic beverage, the Japanese government is considering removing its own tariffs on imported wine. Australia and New Zealand, large wine producers, would benefit from such a decision.[19]

Non-Tariff Barriers Non-tariff, or administrative, trade barriers also restrict imports. These measures may take such forms as quotas on imports, restrictive standards for imports, and export subsidies. Because many countries have recently substantially reduced tariffs or eliminated them entirely, they increasingly use non-tariff barriers to control flows of imported products.

<u>Quotas</u> limit the amounts of particular products that countries can import during specified time periods. Limits may be set as quantities, such as the number of cars or bushels of wheat, or as values, such as dollars' worth of cigarettes. Governments regularly set quotas for agricultural products and sometimes for imported automobiles. The United States, for example, sets a quota on imports of sugar. Imports under the quota amount are subject to a lower tariff than shipments above the quota.[20]

Quotas help prevent <u>dumping</u>. In one form of dumping, a company sells products abroad at prices below its cost of production. In another, a company exports a large quantity of a product at a lower price than the same product in the home market and drives down the price of the domestic product. Dumping

tariffs taxes, surcharges, or duties on foreign products.

quota limit set on the amounts of particular products that countries can import during specified time periods.

dumping selling products abroad at prices below production costs or below typical prices in the home market to capture market share from domestic competitors.

More severe than a quota, an embargo imposes a total ban on importing a specified product or even a total halt to trading with a particular country. One result of the United States' long-standing trade embargo with Cuba is the lack of new cars in the country—as you can see in this Cuban neighborhood.

Assessment Check ☑

1. How might values and attitudes form a barrier to trade, and how can they be overcome?
2. What is a tariff? What is its purpose?
3. Why is dumping a problem for companies marketing goods internationally?

benefits domestic consumers in the importing market, but it hurts domestic producers. It also allows companies to gain quick entry to foreign markets. Tariffs have been imposed on Chinese solar panel makers accused of dumping their products in the United States.[21]

More severe than a quota, an **embargo** imposes a total ban on importing a specified product or even a total halt to trading with a particular country. The United States has a long-standing trade embargo with Cuba. Embargo durations can vary to accommodate changes in foreign policy.

Another form of administrative trade restriction is **exchange control**. Imposed through a central bank or government agency, exchange controls affect both exporters and importers. Firms that gain foreign currencies through exporting are required to sell them to the central bank or another agency. Importers must buy foreign currencies to pay for their purchases from the same agency. The exchange control authorities can then allocate, expand, or restrict foreign exchange in accordance with national policy.

4 Reducing Barriers to International Trade

Although tariffs and administrative barriers still restrict trade, overall the world is moving toward free trade. Several types of organizations ease barriers to international trade, including groups that monitor trade policies and practices and institutions that offer monetary assistance. Another type of federation designed to ease trade barriers is the multinational economic community, such as the European Union. This section looks at the roles these organizations play.

Organizations Promoting International Trade

The **General Agreement on Tariffs and Trade (GATT)**, an international trade accord, has sponsored a series of negotiations, called rounds, which substantially reduced worldwide tariffs and other barriers. Major industrialized nations founded the multinational organization in 1947 to work toward reducing tariffs and relaxing import quotas. The last set of completed negotiations—the Uruguay Round—cut average tariffs by one-third, in excess of $700 billion; reduced farm subsidies; and improved protection for copyright and patent holders. In addition, international trading rules now apply to various service industries. Finally, the new agreement established the **World Trade Organization (WTO)** to succeed GATT. This organization includes representatives from 159 countries.

World Trade Organization Since 1995, the WTO has monitored GATT agreements among the member nations, mediated disputes, and continued the effort to reduce trade barriers throughout the world. Unlike provisions in GATT, the WTO's decisions are binding on parties involved in disputes.

The WTO has become increasingly controversial in recent years as it issues decisions that have implications for working conditions and the environment in member nations. Concerns have been expressed that the WTO's focus on lowering trade barriers encourages businesses to keep costs down through practices that may increase pollution and human rights abuses. Particularly worrisome is the fact that the organization's member countries must agree on policies, and developing countries tend not to be eager to lose their low-cost advantage by enacting stricter labor and environmental laws. Other critics claim that if well-funded U.S. firms such as fast-food chains, entertainment companies, and online retailers can freely enter foreign markets, they will eliminate smaller foreign businesses serving the distinct tastes and practices of other countries.

Trade unions in developed nations complain that the WTO's support of free trade makes it easier to export manufacturing jobs to low-wage countries. But many small and midsize firms have benefited from the WTO's reduction of trade barriers and lowering of the cost of trade. They currently make up 97 percent of all firms that export goods and services, according to the U.S. Department of Commerce.

The most recent round of WTO talks is called the *Doha Round* after the city in Qatar where it began. After more than a decade, discussion still continues on ways to improve global trade among developing countries, with the goal of reducing domestic price supports, eliminating export subsidies, and improving market access for goods. Such changes could help farmers in developing countries compete in the global marketplace.[22]

World Bank Shortly after the end of World War II, industrialized nations formed an organization to lend money to less-developed and developing countries. The <u>World Bank</u> primarily funds projects that build or expand nations' infrastructure, such as transportation, education, and medical systems and facilities. The World Bank and other development banks provide the largest source of advice and assistance to developing nations. Often, in exchange for granting loans, the World Bank imposes requirements intended to build the economies of borrower nations.

The World Bank has been criticized for making loans with conditions that ultimately hurt the borrower nations. When developing nations are required to balance government budgets, they are sometimes forced to cut vital social programs. Critics also say that the World Bank should consider the impact of its loans on the environment and working conditions.

International Monetary Fund Established a year after the World Bank, the <u>International Monetary Fund (IMF)</u> was created to promote trade through financial cooperation and, in the process, eliminate barriers. The IMF makes short-term loans to member nations that are unable to meet their expenses. It operates as a lender of last resort for troubled nations. In exchange for these emergency loans, IMF lenders frequently require significant commitments from the borrowing nations to address the problems that led to the crises. These steps may include curtailing imports or even devaluing currencies. Throughout its existence, the IMF has worked to prevent financial crises by warning the international business community when countries encounter problems meeting their financial obligations. Often, the IMF lends to countries to keep them from defaulting on prior debts.

However, some countries owe far more money than they can ever hope to repay, and the debt payments make it impossible for their governments to deliver needed services to their citizens. Recently, the IMF has come under scrutiny over how much influence and voting power emerging market economies (EMEs) have within the IMF. With the rapid development and expansion of developing economies, some believe that their voice and power in the IMF has not grown proportionately. As emerging markets continue to remain vulnerable to tightened global financial conditions and a turbulent world economy, the issue of governance reform of the IMF remains at the forefront.

International Economic Communities

International economic communities reduce trade barriers and promote regional economic integration. In the simplest approach, countries may establish a *free-trade area* in which they trade freely among themselves without tariffs or trade restrictions. Each maintains its own tariffs for trade outside this area. A *customs union* sets up a free-trade area and specifies a uniform tariff structure for members' trade with nonmember nations. In a *common market*, or economic union, members go beyond a customs union and try to bring all of their trade rules into agreement.

One example of a free-trade area is the <u>North American Free Trade Agreement (NAFTA)</u> enacted by the United States, Canada, and Mexico. Other examples of regional trading blocs include the MERCOSUR customs union (joining Brazil, Argentina, Paraguay, Uruguay, Chile, and Bolivia) and the 10-country Association of South East Asian Nations (ASEAN).

World Bank organization established by industrialized nations to lend money to less-developed countries.

International Monetary Fund (IMF) organization created to promote trade, eliminate barriers, and make short-term loans to member nations that are unable to meet their budgets.

North American Free Trade Agreement (NAFTA) agreement among the United States, Canada, and Mexico to break down tariffs and trade restrictions.

NAFTA

NAFTA became effective in 1994, creating the world's largest free-trade zone with the United States, Canada, and Mexico. With a combined population of more than 471 million and a total GDP of more than $20 trillion, North America represents the world's largest and most attractive free-trade areas. The United States—the single largest market—dominates North America's business environment. Although fewer than 1 person in 20 lives in the United States, the nation's more than $16 trillion GDP represents about one-fifth of total world output.[23]

Canada is far less densely populated but has achieved a similar level of economic development. Over the last decade, Canada's economy has grown at about the same rate as the U.S. economy. Almost 70 percent of Canada's GDP is generated in the services sector, and three of every four Canadian workers are engaged in service occupations. The country's per-capita GDP places Canada among the top 10 nations in terms of its people's spending power. Canada's economy is fueled by trade with the United States, and its home markets are strong as well. About 75 percent of Canada's exports and about 50 percent of its imports are to or from the United States.[24] Ford, General Motors, Toyota, Honda, and Chrysler all have large production facilities in Canada. Mexico is moving from developing nation to industrial nation status, thanks largely to NAFTA. Mexico's trade with the United States and Canada has tripled since the signing of NAFTA, although 15 percent of the country's 119 million people live below the poverty line, and per-capita income is about a third that of the United States. But Mexico's border with the United States is busy with a nearly endless stream of traffic transporting goods from Mexican manufacturing facilities into the United States. The United States is Mexico's largest trading partner by far, accounting for about 78 percent of total exports and 50 percent of all Mexico's imports.[25]

By eliminating all trade barriers and investment restrictions among the United States, Canada, and Mexico over a 15-year period, NAFTA opened more doors for free trade. The agreement also eased regulations governing services, such as banking, and established uniform legal requirements for protection of intellectual property. The three neighboring nations can now trade with one another without tariffs or other trade barriers, simplifying shipments of goods across the partners' borders. Standardized customs and uniform labeling regulations create economic efficiencies and smooth import and export procedures. Trade among the partners has increased steadily, more than doubling since NAFTA took effect.

© Roger Lecuyer/iStockphoto

With NAFTA allowing free trade for the United States, Canada, and Mexico, the amount of goods and services traded is healthy for Canada's economy as well as the United States.

CAFTA-DR

The **Central America–Dominican Republic Free Trade Agreement (CAFTA-DR)** created a free-trade area among the United States, Costa Rica, El Salvador, Guatemala, Honduras, Nicaragua, and the Dominican Republic (the DR of the title). The agreement—the first of its kind between the United States and these smaller, developing economies—ends tariffs on the nearly $56 billion in products traded between the United States and its Latin American neighbors. Agricultural producers such as corn, soybean, and dairy farmers stand to gain under the relaxed trade rules. Overall, CAFTA-DR's effects have increased both exports and imports substantially, much as NAFTA did.[26]

European Union

Perhaps the best-known example of a common market is the **European Union (EU)**. The EU combines 28 countries, over 506 million people, and a total GDP of roughly $16 trillion to form a huge common market representing 20 percent of the world's GDP. Figure 4.4 shows the member countries. Current candidates for membership are Iceland, Montenegro, Serbia, Turkey, and Macedonia.[27]

The EU's goals include promoting economic and social progress, introducing European citizenship as a complement to national citizenship, and giving the EU a significant role in international affairs. To achieve its goal of a borderless Europe, the EU is removing barriers to free trade among its members. This highly complex process involves standardizing business regulations and requirements, standardizing import duties and taxes, and eliminating customs checks so that companies can transport goods from France to Italy or Poland as easily as from New York to Boston.

Unifying standards and laws can contribute to economic growth. But just as NAFTA sparked fears in the United States about free trade with Mexico, some people in Western Europe worried that opening trade with such countries as Poland, Hungary, and the Czech Republic would cause jobs to flow eastward to lower-wage economies.

The EU also introduced the euro to replace currencies such as the French franc and Italian lira. For the 18 member-states that have adopted the euro, potential benefits include eliminating the economic costs of currency exchange and simplifying price comparisons. Businesses and their customers now make electronic and credit card transactions in euros and use euro notes and coins in making cash purchases.

Central America–Dominican Republic Free Trade Agreement (CAFTA-DR) agreement among the United States, Costa Rica, El Salvador, Guatemala, Honduras, Nicaragua, and the Dominican Republic to reduce tariffs and trade restrictions.

European Union (EU) 28-nation European economic alliance.

Assessment Check ✅

1. What international trade organization succeeded GATT, and what is its goal?

2. Compare and contrast the goals of the World Bank and the International Monetary Fund.

3. What are the goals of the European Union, and how do they promote international trade?

FIGURE 4.4 The 28 Nations of the European Union

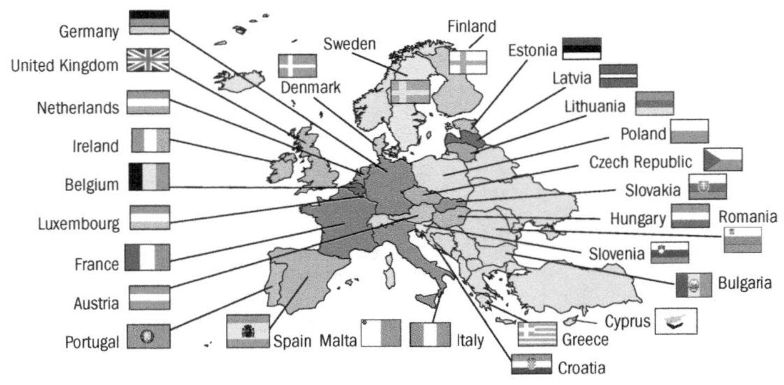

Germany, United Kingdom, Netherlands, Ireland, Belgium, Luxembourg, France, Austria, Portugal, Sweden, Denmark, Spain, Malta, Italy, Finland, Estonia, Latvia, Lithuania, Poland, Czech Republic, Slovakia, Hungary, Slovenia, Romania, Bulgaria, Cyprus, Greece, Croatia

Going Global

Although expanding into overseas markets can increase profits and marketing opportunities, it also introduces new complexities to a firm's business operations. Before deciding to go global, a company faces a number of key decisions, beginning with the following:

- determining which foreign market(s) to enter
- analyzing the expenditures required to enter a new market
- deciding the best way to organize the overseas operations

These issues vary in importance, depending on the level of involvement a company chooses. Education and employee training in the host country would be much more important for an electronics manufacturer building an Asian factory than for a firm that is simply planning to export American-made products.

The choice of which markets to enter usually follows extensive research focusing on local demand for the firm's products, availability of needed resources, and ability of the local workforce to produce quality merchandise. Other factors include existing and potential competition, tariff rates, currency stability, and investment barriers. A variety of government and other sources are available to facilitate this research process. A good starting place is the CIA's *World Factbook*, which contains country-by-country information on geography, population, government, economy, and infrastructure.

U.S. Department of Commerce counselors working at district offices offer a full range of international business advice, including computerized market data and names of business and government contacts in dozens of countries. As Table 4.3 shows, there are numerous online resources for international trade information.

TABLE 4.3 **International Trade Research Resources on the Internet**

WEBSITE AND ADDRESS	GENERAL DESCRIPTION
Europages http://www.europages.com	Directory of and links to Europe's top 500,000 companies in 33 European countries
World Trade Organization http://www.wto.org	Details on the trade policies of various governments
CIA *World Factbook* https://www.cia.gov/library/publications/the-world-factbook/	Basic facts about the world's nations, from geography to economic conditions
United States International Trade Commission http://www.usitc.gov/	The U.S. International Trade Commission administers U.S. trade remedy laws
U.S. Commercial Service http://trade.gov/cs	Information about Commerce Department counseling services, trade events, and U.S. export regulations
U.S. Small Business Advisor http://www.SBA.gov	One-stop access to a range of federal government information, services, and transactions
U.S. State Department http://www.travel.state.gov/travel/cis_pa_tw/tw/tw_1764.html	Listing of the State Department's latest travel warnings about conditions that may affect safety abroad, supplemented by the list of consulate addresses and country information

Levels of Involvement

After a firm has completed its research and decided to do business overseas, it can choose one or more strategies:

- exporting or importing

- entering into contractual agreements such as franchising, licensing, and subcontracting deals

- direct investment in the foreign market through acquisitions, joint ventures, or establishment of an overseas division

Although the company's risk increases with the level of its involvement, so does its overall control of all aspects of producing and selling its goods or services.

For Jeffery Adler, it was an offer too good to refuse. His California-based business, Dlush Beverage Joints, a small chain of shops that served fruit smoothies, tea, and baked goods, was paid a visit one day by several members of the wealthy Alghanim family from Kuwait. The Alghanims liked the experience so much they proposed a sweet business deal to Adler and his firm: Alghanim Sons Group would become the Persian Gulf franchisee of Dlush. Alghanim now has a 20-year franchise agreement to develop an unlimited number of Dlush stores in six countries throughout the region. Adler receives a percentage of the stores' revenues and a steady income, and the Dlush brand had an immediate international presence.[28]

Zazzle, on the other hand, has worked to develop an international presence via the Internet. The California company offers specialized t-shirts, mugs, hats, and other such items. Zazzle has tailored its business to each specific country by building individual websites (in different languages) for 17 countries and offering shipping to another 70. Michael Karns, head of Zazzle's international development, keeps a close watch on all aspects of the company's overseas e-commerce.[29]

Jeffery Adler, head of Dlush Beverage Joints, joined with Alghanim Sons Group, from Kuwait, to expand his business into the Persian Gulf.

Marsaili McGrath/Getty Images, Inc.

Importers and Exporters When a firm brings in goods produced abroad to sell domestically, it is an importer. Conversely, companies are exporters when they produce—or purchase—goods at home and sell them in overseas markets. An importing or exporting strategy provides the most basic level of international involvement, with the least risk and control.

Exports are frequently handled by special intermediaries called export trading companies. These firms search out competitively priced local merchandise and then resell it abroad at prices high enough to cover expenses and earn profits. When a retail chain such as Dallas-based Pier 1 Imports wants to purchase West African products for its store shelves, it may contact an export trading company operating in a country such as Ghana. The local firm is responsible for monitoring quality, packaging the order for transatlantic shipment, arranging transportation, and arranging for completion of customs paperwork and other steps required to move the product from Ghana to the United States.

Firms engage in exporting of two types: indirect and direct. A company engages in *indirect exporting* when it manufactures a product, such as an electronic component, that becomes part of another product sold in foreign markets. The second method, *direct exporting*, occurs when a company seeks to sell its products in markets outside its own country. Often the first step for companies entering foreign markets, direct exporting is the most common form of international business. Firms that succeed at this may then move to other strategies.

In addition to reaching foreign markets by dealing with export trading companies, exporters may choose two other alternatives: export management companies and offset agreements. Rather than simply relying on an export trading company to assist in foreign markets, an exporting firm may turn to an *export management company* for advice and expertise. These international specialists help the exporter complete paperwork, make contacts with local buyers, and comply with local laws governing labeling, product safety, and performance testing. At the same time, the exporting firm retains much more control than would be possible with an export trading company.

An *offset agreement* matches a small business with a major international firm. It basically makes the small firm a subcontractor to the larger one. Such an entry strategy helps a new exporter by allowing it to share in the larger company's international expertise. The small firm also benefits in such important areas as international transaction documents and financing, while the larger company benefits from the local expertise and capabilities of its smaller partner.

Countertrade A sizable share of international trade involves payments made in the form of local products, not currency. This system of international bartering agreements is called countertrade.

A common reason for resorting to international barter is inadequate access to needed foreign currency. To complete an international sales agreement, the seller may agree to accept part or all of the purchase cost in merchandise rather than currency. Because the seller may decide to locate a buyer for the bartered goods before completing the transaction, a number of international buyers and sellers frequently join together in a single agreement.

Countertrade may often be a firm's only opportunity to enter a particular market. Many developing countries simply cannot obtain enough credit or financial assistance to afford the imports that their people want. Countries with heavy debt burdens also resort to countertrade. Russian buyers, whose currency is often less acceptable to foreign traders than the stronger currencies of countries such as the United States, Great Britain, Japan, and EU countries, may resort to trading local products ranging from crude oil to diamonds to vodka as payments for purchases from foreign companies unwilling to accept Russian rubles. Still, other countries such as China may restrict imports. Under such circumstances, countertrade may be the only practical way to win government approval to import needed products.

Contractual Agreements Once a company, large or small, gains some experience in international sales, it may decide to enter into contractual agreements with local parties. These arrangements can include franchising, foreign licensing, and subcontracting.

Franchising Common among U.S. companies, franchising can work well for companies seeking to expand into international markets, too. A **franchise**, as described in detail in Chapter 5, is a contractual agreement in which a wholesaler or retailer (the franchisee) gains the right to sell the franchisor's products under that company's brand name if it agrees to the related operating requirements. The franchisee can also receive training, marketing, management, and business services from the franchisor. While these arrangements are common among leading fast-food brands such as Dunkin' Donuts, McDonald's, and KFC, other kinds of service providers like Cisco also often look to franchising as an international marketplace option.

Domino's Pizza has expanded to more than 10,000 stores in more than 70 international markets around the world. Its largest international market is in Mexico, but wherever it

countertrade barter agreement whereby trade between two or more nations involves payment made in the form of local products instead of currency.

franchise contractual agreement in which a franchisee gains the right to produce and/or sell the franchisor's products under that company's brand name if they agree to certain operating requirements.

operates, the company fine-tunes its menus to meet local tastes with such specialties as its Junkanoo Feast pizza in the Bahamas, which includes pepperoni, barbeque chicken, and banana peppers; squid in Japan; and chorizo in Mexico.[30]

Foreign Licensing In a <u>foreign licensing agreement</u>, one firm allows another to produce or sell its product, or use its trademark, patent, or manufacturing processes, in a specific geographical area. In return, the firm gets a royalty or other compensation.

Licensing can be advantageous for a small manufacturer eager to launch a well-known product overseas. Not only does it get a proven product from another market, but little or no investment is required to begin operating. The arrangement can also allow entry into a market otherwise closed to imports due to government restrictions. Sometimes a licensing agreement can ensure product freshness by allowing manufacturing to take place in the local market. Morinaga, a Japanese food manufacturer, holds licenses to produce Lipton teas, Kraft cheeses, and Sunkist fruit drinks and desserts in Japan.[31]

Subcontracting The third type of contractual agreement, <u>subcontracting</u>, involves hiring local companies to produce, distribute, or sell goods or services. This move allows a foreign firm to take advantage of the subcontractor's expertise in local culture, contacts, and regulations. Subcontracting works equally well for mail-order companies, which can farm out order fulfillment and customer service functions to local businesses. Manufacturers practice subcontracting to save money on import duties and labor costs, and businesses go this route to market products best sold by locals in a given country. Some firms, such as Maryland-based Pacific Bridge Medical, help medical manufacturers find reliable subcontractors and parts suppliers in Asia.

A key disadvantage of subcontracting is that companies cannot always control their subcontractors' business practices. Several major U.S. companies have been embarrassed by reports that their subcontractors used child labor to manufacture clothing.

Offshoring While it is not generally considered a way of initiating business internationally, *offshoring*, or the relocation of business processes to a lower-cost location overseas, has become a widespread practice. Despite increasing labor costs, China is still the top destination for production offshoring and India and the Philippines for services offshoring. Many business leaders argue, in favor of offshoring, that global firms must keep their costs as low as possible to remain competitive. But the apparent link between jobs sent overseas and jobs lost at home has made the practice controversial. Legislatures of various states have tried to slow the tide of offshoring through new laws, but many observers believe the real goal should be to improve corporate research and development efforts in the United States.

Offshoring shows no signs of slowing down, but it is changing, particularly for manufacturers. Mexico, India, and Vietnam are now the countries with the lowest manufacturing costs. Not surprisingly, maintaining flexibility by offshoring to a few different low-cost locations may be U.S. firms' lowest-risk strategy for the future. The rising cost of Chinese labor has created a wave of change. Mexican workers now cost about the same as Chinese workers, and many countries, like Vietnam, have seen gains due to the country's lower wages. India and the Philippines remain top outsourcing destinations.[32]

International Direct Investment Investing directly in production and marketing operations in a foreign country is the ultimate level of global involvement. Over time, a firm may become successful at conducting business in other countries through exporting and contractual agreements. Its managers may then decide to establish manufacturing facilities in those countries, open branch offices, or buy ownership interests in local companies. Apple

foreign licensing agreement international agreement in which one firm allows another to produce or sell its product, or use its trademark, patent, or manufacturing processes, in a specific geographical area in return for royalties or other compensation.

subcontracting international agreement that involves hiring local companies to produce, distribute, or sell goods or services in a specific country or geographical region.

Hit&Miss

Apple Brings Manufacturing Work Back Home

As recently as a decade ago, you could purchase an Apple product made in the USA. Apple, along with numerous other companies, took pride in their "Made in USA" status. But in recent years, Apple and other companies chose a lower-cost labor structure in overseas countries. But that strategy seems to be slowly changing, with a small but gradual boomerang back to the United States—mainly from China. It's called reshoring, and Apple is part of the trend to bring manufacturing back to the U.S.

Recently, the company created 2,000 engineering, manufacturing, and construction jobs in a facility in Arizona, where components for its products will be produced. In addition, Apple is producing its newly redesigned Mac Pro computer in Austin, Texas. The benefits of this move back home include quicker response to production problems and increased quality control.

Significant wage increases in China over the past decade and concerns over protecting intellectual property overseas are two reasons that helped prompt the move. In addition, geographically close-knit design and production teams leave less room for error in the manufacturing process.

For Apple, bringing jobs home is certainly a positive way to help the U.S. economy. With reshoring—and reuniting design and production in one country—Apple will need to change the slogan on some of its products back to "Made in the USA."

Questions for Critical Thinking

1. Are there certain types of products, companies, or industries in which reshoring makes the most sense?

2. Is your decision to purchase a product ever influenced by where it was produced? If so, explain.

Sources: Clare Goldsberry, "As 'Made in USA' Gains in Popularity, Companies Reshore Manufacturing," *Plastics Today*, accessed January 6, 2014, www.plasticstoday.com; Juliette Garside, "Apple Creates 2,000 Jobs Shifting Production Back to US," *The Guardian*, accessed January 6, 2014, www.theguardian.com; Joel Johnson, "Made in America," or How Re-Shoring Can Transform the Global Procurement Landscape," *Spend Matters*, accessed January 6, 2014, http://spendmatters.com.

---

is involved in the trend of reshoring, or bringing jobs back to the United States, mainly from China. See the "Hit & Miss" feature for more.

In an *acquisition*, a company purchases another existing firm in the host country. An acquisition permits a largely domestic business operation to gain an international presence very quickly. Facebook acquired online photo, video, and social media site Instagram for $1 billion in cash and stock. This acquisition allows Facebook users to share photos, and it eliminates Instagram as a Facebook competitor.[33]

Joint ventures allow companies to share risks, costs, profits, and management responsibilities with one or more host country nationals. By setting up an *overseas division*, a company can conduct a significant amount of its business overseas. This strategy differs from that of a multinational company in that a firm with overseas divisions remains primarily a domestic organization with international operations. BMW and Toyota signed a technology-related joint venture to join forces for future products and technology development, which includes developing a platform for a mid-size sports vehicle.[34]

From Multinational Corporation to Global Business

A **multinational corporation (MNC)** is an organization with significant foreign operations. As Table 4.4 shows, firms headquartered in the United States and China make up 4 of the top 10 world's largest multinationals. Other locations include Brazil, China, the Netherlands, and the United Kingdom. Note that the two top industries are banking and oil and gas.

Many U.S. multinationals, including Nike and Walmart, have expanded their overseas operations because they believe that domestic markets are mature and foreign markets offer greater sales and profit potential. Other MNCs are making substantial investments in developing countries in part because these countries provide low-cost labor compared with the United States and Western Europe. In addition, many MNCs are locating high-tech facilities in countries with large numbers of technical school graduates.

joint venture partnership between companies formed for a specific undertaking.

multinational corporation (MNC) firm with significant operations and marketing activities outside its home country.

Assessment Check ✅

1. Name three possible strategies for beginning overseas operations.
2. What is countertrade?
3. Compare and contrast licensing and subcontracting.
4. Describe joint ventures.

TABLE 4.4	The World's Top 10 Leading Companies (Based on a Combined Ranking for Sales, Profits, Assets, and Market Value)		
RANK	COMPANY	INDUSTRY	COUNTRY OF ORIGIN
1	ICBC	Banking	China
2	China Construction Bank	Banking	China
3	JPMorgan Chase	Banking	United States
4	General Electric	Conglomerate	United States
5	Exxon Mobil	Oil & Gas	United States
6	HSBC Holdings	Banking	United Kingdom
7	Royal Dutch Shell	Oil & Gas	Netherlands
8	Agriculture Bank of China	Banking	China
9	Berkshire Hathaway	Conglomerate	United States
10	PetroChina	Oil & Gas	China

Source: "The World's Biggest Companies," *Forbes*, accessed February 8, 2014, www.forbes.com.

 6

Developing a Strategy for International Business

In developing a framework in which to conduct international business, managers must first evaluate their corporate objectives, organizational strengths and weaknesses, and strategies for product development and marketing. They can choose to combine these elements in either a global strategy or a multidomestic strategy.

Global Business Strategies

In a global business (or *standardization*) strategy, a firm sells the same product in essentially the same manner throughout the world. Many companies simply modify their domestic business strategies by translating promotional brochures and product-use instructions into the languages of the host nations.

A global marketing perspective can be appropriate for some goods and services and certain market segments that are common to many nations. The approach works for products with nearly universal appeal, for luxury items such as jewelry, and for commodities like chemicals and metals. Alcoa, for instance, is the world's biggest producer of aluminum for markets that include aerospace, automotive, building and construction, consumer electronics, packaging, and commercial transportation. Because in many applications aluminum's strength and light weight mean there are no good substitutes for it, the company forecasts a long-term increase in global demand, especially in China, India, Russia, the Middle East, and Latin America. It also views itself as committed to a global strategy that incorporates the highest ethical and sustainability practices. Recently, Alcoa was awarded the top spot for its use of basic resources

global business strategy offering a standardized, worldwide product and selling it in essentially the same manner throughout a firm's domestic and foreign markets.

Chapter 4 *Competing in World Markets* | **115**

Solving an Ethical Controversy

Bribery or the Cost of Doing Business?

Roughly translated, *guanxi* is the Chinese word for relationships and involves making business connections with local companies and officials. Some say *guanxi* is a local custom and a generally accepted business practice in China, while others say it is a form of bribery to extort money from companies anxious to do business there.

Should foreign companies practice *guanxi* when doing business in China?

PRO

1. Building mutually beneficial relationships with connected networks of local businesses and government officials provides foreign companies with strategic advantages.

2. The concept of *guanxi* is a local custom, and companies and officials expect foreign companies to seek their advice and expertise to navigate the complicated business environment in China.

CON

1. The concept of *guanxi* is another word for doing whatever it takes (no matter the cost) to make headway in the Chinese business marketplace.

2. Although they are doing business in a foreign land, U.S. companies must abide by the Foreign Corrupt Practices Act, federal legislation that prohibits the exchange of money for obtaining or retaining business.

Summary

Competing in world markets includes understanding local customs and business practices of the countries in which a company plans to operate. At the same time, however, companies must base their business strategy on solid business and ethical foundations. Regardless of the legal implications in the United States, business officials must know how to operate financially and ethically in any business situation.

Sources: Aruna Viswanatha, "U.S. Corporations Beg Clarity on Anti-Bribery Law," accessed January 6, 2014, http://www.reuters.com; "Avon Bribery Scandal in China, Not Really a Big Deal," China Lawyer in Shanghai (blog), accessed January 6, 2014; Kelly Baldwin, "*Guanxi*: The Ethics of Chinese Business Relationships," accessed January 6, 2014, http://myportfolio.usc.edu; David Wolf, "Business Ethics and Culture Clashes in China," accessed January 6, 2014, http://siliconhutong.com.

---

multidomestic business strategy developing and marketing products to serve different needs and tastes of separate national markets.

Assessment Check ☑

1. What is a global business strategy? What are its advantages?

2. What is a multidomestic business strategy? What are its advantages?

by the annual Covalence Ethical Rankings, a prestigious international survey that ranks the ethical performance of multinational companies.[35] Regardless of global business strategies, companies need to be aware of cultural and business customs in the countries in which they do business and of whether certain behaviors are accepted, as the feature "Solving an Ethical Controversy" discusses.

Multidomestic Business Strategies

Under a **multidomestic business** (or *adaptation*) **strategy**, the firm treats each national market in a different way. It develops products and marketing strategies that appeal to the customs, tastes, and buying habits of particular national markets. Companies that neglect the global nature of the Internet can unwittingly cause problems for potential customers by failing to adapt their strategy. At first, European consumers were hesitant to adopt online ordering of products ranging from books to railroad tickets. But in recent years, Internet use in Western Europe has grown dramatically. Companies as diverse as the European divisions of Amazon.com; Egg PLC of London, an online financial services company; and the French national railroad have seen the numbers of visitors to their websites climb, along with Internet revenues.

116

What's Ahead

Examples in this chapter indicate that businesses of all sizes are relying on world trade. Chapter 5 examines the special advantages and challenges that small-business owners encounter. In addition, a critical decision facing any new business is the choice of the most appropriate form of business ownership. Chapter 5 also examines the major ownership structures—sole proprietorship, partnership, and corporation—and assesses the pros and cons of each. The chapter closes with a discussion of recent trends affecting business ownership, such as the growing impact of franchising and business consolidations through mergers and acquisitions.

The global expansion of the Internet has allowed users in most Western European countries to purchase their railway tickets online.

Chapter in Review

Summary of Learning Objectives

1 Explain why nations trade.

The United States is both the world's largest importer and the largest exporter, although less than 5 percent of the world's population lives within its borders. With the increasing globalization of the world's economies, the international marketplace offers tremendous opportunities for U.S. and foreign businesses to expand into new markets for their goods and services. Doing business globally provides new sources of materials and labor. Trading with other countries also reduces a company's dependence on economic conditions in its home market. Countries that encourage international trade enjoy higher levels of economic activity, employment, and wages than those that restrict it.

Nations usually benefit if they specialize in producing certain goods or services. A country has an absolute advantage if it holds a monopoly or produces a good or service at a lower cost than other nations. It has a comparative advantage if it can supply a particular product more efficiently or at a lower cost than it can produce other items.

Assessment Check Answers

1.1 Why do nations trade? Nations trade because trading boosts economic growth by providing a market for products and access to needed resources. This makes production and distribution systems more efficient and reduces dependence on the economy of the home nation.

1.2 Cite some measures of the size of the international marketplace. Although developing countries have lower per-capita incomes than developed nations in North America and Western Europe, their populations are large and growing. China's population is about 1.3 billion, and India's is roughly 1.2 billion.

1.3 How does a nation acquire a comparative advantage? Comparative advantage exists when a nation can supply a product more efficiently and at a lower price than it can supply other goods, compared with the outputs of other countries.

2 Describe how trade is measured between nations.

Countries measure the level of international trade by comparing exports and imports and then calculating whether a trade surplus or a deficit exists. This is the balance of trade, which represents the difference between exports and imports. The term *balance of payments* refers to the overall flow of money into or out of a country, including overseas loans and borrowing, international investments, and profits from such investments. An exchange rate is the value of a nation's currency relative to the currency of another nation. Currency values typically fluctuate relative to the supply and demand for specific currencies in the world market. When the value of the dollar falls compared with other currencies, the cost paid by foreign businesses and households for U.S. products declines, and demand for exports may rise. An increase in the value of the dollar raises the prices of U.S. products sold abroad, but it reduces the prices of foreign products sold in the United States.

Chapter 4 *Competing in World Markets* **117**

2.1 Compare balance of trade and balance of payments. Balance of trade is the difference between a nation's exports and imports. Balance of payments is the overall flow of money into or out of a country.

2.2 Explain the function of an exchange rate. A nation's exchange rate is the rate at which its currency can be exchanged for the currencies of other nations to make it easier for them to trade with one another.

2.3 What happens when a currency is devalued? Devaluation describes a drop in a currency's value relative to other currencies or to a fixed standard.

⎡3⎤ Identify the barriers to international trade.
Businesses face several obstacles in the global marketplace. Companies must be sensitive to social and cultural differences, such as languages, values, and religions, when operating in other countries. Economic differences include standard-of-living variations and levels of infrastructure development. Legal and political barriers are among the most difficult to judge. Each country sets its own laws regulating business practices. Trade restrictions such as tariffs and administrative barriers also present obstacles to international business.

Assessment Check Answers ✓

3.1 How might values and attitudes form a barrier to trade, and how can they be overcome? Marked differences in values and attitudes, such as religious attitudes, can form barriers between traditionally capitalist countries and those adapting new capitalist systems. Many of these can be overcome by learning about and respecting such differences.

3.2 What is a tariff? What is its purpose? A tariff is a tax, surcharge, or duty charged on foreign products. Its purpose is to protect domestic producers of those items.

3.3 Why is dumping a problem for companies marketing goods internationally? Dumping is selling products abroad at prices below the cost of production or exporting products at a lower price than charged in the home market. It drives the cost of products sharply down in the market where they are dumped, thus hurting the domestic producers of those products.

⎡4⎤ Discuss reducing barriers to international trade.
Many international organizations seek to promote international trade by reducing barriers among nations. Examples include the World Trade Organization, the World Bank, and the International Monetary Fund. Multinational economic communities create partnerships to remove barriers to the flow of goods, capital, and people across the borders of members. Three such economic agreements are the North American Free Trade Agreement (NAFTA), CAFTA-DR, and the European Union.

Assessment Check Answers ✓

4.1 What international trade organization succeeded GATT, and what is its goal? The World Trade Organization (WTO) succeeded GATT with the goal of monitoring GATT agreements, mediating disputes, and continuing the effort to reduce trade barriers throughout the world.

4.2 Compare and contrast the goals of the World Bank and the International Monetary Fund. The World Bank funds projects that build or expand nations' infrastructure such as transportation, education, and medical systems and facilities. The International Monetary Fund makes short-term loans to member nations that are unable to meet their expenses. The fund operates as a lender of last resort for troubled nations.

4.3 What are the goals of the European Union, and how do they promote international trade? The European Union's goals include promoting economic and social progress, introducing European citizenship as a complement to national citizenship, and giving the EU a significant role in international affairs. Unifying standards and laws can contribute to economic growth.

⎡5⎤ Explain the decisions to go global.
Exporting and importing, the first level of involvement in international business, involves the lowest degree of both risk and control. Companies may rely on export trading or management companies to help distribute their products. Contractual agreements, such as franchising, foreign licensing, and subcontracting, offer additional options. Franchising and licensing are especially appropriate for services. Companies may also choose local subcontractors to produce goods for local sales. International direct investment in production and marketing facilities provides the highest degree of control but also the greatest risk. Firms make direct investments by acquiring foreign companies or facilities, forming joint ventures with local firms, and setting up their own overseas divisions.

Assessment Check Answers ✓

5.1 Name three possible strategies for beginning overseas business operations. Strategies are exporting or importing; contractual agreements such as franchising, licensing, or subcontracting; and making direct investments in foreign markets through acquisition, joint venture, or establishment of an overseas division.

5.2 What is countertrade? Countertrade consists of payments made in the form of local products, not currency.

5.3 Compare and contrast licensing and subcontracting. In a foreign licensing agreement, one firm allows another to produce or sell its product or use its trademark, patent, or manufacturing process in a specific geographical area in return for royalty payments or other compensation. In subcontracting, a firm hires local companies abroad to produce, distribute, or sell its goods and services in a specific region.

5.4 Describe joint ventures. Joint ventures allow companies to share risks, costs, profits, and management responsibilities with one or more host-country nationals.

⌐6⌐ Discuss developing a strategy for international business.

A company that adopts a global strategy develops a single, standardized product and marketing strategy for implementation throughout the world. The firm sells the same product in essentially the same manner in all countries in which it operates. Under a multidomestic (or adaptation) strategy, the firm develops a different treatment for each foreign market. It develops products and marketing strategies that appeal to the customs, tastes, and buying habits of particular nations.

Assessment Check Answers ✅

6.1 What is a global business strategy? What are its advantages? A global business strategy specifies a standardized competitive strategy in which the firm sells the same product in essentially the same manner throughout the world. It works well for goods and services that are common to many nations.

6.2 What is a multidomestic business strategy? What are its advantages? A multidomestic business strategy allows the firm to treat each foreign market in a different way to appeal to the customs, tastes, and buying habits of particular national markets. It allows the firm to customize its marketing appeals for individual cultures or areas.

◼ Business Terms You Need to Know

exports 94	exchange control 106	European Union (EU) 109
imports 94	General Agreement on Tariffs and	countertrade 112
balance of trade 97	Trade (GATT) 106	franchise 112
balance of payments 97	World Trade Organization (WTO) 106	foreign licensing agreement 113
exchange rate 98	World Bank 107	subcontracting 113
devaluation 99	International Monetary Fund (IMF) 107	joint venture 114
infrastructure 102	North American Free Trade Agreement	multinational corporation (MNC) 114
tariffs 105	(NAFTA) 107	global business strategy 115
quota 105	Central America–Dominican	multidomestic business strategy 116
dumping 105	Republic Free Trade Agreement	
embargo 106	(CAFTA-DR) 109	

◼ Review Questions

1. How does a business decide whether to trade with a foreign country? What are the key factors for participating in the information economy on a global basis?

2. Why have developing countries such as China and India become important international markets?

3. What is the difference between absolute advantage and comparative advantage? Give an example of each.

4. Can a nation have a favorable balance of trade and an unfavorable balance of payments? Why or why not?

5. Identify several potential barriers to communication when a company attempts to conduct business in another country. How might these be overcome?

6. Identify and describe briefly the three dimensions of the legal environment for global business.

7. What are the major nontariff restrictions affecting international business? Describe the difference between tariff and nontariff restrictions.

8. What is NAFTA? How does it work?

9. How has the EU helped trade among European businesses?

10. What are the key choices a company must make before reaching the final decision to go global?

◼ Projects and Teamwork Applications

1. What are some examples of business or personal mishaps that have resulted from cultural misunderstandings? How did they occur, and how were they resolved? Give specific examples and discuss among classmates.

2. The tremendous growth of online business has introduced new elements to the legal climate of international business.

Patents, brand names, copyrights, and trademarks are difficult to monitor because of the boundaryless nature of the Internet. What steps could businesses take to protect their trademarks and brands in this environment? Come up with at least five suggestions, and compare your list with those of your classmates.

Chapter 4 *Competing in World Markets* **119**

3. The WTO monitors GATT agreements, mediates disputes, and continues the effort to reduce trade barriers throughout the world. However, widespread concerns have been expressed that the WTO's focus on lowering trade barriers may encourage businesses to keep costs down through practices that may lead to pollution and human rights abuses. Others argue that human rights should not be linked to international business. Do you think environmental and human rights issues should be linked to trade? Why or why not?

4. Describe briefly the EU and its goals. What are the pros and cons of the EU? Do you predict that the European alliance will hold up over the next 20 years? Why or why not?

5. Use the most recent edition of "The *Fortune* Global 500," which usually is published in *Fortune* magazine in July, or go to *Fortune's* online version at http://money.cnn.com/magazines/fortune/global500/.
   a. On what data is the Global 500 ranking based?
   b. Among the world's 10 largest corporations, list the countries in which they are based.
   c. Identify the top-ranked company, along with its Global 500 ranking and country, for the following industry classifications: Food and Drug Stores; Industrial and Farm Equipment; Petroleum Refining; Utilities: Gas and Electric; Telecommunications; Pharmaceuticals.

▉ Web Assignments

1. **WTO**. Visit the website of the World Trade Organization (http://www.wto.org). Research two current trade disputes. Which countries and products are involved? What, if anything, do the two disputes have in common? What procedures does the WTO follow in resolving trade disputes between member countries?

2. **EU**. Europa.eu is the web portal for the European Union. Go to the following website (http://europa.eu/index_en.htm) and answer the following questions:
   a. What are the steps a country must take to become a member of the EU?
   b. How many EU members have adopted the euro? Which countries will be adopting the euro over the next few years?
   c. What is the combined GDP of EU members? Which EU member has the largest GDP? Which has the smallest GDP?

3. **PepsiCo**. PepsiCo is one of the world's largest global corporations. Visit the firm's website (http://www.pepsi.com). Where is the company headquartered? What are some of its best-known brands? Are these brands sold in specific countries or are they sold worldwide? Make a list of three of four issues Pepsi faces as a global corporation.

Note: Internet web addresses change frequently. If you do not find the exact sites listed, you may need to access the organization's or company's home page and search from there or use a search engine such as Google or Bing.

CASE 4.1	**McDonald's Local Menu Strategy a Hit**

With over 34,000 restaurants in 118 countries, global giant McDonald's is not only the world's largest burger chain, but one of the fastest growing fast-food chains overseas. The company has become an icon of globalization. Part of the company's success lies in its ability to employ a strategy of adapting its menu to local tastes to compete with other local food chains.

Sensitivity to cultural influences and dietary laws is a dominant theme on McDonald's menus worldwide. The company and its staff in each test kitchen keep pace with changing customer tastes and preferences worldwide. In each country, McDonald's management carefully plans its localized menu around its core group of products—its burgers, shakes, and fries.

In India, McDonald's has adapted its burgers to consumers who don't eat meat. The majority of people in India are Hindus, and killing cows to eat beef is against their religious beliefs. McDonald's menu in India includes many vegetarian options, including the McVeggie, a rice, bean, and vegetable patty with breading, and a potato-vegetable burger, also known as the McAloo Tikki. In China, one of McDonald's fastest growing markets, the company recently introduced breaded and fried Spicy Pork McBites, a variation of its popular Chicken McNuggets.

Tailoring the menu to local tastes doesn't only happen overseas. In southern U.S. states, breakfast items include a biscuit smothered with sausage gravy. Healthy lifestyles count too. In many locations, McDonald's has adapted its menu to add more fruit choices to increase healthy choices for children and adults alike. The next time you order a value meal, you may very well have to make the decision between having a side salad or a piece of fruit in lieu of fries.

Questions for Critical Thinking

1. How do other fast-food companies adapt their menus to serve a global market?
2. How might other industries like the automobile industry adapt their products to local consumer tastes and preferences as McDonald's has?

Sources: Company website, "Getting to Know Us," and "World Class Training," www.aboutmcdonalds.com, accessed February 8, 2014; Mike Ives, "McDonald's Opens in Vietnam, Bringing Big Macs to Fans of Bahn Mi," *The New York Times,* February 7, 2014, www.nytimes.com; Amy Qin, "Would You Like Fries with Those Spicy Pork McBites?" *The New York Times,* accessed January 6, 2014, http://sinosphere.blogs.nytimes.com; Stephanie Strom, "With Tastes Growing Healthier, McDonald's Aims to Adapt Its Menu," *The New York Times,* accessed January 6, 2014, www.nytimes.com.

TOMS Shoes Takes One Step at a Time

On a trip to Argentina, a young U.S. entrepreneur named Blake Mycoskie saw firsthand how a simple pair of shoes, beyond the means of many of the world's poor, could provide everything from the ability to attend school to protection from life-threatening infections. Moved by the experience, Mycoskie had a striking insight: that a revenue-based business was more likely than a charity to sustain itself over the long term. And so TOMS Shoes was born.

TOMS Shoes, which stands for "tomorrow's shoes," makes simple, lightweight, but stylish shoes with a unique business model called One for One. For every pair it sells, TOMS gives a pair of shoes away to a child in need somewhere in the world.

To those who have difficulty understanding his business model, Mycoskie tells this story: "I got to meet Bill Gates. And he said, 'You know, 50 percent of the infectious diseases in the world can be prevented by two things. Toilets and shoes. So, keep doing what you're doing.' "

TOMS's current focus is on preventing a debilitating soil-borne disease, common in Ethiopia, which attacks the lymphatic system. Simply wearing shoes prevents its transmission. Donated shoes are also helping to prevent hookworm in Guatemala. And children who wear shoes can more readily walk to school.

Mycoskie, who recently gave away most of his possessions to live on a small sailboat docked on the California coast, keeps his entrepreneurial hand in everything the company does. With only 50 full-time employees and a crew of enthusiastic volunteers, TOMS recently turned its first profit, in a year in which it also gave away 300,000 pairs of shoes. "It turns out doing the things you enjoy and having fun with them often create the best message."

Questions for Critical Thinking

1. Do you think TOMS's One for One business model is sustainable in the long term? Why or why not?
2. Mycoskie says his customers provide "the best type of marketing you can have" because when asked about their footwear, "they say, 'When I bought this pair of shoes, a child got a pair.' " What lesson do you think other socially responsible firms can learn from TOMS's business practices?

Sources: Company website, http://www.toms.com, accessed January 6, 2014; Tamara Schweitzer, "The Way I Work," *Inc.,* accessed January 6, 2014, www.inc.com; Kellie Doligale, "Good for the Sole: Toms Founder Set to Visit UK," *The Kentucky Kernel,* accessed January 6, 2014, http://kykernel.com; Daniel Seberg, "Giving Kids Their First Pair of Shoes," *CBS News,* accessed January 6, 2014, www.cbsnews.com; Karen Leo and Lindsay Goldwert, "TOMS Shoes Saving Lives, One Sole at a Time," *ABC News,* accessed January 6, 2014, www.abcnews.com; Shannon Cook, "These Shoes Help Others Get a Step Up," *CNN,* accessed January 6, 2014, www.cnn.com.

Smart Design: Life Is in the Details

When you peel a potato or run your pizza cutter through to cut a slice, it's likely that you only notice the tool you are using if it doesn't work—if it sticks or snags, gouges the potato, or tears the pizza crust. The team at Smart Design doesn't mind not being noticed. They operate quietly behind the scenes, developing a wide range of designs for products made and sold by companies around the world. They come up with designs that make everything from toothbrushes to automobiles function better in human hands. Smart Design engineers developed the popular OXO Good Grips line of kitchen utensils as well as the SmartGauge instrument cluster for the Ford Fusion Hybrid.

"Smart Design is about designing products for people in their everyday life," explains Richard Whitehall, vice president of industrial design for Smart Design. "There are little things you might see in a product that you'd think, 'I wish I'd thought of that—it's a great idea.'" Sometimes it's the simplest or smallest detail in the engineering of a product that makes a difference in whether consumers will continue to use the product or purchase it again. Smart Design tries to make products that work well universally for a wide range of people in different situations. This is where the global challenge comes in—differences in cultural preferences, product use, language, and other factors can make universal product development difficult. But Smart Design has offices in the United States and abroad, with testing locations in Europe and Asia, and employees representing more than 20 different countries.

Ted Booth, director of interactive design says, "Interactive design is anything with a 'chip' in it. I can't imagine approaching interactive design without a global perspective." Booth explains how Smart Design develops the design for a mobile phone. "The way people use it varies from country to country," he notes. "So what might look like a new feature in one country is really old hat in another." Booth observes that it is very common for consumers in Finland and South Korea to pay for most goods and services from their mobile phones, whereas this is not a common practice among U.S. consumers. Some of this practice is driven by industry standards, but much of it has to do with cultural expectations. "It's important to have a global perspective [in design] so you know the trends in other countries. You need to design and shape the experience to hit the market and bring something new to the market, but also adapt to individual markets," concludes Booth.

Booth describes his company's work on the "Q" control for HP—a single navigation controller that can be used across all HP products, ranging from TV remotes to printers to cameras. Smart Design tested the Q control in the United States, Germany, Spain, and South Korea. Researchers discovered that, while a few local adaptations were necessary, there was one universal preference among all consumers: everyone needed a "back" button in order to go forward. Booth explains that there is a universal need for people to know that there is an escape, undo—or back—for every function in order for users to feel comfortable completing an interactive task.

Smart Design has an impressive list of worldwide clients, including Ford, Bell Canada, ESPN, World Kitchen, Microsoft, Samsung, and Kellogg's, among many others. The firm has won many accolades, including nationally recognized design awards. But Smart Design remains focused on the details. The firm recently developed the Reach Wondergrip children's toothbrush for Johnson & Johnson when it became apparent that traditional children's toothbrushes were just scaled down from the adult models. Kids couldn't hold them easily and were less likely to brush their teeth. The new Wondergrip children's model changed the industry standard for children's toothbrushes—and brushing habits. Smart Design also developed a women's sports watch for Nike—based on needs and preferences of women runners. And there's that line of kitchen tools that make food preparation and cooking just a little bit easier and more fun.

Richard Whitehall, who actually began his career working for a firm that manufactured mountaineering gear, describes the importance of design in every product used by consumers. "We were trying to think of a situation people were in and trying to design a product in a way that people from different countries—whether they were stuck in the Alps or on a boat—could use in all these different situations." Whether you are climbing a mountain in Switzerland or cutting your pizza in Boston, you want your gear to work flawlessly—and that is the goal of Smart Design.

Questions for Critical Thinking

1. Ted Booth and Richard Whitehall mention some of the cultural barriers that Smart Design faces in developing products for worldwide use. Give examples of other barriers the firm might face in international trade.

2. Describe what you believe would be the best level of involvement for Smart Design to have when doing business in Europe. Remember to take into consideration the impact of the European Union on business transactions.

3. Smart Design already has a presence in South Korea. How might the firm best approach developing products for the market in India? In China?

4. Do you believe it is possible to develop truly universal products? Why or why not?

Sources: Company website, http://www.smartdesignworldwide.com, accessed January 6, 2014; "National Design Awards," *Cooper-Hewitt, National Design Museum,* accessed January 6, 2014, www.cooperhewitt.org; Alissa Walker, "Biomimicry Challenge: For IBM, Smart Design Draws Water Conservation Inspiration from Ecosystems," *Fast Company,* accessed January 6, 2014, www.fastcompany.com.

KANSAS

GREENSBURG, KS
New Ways to Be a Better Town

Greensburg, Kansas, had been struggling for years. Located along Highway 54, a major trucking route, the town was merely a pit stop for people on their way somewhere else. It did have a few tourist attractions: the Big Well, the world's largest hand-dug well, and a 1,000-pound meteorite that fell from the sky in 2006.

Lonnie McCollum, the town's mayor, had been looking into ways to breathe new life into the town. McCollum wanted to add a little vintage charm to its quaint Main Street but could not raise the money. And he had launched a campaign to put the "green" back in Greensburg by promoting green building technology. But the idea, which many residents associated with hippies and tree-huggers, did not go over well.

Then everything changed. "My town is gone," announced Town Administrator Steve Hewitt on May 5, 2007, after surveying the damage caused by a devastating tornado. "I believe 95 percent of the homes are gone. Downtown buildings are gone, my home is gone." With a clean slate and 700 homes to replace, Hewitt vowed to rebuild Greensburg using sustainable materials. He believed the town had a unique opportunity to control its environmental impact and reduce operating costs through increased energy efficiency.

"What if we turned this tragedy into something beautiful?" asked resident Dan Wallach in a new business plan he wrote shortly after the disaster. Wallach and his wife had long been interested in sustainable green living. Using their experience in developing nonprofits, the two launched Greensburg GreenTown, an organization designed to support Greensburg's green building efforts through education, fund-raising, and public relations management.

One of Wallach's favorite new projects was BTI Greensburg, the local John Deere dealership. Owners Kelly and Mike Estes had decided to replace their ruined building with an energy-efficient, technologically state-of-the-art showroom featuring radiant heat, solar energy, passive cooling, and wind power. With corporate support from John Deere, BTI Greensburg would become a flagship green dealership.

Long-term plans for Greensburg include a business incubator, to help displaced businesses get back on their feet and bring new businesses to town; a green industrial park, green museum, and green school system; green building codes and zoning restrictions; and a community of green homes and businesses.

Questions
After viewing the video, answer the following questions:

1. In what ways is the town of Greensburg like any other business?

2. In what ways is the town of Greensburg a socially responsible organization?

3. What might be the effects of the town's new green building guidelines on residents and businesses? On the regional economy?

4. What kind of business is Greensburg GreenTown? How does its structure differ from John Deere's?

LAUNCHING YOUR
[Global Business and Economics Career]

In Part 1, "Business in a Global Environment," you learned about the background and current issues driving contemporary business. The part includes four chapters covering such issues as the changing face of business, business ethics and social responsibility, economic challenges facing contemporary business, and competing in world markets. Business has always been an exciting career field, whether you choose to start your own company, work at a local business, or set your sights on a position with a multinational corporation. But today's environment is especially attractive because businesses continue to expand their horizons to compete in a global economy—and they need dedicated and talented people to help them accomplish their goals. In fact, professional and business service jobs are found in some of the fastest-growing industries in the U.S. economy and are projected to grow during this decade.[1] So now is the time to explore several different career options that can lead you to your dream job. Each part in this text profiles the many opportunities available in business. Here are a few related to Chapters 1 through 4.

If you're good at math and are interested in how societies and companies function, then maybe a career as an *economist* is in your future. Economists study how resources are allocated, conduct research by collecting and analyzing data, monitor economic trends, and develop forecasts. They look into such vital areas as the cost of energy, foreign trade and exchange between countries, the effect of taxes, and employment levels—both from a big-picture national or global viewpoint and from the perspective of individual businesses. Economists work for corporations to help them run more efficiently, for consulting firms to offer special expertise, or for government agencies to oversee economic decision making. Typically, advanced degrees are needed to climb to top-level positions. Economists typically earn about $91,860 per year.[2]

Or perhaps you are interested in global business. Companies increasingly search the world for the best employees, supplies, and markets. So you could work in the United States for a foreign-based firm such as Siemens or Toyota; abroad in Australia, Asia, Europe, or Latin America for a U.S.-based firm such as Microsoft; or with overseas co-workers via computer networks to develop new products for a firm such as General Electric. With technology and telecommunications, distance is no longer a barrier to conducting business. Global business careers exist in all the areas you'll be reading about in this text—business ownership, management, marketing, technology, and finance.

Global business leaders are not born but made—so how can you start on that career path? Here are the three areas that businesses consider when selecting employees for overseas assignment:

- *competence*—including technical knowledge, language skills, leadership ability, experience, and past performance

- *adaptability*—including interest in overseas work, communication and other personal skills, empathy for other cultures, and appreciation for varied management styles and work environments

- *personal characteristics*—level of education, experience, and social compatibility with the host country[3]

Solid experience in your field or company ranks at the top of the list of needed skills. Firms want to send employees who have expertise in their business and loyalty to the firm to represent them overseas. Companies are reluctant to send new graduates abroad immediately. Instead, they invest in training to orient employees to the new assignment.

Knowledge of and interest in other languages and cultures is the second-highest priority. Businesspeople need to function smoothly in another society, so they are selected based on their familiarity with other languages and cultures. Because many companies are doing business in China, some people have become fluent in Mandarin Chinese to boost their career prospects. Also, some school systems are offering Chinese language classes in addition to their standard offerings of Spanish, French, German, and Russian.

Finally, employees are evaluated on their personal characteristics to be certain that they will fit well in their new country. A person's talent is still foremost in making assignments, but executives with cross-cultural skills are in high demand.

Career Assessment Exercises in Economics and Global Business

1. With the ups and downs in the U.S. economy, economists have been highlighted in the news. The head of the Federal Reserve, Janet Yellen, is charged with managing the nation's currency, money supply, and interest rates. To get an idea of the role economists play in a federal government agency, research Yellen's background and qualifications. Now make a list of your own skills. Looking at Yellen's background, how can you improve your skill set?

2. To see the effect of the global economy in your community, go to any major retailer. Look at the number of different countries represented in the products on the shelves. Compare your list with those of your classmates to see who found the most countries and what goods those countries provided. Go online to research the career opportunities at the retailer's website.

3. To learn more about other countries, do research online for a country in which you are interested. Here are some sources that may be useful:

   - *The World Factbook*, published by the Central Intelligence Agency, https://www.cia.gov/library/publications/the-world-factbook/. This publication, updated yearly, contains a wealth of information about countries—geography and climate, population statistics, cultural and political information, transportation and communications methods, and economic data.

   - *Bloomberg Businessweek* magazine, www.businessweek.com. The website has links to "Global Economics," where you can explore breaking news or information on global companies.

   - Online news sites Yahoo! News and Google News, http://news.yahoo.com and http://news.google.com. Both of these online news sites have links to global business news.

   Write a one-page summary of what you found. Make a list of abilities you would need to function well as a businessperson in that country. Concentrate on the areas of competence, adaptability, and personal characteristics. How might you formulate a plan to gain those skills?

Learning Objectives

1. Discuss why most businesses are small businesses.
2. Determine the contributions of small businesses to the economy.
3. Discuss why small businesses fail.
4. Describe the features of a successful business plan.
5. Identify the available assistance for small businesses.
6. Explain franchising.
7. Outline the forms of private business ownership.
8. Describe public and collective ownership of business.
9. Discuss organizing a corporation.
10. Explain what happens when businesses join forces.

Chapter 5

Forms of Business Ownership and Organization

© Kali Nine LLC/iStockphoto

Anytime Fitness Takes Top Franchise Spot

Chuck Runyon and Dave Mortensen started Minnesota-based Anytime Fitness, a 24-hour fitness chain, more than a decade ago with a vision of giving franchisees a proven, reasonably priced business model. The approach is simple: provide a safe, secure place for fitness members to work out on their own schedules; keep monthly membership and franchise fees low; and provide ongoing support to franchisees and members. The result? Anytime Fitness has recently been named *Entrepreneur Magazine's* Top Franchise of the year.

With more than 2,400 franchises worldwide, Anytime Fitness has taken advantage of the fast-growing fitness club industry. According to recent statistics, over 1 million people join fitness clubs each year—with more than an estimated 40 million members nationwide. Anytime's low monthly member fees make it easier to sign up new recruits, and members can use other Anytime fitness locations around the world.

With state-of-the art keycard access, videotape surveillance, and panic button security, most locations do not require a staff member on duty at all times, which helps keep labor costs low. And automated services and support from regional corporate offices assist franchisees in keeping overhead and salary costs down. Another advantage to attracting new business owners is Anytime's monthly flat-rate franchise license fee—regardless of the location's size or number of members.

The fitness chain also wants to increase its online presence and get its customers to follow. CEO Runyon believes fitness companies that can bridge the gap between a physical location and a digital presence will become the industry leaders. The company has built an online platform called Anytime Health where members can track their fitness progress, get tips about healthy lifestyles, and connect with other members to share their fitness stories. The company also views the online site as a place where members and operators alike can exchange feedback about the overall Anytime Fitness experience, which will help the company fine-tune its overall business operations.

Anytime's purple running man logo has become a symbol of success—and a tattoo for more than 1,000 members and franchisees. Runyon says the company reimburses franchisees and members who get the running man tattoo—if they can tell a good story about what the running man means to them. For some, the purple runner symbolizes an accomplishment of losing weight and improving overall health. For others, it's a symbol of entrepreneurial success and running one's own business.[1]

Overview

Do you hope to work for a big company or a small one? Do you plan to start your own business? If you're thinking about striking out on your own, you're not alone. On any given day in the United States, more people are in the process of starting a new business than getting married or having a baby. But before you enter the business world—as an employee or an owner—you need to understand the industry in which a company operates, as well as the size and framework of the firm's organization. For example, Anytime Fitness is a fast-growing business in the global fitness industry. It's important to remember that most large businesses—like Ford and Apple—began as small businesses.

Several variables affect the way a business is organized, including how easily it can be set up, access to financing, tolerance of financial risk, and strengths and weaknesses that exist in competing firms, as well as the strengths and weaknesses of your firm.

This chapter begins by focusing on small-business ownership, including the advantages and disadvantages of small-business ventures, the contributions of small business to the economy, and the reasons small businesses fail. The chapter examines the services provided by the U.S. government's Small Business Administration, the role of women and minorities in small business, and alternatives for small businesses such as franchising.

The chapter then moves on to an overview of the forms of private business ownership—sole proprietorships, partnerships, and corporations. In addition, the features of businesses owned by employees and families, as well as not-for-profit organizations, are discussed. Public and collective ownership are examined. The chapter concludes with an explanation of structures and operations typical of larger companies and a review of the major types of business alliances.

⌜1⌝ Most Businesses Are Small Businesses

Although many people associate the term *business* with corporate giants such as Walmart, 3M, and ExxonMobil, 99.7 percent of all U.S. companies are considered small businesses. Small businesses have generated 64 percent of new jobs over the past two decades and employ close to half of all private-sector workers.[2] Small business is also the launching pad for new ideas and products. They hire 43 percent of high-tech workers, such as scientists, engineers, and computer programmers, who devote their time to developing new goods and services.[3]

What Is a Small Business?

small business
independent business with fewer than 500 employees, not dominant in its market.

How can you tell a small business from a large one? The Small Business Administration (SBA), the federal agency most directly involved with this sector of the economy, defines a <u>small business</u> as an "independent business having fewer than 500 employees." However, those bidding for government contracts or applying for government assistance may vary in size according to industry. For example, small manufacturers fall in the 500-worker range, whereas wholesalers must employ fewer than 100. Retailers may generate up to $7 million in annual sales and still be considered small businesses, while farms or other agricultural businesses are designated small if they generate less than $750,000 annually.[4]

Anthony Saladino considers getting fired from his job selling kitchen cabinets one of the worst days in his life. But with $20,000 and some knowledge of kitchen cabinets and design, Saladino launched Kitchen Cabinet Kings, an Internet-only distributor of kitchen and bathroom cabinets in New York City. With a user-friendly website, the company's business has taken off and continues to be successful.[5]

Because government agencies offer benefits designed to help small businesses compete with larger firms, small-business owners want to determine whether their companies meet the standards for small-business designation. If it qualifies, a company may be eligible for government loans or for government purchasing programs that encourage proposals from smaller suppliers. With this type of assistance, companies like Kitchen Cabinet Kings might eventually expand and become a larger business.

Typical Small-Business Ventures

Small businesses have always competed against each other as well as against some of the world's largest organizations. ModCloth, an online clothing, accessories, and home furnishings retailer founded by the husband-and-wife team Eric and Susan Koger, does both. Launched while the owners were still in college, the business, which is located in Pittsburgh, offers trendy and vintage-inspired fashions by independent designers. The company reaches out to consumers via Twitter,

Kitchen Cabinet Kings

Anthony Saladino started New York–based Kitchen Cabinet Kings, an Internet-only distributor of kitchen and bathroom cabinets, after he lost his job.

128 Part 2 *Starting and Growing Your Business*

148

Facebook, and a company blog. Voted by *Fast Company* as one of the top 50 Most Innovative Companies, ModCloth is able to compete against other clothing e-tailers of any size. Once considered a small business, ModCloth's most recent annual revenues reached $100 million.[6]

There has been a steady erosion of small businesses in some industries as larger firms have bought out small, independent businesses and replaced them with larger operations. The number of independent home improvement stores has fallen dramatically as Lowe's and other national discounters have increased the size and number of their stores. But as Table 5.1 reveals, the businesses least likely to be gobbled up are those that sell personalized services, rely on certain locations, and keep their overhead costs low.

Nonfarming-related small firms create more than half the nation's gross domestic product (GDP). In the past, many of these businesses focused on retailing or a service industry, such as insurance. More recently, however, small firms have carved out an important niche for themselves: providing busy consumers with customized services that range from pet-sitting to personal shopping. These businesses cater to the needs of individual customers in a way not possible with big firms.

As Figure 5.1 shows, small businesses provide most jobs in the construction, agricultural services, wholesale trade, services, and retail trade industries. Retailing to the consumer is another important industry for small firms. Online and retailing giants such as Amazon and Macy's may be the best-known firms, but smaller stores and websites outnumber them. And these small firms can be very successful, as the owners of ModCloth illustrate, often because they can keep their overhead expenses low.

Small business also plays a significant role in agriculture. Although most farm acreage is in the hands of large, corporate farms, almost 90 percent of U.S. farms are owned by individual farmers or families, not partners or shareholders.[7] The family farm is a classic example of a small-business operation. It is independently owned and operated, with a limited number of employees, including family members. Cider Hill Farm in Massachusetts is one such farm.

TABLE 5.1 Business Sectors Most Dominated and Least Dominated by Small Firms

MOST LIKELY TO BE A SMALL FIRM	FEWER THAN 20 WORKERS
Home builders	97%
Florists	97%
Hair salons	96%
Auto repair	96%
Funeral homes	94%
LEAST LIKELY TO BE A SMALL FIRM	**FEWER THAN 20 WORKERS**
Hospitals	14%
Nursing homes	23%
Paper mills	33%
Electric utilities	38%
Oil pipelines	38%

Source: U.S. Census Bureau, "Number of Firms, Number of Establishments, Employment, and Annual Payroll by Employment Size of the Enterprise for the United States, All Industries," http://www.census.gov, accessed January 11, 2014.

FIGURE
5.1

Industries Dominated by Small Businesses

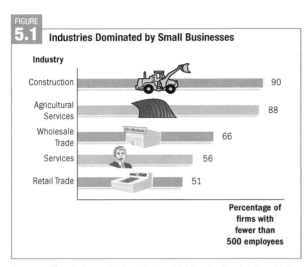

Industry

Construction	90
Agricultural Services	88
Wholesale Trade	66
Services	56
Retail Trade	51

Percentage of firms with fewer than 500 employees

Source: Office of Advocacy, U.S. Small Business Administration, "Small Business Profile: United States," http://www.sba.gov/advocacy, accessed January 11, 2014.

home-based businesses firm operated from the residence of the business owner.

Assessment Check ✅

1. How does the Small Business Administration (SBA) define *small business*?

2. In what industries do small businesses play a significant role?

Together, three generations of the Cook family operate the farm producing fruit and vegetables, including a wide variety of cooking and eating apples from its orchards and honey from its on-site beehives. In addition, Cider Hill makes its own fresh cider and cider doughnuts every day and operates a well-stocked country store on the property. During growing season, the farm hosts field trips for schools, offers hay rides, and creates a corn maze in its fields. All of these activities contribute to the income of the farm. The Cooks are also dedicated to environmentally friendly farming technologies. Cider Hill operates three wind turbines and uses solar cells to help power its buildings.[8]

Fifty-two percent of small businesses in the United States are **home-based businesses**—firms operated from the residence of the business owner. There are about 18 million such businesses in the United States.[9] People who operate home-based firms often do so because this type of work allows them more control over their business as well as their personal time. Whether you're a morning person or a night owl, in many cases you can structure your business hours accordingly. Access to the Internet and availability of mobile computing devices and technology make it convenient to run a home-based business. Reduced overhead costs such as leasing office or warehouse space is another major attraction of home-based businesses. Drawbacks include separating business and personal life, isolation, and less customer visibility—except, of course, if your customers visit you online. In that case, they don't care where your office is located.

Many small-business start-ups are more competitive because of technology and online resources. The Internet does not guarantee success—there are so many sites and tools that a small firm can utilize (including search engine optimization) to make its online presence effective. But establishing an online presence is generally less expensive than opening a retail store while reaching a broader spectrum of potential customers. Connecticut-based eBeanstalk.com is an online toy store. How does this small business compete with the likes of online giants such as Amazon and Toys 'R Us? The company specializes in learning toys that "help plant the seeds that help children grow." Two teams of experts (including 700 moms) hired by eBeanstalk evaluate more than 10,000 toys from manufacturers to narrow the selection down to around 600 of what they consider to be the best learning toys. That group may shrink even further. Only the selected toys are included on the site. Consumers appreciate this screening process, knowing they can go straight to eBeanstalk for the toys they want.[10]

American business history is filled with inspirational stories of great inventors who launched companies in barns, garages, warehouses, and attics. For visionaries such as the late Apple Computer founder Steve Jobs and co-founder Steve Wozniak, the logical option for transforming their technical idea into a commercial reality was to begin work in a family garage. The impact of today's entrepreneurs, including home-based businesses, is discussed in more depth in Chapter 6.

⌐2⌐ Contributions of Small Business to the Economy

Small businesses form the core of the U.S. economy. Businesses with fewer than 500 employees generate more than half the nation's GDP. These companies account for $65 billion in exports, shipping more than 13 percent of all exported goods overseas each year.[11] Small firms are credited with U.S. competitiveness in a number of global markets.[12]

150

INDUSTRY	PREDICTED TREND
Online Marketing	As businesses increase their use of the Internet, including their presence on the web, services to maintain a company's online impact and image will be in demand.
App & Game Development	As smart phone use becomes almost universal, apps for services and games continue to grow.
Online Education	Technological change has allowed for online learning to take place anytime, anywhere.
Consumer Health Technology	To rein in health care costs, both individuals and corporations are focused on health monitoring and assessment.
Specialized Online Retail	Consumers continue to love unique and personalized products.
3D Printing	This technology will revolutionize industries, from automobiles to airplanes, with the ability to bypass parts suppliers and "print" on demand.
Cloud Services or Virtual Data Rooms	As data continues to grow at lightning speed, so will the demand to access, share, and review documents.
Building and Maintenance Services	Home maintenance and renovation have grown as the economy recovers.
Online Travel Agencies	As demand for off-the-beaten-path travel continues, online travel companies will be busy making reservations and creating dream vacations.

Sources: "The Eight Hottest Industries for Startups in 2013," *Washington Post*, accessed January 12, 2014, www.washingtonpost .com; John W. Taylor, "8 Best Industries for Starting a Business Now," *Inc.*, accessed January 12, 2014, www.inc.com; David Nixon, "The 7 Best Industries for Starting a Business," *Insider Monkey,* accessed January 12, 2014, www.insidermonkey.com.

Creating New Jobs

Small businesses make tremendous contributions to the U.S. economy and to society as a whole. One impressive contribution is the number of new jobs created each year by small businesses. While it varies from year to year and remains dependent on the state of the economy, on average two of every three new jobs are created by companies with fewer than 500 employees.[13] A significant share of these jobs is created by the smallest companies, those with four or fewer employees. Over the last several years, the SBA has provided more than $90 billion in loans to small businesses to allow access to capital and increased growth.[14] Table 5.2 illustrates some of the best industries for starting a new business.

Small businesses also contribute to the economy by hiring workers who traditionally have had difficulty finding jobs at larger firms, such as military veterans returning to the workforce, former welfare recipients, and workers with various challenges. The SBA provides incentives for companies to hire these types of workers. Small firms often hire the youngest workers.

Creating New Industries

Small firms give businesspeople the opportunity and outlet for developing new ideas. Sometimes these new ideas become entirely new industries. Many of today's largest and most

Need a Job? Need Employees? Tweet

If you've ever tried to pare down your résumé into a single page, consider the challenge of creating a 140-character Twitter résumé. While this may sound unthinkable, recruiters and job seekers alike are finding value in the Twittersphere.

One talent acquisitions manager says she watches how people interact on the social media site, what their job positions are, who their best friends are on Twitter, and whether they have a sense of humor. Another recruiter says he believes your presence on social media can be considered your résumé, and your participation in social networks your references.

Candidates can develop a rapport by conversing, following, responding, and re-tweeting texts made by hiring managers and employees of targeted companies. After establishing rapport and getting noticed, sending a personal message may feel like a bold and risky move, yet it can be effective. This can lead to more traditional ways of communicating and further exploration—résumé requests, phone calls, or interviews—from both parties.

Candidates are advised to create a Twitter account that basically is an online business card, with a picture, résumé, and even a brief video recapping job skills. Tweet out interesting facts to gain attention from possible employers and other influential followers. A software designer who writes a blog, gives talks, holds meet-ups, and publishes content was approached by a long-time follower with an overture of "I like what you've been saying on Twitter and I agree with your approach. If you're ever looking to hire someone, give me a shout. I'd love to work for you." The newly employed follower may now have something worth tweeting about.

Sources: Rachel Emma Silverman and Lauren Weber, "The New Résumé: It's 140 Characters," *The Wall Street Journal*, accessed January 18, 2014, http://online.wsj.com; Susan Adams, "4 Ways to Use Twitter to Find a Job," *Forbes*, accessed January 18, 2014, www.forbes.com; Suzanne Lucas, "How to Use Twitter to Find a Job," *Money Watch*, accessed January 18, 2014, www.cbsnews.com.

Courtesy ThinkEco, Inc. Reproduced with permission.

New industries can be created when small businesses adapt to shifts in consumer interests and preferences. ThinkEco wants to make it easier for consumers to save money and energy.

successful firms, such as Whole Foods, Google, and Amazon, began as small businesses. When 16-year-old John W. Nordstrom left Sweden for America with $5 in his pocket, he dreamed of something bigger. With enough savings, he opened his first shoe store in Seattle in 1901. Today, Nordstrom is a multi-billion dollar retailer that is well known for its customer service.[15]

New industries are sometimes created when small businesses adapt to provide needed services to a larger corporate community. Corporate downsizing has created a demand for other businesses to perform activities previously handled by in-house employees. These support businesses may become an industry themselves.

New industries can be created when small businesses adapt to shifts in consumer interests and preferences. For example, the idea of offering shaving accessories and services for a man's face, scalp, and body—dubbed "manscaping" by marketers—has taken root in the U.S. economy, with small businesses providing body grooming products and services. Services include facial hair "styling"—beard, mustache, and goatee shaping and scalp and body hair waxing and shaving.[16]

Finally, new industries may be created when both the business world and consumers recognize a need for change. The recent emphasis on environmental responsibility—ranging from recycling and reuse of goods to reducing the amount of energy consumed—has fostered a whole new industry of green products and services, many produced by small companies. ThinkEco is a small firm based in New York City that has created a device that regulates outlet power, allowing its business customers to save as much as 20 percent on their energy bills. ClearEdge Power, based in Hillsboro, Oregon, offers a fuel-cell power energy system that is particularly effective for other small businesses, such as boutique hotels and restaurants.[17]

Innovation

Small businesses are adept at developing new and improved goods and services. Innovation is often the entire reason for the founding of a new business. In a typical year, small firms develop twice as many product innovations per employee as larger firms. They also produce more than 16 times more patents per employee than larger firms.[18]

Key innovations developed by small businesses in the 20th century include the airplane, the personal computer, soft contact lenses, and the zipper.

Innovations, many technology-related, that already drive small businesses in the 21st century include cloud computing, 3D printing, green energy, and social media, to name a few. The "Career Kickstart" feature offers tips on how to use Twitter to find a job or new employees.

Assessment Check ✅

1. What are the three key ways in which small businesses contribute to the economy?

2. How are new industries created?

[3] Why Small Businesses Fail

Small businesses play an integral role in the U.S. economy. But one of the reasons they are so successful is also the reason they might fail—their founders are willing to take a risk. Some of the most common shortcomings that plague a small firm include management inexperience, inadequate financing, and the challenge of meeting government regulations.

As Figure 5.2 shows, nearly 7 out of every 10 new businesses survive at least two years. About 50 percent make it to the five-year mark. But by the tenth year, 82 percent will have closed. However, keep in mind that these statistics can be misleading—they include companies that have changed their names, changed their legal structure, merged into another firm, or have been sold. Let's look a little more closely at why this happens.[19]

Management Shortcomings

One of the most common causes of small-business failure is the shortcomings of management. These may include overconfidence, lack of people skills, inadequate knowledge of finance, inability to track inventory or sales, poor assessment of the competition or customer, or simply poor time management or the lack of time to do everything required. While large firms often have the resources to recruit specialists in areas such as marketing and finance, the owner of a small business often winds up doing too many things at once.

This could result in bad decision making, which could end in the firm's failure. Krispy Kreme was once a small business that expanded too quickly by taking on too much debt. The company's near failure had nothing to do with the quality of its doughnuts. In addition, consumers turned their taste buds toward more healthful snacks and breakfast foods produced by competitors. Krispy Kreme's most recent results show growth, as doughnuts and cronuts, a hybrid of a croissant and a doughnut, experienced a recent revival. With new coffee and beverage offerings, the company is recovering, but many business observers have a wait and see attitude.[20]

Owners of small businesses can increase their chances of success if they become educated in the principles of business and entrepreneurship; know the industry in which they intend to operate; develop good customer service and interpersonal skills; understand their customers; hire and train motivated employees; and seek professional advice on issues such as finance, regulations, and other legal matters.[21]

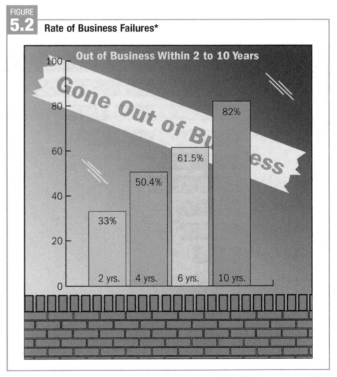

FIGURE 5.2 Rate of Business Failures*

Out of Business Within 2 to 10 Years

Gone Out of Business

	2 yrs.	4 yrs.	6 yrs.	10 yrs.
	33%	50.4%	61.5%	82%

*Data includes companies that have changed their names, changed their legal structure, merged into another firm, or have been sold.

Source: Office of Advocacy, U.S. Small Business Administration, "Frequently Asked Questions: Advocacy Small Business Statistics and Research," http://www.sba.gov, accessed January 11, 2014.

Inadequate Financing

Money provides the growth engine of any business. Every business—large or small—needs a certain amount of financing in order to operate, thrive, and grow. Another leading problem of small businesses is inadequate financing. First-time business owners often overestimate the funds their firms will generate from initial sales to allow for operations to continue. But building a business takes time and perseverance. Products need to be developed, employees have to be hired, a website must be built, distribution strategy has to be determined, office or retail space might have to be secured, and so forth. Most small businesses—even those with minimal start-up costs—sometimes don't turn a profit for months or even years.[22]

Although there are stories about business founders starting firms with just a few hundred dollars loaned by family or with a cash advance from a credit card, commercial banks and other financial institutions are the largest lenders to small businesses, accounting for 58 percent of total traditional credit to small firms. This type of financing includes credit lines and loans for nonresidential mortgages, vehicles, specialized equipment, and leases.[23]

Figure 5.3 shows that despite their relatively high interest rates, credit cards do remain an important source of financing for small businesses. The heaviest users of credit cards for business financing are firms with fewer than 10 employees. Inadequate financing can compound management shortcomings by making it more difficult for small businesses to attract and keep talented people. Typically, a big company can offer more career options, a better benefits package, and a higher salary.

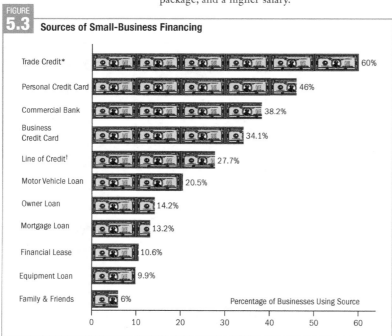

FIGURE 5.3 Sources of Small-Business Financing

Source	Percentage
Trade Credit*	60%
Personal Credit Card	46%
Commercial Bank	38.2%
Business Credit Card	34.1%
Line of Credit†	27.7%
Motor Vehicle Loan	20.5%
Owner Loan	14.2%
Mortgage Loan	13.2%
Financial Lease	10.6%
Equipment Loan	9.9%
Family & Friends	6%

Percentage of Businesses Using Source

*Trade credit is purchasing goods or equipment from a supplier who finances the purchase by delaying the date of payment for those goods.

†A line of credit is an agreement between a bank and a borrower, indicating the maximum amount of credit the bank will extend to the borrower.

Note: Total exceeds 100 percent because businesses typically use more than one source of financing.

Sources: Small Business Administration, Office of Advocacy, "Financing Patterns of Small Firms," http://www.sba.gov/advocacy, January 11, 2014; Susan Coleman, "Free and Costly Trade Credit: A Comparison of Small Firms," *Academy of Entrepreneurial Finance*, accessed January 11, 2014, http://www.google.com.

With less money to spend on employees, marketing, inventory, and other business costs, successful small companies need to be creative. Ann Dickerson and her husband, Bill Zack, of Signal Mountain, Tennessee, are both former sports journalists. They decided to pursue their love of cooking to embark on a new career. When the state of Tennessee changed the law to allow legal moonshine, a once illegal 100-proof liquor, Ann and Bill saw the opportunity to create the first ever moonshine bakery. After diligent experimentation and testing, the two came up with the perfect cake batter. Combining their own concoction of moonshine with homemade cake batter, Tennessee Moonshine Cakes was created. The "witch's brew" glaze on the cakes is where the moonshine comes in, although the alcohol evaporates during the baking process. The cakes are sold through retailers, online, and at Tennessee airports and festivals.[24]

Government Regulation

Small-business owners cite their struggle to comply with government regulations as one of the biggest challenges they face. Some firms fold because of this burden alone. Paperwork costs account for billions of small-business dollars each year. A large company can better cope with requirements for forms and reports. Larger firms often find that it makes economic sense to hire or contract with specialists in specific types of regulation, such as employment law and workplace safety regulations. By contrast, small businesses often struggle to absorb the costs of government paperwork because of their more limited staff and budgets. The smallest firms—those with fewer than 20 employees—spend 45 percent more per employee than larger firms just to comply with federal regulations.[25]

Recognizing the burden of regulation on small businesses, Congress sometimes exempts the smallest companies from certain regulations. For example, small businesses with 49 or fewer employees are exempt from both the Personal Protection and Affordable Care Act and the Family and Medical Leave Act, which gives employees up to 12 weeks of unpaid leave each year to take care of a newborn child, adopt a child, or care for a family member who has serious health problems.[26] Most small-business owners comply with employment and other laws, believing that such compliance is ethically correct and fosters better employee relations than trying to determine which regulations don't apply to a small business.

Taxes are another burdensome expense for a small business. In addition to local, state, and federal income taxes, employers must pay taxes covering workers' compensation insurance, Social Security payments, and unemployment benefits. Although large companies have similar expenses, they generally have more resources to cover them. But there are also tax incentives designed to help small businesses. These incentives cover a broad range, including HUBZones (Historically Underutilized Business), tax credits for use of biodiesel and renewable fuels, increased research activities, pension plan start-up, and access for individuals with disabilities.[27]

Ann Dickerson and her husband, Bill Zack, took a unique cake idea and turned it into a successful business.

Kenney Photography/Tennessee Moonshine Cakes

Assessment Check ☑

1. What percentage of small businesses remain in operation five years after starting? Ten years?

2. What are the three main causes of small-business failure?

[4] The Business Plan: A Foundation for Success

Large or small, every business needs a plan in order to succeed. While there are tales of firms launched from an idea scribbled on a napkin at a restaurant or sketched out on graph paper in a dorm room, the idea has a greater chance of becoming a reality if it is backed by a solid plan. A **business plan** is a written document that provides an orderly statement of a company's goals, the methods by which it intends to achieve these goals, and the standards by which it will measure its achievements. The business plan is often the document that secures financing for a firm and creates a framework for the organization.

Business plans give the organization a sense of purpose. They identify the firm's mission and goals. They create measurable standards and outline a strategy for reaching company objectives. A typical business plan includes the following sections:

- an *executive summary* that briefly answers the who, what, where, when, why, and how questions for the business

- an *introduction* that includes a general statement of the concept, purpose, and objectives of the proposed business

- separate *financial* and *marketing sections* that describe the firm's target market and marketing plan as well as detailed financial forecasts of the need for funds and when the firm is expected to break even—the level of sales at which revenues equal costs

- *résumés of principals*—especially in plans written to obtain financing

business plan written document that provides an orderly statement of a company's goals, methods, and standards.

Chapter 5 *Forms of Business Ownership and Organization*   **135**

© Dimitrije Paunovic/iStockphoto

The business plan is often the document that secures financing for a company and creates a framework for the organization. Business plans identify the firm's missions and goals. They create measurable standards and outline a strategy for reaching company objectives.

Within this structure, an effective business plan contains the written soul of a firm. A good plan addresses the following issues:

- *The company's mission and the vision of its founders.* Look at the home page of any firm's website and you will find its mission. At the website for New York–based Warby Parker, an online subscription eyewear company, visitors learn that "For every pair purchased, a pair is distributed to someone in need. Buy a Pair, Give a Pair." Thanks to its customers, the company has hit a milestone of distributing 500,000 pairs of glasses.[28] This simple declaration states why the company was founded and what it intends to accomplish.

- *An outline of what makes the company unique.* Why start a business that's just like hundreds of others? An effective business plan describes what distinguishes the firm and its products from competitors. Warby Parker illustrates a unique business model with its one-for-one donation program.

- *The customers.* A business plan identifies who the firm's customers will be and how it will serve their needs.

- *The competition.* A business plan addresses its existing and potential competitors with a strategy for creating superior or unique offerings. Studying the competition can provide valuable information about what works and what doesn't in the marketplace.

- *Financial evaluation of the industry and market conditions.* This knowledge helps develop a credible financial forecast and budget.

- *Assessment of the risks.* Every business undertaking involves risks. A solid business plan acknowledges these and outlines a strategy for dealing with them.[29]

Whether a firm's intention is to revolutionize an entire industry on a global scale or improve the lives of individuals by providing them with eyeglasses, the business plan is a major factor in its success. For more detailed information on how to write a business plan, see Appendix D, "Developing a Business Plan."

Assessment Check ☑

1. What are the five main sections of a business plan?

2. Why is an effective business plan important to the success of a firm?

5 Assistance for Small Businesses

An important part of organizing a small business is financing its activities. Once a business plan has been created, various sources can be tapped for loans and other types of financing. These include government agencies as well as private investors.

Small Business Administration

Small Business Administration (SBA)
principal government agency concerned with helping small U.S. firms.

Small businesses can benefit from using the resources provided by the <u>Small Business Administration (SBA)</u>. The SBA is the principal government agency concerned with helping small U.S. firms, and it is the advocate for small businesses within the federal government. Several thousand employees staff the SBA's Washington, D.C. headquarters and its 1,800

136 Part 2 *Starting and Growing Your Business*

regional and field offices. The SBA's mission statement declares that, "Small business is critical to our economic recovery and strength, to building America's future, and to helping the United States compete in today's global marketplace."[30]

Financial Assistance from the SBA Contrary to popular belief, the SBA seldom provides direct business loans. Nor does it provide outright grants to start or expand small businesses. Instead, the SBA *guarantees* small-business loans made by private lenders, including banks and other institutions. To qualify for an SBA-backed loan, borrowers must be "unable to secure conventional commercial financing on reasonable terms and be a 'small business' as defined by SBA size standards."[31] Direct SBA loans are available in only a few special situations, such as natural disaster recovery and energy conservation or development programs.

The SBA also guarantees <u>microloans</u> of up to $35,000 to start-ups and other very small firms. The average loan is $13,000, with a maximum term of six years.[32] Microloans may be used to buy equipment or operate a business but not to buy real estate or pay off other loans. These loans are available from nonprofit organizations located in most states. Other sources of microloans include the federal Economic Development Administration, some state governments, and certain private lenders, such as credit unions. State and local programs offer business grants for creation of energy-efficient technology, child care centers, or marketing campaigns for tourism, for example.

> **microloans** small-business loans often used to buy equipment or operate a business.

Small-business loans are also available through SBA-licensed organizations called *Small Business Investment Companies (SBICs)*, which are run by experienced venture capitalists. SBICs use their own capital, supplemented with government loans, to invest in small businesses. Like banks, SBICs are profit-making enterprises, but they are likely to be more flexible than banks in their lending decisions. Large companies that used SBIC financing when they were small start-ups include Apple, FedEx, and Staples.

Other Specialized Assistance Although government purchases represent a huge market, small companies have difficulty competing for this business with giant firms, which employ specialists to handle the volumes of paperwork involved in preparing proposals and completing bid applications. Today, many government procurement programs set aside portions of government spending for small companies; an additional SBA role is to help small firms secure these contracts. With set-aside programs for small businesses, up to 23 percent of certain government contracts are designated for small businesses.

Every federal agency with buying authority must maintain an Office of Small and Disadvantaged Business Utilization to ensure that small businesses receive a reasonable portion of government procurement contracts. To help connect small businesses with government agencies, the SBA's website offers Central Contractor Registration, which includes a search engine for finding business opportunities as well as a chance for small businesses to provide information about themselves. Set-aside programs are also common in the private sector, particularly among major corporations.

In addition to help with financing and government procurement, the SBA delivers a variety of other services to small businesses. It provides information and advice through toll-free telephone numbers and its website, http://www.sba.gov. Through its Small Business Training Network,

Small Business Investment Companies (SBICs) are for-profit businesses licensed by the Small Business Administration. Using their own capital, SBICs provide loans to small businesses. FedEx used SBIC financing when it was a small start-up company.

Chapter 5 *Forms of Business Ownership and Organization* **137**

Turning Technologies Creates High-Tech Jobs

Turning Technologies, founded in Youngstown, Ohio, has enjoyed substantial growth and brought dozens of new jobs to a city with a high unemployment rate still haunted by the decline of its old steel mills. Turning has already been called the fastest growing privately held software company in the United States. The firm boasts more than 6,500 clients, and more than a million people use its audience-response products.

Audience-response systems are the wireless keypads that spectators use on TV game shows to register their opinions or answers to questions. Teachers from kindergarten through college also use Turning's audience-response technology. Instructors can ask questions in class using other programs; have students key in answers—anonymously or not—using their remotes; and instantly collate the responses to see how many students answered correctly. Says a school principal about applications of the Turning program, "We have some teachers who are working hard to find the many avenues they can go beyond. You're really only limited by your creativity." Government agencies and nonprofit organizations also use the systems for their training programs.

Most of Turning's 200 employees are young Ohioans who enjoy some of the same benefits as their Silicon Valley counterparts. The firm takes pride in being the kind of success story people have long thought "doesn't happen here."

The bottom line? Good products that are affordable, easy to use, and well marketed can help small companies become engines of growth and job creators.

Questions for Critical Thinking

1. Why might a company such as Turning Technologies locate outside the high-tech hotspots where most firms are? List some possible advantages and disadvantages to that strategy.
2. What should a company like Turning Technologies do if, as it grows, it needs to hire people with technical experience or skills?

Sources: Company website, www.turningtechnologies.com, accessed January 18, 2014; Anthony Ponce and Shawna Prince, "Classrooms Evolve Beyond Chalkboards, No. 2 Pencils," *NBC Chicago,* accessed January 18, 2014, www.nbcchicago.com; "Turning Technologies Releases New Polling Tools," *Successful Meetings,* accessed January 18, 2014, www.successfulmeetings.com; Mike Broderick, "4 Easy to Execute Tips for New Entrepreneurs," *Business News Daily,* accessed January 18, 2014, www.businessnewsdaily.com.

---

the SBA offers free online courses; sponsors inexpensive training courses on topics such as taxes, networking, and start-ups in cities and towns throughout the nation; and provides a free online library of more than 200 SBA publications and additional business resources. Business owners can find local resources by logging on to the SBA website and searching for SBA partners in their region. Local resource partners include small-business development centers, women's business centers, U.S. export assistance centers, and veterans business outreach centers.[33]

Local Assistance for Small Businesses

In conjunction with the federal government or on their own, state and local governments often have programs in place to help small businesses get established and grow. One such region is Washington State's Thurston County. The Thurston County Economic Development Council (EDC) was founded more than 30 years ago with the mission of "creating a vital and sustainable economy throughout our County that supports the livelihood and values of our residents." The Thurston County EDC provides information and assistance in business planning, licenses and registrations, taxes, and employment considerations. In addition, the council works to connect local businesses with each other and with industry experts, create marketing messages that attract new businesses and customers, and ensure that Thurston County plays an important role in the region's economy.[34] Organizations like the Thurston County EDC offer important resources and links for small businesses around the country.

business incubator local programs designed to provide low-cost shared business facilities to small start-up ventures.

Business Incubators Some community agencies interested in encouraging business development have implemented a concept called a **business incubator** to provide low-cost shared business facilities to small start-up ventures. See the "Hit and Miss" feature to read about Turning Technologies's incubator experience. A typical incubator might section off space in an abandoned plant and rent it to various small firms. Tenants often share clerical staff, computers,

138 Part 2 *Starting and Growing Your Business*

and other business services. The objective is that, with the incubator as a launch pad, after a few months or years, the fledgling business will be ready to move out and operate on its own.

More than 1,250 business incubator programs operate in the United States, with about 7,000 worldwide. Ninety-four percent are run by not-for-profit organizations focused on economic development. Nearly half of all incubators focus on new technology businesses, and more than half operate in urban areas. Universities house incubators, too. Recently Rice University in Houston, Texas, was named the top global university business incubator.[35]

Private Investors

A small business may start with cash from a personal savings account or a loan from a family member. But small-business owners soon begin to look for greater sums of money in order to continue operating and eventually grow. They may want to continue with assistance from private investors. **Venture capital**—money invested in the small business by another business firm or group of individuals in exchange for an ownership share—can give the small business needed capital to expand. Venture capitalists are likely to focus on several technology trends in the near future. They include cloud computing, cybersecurity, and life science investments. People and companies alike are worried about the security of sensitive information when it resides in the cloud. These investors are strict in their requirements for a solid business plan and expect small-business owners to run lean operations. The largest concentration of U.S. venture capital firms are in California's Silicon Valley; New York; Boston; Washington, D.C.; Seattle; and Austin, Texas.[36]

venture capital money invested in a business by another business firm or group of individuals in exchange for an ownership share.

Small-Business Opportunities for Women and Minorities

Over the last 15 years, the number of women-owned businesses has grown one and a half times the national average. In the United States today, more than 8.6 million firms are owned in part or entirely by women, employing more than 7.8 million workers and generating nearly $1.3 trillion in sales. In fact, 40 percent of all privately held companies are owned by women. Industries with the highest concentration of women-owned firms are health care and social assistance, educational services, and administrative support and waste management services.[37]

Women, like men, have a variety of reasons for starting their own companies. Some have a unique business idea that they want to bring to life. Others decide to strike out on their own when they lose their jobs or become frustrated with the bureaucracies in large companies. Jamie Arundell-Latshaw served as an officer in the U.S. Army for eight years. While in the Middle East, she saw the need for soldiers to learn about the people and customs of the lands where they would be stationed. When she left the service, she founded Lexicon Consulting. Hired by the U.S. Department of Defense and other government agencies, the company helps soldiers learn about foreign cultures before they are deployed, by hiring professional actors and native-speaking immigrants to conduct intensive, realistic training. Arundell-Latshaw was recently honored as one of America's "100 Most Intriguing Entrepreneurs" by Goldman Sachs at its annual Builders + Innovator's Summit.[38]

In other cases, women leave large corporations when they feel blocked from opportunities for advancement. Sometimes this occurs because they hit the so-called glass ceiling. Because women are more likely than men to be the primary caregivers in their families, some may seek

Jamie Arundell-Latshaw, a U.S. Army veteran, founded Lexicon Consulting, a company that helps soldiers learn about foreign countries and customs before they are deployed.

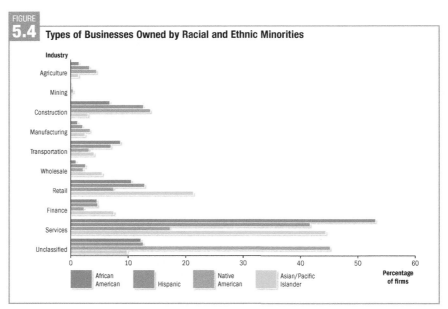

FIGURE 5.4 Types of Businesses Owned by Racial and Ethnic Minorities

Source: Data from Office of Advocacy, U.S. Small Business Administration, "Minorities in Business," http://www.sba.gov/advocacy, accessed January 11, 2014.

self-employment as a way to achieve flexible working hours so they can spend more time with their families.

One of the many nationwide programs to assist women-owned firms offered by the Small Business Administration is the Contract Assistance for Women Business Owners program, which teaches women how to market their businesses to the federal government. Federal contracting opportunities for WOSBs (women-owned small businesses) have been expanded. Organizations such as the Center for Women's Business Research provide information, contacts, and other resources as well.

Business ownership is also an important opportunity for America's racial and ethnic minorities. In recent years, the growth in the number of businesses owned by African Americans, Hispanics, and Asian Americans has far outpaced the growth in the number of U.S. businesses overall. Figure 5.4 shows the percentages of minority ownership in major industries. The relatively strong presence of minorities in the services and retail industries is especially significant because these industries contain the greatest number of businesses.

The Small Business Administration has programs targeted to minority-owned small businesses. SBA's 8(a) Business Development program helps minority-owned firms develop and grow through one-to-one counseling, training, and management and technical guidance, with access to government contracting opportunities.[39]

6 Franchising

Using another company's established business model, **franchising** is a contractual business arrangement between a manufacturer or another supplier and a dealer such as a restaurant operator or a retailer. The contract specifies the methods by which the dealer markets the product of the supplier. Franchises can involve both goods and services, and many well-known brands like 7-Eleven and Wendy's have grown with this model.

Assessment Check ☑

1. What are the various ways the SBA helps small businesses?

2. What are business incubators?

3. Why are small businesses good opportunities for women and minorities?

franchising contractual business arrangement between a manufacturer or other supplier, and a dealer such as a restaurant operator or retailer.

140

Starting a small, independent company can be a risky, time-consuming endeavor, but franchising can reduce the amount of time and effort needed to expand. The parent company has already developed and tested the concept, and the brand is often familiar to prospective customers.

The Franchising Sector

Franchised businesses are a huge part of the U.S. economy, accounting for over 18 million jobs in the U.S. workforce. The International Franchise Association reported that franchising is responsible for close to 825,000 businesses at a gross value forecasted to be over $2 trillion annually. The business sectors currently experiencing the most growth are business services, commercial and residential services, and quick service restaurants.[40]

An increased appetite for Footlongs, Big Macs, and Baskin Robbins ice cream in the developing world coincides with rising levels of household income. With global fast-food giants like Subway, McDonald's, and KFC saturating the U.S. market, expansion overseas in emerging markets like China, India, Africa, Russia, Indonesia, and Vietnam continues at a rapid clip. Yum! Brands, the parent company of Taco Bell, KFC, and Pizza Hut, saw over 70 percent of its most recent annual sales outside the United States. Also becoming more common are other international franchises like Baskin-Robbins. Now owned by Dunkin' Brands, Baskin-Robbins ice cream has more than 7,000 stores worldwide in 51 countries.[41]

International franchises are becoming more common. Baskin-Robbins has stores in nearly 50 countries including Australia, China, Japan, Russia, and Vietnam.

Franchising Agreements

The two principals in a franchising agreement are the franchisee and the franchisor. The individual or business firm purchasing the franchise is called the **franchisee**. This business owner agrees to sell the goods or services of the franchisor under certain terms. The **franchisor** is the firm whose products are sold by the franchisee. For example, McDonald's Corp. is a franchisor. Your local McDonald's restaurant owner is a franchisee.

Franchise agreements can be complex. They involve an initial purchase fee plus agreed-on start-up costs. Because the franchisee is representing the franchisor's brand, the franchisor usually stipulates the purchase of certain ingredients or equipment, pricing, and marketing efforts. The total start-up cost for a SUBWAY franchise may be as low as $116,000.[42] In contrast, McDonald's is one of the more expensive franchises—total start-up costs can run more than $1 million. For this reason, businesspeople interested in purchasing a more expensive franchise often group together.

franchisee individual or business firm purchasing a franchise.

franchisor firm whose products are sold to customers by the franchisee.

Benefits and Challenges of Franchising

Like any other type of business arrangement, franchising has its benefits and drawbacks. Benefits for the franchisor include opportunities for expansion that might not otherwise be available. A franchised business can move into new geographic locations, including those overseas, at less expense and with the advantages of employing local workers and businesspeople who have intimate knowledge of local preferences. A good franchisee can manage a larger and more complex business—with fewer direct employees—than could be handled without the franchise option. In most cases, franchisees will be highly attentive to the management of their franchises because of their stake as business owners. If the business is run efficiently, the

Jim Gensheimer/SAN JOSE MERCURY NEWS/KRT/NewsCom

Chapter 5 *Forms of Business Ownership and Organization*   **141**

Hit&Miss

Starbucks Uses Franchising for UK Expansion

You're in the United Kingdom, and you can get an iced caramel macchiato at one of any corporate-owned Starbucks stores, right? Well, sort of. You can get the iced coffee drink, but the store isn't going to be corporate owned. Starbucks, long known for its expansion strategy through company-owned stores, has taken the leap to capitalize on a franchise business model to expand in the UK and Europe.

Expansion through company-owned stores in Europe hasn't generated the profits the company anticipated. Performance in high-rent shopping districts in major European cities has fallen short. The company hopes to continue its growth trend overseas using a franchise business model. Franchisees provide quick inroads in the more remote parts of Europe where Starbucks is less familiar to the locals. While franchised-owned stores remain a small percentage of all European Starbucks stores, the company plans to expand throughout other parts of Europe using this business model. U.S. stores will continue to be company owned.

To date, Starbucks has almost 50 UK stores, 9 of which are franchised. The company plans to limit its franchisees to fewer than 25, giving UK franchisees the opportunity to become multi-unit owners. Starbucks has wooed the franchisees with trips to its Seattle, Washington, headquarters to immerse them in company culture and the Starbuck's way. Each Starbucks franchisee who signs a 10-year contract is expected to open a minimum of 10 stores.

Getting selected by Starbucks to become a franchise owner is no easy feat. The company scrutinizes each applicant to make sure he or she has a significant financial net worth, which includes liquidity of $700,000; multi-unit food and beverage experience; and a residence in Europe. Going to the UK anytime soon? Look for your Starbucks latte to be served up by a franchisee.

Questions for Critical Thinking

1. Why do you suppose a global brand like Starbucks is so particular about whom they choose as franchisees?

2. U.S. restaurant chains have long worked with overseas franchise partners to expand. What are some of the reasons it took Starbucks so long to consider this form of expansion?

Sources: Company website, "Franchised Stores," http://investor.starbucks.com, accessed January 17, 2014; Julie Jargon, "Starbucks Tries Franchising to Perk Up Europe Business," *The Wall Street Journal*, accessed January 17, 2014, http://online.wsj.com; Emily Coyle, "Starbucks Tries to Caffeinate Europe with Franchising," *Wall St. Cheat Sheet*, accessed January 17, 2014, www.wallstcheatstreet.com.

---

franchisor will probably experience a greater return on investment than if the firm were run entirely as a company-owned chain of retail shops, restaurants, or service establishments.

Finally, a successful franchisor can usually negotiate better pricing for ingredients, supplies, even real estate, because of its financial strength and large volume purchases. This benefits the franchisees if the savings are passed along to them.[43]

Franchising can be the quickest way to become a business owner. Some people contend that it's also the least risky. Franchisees have the benefit of name recognition—Papa John's, LA Fitness, Great Clips, and Days Inn—that usually includes a loyal following of customers. The management system of the franchisor has already been established and a performance record is readily available. In addition, franchisors provide a wide range of support to franchisees, including financing, assistance in obtaining a location, business training, supplies, and marketing programs.[44]

Franchisees themselves say they are drawn to the idea of franchising because it combines the freedom of business ownership with the support of a large company. Like other small-business owners, franchisees want to make their own business decisions and determine their own work hours. And they want to have more control over the amount of wealth they can possibly accumulate, as opposed to what they might earn in a salaried job. In an economic slowdown, franchisees might very well be executives who have been laid off during a downsizing or reorganization effort by previous employers. These are highly trained and motivated businesspeople looking for a way to advance their careers.[45] Sometimes a company decides that franchising may be a good business model after all. See the "Hit & Miss" feature for more details.

Franchising can have its downside—for both franchisors and franchisees. For the franchisor, if its franchisees fail in any way, that failure reflects poorly on the overall brand as well as the bottom line. The same holds true for the franchisee: A firm that is mismanaged at the top

Part 2 *Starting and Growing Your Business*

level can spell doom for the smaller business owners who are actually running the individual units. Krispy Kreme, mentioned earlier, is an example of a franchised company that stumbled due to overexpansion. When a firm initially decides to offer franchise opportunities, the company overall may lose money for several years. Of course, in offering franchise opportunities, the franchisor—often the founder of what was once a small business—loses absolute control over every aspect of the business. This uncertainty can make the process of selecting the right franchisees to carry out the company's mission an important task.[46]

The franchisee faces an outlay of cash in the form of an initial investment, franchise fees, supplies, maintenance, leases, and the like. The most expensive franchises generally are those that involve hotels and resorts, which can run in the millions.[47] For this reason, it is not unusual for groups of businesspeople to purchase a franchise (or several franchise locations). Payments to the franchisor can add to the burden of keeping the business afloat until owners begin to earn a profit. Choosing a low-cost start-up such as Heaven's Best might be a good alternative. Heaven's Best is a cleaning company that specializes in business and residential carpet and upholstery. The firm offers top-quality methods, equipment, and products along with training, brand awareness, and marketing tools. Businesspeople can purchase a franchise for an investment of as little as $29,800.[48] As in any business, it is important for franchisees to evaluate carefully how much profit they can make once their cost obligations are met.

Because franchises are so closely linked to their brand, franchisors and franchisees must work well together to maintain standards of quality in their goods and services. If customers are unhappy with their experience at one franchise location, they might avoid stopping at another one several miles away, even if the second one is owned and operated by someone else. This is especially true where food is involved. The discovery of tainted meat or produce at one franchise restaurant can cause panic to spread throughout the entire chain. A potential franchisee would be wise to thoroughly research the financial performance and reputation of the franchisor, using resources such as other franchisees and the Federal Trade Commission. A prospective franchisee typically receives the franchisor's franchise disclosure document, a presale document presented to any prospective franchisee, prior to signing a contract or submitting payment.

Some franchisees have found the franchising agreement to be too confining. As the saying goes, you can't add a tuna salad sandwich to the menu at McDonald's no matter how many stores you own. The agreements are usually fairly strict, and that generally helps to maintain the integrity of and uniformity of the brand. Toward this end, some franchise companies control promotional activities, select the site location, or even become involved in hiring decisions. But these activities may seem overly restrictive to some franchisees, especially those seeking independence and autonomy.

Restrictions can also cost franchisees more than they feel is fair. The National Franchise Association, a group that represents more than 80 percent of Burger King's U.S. franchisees, sued the hamburger company for forcing its members to offer consumers a $1 double cheeseburger on its menu. While the $1 burger offering may seem like a great way to attract and serve hungry consumers, BK franchisees claimed that the promotion cost them a loss of at least 10 cents per burger. In other words, it cost most franchises $1.10 to make and serve a cheeseburger for which they had to charge $1. However, a judge dismissed the lawsuit, siding with Burger King.[49]

[7] Forms of Private Business Ownership

Regardless of its size, every business is organized according to one of three categories of legal structure: sole proprietorship, partnership, or corporation. As Figure 5.5 shows, sole proprietorships are the most common form of business ownership, accounting for more than 70 percent of all firms in the United States. Although far fewer firms are organized as corporations, the revenues earned by these companies are 19 times greater than those earned by sole proprietorships.

Assessment Check ☑

1. What is the difference between a franchisor and a franchisee?

2. What are the benefits to both parties of franchising?

3. What are the potential drawbacks of franchising for both parties?

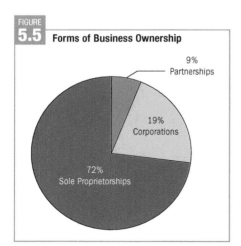

FIGURE 5.5 Forms of Business Ownership

9% Partnerships

19% Corporations

72% Sole Proprietorships

Source: Data from U.S. Census Bureau, "Business Enterprise: Sole Proprietorships, Partnerships, Corporations, Table 744," *Statistical Abstract of the United States,* http:/www.uscensus.gov, accessed January 17, 2014.

sole proprietorship business ownership in which there is no legal distinction between the sole proprietor's status as an individual and his or her status as a business owner.

Each legal structure offers unique advantages and disadvantages. But because there is no universal formula for every situation, some business owners prefer to organize their companies further as S corporations, limited-liability partnerships, and limited-liability companies. In some cases, corporations are owned by their employees.

In addition to the three main legal structures, several other options for ownership exist. These include employee-owned businesses, family-owned businesses, and not-for-profit organizations.

Sole Proprietorships

The most common form of business ownership, the **sole proprietorship** is also the oldest and the simplest. In a sole proprietorship, no legal distinction separates the sole proprietor's status as an individual from his or her status as a business owner. Although sole proprietorships are common in a variety of industries, they are concentrated primarily among small businesses such as repair shops, small retail stores, and service providers such as plumbers, hair stylists, and photographers.

Sole proprietorships offer some unique advantages. Because such businesses involve a single owner, they are easy to form *and* dissolve. A sole proprietorship gives the owner maximum management flexibility, along with the right to all profits after payment of business-related bills and taxes. A highly motivated owner of a sole proprietorship directly reaps the benefits of his or her hard work.

Minimal legal requirements simplify entering and exiting a sole proprietorship. The owner registers the business or trade name—to guarantee that two firms do not use the same name—and takes out any necessary licenses. Local governments require certain licenses for businesses such as restaurants, motels or hotels, and retail stores. In addition, some occupational licenses require business owners to obtain specific insurance such as liability coverage.

Sole proprietorships are also easy to dissolve. This advantage is particularly important to temporary or seasonal businesses that set up for a limited period of time. It's also helpful if the owner needs or wants to close the business for any reason—say, to relocate or to accept a full-time position with a larger firm.

Management flexibility is another advantage of a sole proprietorship. The owner can make decisions without reporting to a manager, take quick action, and keep trade secrets. A sole proprietorship always bears the individual stamp or flair of its owner, whether it's a certain way of styling hair or the way a store window is decorated.

The greatest disadvantage of the sole proprietorship is the owner's personal financial liability for all debts of the business. Also, the business must operate with financial resources limited to the owner's personal funds and money that he or she can borrow. Such financing limitations can keep the business from expanding.

Another disadvantage is that the owner must wear many hats, handling a wide range of management and operational responsibilities. He or she may not have expertise in every area, which may inhibit the firm's growth or even cause the firm damage. In addition, a sole proprietorship usually lacks long-term continuity, because a change in personal circumstances or finances can terminate the business on short notice.

Partnerships

partnership association of two or more persons who operate a business as co-owners by voluntary legal agreement.

Another option for organizing a business is to form a partnership. The Uniform Partnership Act, which regulates this ownership form in most states, defines a **partnership** as an association of two or more persons who operate a business as co-owners by voluntary legal agreement. Many small businesses begin as partnerships between co-founders.

Partnerships are easy to form. All the partners need to do is register the business name and obtain any necessary licenses. Having a partner generally means greater financial capability and someone to share in the operations and decision making of a business. It is even better if one partner has a particular skill, such as design, while the other has a knack for financials.

Most partnerships have the disadvantage of being exposed to unlimited financial liability. Each partner bears full responsibility for the debts of the firm, and each is legally liable for the actions of the other partners. If the firm fails and is left with debt—no matter who is at fault—every partner is responsible for those debts. If one partner defaults, the others are responsible for the firm's debts, even if it means dipping into personal funds. To avoid these problems, many firms establish a limited-liability partnership, which limits the liability of partners to the value of their interests in the company.

Breaking up a partnership is more complicated than dissolving a sole proprietorship. Rather than simply withdrawing funds from the bank, the partner who wants out may need to find someone to buy his or her interest in the firm. The death of a partner also threatens the survival of a partnership. A new partnership must be formed, and the estate of the deceased is entitled to a share of the firm's value. To ease the financial strains of such events, business planners often recommend life insurance coverage for each partner, combined with a buy–sell agreement. The insurance proceeds can be used to repay the deceased partner's heirs and allow the surviving partner to retain control of the business. Because partnerships are vulnerable to personal conflicts that can escalate quickly, it is important for partners to choose each other carefully—not just because they are friends—and try to plan for the future.

Corporations

A **corporation** is a legal organization with assets and liabilities separate from those of its owner(s). A corporation can be a large or small business. It can be Ford Motor Company or a local auto repair shop.

Corporate ownership offers considerable advantages. Because a corporation is a separate legal entity, its stockholders have limited financial risk. If the firm fails, they lose only the money they have invested. This applies to the firm's managers and executives as well. Because they are not the sole proprietors or partners in the business, their personal savings are not at risk if the company folds or goes bankrupt. This protection also extends to legal risk. Class-action suits involving automakers, drug manufacturers, and food producers are filed against the companies, not the owners of those companies. Target recently experienced a class-action lawsuit due to a data breach; however, their employees and stockholders are not required to pay the settlements from their own bank accounts.[50]

Corporations offer other advantages. They gain access to expanded financial capabilities based on the opportunity to offer direct outside investments such as stock sales. A large corporation can legally generate internal financing for many projects by transferring money from one part of the corporation to another.

One major disadvantage for a corporation is the double taxation of corporate earnings. After a corporation pays federal, state, and local income taxes on its profits, its owners (stockholders) also pay personal taxes on any distributions of those profits they receive from the corporation in the form of dividends.

S Corporations and Limited Liability Corporations To avoid double taxation of business income while minimizing financial liability for their owners, many smaller firms (those with fewer than 100 stockholders) organize as **S corporations**. These companies can elect to pay federal income taxes as partnerships while retaining the liability limitations typical of corporations. S corporations are taxed only once. Unlike regular corporations, S corporations do not pay corporate taxes on their profits. Instead, the untaxed profits of S corporations are paid directly as dividends to shareholders, who then pay the individual tax rate. This tax advantage has resulted in a tremendous increase in the number of S corporations. Consequently, the IRS

corporation legal organization with assets and liabilities separate from those of its owner(s).

S corporations corporations that do not pay corporate taxes on profits; instead, profits are distributed to shareholders, who pay individual income taxes.

GoingGreen

B Corporations Support Social and Environmental Goals

What do companies like Numi Organic Tea, Method Soap, Patagonia, Etsy, and Warby Parker have in common? All are certified Benefit Corporations—or B Corporations for short—and must meet high standards in how they treat employees, their impact on the environment, and how they benefit the communities in which they operate.

A newer form of corporate ownership, B Corporations differ from traditional corporations in that a third-party auditor must verify that the corporation stands behind its goals—those that go beyond earning a profit. B Corporations must state their social and environmental goals in their bylaws—the rules a corporation uses to regulate itself. An annual benefit report, which differs from a company's traditional annual report, must be published in order to accurately measure its actual versus stated goals.

B Corporations are taxed in the same way as their traditional C Corporation counterparts. Companies become B Corporations as part of a larger mission. Method, an eco-friendly home and personal care products company, became a B Corporation rather than just being a business that talks about "people, planet, and profit," according to its co-founder.

Patagonia's CEO doesn't believe traditional corporate structures encourage a company's board of directors to possibly lessen shareholder value for the public good. To date, 20 states have passed B Corporation legislation with hopes of more businesses enhancing not only their profits but also society.

Questions for Critical Thinking

1. Will all shareholders, particularly those with a primary goal of earning a profit, agree with a company's decision to become a B Corp? Why or why not?

2. How might B Corporation status impact a company's sales? Discuss the implications, both positive and negative.

Sources: Organization website, www.bcorporation.net, accessed January 18, 2014; Mark Kohler, "Benefit Corporations: Doing Good (and Potentially) Boosting Profits," *Entrepreneur,* accessed January 17, 2014, www.entrepreneur.com; Michelle Goodman, "Everything You Need to Know About B Corporation Certification," *Entrepreneur,* accessed January 16, 2014, www.entrepreneur.com.

---

limited-liability corporation (LLC) corporation that secures the corporate advantage of limited liability while avoiding the double taxation characteristic of a traditional corporation.

closely monitors S corporations because some businesses don't meet the legal requirements to form S corporations.[51]

Business owners may also form **limited-liability corporations (LLCs)** to secure the corporate advantage of limited liability while avoiding the double taxation characteristic of corporations. An LLC combines the pass-through taxation of a partnership or sole proprietorship with the limited liability of a corporation.

An LLC is governed by an operating agreement that resembles a partnership agreement, except that it reduces each partner's liability for the actions of the other owners. Corporations of professionals, such as lawyers, accountants, and physicians, use a similar approach, with the letters *PC* (professional corporation) attached to the business name. LLCs appear to be the wave of the future. Immediately after the first LLC law was passed, most major CPA (certified public accountant) firms in the U.S. converted to LLC status. Today you'll see the LLC or PC designation attached to businesses ranging from bowling alleys to veterinary hospitals.

Benefit Corporations Some for-profit organizations are choosing a newer corporate form called a Benefit Corporation, or B corporation for short. Companies with a culture, structure, and decision making centered around creating a meaningful impact on the environment have chosen this form of business ownership. The purpose of a B corporation is to create a qualitative benefit to the public beyond financial gains for its shareholders.[52] See the "Going Green" feature for more on the story.

Employee-Owned Corporations

employee ownership business ownership in which workers own shares of stock in the company that employs them.

Another alternative for creating a corporation is **employee ownership**, in which workers own shares of stock in the company that employs them. The corporate organization stays the same, but most stockholders are also employees.

The popularity of this form of corporation is growing. The number of employee ownership plans has increased dramatically. Today about 20 percent of all employees of for-profit companies report owning stock in their companies; approximately 25 million Americans own

146   **Part 2** *Starting and Growing Your Business*

employer stock through *employee stock ownership plans (ESOPs)*, options, stock purchase plans, 401(k) plans, and other plans.[52]

Several trends underlie the rise in employee ownership. One is that employees want to share in whatever profit their company earns. Another is that management wants employees to care deeply about the firm's success and contribute their best effort. These firms remain committed to this kind of involvement and compensation for their workers. Because human resources are so essential to the success of a modern business, employers want to build their employees' commitment to the organization. However, some managers also admit that often employees are not as informed about the programs as they should be, and their companies could do a better job of educating employees at all levels.[53] Some of the country's most successful public corporations, including Procter & Gamble, Publix Super Markets, and Southwest Airlines, have embraced employee ownership.

Family-Owned Businesses

Family-owned firms are considered by many to be the backbone of American business. The Waltons and the Fords are viewed as pioneers because each of these firms—Walmart and Ford Motor Company—was once a small, family-owned company. Family-owned firms come in a variety of sizes and legal structures. But because of the complex nature of family relationships, family-owned firms experience some unique challenges.

Whether a family-owned business is structured as a partnership, limited liability corporation, or traditional corporation, its members must make decisions regarding succession, marriages and divorces, compensation, hierarchy and authority, shareholder control, and the like. Whereas some family members may prefer a loose structure—perhaps not even putting certain agreements in writing—experienced businesspeople caution that failing to choose the right legal structure for a family-owned firm can doom the business from the start.[54]

Succession is a major benefit—and drawback—to family-owned firms. On the one hand, a clearly documented plan for succession from one generation to the next is a huge source of security for the firm's continuity. But lack of legal planning, or situations in which succession is challenged, can cause chaos. In fact, only a small percentage of family-owned businesses survive into the second or third generation.

A small family firm that has managed to thrive for five generations is Squamscot Beverages. Originally called Connermade, the company was founded in 1883 when William H. Conner began producing his own "tonic" beverage—a spruce beer that came in glass bottles with porcelain-and-wire stoppers. Conner ran the company until his son Alfred took over in 1911. Alfred remained in charge until 1948, when he handed the reins to his own son, Alfred Jr. Today, Tom Conner and his son Dan manage most aspects of running the firm, which is still headquartered on the family's rural property in New Hampshire. Squamscot Beverages produces soda drinks in a variety of flavors, including birch beer, cola, cream, orange, grape, and ginger ale. Bottles are distributed to small grocery outlets, or customers can visit the bottling plant to select whichever flavors they want.[55]

not-for-profit corporations organization whose goals do not include pursuing a profit.

Family-owned companies are considered by many to be the backbone of American business. Sam Walton started the family business with Walton's 5 &10 store, which later became Walmart.

Not-for-Profit Corporations

The same business concepts that apply to commercial companies also apply to <u>not-for-profit corporations</u>—organizations whose goals do not include pursuing a profit. About 1.5 million

Jb Reed/Bloomberg/Getty Images, Inc.

not-for-profits operate in the United States, including charitable groups, social-welfare organizations, government agencies, and religious congregations. This sector also includes museums, libraries, hospitals, conservation groups, private schools, and the like.

Most states set out separate legal provisions for organizational structures and operations of not-for-profit corporations. These organizations do not issue stock certificates, because they pay no dividends to owners, and ownership rarely changes. They are also exempt from paying corporate taxes. However, they must meet strict regulations in order to maintain their not-for-profit status.

City Year Inc. is a not-for-profit organization that supports community service efforts by young people in their late teens and early twenties. Headquartered in Boston, City Year has a number of programs in which volunteers can participate. Its signature program, the City Year Youth Corps, invites 6,000 volunteers between the ages of 17 and 24 to commit to a year of full-time community service in activities such as mentoring and tutoring inner-city school children, helping to restore and reclaim public spaces, and staffing youth summer camps. The organization also partners with for-profit corporations such as Microsoft, Cisco, and Pepsi to fund and implement its efforts.[56]

[8] Public and Collective Ownership of Business

Though most businesses in the United States are in the private sector, some firms are actually owned by local, state, or the federal government. Alaskan Railroad Corp., East Alabama Medical Center, and Washington State Ferries are all government-owned businesses.[57]

In another type of ownership structure, groups of customers may collectively own a company. Recreational Equipment Inc. (REI) is a collectively owned retailer that sells outdoor gear and apparel. Finally, groups of smaller firms may collectively own a larger organization. Both of these collective ownership structures are also referred to as cooperatives.

Public (Government) Ownership

One alternative to private ownership is some form of *public ownership*, in which a unit or agency of government owns and operates an organization. In the United States, local governments often own parking structures and water systems. The Pennsylvania Turnpike Authority operates a vital highway link across the Keystone State. The federal government operates Hoover Dam in Nevada to provide electricity over a large region.

Sometimes public ownership results when private investors are unwilling to invest in a high-risk project—or find that operating an important service is simply unprofitable. The National Railroad Passenger Corporation—better known as Amtrak—is a for-profit corporation that operates 2,100 route miles of intercity passenger rail service in 46 states and the District of Columbia. Congress created Amtrak in the Rail Passenger Service Act of 1970, thereby removing from private railroads the obligation of transporting passengers, because passenger rail travel was generally unprofitable. In exchange, the private railroads granted Amtrak access to their existing tracks at a low cost. The Amtrak board of directors is made up of seven voting members appointed for five-year terms by the president of the United States.[58]

Collective (Cooperative) Ownership

Collective ownership establishes an organization referred to as a *cooperative* (or *co-op*), whose owners join forces to operate all or part of the activities in their firm or industry. Currently,

Assessment Check ☑

1. What are the key differences between sole proprietorships and partnerships?
2. What is a corporation?
3. What are the main characteristics of a not-for-profit corporation?

there are about 100 million people worldwide employed by cooperatives.[59] Cooperatives allow small businesses to pool their resources on purchases, marketing, equipment, distribution, and the like. Cooperatives can share equipment and expertise, and discount savings can be split among members.

Cooperatives are frequently found among agricultural businesses. Cabot Creamery is a cooperative of 1,200 small dairy farms spread throughout New England and upstate New York. Cabot is owned and operated by its members—farmers and their families. In addition, Cabot works with other cooperatives around the country to produce and distribute high-quality cheese, butter, and other dairy products.[60]

Assessment Check ☑

1. What is public ownership?

2. What is collective ownership? Where are cooperatives typically found, and what benefits do they provide small businesses?

[9] Organizing a Corporation

A corporation is a legal structure, but it also requires a certain organizational structure that is more complex than the structure of a sole proprietorship or a partnership. This is why people often think of a corporation as a large entity, even though it does not have to be a specific size. In rare instances, there are one-person corporations.

Types of Corporations

Corporations fall into three categories: domestic, foreign, and alien. A firm is considered a *domestic corporation* in the state where it is incorporated. When a company does business in states other than the one where it has filed incorporation papers, it is registered as a *foreign corporation* in each of those states. A firm incorporated in one nation that operates in another is known as an *alien corporation* where it operates. Many firms—particularly large corporations with operations scattered around the world—may operate under all three of these designations.

Where and How Businesses Incorporate

Businesses owners who want to incorporate must decide where to locate their headquarters and follow the correct procedure for submitting the legal document that establishes the corporation.

Although most small- and medium-sized businesses are incorporated in the states in which they operate, a U.S. firm can actually incorporate in any state it chooses. The founders of large corporations, or those that will do business nationwide, often compare the benefits—such as tax incentives—provided by each state. Some states are considered to be more "business friendly" than others. Delaware is one of the easiest states in which to incorporate.

The Corporate Charter Each state has a specific procedure for incorporating a business. Most states require at least three *incorporators*—the individuals who create the corporation. In addition, the new corporation must select a name that is different from names used by other businesses. Figure 5.6 lists the 10 elements that most states require for chartering a corporation.

The information provided in the articles of incorporation forms the basis on which a state grants a *corporate charter*, which is the legal document that formally establishes a corporation. After securing the charter, the owners prepare the company's bylaws, which describe the rules and procedures for its operation.

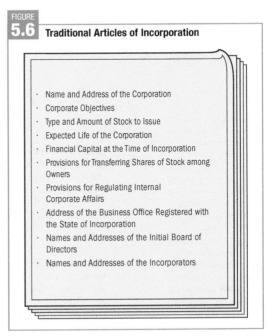

FIGURE **5.6** Traditional Articles of Incorporation

- Name and Address of the Corporation
- Corporate Objectives
- Type and Amount of Stock to Issue
- Expected Life of the Corporation
- Financial Capital at the Time of Incorporation
- Provisions for Transferring Shares of Stock among Owners
- Provisions for Regulating Internal Corporate Affairs
- Address of the Business Office Registered with the State of Incorporation
- Names and Addresses of the Initial Board of Directors
- Names and Addresses of the Incorporators

Chapter 5 *Forms of Business Ownership and Organization*   **149**

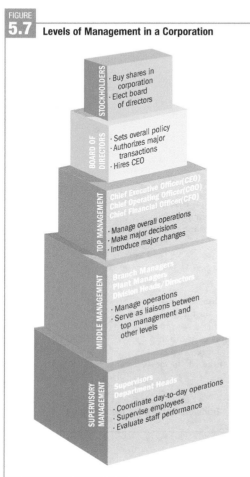

FIGURE 5.7 Levels of Management in a Corporation

STOCKHOLDERS
· Buy shares in corporation
· Elect board of directors

BOARD OF DIRECTORS
· Sets overall policy
· Authorizes major transactions
· Hires CEO

TOP MANAGEMENT
Chief Executive Officer (CEO)
Chief Operating Officer (COO)
Chief Financial Officer (CFO)
· Manage overall operations
· Make major decisions
· Introduce major changes

MIDDLE MANAGEMENT
Branch Managers
Plant Managers
Division Heads/Directors
· Manage operations
· Serve as liaisons between top management and other levels

SUPERVISORY MANAGEMENT
Supervisors
Department Heads
· Coordinate day-to-day operations
· Supervise employees
· Evaluate staff performance

stockholders owners of a corporation due to their purchase of stock in the corporation.

preferred stock shares that give owners limited voting rights, and the right to receive dividends or assets before owners of common stock.

common stock shares that give owners voting rights but only residual claims to the firm's assets and income distributions.

board of directors governing body of a corporation.

Corporate Management

Regardless of its size, every corporation has levels of management and ownership. Figure 5.7 illustrates those that are typical—although a smaller firm might not contain all five of these. Levels range from stockholders down to supervisory management.

Stock Ownership and Stockholder Rights At the top of Figure 5.7 are stockholders. They buy shares of stock in the corporation, becoming part owners of it. Some companies, such as family businesses, are owned by relatively few stockholders, and the stock is generally unavailable to outsiders. In such a firm, known as a *closed* or *closely held corporation*, the stockholders also control and manage all of the company's activities. S.C. Johnson & Son, makers of household products like Pledge and Windex, is one such firm.

In contrast, an open corporation, also called a *publicly held corporation*, sells stock to the general public, establishing diversified ownership and often leading to a broader scope of operations than those of a closed corporation. Publicly held corporations usually hold annual stockholders' meetings. During these meetings, managers report on corporate activities, and stockholders vote on any decisions that require their approval, including elections of officers. Walmart holds the nation's largest stockholder meeting at the University of Arkansas Bud Walton Arena. Approximately 16,000 people attend. In addition to standard shareholder business, the Walmart meeting has featured celebrities and entertainers such as Hugh Jackman, Kelly Clarkson, Jennifer Hudson, and John Legend.

Stockholders' role in the corporation depends on the class of stock they own. Shares are usually classified as common or preferred stock. Although owners of preferred stock have limited voting rights, they are entitled to receive dividends before holders of common stock. If the corporation is dissolved, they have first claims on assets, once debtors are repaid. Owners of common stock have voting rights but only residual claims on the firm's assets, which means they are last to receive any distributions. Because one share is typically worth only one vote, small stockholders generally have little influence on corporate management actions.

Board of Directors Stockholders elect a board of directors—the governing body of a corporation. The board sets overall policy, authorizes major transactions involving the corporation, and hires the chief executive officer (CEO). Most boards include both inside directors (corporate executives) and outside directors—people who are not otherwise employed by the organization. Sometimes the corporation's top executive also chairs the board. Generally, outside directors are also stockholders, so they have a financial stake in the company's performance.

Corporate Officers and Managers The CEO and other members of top management, such as the chief operating officer (COO), chief financial officer (CFO), and the chief information officer (CIO), make most major corporate decisions. Managers at the next level down the hierarchy, middle management, handle the ongoing operational functions of the company. At the first tier of management, supervisory personnel coordinate day-to-day operations, assign specific tasks to employees, and evaluate job performance.

150   **Part 2** *Starting and Growing Your Business*

Solving an Ethical Controversy

Do Some CEOs Earn Too Much?

Median CEO pay reached $9.7 million recently, up 6.5 percent from the previous year. Enormous pay packages are meant to reward stellar company performance, but this has not always been the case. Some CEOs in recent years have been paid large amounts of money as part of their compensation packages, yet their companies have not demonstrated strong business gains.

Is executive pay excessive?

PRO

1. CEO compensation should reflect the overall state of the company and should be adjusted accordingly.

2. CEOs do not merit high rewards when their company stocks demonstrate lackluster performance.

CON

1. CEOs must take huge personal and professional risks to successfully manage their firms, and they should be well rewarded.

2. High pay ensures that firms attract and keep talented CEOs.

Summary

As CEO salaries have continued to skyrocket to more than 300 times the average U.S. worker's pay in recent years, Congress handed shareholders new legislation, which allows them to vote "no" on executives' excessive pay. So far, however, "no" votes have only occurred at fewer than 2 percent of almost 2,000 publicly traded companies.

Sources: Daily Viewpoint, "GMI Ratings' 2013 CEO Pay Survey Reveals CEO Pay Is Still on the Rise," accessed January 17, 2014, http://www3.gmiratings.com/home; Rob Silverblatt, "New Report Condemns Trends in CEO Compensation," *U.S. News and World Report*, accessed January 17, 2014, http://money.usnews.com; Christina Rexrode, "Median CEO Pay Rises to $9.7 million in 2012," *USA Today*, accessed January 17, 2014, www.usatoday.com.

Today's CEOs and CFOs are bound by stricter regulations than in the past. They must verify in writing the accuracy of their firm's financial statements, and the process for nominating candidates for the board has become more complex. In short, more checks and balances are in place for the governance of corporations. A continuing controversy surrounds the rising pay levels of CEOs, however; see the "Solving an Ethical Controversy" feature.

[10] When Businesses Join Forces

Today's business environment contains many complex relationships among businesses as well as not-for-profit organizations. Two firms may team up to develop a product or co-market products. One company may buy out another. Large corporations may split into smaller units. The list of alliances is as varied as the organizations themselves, but the major trends in corporate ownership include mergers and acquisitions and joint ventures.

Mergers and Acquisitions (M&A)

In recent years, mergers and acquisitions among U.S. corporations have hit an all-time high. Airlines, financial institutions, telecommunications companies, and media corporations are just a few of the types of businesses that have merged into giants. Recently, American Airlines merged with US Airways, giving the new airline the opportunity to compete against Delta, United, and others.[61]

The terms *merger* and *acquisition* are often used interchangeably, but their meanings are different. In a **merger**, two or more firms combine to form one company. In an **acquisition**, one

1. What are the two key elements of the incorporation process?
2. Identify the five main levels of corporate ownership and management.

merger agreement in which two or more firms combine to form one company.

acquisition agreement in which one firm purchases another.

Chapter 5 *Forms of Business Ownership and Organization*   **151**

firm purchases the other. This means that not only does the buyer acquire the firm's property and assets, it also takes on any debt obligations. Acquisitions also occur when one firm buys a division or subsidiary from another firm. Not all such attempts are successful. When AT&T attempted to buy T-Mobile USA, an acquisition that would have combined the second- and fourth-largest American wireless companies, the government filed a lawsuit to block the deal. They said it said would be a violation of antitrust law and substantially lessen competition. Because of the high fees AT&T would have to pay T-Mobile's parent company if the deal fell through, AT&T decided to fight the government's claim. In the end, AT&T gave up its attempt to buy the smaller company and instead negotiated an agreement with T-Mobile on roaming charges for phone users.[62]

Mergers can be classified as vertical, horizontal, or conglomerate. A **vertical merger** combines firms operating at different levels in the production and marketing process—the combination of a manufacturer and a large retailer, for instance. A vertical merger pursues one of two primary goals: (1) to ensure adequate flows of raw materials and supplies needed for a firm's products or (2) to increase distribution.

A **horizontal merger** joins firms in the same industry. This is done for the purpose of diversification, increasing customer bases, cutting costs, or expanding product lines. This type of merger is particularly popular in the auto and health care industries. Volkswagen now owns the Porsche brand, while CVS Caremark recently purchased another firm's Medicaid prescription business.

A **conglomerate merger** combines unrelated firms. The most common reasons for a conglomerate merger are to diversify, spur sales growth, or spend a cash surplus that might otherwise make the firm a tempting target for a takeover effort. Conglomerate mergers may join firms in totally unrelated industries. General Electric is well known for its conglomerate mergers—including its ownership of health care services and household appliances. Experts debate whether conglomerate mergers are beneficial. The usual argument in favor of such mergers is that a company can use its management expertise to succeed in a variety of industries. But the obvious drawback is that a huge conglomerate can spread its resources too thin to be dominant in any one market.

Joint Ventures: Specialized Partnerships

A **joint venture** is a partnership between companies formed for a specific undertaking. Sometimes a company enters into a joint venture with a local firm, sharing the operation's costs, risks, management, and profits with its local partner. This is particularly common when

vertical merger merger that combines firms operating at different levels in the production and marketing process.

horizontal merger merger that joins firms in the same industry for the purpose of diversification, increasing customer bases, cutting costs, or expanding product lines.

conglomerate merger merger that combines unrelated firms, usually with the goal of diversification, spurring sales growth, or spending a cash surplus in order to avoid a takeover attempt.

joint venture partnership between companies formed for a specific undertaking.

Courtesy City Year Miami

Joint ventures between for-profit firms and not-for-profit organizations provide great benefits for both parties. Starbucks partnered with City Year Miami and Rebuilding Together Miami Dade to repair a veteran's home in appreciation for his military service, as part of Sears's Operation Rebuild for Heroes at Home program.

a firm wants to enter into business in a foreign market. French carmaker Renault recently won approval from Chinese authorities to begin production of SUVs in China in a joint venture with Dongfeng Motor Group, allowing Renault entry into the world's largest auto market.[63]

Joint ventures between for-profit firms and not-for-profit organizations are becoming more and more common. These partnerships provide great benefits for both parties. Not-for-profit organizations receive the funding, marketing exposure, and sometimes manpower they might not otherwise generate. City Year, mentioned earlier, enjoys these benefits from partnerships with Timberland, Pepsi, and Comcast along with other firms such as Starbucks and Sears. Recently, Starbucks partnered with City Year Miami and Rebuilding Together Miami Dade to repair a veteran's home in appreciation for his military service. The effort was made possible as part of Sears's Operation Rebuild for Heroes at Home program.[64]

What's Ahead

The next chapter focuses on entrepreneurs, the driving force behind the formation of new businesses. It examines the differences between a small-business owner and an entrepreneur and identifies certain personality traits typical of entrepreneurs. The chapter also details the process of launching a new venture, including identifying opportunities, locating needed financing, and turning good ideas into successful businesses. Finally, the chapter explores a method for infusing the entrepreneurial spirit into established businesses—intrapreneurship.

Assessment Check ✔

1. Distinguish between a merger and an acquisition.
2. What are the different kinds of mergers?
3. What is a joint venture?

Chapter in Review

▮ Summary of Learning Objectives

⌐1⌐ Discuss why most businesses are small businesses.

A small business is an independently owned business having fewer than 500 employees. Generally, it is not dominant in its field and meets industry-specific size standards for income or number of employees. A business is classified as large when it exceeds these specifications.

Assessment Check Answers ✔

1.1 How does the Small Business Administration (SBA) define *small business*? A small business is defined as an independent business having fewer than 500 employees. However, those bidding for government contracts or applying for government assistance may vary in size according to industry.

1.2 In what industries do small businesses play a significant role? Small businesses provide most jobs in construction, agriculture, wholesale trade, services, and retail trade. In addition, home-based businesses make up 52 percent of American small businesses.

⌐2⌐ Determine the contributions of small businesses to the economy.

Small businesses create new jobs and new industries. They often hire workers who traditionally have had

difficulty finding employment at larger firms. Small firms give people the opportunity and outlet for developing new ideas, which can turn into entirely new industries. Small businesses also develop new and improved goods and services.

Assessment Check Answers ✔

2.1 What are the three key ways in which small businesses contribute to the economy? Small businesses create new jobs and new industries, and provide innovation.

2.2 How are new industries created? New industries are created when small businesses adapt to shifts in consumer interests and preferences. Innovation and new technology can play a significant role. In addition, new industries may be created when both the business world and consumers recognize a need for change.

⌐3⌐ Discuss why small businesses fail.

About 7 of every 10 new (small) businesses survive at least two years. But by the tenth year, 82 percent have closed. Failure is often attributed to management shortcomings, inadequate financing, and difficulty meeting government regulations.

Assessment Check Answers ✓

3.1 What percentage of small businesses remain in operation five years after starting? Ten years? About 50 percent are in business after five years; about 82 percent have folded by the 10-year mark.

3.2 What are the three main causes of small-business failure? The three main causes of small-business failure are management shortcomings, inadequate financing, and difficulty complying with government regulations.

⌐4⌐ Describe the features of a successful business plan.

A complete business plan contains an executive summary, an introduction, financial and marketing sections, and résumés of the business principals. Within this structure, an effective business plan includes the company's mission, an outline of what makes the company unique, identification of customers and competitors, financial evaluation of the industry and market, and an assessment of the risks.

Assessment Check Answers ✓

4.1 What are the five main sections of a business plan? The five sections are the executive summary, introduction, financial section, marketing section, and résumés of principals.

4.2 Why is an effective business plan important to the success of a firm? The business plan is a written document that provides an orderly statement of a company's goals, methods, and standards. It is the document that secures financing and creates a framework for the organization.

⌐5⌐ Identify the available assistance for small businesses.

The SBA guarantees loans made by private lenders, including microloans and those funded by Small Business Investment Companies (SBICs). It offers training and information resources, so business owners can improve their odds of success. The SBA also provides specific support for businesses owned by women and minorities. State and local governments also have programs designed to help small businesses get established and grow. Venture capitalists are firms that invest in small businesses in return for an ownership stake.

Assessment Check Answers ✓

5.1 What are the various ways the SBA helps small businesses? The SBA guarantees business loans; helps small businesses compete for government set-aside programs; and provides business information, advice, and training to owners of small businesses. It also advocates for small-business interests within the federal government.

5.2 What are business incubators? Business incubators are local programs organized by community agencies that provide low-cost shared business facilities in an effort to help small businesses get started.

5.3 Why are small businesses good opportunities for women and minorities? Many women feel they can achieve more as small-business owners and can balance family and work more easily if they own their own firms. Minority business owners can receive special assistance from programs such as the SBA's 8(a) Business Development program.

⌐6⌐ Explain franchising.

A franchisor is a large firm that permits another business (the franchisee) to sell its products under its brand name in return for a fee. Benefits to the franchisor include opportunities for expansion and greater profits. Benefits to the franchisee include name recognition, quick start-up, support from the franchisor, and the freedom of small-business ownership.

Assessment Check Answers ✓

6.1 What is the difference between a franchisor and a franchisee? A franchisor permits a franchisee to market and sell its products under its brand name, in return for a fee.

6.2 What are the benefits to both parties of franchising? Benefits to the franchisor include opportunities for expansion and greater profits. Benefits to the franchisee include name recognition, quick start-up, support from the franchisor, and the freedom of small-business ownership.

6.3 What are the potential drawbacks of franchising for both parties? The drawbacks for the franchisor include mismanagement and failure on the part of any of its franchisees, overexpansion, and loss of absolute control over the business. Drawbacks for the franchisee include an initial outlay of expenses, problems due to failure on the part of the franchisor or other franchisees, and restrictive franchise agreements.

⌐7⌐ Outline the forms of private business ownership.

A sole proprietorship is owned and operated by one person. While sole proprietorships are easy to set up and offer great operating flexibility, the owner remains personally liable for all of the firm's debts and legal settlements. In a partnership, two or more individuals share responsibility for owning and running the business. Partnerships are relatively easy to set up, but they do not offer protection from liability. When a business is set up as a corporation, it becomes a separate legal entity. Investors receive shares of stock in the firm. Owners have no legal and financial liability beyond their individual investments. In an employee-owned business, most stockholders are also employees. Family-owned businesses may be structured legally in any of these three ways but face unique challenges, including succession and complex relationships. The legal structure of a not-for-profit corporation stipulates that its goals do not include earning a profit.

Assessment Check Answers ✓

7.1 What are the key differences between sole proprietorships and partnerships? Sole proprietorships and partnerships expose their owners to unlimited financial liability from their businesses. Sole proprietorships are more flexible and easier to dissolve than partnerships. Partnerships involve shared work load and decision making, whereas sole proprietorships are entirely the responsibility of one business owner.

7.2 What is a corporation? A corporation is a legal organization with assets and liabilities separate from those of its owners. A corporation can be a large or small business.

7.3 What is the main characteristic of a not-for-profit corporation? A not-for-profit organization is set up legally so that its goals do not include pursuing a profit. Most states set out specific legal provisions for organizational structures and operations of not-for-profit corporations. They are exempt from paying corporate taxes.

⌐8⌐ Describe public and collective ownership of business.

Public ownership occurs when a unit or agency of government owns and operates an organization. Collective ownership establishes an organization referred to as a cooperative, whose owners join forces to operate all or part of the functions in their firm or industry.

Assessment Check Answers ✓

8.1 What is public ownership? Public ownership occurs when a unit or agency of government owns and operates an organization.

8.2 What is collective ownership? Where are cooperatives typically found, and what benefits do they provide small businesses? Collective ownership establishes an organization referred to as a cooperative (co-op), whose owners join forces to operate all or part of the functions in their firm or industry. Cooperatives are frequently found among agricultural businesses. Cooperatives allow small firms to pool their resources, share equipment and expertise, and split discount savings among members.

⌐9⌐ Discuss organizing a corporation.

There are three types of corporations: domestic, foreign, and alien. Stockholders, or shareholders, own a corporation. In return for their financial investments, they receive shares of stock in the company. Stockholders elect a board of directors, who set overall policy. The board hires the chief executive officer (CEO), who then hires managers.

Assessment Check Answers ✓

9.1 What are the two key elements of the incorporation process? The two key elements are where to incorporate and the corporate charter.

9.2 Identify the five main levels of corporate ownership and management. The five levels are stockholders, board of directors, top management, middle management, and supervisory management.

⌐10⌐ Explain what happens when businesses join forces.

In a merger, two or more firms combine to form one company. A vertical merger combines firms operating at different levels in the production and marketing process. A horizontal merger joins firms in the same industry. A conglomerate merger combines unrelated firms. An acquisition occurs when one firm purchases another. A joint venture is a partnership between companies formed for a specific undertaking.

Assessment Check Answers ✓

10.1 Distinguish between a merger and an acquisition. In a merger, two or more firms combine to form one company. In an acquisition, one firm purchases the property and assumes the obligations of another. Acquisitions also occur when one firm buys a division or subsidiary from another firm.

10.2 What are the different kinds of mergers? Mergers can be classified as vertical, horizontal, or conglomerate.

10.3 What is a joint venture? A joint venture is a partnership between organizations formed for a specific undertaking.

▮ Business Terms You Need to Know

small business 128	franchisor 141	preferred stock 150
home-based businesses 130	sole proprietorship 144	common stock 150
business plan 135	partnership 144	board of directors 150
Small Business Administration (SBA) 136	corporation 145	merger 151
microloans 137	S corporations 145	acquisition 151
business incubator 138	limited-liability corporation (LLC) 146	vertical merger 152
venture capital 139	employee ownership 146	horizontal merger 152
franchising 140	not-for-profit corporations 147	conglomerate merger 152
franchisee 141	stockholders 150	joint venture 152

Review Questions

1. Describe how a small business might use innovation to create new jobs.
2. Why do so many small businesses fail before they reach their tenth year?
3. What are the benefits of developing and writing an effective business plan?
4. What is the Small Business Administration? How does it assist small companies, financially and in other specialized ways?
5. Describe how local governments and business incubators help small firms get established and grow.
6. Why are so many small-business owners attracted to franchising? Under what circumstances might it be better to start an entirely new business instead of purchasing a franchise?
7. What are the benefits and drawbacks to traditional corporate structure? How do S corporations and limited liability corporations enhance the corporate legal structure?
8. Cooperatives appear frequently in agriculture. Describe another industry in which you think collective ownership would be beneficial, and explain why.
9. In a proprietorship and in partnerships the owners and the managers of the business are the same people. How are ownership and management separated in corporations?
10. How might a joint venture between a commercial firm and a not-for-profit organization help both achieve their goals?

Projects and Teamwork Applications

1. Research a large firm to find out more about its beginnings as a start-up or small business. Who founded the company? What were the firm's original offerings and how do they differ today?
2. Go to the website for *Entrepreneur* and research information on "Franchise 500," the magazine's top franchises. Choose one that interests you and evaluate the information about its start-up requirements. Discuss whether you would consider a partnership in your franchise with someone you know. Why or why not? Present your findings in class.
3. Think of your favorite small business—you know, the one where they know you by name. Maybe it's your hair salon, coffee shop, or corner market. Interview the owner of the business and ask how the current form of ownership was chosen. Present your findings in class.
4. Identify an organization—such as AmeriCorps or the United States Postal Service—that is owned by a unit or agency of government. Discuss the pros and cons of whether the organization should remain publicly owned. Research its successes and failures, and create an outline explaining your conclusion.
5. Identify a business and a not-for-profit organization that could form a joint venture beneficial to both. Draft a written proposal for this venture.

Web Assignments

1. **Small-business successes.** Do some online research to find a few recent small-business success stories. Visit the websites of *Entrepreneur* and *Inc.* magazines, which are both good places to start. Find a company of interest and prepare a brief report answering these questions:
   a. What does the firm do?
   b. Where did the idea originate?
   c. What expertise does the owner have?
   d. How did the business begin?
   e. Who are its competitors?
2. **Venture capital firms.** Kleiner Perkins Caufield & Byers is regarded by Wall Street as one of the largest and most established venture capital firms in the country. Go to the company's website (www.kpcb.com) and click on "companies" to review "focus areas." Choose one focus area and describe its initiatives and categories.
3. **Family-business tips for success.** Go to the website for *Family Business Magazine* at http://www.familybusinessmagazine.com and click on the free feature article. Discuss the feature article in class. Alternatively, choose a family-owned business such as S.C. Johnson (large) or Cider Hill Farm (small) and visit the firm's website to learn how the company has grown over the years and achieved success.

Note: Internet web addresses change frequently. If you do not find the exact sites listed, you may need to access the organization's or company's home page and search from there or use a search engine like Google or Bing.

Ideeli Gives Members (and Suppliers) Daily Deals

If you like to shop online and love a bargain, you may already be among the almost 6 million members of Ideeli.com, a flash-sale website. Every day at noon, Ideeli unveils over a dozen new, members-only sales of high-fashion clothing for men, women, and children, along with home furnishings and travel. Items move fast and sales end quickly, but joining the site is easy and discounts can reach 80 percent off retail.

Ideeli members obviously love surprises and great deals, but what attracts more than 1,000 suppliers to Ideeli's website? It's the ability to either speedily unload excess inventory or find new markets for up-and-coming brands, with reduced prices sheltered behind the members-only shopping concept. "Membership helps protect the brand," says one industry expert. "You can't find a sale on Prada or whatever just by Googling. It's behind a wall."

Ideeli was recently purchased by Groupon for $43 million and will continue to operate as a separate company. While flash shopping has been popular in Europe for a decade, Ideeli's founder Paul Hurley feels it still has room to grow. Groupon agrees. Its purchase of Ideeli increases Groupon's presence among the flash-shopping segment and mobile users. Groupon hopes to capitalize on the use of mobile devices to increase both its revenues and cache among Ideeli users.

Questions for Critical Thinking

1. Do you agree with Paul Hurley that future retailers will adopt Ideeli's flash-sale model? Why or why not?
2. What effects, if any, do you think the Groupon purchase will have on Ideeli?

Sources: Company website, www.ideeli.com, accessed January 17, 2014; Ingrid Lunden, "Groupon Moves into Flash Fashion for $43 Million in Cash," *Tech Crunch*, accessed January 17, 2014, http://techcrunch.com; Jill Krasny, "Groupon Buys Ideeli in a Sign of Retailer's Reliance on Mobile," *Inc.*, accessed January 16, 2014, www.inc.com; Katie Roof, "Groupon Buys Ideeli at a Discount," *Forbes*, January 13, 2014, www.forbes.com.

GoPro Your Next Big Wave or Snowboard Run

A little over a decade ago, Nicholas Woodman, an avid surfer and adventure sports lover, strapped a camera onto his wrist with some rubber bands and Velcro so that he could show his friends actual surfing footage. Today, his company, Woodman Labs, based in San Mateo, California, makes the GoPro camera, which can be attached to a car rooftop, bike helmet and handlebars, surfboards, and snowboards. Woodman refers to his GoPro camera, which sells for $200 and up, as a "life" camera.

After two failed start-ups and the experience of losing other people's money, he decided to bootstrap his company. With $30,000 in savings, and a $235,000 loan from his parents, he started Woodman Labs. His earliest sales effort involved peddling the small camera at surf and trade shows along the California coast. Eventually, he developed a following in a small niche of sports enthusiasts. Soon Woodman was noticed by the likes of buyers at Best Buy and REI, who were well aware of his cultlike following.

Since the camera initially arrived on the surfing scene, sales have doubled annually, with sales in excess of $500 million. GoPro recently exceeded Sony in video camcorder sales and claims a 21 percent market share in the video camcorder segment nationwide. The company's phenomenal growth has attracted investors, including Foxconn, a Chinese electronics manufacturer and maker of Apple's iPhones, and GoPro recently went public.

Before GoPro, only professional photographers could capture pictures and videos. But GoPro's small size and durability, not to mention its high-quality footage, allows anyone to capture an activity easily.

Surfers, skaters, skydivers, and adventure seekers are not the only ones with an attachment to Woodman's gadget. GoPro products are used in a wide range of settings. Film industry veterans and Hollywood directors keep GoPros on set. The military uses GoPro in its training exercises. Even professional athletes like snowboarder Shaun White, who once taped cameras to his hands to film his runs, regularly use GoPros. Woodman's GoPro camera captures the special thrill-seeking moments that would be difficult to recreate.

Questions for Critical Thinking

1. If you were in Woodman's shoes, what creative ways could you think of to promote and gain traction for your new gadget?

2. Discuss your thoughts on Google Glass and the wearable computer that can record everything. What are the pros and cons of this type of recording ability? What would be additional uses for the GoPro camera?

Sources: Brian Solomon, "Surf's Up! GoPro Goes Public, Pops 30% in Debut," *Forbes*, accessed July 2, 2014, www.forbes.com; Lizette Chapman, "How Family Ties Helped Nick Woodman Make GoPro Click," *The Wall Street Journal*, accessed January 17, 2014, http://blogs.wsj.com; Lizette Chapman, "How I Built GoPro Extreme Sports Camera," *The Wall Street Journal*, accessed January 17, 2013, http://online.wsj.com; Ryan Mac, "The Mad Billionaire Behind GoPro: The World's Hottest Camera Company," *Forbes*, accessed January 17, 2014, www.forbes.com; "The World's Newest Billionaire—GoPro's Inventor Nick Woodman," accessed January 17, 2014, http://addicted2success.com.

CASE 5.3 ▶ The Mei Mei Group: A Family Affair in Boston

Many consider family-owned businesses the backbone of American business. "Mei Mei" translates to "little sister" in Chinese, and its name aptly represents a family business of three siblings, Andy, Margaret (Mei), and Irene Li. When Andy, the oldest sibling, formed the Mei Mei Group, it was only appropriate to name it after his two little sisters, Margaret and Irene. Together as the Mei Mei Group, the Lis operate Mei Mei Street Kitchen, a food truck on the streets of Boston, and more recently, Mei Mei restaurant near the Boston University campus. When the siblings decided to go into business together, they realized that despite their distinctly different backgrounds, what they have all shared since childhood was a love of food.

With a passion for food instilled in them by their parents, the Li siblings began brainstorming about how to utilize their complimentary skills to create a family business. With restaurant management experience, Andy oversees the restaurant. Mei studied social entrepreneurship in London. While in London, she created a number of pop-up restaurants in unique locations, including one underneath the railway arches of the Thames River. Mei also attended business school, so she focuses on finances, marketing, business development, and the company's social media platform. Irene, the youngest sibling, attended Cornell University and has worked and lived on organic farms. Her experience helps the company ethically source food ingredients from local vendors. While in college Irene also began her own pop-up restaurant. The siblings were unanimous in their goal to bring authentic Chinese dishes with an American twist to Boston consumers, using seasonal, locally sourced ingredients.

One impressive contribution of small businesses like the Mei Mei Group is its creation of jobs in the local Boston area. Between its food truck and restaurant, the Mei Mei Group now employs more than 35 workers. In addition, the Lis firmly believe that supporting the local food system and

area farms provides fresher products to its customers. As a result, they are able to create jobs and provide revenue to the local Boston area economy.

The Mei Mei Group is an example of a small business that has provided an outlet for creative new ideas as business and consumers recognize a need for change. In this case, making a difference in the local food system is part of Mei Mei's core values. Since opening less than five years ago, the Mei Mei Group has brought 120,000 pounds of local and regional food from nearby farms in the Northeast to the consumers of Boston.

Menu items begin with traditional Chinese cuisine, and based on the supply of produce from local growers, menus are constantly changed and updated. Dumplings, for example, might be filled with sweet potato and sage, based on what's local and in season. With hundreds sold daily, Mei Mei's signature Double Awesome is an egg sandwich with pesto made from local growers and Vermont cheese on a scallion pancake. All eggs are purchased from a local free-range farm in nearby Providence, Rhode Island, and after a few years in business, the Lis are beginning to realize the impact of local sourcing on the local economy and the Boston food scene.

Although it may feel like David versus Goliath, the Mei Mei Group wants to do its part to innovate by working with local and regional growers to change the startling statistic that only 1 percent of food consumed is grown locally. Most food is produced on a massive or industrialized scale, which includes growing food on farms as cheaply as possible, many times resulting in the inhumane treatment of animals solely for profit. The Lis' business model has proved that providing healthy, locally grown food and meats to customers is both responsible and financially sustainable.

The growth of the Mei Mei Group has had a direct impact on the prosperity of the 40 local farmers with whom they work. Irene has built strong and enduring partnerships with their suppliers who range from pig, poultry, and beef farmers to local and regional growers. One farmer is building two new chicken coops for the Mei Mei Group, which purchased every one of his chickens last year. Since the demand for greens like kale and swiss chard remains strong, Mei Mei Group's suppliers are working on ways to continue greenhouse operations during winter months.

The Lis wrote a business plan, which was a helpful way for them to learn more about the industry and to think about the different aspects of their business, from marketing, to finance, to operations. Knowing very well that industries and markets continually change, the Lis used the business plan as a dynamic and changing road map. In addition, the Lis decided to create their form of ownership as an S corporation. This decision was made to avoid double taxation of business income while minimizing financial liability for the siblings.

The challenge of financing remains an obstacle for many small businesses and without adequate funds generated from initial sales, failure can occur. Through personal loans and some help from family members, the Lis launched their first venture, the food truck, a little more than three years ago. Partial financing for their restaurant came in the form of donations of $35,000 from Kickstarter, a crowdsourcing website.

Some of the biggest challenges faced by the Mei Mei Group are regulatory in nature. The city of Boston has many food truck regulations that Mei Mei and other businesses must follow. Issues range from the threat of fewer public parking spaces, truck hours and locations, and the types of food and meals the trucks are allowed to serve. In addition, the Mei Mei Group has been persistent about trying to obtain a liquor license for its restaurant operation.

Without thinking too much about future plans, the siblings are enjoying their firm's success and the fruits of their labor. Unsure of just exactly how, the siblings know the Mei Mei Group will continue to grow. While there's always the possibility of opening more restaurants, the company's core value of making a difference in the local food system may take them in a different direction that could involve farming. For now, the Li siblings are sure of one business goal: continuing to bring good food to the people of Boston.

Questions for Critical Thinking

1. Discuss and outline the unique ways the Mei Mei Group contributes to the local Boston area economy. Provide additional ideas and examples of how the Mei Mei Group can continue making a contribution to the local food scene in Boston.

2. Only a small number of family businesses survive into the second or third generation. What factors do you think contribute to this statistic? How might this impact succession planning for the Mei Mei Group?

3. Small businesses contribute to the economy by creating new jobs and industries and providing innovation. Provide examples of how the Mei Mei Group has achieved each of the contributions typically made by small businesses.

4. Discuss some of the biggest challenges for the Mei Mei Group as a small business. How do these challenges differ from other types of small businesses?

Sources: Company website, http://meimeiboston.com, accessed June 9, 2014; Mei Mei Street Kitchen Facebook page, https://www.facebook.com/meimeibostoon, accessed June 9, 2014; "Meet Young Guns Semi-Finalists Irene Li and Max Hull of Boston's Mei Mei," *Eater.com*, accessed June 9, 2014, www.eater.com; Sascha Garey, "Lunch Anyone? Mei Mei," *BU Today*, accessed June 9, 2014, www.bu.edu; Rachel Leah Blumenthal, "Mei Mei Could Get a Beer & Wine License After All," *Boston Eater*, accessed June 9, 2014, http://boston.eater.com; "Changing the Way the World Eats: Mei Mei Street Kitchen at TED," YouTube, accessed June 9, 2014, www.youtube.com; Christopher Hughes, "Five Reasons You Should Be Eating at Mei Mei Street Kitchen," *Boston Magazine*, accessed June 9, 2014, www.bostonmagazine.com; Devya First, "Mei Mei Crew Inventively Spins Off Its Truck Menu," *Boston Globe*, accessed June 3, 2014, www.bostonglobe.com; Jon Giardiello, "Mei Mei Street Kitchen Opens New Location," *Boston.com*, accessed June 9, 2014, www.boston.com; Morgan Rousseau, "Cray Cray for Mei Mei: Boston Food Truck to Open Green Eatery," *Metro US Magazine*, accessed June 9, 2014, www.metro.us; Rachel Travers, "Rolling with the Mei Mei Street Kitchen," *Boston.com*, accessed June 9, 2014, www.boston.com; Brian Samuels, "Serving Local on the Road: Mei Mei Street Kitchen," *Edible Boston*, accessed June 9, 2014, http://edibleboston.com.

Learning Objectives

1. Define *entrepreneur*.
2. Identify the different categories of entrepreneurs.
3. Explain why people choose entrepreneurship as a career path.
4. Discuss the environment for entrepreneurs.
5. Identify the characteristics of entrepreneurs.
6. Summarize the process of starting a new venture.
7. Explain intrapreneurship.

Chapter 6

Starting Your Own Business: The Entrepreneurship Alternative

© artpipi / iStockphoto

Sharing Economy Sparks Start-Ups

Find a need and fill it is the age-old way to start a new business venture. Finding a need is exactly what San Francisco entrepreneurs Kevin Petrovic, Rujul Zaparde, and Shri Ganeshram have done. The need these three teens identified is one familiar to most airline travelers: What do you do with your car when you are away on a trip? For most travelers, parking at the airport is the easiest, although not the least expensive, option. If you head to a typical large airport, you will see parking lots filled with private cars. Upon closer inspection, you will also see lots filled with rental cars waiting for customers. These entrepreneurs thought, "what if we could connect the owners of these parked cars with travelers who want to rent cars?" In this way, cars would not sit idle while travelers are away, there would be no need for large fleets of rental cars to own and maintain, and FlightCar rentals would be covered by a $1 million insurance policy.

Their venture, FlightCar, is just one of a growing number of peer-to-peer businesses that offer sharing services. Airbnb is probably the best-known sharing business. Started a little more than five years ago, this firm offers a web-based service linking travelers who want to rent rooms with individuals who have space in their homes or apartments. Airbnb charges owners 3 percent of the nightly room charge and renters 10 percent.

The company prescreens individuals to ensure guests and owners have a good experience and even suggests that individuals check each other's information on social media sites such as Facebook. For the room owners, it is a good deal because they can make some money from their unused rooms; and for the travelers, they can stay in private homes for a fraction of the cost of a hotel room. More than 9 million people have used Airbnb's services, with more than a half a million listings worldwide.

Peer-to-peer sharing is part of a fast-growing trend toward renting and not owning. *Forbes* estimates that this new "share economy" will be greater that $3.5 billion and grow at over 25 percent per year. What is fueling this trend? For one thing, it is the access to information via the Internet, which provides search engines, mobile devices, and social media pages and profiles. There is also the idea that spending money for little-used goods may not make much sense. So, the next time you drive by airport parking, open your closet, or store holiday decorations in an unused room, think about the items you own that could be shared with others—for a fee. You might be able to make a few dollars renting these items out, or, like the FlightCar founders, maybe millions, by starting a company to help others do the same.[1]

Overview

You think you want to start and run your own company. Like the founders of FlightCar, you have a great idea for a new business. Maybe you even dream of achieving fame and fortune. If you have been bitten by the entrepreneurial bug, you are not alone. More than ever, people like you, your classmates, and your friends are choosing the path of entrepreneurship.

How do you become an entrepreneur? Experts advise aspiring entrepreneurs to learn as much as possible about business by completing academic programs such as the one in which you are currently enrolled and by gaining practical experience by working part- or full-time for businesses. In addition, you can obtain valuable insights about the pleasures and pitfalls of entrepreneurship by reading newspaper and magazine articles and biographies of successful entrepreneurs. These sources will help you learn how entrepreneurs handle the challenges of starting their businesses. For advice on how to launch and grow a new venture, turn to magazines such as *Entrepreneur*, *Forbes*, *Fast Company*, *Success*, *Black Enterprise*, *Hispanic*, and *Inc*. Entrepreneurship associations such as the African-American Women Business Owners Association and the Entrepreneurs' Organization also provide valuable assistance. Finally, any aspiring entrepreneur should visit these websites:

- U.S. Chamber of Commerce
  (http://www.uschamber.com)

- Entrepreneur.com
  (http://www.entrepreneur.com)

- Kauffman Foundation
  (http://www.kauffman.org)

- The Small Business Administration
  (http://www.sba.gov)

- The Wall Street Journal Small Business
  (http://online.wsj.com/small-business)

In this chapter, we focus on pathways for entering the world of entrepreneurship, describing the activities, the different kinds of small-business owners, and the reason a growing number of people choose to be entrepreneurs. It discusses the business environment in which business owners work, the characteristics that help them succeed, and the ways they start new ventures. The chapter ends with a discussion of methods by which large companies try to incorporate the entrepreneurial spirit.

[1] What Is an Entrepreneur?

An **entrepreneur** is a risk taker in the private enterprise system, a person who seeks a profitable opportunity and takes the necessary risks to set up and operate a business. Consider Sam Walton, Walmart's founder, who started by franchising a few small Ben Franklin variety stores and then opened his own Walton Five and Dime stores. Today, Walmart has grown into a multibillion-dollar global business that is also one of the world's largest companies.

Entrepreneurs differ from many small-business owners. Although many small-business owners possess the same drive, creative energy, and desire to succeed, what makes entrepreneurs different is that one of their major goals is expansion and growth. Sam Walton was not satisfied with just one successful Ben Franklin franchise, so he purchased others. And when that was not enough, he started and grew his own stores. Entrepreneurs combine their ideas and drive with money, employees, and other resources to create a business that fills a market need. That entrepreneurial role can make something significant out of a small beginning. Walmart, the company that Sam Walton started, reported net sales in excess of $469 billion for one recent year.[2]

Entrepreneurs also differ from managers. Managers are employees who direct the efforts of others to achieve organizational goals. Owners of some small start-up firms serve as owner-managers to implement their plans for their businesses and to offset human resource limitations at their fledgling companies. Entrepreneurs may also perform a managerial role, but their overriding responsibility is to use the resources of their organizations—employees, money, equipment, and facilities—to accomplish their goals. When Bobbie Weiner found herself divorced and struggling for cash, she signed up for a special-effects makeup course, hoping that she could acquire some new skills and support herself by working in the movie industry. Her hard work has resulted in a successful business. She realized that specialized makeup is needed by many categories of people—actors, Halloween revelers, sports fans, funeral directors, and the military. After doing a few makeup jobs on horror films, Weiner was recruited to work on the blockbuster *Titanic*. That led to many other movies, a contract with the military for camouflage paint, worldwide requests from funeral homes, and her own product line, called Bloody Mary. Although Weiner is now worth millions and employs 250 people at her company, Bobbie Weiner Enterprises, based in Fort Worth, Texas, she is still very much in charge of the firm's mission, goals, and image.[3]

Studies have identified certain personality traits and behaviors common to entrepreneurs that differ from those required for managerial success. One of these traits is the willingness to assume the risks involved in starting a new venture. Some, like Bobbie Weiner, take that risk out of necessity—they have left or lost previous jobs or simply need a way to generate cash. Others want a challenge or a different quality of life. Entrepreneurial characteristics are examined in detail in a later section of this chapter.

Assessment Check ☑

1. How do entrepreneurs create new businesses?
2. How do entrepreneurs differ from managers?

Part 2 *Starting and Growing Your Business*

`2` Categories of Entrepreneurs

Entrepreneurs apply their talents in different situations. These differences can be classified into distinct categories: classic entrepreneurs, serial entrepreneurs, and social entrepreneurs.

Classic entrepreneurs identify business opportunities and allocate available resources to tap those markets. Tim Haskell is a classic entrepreneur. When the theater producer was unable to find a haunted house experience in New York City, he created his own. Over a decade later, during the months of September and October, Haskell mischievously frightens guests who walk through his theatrical haunted house, aptly named *Nightmare*. Haskell creates a new theme annually. His most recent, Killer 2, drew 30,000 to 35,000 thrill-seekers at ticket prices of $30 to $60 each. Today, Haskell is responsible for more than just the production of his scare-fest. As an entrepreneur, he oversees room planning, acquires building permits, and manages over 100 people involved in the production.[4]

A classic entrepreneur starts a new company by identifying a business opportunity and allocating resources to tap a new market; **serial entrepreneurs** start one business, run it, and then start and run additional businesses in succession. Elon Musk, the founder of such businesses as PayPal, Tesla Motors, Solar City, and SpaceX, is a serial entrepreneur. Jessica Herrin is also a serial entrepreneur. When Herrin graduated from college with an economics degree, she joined a software start-up firm where she got hooked on the idea of "unlimited potential." At age 24, Herrin co-founded WeddingChannel.com in Los Angeles, which grew within a few years to 100 employees and $21 million in revenues. When her firm was purchased by The Knot, Herrin went on to start Stella & Dot, a high-quality, fashion jewelry business sold by more than 14,000 independent representatives at parties and online. Stella & Dot now has $200 million in revenues, and the jewelry has been featured in business and fashion press—and perhaps more importantly, on celebrities.[5]

Some entrepreneurs focus on solving society's challenges through their businesses. **Social entrepreneurs** recognize a societal problem and use business principles to develop innovative solutions. Social entrepreneurs are pioneers of innovations that benefit humanity. Conscious Commerce, co-founded by actress and social entrepreneur Olivia Wilde, encourages corporations to become better corporate citizens. Conscious Commerce pairs a company's brand with a cause. Consumers may choose from among a number of participating companies, such as TOMS Shoes, Method cleaning products, Aveda, and Kiehl's. For example, when you purchase a red Morphie smart phone charger, Morphie helps combat HIV in Africa. Wilde's company recently raised $100,000 for New Light India, a community-development project serving women and children in Kolkata, India.[6]

classic entrepreneur
person who identifies a business opportunity and allocates available resources to tap that market.

serial entrepreneur
person who starts one business, runs it, and then starts and runs additional businesses in succession.

social entrepreneur
person who recognizes societal problems and uses business principles to develop innovative solutions.

Assessment Check ✓

1. What is the difference between a classic entrepreneur and a serial entrepreneur?

2. Describe a social entrepreneur.

After selling WeddingChannel.com to The Knot, serial entrepreneur Jessica Herrin founded Stella & Dot, a high-quality jewelry business.

Courtesy Stella & Dot

Reasons to Choose Entrepreneurship as a Career Path

If you want to run your own business someday, you'll have plenty of company. During one recent year, about 543,000 new businesses were created each month in the United States, with the construction and service industries experiencing the highest rates of activity.[7]

The past few decades have witnessed a heightened interest in entrepreneurial careers, spurred in part by publicity celebrating the successes of entrepreneurs such as Elon Musk, who launched the first electric sports car; Larry Page and Sergey Brin of Google; and Bill Gates, who left Harvard to start Microsoft with friend Paul Allen.

People choose to become entrepreneurs for many different reasons. Some are motivated by dissatisfaction with the traditional work setting—they want a more flexible schedule or freedom to make all the decisions. Others launch businesses to fill a gap in goods or services that they could use themselves. Still others start their own firms out of financial necessity, like Bobbie Weiner did with her makeup business. Carol Craig is another such entrepreneur. Craig was a flight officer and computer engineer, specializing in anti-submarine and subsurface warfare for the U.S. Navy. When unsuccessful knee surgery left her with a disabled veteran discharge, she was forced to reevaluate her career plans. So she founded Craig Technologies, headquartered in Orlando, Florida, which provides system engineering, software development, project management, courseware and training applications, modeling and simulation, and database and information technology services to the federal government and other commercial entities. In over a decade, the firm has grown to 285 employees and more than $25 million in sales. Although Craig didn't plan this to be her career, she says, "I was never afraid of trying new things. I'm an accidental entrepreneur."[8]

As pointed out in Figure 6.1, people become entrepreneurs for one or more of four major reasons: a desire to be their own boss, to succeed financially, to attain job security, and to improve their quality of life. Each of these reasons is described in more detail in the following sections.

Being Your Own Boss

The freedom to make all the decisions—being your own boss—is one of the biggest lures of entrepreneurship. When Michael Grondahl purchased a struggling gym, little did he know that more than two decades later, he'd be disrupting the fitness industry's model of locked-in annual membership contracts and high monthly fees. Based in New Hampshire, Planet Fitness offers its members a no "gymtimidation," judgment-free zone, and a unique environment where anyone can be comfortable. With the same equipment and amenities as its competitors, Planet Fitness does not require a contract for sometimes-fickle gym members. For a $10 monthly fee, members join without the pressure of an annual commitment. As a national sponsor of NBC's reality TV hit, *The Biggest Loser*, Planet Fitness has tripled in size to 700 locations.[9]

Being your own boss generally means getting to make all the important decisions. It also means engaging in much—if not all—of the communication related to your business, including customers, suppliers, distributors, retailers, and the like. The "Career Kickstart" feature offers tips for professional-style communication—even if you are on the run and using your thumbs.

Financial Success

Entrepreneurs are wealth creators. Some start their ventures with the specific goal of becoming rich—or at least financially successful. Often they believe they have an idea for a superior product and they want to be the first to bring it to market, reaping the financial rewards as a result. Entrepreneurs believe they will not achieve their greatest success by working for someone else,

Former Naval flight officer Carol Craig considers herself an accidental entrepreneur. After being discharged as a disabled veteran, Craig started a technology company that provides avionic software development and project management to various clients.

FIGURE 6.1 Why People Become Entrepreneurs

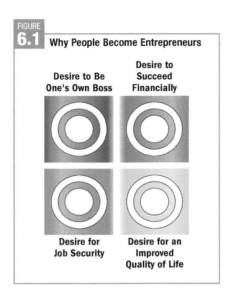

- Desire to Be One's Own Boss
- Desire to Succeed Financially
- Desire for Job Security
- Desire for an Improved Quality of Life

and they are generally right. Of course, the downside is that when they fail, entrepreneurs do not have the cushion of employment.

Online shoe and clothing retailer Zappos was started by Nick Swinmurn, whose inspiration struck when he was unable to find a pair of brown Airwalk shoes at his local mall. Swinmurn approached Tony Hsieh and Alfred Lin to invest, which they did—and shoesite.com, later renamed Zappos, was born. Ten years later, Amazon purchased the company for more than $1 billion.[10]

CareerKickstart

How to Be a Pro at Electronic Communications

Most entrepreneurs rely heavily on electronic communication to reach the people in their network. They're on the run, busy multitasking. Although you may be adept with your smart phone, it's wise to review a few tips about messaging.

- Don't write in all caps. It makes your message look as if you're yelling at the recipient.
- Avoid subject lines like "Important—Please Read." Such e-mails end up in the spam folder, unread. Instead, use short, descriptive subject lines that help your recipient know what the message is about—for example, "Review of Tuesday's Meeting."
- Don't use slang or shorthand like "LOL," "ru," and "L8." Also avoid smiley or sad-face emoticons.
- Be friendly, but not overly familiar. Never include jokes in a business e-mail or text message.
- Keep it brief. Short messages are more helpful than long ones. If more discussion is necessary, conclude by saying you'll follow up with a phone call.
- Remember: Computers and phones are like tape recorders. Messages can be saved—and could come back to haunt you. Never include personal messages within professional ones, and refrain from comments that could damage your company's image or the reputation of others.

Sources: Mark Grossman, "Email Etiquette Is Important," *Grossman Law Group,* accessed January 18, 2014, www.ecomputerlaw.com; Alina Tugend, "What to Think About Before You Hit Send," *The New York Times,* accessed January 18, 2014, www.nytimes.com; Karl Stolley and Allen Brizee, "Email Etiquette," *Purdue Owl,* accessed January 18, 2014, http://owl.english .purdue.edu; Nina Kaufman, "Making It Legal," *Entrepreneur,* accessed January 18, 2014, http://legal.entrepreneur.com.

Job Security

As you probably know, working for a company, even a well-known *Fortune* 500 firm, is no guarantee of job security. In fact, over the past 10 years, large companies sought efficiency by downsizing and eliminated more jobs than they created. As a result, a growing number of American workers—both first-time job seekers and laid-off long-term employees—are deciding to create their own job security by starting their own businesses. Although running your own business doesn't guarantee job security, the U.S. Small Business Administration has found that most newly created jobs come from small businesses, with a significant share of those jobs coming from new companies.[11]

As economies around the world are changing, workers are discovering the benefits of entrepreneurship compared with employment by big firms. In some countries, where entire industries, such as banking, steel, and telecommunications, are government-owned, young businesspeople are starting their own small firms. There are nearly 500 million people under the age of 30 in China, and their role models are Bill Gates and other famous U.S. technology entrepreneurs.[12]

Quality of Life

Entrepreneurship is an attractive career option for people seeking to improve their quality of life. Starting a business gives the founder independence and some freedom to decide

Chapter 6 *Starting Your Own Business: The Entrepreneurship Alternative*   **165**

lifestyle entrepreneur person who starts a business to gain flexibility in work hours and control over his or her life.

when, where, and how to work. A lifestyle entrepreneur is a person who starts a business to gain flexibility in work hours and control over his or her life. But this does *not* mean working fewer hours or with less intensity. Generally, it is the opposite—people who start their own businesses often work longer and harder than ever before, at least in the beginning. But they enjoy the satisfaction of success, both materially and in the way they live their lives.

Tim Ferriss, best-selling author of the *4-Hour* self-help series (*The 4-Hour Workweek, The 4-Hour Body,* and *The 4-Hour Chef*), is considered by many to be an example of a lifestyle entrepreneur. He ran a dietary supplement company, which made him wealthy but also had him working 24/7. Ferriss took a month off to travel and ended up traveling the world for almost a year and a half. While he was traveling, his company thrived without him. When he returned home, he went back to work but made time to write his first book, which advised people to maximize their business results while minimizing the time to do it. After being rejected by 27 publishers, Ferriss hit the jackpot: one publisher finally took a risk and published his book. The book became a huge hit. He sold his company and became a successful author, consultant, and investor in many tech start-ups.[13]

Assessment Check ☑

1. What are the four main reasons people choose to become entrepreneurs?

2. What is a lifestyle entrepreneur?

[4] # The Environment for Entrepreneurs

Are you ready to start your own company? Do some research about the environment in which you will be conducting business. There are several important overall factors to consider. There's the economy—whether it is lagging or booming, you may find opportunities. Consider where you want to locate your business. Currently, the states with the highest rate of entrepreneurial activity are Montana, Vermont, New Mexico, Alaska, Mississippi, California, Idaho, Hawaii, Louisiana, and Nevada. And the metropolitan area with the highest rate of activity is Miami.[14]

Overall, the general attitude toward entrepreneurs in the United States is positive. In addition to favorable public attitudes toward entrepreneurs and the growing number of financing options, several other factors—identified in Figure 6.2—also support and expand opportunities for entrepreneurs: globalization, education, information technology, and demographic and economic trends. Each of these factors is discussed in the following sections.

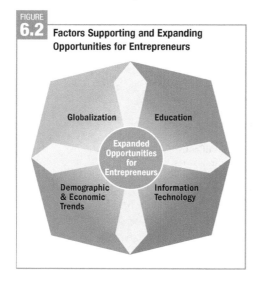

FIGURE 6.2 Factors Supporting and Expanding Opportunities for Entrepreneurs

Globalization

The rapid globalization of business has created many opportunities for entrepreneurs. Entrepreneurs market their products abroad and hire international workers. Among the fastest-growing small U.S. companies, almost two of every five have international sales. Over two decades ago, Turkey native Anisa Telwar started Anisa International, a manufacturer of cosmetic brushes and makeup tools and accessories. Her mother's business selling food, furniture, and consumer products gave Telwar the courage to start her own makeup brush company. To date, her company has global sales of $30 million and more than 600 employees.[15]

Growth in entrepreneurship is a worldwide phenomenon. The role of entrepreneurs is growing in most industrialized and newly industrialized nations, as well as in the emerging free-market countries in Eastern Europe. However, as shown in Figure 6.3, the business ownership rate is highest in economies that compete based on unskilled labor and natural resources—like those in Sub-Saharan Africa, Latin America, and the Caribbean. Established business ownership rates are lower in places like Italy, Japan, and France—countries whose economies are driven by innovation.[16]

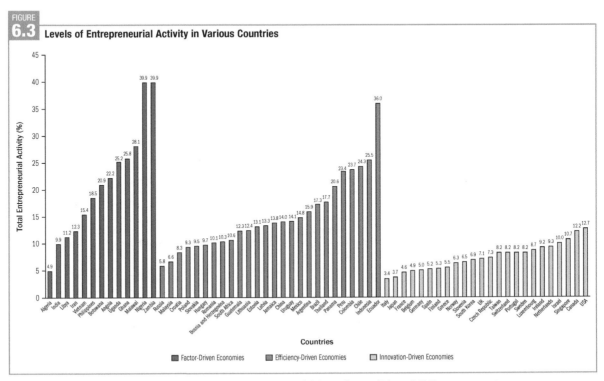

FIGURE 6.3 Levels of Entrepreneurial Activity in Various Countries

Source: José Ernesto Amorós and Niels Bosma, "Global Entrepreneurship Monitor 2013 Global Report," accessed February 5, 2014, www.gemconsortium.org.

Organizations worldwide recognize the importance of developing the next generation of entrepreneurs. Global Entrepreneurship Week (GEW) is one way of reaching out to innovators and job creators as well as recent graduates to encourage entrepreneurship and drive economic growth. Founded by the Kauffman Organization and Enterprise UK, GEW holds thousands of events, activities, and competitions in more than 138 countries for nearly 20 million participants. More than 24,000 companies and organizations plan youth-oriented business events in countries ranging from the United States to South Africa.[17]

Education

The past two decades have brought tremendous growth in the number of educational opportunities for would-be entrepreneurs. Today, many U.S. universities offer full-fledged majors in entrepreneurship, dozens of others offer an emphasis in entrepreneurship, and hundreds more offer one or two courses in how to start a business.

In addition to traditional classroom experience, a number of schools offer opportunities to intern with a start-up or actually work toward launching a company. The Entrepreneurship and Innovation Group at Northeastern University in Boston, which is staffed by professors who are entrepreneurs themselves, provides students with the chance to work in entrepreneurial settings in a variety of industries, including retail, commercial real estate development, financial services, health care, and high-growth technology.[18]

Besides schools, many organizations have sprouted up in recent years to teach entrepreneurship to young people. The Kauffman Center for Entrepreneurial Leadership in Kansas City, Missouri, offers training programs for learners from kindergarten through community college. Students in Free Enterprise (SIFE) is a worldwide, not-for-profit organization in which college students, working with faculty advisors, teach grade school and high school students and other community members the value of private enterprise and entrepreneurship.[19] The Association of Collegiate Entrepreneurs has chapters on many college campuses in the United States and Canada.

You don't have to major in business to become an entrepreneur, but students who do major in entrepreneurship or take entrepreneurship courses are three times more likely to start their own business or help someone else start a business.[20] In fact, you don't have to wait for graduation to launch your first start-up, and your business idea doesn't have to change the world. Ge Wang finished college before starting his business, but he never intended to be an entrepreneur. Wang was a music professor who had earned a bit of notoriety by creating the first orchestra composed entirely of mobile phones. One of Wang's students, Jeff Smith, had started a small tech company before returning to teaching. When Smith met Wang he thought, "This dude is going to change music." So Wang began to create iPhone apps for Smith's new venture, including Sonic Lighter and Ocarina (which turns an iPhone into a flute and has sold more than 3 million downloads).[21]

Information Technology

The explosion in information technology (IT) has provided one of the biggest boosts for entrepreneurs, such as Jack Dorsey of Twitter. As computer and communications technologies have merged and dropped dramatically in cost, entrepreneurs have gained tools that help them compete with large companies. Information technology helps entrepreneurs work quickly and efficiently, provide immediate and attentive customer service, and increase sales. In fact, technology has leveled the playing field to the point that, with the use of smart phones and other wireless devices, along with instant web distribution, a dorm-room innovator can compete with a much larger firm. Despite the technological advances that occur every day, sometimes a simple idea—and lots of hard work—can make an unlikely individual a successful entrepreneur. See the story in the "Hit & Miss" feature.

Social networking continues to transform the business environment for entrepreneurs. According to a recent study, more than 90 percent of successful companies now use at least one social media tool. One entrepreneur who embraces the full impact of social media on his business is Adam Kidron, who created New York City–based 4food, and whose mission is to make fast food healthier. Customers design their own burgers on one of the iPads in the restaurant or on their home computers or smart phones. Then they save the burger recipe to 4food's database. They can also post their creation on Twitter or Facebook, or they can create their own YouTube commercial about it.[22]

Demographic and Economic Trends

Who might be starting a business alongside you? Immigrants to the United States are the most likely to start their own businesses, as well as those between the ages of 55 and 64.[23] As Baby Boomers continue to age and control a large share of wealth in this country, the trend can only be expected to continue. Older entrepreneurs will also have access to their retirement funds and home equity for financing. Many Boomers also plan to work after retirement from traditional jobs or careers, either because they want to continue to work or in order to boost income and savings.

As mentioned earlier, college students are jumping on the entrepreneurial wagon in greater numbers, too. Four students from Carnegie Mellon University in Pittsburgh created

Hit&Miss

The Millionaire Rubber Band Man

At one time or another, you may have noticed kids wearing intricately woven patterns of colorful rubber band bracelets. Kids and parents alike can thank a former Detroit-based Nissan crash safety engineer, Cheong-Choon Ng, for his invention of a rubber band jewelry-making kit—called the Rainbow Loom.

While making friendship bracelets using tiny rubber bands with his two young daughters, Ng, a Malaysian immigrant, stumbled upon the idea for his company. His hands were too large to stitch the rubber bands together, so he devised a solution using an old, wooden scrub board with rows of pushpins to create a loom. Soon, he was experimenting with interesting geometric shapes woven in colorful patterns.

Ng convinced his wife to let him spend the $10,000 they had in college savings for their daughters to make a prototype loom and order rubber bands from China. In business for less than five years, the company has exceeded more than $15 million in revenues and sold more than 3 million units at Michael's Crafts, Learning Express, and through the company's website. Ng says that in today's 24/7 world, with everyone glued to their mobile devices, Rainbow Loom, a manual craft activity, offers both a creative and social outlet. About his phenomenal success:

"Actually, it's mind blowing. Every day I wake up and tell myself this is for real, it's not a dream."

Questions for Critical Thinking

1. As an entrepreneur, Ng has faced many challenges. What ideas do you have for Ng to expand his business? Are there additional product lines he might consider?

2. One downside of Ng's success is the copycats who have taken his idea—including his product photos and packaging designs—to sell almost identical products. What can Ng do to prevent others from making money off of his product?

Sources: Company website, www.rainbowloom.com, accessed January 21, 2014; Adrienne Burke, "Rainbow Loom Leads to Entrepreneurial Gold for Many," *Yahoo! Small Business,* accessed January 21, 2014, http://smallbusiness.yahoo.com; Catherine Clifford, "Inventor of the Wildly Popular 'Rainbow Loom' Weaves the American Dream with Rubber Bands in a Detroit Basement," *Entrepreneur,* accessed January 21, 2014, www.entrepreneur.com; Claire Martin, "Rainbow Loom's Success, From 2,000 Pounds of Rubber Bands," *The New York Times,* accessed January 21, 2014, www.nytimes.com.

---

a fingerprint-based payment identification system. PayTango, a unique biometric product, allows users to register their identity and credit cards by touching two fingertips to a screen that reads their information. PayTango was recently named one of America's Coolest College Start-Ups by *Inc.* magazine.[24]

Demographic trends—including the aging of the U.S. population, increasingly diverse ethnic groups, and the predominance of two-income families—create opportunities for entrepreneurs. Convenience products for busy parents, ethnic foods that cater to individuals, and services designed specifically for older consumers all enjoy opportunities for success. And as the economy fluctuates, entrepreneurs who are flexible enough to adapt quickly stand the best chance for success. Bobby Flam, owner of Jumbo's Restaurant in Miami, has kept his restaurant in the same location for 46 years despite hurricanes, riots, economic downturns, and the flight of other business. "I stayed because I wanted to be an example that business could succeed here," says Flam. He admits that not much has changed. Flam never turns away someone who is hungry, and he feeds an average of 10 homeless people a day. He also helps new local entrepreneurs get started in the neighborhood—and enjoys regular visits by sports stars from the Miami Heat and Miami Dolphins.[25]

[5] Characteristics of Entrepreneurs

People who strike out on their own are pioneers in their own right. They aren't satisfied with the status quo and want to achieve certain goals on their own terms. Successful entrepreneurs are often likely to have had parents who were entrepreneurs—or dreams of starting their own business. They also tend to possess specific personality traits. Researchers who study successful entrepreneurs report that they are more likely to be curious, passionate, self-motivated,

Assessment Check ✓

1. What opportunities does globalization create for today's entrepreneurs?

2. Identify the educational factors that help expand current opportunities for entrepreneurs.

3. Describe current demographic trends that present opportunities for entrepreneurial businesses.

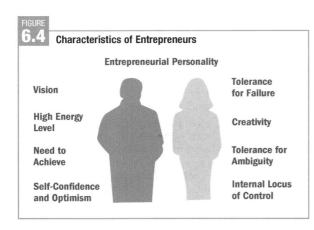

FIGURE 6.4 — Characteristics of Entrepreneurs

Entrepreneurial Personality

Vision

High Energy Level

Need to Achieve

Self-Confidence and Optimism

Tolerance for Failure

Creativity

Tolerance for Ambiguity

Internal Locus of Control

honest, courageous, and flexible. The eight traits summarized in Figure 6.4 are especially important for people who want to succeed as entrepreneurs.

Vision

Entrepreneurs generally begin with a *vision*—an overall idea for how to make their business idea a success. Then they pursue that vision with relentless passion. Russell Simmons, a successful entrepreneur, is credited with bringing hip-hop culture to the mainstream. His company, Rush Communications, has grown to include music, film, video games, publishing, fashion, television, and even financial services. It is one of the largest African American–owned entertainment companies in the United States.[26]

Arguably, every invention from the light bulb to the smart phone originated from a person with vision—someone who viewed the world in a slightly different way. Sometimes inventions have occurred out of necessity or even a mistake. True entrepreneurs know how to turn these situations into opportunities. It's well known that penicillin was created by accident; so was champagne. The heating potential for microwaves was discovered by its inventor while working on another project. Play-Doh was intended to be a cleaning product, and Velcro was created by a hunter who noticed that burrs stuck to his socks as he walked through the wilderness.[27]

High Energy Level

Entrepreneurs work long and hard to realize their visions. Many entrepreneurs work full-time at their regular day jobs and spend weeknights and weekends launching their start-ups. Many entrepreneurs work alone or with a very small staff, which means that they often wear most—if not all—of the hats required to get the business going, filling design, marketing, sales, and financial roles. Most entrepreneurs spend at least 70 hours a week on their new business, which can affect their other job (if they have one) and the quality of their personal life—at least in the beginning.[28] Thus, they need a high level of energy in order to succeed.

Need to Achieve

Entrepreneurs work hard because they want to excel. Their strong competitive drive helps them enjoy the challenge of reaching difficult goals and promotes dedication to personal success. In a recent interview, Virgin Group founder Richard Branson said Steve Jobs is the entrepreneur he most admires. Branson explains that what allowed Jobs to create the most respected brand in the world was his ability to, as Apple's advertising once claimed, "think different." "Steve Jobs wasn't known for his sense of fun, but he was always at the center of everything Apple did. Jobs was a great comeback artist who fought his way back up to create the greatest global brand ever."[29]

Self-Confidence and Optimism

Entrepreneurs believe in their ability to succeed, and they instill their optimism in others. Often their optimism resembles fearlessness in the face of difficult odds. They see opportunities where others see danger lurking. Robbie Vitrano is one such entrepreneur. Owner of Trumpet, a marketing agency based in New Orleans,

Frazer Harrison / Getty Images

Entrepreneurs need to have a vision—how to make their business idea a success. Russell Simmons is one of the top African-American entrepreneurs in the country. His Rush Communications entertainment empire includes music, film, fashion, and even financial services.

170   **Part 2** *Starting and Growing Your Business*

Solving an Ethical Controversy

Entrepreneurs and Ethics: It's Good Business

It's easy to get caught up in the excitement when launching a business, and while it might seem harmless to be overly optimistic or vague about details, experts warn against a lack of transparency. Not only might your venture fall flat as a result, but failure may have ethical or legal ramifications.

Should every business have a code of ethics?

PRO

1. A code of ethics reflects who your organization is, what you stand for, and how others can expect you to behave.

2. A code of ethics is a necessity today. Without it, businesses risk serious legal exposure.

CON

1. Not every entrepreneurial enterprise needs a formal code of ethics. What's important is conveying integrity about how you do business.

2. Accounts of ethics scandals are overblown in the media. In fact, the majority of entrepreneurs conduct their business ethically. A code of ethics won't make a bad person good, nor will the lack of one turn a good person bad.

Summary

Although it's time-consuming to create a formal code of ethics, business experts strongly recommend having one. Entrepreneurs face many challenges and sometimes a few failures; but none should be a failure of ethics.

Sources: U.S. Small Business Administration, "Business Ethics," accessed January 18, 2014, www.sba.gov; Carter McNamara, "Complete Guide to Ethics Management," *Management Help*, accessed January 18, 2014, www.managementhelp.org; Chris MacDonald, "Considerations for Writing a Code of Ethics," *Streetwise Small Business Book of Lists*, accessed January 18, 2014; Josh Spiro, "How To Write a Code of Ethics for Business," *Inc.*, accessed January 18, 2014, www.inc.com; Don Knauss, "The Role of Business Ethics in Relationships with Customers," *Forbes*, accessed January 18, 2014, www.forbes.com.

Vitrano refuses to give up on the small businesses that were wiped out by Hurricane Katrina. After other types of aid disappeared, Vitrano continued to support his business neighbors—believing that his investment would pay off in the revitalization of the city. Trumpet is now headquartered in the Icehouse, a 12,000-square-foot commercial real estate development in a building that once was under water. The Icehouse is home to numerous small business and start-ups, organizations that otherwise would have been left without office space. Elsewhere in town, Vitrano jump-started Naked Pizza, which has become so popular that Vitrano sells franchises.[30]

Tolerance for Failure

Entrepreneurs often succeed by sheer will and the ability to try and try again when others would give up. They also view setbacks and failures as learning experiences and are not easily discouraged or disappointed when things don't go as planned. Bobbi Brown built a big name in the cosmetics industry. Estée Lauder bought her company, and Brown stayed on in an active role. The brand faced some setbacks after its acquisition and sales went flat, but Brown never gave up. She met with the CEO, who said the problem was that the cosmetics were not setting themselves apart from the competition. Brown took the criticism in stride, learned from the setback, and decided to change the culture of the company. She moved out of the GM building to a loft in the SoHo section of Manhattan, made advertising photographs more editorial, and approached the cosmetics business as if it were a magazine. The company's numbers vastly improved, and today the Bobbi Brown empire is valued at over a billion dollars. [31]

When things go well, it's easy to take personal credit. But when poor business decisions result in failure, it's a bit more difficult. Truly successful entrepreneurs are willing to take responsibility for their mistakes. That is why an important part of launching any new business is establishing a code of ethics, as discussed in the "Solving an Ethical Controversy" feature.

Creativity

Entrepreneurs typically conceive new ideas for goods and services, and they devise innovative ways to overcome difficult problems and situations. If we look at the top entrepreneurs in the world, we can see that creativity is the common denominator. *Inc.* magazine presents an annual list of the 500 top small businesses, most of which were started by entrepreneurs. The word *solution* is one of the most common to appear in the names of these companies.

Some entrepreneurs find creative solutions to problems; others find creative ways to accomplish a task or provide a service. Still others create entirely new products. More than 20 years ago, Jimmy Ray sketched his idea for an affordable telephone system for private airplanes on a paper napkin. Today, Illinois-based Gogo provides in-flight Internet access services using wi-fi. Many business travelers, desperate to send e-mails during long flights, have paid the additional fees for in-flight service. Recent approval by the Federal Aviation Administration gives customers in-flight use of electronic devices. As more airlines use wi-fi access as an additional revenue source, competition will increase to attract more passengers willing to pay for these services.[32]

When his grandmother died, college student Curtis Funk got the idea to record the proceedings and memories of funerals onto CDs and sell them to families through funeral homes. Families of deceased loved ones appreciated the CDs so much that Funk's company, Utah-based FuneralRecording.com, provides live streaming audio and video, transcripts, CDs, and other services. The firm also offers Twitter updates under the name "funeraltech."[33]

Tolerance for Ambiguity

Entrepreneurs take in stride the uncertainties associated with launching a venture. Dealing with unexpected events is the norm for most entrepreneurs. Tolerance for ambiguity is different from the love of risk taking that many people associate with entrepreneurship. Successful entrepreneurship is a far cry from gambling because entrepreneurs look for strategies that they believe have a good chance of success, and they quickly make adjustments when a strategy isn't working. An important way entrepreneurs manage ambiguity is by staying close to customers so that they can adjust their offerings to customer desires. When Netflix's founder Reed Hastings tried to phase out the DVD-by-mail offering in favor of a more up-and-coming streaming service, he was met with intense customer resistance. Hasting's decision cost Netflix a loss of 800,000 subscribers and $12 billion in market value. Netflix continues to offer DVDs by mail as well as its streaming services.[34]

Internal Locus of Control

Entrepreneurs have an internal locus of control, which means they believe that they control their own destinies. You will not find entrepreneurs blaming others or outside events for their successes or failures—they own it all.

Diagnosed with a degenerative illness at age 6, Ralph Braun was confined to a wheelchair by the time he was 14. College became too difficult for Braun to navigate in his traditional wheelchair, so he decided to design his own transportation. Within about four months, he had built his first scooter. Braun later redesigned the interior of his van and created a wheelchair lift. Braun's increased mobility attracted the attention of the community of people with disabilities, and he began to receive requests for scooters, wheelchair-enabled vans, wheelchair lifts, and other products that aid the wheelchair-bound. Indiana-based Braun Corporation has 500 employees and manufactures a full line of mobility products.[35]

After reading this summary of typical personality traits, maybe you're wondering if you have what it takes to become an entrepreneur. Take the test in Figure 6.5 to find out. Your results may help you determine whether you would succeed in starting your own company.

Assessment Check ✓

1. What is meant by an entrepreneur's vision?
2. Why is it important for an entrepreneur to have a high energy level and a strong need for achievement?
3. How do entrepreneurs generally feel about the possibility of failure?

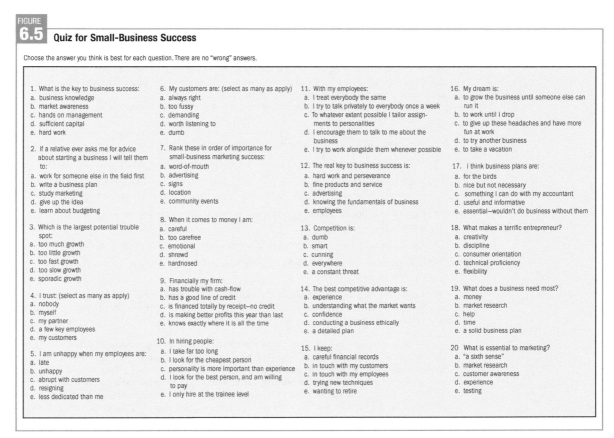

FIGURE 6.5 Quiz for Small-Business Success

Choose the answer you think is best for each question. There are no "wrong" answers.

1. What is the key to business success:
   a. business knowledge
   b. market awareness
   c. hands on management
   d. sufficient capital
   e. hard work

2. If a relative ever asks me for advice about starting a business I will tell them to:
   a. work for someone else in the field first
   b. write a business plan
   c. study marketing
   d. give up the idea
   e. learn about budgeting

3. Which is the largest potential trouble spot:
   a. too much growth
   b. too little growth
   c. too fast growth
   d. too slow growth
   e. sporadic growth

4. I trust: (select as many as apply)
   a. nobody
   b. myself
   c. my partner
   d. a few key employees
   e. my customers

5. I am unhappy when my employees are:
   a. late
   b. unhappy
   c. abrupt with customers
   d. resigning
   e. less dedicated than me

6. My customers are: (select as many as apply)
   a. always right
   b. too fussy
   c. demanding
   d. worth listening to
   e. dumb

7. Rank these in order of importance for small-business marketing success:
   a. word-of-mouth
   b. advertising
   c. signs
   d. location
   e. community events

8. When it comes to money I am:
   a. careful
   b. too carefree
   c. emotional
   d. shrewd
   e. hardnosed

9. Financially my firm:
   a. has trouble with cash-flow
   b. has a good line of credit
   c. is financed totally by receipt—no credit
   d. is making better profits this year than last
   e. knows exactly where it is all the time

10. In hiring people:
    a. I take far too long
    b. I look for the cheapest person
    c. personality is more important than experience
    d. I look for the best person, and am willing to pay
    e. I only hire at the trainee level

11. With my employees:
    a. I treat everybody the same
    b. I try to talk privately to everybody once a week
    c. To whatever extent possible I tailor assignments to personalities
    d. I encourage them to talk to me about the business
    e. I try to work alongside them whenever possible

12. The real key to business success is:
    a. hard work and perseverance
    b. fine products and service
    c. advertising
    d. knowing the fundamentals of business
    e. employees

13. Competition is:
    a. dumb
    b. smart
    c. cunning
    d. everywhere
    e. a constant threat

14. The best competitive advantage is:
    a. experience
    b. understanding what the market wants
    c. confidence
    d. conducting a business ethically
    e. a detailed plan

15. I keep:
    a. careful financial records
    b. in touch with my customers
    c. in touch with my employees
    d. trying new techniques
    e. wanting to retire

16. My dream is:
    a. to grow the business until someone else can run it
    b. to work until I drop
    c. to give up these headaches and have more fun at work
    d. to try another business
    e. to take a vacation

17. I think business plans are:
    a. for the birds
    b. nice but not necessary
    c. something I can do with my accountant
    d. useful and informative
    e. essential—wouldn't do business without them

18. What makes a terrific entrepreneur?
    a. creativity
    b. discipline
    c. consumer orientation
    d. technical proficiency
    e. flexibility

19. What does a business need most?
    a. money
    b. market research
    c. help
    d. time
    e. a solid business plan

20. What is essential to marketing?
    a. "a sixth sense"
    b. market research
    c. customer awareness
    d. experience
    e. testing

Source: U.S. Small Business Administration, "Quiz for Small Business Success," accessed January 20, 2014, at www.ltbn.com/biz_quiz.htm.

6 Starting a New Venture

The examples of entrepreneurs presented so far have introduced many ways to start a business. This section discusses the process of choosing an idea for a new venture and transforming the idea into a working business.

Selecting a Business Idea

In choosing an idea for your business, the two most important considerations are (1) finding something you love to do and are good at doing, and (2) determining whether your idea can satisfy a need in the marketplace. People willingly work hard doing something they love, and the experience will bring personal fulfillment. The old adages "Do what makes you happy" and "Be true to yourself" are the best guidelines for deciding on a business idea.

Success also depends on customers, so would-be entrepreneurs must also be sure that the idea they choose fills a need in the marketplace. The most successful entrepreneurs tend to operate in industries in which change is ongoing and in which customers have difficulty pinpointing their precise needs. These industries allow entrepreneurs to capitalize on their strengths, such as creativity, hard work, and tolerance of ambiguity, to build customer relationships. Nevertheless, examples of outstanding entrepreneurial success occur in every industry. Whether you want to build a business based on your grandmother's cookie recipes or know that you have a better idea for tax-preparation software, you are more likely to succeed if you ask yourself the right questions from the beginning.

Consider the following guidelines as you think about your business ideas:

- List your interests and abilities. Include your values and beliefs, your goals and dreams, things you like and dislike doing, and your job experiences.

- Make another list of the types of businesses that match your interests and abilities.

- Read business and consumer magazines and websites to learn about demographic and economic trends that identify future needs for products that no one yet offers.

- Carefully evaluate existing goods and services, looking for ways you can improve them.

- Decide on a business that matches what you want and offers profit potential.

- Conduct marketing research to determine whether your business idea will attract enough customers to earn a profit.

- Learn as much as you can about the industry in which your new venture will operate, your merchandise or service, and your competitors. Read surveys that project growth in various industries.

Many entrepreneurs who start new businesses invent new products or processes. When that happens, the inventor–entrepreneur needs to protect the rights to his or her invention by securing a patent. The U.S. Patent and Trademark Office's website (http://www.uspto.gov) provides information about this process, along with forms to apply for a patent. Inventors can also apply for a patent online. The same suggestions apply to entrepreneurs who are interested in copyright protection for their product names or processes. The U.S. Copyright Office's website (http://www.copyright.com) provides information about this process, along with forms to apply for copyright protection. Other entrepreneurial firms come up with innovative ways to build new markets, as the California solar energy company Sungevity is doing. See the "Going Green" feature for the story.

Buying an Existing Business Some entrepreneurs prefer to buy established businesses rather than assume the risks of starting new ones. Buying an existing business brings many advantages: employees are already in place to serve established customers and deal with familiar suppliers, the good or service is known in the marketplace, and the necessary permits and licenses have already been secured. Getting financing for an existing business can be easier than it is for most start-ups. Some sellers may even help the buyers by providing financing and offering to serve as consultants. Most people want to buy a healthy business so that they can build on its success, but an experienced entrepreneur might purchase a struggling business with the intent of turning it around. There are many resources for entrepreneurs who are considering the purchase of a business, ranging from information provided by government agencies such as the Small Business Administration to websites listing actual companies for sale.

Buying a Franchise Like buying an established business, buying a franchise offers a less risky way to begin a business than starting an entirely new firm. But franchising, which was discussed in detail in Chapter 5, still involves risks, and it is wise to do thorough research

GoingGreen

Sungevity Follows the Sun

If you're considering solar power, a California company called Sungevity, which makes home rooftop solar systems, has a solution for you.

The firm's vision, that "everyone should be able to go solar," is supported by its innovative business model intended to make solar energy affordable. In addition to selling them, Sungevity also leases solar panels that it owns, installs, and maintains for a monthly fee. Customers' electricity bills go down, along with their consumption of nonrenewable fossil fuels. Using satellite images of roofs and measures of sun intensity, Sungevity can also offer customers accurate online price quotes, via home computer or through a partnership with Lowe's at its stores.

The fastest-growing residential solar company in the United States, Sungevity currently operates in nine states, Australia, and the Netherlands. A recent capital investment from several sources, including GE Energy Ventures, will help Sungevity continue to grow.

Questions for Critical Thinking

1. What innovative Sungevity strategies might appeal to middle-class buyers?
2. Discuss the difference between companies that sell solar energy and those like Sungevity that sell solar hardware. What are the challenges for each?

Sources: Company website, www.sungevity.com, accessed January 21, 2014; Charles W. Thurston, "Partnering with Big Box Stores Allows Solar Installers to Increase Job Prospects," *Solar Builder Magazine,* accessed January 21, 2014, http://solarbuildermag.com; Cassandra Sweet, "Update: Sungevity Raises $15 Million in Venture Capital from GE, Others," *The Wall Street Journal,* accessed January 21, 2014, http://online.wsj.com; Martin La Monica, "Sungevity Socks Away Cash for Solar Leasing," *CNET News,* accessed January 21, 2014, http://news.cnet.com; Osha Gray Davidson, "Lowe's and Sungevity Announce Solar Partnership," *Forbes,* accessed January 21, 2014, www.forbes.com.

---

before taking the plunge. Although there are a multitude of franchises from which to choose, one area that is experiencing tremendous growth is firms whose goods and services are targeted to children and their parents. These businesses offer everything from photography to tutoring to security.

Creating a Business Plan

In the past, many entrepreneurs launched their ventures without creating formal business plans. Although planning is an integral part of managing in contemporary business, entrepreneurs typically seize opportunities as they arise and change course as necessary. Flexibility seems to be the key to business start-ups, especially in rapidly changing markets. But because of the risks inherent in starting a business, it has become apparent that at least some planning is not only advisable but necessary, particularly if an entrepreneur is seeking funds from outside sources.

Before Shez Zamrudeen opened her own high-fashion boutique called Deen, she built a business plan. A major part of Zamrudeen's plan involved finding a way to distinguish her shop from many others in her New Jersey area. She decided to place her flagship store in New Jersey's Powerhouse Arts District in Jersey City—complete with original artwork decorating the walls. When a recession hit, Zamrudeen was undaunted. "I had to adjust my current business plan and long-term goals," she admits. "I had to be smarter and more careful with my inventory." But Zamrudeen says she still plans to achieve all her business goals.[36]

Chapter 5 and Appendix D discuss business plans in more detail. The Internet also offers a variety of resources for creating business plans. Table 6.1 lists some of these online resources.

Buying a franchise, such as a SUBWAY store, offers entrepreneurs a less risky way to begin a business than starting an entirely new firm.

Brendan Howard / Shutterstock

TABLE

└6.1┘ Online Resources for Preparing a Business Plan

AllBusiness.com http://www.allbusiness.com	Enter "Business Plan" in the search query to learn more about writing a business plan.
Inc. http://www.inc.com	Under "Start Ups," click "Business Plans."
MoreBusiness.com http://www.morebusiness.com	To see a sample plan, select "Write a Business Plan" from the list of templates.
Small Business Administration http://sba.gov	Go to "Create Your Business Plan" under "Starting and Managing."

Finding Financing

seed capital
initial funding used to launch a company.

A key issue in any business plan is financing. Requirements for **seed capital**, funds used to launch a company, depend on the nature of the business. Nibbol is a San Francisco–based start-up founded by two friends who met at community college. Nibbol is a unique online platform for animal owners to search for and schedule appointments instantly with veterinarians based on ratings, reviews, prices, specialty, and distance from home. Before seeking investors, the two entrepreneurs are funding their business idea from their savings until they find a product market fit and a viable revenue model.[37] Table 6.2 lists the common sources of start-up capital.

debt financing
borrowed funds that entrepreneurs must repay.

Debt Financing When entrepreneurs use **debt financing**, they borrow money that they must repay. Loans from banks, finance companies, credit card companies, and family or friends are all sources of debt financing. Although some entrepreneurs charge business expenses to personal credit cards because they are relatively easy to obtain, high interest rates make this source of funding expensive, and the Small Business Administration (SBA) recommends finding less expensive credit.

Many banks turn down requests for loans to fund start-ups, fearful of the high risk such ventures entail. This has been particularly true over the past several years. Only a small percentage of start-ups raise seed capital through bank loans, although some new firms can get SBA-backed

TABLE

└6.2┘ Funding Used by Entrepreneurs for Start-Ups

SOURCE	PERCENTAGE OF ENTREPRENEURS*
Self-financing	82%
Loans from family, friends, or business associates	22%
Bank loans	18%
Lines of credit	18%
Venture capital	8%
SBA or other government funds	4%

*Percentages do not total 100 because entrepreneurs often use multiple sources to finance start-ups.

Source: "Entrepreneurial America: A Comprehensive Look at Today's Fastest-Growing Private Companies," *Inc., The Handbook of the American Entrepreneur,* accessed January 20, 2014, http://www.inc.com.

loans, as discussed in Chapter 5. Applying for a bank loan requires careful preparation. Bank loan officers want to see a business plan and will evaluate the entrepreneur's credit history. Because a start-up has not yet established a business credit history, banks often base lending decisions on evaluations of entrepreneurs' personal credit histories. Banks are more willing to make loans to entrepreneurs who have been in business for a while, show a profit on rising revenues, and need funds to finance expansion. Some entrepreneurs have found that local community banks are more interested in their loan applications than are the major national banks.

Even entrepreneurs who have previously received funding from banks—and have maintained a good relationship with their lenders—have experienced a credit crunch in recent years. After several years in business, entrepreneur Kevin Semcken learned his bank would no longer fund his $2.5 million line of credit. A line of credit is an approved loan that a business can borrow from when funds are needed. Without that money Semcken's firm, Colorado-based Able Planet, could not buy the raw materials or manufacture its products—headsets, headphones, and assistive listening devices for people with hearing issues. Large retailers such as Costco and Walmart had already placed orders; Semcken reevaluated his business plan and found alternative funding.[38]

Equity Financing To secure equity financing, entrepreneurs exchange a share of ownership in their company for money supplied by one or more investors. Entrepreneurs invest their own money along with funds supplied by other people and firms that become co-owners of the start-ups. An entrepreneur does not have to repay equity funds. Rather, the investors share in the success of the business. Sources of equity financing include family and friends, business partners, venture capital firms, and private investors. Able Planet's CEO Kevin Semcken was able to secure equity funding.[39]

Teaming up with a partner who has funds to invest may benefit an entrepreneur with a good idea and skills but little or no money. Investors may also have business experience, which they will be eager to share because the company's prosperity will benefit them. Like borrowing, however, equity financing has its drawbacks. One is that investment partners may not agree on the future direction of the business, and in the case of partnerships, if they cannot resolve disputes, one partner may have to buy out the other to keep operating.

Some entrepreneurs find creative ways to obtain equity financing. Gavin McClurg did that when he came up with a timeshare business model for his start-up. His venture, called Offshore Odysseys, is actually a multi-year sailing expedition aboard a $1.2 million catamaran named *Discovery* that sails the world. Investors buy timeshare segments for between $20,000 and

equity financing
funds invested in new ventures in exchange for part ownership.

Jody MacDonald Photography

Some entrepreneurs find creative ways to obtain equity financing. Gavin McClurg's venture, Offshore Odysseys, is a sailing expedition aboard a catamaran named *Discovery*. Investors buy timeshare segments for between $20,000 and $30,000 on the journey, during which they might swim, snorkel, kite surf, or paraglide in beautiful, remote parts of the world.

$30,000, during which they might snorkel near the Equator, kite surf off Fiji, or paraglide above Tahiti. Shareholders may purchase more than one segment and trade their time with other members. Annual fees cover the firm's operating expenses as well as food and beverages on the trip.[40]

Venture capitalists are business organizations or groups of private individuals that invest in early-stage, high-potential growth companies. Venture capitalists typically back companies in high-technology industries such as biotechnology. In exchange for taking a risk with their own funds, these investors expect high rates of return, along with a stake in the company. Typical terms for accepting venture capital include agreement on how much the company is worth, how much stock both the investors and the founders will retain, control of the company's board, payment of dividends, and the period of time during which the founders are prohibited from "shopping" for additional investors.[41] Venture capitalists require a combination of qualities, such as innovative technology, potential for rapid growth, a well-developed business model, and an experienced management team.

Angel investors, wealthy individuals who invest money directly in new ventures in exchange for equity, are a larger source of investment capital for start-up firms. In contrast to venture capitalists, angels focus primarily on new ventures. Many angel investors are successful entrepreneurs who help aspiring business owners through the familiar difficulties of launching their businesses. Angel investors back a wide variety of new ventures. Because most entrepreneurs have trouble finding wealthy private investors, angel networks are formed to match business angels with start-ups in need of capital. New York Angels is an organization that invests in early-stage technology companies in the Northeast.

The Small Business Administration's Active Capital provides online listings to connect would-be angels with small businesses seeking financing. Venture capitalists that focus on women include Women's Venture Capital Fund (http://www.womensvcfund.com) and Springboard Enterprises (https://sb.co). Those interested in minority-owned business include, for example, the U.S. Hispanic Chamber of Commerce (http://www.ushcc.com).

Government Support for New Ventures

Federal, state, and local governments support new ventures in a number of ways, as discussed in Chapter 5. The Small Business Administration (SBA), state and local agencies, and business incubators all offer information, resources, and sometimes access to financing for entrepreneurs.

Another way to encourage entrepreneurship is through *enterprise zones*, specific geographic areas designated for economic revitalization. Enterprise zones encourage investment, often in distressed areas, by offering tax advantages and incentives to businesses locating within the boundaries of the zone. The state of Florida, for example, has 63 enterprise zones and allows a business located within urban zones to take tax credits for 20 or 30 percent of wages paid to new employees who reside within the urban enterprise zone. Colorado has 16 zones, while Ohio has more than 360 active zones.[42]

Government legislation can also encourage investment in the U.S. economy. The Immigration Act of 1990 (IMMACT 90) recognizes the growing globalization of business. It contains a provision that sets aside visas for immigrants wishing to invest money in a new venture in a *targeted employment area*—a rural area or an area that has experienced an unemployment rate of at least 150 percent of the national average. In addition, IMMACT 90 enables more experts in the fields such as science, engineering, and computer programming to be hired by U.S. firms.[43]

⌐7⌐ Intrapreneurship

Established companies try to retain the entrepreneurial spirit by encouraging **intrapreneurship**, the process of promoting innovation within their organizational structures. Today's fast-changing business climate compels established firms to innovate continually to maintain

Hit&Miss

3D Printing Takes Off

Chuck Hull may not be a household name, but he has forever changed the way things are designed, manufactured, and sold. Hull, an engineer by trade, worked for a systems manufacturing company back in the early 1980s and went to his boss with an idea to build a machine that printed out objects you could hold in your hand. While his boss was not encouraging, he did make a deal with Hull that he could work on his "dream machine" after hours.

While working on his project, Hull discovered that he could use ultraviolet lights to etch plastic layers into different shapes by stacking the layers to form a 3D object—and 3D printing was born. Shortly thereafter, Hull started a company called 3D Systems, headquartered in Valencia, California. Hull's company came to the rescue of Detroit automobile manufacturers who were desperate to shorten the design process due to increased competition from Japanese automakers. Using Hull's technology, automobile engineers could create their own prototypes for door handles or stick-shift knobs to eliminate the time-consuming process of sending drawings to a tool-and-die shop. The technology is now used in many other industries, including medical equipment, toy, and furniture manufacturing.

Hull knew his invention would take some time to catch on, but little did he know that instead of waiting months for replacement parts from Earth, one day astronauts would bring along a 3D printer to fabricate the tools and materials they needed in space.

Questions for Critical Thinking

1. Although new technology is always exciting, it could also have some downsides. What do you think could be some of the negative effects of 3D printing technology?
2. What are some of the ways a 3D printer could serve the consumer market? When do you foresee the use of a 3D printer in your home?

Sources: Company website, www.3dsystems.com, accessed January 20, 2014; Pagan Kennedy, "Who Made That 3D Printer?" *The New York Times,* accessed January 20, 2014, www.nytimes.com; "How NASA Will Use 3D Printers in Space," www.space.com, accessed January 20, 2014; Travis Hessman, "Take 5: Q&A with Chuck Hull, Co-Founder, 3D Systems," *Industry Week,* accessed January 20, 2014, www.industryweek.com.

---

their competitive advantages. Another form of intrapreneurship is a **skunkworks**, a project initiated by an employee who conceives an idea, convinces top management of its potential, and then recruits human and other resources from within the company to turn that idea into a commercial project.

Many companies encourage intrapreneurship—30 percent of large firms now allocate funds toward intrapreneurship.[44] 3M is a firm that has long been known for its innovative products. Ranging from Post-It Notes and Scotch Tape to Nutri-Dog Chews and Thinsulate insulation, there are more than 55,000 3M products either on store shelves or embedded in other firms' goods.[45] Sometimes a good idea takes a long time to turn into a successful innovation. See the "Hit & Miss" feature for the story.

Coming up with the ideas for these products, developing them, and testing them before bringing them to market takes time and resources. Former 3M CEO George Buckley believes that the only way to do this is to allocate both time and money in support of intrapraneurship. 3M, along with Apple, Google, Facebook, and LinkedIn allow its researchers to devote 15 to 20 percent of their time to pursue their own ideas. A group of five employees at MRY, a global branding and technology company, became tired of long coffee lines at the company's in-house café. They released an app that allows staff to order beverages on their mobile devices and be notified when the beverages are ready.[46]

What's Ahead

In upcoming chapters, we look at other trends that are reshaping the business world of the 21st century. For example, in the next part of *Contemporary Business* we explore the critical issues of how companies organize, lead, and manage their work processes; manage and motivate their employees; empower their employees through teamwork and enhanced communication; handle labor and workplace disputes; and create and produce world-class goods and services.

skunkworks
project initiated by an employee who conceives an idea, convinces top management of its potential, and then recruits human and other resources from within the company to turn the idea into a commercial project.

Assessment Check ☑

1. Why do large, established companies support intrapreneurship?
2. What is a skunkworks?

Chapter 6 *Starting Your Own Business: The Entrepreneurship Alternative*

179

Chapter in Review

■ Summary of Learning Objectives

⌐1⌐ Define *entrepreneur*.

Unlike some small-business owners, entrepreneurs are risk takers who run their business with a major goal of expansion and growth. They are visionaries who seek profitable opportunities and take the initiative to gather the resources they need to start their businesses quickly.

Assessment Check Answers ✓

1.1 How do entrepreneurs create new businesses? Entrepreneurs combine their ideas and drive with money, employees, and other resources to create a business that fills a market need.

1.2 How do entrepreneurs differ from managers? Managers are employees who direct the efforts of others to achieve an organization's goals. The drive and impatience that entrepreneurs have to make their companies successful may hurt their ability to manage.

⌐2⌐ Identify the different categories of entrepreneurs.

A classic entrepreneur identifies a business opportunity and allocates available resources to tap that market. A serial entrepreneur starts one business, runs it, and then starts and runs additional businesses in succession. A social entrepreneur uses business principles to solve social problems.

Assessment Check Answers ✓

2.1 What is the difference between a classic entrepreneur and a serial entrepreneur? A classic entrepreneur identifies a business opportunity and allocates available resources to tap that market. A serial entrepreneur starts one business, runs it, and then starts and runs additional businesses in succession.

2.2 Describe a social entrepreneur. A social entrepreneur recognizes a societal problem and uses business principles to develop innovative solutions.

⌐3⌐ Explain why people choose entrepreneurship as a career path.

There are many reasons people choose to become entrepreneurs. Some reasons are desire to be one's own boss, desire to achieve financial success, desire for job security, and desire to improve one's quality of life.

Assessment Check Answers ✓

3.1 What are the four main reasons people choose to become entrepreneurs? People generally choose to become entrepreneurs because they want to be their own boss, they believe they will achieve greater financial success, they believe they have more control over job security, and they want to enhance their quality of life.

3.2 What is a lifestyle entrepreneur? A lifestyle entrepreneur is a person who starts a business to gain flexibility in work hours and control over his or her own life.

⌐4⌐ Discuss the environment for entrepreneurs.

A favorable public perception, availability of financing, the falling cost and widespread availability of information technology, globalization, entrepreneurship education, and changing demographic and economic trends all contribute to a fertile environment for people to start new ventures.

Assessment Check Answers ✓

4.1 What opportunities does globalization create for today's entrepreneurs? The rapid globalization of business has created many opportunities for entrepreneurs. They market their products abroad and hire international workers. Among the fastest-growing small U.S. companies, almost two of every five have international sales.

4.2 Identify the educational factors that help expand current opportunities for entrepreneurs. Many U.S. universities offer majors in entrepreneurship, dozens of others offer an entrepreneurship emphasis, and hundreds more offer courses in how to start a business. Also, organizations such as the Kauffman Center for Entrepreneurial Leadership and Students in Free Enterprise encourage and teach entrepreneurship.

4.3 Describe current demographic trends that present opportunities for entrepreneurial businesses. The aging of the U.S. population, increasingly diverse ethnic groups, and the predominance of two-income families are creating opportunities for entrepreneurs to market new goods and services.

⌐5⌐ Identify the characteristics of entrepreneurs.

Successful entrepreneurs share several typical traits, including vision, high energy levels, the need to achieve, self-confidence and optimism, tolerance for failure, creativity, tolerance for ambiguity, and an internal locus of control.

Assessment Check Answers ✓

5.1 What is meant by an entrepreneur's vision? Entrepreneurs begin with a vision, which is an overall idea for how to make their business idea a success, and then passionately pursue it.

5.2 Why is it important for an entrepreneur to have a high energy level and a strong need for achievement? Because start-up companies typically have a small staff and struggle to raise enough capital, the entrepreneur has to make up the difference by working long hours. A strong need for achievement helps entrepreneurs enjoy the challenge of reaching difficult goals and promotes dedication to personal success.

5.3 How do entrepreneurs generally feel about the possibility of failure? They view failure as a learning experience and are not easily discouraged or disappointed when things don't go as planned.

⌐6⌐ Summarize the process of starting a new venture.
Entrepreneurs must select an idea for their business, develop a business plan, and obtain financing.

Assessment Check Answers ✔

6.1 What are the two most important considerations in choosing an idea for a new business? Two important considerations are finding something you love to do and are good at doing and determining whether your idea can satisfy a need in the marketplace.

6.2 What is seed capital? Seed capital is the money that is used to start a company.

6.3 What is the difference between debt financing and equity financing? Debt financing is money borrowed that must be repaid. Equity financing is an exchange of ownership shares in a company for money supplied by one or more investors.

⌐7⌐ Explain intrapreneurship.
Intrapreneurship is the process of promoting innovation within the structure of an established company.

Assessment Check Answers ✔

7.1 Why do large, established companies support intrapreneurship? Large firms support intrapreneurship to retain an entrepreneurial spirit and to promote innovation.

7.2 What is a skunkworks? A skunkworks project is initiated by an employee who conceives an idea and then recruits resources from within the company to turn that idea into a commercial product.

■ Business Terms You Need to Know

entrepreneur 162
classic entrepreneur 163
serial entrepreneur 163
social entrepreneur 163

lifestyle entrepreneur 166
seed capital 176
debt financing 176
equity financing 177

venture capitalists 178
angel investors 178
intrapreneurship 178
skunkworks 179

■ Review Questions

1. Identify the three categories of entrepreneurs. How are they different from each other? How might an entrepreneur fall into more than one category?

2. People often become entrepreneurs because they want to be their own boss and be in control of most or all of the major decisions related to their business. How might this relate to potential financial success? If there are downsides, what might they be?

3. How have globalization and information technology created new opportunities for entrepreneurs? Describe current demographic trends that suggest new goods and services for entrepreneurial businesses.

4. Identify the eight characteristics that are attributed to successful entrepreneurs. Which trait or traits do you believe are the most important for success? Why? Are there any traits that you think might actually contribute to potential failure? If so, which ones—and why?

5. When selecting a business idea, why is the advice to "do what makes you happy" and "be true to yourself" so important?

6. Suppose an entrepreneur is considering buying an existing business or franchise. Which of the eight entrepreneurial traits do you think would most apply to this person, and why?

7. Imagine that you and a partner are planning to launch a business that sells backpacks, briefcases, and soft luggage made out of recycled materials. You'll need seed capital for your venture. Outline how you would use that seed capital.

8. Describe the two main types of financing that entrepreneurs may seek for their businesses. What are the risks and benefits involved with each?

9. What is an enterprise zone? Describe what types of businesses might benefit from opening in such a zone—and how their success might be interconnected.

10. What is intrapreneurship? How does it differ from entrepreneurship?

■ Projects and Teamwork Applications

1. You got the entrepreneurial bug after taking an entrepreneurship class. You are at the point of deciding whether to leave college to launch a business. After all, some famous entrepreneurs—for example, Mark Zuckerberg of Facebook and Steve Jobs of Apple—were college dropouts. What are the arguments for and against leaving school to launch your new business venture? Form two teams to debate this issue.

2. Certain demographic trends can represent opportunities for entrepreneurs—the aging of the U.S. population, the increasing diversity of the U.S. population, the growth in population of some states, and the predominance of two-income families, to name a few. On your own or with a classmate, choose a demographic trend and brainstorm for business ideas that could capitalize on the trend. Present your idea—and its relationship to the trend—to your class.

3. Are entrepreneurs born? Or are they made? Evaluate yourself on the basis of the eight characteristics of successful entrepreneurs outlined in the chapter. Share your self-assessment with a classmate.

4. Many entrepreneurs turn a hobby or area of interest into a business idea. Others get their ideas from situations or daily problems for which they believe they have a solution—or a better solution than those already offered. Think about an area of personal interest—or a problem you think you could solve with a new good or service—and create the first part of a potential business plan, the introduction to your new company and its offerings. Then outline briefly the kind of financing you think would work best for your business and the steps you would take to secure the funds.

5. You've recently graduated, and you're trying to decide whether to take a job at a large company or start your own company. Form two teams to evaluate, compare, and contrast the risk of entrepreneurship and business ownership versus working for a large company. Outline and debate the risks and rewards of each.

Web Assignments

1. **Using data to make decisions.** You're starting a new venture, and to make an informed decision, you'd like to begin with a few surveys to determine if your idea fills a need. A friend has told you about SurveyMonkey, a website that allows users to create and send their own web-based surveys. Go to www .surveymonkey.com and evaluate how you as an entrepreneur would use the service to connect with your customers. How would the business you would like to create use the survey site? What types of questions would you ask and to whom?

2. **Venture capitalists.** Venture capital firms are an important source of financing for entrepreneurs. Most actively solicit funding proposals from entrepreneurs. Go to the website of the National Venture Capital Association (www.nvca.org) to learn more about venture capital. What are some of the famous businesses that were originally financed by venture capitalists?

3. **Getting started.** Each year, *Fast Company* magazine publishes its "50 Most Innovative Companies" issue. Visit the company's website (www.fastcompany.com) and search for "50 Most Innovative Companies." Choose one of the companies and discuss the steps involved from business idea to market launch. Go to the company's website to determine how the company is doing today.

Note: Internet web addresses change frequently. If you don't find the exact sites listed, you may need to access the organization's home page and search from there or use a search engine such as Google or Bing.

CASE 6.1 | **Glassybaby Sees the Light**

When cancer patient Lee Rhodes was unexpectedly soothed by reflective light of a simple candle, a business was born. Today, Glassybaby produces hand-blown votive candles that require four glassblowers, three layers of glass, and a 24-hour process to make. Coming in 450 colors, with names like Wet Dog and Begin Again, they sell for $44 each, and sales are expected to top $8 million at four retail storefronts.

As integral to Glassybaby as its Seattle glass-blowing studios, which are open to customers, is its commitment to donate 10 percent of revenues to help cancer patients cover noninsured expenses. Rhodes has given more than $1.5 million to charitable organizations dedicated to healing.

Despite suggestions to expand her product line, Rhodes, who is now healthy, is keeping the business simple.

"There's something to be said for sticking to what you're good at," she says. "We make one thing really, really well."

Recently, Rhodes opened a store in San Francisco, increasing the total number of retail outlets to four. While many told Rhodes that she would never succeed selling a single American-made product, she refused to believe she could not. In fact, a few years ago, Amazon's Jeff Bezos contacted her to become a silent investor. Today, Bezos owns 22 percent of Glassybaby and fully supports its product and mission.

Questions for Critical Thinking

1. Rhodes says she wasn't intending to start a business. Which qualities of a successful entrepreneur does Rhodes probably have?

2. If you were an entrepreneur like Rhodes, would you expand Glassybaby's product line? Why or why not?

Sources: Company website, www.glassybaby.com, accessed January 18, 2014; Sophia Markoulakis, "Glassybaby's Lee Rhodes Lights the Way in SF," *San Francisco Chronicle*, accessed January 18, 2014, www.sfgate.com; Carolyn Horowitz, "Meet the Entrepreneur of 2011 Award Winners," *Entrepreneur*, accessed January 18, 2014, www.entrepreneur.com; Gwen Moran, "From Cancer Patient to Successful Beacon of Hope," *Second Act.com*, www.secondact.com, accessed January 18, 2014, www.secondact.com; Blythe Lawrence, "Glassybaby Founder Lee Rhodes Was Inspired by Adversity," *The Seattle Times*, accessed January 18, 2014, http://seattletimes.nwsource.com; Julie Weed, "Seattle Firm Struggles in the Biggest Market," *The New York Times*, accessed January 18, 2014, www.nytimes.com.

Unreal Brands "Unjunks" Candy

On Halloween a few years ago, 13-year-old Nicky Bronner's dad Michael confiscated his candy for being too unhealthy. Irate, young Bronner researched how to "unjunk" the same type of candy found in his Halloween loot. Most large candy manufacturers, he learned, use corn syrup, hydrogenated fats, GMOs, preservatives, and artificial colors and flavors to make the candy. This makes it less expensive to manufacture the candy and extends its shelf life. With loads of experimentation and testing, and help from food scientists and a trained chef, Unreal was born.

Today, Unreal Brands produces healthier products that compete with well-known candies like M&Ms, peanut M&Ms, Snickers, Milky Way, and Reese's peanut butter cups. The company has received venture funding from a few well-known firms and from his dad, the founder of Digitas, a successful global marketing and technology agency. With 23 percent fewer calories, 45 percent less sugar, and 13 percent less fat, Unreal candy is made with responsibly sourced natural ingredients. The candy contains almost double the amount of protein and fiber than its well-known counterparts. Unreal uses cacao, real caramel, cane sugar, and organic blue agave—and no corn syrup, hydrogenated oils, artificial flavors, or GMOs.

Unreal's products are sold through retailers like Walgreens, Target, Kroger, and CVS. "The reason this company exists is to be a catalyst for change," Bronner says. Part of his motivation is to get big candy manufacturers to take notice and to follow suit by getting the junk out. What's next for Unreal? The company's next plan is to "unjunk" snack foods, breakfast cereal, and sweetened beverages.

Questions for Critical Thinking

1. Even though Unreal's products have fewer calories and healthier ingredients, they are more expensive than other candy products. Do you think the novelty of eating healthier candy will wear off as consumers pay more for the product? Why or why not?

2. What other products can you think of with a mission similar to that of Unreal Brands? Would you make it a priority to purchase products from a mission-driven company? Why or why not?

Sources: Company website, http://getunreal.com, accessed January 20, 2014; Megan Rose Dickey, "The Story of a Boy Whose Temper Tantrum Led to a Venture-Backed Food Startup," *Business Insider*, accessed January 20, 2014, www.businessinsider.com; Brad Stone, "Venture Capital Sees Promise in Lab-Created Eco-Foods," *Bloomberg Businessweek*, accessed January 20, 2014, www.businessweek.com.

Comet Skateboards: It's a Smooth Ride

Jason Salfi loves skateboarding. This is how many small businesses begin. The founder has a passion for something—whether it's cooking or surfing or creating video games—and wants to turn it into a business. In Salfi's case, it's skateboarding. The company, now in business for more than 15 years, is Comet Skateboards. After Salfi graduated from college, he lived on a boat off the coast of California for a while and partnered with a friend,

tinkering around with skateboards, which the pair sold to other skateboard fans among their circle of friends. Salfi desired something more. He wanted to find a better way to manufacture skateboards as well as the means to support his newly started family. "Back then, skateboards were made with seven layers of maple and sprayed with a lacquer based coating," he recalls. "Skateboards were accounting for 35 to 40 percent of the natural maple being harvested each year." Salfi loved skateboarding, but he didn't like the way boards were made. He believed that a skateboard could be built with more environmentally sustainable processes and materials. "I wanted to start a company that would make an impression on people and build an awareness around the use of natural resources," Salfi says.

Not long after he established Comet Skateboards, Salfi moved his company and his family back east to Ithaca, New York, where he partnered with e2e Materials, another small start-up. The firm specializes in regionally sourced bio-composite materials; they manufacture their own soy-based resin and bio-composites that Salfi describes as "incredibly strong *and* biodegradable." The formula was exactly what Salfi was looking for. He set up shop and hired several employees, including Bob Rossi, who is head of web development for Comet as well as president of the Green Resource Hub, an organization that focuses on finding ways for businesses to practice sustainability.

Rossi is impressed with Salfi's total commitment to finding the best way to manufacture his products, even if it means moving cross country. "To move your business into the opportunity, to create a greener product, that is pretty impressive to me," observes Rossi. "There's a lot of green-washing out there," says Rossi. He knows the difference. Comet goes much farther than simply purchasing e2e's materials; the firm has adopted a closed-loop manufacturing process, which means that it reduces or eliminates waste by examining the life cycle of all the materials used in its manufacturing process.

It might seem as if Salfi and Rossi aren't cut from the same cloth as the previous generation of skateboarders—they're busy doing good things for the environment and for their community instead of rolling along the fringes of society like the bad boys of original skateboarding. But Salfi remains true to his skateboarding heritage. (Rossi admits to being new to the sport.) Comet boards have names such as The Voodoo Doll and Shred City, and are built for specialists who prefer downhill or free riding. Riders are invited to contribute ideas for the shapes, graphics, and names of new boards. Comet, which has found a way to actually increase profit potential by using green materials, receives kudos from business bloggers as well as diehard boarding bloggers. It appears that Salfi has found a way to blend doing good with doing good business—in a sport that was once considered far out of the mainstream.

Salfi hopes that Comet Skateboards will ultimately serve as an example of a small business that can make a big difference—while making products that provide fun. "We look at everything we do through the lens of how we can create a model that people can replicate in the future," he says. Salfi observes proudly that although Comet has only been in Ithaca for a few years, so far the company has a 100 percent retention rate of employees. He wants Comet to be a company that is known for its positive working environment, a place where people can develop long-term careers.

"We know that in the grand scheme of things, we're a small company, but through the many means of getting the message out—the Internet, video, music, and photography—we can actually have a broad footprint and make the idea of sustainability and social justice appealing to a broader market," predicts Salfi. While the bottom line—turning a profit—is vital to Comet's survival and growth, Salfi believes that this new way of doing business is more important in the long run. "We like to think we're creating a blueprint for the kind of company that will be around for 100 or 200 years," he muses. Then the skateboarder emerges. With a grin Salfi adds, "At the end of the day we're making skateboards, and we don't want to bum anybody out."

Questions for Critical Thinking

1. In which category (or categories) would you place Jason Salfi as an entrepreneur? Why? Give examples.
2. Salfi notes that the use of information technology—part of the environment for entrepreneurs—can help Comet Skateboards reach a broader audience. Can you identify any demographic and economic trends that might provide opportunities for Comet Skateboard's growth as a business?
3. Which of the traditional characteristics of entrepreneurs do you believe best describe Jason Salfi? Why?
4. As Comet Skateboards reaches the next level of growth, where might the firm have the best chance of obtaining further financing? Why?

Sources: Company website, www.cometskateboards.com, accessed January 21, 2014; Video: Liam Morgan's Air-Frame Deck: Comet Skateboards, *Wheelbase Magazine*, accessed January 21, 2014, www.wheelbasemag.com; organization website, "Comet Skateboards," www.bcorporation.net, accessed January 21, 2014; Nadia Hosni, "Triple Bottom Line: Comet Skateboards," *Tonic*, accessed January 21, 2014, www.tonic.com.

GREENSBURG, KS
A Great Place to Start

Ashley Petty started taking massage therapy classes while studying for her business degree. After graduating, she worked for several years as a massage therapist, until the spa where she worked closed. Petty was job hunting when the tornado hit her hometown of Greensburg, Kansas. Watching volunteers, residents, and relief workers exhaust themselves cleaning up the devastated town, she saw an opportunity. She would return home to start her own spa in Greensburg.

It was definitely a risky venture—the last thing she would have expected to find in Greensburg before the storm. Armed with a business plan she had written in college, Petty drove to town hall and applied for one of the temporary trailers that were brought in to house displaced businesses. She got her trailer—a 1970s singlewide, complete with imitation wood paneling, stinky carpet, and a leaky roof. Not exactly the lux spa she had envisioned in her business plan, but a good enough start. With a fresh coat of paint, some scented candles, and new drapes, she opened Elements Therapeutic Massage and Day Spa.

Petty had expected that her spa would be a hard sell. The storm had destroyed the town's communications, so traditional advertising was out. To build a client base, Petty turned to word of mouth. She went to town meetings, talked to old friends, met with volunteers from all over the country. Still, months went by and she still had barely enough clients to pay her expenses.

Winter hit. It was cold, the ancient furnace ran constantly, drafts blew in the new curtains, and rain soaked the freshly steamed carpet. Elements was the last place anyone would want to go to escape the stress of rebuilding—even Petty couldn't stand to be there. Under normal circumstances, she would have considered more extensive capital improvements, but the trailer was only temporary and she was out of money.

At one town meeting, green architecture firm BNIM presented a plan for the new Downtown Greensburg, including a business incubator to sustain old businesses and promote new ones. Traditionally, a business incubator is reserved for start-ups, but in Greensburg, once-successful businesses needed help getting back on their feet. The incubator would be housed in a totally energy-efficient retail/office building with space for approximately 10 new businesses. The rent would be reasonable, and the utility costs next to nothing. Petty jumped at the chance to apply for a place in the building.

Questions

After viewing the video, answer the following questions:

1. What major challenges does Ashley Petty face in starting her business?

2. How will Greensburg's business incubator stimulate economic development?

3. What are some of the challenges Greensburg faces in recruiting new businesses? What incentives would you offer to encourage new business development there?

4. Would you start a new business in Greensburg? Why or why not?

LAUNCHING YOUR
[Entrepreneurial Career]

In Part 2, "Starting and Growing Your Business," you learned about the many ways that business owners have achieved their dreams of owning their own company and being their own boss. The part's two chapters introduced you to the wide variety of entrepreneurial or small businesses; the forms they can take—sole proprietorship, partnership, or corporation—and the reasons that some new ventures succeed and others fail. You learned that entrepreneurs are visionaries who build firms that create wealth and that they share traits such as vision and creativity, high energy, optimism, a strong need to achieve, and a tolerance for failure. By now you might be wondering how you can make all this information work for you. Here are some career ideas and opportunities in the small-business and e-business areas.

First, whatever field attracts you as a future business owner, try to acquire experience by working for someone else in the industry initially. The information and skills you pick up will be invaluable when you start out on your own. Lack of experience is often cited as a leading reason for small-business failure.[1]

Next, look for a good fit between your own skills, abilities, and characteristics and a market need or niche. For instance, the U.S. Department of Labor reports that opportunities in many health care fields are rising with the nation's increased demand for health services.[2] As the population

of older people rises, and as young families find themselves increasingly pressed for time, the need for childcare and elder services will also increase—and so will the opportunities for new businesses in those areas. So keep your eyes on trends to find ideas that you can use or adapt.

Another way to look for market needs is to talk to current customers or business associates. When the owner of Michigan-based Moon Valley Rustic Furniture wanted to retire, he went to see Rick Detkowski, who was in the real estate business. The owner intended to offer the buildings to Detkowski and close the business down. But the real estate agent, who owned several pieces of Moon Valley furniture himself, instead decided to buy, not just the buildings, but the furniture business, too. Before the sale was completed—and to determine whether he could run Moon Valley profitably—Detkowski talked with existing customers and furniture dealers, who had been hoping for years that the company would expand its line of sturdy cedar and pine items from the traditional summer lawn furniture into more innovative designs. Further research showed that the general environmental trend among consumers was boosting demand for rustic furniture. So Detkowski took the plunge and is now in the furniture manufacturing business. He has expanded the company's product lines and reorganized the factory floor for more efficiency—and cost savings.[3]

Are you intrigued by the idea of being your own boss but worried about risking your savings to get a completely new and untried business off the ground? Then owning a franchise, such as SUBWAY or Dunkin' Donuts, might be for you. The Small Business Administration advises aspiring entrepreneurs that while franchising can be less risky than starting a new business from scratch, it still requires hard work and sacrifice. In addition, you need to completely understand both the resources to which you will be entitled and the responsibilities you will assume under the franchise agreement. Again, filling a market need is important for success. To find more information about franchising, access the Federal Trade Commission's consumer guide to buying a franchise at http://www.ftc .gov/bcp/edu/pubs/consumer/invest/ inv05.shtm.

Are you skilled in a particular area of business, technology, or science? The consulting industry will be a rapidly growing area for several years, according to the Bureau of Labor Statistics.[4] Consulting firms offer their expertise to clients in private, government, not-for-profit, and even foreign business operations. Business consultants influence clients' decisions in marketing, finance, manufacturing, information systems, e-business, human resources, and many other areas including corporate strategy and organization. Technology consultants support businesses in all fields, with services ranging from setting up a secure website or training employees in the use of new software to managing an off-site help desk or planning for disaster recovery. Science consulting firms find plenty of work in the field of environmental consulting, helping businesses deal with pollution clean up and control, habitat protection, and compliance with government's environmental regulations and standards.

But perhaps none of these areas appeals to you quite so much as tinkering with gears and machinery or with computer graphics and code. If you think you have the insight and creativity to invent something completely new, you need to make sure you're informed about patents, trademarks, and copyright laws to protect your ideas. Each area offers different protections for your work, and none will guarantee success. Here again, hard work, persistence, and a little bit of luck will help you succeed.

Career Assessment Exercises in Entrepreneurship and Business Ownership

1. Find out whether you have what it takes to be an entrepreneur. Review the material on the SBA's website, http://www .sba.gov/smallbusinessplanner/index .html or take the *Crain's Chicago Business* Entrepreneurial Test at http://www.chicagobusiness .com/article/20130928/ISSUE02/ 130829939/do-you-have-the-mind -of-an-entrepreneur#. After you've finished, use the guides to determine how ready you are to strike out on your own. What did your results disclose? What can you do to increase your chance of success?

2. Find an independent business or franchise in your area, and make an appointment to talk to the owner about his or her start-up

experience. Prepare a list of questions for a 10- to 15-minute interview, and remember to ask about details such as the number of hours worked per week, approximate start-up costs, goals of the business, available resources, lessons learned since opening, and rewards of owning the business. How different are the owner's answers from what you expected?

3. Search online for information about how to file for a patent, trademark, or copyright. A good starting point is http://www.uspto .gov. Assume you have an invention you want to protect. Find out which forms are required; the necessary fees; how much time is typically needed to complete the legal steps; and what rights and protections you may gain.

Part 3 | Management: Empowering People to Achieve Business Success

Chapter 7

Learning Objectives

[1] Define *management*.

[2] Explain the role of setting a vision and ethical standards for the firm.

[3] Summarize the importance of planning.

[4] Describe the strategic planning process.

[5] Discuss managers as decision makers.

[6] Evaluate managers as leaders.

[7] Discuss corporate culture.

[8] Identify organizational structures.

Management, Leadership, and the Internal Organization

© mediaphotos/iStockphoto

Quicken Loans Is a Great Place to Work

Detroit-based Quicken Loans is a great place to work, according to an annual list compiled by *Fortune Magazine*. The online mortgage lender has consistently made an appearance in the top 30 companies, thanks to a strong commitment to its employees and its community.

Dan Gilbert, Quicken Loans's founder and chairman, grew up in Detroit and is working to bring this area back from bankruptcy and to restore portions of the city to become a good place to live and work. And the employees support his efforts. Gilbert has moved the company headquarters to downtown Detroit from a suburban location—with the support of the more than 700 employees who work at the corporate offices.

As part of the corporate move, Quicken Loans partnered with local businesses to offer incentives to employees willing to move to the city, including $20,000 in forgivable home loans. Some of the other employee benefits offered by Quicken Loans include onsite child care and fitness centers, health care coverage, a compressed workweek, and telecommuting.

Gilbert and his management team also believe in having fun while working. During college basketball's annual tournament, Nerf basketballs appear and school pennants are draped over office cubicles. During spring break week, the preferred office wardrobe includes shorts, hats, and sandals. And Gilbert, always a prankster, brought in dozens of farm animals to decorate the office of a colleague who was celebrating a big birthday.

Bill Emerson, the company's CEO, is proud of Quicken Loans's spot on the "Best Companies to Work For" list and credits employees for the company's recognition. "It's incredible to see what's possible when you hire great people, empower them, and set them loose to innovate and create," he says. The employees share his pride—more than 98 percent of the employees surveyed for the *Fortune* poll said they feel good about how the company gives back to the community and provides them with the opportunity to have fun while working.[1]

Overview

When asked about their professional objectives, some students say, "I want to be a manager." You may think that the role of a manager is basically being the boss. But in today's business environment, companies are looking for much more than bosses. They want managers who understand technology, can adapt quickly to change, can skillfully motivate employees, and realize the importance of satisfying customers. Managers who can master those skills will continue to be in great demand because their commitment strongly affects their firms' performance. And Dan Gilbert's management approach at Quicken Loans ensures the continued growth of the company in the competitive mortgage-lending business.

This chapter begins by examining how successful organizations use management to turn visions into reality. It describes the levels of management, the skills that managers need, and the functions that managers perform. The chapter explains how the first of these functions, planning, helps managers meet the challenges of a rapidly changing business environment and develop strategies that guide a company's future. Other sections of the chapter explore the types of decisions that managers make, the role of managers as leaders, and the importance of corporate culture. The chapter concludes by examining the second function of management—organizing.

What Is Management?

management process of achieving organizational objectives through people and other resources.

Management is the process of achieving organizational objectives through people and other resources. The manager's job is to combine human and technical resources in the best way possible to achieve the company's goals.

Management principles and concepts apply to not-for-profit organizations as well as profit-seeking firms. A city mayor, the executive director of Goodwill Industries International, and a superintendent of schools all perform the managerial functions described later in this chapter. Management happens at many levels, from that of the manager of a family-owned restaurant to a national sales manager for a major manufacturer.

The Management Hierarchy

Your local supermarket works through a fairly simple organization that consists of a store manager, several assistant or department managers, and employees who may range from baggers to cashiers to stock clerks. However, if your supermarket is part of a regional or national chain, there will be corporate managers above the store manager. The Stop & Shop Supermarket Company has more than 400 supermarkets located from New Hampshire to New Jersey. It is headquartered in Massachusetts. Within each store there are managers for everything from the meat department to human resources. But at Stop & Shop headquarters, you'll find top-level managers for such functions as finance, customer service, real estate, information technology, sales and operations, and pharmacy among others.[2]

All of these people are managers because they combine human and other resources to achieve company objectives. Their jobs differ, however, because they work at different levels of the organization.

A firm's management usually has three levels: top, middle, and supervisory. These levels of management form a management hierarchy, as shown in Figure 7.1. The hierarchy is the traditional structure found in most organizations. Managers at each level perform different activities.

The highest level of management is *top management*. Top managers include such positions as chief executive officer (CEO), chief financial officer (CFO), and executive vice president. Top managers devote most of their time to developing long-range plans for their organizations. They make decisions such as whether to introduce new products, purchase other companies, or enter new geographical markets. Top managers set a direction for their organization and inspire the company's executives and employees to achieve their vision for the company's future.

The job is intense and demanding. Many top managers must lead their companies through challenging economic times, a quality crisis, and the like. Sometimes this involves selling a positive outlook to investors, stockholders, and managers during a weak economy. John Idol, CEO of Michael Kors, turned a once-struggling fashion company into a profitable retailer with stores worldwide. Idol, a veteran in the fashion industry, is also known as an executive with both marketing and management skills who restored the company's sales and profitability. When Idol repositioned the Michael Kors brand, it attracted international attention as a classic, American lifestyle company.[3]

Middle management, the second tier in the management hierarchy, includes positions such as general managers, plant managers, division managers, and unit managers. Middle managers' attention focuses on specific operations, products, or customer groups within an organization. They are responsible for developing detailed plans and procedures to implement

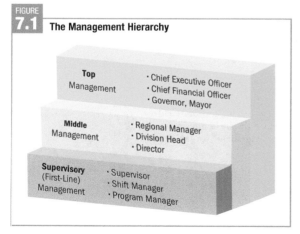

FIGURE 7.1 The Management Hierarchy

- **Top Management**
  - Chief Executive Officer
  - Chief Financial Officer
  - Governor, Mayor
- **Middle Management**
  - Regional Manager
  - Division Head
  - Director
- **Supervisory (First-Line) Management**
  - Supervisor
  - Shift Manager
  - Program Manager

190 Part 3 *Management: Empowering People to Achieve Business Success*

the firm's strategic plans. If top management decided to broaden the distribution of a product, a sales manager would be responsible for determining the number of sales personnel required. Middle managers are responsible for targeting the products and customers who are the source of the sales and profit growth expected by their CEOs. To achieve these goals, middle managers might budget money for product development, identify new uses for existing products, and improve the ways they train and motivate salespeople. Because they are more familiar with day-to-day operations than CEOs, middle managers often come up with new ways to increase sales or solve company problems.

Supervisory management, or first-line management, includes positions such as supervisor, section chief, and team leader. These managers are directly responsible for assigning nonmanagerial employees to specific jobs and evaluating their performance. Managers at this first level of the hierarchy work directly with the employees who produce and sell the firm's goods and services. They are responsible for implementing middle managers' plans by motivating workers to accomplish daily, weekly, and monthly goals. A recent survey by the marketing research firm Temkin Group rated customer service at U.S. companies. All of the top-ranked firms have first-line managers who implement the firms' strategies to provide superior customer service. Trader Joe's, Dollar Tree, Sonic Drive-Ins, and Costco all have in common first-line managers who see that customer service is a top priority among its employees.[4]

Dollar Tree Stores ranks in the top tier of the Temkin Group's annual list of companies providing top-notch customer service. First-line managers make sure that customer service is a priority for all employees.

Skills Needed for Managerial Success

Managers at every level in the management hierarchy must exercise three basic types of skills: technical, human, and conceptual. All managers must acquire these skills in varying proportions, although the importance of each skill changes at different management levels.

Technical skills are the manager's ability to understand and use the techniques, knowledge, tools, and equipment of a specific discipline or department. Technical skills are especially important for first-line managers and become less important at higher levels of the management hierarchy. But most top executives started out as technical experts. The résumé of a vice president for information systems probably lists experience as a computer analyst and that of a vice president for marketing usually shows a background in sales. Many firms, including Procter & Gamble and Marriott International, have increased training programs for first-line managers to boost technical skills and worker productivity. Cold Stone Creamery, which operates franchises for its premium ice-cream stores nationwide, carefully trains managers and crew members in the art of preparing its specialty ice cream for hungry customers. "We don't interview potential crew members, we audition them," says the company.[5]

Human skills are interpersonal skills that enable managers to work effectively with and through people. Human skills include the ability to communicate with, motivate, and lead employees to complete assigned activities. Managers need human skills to interact with people both inside and outside the organization. It would be tough for a manager to succeed without such skills, even though they must be adapted to different forms—for instance, mastering and communicating effectively with staff through e-mail, smart phones, videoconferencing, and text messaging, all of which are widely used in today's offices. As you can imagine, it is important for managers of Cold Stone Creamery ice-cream stores to have excellent human skills not only with customers but also with employees.

Conceptual skills determine a manager's ability to see the organization as a unified whole and to understand how each part of the overall organization interacts with other

Chapter 7 *Management, Leadership, and the Internal Organization*   **191**

parts. These skills involve an ability to see the big picture by acquiring, analyzing, and interpreting information. Conceptual skills are especially important for top-level managers, who must develop long-range plans for the future direction of their organizations. At New York–based Pfizer, CEO Ian Read has implemented long-range plans for the pharmaceutical company that include narrowing the focus of its research programs to blockbuster new drugs. The company's recent successes include a drug to treat rheumatoid arthritis and one that thins the blood. In addition, Read has streamlined company operations in an effort to combat less-expensive generic drugs that have come to market as a result of the company's expiring patents.[6]

Managerial Functions

In the course of a typical day, managers spend time meeting and talking with people, reading, evaluating, analyzing, and communicating. As they perform all these activities, managers are carrying out four basic functions: planning, organizing, directing, and controlling. Planning activities lay the groundwork, and the other functions are aimed at carrying out the plans.

planning process of anticipating future events and conditions and determining courses of action for achieving organizational objectives.

Planning Planning is the process of anticipating future events and conditions and determining courses of actions for achieving organizational objectives. Effective planning helps a business focus its vision, avoid costly mistakes, and seize opportunities. Planning should be flexible and responsive to changes in the business environment, and should involve managers from all levels of the organization. As global competition intensifies, technology expands, and the speed at which firms bring new innovations to market increases. Thus, planning for the future becomes even more critical. For example, a CEO and other top-level managers need to plan for succession—those who will follow in their footsteps. Some CEOs resist this kind of planning, fearing that doing so might shorten their time at the helm of a company. But management experts encourage planning ahead for the next generation of management, in order to keep the company's position in the marketplace strong.[7]

Business mogul Warren Buffet is now in his 80s and showing few signs of slowing down. But it's clear that someone (or several people) must be in place to take the reins of his huge diversified company, Berkshire Hathaway, which has significant holdings in businesses ranging from Geico Insurance to Dairy Queen to Benjamin Moore Paints. Buffet tapped Todd Combs, who is half Buffet's age, as an investment manager and potential successor to manage Berkshire's nearly $100 billion investment portfolio in more than 40 companies. Although Buffet has no immediate plans to retire from Berkshire Hathaway, when he does, he has named his son Howard to become the company's chairman.[8]

organizing process of blending human and material resources through a formal structure of tasks and authority; arranging work, dividing tasks among employees, and coordinating them to ensure implementation of plans and accomplishment of objectives.

Organizing Once plans have been developed, the next step in the management process typically is organizing—the process of blending human and material resources through a formal structure of tasks and authority; arranging work, dividing tasks among employees, and coordinating them to ensure implementation of plans and accomplishment of objectives. Organizing involves classifying and dividing work into manageable units with a logical structure. Managers staff the organization with the best possible employees for each job. Sometimes the organizing function requires studying a company's existing structure and determining whether to restructure it in order to operate more efficiently, cost effectively, or sustainably.

directing guiding and motivating employees to accomplish organizational objectives.

Directing Once an organization has been established, managers focus on directing, or guiding and motivating employees to accomplish organizational objectives. Directing might include training (or retraining), setting up schedules, delegating certain tasks, and monitoring progress. To accomplish the objective of reducing the office electricity bill, an office manager might have incandescent light bulbs replaced by compact fluorescents,

192

ask employees to turn off the lights when they leave a room or use occupancy sensors, and direct the IT staff to program all the office computer screens to turn off after 10 or 15 minutes of inactivity.[9]

Often when managers take time to listen to their employees, the manager gains insight and the employee gets a motivational boost. Fashion designer Eileen Fisher says, "Share information and your own ideas. Be present. Be accessible. Listen."[10]

Controlling The controlling function evaluates an organization's performance against its objectives. Controlling assesses the success of the planning function and provides feedback for future rounds of planning.

The four basic steps in controlling are to establish performance standards, monitor actual performance, compare actual performance with established standards, and make corrections if necessary. Under the provisions of the Sarbanes-Oxley Act, for example, CEOs and CFOs must monitor the performance of the firm's accounting staff more closely than typically had been done in the past. They must personally attest to the truth of financial reports filed with the Securities and Exchange Commission.

2 Setting a Vision and Ethical Standards for the Firm

A business begins with a vision, its founder's perception of marketplace needs and the ways a firm can satisfy them. Vision serves as the target for a firm's actions, helping direct the company toward opportunities and differentiating it from its competitors. When Joe Fernandez had his jaw wired shut from surgery, the only way he could communicate was through online social networks like Facebook and Twitter. As a result of his experience, Fernandez created Klout, a website and mobile app that measures the overall influence of social media users according to their number of followers, the content they create, and their tweets and retweets. Fernandez recently sold Klout to Lithium Technologies.[11]

A company's vision must be focused and yet flexible enough to adapt to changes in the business environment. Also critical to a firm's long-term relationship with its customers, suppliers, and the general public are the ethical standards that top management sets. Sometimes ethical standards are set in compliance with industry or federal regulations, such as safety or quality standards. Sometimes new standards are set in response to a crisis. Some states and corporations have had a difficult time paying their pension obligations for employees in recent years. New standards have been put in place to improve accounting requirements and disclosures related to financial reporting of pensions. The state of Illinois recently passed pension reform legislation that will trim benefits to state retirees and increase state pension contributions.[12]

The ethical tone that a top management team establishes can reap monetary as well as nonmonetary rewards. Setting a high ethical standard does not merely discourage employees from doing wrong, but it motivates and inspires them to achieve goals they never thought possible. Such satisfaction creates a more productive, stable workforce—one that can create a long-term competitive advantage for the organization. In practice, ethical decisions are not always clear-cut, and managers must make difficult decisions. Sometimes a firm operates in a country where standards differ from those in the United States. In other situations, a manager might have to make an ethical decision that undermines profits or even causes people to lose their jobs. And while it's tempting to think that a large firm—by virtue of its size—will have a harder time adopting ethical practices than a small firm, consider the retail giant Gap, which recently earned recognition for its ethical standards. Named one of the World's Most Ethical Companies by the Ethisphere Institute, San Francisco-based Gap consistently demonstrates high standards in a number of areas.

controlling function of evaluating an organization's performance against its objectives.

Assessment Check ✔

1. What is management?
2. How do the jobs of top managers, middle managers, and supervisory managers differ?
3. What is the relationship between the manager's planning and controlling functions?

vision perception of marketplace needs and the ways a firm can satisfy them.

© FocusTechnology/Alamy

With his jaw wired shut after surgery, Joe Fernandez could only communicate through online social networks. As a result of this experience, he founded Klout, an online business that measures the overall influence of social media users.

Assessment Check ✓

1. What is meant by a vision for the firm?
2. Why is it important for a top executive to set high ethical standards?

Alex Brigham, executive director of the New York–based Ethisphere Institute, observes the connection between ethics and good business. He states a company's ethical environment "shows a clear understanding that operating under the highest standards for business behavior goes beyond goodwill and 'lip-service' and is linked to performance and profitability."[13]

Sometimes taking an ethical stand can actually cost a firm in lost revenues and other support. When Google announced a reversal of its original stance on censorship in China—essentially shutting down operations there and rerouting traffic to an uncensored site in Hong Kong—not only did the company lose business, it found itself standing eerily alone on the issue. Sometimes, however, firms' actions raise more ethical questions than they answer, as the example in the "Solving an Ethical Controversy" feature shows.

[3] Importance of Planning

Although some firms manage to launch without a clear strategic plan, they won't last long if they don't map out a future. Nintendo's senior management is rethinking the company's console strategy as gaming on smart phones continues to grow. With more free game offerings for mobile devices from other companies, Nintendo recently sold fewer Wii U game consoles than it originally estimated. The company is considering a new business structure amidst a fast-changing gaming market.[14]

Types of Planning

Planning can be categorized by scope and breadth. Some plans are very broad and long range, whereas others are short range and very narrow, affecting selected parts of the organization rather than the company as a whole. Planning can be divided into the following categories: strategic, tactical, operational, and contingency, with each step including more specific information than the last. From the mission statement (described in the next section) to objectives

Solving an Ethical Controversy

MF Global: Where Did Customers' Money Go?

MF Global Holdings, a brokerage firm and derivatives trader, began its slide toward bankruptcy in late 2011 when Wall Street ratings agencies lost confidence in its heavy purchases of risky European debt. When the dust cleared a few weeks later, some of the $6 billion the firm was supposed to manage for its clients was missing. About $5.3 billion has since been found, but despite Congressional hearings into what went wrong, some $1.2 billion in customers' money is still unaccounted for, and some fear it may never be recovered.

Should senior management be legally responsible for clients' money losses?

PRO

1. When management knowingly takes unwarranted risk—or breaks the law—executives should make good on resulting customer losses.

2. If managers deliberately profit from lack of oversight, they are culpable and should pay customers for losses.

CON

1. If customers are exposed to illegal risks, it is regulators, not managers, who aren't doing their jobs.

2. Customers who can't afford big losses shouldn't be in high-risk markets.

Summary

A federal bankruptcy judge recently approved a settlement that would return at least 93 percent of customers' investments, with the possibility of additional payouts from the company's general funds.

Sources: Nate Raymond, "Corzine Fails to Win Dismissal of MF Customers' Lawsuit," *Reuters,* accessed February 27, 2014, www.reuters.com; Ben Protess, "MF Global Customers Will Recover All They Lost," *The New York Times,* accessed January 25, 2014, http://dealbook.nytimes.com; "Judge Approves Payout to MF Global Customers," *The New York Times,* accessed January 25, 2014, www.nytimes.com; Tiffany Kary, "Corzine Appeals Ruling Allowing Full MF Global Repayment," *Bloomberg News,* accessed January 25, 2014, www.bloomberg.com; "Much of Missing MF Global Money Might Never Be Found, Officials Think," *Chicago Business,* accessed January 25, 2014, www.chicagobusiness.com; "Jon Corzine (MF Holdings)," *The New York Times,* accessed January 25, 2014, www.nytimes.com.

to specific plans, each phase must fit into a comprehensive planning framework. The framework also must include narrow, functional plans aimed at individual employees and work areas relevant to individual tasks. These plans must fit within the firm's overall planning framework and help it reach objectives and achieve its mission.

Strategic Planning The most far-reaching level of planning is *strategic planning*—the process of determining the primary objectives of an organization and then acting and allocating resources to achieve those objectives. Generally, strategic planning is undertaken by top executives in a company. As customers use multiple channels for retail shopping, Home Depot has implemented a strategy called "interconnected retailing." The company wants to create a seamless experience for customers—whether they browse online, open promotional e-mails on their smart phones, or visit brick-and-mortar locations in person.[15]

Tactical Planning *Tactical planning* involves implementing the activities specified by strategic plans. Tactical plans guide the current and near-term activities required to implement overall strategies. As part of Home Depot's strategy to create a multi-channel customer shopping experience, the company has recently introduced an optimized mobile redesign, which integrates location-based technology in smart phones. The technology allows promotions to

215

As part of its strategic planning, Home Depot has introduced mobile apps with location-based technology that provides shoppers with real-time inventory, pricing, and information about where to find products in a specific store.

be sent to in-store shoppers while giving them access to real-time inventory, location, and pricing by store. How-to videos are offered for mobile shoppers doing research on products. The tactical plan keeps customers in contact with the retailer across multiple points of the shopping process.[16]

Operational Planning *Operational planning* creates the detailed standards that guide implementation of tactical plans. This activity involves choosing specific work targets and assigning employees and teams to carry out plans. Unlike strategic planning, which focuses on the organization as a whole, operational planning deals with developing and implementing tactics in specific functional areas. If customers make purchases online and pick up or return merchandise to the retailer, Home Depot will need staff at its stores to take care of these transactions. This will require additional planning on the part of management that might include additional staffing in shipping, separate customer service teams, and different delivery strategies.

Contingency Planning Planning cannot foresee every possibility. Major accidents, natural disasters, and rapid economic downturns can throw even the best-laid plans into chaos. To handle the possibility of business disruption from events of this nature, many firms use *contingency planning*, which allows them to resume operations as quickly and as smoothly as possible after a crisis while openly communicating with the public about what happened. This planning activity involves two components: business continuation and public communication. Many firms have developed management strategies to speed recovery from accidents such as loss of data, breaches of security, product failures, and natural disasters such as floods or fire. If a major disaster or business disruption occurs, a company's contingency plan usually designates a chain of command for crisis management, assigning specific functions to particular managers and employees in an emergency. But crisis more often occurs on a less global scale. For example, a product delivery might go astray, a key person might be sick and unable to attend an important customer meeting, or the power might go out for a day. These instances require contingency planning as well.

Shortly after the introduction of Tesla's Model S luxury electric car, a series of fires broke out in several of the cars—one involved an overheated charging system and three other fires occurred on the road. Tesla has given customers upgraded wall adapters to prevent overheating of the charging system. In addition, Tesla is working with the U.S. National Highway Traffic Safety Administration on testing. In response to the road fires, the company has modified the ground clearance for the car and provided customers with extended warranties to cover fire damage.[17]

Planning at Different Organizational Levels

Although managers spend some time on planning virtually every day, the total time spent and the type of planning done differ according to the level of management. As Table 7.1 points out, top managers, including a firm's board of directors and CEO, spend a great deal of time on long-range planning, while middle-level managers and supervisors focus on short-term, tactical, and operational planning. Employees at all levels can benefit themselves and their company by making plans to meet their own specific goals.

Assessment Check ☑

1. Outline the planning process.

2. Describe the purpose of tactical planning.

3. Compare the kinds of plans made by top managers and middle managers. How does their focus differ?

196

7.1 Planning at Different Management Levels

PRIMARY TYPE OF PLANNING	MANAGERIAL LEVEL	EXAMPLES
Strategic	Top management	Organizational objectives, fundamental strategies, long-term plans
Tactical	Middle management	Quarterly and semiannual plans, departmental policies and procedures
Operational	Supervisory management	Daily and weekly plans, rules, and procedures for each department
Contingency	Primarily top management, but all levels contribute	Ongoing plans for actions and communications in an emergency

4 The Strategic Planning Process

Strategic planning often makes the difference between an organization's success and failure. Strategic planning has formed the basis of many fundamental management decisions. Successful strategic planners typically follow the six steps shown in Figure 7.2: defining a mission, assessing the organization's competitive position, setting organizational objectives, creating strategies for competitive differentiation, implementing the strategy, and evaluating the results and refining the plan.

Defining the Organization's Mission

The first step in strategic planning is to translate the firm's vision into a **mission statement**. A mission statement is a written explanation of an organization's business intentions and aims. It is an enduring statement of a firm's purpose, possibly highlighting the scope of operations, the market it seeks to serve, and the ways it will attempt to set itself apart from competitors. A mission statement guides the actions of employees and publicizes the company's reasons for existence.

mission statement
written explanation of an organization's business intentions and aims.

FIGURE
7.2 Steps in the Strategic Planning Process

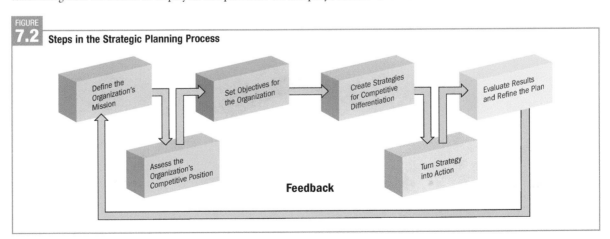

Mission statements can be short or long:

- Starbucks: "To inspire and nurture the human spirit—one person, one cup, and one neighborhood at a time."

- Disney: "To be one of the world's leading producers and providers of entertainment and information, using its portfolio of brands to differentiate its content, services, and consumer products."

- Nike: "To bring inspiration and innovation to every athlete in the world."

- Sony: "To experience the joy of advancing and applying technology for the benefit of the public."

A good mission statement states the firm's purpose for being in business and its overall goal. The most effective mission statements are memorable as well. The "Going Green" feature describes the mission of Johnson & Johnson, a global manufacturer of pharmaceuticals and health care products.

Assessing Your Competitive Position

SWOT analysis SWOT is an acronym for *strengths, weaknesses, opportunities,* and *threats.* By systematically evaluating all four of these factors, a firm can then develop the best strategies for gaining a competitive advantage.

Once a mission statement has been created, the next step in the planning process is to determine the firm's current—or potential—position in the marketplace. The company's founder or top managers evaluate the factors that may help it grow or could cause it to fail. A frequently used tool in this phase of strategic planning is the **SWOT analysis**. SWOT is an acronym for *strengths, weaknesses, opportunities,* and *threats.* By systematically evaluating all four of these factors, a firm can then develop the best strategies for gaining a competitive advantage. The framework for a SWOT analysis appears in Figure 7.3.

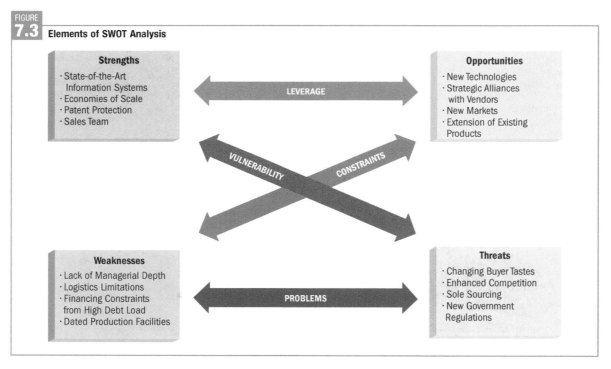

FIGURE 7.3 Elements of SWOT Analysis

Strengths
- State-of-the-Art Information Systems
- Economies of Scale
- Patent Protection
- Sales Team

Opportunities
- New Technologies
- Strategic Alliances with Vendors
- New Markets
- Extension of Existing Products

LEVERAGE

VULNERABILITY

CONSTRAINTS

Weaknesses
- Lack of Managerial Depth
- Logistics Limitations
- Financing Constraints from High Debt Load
- Dated Production Facilities

Threats
- Changing Buyer Tastes
- Enhanced Competition
- Sole Sourcing
- New Government Regulations

PROBLEMS

218

GoingGreen

Johnson & Johnson: Caring for the World

In its company statement of values and company credo, Johnson & Johnson promises, "We must maintain in good order the property we are privileged to use, protecting the environment and natural resources." Johnson & Johnson makes consumer products such as Band-Aids, Listerine, and Johnson's Baby Lotion, as well as medical devices and prescription drugs. Doing so can result in a giant carbon footprint made by manufacturing emissions, chemicals in products and processes, and a tremendous use of energy. Yet Johnson & Johnson has put strategies in place to reach its environmental goals.

The firm sets new long-term goals every five years, under its "Healthy Planet" program, for example, using direct purchase of low-impact hydro and wind power, on-site solar power and landfill gas, and purchasing renewable energy certificates. Johnson & Johnson also operates the largest fleet of hybrid and alternative fuel vehicles owned by any corporation in the world.

Part of the "Healthy Planet" program also involves being truthful about green advertising and being specific about sustainability measures. The company is the second-largest producer of solar panels in the United States, and it has received the Leadership in Energy and Environmental

Design (LEED) Gold certification for its Spring House research facility in Pennsylvania.

None of these goals could be achieved without support from Johnson & Johnson's leadership. Chairman and CEO Alex Gorsky writes, "I am proud to continue to lead our legacy of commitment to sustainable ideals, born from our Credo commitments and in line with our purpose of caring for the world, one person at a time."

Questions for Critical Thinking

1. What role does the CEO's leadership play in accomplishing Johnson & Johnson's green goals?

2. How does the company's mission relate to sustainability?

Sources: Company website, www.jnj.com, accessed February 11, 2014; Michael Christel, "J&J's New Lean, Green Lab to Be Key R&D Hub," *PharmaLive*, accessed January 25, 2014, http://blog.rddirections.com; "To Our Shareholders," *Annual Report*, accessed January 25, 2014, www.investore.jnj.com; organization website, "Partner Profile," *Green Power Partnership*, accessed January 25, 2014, www.epa.gov.

To evaluate a firm's strengths and weaknesses, its managers may examine each functional area such as finance, marketing, information technology, and human resources. Or they might evaluate strengths and weaknesses of each office, plant, or store. Entrepreneurs may focus on the individual skills and experience they bring to a new business.

For Starbucks, a key strength is consumers' positive image of the company's brand, which gets them to stand in line to pay premium prices for coffee, its market dominance, and strong financial position. That positive image comes from Starbucks being one of *Fortune's* best 100 companies to work for in the United States and from its socially responsible corporate policies. The company's strategic plans have included various ways to build on Starbucks's strong brand loyalty by attaching it to new products and expanding into new markets. The expansion efforts have included the purchase of Evolution Fresh cold-pressed juices, La Boulange Café and Bakery, and Teavana, a high-end tea store found in shopping malls. Starbucks remains focused on overseas retail expansion; its online, mobile, and digital loyalty program; and its gift card business. Weaknesses include a premium-priced product in a challenging economy, saturating some markets with too many stores, and not paying attention to store design. Starbucks eventually addressed these weaknesses by lowering the price of bagged coffee, closing some stores, and redesigning others.[18]

SWOT analysis continues with an attempt to define the major opportunities and threats the firm is likely to face. Threats might include rising coffee bean prices, trademark infringements, increased competition from local cafes and lower priced fast-food chains, and increased online shopping, particularly during holiday seasons, thus reducing foot traffic in stores. Starbucks addressed the threat of the challenging economy and lower-priced competitors by beginning to offer less-expensive, instant coffee in its stores and through retailers such as Costco and Target. An additional threat includes single coffee brewers like Keurig, part of competitor Green Mountain Roasters. Opportunities include expansion of retail stores' operations, increased product offerings, expansion to emerging economies, and connections to customers by continuing to build online communities.[19]

Chapter 7 *Management, Leadership, and the Internal Organization*

199

A SWOT analysis isn't carved in stone. Strengths and weaknesses, like opportunities and threats, may shift over time. A strength may eventually become a weakness and a threat may turn into an opportunity. But the analysis gives managers a place to start.

Setting Objectives for the Organization

The next step in planning is to develop objectives for the firm. **Objectives** set guideposts by which managers define the organization's desired performance in such areas as new-product development, sales, customer service, growth, environmental and social responsibility, and employee satisfaction. While the mission statement identifies a company's overall goals, objectives are more concrete.

As part of its growth strategy, Marriott Corporation recently opened its first boutique hotel named *Edition* in London. "We're trying to get some flash," says J.W. Marriott, the 80-something year old son of the company's founder. Arne M. Sorenson, Marriott's first non-family CEO, says he is committed to broadening the company's overall business portfolio.[20]

Creating Strategies for Competitive Differentiation

Developing a mission statement and setting objectives point a business in a specific direction. But the firm needs to identify the strategies it will use to reach its destination ahead of the competition. The underlying goal of strategy development is *competitive differentiation*—the unique combination of a company's abilities and resources that set it apart from its competitors. A firm might differentiate itself by being the first to introduce a service, such as online video streaming to a widespread market, or by offering value as Costco does. College student Jack McDermott launched Balbus Speech, which includes two apps with proven speech therapy technology to help those with speech impediments. Downloaded nearly 10,000 times, the apps cost between $10 and $15—a fraction of what traditional competitors have charged in the past.[21]

Implementing the Strategy

Once the first four phases of the strategic planning process are complete, managers are ready to put those plans into action. Often, it's the middle managers or supervisors who actually implement a strategy. But studies show that top company officials are still reluctant to empower these managers with the authority to make decisions that could benefit the company. Companies that are willing to empower employees generally reap the benefits.[22]

Zappos values customer service and empowers its employees to take care of each customer's needs.

When Tony Hsieh, the CEO of Zappos, decided to sell the company to Amazon, he wanted to keep in place the customer-service strategies that had made Zappos a success. Among these strategies is hiring people who want to "create fun and a little weirdness." Unlike most other companies, Zappos sets no time limit on how long customer service reps speak with customers; the chief goal is to empathize and take care of each customer's needs. The company values excellent customer service over the number of calls taken by its customer service staff.[23]

Monitoring and Adapting Strategic Plans

The final step in the strategic planning process is to monitor and adapt plans when the actual performance fails to meet goals. Monitoring involves securing feedback about performance. Managers might compare actual sales against forecasts; compile information from surveys; listen to complaints from the customer hot line; interview employees who are involved; and review reports prepared by production, finance, marketing, or other company units. If an Internet advertisement doesn't result in enough response or sales, managers might evaluate whether to continue the advertisement, change it, or discontinue it. If a retailer observes customers buying more jeans when they are displayed near the front door, likely the display area will stay near the door—and perhaps be enlarged. Ongoing use of such tools as SWOT analysis and forecasting can help managers adapt their objectives and functional plans as changes occur.

Assessment Check ☑

1. What is the purpose of a mission statement?

2. Which of the firm's characteristics does a SWOT analysis compare?

3. How do managers use objectives?

⌐5⌐ Managers as Decision Makers

Managers make decisions every day, whether it involves shutting down a manufacturing plant or adding grilled cheese sandwiches to a lunch menu. **Decision making** is the process of recognizing a problem or opportunity, evaluating alternative solutions, selecting and implementing an alternative, and assessing the results. Managers make two basic kinds of decisions: programmed decisions and nonprogrammed decisions.

decision making process of recognizing a problem or opportunity, evaluating alternative solutions, selecting and implementing an alternative, and assessing the results.

Programmed and Nonprogrammed Decisions

A *programmed decision* involves simple, common, and frequently occurring problems for which solutions have already been determined. Examples of programmed decisions include reordering office supplies, renewing a lease, and referring to an established discount for bulk orders. Programmed decisions are made in advance—the firm sets rules, policies, and procedures for managers and employees to follow on a routine basis. Programmed decisions actually save managers time and companies money because new decisions don't have to be made each time the situation arises.

A *nonprogrammed decision* involves a complex and unique problem or opportunity with important consequences for the organization. Examples of nonprogrammed decisions include entering a new market, deleting a product from the line, or developing a new product. Pepsi's recent decision to invest an additional $5 billion in Mexico over the next few years is designed to further strengthen the company's food and beverage business in that country. With its growing middle class, Mexico remains an attractive market for PepsiCo's snacks and beverages.[24]

How Managers Make Decisions

In a narrow sense, decision making involves choosing among two or more alternatives, with the chosen alternative becoming the decision. In a broader sense, decision making involves a systematic, step-by-step process that helps managers make effective choices. This process begins when someone recognizes a problem or opportunity, develops possible courses of action, evaluates the alternatives, selects and implements one of them, and assesses the outcome. It's important to keep in mind that managers are *human* decision makers, and while they can follow the decision-making process step-by-step as shown in Figure 7.4, the outcome of their decisions depends on many factors, including the accuracy of their information and the

© Alpha and Omega Collection/Alamy

Global snack and beverage giant PepsiCo recently announced a $5 billion investment in Mexico to strengthen its business in that country. The move is considered a *nonprogrammed decision* because it involves an opportunity with important consequences for the overall organization.

Hit&Miss

Hands-Off Approach Works for Buffett

Warren Buffett, billionaire investor and CEO of Berkshire Hathaway, is known for his hands-off management style. Buffett prefers to give his chief lieutenants the autonomy to make decisions on their own about the companies they run—even if he doesn't agree with them.

Buffett believes that giving people autonomy motivates them to do the best possible job. In his company's annual letter to shareholders, he writes, "there are managers to whom I have not talked in the last year, while there is one with whom I talk almost daily. Our trust is in people rather than process. A 'hire well, manage little' code suits both them and me."

In Berkshire Hathaway's more than 40 businesses, the CEOs are experienced, competent, and understand Buffett's management approach. Tracy Cool, a 29-year-old business school graduate, is one of Buffett's most recent recruits and has become one of his most trusted advisors. Cool chairs four of Buffett's subsidiaries, with combined sales exceeding $4 billion and more than 10,000 employees. When Cool hires employees, she tries to hire individuals who are committed to the job, who understand Berkshire's unique culture, and who can function in a hands-off environment. She also believes that making mistakes is a great way to learn, and Buffett is very supportive of his management team.

Buffett echoes Cool's comments. He believes in hiring self-starters who love what they do. "Talented people can accomplish a whole lot," he says.

Questions for Critical Thinking

1. What are the advantages and disadvantages of a hands-off management style like Buffett's approach?

2. Buffett states there are managers to whom he has not talked with over the last year, and those with whom he talks almost daily. As one of Buffett's lieutenants, how often would you communicate with your boss? Explain your reasoning.

Sources: Company website, http://berkshirehathaway.com, accessed January 26, 2014; Anupreeta Das, "Tracy Britt Cool on Management Lessons from Warren Buffett," *The Wall Street Journal*, accessed January 26, 2014, http://blogs.wsj.com; Noah Buhayar and Laura Colby, "Buffett Leans on 29-Year-Old Cool to Oversee Problems," *Bloomberg News*, accessed January 21, 2014, www.bloomberg.com; Andrew Ross Sorkin, "Warren Buffett Delegator in Chief," *The New York Times*, accessed January 25, 2014, www.nytimes.com; Timothy R. Clark, "Why We Trust Warren Buffett," *Deseret News*, accessed January 26, 2013, www.deseretnews.com.

---

experience, creativity, and wisdom of the person. Warren Buffett, billionaire investor and CEO of Berkshire Hathaway, empowers his managers to make decisions without his input. See the "Hit & Miss" feature for more on Buffet's management style.

Making good decisions is never easy. A decision might hurt or help the sales of a product; it might offend or disappoint a customer or co-worker; it might affect the manager's own career or reputation. Managers' decisions can have complex legal and ethical dimensions. *CRO Magazine* publishes an annual list of the "100 Best Corporate Citizens." These companies make decisions that are ethical, environmentally responsible, fair toward employees, and accountable to local communities and that provide responsible goods and services to customers and a healthy return to investors. These organizations prove that good corporate citizenship is good behavior. The top 10 corporate citizens named one recent year were AT&T, Mattel, Bristol-Myers Squibb, Eaton, Intel, Gap, Hasbro, Merck & Co., Campbell Soup, and Coca-Cola Enterprises.[25]

Assessment Check ☑

1. Distinguish between programmed and non-programmed decisions.

2. What are the steps in the decision-making process?

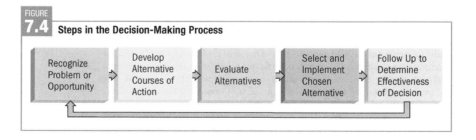

FIGURE 7.4 **Steps in the Decision-Making Process**

Recognize Problem or Opportunity → Develop Alternative Courses of Action → Evaluate Alternatives → Select and Implement Chosen Alternative → Follow Up to Determine Effectiveness of Decision

Part 3 *Management: Empowering People to Achieve Business Success*

6 Managers as Leaders

A manager must demonstrate **leadership**, directing or inspiring people to attain certain goals. Great leaders do not all share the same qualities, but three traits are often mentioned: empathy (the ability to imagine yourself in someone else's position), self-awareness, and objectivity. While it might seem as though empathy and objectivity are opposite traits, they do balance each other. Many leaders share other traits—courage, passion, commitment, innovation, and flexibility to name a few.

Leadership involves the use of influence or power. This influence may come from one or more sources. One source of power is the leader's position in the company. A national sales manager has the authority to direct the activities of the sales force. Another source of power is a leader's expertise and experience. A first-line supervisor with expert machinist skills will most likely be respected by employees in the machining department. Some leaders derive power from their personalities. Employees may admire a leader because they recognize an exceptionally kind and fair, humorous, energetic, or enthusiastic person. Admiration, inspiration, and motivation are especially important during difficult economic times or when a leader has to make tough decisions for the company, as was recently the case at General Motors. See the accompanying "Hit & Miss" feature for an introduction to that company's first female CEO.

With more than 30 years of experience at GM, Mary Barra recently became the company's first female CEO.

Apple recently tapped Angela Ahrendts to head the company's retail operations. Former CEO of Burberry, the British luxury retailer, Ahrendts oversees the strategic direction, expansion, and operation of Apple retail stores, as well as its online retail sales. Credited with Burberry's success in China, Ahrendts will also be responsible for growing Apple's Chinese retail business. Apple is confident that Ahrendts will provide the necessary leadership to increase global retail sales, which have been lagging.[26]

> **leadership** ability to direct or inspire people to attain certain goals.

Leadership Styles

The way a person uses power to lead others determines his or her leadership style. Leadership styles range along a continuum with autocratic leadership at one extreme end and free-rein leadership at the other. *Autocratic leadership* is centered on the boss. Autocratic leaders make decisions on their own without consulting employees. They reach decisions, communicate them to subordinates, and expect automatic implementation.

Democratic leadership includes subordinates in the decision-making process. This leadership style centers on employees' contributions. Democratic leaders delegate assignments, ask employees for suggestions, and encourage participation. An important outgrowth of democratic leadership in business is the concept of **empowerment**, in which employees share authority, responsibility, and decision making with their managers.

At the other end of the continuum from autocratic leadership is *free-rein leadership*. Free-rein leaders believe in minimal supervision. They allow subordinates to make most of their own decisions. Free-rein leaders communicate with employees frequently, as the situation warrants. For the first decade of its existence, Google was proud of its free-rein leadership style. Engineers were encouraged to pursue any and all ideas; teams formed or disbanded on their own; employees spent as much or as little time as they wanted to on any given project. But as the firm entered its second decade, it became apparent that not every innovation was worth pursuing—and some valuable ideas were getting lost in the chaos. Concerned that some of the biggest ideas were getting squashed, the firm established a process for reviewing new project ideas in order to identify those most likely to succeed.[27]

> **empowerment** giving employees shared authority, responsibility, and decision making with their managers.

Chapter 7 *Management, Leadership, and the Internal Organization*   **203**

Hit&Miss

GM's First Female CEO Faces Challenges and Opportunities

Mary Barra, GM's first female CEO, knows cars. She has worked for the Detroit automaker for more than 30 years in a variety of positions. She began her GM career as an intern while in college. After graduation, Barra's first job was a plant engineer at the assembly factory in Pontiac, Michigan.

Before being tapped for the CEO post, Barra spent time in several different divisions of the company, including global manufacturing, purchasing, supply chain management, and human resources. Most recently, she headed up the $15 billion global product development group, where she and her team were responsible for the design and engineering of GM vehicles worldwide. *Motor Trend* Magazine recently named the Cadillac CTS Car of the Year, and *Consumer Reports* named the Chevy Impala the best sedan and the Silverado the best pickup truck.

In her new position as CEO, Barra has already faced several challenges, including a safety recall of millions of GM vehicles caused by a faulty ignition switch that resulted in multiple deaths. She appeared before a Congressional committee to discuss the recall, authorized an in-depth internal investigation by a former federal prosecutor, and subsequently fired 15 employees for misconduct and incompetence.

Despite the recall and associated issues, Barra continues to see opportunities for GM, particularly in Asia. Of the 2.4 million cars sold in GM's most recent financial quarter, more than 30 percent were sold in China. She plans to continue the company's global expansion with sales of the Chevrolet and Cadillac brands and is optimistic that new product launches will keep the auto giant on a successful business path.

Questions for Critical Thinking

1. How do Barra's previous job experiences at GM help her in her role as the company's CEO?

2. What challenges will Barra encounter as she guides the company's global expansion into other markets?

Sources: Kyle Stock, "GM's Mary Barra Fires 15, Says More Recalls Are Coming," *Bloomberg Businessweek*, accessed June 6, 2014, www.businessweek.com; Chris Isidore and Katie Lobosco, "GM CEO Barra: 'I Am Deeply Sorry,'" *CNN Money*, accessed June 6, 2014, http://money.cnn.com; Joann Muller, "Exclusive Q&A: GM CEO Mary Barra on Crisis Management, Culture Change and the Future of GM," *Forbes*, accessed June 6, 2014, www.forbes.com; company website, www.gm.com, accessed February 11, 2014; Sherri Welch, "By Naming Mary Barra CEO, GM Sends Strong Message about Talent, Opportunity," *Crain's Chicago Business*, accessed February 11, 2014, www.crainsdetroit.com; Tim Higgins, "GM CEO Barra Aims to Accelerate Strategies Set Under Akerson," *Bloomberg Businessweek*, accessed January 26, 2014, www.businessweek.com; Tim Higgins and Brian Urstadt, "Exclusive: The Inside Story of GM's Comeback and Mary Barra's Rise," *Bloomberg Businessweek*, accessed January 26, 2014, www.businessweek.com.

Which Leadership Style Is Best?

No single leadership style is best for every firm in every situation. Sometimes leadership styles require change in order for a company to grow, as has been the case for Google. In a crisis, an autocratic leadership style might save the company—and sometimes the lives of customers and employees. This was the case when US Airways flight 1549 was forced to ditch into the Hudson River after hitting a wayward flock of Canada geese. Quick, autocratic decisions made by the pilot, Capt. Chesley Sullenberger, resulted in the survival of everyone on board the flight. But US Airways management on the ground demonstrated a democratic style of leadership in which managers at many levels were empowered to take actions to help the passengers and their families. For example, one executive arrived on the scene with a bag of emergency cash for passengers and credit cards for employees so they could purchase medicines, food, or anything else they needed.[28] A company that recognizes which leadership style works best for its employees, customers, and business conditions is most likely to choose the best leaders for its particular needs.

Assessment Check ☑

1. How is *leadership* defined?

2. Identify the styles of leadership as they appear along a continuum of greater or lesser employee participation.

⌐7⌐ Corporate Culture

corporate culture organization's system of principles, beliefs, and values.

An organization's **corporate culture** is its system of principles, beliefs, and values. The leadership style of its managers, the way it communicates, and the overall work environment influence a firm's corporate culture. A corporate culture is typically shaped by the leaders who founded and developed the company and by those who have succeeded them. Although

Google has grown by leaps and bounds since its launch, the firm still tries to maintain the culture of innovation, creativity, and flexibility that its co-founders, Larry Page and Sergey Brin, promoted from the beginning. Google now has offices around the world, staffed by thousands of workers who speak a multitude of languages. "We hire people who are smart and determined, and we favor ability over experience. Although Googlers share common goals and visions for the company, we hail from all walks of life and speak dozens of languages, reflecting the global audience that we serve," the website states. "When not at work, Googlers pursue interests ranging from cycling to beekeeping, from frisbee to foxtrot."[29]

Managers use symbols, rituals, ceremonies, and stories to reinforce corporate culture. The corporate culture at the Walt Disney Company is almost as famous as the original Disney characters themselves. In fact, Disney employees are known as cast members. All new employees attend training seminars in which they learn the language, customs, traditions, stories, product lines—everything there is to know about the Disney culture and its original founder, Walt Disney.[30]

Google maintains a culture of innovation, creativity, and flexibility that company founders promoted from the beginning. The Google office in Paris, France, features a photo booth for employees..

JACQUES BRINON/AFP/Getty Images, Inc.

Corporate cultures can be very strong and enduring, but sometimes they are forced to change to meet new demands in the business environment. A firm that is steeped in tradition and bureaucracy might have to shift to a leaner, more flexible culture in order to respond to shifts in technology or customer preferences. A firm that grows quickly—like Google—generally has to make some adjustments in its culture to accommodate more customers and employees.

[8] Organizational Structures

An <u>organization</u> is a structured group of people working together to achieve common goals. An organization features three key elements: human interaction, goal-directed activities, and structure. The organizing process, much of which is led by managers, should result in an overall structure that permits interactions among individuals and departments needed to achieve company goals.

The steps involved in the organizing process are shown in Figure 7.5. Managers first determine the specific activities needed to implement plans and achieve goals. Next, they group these work activities into a logical structure. Then they assign work to specific employees and give the people the resources they need to complete it. Managers coordinate the work of different groups and employees within the firm. Finally, they evaluate the results of the organizing process to ensure effective and efficient progress toward planned goals. Evaluation sometimes results in changes to the way work is organized.

Many factors influence the results of organizing. The list includes a firm's goals and competitive strategy, the type of product it offers, the way it uses technology to accomplish work, and its size. Small firms typically create very simple structures. The owner of a dry-cleaning business generally is the top manager, who hires several employees to process orders, clean the clothing, and make deliveries. The owner handles the functions of purchasing supplies such as detergents and hangers, hiring and training employees and coordinating their work, preparing advertisements for the local newspaper, and keeping accounting records.

Assessment Check ☑

1. What is the relationship between leadership style and corporate culture?

2. How do managers reinforce corporate culture?

organization structured group of people working together to achieve common goals.

Chapter 7 *Management, Leadership, and the Internal Organization*

205

FIGURE
7.5
Steps in the Organizing Process

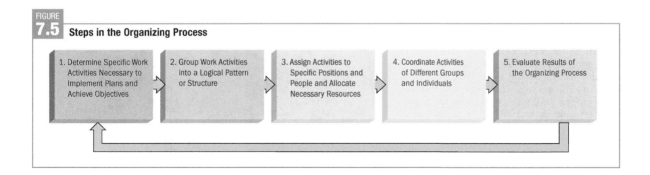

As a company grows, its structure increases in complexity. With increased size comes specialization and growing numbers of employees. A larger firm may employ many salespeople, along with a sales manager to direct and coordinate their work, or organize an accounting department.

An effective structure is one that is clear and easy to understand: Employees know what is expected of them and to whom they report. They also know how their jobs contribute to the company's mission and overall strategic plan. An *organization chart* is a visual representation of a firm's structure that illustrates job positions and functions. Figure 7.6 illustrates a sample organization chart.

Not-for-profit organizations also organize through formal structures so they can function efficiently and carry out their goals. These organizations, such as the Salvation Army and the American Society for Prevention of Cruelty to Animals (ASPCA), sometimes have a blend of paid staff and volunteers in their organizational structure.

departmentalization
process of dividing work
activities into units within
the organization.

Departmentalization

<u>Departmentalization</u> is the process of dividing work activities into units within the organization. In this arrangement, employees specialize in certain jobs—such as marketing, finance, or

FIGURE
7.6
Sample Organization Chart

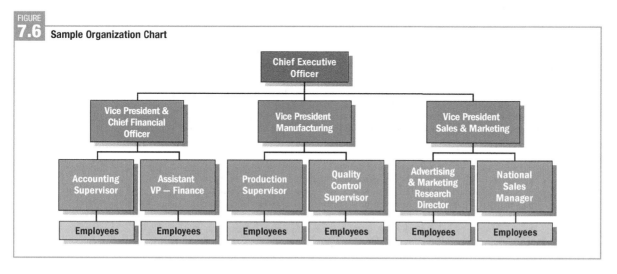

Part 3 *Management: Empowering People to Achieve Business Success*

These familiar office products represent only one of 3M Corporation's many product lines. Because 3M serves such a broad spectrum of customers, it is organized on the basis of customer departmentalization.

design. Depending on the size of the firm, usually an executive runs the department, followed by middle-level managers and supervisors. The five major forms of departmentalization subdivide work by product, geographical area, customer, function, and process.

- *Product departmentalization.* This approach organizes work units based on the goods and services a company offers. California's Activision Blizzard Inc. is organized by product. The video game publisher is divided into four divisions: Call of Duty, Skylanders, Diablo, and World of Warcraft.[31]

- *Geographical departmentalization.* This form organizes units by geographical regions within a country or, for a multinational firm, by region throughout the world. The website Petswelcome.com makes it easy for traveling pet owners to locate hotel chains, rentals, amusement parks, and other recreational locations around the country that welcome pets. Users can search by type of lodging, route planned, and destination.[32]

- *Customer departmentalization.* A firm that offers a variety of goods and services targeted at different types of customers might structure itself based on customer departmentalization. Management of Procter & Gamble's wide array of products is divided among four business units: Beauty (CoverGirl, Old Spice, and Pantene); Baby, Feminine, and Family Care (Pampers and Charmin); Fabric and Home Care (Swiffer, Tide, and Duracell); and Health and Grooming (Crest, Gillette, and Oral-B).[33]

- *Functional departmentalization.* Some firms organize work units according to business functions such as finance, marketing, human resources, and production. An advertising agency may create departments for creative personnel (say, copywriters), media buyers, and account executives.

- *Process departmentalization.* Some goods and services require multiple work processes to complete their production. A manufacturer may set up separate departments for cutting material, heat-treating it, forming it into its final shape, and painting it.

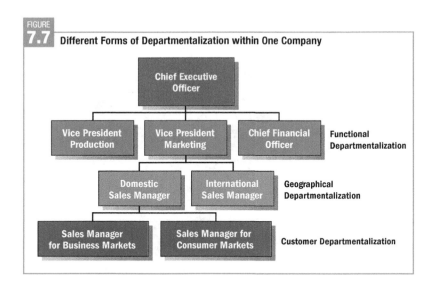

FIGURE 7.7 Different Forms of Departmentalization within One Company

Chief Executive Officer

Vice President Production — Vice President Marketing — Chief Financial Officer — **Functional Departmentalization**

Domestic Sales Manager — International Sales Manager — **Geographical Departmentalization**

Sales Manager for Business Markets — Sales Manager for Consumer Markets — **Customer Departmentalization**

As Figure 7.7 illustrates, a single company may implement several different departmentalization schemes. In deciding on a form of departmentalization, managers take into account the type of product they produce, the size of their company, their customer base, and the locations of their customers.

Delegating Work Assignments

delegation managerial process of assigning work to employees.

Managers assign work to employees, a process called <u>delegation</u>. Employees might be responsible for answering customer calls, scooping ice cream, processing returns, making deliveries, opening or closing a store, cooking or serving food, contributing to new-product design, calculating a return on investment, or any of thousands of other tasks. Just as important, employees are given a certain amount of authority to make decisions.

Companies like Zappos, the online shoe retailer, that empower their workers to make decisions that could better serve their customers generally have happier employees and more satisfied customers.[34] As employees receive greater authority, they also must be accountable for their actions and decisions—they receive credit when things go well, and must accept responsibility when they don't. Managers also must figure out the best way to delegate responsibilities to employees who belong to different age groups, including Millennials, as discussed in the "Career Kickstart" feature.

Span of Management The *span of management*, or span of control, is the number of employees a manager supervises. These employees are often referred to as direct reports. First-line managers have wider spans of management, monitoring the work of many employees. The span of management varies depending on many factors, including the type of work performed and employees' training. In recent years, a growing trend has brought wider spans of control, as companies have reduced their layers of management to flatten their organizational structures, in the process increasing the decision-making responsibility they give employees.

Centralization and Decentralization How widely should managers disperse decision-making authority throughout an organization? A company that emphasizes *centralization* retains decision making at the top of the management hierarchy. A company that emphasizes *decentralization* locates decision making at lower levels. A trend toward decentralization has

208

Part 3 *Management: Empowering People to Achieve Business Success*

228

pushed decision making down to operating employees in many cases. Firms that have decentralized believe that the change can improve their ability to serve customers. For example, the front-desk clerk at a hotel is much better equipped to fulfill a guest's request for a crib or a wake-up call than the hotel's general manager.

Types of Organization Structures

The four basic types of organization structures are line, line-and-staff, committee, and matrix. While some companies do follow one type of structure, most use a combination.

Line Organizations A *line organization*, the oldest and simplest organization structure, establishes a direct flow of authority from the chief executive to employees. The line organization defines a simple, clear *chain of command*—a hierarchy of managers and workers. With a clear chain of command, everyone knows who is in charge and decisions can be made quickly. This structure is particularly effective in a crisis situation. But a line organization has its drawbacks. Each manager has complete responsibility for a range of activities; in a medium-sized or large organization, however, this person can't possibly be expert in all of them. In a small organization such as a local hair salon or a dentist's office, a line organization is probably the most efficient way to run the business.

Line-and-Staff Organizations A *line-and-staff organization* combines the direct flow of authority of a line organization with staff departments that support the line departments. Line departments participate directly in decisions that affect the core operations of the organization. Staff departments lend specialized technical support. Figure 7.8 illustrates a line-and-staff organization. Accounting, engineering, and human resources are staff departments that support the line authority extending from the plant manager to the production manager and supervisors.

A line manager and a staff manager differ significantly in their authority relationships. A line manager forms part of the primary line of authority that flows throughout the organization. Line managers interact directly with the functions of production, financing, or marketing—the functions needed to produce and sell goods and services. A staff manager provides information, advice, or technical assistance to aid line managers. Staff managers do not have authority to give orders outside their own departments or to compel line managers to take action.

The line-and-staff organization is common in midsize and large organizations. It is an effective structure because it combines the line organization's capabilities for rapid decision making and direct communication with the expert knowledge of staff specialists.

Committee Organizations A *committee organization* is a structure that places authority and responsibility jointly in the hands of a group of individuals rather than a single manager. This model typically appears as part of a regular line-and-staff structure.

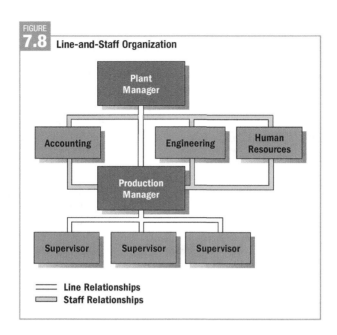

FIGURE 7.8 Line-and-Staff Organization

Plant Manager

Accounting

Engineering

Human Resources

Production Manager

Supervisor

Supervisor

Supervisor

Line Relationships
Staff Relationships

Committees also work in areas such as new-product development. A new-product committee may include managers from such areas as accounting, engineering, finance, manufacturing, marketing, and technical research. By including representatives from all areas involved in creating and marketing products, such a committee generally improves planning and employee morale because decisions reflect diverse perspectives.

Committees tend to act slowly and conservatively, however, and may make decisions by compromising conflicting interests rather than by choosing the best alternative. The definition of a camel as "a racehorse designed by committee" provides an apt description of some limitations of committee decisions.

Matrix Organizations Some organizations use a matrix or product management design to customize their structures. The *matrix structure* links employees from different parts of the organization to work together on specific projects. Figure 7.9 diagrams a matrix structure. A project manager assembles a group of employees from different functional areas. The employees keep their ties to the line-and-staff structure, as shown in the vertical white lines. As the horizontal gold lines show, employees are also members of project teams. When the project is completed, employees return to their regular jobs.

In the matrix structure, each employee reports to two managers: one line manager and one project manager. Employees who are chosen to work on a special project receive instructions from the project manager (horizontal authority), but they continue as employees in their permanent functional departments (vertical authority). The term *matrix* comes from the intersecting grid of horizontal and vertical lines of authority.

The matrix structure is popular at high-technology and multinational corporations, as well as hospitals and consulting firms. Dow Chemical and Procter & Gamble have both used matrix structures. The major benefits of the matrix structure come from its flexibility in adapting quickly to rapid changes in the environment and its capability of focusing resources on major problems or products. It also provides an outlet for employees' creativity and initiative. However, it challenges project managers to integrate the skills of specialists from many

FIGURE 7.9 Matrix Organization

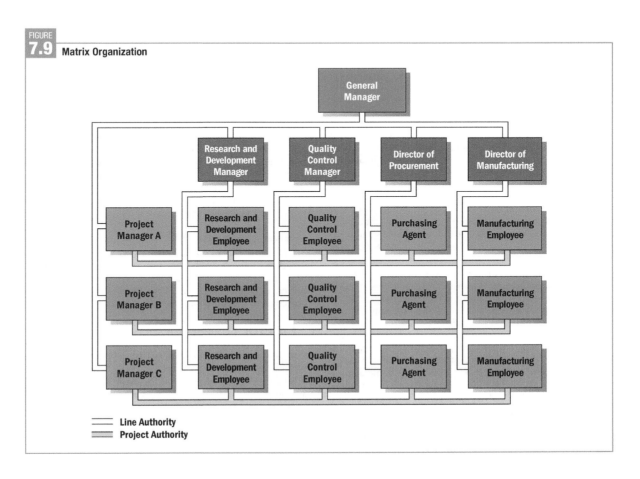

departments into a coordinated team. It also means that team members' permanent functional managers must adjust their employees' regular workloads.

The matrix structure is most effective when company leaders empower project managers to use whatever resources are available to achieve the project's objectives. Good project managers know how to make the project goals clear and keep team members focused. A firm that truly embraces the matrix structure also nurtures a project culture by making sure staffing is adequate, the workload is reasonable, and other company resources are available to project managers.[35]

What's Ahead

In the next chapter, we sharpen our focus on the importance of people—the human resource— in shaping the growth and profitability of the organization. We examine how firms recruit, select, train, evaluate, and compensate employees in their attempts to attract, retain, and moti- vate a high-quality workforce. The concept of motivation is examined, and we will discuss how managers apply theories of motivation in the modern workplace. The next chapter also looks at the important topic of labor–management relations.

Assessment Check ✓

1. What is the purpose of an organization chart?
2. What are the five major forms of departmental- ization?
3. What does *span of man- agement* mean?

Chapter in Review

■ Summary of Learning Objectives

⌜1⌟ Define *management*.

Management is the process of achieving organizational objectives through people and other resources. The management hierarchy is generally as follows: top managers provide overall direction for company activities, middle managers implement the strategies of top managers and direct the activities of supervisors, and supervisors interact directly with workers. The three basic managerial skills are: technical, human or interpersonal, and conceptual.

Assessment Check Answers ✅

1.1 What is management? Management is the process of achieving organizational objectives through people and other resources. The manager's job is to combine human and technical resources in the best way possible to achieve the company's goals.

1.2 How do the jobs of top managers, middle managers, and supervisory managers differ? Top managers develop long-range plans, set a direction for their organization, and inspire all employees to achieve the company's vision. Middle managers focus on specific operations, products, or customers. They develop procedures to implement the firm's strategic plans. Supervisory managers interact directly with nonmanagerial employees who produce and sell the firm's goods and services. They are responsible for implementing the plans developed by middle managers and motivating workers to accomplish daily, weekly, and monthly goals.

1.3 What is the relationship between the manager's planning and controlling functions? The basic purpose of controlling is to assess the success of the planning function. Controlling also provides feedback for future rounds of planning.

⌜2⌟ Explain the role of setting a vision and ethical standards for the firm.

Vision is the founder's perception of the marketplace needs and the firm's methods for meeting them. Vision helps clarify a firm's purpose and the actions it can take to make the most of opportunities. High ethical standards can help build success for a firm through job satisfaction and customer loyalty.

Assessment Check Answers ✅

2.1 What is meant by a vision for the firm? A vision serves as the target for a firm's actions, helping direct the company toward opportunities and differentiating it from its competitors.

2.2 Why is it important for a top executive to set high ethical standards? High ethical standards often result in a stable workforce, job satisfaction, and customer loyalty.

⌜3⌟ Summarize the importance of planning.

The planning process identifies organizational goals and develops the actions necessary to reach them. Planning helps a company turn vision into action, take advantage of opportunities, and avoid costly mistakes. Strategic planning is a far-reaching process. It views the world through a wide-angle lens to determine the long-range focus and activities of the organization. Tactical planning focuses on the current and short-range activities required to implement the organization's strategies. Operational planning sets standards and work targets for functional areas such as production, human resources, and marketing.

Assessment Check Answers ✅

3.1 Outline the planning process. Some plans are very broad and long range, focusing on key organizational objectives; others are more detailed and specify how particular objectives will be achieved. From the mission statement to objectives to specific plans, each phase must fit into a comprehensive planning framework.

3.2 Describe the purpose of tactical planning. The purpose of tactical planning is to determine which short-term activities should be implemented to accomplish the firm's overall strategy.

3.3 Compare the kinds of plans made by top managers and middle managers. How does their focus differ? Top managers focus on long-range, strategic plans. In contrast, middle-level managers focus on short-term, tactical planning.

⌜4⌟ Describe the strategic planning process.

The first step of strategic planning is to translate the firm's vision into a mission statement that explains its overall intentions and aims. Next, planners must assess the firm's current competitive position using tools such as SWOT analysis. Managers then set specific objectives. The next step is to develop strategies for reaching objectives that will differentiate the firm from its competitors. Managers then develop an action plan that outlines the specific methods for implementing the strategy. Finally, the results achieved by the plan are evaluated, and the plan is adjusted as needed.

Assessment Check Answers ✅

4.1 What is the purpose of a mission statement? A mission statement is a written explanation of a firm's purpose, the reason it exists, the customers it will serve, and how it is different from competitors. A mission statement guides the actions of company managers and employees.

4.2 Which of the firm's characteristics does a SWOT analysis compare? A SWOT analysis determines a firm's strengths, weaknesses, opportunities, and threats relative to its competitors.

4.3 How do managers use objectives? Objectives set guideposts by which managers define the organization's desired performance in such areas as new-product development, sales, customer service, and employee satisfaction.

⌐5⌐ Discuss managers as decision makers.

A programmed decision applies a company rule or policy to solve a frequently occurring problem. A nonprogrammed decision forms a response to a complex and unique problem with important consequences for the organization. The five-step approach to decision making includes recognizing a problem or opportunity, developing alternative courses of action, evaluating the alternatives, selecting and implementing an alternative, and following up the decision to determine its effectiveness.

Assessment Check Answers ✓

5.1 Distinguish between programmed and nonprogrammed decisions. Programmed decisions, such as reordering office supplies, are simple and happen frequently, so procedures for them can streamline the process. Nonprogrammed decisions, such as entering a new market or developing a new product, require more individual evaluation.

5.2 What are the steps in the decision-making process? The decision-making steps are recognition of a problem or opportunity, development of alternatives, evaluation of alternatives, selection and implementation of the chosen alternative, and follow-up to determine effectiveness of the decision.

⌐6⌐ Evaluate managers as leaders.

Leadership is the act of motivating others to achieve certain goals. The basic leadership styles are autocratic, democratic, and free-rein leadership. The best leadership style depends on three elements: the leader, the followers, and the situation.

Assessment Check Answers ✓

6.1 How is *leadership* defined? Leadership means directing or inspiring people to attain certain organizational goals. Effective leaders share several traits, such as empathy, self-awareness, and objectivity in dealing with others. Leaders also use the power of their jobs, expertise, and experience to influence others.

6.2 Identify the styles of leadership as they appear along a continuum of greater or lesser employee participation. At one end of the continuum, autocratic leaders make decisions without consulting employees. In the middle of the continuum, democratic leaders ask employees for suggestions and encourage participation. At the other end of the continuum, free-rein leaders leave most decisions to their employees.

⌐7⌐ Discuss corporate culture.

Corporate culture refers to an organization's principles, beliefs, and values. It is typically shaped by a firm's founder and perpetuated through formal programs such as training, rituals, and ceremonies, as well as through informal discussions among employees. Corporate culture can influence a firm's success by giving it a competitive advantage.

Assessment Check Answers ✓

7.1 What is the relationship between leadership style and corporate culture? The best leadership style to adopt often depends on the organization's corporate culture and its system of principles, beliefs, and values. Managerial philosophies, communications networks, and workplace environments and practices all influence corporate culture.

7.2 How do managers reinforce corporate culture? Managers use symbols, rituals, ceremonies, and stories to reinforce corporate culture.

⌐8⌐ Identify organizational structures.

The subdivision of work activities into units within the organization is called *departmentalization*. It may be based on products, geographical locations, customers, functions, or processes. Most firms implement one or more of four structures: line, line-and-staff, committee, and matrix structures.

Assessment Check Answers ✓

8.1 What is the purpose of an organization chart? An organization chart is a visual representation of a firm's structure that illustrates job positions and functions.

8.2 What are the five major forms of departmentalization? Product departmentalization organizes units by the different goods and services a company offers. Geographical departmentalization organizes units by geographical regions. Customer departmentalization organizes units by different types of customers. Functional departmentalization organizes units by business activities such as finance, marketing, human resources, and production. Process departmentalization organizes units by the steps or work processes it takes to complete production or provide a service.

8.3 What does *span of management* mean? The span of management, or span of control, is the number of employees a manager supervises.

Business Terms You Need to Know

management 190
planning 192
organizing 192
directing 192
controlling 193
vision 193

mission statement 197
SWOT analysis 198
objectives 200
decision making 201
leadership 203
empowerment 203

corporate culture 204
organization 205
departmentalization 206
delegation 208

Review Questions

1. What are the three levels of management hierarchy? For each level, which management skills might be considered most important, and why?

2. Identify the four basic managerial functions. Suppose you were hired to be the manager of a local restaurant. Which managerial functions would likely be the biggest part of your job? In what ways?

3. Describe the link between a company's vision and its ethical standards. Why is it important for top management to put forth a clear vision and ethical standards for a company?

4. Identify the four types of planning, then think about the following scenario. Suppose you planned a large cookout with your friends, but when you woke up on the morning of the party, it was pouring rain. What type of planning would you use prior to the storm? What type of planning would allow you to cope with the rain? Specifically, what could you do?

5. What is the link between a firm's vision and its mission statement? Think about your own career as a start-up venture. What is your vision? What might be your mission statement?

6. Define *objectives*. Outline objectives you might have for your own college education and career. How might this outline help you implement your own career strategy?

7. Identify each of the following as a programmed or nonprogrammed decision:
   a. reordering printer cartridges
   b. buying a new smart phone
   c. buying your favorite toothpaste or shampoo at the supermarket
   d. selecting a college to attend
   e. filling your car with gasoline

8. From what sources might a leader derive power? Which leadership style might work best for a manager whose firm is forced to make cost-cutting decisions? Why?

9. Why is a strong corporate culture important to a company's success? How might the corporate culture be linked to leadership style?

10. Which type of organization structure provides a firm with the most flexibility to respond to changes in the marketplace and engage in innovation? What might be the drawbacks of this structure?

Projects and Teamwork Applications

1. Imagine that you've been hired as a supervisor by a bakery shop called Clare's Cakes that is beginning to grow. Clare—the founder—is looking for ways to increase production capacity, expand its deliveries, and eventually open several more shops in the area. Create a job description for yourself, including the managerial functions you think you'll need and skills you believe you'll need for success.

2. Search your personal or professional network to find a supervisor or manager to interview. Find out more about how he or she performs each of the four management functions discussed in this chapter. Which of the technical, conceptual, and human skills are important for on-the-job performance?

3. Contingency planning requires a combination of foresight and adaptability. Josh James, founder of Omniture, the web analytics firm he sold to Adobe, recalls the importance of being able to adapt when his company seemed on the brink

of disaster. "There were times when I lay down on the floor at night, close to crying. Then my wife would come over and kick me and say, 'Get up and figure it out.'"[36] Research the news headlines for situations that could (or did) require contingency planning. Report to the class what the challenge was, and how the managers involved handled it. Remark on whether the planning was effective or successful.

4. Identify someone who you think is a good leader—it can be someone you know personally or a public figure. Describe the traits that you think are most important in making this person an effective leader. Would this person's leadership style work in situations other than his or her current position? Why or why not?

5. Research a firm whose goods or services you purchase or admire. Learn what you can about the organization's culture. Do you think you would be an effective manager in this culture? Why or why not? Share your findings with the class.

Web Assignments

1. **SWOT analysis.** Create your own personal SWOT analysis as part of your career plan by going to the website listed below. Evaluate your personal strengths, weaknesses, opportunities, and threats. Either with a partner or in a small group, discuss your personal assessment and its impact on your career.

   www.quintcareers.com/SWOT_Analysis.html

2. **Mission statements.** Go to the websites of two organizations, a for-profit firm and a not-for-profit organization. Print out both organizations' mission statements. Bring the material with you to class to participate in a discussion on mission statements.

3. **Management structure.** Visit the website listed below and answer the following questions.

   www.pfizer.com/about/leadership_and_structure/leadership_structure

   a. How would you characterize Pfizer's organizational structure?

   b. What is the composition of Pfizer's board of directors?

Note: Internet web addresses change frequently. If you don't find the exact sites listed, you may need to access the organization's home page and search from there or use a search engine such as Google or Bing.

Strong Leadership Keeps Ford on Track

CASE 7.1

When the other major U.S. automakers accepted federal funds in order to stay in business, Ford Motor Company—in the voice of then CEO Alan R. Mulally—said no. The federal funds were to come in the form of short-term loans, which Ford determined it didn't need at the time. Several years earlier, the firm had restructured its debt so that when the economy slowed down, Ford didn't.

Mulally observes that this timing was a bit of luck and a bit of strategic planning. To implement this overall strategy, Ford sold off its luxury brands Aston Martin, Jaguar, and Land Rover and invested in the development of moderately priced, fuel-efficient cars and trucks. Ford took on some extra debt as a hedge against a recession—and had the cash on hand when other U.S. automakers didn't.

Decisions like these require strong leadership qualities that include a will to persevere during tough times. Mulally's first management position was at Boeing. He overmanaged his employees so closely that one engineer finally quit. Mulally says that this early experience taught him that his job as a manager was "to help connect people to a bigger goal, a bigger program and help them move forward to even bigger contributions. That experience stayed with me forever on what it really means to manage and lead."

Mulally recently retired from Ford and was succeeded by long-time Ford executive, Mark Fields. Mulally believes that every employee has something to offer and that each worker must be clear about the firm's mission. He says that his job at Ford was to focus on four things: (1) the process of connecting his firm to the outside world, (2) keeping track of the firm's identity in the marketplace, (3) balancing short-term objectives with long-term goals, and (4) the values and standards of the organization. When asked what career advice he would give to young recruits to the business world, Mulally answers without hesitation, "Don't manage your career. Follow your dream and contribute."

Questions for Critical Thinking

1. How did Alan Mulally's "focus on four things" help him with strategic planning for Ford? Do you believe it made a difference in the firm's decision to decline the federal loan?

2. Mulally emphasizes the importance of having every employee understand the firm's mission. How might this understanding help employees contribute to the company's performance?

Sources: James R. Healey, "Fields Named New Ford CEO, Mulally Retires July 1," *USA Today*, accessed June 2, 2014, www.usatoday.com; Paul Ingrassia, "Ford's Renaissance Man," *The Wall Street Journal*, accessed January 25, 2014, http://online.wsj.com; Keith Naughton and Ian King, "Mulally: Ford Making 'Tremendous Progress,'" *Bloomberg Businessweek*, accessed January 25, 2014, www.businessweek.com; Adam Bryant, "Planes, Cars, and Cathedrals," *The New York Times*, accessed January 25, 2014, www.nytimes.com; John Hockenberry, "Interview with Ford CEO Alan Mulally," PRI/WNYC, accessed January 24, 2014, www.pri.org; excerpt from "Interview with Ford CEO Alan Mulally," from The Takeaway, a co-production of Public Radio International and WNYC. Reprinted with permission.

No Workaholics Allowed at BambooHR

To say that Utah-based start-up BambooHR has a work culture that includes consequences for working too many hours might sound peculiar. But while some start-up businesses demand long work hours, BambooHR, maker of online human resources software, has a strict policy against it. As work–life balance remains an issue for many companies and employees, BambooHR has created a unique culture for its 53 workers with definitive work time policies.

Recently voted by *Utah Business* as a "Best Company for Work For," BambooHR is well known for its workplace culture. Co-founders Ryan Sanders and Ben Peterson have created a unique approach to enforcing a strict policy that work–life balance is not just lip service and reminding employees that a 40-hour workweek does not limit creativity. The company's "anti-workaholics" policy means that all employees must leave the office at 5 pm. Breaks are mandatory, and employees are admonished for not taking them.

Why the fuss? The guidelines, part of the co-founders' core beliefs, have developed from witnessing and hearing firsthand about other business cultures where their friends worked. Sleep deprivation, rewards for working long hours, failed marriages, and stress-related illnesses were just some of the things they observed.

Sanders says working a lot of hours might seem great on the surface, but ultimately it affects the business—in a negative way. One employee, who used to work 70 to 80 hours a week, nearly lost her job because she was sleep deprived, increasingly difficult to work with, and not very productive. Confronted by the company's two owners, she was told she needed to scale back to a 40-hour workweek or risk losing her job.

The company's "no workaholics" strategy has not hurt the bottom line. In its most recent year, the young company posted sales in the millions. BambooHR employees—and their bosses—are united in the belief that one's home life does not need to be sacrificed to build a great company.

Questions for Critical Thinking

1. Discuss the impact on employees of working long hours. What is the impact on productivity? Morale?

2. Defend the merits of a 40-hour workweek to someone who doesn't agree with the concept, particularly in a start-up environment.

Sources: Company website, http://bamboohr.com, accessed February 11, 2014; Devin Felix, Rachel Madison, and Heather Stewart, "Best Companies to Work For," *Utah Business*, accessed January 25, 2014, www.utahbusiness.com; Jennifer Alsever, "Why This Startup Has a No-Workaholics Policy," *Inc.*, accessed January 25, 2014, www.inc.com.

▶ Dan Formosa: At the Forefront of Smart Design

Like many new businesses, Smart Design was founded by a collection of college classmates who wanted to change something. Dan Formosa, along with several college friends, had a background in design and ergonomics. The group believed that design should be about people, not things—and Smart Design was born. In the beginning, it was a hard sell—not the designs themselves, but the idea that the needs of individual *people* should be involved in the development of design. Formosa was interested in "how design can affect our quality of life, improve performance, and affect behavior." Based in San Francisco, the original Smart Design team "pulled together techniques in biomechanics and cognitive psychology," recalls Formosa. "This was a type of an approach that no other design group was undertaking in the U.S. at the time, so it was an early test of our beliefs about what and where design should be." Smart Design was successful throughout the 1980s, but Formosa admits that it was an uphill battle to convince clients that design was, indeed, for everyone.

Then came OXO. Around 1990, Smart Design acquired the manufacturing firm OXO as a client, giving Formosa's team a chance to re-invent the design of common household products ranging from can openers to scissors, resulting in the OXO Good Grips line of kitchen utensils. Because of the mundane nature of these products—consumers weren't accustomed to shopping for a potato peeler that actually felt comfortable in the hand—once they caught on, the idea that everyday design matters began to take hold in the marketplace. Smart Design's client base grew significantly, as did the company. Firms such as Ford, ESPN,

Samsung, Nike, and Microsoft began to request Smart Design's services, and the number of employees increased.

No matter how much talent lies in the firm, though, managing a company of designers can be like trying to herd cats. Everyone has an idea, and everyone is running headlong in a different direction. So leadership is critical to the firm's success. Paulette Bluhm-Sauriol, director of brand communication, observes that while most designers are detail oriented, "Someone has to make sure that the team is keeping the big picture in mind, not just the details." That's part of her job as well as Formosa's: maintaining the overall vision. She also notes that, as a leader, Formosa has the natural gift of connecting and empathizing with people, whether it is employees or potential end-users of Smart Design's products. "Dan has the ability to make going into people's lives and becoming part of their lives comfortable," she observes.

This was particularly true during the development of a new type of pre-filled medical syringe that Smart Design undertook for UCB/OXO Cimzia. The medication Cimzia is a solution that alleviates chronic pain in patients with certain conditions. If patients could administer the solution themselves in a comfortable way, it would enhance their lives. When the pharmaceutical maker UCB and OXO partnered to develop the new product, they went to Smart Design for the design. Formosa asked his team to go straight to the patients themselves to ask them what they needed. Designers met and observed patients in their own environment, giving them a chance to express their wishes. "It can be uncomfortable, but it's amazing how you can get to the big ideas by approaching the project his way," says Bluhm-Sauriol.

The syringe has met with marketplace success, and has even won an International Design Excellence Award.

Most important, patients are getting what they need, which is exactly what Formosa strives for in each product his firm designs. "If someone buys a product or signs up for a service, they expect it to work. If you actually encounter a product or service that exceeds expectations, that is the sign of a great design," he says. Formosa also contends that the same principles can be applied to the design of a delicate hospital instrument as are applied to a pizza cutter.

At Smart Design, the corporate culture supports the notion that the ideas of every employee are important. Regardless of job title, each person is considered a designer, with something valuable to contribute to the process. Formosa doesn't mind the potential chaos of this kind of organization—it's how he operates. "When we have everybody thinking everything, it's a positive sign," he says. It's a formula that works.

Questions for Critical Thinking

1. Describe Dan Formosa's vision for Smart Design. Why do you think it took so long to gain popularity in the marketplace?
2. Identify Smart Design's strategy for competitive differentiation.
3. How would you describe Dan Formosa's leadership style? Do you think it is the best style for Smart Design? Why or why not?
4. Discuss Smart Design's corporate culture. Do you think it is effective for the kind of business the company engages in? Why or why not?

Sources: Company website, http://smartdesignworldwide.com, accessed February 11, 2014; Molly Petrilla, "Q&A: Dan Formosa, Award-Winning Product Designer," *Smart Planet*, accessed February 11, 2014, www.smartplanet.com; "Smart Design," *National Design Awards*, accessed January 25, 2014, www.cooperhewitt.org.

Chapter 8

Learning Objectives

[1] Explain the role of human resources: the people behind the people.

[2] Describe recruitment and selection.

[3] Discuss orientation, training, and evaluation.

[4] Describe compensation.

[5] Discuss employee separation.

[6] Explain the different methods for motivating employees.

[7] Discuss labor–management relations.

Human Resource Management: From Recruitment to Labor Relations

Steve Debenport/iStockphoto

Glassdoor Helps Job Seekers and Employers

Technology and the use of online data have helped change the job search for the better, and Glassdoor is leading the way. Glassdoor is an online job site that assists people seeking work to find the right fit with the right employer. Based in Sausalito, California, the company provides employer information, compensation data, and reviews by current employees—specifics that come in handy when applicants are looking for potential employers.

Started less than a decade ago, Glassdoor has more than 5 million company reviews, salary reports, and interview reviews for 300,000 companies—all used by job seekers as part of their search. A recent survey by Software Advice, a company that reviews recruiting software, suggests that almost 50 percent of people looking for jobs use Glassdoor during their search, and half of the visitors to the Glassdoor site use the posted data to narrow their job search to specific employers. Another 15 percent use Glassdoor after getting an offer, to help them to decide whether to accept the job offer based on information about the prospective employer posted online.

When people go online to post reviews, they are asked to rate companies in five categories: culture and values, work–life balance, senior management, compensation and benefits, and career opportunities. Of the five categories, positive reviews about a company's compensation and benefits are the number one driver of applications to that company, while negative reviews about compensation and benefits are the main reason why candidates don't apply for jobs with that organization.

With a community of 23 million members across 190 countries, Glassdoor also provides employers with a large audience of potential employees. More than 1,000 employers worldwide, including Walmart and Facebook, use the site to support their recruiting and branding efforts. These companies and others encourage their employees to post positive reviews about their work experiences in an effort to keep potential job candidates interested in their companies' brands.

The company has recently introduced a free tool called Glassdoor Employer Center, which allows employers to see who is researching their company and viewing job openings and their employment data. Information made available to employers includes searchers' education level, years of experience in the workplace, gender, and job title. This type of information will help employers determine how better to target potential employees and whether they are attracting the workers they need.[1]

Overview

The importance of employees to the success of any organization is the very basis of management. In this chapter, we explore the important issues of human resource management and motivation. We begin with a discussion of the ways organizations attract, develop, and retain employees. Topics covered include finding qualified candidates; selecting and hiring employees; creating effective training programs; conducting performance evaluations; and implementing compensation and benefits strategies. Then we describe the concepts behind motivation and the way human resource managers apply them to increase employee satisfaction and organizational effectiveness.

We also discuss the reasons why labor unions exist and focus on legislation that affects labor–management relations. The process of collective bargaining is then discussed, along with tools used by unions and management in seeking their objectives.

Human Resources: The People Behind the People

human resource management function of attracting, developing, and retaining employees who can perform the activities necessary to accomplish organizational objectives.

A company is only as good as its workers. If people come to work each day eager to see each other, to do their very best on the job, to serve their customers, and to help their firm compete, then it's very likely that company will be a success. The best companies value their employees just as much as their customers—without workers, there would be no goods or services to offer customers. Companies like Glassdoor, Walmart, and Google understand this. Management at these companies know that hiring good workers is vital to their overall success. Achieving the highest level of job satisfaction and dedication among employees is the goal of **human resource management**, which attracts, develops, and retains the employees who can perform the activities necessary to accomplish organizational objectives.

Not every firm is large enough to have an entire human resources department. But whoever performs this function generally does the following: plans for staffing needs, recruits and hires workers, provides for training and evaluates performance, determines compensation and benefits, and oversees employee separation. In accomplishing these five tasks, shown in Figure 8.1, human resource managers achieve their objectives of

1. providing qualified, well-trained employees for the organization;

2. maximizing employee effectiveness in the organization; and

3. satisfying individual employee needs through monetary compensation, benefits, opportunities to advance, and job satisfaction.

Human resource plans must be based on an organization's overall competitive strategies. In conjunction with other managers, human resource managers predict how many employees a firm or department will need and what skills those workers should bring to the job—along with what skills they might learn on the job. Human resource managers are often consulted when a firm is considering reducing costs by laying off workers or increasing costs by hiring new ones. They may be involved in both long-term and short-term planning.

human resource
management function of
attracting, developing, and
retaining employees who
can perform the activities
necessary to accomplish
organizational objectives.

Assessment Check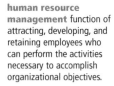

1. What are the five main tasks of a human resource manager?

2. What are the three overall objectives of a human resource manager?

FIGURE 8.1 Human Resource Management Responsibilities

Recruitment and Selection

Human resource managers recruit and help select the right workers for a company. To ensure that job candidates bring the necessary skills to the job or have the desire and ability to learn them, most firms implement the recruitment and selection process shown in Figure 8.2.

Finding Qualified Candidates

When the economy dips and jobs are lost, many people compete for a limited number of positions. When a company develops a great reputation for benefits or working conditions, it might be inundated with résumés. But even with a large number of job candidates competing for a small number of openings, companies sometimes have trouble finding the right person for each position. According to a recent survey by career website Brandresume.com, firms are currently looking for candidates with these skills: social media management, marketing research, mobile application development, data engineering, and talent acquisition.[2]

In addition to traditional methods of recruiting, such as college job fairs and personal referrals, most companies now rely on their websites. A firm's website might contain a career section with general employment information and a listing of open positions. Applicants are often able to submit a résumé and apply for an open position online. When applying for jobs online, it's helpful to use the key words in the job description as part of the application. Also, if a current résumé is required as part of the job application, tailor the wording of the résumé to reflect the key components of the job you are seeking.

Internet recruiting is such a quick, efficient, and inexpensive way to reach a large pool of job seekers that the vast majority of companies currently use the Internet, including social networking sites, to fill job openings. This is also the best way for firms to reach new graduates and workers of all ages. Using a social media site such as Twitter, LinkedIn, or Facebook allows firms to communicate directly with candidates. The "Hit & Miss" feature describes the growth of employee recruitment via mobile devices.

It's also important for job seekers to be as specific as possible when using the Internet to look for a job. For example, if possible, they should apply through the firm's website instead of one of the large, third-party job sites. "Employers see that the vast majority of applicants coming through these [third-party] sites have not done sufficient research, and often are questionable fits for the advertised positions," notes one human resource expert.[3]

Recruiting techniques continue to evolve as technology advances. JobsinPods.com is an online library of podcast interviews with hiring managers and employees at a variety of U.S. companies, including AT&T, Intel, and IBM. New podcasts, also called jobcasts, are posted in a blog format and older podcasts are archived. Some describe employers' hiring needs, while others talk about what it's like to work at a particular company. Job seekers can also download the podcasts to an iPod and listen to them at their leisure.[4]

Selecting and Hiring Employees

It's the human resource manager's job to select and hire employees, often in conjunction with department managers or supervisors. Every firm must follow state and federal employment laws. Title VII of the Civil Rights Act of 1964 prohibits employers from discriminating against applicants based on their race, religion, color, sex, or national origin. The Americans with Disabilities Act of 1990 prohibits employers from discriminating against disabled applicants. The Civil Rights Act created the *Equal Employment Opportunity Commission (EEOC)* to investigate discrimination complaints. The Uniform Employee Selection Guidelines were adopted by the EEOC in 1978 to further clarify ways in which employers must ensure that their employees will be hired and managed without discrimination.[5] The EEOC also helps employers set up *affirmative action programs* to increase job opportunities for women, minorities, people with disabilities, and other protected groups. The Civil Rights Act of 1991 expanded the alternatives available to victims of employment discrimination by including the right to a jury trial, punitive damages, and damages for emotional distress. At the same time, opponents to such laws have launched initiatives to restrict affirmative action standards and protect employers against unnecessary litigation.

These laws have been the basis for thousands of legal cases over the years. Recently Cargill's meat-processing division agreed to pay $2.2 million to job applicants who were rejected based on gender and race. The company agreed to pay money to nearly 3,000 applicants and to offer about 350 new jobs to them as positions become available.[6] Failure to comply with equal employment opportunity legislation can result in costly legal fees, expensive fines, bad publicity, and poor employee morale.

Because of the high cost of such lawsuits and settlements, human resource managers must understand the laws in order to prevent unintended violations. Even the process of interviewing a job candidate is covered by law. An interviewer may not ask any questions about marital status, children, race or nationality, religion, age, criminal records, mental illness,

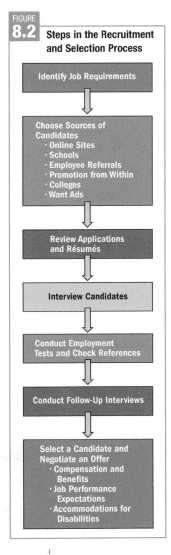

FIGURE 8.2 Steps in the Recruitment and Selection Process

- Identify Job Requirements
- Choose Sources of Candidates
  - Online Sites
  - Schools
  - Employee Referrals
  - Promotion from Within
  - Colleges
  - Want Ads
- Review Applications and Résumés
- Interview Candidates
- Conduct Employment Tests and Check References
- Conduct Follow-Up Interviews
- Select a Candidate and Negotiate an Offer
  - Compensation and Benefits
  - Job Performance Expectations
  - Accommodations for Disabilities

Hit&Miss

Accenture's Mobile Recruitment Strategy

How would you like to use a mobile app to shop for a new career in much the same way that you shop online for shoes? With more job seekers using mobile devices to search for positions, Chicago-based Accenture, a global management consulting firm, uses mobile career pages and social platforms to compete for workforce talent.

Accenture's career app allows mobile users to receive notifications, read job descriptions, ask questions, sign up for alerts, and search for jobs by location. The app provides published podcasts, insights, and company information for job seekers. Accenture's mobile-friendly approach is a good branding strategy, and it increases the chance that candidates will engage with the company directly.

Using location-based services, Accenture targets and connects with qualified candidates by geographic location. Accenture can deliver personal messages to candidates with the interface they use most: mobile devices. For a faster, more intuitive experience, candidates can video record answers to written interview questions from their mobile devices. Accenture recruiters can watch the videos any time or any where, which helps when working around busy schedules. As mobile surpasses desktop in terms of usage, your next job interview might well be on your mobile device.

Questions for Critical Thinking

1. In the competitive world of recruitment, what are the benefits to Accenture of using a mobile approach?

2. Do you believe that mobile recruiting increases hiring success rates and choosing the right candidate for the job? Discuss its pros and cons.

Sources: Company website, "Accenture App for iPhone," http://careers.accenture.com, accessed February 9, 2014; Selena Kerley, "Mobile Recruiting: It's Here to Stay," *The Undercover Recruiter*, accessed February 9, 2014, http://theundercoverrecruiter.com; Meghan Biro, "Leadership Is Catching a Mobile Recruiting Wave," *Forbes*, accessed February 9, 2014, www.forbes.com; Lauren Weber, "How Your Smartphone Can Get You a Job," *The Wall Street Journal*, accessed February 9, 2014, http://online.wsj.com; Jessica Miller-Merrell, "25 Companies with Careers & Recruiting Apps," *Blogging for Jobs*, accessed February 9, 2014, www.blogging4jobs.com.

More and more companies are using the Internet to recruit potential employees. Posting job openings online (including social networking sites) is a quick, efficient, and inexpensive way for companies to reach a large pool of job seekers.

medical history, or alcohol and substance abuse problems. For more information about employment law, visit the websites of the Society for Human Resource Management (http://www.shrm.org) and the EEOC (http://www.eeoc.gov).

Navigating the maze of hiring restrictions is a challenge. Some firms try to screen out high-risk employees by requiring drug testing for job applicants, particularly in industries that deal with public safety—such as air travel or truck driving. But drug testing is controversial because of privacy issues. Also, positive test results may not be accurate. Another issue is whether employees can be required to speak a particular language—usually English—in the workplace. Although the EEOC views this as discrimination, one state recently legalized the practice. And some employers in other states are seeking guidance on whether they can lawfully require English to be spoken in the workplace.[7] Employers may legally establish requirements for specific jobs—a bona fide occupational qualification (BFOQ)—that may cut across EEOC protected classes. For example, a designer of women's clothes by necessity is permitted to hire only female models to show off new designs.

Recruitment and selection are expensive. There are costs for advertising, interviewing, administering employment tests and even medical exams. Once an applicant is hired, there are costs for training and equipment such as a computer. But a bad hiring decision is even more expensive, because the firm has to go through the whole process again to find the right person. One estimate states that the cost of hiring the wrong top-level manager amounts to 24 times the candidate's annual pay. To avoid bad hiring decisions, some companies require job candidates to perform tasks related to the job they're seeking as part of the job application process. For example, a company might ask job candidates for a sales position to work with a company salesperson in the local sales region before making a final decision on which candidate to hire.

To avoid these mistakes—and to get the right person for the job—many employers require applicants to complete employment tests. These tests may verify certain skills, including mechanical, technical, language, and computer skills. One example is the Wonderlic Basic Skills Test, which is a cognitive ability test that measures a person's abilities in understanding words, numbers, and logic. Cognitive ability tests accurately predict job performance on many types of jobs.

3

Orientation, Training, and Evaluation

Assessment Check ☑

1. Describe several recruiting techniques used by human resource managers.

2. What is the function of the Equal Employment Opportunity Commission (EEOC)?

Once hired, employees need to know what is expected of them and how well they are performing. Companies provide this information through orientation, training, and evaluation. A new hire may complete an orientation program administered jointly by the human resource personnel and the department in which the employee will work. During orientation, employees learn about company policies regarding their rights and benefits. They might receive an employee manual that includes the company's code of ethics and code of conduct. And they'll usually receive some form of training.

Training Programs

Training is a good investment for both employers and employees. Training provides workers with an opportunity to build their skills and knowledge, preparing them for new job opportunities within the company. It also provides employers with a better chance at retaining long-term, loyal, high-performing workers. Companies of all sizes take creative approaches to training. Information technology giant Cisco, one of *Fortune's* "100 Best Companies to Work For," provides employees with an online learning and development community that offers access to educational materials and tasks, which employees can rate after using. The company also has an e-mentoring platform that pairs employees at all levels of the organization and a job performance portal where workers can request and give feedback year-round.[8]

On-the-Job Training One popular teaching method is *on-the-job training*, which prepares employees for job duties by allowing them to perform tasks under the guidance of experienced employees. A variation of on-the-job training is apprenticeship training, in which an employee learns a job by serving for a time as an assistant to a trained worker. To bridge the gap between what students learn in the classroom and what companies require, BMW's Spartanburg, South Carolina, plant works with students from nearby technical colleges who train and study 25 hours a week at the manufacturing plant while earning two-year degrees.[9]

Classroom and Computer-Based Training Many firms offer some form of classroom instruction such as lectures, conferences, and workshops or seminars. Ernst & Young, a global professional services firm, offers a training program called Ernst & Young and You (EYU), focusing on classroom learning, experiential learning, and coaching.[10]

Many firms are replacing classroom training with computer-based training programs, which can significantly reduce the cost of training. Computer-based training offers consistent presentations, along with videos that can simulate the work environment. Employees can learn at their own pace without having to sign up for a class. Through online training programs, employees can engage in interactive learning—they might conference with a mentor or instructor who is located elsewhere or they might participate in a simulation requiring them to make decisions related to their work. An extension of computer-based training is multimedia training, which may combine text with sound, 3D animation, high-resolution graphics, games, simulations, and the like.

Management Development A *management development program* provides training designed to improve the skills and broaden the knowledge of current or future managers and executives. Training may be aimed at increasing specific technical knowledge or more general knowledge in areas such as leadership and interpersonal skills. Glimmerglass Consulting

Employees value face-to-face feedback on their performance. Evaluations that are fair and consistent can improve an organization's productivity and profitability.

Group, based in New Hampshire, provides management training in leadership, team development, and strategic implementation. After assessing a client's work environment as well as the strengths and weaknesses of its management team, Glimmerglass coaches design a program intended to strengthen management's leadership and team skills. The program may involve an outdoor learning experience such as rock climbing. Glimmerglass's client list includes such firms as American Express, Big Brothers/Big Sisters, Pfizer, and Shell International.[11]

Despite the importance of training talented employees for managerial jobs, many companies are searching for new hires to fill gaps in their executive ranks because they failed to develop future managers. In a move that surprised the international banking world, David de Rothschild appointed a successor from outside his family—the first in 200 years—to become CEO of the Rothschild banking empire. Nigel Higgins was no stranger to the firm; he had worked there for 27 years. But Rothschild chose Higgins because there was no family member ready to handle the job.[12]

Performance Appraisals

performance appraisals evaluation of and feedback on an employee's job performance.

Feedback about performance is the best way for a company—and its employees to improve. Most firms use annual **performance appraisals** to evaluate an employee's job performance and provide feedback about it. A performance appraisal can include assessments of everything from attendance to goals met. Based on this evaluation, a manager will make decisions about compensation, promotion, additional training needs, transfers, or even termination. See the "Career Kickstart" feature for tips on how to prepare for a performance review.

Some management experts argue that a performance review is skewed in favor of a single manager's subjective opinion—whether it's positive or negative—and that most employees are afraid to speak honestly to their managers during a performance review. If a performance review is to be at all effective, it should meet the following criteria:

- be linked to organizational goals;
- be based on objective criteria;
- take place in the form of a two-way conversation.[13]

Some firms conduct peer reviews, in which employees assess the performance of their co-workers, while other firms ask employees to review their supervisors and managers. One such performance appraisal is the *360-degree performance review*, a process that gathers feedback from a review panel of 8 to 12 people, including co-workers, supervisors, team members, subordinates, and sometimes even customers. The idea is to get as much frank feedback from as many perspectives as possible. By its very nature, this kind of review involves a lot of work, but employees benefit from it because they are more involved with the process and ultimately better understand their own strengths, weaknesses, and roles in the company. Managers benefit because they get much more in-depth feedback from all parts of the organization. Companies such as Halogen Software offer cloud-based performance appraisal software to help firms evaluate employee performance. Organizations as diverse as Dole, Jelly Belly, Princess Cruises, and the San Diego Zoo use products from Canada-based Halogen. However, a potential weakness of this type of review is its anonymous nature.[14]

Assessment Check ☑

1. What are the benefits of computer-based training?
2. What is a management development program?
3. What are the three criteria of an effective performance appraisal?

224

[4] Compensation

Compensation—how much employees are paid in money and benefits—is one of the most highly charged issues faced by human resource managers. The amount employees are paid, along with whatever benefits they receive, has a tremendous influence on where they live, what they eat, and how they spend their leisure time. It also has an effect on job satisfaction. Balancing compensation for employees at all job levels can be a challenge for human resource managers. And while compensation certainly is a factor in job satisfaction, it isn't the only one, as discussed in the "Hit & Miss" feature.

Everyone likes to read about the companies that provide generous employee salaries and benefits. *Fortune* magazine's annual "100 Best Companies to Work For" list includes cash and benefits information as well as other interesting perks. For example, when employees at Cooley, a law firm based in Palo Alto, California, do a good job, they are rewarded with "Snooze or Cruise" certificates, which allow them to come in two hours late or leave two hours early on a day of their choosing.[15]

The terms *wages* and *salary* are often used interchangeably, but actually are different. Wages are based on an hourly pay rate or the amount of work accomplished. Typical wage earners are factory workers, construction workers, auto mechanics, retail salespeople, and restaurant wait staff. Salaries are calculated periodically, such as weekly or monthly. Salaried employees receive a set amount of pay that does not fluctuate with the number of hours worked. Whereas wage earners receive overtime pay, salaried workers do not. Office managers, executives, and professional employees usually receive salaries.

An effective compensation system should attract well-qualified workers, keep them satisfied in their jobs, and inspire them to succeed. It's also important to note that certain laws, including minimum wage, must be taken into account. The Lilly Ledbetter Fair Pay Act of 2009 is one such law, which gives workers more time to file a complaint for pay discrimination.[16]

Most firms base their compensation policies on the following factors: (1) what competing companies are paying, (2) government regulation, (3) cost of living, (4) company profits, and (5) an employee's productivity or performance. Many firms try to balance rewarding workers with maintaining profits by linking more of their pay to superior performance. Firms try to motivate employees to excel by offering some type of incentive compensation in addition to salaries or wages. These programs include the following:

- profit sharing, which awards bonuses based on company profits;
- gain sharing, when companies share the financial value of productivity gains, cost savings, or quality improvements with their workers;

CareerKickstart

How to Prepare for a Performance Review

Performance reviews can bring about feelings of anxiety and uncertainty for both employees and supervisors. Here are some tips for preparing for a performance review.

- *Know yourself.* Evaluate your performance as if you were an outside observer. If applicable, review your performance improvements and accomplishments since your last review. Asking for feedback regularly—from your supervisor as well as from colleagues—will help in your self-assessment to see if you're on track to meet career goals.

- *Think about your future.* The performance review is a perfect opportunity to talk about your future and your career goals—namely, what you might need from the company in terms of training or professional development. Clearly state your goals as part of the discussion. You may want to prepare a career wish list for this part of the review.

- *Provide details.* Annual performance reviews can be based upon most recent work behavior rather than year-round performance. Be sure to provide evidence of meeting or exceeding performance goals in the form of dates and figures, accolades, professional accomplishments, and situations where you believe you have done above and beyond expectations. Be realistic—if you fell short, acknowledge the shortfalls and detail how they will be remedied.

- *The truth can be hard.* Even top performers have room for improvement, so be prepared to stay professional without becoming defensive or angry during the performance discussion. Showing you can stay professional while receiving constructive criticism is important. Come away with items that need improvement. Most importantly, follow up on those items as part of your everyday work performance.

Sources: Josh Patrick, "Ten Reasons Performance Reviews Don't Work," *The New York Times*, accessed February 10, 2014, http://boss.blogs.nytimes.com; Chrissy Scivicque "How to Prepare for Your Next Performance Review," *US News and World Report*, accessed February 10, 2014, http://money.usnews.com; "How to Ace a Performance Review," accessed February 10, 2014, *The Wall Street Journal*, http://guides.wsj.com.

compensation amount employees are paid in money and benefits.

wage pay based on an hourly rate or the amount of work accomplished.

salary pay calculated on a periodic basis, such as weekly or monthly.

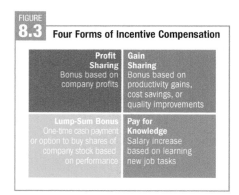

FIGURE 8.3 Four Forms of Incentive Compensation

Profit Sharing	Gain Sharing
Bonus based on company profits	Bonus based on productivity gains, cost savings, or quality improvements
Lump-Sum Bonus One-time cash payment or option to buy shares of company stock based on performance	**Pay for Knowledge** Salary increase based on learning new job tasks

- lump-sum bonuses and stock options, which include one-time cash payments and the right to purchase stock in the company based on performance;

- pay for knowledge, which distributes wage or salary increases as employees learn new job tasks.

Figure 8.3 summarizes the four types of incentive compensation programs.

Employee Benefits

In addition to wages and salaries, firms provide benefits to employees and their families as part of their compensation. **Employee benefits**—such as vacation, retirement plans, profit-sharing, health insurance, gym memberships, child and elder care, and tuition reimbursement—are sometimes offered by the company. Benefits represent a large component of an employee's total compensation. Although wages and salaries account for around 70 percent of the typical employee's earnings, the other 30 percent takes the form of employee benefits.[17] Table 8.1 shows the breakdown of an average worker's benefits as compared to wages or salary.

Some benefits are required by law. U.S. firms are required to make Social Security and Medicare contributions, as well as payments to state unemployment insurance and workers' compensation programs, which protect workers in case of job-related injuries or illnesses. The Family and Medical Leave Act of 1993 requires covered employers to offer up to 12 weeks of unpaid, job-protected leave to eligible employees. Firms voluntarily provide other employee benefits, such as child care and health insurance, to help them attract and retain employees. Some states, such as California, New Jersey, and Washington, have laws mandating paid family leave.

In the past, companies have paid the greater share of the cost of health care benefits, with employees paying a much smaller share. However, as health care costs rise, employers are passing along premium increases to employees. Many companies now offer incentives for workers

employee benefits additional compensation such as vacation, retirement plans, profit-sharing, health insurance, gym memberships, child and elder care, and tuition reimbursement, paid entirely or in part by the company.

226 Part 3 *Management: Empowering People to Achieve Business Success*

8.1 Average Costs for Employee Compensation

TYPE OF COMPENSATION	PERCENTAGE OF TOTAL COMPENSATION
Wages and salaries	69.1%
Benefits	30.9
Paid leave	7.0
Supplemental pay	2.4
Insurance	9.0
Health benefits	8.5
Retirement and savings	4.8
Legally required benefits	7.8

Source: Bureau of Labor Statistics, "Employer Costs for Employee Compensation," press release, http://www.bls.gov, accessed February 15, 2014.

to live healthier lives. Gym memberships, nutrition programs, wellness visits to the doctor, and smoking-cessation classes are all examples of these incentives. At Qualcomm, a global mobile technologies firm, employee benefits include unlimited sick days, on-site gyms, tuition assistance, and work–life balance programs like job sharing, compressed workweeks, and telecommuting. In addition, Qualcomm provides a generous company match on its retirement savings plan and pays 100 percent of the monthly health insurance premium.[18]

Retirement plans make up a chunk of employee benefits. Some companies have reduced the contributions they make to workers' *401(k) plans*—retirement savings plans to which employees can make pretax contributions. Some firms have cut back on cash contributions to the plans and contribute company stock instead. However, others provide a high level of funding. Raytheon Solipsys offers a 401(k) with company match of up to 200 percent on employee contributions.[19]

Flexible Benefits

In response to increasing diversity in the workplace, firms are developing creative ways to tailor their benefit plans to the needs of employees. One approach sets up *flexible benefit plans*, also called cafeteria plans. This system offers employees a choice of benefits, including different types of medical insurance, dental and vision plans, and life and disability insurance. This flexibility allows one working spouse to choose medical coverage for the entire family, while the other spouse uses benefit dollars to buy other types of coverage. Typically, each employee receives a set allowance (called flex dollars or credits) to pay for benefits depending on his or her needs. Contributions to cafeteria accounts can be made by both the employee and employer. Cafeteria plans also offer tax benefits to both employees and employers.

Benefits such as on-site fitness facilities improve both a company's health and that of its employees.

Ryan McVay/Photodisc/Alamy

A two-career couple heads for the daycare center and work. Many employees use flextime to coordinate their work schedules with opening and closing times at schools and daycare programs.

Another way of increasing the flexibility of employee benefits involves time off from work. Instead of establishing set numbers of holidays, vacation days, and sick days, some employers give each employee a bank of *paid time off (PTO)*. Employees use days from their PTO account without having to explain why they need the time. The greatest advantage of PTO is the freedom it gives workers to make their own choices; the greatest disadvantage is that it is an expensive benefit for employers.

Flexible Work

Many firms have moved toward the option of *flexible work plans*, which are benefits that allow employees to adjust their working hours or places of work according to their needs. Flexible work plan options include flextime, compressed workweeks, job sharing, and home-based work (telecommuting). These benefit programs have reduced employee turnover and absenteeism, and boosted productivity and job satisfaction. Flexible work has become critical in attracting and keeping talented human resources.

Flextime allows employees to set their own work hours within certain parameters. Rather than mandating that all employees work, say, from 8:00 A.M. to 5:00 P.M., a manager might stipulate that everyone works between the core hours of 10:00 A.M. and 3:00 P.M. Outside the core hours, employees could choose to start and end early, or start and end late. Flextime works well in jobs that are independent, but not so well when teams or direct customer service are involved. Flextime has gained popularity in the accounting industry. Ernst & Young builds flexibility into its workplace, believing it fosters greater productivity in the long run.[20]

For workplaces that require continuous staffing, cloud-based scheduling software can simplify scheduling and staffing tasks. One such software program, called ShiftBoard.com, lets managers post schedules online; employees log in and request certain shifts or schedule changes.[21]

Some companies offer a *compressed workweek*, which allows employees to work longer hours on fewer days. Employees might work four 10-hour days and then have three days off each week. Such arrangements not only reduce the number of hours employees spend commuting each week, but can stretch out the company's overall workday, providing more availability to customers in other time zones. Hospitals, police and fire departments, and airlines often offer work schedules that allow several long days matched by several days off. Employees at AFLAC, an insurance company, have the option of a three-day (12-hour a day) or a four-day (10-hour a day) compressed workweek. At TreeHouse Island, a technical educator in Orlando, Florida, all employees work a compressed four-day workweek.[22]

A *job sharing program* allows two or more employees to divide the tasks of one job. This plan appeals to a growing number of people who prefer to work part-time rather than full-time—such as students, working parents, and people of all ages who want to devote time to personal interests or leisure. Job sharing requires a lot of cooperation and communication between the partners, but an employer can benefit from the talents of both people.

Home-based work programs allow employees to perform their jobs from home instead of at the workplace. These *telecommuters* are connected to their employers via the Internet, voice and video conferencing, and mobile devices. Working from home generally appeals to employees who want freedom, but also to persons with disabilities, older workers, and parents. Companies benefit from telecommuting arrangements because they can expand their pool of talent and increase productivity without increasing costs. Telecommuters need to be self-disciplined and reliable employees. They also need managers who are comfortable with setting goals and managing from afar. Telecommuting continues to grow, and currently one in five people work remotely. Many workers are interested in continuing to work but on their own terms and on their own schedule. This allows for greater flexibility for workers juggling multiple responsibilities.[23]

More than 70 percent of Generation Y professionals—those just entering the workforce—are concerned with balancing career with personal life. Most simply reject the idea of sitting in an office cubicle for 8 to 10 hours a day. They want the flexibility to do their jobs anywhere, any time. This is placing increasing pressure on companies to offer options such as job sharing, compressed workweeks, and telecommuting.[24]

[5] ## Employee Separation

Employee separation is a broad term covering the loss of an employee for any reason, voluntary or involuntary. Voluntary separation includes workers who resign to take a job at another firm or start a business. Involuntary separation includes downsizing and outsourcing.

Voluntary and Involuntary Turnover

Turnover occurs when an employee leaves a job. Voluntary turnover occurs when the employee resigns—perhaps to take another job, start a new business, or retire. The human resource manager might conduct an exit interview with the employee to learn why he or she is leaving; this conversation can provide valuable information to a firm. An employee might decide to resign because of lack of career opportunities. Learning this, the human resource manager might offer ongoing training. Sometimes employees choose to resign and accept jobs at other firms because they fear upcoming layoffs. In this case, the human resource manager might be able to allay fears about job security.

Occasionally, an employee resigns because of low pay. In some cases, to keep a high-performing employee, the human resource manager might offer a raise.

Involuntary turnover occurs when employees are terminated because of poor job performance or unethical behavior. No matter how necessary a termination may be, it is never easy for the manager or the employee. The employee may react with anger or tears; co-workers may take sides. Managers should remain calm and professional, and must be educated in employment laws. Protests against wrongful dismissal are often involved in complaints filed by the EEOC or by lawsuits brought by fired employees. Involuntary turnover also occurs when firms are forced to eliminate jobs as a cost-cutting measure, as in the case of downsizing or outsourcing.

Downsizing

As the economy tightens, companies are often faced with the hard choice of terminating employees in order to cut costs or streamline the organization. **Downsizing** is the process of reducing the number of employees within a firm by eliminating jobs. Downsizing can be accomplished through early retirement plans or voluntary severance programs.

Although some firms report improvements in profits, market share, employee productivity, quality, and customer service after downsizing, research shows that downsizing doesn't guarantee those improvements. And while in some cases downsizing is necessary and justified, it can have the following negative effects:

- Anxiety, health problems, low morale, and reduced productivity among remaining workers.

- Diminished trust in management.

- Expensive severance packages paid to laid-off workers.

- Loss of institutional memory and knowledge

Assessment Check ☑

1. Explain the difference between *wage* and *salary*.
2. What are flexible benefit plans? How do they work?

employee separation broad term covering the loss of an employee for any reason, voluntary or involuntary.

downsizing process of reducing the number of employees within a firm by eliminating jobs.

- A domino effect on the local economy—unemployed workers have less money to spend, creating less demand for consumer goods and services, increasing the likelihood of more layoffs and other failing businesses.[25]

When downsizing is the only alternative for company survival, there are steps managers can take to make sure it is done the best way possible. A firm committed to its workforce as part of its mission will do everything it can to support the workers who must leave and those who will stay.

Sometimes firms downsize in the hope of attracting a buyer, as in the case of Memorex, the once-iconic magnetic tape brand. About 20 percent of its workforce was let go before the company was sold.[26]

Outsourcing

Another way that firms shrink themselves into leaner organizations is by **outsourcing**. Outsourcing involves transferring jobs from inside a firm to outside the firm. Jobs that are typically outsourced include office maintenance, deliveries, food service, and security. However, other job functions can be outsourced as well, including manufacturing, design, information technology (IT), and accounting. In general, in order to save expenses and remain flexible, companies will try to outsource functions that are not part of their core business.

Although outsourcing might work on paper, often the reality is quite different. Industry observers claim aggressive outsourcing was the reason Boeing's highly touted 787 Dreamliner arrived three years behind schedule and billions of dollars over budget. Boeing outsourced the manufacture of 30 percent of the plane's parts; by contrast, it had outsourced only 5 percent of its iconic 747 aircraft. China's low wages lured many electronics firms and appliance makers to outsource the manufacturing of their goods overseas. However, as wages and shipping costs have increased in China, while energy costs in the U.S. have stabilized, many companies are rethinking their strategies. A recent reversal of the outsourcing trend, called *reshoring*, has slowly occurred, with companies bringing back work to the United States.[27]

⌈6⌉ Motivating Employees

Everyone wants to enjoy going to work. Smart employers know that and look for ways to motivate workers to commit to their company's goals and perform their best. Motivation starts with high employee morale—a positive attitude towards the job. Each year, *Fortune* announces its rankings for the "100 Best Companies to Work For." The most recent top 10 are listed in Table 8.2. Employees at these companies have high morale because they feel valued and empowered.

TABLE
⌈8.2⌋ *FORTUNE's®* Top 10 Best Companies to Work For

1. Google	**6.** Genentech
2. SAS	**7.** Salesforce.com
3. Boston Consulting Group	**8.** Intuit
4. Edward Jones	**9.** Robert W. Baird & Co.
5. Quicken Loans	**10.** DPR Construction

Source: "100 Best Companies to Work For 2014," *Fortune,* accessed February 16, 2014, http://fortune.com.

Solving an Ethical Controversy

Monitoring Employees' Social Media Activities

A study by the Society for Human Resource Managers (SHRM) reveals that more than half of hiring managers report using social media sites to screen and research job applicants. But what happens when companies check out their employees' presence and comments on social media and use this information in the work setting?

Is everything an employee posts online fair game?

PRO

1. In many cases, screening social media information can be helpful in seeing what workers are up to during their tenure with an employer. A well-crafted online profile, a professional presentation, well-written blogs, tweets, and posts can actually make an employee look more favorable and represent his or her employer in a positive light.

2. Employers are using all available tools as part of their HR practices to ensure they have hired the best possible employees. Whatever is found online is fair game—a public profile is just that. It is acceptable for HR managers to search for employees online to learn more about whether they represent the company's best interests.

CON

1. Employers are apt to misinterpret employees' online postings. Information and decisions made about an employee's off-duty behavior can be misleading and irrelevant.

2. It is inappropriate to obtain information that is unlawful to consider in any workplace or employment decision, such as the applicant's race, marital status, disability, or sexual orientation.

Summary

Social media issues continue to blur the lines between a candidate's private and work life. While social media sites can help confirm an employer's decision with regard to hiring and promoting workers, they can also provide information that confirms an employer's decision not to hire a candidate or to let go an employee if downsizing becomes necessary. Employees need to be mindful that their social media behavior can be viewed by anyone—even their employer.

Sources: Jacquelyn Smith, "How Social Media Can Help (or Hurt) You in Your Job Search," *Forbes,* accessed January 28, 2014, www.forbes.com; Sara Jodka, "The Dos and Don'ts of Conducting a Legal, Yet Helpful, Social Media Background Screen," *Law Practice Today,* accessed January 28, 2014, www.americanbar.org; "More Employers Finding Reasons Not to Hire Candidates on Social Media, Finds CareerBuilder Survey," *Career Builder,* accessed January 28, 2014, http://careerbuilder.com; Robert McHale, "Using Facebook to Screen Potential Hires Can Get You Sued," *Fast Company,* accessed January 28, 2014, www.fastcompany.com.

High morale generally results from good management, including an understanding of human needs and an effort to satisfy those needs in ways that move the company forward. Low employee morale, on the other hand, usually signals a poor relationship between managers and employees and often results in absenteeism, voluntary turnover, and a lack of motivation. Sometimes employees use social media to express frustration with management. See the "Solving an Ethical Controversy" feature about the pros and cons of posting comments online about your workplace.

Generally speaking, managers use rewards and punishments to motivate employees. Extrinsic rewards are external to the work itself, such as pay, fringe benefits, and praise. Intrinsic rewards are feelings related to performing the job, such as feeling proud about

Chapter 8 *Human Resource Management: From Recruitment to Labor Relations*

231

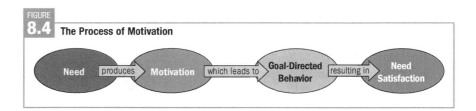

FIGURE 8.4 The Process of Motivation

Need — produces → Motivation — which leads to → Goal-Directed Behavior — resulting in → Need Satisfaction

meeting a deadline or achieving a sales goal. Punishment involves a negative consequence for such behavior as being late, skipping staff meetings, or treating a customer poorly.

There are several theories of motivation, all of which relate back to the basic process of motivation itself, which involves the recognition of a need, the move toward meeting that need, and the satisfaction of that need. For instance, if you are hungry you might be motivated to make yourself a peanut butter sandwich. Once you have eaten the sandwich, the need is satisfied and you are no longer hungry. Figure 8.4 illustrates the process of motivation.

Maslow's Hierarchy of Needs Theory

The studies of psychologist Abraham H. Maslow suggest how managers can motivate employees. **Maslow's hierarchy of needs** has become a widely accepted list of human needs based on these important assumptions:

- People's needs depend on what they already possess.

- A satisfied need is not a motivator; only needs that remain unsatisfied can influence behavior.

- People's needs are arranged in a hierarchy of importance; once they satisfy one need, at least partially, another emerges and demands satisfaction.

In his theory, Maslow proposed that all people have basic needs such as hunger and protection that they must satisfy before they can consider higher-order needs such as social relationships or self-worth. He identified five types of needs:

1. *Physiological needs*. These basic human needs include food, shelter, and clothing. On the job, employers satisfy these needs by paying salaries and wages and providing a temperature-controlled workspace.

2. *Safety needs*. These needs refer to desires for physical and economic protection. Companies satisfy these needs with benefits such as health insurance and meeting safety standards in the workplace.

3. *Social (belongingness) needs*. People want to be accepted by family, friends and co-workers. Managers might satisfy these needs through teamwork and group lunches.

4. *Esteem needs*. People like to feel valued and recognized by others. Managers can meet these needs through special awards or privileges.

5. *Self-actualization needs*. These needs drive people to seek fulfillment of their dreams and capabilities. Employers can satisfy these needs by offering challenging or creative projects, along with opportunities for education and advancement.[28]

According to Maslow, people must satisfy the lower-order needs in the hierarchy (physiological and safety needs) before they are motivated to satisfy higher-order needs (social, esteem, and self-actualization needs).

Maslow's hierarchy of needs theory of motivation proposed by Abraham Maslow. According to the theory, people have five levels of needs that they seek to satisfy: physiological, safety, social, esteem, and self-actualization.

Part 3 *Management: Empowering People to Achieve Business Success*

Herzberg's Two-Factor Model of Motivation

More than 50 years ago, Frederick Herzberg—a social psychologist and consultant—came up with a theory of motivation and work that is still popular today. Herzberg surveyed workers to find out when they felt good or bad about their jobs. He learned that certain factors were important to job satisfaction though they might not contribute directly to motivation. These *hygiene factors* (or maintenance factors) refer to aspects of work that are not directly related to a task itself but instead related to the job environment, including pay, job security, working conditions, status, interpersonal relations, technical supervision, and company policies.

Motivator factors, on the other hand, can produce high levels of motivation when they are present. These relate directly to the specific aspects of a job, including job responsibilities, achievement and recognition, and opportunities for growth. Hygiene factors are extrinsic, while motivators are intrinsic. Managers should remember that hygiene factors, though not motivational, can result in satisfaction. But if managers want to motivate employees, they should emphasize recognition, achievement, and growth. Regardless of their size, companies that make the various lists of "best places to work" have managers who understand what it takes to motivate employees.

Expectancy Theory and Equity Theory

Victor Vroom's **expectancy theory** of motivation describes the process people use to evaluate the likelihood that their efforts will yield the results they want, along with the degree to which they want those results. Expectancy theory suggests that people use three factors to determine how much effort to put forth. First is a person's subjective prediction that a certain effort will lead to the desired result. This is the "can do" component of an employee's approach to work. Second is the value of the outcome (reward) to the person. Third is the person's assessment of how likely a successful performance will lead to a desirable reward. Vroom's expectancy theory is summarized in Figure 8.5. In short, an employee is motivated if he or she thinks he or she can complete a task. Next, the employee assesses the reward for accomplishing the task and is motivated if the reward is worth the effort.

Equity theory is concerned with an individual's perception of fair and equitable treatment. In their work, employees first consider their effort and then their rewards. Next,

expectancy theory the process people use to evaluate the likelihood that their efforts will yield the results they want, along with the degree to which they want those results.

equity theory an individual's perception of fair and equitable treatment.

FIGURE 8.5 Vroom's Expectancy Theory

Chapter 8 *Human Resource Management: From Recruitment to Labor Relations*

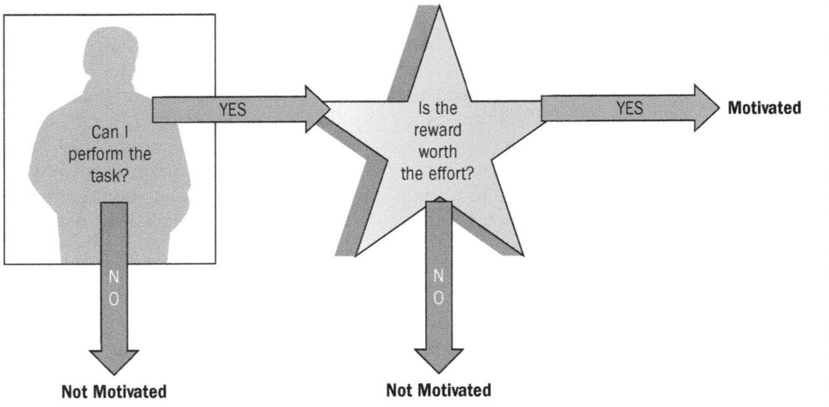

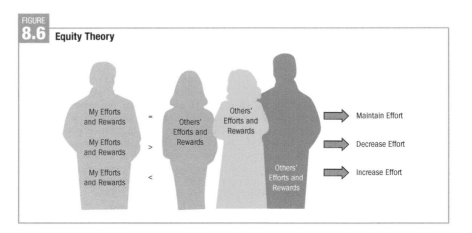

Equity Theory

My Efforts and Rewards = Others' Efforts and Rewards → Maintain Effort

My Efforts and Rewards > Others' Efforts and Rewards → Decrease Effort

My Efforts and Rewards < Others' Efforts and Rewards → Increase Effort

employees compare their results against those of their co-workers. As shown in Figure 8.6, if employees feel they are under-rewarded for their effort in comparison with others doing similar work, equity theory suggests they will decrease their effort to restore the balance. Conversely, if employees feel they are over-rewarded, they will feel guilty and put more effort into their job to restore equity and reduce guilt.

Many workers are willing to work hard as long as the burden is shared. Income inequality is higher in the United States than in any other developed society in the world. For example, today the CEO of a large company in America makes about 354 times more than the average worker. This remains a topic of intense debate. Legislation has been introduced several times in Congress to cap CEO compensation but has been defeated.[29]

Goal-Setting Theory and Management by Objectives

Needs motivate people to direct their behavior toward something that will satisfy those needs. That something is a goal. A goal is a target, objective, or result that someone tries to accomplish. **Goal-setting theory** says that people will be motivated to the extent to which they accept specific, challenging goals and receive feedback that indicates their progress toward goal achievement. As shown in Figure 8.7, the basic components of goal-setting theory are goal specificity, goal difficulty, goal acceptance, and performance feedback.

Goal specificity is the extent to which goals are clear and concrete. A goal such as "we want to reduce carbon emissions" is vague and hard to pin down. But, "we want to reduce carbon emissions by 2 percent" gives employees a clear target. Goal difficulty outlines how hard the goal is to reach. A more difficult goal, such as "we want to reduce carbon emissions by 5 percent in three years" can actually be more motivating than the easier goal.

Goal acceptance is the extent to which people understand and agree to the goal. If a goal is too challenging—such as reducing the firm's carbon emissions by 20 percent in two years—people are likely to reject it. Finally, performance feedback is information about performance and how well the goal has been met. Goal setting typically won't work unless performance feedback is provided.

Goals help focus workers' attention on the important parts of their jobs. Goals also energize and motivate people. They create a positive tension between the current state of affairs and the desired state. This tension is satisfied by meeting the goal or abandoning it.

More than 60 years ago, Peter Drucker introduced a goal-setting technique called **management by objectives (MBO)** in his book, *The Practice of Management*. MBO is a systematic approach that allows managers to focus on attainable goals and to achieve the best results based on the organization's resources. MBO helps motivate individuals by aligning their objectives

goal-setting theory says that people will be motivated to the extent to which they accept specific, challenging goals and receive feedback that indicates their progress toward goal achievement.

management by objectives (MBO) systematic approach that allows managers to focus on attainable goals and to achieve the best results based on the organization's resources.

234 Part 3 *Management: Empowering People to Achieve Business Success*

with the goals of the organization, increasing overall organizational performance. MBO clearly outlines people's tasks, goals, and contributions to the company. MBO is a collaborative process between managers and employees. MBO principles include the following:

- a series of related organizational goals and objectives;
- specific objectives for each person;
- participative decision making;
- a set time period to accomplish goals; and
- performance evaluation and feedback.

Job Design and Motivation

Today's human resource managers constantly search for ways to motivate employees through their jobs. Three ways that jobs can be restructured to be more motivating are through job enlargement, job enrichment, and job rotation.

Job enlargement is a job design that expands an employee's responsibilities by increasing the number and variety of tasks. Redesigning the production process is one way to accomplish this. Instead of having an assembly line on which each worker repeatedly completes the same task, modular work areas allow employees to complete a variety of tasks, which may result in the construction of an entire product.

Job enrichment involves an expansion of job duties that empowers an employee to make decisions and learn new skills leading toward career growth. The Pampered Chef is a direct seller of kitchen tools and housewares that gives its managers and sales consultants the power to make decisions about many aspects of their work. Pampered Chef consultants, who organize home sales parties, can decide how much or how little they want to work and receive various incentive rewards for performance. The company's mission is to provide "opportunities for individuals to develop their talents and skills to their fullest potential for the benefit of themselves, their families, our customers, and the company."[30]

Job rotation involves systematically moving employees from one job to another. Job rotation increases the range of activities by introducing workers to more jobs and therefore more tasks. The goal is to increase employees' interest in their jobs and allow them to learn more about the company. Nurses might rotate from oncology to the ICU in a hospital. Job rotation is often part of a training program, as is the case at EMC, a global provider of business solutions for data backup and storage, information security, infrastructure management, and many other products. EMC offers motivated employees the chance to participate in rotational training programs in business, leadership, finance, marketing, and other areas.[31]

Managers' Attitudes and Motivation

A manager's attitude toward his or her employees greatly influences their motivation. Maslow's theory, described earlier, has helped managers understand that employees have a range of needs beyond their paychecks. Psychologist Douglas McGregor, a student of Maslow, studied motivation from the perspective of how managers view employees. After observing managers' interactions with employees, McGregor created two basic labels for the assumptions that different managers make about their workers' behavior, and how these assumptions affect management styles.

FIGURE 8.7 **Components of Goal-Setting Theory**

Goal Specificity

Goal Difficulty

Performance Feedback

Goal Acceptance

- *Theory X* assumes that employees dislike work and try to avoid it whenever possible, so management must coerce them to do their jobs. Theory X managers believe that the average worker prefers to receive instructions, avoid responsibility, take little initiative, and views money and job security as the only valid motivators—Maslow's lower order of needs.

- *Theory Y* assumes that the typical person actually likes work and will seek and accept greater responsibility. Theory Y managers assume that most people can think of creative ways to solve work-related problems, and should be given the opportunity to participate in decision making. Unlike the traditional management philosophy that relies on external control and constant supervision, Theory Y emphasizes self-control and self-direction—Maslow's higher order of needs.

Another perspective on management, proposed by management professor William Ouchi, has been labeled *Theory Z.* Organizations structured on Theory Z concepts attempt to blend the best of American and Japanese management practices. This approach views worker involvement as the key to increased productivity for the company and improved quality of work life for employees. Many U.S. firms have adopted the participative management style used in Japanese firms by asking workers for suggestions to improve their jobs and then giving them the authority to implement proposed changes.

Assessment
Check ✅

1. What are the four steps in the process of motivation?

2. Explain goal-setting theory.

3. Describe three ways that managers restructure jobs to increase employee motivation.

⌐7⌐ Labor–Management Relations

The U.S. workplace is far different from what it was a century ago, when child labor, unsafe working conditions, and a 72-hour workweek were common. The development of labor unions, labor legislation, and the collective bargaining process have contributed to the changed environment. Today's human resource managers must be educated in labor–management relations, the settling of disputes, and the competitive tactics of unions and management.

Development of Labor Unions

labor union group of workers who have banded together to achieve common goals in the areas of wages, hours, and working conditions.

A **labor union** is a group of workers who have banded together to achieve common goals in the areas of wages, hours, and working conditions. The organized efforts of Philadelphia printers in 1786 resulted in the first U.S. agreed-upon wage—$1 a day. One hundred years later, New York City streetcar conductors were able to negotiate a reduction in their workday from 17 to 12 hours.

Labor unions can be found at the local, national, and international levels. A *local union* represents union members in a specific area, such as a single community, while a *national union* is a labor organization consisting of numerous local chapters. An *international union* is a national union with membership outside the United States, usually in Canada. About 14.5 million U.S. workers—just over 11 percent of the nation's full-time workforce—belong to labor unions.[32] Although only about 6 percent of workers in the private sector are unionized, more than one-third of government workers belong to unions. The largest union in the United States is the 3 million-member National Education Association (NEA), representing public school teachers and other support personnel. Other large unions include the 2.1 million members of the Service Employees International Union (SEIU), the 1.6 million members of the American Federation of State, County & Municipal Employees, the 1.4 million members of the International Brotherhood of Teamsters, the 1.3 million members of the United Food and Commercial Workers, and the 390,000 members of the United Automobile, Aerospace and Agricultural Implement Workers of America.[33]

Labor Legislation

Over the past century, some major pieces of labor legislation have been enacted, including the following:

- *National Labor Relations Act of 1935 (Wagner Act)*. Legalized collective bargaining and required employers to negotiate with elected representatives of their employees. Established the National Labor Relations Board (NLRB) to supervise union elections and prohibit unfair labor practices such as firing workers for joining unions, refusing to hire union sympathizers, threatening to close if workers unionize, interfering with or dominating the administration of a union, and refusing to bargain with a union.

- *Fair Labor Standards Act of 1938*. Set the first federal minimum wage (25 cents an hour), and maximum basic workweek for certain industries. Also outlawed child labor.

- *Taft-Hartley Act of 1947 (Labor–Management Relations Act)*. Limited unions' power by banning such practices as coercing employees to join unions, coercing employers to discriminate against employees who are not union members, discrimination against nonunion employees, picketing or conducting secondary boycotts or strikes for illegal purposes, and excessive initiation fees.

- *Landrum-Griffin Act of 1959 (Labor–Management Reporting and Disclosure Act)*. Amended the Taft-Hartley Act to promote honesty and democracy in running unions' internal affairs. Required unions to set up a constitution and bylaws and to hold regularly scheduled elections of union officers by secret ballot. Set forth a bill of rights for members. Required unions to submit certain financial reports to the U.S. Secretary of Labor.

The Collective Bargaining Process

Labor unions work to increase job security for their members and to improve wages, hours, and working conditions. These goals are achieved primarily through **collective bargaining**, the process of negotiation between management and union representatives.

collective bargaining
process of negotiation between management and union representatives.

Union contracts, which typically cover a two- or three-year period, are often the result of weeks or months of discussion, disagreement, compromise, and eventual agreement. Once agreement is reached, union members must vote to accept or reject the contract. If the contract is rejected, union representatives may resume the bargaining process with management representatives, or union members may strike to obtain their demands.

Settling Labor–Management Disputes

Strikes make the headlines, but most labor–management negotiations result in a signed contract. If a dispute arises, it is usually settled through a mechanism such as a grievance procedure, mediation, or arbitration. Any of these alternatives is quicker and less expensive than a strike.

The union contract serves as a guide to relations between the firm's management and its employees. The

Union workers stage a sit-down protest inside a Las Vegas casino in an effort to secure a new contract.

Julie Jacobson/AP Photos

Chapter 8 *Human Resource Management: From Recruitment to Labor Relations* **237**

rights of each party are stated in the agreement. But no contract, regardless of how detailed, will eliminate the possibility of disagreement. Such differences can be the beginning of a *grievance*, a complaint—by a single employee or by the entire union—that management is violating some portion of the contract. Almost all union contracts require these complaints to be submitted through a formal grievance procedure similar to the one shown in Figure 8.8. A grievance might involve a dispute about pay, working hours, or the workplace itself. The grievance procedure usually begins with an employee's supervisor and then moves up the company's hierarchy. If the highest level of management can't settle the grievance, it is submitted to an outside party for mediation or arbitration.

Mediation is the process of settling labor–management disputes through an impartial third party. Although the mediator does not make the final decision, he or she can hear the whole story and make objective recommendations. If the dispute remains unresolved, the two parties can turn to *arbitration*—bringing in an outside arbitrator, who renders a legally binding decision. The arbitrator must be acceptable both to the union and to management, and his or her decision is final. Most union negotiations go to arbitration if union and management representatives fail to reach a contract agreement.

Competitive Tactics of Unions and Management

Both unions and management use tactics to make their views known and to win support.

Union Tactics The chief tactics of unions are strikes, picketing, and boycotts. The *strike*, or walkout, is one of the most effective tools of the labor union. It involves a temporary work stoppage by workers until a dispute has been settled or a contract signed. A strike generally seeks to disrupt business as usual, calling attention to workers' needs and union demands. Strikes can last for days or weeks and can be costly to both sides. Although a strike is powerful, it can also be damaging to the very people it is trying to help. Surrounding businesses may suffer too. If striking workers aren't eating at their usual lunch haunts, those businesses will lose profits.

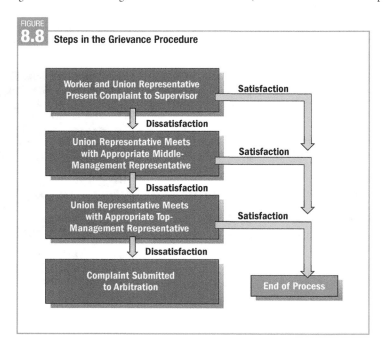

FIGURE 8.8 Steps in the Grievance Procedure

GoingGreen

Labor Unions and Green Construction

The construction industry has nearly unlimited opportunities to make the world greener. One labor union, the Operative Plasterers and Cement Masons International Association (OPCMIA), has already recognized this and is training its members in the use of new green technologies and processes.

The OPCMIA training program, called Green Five, is being incorporated into existing training curricula to reach about 5,400 participants in 70 programs across local chapters, community colleges, vocational/technical schools, and OPCMIA Joint Apprenticeship and Training Centers. The Green Five program trains plasterers and cement masons in the sustainable use and application of concrete, exterior insulation finish systems, and American Clay. The Green Five program includes Green Awareness Training, which deals with energy-efficient building construction in general, addresses the process of energy assessment and retrofitting existing buildings, and provides an overview of environmentally sustainable products and manufacturing processes. Leadership training and "train-the-trainer" courses are offered as well.

Questions for Critical Thinking

1. How does a progressive stance toward green training help secure an important industry role for OPCMIA going forward?

2. Besides construction, what other industries might benefit from unions taking a leadership role in sustainability training? How might these steps benefit workers, unions, and management?

Sources: Organization website, "About OPCMIA," www.opcmia.org, accessed February 16, 2014; Gerry Ryan, "Plasterers and Cement Masons Implement Green Construction Technologies and Training," *OPCMIA News*, accessed February 16, 2014, www.plasterers31.org; Gerry Ryan, "The Green Five Program," *Green Labor Journal*, accessed February 16, 2014, http://greenlaborjournal.com; David Bradley, "TR10: Green Concrete," *Technology Review*, accessed February 16, 2014, www.technologyreview.com.

Strikes seem to be on the decline, however. During the past decade, there have been only 15 major work stoppages on average per year, half the number that took place in the 1990s.[34]

Picketing, which involves workers marching in a public protest against their employer, is another effective form of union pressure. As long as picketing does not involve violence or intimidation, it is protected under the U.S. Constitution as freedom of speech. Picketing may accompany a strike, or it may be a protest against alleged unfair labor practices. Recently culinary union members in Las Vegas picketed for a new contract.[35]

A *boycott* is an organized attempt to keep the public from purchasing the goods or services of a firm. Some unions have been quite successful in organizing boycotts, and some unions even fine members who defy a boycott.

Management Tactics Management also has tactics for competing with organized labor when negotiations break down. In the past, it has used the lockout—a management "strike" to put pressure on union members by closing the firm. However, companies more commonly try to recruit strikebreakers in highly visible fields such as professional sports, or transfer supervisors and other nonunion employees to continue operations during strikes.

The Future of Labor Unions

Union membership and influence grew through most of the 20th century by giving industrial workers a voice in decisions about their wages, benefits, and working conditions. However, as the United States, western Europe, and Japan have shifted from manufacturing economies to information and service economies, union membership and influence has declined. Today, about 40 percent of all union members are government employees.[36]

How can labor unions change to maintain their relevance? They can be more flexible and adapt to a global economy and diverse workforce. They can respond to the growing need for environmentally responsible business and manufacturing processes, as the Operative Plasterers and Cement Masons International Association (OPCMIA) is doing, described in the "Going Green" feature. Unions can establish collaborative relationships with human resource managers and other managers. And they can recognize the potential for prosperity for all—management and union workers included.

Assessment Check ☑

1. What is a labor union? What is collective bargaining?

2. What are the three main tactics used by unions to win support for their demands?

What's Ahead

Treating employees well by enriching the work environment will continue to gain importance as a way to recruit and retain a highly motivated workforce. In addition, managers can tap the full potential of their employees by empowering them to make decisions, leading them to work effectively as teams, and fostering clear, positive communication. The next chapter covers these three means of improving performance. By involving employees more fully through empowerment, teamwork, and communication, companies can benefit from their knowledge while employees enjoy a more meaningful role in the company.

Chapter in Review

■ Summary of Learning Objectives

⌐1⌐ Explain the role of human resources: the people behind the people.

Human resource managers are responsible for attracting, developing, and retaining the employees who can perform the activities necessary to accomplish organizational objectives. They plan for staffing needs, recruit and hire workers, provide for training, evaluate performance, determine compensation and benefits, and oversee employee separation.

Assessment Check Answers ✅

1.1 What are the five main tasks of a human resource manager? The five main tasks are planning for staffing needs, recruiting and hiring workers, providing for training and evaluating performance, determining compensation and benefits, and overseeing employee separation.

1.2 What are the three overall objectives of a human resource manager? They are providing qualified, well-trained employees for the organization; maximizing employee effectiveness; and satisfying individual employee needs through monetary compensation, benefits, opportunities to advance, and job satisfaction.

⌐2⌐ Describe recruitment and selection.

Human resource managers use internal and external methods to recruit qualified employees. They may use college job fairs, personal referrals, want ads, and other resources. Internet recruiting is now the fastest, most efficient, and inexpensive way to reach a large pool of job seekers. Firms must abide by employment laws during selection. Before hiring candidates, human resource managers may require employment tests that evaluate certain skills or aptitudes. When all of this is complete, there is a better chance that the right person will be hired for the job.

Assessment Check Answers ✅

2.1 Describe several recruiting techniques used by human resource managers. Techniques include college job fairs, personal referrals, want ads, company websites, online job sites, and social networking sites.

2.2 What is the function of the Equal Employment Opportunity Commission (EEOC)? The EEOC investigates discrimination complaints and helps employers set up affirmative action programs.

⌐3⌐ Discuss orientation, training, and evaluation.

New employees often participate in an orientation where they learn about company policies and practices. Training programs provide opportunities for employees to build their skills and knowledge and prepare them for new job opportunities within the company. They also give employers a better chance of retaining employees. Performance appraisals give employees feedback about their strengths and weaknesses and how they can improve.

Assessment Check Answers ✅

3.1 What are the benefits of computer-based training? Computer-based training offers consistent presentations, interactive learning, and employees can learn at their own pace. It is also less expensive than other types of training.

3.2 What is a management development program? A management development program provides training designed to improve the skills and broaden the knowledge of current or future managers and executives.

3.3 What are the three criteria of an effective performance appraisal? A performance appraisal be linked to organizational goals, be based on objective criteria, and be a two-way conversation.

⌐4⌐ Describe compensation.

Firms compensate employees with wages, salaries, incentive pay systems, and benefits. Benefit programs vary among firms, but most companies offer health care programs, insurance, retirement plans, paid time off, and sick leave. A growing number of companies are offering flexible benefit plans and flexible work plans, such as flextime, compressed workweeks, job sharing, and home-based work.

Assessment Check Answers ✔️

4.1 Explain the difference between _wage_ and _salary_. Wages are based on an hourly pay rate or the amount of work accomplished. Salaries are paid periodically, such as weekly or monthly. Salaries do not fluctuate with hours worked.

4.2 What are flexible benefit plans? How do they work? Flexible benefit plans offer employees a choice of benefits, including different types of medical insurance, dental and vision plans, and life and disability insurance. Typically, each employee receives a set allowance to pay for these benefits depending on his or her needs.

⌜5⌟ Discuss employee separation.

Employee separation occurs when a worker leaves his or her job, voluntarily or involuntarily. Sometimes an employee is terminated because of poor job performance or unethical behavior. Downsizing is the process of reducing the number of employees within a firm in order to cut costs and achieve a leaner organization. However, some negative effects include anxiety and lost productivity among remaining workers; expensive severance packages; and a domino effect in the local economy. Outsourcing involves transferring jobs from inside a firm to outside the firm. While some expenses may be cut, a firm may experience a backlash in performance and public image.

Assessment Check Answers ✔️

5.1 What is the difference between voluntary and involuntary turnover? Voluntary turnover occurs when employees resign and leave firms to start their own businesses, take jobs with other firms, move to another community, or retire. Involuntary turnover occurs when employees are terminated because of poor job performance or unethical behavior. It can also occur when a company is forced to eliminate jobs.

5.2 What is downsizing? How is it different from outsourcing? Downsizing is the process of reducing the number of employees within a firm by eliminating jobs. Downsizing is done to cut overhead costs and streamline the organizational structure. With outsourcing, companies contract with other firms to perform noncore jobs or business functions, such as maintenance or accounting. This allows companies to focus on what they do best and can result in a downsized workforce.

⌜6⌟ Explain the different methods for motivating employees.

Employee motivation starts with high employee morale. According to Maslow's hierarchy of needs, people satisfy lower-order needs (such as food and safety) before moving to higher-order needs (such as esteem and fulfillment). Herzberg's two-factor model of motivation is based on the fulfillment of hygiene factors and motivation factors. Expectancy theory suggests that people use those factors to determine whether to put forth the effort to complete a task. Equity theory refers to a person's perception of fair and equitable treatment. Goal-setting theory says that people will be motivated to the extent to which they accept specific, challenging goals. Job design is also used by managers for motivation.

Assessment Check Answers ✔️

6.1 What are the four steps in the process of motivation? The four steps are need, motivation, goal-directed behavior, and need satisfaction.

6.2 Explain goal-setting theory. People will be motivated to the extent to which they accept specific, challenging goals and receive feedback that indicates their progress toward goal achievement.

6.3 Describe three ways that managers restructure jobs to increase employee motivation. Three ways that employers apply motivational theories to restructure jobs are job enlargement, job enrichment, and job rotation. Job enlargement is a job design that expands an employee's responsibilities by increasing the number and variety of tasks the person works on. Job enrichment is an expansion of job duties that empowers employees to make decisions and learn new skills leading toward career growth. Job rotation involves systematically moving employees from one job to another.

⌜7⌟ Discuss labor–management relations.

Labor unions have resulted in the improvement of wages and working conditions for many workers over the past century, along with the passage of significant labor laws. Unions achieve these improvements through the collective bargaining process, resulting in an agreement. Most labor–management disputes are settled through the grievance process, in which mediation or arbitration sometimes is necessary.

Assessment Check Answers ✔️

7.1 What is a labor union? What is collective bargaining? A labor union is a group of workers who have banded together to achieve common goals in the areas of wages, hours, and working conditions. Collective bargaining is the process of negotiation between management and union representatives.

7.2 What are the three main tactics used by unions to win support for their demands? Unions use strikes (walkouts), picketing, and boycotts.

Business Terms You Need to Know

human resource management 220	employee separation 229	goal-setting theory 234
performance appraisal 224	downsizing 229	management by objectives
compensation 225	outsourcing 230	(MBO) 234
wage 225	Maslow's hierarchy of needs 232	labor union 236
salary 225	expectancy theory 233	collective bargaining 237
employee benefits 226	equity theory 233	

Review Questions

1. Why has Internet recruiting become such an important tool for human resource managers?

2. Recruitment and selection are expensive. So, what precautions do human resource managers take to make sure they are hiring the right person for each job?

3. Give an example of a type of job that would be appropriate for on-the-job training. Then describe specifically how you think that type of training would work for your selected job, including types of tasks a new hire might learn this way.

4. On what five factors are compensation policies usually based? Name at least three employee benefits that are required by law and three more that are provided voluntarily by some firms.

5. Describe four types of flexible work plans. Identify an industry that would be well suited to each type of plan, and explain why.

6. Why do companies downsize? What are some of the drawbacks to downsizing? Why do companies outsource? What are some of the drawbacks to outsourcing?

7. Select three different theories of motivation, and explain how each can be used by managers to motivate employees.

8. Suppose a manager of a popular sandwich shop maintains a Theory X assumption about employees. At the beginning of each workweek, what types of things might the manager tell his or her employees? Now suppose the manager has a Theory Y assumption; then Theory Z. Describe what he or she might say to employees.

9. In what major ways has labor legislation changed the workplace over the past century? How might the workplace be different today without this legislation?

10. What are mediation and arbitration? Describe a situation that you think might result in arbitration.

Projects and Teamwork Applications

1. On your own or with a classmate, research consulting firms that provide management training programs, such as Glimmerglass Consulting Group, described in the chapter. Prepare a presentation about one of these firms, describing the approach it takes as well as some of the specific elements of the program.

2. Choose one of the following companies, or one that you think you might like to work for sometime in the future. Using the firm's website and one of the job websites such as Monster.com (if applicable), research the company's benefits. Outline the firm's benefits and then determine if you still want to work for that company, and why. Suggested firms:
   a. Timberland
   b. SAS
   c. IBM

   d. Procter & Gamble
   e. FedEx

3. With a classmate, choose an on-campus job and outline how you would share that job. Create a schedule and division of tasks.

4. Choose what you think would be your dream job five years from now. Then create a chart according to Maslow's hierarchy of needs, and identify the ways in which you envision this job fulfilling each level of need.

5. Some employees might question the need for company policies related to workers' appearances. As tattoos and piercings have become more mainstream, discuss the pros and cons of putting appearance-related policies in place in the work setting.

Web Assignments

1. **Human resources (HR) as a profession.** Go to the website listed below and review the data about HR managers.

   http://www.bls.gov/ooh/management/human-resources-managers.htm

   Answer the following questions:

   a. What do HR managers do?

   b. What is the job outlook for HR managers?

   c. Review and discuss the "How to Become a Human Resource Manager" link on the website.

2. **Society for Human Resource Professionals.** If you are interested in working in human resources, you might want to learn about the Society for Human Resource Management (SHRM). An industrywide organization, SHRM supports its members with advocacy, education, seminars, career search, and more. Go to the websites listed below to find out more about the organization. How would becoming a student member help you decide if HR management is a field for you?

   www.shrm.org/Communities/SHRMChapters/ProfessionalChapters/Pages/default.aspx#search

   www.shrm.org/Communities/SHRMChapters/StudentChapters/Pages/default.aspx

3. **Teamsters.** The Teamsters is one of the nation's largest and oldest labor unions. Go to the union's website and review the material. When was the union founded? Originally, the union represented workers in what industry? How many members do the Teamsters currently have? Other than the United States, in what other country does the union represent workers?

   http://www.teamster.org

   Note: Internet web addresses change frequently. If you don't find the exact sites listed, you may need to access the organization's home page and search from there or use a search engine such as Google or Bing.

Evernote's Message to Employees: Go on Vacation

CASE 8.1

Evernote, a California-based maker of note-taking and archiving technology apps, lets its 300 or so employees know that taking vacation is part of the job requirement. The company has made an effort to go beyond the typical two weeks of vacation offered by most companies. At Evernote, there is no limit on the number of vacation days an employee can take.

Initially, CEO Phil Libin worried that workers would take fewer days off, so as not to abuse the unlimited vacation policy. As an added incentive, he instituted a once-a-year $1,000 vacation subsidy to encourage employees, predominantly programmers and engineers, to go on vacation for at least one week. The only proof required to claim the subsidy is an airline ticket or vacation pictures.

Libin extols the virtues of treating employees as adults and measuring them on what they've accomplished in the workplace. He believes that an employer should do whatever it takes to make employees as productive as possible. Evernote is among a growing number of companies providing employees with unlimited paid vacation to ease stress and encourage employees' best work. Evernote's employees are committed self-starters, who need to be reminded that time away from the office is essential to refresh and replenish their energy and productivity.

With burnout and 24/7 connectedness pervasive among many tech workers, Libin implemented the policy to emphasize that workers could take as much time as they want as long as they get their job done. "You're not going to get a lot of work out of someone if they haven't taken a vacation in a while," he says.

Evernote's employees have responded favorably to the vacation policy, and there has been very little reported abuse. Of course, there remain a few employees who could be better at their jobs by taking more vacation. Evernote's CEO believes his employees perform better after they have taken some time off from their work responsibilities.

Questions for Critical Thinking

1. Discuss the impact of an unlimited vacation policy on employees who have to cover for their colleagues taking several weeks off at a time. What strategies need to be implemented to avoid burnout for those covering others' projects?

2. In this ever-connected world, how can employers encourage their workers to "turn off" the workweek?

Sources: Alison Griswold, "The Pros and Cons of Unlimited Vacation Policies," *Business Insider*, accessed February 9, 2014, http://www.businessinsider.com; Peter Weber, "Who Wouldn't Want Unlimited Vacation Days? (You, Probably)," *The Week*, accessed February 9, 2014, http://theweek.com; Adam Bryant, "The Phones Are Out, but the Robot Is In," *The New York Times*, accessed February 9, 2014, www.nytimes.com.

Winning HR Practices at the Cheesecake Factory

There's more to a successful restaurant than good food and mouth-watering desserts. That's why the Cheesecake Factory's culture is built around employee strengths. Managers at the 175-store chain not only focus on improving skills through the employee development plan; they also develop employees' existing talents, such as analysis or collaboration, with enriched assignments and responsibilities. Cheesecake Factory job descriptions are standardized, but they're also flexible so managers can tweak the balance of, say, administrative and field work for individual employees.

While most firms conduct exit interviews to quiz departing employees, the Cheesecake Factory holds innovative "stay interviews." Says its senior vice president for HR, "You talk with them about how happy they are, how satisfied they are at work, and what would it take for somebody to take them away from us. And what is the one thing we could do to improve their work experience."

The chain's strategies show up in its bottom line as well. The Cheesecake Factory was recently voted consumers' favorite casual dining restaurant by *Nation's Restaurant News.*

Questions for Critical Thinking

1. How can the Cheesecake Factory's "stay interviews" affect its bottom line?
2. Do you see any downside to managers' ability to tailor jobs to employees' strengths? Explain.

Sources: Company website, www.thecheesecakefactory.com, accessed February 16, 2014; "Inside the Cheesecake Factory Culture," *Nation's Restaurant News,* accessed February 16, 2014, http://nrn.com; Sherry Benjamin, "How (and Why) the Cheesecake Factory Builds a Strength-Based Culture," *Real Talent* newsletter, accessed February 16, 2014, http://sbenjamin.virtualadminsplus.com; Ron Ruggless, "People Report Recognizes Workplace Excellence," *Nation's Restaurant News,* accessed February 16, 2014, http://nrn.com.

 Timberland's Culture Rooted in Community Building

Timberland's employees agree that what makes the firm unique is the way its culture is brought to life every day, supported by company values of humanity, humility, integrity, and excellence. The role of the human resources department, closely aligned with the company's social responsibility team, is to ensure all events and programs reinforce and support the company's culture of giving, which is at the very foundation of this New Hampshire-based global lifestyle company.

The roots of Timberland's tree logo have often been compared to the foundation of its rich culture of community building. Founded in Boston as a private-label shoe company by Nathan Swartz, it wasn't until the 1970s that his son, Sydney, put the company on the map with its iconic yellow boot. Waterproof and able to withstand the harsh New England winters, the boot's brand name, "Timberland," soon became the name of the company.

The connection between corporate social responsibility and human resources is at the core of Timberland's values. Community involvement not only enhances a community outside of Timberland but also creates one within. As a result of the company's community involvement, workplace collaboration is enhanced, and associates have a unique

opportunity to build relationships with leaders and managers throughout the organization, regardless of rank. It's also an opportunity for all employees to demonstrate leadership and team-building skills.

Timberland's team-building events happen away from its workplace, and they're not in the form of a company picnic or an awards dinner. Timberland's Path of Service™ program, in which all employees are offered up to 40 hours of paid time to use in community service, also provides a team-building vehicle. Its two global annual events include Earth Day in the spring, and "Serv-a-palooza," a day of annual service in the fall. On both days, in an effort to give back and make a difference in the communities where its employees live and work, the company closes its main offices.

In addition to analyzing ways to keep employees productive and motivated, the human resources function at Timberland includes training and development. When associates assume a leadership and development role to put together a community service project, "they get to exercise that leadership muscle." Many employees are motivated by their experiences outside the organization and are helped by helping others.

Timberland's culture of service touches many different aspects of its human resources functions, including training, development, and orientation. At Timberland, community service provides a way to foster learning, create leaders, motivate employees, and increase employee morale. New recruits, as part of their orientation process, participate in a new-hire service event, where they engage and get to know one another. While Timberland does its best to hire motivated self-starters, keeping them motivated is largely a function of the opportunities available inside and outside of its workplace environment. The culture is described as empowering and motivating, and employees agree that growth is a direct result of the company's investment and commitment to its people.

Human resource departments typically deal with issues of employee loyalty, retention, absenteeism, and morale. Timberland's culture of giving has a residual effect of increasing loyalty among its associates. The company also makes commitments in developing countries to help workers, employed by third-party manufacturers, who are engaged in the manufacture of its products with factories scattered across 30 countries. After recognizing the needs of factory workers with children in India, Timberland helped establish a community-based day care center. Investing in factory workers and their well-being has paid incredible dividends in the form of higher morale, increased loyalty, greater retention, and less absenteeism.

Whether it's doing some gardening in the company's "Victory Garden," which sells its organically grown produce and donates proceeds to the local food bank, or helping with a reading program at a local elementary school, Timberland employees work together to forge lasting bonds in and out of the workplace. In addition, employees can use service hours any way they see fit.

An integral part of human resource management is talent acquisition, learning and development, and management of compensation and benefits. Talent acquisition at Timberland is about finding the best people in the industry and helping them grow in their careers. Equally important to an associate's skills set is cultural fit. Talent is scouted primarily using social media sites such as LinkedIn, and the employee referral program has become widely used. The company's policy is to fill openings first with internal candidates. Timberland's human resources group manages its unique and exciting wellness programs, along with its competitive compensation and benefits programs. Onsite wellness programs include the use of a fitness center, soccer games, yoga, and boot camp style exercise. Learning and development are critical to the success of the Timberland brand, and the company is committed to making sure that associates are growing in the same direction, and as quickly as the company.

As an outdoor lifestyle company, Timberland embraces the crucial nature of work–life balance, and the perks the company offers are again connected to its values. Intent on making sure employees connect with the outdoor lifestyle promoted by its brand, Timberland provides kayaks to employees during the summer and snowshoes during the winter. The cafeteria prides itself on healthy food choices at reasonable prices. In addition, there are incentives for biking to work and other wellness activities.

For those who place a high value on community, Timberland is an incredibly unique and special place to work. Its human resource department has spent decades reinforcing the company's unique culture through events and programs that connect associates in a meaningful way. When associates are connected to loving the work they do, they're also connected to the community in which they're doing the work. At Timberland, the company's corporate culture has proved to be as durable as its iconic yellow work boot.

Questions for Critical Thinking

1. Volunteerism and service are key components of Timberland's corporate values. For each of the human resource functions outlined in the chapter, provide examples of the skills employees gain through the company's culture of volunteerism and community service.

2. Provide specific examples of how Timberland's values of humanity, humility, integrity, and excellence come to life within the organization.

3. Discuss Timberland's flexible schedule options and the benefits to employees. Does the company support telecommuting and flexible schedule options? What impact, if any, does this have on company results?

4. Discuss the various ways Timberland keeps its employees motivated. Discuss the ways employees are encouraged to seek out opportunities on their own and to pursue their own path for career development.

Sources: Company website, www.vfc.com, accessed June 25, 2014; company website, "About Us," www.timberland.com, accessed June 25, 2014; company website, http://responsibility.timberland.com, accessed June 25, 2014; company website, www.timberland.com/en/yellow-boot, accessed June 25, 2014; Fawnia Soo Hoo, "Will the Return of Timberland's Classic Boot Help Sell Its Other Styles?" *Fashionista*, accessed June 25, 2014, http://fashionista.com; Natalie Burg, "Timberland and Its Corporate Transparency," *Business Insider*, accessed June 25, 2014, www.businessinsider.com; Karizza Sanchez, "Trend Watch: Celebrities Wearing Timberlands This Winter," *Complex Style*, accessed June 25, 2014, www.complex.com; Leon Kaye, "How Timberland Is Building a Better Life for Factory Workers in China," *The Guardian*, accessed June 25, 2014, www.theguardian.com; Melissa Korn and Audria Cheng, "VF to Buy Timberland, Build Up Outdoor Lines," *The Wall Street Journal*, accessed June 24, 2014, http://online.wsj.com.

Learning Objectives

[1] Discuss empowering employees.

[2] Distinguish the five types of teams.

[3] Identify team characteristics.

[4] Evaluate team cohesiveness and norms.

[5] Describe team conflict.

[6] Explain the importance of effective communication.

[7] Compare the basic forms of communication.

[8] Explain external communication and crisis management.

Chapter 9

Top Performance through Empowerment, Teamwork, and Communication

© mediaphotos/iStockphoto

Yahoo Brings Employees Back to the Office

Working from home might seem like a great idea—lots of flexibility, the opportunity to care for young children or aging relatives, and best of all, no commute to the office. Sounds like an ideal situation. Studies have shown that employees who work from home are more productive than workers in an office. If this is true, then why have Yahoo, Bank of America, Zappos, and Hewlett-Packard, among others, recently decided that many of their workers can no longer work exclusively from home and must come to the office? In the highly competitive business world, these companies believe that innovation springs from employee interaction and collaboration.

Yahoo's CEO Marissa Mayer may have had this in mind when she abolished Yahoo's work-at-home policy and ordered almost everyone back to the office. Mayer believes that people are more productive when they are alone, but are more collaborative and innovative when they work together. And innovation is precisely what companies like Yahoo need to stay relevant in the highly competitive Internet world.

Mayer's decision was not taken lightly. In the technology community, it reignited the debate about the merits of working from home. Some business leaders thought this seemed like a step backwards in an era when working remotely is easier because the business world is so highly connected. Others thought it was a terrible business decision, while some even thought Mayer was trying to get some employees to quit their jobs.

Despite employee objections and competitors' comments, Mayer followed through on her policy change, and less than a year later, the company says that employee engagement has improved, product launches have increased, and work teams are thriving. Will getting workers to come to the office every day make the difference between Yahoo's success and failure? Probably not. However, to be a leader often means making unpopular decisions, ones that are in the best interest of the company. And maybe a change of scenery will help Yahoo's workers spur the innovation and growth that Mayer hopes to create.[1]

Overview

Top managers at organizations such as Yahoo recognize that teamwork and communication are essential for empowering employees to perform their best. This chapter focuses on how organizations involve employees by sharing information and empowering them to make critical decisions, allowing them to work in teams, and fostering communication.

We begin by discussing the ways managers can empower their employees' decision-making authority and responsibility. Then we explain why and how a growing number of firms rely on teams of workers rather than individuals to make decisions and carry out assignments. We discuss the five basic types of teams found in the business environment and provide real-world examples of each type. We also highlight the characteristics shared by effective teams and discuss the five stages of team development.

Finally, we discuss how effective communication allows workers to share information that improves the quality of decision making.

[1]

Empowering Employees

empowerment giving employees authority and responsibility to make decisions about their work.

An important component of effective management is the **empowerment** of employees. Managers promote this goal by giving employees the authority and responsibility to make decisions about their work. Empowerment seeks to tap the brainpower of all workers to find improved ways of doing their jobs, better serving customers, and achieving organizational goals. It also motivates workers by adding challenges to their jobs and giving them a feeling of ownership. Managers empower employees by sharing company information and decision-making authority and by rewarding them for their performance—as well as the company's.

Sharing Information and Decision-Making Authority

One of the most effective methods of empowering employees is to keep them informed about the company's performance. Companies such as Kind Healthy Snacks, a New York–based maker of whole nut and fruit bars, believes that a transparent work environment is one where employees are kept informed and taught to think like owners. It's up to leaders to mentor their teams to develop this type of thinking and to consistently demonstrate how employees can make decisions as an owner in real time. The company's senior vice president of marketing believes that the benefits of this type of work environment are endless and lead to employee loyalty and trust and a flat organizational structure. When a company's employees begin to question the authenticity of company results and information, this can greatly affect the growth of its brand. While some decisions will continue to be made at the top, transparency about why and how decisions are made and listening to employee feedback allows for all team members to feel a part of, and more invested in, company results. Using information technology to empower employees does carry some risks. One is that information may reach competitors. Kind Healthy Snacks knows that setting up systems to share information and providing training to allow employees to understand such information is integral to its core values—a work environment in which the team dynamic and decisions genuinely reflect the company's brand.[2]

The second way in which companies empower employees is to give them broad authority to make workplace decisions that implement a firm's vision and its competitive strategy. Even among non-management staff, empowerment extends to decisions and activities traditionally handled by managers. In a work environment that includes decision-making tools and managerial support, Toyota's frontline assembly workers are challenged to identify and solve problems as they arise on the assembly line.[3]

This can be an especially powerful tool in many health care environments. At Lebanon Valley Brethren Home, a long-term care facility in Pennsylvania, workers at all levels are empowered to do whatever it takes to improve the quality of their elderly residents' lives. Each care worker attends to the same residents every day, so caregivers and residents form a strong personal bond. Caregivers are responsible for the overall management of their households, including meals and housekeeping. They make decisions for individual

Jacob Wackerhausen/iStockphoto

A way in which companies empower employees is to give them broad authority to make workplace decisions that implement a firm's vision and its competitive strategy without seeking managerial input. At Lebanon Valley Brethren Home, a long-term care facility in Pennsylvania, workers at all levels are empowered to do whatever it takes to improve the quality of their elderly residents' lives.

Hit&Miss

Cisco Plays Games as Part of Employee Training

If you like the thrill of reviewing your spot on a leaderboard, completing achievement levels, and earning prizes when playing mobile or video games like "Candy Crush Saga," you may be able to have the same experience right in the workplace. It's called gamification, and companies like Cisco Systems are using the same features found in video games for training, education, and skill-based learning.

Cisco Systems, a network equipment manufacturer, uses an advanced simulation game in which players manage an interactive business as it evolves through the various stages of the Internet over the past 25 years: from the stone age of dial-up modems, through the broadband and mobile connected eras, and into the dawning of the "medianet" age—where all consumer experiences are video based and interactive. The game provides the user with an experience of managing and guiding citizens into the "Connected Life," using Cisco's core visual networking products. The company has also adopted gaming strategies to enhance its virtual global sales meeting and call center operations, made up of more than 19,000 employees. The result? Call times were reduced by 15 percent, and sales improved between 8 and 12 percent.

Questions for Critical Thinking

1. What are your thoughts about gamification strategies for increasing employee productivity? Discuss the pros and cons.

2. How can gamification techniques drive business performance through increased sales, improved learning, and greater employee collaboration?

Sources: Company website, "Celebrate Cisco's 25th Anniversary by Playing Cisco myPlanNet 1.0," http://blogs.cisco.com, accessed February 19, 2014; Farhad Manjoo, "High Definition: The 'Gamification' of the Office Approaches," *The Wall Street Journal*, accessed February 19, 2014, http://online.wsj.com; Justin Bachman, "Playing Games at Work: Just Like Your Boss Wants," *Bloomberg Businessweek*, accessed February 19, 2014, www.businessweek.com; Dan Schawbel, "Adam Penenberg: How Gamification Is Going To Change the Workplace," *Forbes*, accessed February 19, 2014, www.forbes.com; Rob Petersen, "21 Companies Use Gamification to Get Better Business Results," *Barn Raisers*, accessed February 1, 2014, http://barnraisersllc.com.

---

residents ranging from sleep schedules to room lighting. As a result, each Green House—or household within the larger community—feels like a home.[4]

Empowerment can take other forms as well. Cisco is using many features found in video games to motivate and train employees as described in the "Hit & Miss" feature.

Linking Rewards to Company Performance

Perhaps the ultimate step in convincing employees of their stake in the prosperity of their firm is employee ownership. Two widely used ways that companies provide such ownership are employee stock ownership plans and stock options. Table 9.1 compares these two methods of employee ownership.

TABLE

9.1 Employee Stock Ownership Plans and Stock Options

EMPLOYEE STOCK OPTION PLANS	STOCK OPTIONS
Company-sponsored trust fund holds shares of stock for employees	Company gives employees the option to buy shares of its stock
Usually covers all full-time employees	Can be granted to one, a few, or all employees
Employer pays for the shares of stock	Employees pay a set price to exercise the option
Employees receive stock shares (or value of stock) upon retiring or leaving the company	Employees receive shares of stock when (and if) they exercise the option, usually during a set period

Sources: "Employee Stock Options and Ownership (ESOP)," Reference for Business, http://www.referenceforbusiness.com, accessed February 15, 2014; "Employee Stock Options Fact Sheet," National Center for Employee Ownership, http://www.nceo.org, accessed February 15, 2014.

Chapter 9 *Top Performance through Empowerment, Teamwork, and Communication* **249**

Employee Stock Ownership Plans More than 11 million workers participate in 12,000 *employee stock ownership plans (ESOPs)* worth almost $858 billion.[5] These plans benefit employees by giving them ownership stakes in their companies, leading to potential profits as the value of their firm increases. Under ESOPs, the employer buys shares of the company stock on behalf of the employee as a retirement benefit. The accounts continue to grow in value tax-free, and when employees leave the company, they can cash in their stock shares. Employees are motivated to work harder and smarter than they would without ESOPs because as part owners, they share in their firm's financial success. More than 84 percent of companies surveyed that offer ESOPs report an increase in employee productivity.[6]

As retirement plans, ESOPs must comply with government regulations designed to protect pension benefits. Because ESOPs can be expensive to set up, they are more common in larger firms than in smaller ones. Public companies with ESOPs average around 14,000 employees, and private companies average about 2,100 employees.[7] One danger with ESOPs is that if the majority of an employee's retirement funds are in company stock and the value falls dramatically, the employee—like other investors—will be financially harmed.[8]

Stock Options Another popular way for companies to share ownership with their employees is through the use of *stock options*, or the right to buy a specified amount of company stock at a given price within a given time period. In contrast to an ESOP, in which the company holds stock for the benefit of employees, stock options give employees a chance to own the stock themselves if they exercise their options by completing the stock purchase. If an employee receives an option on 100 shares at $10 per share and the stock price goes up to $25, the employee can exercise the option to buy those 100 shares at $10 each, sell them at the market price of $25, and pocket the difference. If the stock price never goes above the option price, the employee isn't required to exercise the option.[9]

Although options were once limited to senior executives and members of the board of directors, some companies now grant stock options to employees at all levels. Federal labor laws allow stock options to be granted to both hourly and salaried employees. It is estimated that 11 million employees in thousands of companies hold stock options.[10] About one-third of all stock options issued by U.S. corporations go to the top five executives at each firm. Much of the remainder goes to other executives and managers, who make up only about 2 percent of the U.S. workforce. Yet there is solid evidence that stock options motivate regular employees to perform better. Some argue that to be most effective as motivators, stock options need to be granted to a much broader base of employees.

Over the past few decades, there have been many stories of stock-options millionaires. After five years at Google, Bonnie Brown—the company's 40th employee and in-house masseuse—cashed out millions of dollars in stock options and retired.[11] But today, such success stories are no guarantee, especially with the volatility of stock prices during a volatile economy. As with ESOPs, employees face risks when they rely on a single company's stock to provide them. In addition to stock options and ESOPs, many firms offer their executives other perks or special privileges.

Restricted stock awards are a popular alternative to stock options. Restricted stock gives employees the full value of a company's stock at a future date when, for example, a performance target or continued employment time is met. These awards are growing in popularity because of favorable accounting rules and income tax treatment.[12]

`2` Teams

A <u>team</u> is a group of people with certain skills who are committed to a common purpose, approach, and set of performance goals. All team members hold themselves mutually responsible and accountable for accomplishing their objectives. Teams are widely used in business

Assessment Check ☑

1. What is empowerment?

2. How can managers empower employees?

3. How do employee stock ownership plans and stock options reward employees and encourage empowerment?

team group of people with certain skills who are committed to a common purpose, approach, and set of performance goals.

and in many not-for-profit organizations such as hospitals and government agencies. Teams are one of the most frequently discussed topics in employee training programs, because teams require that people learn how to work effectively together. Many firms emphasize the importance of teams during their hiring processes, asking job applicants about their previous experiences as team members. Why? Because companies want to hire people who can work well with other people and pool their talents and ideas to achieve more together than they could achieve working alone. Figure 9.1 outlines five basic types of teams: work teams, problem-solving teams, self-managed teams, cross-functional teams, and virtual teams.

About two-thirds of U.S. firms currently use **work teams**, which are relatively permanent groups of employees. In this approach, people with complementary skills perform the day-to-day work of the organization. A work team might include all the workers involved in assembling and packaging a product—it could be anything from cupcakes to cars. Most of Walmart's major vendors maintain offices near its headquarters in Bentonville, Arkansas. Typically, the vendor offices operate as work teams, and the heads of these vendor offices often have the title of "team leader."

In contrast to work teams, a **problem-solving team** is a temporary combination of workers who gather to solve a specific problem and then disband. They differ from work teams in important ways, though. Work teams are permanent units designed to handle any business problem that arises, but problem-solving teams pursue specific missions. When consumer products giant Johnson & Johnson discovered that 200,000 bottles of liquid Motrin for infants might contain small particles of plastic, the company immediately issued a product recall. The company then created supply chain and quality work teams to implement a single streamlined supply chain, shifting its focus to earlier detection of potential problems. More than $100 million has been spent to upgrade plant equipment at one of the company's facilities where the problems originated. In addition, an outside consulting firm has been brought in to evaluate procedures and systems on an ongoing basis.[13] Typically, when a problem is solved, the team disbands—but in some cases, the team may develop or take on a more permanent role within the firm, as is the case at Johnson & Johnson.

A work team empowered with the authority to decide how its members complete their daily tasks is called a **self-managed team**. A self-managed team works most effectively when it combines employees with a range of skills and functions. Members are cross-trained to perform each other's jobs as needed. Distributing decision-making authority in this way can free members to concentrate on satisfying customers. Whole Foods Market has a structure based on self-managed work teams. Company managers decided that Whole Foods could be most innovative if employees made decisions themselves. Every employee is part of a team, and each store has about ten teams handling separate functions, such as groceries, bakery, and customer service. Each team handles responsibilities related to setting goals, hiring and training employees, scheduling team members, and purchasing goods to stock. Teams meet at least monthly to review goals and performance, solve problems, and explore new ideas. Whole Foods awards bonuses based on the teams' performance relative to their goals.[14]

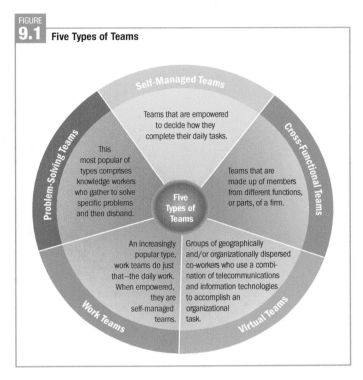

FIGURE 9.1 Five Types of Teams

Five Types of Teams

Self-Managed Teams — Teams that are empowered to decide how they complete their daily tasks.

Problem-Solving Teams — This most popular of types comprises knowledge workers who gather to solve specific problems and then disband.

Cross-Functional Teams — Teams that are made up of members from different functions, or parts, of a firm.

Work Teams — An increasingly popular type, work teams do just that—the daily work. When empowered, they are self-managed teams.

Virtual Teams — Groups of geographically and/or organizationally dispersed co-workers who use a combination of telecommunications and information technologies to accomplish an organizational task.

work team relatively permanent group of employees with complementary skills who perform the day-to-day work of organizations.

problem-solving team temporary or permanent combination of workers who gather to solve a specific problem.

self-managed team work team that has the authority to decide how its members complete their daily tasks.

Although members of a virtual team rarely meet in person, they stay in touch through technologies such as videoconferencing. In today's global marketplace, the flexibility of virtual teams is a distinct advantage

cross-functional team a team made up of members from different functions, such as production, marketing, and finance.

virtual team group of geographically or organizationally dispersed co-workers who use a combination of telecommunications and information technologies to accomplish an organizational task.

Assessment Check ☑

1. What is a team?

2. What are the five types of teams, and how are they different?

A team made up of members from different functions, such as production, marketing, and finance, is called a **cross-functional team**. Most often, cross-functional teams work on specific problems or projects, but they can also serve as permanent work team arrangements. The value of cross-functional teams comes from their ability to bring different perspectives— as well as different types of expertise—to a work effort. Communication is key to the success of cross-functional teams. Chatter is a networking tool developed by Salesforce.com that allows internal information sharing across different business units and divisions of companies. Chatter "is an integrated view into your entire business," says Marc Benioff, Salesforce.com's co-founder.[15]

Virtual teams are groups of geographically or organizationally dispersed co-workers who use a combination of telecommunications and information technologies to accomplish an organizational task. Because of the availability of e-mail, videoconferencing, and group-communication software, members of virtual teams rarely meet face to face. The principal advantage of virtual teams is that they are very flexible. Employees can work with each other regardless of physical location, time zone, or organizational affiliation. Because of their very nature, virtual teams that are scattered across the globe can be difficult to manage. But firms that are committed to them believe that the benefits outweigh the drawbacks. See the "Solving an Ethical Controversy" feature for a discussion of both sides.

⌐3⌐ Team Characteristics

Effective teams share a number of characteristics. They must be an appropriate size to accomplish their work. In addition to size, teams also can be categorized according to the similarities and differences among team members, called *level* and *diversity*. We discuss these three characteristics next.

252 Part 3 *Management: Empowering People to Achieve Business Success*

Solving an Ethical Controversy

Who Benefits from Virtual Teamwork?

Virtual teams are teams of professionals, some or all of whose members work from home or in various off-site locations, to reach a common objective or goal. They work and keep in touch using web-based technology tools, project management software, and voice-over-Internet services such as Skype. By reducing the need for office space and overhead, they can generate lower costs. But some companies fear that geographically dispersed employees pose greater management challenges.

Are virtual teams good for business and for employees?

PRO

1. Virtual teams let managers tap the most skilled and most diverse members regardless of their location.

2. Team members who don't commute can enjoy better work–life balance and flexible schedules with fewer interruptions.

CON

1. Communication among team members can be difficult across different cultures, time zones, and technologies, so misunderstandings and errors can occur.

2. Virtual teamwork calls for everyone to learn new skills and behaviors.

Summary

Virtual teams can't solve all problems, but with the right members, they can often achieve more than other teams and at lower cost. For best results, managers should hire people suited to working virtually, choose an experienced team leader, set clear goals, and make sure the right technology is in place. Occasional in-person team meetings help too.

Sources: Michael Wood, "Virtual Teams: Do the Challenges Outweigh the Benefits?" *Project Management,* accessed February 19, 2014, www.projectmanagement.com; "5 Tips to Establishing a Successful Virtual Team," *Virtual Teams,* accessed February 12, 2014, http://virtualteamsblog.com; "Virtual Teams: Pros, Cons & Best Practices," *Fast Fedora,* accessed February 12, 2014, http://fastfedora.com; Maan Laxa, "Pros & Cons of Working with Virtual Teams," *Pepper Virtual Assistant,* accessed February 12, 2014, www.peppervirtualassistant.com.

Team Size

Teams can range in number from as few as two people to as many as 150 people. In practice, however, most teams have fewer than 12 members. Although no ideal size limit applies to every team, research on team effectiveness indicates that they achieve their best results with about six or seven members. A group of this size is big enough to benefit from a variety of diverse skills, yet small enough to allow members to communicate easily and feel part of a close-knit group.

Certainly, groups smaller or larger than this can be effective, but they also create added challenges for team leaders. Participants in small teams of two to four members often show a desire to get along with each other. They tend to favor informal interactions marked by discussions of personal topics, and they make only limited demands on team leaders. A large team with more than 12 members poses a different challenge for team leaders because decision making may work slowly and participants may feel less committed to team goals. Larger teams also tend to foster disagreements, absenteeism, and membership turnover. Subgroups may form, leading to possible conflicts among various functions. As a general rule, a team of more than 20 people should be divided into subteams, each with its own members and goals.

Strong teams not only have talented members but members who are different in terms of ability, experience, personality, and cultural backgrounds. For example, cosmetics maker L'Oréal USA capitalizes on team members' different perspectives to create products that cater to specific ethnic concerns.

Team Level and Team Diversity

team level average level of ability, experience, personality, or any other factor on a team.

team diversity variances or differences in ability, experience, personality, or any other factor on a team.

Team level is the average level of ability, experience, personality, or any other factor on a team. Businesses consider team level when they need teams with a particular set of skills or capabilities to do their jobs well. For example, an environmental engineering firm might put together a team with a high level of experience to write a proposal for a large contract.

While team level represents the average level or capability on a team, **team diversity** represents the differences in ability, experience, personality, or any other factor on a team. Strong teams not only have talented members—as demonstrated by their team level—but also members who are different in terms of ability, experience, or personality. Team diversity is an important consideration for teams that must complete a wide range of different tasks or particularly complex tasks. Using a diverse teams approach, L'Oréal USA worked on a project designed to understand the problems non-Caucasian women face when it comes to buying the appropriate shade of cosmetics for their skin tones. The team's work helped the company create a brand that caters to specific ethnic concerns. The diversity and industry experience of the team's members has had a direct impact on L'Oréal's success in new product innovation.[16]

Team diversity is an important component of many successful companies. Read how Sheryl Sandberg and Facebook put this strategy to good use as described in the "Hit & Miss" feature.

Stages of Team Development

Teams typically progress through five stages of development: forming, storming, norming, performing, and adjourning. Although not every team passes through each of these stages, those teams that do are usually better performers. These stages are summarized in Figure 9.2.

Stage 1: Forming Forming is an orientation period during which team members get to know each other and find out the behaviors that are acceptable to the group. Team members begin with curiosity about expectations of them and whether they will fit in with the group. An effective team leader provides time for members to become acquainted.

Stage 2: Storming The personalities of team members begin to emerge during the storming stage, as members clarify their roles and expectations. Conflicts may arise, as people disagree over the team's mission and jockey for position and control of the group. Subgroups may form based on common interests or concerns. At this stage, the team leader must encourage everyone to participate, allowing members to work through their uncertainties and conflicts. Teams must move beyond this stage to achieve real productivity.

Stage 3: Norming During the norming stage, members resolve differences, accept each other, and reach broad agreement about the roles of the team leader and other participants. This stage is usually brief, and the team leader should use it to emphasize the team's unity and the importance of its objectives.

Stage 4: Performing While performing, members focus on solving problems and accomplishing tasks. They interact frequently and handle conflicts in constructive ways. The team leader encourages contributions from all members. He or she should attempt to get any nonparticipating team members involved.

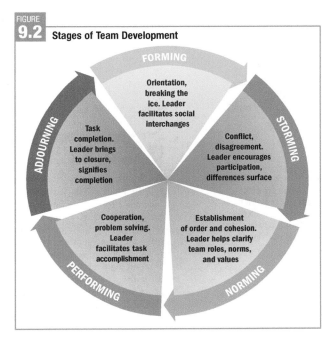

FIGURE 9.2 Stages of Team Development

Stage 5: Adjourning The team adjourns after members have completed the assigned task or solved the problem. During this phase, the focus is on wrapping up and summarizing the team's experiences and accomplishments. The team leader may recognize the team's accomplishments with a celebration, perhaps handing out plaques or awards.

Assessment Check ✓

1. Explain team level and team diversity.

2. Explain how teams progress through the stages of team development.

Chapter 9 *Top Performance through Empowerment, Teamwork, and Communication*

255

Team Cohesiveness and Norms

team cohesiveness
extent to which team
members feel attracted to
the team and motivated to
remain part of it.

Teams tend to maximize productivity when they form into highly cohesive units. **Team cohesiveness** is the extent to which members feel attracted to the team and motivated to remain part of it. This cohesiveness typically increases when members interact frequently, share common attitudes and goals, and enjoy being together. Cohesive groups have a better chance of retaining their members than those that do not achieve cohesiveness. As a result, cohesive groups typically experience lower turnover. In addition, team cohesiveness promotes cooperative behavior, generosity, and a willingness on the part of team members to help each other. When team cohesiveness is high, team members are more motivated to contribute to the team, because they want the approval of other team members. Not surprisingly, studies have clearly established that cohesive teams quickly achieve high levels of performance and consistently perform better.

Team-building retreats are one way to encourage cohesiveness and improve satisfaction and retention. Firms that specialize in conducting these retreats offer a wide range of options. Massachusetts–based TeamBonding is a company specializing in creating customized corporate retreats and team-building experiences. Clients like American Express, Disney, and Apple can choose among a variety of events, including a high-tech scavenger hunt using tablets and smart phones, location-based trivia, and photo and video challenges.[17]

team norm standard of conduct shared by team members that guides their behavior.

A **team norm** is a standard of conduct shared by team members that guides their behavior. Norms are not formal written guidelines; they are informal standards that identify key values and clarify team members' expectations. In highly productive teams, norms contribute to constructive work and the accomplishment of team goals. At Texas–based retailer The Container Store, employees come first. CEO Kip Tindell believes strongly that if his employees are paid better and given excellent training, they will take care of their customers. Each new employee receives one week of intensive training and more than 263 hours of formal training during his or her first year with the company. Team norms include supportive and spontaneous ways in which employees take time to recognize and support the efforts of co-workers.[18]

Assessment Check ✅

1. How does cohesiveness affect teams?
2. What is a team norm?

Team Conflict

conflict situation in which one person's or group's needs do not match those of another, and attempts may be made to block the opposing side's intentions or goals.

Conflict occurs when one person's or group's needs do not match those of another, and attempts may be made to block the opposing side's intentions or goals. Conflict and disagreement are inevitable in most teams. But this shouldn't surprise anyone. People who work together are naturally going to disagree about what and how things are done. What causes conflict in teams? Although almost anything can lead to conflict—casual remarks that unintentionally offend a team member or fighting over scarce resources—the primary cause of team conflict is disagreement over goals and priorities. Other common causes of team conflict include disagreements over task-related issues, interpersonal incompatibilities, simple fatigue, and team diversity.

Earlier in this chapter we noted how teams can experience diversity among members. While diversity brings stimulation, challenge, and energy, it can also lead to conflict. The job of the manager is to create an environment in which differences are appreciated and in which a team of diverse individuals works productively together. Diversity awareness training programs can reduce conflict by bringing these differences out in the open and identifying the unique talents of diverse individuals.

cognitive conflict disagreement that focuses on problem- and issue-related differences of opinion.

Although most people think conflict should be avoided, management experts note that conflict can actually enhance team performance. The key to dealing with conflict is making sure that the team experiences the right kind of conflict. **Cognitive conflict** focuses on problem-related differences of opinion, and reconciling those differences strongly improves team performance. With cognitive conflict, team members disagree because their different experiences and expertise lead them to different views of the problem and its solutions.

256

Cognitive conflict is also characterized by a willingness to examine, compare, and reconcile differences to produce the best possible solution. By contrast, affective conflict refers to the emotional reactions that can occur when disagreements become personal rather than professional, and these differences strongly decrease team performance. Because affective conflict often results in hostility, anger, resentment, distrust, cynicism, and apathy, it can make people uncomfortable, cause them to withdraw, decrease their commitment to a team, lower the satisfaction of team members, and decrease team cohesiveness. So, unlike cognitive conflict, affective conflict undermines team performance by preventing teams from engaging in activities that are critical to team effectiveness.

What can managers do to manage team conflict—and even make it work for them? Perhaps the team leader's most important contribution to conflict resolution can be facilitating good communication so that teammates respect each other and are free to disagree with each other. Ongoing, effective communication ensures that team members perceive each other accurately, understand what is expected of them, and obtain the information they need. Taking this a step further, organizations should evaluate situations or conditions in the workplace that might be causing conflict. Solving a single conflict isn't helpful if there are problems systemic to the team or to the company. Team-building exercises, listening exercises, and role-playing can help employees learn to become better team members.[19]

affective conflict disagreement that focuses on individuals or personal issues.

Assessment Check

1. What is cognitive conflict, and how does it affect teams?
2. Explain affective conflict and its impact on teams.

6 The Importance of Effective Communication

Countries such as China, India, and Mexico are home to businesses that provide goods and services to companies or consumers in the United States. But the more parties involved in the production process, the harder it is to coordinate communication. American Giant, a South Carolina–based maker of sweatshirts and other clothing, experienced miscommunications with its Indian fabric suppliers that caused manufacturing issues, shipment delays, and increased costs. After unsuccessful attempts to get fabric made according to its specifications, the company decided to bring manufacturing back to the United States.[20]

Communication can be defined as a meaningful exchange of information through messages. Few businesses can succeed without effective communication. In fact, miscommunication can result in damage to the company and can be costly. Starbucks terminated its contract with Kraft for distribution of its packaged coffee in retail stores. Starbucks said that Kraft (now Mondelez International) did not deliver on its responsibilities to the Starbucks brand under the agreement—working closely with Starbucks on marketing decisions and customer contact. The miscommunication cost Starbucks an early contract termination fee of $2.76 billion paid to Mondelez.[21]

Managers spend about 80 percent of their time—nearly six and a half hours of every eight-hour day—in direct communication with others, whether on the telephone, in meetings, via e-mail, or in individual conversations. Company recruiters consistently rate effective communication, such as listening, conversing, and giving feedback, as the most important skill they look for when hiring new employees. In the last part of this chapter, you'll learn about the communication process, the basic forms of communication, and ways to improve communication within organizations.

communication meaningful exchange of information through messages.

The Process of Communication

Every communication follows a step-by-step process that involves interactions among six elements: sender, message, channel, audience, feedback, and context. This process is illustrated in Figure 9.3.

In the first step, the *sender* composes the message and sends it through a communication carrier, or channel. Encoding a message means that the sender translates its meaning into

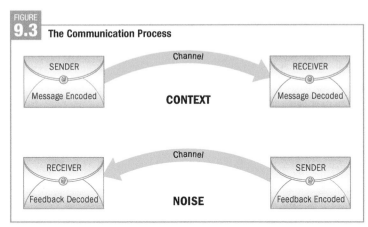

FIGURE 9.3 The Communication Process

```
SENDER          Channel          RECEIVER
  @                                  @
Message Encoded                  Message Decoded

            CONTEXT

RECEIVER         Channel          SENDER
  @                                  @
Feedback Decoded                 Feedback Encoded

            NOISE
```

understandable terms and a form that allows transmission through a chosen channel. The sender can communicate a particular message through many different channels, including face-to-face conversations, phone calls, and e-mail or texting. A promotional message to the firm's customers may be communicated through such forms as radio and television ads, billboards, magazines and newspapers, sales presentations, and social media such as Facebook and Twitter. The audience consists of the people who receive the message. In decoding, the receiver of the message interprets its meaning. Feedback from the audience—in response to the sender's communication—helps the sender determine whether the audience has correctly interpreted the intended meaning of the message.

Every communication takes place in some sort of situational or cultural context. The *context* can exert a powerful influence on how well the process works. A conversation between two people in a quiet office, for example, may be a very different experience from the same conversation held at a noisy party. An American who orders chips in an English tavern will receive French fries.

Anthropologists classify cultures as low context and high context. Communication in *low-context cultures* tends to rely on explicit written and verbal messages. Examples include Switzerland, Austria, Germany, and the United States. In contrast, communication in *high-context cultures*—such as those of Japan, Latin America, and India—depends not only on the message itself but also on the conditions that surround it, including nonverbal cues, past and present experiences, and personal relationships among the parties. Westerners must carefully temper their low-context style to the expectations of colleagues and clients from high-context countries. Although Americans tend to favor direct interactions and want to "get down to business" soon after shaking hands or sitting down to a business dinner, businesspeople in Mexico and Asian countries prefer to become acquainted before discussing details. When conducting business in these cultures, wise visitors allow time for relaxed meals during which business-related topics are avoided.

Senders must pay attention to audience feedback, even requesting it if none is forthcoming, because this response clarifies whether the communication has conveyed the intended message. Feedback can indicate whether the receiver heard the message and was able to decode it accurately. Even when the receiver tries to understand, the communication may fail if the message contained jargon or ambiguous words.

Noise during the communication process is some type of interference that influences the transmission of messages and feedback. It can result from simple physical factors such as poor reception of a cell phone message or it can be caused by complex differences in people's attitudes and perceptions. Consequently, even when people are exposed to the same communications, they may end up with very different levels of perception and understanding because of communication noise.

and feedback. Noise can result from simple physical factors such as poor reception of a cell phone message or static that drowns out a radio commercial. It can also be caused by more complex differences in people's attitudes and perceptions. Consequently, even when people are exposed to the same communications, they can end up with very different perceptions and understandings because of communication noise.

Noise can be present at any point in the communication process. This is why managers must learn how to cut through noise when communicating with employees. Every day throughout its worldwide luxury hotels, Ritz-Carlton holds 15-minute departmental meetings at which managers share "wow stories," examples of outstanding service by department employees. The meetings are also a way to reinforce important skills and to demonstrate through storytelling the value of exceptional customer service.[22]

[7] Basic Forms of Communication

Managers and co-workers communicate in many different ways—by making a phone call, sending an e-mail or text message, holding a staff meeting, or chatting in the hallway. They also communicate with facial expressions, gestures, and other body language. Subtle variations can significantly influence the reception of a message. As Table 9.2 points out, communication takes various forms: oral and written, formal and informal, and nonverbal.

Oral Communication

Managers spend a lot of time engaged in oral communication, both in person and on the phone. Some people prefer to communicate this way, believing that oral channels convey messages more accurately. Face-to-face oral communication allows people to combine words with such cues as facial expressions, body language, and tone of voice. Oral communication over the telephone lacks visual cues, but it does allow people to hear the tone of voice and provide immediate feedback by asking questions or restating the message. Because of its immediacy,

TABLE
9.2 Forms of Communication

FORM	DESCRIPTION	EXAMPLES
Oral communication	Communication transmitted through speech	Personal conversations, speeches, meetings, voice mail, telephone conversations, video or web conferences
Written communication	Communication transmitted through writing	e-mails, letters, memos, formal reports, news releases, online discussion groups, text messages
Formal communication	Communication transmitted through the chain of command within an organization to other members or to people outside the organization	Internal—memos, reports, meetings, written proposals, oral presentations, meeting minutes; external—letters, written proposals, oral presentations, speeches, news releases, press conferences
Informal communication	Communication transmitted outside formal channels without regard for the organization's hierarchy of authority	Rumors spread informally among employees via the grapevine
Nonverbal communication	Communication transmitted through actions and behaviors rather than through words	Gestures, facial expressions, posture, body language, dress, makeup

Chapter 9 *Top Performance through Empowerment, Teamwork, and Communication*

259

Assessment Check ✓

1. What is the difference between communication in low-context and high-context cultures?
2. In the context of the communication process, what is noise?

Joshua Hodge Photography/iStockphoto

Listening may seem easy, because the listener appears to make no effort. But the average person talks much slower than the amount of information the brain can handle at any given time. This gap may lead to boredom, inattention, and misinterpretation on the part of the listener.

listening receiving a message and interpreting its intended meaning by grasping the facts and feelings it conveys.

oral communication has drawbacks. If one person is agitated or nervous during a conversation, noise enters the communication process. A hurried manager might brush off an employee who has an important message to deliver. A frustrated employee might feel compelled to fire a harsh retort at an unsupportive supervisor instead of thinking before responding.

In any medium, a vital component of oral communication is **listening** —receiving a message and interpreting its genuine meaning by accurately grasping the facts and feeling conveyed. Although listening may be the most important communication skill, most of us don't use it enough—or as well as we should.

Listening may seem easy, because the listener appears to make no effort. But the average person talks at a rate of roughly 150 words per minute, while the brain can handle up to 400 words per minute. This gap can lead to boredom, inattention, and misinterpretation. In fact, immediately after listening to a message, the average person can recall only half of it. After several days, the proportion of a message that a listener can recall falls to 25 percent or less.

Certain types of listening behaviors are common in both business and personal interactions:

- *Cynical or defensive listening.* This type of listening occurs when the receiver of a message feels that the sender is trying to gain some advantage from the communication.

- *Offensive listening.* In this type of listening, the receiver tries to catch the speaker in a mistake or contradiction.

- *Polite listening.* In this mechanical type of listening, the receiver listens to be polite rather than to contribute to communication. Polite listeners are usually inattentive and spend their time rehearsing what they want to say when the speaker finishes.

- *Active listening.* This form of listening requires involvement with the information and empathy with the speaker's situation. In both business and personal life, active listening is the basis for effective communication.

Learning how to be an active listener is an especially important goal for business leaders because effective communication is essential to the effectiveness of their role. Listening is hard work, but it pays off with increased learning, better interpersonal relationships, and greater influence.[23] Both managers and employees can develop skills to make them better listeners, as described in the "Career Kickstart" feature.

Written Communication

Channels for written communication include reports, letters, memos, online discussion boards and social media, e-mails, and text messages. Many of these channels permit only delayed feedback and create a record of the message. So it is important for the sender of a written communication to prepare the message carefully and review it to avoid misunderstandings—particularly before pressing that "send" button.

Effective written communication reflects its audience, the channel carrying the message, and the appropriate degree of formality. When writing a formal business document such as a complex marketing research report, a manager must plan in advance and carefully construct the document. The process of writing a formal document involves planning, research,

260 | **Part 3** *Management: Empowering People to Achieve Business Success*

organization, composition and design, and revision. Written communication via e-mail may call for a less-formal writing style, including short sentences, phrases, and lists.

E-mail is a very effective communication channel, especially for delivering straightforward messages and information. But e-mail's effectiveness also leads to its biggest problem: too much e-mail! Many workers find their valuable time being consumed with e-mail. To relieve this burden and leave more time for performing the most important aspects of the job, some companies are looking into ways to reduce the time employees spend sending and reading e-mail. To fulfill this need, there are now firms that provide e-mail management services. One such company is Boston–based SaneBox, which provides customized e-mail solutions for firms that have been struggling to keep up with the volume of e-mail they receive and the time it takes to operate an in-house server.[24]

Other e-mail issues are security and retention. Because e-mail messages are often informal, senders occasionally forget that they are creating a written record. Even if the recipient deletes an e-mail message, other copies exist on company e-mail servers. E-mails on company servers can be used as evidence in a legal case or disciplinary action.

Formal Communication

A *formal communication channel* carries messages that flow within the chain of command structure defined by an organization. The most familiar channel, downward communication, carries messages from someone who holds a senior position in the organization to subordinates. Managers may communicate downward by sending employees e-mail messages, presiding at department meetings, giving employees policy manuals, posting notices online or on bulletin boards, and reporting news in company newsletters. The most important factor in formal communication is to be open and honest. "Spinning" bad news to make it look better almost always backfires. In a work environment characterized by open communication, employees feel free to express opinions, offer suggestions, and even voice complaints. Research has shown that open communication has the following seven characteristics:

1. *Employees are valued.* Employees are happier and more motivated when they feel they are valued and their opinions are heard.

2. *A high level of trust exists.* Telling the truth maintains a high level of trust; this forms the foundation for open communication and employee motivation and retention.

3. *Conflict is invited and resolved positively.* Without conflict, innovation and creativity are stifled.

4. *Creative dissent is welcomed.* By expressing unique ideas, employees feel they have contributed to the company and improved performance.

5. *Employee input is solicited.* The key to any company's success is input from employees, which establishes a sense of involvement and improves working relations.

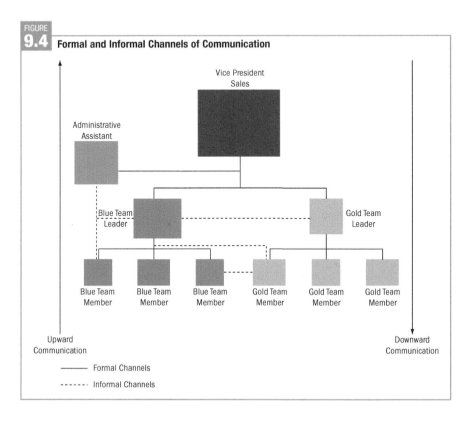

FIGURE 9.4 Formal and Informal Channels of Communication

Vice President
Sales

Administrative
Assistant

Blue Team
Leader

Gold Team
Leader

Blue Team
Member

Blue Team
Member

Blue Team
Member

Gold Team
Member

Gold Team
Member

Gold Team
Member

Upward
Communication

Downward
Communication

——— Formal Channels

------ Informal Channels

6. *Employees are well informed.* Employees are kept informed about what is happening within the organization.

7. *Feedback is ongoing.* Both positive and negative feedback must be ongoing and provided in a manner that builds relationships rather than assigns blame.[25]

Many firms also define formal channels for upward communications. These channels encourage communication from employees to supervisors and upward to top management levels. Some examples of upward communication channels are employee surveys, suggestion boxes, and other online systems that allow employees to propose ideas for new products or express concerns. Upward communication is also necessary for managers to evaluate the effectiveness of downward communication. Figure 9.4 illustrates the forms of organizational communication, both formal and informal.

Informal Communication

Informal communication channels carry messages outside formally authorized channels within an organization's hierarchy. A familiar example of an informal channel is the **grapevine**, an internal channel that passes information from unofficial sources. All organizations, large or small, have grapevines. Grapevines disseminate information with speed and economy and are surprisingly reliable. But company communications must be managed effectively so that the grapevine is not the main source of information. When properly nurtured, the grapevine can

grapevine internal information channel that transmits information from unofficial sources.

Part 3 *Management: Empowering People to Achieve Business Success*

help managers get a feel for the morale of companies, understand the anxieties of the work-force, and evaluate the effectiveness of formal communications. Managers can improve the quality of information circulating through the company grapevine by sharing what they know, even if it is preliminary or partial information. By feeding information to selected people, smart leaders can harness the power of the grapevine.

Gossip—which usually travels along the grapevine—is the main drawback of this communication channel. Because gossip can spread misinformation quickly—particularly if it is discovered online—a manager should address the issue quickly so the grapevine can become a legitimate source of information once again. Conversely, employees can nurture informal communication by taking the time to learn more about the communication needs of their managers.[26]

As organizations become more decentralized and more globally dispersed, informal communication—more than ever before—provides an important source of information, through e-mail, texting, and social media.

Nonverbal Communication

So far, this section has considered different forms of verbal communication, or communication that conveys meaning through words. Equally important is *nonverbal communication*, which transmits messages through actions and behaviors. Gestures, posture, eye contact, tone and volume of voice, and even clothing choices are all nonverbal actions that become communication cues. Nonverbal cues can have a far greater impact on communications than many people realize. In fact, it is estimated that 70 percent of interpersonal communication is conveyed through nonverbal cues. Top salespeople are particularly adept at reading and using these cues. For example, they practice "mirroring" a customer's gestures and body language in order to indicate agreement.[27]

Even personal space—the physical distance between people who are engaging in communication—can convey powerful messages. Figure 9.5 shows a continuum of personal space and social interaction with four zones: intimate, personal, social, and public. In the United States, most business conversations occur within the social zone, roughly between 4 and 12 feet apart.

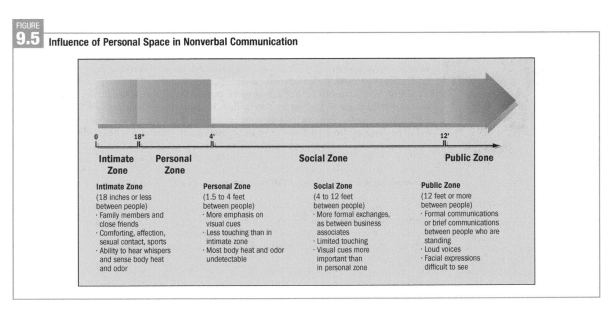

FIGURE 9.5 Influence of Personal Space in Nonverbal Communication

Intimate Zone	Personal Zone	Social Zone	Public Zone
(18 inches or less between people)	(1.5 to 4 feet between people)	(4 to 12 feet between people)	(12 feet or more between people)
· Family members and close friends	· More emphasis on visual cues	· More formal exchanges, as between business associates	· Formal communications or brief communications between people who are standing
· Comforting, affection, sexual contact, sports	· Less touching than in intimate zone	· Limited touching	· Loud voices
· Ability to hear whispers and sense body heat and odor	· Most body heat and odor undetectable	· Visual cues more important than in personal zone	· Facial expressions difficult to see

If one person tries to approach closer than that, the other individual will likely feel uncomfortable or even threatened.

Interpreting nonverbal cues can be especially challenging for people with different cultural backgrounds. Concepts of appropriate personal space differ dramatically throughout most of the world. Latin Americans conduct business discussions in positions that most Americans and northern Europeans would find uncomfortably close. Americans often back away to preserve their personal space, a gesture that Latin Americans perceive as a sign of cold and unfriendly relations. To protect their personal space, some Americans separate themselves across desks or tables from their Latin American counterparts—at the risk of challenging their colleagues to maneuver around those obstacles to reduce the uncomfortable distance.

People send nonverbal messages even when they consciously try to avoid doing so. Sometimes nonverbal cues convey a person's true attitudes and thoughts, which may differ from spoken meanings. Generally, when verbal and nonverbal cues conflict, receivers of the communication tend to believe the nonverbal content. This is why firms seeking to hire people with good attitudes and a team orientation closely watch nonverbal behavior during job interviews in which job applicants participate in group sessions with other job candidates applying for the same job. If in those group interviews an applicant frowns or looks discouraged when a competing candidate gives a good answer, that nonverbal behavior suggests that this person may not be strongly team oriented.

Assessment Check ☑

1. Define the four common listening behaviors.
2. What are the differences between formal and informal communication?

external communication meaningful exchange of information through messages transmitted between an organization and its major audiences.

[8] External Communication and Crisis Management

External communication is a meaningful exchange of information through messages transmitted between an organization and its major audiences, such as customers, suppliers, other firms, the general public, and government officials. Businesses use external communication to keep their operations functioning, to maintain their positions in the marketplace, and to build customer relationships by supplying information about topics such as product modifications and price changes. Every communication with customers—including sales presentations and advertisements—should create goodwill and contribute to customer satisfaction. SC Johnson uses its annual report, its website, its product packaging, and even the phone to communicate good news about the company, as described in the "Going Green" feature. Letting the public know about new initiatives for environmentally friendly processes as well as community projects and other socially responsible activities in which the firm is involved is an important function of external communication.

However, all of this is threatened when companies experience a public relations crisis that threatens their reputation or goodwill, as in the case of Florida-based Carnival Cruise Lines. In a recent crisis, an engine room fire aboard the *Carnival Triumph* left the ship's 4,200 passengers and crew floating adrift in the Gulf of Mexico. A scheduled four-day cruise lasted eight days, as passengers were left without air conditioning, lights, food, water, and working toilets. While the company insists that what happened on the ship was an accident and that its ticket contract with passengers makes no legal guarantee for safe passage, Carnival has since instituted a 110 percent money-back "Great Vacation Guarantee" on its cruises.[28]

How companies such as Carnival Cruise Lines and Johnson & Johnson handle such events can determine whether the company's reputation can be restored. Putting together a plan of action and dealing with facts and rumors immediately could be the difference between regaining trust and disaster. The following communication steps can help calm a public relations crisis:

1. When a crisis occurs, a firm should respond quickly. Executives should prepare a written statement—and stick to it. The statement should mention the time, place,

Businesses use external communication to keep their operations functioning, to maintain their positions in the marketplace, and to build customer relationships. Every communication with customers—including sales presentations and advertisements—should create goodwill and contribute to customer satisfaction.

© Steve Debenport/iStockphoto

264 Part 3 *Management: Empowering People to Achieve Business Success*

GoingGreen

SC Johnson Company Goes Green and Beyond

When a company as big as SC Johnson & Son, Inc., maker of cleaning products Glade, Pledge, and Windex, reaches its sustainability goals, it's good news for the environment. SC Johnson recently announced it had increased its use of renewable energy with the launch of two wind turbines at its largest global manufacturing facility in Waxdale, Wisconsin.

SC Johnson, based in Racine, Wisconsin, was even recognized by the U.S. Environmental Protection Agency (EPA) for being a top voluntary user of "green" energy and received the agency's Climate Leadership Award for aggressive goal setting. Seven of the company's manufacturing sites are now zero landfill.

The family-owned company has publicly reported its progress in meeting environmental goals for over 20 years. Says CEO Fisk Johnson, "We've reduced both global manufacturing waste by 62 percent, and greenhouse gases nearly 40 percent since 2000, and we'll continue to push the needle." Two new "Green Choice" products were introduced to reduce landfill waste of plastic trigger bottles: Smart Twist™ cleaning system, a refillable system for concentrated cleaners, and a compostable Ziploc® Brand bag. SC Johnson also continues to improve the impact of its product ingredients on the environment under its patented

Greenlist™ process, and it makes that information public too—online, on its packages, and by phone in English, Spanish, and French.

"At SC Johnson, we work hard every day to create winning products that use fewer resources, ensure less waste, and serve the greater good," said Johnson.

Questions for Critical Thinking

1. Is SC Johnson doing a good enough job communicating its green efforts to customers? Why or why not?

2. How do you think the company's regular reporting about these efforts affects the results?

Sources: Company website, "SC Johnson Sustainability Report," "SC Johnson Awarded Goal Setting Certificate by EPA's Climate Leadership Program," "Green Choices Marketplace," "SC Johnson Helps Families Learn More about the Products They Use Every Day," www.scjohnson.com, accessed February 1, 2014; David Schuyler, "Kohl's and SC Johnson Among Top Green Power Users," *Milwaukee Business Journal*, accessed February 1, 2014, www.bizjournals.com; "SC Johnson Receives EPA Green Power Leadership Award," *PR Newswire*, accessed February 1, 2014, www.prnewswire.com; "10 Green Giants: S.C. Johnson," *CNN Money*, accessed February 1, 2014, http://money.cnn.com.

---

initial description of what occurred (not the cause), and the number and status of the people involved.

2. As soon as possible, top company management should appear in public—if possible, to the press. Because the public will hold top management accountable, it's best to have top managers responding to reporters' questions.

3. When answering questions at an initial press conference or in an interview, the management representative must stick to the facts. It's likely that details about the event, the cause, and people's roles will not yet be known; the spokesperson shouldn't speculate. As information becomes available, the firm can provide accurate updates.

4. If a question is currently unanswerable, the executive can offer to find out the answer, which should be delivered in a timely manner. It's not advisable to answer a question by saying, "No comment." It's much better to say, "I don't know."

5. The firm should acknowledge problems, explain solutions, and welcome feedback. If a question or factual statement puts the organization in a negative light, the manager should acknowledge the problem, and then explain how the firm is correcting it.

6. The press conference or interview will be most effective if the executive speaks briefly, clearly and provides positive visual images.[29]

Crises faced by firms such as Johnson & Johnson and Carnival Cruise Lines are generally exacerbated by widespread criticism on social media sites. By the time they have a chance to reply, the damage to their reputations is significant. Although Johnson & Johnson took steps to better its manufacturing efforts, the company continues to deal with negative publicity. Carnival Cruise Lines has invested $300 million to update its on-board generators and fire suppression equipment. In addition to a money-back guarantee, Carnival also offers on-board ship credits and transportation home to its passengers. Management experts warn that companies should continue to take the use of social media seriously.[30]

Assessment Check ✅

1. What is external communication?

2. What is the first thing a company should do when a public crisis occurs?

What's Ahead

Today's consumers expect the products they buy to be of the highest value for the price. Firms ensure this value by developing efficient systems for producing goods and services, as well as maintaining high quality. The next chapter examines the ways in which businesses produce world-class goods and services, efficiently organize their production facilities, purchase what they need to produce their goods and services, and manage large inventories to maximize efficiency and reduce costs.

Chapter in Review

Summary of Learning Objectives

1 Discuss empowering employees.

Managers empower employees by giving them the authority and responsibility to make decisions about their work. Empowerment seeks to tap the brainpower of all workers to find improved ways of doing their jobs, better serving customers, and achieving organizational goals. Empowerment often includes linking rewards to company performance through employee stock ownership plans (ESOPs) and stock options.

Assessment Check Answers

1.1 What is empowerment? Empowerment comes from giving employees authority and responsibility to make decisions about their work.

1.2 How can managers empower employees? Managers empower employees by sharing company information and decision-making authority and by rewarding them for their performance as well as the company's.

1.3 How do employee stock ownership plans and stock options reward employees and encourage empowerment? Employee stock ownership plans (ESOPs) benefit employees by giving them ownership stakes in their companies. Employees are motivated to work harder and smarter than they would without ESOPs, because they share in their firm's financial success. In contrast to an ESOP, in which the company holds stock for the benefit of employees (when employees leave the company, they cash in their stock), stock options give employees a chance to own the stock themselves if they exercise their options by completing the stock purchase.

2 Distinguish the five types of teams.

The five basic types of teams are work teams, problem-solving teams, self-managed teams, cross-functional teams, and virtual teams. Work teams are permanent groups of co-workers who perform the day-to-day tasks necessary to operate the organization. Problem-solving teams are temporary groups of employees who gather to solve specific problems and then disband. Self-managed teams have the authority to make decisions about how their members complete their daily tasks. Cross-functional teams are made up of members from different units, such as production, marketing, and finance. Virtual teams are groups of geographically or organizationally dispersed co-workers who use a combination of telecommunications and information technologies to accomplish an organizational task.

Assessment Check Answers

2.1 What is a team? A team is a group of people with certain skills who are committed to a common purpose, approach, and set of performance goals.

2.2 What are the five types of teams, and how are they different? Work teams are permanent, while problem-solving teams are temporary. Unlike work teams, self-managed teams have the authority to change how they get their work done. Cross-functional teams are composed of people from different backgrounds, while virtual teams are composed of people from different locations.

3 Identify team characteristics.

Three important characteristics of a team are its size, team level, and team diversity. The ideal team size is about six or seven members. Team level is the average level of ability, experience, personality, or any other factor on a team. Team diversity is the variances or differences in ability, experience, personality, or any other factor on a team. Team diversity is an important consideration for teams that must complete a wide range of different tasks or particularly complex tasks. Teams pass through five stages of development: (1) Forming is an orientation period during which members get to know each other and find out the behaviors that are acceptable to the group. (2) Storming is the stage during which individual personalities emerge as members clarify their roles and expectations. (3) Norming is the stage at which differences are resolved, members accept each other, and consensus emerges about the roles of the team leader and other participants. (4) Performing is characterized by problem solving and a focus on task accomplishment. (5) Adjourning is the final stage, with a focus on wrapping up and summarizing the team's experiences and accomplishments.

Assessment Check Answers ☑

3.1 Explain team level and team diversity. Team level is the average level of ability, experience, personality, or other factors on a team. Team diversity represents differences in ability, experience, personality, or any other factor on a team.

3.2 Explain how teams progress through the stages of team development. Teams pass through five stages of development: forming, storming, norming, performing, and adjourning.

⌈4⌉ Evaluate team cohesiveness and norms.

Team cohesiveness is the extent to which team members feel attracted to the team and motivated to remain on it. Team norms are standards of conduct shared by team members that guide their behavior. Highly cohesive teams whose members share certain standards of conduct tend to be more productive and effective.

Assessment Check Answers ☑

4.1 How does cohesiveness affect teams? Members of cohesive teams interact more often, share common attitudes and goals, have higher morale, and are more likely to help each other. Cohesive teams also perform better.

4.2 What is a team norm? A team norm is a standard of conduct shared by team members that guides their behavior. Norms are informal standards that identify key values and clarify team members' expectations.

⌈5⌉ Describe team conflict.

Conflict and disagreement are inevitable in most teams. Conflict can stem from many sources: disagreements about goals and priorities, task-related issues, interpersonal incompatibilities, scarce resources, and simple fatigue. The key to dealing with team conflict is not avoiding it, but making sure that the team experiences the right kind of conflict. Cognitive conflict focuses on problem-related differences of opinion and, when reconciled, strongly improves team performance. By contrast, affective conflict refers to the emotional reactions that can occur when disagreements become personal rather than professional, and these differences strongly decrease team performance. A team leader can manage team conflict

by fostering good communication so team members perceive each other accurately, understand what is expected of them, and obtain the information they need.

Assessment Check Answers ☑

5.1 What is cognitive conflict, and how does it affect teams? In cognitive conflict, team members disagree because their different experiences and expertise lead them to different views of the problem and its solutions. Cognitive conflict is characterized by a willingness to examine, compare, and reconcile differences to produce the best possible solution.

5.2 Explain affective conflict and its impact on teams. Affective conflict refers to the emotional reactions that can occur when disagreements become personal rather than professional. These differences strongly decrease team performance.

⌈6⌉ Explain the importance of effective communication.

Managers spend about 80 percent of their time in direct communication with others. Company recruiters consistently rate effective communication—such as listening, conversing, and giving feedback—as the most important skill they look for when hiring new employees. The communication process follows a step-by-step process that involves interactions among six elements: sender, message, channel, audience, feedback, and context. The sender composes the message and sends it through the channel. The audience receives the message and interprets its meaning. The receiver gives feedback to the sender. The communication takes place in a situational or cultural context.

Assessment Check Answers ☑

6.1 What is the difference between communication in low-context and high-context cultures? Communication in low-context cultures tends to rely on explicit written and verbal messages. By contrast, communication in high-context cultures depends not only on the message itself but also on the conditions that surround it, including nonverbal cues, past and present experiences, and personal relationships among the parties.

6.2 In the context of the communication process, what is noise? Noise is some type of interference that influences the transmission of messages and feedback. It can result from physical factors such as poor reception of a cell phone message or from differences in people's attitudes and perceptions.

⌈7⌉ Compare the basic forms of communication.

People exchange messages in many ways: oral and written, formal and informal, verbal and nonverbal communication. Effective written communication reflects its audience, its channel, and the appropriate degree of formality. Formal communication channels carry messages within the chain of command.

Informal communication channels, such as the grapevine, carry messages outside the formal chain of command. Nonverbal communication plays a larger role than most people realize. Generally, when verbal and nonverbal cues conflict, the receiver of a message tends to believe the meaning conveyed by nonverbal cues.

Assessment Check Answers ✔

7.1 Define the four common listening behaviors. Cynical listening occurs when the receiver of a message feels that the sender is trying to gain some advantage from the communication. Offensive listening occurs when the receiver tries to catch the speaker in a mistake or contradiction. Polite listening occurs when the receiver is rehearsing what he or she wants to say when the speaker finishes. Active listening requires involvement with the information and empathy with the speaker's situation.

7.2 What are the differences between formal and informal communication? Formal communication occurs within the formal chain of command defined by an organization. Informal communication occurs outside formally authorized channels within an organization's hierarchy.

⌐8⌐ Explain external communication and crisis management.

External communication is a meaningful exchange of information through messages transmitted between an organization and its major audiences, such as customers, suppliers, other firms, the general public, and government officials. Every communication with customers should create goodwill and contribute to customer satisfaction. However, all of this is threatened when companies experience a public crisis that threatens their reputations or goodwill. To manage a public crisis, businesses should respond quickly and honestly, with a member of top management present.

Assessment Check Answers ✔

8.1 What is external communication? External communication is a meaningful exchange of information through messages transmitted between an organization and its major audiences.

8.2 What is the first thing a company should do when a public crisis occurs? The firm should respond quickly by preparing a written statement that includes the time, place, description of the event, and the number and status of people involved.

▦ Business Terms You Need to Know

empowerment 248	virtual team 252	cognitive conflict 256
team 250	team level 254	affective conflict 257
work team 251	team diversity 254	communication 257
problem-solving team 251	team cohesiveness 256	listening 260
self-managed team 251	team norm 256	grapevine 262
cross-functional team 252	conflict 256	external communication 264

▦ Review Questions

1. How do companies benefit from empowering their employees? How do employees benefit from empowerment?

2. How might a firm that manufactures shoes use teams to determine ways to improve its environmental standards in terms of products and processes? What type (or types) of teams would be best for this initiative? Why?

3. How do team level and team diversity affect team performance?

4. What are the characteristics of an effective team? Why are these features so significant?

5. At what stages of development might a team *not* be able to move forward? How might a team leader or manager resolve the situation?

6. Describe the norms associated with your business class. How do these norms influence the way students behave in class?

7. What steps can managers take to resolve team conflict?

8. In what ways is context a powerful influence on the effectiveness of communication? Describe an instance in which situational or cultural context has influenced one of your communication processes.

9. What are the benefits and drawbacks of oral and written communication?

10. What is the role of external communication? Why is it so important to companies?

▦ Projects and Teamwork Applications

1. Discuss the concepts of authority, accountability, and responsibility. Who has the authority in a school setting? In the classroom? What is the difference between accountability and responsibility as a student? Provide several examples.

2. Is teamwork more important than skill? In pairs or in groups, discuss the importance of an organizational culture that includes teamwork and collaboration over an organization that lacks such traits. Using sports as an analogy, why is it

that a team with weaker players but stronger cohesiveness and collaboration can beat a team with stronger, more-skilled players? If you had to choose, would you select the team with stronger collaboration or the one with more skilled players? Discuss your reasoning.

3. Try this listening exercise with a partner. First, spend a few minutes writing a paragraph or two about the most important thing that happened to you this week. Second, read your paragraph out loud to your partner. Next, have your partner read his or her paragraph. Finally, take turns summarizing the most important points in one another's stories. How well did you listen to one another?

4. On your own or with a classmate, visit the college library, a mall, or anywhere else people gather. For about 10 or 15 minutes, observe the nonverbal cues that people give each other: Does the librarian smile at students? What is the body language of students gathered in groups? When you leave the venue, jot down as many of your observations as you can. Notice things such as changes in nonverbal communication when someone joins a group or leaves it.

5. Every day we hear news about companies in crisis. Either online or through media reports, find and research a recent event and how the company used external communication to address the crisis. Review the communication steps outlined in the chapter and discuss whether the company followed these steps.

Web Assignments

1. **Team-building exercises.** The website Team-Building-Bonanza.com calls itself "the motherlode of corporate team building ideas." You want to select a team-building exercise to help resolve conflicts. What are some of the suggested activities?

   http://www.team-building-bonanza.com

2. **Writing better business letters.** Assume you'd like to improve your business letter–writing ability. Using a search engine such as Google or Bing, search the web for sites with tips and suggestions to improve letter-writing skills. (An example site is listed below.) Select two of these sites and review the material. Prepare a brief summary.

   http://writingcenter.unc.edu/handouts/business-letters/

   https://owl.english.purdue.edu/owl/resource/653/01/

3. **Teamwork at Whole Foods.** Go to the Whole Foods website and learn more about the importance of teams and teamwork on the "Company Values and Mission" page. Discuss, along with additional research, if necessary, the company's organizational structure and the importance of collaboration and teamwork.

   www.wholefoodsmarket.com

   Note: Internet web addresses change frequently. If you don't find the exact sites listed, you may need to access the organization's home page and search from there or use a search engine such as Google or Bing.

Southwest Airlines Thrives on Customer Service	CASE 9.1

For anyone doubting that customer service affects the bottom line, Southwest Airlines, with a reputation for "fast, fun, and friendly," has an answer. The Dallas-based carrier has been top ranked in customer satisfaction for 20 straight years and is the only major airline that consistently is profitable. Its 46,000 employees also voted the airline into the top 50 best places to work in Glassdoor's annual Employee Choice Awards, based on company culture, benefits and pay, and communication.

Sometimes Southwest's service is extraordinary, as when a pilot held a plane to allow a family member of a murdered child to make the flight. To the passenger's thanks the pilot responded, "They can't go anywhere without me and I wasn't going anywhere without you." On more routine trips, passengers appreciate Southwest's "Bags Fly Free" policy of two free checked bags. Southwest recently earned the Quest for Quality Award, the gold standard for customer satisfaction and performance excellence for the logistics industry.

Says the airline's executive vice president, "Here at Southwest, every ONE matters. We have the best workforce in the aviation industry and we are not afraid to show it. Our employees are filled with passion; we work hard and we learn from our mistakes. This makes us stronger as a company and the best place to work."

Chapter 9 *Top Performance through Empowerment, Teamwork, and Communication*   **269**

Questions for Critical Thinking

1. How does Southwest's customer service affect its bottom line?
2. Among 47 industries, airlines overall continue to earn the lowest customer satisfaction score. What could they learn from Southwest?

Sources: Company website, "Southwest Corporate Fact Sheet," www.swamedia.com, accessed February 19, 2014; company website, "Glassdoor's Employee Choice Awards 2014," www.glassdoor.com, accessed February 19, 2014; company website, "Southwest Airline's Cargo Honored for Outstanding Performance," http://southwest.investorroom.com, accessed February 19, 2014; "Southwest Airlines Reports Record Fourth Quarter and Full Year Profit; 41st Consecutive Year of Profitability," *Yahoo Finance,* accessed February 19, 2014, http://finance.yahoo.com; Jack Nicas and Susan Carey, "Southwest CEO Opens Door to Baggage Fees," *The Wall Street Journal,* accessed February 1, http://online.wsj.com, accessed February 1, 2014; Sylvia Vorhauser-Smith, "How the Best Places to Work Are Nailing Employee Engagement," *Forbes,* accessed February 1, 2014, www.forbes.com; Christopher Elliott, "Southwest Airlines Pilot Holds Plane for Murder Victim's Family," *Elliott Blog,* accessed February 1, 2014, www.elliott.org.

CASE 9.2 — Merrill Lynch Tells Its Advisers: Join a Team

The Merrill Lynch Client Experience Achievement Award may sound more like a sales award than the company's latest effort to inspire and compensate team building within its ranks. To encourage teams, Bank of America–owned brokerage firm Merrill Lynch has offered its 14,000 financial advisers a bonus equivalent to 10 percent of increased revenues if they double it over the next five years—and if they join a team.

Why the push to join a team? Merrill Lynch, the country's largest brokerage firm by assets, wants to provide its clients with a more holistic approach and increased interaction through a team structure. As clients' needs continue to change, Merrill Lynch hopes to provide investment management, lending, financial planning, and trust services through its updated team approach. When clients have a question, Merrill Lynch wants to make sure that someone on the team knows the answer rather than relying on a single individual.

Over half of the company's financial advisers currently operate in teams, but in the past, with stiff competition for clients, advisers worked diligently as sole practitioners, caring for and nurturing their high net-worth client accounts. The new bonus, which requires a five-year span of revenue growth, also serves as a way to help retain valued wealth managers, many of whom might be at risk of jumping to a competitor.

The new bonus plan comes with an internal benefit for Merrill Lynch. Feeling the effects of an aging workforce, the company allows advisers aged 55 and over to retain a two- to four-year consultant's role on their team when they retire. This makes succession planning and account transitioning more seamless for valued clients. While the team approach is highly encouraged, it isn't required. There will always be advisers who prefer to fly solo rather than share coveted clients—and commissions—with team members.

Questions for Critical Thinking

1. What incentive is there for an adviser who has an established clientele to join a team?
2. What are the benefits for the client and for Merrill Lynch of a team approach to managing investments?

Sources: Corrie Driebusch, "Financial Advisers Are Lured to Stay with Perks That Pay Off Later," *The Wall Street Journal,* accessed February 19, 2014, http://online.wsj.com; Trevor Hunnicutt, "New Merrill Lynch Comp Plan Rewards Teams," *Investment News,* accessed February 19, 2014, www.investmentnews.com; "Merrill Lynch to Offer Teamwork Bonuses to Advisers," *The Wall Street Journal,* accessed February 19, 2014, http://online.wsj.com.

CASE 9.3 — Necco Empowers and Engages Employees

If you've ever received a box of candy hearts imprinted with cute sayings for Valentine's Day, you know about the New England Confectionery Company, or Necco, for short. Behind the scenes of the 150-year tradition of "Conversation Hearts" is a collaborative and empowered group of 500 employees who work in teams at Necco's headquarters in Revere, Massachusetts.

Facilitating change at the oldest candy-making company in the United States is no easy feat. A company executive with the title of lean champion works tirelessly to engage and empower the workforce, build awareness, and capture energy and passion among employees. In addition, the lean champion tries to find the root cause of wasteful activities and to eliminate anything that does not add value to the company's products. Eliminating waste, whether it be materials, supplies, or production processes, is Necco's overall goal. For example, once the circles used to make Necco wafers are printed, the remaining dough is automatically reused and sent through the machine to produce more product.

In addition to reducing waste, part of the company's initiative is to add value. This includes determining employee training needs, identifying tools to do jobs more efficiently, and working collaboratively to determine strategies for improvement. Necco has reduced scrap and reworks, which has resulted in improved quality and production lead times. However, none of this can be accomplished without Necco employees, all of whom are members of the company's various teams.

Necco's lean initiative, pervasive throughout its culture of expansion, rebuilding, and improvement, is practiced from the top down. One recent change was the decision to discontinue its all-natural wafers. In a move to meet consumer demand, Necco decided to produce its centuries-old wafer as all natural, substituting corn syrup for sugar and using beet juce and purple cabbage in place of colorings and sweeteners. Customers were not happy with the change, and management made the decision to revert back to the original ingredients, which resulted in a sales rebound of 20 percent. In addition, the Sweetheart candies were introduced in new, trendier flavors. These steps are part of Necco's long-term vision for innovation, new products, and new markets.

Integral to the growth and transformation of Necco's products is employee engagement. The company solicits input from employees, all of whom are considered "experts" in their respective work areas. When employees know there is someone within the organization to champion their efforts, they want to come to work, and the more support they have, they more they do for the company. For improvement to occur, Necco's leadership team not only talks the talk but walks the walk. Goals and values, referred to as key performance indicators or KPIs, are developed by top management and supported at every level of the company.

Rewards are linked to both company and department performance. When goals are met, manufacturing workers on a single production line are given monetary incentives. Within the wafers team—the company's largest—various departments work together, including sales, marketing, production, and engineering. In addition to each product team,

Necco assembles cross-functional teams to problem solve and improve processes. Staying involved in all phases of the business keeps employees engaged and interested.

Necco's focus on product quality requires teamwork and collaboration, and it doesn't end after the candy is produced. Teams in sales, packaging, distribution, and shipping play an integral role in managing everything from the purchase of raw materials to product delivery. The company's improvement plan is fueled by the trust and cohesiveness among team members in each of Necco's units.

Necco's recipe for empowerment includes the key ingredients of knowledge and education for employees to perform their jobs effectively. If things don't go as planned, employees have the authority to stop the process to make the proper adjustments. Necco's open door policy encourages employees at all levels to meet and speak with others throughout the organization, regardless of rank or hierarchy.

At Necco, continuing to woo the next generation of customers requires knowledge, support, engagement, and collaboration among its employees and work teams. With its focus on innovation, product development, and employee empowerment, Necco continues to be on a successful business path.

Questions for Critical Thinking

1. Give three specific reasons why empowerment is key to Necco's success. Provide examples of how Necco empower its employees.

2. Select the concept of a problem-solving team or a self-managed team. How might this team function at Necco? Who might be on the team, and what role might the team have in the running of the company?

3. Give an example of a situation in which informal communication would work well among Necco employees—either on the production floor or among its top leadership team.

4. Describe the five stages of team development, and provide an example of what each stage might look like at Necco.

Sources: Company website, http://necco.com, accessed June 3, 2014; Seth Daniel, "Attraction to Necco Much Sweeter This Year," *Revere Journal*, accessed May 31, 2014, www.reverejournal.com; "Candy Company Necco Offers Custom #Tweethearts for Valentine's Day," *ClickZ*, accessed May 31, 2014, www.clickz.com; Jonathan Berr, "Necco's Iconic Sweethearts Show Their Sassy Side," *CBS News*, accessed May 30, 2014, www.cbsnews.com; Claire Suddath, "How Do They Get Those Tiny Words on Sweethearts Candy?," *Time*, accessed May 31, 2014, http://content.time.com; Associated Press "Necco Wafers Scrapping Artificial Additives," *The Daily Beast*, accessed May 31, 2014, www.thedailybeast.com.

Learning Objectives

[1] Explain the strategic importance of production.

[2] Identify and describe the production processes.

[3] Explain the role of technology in the production process.

[4] Identify the factors involved in a location decision.

[5] Explain the job of production managers.

[6] Discuss controlling the production process.

[7] Determine the importance of quality.

Chapter
10

Production and Operations Management

© MachineHeadz/iStockphoto

Building a 3D Future at GE

General Electric, one of the world's largest manufacturers, is creating parts for its jet engines using a new technology called 3D printing or additive manufacturing. Unlike many conventional manufacturing processes that are subtractive—for example, drilling a hole in a block of metal—3D printing is an additive manufacturing process that creates the metal block around the hole. Expected to be one of the biggest changes in industrial production methods in decades, 3D printing is a process that is capable of creating almost any solid shape.

As with a 2D printer, the 3D printing process begins with the creation of a product design on a computer. Designers use computer-aided design (CAD) programs to specify the product size, shape, tolerances, color, and materials. This information is then transferred to a 3D printer, which creates the shape from plastic or metal material one layer at a time. One method uses thin layers of powdered metals or plastics with an epoxy to adhere the powder particles together. Other methods use extruded plastics or a liquid material that solidifies when exposed to ultraviolet light to make the desired solid shapes.

This process allows firms like GE to create structures that were unimaginable just a few years ago. For its advanced jet engine, the LEAP-1, GE has created a new fuel nozzle using 3D printing. What had been a 20-piece assembly is now a single metal part printed in one piece that is 25 percent lighter than the original version. Printing in one piece also gives the new fuel nozzle a life estimated to be five times greater than the 20-piece assembly. And the design and prototyping time required for building these types of structures is greatly reduced, as engineers can design and fabricate test products in a matter of hours.

Maybe best of all, the cost of producing complex fuel nozzles via 3D printing is 20 percent less than a conventionally made one, according to GE. This translates into lower labor costs because less time is spent assembling and inspecting the various parts of the fuel nozzles. GE believes that 3D printing is the manufacturing technology of the future and estimates it will produce more than 40,000 fuel nozzles annually using this new process.[1]

Overview

By producing and marketing the goods and services that people want, businesses satisfy their commitment to society as a whole. They create what economists call *utility*—the want-satisfying power of a good or service. Businesses can create or enhance four basic kinds of utility: time, place, ownership, and form. A firm's marketing operation generates time, place, and ownership utility by offering products to customers at a time and place that is convenient for purchase.

Production creates form utility by converting raw materials and other inputs into finished products, such as GE's 3D fuel nozzles. Production uses resources, including workers and machinery, to convert materials into finished goods and services. This conversion process may result in major changes in raw materials or simply combine already finished parts into new products. The task of production and operations management in a firm is to oversee the production process by managing people and machinery in converting materials and resources into finished goods and services, which is illustrated by Figure 10.1.

People sometimes use the terms *production* and *manufacturing* interchangeably, but the two are actually different. Production spans both manufacturing and nonmanufacturing industries. For instance, companies that engage in fishing or mining engage in production, as do firms that provide package deliveries or lodging. Figure 10.2 lists five examples of production systems for a variety of goods and services.

But whether the production process results in a tangible good such as a car or an intangible service such as cable television, it always converts inputs into outputs. A cabinetmaker combines wood, tools, and skill

FIGURE
10.1 The Production Process: Converting Inputs to Outputs

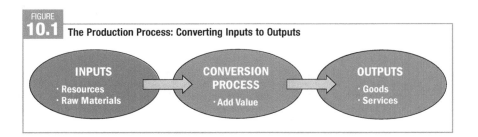

to create finished kitchen cabinets for a new home. A transit system combines buses, trains, and employees to create its output: passenger transportation. Both of these production processes create utility.

This chapter describes the process of producing goods and services. It looks at the importance of production and operations management and discusses the new technologies that are transforming the production function. It then discusses the tasks of the production and operations manager, the importance of quality, and the methods businesses use to ensure high quality.

FIGURE
10.2 Typical Production Systems

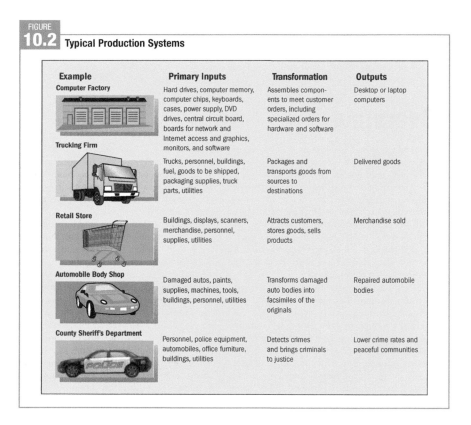

Example	Primary Inputs	Transformation	Outputs
Computer Factory	Hard drives, computer memory, computer chips, keyboards, cases, power supply, DVD drives, central circuit board, boards for network and Internet access and graphics, monitors, and software	Assembles components to meet customer orders, including specialized orders for hardware and software	Desktop or laptop computers
Trucking Firm	Trucks, personnel, buildings, fuel, goods to be shipped, packaging supplies, truck parts, utilities	Packages and transports goods from sources to destinations	Delivered goods
Retail Store	Buildings, displays, scanners, merchandise, personnel, supplies, utilities	Attracts customers, stores goods, sells products	Merchandise sold
Automobile Body Shop	Damaged autos, paints, supplies, machines, tools, buildings, personnel, utilities	Transforms damaged auto bodies into facsimiles of the originals	Repaired automobile bodies
County Sheriff's Department	Personnel, police equipment, automobiles, office furniture, buildings, utilities	Detects crimes and brings criminals to justice	Lower crime rates and peaceful communities

The Strategic Importance of Production

Along with marketing and finance, **production** is a vital business activity. Without products to sell, companies cannot generate money to pay their employees, lenders, and stockholders. And without the profits from products, firms quickly fail. The production process is just as crucial in nonprofit organizations such as St. Jude Children's Research Hospital or Goodwill Industries because the goods or services they offer justify their existence. Effective **production and operations management** can lower a firm's costs of production, boost the quality of its goods and services, allow it to respond dependably to customer demands, and enable it to renew itself by providing new products. Let's look at the differences among mass, flexible, and customer-driven production.

Mass Production

From its beginnings as a colonial supplier of raw materials to Europe, the United States has evolved into an industrial giant. Much of this change has resulted from **mass production**, a system for manufacturing products in large quantities through effective combinations of employees with specialized skills, mechanization, and standardization. Mass production makes outputs (goods and services) available in large quantities at lower prices than individually crafted items would cost. Mass production brought cars, computers, televisions, books, and even homes to the majority of the population. William Levitt made homes affordable to the average American from the 1940s to the 1960s by removing the most expensive item—the basement—and mass-producing houses at the rate of one every 16 minutes. Levitt's first planned housing community in Levittown, New York, brought his company a profit of about $5 million more than 60 years ago.[2]

Mass production begins with the specialization of labor, dividing work into its simplest components so that each worker can concentrate on performing one task. By separating jobs into small tasks, managers create conditions for high productivity through mechanization, in which machines perform much of the work previously done by people. Standardization, the third element of mass production, involves producing uniform, interchangeable goods and parts. Standardized parts simplify the replacement of defective or worn-out components. For instance, if your room's light bulb burns out, you can easily buy a replacement at a local hardware store or supermarket.

A logical extension of these principles of specialization, mechanization, and standardization led to development of the *assembly line*. This manufacturing method moves the product along a conveyor belt past a number of workstations, where workers perform specialized tasks such as welding, painting, installing individual parts, and tightening bolts. Henry Ford's application of this concept revolutionized auto assembly. Before the assembly line, it took Ford's workers 12 hours to assemble a Model T car. But with an assembly line, it took just 1.5 hours to make the same car. Not surprisingly, dozens of other industries soon adopted the assembly-line process.

Although mass production has important advantages, it has limitations, too. While mass production is highly efficient for producing large numbers of similar products, it is highly inefficient when producing small batches of different items. This trade-off might tempt some companies to focus on efficient production methods rather than on making what customers really want. In addition, the labor specialization associated with mass production can lead to boring jobs, because workers keep repeating the same task. To improve their competitive capabilities, many firms adopt flexible production and customer-driven production systems. These methods won't replace mass production in every case, but in many instances might lead to improved product quality and greater job satisfaction. It might also enhance the use of mass production.

production use of resources, such as workers and machinery, to convert materials into finished goods and services.

production and operations management oversee the production process by managing people and machinery in converting materials and resources into finished goods and services.

mass production a system for manufacturing products in large quantities through effective combinations of employees, with specialized skills, mechanization, and standardization.

Chapter 10 *Production and Operations Management*

275

This Honda auto plant uses flexible production techniques to turn out several different models. The auto industry, which developed mass-production methods, now finds flexible production to be more efficient.

Flexible Production

While mass production is effective for creating large quantities of one item, *flexible production* is usually more cost-effective for producing smaller runs. Flexible production can take many forms, but it generally involves using information technology to share the details of customer orders, programmable equipment to fulfill the orders, and skilled people to carry out whatever tasks are needed to fill a particular order. This system is even more beneficial when combined with lean production methods that use automation and information technology to reduce requirements for workers and inventory. Flexible production requires a lot of communication among everyone in the organization.

Flexible production is now widely used in the auto industry. While Henry Ford revolutionized auto production in the early 20th century, automakers such as Toyota and Honda are innovating with new methods of production. Changing from mass production to flexible production has enabled these companies to produce different kinds of cars at the same plant. Honda's flexible manufacturing plant in East Liberty, Ohio, builds cars and light trucks on the same assembly line. The facility accomplishes this through team-based operations, relying on the expertise and knowledge of individual workers to innovate and improve manufacturing processes.[3]

Customer-Driven Production

A *customer-driven* production system evaluates customer demands in order to make the connection between products manufactured and products bought. Many firms use this approach with great success. One method is to establish information systems between factories and retailers using sales data as the basis for creating short-term forecasts and production schedule designs to meet those forecasts. Another approach to customer-driven production systems is simply to make the product only when a customer orders it—whether it's a taco or a tablet. Massachusetts–based Custom Made is an online marketplace connecting buyers who want one-of-a-kind creations with makers of a large variety of goods, including furniture and jewelry. By submitting a budget, photo, or description of what they would like to purchase, buyers connect with makers interested in producing the item. Buyers can also browse maker portfolios on the website and contact them directly.[4]

2 Production Processes

Not surprisingly, the production processes and time required to make an Apple iPad and a gallon of gasoline are different. Production processes use either an analytic or synthetic system; time requirements call for either a continuous or an intermittent process.

An analytic production system reduces a raw material to its component parts in order to extract one or more marketable products. Petroleum refining breaks down crude oil into several marketable products, including gasoline, heating oil, and aviation fuel. When corn is processed, the resulting marketable food products include animal feed and corn sweetener.

Assessment Check ✅

1. What is mass production?
2. What is the difference between flexible production and customer-driven production?

Part 3 *Management: Empowering People to Achieve Business Success*

A synthetic production system is the reverse of an analytic system. It combines a number of raw materials or parts or transforms raw materials to produce finished products. Canon's assembly line produces a camera by assembling various parts such as a shutter or a lens cap. Other synthetic production systems make prescription drugs, chemicals, computer chips, and canned soup.

A continuous production process generates finished products over a lengthy period of time. The steel industry provides a classic example. Its blast furnaces never completely shut down except for malfunctions. Petroleum refineries, chemical plants, and nuclear power facilities also practice continuous production. A shutdown can damage sensitive equipment, with extremely costly results.

An intermittent production process generates products in short production runs, shutting down machines frequently or changing their configurations to produce different products. Most services result from intermittent production systems. For instance, accountants, plumbers, and dentists traditionally have not attempted to standardize their services because each service provider confronts different problems that require individual approaches. However, some companies, such as Jiffy Lube and H&R Block, offer standardized services as part of a strategy to operate more efficiently and compete with lower prices. McDonald's, well-known for its nearly continuous production of food, has moved toward a more intermittent production model. The fast-food chain invested millions in new cooking equipment to set up kitchens for preparing sandwiches quickly to order, rather than producing large batches ahead of time and keeping them warm under heat lamps.

Assessment Check ☑

1. What are the two main production systems?
2. What are the two time-related production processes?

[3] Technology and the Production Process

Technological advances continue to change the production process. Some manufacturing plants are now "lights out" facilities that are completely automated—meaning no workers are required to build or make the products. While this signals a change in the types of jobs available in manufacturing, it also means that companies can design, produce, and adapt products more quickly to meet customers' changing needs.

Green Manufacturing Processes

More and more firms are investing in the development of manufacturing processes that result in a reduction of waste, energy use, and pollution. Companies ranging in size from Walmart to the local café are finding ways to operate in a more sustainable manner. Whether it is using a fleet of electric delivery trucks or eliminating unnecessary packaging, firms have begun to view the steps they take with pride. Toy manufacturer LEGO Group has recently entered into a partnership with the World Wildlife Fund to improve its performance on a range of environmental issues, including test projects with suppliers to create the best solutions for reducing the company's supply chain impact on carbon emissions.[5] eBay's business model includes a built-in element of environmental sustainability by connecting potential buyers and sellers. See the "Going Green" feature for details.

Firms that are involved in construction—or are thinking of building new offices or manufacturing plants—are turning their attention to LEED (Leadership in Energy and Environmental Design) certification for their facilities. LEED is a voluntary certification program administered by the U.S. Green Building Council, aimed at promoting the most sustainable construction processes available. The LEED certification process is rigorous

LEED (Leadership in Energy and Environmental Design) voluntary certification program administered by the U.S. Green Building Council, aimed at promoting the most sustainable construction processes available.

Chapter 10 *Production and Operations Management*   **277**

GoingGreen

eBay and Its Green Commerce Push

If you've ever bought something used on eBay, you probably not only saved money, but indirectly you helped recycle. eBay, the world's largest online and shopping consumer-to-consumer site, claims to be powering a global "recommerce" or green commerce revolution, helping people think differently not just about what they buy but how they buy.

Using the web's connectivity, potential buyers and sellers are able to exchange and reuse goods rather than purchase new ones. With more than 112 million active users, eBay's business model has a built-in environmental sustainability element—extending products' lifespan by finding new homes for used goods. While some consumers prefer to purchase new goods, one reason for purchasing used goods is to save money.

Another less obvious reason is to reduce landfill waste. A global secondary market, now valued at $500 billion, has long been a mainstay for larger, more expensive items like automobiles. Thanks to eBay's green commerce efforts, the secondary market now includes everything from car parts to shoes to electronics.

As part of its recommerce efforts, eBay recently launched classifieds within local online communities, where individuals can buy and sell used

appliances, furniture, and other hard-to-ship items. Its Green Deals page states, "Get the most out of your resources and the planet's by shopping refurbished, resource-saving, and sustainably made deals." With eBay's recommerce platform thriving, your next new purchase may actually be used.

Questions for Critical Thinking

1. Do you think eBay sells more new goods or used goods? Why or why not?

2. In what other ways have you witnessed technology creating a green exchange effort for individuals and companies? Provide examples.

Sources: "eBay's Recommerce Revolution," *Collaborative Consumption*, accessed February 22, 2014, www.collaborativeconsumption.com; company website, http://green.ebay.com, accessed February 22, 2014; "eBay Releases Three-Year Sustainability Goals: Enabling Greener Commerce," *Corporate Social Responsibility Newswire*, accessed February 22, 2014, www.csrwire.com; Mickey Meece, "A Second Chance for Idle Electronics," *The New York Times*, accessed February 22, 2014, www.nytimes.com.

---

and involves meeting standards in energy savings, water efficiency, CO2 emissions reduction, improved indoor environmental quality (including air and natural light), and other categories.[6]

Robots

A growing number of manufacturers have freed workers from boring, sometimes dangerous jobs by replacing them with robots. A *robot* is a reprogrammable machine capable of performing a variety of tasks that require the repeated manipulation of materials and tools. Robots can repeat the same tasks many times without varying their movements. Many factories use robots today for welding, painting, assembly, product inspection, testing, stacking products on pallets, and shrink-wrapping for shipping. Boston Scientific, a firm that makes medical devices, uses robots made by Kiva (an Amazon company) to automate order fulfillment in two of its distribution centers. Gilt Groupe, a flash sale website, uses Kiva robots at its distribution center in Shepherdsville, Kentucky.[7]

Historically, robots were most common in automotive and electronics manufacturing, but growing numbers of industries are adding robots to production lines as technological advances make them less expensive and more useful. Firms operate many different types of robots, depending on their application and use. Different robot types include industrial, domestic or household, medical, service, military, space, and the like. The simplest kind, a pick-and-place robot, moves in only two or three directions as it picks up something from one spot and places it in another. So-called field robots assist people in nonmanufacturing, often hazardous, environments such as nuclear power plants, the international space station, and even military battlefields. Police use robots to remotely dispose of suspected bombs. However, the same technology can be used in factories. Using vision systems, infrared sensors, and bumpers on mobile platforms, robots can automatically move parts or finished goods from one place to another, while either following or avoiding people, whichever is necessary to do the job. For instance, machine vision systems are being used more frequently for complex applications such

Part 3 *Management: Empowering People to Achieve Business Success*

as quality assurance in the manufacturing of medical devices. The advancements in machine vision components such as cameras, illumination systems, and processors have greatly improved their capabilities. Companies such as Texas-based National Instruments help customers around the work boost productivity, simplify development, and reduce time to market.[8]

Computer-Aided Design and Manufacturing

A process called **computer-aided design (CAD)** allows engineers to design components as well as entire products on computer screens faster and with fewer mistakes than they could achieve working with traditional drafting systems. Using an electronic pen, an engineer can sketch three-dimensional (3-D) designs on an electronic drafting board or directly on the screen. The computer then provides tools to make major and minor design changes and to analyze the results for particular characteristics

Robots are used in manufacturing as well as in many other fields. In auto manufacturing, robots can perform a variety of tasks that have freed workers from boring and sometimes dangerous jobs.

or problems. Engineers can put a new car design through a simulated road test to project its real-world performance. If they find a problem with weight distribution, for example, they can make the necessary changes virtually—without actually test-driving the car. With advanced CAD software, prototyping is as much "virtual" as it is "hands-on." Actual prototypes or parts aren't built until the engineers are satisfied that the required structural characteristics in their virtual designs have been met. Dentistry has benefited from CAD, which can design and create on-site such products as caps and crowns that precisely fit a patient's mouth or jaw.[9]

The process of **computer-aided manufacturing (CAM)** picks up where the CAD system leaves off. Computer tools enable a manufacturer to analyze the steps that a machine must take to produce a needed product or part. Electronic signals transmitted to processing equipment provide instructions for performing the appropriate production steps in the correct order. Both CAD and CAM technologies are now used together at most modern production facilities. These so-called CAD/CAM systems are linked electronically to automatically transfer computerized designs into the production facilities, saving both time and effort. They also allow more precise manufacturing of parts.

Flexible Manufacturing Systems

A **flexible manufacturing system (FMS)** is a production facility that workers can quickly modify to manufacture different products. The typical system consists of computer-controlled machining centers to produce metal parts, robots to handle the parts, and remote-controlled carts to deliver materials. All components are linked by electronic controls that dictate activities at each stage of the manufacturing sequence, even automatically replacing broken or worn-out drill bits and other implements.

Flexible manufacturing systems have been enhanced by powerful new software that allows machine tools to be reprogrammed while they are running. This capability allows the same machine to make hundreds of different parts without the operator having to shut the machine down each time to load new programs. The software also connects to the Internet to receive updates or to control machine tools at other sites. And because the software resides on a company's computer network, engineers can use it to diagnose production problems any time, from anywhere they can access the network. Pharmaceutical companies are constantly looking for new ways to use flexible manufacturing. Flexible manufacturing has also become important for minimizing supply chain disruptions from natural disasters. India, China, Singapore, and Latin America have become important locations for this and other innovations in manufacturing.[10]

computer-aided design (CAD) process that allows engineers to design components as well as entire products on computer screens faster and with fewer mistakes than they could achieve working with traditional drafting systems.

computer-aided manufacturing (CAM) computer tools to analyze CAD output and enable a manufacturer to analyze the steps that a machine must take to produce a needed product or part.

flexible manufacturing system (FMS) production facility that workers can quickly modify to manufacture different products.

Chapter 10 *Production and Operations Management*   **279**

Computer-Integrated Manufacturing

Companies integrate robots, CAD/CAM, FMS, computers, and other technologies to implement **computer-integrated manufacturing (CIM)**, a production system in which computers help workers design products, control machines, handle materials, and control the production process in an integrated fashion. This type of manufacturing does not necessarily imply more automation and fewer people than other alternatives. It does, however, involve a new type of automation organized around the computer. The key to CIM is a centralized computer system running software that integrates and controls separate processes and functions. The advantages of CIM include increased productivity, decreased design costs, increased equipment utilization, and improved quality.

CIM is widely used in the printing industry to coordinate thousands of printing jobs, some very small. CIM saves money by combining many small jobs into one larger one and by automating the printing process from design to delivery.[11]

4 The Location Decision

The decision of where to locate a production facility hinges on transportation, human, and physical factors, as shown in Table 10.1. Transportation factors include proximity to markets and raw materials, along with availability of alternative modes for transporting both inputs and outputs. Automobile assembly plants are located near major rail lines. Inputs—such as engines, plastics, and metal parts—arrive by rail, and the finished vehicles are shipped out by

TABLE

10.1 Factors in the Location Decision

LOCATION FACTOR	EXAMPLES OF AFFECTED BUSINESSES
Transportation	
Proximity to markets	Baking companies and manufacturers of other perishable products, dry cleaners, hotels, other services
Proximity to raw materials	Paper mills
Availability of transportation alternatives	Brick manufacturers, retail stores
Physical Factors	
Water supply	Computer chip fabrication plants
Energy	Aluminum, chemical, and fertilizer manufacturers
Hazardous wastes	All businesses
Human Factors	
Labor supply	Auto manufacturers, software developers, and engineers
Local zoning regulations	Manufacturing and distribution companies
Community living conditions	All businesses
Taxes	All businesses

Part 3 *Management: Empowering People to Achieve Business Success*

Deciding where to locate a production facility can often depend on the weather. Some theme parks, such as Walt Disney World, are located in warm climates so they can be open and attract visitors year-round.

rail. Shopping malls are often located next to major streets and freeways in suburban areas, because most customers arrive by car.

Physical variables involve such issues as weather, water supplies, available energy, and options for disposing of hazardous waste. Theme parks like Walt Disney World are often located in warm climates so they can be open and attract visitors year-round. A manufacturing business that wants to locate near a community must prepare an *environmental impact study* that analyzes how a proposed plant would affect the quality of life in the surrounding area. Regulatory agencies typically require these studies to cover topics such as the impact on transportation facilities; energy requirements; water and sewage treatment needs; natural plant life and wildlife; and water, air, and noise pollution.

Human factors in the location decision include an area's labor supply, local regulations, taxes, and living conditions. Management considers local labor costs, as well as the availability of workers with needed skills. Technology companies concentrate in areas with the technical talent they need, including California's Silicon Valley, Seattle, New York City, Boston, and Austin, Texas. By contrast, some labor-intensive industries have located plants in rural areas with readily available labor pools and limited high-wage alternatives. And some firms with headquarters in the United States and other industrialized countries have moved production off-shore in search of low wages, although that trend may be changing, with some U.S. firms bringing jobs back home. But no matter what type of industry a firm is in, a production and operations manager's facility location decision must consider the following factors:

- proximity to suppliers, warehouses, and service operations
- insurance and taxes
- availability of such employee needs as housing, schools, mass transportation, daycare, shopping, and recreational facilities
- size, skills, and costs of the labor force
- ample space for current and future needs of the firm

Hit&Miss

Mexico Becomes a Major Hub for Auto Manufacturing

When it comes to automobile manufacturing, you probably do not think about Mexico as the destination for billions of investment dollars—but it is. Most automakers, including Ford, General Motors, and Chrysler, have increased their manufacturing assembly lines in Mexico. The country's proximity to the United States and its highly skilled workers match their American counterparts at a fraction of the wage cost.

Mexico has become the fastest-growing country worldwide for auto assembly and parts production. General Motors is making its iconic Silverado pickup trucks in central Mexico's Guanajuato state. Audi will invest $1.3 billion to build its assembly plant in the state of Puebla, where it will build its luxury vehicles—a first for Mexico. And Mexico is ground zero for Nissan's expansion plans in the Americas. Honda and Mazda are also adding manufacturing facilities in the country, which has shot past Canada to become the second-largest auto producer in North America.

A German-engineered BMW made in Mexico? The company recently announced a billion-dollar investment to build a new plant there to produce 150,000 vehicles annually.

Questions for Critical Thinking

1. How does this business boom in Mexico impact the future of autoworkers in the United States?

2. About 80 percent of the cars made in Mexico are for export to the United States. Do you foresee Mexico's growth trend continuing? Why or why not?

Sources: Nick Parker, "BMW's Billion-Dollar Bet on Mexico," *CNN Money,* accessed July 13, 2014, http://money.cnn.com; Chris Anderson, "Mexico: The New China," *The New York Times,* accessed February 24, 2014, www.nytimes.com; Harold L. Sirkin, "The New Mexico," *Bloomberg Businessweek,* accessed February 24, 2014, www .businessweek.com; Philip LeBeau, "Mexico Stakes Claim as Hottest Hub for Auto Production," *CNBC,* accessed February 24, 2014, www.cnbc.com; Ben Klayman, "Auto Industry Love for Mexico Grows with New Audi Plant," *Reuters,* accessed February 24, 2014, www.reuters.com; Juan Montes, "BMW Considers First Plant in Mexico," *The Wall Street Journal,* accessed February 24, 2014, http://online.wsj.com.

- distance to market for goods

- receptiveness of the community

- economical transportation for materials and supplies, as well as for finished goods

- climate and environment that matches the industry's needs and employees' lifestyle

- amount and cost of energy services

- government incentives.

Assessment Check ✓

1. How does an environmental impact study influence the location decision?

2. What human factors are relevant to the location decision?

A continuing trend in location strategy is bringing production facilities closer to the final markets where the goods will be sold. One reason for this is reduced time and cost for shipping. Another reason is a closer cultural affinity between the parent company and supplier (in cases where production remains overseas). Global snack food company Mondelez International, maker of such products as Oreos, Cadbury candy, and Trident chewing gum, recently invested $190 million as part of its ongoing supply chain plan, which will address growth demands in emerging markets like India, as well as improving productivity and reducing costs.[12] Mexico has become the newest location for automobile manufacturing. See the "Hit & Miss" feature for more details.

⌐5⌐ The Job of Production Managers

Production and operations managers oversee the work of people and machinery to convert inputs (materials and resources) into finished goods and services. As Figure 10.3 shows, these managers perform four major tasks:

1. Plan the overall production process.

2. Determine the best layout for the firm's facilities.

282   Part 3 *Management: Empowering People to Achieve Business Success*

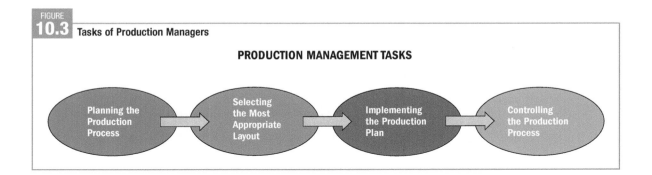

FIGURE 10.3 Tasks of Production Managers

PRODUCTION MANAGEMENT TASKS

Planning the Production Process → Selecting the Most Appropriate Layout → Implementing the Production Plan → Controlling the Production Process

3. Implement the production plan.

4. Control the manufacturing process to maintain the highest possible quality.

Part of the control process involves continuous evaluation of results. If problems occur, managers return to the first step and make adjustments.

Planning the Production Process

Production planning begins by choosing what goods or services to offer to customers. This decision is the essence of every company's reason for operating. Other decisions such as machinery purchases, pricing decisions, and selection of retail outlets all grow out of product planning. But with product planning, it's not enough to plan products that satisfy customers. Products must satisfy customers *and* be produced as efficiently and inexpensively as possible. So while marketing research studies determine consumer reactions to proposed products and estimate potential sales and profitability levels, production departments focus on planning the production process when they (1) convert original product ideas into final specifications and (2) design the most efficient facilities to produce those products.

It is important for production managers to understand how a project fits into the company's structure because this will affect the success of the project. In a traditional manufacturing organization, each production manager is given a specific area of authority and responsibility such as purchasing or inventory control. One drawback to this structure is that it may actually pit the purchasing manager against the inventory control manager. As more organizations have moved toward team-oriented structures, some organizations assign team members to specific projects reporting to the production manager. Each team is responsible for the quality of its products and has the authority to make changes to improve performance and quality. The major difference between the two approaches is that all workers on teams are responsible for their output, and teamwork avoids the competitiveness between managers often found in traditional structures.

Determining the Facility Layout

The next production management task is determining the best layout for the facility. An efficient facility layout can reduce material handling, decrease costs, and improve product flow through the facility. This decision requires managers to consider all phases of production and the necessary inputs at each step. Figure 10.4 shows three common layout designs: process, product, and fixed-position layouts. It also shows a customer-oriented layout typical of service providers' production systems.

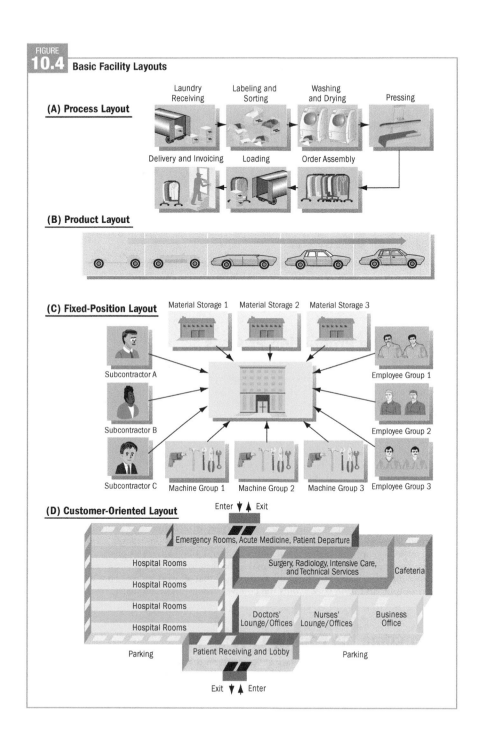

FIGURE 10.4 Basic Facility Layouts

(A) Process Layout

Laundry Receiving · Labeling and Sorting · Washing and Drying · Pressing

Delivery and Invoicing · Loading · Order Assembly

(B) Product Layout

(C) Fixed-Position Layout

Material Storage 1 · Material Storage 2 · Material Storage 3

Subcontractor A · Subcontractor B · Subcontractor C

Employee Group 1 · Employee Group 2 · Employee Group 3

Machine Group 1 · Machine Group 2 · Machine Group 3

(D) Customer-Oriented Layout

Enter ▼ ▲ Exit

Emergency Rooms, Acute Medicine, Patient Departure

Hospital Rooms · Hospital Rooms · Hospital Rooms · Hospital Rooms

Surgery, Radiology, Intensive Care, and Technical Services · Cafeteria

Doctors' Lounge/Offices · Nurses' Lounge/Offices · Business Office

Parking · Patient Receiving and Lobby · Parking

Exit ▼ ▲ Enter

A *process layout* groups machinery and equipment according to their functions. The work in process moves around the plant to reach different workstations. A process layout often facilitates production of a variety of nonstandard items in relatively small batches. Its purpose is to process goods and services that have a variety of functions. For instance, a typical machine shop generally has separate departments where machines are grouped by functions such as grinding, drilling, pressing, and lathing. Process layouts accommodate a variety of production functions and use general-purpose equipment that can be less costly to purchase and maintain than specialized equipment.

A *product layout*, also referred to as an assembly line, sets up production equipment along a product-flow line, and the work in process moves along this line past workstations. This type of layout efficiently produces large numbers of similar items, but it may prove inflexible and able to accommodate only a few product variations. Although product layouts date back at least to the Model T assembly line, companies are refining this approach with modern touches. Many auto manufacturers continue to use a product layout, but robots perform many of the activities that humans once performed. Automation overcomes one of the major drawbacks of this system—unlike humans, robots don't get bored doing a dull, repetitive job. European automaker Holland Car PLC uses an assembly-line approach called complete knockdown (CKD), in which all the parts of an auto are imported in pieces to be welded, painted, and assembled at its facility in Ethiopia.[13]

A *fixed-position layout* places the product in one spot, and workers, materials, and equipment come to it. This approach suits production of very large, bulky, heavy, or fragile products. For example, a bridge cannot be built on an assembly line. Fixed-position layouts dominate several industries including construction, shipbuilding, aircraft and aerospace, and oil drilling, to name a few. In all of these industries, the nature of the product generally dictates a fixed-position layout.

Service organizations also must decide on appropriate layouts for their production processes. A service firm should arrange its facilities to enhance the interactions between customers and its services—also called *customer-oriented layout*. If you think of patients as inputs, a hospital implements a form of the process layout. Banks, libraries, dental offices, and hair salons also use process layouts. Sometimes the circumstances surrounding a service require a fixed-position layout. For instance, doctors, nurses, and medical devices are brought to patients in a hospital emergency room.

Implementing the Production Plan

After planning the production process and determining the best layout, a firm's production managers begin to implement the production plan. This activity involves (1) deciding whether to make, buy, or lease components; (2) selecting the best suppliers for materials; and (3) controlling inventory to keep enough, but not too much, on hand.

Make, Buy, or Lease Decision One of the fundamental issues facing every producer is the make, buy, or lease decision—choosing whether to manufacture a product or component in-house, purchase it from an outside supplier, or lease it. This decision is critical in many contemporary business situations.

Several factors affect the make, buy, or lease decision, including the costs of leasing or purchasing parts from vendors compared with the costs of producing them in-house. The decision sometimes hinges on the availability of outside suppliers that can dependably meet a firm's standards for schedule, quality, and quantity. The need for confidentiality sometimes affects the decision, as does the short- or long-term duration of the firm's need for supplies. A firm might not yet have the technology to produce certain components or materials, or the technology might be too costly. The "Hit & Miss" feature describes some of the difficult production decisions Harley-Davidson had to make to help it rebound from a sluggish economy.

make, buy, or lease decision choosing whether to manufacture a product or component in-house, purchase it from an outside supplier, or lease it.

Harley-Davidson Turns Lean

For more than a century, Harley-Davidson, the iconic motorcycle brand, has embodied everything American. In its heyday, Harley-Davidson had such a following that consumers would wait patiently for 18 months to get their hands on a new bike. More recently, however, a combination of a slow economy and global competition created some tough decisions for the company. Like other manufacturers that opted for low-cost overseas or domestic nonunion production, the company was forced to decide whether to eliminate its union. Rather than scrap the union, the company redesigned the production system to allow for fewer workers in its York, Pennsylvania, plant—with the union's blessing. In addition, Harley-Davidson tore down the York plant and built a brand-new one. Instead of replacing experienced employees with state-of-the-art robotic technology, the company developed a lean manufacturing operation, complete with teams of five to six workers who manually build each of its core four motorcycle styles, complete with more than 1,200 customizable options.

With its lean manufacturing process and new facility, the company has reduced costs by $100 million while increasing quality and customer demand. In addition, it retained the union—experienced workers who are able to solve problems and search for better ways to make motorcycles that robots cannot. With a new motorcycle starting on the assembly line every 80 seconds, Harley-Davidson remains optimistic that its H.O.G. members (Harley Owner's Group) worldwide will continue to be happy, while now only waiting a few weeks for a new bike.

Questions for Critical Thinking

1. What do you think might have been the outcome had the company decided to follow other manufacturers overseas in pursuit of lower production costs?

2. Discuss the relationship between the iconic Harley-Davidson brand and the company's production decisions.

Sources: Company website, "Harley Owners Group," www.harley-davidson.com, accessed February 5, 2014; Adam Davidson, "Building a Harley Faster," *The New York Times*, accessed February 5, 2014, www.nytimes.com; Ginger Christ-Martin, "2013 IW Best Plants Winner: Harley-Davidson—Driving a Future of Excellence," *Industry Week*, accessed February 5, 2014, www.industryweek.com; James Hagerty, "Harley Goes Lean to Build Hogs," *The Wall Street Journal*, accessed February 5, 2014, http://online.wsj.com.

Even when the firm decides to purchase from outside vendors, production managers should maintain access to multiple supply sources. An alternative supplier ensures that the firm can obtain needed materials despite strikes, quality-assurance problems, or other situations that may affect inputs. Outsourcing has its disadvantages. The main reasons companies say they use outsourcing is to reduce costs and focus on their core business activities, but outsourcing also may trigger layoffs and compromise quality.

In an industry where outsourcing is common, American Apparel chooses to keep all of its clothing production in the metropolitan Los Angeles area. Though the firm pays higher wages than rivals who outsource to other countries, American Apparel is able to offer quicker response times and maintain higher quality and better inventory control.[14]

Selection of Suppliers Once a company decides what inputs to purchase, it must choose the best vendors for its needs. To make this choice, production managers compare the quality, prices, dependability of delivery, and services offered by competing companies. Different suppliers may offer virtually identical quality levels and prices, so the final decision often rests on factors such as the firm's experience with each supplier, speed of delivery, warranties on purchases, and other services.

For a major purchase, negotiations between the purchaser and potential vendors may stretch over several weeks or even months, and the buying decision may rest with a number of colleagues who must say yes before the final decision is made. The choice of a supplier for an industrial drill press, for example, may require a joint decision by the production, engineering, purchasing, and quality-control departments. These departments often must reconcile their different views to settle on a purchasing decision.

The Internet has given buyers powerful tools for finding and comparing suppliers. Buyers can log on to business exchanges to compare specifications, prices, and availability. Ariba, recently acquired by German software maker SAP, provides cloud-based applications to the world's largest business-to-business community of more than 1.2 million businesses. This allows companies to collaborate with a global network of suppliers and partners valued at more than $500 billion in commerce.[15]

Firms often purchase raw materials and component parts on long-term contracts. If a manufacturer requires a continuous supply of materials, a one-year or two-year contract with a vendor helps ensure availability. Today, many firms are building long-term relationships with suppliers and slashing the number of companies with which they do business. At the same time, they are asking their vendors to expand their roles in the production process.

Networking provides a way for production managers to learn about suppliers and get to know them personally. Trade shows, conferences, seminars, and other meetings enable managers to meet vendors, competitors, and colleagues.

Inventory Control Production and operations managers' responsibility for inventory control requires them to balance the need to keep stock on hand to meet demand against the costs of carrying inventory. Among the expenses involved in storing inventory are warehousing costs, taxes, insurance, and maintenance. Firms waste money if they hold more inventory than they need. On the other hand, having too little inventory on hand may result in a shortage of raw materials, parts, or goods for sale that could lead to delays and unhappy customers.

Firms stand to lose business when they miss promised delivery dates or turn away orders. Having an efficient inventory control system can save customers and money. Many firms maintain *perpetual inventory* systems to continuously monitor the amounts and locations of their stock. Such inventory control systems typically rely on computers, and many automatically generate orders at the appropriate times. Many companies link their scanning devices to perpetual inventory systems that reorder needed merchandise without human interaction. As the system records a shopper's purchase, it reduces the inventory count stored in the computer. Once inventory on hand drops to a predetermined level, the system automatically reorders the merchandise. New Jersey–based Toys 'R Us, the nation's largest toy retailer, has a dual inventory management challenge, particularly during the critical holiday season. Not only must its stores be supplied with goods to be sold, but also customer orders entered on its website must be fulfilled by the Christmas deadline. The company uses a software system responsible for ordering and receiving inventory as well as counting and selecting inventory in stockrooms and distribution centers. In addition, the system updates and verifies perpetual inventory balances and keeps inventory at optimal levels to prevent the retail chain from running out of in-store and online items.[16]

Some companies go further and hand over their inventory control functions to suppliers. This concept is known as *vendor-managed inventory*. Dow Chemical uses a vendor-managed inventory service for its customers with predictable and consistent product supply needs. Dow uses the latest technology to manage its customers' inventory levels and consumption rates to automatically place product re-orders for just-in-time supply.[17]

Just-in-Time Systems A just-in-time (JIT) system implements a broad management philosophy that reaches beyond the narrow activity of inventory control to influence the entire system of production and operations management. A JIT system seeks to eliminate anything that does not add value in operations activities by providing the right part at the right place at just the right time—right before it is needed in production.

JIT systems are being used in a wide range of industries, including medical supplies. Seattle Children's Hospital uses a two bin system called Demand Flow to manage the distribution of its supplies, equipment, and clinical materials. The Demand Flow system distributes supplies in a two bin, low unit of measure (LUM) system, where supplies are delivered in the right quantity and at the right time, removing the clinician from the ordering process. Unlike other distribution systems, Demand Flow monitors inventory turns of the supply bins at the point of use, while a more traditional distribution system monitors usage at the warehouse. Demand Flow enables Seattle Children's to monitor performance of the supplies within the bins so the bins can be right sized at the point of use, eliminating supply stock-outs and stale inventory. The hospital partners with its key distributors to deploy the system. While the

inventory control function requiring production and operations managers to balance the need to keep stock on hand to meet demand against the costs of carrying inventory.

just-in-time (JIT) system broad management philosophy that reaches beyond the narrow activity of inventory control to influence the entire system of production and operations management.

JIT inventory systems are used in a wide range of industries, including the healthcare field. Seattle Children's Hospital uses a JIT system to manage distribution of its supplies and other materials.

hospital does keep an inventory of certain emergency supplies on hand, the rest are distributed on a JIT basis, saving the hospital more than $2.5 million in its first year.[18]

Production using JIT shifts much of the responsibility for carrying inventory to vendors, which operate on forecasts and keep stock on hand to respond to manufacturers' needs. Suppliers that cannot keep enough high-quality parts on hand may be assessed steep penalties by purchasers. Another risk of using JIT systems is what happens if manufacturers underestimate demand for a product. Strong demand will begin to overtax JIT systems, as suppliers and their customers struggle to keep up with orders with no inventory cushion to tide them over. Natural disasters can also have a negative impact on JIT systems, preventing materials from reaching manufacturing facilities in a timely manner.

Materials Requirement Planning Besides efficiency, effective inventory control requires careful planning to ensure the firm has all the inputs it needs to make its products. How do production and operations managers coordinate all of this information? They rely on <u>materials requirement planning (MRP)</u>, a computer-based production planning system that lets a firm ensure that it has all the parts and materials it needs to produce its output at the right time and place and in the right amounts.

Production managers use MRP programs to create schedules that identify the specific parts and materials required to produce an item. These schedules specify the exact quantities needed and the dates on which to order those quantities from suppliers so that they are delivered at the correct time in the production cycle. A small company might get by without an MRP system. If a firm makes a simple product with few components, a telephone call may ensure overnight delivery of crucial parts. For a complex product, however, such as a high-definition TV or an aircraft, longer lead times are necessary.

Turtle Wax Ltd., an Illinois manufacturer of car care products including Turtle Wax, Color Magic, and Clear Vue, uses MRP software for a better picture of its operations. The software provides immediate production summaries, inventory levels, and sales and stock forecasts.[19]

materials requirement planning (MRP) computer-based production planning system that lets a firm ensure that it has all the parts and materials it needs to produce its output at the right time and place and in the right amounts.

Assessment Check ☑

1. List the four major tasks of production and operations managers.

2. What is the difference between a traditional manufacturing structure and a team-based structure?

3. What factors affect the make, buy, or lease decision?

288

6 │ Controlling the Production Process

The final task of production and operations managers is controlling the production process to maintain the highest possible quality. **Production control** creates a well-defined set of procedures for coordinating people, materials, and machinery to provide maximum production efficiency. Suppose that a watch factory must produce 80,000 watches during October. Production control managers break down this total into a daily production assignment of 4,000 watches for each of the month's 20 working days. Next, they determine the number of workers, raw materials, parts, and machines the plant needs to meet the production schedule. Similarly, a manager in a service business such as a restaurant must estimate how many dinners the outlet will serve each day and then determine how many people are needed to prepare and serve the food, as well as what food to purchase.

Figure 10.5 illustrates production control as a five-step process composed of planning, routing, scheduling, dispatching, and follow-up. These steps are part of the firm's overall emphasis on total quality management.

production control creates a well-defined set of procedures for coordinating people, materials, and machinery to provide maximum production efficiency.

Production Planning

The phase of production control called *production planning* determines the amount of resources (including raw materials and other components) an organization needs to produce a certain output. The production planning process develops a bill of materials that lists all needed parts and materials. By comparing information about needed parts and materials with the firm's perpetual inventory data, purchasing staff can identify necessary purchases. Employees or automated systems establish delivery schedules to provide needed parts and materials when required during the production process. Production planning also ensures the availability of needed machines and personnel. Workers at a Wilson Sporting Goods Company factory in Ohio have made every football ever used in a Super Bowl game. Each January, production begins; the footballs are about 70 percent complete before the final playoff games are decided. Once the Super Bowl teams emerge and workers know which two team names will be printed on the balls, production goes into overdrive. The plant makes 228 official game balls and around 15,000 replicas for sale to fans.[20]

Although material inputs contribute to service-production systems, production planning for services tends to emphasize human resources more than materials.

Routing

Another phase of production control, called *routing*, determines the sequence of work throughout the facility and specifies who will perform each aspect of the work at what location. Routing choices depend on two factors: the nature of the good or service and the facility layouts discussed earlier in the chapter—product, process, fixed position, or customer oriented.

FIGURE
10.5 Steps in Production Control

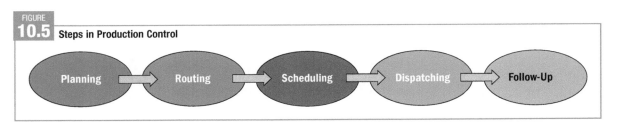

Planning → Routing → Scheduling → Dispatching → Follow-Up

Chapter 10 *Production and Operations Management*   **289**

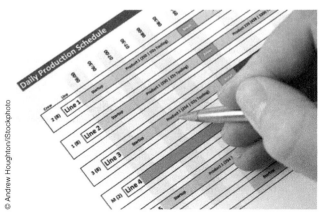

In the scheduling phase of production control, managers develop timetables that specify how long each operation in the production process takes and when workers should perform it.

JETCAM is a firm headquartered in Monaco that provides routing software to the aerospace composite industry, in which quality and accuracy are absolutely critical. One feature of the software is that it allows instructions for processes to be provided automatically instead of keyed in by workers—thus avoiding errors.[21]

Scheduling

In the *scheduling* phase of production control, managers develop timetables that specify how long each operation in the production process takes and when workers should perform it. Efficient scheduling ensures that production will meet delivery schedules and make efficient use of resources.

Scheduling is important whether the product is complex or simple to produce and whether it is a tangible good or a service. A pencil is simpler to produce than a computer, but each production process has scheduling requirements. A stylist may take 25 minutes to complete each haircut with just one or two tools, whereas every day a hospital has to schedule procedures and treatments ranging from X-rays to surgery to follow-up appointments. Oregon–based Swanson Group manufactures lumber, plywood, and wood veneers. MRP software made a dramatic difference in the company's productivity, cost savings, and on-time delivery. The software helped the company control scheduling, which can be challenging because of the intricacies of the wood manufacturing process. Knowing when machinery would be needed for manufacturing the various wood products helped the company reduce labor costs. Best of all, on-time shipments increased as a result of using the software, which provided advanced information about potential bottlenecks in the mill.[22]

Production managers use a number of analytical methods for scheduling. One of the oldest methods, the *Gantt chart*, tracks projected and actual work progress over time. Gantt charts like the one in Figure 10.6 remain popular because they show at a glance the status of a particular project. However, they are most effective for scheduling relatively simple projects.

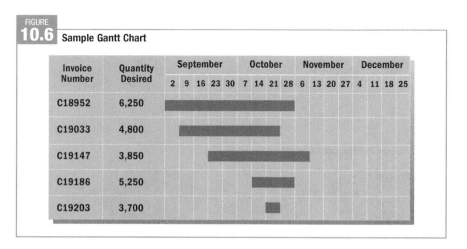

FIGURE 10.6 Sample Gantt Chart

Invoice Number	Quantity Desired	September					October				November				December			
		2	9	16	23	30	7	14	21	28	6	13	20	27	4	11	18	25
C18952	6,250																	
C19033	4,800																	
C19147	3,850																	
C19186	5,250																	
C19203	3,700																	

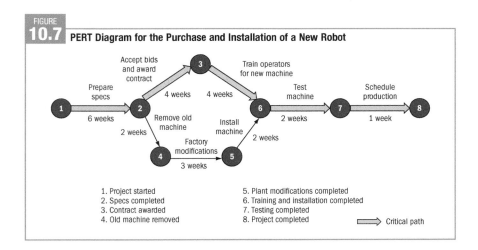

FIGURE 10.7 PERT Diagram for the Purchase and Installation of a New Robot

1. Project started
2. Specs completed
3. Contract awarded
4. Old machine removed
5. Plant modifications completed
6. Training and installation completed
7. Testing completed
8. Project completed

→ Critical path

A complex project might require a *PERT (program evaluation and review technique)* chart, which seeks to minimize delays by coordinating all aspects of the production process. First developed for the military, PERT has been modified for industry. The simplified PERT diagram in Figure 10.7 summarizes the schedule for purchasing and installing a new robot in a factory. The heavy gold line indicates the *critical path*—the sequence of operations that requires the longest time for completion. In this case, the project cannot be completed in fewer than 17 weeks.

In practice, a PERT network may consist of thousands of events and cover months of time. Complex computer programs help production managers develop such a network and find the critical path among the maze of events and activities. The construction of a huge office building requires complex production planning of this nature.

Dispatching

Dispatching is the phase of production control in which management instructs each department on what work to do and the time allowed for its completion. The dispatcher authorizes performance, provides instructions, and lists job priorities. Dispatching may be the responsibility of a manager or a self-managed work team.

Follow-Up

Because even the best plans sometimes fail, production managers need to be aware of any problems. *Follow-up* is the phase of production control in which managers and employees or team members spot problems in the production process and come up with solutions. Problems take many forms: machinery malfunctions, delayed shipments, and employee absenteeism can all affect production. The production control system must detect and report these delays to managers or work teams so they can adjust schedules and correct the underlying problems.

If your interest in any of the production planning and control functions has been piqued, you might be thinking about possible jobs in these areas. See the "Career Kickstart" feature for some tips about handling the first day on a new job.

Assessment Check ☑

1. What five steps are involved in controlling the production process?

2. What is the difference between a Gantt chart and a PERT chart?

Chapter 10 *Production and Operations Management*

291

CareerKickstart

Tips for Starting That New Job

It's natural to be a little nervous about starting a new job. But nerves shouldn't hamper your performance. Here are some tips to build your confidence on the first day.

1 *Look professional.* Be a little overdressed rather than underdressed in the beginning, to make a good first impression.

2 *Ask lots of questions.* Be sure you know what your boss expects you to do, both long-term and day-to-day. Check in periodically to confirm your understanding.

3 *Be innovative and creative.* But listen, too, and know when to offer your opinion and when not to.

4 *Build relationships from day one, and don't restrict yourself to co-workers at your own level or in your own department.* Network in every direction and nurture connections with people you click with.

5 *Don't know how to build relationships?* Start by offering to help someone.

6 *Show your confidence.* Don't be cocky or smug, but be positive and smile.

7 *Keep work and home separate.* Avoid personal phone calls, texts, and e-mails while on the job.

8 *Continue the company research you started before your interview.* You can never know enough about the organization you work for, its history, its culture, and its goals.

Good luck!

Sources: Kristi Hedges, "Start Your New Job Like a Rock Star," *Forbes*, accessed February 23, 2014, www.forbes.com; Miriam Salpeter, "First Day on the Job: 9 Ways to Make a Great Impression," *AOL.com*, accessed February 23, 2014, http://jobs.aol.com; "Welcome to Your New Job," *First 30 Days*, accessed February 23, 2014, www.first30days.com; William Donckets, "Starting a New Job: Some Tips for Early Success, *Technorati*, accessed February 23, 2014, www.technorati.com.

Importance of Quality

Quality—as it relates to the production of goods and services—is defined as being free of deficiencies. Quality matters because fixing, replacing, or redesigning defective products is costly. If Seagate makes a defective computer hard drive, it has to either fix the drive or replace it to keep a customer happy. If Delta Airlines books too many passengers for a flight, it has to offer vouchers worth hundreds of dollars to encourage passengers to give up their seats and take a later flight.

For most companies, the costs of poor quality can amount to 20 percent of sales revenue, if not more. Some typical costs of poor quality include downtime, repair costs, rework, and employee turnover. Poor quality can also result in lost sales and a tarnished image. Lululemon, the Vancouver, Canada–based athletic apparel company, recently experienced quality issues with some of its yoga pants, which consumers complained were too sheer. Product recalls cost Lululemon millions, and the company suffered bad publicity when the situation was not handled promptly.[23]

One process that companies use to ensure that they produce high-quality products from the start is **benchmarking**—determining how well other companies perform business functions or tasks. In other words, benchmarking is the process of comparing other firms' standards, performance metrics, and best practices, usually in terms of quality, costs, and time. Automobile companies routinely purchase each other's cars and take them apart to examine and compare the design, components, and materials used to make even the smallest part. They then make improvements to match or exceed the quality found in their competitors' cars. Companies may use many different benchmarks, depending on their objectives. For instance, organizations that want to make more money may compare their operating profits or expenses to those of other firms. Retailers concerned with productivity may benchmark sales per square foot. Manufacturers interested in productivity may benchmark using output per workers.

It's important when benchmarking for a firm to establish what it wants to accomplish, what it wants to measure, and which company can provide the most useful benchmarking information. A firm might choose a direct competitor for benchmarking, or it might select a company in an entirely different industry—but one that has processes the firm wants to study and emulate.

quality good or service that is free of deficiencies.

benchmarking process of determining how well other companies perform business functions or tasks.

---

292 Part 3 *Management: Empowering People to Achieve Business Success*

Solving an Ethical Controversy

Multivitamins Produced in China: Are Stricter Quality Controls Necessary?

Chinese-made multivitamins reportedly contain dangerous levels of lead and toxic bacteria—and are showing up in U.S. stores. Some people have called for stricter quality standards.

Should tighter quality controls be placed on Chinese-made goods?

PRO

1. According to the Chinese Ministry of Commerce, 85 percent of Chinese citizens rank quality concerns high for food and drugs made in their own country. Tighter controls would also benefit Chinese consumers.

2. Vitamins stamped "Made in Germany" or "Made in the USA" might still contain ingredients from China. Because it has already been demonstrated that these products contain high levels of toxic substances, tighter quality controls must be put into place.

CON

1. Many vitamins contain ingredients from multiple sources, so it is impossible to target China as the sole source of contamination.

2. Chinese production offers companies good value. With lower-cost labor and other services, savings can be passed along to the consumer.

Summary

Despite ongoing concerns, Swiss manufacturer Lonza recently announced it would locate its vitamin B3 manufacturing in China. Meanwhile, China is considering new production regulations on vitamin C—but with an emphasis on pricing power.

Sources: Steve Kelman, "Secret Chinese Vitamins," *Federal Computer Week*, accessed February 4, 2014, www.fcw.com; "Lonza to Build Vitamin B3 Plant in China," *All about Feed*, accessed February 4, 2014, www.allaboutfeed.net; "New Multivitamins Target Concern over China's Quality Problems," *Bio-Medicine*, accessed February 4, 2014, http://news.bio-medicine.org.

Quality Control

Quality control involves measuring output against established quality standards. Firms need such checks to spot defective products and to avoid delivering inferior shipments to customers. Standards should be set high enough to meet customer expectations. A 90 or 95 percent success rate might seem to be a good number, but consider what your phone service or ATM network would be like if it worked only 90 percent of the time. You would feel frustrated and inconvenienced and would probably switch your account to another service provider or bank.

Manufacturing firms can monitor quality levels through visual inspections, electronic sensors, robots, and X-rays. Surveys can provide quality-control information to services. Negative feedback from customers or a high rejection rate on a product or component sends a signal that production is not achieving quality standards. Firms that outsource operations may face a greater challenge in monitoring quality and assuring customers of the quality of their goods or services, especially if they are highly visible companies such as airlines. The "Solving an Ethical Controversy" feature discusses concerns over the quality of multivitamins manufactured for U.S. companies in China.

Because the typical factory can spend up to half its operating budget identifying and fixing mistakes, a company cannot rely solely on inspections to achieve its quality goals. Instead, quality-driven production managers identify all processes involved in producing goods and services and work to maximize their efficiency. The causes of problems in the processes must be found and eliminated. If a company concentrates its efforts on better designs of products and processes with clear quality targets, it can ensure virtually defect-free production.

quality control
measuring output against established quality standards.

Many businesses and consumers prefer to buy from companies that are ISO certified.

International Organization for Standardization, ISO organization whose mission is to develop and promote international standards for business, government, and society to facilitate global trade and cooperation.

Assessment Check ✅

1. What are some ways in which a company can monitor the quality level of its output?

2. List some of the benefits of acquiring ISO 9000 certification.

General Electric, Heinz, 3M, Sears, and the U.S. military are among the organizations that use the Six Sigma concept to achieve quality goals. *Six Sigma* means a company tries to make error-free products 99.9997 percent of the time—a tiny 3.4 errors per million opportunities. The goal of Six Sigma programs is for companies to eliminate virtually all defects in output, processes, and transactions. Motorola Solutions—also a Six Sigma firm—recently completed an initiative to redesign and simplify much of its software architecture in order to improve operational efficiencies and cut costs by reducing redundant IT applications.[24]

ISO Standards

For many goods and services, an important measure of quality is to meet the standards of the **International Organization for Standardization**, known as ISO for short—not an acronym but a shorter name derived from the Greek word *isos*, meaning "equal." Operating since 1947, ISO is a network of national standards bodies from 162 countries. Its mission is to develop and promote international standards for business, government, and society to facilitate global trade and cooperation. ISO has developed voluntary standards for everything from the format of banking and telephone cards to freight containers to paper sizes to metric screw threads. The U.S. member body of ISO is the American National Standards Institute.

The ISO 9000 family of standards gives requirements and guidance for quality management to help organizations ensure that their goods and services achieve customer satisfaction and also provide a framework for continual improvement. The ISO 14000 family of standards for environmental management helps organizations to ensure that their operations cause minimal harm to the environment and to achieve continual improvement of their environmental performance.

ISO 9001:2008 and ISO 14001:2004 respectively give the requirements for a quality management system and an environmental management system. Both can be used for certification, which means that the organization's management system (the way it manages its processes) is independently audited by a certification body (also known in North American as a registration body, or registrar) and confirmed as conforming to the requirements of the standard. The organization is then issued with an ISO 9001:2008 or an ISO 14001:2004 certificate.

It should be noted that certification is not a requirement of either standard, which can be implemented solely for the benefits it provides the organization and its customers. However, many organizations opt to seek certification because of the perception that an independent audit adds confidence in its abilities. Business partners, customers, suppliers, and consumers may prefer to deal with or buy products from a certified organization. Certifications have to be periodically renewed through accompanying audits.

A second point is that ISO itself develops standards but does not itself carry out auditing and certification. This is done independently of ISO by hundreds of certification bodies around the world. The certificates they issue carry their own logo, but not ISO's because the latter does not approve or control their activities.

Whether or not an organization decides to seek certification of its management system, many have reported significant benefits from implementing ISO's management system standards, such as increased efficiency, better teamwork, improved customer satisfaction, and reduced consumption of resources.[25]

What's Ahead

Maintaining high quality is an important part of satisfying customers. Product quality and customer satisfaction are also objectives of the business function of marketing. The next part consists of three chapters that explore the many activities involved in customer-driven marketing. These activities include product development, distribution, promotion, and pricing.

Chapter in Review

■ Summary of Learning Objectives

⌐1¬ Explain the strategic importance of production.

Production and operations management is a vital business function. Without a quality good or service, a company cannot create profits, and it soon fails. The production process is also crucial in a not-for-profit organization, because the good or service it produces justifies the organization's existence. Production and operations management plays an important strategic role by lowering the costs of production, boosting output quality, and allowing the firm to respond flexibly and dependably to customers' demands.

Assessment Check Answers ☑

1.1 What is mass production? Mass production is a system for manufacturing products in large quantities through effective combinations of employees with specialized skills, mechanization, and standardization.

1.2 What is the difference between flexible production and customer-driven production? Flexible production generally involves using technology to receive and fulfill orders and skilled people to carry out tasks needed to fill a particular order. Customer-driven production evaluates buyer demands in order to make the connection between products manufactured and products bought.

⌐2¬ Identify and describe the production processes.

The four main categories of production processes are the analytic production system, which reduces a raw material to its component parts in order to extract one or more marketable products; the synthetic production system, which combines a number of raw materials or parts to produce finished products; the continuous production process, which generates finished items over a lengthy period of time; and the intermittent production process, which generates products in short production runs.

Assessment Check Answers ☑

2.1 What are the two main production systems? The two systems are analytic production and synthetic production.

2.2 What are the two time-related production processes? The two time-related production processes are the continuous production process and the intermittent production process.

⌐3¬ Explain the role of technology in the production process.

Computer-driven automation allows companies to design, create, and modify products rapidly and produce them in ways that effectively meet customers' changing needs. Important design and production technologies include robots, computer-aided design (CAD), computer-aided manufacturing (CAM), and computer-integrated manufacturing (CIM). Many firms are pouring resources into the development of manufacturing processes that result in a reduction of waste, energy use, and pollution.

Assessment Check Answers ☑

3.1 List some of the reasons businesses invest in robots. Businesses use robots to free people from boring, sometimes dangerous assignments and to perform tasks that require repeated manipulation of materials and tools.

3.2 What is a flexible manufacturing system (FMS)? An FMS is a production facility that workers can quickly modify to manufacture different products.

3.3 What are the major benefits of computer-integrated manufacturing (CIM)? The main benefits are increased productivity, decreased design costs, increased equipment utilization, and improved quality.

⌐4¬ Identify the factors involved in a location decision.

Criteria for choosing the best site for a production facility fall into three categories: transportation, physical, and human factors. Transportation factors include proximity to markets and raw materials, along with availability of transportation alternatives. Physical variables involve such issues as water supply, available energy, and options for disposing of hazardous wastes. Human factors include the area's labor supply, local regulations, taxes, and living conditions.

Assessment Check Answers ☑

4.1 How does an environmental impact study influence the location decision? An environmental impact study influences the location decision because it outlines how transportation, energy use, water and sewer treatment needs, and other factors will affect plants, wildlife, water, air, and other features of the natural environment.

4.2 What human factors are relevant to the location decision? Human factors include an area's labor supply, labor costs, local regulations, taxes, and living conditions.

⌐5¬ Explain the job of production managers.

Production and operations managers use people and machinery to convert inputs (materials and resources) into finished goods and services. Four major tasks are involved. First, the managers must plan the overall production process. Next, they must pick the best layout for their facilities. Then they implement their production plans. Finally, they control the production process and evaluate results to maintain the highest possible quality.

Implementation involves deciding whether to make, buy, or lease components; selecting the best suppliers for materials; and controlling inventory to keep enough, but not too much, on hand.

Assessment Check Answers ☑

5.1 List the four major tasks of production and operations managers. The four tasks are planning the overall production process, determining the best layout for the firm's facilities, implementing the production plan, and controlling manufacturing to maintain the highest quality.

5.2 What is the difference between a traditional manufacturing structure and a team-based structure? In the traditional structure, each manager is given a specific area of authority. In a team-based structure, all workers are responsible for their output.

5.3 What factors affect the make, buy, or lease decision? The costs of leasing or purchasing parts from vendors, versus producing them in-house, the availability of dependable outside suppliers, and the need for confidentiality affect this decision.

⌈6⌉ Discuss controlling the production process.

The production control process consists of five steps: planning, routing, scheduling, dispatching, and follow-up. Quality control is an important consideration throughout this process. Coordination of each of these phases should result in high production efficiency and low production costs.

Assessment Check Answers ☑

6.1 What five steps are involved in controlling the production process? The five steps are planning, routing, scheduling, dispatching, and follow-up.

6.2 What is the difference between a Gantt chart and a PERT chart? Gantt charts, which track projected and actual work progress over time, are used for scheduling relatively simple projects. PERT charts, which seek to minimize delays by coordinating all aspects of the production process, are used for more complex projects.

⌈7⌉ Determine the importance of quality.

Quality control involves evaluating goods and services against established quality standards. Such checks are necessary to spot defective products and to see that they are not shipped to customers. Devices for monitoring quality levels of the firm's output include visual inspection, electronic sensors, robots, and X-rays. Companies are increasing the quality of their goods and services by using Six Sigma techniques and by becoming ISO 9000 and ISO 14000 certified.

Assessment Check Answers ☑

7.1 What are some ways in which a company can monitor the quality level of its output? Benchmarking, quality control, Six Sigma, and ISO standards are ways of monitoring quality.

7.2 List some of the benefits of acquiring ISO 9000 certification. These standards define how a company should ensure that its products meet customers' requirements. Business partners, customers, suppliers, and consumers may prefer to deal with or buy products from a certified organization.

■ Business Terms You Need to Know

production 275
production and operations management 275
mass production 275
LEED (Leadership in Energy and Environmental Design) 277
computer-aided design (CAD) 279
computer-aided manufacturing (CAM) 279
flexible manufacturing system (FMS) 279
computer-integrated manufacturing (CIM) 280
make, buy, or lease decision 285
inventory control 287
just-in-time (JIT) system 287
materials requirement planning (MRP) 288
production control 289
quality 292
benchmarking 292
quality control 293
International Organization for Standardization, ISO 294

■ Review Questions

1. What is utility? How does production create utility?

2. Why is production such an important business activity? In what ways does it create value for the company and its customers?

3. Why are firms now moving more toward flexible production and customer-driven production instead of mass production? Describe a product that you think would be better suited to flexible production or customer-driven production than mass production. Explain your choice.

4. Identify which production system—analytic or synthetic—applies to each of the following products:
   a. logging
   b. medical care
   c. soybean farming
   d. fishing
   e. microchips

5. Industries such as home construction and dentistry benefit from the use of CAD. In both of these, CAM could be used as well—in the manufacture of home components as well as dental implants, crowns, and the like. Choose another industry that seems like a candidate for the use of both CAD and CAM systems. Explain how the industry could use both.

6. SeaWorld has facilities in Florida, Texas, and California. What specific factors might have contributed to those choices?

7. What would be the best facility layout for each of the following?

   a. a physical therapy business

   b. nail salon

   c. car wash

   d. sandwich shop

8. What might be the factors involved in the selection of suppliers for a steakhouse restaurant?

9. What is inventory control? Why is the management of inventory crucial to a company's success?

10. What is benchmarking? How can it help a firm improve the quality of its goods and services?

Projects and Teamwork Applications

1. In groups or in pairs, compare your backpacks, handbags, and any articles of clothing or shoes. Can you determine from the item's label where it was manufactured? What type of production process do you think was used to make the item? Is anyone wearing an item made in the United States? If so, how does it differ from the items made elsewhere?

2. On your own or with a classmate, imagine that you've been hired to help a business group design a shopping mall. Taking into account the factors discussed in the chapter, come up with recommendations for where the mall should be located—and why. Present your plan to the class.

3. On your own or with a classmate, select one of the following businesses and sketch or describe the layout that you think would be best for attracting and serving customers:

   a. Mexican restaurant

   b. home furnishings store

   c. pet store

   d. motorcycle dealership

   e. attorney's office

4. Suppose you and your best friend decided to operate a coffee café. Draft a production plan for your business, including the following decisions: (a) make, buy, or lease; (b) suppliers; and (c) inventory control.

5. Choose two firms for comparison (one firm should provide a good benchmarking opportunity for its production processes). Keep in mind that the benchmarking firm doesn't necessarily have to be in the same industry as the other selected firm. Present your decisions to the class and explain why you made both choices. What criteria would you use in your comparison?

Web Assignments

1. **Just-in-time inventory management.** Go online to learn more about just-in-time inventory management. Form two teams. One will discuss the advantages of just-in-time inventory management, and the other team will discuss its disadvantages. Be sure to discuss the implications of each for a global manufacturer.

   www.wisegeek.com/what-is-a-just-in-time-inventory.htm

   http://smallbusiness.chron.com/pros-cons-jit-inventory-system-3195.html

2. **Plant location decision.** Using an Internet business news service, search for information on a recent plant location decision. One example is Nissan's plant in Smyrna, Tennessee. Research the decision and then prepare a brief report outlining the factors that went into the firm's decision to locate the plant where it did.

   http://nissannews.com/en-US/nissan/usa/releases/nissan-celebrates-30th-anniversary-of-u-s-manufacturing-with-creation-of-900-jobs

3. **Reshoring.** Discuss and give examples of the benefits realized by companies involved in reshoring—bringing manufacturing and production work back to the United States. Study the website below and discuss some of the reasons this movement has begun to take shape. Outline, individually or in groups, the initiatives listed on this website.

   www.reshorenow.org

Note: Internet web addresses change frequently. If you don't find the exact sites listed, you may need to access the organization's home page and search from there or use a search engine such as Google or Bing.

CASE 10.1 Home Depot Customers Feel the Need for Speed

Picture yourself in the middle of a home improvement project and in need of additional paint, nails, or lumber. Home improvement retail giant Home Depot is well aware of customers and do-it-yourselfers who find themselves in this situation. As online retail sales continue to grow, delivery times and "want-it-now" attitudes have created a newer, same-day delivery model. Customers' need for speed has, in some cases, deemed traditional one- or two-day delivery too slow.

Although initially reluctant to embrace the web and its technology, Home Depot admits its mistake. In its most recent year, the company's online sales are expected to increase by 50 percent. With retail online sales tripling over the last decade, Home Depot has recently invested over $300 million on supply chain, technology, and online improvements, including building new fulfillment centers and updating warehouse technology systems. In addition to using its retail stores as distribution centers, over the next few years Home Depot plans to open three additional fulfillment centers for online and same-day delivery of more than 100,000 items. With a focus on growing its online business, Home Depot has limited further construction of its brick and mortar stores.

With its current delivery process, Home Depot takes between two and seven days to deliver most orders. Using its stores for online fulfillment will shorten delivery times to two days or less for 90 percent of orders. Customer orders placed by 5 P.M. will be shipped out that same evening, and customers will receive real-time delivery updates via mobile devices. The company is counting on a continued recovery in the housing market, as well as the inevitability that customers and contractors will continue to run short of lumber and nails in the midst of that all-important home improvement project.

Questions for Critical Thinking

1. Do you agree with Home Depot's supply chain investment based upon a customer's need for speed when it comes to purchasing home improvement items?

2. How can Home Depot ensure that its online fulfillment strategy keeps the retail chain competitive?

Sources: Company website, "Hassle-Free Online Shopping," www .homedepot.com, accessed February 8, 2014; Courtney Regan, "Home Depot CEO: Supply Chain Very Flexible," *CNBC*, accessed February 8, 2014, http://video.cnbc.com; Courtney Regan, "Same-Day Delivery Wars: The Need for Speed," *CNBC*, accessed February 8, 2014, www.cnbc.com; Stacy Jones, "Online Retail Still Very Small Compared to Brick and Mortar," *New Jersey News*, accessed February 8, 2014, www.nj.com; Shelly Banjo, "Home Depot Looks to Offer Same-Day Shipping," *The Wall Street Journal*, accessed February 8, 2014, http://online.wsj.com.

CASE 10.2 The F-35 Fighter Jet Flies over Budget

What would you think if a product you ordered was delivered late, at twice the estimated cost, with testing only 20 percent complete, and the necessary software delayed four years? What if it also proved to have structural flaws?

That's what happened to the U.S. government when it started taking delivery of F-35 fighter planes built by Lockheed Martin, using thousands of parts sourced from nine different countries and 48 states. The $133 million F-35 uses sophisticated stealth technology and is intended to serve the Air Force, the Marine Corps, the Navy, and several U.S. allies. However, many believe production delays, cost overruns, and quality problems have made it a prime candidate for Congressional budget cuts, which could further delay production and damage Lockheed Martin's revenue projections. The $47 billion manufacturer has been expecting to earn about 20 percent of its revenues from the F-35.

Although company profits are down, the F-35 is seeing more progress than problems. The Pentagon estimates that it will spend $392 billion for more than 2,440 F-35s over the next few decades. The F-35 is crucial to Lockheed Martin's bottom line. Britain is considering ordering 14 F-35s, and South Korea has chosen the F-35 over Boeing's F-15, a contract worth more than $7 billion. Still, investors are keeping a watchful eye on the F-35, should any more problems be reported.

Questions for Critical Thinking

1. Why did Lockheed Martin choose a concurrent production strategy, building planes while testing was still ongoing?

2. What can Lockheed Martin do to compensate for government-mandated production delays that hamper its efforts to achieve cost-saving economies of scale?

Sources: Katie Spence, "Will the $392 Billion F-35 Make or Break Lockheed Martin?" *Motley Fool,* accessed February 6, 2014, www.fool.com; Loren Thomson, "2013 Was the Year Everything Went Right for Lockheed Martin's F-35 Fighter," *Forbes,* accessed February 6, 2014, www.forbes.com; Andrea Shalai-Esa, "Government Sees Lifetime Cost of F-35 Fighter at $1.51 Trillion," *Reuters,* accessed February 6, 2014, www.reuters.com; "F-35 Airplane Joint Strike Fighter," *The New York Times,* accessed February 6, 2014; Exclusive: Parachute Issue Grounds Some Lockheed F-35 Jets," *Reuters,* accessed February 6, 2014, www.reuters.com.

Necco Produces Classic Valentine's Day Treats CASE 10.3

Not long ago, New England Confectionery Company, or Necco for short, marked the production of its one *trillionth* candy wafer. The humble roots of Necco, the country's oldest continuously operating candy company, began in Cambridge, Massachusetts in 1847. In fact, during the Civil War, Union soldiers carried Necco "hub wafers." Over the years, the candy maker has expanded production and become famous for more than just its wafers. Its product line includes the world famous Sweethearts, a favorite for Valentine's Day, Clark Bar, Candy Buttons, Mighty Malts, and Haviland Thin Mints.

In addition to inventing a machine to print sayings onto candy, Necco founder Oliver Chase invented and patented the first American candy machine, a lozenge cutter. The result is Necco's iconic pastel-colored wafers, made mainly from sugar, corn syrup, gelatin, colorings, and flavoring. In its most recent year, the company produced over 4 billion wafers. Integral to the timely production and delivery of Necco's sweet treats is an ongoing strategic planning and production process. Production for Valentine's Day, an annual event lasting 24 hours, consists of 11 months of work. During this time, the company produces roughly 15 million pounds of Sweetheart hearts and close to 8 billion of them are sold in a six-week window. After Valentine's Day, the demand for Sweethearts falls off dramatically.

For more than 150 years, the production process for Necco's hearts has remained unchanged. The ingredients to make the dough are mixed and then thrown on a machine for stretching and rolling. Sweethearts are embossed, rather than laser printed, in red ink with an old-fashioned print plate, including letters that can be rearranged and moved. It is during embossing that the dough gets cut into the shape of a heart. Two to three days later, after the drying (not baking) process, the hearts are placed into what Necco calls its rocket launcher, which mixes them together so that no one box has too many hearts of the same color. There are 72 different affectionate sayings like "Kiss Me," "Be True," and, "XOXO," and each year, 12 new sayings are added.

Newer sayings include "Text Me," or "Tweet Me." In fact, on the company's website, consumers can order personalized hearts and Necco wafers.

As a production company, Necco focuses its strategies on identifying opportunities for process improvement. The task of the company's executive called the lean champion is to identify, through observation and dialogue with employees, areas throughout the company in need of improvement. A cross-functional team is assembled to address many different kinds of process improvements, which can range from safety issues to eliminating waste and re-works of any kind. Often times, this process improvement may include managing people and machinery.

In addition to process improvement, Necco focuses intently on quality. At the heart of its operation is balancing the production process, which includes projecting the time required to produce its various products while meeting delivery schedules. A Necco production supervisor firmly states there are no shortcuts to making a product that should have gone out the door yesterday. Each step in the production process requires a certain amount of time, and there are procedures followed to ensure that a quality food product is delivered to the customer. Necco also remains well aware that without its customers, the company would not be in business. The company strives for freshness and consistency by weighing, measuring, and timing each of the 10 steps in the production of its wafers, for example.

About a decade ago, in order to expand, Necco was faced with a location decision after many years at its original 500,000 square foot location and longtime home in Cambridge, Massachusetts. The company made the decision to move to a suburb about eight miles away—a location that boasts an 800,000+ square foot facility for its 500 employees. One of the location factors in Necco's decision was to remain close to its roots in Cambridge. In addition, the company has plans to expand and house production of multiple products under one roof while retaining and growing its longtime base of coveted employees and nearby suppliers. Despite moves

Chapter 10 *Production and Operations Management*   **299**

to Mexico by most candy companies where sugar is less expensive, Necco refused to even consider the consequence of such a move on its loyal employees.

Part of Necco's production process involves monitoring and controlling inventory. Necco must pay constant attention to products such as sugar, corn syrup, gelatin, colorings, and flavoring to avoid wasting dollars in carrying inventory on its warehouse floor. Its methods include carrying enough "safety stock" and controlling the inventory it does keep on hand without having to tie up a lot of money with product "sitting on the warehouse that's not going to move." Ideally, Necco would prefer not to keep any inventory on hand, although that's next to impossible until the company is able to improve its processes that would allow raw materials to be delivered just in time for production. However, for a company producing 8 billion individually embossed Sweetheart candies annually, Valentine's Day, for years gone by and those to come, would not be the same without Necco's miniature proclamations of romantic intentions.

Questions for Critical Thinking

1. What is the key role of a production supervisor at Necco, how might it change during peak production times, and with which departments and employees might the supervisor interface? How might the role of a production supervisor at Necco differ from that of a company with a steadier production process?

2. A daily staff meeting at Necco can be considered part of production control, contributing to the smooth running of the candy production process. Who might attend such a meeting? What kinds of topics might they discuss, and how might the discussion change during peak production times?

3. What steps does a supervisor at Necco take to balance quality and doing a job well? As a player in the food business, discuss and provide examples of the ways and the processes Necco uses to monitor quality throughout its supply chain. Evaluate and discuss Necco's quality control process and list any changes you might make.

4. Discuss Necco's efforts to remain relevant in today's environment. How do its efforts to remain relevant impact its production processes and decisions? Discuss the role of mass customization in the production of Necco's Sweetheart candies.

Sources: Company website, http://necco.com, accessed June 3, 2014; Seth Daniel, "Attraction to Necco Much Sweeter This Year," *Revere Journal*, accessed May 31, 2014, www.reverejournal.com; "Candy Company Necco Offers Custom #Tweethearts for Valentine's Day," *ClickZ*, accessed May 31, 2014, www.clickz.com; Jonathan Berr, "Necco's Iconic Sweethearts Show Their Sassy Side," *CBS News*, accessed May 30, 2014, www.cbsnews .com; Claire Suddath, "How Do They Get Those Tiny Words on Sweethearts Candy?," *Time*, accessed May 31, 2014, http://content.time.com.

KANSAS

GREENSBURG, KS
No Time to Micromanage

"This is a stepping stone for me," thought Greensburg's town administrator, Steve Hewitt. Hewitt, who had grown up in Greensburg, had moved back home and taken a position in the tiny rural town of 1,500. Standing in what was left of his kitchen on the night of Friday, May 4, 2007, he realized he had gotten more than he bargained for.

Across town, Mayor Lonnie McCollum and his wife had survived by clinging to a mattress as the storm ravaged their home. A write-in candidate in the past election, McCollum had accepted the job and set out to revive the dying town. Among his many ideas, the most innovative had been green building. McCollum was no tree-hugger; he was simply looking for a way to save money on fuel and utilities, to conserve the town's resources.

Like many people in town, Hewitt and McCollum had no idea of the extent of the damage. They would later learn that the two-mile-wide F5 tornado drove right through the two-mile-wide town. By the end of the weekend, though, they knew that Greensburg was gone. At a press conference, McCollum announced that the town would rebuild, and would do it using green technology.

By May 2008, the town was on its third mayor since the disaster, but Hewitt was still the town administrator. He had expanded his staff from 20 to 35 people, establishing a full-time fire department, a planning department, and a community development department. Each week Hewitt spent hours giving interviews to reporters from all over the world. "He's very open as far as information," said Recovery Coordinator and Assistant Town Administrator Kim Alderfer. "He's very good about delegating authority. He gives you the authority to do your job. He doesn't have time to micromanage."

Meanwhile, residents Janice and John Haney had rebuilt their family farm on the outskirts of town. Although their new home, an earth berm structure, was full of energy-efficient features, Janice wasn't convinced that the plan to rebuild Greensburg using green technology was the right one. "I do worry that it will be a T-shirt slogan," said Haney. "I personally don't think the persons that are living in Greensburg right now are really committed to it. We didn't have a choice. You MUST go green. That's really not everybody's option." She added that many people feared higher taxes would force some families out of town.

Questions

After viewing the video, answer the following questions:

1. What kind of leader is Steve Hewitt?
2. How would you describe Greensburg's culture?
3. Do you believe that as town administrator, Hewitt had the right to impose green building codes on residents and businesses?
4. Perform a SWOT analysis of Greensburg's green initiative.

321

LAUNCHING YOUR
[Management Career]

Part 3, "Management: Empowering People to Achieve Business Success," covers Chapters 7 through 10, which discuss management, leadership, and the internal organization; human resource management, motivation, and labor–management relations; improving performance through empowerment, teamwork, and communication; and production and operations management. In those chapters, you read about top executives and company founders who not only direct their companies' strategy but lead others in their day-to-day tasks to keep them on track, middle managers who devise plans to turn the strategies into realities, and supervisors who work directly with employees to create strong teams that satisfy customers. An incredible variety of jobs is available to those choosing management careers. And the demand for managers will continue to grow. The U.S. Department of Labor estimates that managerial jobs will grow by about 7 percent over the next decade.[1]

So what kinds of jobs might you be able to choose from if you launch a management career? As you learned in Chapter 7, three types of management jobs exist: supervisory managers, middle managers, and top managers. Supervisory management, or first-line management, includes positions such as supervisor, office manager, department manager, section chief, and team leader. Managers at this level work directly with the employees who produce and sell a firm's goods and services.

Middle management includes positions such as general managers, plant managers, division managers, and regional or branch managers. They are responsible for setting objectives consistent with top management's goals and planning and implementing strategies for achieving those objectives.

Top managers include such positions as chief executive officer (CEO), chief operating officer (COO), chief financial officer (CFO), chief information officer (CIO), and executive vice president. Top managers devote most of their time to developing long-range plans, setting a direction for their organization, and inspiring a company's executives and employees to achieve their vision for the company's future. Top managers travel frequently between local, national, and global offices as they meet and work with customers, vendors, and company managers and employees.

Most managers start their careers in areas such as sales, production, or finance, so you likely will start in a similar entry-level job. If you do that job and other jobs well, you may be considered for a supervisory position. Then, if you are interested and have the technical, human, and conceptual skills to succeed, you'll begin your management career path. But what kinds of supervisory management jobs are typically available? Let's review the exciting possibilities.[2]

Administrative services managers manage basic services—such as clerical work, payroll, travel, printing and copying, data records, telecommunications, security, parking, and supplies—without which no organization could operate. On average, administrative service managers earn $81,000 a year.

Construction managers plan, schedule, and coordinate the building of homes, commercial buildings such as offices and stores, and industrial facilities such as manufacturing plants and distribution centers. Unlike administrative service managers, who work in offices, construction managers typically work on building sites with architects, engineers, construction workers, and suppliers. On average, construction managers earn $82,790 a year.

Food service managers run restaurants and services that prepare and offer meals to customers. They coordinate workers and suppliers in kitchens, dining areas, and banquet operations; are responsible for those who order and purchase food inventories; maintain kitchen equipment; and recruit, hire, and train new workers. Food service managers can work for chains such as Ruby Tuesday or Olive Garden, for local restaurants, and for corporate food service departments in organizations. On average, food service managers earn more than $47,960 a year.

Human resource managers help organizations follow federal and local labor laws; effectively recruit, hire, train, and retain talented workers; administer corporate pay and benefits plans; develop and administer organizational human resource policies; and, when necessary, participate in contract negotiations or handle disputes. Human resource management jobs vary widely, depending on how specialized the requirements are. On average, human resource managers earn $99,720 a year.

Lodging managers work in hotels and motels but also help run camps, ranches, and recreational resorts. They may oversee guest services, front desk, kitchen, restaurant, banquet, house cleaning, and maintenance workers. Because they are expected to help satisfy customers around the clock, they often work long hours and may be on call when not at work. On average, lodging managers earn about $46,810 a year.

Medical and health services managers work in hospitals, nursing homes, doctors' offices, and corporate and university settings. They run departments that offer clinical services; ensure that state and federal laws are followed; and handle decisions related to the management of patient care, nursing, surgery, therapy, medical records, and financial payments. On average, medical and health service managers earn $88,580 a year.

Sales managers direct organizations' sales teams. They set sales goals, analyze data, and develop training programs for organizations' sales representatives. On average, sales managers earn roughly $105,260 a year. Industrial production managers oversee the daily operations of manufacturing and related plants. They coordinate, plan, and direct the activities used to create a wide range of goods, such as cars, computer equipment, or paper products. On average, industrial production managers earn almost $89,190 a year.

Career Assessment Exercises in Management

1. The American Management Association is a global, not-for-profit professional organization that provides a range of management development and educational services to individuals, companies, and government agencies. Access the AMA's web site at http://www.amanet.org. Explore under "Individuals" and then "Articles and White Papers." Pick an article or research area that interests you. Provide a one-page summary of the management issues discussed in the feature.

2. Go online to a business news website like *Wall Street Journal, Forbes, Fortune, or Bloomberg Businessweek.* Find a story relating to a first-line supervisor, middle manager, or top executive. Summarize that person's duties. What decisions does that person make and how do those decisions impact his or her organization?

3. Pick a supervisory management position from the descriptions provided here that interests you. Research the career field. What skills do you possess that would make you a good candidate for a management position in that field? What work and other experience do you need to help you get started? Create a list of both your strengths and weaknesses and formulate a plan to add to your strengths.

Part 4 Marketing Management

Chapter 11

Learning Objectives

1. Define *marketing*.
2. Discuss the evolution of the marketing concept.
3. Describe not-for-profit marketing and nontraditional marketing.
4. Outline the basic steps in developing a marketing strategy.
5. Describe marketing research.
6. Discuss market segmentation.
7. Summarize consumer behavior.
8. Discuss relationship marketing.

Customer-Driven Marketing

© catchlights_sg /iStockphoto

(N)ASCAR's Strategy to Connect with Fans

Connecting with consumers is a challenge for any business. Whether it is the local convenience store or a Fortune 500 company, creating a lasting relationship with customers can mean the difference between success and failure. When it comes to connecting with consumers, no organization has done it better than NASCAR. The sport's popularity skyrocketed in the late 1990s and early 2000s. However, the recent recession dealt the sport a major hit. NASCAR officials saw TV ratings fall for five years in a row, and ticket revenues were also down by more than 40 percent.

Working with team owners, drivers, tracks, and sponsors, NASCAR came up with an action plan to help the sport come back from a sluggish economy and influence consumer behavior. Their goals include ramping up digital and social media offerings, appealing to broader demographic groups, and even making changes to the race cars to make the sport more exciting. NASCAR's chief marketing officer says that although the sport experienced explosive growth in the past, the slower economy and the way consumers now use their leisure time to watch sports and other entertainment has fueled the organization's proposed changes.

NASCAR is now busy implementing its plan. First, it entered into an agreement with Lifefyre, the leading provider of real-time social software. This collaboration allows fans to have conversations in real time via PC, tablet, or mobile device across NASCAR's racing website to discuss the latest news or live action on the track. NASCAR fans will also be able to bring others into the conversation by tagging friends on social media networks like Twitter and Facebook.

According to NASCAR's vice president of digital media, utilizing technology such as Livefyre's was an extension of fan engagement and adds a new dimension to fans' NASCAR experience. "NASCAR's digital platform is all about deeper engagement and providing the ultimate second screen experience for our fans," he says. NASCAR officials hope these changes will keep their product fresh and relevant to the current and next generation of racing fans.[1]

Overview

Business success in the 21st century is directly tied to a company's ability to identify and serve its target markets. In fact, all organizations—profit-oriented and not-for-profit, manufacturing and retailing—*must* serve customer needs to succeed, just as NASCAR increases its visibility with racing fans. Marketing is the link between the organization and the people who buy and use its goods and services. It is the way organizations determine buyer needs and inform potential customers that their firms can meet those needs by supplying a quality product at a reasonable price. And it is the path to developing loyal, long-term customers.

Consumers who purchase goods for their own use and business purchasers seeking products to use in their firm's operation may seem to fall in the same category, but marketers see distinct wants and needs for each group. To understand buyers—from manufacturers to web surfers to shoppers in the grocery aisles—companies gather mountains of data on every aspect of consumer lifestyles and buying behaviors. Marketers use the data to understand the wants and needs of both final customers and business buyers. Satisfying customers goes a long way toward building relationships with them. It's not always easy.

This chapter begins with an examination of the marketing concept and the way businesspeople develop a marketing strategy. We then turn to marketing research techniques and how businesses apply data to market segmentation and understanding customer behavior. The chapter closes with a detailed look at the important role customer relationships play in today's highly competitive business world.

[1] What Is Marketing?

Every organization—from profit-seeking firms such as Jimmy John's and Zappos to such not-for-profits as the Make-A-Wish Foundation and the American Cancer Society—must serve customer needs to succeed. Perhaps the retail pioneer J. C. Penney best expressed this priority when he told his store managers, "Either you or your replacement will greet the customer within the first 60 seconds."

marketing activity, set of institutions, and processes for creating, communicating, delivering, and exchanging offerings that have value for customers, clients, partners, and society at large.

According to the American Marketing Association, **marketing** is the activity, set of institutions, and processes for creating, communicating, delivering, and exchanging offerings that have value for customers, clients, partners, and society at large.[2] In addition to selling goods and services, marketing techniques help people advocate ideas or viewpoints and educate others. The American Heart Association has an online heart attack risk calculator and prevention guideline tools, along with a spreadsheet for health care providers and patients to estimate ten-year and lifetime risks for heart disease. Such tools help educate the general public about this widespread condition by listing its risk factors and common symptoms and describing the work of the association.[3]

Department store founder Marshall Field explained marketing quite clearly when he advised one employee to "give the lady what she wants." The phrase became the company motto, and it remains a business truism today. The best marketers not only give consumers what they want but even anticipate consumers' needs before those needs surface. Ideally, they can get a jump on the competition by creating a link in consumers' minds between the new need and the fulfillment of that need by the marketers' products. CVS Caremark, with headquarters in Rhode Island, is a retail pharmacy, and with its "MinuteClinic" service, customers can get quick, in-store medical consultations without going to the doctor. NetJets offers fractional jet ownership to executives who want the luxury and flexibility of private ownership without the cost of owning their own plane. Airbnb is an online vacation rental site where people can list or lease spare rooms, apartments, homes, and other accommodations.[4]

exchange process activity in which two or more parties give something of value to each other to satisfy perceived needs.

As these examples illustrate, marketing is more than just selling. It is a process that begins with discovering unmet customer needs and continues with researching the potential market; producing a good or service capable of satisfying the targeted customers; and promoting, pricing, and distributing that good or service. Throughout the entire marketing process, a successful organization focuses on building customer relationships.

utility power of a good or service to satisfy a want or need.

When two or more parties benefit from trading things of value, they have entered into an **exchange process**. When you purchase a cup of coffee, the other party may be a convenience store clerk, a vending machine, or a Seattle's Best server. The exchange seems simple—some money changes hands, and you receive your cup of coffee. But the exchange process is more complex than that. It could not occur if you didn't feel the need for a cup of coffee or if the convenience store or vending machine were not available. You wouldn't choose Seattle's Best Coffee unless you were aware of the brand. Because of marketing, your desire for a flavored blend, plain black coffee, or decaf is identified, and the coffee manufacturer's business is successful.

© sjscreens/Alamy Inc.

California-based Airbnb is an online marketplace where consumers can list, explore, and book rental accommodations around the world at various price points from their computers or mobile devices.

How Marketing Creates Utility

Marketing affects many aspects of an organization and its dealings with customers. The ability of a good or service to satisfy the wants and needs of customers is called **utility**. A company's production function creates *form utility* by converting raw materials, component parts, and other inputs into finished goods and services. But the marketing function creates time, place, and ownership utility. *Time utility* is created by making a good

Hit&Miss

or service available when customers want to purchase it. *Place utility* is created by making a product available in a location convenient for customers. *Ownership utility* refers to an orderly transfer of goods and services from the seller to the buyer. Firms may be able to create all three forms of utility. Target was the first nationwide retailer to offer bar-coded, scannable mobile coupons direct to cell phones. Guests can sign on to the program either on their personal computers or on their cell phones. Each month, they receive a text message with a link to a mobile web site page where they will find offers for various products. They can use the mobile coupons at any Target store nationwide because Target is the first retailer to have point-of-sale scanning technology for the coupons in all of its stores.[5] Technology is also having a major impact on the entertainment industry. See the "Hit & Miss" feature for more details.

[2] Evolution of the Marketing Concept

Marketing has always been a part of business, from the earliest village traders to large 21st-century organizations producing and selling complex goods and services. Over time, however, marketing activities evolved through the five eras shown in Figure 11.1: the production, sales, marketing, and relationship eras, and now the social era. Note that these eras parallel some of the time periods discussed in Chapter 1.

For centuries, organizations of the *production era* stressed efficiency in producing quality products. Their philosophy could be summed up by the remark, "A good product will sell itself." Although this production orientation continued into the 20th century, it gradually gave way to the *sales era*, in which businesses assumed that consumers would buy as a result of energetic sales efforts. Organizations didn't fully recognize the importance of their customers until the *marketing era* of the 1950s, when they began to adopt a consumer orientation. This focus intensified, leading to the emergence of the *relationship era* in the 1990s. In the relationship era, companies emphasized customer satisfaction and building long-term business relationships. Today, the social era continues to grow exponentially, thanks to the Internet and social media sites like Facebook, Twitter, and LinkedIn. Companies now routinely use mobile, social media, and the web as a way of marketing their goods and services to consumers.

Emergence of the Marketing Concept

The term **marketing concept** refers to a companywide customer orientation with the objective of achieving long-run success. The basic idea of the marketing concept is that marketplace success begins with the customer. A firm should analyze each customer's needs and then work

Assessment Check ✅

1. What is utility?
2. Identify three ways in which marketing creates utility.

marketing concept
companywide consumer orientation to promote long-run success.

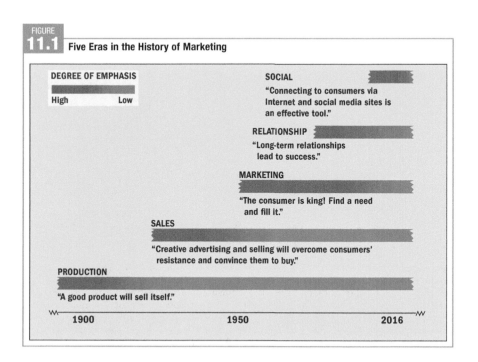

FIGURE 11.1 Five Eras in the History of Marketing

DEGREE OF EMPHASIS

High ▬▬▬▬ Low

SOCIAL ▬▬▬▬▬
"Connecting to consumers via Internet and social media sites is an effective tool."

RELATIONSHIP ▬▬▬▬▬▬▬
"Long-term relationships lead to success."

MARKETING ▬▬▬▬▬▬▬▬▬▬
"The consumer is king! Find a need and fill it."

SALES ▬▬▬▬▬▬▬▬▬▬▬▬▬
"Creative advertising and selling will overcome consumers' resistance and convince them to buy."

PRODUCTION ▬▬▬▬▬▬▬▬▬▬▬▬▬▬▬
"A good product will sell itself."

1900   1950   2016

backward to offer products that fulfill them. The emergence of the marketing concept can be explained best by the shift from a *seller's market*, one with a shortage of goods and services, to a *buyer's market*, one with an abundance of goods and services. During the 1950s, the United States became a strong buyer's market, forcing companies to satisfy customers rather than just producing and selling goods and services.

Today, much competition among firms centers on the effort to satisfy customers. While Facebook, LinkedIn, and Twitter dominate the world of social media apps, competitors continue to grow in numbers. The increased popularity of photo and video sharing is due in part to apps like Instagram, which is owned by Facebook. Vine (launched by Twitter), WhatsApp (recently bought by Facebook), and Snapchat are messaging apps, each with photo, audio, or video sharing capabilities. Yahoo's purchase of Tumblr, an online site that is part social network and part microblog, allows Yahoo to be part of the social media apps market as well. Google's most recent creation, Google+, is considered a competitor to Facebook.[6]

Assessment Check ☑

1. What is the marketing concept?

2. How is the marketing concept tied to the relationship and social eras of marketing?

[3] Not-for-Profit and Nontraditional Marketing

The marketing concept has traditionally been associated with products of profit-seeking organizations. Today, however, it is also being applied to not-for-profit sectors and other nontraditional areas ranging from religious organizations to political campaigns.

Not-for-Profit Marketing

Residents of every continent benefit in various ways from the approximately 20 million not-for-profit organizations currently operating around the globe. Nearly 1.5 million of them are located in the United States, where they employ 13.5 million workers and benefit from volunteers representing the equivalent of 9 million full-time employees.[7] Women tend to volunteer at a higher rate than men, and 35- to 44-year-olds and 45- to 54-year-olds are also the most likely to volunteer.[8] The largest not-for-profit organization in the world is the Red Cross/Red Crescent. Other not-for-profits range from Habitat for Humanity to the Boys & Girls Clubs of America to the Juvenile Diabetes Research Foundation. These organizations all benefit by applying many of the strategies and business concepts used by profit-seeking firms. They apply marketing strategies to reach audiences, secure funding, and accomplish their overall missions. Marketing strategies are important for not-for-profit organizations because they are all competing for dollars—from individuals, foundations, and corporations—just as commercial businesses are.

ONE is a not-for-profit organization co-founded by Irish rock celebrity Bono. It partners with firms such as Motorola, Starbucks, and Apple to sell RED-branded products and raise funds to fight AIDS in Africa.

Not-for-profit organizations operate in both public and private sectors. Public groups include federal, state, and local government units as well as agencies that receive tax funding. A state's department of natural resources, for instance, regulates land conservation and environmental programs; the local animal control officer enforces ordinances protecting people and animals; a city's public health board ensures safe drinking water for its citizens. The private not-for-profit sector comprises many different types of organizations, including the Philadelphia Zoo, the United States Olympic Committee, and the American Academy of Orthopaedic Surgeons. Although some private not-for-profits generate surplus revenue, their primary goals are not earning profits. If they earn funds beyond their expenses, they invest the excess in their organizational missions.

In some cases, not-for-profit organizations form a partnership with a profit-seeking company to promote the firm's message or distribute its goods and services. This partnership usually benefits both organizations. The National Football League and the United Way recently celebrated 40 years as one of the longest-running public-service partnerships in the United States. NFL athletes and other personalities appear in public-service advertisements and in person to promote community service and fundraising. Since 1999, the "Hometown Huddle" has been an NFL-wide day of service when team members, their families, coaches, and staff members participate in local community service activities.[9]

Celebrities are particularly visible campaigning for not-for-profit organizations—their own as well as others. ONE is a not-for-profit organization co-founded by Bono, lead singer of the Irish rock band U2. Working with more than 3.5 million people around the world, ONE spearheads activities to end extreme poverty and preventable diseases, primarily in Africa. As part of its strategy, the organization uses its division called RED to partner with brands like Starbucks and Apple, which contribute profits from the sale of RED-branded products. RED has raised more than $215 million to fight AIDS in Africa.[10]

Nontraditional Marketing

Not-for-profit organizations often engage in one or more of five major categories of nontraditional marketing: person marketing, place marketing, event marketing, cause marketing, and organization marketing. Figure 11.2 provides examples of these types of marketing. As described in the "Going Green" feature, through each of these types of marketing, an organization seeks to connect with the audience that is most likely to offer time, money, or other resources. In the case of ice cream maker Häagen-Dazs, the company has chosen to support research related to the disappearing honey bee.

Person Marketing Efforts designed to attract the attention, interest, and preference of a target market toward a person are called **person marketing**. Campaign managers for a political candidate conduct marketing research, identify groups of voters and financial supporters,

person marketing
use of efforts designed to attract the attention, interest, and preference of a target market toward a person.

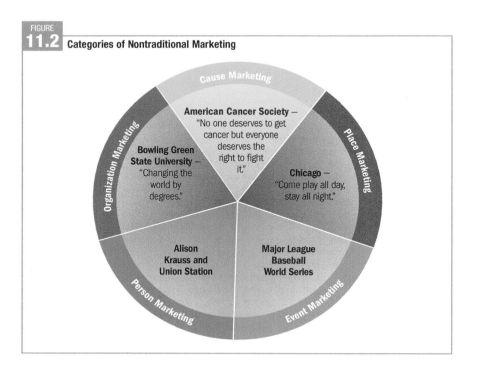

FIGURE 11.2 Categories of Nontraditional Marketing

Cause Marketing

American Cancer Society – "No one deserves to get cancer but everyone deserves the right to fight it."

Organization Marketing

Bowling Green State University – "Changing the world by degrees."

Place Marketing

Chicago – "Come play all day, stay all night."

Person Marketing

Alison Krauss and Union Station

Event Marketing

Major League Baseball World Series

and then design advertising campaigns, fund-raising events, and political rallies to reach them. Nike's advertising campaign and his namesake shoes have helped establish LeBron James as one of the biggest NBA stars since Michael Jordan.[11]

Many successful job seekers apply the tools of person marketing. They research the wants and needs of prospective employers, and they identify ways they can meet them. They seek employers through a variety of channels, sending messages that emphasize how they can benefit the employer.

place marketing
attempt to attract people to a particular area, such as a city, state, or nation.

Place Marketing As the term suggests, place marketing attempts to attract people to a particular area, such as a city, state, or nation. It may involve appealing to consumers as a tourist destination or to businesses as a desirable business location. A strategy for place marketing often includes advertising.

Place marketing may be combined with event marketing, such as the Super Bowl. Each year on its official Super Bowl website, the NFL lists local host-city events, lodging, restaurants, travel packages, and even what to wear. Well before the actual game, the website captures the energy and spirit of the upcoming competition.[12]

event marketing
marketing or sponsoring short-term events such as athletic competitions and cultural and charitable performances.

Event Marketing Marketing or sponsoring short-term events such as athletic competitions and cultural and charitable performances is known as event marketing. The American Diabetes Association sponsors the "Tour de Cure," a series of fund-raising cycling events held across the United States to raise funds to support its mission to prevent and cure diabetes.[13]

Event marketing often forges partnerships between not-for-profit and profit-seeking organizations. Many businesses sponsor events such as 10K runs to raise funds for health-related

GoingGreen

Häagen-Dazs Focuses on Honey Bee Research

You may not immediately make an association between premium ice cream and honey bees. Pollinating many of the fruits, vegetables, and nuts we eat, honey bees are integral to more than half of the all-natural fruits, nuts, and berries used to produce Häagen-Dazs ice creams, sorbets, and frozen yogurts. Mysteriously, honey bees have been disappearing over the last decade.

Häagen-Dazs decided to take action by contributing to research to preserve honey bee colonies. The company has created the Häagen-Dazs Ice Cream Bee Board to provide insight and consultation into the causes of colony collapse disorder (CCD), which occurs when bees mysteriously die after leaving their hives.

Scientists and researchers are not certain what causes CCD. Environmental factors like chemical exposure, parasites, and pesticides are believed to be contributors, along with viruses, mites, and poor nutrition.

To date, Häagen-Dazs has contributed over $700,000 to support a California-based honey bee research facility, one of the largest of its kind in North America. In addition, the company has made a gift of $250,000 to Penn State University to provide funds for research, education,

outreach, and student training. "We want to keep these little heroes buzzing. We hope you'll join our mission," reads the Häagen-Dazs website.

Questions for Critical Thinking

1. Häagen-Dazs has introduced an ice cream flavor called Vanilla Honey Bee, and partial proceeds go to CCD research. How can the company make consumers aware of its efforts to save the bees?

2. Discuss how Häagen-Dazs is attempting to use cause marketing. Whose interests are being served in the company's attempt to save honey bees?

Sources: Company website, "Honey, Please Don't Go," www.haagendazs.com, accessed February 9, 2014; organization website, "Laidlaw Facility: Häagen-Dazs Honey Bee Haven," http://beebiology.ucdavis.edu, accessed February 9, 2014; Michael Wines, "Bee Deaths May Stem from Virus, Study Says," *The New York Times*, accessed February 9, 2014, www.nytimes.com; Parija B. Kavilanz, "Disappearing Bees Threaten Ice Cream Sellers," *CNNMoney*, accessed February 9, 2014, http://money.cnn.com.

---

charities. These occasions require a marketing effort to plan the event and attract participants and sponsors. Events may be intended to raise money or awareness, or both.

Cause Marketing Marketing that promotes awareness of, or raises money for, a cause or social issue, such as drug abuse prevention or childhood hunger is cause marketing. Cause marketing seeks to educate the public and may or may not attempt to directly raise funds. An advertisement often contains a phone number, a website address, or QR (quick response) code through which people can obtain more information about the organization or issue. Then they can either donate money or take other actions of support. Upscale retailer Nordstrom awards $10,000 scholarships for academic achievement and community involvement to high school students nationwide to cover some of their college expenses.[14]

Profit-seeking companies look for ways to contribute to their communities by joining forces with charities and causes, providing financial, marketing, and human resources. For-profit firms can also combine their goods and services with a cause. After spending time in Kenya drilling clean water wells, Josh Weingart partnered with an African manufacturer to produce sandals made from recycled materials like old tires that are sold in the U.S. market. Called WaterDrop Shop, the company plans to use its profits to build more water wells in African communities.[15]

Organization Marketing The final category of nontraditional marketing, organization marketing, influences consumers to accept the goals of, receive the services of, or contribute in some way to an organization. The U.S. Postal Service, the ALS Association, and the NBA are all examples of organizations that engage in marketing. Recently the NBA has turned to social media for much of its marketing. The NBA continues to have great success with social media for much of its marketing as avid fans turn to social media sites, especially on game day. Of all the NBA teams, the Los Angeles Lakers have the most fans on Facebook with 17 million, followed by the Chicago Bulls with just under 10 million, and the Miami Heat with almost 9 million.[16]

cause marketing marketing that promotes a cause or social issue, such as preventing child abuse, anti-littering efforts, and stop-smoking campaigns.

organization marketing marketing strategy that influences consumers to accept the goals of, receive the services of, or contribute in some way to an organization.

Assessment Check ☑

1. Why do not-for-profit organizations engage in marketing?

2. What are the five types of nontraditional marketing used by not-for-profit organizations?

Chapter 11 *Customer-Driven Marketing*   **311**

331

[4] Developing a Marketing Strategy

Decision makers in any successful organization, for-profit or not-for-profit, follow a two-step process to develop a *marketing strategy*. First, they study and analyze potential target markets and choose among them. Second, they create a marketing mix to satisfy the chosen market. Figure 11.3 shows the relationships among the target market, the marketing mix variables, and the marketing environment. Later discussions refer back to this figure as they cover each topic. This section describes the development of a marketing strategy designed to attract and build relationships with customers. Sometimes, in an effort to do this, marketers use questionable methods, as described in the "Solving an Ethical Controversy" feature.

Earlier chapters of this book introduced many of the environmental factors that affect the success or failure of a firm's business strategy, including today's rapidly changing and highly competitive world of business, a vast array of social and cultural factors, economic challenges, political and legal factors, and technological innovations. Although these external forces frequently operate outside managers' control, marketers must still consider the impact of environmental factors on their decisions.

A marketing plan is a key component of a firm's overall business plan. The marketing plan outlines its marketing strategy and includes information about the target market, sales and revenue goals, the marketing budget, and the timing for implementing the elements of the marketing mix.

FIGURE 11.3 Target Market and Marketing Mix within the Marketing Environment

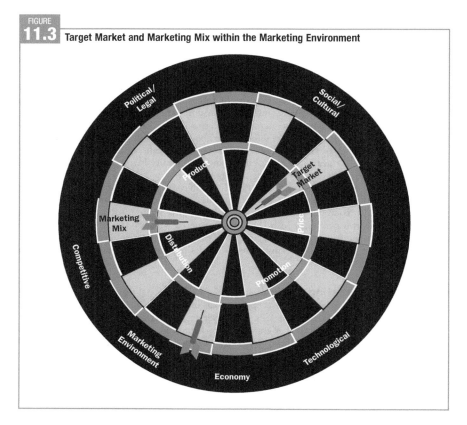

Solving an Ethical Controversy

When Free Credit Reports Aren't Free

When times are tough and credit is tight, consumers are more likely to search for and monitor their credit scores. The Fair Credit Reporting Act (FCRA) requires the three major consumer reporting companies—Equifax, Experian, and TransUnion—to provide consumers a free copy of their credit reports once a year. Consumers must request the report through the official Annual Credit Report Request Service by phone or mail, or online at AnnualCreditReport.com. Credit report companies claim to offer free credit reports—but many offers contain hidden charges. Also, Experian has profited because consumers confuse its FreeCreditReport.com division with the federal government's AnnualCreditReport.com, the only truly free web site.

Should firms be allowed to use the word "free" in advertising for credit reports if the service contains hidden charges?

PRO

1. If the credit score itself is free, but related services are not, then the advertising is truthful.

2. Some promotional offers contain free credit scores, with a tie-in to additional services for a fee.

CON

1. Some companies provide "free" reports, then bill consumers for services they have to cancel.

2. Consumer advocates say firms exploit people's fears.

Summary

The Federal Trade Commission's Free Credit Reports Rule requires credit report web sites to carry the following across the top of each page: "THIS NOTICE IS REQUIRED BY LAW. Read more at FTC.GOV. You have the right to a free credit report from AnnualCreditReport.com or 877-322-8228, the ONLY authorized source under federal law." Very recently, rather than including this disclosure, Experian began charging $1 for a credit report and donating the fee to charity.

Sources: Federal Trade Commission, "Free Annual Credit Reports," www.ftc.gov, accessed February 11, 2014; Ron Lieber, "Free Credit on Credit? No Longer," *The New York Times,* accessed February 11, 2014, www.nytimes.com; Joe Taylor Jr., "New Laws Crack Down on Free Credit Report Marketing," *CardRatings,* accessed February 11, 2014, www.cardratings.com; Michelle Singletary, "Free Credit Reports Get Easier to Find," *Washington Post,* accessed February 11, 2014, www.washingtonpost.com.

Selecting a Target Market

The expression "find a need and fill it" is perhaps the simplest explanation of the two elements of a marketing strategy. A firm's marketers find a need through careful and continuing study of the individuals and business decision makers in its potential market. A market consists of people with purchasing power, willingness to buy, and authority to make purchase decisions.

Markets can be classified by type of product. **Consumer products**—often known as business-to-consumer (B2C) products—are goods and services, such as GPS systems, tomato sauce, and a haircut, that are purchased by end users. **Business products**—or business-to-business (B2B) products—are goods and services purchased to be used, either directly or indirectly, in the production of other goods for resale. Some products can fit either classification depending on who buys them and why. A computer or credit card can be used by a business or a consumer.

An organization's **target market** is the group of potential customers toward whom it directs its marketing efforts. Customer needs and wants vary considerably, and no single organization has the resources to satisfy everyone. *Popular Science* is geared toward readers who are interested in science and technology, whereas *Bon Appétit* is aimed at readers who are interested in fine food and cooking.

Decisions about marketing involve strategies for four areas of marketing activity: product, distribution, promotion, and pricing. A firm's **marketing mix** blends the four strategies to fit the needs and preferences of a specific target market. Marketing success depends not on the four individual strategies but on their unique combination.

consumer (B2C) product good or service that is purchased by end users.

business (B2B) product good or service purchased to be used, either directly or indirectly, in the production of other goods for resale.

target market group of people toward whom an organization markets its goods, services, or ideas with a strategy designed to satisfy their specific needs and preferences.

marketing mix blending of the four elements of marketing strategy—product, distribution, promotion, and pricing—to fit the needs and preferences of a specific target market.

Product strategy involves more than just designing a good or service with needed attributes. It also includes decisions about package design, brand names, trademarks, warranties, product image, new-product development, and customer service. Think about your favorite pair of jeans. Do you like them because they fit the best, or do other attributes—such as styling and overall image—also contribute to your brand preference? *Distribution strategy*, the second marketing mix variable, ensures that customers receive their purchases in the proper quantities at the right times and locations. *Promotional strategy*, another marketing mix element, effectively blends advertising, personal selling, sales promotion, and public relations to achieve its goals of informing, persuading, and influencing purchase decisions.

Pricing strategy, the final mix element, is also one of the most difficult areas of marketing decision making in setting profitable and justifiable prices for the firm's product offerings. Such actions are sometimes subject to government regulation and considerable public scrutiny. They also represent a powerful competitive weapon and frequently produce responses by the other firms in the industry, who match price changes to avoid losing customers. Think about your jeans again. Would you continue to purchase them if they were priced either much higher or much lower?

Retail health clinics are low-cost, walk-in medical facilities usually found in supermarkets, chain drugstores, and retailers like Walmart and Target. Patients typically see nurse practitioners or physician assistants, who can diagnose and treat minor medical conditions and prescribe some medications. The clinics are open late in the evenings and on weekends and also offer appropriate vaccinations and inexpensive sports and summer-camp physicals for children. They have proved to be a popular alternative to primary care in areas where primary-care physicians are scarce and because of their low cost, usually about 40 percent less than a physician office visit, or $60 per visit. A recent survey found that there were about 1,500 retail clinics throughout the United States, and that number appears to be growing. One important problem with walk-in clinics is that often the patients don't tell their primary-care doctors about the visits—or about any medications they were prescribed. In an attempt to solve these problems, drugstore chain CVS has been marketing its Minute Clinics with some nationwide health-care organizations. Other challenges include the seasonality of such products as flu shots and summer-camp physicals, oversaturation of the market in some areas, and difficulty in reaching potential patients who don't shop at the particular store. Retail clinics are evolving with the changing economic and health care landscape, and how the operators of the clinics will solve these marketing problems remains to be seen.[17]

Developing a Marketing Mix for International Markets

Marketing a good or service in foreign markets means deciding whether to offer the same marketing mix in every market *(standardization)* or to develop a unique mix to fit each market *(adaptation)*. The advantages of standardizing the marketing mix include reliable marketing performance and low costs. This approach works best with B2B goods, such as steel, chemicals, and aircraft, which require little sensitivity to a nation's culture.

Adaptation, on the other hand, lets marketers vary their marketing mix to suit local competitive conditions, consumer preferences, and government regulations. Consumer tastes are often shaped by local cultures. Because consumer products generally tend to be more culture dependent than business products, they more often require adaptation. SUBWAY already has over 425 stores in China, with more than 100 in Beijing alone. In the next few years, the company plans to have 180 stores in Beijing and more than 600 throughout China. Surpassing McDonald's, SUBWAY has over 40,000 stores worldwide compared to McDonald's 33,000 units. As SUBWAY opens stores in different regions, it plans to adapt its menu to local tastes with such offerings as Beijing roast duck sandwiches and "hot spicy Szechuan sauce." Why do these firms go out of their way to adapt to Chinese preferences? China is a market with a growing middle class and 1.3 billion potential consumers.[18]

Marketers also try to build adaptability into the designs of standardized goods and services for international and domestic markets. *Mass customization* allows a firm to mass produce goods and services while adding unique features to individual or small groups of orders. For

Karen Cowled/Alamy

Adaptation allows marketers to vary their marketing mix to suit local competitive conditions, consumer preferences, and government regulations. Because consumer products, particularly food items, tend to be more culture dependent than business products, they often require adaptation.

Assessment Check ✅

1. Distinguish between consumer products and business products.
2. What are the steps in developing a marketing strategy?

example, the online firm Blank Label specializes in custom men's dress shirts and allows customers to choose their own fabric, style, individual features, and size. Spreadshirt, with U.S. headquarters in Boston, specializes in customized casual wear, accessories, and even personalized underwear.[19]

5 Marketing Research

Marketing research involves more than just collecting data. Researchers must decide how to collect data, interpret the results, convert the data into decision-oriented information, and communicate those results to managers for use in decision making. **Marketing research** is the process of collecting and evaluating information to help marketers make effective decisions. It links business decision makers to the marketplace by providing data about potential target markets that help them design effective marketing mixes.

The technological advances of the past two decades—the Internet, social media, mobile devices, and the like—have given rise to what's been called **big data**, information collected in massive amounts and at unprecedented speed from both traditional and digital sources. These advances make it possible for businesses to gather and analyze information from customers, visitors to company websites, social media sites, and more. Big data has the potential to increase revenue, create new business and marketing strategies, and build market share. The greatest challenge for marketers, however, is the ability to manage and analyze all of this data. According to IBM, more than 2.5 *quintillion* bytes of data are created worldwide every day.[20]

marketing research collecting and evaluating information to help marketers make effective decisions.

big data information collected in massive amounts and at unprecedented speed from both traditional and digital sources that is used in business decision making.

Obtaining Marketing Research Data

Marketing researchers need both internal and external data. Firms generate *internal data* within their organizations. Financial records provide a tremendous amount of useful information,

Chapter 11 *Customer-Driven Marketing*

315

such as inventory levels; sales generated by different categories of customers or product lines; profitability of particular divisions; or comparisons of sales by territories, salespeople, customers, or product lines; or unpaid bills.

Researchers gather *external data* from outside sources, including previously published data. Trade associations publish reports on activities in particular industries. Advertising agencies collect information on the audiences reached by various media. National marketing research firms offer information through subscription services. Some of these professional research firms specialize in specific markets, such as teens or ethnic groups. This information helps companies make decisions about developing or modifying products.

A recent report by the marketing research firm comScore indicates that consumers now view website, video, and app content across a variety of platforms, including mobile. In today's multiplatform digital media environment, understanding digital consumer behavior across desktop computers, smartphones, and tablets is critical information to marketers.

For a device introduced less than five years ago, tablets are now driving more digital traffic than smart phones. For the first time, tablets recently topped traditional desktop devices for purchases. Mobile channels now account for one out of every three digital media consumption minutes. The increased popularity of smart phones and the introduction of tablets and other web-enabled devices have contributed to the explosion in digital media consumption. Such big data can provide very clear indications of what consumers are looking for in a product.[21]

The largest consumer-goods manufacturer in the world, Procter & Gamble, has excelled in marketing research for a long time; it created its own marketing research department in 1923 and began conducting its research online in 2001. To help the company recover from the global recession and focus on the future, the company's CEO, A.G. Lafley, continues to rely on his inquisitive nature and commitment to understanding how consumers live. Early in his career, Lafley spent time in households in various countries to observe and listen and to understand what delights customers. As the consumer products giant moves forward with expansion plans to reach customers in developing regions, Procter & Gamble continues its sharply focused marketing research efforts.[22]

Secondary data, or previously published data, are low cost and easy to obtain. Federal, state, and local government publications are excellent data sources, and most are available online. The most frequently used government statistics include census data, which contain the population's age, gender, education level, household size and composition, occupation, employment status, and income. Even private research firms such as TRU (formerly Teenage Research Unlimited), which studies the purchasing habits of teens, provide some free information on their web sites. This information helps firms evaluate consumers' buying behavior, anticipate possible changes in the marketplace, and identify new markets.

Even though secondary data are a quick and inexpensive resource, marketing researchers sometimes discover that this information isn't specific or current enough for their needs. If so, researchers may conclude that they must collect *primary data*—data collected firsthand through such methods as observation and surveys. Online survey sites, such as Survey Monkey, are quick and effective ways to collect primary data.

Observational studies view the actions of consumers either directly or through other devices. As more retailers watch their customers via video cameras, they can solve problems such as widening a too-narrow aisle to allow shoppers easier access, but such close monitoring has also raised privacy concerns.[23]

As fresh soups have become more available in supermarkets, canned soup consumption is down. Campbell Soup Company undertook a marketing research study that involved eating, cooking, and shopping with Millennials to understand their food and shopping habits. The company thinks this type of research will help it create new food choices for younger consumers.[24]

Simply observing customers cannot provide some types of information. A researcher might observe a customer buying a red sweater, but have no idea why the purchase was made—or for whom. When researchers need information about consumers' attitudes, opinions, and motives, they need to ask the consumers themselves. They may conduct surveys by telephone, in person, online, or in focus groups.

A *focus group* gathers 8 to 12 people in a room or over the Internet to discuss a particular topic. A focus group can generate new ideas, address consumers' needs, and even point out flaws in existing products. Campbell Soup Company held nationwide focus groups in which respondents reviewed ingredients from two soups. Two of three focus group participants overwhelmingly chose the Campbell's brand.[25] Marketing researchers continue to take advantage of social media such as Facebook, Twitter, Pinterest, Tumblr, and blogs, as well as mobile marketing.

Applying Marketing Research Data

As the accuracy of information collected by researchers increases, so does the effectiveness of resulting marketing strategies. One field of research is known as **business intelligence**, which uses various activities and technologies to gather, store, and analyze data to make better competitive decisions. Unilever, maker of consumer products including Dove soap, Axe deodorant, and Ben and Jerry's ice cream, has a highly regarded global research staff and values input from outside sources. The company has adopted a crowdsourced, open-idea platform, where external contributions are sought for diverse projects. Unilever's "challenges and wants" web page solicits ideas for new designs and technologies to help improve the way its products are made. If Unilever decides to pursue a submitted idea, the originator might benefit financially.[26]

business intelligence activities and technologies for gathering, storing, and analyzing data to make better competitive decisions.

Data Mining

Once a company has built a database, marketers must be able to analyze the data and use the information it provides. **Data mining**, part of the broader field of business intelligence, is the task of using computer-based technology to evaluate data in a database and identify useful trends. These trends or patterns may suggest predictive models of real-world business activities. Accurate data mining can help researchers forecast economic trends and pinpoint sales prospects.

data mining the task of using computer-based technology to evaluate data in a database and identify useful trends.

Data mining uses **data warehouses**, which are sophisticated customer databases that allow managers to combine data from several different organizational functions. In an effort to recruit consumers with specific conditions for clinical drug trials, pharmaceutical companies hire firms like Blue Chip Marketing Worldwide. Based in suburban Chicago, Blue Chip Marketing uses data from social networks, data brokers, and pharmacies to identify potential participants. Among the issues arising from data mining are ownership of web user data, the targeting capabilities of web research, government intervention, and privacy.[27]

data warehouse customer database that allows managers to combine data from several different organizational functions.

Google intended its social network Google Buzz to compete with Twitter, with members sharing status updates, photos and videos, and links with "friends" via Gmail. The platform also mined users' Gmail contacts, automatically letting users follow the people with whom they had the most contact. But this meant that lists of followers had to be public. Also, there was no way to block anyone—even someone who did *not* have a Gmail public profile—from following any user. After numerous complaints, Google agreed to sweeping privacy-protection measures. Despite these fixes, Google Buzz never really took off and is no longer operating, largely because it didn't differentiate itself from other more popular social media sites such as Facebook and Twitter. Some observers feel that privacy norms are changing, with confidentiality giving way to increasing openness.[28]

Playnomics' segmentation technology and predictive analysis mine and analyze the behavior of online and app game players by tracking the number of hours they spend on games and creating behavioral profiles. App and game developers pay a monthly fee for the resulting data. The company's CEO says providing information about user activity gives marketers a way to find and engage the right player for greater retention and increased revenues.[29]

Assessment Check ✅

1. What is the difference between primary data and secondary data?
2. What is data mining?

Market Segmentation

Market segmentation is the process of dividing a market into several relatively homogeneous groups. Both profit-seeking and not-for-profit organizations use segmentation to help them reach desirable target markets. Market segmentation is often based on the results of research, which attempts to identify trends among certain groups of people. For instance, one recent survey revealed that social media use among Internet-using Baby Boomers—those Americans between 50 and 64 years old—grew from 52 to 65 percent. Younger adults—those under age 30—are still the heaviest users, with 90 percent visiting a social networking site on any given day. Overall, 73 percent of adult Internet users visit social networking sites, but the rise in use by older consumers is important information for businesses.[30] This kind of information can help marketers decide what types of products to develop and to whom they should be marketed.

Market segmentation attempts to isolate the traits that distinguish a certain group of customers from the overall market. However, segmentation doesn't automatically produce marketing success. Table 11.1 lists several criteria that marketers should consider. The effectiveness of a segmentation strategy depends on how well the market meets these criteria. Once marketers identify a market segment to target, they can create an appropriate marketing strategy.

Companies that can identify trends in consumer preferences before their rivals do can benefit greatly; those that miss the boat generally suffer the consequences. There is an expanding opportunity for mobile apps and Internet-based services to make their way into consumers' cars. Pandora Internet Radio is now being used in 5 million cars and 100 models through its partnerships with auto brands and stereo manufacturers. Apple hopes to integrate Siri technology and maps into car navigation systems, and Ford already uses voice, steering wheel, or touchscreen-activated controls for mobile apps.[31]

How Market Segmentation Works

An immediate segmentation distinction involves whether the firm is offering goods and services to customers for their own use or to purchasers who will use them directly or indirectly in providing other products for resale (the so-called B2B market). Depending on whether their firms offer consumer or business products, marketers segment their target markets differently. Four common bases for segmenting consumer markets are geographical segmentation, demographic segmentation, psychographic segmentation, and product-related segmentation. By contrast, business markets can segment on three criteria: customer-based segmentation, end-use segmentation, and geographical segmentation. Figure 11.4 illustrates the segmentation methods for these two types of markets.

TABLE
⌐11.1¬ Criteria for Market Segmentation

CRITERION	EXAMPLE
A segment must be a measurable group.	Data can be collected on the dollar amount and number of purchases by college students.
A segment must be accessible for communication.	A growing number of seniors are going online, so they can be reached through Internet channels.
A segment must be large enough to offer profit potential.	In a small community, a store carrying only large-size shoes might not be profitable. Similarly, a specialty retail chain may not locate in a small market.

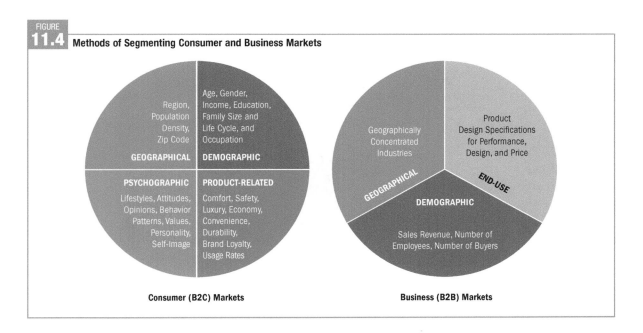

FIGURE 11.4 Methods of Segmenting Consumer and Business Markets

Consumer (B2C) Markets

GEOGRAPHICAL	DEMOGRAPHIC
Region, Population Density, Zip Code	Age, Gender, Income, Education, Family Size and Life Cycle, and Occupation
PSYCHOGRAPHIC	PRODUCT-RELATED
Lifestyles, Attitudes, Opinions, Behavior Patterns, Values, Personality, Self-Image	Comfort, Safety, Luxury, Economy, Convenience, Durability, Brand Loyalty, Usage Rates

Business (B2B) Markets

GEOGRAPHICAL — Geographically Concentrated Industries

END-USE — Product Design Specifications for Performance, Design, and Price

DEMOGRAPHIC — Sales Revenue, Number of Employees, Number of Buyers

Segmenting Consumer Markets

Market segmentation has been around since people first began selling products. Tailors made some clothing items for men and others for women. Tea was imported from India for tea drinkers in England and other European countries. In addition to demographic and geographical segmentation, today's marketers also define customer groups based on psychographic—lifestyle and values—criteria as well as product-related distinctions.

Geographical Segmentation The oldest segmentation method is <u>geographical segmentation</u>—dividing a market into homogeneous groups on the basis of their locations. Geographical location does not guarantee that consumers in a certain region will all buy the same kinds of products, but it does provide some indication of needs. For instance, suburbanites buy more lawn-care products than central-city dwellers. However, many suburbanites choose instead to purchase the services of a lawn maintenance firm. Consumers who live in northern states, where winter is more severe, are more likely to buy ice scrapers, snow shovels, and snow blowers than those who live in warmer climates. They are also more likely to contract with firms who remove the snow from driveways. Marketers also look at the size of the population of an area, as well as who lives there—are residents old or young? Do they reflect an ethnic background? What is the level of their income?

Job growth and migration patterns are important considerations as well. Some businesses combine areas or even entire countries that share similar population and product-use patterns instead of treating each as an independent segment.

Demographic Segmentation By far the most common method of market segmentation, <u>demographic segmentation</u> distinguishes markets on the basis of various demographic or socioeconomic characteristics. Common demographic measures include gender, income, age, occupation, household size, stage in the family life cycle, education, and racial or ethnic group. The U.S. Census Bureau is one of the best sources of demographic information for the domestic market. Figure 11.5 lists some of the measures used in demographic segmentation.

geographical segmentation dividing a market into homogeneous groups on the basis of their locations.

demographic segmentation distinguishes markets on the basis of various demographic or socioeconomic characteristics.

Chapter 11 *Customer-Driven Marketing* **319**

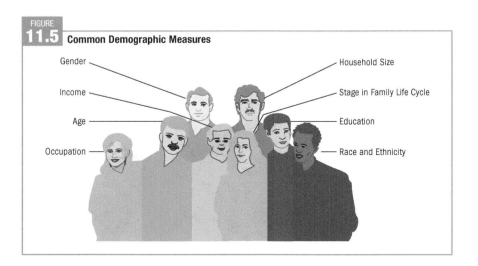

FIGURE 11.5 Common Demographic Measures

Gender

Income

Age

Occupation

Household Size

Stage in Family Life Cycle

Education

Race and Ethnicity

Police departments around the United States constitute a highly specialized occupational demographic group. Popular for its durability, the Ford Crown Victoria has long held 75 percent of the patrol-car market share. Ford has phased out the "Crown Vic," replacing it with the Police Interceptor, modeled on the Taurus sedan but modified for the extreme circumstances of police work. The Interceptor's fuel efficiency is 25 percent better than the Crown Vic's. Its 365-horsepower engine outguns the Crown Vic's by 115 horsepower. Its newest model, the Explorer Police Interceptor, has a 3.5-liter, twin turbocharged engine, which helps the company compete with similar models from GM and Dodge.[32]

Gender used to be a simple way to define markets for certain products—jewelry and skin care products for women; tools and motorcycles for men. Much of that has changed—dramatically. Men now buy jewelry and skin care products, and women buy tools and motorcycles. But marketers have also found that even though these shifts have blurred the lines between products, there are still differences in the *way* that women and men shop. A recent study of online shopping habits revealed that men are more likely to make a purchase from a desktop or laptop computer, while women are more likely to use a mobile device to complete a purchase. Marketers should be sure a website has an easy-to-use mobile interface. Other data suggests that women were slightly more intent on getting the best available price, so easy page-browsing and in-page price comparisons from a mobile device should be a top priority.[33]

Another shift involves purchasing power. Women now control an estimated 80 percent of consumer spending, estimated between $5 and $15 trillion per year.[34] With this knowledge in hand, Amazon purchased online retailer Zappos and launched a program called Amazon Mom, a free membership program for parents of small children.[35]

With our rapidly aging population, age is perhaps the most volatile factor in demographic segmentation in the United States. Of the 325-plus million people estimated to be living in the United States over the next few years, almost 87 million will be age 55 or older.[36] Working from these statistics, marketers for travel and leisure products, as well as retirement and business investments, are working hard to attract the attention of this age group, the aging Baby Boomers—those born between 1946 and 1964. Active-adult housing communities are one result of these efforts. Some developers have built communities with a resort-style atmosphere in desirable locations such as Colorado ski country or the outskirts of a large cities such as Chicago and San Francisco. However, because of the recent recession,

Marketers know that there are still differences in the way men and women shop. A recent study revealed that men are more likely than women to make a purchase from a desktop or laptop computer.

many older Americans will have to work longer, and many others have been forced to take early retirement. A recent report by the Government Accountability Office states, "While the recession has affected all age groups, older adults—particularly those close to or in retirement—may face a greater burden because they may not have the same opportunities to recover from its effects."[37]

Generation Y—those born between 1976 and 1997—encompasses about 113 million young Americans, or a little more than one-third of the population. Often called the Millennials, these consumers are tech-savvy shoppers who influence not only their own purchases but also those of their families and friends. They are educated consumers who comparison shop and usually avoid impulse purchases, partly because of the recession and partly because they are spending their own money. According to a Nielsen survey, compared with older generations, such as the so-called Greatest Generation (those who lived through World War II) and the Baby Boomers, Generation Y consumers shop less often but buy more when they do, preferring megastores and big box-retailers.[38]

The Millennials are a rapidly growing consumer market. They are characterized as tech-savvy shoppers who influence the purchases of their families and friends.

Statistics can be helpful, but they don't tell the whole story. Marketers must learn where people live, how old they are, what language or languages they speak, and how much income they have in order to serve them well. They must learn cultural tastes and preferences, too. Smart marketers also follow technology trends, as Redbox has done to cater to consumers' changing video-viewing habits and buying preferences with new offerings. See the "Hit & Miss" feature for the story.

Above all, companies must avoid stereotyping if they are going to market successfully to a diverse group of consumers. One way to do this is to break a large group into smaller segments. For instance, the Hispanic market is made up of many smaller segments, based on country of origin, language, lifestyle, and cultural values. In an attempt to target a younger Hispanic audience, three television networks have begun to offer bilingual, Spanish, and English-language programming with Hispanic themes. Because many Hispanic American teens and young adults are bilingual, the networks are trying to capture their attention while their parents and grandparents continue to watch Spanish-only programming. The Spanish-language network Telemundo recently launched an app for downloading its wildly popular *telenovelas* (nightly soap operas) onto a user's iPhone or tablet. The app also features interviews, news, and the chance to rate episodes. Another Spanish-language network, Univision, recently launched a radio app that lets users search for local Univision stations by name, location, or genre. The Univision radio app has a bilingual interface in Spanish and English. Users can buy songs they hear on the app via iTunes. The president of Univision says the radio app provides Hispanic audiences with high-quality content across all media platforms.[39]

Entrepreneurs who are members of minority groups may start their own businesses out of frustration at not being able to find food, clothing, entertainment, or other goods and services that fit their tastes and needs. In fact, almost 10 percent of all business owners in the United States are immigrants. Mexicans are the largest group, with 6.5 percent of immigrant-owned businesses. Motivated by the American dream that hard work will bring success and the good life, extended families often work in these businesses, which also support their ethnic communities. This localization makes them particularly vulnerable during hard times, but many immigrant entrepreneurs remain optimistic. In fact, during the recent economic downturn, immigrants started businesses at more than twice the rate of citizens born in America.[40]

Psychographic Segmentation Lifestyle is the sum of a person's needs, preferences, motives, attitudes, social habits, and cultural background. In recent years, marketing researchers

Hit&Miss

Redbox Teams with Verizon to Offer Streaming

Even as competitor Netflix continues to deemphasize DVD rentals in favor of streaming content over the Internet, Redbox's video streaming partnership with Verizon will retain all the firm's 42,000 rental kiosks for customers who still want DVDs rather than downloading videos over the Internet. "We have to stay focused on giving the customers what they want," said the CFO of Redbox parent, Outerwall, which changed its name from Coinstar.

Redbox kiosks currently serve about 30 million DVD and game renters, compared to almost 25 million Netflix users. Its combination of physical and digital video will be competitively priced and customer focused. Called Redbox Instant, streaming is available nationwide, and not just to Verizon customers. It recently debuted on Sony PlayStation 3 consoles.

None of Netflix's streaming competitors—Amazon, Hulu, or Walmart—offers DVD rentals. Redbox and Verizon hope that the nearly 35 million U.S. homes with at least one TV connected to the Internet will become Redbox Instant customers.

Questions for Critical Thinking

1. Outerwall recently acquired Blockbuster assets including 9,000 additional rental kiosks because the company thinks there is still a bright future in renting DVDs to consumers. Do you agree? Why or why not?

2. Redbox counts on Verizon to negotiate successfully with Hollywood for more video content. How will Verizon profit from the partnership?

Sources: Alan Buckingham, "Redbox Instant Debuts on Sony PS3," *Beta News,* accessed February 9, 2014, http://betanews.com; Clark Fredrickson, "A Quarter of U.S. Households Now Have a TV Connected to the Internet," *eMarketer,* accessed February 9, 2014, www.emarketer.com; Amy Chozick, "Verizon Teaming with Redbox for DVD and Streaming Service," *The New York Times,* accessed February 9, 2014, www.nytimes.com; Austin Carr, "New Details on Redbox-Verizon Streaming Service, Netflix Competition," *Fast Company,* accessed February 9, 2014, www.fastcompany.com.

---

psychographic segmentation dividing consumer markets into groups with similar psychological characteristics, values, and lifestyles.

have tried to formulate lifestyle portraits of consumers. This effort has led to another strategy for segmenting target markets, **psychographic segmentation**, which divides consumer markets into groups with similar psychological characteristics, values, and lifestyles.

Psychographic studies have evaluated motivations for purchases of hundreds of goods and services, ranging from soft drinks to health care services. Using the resulting data, firms tailor their marketing strategies to carefully chosen market segments. A frequently used method of developing psychographic profiles involves the use of *AIO statements*—people's verbal descriptions of various attitudes, interests, and opinions. Researchers survey a sample of consumers, asking them whether they agree or disagree with each statement. The answers are then tabulated and analyzed for use in identifying various lifestyle categories.

Another way to get current information from consumers about their lifestyles is to create *blogs* to which consumers can respond. Companies including Stonyfield Farm, Verizon, and Microsoft have hired bloggers to run online web journals as a way to connect with and receive information from consumers. Other firms encourage employees at all levels to use blogs to communicate with consumers. General Motors has a social hub web page that invites users to connect with its social media channels, each tailored to a specific brand or consumer interest. The FastLane blog discusses GM cars and trucks, inviting consumers to offer their thoughts and ideas. Chevrolet Voltage is aimed at fans of the Volt and other electric vehicles. The Lab is where GM's advanced design team talks about its work and invites feedback from community members.[41]

Although demographic classifications such as age, gender, and income are relatively easy to identify and measure, researchers also need to define psychographic categories. Often marketing research firms conduct extensive studies of consumers and then share their psychographic data with clients. In addition, businesses look to studies done by sociologists and psychologists to help them understand their customers. For instance, while children may fall into one age group and their parents in another, they also live certain lifestyles together. Recent marketing research reveals that today's parents are willing and able to spend more on goods and services for their children than parents were a generation or two ago. Spending on toys and video games for children topped $38 billion for a recent year in the United States.[42] These are just a few trends identified by the researchers, but they provide valuable information to firms that may be considering developing toys and games, designing the interiors of family vehicles, or implementing new wireless plans.

Product-Related Segmentation Using product-related segmentation, sellers can divide a consumer market into groups based on buyers' relationships to the good or service. The three most popular approaches to product-related segmentation are based on benefits sought, usage rates, and brand-loyalty levels.

Segmenting by *benefits sought* focuses on the attributes that people seek in a good or service and the benefits they expect to receive from it. As more firms shift toward consumer demand for products that are eco-friendly, marketers find ways to emphasize the benefits of these products. The Swedish home-goods retailer IKEA follows strict guidelines for sourcing its solid-wood furniture products. For example, the worldwide company does not accept any illegally felled wood. IKEA's own forest specialists trace batches of timber to their origins to ensure that the lumber is properly documented and certified by the Forest Stewardship Council (FSC). In addition, these specialists work with suppliers to promote more sustainably managed forests worldwide. IKEA uses its web site and signage in its stores to educate consumers about its wood-source policies.[43]

Consumer markets can also be segmented according to the amounts of a product that people buy and use. Segmentation by *product usage rate* usually defines such categories as heavy users, medium users, and light users. The 80/20 principle states that roughly 80 percent of a product's revenues come from only 20 percent of its buyers. Companies can now pinpoint which of their customers are the heaviest users—and even the most profitable customers—and direct their heaviest marketing efforts to those customers.

The third technique for product-related segmentation divides customers by *brand loyalty*— the degree to which consumers recognize, prefer, and insist on a particular brand. Marketers define groups of consumers with similar degrees of brand loyalty. They then attempt to tie loyal customers to a good or service by giving away premiums, which can be anything from a logo-emblazoned T-shirt to a pair of free tickets to a concert or sports event.

Segmenting Business Markets

In many ways, the segmentation process for business markets resembles that for consumer markets. However, some specific methods differ. Business markets can be divided through geographical segmentation; demographic, or customer-based, segmentation; and end-use segmentation.

Geographical segmentation methods for business markets resemble those for consumer markets. Many B2B marketers target geographically concentrated industries, such as aircraft manufacturing, automobiles, and oil field equipment. Especially on an international scale, customer needs, languages, and other variables may require differences in the marketing mix from one location to another.

Demographic, or *customer-based, segmentation* begins with a good or service design intended to suit a specific organizational market. Sodexo is the largest provider of food services in North America. Its customers include health care institutions, business and government offices, schools, and colleges and universities. Within these broad business segments, Sodexo identifies more specific segments, which might include colleges in the South or universities with culturally diverse populations—and differing food preferences or dining styles. Sodexo uses data obtained from surveys that cover students' lifestyles, attitudes, preferences for consumer products in general, services, and media categories. In addition, it uses targeted surveys that identify preferences for restaurant brands or certain foods, meal habits, amount of spending, and the like. Marketers evaluate the data, which sometime reveal surprising trends. Noting the rise of food trucks across the country, Sodexo recently started a food-truck program at a university. The truck visits the campus several times a month, offering lunch items such as grilled-cheese sandwiches and a Korean-style sandwich wrap with pulled pork.[44]

To simplify the process of focusing on a particular type of business customer, the federal government has developed a system for subdividing the business marketplace into detailed segments. The six-digit *North American Industry Classification System (NAICS)* provides a common classification system used by the member nations of NAFTA (the United States, Canada, and

product-related segmentation dividing consumer markets into groups based on buyers' relationships to the good or service.

end-use segmentation
marketing strategy that focuses on the precise way a B2B purchaser will use a product.

Assessment Check ☑️

1. What is the most common form of segmentation for consumer markets?

2. What are the three approaches to product-related segmentation?

3. What is end-use segmentation in the B2B market?

consumer behavior
actions of ultimate consumers directly involved in obtaining, consuming, and disposing of products and the decision processes that precede and follow these actions.

Mexico). It divides industries into broad categories such as agriculture, forestry, and fishing; manufacturing; transportation; and retail and wholesale trade. Each major category is further subdivided into smaller segments—such as gas stations with convenience food and warehouse clubs—for more detailed information and to facilitate comparison among the member nations.

Another way to group firms by their demographics is to segment them by size based on their sales revenues or numbers of employees. Some firms collect data from visitors to its web site and use the data to segment customers by size. Modern information processing also enables companies to segment business markets based on how much they buy, not just how big they are. **End-use segmentation** focuses on the precise way a B2B purchaser will use a product. Resembling benefits-sought segmentation for consumer markets, this method helps small and mid-size companies target specific end-user markets rather than competing directly with large firms for wider customer groups. A company might also design a marketing mix based on certain criteria for making a purchase.

7 Consumer Behavior

A fundamental marketing task is to find out why people buy one product and not another. The answer requires an understanding of consumer behavior, the actions of ultimate consumers directly involved in obtaining, consuming, and disposing of products and the decision processes that precede and follow these actions.

Determinants of Consumer Behavior

By studying people's purchasing behavior, businesses can identify consumers' attitudes toward and uses of their products. This information also helps marketers reach their targeted customers. Both personal and interpersonal factors influence the way buyers behave. Personal influences on **consumer behavior** include individual needs and motives, perceptions, attitudes, learned experiences, and self-concept. For instance, today people are constantly looking for ways to save time, so firms do everything they can to provide goods and services designed for convenience. However, when it comes to products such as dinner foods, consumers want convenience, but they also want to enjoy the flavor of a home-cooked meal and spend quality time with their families. So companies such as Stouffer's offer frozen lasagna or manicotti in family sizes, and supermarkets have entire sections devoted to freshly prepared take-out meals that range from roast turkey to filet mignon. A recent survey revealed that almost half of U.S. consumers who eat nutritional food and drinks do so because the products are easy to consume on the go.[45]

The interpersonal determinants of consumer behavior include cultural, social, and family influences. In the area of convenience foods, cultural, social, and family influences come into play as much as an individual's need to save time. Understanding that many consumers value the time they spend with their families and want to care for them by providing good nutrition, marketers often emphasize these values in advertisements for fast and easy-to-prepare food products.

Sometimes external events influence consumer behavior. One study suggests that as a result of the recent recession, consumers may have permanently altered their buying and spending behavior. Industry analysts believe the increasing importance and growth of private label brands and consumers' focus on product value will continue. Manufacturers and retailers—and especially small businesses—will need to create new marketing strategies in response to these challenges.[46]

Determinants of Business Buying Behavior

Because a number of people can influence purchases of B2B products, business buyers face a variety of organizational influences in addition to their own preferences. A design engineer

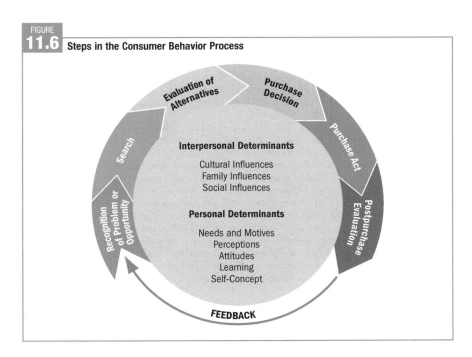

FIGURE 11.6 Steps in the Consumer Behavior Process

Evaluation of Alternatives

Purchase Decision

Search

Purchase Act

Recognition of Problem or Opportunity

Postpurchase Evaluation

Interpersonal Determinants

Cultural Influences
Family Influences
Social Influences

Personal Determinants

Needs and Motives
Perceptions
Attitudes
Learning
Self-Concept

FEEDBACK

may help set the specifications that potential vendors must satisfy. A procurement manager may invite selected companies to bid on a purchase. A production supervisor may evaluate the operational aspects of the proposals that the firm receives, and the vice president of manufacturing may head a committee making the final decision.

Steps in the Consumer Behavior Process

Consumer decision making follows the sequential process outlined in Figure 11.6, with interpersonal and personal influences affecting every step. The process begins when the consumer recognizes a problem or opportunity. If someone needs a new pair of shoes, that need becomes a problem to solve. If you receive a promotion at work and a 20 percent salary increase, that change may also become a purchase opportunity.

To solve the problem or take advantage of the opportunity, the consumer seeks information about his or her intended purchase and evaluates alternatives, such as available brands. The goal is to find the best response to the problem or opportunity.

Eventually, the consumer reaches a decision and completes the transaction. Later, he or she evaluates the experience by making a postpurchase evaluation. Feelings about the experience serve as feedback that will influence future purchase decisions. The various steps in the sequence are affected by both interpersonal and personal factors.

Assessment Check ✓

1. Define *consumer behavior.*
2. What are some determinants of consumer behavior?

[8] **Relationship Marketing**

The past decade has brought rapid change to most industries, as customers have become better-informed and more-demanding purchasers through closely comparing competing goods and services. They expect, even demand, new benefits from the companies that supply them, making it harder for firms to gain a competitive advantage based on product features alone.

Chapter 11 *Customer-Driven Marketing*   **325**

In today's hypercompetitive era, businesses need to find new ways of relating to customers if they hope to maintain long-term success. Businesses are developing strategies and tactics that draw them into tighter connections with their customers, suppliers, and even employees. As a result, many firms are turning their attention to the issues of relationship marketing. **Relationship marketing** goes beyond an effort toward making the sale. Instead, it develops and maintains long-term, cost-effective exchange relationships with partners. These partners include individual customers, suppliers, and employees. As its ultimate goal, relationship marketing seeks to achieve customer satisfaction.

Managing relationships instead of simply completing transactions often leads to creative partnerships. However, customers enter into relationships with firms only if they are assured that the relationship will somehow benefit them. As the intensity of commitment increases, so does the likelihood of a business continuing a long-term relationship with its customers. Businesses are building relationships by partnering with customers, suppliers, and other businesses. Timberland, maker of footwear and clothing, creates many partnerships that foster long-term relationships. The firm partners with not-for-profit organizations such as City Year and the Planet Water Foundation to complete service projects for communities and the environment. Through its Serv-a-Palooza, hundreds of Timberland employees engage in volunteer tasks in their communities. Those opportunities even extend to customers who have expressed an interest in participating in programs in their own regions. If you want to volunteer for a food drive or to help restore a marsh, just log on to the Timberland web site to see what's available. All of these activities help build relationships with customers, communities, and other organizations.[47]

Benefits of Relationship Marketing

Relationship marketing helps all parties involved. In addition to providing mutual protection against competitors, businesses that forge solid links with vendors and customers are often rewarded with lower costs and higher profits than they would generate on their own. Long-term agreements with a few high-quality suppliers frequently reduce a firm's production costs. Unlike one-time sales, ongoing relationships encourage suppliers to offer customers preferential treatment, quickly adjusting shipments to accommodate changes in orders and correcting any quality problems that might arise.

Good relationships with customers can be vital strategies for a firm. By identifying current purchasers and maintaining positive relationships with them, organizations can efficiently target their best customers. Studying current customers' buying habits and preferences can help marketers identify potential new customers and establish ongoing contact with them. Attracting a new customer can cost five times as much as keeping an existing one. Not only do marketing costs go down, but long-term customers usually buy more, require less service, refer other customers, and provide valuable feedback. Together, these elements contribute to a higher **lifetime value of a customer**—the revenues and intangible benefits (referrals and customer feedback) from the customer over the life of the relationship, minus the amount the company must spend to acquire and serve that customer. Keeping that customer may occasionally require some extra effort, especially if the customer has become upset or dissatisfied with a good or service. But good marketers can overcome this particular challenge, as described in the "Career Kickstart" feature.

Businesses also benefit from strong relationships with other companies. Purchasers who repeatedly buy from one business may find that they save time and gain service quality as the business learns their specific needs. Some relationship-oriented companies also customize items based on customer preferences. Because many businesses reward loyal customers with discounts or bonuses, some buyers may even find that they save money by developing long-term relationships. Alliances with other firms to serve the same customers also can be rewarding. The partners combine their capabilities and resources to accomplish goals that they could not reach on their own. In addition, alliances with other firms may help businesses develop the skills and experience they need to successfully enter new markets or improve service to current customers.

Tools for Nurturing Customer Relationships

Although relationship marketing has important benefits for both customers and businesses, most relationship-oriented businesses quickly discover that some customers generate more profitable business than others. If 20 percent of a firm's customers account for 80 percent of its sales and profits—the 80/20 principle mentioned earlier in the chapter—a customer in that category undoubtedly has a higher lifetime value than a customer who buys only once or twice or who makes small purchases.

While businesses shouldn't ignore any customer, they need to allocate their marketing resources wisely. A firm may choose to customize goods or services for high-value customers while working to increase repeat sales of stock products to less-valuable customers. Differentiating between these two groups also helps marketers focus on each in an effort to increase their commitment.

Frequency Marketing and Affinity Marketing Programs Popular techniques through which firms try to build and protect customer relationships include frequent-buyer or -user programs. These so-called **frequency marketing** programs reward purchasers with cash, rebates, merchandise, or other premiums. Frequency programs have grown more sophisticated over the years. They offer more personalization and customization than in the past. Airlines, hotel groups, restaurants, and many retailers including supermarkets offer frequency programs. For example, vacationers who book a certain number of nights at the Atlantis resort in the Bahamas may earn airfare credit for their trip.[48]

Affinity programs are another tool for building emotional links with customers. An affinity program is a marketing effort sponsored by an organization that solicits involvement by individuals who share common interests and activities. Affinity programs are common in the credit-card industry. For instance, a person can sign up for a credit card emblazoned with the logo of a favorite charity, a sports or entertainment celebrity, or an image of his or her college. Bank of America offers credit cards featuring the logos of all the 30 Major League Baseball clubs.

Many businesses also use comarketing and cobranding. In a **comarketing** deal, two businesses jointly market each other's products. When two or more businesses link their names to a single product, **cobranding** occurs. When two seemingly unlikely businesses team up, the marketing sparks fly—and two very different groups of consumers may come together to buy the same product. Hershey has teamed up with Betty Crocker to introduce a new line of co-branded desserts, including cookies, cupcakes, and frostings, based on Reese's Peanut Butter Cups, Almond Joy, and Hershey's Milk Chocolate Bars.[49]

Calming the Angry Customer

An angry customer is a challenge representing not only an immediate problem but also a potential loss of future business. You, the businessperson, should view this customer not as a disruption but as an opportunity to see your company from the outside. With common sense, good personal skills, and knowledge of your company and its products, you can very likely turn the customer's dissatisfaction into satisfaction.

- *Remain calm and professional.* The customer isn't angry with you personally. Let the customer speak first, and listen carefully. Make written notes. Acknowledge the customer's anger, then assure him or her that you will correct the situation.

- *Repeat the customer's stated problem.* Using your own words assures the customer that you have been listening. For example, you might say, "The shoes you received were the right color but the wrong size." Make sure you understand the problem before offering a solution.

- *Focus on the solution.* Having procedures in place can help you resolve a problem quickly. If you can't solve the problem yourself, immediately refer it to someone who can.

- *Thank the customer for his or her patience.* By bringing the problem to your attention, the customer is actually giving you an opportunity to improve service to all your clients.

- *Follow up.* If appropriate, send an e-mail, make a phone call, or communicate via social media to make sure the correct pair of shoes arrived. Your professionalism will strengthen the customer's relationship with your firm—and positive word of mouth may even bring you new customers.

Sources: Lynne McClure, "Handling Angry Customers," *Impact Publications,* accessed February 25, 2014, www.impactpublications.com; Katy Tynan, "Conflict Management Part 2—Calming an Irate Customer," *Ezinearticles.com,* accessed February 25, 2014, http://ezinearticles.com; "How to Calm an Angry Customer," *Business Knowledge Source,* accessed February 25, 2014, www.businessknowledgesource.com.

affinity programs marketing effort sponsored by an organization that solicits involvement by individuals who share common interests and activities.

comarketing cooperative arrangement in which two businesses jointly market each other's products.

cobranding cooperative arrangement in which two or more businesses team up to closely link their names on a single product.

Affinity programs are another tool for building emotional links with customers and are common in the credit-card industry. For instance, Bank of America offers credit cards featuring Major League Baseball logos, like the one pictured here, as well as the logos of all 30 MLB clubs.

Assessment Check ✓

1. What is the lifetime value of a customer?

2. Discuss the increasing importance of one-on-one marketing efforts.

One-on-One Marketing The ability to customize products and rapidly deliver goods and services has become increasingly dependent on technology such as computer-aided design and manufacturing (CAD/CAM). The Internet offers a way for businesses to connect with customers in a direct and intimate manner. Companies can take orders for customized products, gather data about buyers, and predict what items a customer might want in the future. Computer databases provide strong support for effective relationship marketing. Marketers can maintain databases on customer tastes, price-range preferences, and lifestyles, and they can quickly obtain names and other information about promising prospects. Amazon.com greets each online customer with a list of suggested products he or she might like to purchase. Many online retailers send their customers e-mails about upcoming sales, new products, and special events.

Small and large companies often rely on *customer relationship management (CRM)* software technology that helps them gather, sort, and interpret data about customers. Software firms develop this software in order to help businesses build and manage their relationships with customers. QueueBuster is one such product. The software offers callers the choice of receiving an automated return call at a convenient time instead of waiting on hold for the next available representative. After implementing the software to support its central reservations team, the Apex Hotel chain minimized the number of dropped customer calls and increased the level of service to its guests. This simple solution to customers' frustration not only helped build customer loyalty and improve employee morale but also helped save Apex Hotels from losing business as well.[50]

What's Ahead

The next two chapters examine each of the four elements of the marketing mix that marketers use to satisfy their selected target markets. Chapter 12 focuses on products and their distribution through various channels to different outlets. Chapter 13 covers promotion and the various methods marketers use to communicate with their target customers, along with strategies for setting prices for different products.

Chapter in Review

Summary of Learning Objectives

⌐1⌐ Define *marketing*.
Marketing is the activity, set of institutions, and processes for creating, communicating, delivering, and exchanging offerings that have value for customers, clients, partners, and society at large. Marketing creates time, place, and ownership utility by making the product available when and where consumers want to buy and by arranging for orderly transfers of ownership.

Assessment Check Answers ✓
1.1 What is utility? Utility is the ability of a good or service to satisfy the wants and needs of customers.

1.2 Identify three ways in which marketing creates utility.
Marketing creates time utility by making a good or service available when customers want to purchase it, place utility by making the product available in a convenient location, and ownership utility by transferring the product from the seller to the buyer.

⌐2⌐ Discuss the evolution of the marketing concept.
The marketing concept refers to a companywide customer orientation with the objective of achieving long-run success. This concept is essential in today's marketplace, which is

328   **Part 4** *Marketing Management*

primarily a buyer's market, meaning buyers can choose from an abundance of goods and services. Marketing now centers on the satisfaction of customers and building long-term relationships with those customers.

Assessment Check Answers ☑

2.1 What is the marketing concept? The marketing concept is a companywide customer orientation with the objective of achieving long-run success. According to the marketing concept, marketplace success begins with the customer.

2.2 How is the marketing concept tied to the relationship and social eras of marketing? Most marketing now centers on the satisfaction of customers and building long-term relationships with them through several channels including the Internet and social media, rather than simply producing and selling goods and services.

⌐3⌐ Describe not-for-profit marketing and nontraditional marketing.

Not-for-profit organizations must engage in marketing just as for-profit firms do. Not-for-profit organizations operate in both the public and private sectors and use marketing to obtain volunteers and donations, make people aware of their existence, achieve certain goals for society, and so on. Not-for-profit organizations may engage in several types of nontraditional marketing—person, place, event, cause, or organization marketing. They may rely on one type or a combination.

Assessment Check Answers ☑

3.1 Why do not-for-profit organizations engage in marketing? Not-for-profit organizations use marketing to reach audiences, secure funding, and accomplish their overall missions.

3.2 What are the five types of nontraditional marketing used by not-for-profit organizations? The five types of nontraditional marketing are person, place, event, cause, and organization marketing.

⌐4⌐ Outline the basic steps in developing a marketing strategy.

All organizations develop marketing strategies to reach customers. This process involves analyzing the overall market, selecting a target market, and developing a marketing mix that blends elements related to product, distribution, promotion, and pricing decisions.

Assessment Check Answers ☑

4.1 Distinguish between consumer products and business products. Consumer products are goods and services purchased by end users. Business products are goods and services purchased to be used, either directly or indirectly, in the production of other goods for resale.

4.2 What are the steps in developing a marketing strategy? The two steps are (1) studying and analyzing potential target markets and choosing among them; and (2) creating a marketing mix to satisfy the chosen market.

⌐5⌐ Describe marketing research.

Marketing research is the information-gathering function that links marketers to the marketplace. It provides valuable information about potential target markets. Firms may generate internal data or gather external data. They may use secondary data or conduct research to obtain primary data. Data mining, which involves computer searches through customer data to detect patterns or relationships, is one helpful tool in forecasting various trends such as sales revenues and consumer behavior.

Assessment Check Answers ☑

5.1 What is the difference between primary data and secondary data? Primary data are collected firsthand through observation or surveys. Secondary data are previously published facts that are inexpensive to retrieve and easy to obtain.

5.2 What is data mining? Data mining is the task of using computer technology to evaluate data in a database and identify useful trends.

⌐6⌐ Discuss market segmentation.

Consumer markets can be divided according to four criteria: geographical factors; demographic characteristics, such as age and family size; psychographic variables, which involve behavioral and lifestyle profiles; and product-related variables, such as the benefits consumers seek when buying a product or the degree of brand loyalty they feel toward it. Business markets are segmented according to three criteria: geographical characteristics, customer-based specifications for products, and end-user applications.

Assessment Check Answers ☑

6.1 What is the most common form of segmentation for consumer markets? Demographics is the most commonly used consumer market segmentation method.

6.2 What are the three approaches to product-related segmentation? The three approaches to product-related segmentation are by benefits sought, product usage rate, and brand loyalty levels.

6.3 What is end-use segmentation in the B2B market? End-use segmentation focuses on the precise way a B2B purchaser will use a product.

⌐7⌐ Summarize consumer behavior.

Consumer behavior refers to the actions of ultimate consumers with direct effects on obtaining, consuming, and disposing of products, as well as the decision processes that precede and follow these actions. Personal influences on consumer behavior include an individual's needs and motives, perceptions, attitudes, learned experiences, and self-concept. The interpersonal determinants include cultural influences, social influences, and family influences. A number of people within a firm may participate in business purchase decisions, so business buyers must consider a variety of organizational influences in addition to their own preferences.

Chapter 11 *Customer-Driven Marketing*   **329**

7.1 Define *consumer behavior*. Consumer behavior refers to the actions of ultimate consumers directly involved in obtaining, consuming, and disposing of products, along with the decision processes that precede and follow these actions.

7.2 What are some determinants of consumer behavior? Both personal and interpersonal factors influence the way buyers behave. Personal influences include an individual's needs and motives; perceptions, attitudes, and learned experiences; and self-concept. Interpersonal influences include cultural, social, and family influences.

⌐8¬ Discuss relationship marketing.

Relationship marketing is an organization's attempt to develop long-term, cost-effective links with individual customers for mutual benefit. Good relationships with customers can be a vital strategic weapon for a firm. By identifying current purchasers and maintaining a positive relationship with them, an organization can efficiently target its best customers, fulfill their needs, and create loyalty. Information technologies, frequency and affinity programs, and one-on-one efforts all help build relationships with customers.

Assessment Check Answers ✅

8.1 What is the lifetime value of a customer? The lifetime value of a customer incorporates the revenues and intangible benefits from the customer over the life of the relationship with a firm, minus the amount the company must spend to acquire and serve the customer.

8.2 Discuss the increasing importance of one-on-one marketing efforts. One-on-one marketing is increasing in importance as consumers demand more customization in goods and services. It is also increasingly dependent on technology such as computer-aided design and manufacturing (CAD/CAM). The Internet also offers a way for businesses to connect with customers in a direct and personal manner.

▨ Business Terms You Need to Know

marketing 306	target market 313	product-related
exchange process 306	marketing mix 313	segmentation 323
utility 306	marketing research 315	end-use segmentation 324
marketing concept 307	big data 315	consumer behavior 324
person marketing 309	business intelligence 317	relationship marketing 326
place marketing 310	data mining 317	lifetime value of a customer 326
event marketing 310	data warehouse 317	frequency marketing 326
cause marketing 311	market segmentation 318	affinity program 327
organization marketing 311	geographical segmentation 319	comarketing 327
consumer (B2C) product 313	demographic segmentation 319	cobranding 327
business (B2B) product 313	psychographic segmentation 322	

▨ Review Questions

1. Define the four different types of utility and explain how marketing contributes to the creation of utility. Then choose one of the following companies and describe how it creates each type of utility with its goods or services:

   a. Taco Bell

   b. Polo Ralph Lauren

   c. Seattle Seahawks

   d. Supercuts hair salons

   e. Adobe Systems

2. Describe the shift from a seller's market to a buyer's market. Why was this move important to marketers?

3. Describe how an organization might combine person marketing and event marketing. Give an example.

4. Describe how an organization might combine cause marketing and organization marketing. Give an example.

5. Identify each of the following as a consumer product or a business product, or classify it as both:

   a. cup of coffee

   b. iPad

   c. gasoline

   d. boat trailer

   e. hand sanitizer

   f. Post-its

6. Identify and describe the four strategies that blend to create a marketing mix.

7. What is a target market? Why is target-market selection usually the first step in the development of a marketing strategy?

8. Identify the two strategies that a firm could use to develop a marketing mix for international markets. What are the advantages and disadvantages of each?

9. Describe the types of data that someone who is thinking of starting an accounting practice might choose to gather. How might this businessperson use the data in making the start-up decision?

10. Explain each of the methods used to segment consumer and business markets. Which methods do you think would be most effective for each of the following? Why? (Note that a combination of methods might be applicable.)

   a. supermarket featuring organic foods

   b. hair-care products

Projects and Teamwork Applications

1. On your own or with a classmate, choose one of the following products and create an advertisement that illustrates how your firm creates time, place, and form utility in its delivery of the product to the customer.

   a. auto-repair service

   b. outdoor adventure tours

   c. craft supply store

   d. dog-walking service

2. Celebrities like Angelina Jolie, Bono, and Selena Gomez are particularly visible campaigning for not-for-profit organizations—their own as well as others. Choose two other celebrities and discuss the cause each has chosen to support. What is the impact of their support for the visibility of the cause?

3. As a marketer, if you can find ways to classify your firm's goods and services as both business and consumer products, most likely your company's sales will increase as you build relationships with a new category of customers. On your own or with a classmate, choose one of the following products and

Web Assignments

1. **Marketing research.** You have probably taken a marketing survey at one time or another. Go to SurveyMonkey.com, an online survey tool, to learn more about how it works. What are some of the different ways surveys are used? How would you reach the right consumers and collect relevant results? What types of questions would you ask if you were opening a coffee shop near your campus?

2. **Market segmentation.** VALS™ (Values, Attitudes, and Lifestyles) is a proprietary psychographic research software used to segment U.S. adults into eight distinct types using a specific set of psychological traits and key demographics that drive consumer behavior.[51] Go to the website below to take the survey. In pairs or groups, summarize and compare the results of your primary and secondary VALS type. Do you agree or disagree with the results?

   http://www.strategicbusinessinsights.com/vals/presurvey.shtml

   c. tour bus company

   d. line of baby food

   e. pet insurance

   f. dry cleaner

11. What are the three major determinants of consumer behavior? Give an example of how each one might influence a person's purchasing decision.

12. What are the benefits of relationship marketing? Describe how frequency and affinity programs work toward building relationships.

outline a marketing strategy for attracting the classification of customer that is *opposite* the one listed in parentheses.

   a. hybrid car (consumer)

   b. LCD TV (consumer)

   c. limousine service (business)

   d. office furniture (business)

4. Think of two situations in which you have been a customer: one in which you were satisfied with the merchandise you received and one in which you were not. Make a list of the reasons you were satisfied in the first case and a list of the reasons you were not satisfied in the second case. Would you say that the failure was the result of the seller's not understanding your needs?

5. Comarketing and cobranding are techniques that firms often use to market their own and each other's products, such as Amazon's Kindle with an Intel processor. On your own or with a classmate, choose two companies with products you think would work well together for comarketing separate products or cobranding a single product. Then create an advertisement for your comarketing or cobranding effort.

3. **Customer loyalty programs.** Airlines and hotel chains have extensive customer loyalty programs. Pick an airline and hotel chain and print out information on the firm's customer loyalty program. (Two examples can be found at the web sites listed below.) Bring the material to class to participate in a discussion on this topic.

   http://www.southwest.com/rapid_rewards/

   http://www.marriott.com/rewards/rewards-program.mi

Note: Internet web addresses change frequently. If you don't find the exact sites listed, you may need to access the organization's home page and search from there or use a search engine such as Google or Bing.

Louis Vuitton: From Luxury to Ultra Luxury

Louis Vuitton is a luxury goods maker whose goal is to sell massive amounts of its products, which include luggage, shoes, purses, wallets, watches, jewelry, and sunglasses. But an aura of exclusivity can quickly diminish with commercial success—with too many consumers walking around with LV's famous monogram.

Named the world's most valuable luxury brand, Louis Vuitton began in 1854 in Paris, France, selling its luggage trunks to the wealthy. Now owned by LVMH Moet Hennessy, LV is trying to decide whether it can shift its market from the affluent to the *really* affluent consumer. While recent revenues are up, profits are down, and the company, long known for its craftsmanship, exceptional quality, and creativity, is in the process of creating an ultra-luxury line to attract an even higher-end customer.

LV is promoting its more expensive leather bags rather than its entry-level canvas bags. To produce the ultra-luxury line, the company has brought back a designer who previously worked at the company. In addition, it just spent $2.6 billion to purchase 80 percent of Loro Piana, an Italian textile producer specializing in ultra-rare materials, like wool from llamas found only in the Peruvian mountains.

While there's been tremendous growth from the millions of customers who have purchased a canvas logo bag as a symbol of LV's coveted luxury, the profit margins are far lower than its ultra-high-end goods. The company is hoping that a price hike and increased profits through its new ultra-luxury line can help restore the company's worldwide exclusivity in the face of a brand that's become overexposed.

Questions for Critical Thinking

1. Will increasing prices for its luxury items help LV attract an even more upscale market segment? Will higher prices attract a different type of customer?
2. The challenge for sellers of luxury goods is to reach out to new markets, which includes younger customers. Based upon what you've read in the chapter, what should be LV's segmentation strategy when it comes to the various consumer markets it serves?

Sources: Company website, www.lvmh.com, accessed February 14, 2014; Kyle Stock, "Louis Vuitton Shops for Even Richer Customers," *Bloomberg Businessweek*, accessed February 14, 2014, www.businessweek.com; "Has Louis Vuitton Discovered the 'New Normal' in the Consumer Market," *PR Web*, accessed February 14, 2014, www.prweb.com; Christina Passariello, "Louis Vuitton Sports a Richer Price Tag," *The Wall Street Journal*, accessed February 14, 2014, http://online.wsj.com.

Arthritis Foundation Takes Aim at Pain

If you believe medication is the best way to alleviate arthritis pain, the Arthritis Foundation and the Ad Council have a message for you: Exercise.

Ads in a print, television, and online campaign created pro bono by New York's Young & Rubicam Agency feature former tennis star Billie Jean King, who promotes pain relievers such as swimming, walking, running, biking, and of course tennis. After the campaign's light-hearted introduction, "We want it to be more urgent and hard hitting, to aim at Baby Boomers 55 and older, to have them take action today to prevent the progression of arthritis," says a vice president for the Arthritis Foundation.

Arthritis affects one in five adults and is the leading cause of disability in the United States. "We're really proud of our work with the Arthritis Foundation," says Y&R's president. "Helping raise awareness for such a prevalent disease and empowering those with arthritis to take action is incredibly important." King was chosen for the campaign because she suffers from osteoarthritis, and because tennis is a sport for all ages.

Questions for Critical Thinking

1. King says of her spokesperson role, "I'm a little chubby, I think people are going to relate." Do you agree? Why or why not?
2. One critic called the campaign "too rational. Most effective ads are emotional." Do you agree? Why or why not?

Sources: Organization website, "Fight Arthritis Pain: Managing OA," www.arthritis.org, accessed February 25, 2014; U.S. Open corporate website, "Billie Jean King in New Arthritis Campaign," www.usopen.org, accessed February 8, 2014; organization website, "Billie Jean King, Arthritis Foundation, Ad Council and USTA Launch Arthritis Campaign," press release, www.arthritis.org, accessed February 8, 2014, Jane L. Levere, "On the Move, Athletically, Against Arthritis," *The New York Times*, accessed February 8, 2014, www.nytimes.com.

The owners of Boston-based food truck Mei Mei Street Kitchen and Mei Mei restaurant, collectively known as the Mei Mei Group, imaginatively provide context to the definition of marketing by creating, communicating, and delivering value to their guests while managing customer relationships. The very nature of its mobile food truck creates visibility for the unique Mei Mei brand, which is making a difference on the local food scene by serving creative Chinese American cuisine.

The sibling threesome, older brother Andy, and his younger sisters, Irene and Margaret (Mei), came up with the idea of a food truck to share their passion for new and exciting cuisine based on what they ate as children. Almost as important as the food itself, the siblings have incorporated practices integral to their marketing strategy and target market, which fit their vision of how to conduct business with a sustainable future. Mei Mei is Mandarin for "little sister," and Mei Mei Group's owners use their combined experience in fine dining, farming, and entrepreneurship to develop marketing strategies, including relationship marketing, marketing research, place marketing, and target marketing.

To differentiate their food from competitors, the siblings strive to be the "best out there," by sourcing local ingredients and working closely with farmers in the Northeast. Also important for a food truck is place marketing, which attempts to attract people to a particular area or location. Mei Mei utilizes its website, social media, Twitter, and a StreetFood app to engage customers and make them aware of the truck's location.

Mei Mei Group's 40 employees, many of whom are professed foodies, represent its brand with passion, knowledge, and pride. Similar to creating new menu items, the company develops fun and engaging promotions to keep customers coming back to its food truck and restaurant.

The success of Mei Mei Group's food truck and restaurant evolved by effectively utilizing a series of marketing research tools. To gain a deeper understanding of how guests perceive and enjoy Mei Mei's food, the owners believe that in-the-moment feedback is crucial. Improvements and changes have been made based upon online and offline feedback from customers. Before the Street Kitchen began, the Li siblings asked themselves about the types of meals they'd be interested in eating. Their research also included a competitive analysis of the types of cuisine available in the Boston-area food truck scene. And they researched food trucks throughout the country to see what was going on and to learn more about the constantly evolving mobile food truck industry.

Mei Mei's food truck and restaurant serve different market segments. On weekdays, the food truck caters to those who want a quick, healthy, and affordable meal at lunchtime. Depending on the truck's location, customers range from students to professionals. The restaurant, which is located next to Boston University, serves college students who may want to grab a quick bite in between classes. In the evening, the restaurant attracts more than just college students because of its creative and contemporary dinner menu. Mei Mei's business practices of using locally sourced produce and sustainably raised meats from small family farms resonate with its animal-loving, health conscious, eco-friendly customers.

Maintaining ongoing relationships with customers through social media and in person allows the Li siblings to develop even deeper connections. Listening to and responding to guests creates a better dining experience and consequently improves business for Mei Mei. It's no surprise that Mei Mei Street Kitchen has been awarded Boston's Best Meal on Wheels and Boston's Best Food Truck.

Questions for Critical Thinking

1. Discuss Mei Mei's target market based on the fact that they source, cook, and serve food that respects animals in the environment. What other unique features of Mei Mei's food truck or restaurant can be used to further segment the company's target market? Discuss.

2. Discuss and list ways Mei Mei Street Kitchen creates time, place, and ownership utility. How does this differ between its food truck and its brick-and-mortar restaurant?

3. Apply the basic steps to develop a marketing strategy to Mei Mei Street Kitchen and Mei Mei Restaurant.

4. What additional marketing research or information gathering might you conduct to increase business for Mei Mei Street Kitchen? How would this differ from data gathered for its restaurant? Discuss how you would utilize both primary and secondary research for each.

Sources: Company website, http://meimeiboston.com, accessed June 3, 2014; Mei Mei Street Kitchen Facebook page, https://www.facebook.com/meimeiboston, accessed June 3, 2014; "Meet Young Guns Semi-Finalists Irene Li and Max Hull of Boston's Mei Mei," Eater.com, accessed June 3, 2014, www.eater.com; Rachel Leah Blumenthal, "Mei Mei Could Get a Beer & Wine License After All," *Boston Eater*, accessed June 9, 2014, http://boston.eater.com; Christopher Hughes, "Five Reasons You Should Be Eating at Mei Mei Street Kitchen," *Boston Magazine*, accessed June 9, 2014, www.bostonmagazine.com; Morgan Rousseau, "Cray Cray for Mei Mei: Boston Food Truck to Open Green Eatery," *Metro US Magazine*, accessed June 9, 2014, www.metro.us; Rachel Travers, "Rolling with the Mei Mei Street Kitchen," *Boston.com*, accessed June 9, 2014, www.boston.com.

Learning Objectives

1. Explain product strategy and how to classify goods and services.
2. Briefly describe the four stages of the product life cycle.
3. Discuss product identification.
4. Outline the major components of an effective distribution strategy.
5. Explain the concept of wholesaling.
6. Describe how to develop a competitive retail strategy.
7. Identify distribution channel decisions and logistics.

Chapter 12

Product and Distribution Strategies

© Patrick Heagney/iStockphoto

Mattel Takes Control of Its Brands

As technology pushes more consumers to mobile and Internet entertainment platforms, Mattel has taken a larger role in managing its toy brands featured in movies, TV, and other media. The California-based company created Playground Productions, an in-house studio that will produce original films, TV shows, web series, live events, and games. According to management, the goal of Playground is to create and develop entertainment on multiple platforms that will influence consumers to shop the toy aisle and provide additional revenue streams for Mattel.

Prior to creating Playground, Mattel focused more on its core toy-making and distribution business, letting others take the lead on managing the media outlets using its brands. While Mattel was concentrating on toys, competitor Hasbro parlayed its franchise Transformers into $2.6 billion in robot-to-car shifting toys and movie tickets. Disney, no stranger to toy and movie combinations, launched its successful Cars toy and movie products. And Marvel has teamed up with Paramount to produce Sponge Bob Square Pants and Avengers movie–toy combinations.

Mattel has several projects already in production through its Playground division, including "Team Hot Wheels: The Origin of Awesome," an animated feature followed by a live-action Hot Wheels direct-to-video movie. Character Max Steel is set to get a feature movie as well as a new line of action figures. He-Man is also up for a new movie. And a new feature is in the works for a Mattel doll line based on Monster High, Mattel's successful gothic-themed brand geared to teenagers, which accounts for more than $1 billion annually in revenues. Taking control of its brands will help Mattel not only manage its business but also extend its storytelling expertise across multiple entertainment platforms.[1]

Overview

In this chapter we examine ways in which organizations design and implement marketing strategies that address customers' needs and wants. Two of the most powerful such tools are strategies that relate to products, which include both goods and services, and those that relate to the distribution of those products.

As the story of Mattel illustrates, successful organizations stay ahead of changes in their business environment and anticipate their customers' needs. Expanding its business beyond toys by integrating product and distribution strategies has allowed Mattel to remain competitive.

This chapter focuses on the first two elements of the marketing mix: product and distribution. Our discussion of product strategy begins by describing the classifications of goods and services, customer service, product lines and the product mix, and the product life cycle. Companies often shape their marketing strategies differently when they are introducing a new product, when the product has established itself in the marketplace, and when it is declining in popularity. We also discuss product identification through brand name and distinctive packaging, and the ways in which companies foster loyalty to their brands to keep customers coming back for more.

Distribution, the second marketing mix variable discussed, focuses on moving goods and services from producer to wholesaler to retailer to buyers. Managing the distribution process includes making decisions such as what kind of wholesaler to use and where to offer products for sale. Retailers can range from specialty stores to factory outlets and everything in between, and they must choose appropriate customer service, pricing, and location strategies in order to succeed. The chapter concludes with a look at logistics, the process of coordinating the flow of information, goods, and services among suppliers and on to consumers.

Product Strategy

product bundle of physical, service, and symbolic characteristics designed to satisfy consumer wants.

Most people respond to the question "What is a product?" by listing its physical features. By contrast, marketers take a broader view. To them, a **product** is a bundle of physical, service, and symbolic characteristics designed to satisfy consumer wants. The chief executive officer of a major tool manufacturer once startled his stockholders with this statement: "Last year our customers bought over 1 million quarter-inch drill bits, and none of them wanted to buy the product. They all wanted quarter-inch holes." Product strategy involves considerably more than just producing a good or service; instead, it focuses on benefits. The marketing conception of a product includes decisions about package design, brand name, trademarks, warranties, product image, new-product development, and customer service. Think, for instance, about your favorite beverage. Do you like it for its taste alone? Or do other attributes, such as clever ads, attractive packaging, ease of purchase from vending machines and other convenient locations, and overall image, also attract you? These other attributes may influence your choice more than you realize.

Classifying Goods and Services

Marketers have found it useful to classify goods and services as either B2C or B2B, depending on whether the purchasers of the particular item are consumers or businesses. These classifications can be subdivided further, and each type requires a different competitive strategy.

Classifying Consumer Goods and Services
The classification typically used for ultimate consumers who purchase products for their own use and enjoyment and not for resale is based on consumer buying habits. *Convenience products* are items the consumer seeks to purchase frequently, immediately, and with little effort. Items stocked in gas-station markets, vending machines, and local newsstands are usually convenience products—for example, newspapers, snacks, candy, coffee, and bread.

Shopping products are those typically purchased only after the buyer has compared competing products in competing stores. A person intent on buying a new sofa or dining room table may visit many stores, examine perhaps dozens of pieces of furniture, and spend days making the final decision. *Specialty products*, the third category of consumer products, are those that a purchaser is willing to make a special effort to obtain. The purchaser is already familiar with the item and considers it to have no reasonable substitute. The nearest Lexus dealer may be 75 miles away, but if you have decided you want one, you will make the trip.

Note that a shopping product for one person may be a convenience item for someone else. Each item's product classification is based on buying patterns of the majority of people who purchase it.

The interrelationship of the marketing mix factors is shown in Figure 12.1. By knowing the appropriate classification for a specific product, the marketing decision maker knows quite a bit about how the other mix variables will adapt to create a profitable, customer-driven marketing strategy.

Classifying Business Goods
Business products are goods and services such as payroll services and huge multifunction copying machines used in operating an organization; they also include machinery, tools, raw materials, components, and buildings used to produce other items for resale. While consumer products are classified

Buying a *specialty product* takes extra effort. The Fiat 500 is sold in a limited number of places.

Kristoffer Tripplaar/Sipa/NewsCom

FIGURE 12.1 Marketing Impacts of Consumer Product Classification

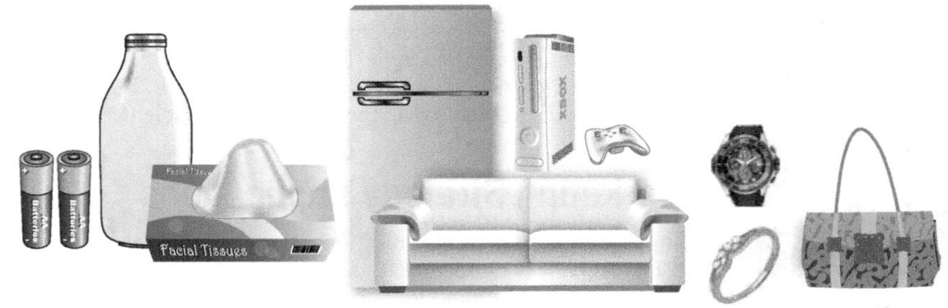

Marketing Strategy Factor	Convenience Product	Shopping Product	Specialty Product
· Purchase Frequency	· Frequent	· Relatively infrequent	· Infrequent
· Store Image	· Unimportant	· Very important	· Important
· Price	· Low	· Relatively high	· High
· Promotion	· By manufacturer	· By manufacturer and retailers	· By manufacturer and retailers
· Distribution Channel	· Many wholesalers and retailers	· Relatively few wholesalers and retailers	· Very few wholesalers and retailers
· Number of Retail Outlets	· Many	· Few	· Very small number; often one per market area

by buying habits, business products are classified based on how they are used and by their basic characteristics. Products that are long-lived and relatively expensive are called *capital items*. Less costly products that are consumed within a year are referred to as *expense items*.

Five basic categories of B2B products exist: installations, accessory equipment, component parts and materials, raw materials, and supplies. *Installations* are major capital items, such as new factories, heavy equipment and machinery, and custom-made equipment. Installations are expensive and often involve buyer and seller negotiations that may last for more than a year before a purchase actually is made. Purchase approval frequently involves a number of different people—production specialists, representatives from the purchasing department, and members of top management—who must agree on the final choice.

Although *accessory equipment* also includes capital items, they are usually less expensive and shorter lived than installations and involve fewer decision makers. Examples include hand tools and printers. *Component parts and materials* are finished business goods that become part of a final product, such as disk drives that are sold to computer manufacturers or batteries purchased by automakers. *Raw materials* are farm and natural products used in producing other final products. Examples include milk, wood, leather, and soybeans. *Supplies* are expense items used in a firm's daily operation that do not become part of the final product. Often referred to as MRO (maintenance, repair, and operating supplies), they include paper clips, light bulbs, and copy paper.

Classifying Services Services can be classified as either B2C or B2B. Child and elder care centers and auto detail shops provide services for consumers, while the Pinkerton security patrol at a local factory and Kelly Services' temporary office workers are examples of business services. In some cases, a service can accommodate both consumer and business markets. For

PepsiCo product mix includes Rockstar Energy drinks, which are distributed in the United States and Canada by various Pepsi Bottling enterprises.

product line group of related products marked by physical similarities or intended for a similar market.

product mix the assortment of product lines and individual goods and services that a firm offers to consumers and business users.

Assessment Check ☑

1. How do consumer products differ from business products?

2. Differentiate among convenience, shopping, and specialty products.

product life cycle four basic stages—introduction, growth, maturity, and decline—through which a successful product progresses.

example, when ServiceMaster cleans the upholstery in a home, it is a B2C service, but when it provides disaster restoration services at a manufacturing plant, it is a B2B service.

Like tangible goods, services can also be convenience, shopping, or specialty products depending on the buying patterns of customers. However, they are distinguished from goods in several ways. First, services, unlike goods, are intangible. In addition, they are perishable because firms cannot stockpile them in inventory. They are also difficult to standardize, because they must meet individual customers' needs. Finally, from a buyer's perspective, the service provider is the service; the two are inseparable in the buyer's mind.

Marketing Strategy Implications

The consumer product classification system is a useful tool in marketing strategy. As described in Figure 12.1, because a new refrigerator is classified as a shopping good, its marketers have a better idea of its promotion, pricing, and distribution needs.

Each group of business products, however, requires a different marketing strategy. Because most installations and many component parts are frequently marketed directly from manufacturer to business buyer, the promotional emphasis is on personal selling rather than on advertising. By contrast, marketers of supplies and accessory equipment rely more on advertising, because their products are often sold through an intermediary, such as a wholesaler. Producers of installations and component parts may involve their customers in new-product development, especially when the business product is custom made. Finally, firms selling supplies and accessory equipment place greater emphasis on competitive pricing strategies than do other B2B marketers, who tend to concentrate more on product quality and customer service.

Product Lines and Product Mix

Few firms operate with a single product. If their initial entry is successful, they tend to increase their profit and growth chances by adding new offerings. The iPhone and iPad, with their touchscreen technology and apps, have expanded Apple's product line. Although most mainstream knowledge workers will probably continue to use conventional computers for some time, touchscreen technology is fast becoming a standard feature in consumer electronics.[2]

A company's **product line** is a group of related products marked by physical similarities or intended for a similar market. A **product mix** is the assortment of product lines and individual goods and services that a firm offers to consumers and business users. The Coca-Cola Company and PepsiCo both have product lines that include old standards—Coke Classic and Diet Coke, Pepsi and Diet Pepsi. But recently, Rockstar energy drink switched distributors from The Coca-Cola Company to PepsiCo, as a result of The Coca-Cola Company's distribution agreement with competitor Monster energy drink. As part of a multiyear agreement, Rockstar energy drinks are distributed in the United States and Canada by Pepsi Bottling Group, PepsiAmericas, and Pepsi Bottling Ventures, as well as other independent Pepsi bottlers.[3]

Marketers must assess their product mix continually to ensure company growth, to satisfy changing consumer needs and wants, and to adjust to competitors' offerings. To remain competitive, marketers look for gaps in their product lines and fill them with new offerings or modified versions of existing ones. A helpful tool that is frequently used in making product decisions is the product life cycle.

⌐2⌐ Product Life Cycle

Once a product is on the market, it usually goes through four stages known as the **product life cycle**: introduction, growth, maturity, and decline. As Figure 12.2 shows, industry sales and profits vary depending on the life cycle stage of an item.

338 Part 4 *Marketing Management*

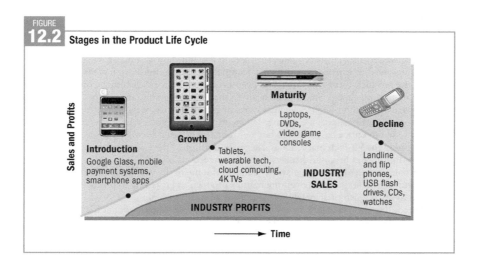

FIGURE

12.2 **Stages in the Product Life Cycle**

Product life cycles are not set in stone; not all products follow this pattern precisely, and different products may spend different periods of time in each stage. The concept, however, helps the marketing planner anticipate developments throughout the various stages of a product's life. Profits assume a predictable pattern through the stages, and promotional emphasis shifts from dispensing product information in the early stages to heavy brand promotion in the later ones.

Stages of the Product Life Cycle

In the *introduction stage*, the firm tries to promote demand for its new offering; inform the market about it; give free samples to entice consumers to make a trial purchase; and explain its features, uses, and benefits. Sometimes companies partner at this stage to promote new products. California-based Fuhu is the maker of the Nabi, a first-of-its-kind Android tablet for children. The company sees the Nabi as a distribution channel for content geared to children and has signed agreements with Nickelodeon and Disney. With retailers Walmart, Target, and Best Buy on board to sell the tablet, the company is developing an audio dock attachment that converts the Nabi into a karaoke machine. Fuhu has announced it will produce an original animated TV series on the BabyFirst cable network that will feature a character modeled after its Nabi tablet.[4]

New-product development costs and extensive introductory promotional campaigns to acquaint prospective buyers with the merits of the innovation, though essential to later success, are expensive and commonly lead to losses in the introductory stage. Some firms are seeking to lower these costs through ultra-low-cost product development, which involves meeting customer needs with the lowest-cost innovations possible, designing from scratch with a stripped-down budget, and the simplest engineering possible. But all these expenditures are necessary if the firm is to profit later.

During the *growth stage*, sales climb quickly as new customers join early users who now are repurchasing the item. Word-of-mouth referrals and continued advertising and other special promotions by the firm induce others to make trial purchases. At this point, the company begins to earn profits on the new product. This success encourages competitors to enter the field with similar offerings, and price competition develops. After its initial success with the Kindle, Amazon faced competition from Barnes & Noble's Nook. Amazon rushed to launch its Kindle for the iPad app, then Barnes & Noble countered with its NOOK Color. Since then, the tablet market has become increasingly crowded, with the iPad still dominating the sector. Recent statistics reveal Apple with a 37 percent share of the tablet market, Samsung with 18 percent, and Amazon with 3 percent.[5]

In the *maturity stage*, industry sales at first increase, but they eventually reach a saturation level at which further expansion is difficult. Competition also intensifies, increasing the availability of the product. Firms concentrate on capturing competitors' customers, often dropping prices to further the appeal. Smart phones are in the maturity stage: competitors compete not only on price but also on features such as operating systems, size, weight, battery life, camera and video specifications, and messaging. When flat-screen TVs reached the maturity stage, companies tried to entice customers to buy new ones by offering even bigger screen sizes than before, topping the 90-inch mark. Today, there are continuing developments in color accuracy, higher resolution, and brighter displays for better screen visibility.[6]

Sales volume fades late in the maturity stage, and some of the weaker competitors leave the market. During this stage, firms promote mature products aggressively to protect their market share and to distinguish their products from those of competitors.

Sales continue to fall in the *decline stage*, the fourth phase of the product life cycle. Profits decline and may become losses as further price-cutting occurs in the reduced overall market for the item. Competitors gradually exit, making some profits possible for the remaining firms in the shrinking market. The decline stage usually is caused by a product innovation or a shift in consumer preferences. Sometimes technology change can accelerate the decline stage for a product. For example, at one time more than 90 percent of U.S. homes contained at least one DVD player. Once touted as the ultimate in DVD technology, high-definition DVDs have now been superseded by Blu-ray technology and online streaming sites. Online sites like Amazon, Netflix, and Hulu, where consumers can watch movies, television shows, or other original programming, have become another major competitor for entertainment as the link between technology and distribution has become faster and more reliable.[7]

Marketing Strategy Implications of the Product Life Cycle

Like the product classification system, the product life cycle is a useful concept for designing a marketing strategy that will be flexible enough to accommodate changing marketplace characteristics. These competitive moves may involve developing new products, lowering prices, increasing distribution coverage, creating new promotional campaigns, or any combination of these approaches. In general, the marketer's objective is to extend the product life cycle as long as the item is profitable. Some products can be highly profitable during the later stages of their life cycle, because all the initial development costs have already been recovered. Ava Anderson Non-Toxic, in the growth stage of the product life cycle, is a company that sells directly to consumers. See the "Going Green" feature for more details.

A commonly used strategy for extending the life cycle is to increase customers' frequency of use. Walmart and Target offer grocery sections in many of their stores to increase the frequency of shopper visits. Another strategy is to add new users. To gain new customers, fast-food companies have added healthy meal choices with more fruits and vegetables and less salt, sugar, and fat to their menus. Burger King recently rolled out "Satisfries," a healthier version of its traditional fries with 40 percent less fat and 30 percent fewer calories. The company also offers fat-free milk, apple juice, and apple fries—fresh cut apples in the shape of french fries.[8]

A third product life cycle extension strategy is to find new uses for products. 3M's Post-it Notes have made successful use of this strategy. One recent blog posting lists 20 innovative ways students can use them, including wrapping the sticky edge around a cable to identify it and using the sticky edge to clean between the keys of a computer keyboard.[9] Finally, a firm may decide to change package sizes, labels, and product designs. Mattel has done this several times with its iconic Barbie doll.

Ava Anderson Non-Toxic Excels via Direct Distribution

Ava Anderson's cosmetics company, Ava Anderson Non-Toxic, grew from a teenager's alarm at discovering that most personal care products contain harmful ingredients, including carcinogens and endocrine disrupters. Then just 14, Anderson set out to find manufacturers who could develop and manufacture cosmetics to her own green standards. Only a few years later, the privately held company she founded with her mother was a finalist in *Entrepreneur* magazine's "Entrepreneur of the Year" competition, selected for its innovation, impact, and community.

The firm produces cosmetics, sunscreen, body, and home care products without harmful chemicals. The products are sold by independent part- and full-time consultants who host parties and seminars and schedule individual customer appointments, providing direct distribution. The company offers ongoing training and rewards consultants with a percentage of their total sales, plus a percentage of the sales of any new consultants they recruit.

Anderson says she is thrilled to watch the company's consultants be successful, really enjoy their jobs, and share her passion to provide safer alternatives to consumers.

Questions for Critical Thinking

1. Is direct distribution appropriate for a product like Non-Toxic's cosmetics? Why or why not?
2. The company offers consultants their own personal online office and website. How would a consultant make the best use of these tools?

Sources: Company website, www.avaandersonnontoxic.com, accessed March 11, 2014; Samantha Escobar, "Meet Ava Anderson, the Teen CEO of an All-Natural Cosmetics Company," *Bliss Tree,* accessed March 11, 2014, www.blisstree.com; Sara Bagwell, "Ava Anderson Non-Toxic Is a Finalist in *Entrepreneur* 2011 Contest," *Bristol-Warren Patch,* accessed February 28, 2014, http://bristol-warrenpatch.com; Sarah Cook, "It's Not Kids Business: Interview with Ava Anderson, Founder of Ava Anderson Non-Toxic," *Raising CEO Kids,* accessed February 28, 2014, www.raisingceokids.com.

Stages in New-Product Development

New-product development is costly, time consuming, and risky, because only about one-third of new products become success stories. Products can fail for many reasons. Some are not properly developed and tested, some are poorly packaged, and others lack adequate promotional support or distribution or do not satisfy a consumer need or want. Even successful products eventually reach the end of the decline stage and must be replaced with new-product offerings.

Most of today's newly developed items are aimed at satisfying specific consumer demands. New-product development is becoming increasingly efficient and cost-effective because marketers use a systematic approach in developing new products. As Figure 12.3 shows, the new-product development process has six stages. Each stage requires a "go/no-go" decision by management before moving on to subsequent stages. Because items that go through each development stage only to be rejected at one of the final stages involve significant investments in both time and money, the sooner decision makers can identify a marginal product and drop it from further consideration, the less time and money will be wasted.

The starting point in the new-product development process is generating ideas for new offerings. Ideas come from many sources, including customer suggestions, suppliers, employees, research scientists, marketing research, inventors outside the firm, and competitive products. The most successful ideas are directly related to satisfying customer needs. California-based Future Motion has created Onewheel, a self-balancing, single-wheel skateboard with speeds of up to 12 miles per hour. Using self-balancing technology, leaning

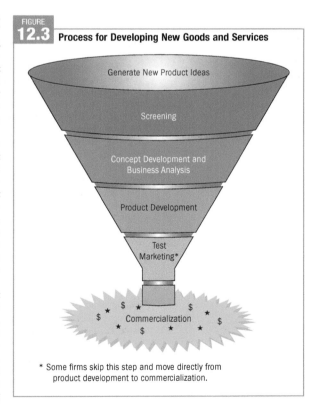

FIGURE 12.3 Process for Developing New Goods and Services

Generate New Product Ideas

Screening

Concept Development and Business Analysis

Product Development

Test Marketing*

Commercialization

* Some firms skip this step and move directly from product development to commercialization.

forward speeds up the skateboard and leaning back slows it down. Features include a rechargeable lithium battery and iPhone and Android apps to monitor speed, acceleration, and range.[10]

In the second stage, screening eliminates ideas that do not mesh with overall company objectives or that cannot be developed given the company's resources. Some firms hold open discussions of new-product ideas with specialists who work in different functional areas in the organization.

During the concept development and business analysis phase, further screening occurs. The analysis involves assessing the new product's potential sales, profits, growth rate, and competitive strengths and determining whether it fits with the company's product, distribution, and promotional resources. *Concept testing*—marketing research designed to solicit initial consumer reaction to new-product ideas—may be used at this stage. For example, potential consumers might be asked about proposed brand names and other methods of product identification. *Focus groups* are sessions in which consumers meet with marketers to discuss what they like or dislike about current products and perhaps test or sample a new offering to provide some immediate feedback.

Next, an actual product is developed, subjected to a series of tests, and revised. Functioning prototypes or detailed descriptions of the product may be created. These designs are the joint responsibility of the firm's development staff and its marketers, who provide feedback on consumer reactions to the proposed product design, color, and other physical features. Sometimes prototypes do not meet the stated requirements. In search of a quick-drying camouflage uniform for tropical environments, the U.S. Marines are back to the drawing board after testing four prototypes at the jungle warfare training center in Okinawa, Japan. Although the uniforms provide ample protection and durability, they need to dry in 20 minutes rather than the usual 40 minutes.[11]

Test marketing introduces a new product supported by a complete marketing campaign to a selected city or TV coverage area. Marketers look for a location with a manageable size, where residents match their target market's demographic profile, to test their product. During the test marketing stage, the item is sold in a limited area while the company examines both consumer responses to the new offering and the marketing effort used to support it. Test market results can help managers determine the product's likely performance in a full-scale introduction. Some firms skip test marketing, however, because of concerns that the test could reveal their strategies to the competition. Also, the expense of doing limited production runs of complex products such as a new auto or refrigerator is sometimes so high that the test marketing stage is skipped and the development process moves directly to the next stage.

In the final stage, commercialization, the product is made available in the marketplace. Sometimes this stage is referred to as a product launch. Considerable planning goes into this stage, because the firm's distribution, promotion, and pricing strategies must all be geared to support the new product offering. Mercedes Benz recently announced plans to launch 30 new models over the next several years as part of an ongoing effort to revitalize its product lines. The S600 is the first Mercedes to have a jet fighter–inspired display for the driver that includes navigation instructions, vehicle speed, and cruise control settings. The car will also have a touchpad controller for the onboard "infotainment" system, which will function like a smart phone or tablet. Back seats will recline, and there is even a refrigerator in the trunk.[12]

The need for a steady stream of new products to offer the firm's customers, the chances of product failure, and the tens of millions of dollars needed to complete a successful new-product launch make new-product development a vital process for 21st-century firms. However, as Table 12.1 illustrates, success is not guaranteed until the new-product offering achieves customer acceptance. Laser virtual keyboards, which project a keyboard on any flat surface, were introduced a few years ago. Reports say not only is the keyboard inaccurate, but it also feels unnatural. With a keyboard on your smart phone or tablet, along with many different accessory options available, critics say that lugging around a device that projects a virtual keyboard is no longer practical.[13]

test marketing introduction of a new product supported by a complete marketing campaign to a selected city or TV coverage area.

12.1 Examples of Products That Failed

PRODUCT	WHY IT FLOPPED
New Coke	Facing stiff competition from other soft drink producers in the mid-1980s, executives at The Coca-Cola Company stopped production on the original Coke and introduced a new, sweeter formula of the soft drink. Consumers were outraged and flooded the company with complaints. Three months later, the company went back to the original Coke formula.
Sony Betamax	Sony's Betamax video recorder was introduced in the mid-1970s. Soon after, a rival company introduced VHS technology, which became the standard for video recordings, and several other competitors introduced VHS machines quickly. Because Sony chose not to license its Betamax technology, and the two technologies were not compatible, consumers needed to choose between Betamax and VHS. As a result, Sony lost its market share.
Pepsi A.M. and Crystal Pepsi	In the late 1980s, Pepsi A.M. was marketed as an alternative to coffee for people who wanted a caffeinated beverage in the morning. Crystal Pepsi was introduced about the same time and was a clear cola drink. Neither product caught on with consumers.
Harley-Davidson Perfume	Fans of the Harley-Davidson brand are considered very loyal to the motorcycle maker. Trying to leverage this loyalty and extend its brand, the company introduced perfume, but consumers didn't buy it.
Colgate Kitchen Entrees	Colgate tried to capitalize on its popular brand by introducing a line of frozen dinners in the early 1980s. Unfortunately, consumers thought of Colgate as a toothpaste brand and not a food company.

Source: "Top 25 Biggest Product Flops of All Time," *Daily Finance*, accessed March 12, 2014, www.dailyfinance.com; Len Penzo, "10 Grocery Products That Flopped," *MSN Money*, accessed March 12, 2014, http://money.msn.com; "Top 10 Bad Beverage Ideas," *Time*, accessed March 12, 2014, http://content.time.com.

3 Product Identification

A major aspect of developing a successful new product involves methods used for identifying a product and distinguishing it from competing offerings. Both tangible goods and intangible services are identified by brands, brand names, and trademarks. A **brand** is a name, term, sign, symbol, design, or some combination that identifies the products of one firm and differentiates them from competitors' offerings. Tropicana, Pepsi, and Gatorade are all made by PepsiCo, but a unique combination of name, symbol, and package design distinguishes each brand from the others.

A **brand name** is that part of the brand consisting of words or letters included in a name used to identify and distinguish the firm's offerings from those of competitors. The brand name is the part of the brand that can be vocalized. Many brand names, such as Coca-Cola, McDonald's, American Express, Google, and Nike, are famous around the world. Likewise, the golden arches brand mark of McDonald's also is widely recognized.

A **trademark** is a brand that has been given legal protection. The protection is granted solely to the brand's owner. Trademark protection includes not only the brand name but also design logos, slogans, packaging elements, and product features such as color and shape. A well-designed trademark, such as the Nike swoosh, can make a difference in how positively consumers perceive a brand.

Assessment Check ☑

1. What are the stages of the product life cycle?
2. What are the marketing implications of each stage?

brand name, term, sign, symbol, design, or some combination that identifies the products of one firm and differentiates them from competitors' offerings.

brand name part of the brand consisting of words or letters included in a name used to identify and distinguish the firm's offerings from those of competitors.

trademark brand that has been given legal protection.

Selecting an Effective Brand Name

Good brands are easy to pronounce, recognize, and remember: Crest, Visa, and Pepsi are examples. Global firms face a real problem in selecting brand names, because an excellent brand name in one country may prove disastrous in another. Most languages have a short *a*, so Coca-Cola is pronounceable almost anywhere. But an advertising campaign for E-Z washing machines failed in the United Kingdom because the British pronounce z as "zed."

Brand names should also convey the right image to the buyer. One effective technique is to create a name that links the product with its positioning strategy. The name Purell reinforces the concept of sanitizing hands to protect against germs, Dove soap and beauty products give an impression of mildness, and Taster's Choice instant coffee supports the promotional claim "Tastes and smells like ground roast coffee."

Brand names also must be legally protectable. Trademark law specifies that brand names cannot contain words in general use, such as *television* or *automobile*. Generic words—words that describe a type of product—cannot be used exclusively by any organization. On the other hand, if a brand name becomes so popular that it passes into common language and turns into a generic word, the company can no longer use it as a brand name. Once upon a time, aspirin, linoleum, and zipper were exclusive brand names, but today they have become generic terms and are no longer legally protectable.

Brand Categories

A brand offered and promoted by a manufacturer is known as a *manufacturer's* (or *national*) *brand*. Examples are Tide, Cheerios, Windex, North Face, and Nike. But not all brand names belong to manufacturers; some are the property of retailers or distributors. A *private* (or *store*) *brand* identifies a product that is not linked to the manufacturer but instead carries a wholesaler's or retailer's label. Sears's Craftsman tools and Walmart's Ol' Roy dog food are examples.

Another branding decision marketers must make is whether to use a family branding strategy or an individual branding strategy. A *family brand* is a single brand name used for several related products. KitchenAid, Johnson & Johnson, Hewlett-Packard, and Arm & Hammer use a family name for their entire line of products. When a firm using family branding introduces a new product, both customers and retailers recognize the familiar brand name. The promotion of individual products within a line benefits all the items because the family brand is well known.

Other firms use an *individual branding* strategy by giving each product within a line a different name. For example, Procter & Gamble has individual brand names for its different laundry detergents, including Tide, Cheer, and Gain. Each brand targets a unique market segment. Consumers who want a cold-water detergent can choose Cheer over Tide or Gain, instead of purchasing a competitor's brand. Individual branding also builds competition within a firm and enables the company to increase overall sales.

Brand Loyalty and Brand Equity

Brands achieve varying consumer familiarity and acceptance. While a homeowner may insist on Andersen windows when renovating, the consumer buying a loaf of bread may not prefer any brand. Consumer loyalty increases a brand's value, so marketers try to strengthen brand loyalty. When a brand image suffers, marketers try to recreate a positive image.

Brand Loyalty Marketers measure brand loyalty in three stages: brand recognition, brand preference, and brand insistence. *Brand recognition* is brand acceptance strong enough that the consumer is aware of the brand, but not strong enough to cause a preference over other brands. A consumer might have heard of L'Oréal hair care products, for instance, without necessarily preferring them to Redken. Advertising, free samples, and discount coupons are among the most common ways to increase brand recognition.

To be effective, *brand names* must be easy for consumers to pronounce, recognize, and remember.

Helen Sessions/Alamy

344   **Part 4** *Marketing Management*

Brand preference occurs when a consumer chooses one firm's brand over a competitor's. At this stage, the consumer usually relies on previous experience in selecting the product. Furniture and other home furnishings fall into this category. A shopper who purchased an IKEA dining room table and chairs and was satisfied with them is likely to return to purchase a bedroom set. While there, this shopper might pick up a set of mixing bowls for the kitchen or a lamp for the family room—because he or she knows and likes the IKEA brand.

Brand insistence is the ultimate degree of brand loyalty, in which the consumer will look for it at another outlet, special-order it from a dealer, order by mail, or search the Internet. Shoppers who insist on IKEA products for their homes may drive an hour or two—making a day excursion of the venture—to visit an IKEA store. The combination of value for the money and the concept of IKEA as a shopping destination have given the brand a unique allure for shoppers.[14]

Brand-building strategies were once limited to the consumer realm, but now they are becoming more important for B2B brands as well. Intel, Xerox, IBM, and service providers such as ServiceMaster and Cisco are among the suppliers who have built brand names among business customers.

IKEA installed this clever showpiece, meant to look like a bus stop, in New York City during Design Week. The retailer of affordable, well-designed contemporary furniture enjoys *brand insistence*—the ultimate expression of brand loyalty. For devoted IKEA fans, no other brand will do.

Brand Equity Brand loyalty is at the heart of <u>brand equity</u>, the added value that a respected and successful name gives to a product. This value results from a combination of factors, including awareness, loyalty, and perceived quality, as well as any feelings or images the customer associates with the brand. High brand equity offers financial advantages to a firm, because the product commands a relatively large market share and sometimes reduces price sensitivity, generating higher profits. Figure 12.4 shows the world's 10 most valuable brands.

Brand awareness means the product is the first one that comes to mind when a product category is mentioned. If someone says "coffee," do you think of Starbucks, Dunkin' Donuts, or Folgers? Brand association is the link between a brand and other favorable images. A recent survey of recognizable logos with strong brand identities includes Starbucks, McDonald's, Target, Disney, Apple, and eBay.[15]

Large companies have typically assigned the task of managing a brand's marketing strategies to a *brand manager*, who may also be called a *product manager* at some firms. This marketer plans and implements the balance of promotional, pricing, distribution, and product arrangements that leads to strong brand equity. A *category manager*, a newer type of marketer, oversees an entire group of products. Unlike traditional brand or product managers, category managers have profit responsibility for their product group. These managers are assisted by associates, usually called *analysts*. Part of the shift to category management was initiated by large retailers, when they realized there could be a benefit from the marketing muscle of large grocery and household goods producers such as General Mills and Procter & Gamble. As a result, producers began to focus their attention on in-store merchandising

brand equity added value that a respected and successful name gives to a product.

FIGURE 12.4 The World's 10 Most Valuable Brands (sales in billions)

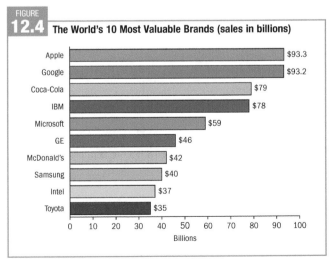

Brand	Billions
Apple	$93.3
Google	$93.2
Coca-Cola	$79
IBM	$78
Microsoft	$59
GE	$46
McDonald's	$42
Samsung	$40
Intel	$37
Toyota	$35

Source: "Best Global Brands 2013," *Interbrand*, accessed March 11, 2014, www.interbrand.com.

Chapter 12 *Product and Distribution Strategies*   **345**

Creating an Identity for Brand X

Does influencing how a consumer's emotional perception, experience, or connection with a brand interest you? Would it be exciting to enhance a consumer's relationship to a brand by developing a product's look, price, and packaging? If so, becoming a brand manager might be for you.

The career path to a brand manager typically includes an entry-level position as a marketing analyst or sales representative, which requires a college degree. To become an assistant brand manager, with the responsibility for developing a brand's strategy, several years of experience or a degree may be required. The skills most sought after for brand managers include strategic vision and the intuition and ability to react. Most brand managers also have some background in marketing or sales. So, what exactly does a brand manager do?

- Monitors the competitive landscape of a brand's category or segment
- Develops strategies to take advantage of opportunities in the marketplace
- Executes those strategies with the help of a cross-functional marketing team
- Delivers the sales volume, market share, and profit projections forecasted by company management

As part of a company's marketing function, a brand manager sets the strategic direction of a brand and works with various departments within the organization to execute the strategy. This includes product and strategy development, manufacturing, product extension, package design, marketing research, business and financial forecasts and analysis, and, of course, promotion.

Sources: "A Day in the Life: Assistant Brand Manager," *Vault*, accessed March 12, 2014, www.vault.com; "Career Overview: Brand Management," *Wet Feet*, accessed March 12, 2014, www.wetfeet.com; "What Does a Brand Manager Do?," *wiseGEEK*, accessed March 12, 2014, www.wisegeek.org; Victoria Black, "A Day in the Life: Assistant Brand Manager," *Bloomberg Businessweek*, accessed March 12, 2014, www.businessweek.com.

instead of mass-market advertising. See the "Career Kickstart" feature for more details on how to be a brand manager.

A **category advisor** functions in the B2B context. This vendor is the major supplier designated by a business customer to assume responsibility for dealing with all the other vendors for a project and presenting the entire package to the business buyer.

Packages and Labels

Packaging and labels are important in product identification. They also play an important role in a firm's overall product strategy. Packaging affects the durability, image, and convenience of an item and is responsible for one of the biggest costs in many consumer products. Due to a growing demand to produce smaller, more environmentally friendly packages, box manufacturers and chemical companies are now working harder to create more compact packaging that is made from renewable sources and is recyclable. One-third of America's waste consists of containers and packaging, much of it from fast-food chains. New York–based Just Salad offers reusable salad bowls, and free toppings are given to customers who bring back the bowls for subsequent use. Whole Foods gives customers a five-cent refund for each bag they bring in to pack their purchases, or customers can donate the money to a local not-for-profit organization.[16]

Choosing the right package is especially crucial in international marketing because marketers must be aware of such factors as language variations and cultural preferences. Consumers in African nations often prefer bold colors, but use of the country's flag colors may be problematic. Some countries frown on other uses of their flag. Also, in Africa red is often associated with death or witchcraft. Package size can vary according to the purchasing patterns and

category advisor
vendor that is designated by the business customer as the major supplier to assume responsibility for dealing with all the other vendors for a project and presenting the entire package to the business buyer.

market conditions of a country. In countries with small refrigerators, people may want to buy their beverages one at a time rather than in six-packs. Package weight is another important issue, because shipping costs are often based on weight.

Labeling is an integral part of the packaging process as well. In the United States, labeling must meet federal laws requiring companies to provide enough information to allow consumers to make value comparisons among competitive products and, in the case of food packaging, provide nutrition information on the label. Marketers who ship products to other countries have to comply with labeling requirements in those nations. This means knowing the answers to such questions as the following:

- Should the labels be in more than one language?
- Should ingredients be specified?
- Do the labels give enough information about the product to meet government standards?

The U.S. Food and Drug Administration (FDA) regulates the labeling of food and drug products, investigates violations, and enforces compliance with the Food, Drug, and Cosmetic Act. Typical violations include unauthorized health claims, unauthorized nutrient content claims, and unauthorized use of such terms as "healthy" and others that have strict regulatory definitions. The FDA is working on revising and updating food label requirements to emphasize calories and sugar content.[17]

Another important aspect of packaging and labeling is the *universal product code (UPC)*, the bar code read by optical scanners that print the name of the item and the price on a receipt. For many stores, these identifiers are useful not just for packaging and labeling but also for simplifying and speeding retail transactions and for evaluating customer purchases and controlling inventory. Radio-frequency identification (RFID) technology—embedded chips that can broadcast their product information to receivers—may also serve as a way to track items effectively. It is unlikely, however, that they will replace bar codes.

Due to a growing demand to produce more environmentally friendly packages, manufacturers are working harder to create more compact packaging that is made from renewable sources and is recyclable.

[4] Distribution Strategy

The next element of the marketing mix, **distribution strategy**, deals with the marketing activities and institutions involved in getting the right good or service to the firm's customers. Distribution decisions involve modes of transportation, warehousing, inventory control, order processing, and selection of marketing channels. Marketing channels typically are made up of intermediaries such as retailers and wholesalers that move a product from producer to final purchaser.

The two major components of an organization's distribution strategy are distribution channels and physical distribution. **Distribution channels** are the paths that products—and legal ownership of them—follow from producer to consumer or business user. They are the means by which all organizations distribute their goods and services. **Physical distribution** is the actual movement of products from producer to consumers or business users. Physical distribution covers a broad range of activities, including customer service, transportation, inventory control, materials handling, order processing, and warehousing. Amazon is creating innovative distribution solutions by piggybacking with its suppliers, as described in the "Hit & Miss" feature.

Distribution Channels

In their first decision for distribution channel selection, marketers choose which type of channel will best meet both their firm's marketing objectives and the needs of their customers. As shown in Figure 12.5, marketers can choose either a *direct distribution channel*, which carries goods directly from producer to consumer or business user, or distribution channels that involve several different marketing intermediaries. A *marketing intermediary* (also called a *middleman*) is a business firm that moves goods between producers and consumers or business users. Marketing intermediaries perform various functions that help the distribution channel operate smoothly, such as buying, selling, storing, and transporting products; sorting and grading bulky items; and providing information to other channel members. The two main categories of marketing intermediaries are wholesalers and retailers.

Assessment Check ✓

1. Differentiate among a brand, a brand name, and a trademark.

2. Define *brand equity*.

distribution strategy deals with the marketing activities and institutions involved in getting the right good or service to the firm's customers.

distribution channels path that products—and legal ownership of them— follow from producer to consumers or business user.

physical distribution actual movement of products from producer to consumers or business users.

Hit&Miss

Amazon and P&G Share Warehouses

For the past few years, Procter & Gamble has been quiet about sharing some of its warehouse space. E-commerce giant Amazon wants a bigger piece of the consumer packaged goods market, projected to grow 25 percent a year for the next few years, and hopes to achieve that growth with a little help from its suppliers and a program it calls Vendor Flex, currently in place in seven of P&G's distribution warehouses.

By piggybacking on the distribution networks and warehouses of its suppliers, Amazon is able to reduce shipping, warehouse, and distribution costs, and equally important, the time it takes to get a package to a consumer's doorstep. P&G's distribution system, along with consumers' moving online to purchase everyday products, is good news for Amazon, which is looking for new ways to grow among the intense competition from the likes of Walmart, Costco, and Target.

P&G loads products onto pallets and brings them over to Amazon's side, where employees package, label, and ship to customers. While Amazon can ship from its own fulfillment centers, the company prefers to reserve its warehouse space for its higher margin, e-commerce items.

Amazon's entry into the consumer packaged goods market began with its $500 million purchase of Quidsi, parent company of Diaper.com, BeautyBar.com, and Soap.com. Sharing warehouses is a win for both companies. For P&G, it is an opportunity to see Amazon's fine-tuned fulfillment know-how in action and to learn more about online selling. For Amazon, the sharing strategy translates to more distribution locations for its lower margin items, reduced costs, and quicker delivery.

Questions for Critical Thinking

1. How should Amazon respond to third-party sellers when asked about the shared arrangement with Procter & Gamble?

2. What are some disadvantages of two companies sharing warehouse space?

Sources: Serena Ng, "Soap Opera: Amazon Moves in with P&G," *The Wall Street Journal,* accessed February 16, 2014, http://online.wsj.com; company website, www.quidsi.com, accessed February 16, 2014; "Amazon's Vendor Flex Supply Chain Innovation," *Technology Evaluation Centers,* accessed February 16, 2014, www.technologyevaluation.com; Jeffrey Grau, "US Retail eCommerce Outlook—What's Driving Growth," *eMarketer,* accessed February 16, 2014, www.emarketer.com.

No one channel suits every product. The best choice depends on the circumstances of the market and on customer needs. The most appropriate channel choice may also change over time as new opportunities arise and marketers strive to maintain their competitiveness. Currently, most smart phones sold in the United States are tied to a specific wireless carrier that controls all distribution of its particular phone. Consumers can choose a smart phone but can't choose the carrier. Google offers an unlocked smart phone, the Samsung Galaxy Nexus, which works on networks worldwide through its Google Play store. The company wants to give consumers the option to choose a distribution channel that is not tied directly to a wireless carrier. In this type of business model, buyers would be able to select a phone first and then sign up with a carrier, much as they can now buy any brand of computer regardless of their Internet service provider.[18]

Direct Distribution The shortest and simplest means of connecting producers and customers is direct contact between the two parties. This approach is most common in the B2B market. Consumers who buy fresh fruits and vegetables at rural roadside stands or farmers markets use direct distribution, as do services ranging from banking and 10-minute oil changes to ear piercing and Mary Kay Cosmetics.

Direct distribution is commonly found in the marketing of relatively expensive, complex products that may require demonstrations. Most major B2B products such as installations, accessory equipment, component parts, business services, and even raw materials are typically marketed through direct contacts between producers and business buyers. The Internet has also made direct distribution an attractive option for many retail companies and service providers. In an effort to bypass the traditional wholesale route of selling through multibrand boutiques and department stores, online companies like Bonobos and Wayfair have found alternative ways to sell directly to consumers. Several years ago, Bayard Winthrop started San Francisco–based American Giant, a web-only apparel business, in an effort to eliminate

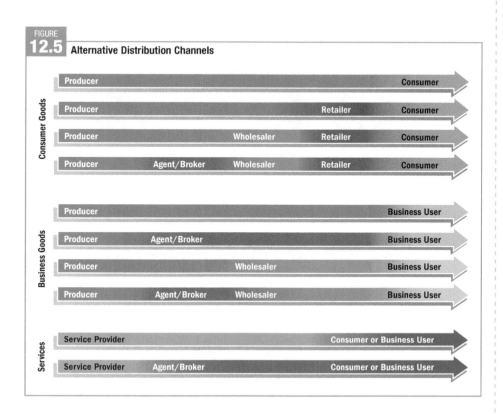

FIGURE 12.5 Alternative Distribution Channels

Consumer Goods

Producer → Consumer

Producer → Retailer → Consumer

Producer → Wholesaler → Retailer → Consumer

Producer → Agent/Broker → Wholesaler → Retailer → Consumer

Business Goods

Producer → Business User

Producer → Agent/Broker → Business User

Producer → Wholesaler → Business User

Producer → Agent/Broker → Wholesaler → Business User

Services

Service Provider → Consumer or Business User

Service Provider → Agent/Broker → Consumer or Business User

excessive markups by intermediaries, maintain decent margins, and provide superior customer service.[19]

Distribution Channels Using Marketing Intermediaries Although direct channels allow simple and straightforward connections between producers and their customers, the list of channel alternatives in Figure 12.5 suggests that direct distribution is not the best choice in every instance. Some products sell in small quantities for relatively low prices to thousands of widely scattered consumers. Makers of such products cannot cost effectively contact each of their customers, so they distribute products through marketing intermediaries called *wholesalers* and *retailers*.

Although you might think that adding intermediaries to the distribution process would increase the final cost of products, more often than not this choice actually lowers consumer prices. Intermediaries such as wholesalers and retailers often add significant value to a product as it moves through the distribution channel. They do so by creating utility, providing additional services, and reducing costs.

Marketing utility is created when intermediaries help ensure that products are available for sale when and where customers want to purchase them. If you want something warm to eat on a cold winter night, you don't call up Campbell's Soup and ask them to ship a can of chicken noodle soup. Instead, you go to the nearest grocery store, where you find utility in the form of product availability. In addition, intermediaries perform such important services as transporting merchandise to convenient locations. Finally, by representing numerous producers, a

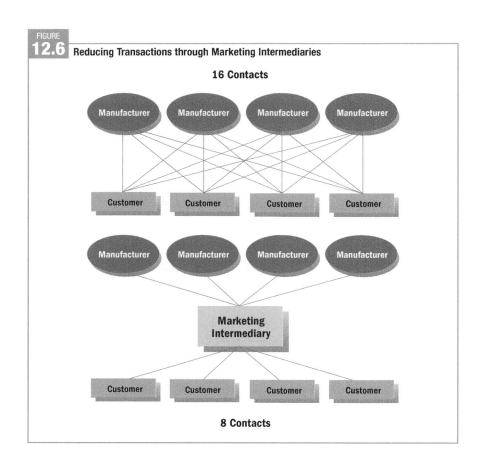

FIGURE 12.6 Reducing Transactions through Marketing Intermediaries

16 Contacts

Manufacturer   Manufacturer   Manufacturer   Manufacturer

Customer   Customer   Customer   Customer

Manufacturer   Manufacturer   Manufacturer   Manufacturer

Marketing Intermediary

Customer   Customer   Customer   Customer

8 Contacts

Assessment Check ✓

1. Define *distribution channels.*

2. What is a marketing intermediary?

wholesaler distribution channel member that sells primarily to retailers, other wholesalers, or business users.

marketing intermediary can cut the costs of buying and selling. As Figure 12.6 shows, if four manufacturers each sold directly to four consumers, this would require 16 separate transactions. Adding a marketing intermediary, such as a retailer, to the exchange cuts the number of necessary transactions to eight.

[5] Wholesaling

A **wholesaler** is a distribution channel member that sells primarily to retailers, other wholesalers, or business users. For instance, Sysco is a wholesaler that buys food products from producers and then resells them to restaurants, hotels, and other institutions in the United States and Canada.

Wholesaling is a crucial part of the distribution channel for many products, particularly consumer goods and business supplies. Wholesaling intermediaries can be classified on the basis of ownership; some are owned by manufacturers, some are owned by retailers, and others are independently owned. The United States has about 486,000 wholesalers, two-thirds of which have fewer than 20 employees.[20]

350   **Part 4** *Marketing Management*

Manufacturer-Owned Wholesaling Intermediaries

A manufacturer's marketing manager may decide to distribute goods directly through company-owned facilities to control distribution or customer service. Firms operate two main types of manufacturer-owned wholesaling intermediaries: sales branches and sales offices.

Sales branches stock the products they distribute and fill orders from their inventories. They also provide offices for sales representatives. Sales branches are common in the chemical, petroleum products, motor vehicle, and machine and equipment industries.

A *sales office* is exactly what its name implies: an office for a producer's salespeople. Manufacturers set up sales offices in various regions to support local selling efforts and improve customer service. Some kitchen and bath fixture manufacturers maintain showrooms to display their products. Builders and decorators can visit these showrooms to see how the items would look in place. Unlike sales branches, however, sales offices do not store any inventory. When a customer orders from a showroom or other sales office, the merchandise is delivered from a separate warehouse.

Independent Wholesaling Intermediaries

An independent wholesaling intermediary is a business that represents a number of different manufacturers and makes sales calls on retailers, manufacturers, and other business accounts. Independent wholesalers are classified as either merchant wholesalers or agents and brokers, depending on whether they take title to the products they handle.

Merchant wholesalers, like apparel wholesaler WholesaleSarong.com, are independently owned wholesaling intermediaries that take title to the goods they handle. Within this category, a *full-function merchant wholesaler* provides a complete assortment of services for retailers or industrial buyers, such as warehousing, shipping, and even financing. A subtype of full-function merchant is a *rack jobber*, such as Virginia-based Choice Books, which handles distribution of inspirational books to retail stores. This type of firm stocks, displays, and services particular retail products, such as calendars, books, and note cards, in drug stores and gift shops. Usually, the retailer receives a commission based on actual sales as payment for providing merchandise space to a rack jobber.

A *limited-function merchant wholesaler* also takes legal title to the products it handles, but it provides fewer services to the retailers to which it sells. Some limited-function merchant wholesalers only warehouse products but do not offer delivery service. Others warehouse and deliver products but provide no financing. One type of limited-function merchant wholesaler is a *drop shipper* such as Kate Aspen, an Atlanta-based wholesaler of wedding favors. Drop shippers also operate in such industries as coal and lumber, characterized by bulky products for which no single producer can provide a complete assortment. They give access to many related goods by contacting numerous producers and negotiating the best possible prices. Cost considerations call for producers to ship such products directly to the drop shipper's customers.

Another category of independent wholesaling intermediaries consists of *agents* and *brokers*. They may or may not take possession of the goods they handle, but they never take title, working mainly to bring buyers and sellers together. Stockbrokers such as Charles Schwab and real estate agents such as RE/MAX perform functions similar to those of agents and brokers, but at the retail level. They do not take title to the sellers' property; instead, they create time and ownership utility for both buyer and seller by helping carry out transactions.

Manufacturers' reps act as independent sales forces by representing the manufacturers of related but noncompeting products. These agent intermediaries, sometimes referred to as *manufacturers' agents*, receive commissions based on a percentage of the sales they make.

Retailer-Owned Cooperatives and Buying Offices

Retailers sometimes band together to form their own wholesaling organizations. Such organizations can take the form of either a buying group or a cooperative. The participating retailers set up the new operation to reduce costs or to provide some special service that is not readily available in the marketplace. To achieve cost savings through quantity purchases,

Assessment Check ☑

1. Define *wholesaling*.
2. Differentiate between a merchant wholesaler and an agent or broker in terms of title to the goods.

retailer distribution channel member that sells goods and services to individuals for their own use rather than for resale.

independent retailers may form a buying group that negotiates bulk sales with manufacturers. Ace Hardware is a retailer-owned cooperative. The independent owners of its 4,600 stores have access to bulk merchandise purchases that save them—and their customers—money.[21] In a cooperative, an independent group of retailers may decide to band together to share functions such as shipping or warehousing.

6 Retailing

Retailers, in contrast to wholesalers, are distribution channel members that sell goods and services to individuals for their own use rather than for resale. Consumers usually buy their food, clothing, shampoo, furniture, and appliances from some type of retailer. The supermarket where you buy your groceries may have bought some of its items from a wholesaler such as Unified Grocers and then resold them to you.

Retailers are the final link—the so-called last three feet—of the distribution channel. Because they are often the only channel members that deal directly with consumers, it is essential that retailers remain aware of changing shopping trends. For instance, soaring gas prices affect consumers' budgets, so they may make fewer trips to the mall or cut back on nonessential purchases. As a result, retailers may need to offer special sales or events to lure customers to their outlets. It is also important for retailers to keep pace with developments in the fast-changing business environment, such as the disruption in delivery of supplies from natural disasters like wildfires or storms.

Nonstore Retailers

Two categories of retailers exist: store and nonstore. As Figure 12.7 shows, nonstore retailing includes four forms: direct-response retailing, Internet retailing, automatic merchandising, and direct selling. *Direct-response retailing* reaches prospective customers through catalogs; telemarketing; and even magazine, newspaper, and television ads. Shoppers order merchandise by mail, telephone, computer, or mobile device and then receive home delivery or pick the merchandise up at a local store. Lands' End has long stood out as a highly successful direct-response retailer; its well-known clothing catalog and stellar customer service have set the standard for this type of distribution channel.

Internet retailing, the second form of nonstore retailing, has grown rapidly. Tens of thousands of retailers have set up shop online, with sales growing at a rate of about 5 percent a year (as compared with declines in total retail sales). Today, online sales account for almost 6 percent of total retail sales.[22] A severe shakeout saw hundreds of Internet enterprises shut down during the first decade of the 21st century, but firms that survived have stronger business models than those that failed. Two examples of successful pure dot-com companies are Amazon and eBay. A major shift in retailing has seen traditional brick-and-mortar retailers competing with e-commerce start-ups by building their own websites as an option for shoppers. Nordstrom, Macy's, and Walmart report strong online sales. Shopping sites are among the most popular Internet destinations, and the most common products purchased online include electronics, clothing, household goods, and office supplies.

FIGURE 12.7 Types of Nonstore Retailing

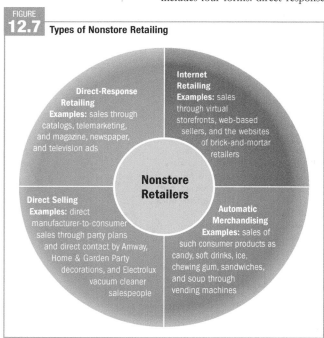

Direct-Response Retailing Examples: sales through catalogs, telemarketing, and magazine, newspaper, and television ads

Internet Retailing Examples: sales through virtual storefronts, web-based sellers, and the websites of brick-and-mortar retailers

Nonstore Retailers

Direct Selling Examples: direct manufacturer-to-consumer sales through party plans and direct contact by Amway, Home & Garden Party decorations, and Electrolux vacuum cleaner salespeople

Automatic Merchandising Examples: sales of such consumer products as candy, soft drinks, ice, chewing gum, sandwiches, and soup through vending machines

The last two forms of nonstore retailing are automatic merchandising and direct selling. *Automatic merchandising* provides convenience through the use of vending machines. ATMs may soon join the ranks of vending machines as banks find new ways to compete for customers. NCR Corporation, a leading manufacturer of ATMs, will soon be putting human tellers on its screens. The new interactive teller includes human help to assist customers with transactions in English or Spanish, with more languages to be added in the future. Bank of America hopes the use of remote tellers at its ATMs will help build deeper customer relationships.[23] *Direct selling* includes direct-to-consumer sales by Pampered Chef kitchen consultants and salespeople for Silpada sterling silver jewelry through party-plan selling methods. Both are forms of direct selling.

Companies that previously relied heavily on telemarketing to generate new customers have encountered consumer resistance to intrusive phone calls. Among the growing barriers are caller ID, call-blocking devices such as the TeleZapper, and the National Do Not Call list, which made it illegal for most companies to call people who are registered. As a result, dozens of companies, including telecommunications and regional utilities, have sent direct-mail pieces to promote such services as phones, cable television, and natural gas distributors.

Bank of America hopes the use of remote human tellers at its ATMs will build stronger customer relationships.

Store Retailers

In-store sales still outpace nonstore retailing methods such as direct-response retailing and Internet selling. Store retailers range in size from tiny newsstands to multistory department stores and multiacre warehouse-like retailers such as Sam's Club. Table 12.2 lists the different

TABLE
12.2 Types of Retail Stores

STORE TYPE	DESCRIPTION	EXAMPLE
Specialty store	Offers complete selection in a narrow line of merchandise	Bass Pro Shops, Dick's Sporting Goods, Williams-Sonoma
Convenience store	Offers staple convenience goods, easily accessible locations, extended store hours, and rapid checkouts	7-Eleven, Mobil Mart, QuikTrip
Discount store	Offers wide selection of merchandise at low prices; off-price discounters offer designer or brand-name merchandise	Target, Walmart, Dollar General, Marshalls
Warehouse club	Large, warehouse-style store selling food and general merchandise at discount prices to membership cardholders	Costco, Sam's Club, BJ's
Factory outlet	Manufacturer-owned store selling seconds, production overruns, or discontinued lines	Adidas, Coach, Pottery Barn, Ralph Lauren
Supermarket	Large, self-service retailer offering a wide selection of food and nonfood merchandise	Publix, Whole Foods Market, Kroger
Supercenter	Giant store offering food and general merchandise at discount prices	Walmart Supercenter, Super Target, Meijer
Department store	Offers a wide variety of merchandise selections (furniture, cosmetics, housewares, clothing) and many customer services	Macy's, Nordstrom, Neiman Marcus

Chapter 12 *Product and Distribution Strategies*

353

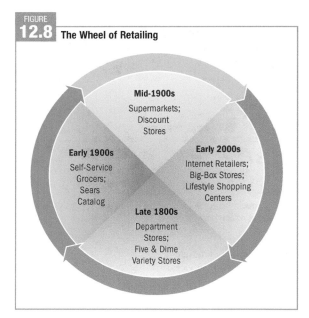

FIGURE
12.8 The Wheel of Retailing

Mid-1900s
Supermarkets;
Discount
Stores

Early 2000s
Internet Retailers;
Big-Box Stores;
Lifestyle Shopping
Centers

Early 1900s
Self-Service
Grocers;
Sears
Catalog

Late 1800s
Department
Stores;
Five & Dime
Variety Stores

types of store retailers, with examples of each type. Clearly, there are many approaches to retailing and a variety of services, prices, and product lines offered by each retail outlet.

The Wheel of Retailing Retailers are subject to constant change as new stores replace older establishments. In a process called the *wheel of retailing*, new retailers enter the market by offering lower prices made possible through reductions in service. Supermarkets and discount houses, for example, gained their initial market footholds through low-price, limited-service appeals. These new entries gradually add services as they grow and ultimately become targets for new retailers.

As Figure 12.8 shows, most major developments in retailing appear to fit the wheel pattern. The low-price, limited-service strategy characterized supermarkets, catalog retailers, discount stores, and, most recently, Internet retailers and giant big-box stores, such as PetSmart, Lowe's, and Office Depot. Corner grocery stores gave way to supermarkets and then to warehouse clubs such as Costco or BJ's. Department stores lost market share to discount clothing retailers such as Target and Marshalls. Independent bookstores have lost business to giant chains such as Barnes & Noble and such online-only sellers such as Amazon.com and Buy.com.

Even though the wheel of retailing does not fit every pattern of retail evolution—for example, automatic merchandising has always been a relatively high-priced method of retailing—it does give retail managers a general idea of what is likely to occur during the evolution of retailing. It also shows that business success involves the "survival of the fittest." Retailers that fail to change fail to survive.

How Retailers Compete

Retailers compete with each other in many ways. Nonstore retailers focus on making the shopping experience as convenient as possible. Shoppers at stores such as Saks Fifth Avenue enjoy a luxurious atmosphere and personal service. In fact, those who visit the new shoe department at the flagship store in New York have the run of the entire eighth floor, devoted entirely to shoes—with its own zip code. The elite shopping experience includes a private VIP room, a repair service, and a chocolate café.[24]

Like manufacturers, retailers must develop marketing strategies based on goals and strategic plans. Successful retailers convey images that alert consumers to the stores' identities and the shopping experiences they provide. To create that image, all components of a retailer's strategy must complement each other. After identifying their target markets, retailers must choose merchandising, customer service, pricing, and location strategies that will attract customers in those market segments.

Identifying a Target Market The first step in developing a competitive retailing strategy is to select a target market. This choice requires careful evaluation of the size and profit potential of the chosen market segment and the current level of competition for the segment's business. Bargain stores such as Dollar General target the price-conscious consumer, for example, while convenience stores like 7-Eleven target consumers who want an easy way to purchase items they buy frequently. As Baby Boomers get older, many suffer from mild-to-moderate hearing loss. California-based Soundhawk is a wearable ear computer created by a physician. The device is a polished curve piece of black plastic, indistinguishable from a Bluetooth phone headset, and carries no stigma of the old-fashioned hearing aids worn by previous generations. A Soundhawk wearer can create a personalized auditory profile with a smart phone app to adjust phone frequencies for better short-range conversations and less background noise.[25]

Selecting a Product Strategy After identifying a target market, the retailer must next develop a product strategy to determine the best mix of merchandise to carry to satisfy that market. Retail strategists must decide on the general product categories, product lines, and variety to offer. Sometimes that involves expanding the product mix and sometime it involves contracting it. Almost 20 years ago, Under Armour began making tee shirts to help athletes stay cool and dry. Since then, the company has expanded its brand to include women's and children's clothing, as well as football cleats and running shoes.[26]

Peapod's service strategy of selecting, packing, and delivering groceries has helped attract and retain customers.

Shaping a Customer Service Strategy A retailer's customer service strategy focuses on attracting and retaining target customers to maximize sales and profits. Some stores offer a wide variety of services, such as gift wrapping, alterations, returns, interior design services, and delivery. Other stores offer bare-bones customer service, stressing low price instead. Some grocery shoppers, for instance, find convenience online through a service such as Peapod, which handles product selection, packing, and delivery. Other shoppers choose to visit a supermarket and make their own selections. Or they can go to a discount supermarket like Iowa-based ALDI, where they not only assemble their orders but also bag their purchases.

Selecting a Pricing Strategy Retailers base their pricing decisions on the costs of purchasing products from other channel members and offering services to customers. Pricing can play a major role in consumers' perceptions of a retailer, and not just because they appreciate low prices. The grocery retailer Trader Joe's offers organic and gourmet foods under its own private labels at rock-bottom prices. Customers enjoy shopping for Trader Jose's Mexican specialties and Trader Darwin's nutritional supplements at prices lower than other gourmet or organic markets.[27] Pricing strategy is covered in more detail in Chapter 13.

Choosing a Location A good location often marks the difference between success and failure in retailing. The location decision depends on the retailer's size, financial resources, product offerings, competition, and, of course, its target market. Traffic patterns, the visibility of the store's signage, parking, and the location of complementary and competing stores also influence the choice of a retail location.

A *planned shopping center* is a group of retail stores planned, coordinated, and marketed as a unit to shoppers in a geographical trade area. By providing convenient locations with free parking, shopping centers have replaced downtown shopping in many urban areas. But time-pressed consumers are increasingly looking for more efficient ways to shop, including catalogs, online retailers, and one-stop shopping at large free-standing stores such as Walmart Supercenters. To lure more customers, shopping centers are recasting themselves as entertainment destinations, with movie theaters, art displays, carousel rides, and musical entertainment. The giant Mall of America in Bloomington, Minnesota, features a seven-acre amusement park and an aquarium.

Solving an Ethical Controversy

Teens at the Mall: Good or Bad for Business?

Some shopping malls have banned unsupervised minors on weekend evenings. Others have initiated a total ban on unaccompanied teens. However, teenagers also spend money at malls. Some merchants who once complained about groups of unsupervised teens have now pinned their revenue hopes on these young spenders.

Should malls lift curfews on teenagers to boost business?

PRO

1. Some studies suggest teenage spending has increased, contrary to expectations after several years of declining figures.

2. Most teenagers are well behaved and should not be banned as a group because of the bad behavior of a few.

CON

1. Some merchants are still wary because some parents ignore their children's bad behavior.

2. The attractiveness of teenage spending has to be weighed against the reality of crowd behavior. Malls provide a venue for teen fights, flash mobs, and other disturbances.

Summary

Just as adults spent much less during the recent recession, so did their children. Teenagers have now returned in some measure to previous spending habits, particularly if they are carrying credit cards. Mall owners and civic leaders will need to find a balance between maintaining order and encouraging tomorrow's consumers.

Sources: Thomas Tracy and Mark Morales, "Brooklyn Mall Lifts Ban on Teens after Post-Christmas Flash Mob Trouble," *New York Daily News*, accessed February 15, 2014, www.nydailynews.com; Pattie Kate, "What Are the Characteristics of Teenage Spending?," *wiseGEEK*, accessed February 14, 2014, www.wisegeek.com; Andrea Chang, "Free-Spending Teens Return to Malls," *Los Angeles Times*, accessed February 14, 2014, http://articles.latimes.com; Erica Shaffer, "City Leaders Recommend Total Ban of Unsupervised Teens at Mall," *WTOL*, accessed February 14, 2014, www.wtol.com; Fran Daniel, "Mall May Limit Teens: Policy Expected to Require Parental Supervision on Friday, Saturday Evenings," *Winston-Salem Journal*, accessed February 14, 2014, www2.journalnow.com.

Shopping malls are well-known magnets for teens, who often meet there to socialize with friends. Businesses want to welcome their teen customers, but sometimes the cluster of teens hanging around the mall causes difficulties for other customers and some retailers, as described in the "Solving an Ethical Controversy" feature.

Large regional malls have witnessed a shift in shopping center traffic to smaller strip centers, name-brand outlet centers, and *lifestyle centers*, open-air complexes containing retailers that often focus on specific shopper segments and product interests. In recent years, lifestyle centers grew at a rate of more than 30 percent.[28]

Building a Promotional Strategy A retailer designs advertisements and develops other promotions to stimulate demand and to provide information such as the store's location, merchandise offerings, prices, and hours. When a recent year proved to be difficult, Starbucks turned to social media for a new promotional strategy. The chain launched MyStarbucksIdea .com, a forum where customers could ask questions, offer suggestions, and even voice their dislikes. The site's more than 180,000 registered users have offered more than 100,000 ideas, of which 150 have been implemented. The Starbucks Facebook page has a staggering 36 million fans; the chain also has nearly 7 million Twitter followers.[29]

Nonstore retailers provide their phone numbers and website addresses. More recently, online retailers have scaled back their big advertising campaigns and worked to build traffic through word of mouth and clever promotions. Promotional strategy is also discussed in depth in Chapter 13.

Creating a Store Atmosphere A successful retailer closely aligns its merchandising, pricing, and promotion strategies with *store atmospherics*, the physical characteristics of a store and its amenities, to influence consumers' perceptions of the shopping experience. Atmospherics begin with the store's exterior, which may use eye-catching architectural elements and signage to attract customer attention and interest. Interior atmospheric elements include store layout, merchandise presentation, lighting, color, sound, and cleanliness. A high-end store such as Nordstrom, for instance, features high ceilings in selling areas that spotlight tasteful and meticulously cared-for displays of carefully chosen items of obvious quality. Dick's Sporting Goods, on the other hand, carries an ever-changing array of moderately priced clothing and gear in its warehouse-like settings furnished with industrial-style display hardware.

Assessment Check ☑

1. Define *retailer*.
2. What are the elements of a retailer's marketing strategy?

⌐7⌐ Distribution Channel Decisions and Logistics

Every firm faces two major decisions when choosing how to distribute its goods or services: selecting a specific distribution channel and deciding on the level of distribution intensity. In deciding which distribution channel is most efficient, business managers need to consider four factors: the market, the product, the producer, and the competition. These factors are often interrelated and may change over time. In today's global business environment, strong relationships with customers and suppliers are important for survival. PortionPac, maker of concentrated cleaning solutions, distributes its products only to organizations. See the "Hit & Miss" feature for more details.

Selecting Distribution Channels

Market factors may be the most important consideration in choosing a distribution channel. To reach a target market with a small number of buyers or buyers concentrated in a geographical area, the most feasible alternative may be a direct channel. In contrast, if the firm must reach customers who are dispersed or who make frequent small purchases, then the channel may need to incorporate marketing intermediaries to make goods available when and where customers want them.

In general, standardized products or items with low unit values usually pass through relatively long distribution channels. On the other hand, products that are complex, expensive, custom made, or perishable move through shorter distribution channels involving few—or no—intermediaries. The increasing prevalence of e-commerce is resulting in changes in traditional distribution practices. The European Commission recently issued a set of rules, effective until 2022, that permit makers of goods with less than a 30 percent market share—usually high-end manufacturers—to block Internet-only retailers from carrying their products. The European Alliance—representing such luxury goods manufacturers as LVMH (Louis Vuitton Moët Hennessey), Gucci, and Burberry—lobbied for and welcomed the new rules as a way to protect the quality image of their products. Online-only retailers, such as Amazon, eBay, and their European counterparts, called for repeal of the bricks-and-mortar requirement and warned that some manufacturers would use the new rules to "restrict the availability" of their products online and thus keep prices high.[30]

Producers that offer a broad product line, with the financial and marketing resources to distribute and promote it, are more likely to choose a shorter channel. Instead of depending on marketing intermediaries, financially strong manufacturers with broad product lines typically use their own sales representatives, warehouses, and credit departments to serve both retailers and consumers.

In many cases, start-up manufacturers turn to direct channels because they can't persuade intermediaries to carry their products or because they want to extend their sales reach. Some

Chapter 12 *Product and Distribution Strategies*   **357**

Hit&Miss

PortionPac Makes More By Selling Less

Founded in 1964, Chicago-based PortionPac is committed to its business model of selling less. PortionPac manufactures cleaning products for commercial use. It sells its cleaning systems of environmentally friendly cleaning solutions in concentrated premeasured "doses" to ensure accurate and controlled use. Instead of producing cleaning solutions in large bottles that contain water as an ingredient, PortionPac delivers concentrated solutions in smaller bottles with instructions for dilution. Customers reuse the original bottle, refilling it each time with a packet of cleaning solution.

The company believes using less of a product is akin to recycling, and it has won several green business awards for its business practices, and sustainability awards for 13 of its 22 products. PortionPac customers—school districts, office managers, health care facilities, and state agencies—like the company's philosophy. They save money and minimize the health hazards associated with cleaning products. While PortionPac currently sells only to organizations, the firm's long-term strategy includes a plan for retail sales.

Questions for Critical Thinking

1. How does PortionPac's practice of selling a product in small, premeasured doses contribute to its product strategy?
2. What issues should PortionPac consider before making the decision to sell in the retail market?

Sources: Company website, www.portionpaccorp.com, accessed March 12, 2014; Hosea Sanders, "Less Is More for Green Business," *ABC News*, accessed March 12, 2014, http://abclocal.com; Leigh Buchanan, "The Un-Factory," *Inc.*, accessed March 12, 2014, www.inc.com.

---

companies employ direct channels to carry intangible goods as well. Based in New York City, Art Meets Commerce uses the Internet and social networking to promote small Broadway and off-Broadway shows with tight marketing budgets. The company posts short videos of its client shows on YouTube and takes advantage of Facebook and Twitter to amplify traditional word-of-mouth publicity. When celebrities see the shows and post favorable tweets, their followers may feel encouraged to see the shows too.[31]

Competitive performance is the fourth key consideration when choosing a distribution channel. A producer loses customers when an intermediary fails to achieve promotion or product delivery. Channels used by established competitors as well as new market entries also can influence decisions. Sometimes a joint venture between competitors can work well. Topshop, a trendy UK-based multinational retailer, has partnered with Nordstrom to sell clothing, shoes, and cosmetics through the department store as a store-within-a-store concept. There will be close to 70 Topshop stores within Nordstrom in key markets over the next several years. Topshop management cites Nordstrom's multichannel retail presence as the reason for the partnership.[32]

Selecting Distribution Intensity

A second key distribution decision involves *distribution intensity*—the number of intermediaries or outlets through which a manufacturer distributes its goods. Only one BMW dealership may be operating in your immediate area, but you can find Coca-Cola everywhere—in supermarkets, convenience stores, gas stations, vending machines, and restaurants. BMW has chosen a different level of distribution intensity than that used for Coca-Cola. In general, market coverage varies along a continuum with three different intensity levels:

1. *Intensive distribution* involves placing a firm's products in nearly every available outlet. Generally, intensive distribution suits low-priced convenience goods such as milk, newspapers, and soft drinks. This kind of market saturation requires cooperation by many intermediaries, including wholesalers and retailers, to achieve maximum coverage.

2. *Selective distribution* is a market-coverage strategy in which a manufacturer selects only a limited number of retailers to distribute its product lines. Selective distribution can reduce total marketing costs and establish strong working relationships within the channel.

358   **Part 4** *Marketing Management*

3. *Exclusive distribution*, at the other end of the continuum from intensive distribution, limits market coverage in a specific geographical region. The approach suits relatively expensive specialty products such as Rolex watches. Retailers are carefully selected to enhance the product's image to the market and to ensure that well-trained personnel will contribute to customer satisfaction. Although producers may sacrifice some market coverage by granting an exclusive territory to a single intermediary, the decision usually pays off in developing and maintaining an image of quality and prestige.

When companies are offloading excess inventory, even high-priced retailers may look to discounters to help them clear the merchandise from their warehouses. To satisfy consumers' taste for luxury goods, designer outlet malls offer shoppers a chance to buy status items at lower prices. Chicago Premium Outlets features 120 stores carrying such upscale brands as Michael Kors, Armani Exchange, and Diesel. Similar centers include Desert Hills Premium Outlets in California, Las Vegas Premium Outlets, and Seattle Premium Outlets.[33]

Selective distribution is a market-coverage strategy in which a manufacturer selects only a limited number of retailers to distribute its product lines. This strategy is used by Honda to distribute its ATVs.

Logistics and Physical Distribution

A firm's choice of distribution channels creates the final link in the **supply chain**, the complete sequence of suppliers that contribute to creating a good or service and delivering it to business users and final consumers. The supply chain begins when the raw materials used in production are delivered to the producer and continues with the actual production activities that create finished goods. Finally, the finished goods move through the producer's distribution channels to end customers.

The process of coordinating the flow of goods, services, and information among members of the supply chain is called **logistics**. The term originally referred to strategic movements of military troops and supplies. Today, however, it describes all of the business activities involved in the supply chain with the ultimate goal of getting finished goods to customers.

Physical Distribution A major focus of logistics management—identified earlier in the chapter as one of the two basic dimensions of distribution strategy—is *physical distribution*, the activities aimed at efficiently moving finished goods from the production line to the consumer or business buyer. As Figure 12.9 shows, physical distribution is a broad concept that includes transportation and numerous other elements that help link buyers and sellers. An effectively managed physical distribution system can increase customer satisfaction by ensuring reliable movements of products through the supply chain. For instance, Walmart studies the speed with which goods can be shelved once they arrive at the store because strategies that look efficient at the warehouse, such as completely filling pallets with goods, can actually be time-consuming or costly in the aisles.

Radio-frequency identification (RFID) technology relies on a computer chip implanted somewhere on a product or its packaging that emits a low-frequency radio signal identifying the item. The radio signal doesn't require a line of sight to register on the store's computers the way a bar code does, so a hand-held RFID reader can scan crates and cartons before they are unloaded. Because the chip can store information about the product's progress through the distribution channel, retailers can efficiently manage inventories, maintain stock levels, reduce loss, track stolen goods, and cut costs. The technology is similar to that already used to identify

supply chain complete sequence of suppliers that contribute to creating a good or service and delivering it to business users and final consumers.

logistics process of coordinating the flow of goods, services, and information among members of the supply chain.

Chapter 12 *Product and Distribution Strategies*   **359**

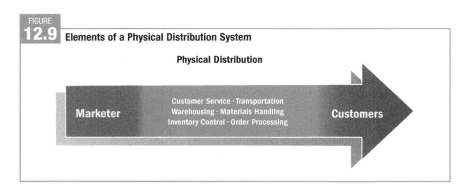

FIGURE 12.9 Elements of a Physical Distribution System

Physical Distribution

Marketer

Customer Service · Transportation
Warehousing · Materials Handling
Inventory Control · Order Processing

Customers

lost pets and speeding vehicles through toll booths. Walmart, Target, the U.S. Department of Defense, and the German retailer Metro Group already require their suppliers to use RFID technology. The U.S. Army is now using solar power to activate battery-powered RFIDs, which are particularly useful in remote areas. Automakers are also using RFID technology to improve their production processes by tracking parts and other supplies. A new version of the RFID chip can be printed on paper or plastic. RFID technology brings with it privacy and counterfeiting concerns. However, one company has developed a process that uses unique silicon "fingerprints" to generate unclonable RFID chips.[34]

Warehousing is the physical distribution activity that involves the storage of products. *Materials handling* is moving items within factories, warehouses, transportation terminals, and stores. Inventory control involves managing inventory costs, such as storage facilities, insurance, taxes, and handling. The physical distribution activity of *order processing* includes preparing orders for shipment and receiving orders when shipments arrive.

The wide use of electronic data interchange (EDI) and the constant pressure on suppliers to improve their response time have led to **vendor-managed inventory**, in which the producer and the retailer agree that the producer (or the wholesaler) will determine how much of a product a buyer needs and automatically ship new supplies when needed.

The form of transportation used to ship products depends primarily on the kind of product, the distance involved, and the cost. The logistics manager can choose from a number of companies and modes of transportation. As Table 12.3 shows, the five major transport modes are—in order of total expenditures—trucks (with about 75 percent of total expenditures), railroads (approximately 12 percent), water carriers (6 percent), air freight (4 percent), and

vendor-managed inventory process in which the producer and the retailer agree that the producer (or the wholesaler) will determine how much of a product a buyer needs and automatically ship new supplies when needed.

TABLE 12.3 Comparison of Transportation Modes

MODE	SPEED	DEPENDABILITY IN MEETING SCHEDULES	FREQUENCY OF SHIPMENTS	AVAILABILITY IN DIFFERENT LOCATIONS	FLEXIBILITY IN HANDLING	COST
Truck	Fast	High	High	Very extensive	Average	High
Rail	Average	Average	Low	Low	High	Average
Water	Very slow	Average	Very low	Limited	Very high	Very low
Air	Very fast	High	Average	Average	Low	Very high
Pipeline	Slow	High	High	Very limited	Very Low	Low

pipelines (3 percent). The faster methods typically cost more than the slower ones. Speed, reliable delivery, shipment frequency, location availability, handling flexibility, and cost are all important considerations when choosing the most appropriate mode of transportation.

About 26.4 million trucks operate in the United States, carrying most finished goods all or part of the way to the consumer. Nearly 3 million of these are tractor trailers.[35] But railroads, which compete with many truck routes despite their recent loss of market share, are a major mode of transportation. The 565 freight railroads in the United States operate across more than 162,000 miles of track and earned more than $67 billion in revenues. A freight train needs only 1 gallon of diesel fuel to transport 1 ton of cargo almost 484 miles.[36]

Customer Service Customer service is a vital component of both product and distribution strategies. *Customer service standards* measure the quality of service a firm provides to its customers. Managers frequently set quantitative guidelines—for example, that all orders be processed in less than 24 hours after they are received or that salespeople approach shoppers within two minutes after they enter the store. Sometimes customers set their own service standards and choose suppliers that meet or exceed them.

The customer service components of product strategy include warranty and repair service programs. *Warranties* are firms' promises to repair a defective product, refund money paid, or replace a product if it proves unsatisfactory. Repair services are also important. Consumers want to know that help is available if something goes wrong. Those who shop for computers or tablets, for example, often choose retailers that not only feature low prices but also offer repair services and tech support centers. Products with inadequate service backing quickly disappear from the market as a result of word-of-mouth criticism.

Consumers' complaints of the impersonal service they received at websites led e-commerce retailers to take a number of steps to "humanize" their customer interactions and deal with complaints. Many websites contain "live chat" features that link companies to visitors in real time with the ability to answer customer questions and provide support.

Assessment Check ✓

1. What is distribution intensity?
2. Define *supply chain.*
3. What do customer service standards measure?

What's Ahead

This chapter covered two of the elements of the marketing mix: product and distribution. It introduced the key marketing tasks of developing, marketing, and packaging want-satisfying goods and services. It also focused on the three major components of an organization's distribution strategy: the design of efficient distribution channels; wholesalers and retailers who make up many distribution channels; and logistics and physical distribution. We now turn to the remaining two—promotion and pricing—in Chapter 13.

Chapter in Review

▊ Summary of Learning Objectives

⌐1¬ **Explain product strategy and how to classify goods and** └ ┘ **services.**

A product is a bundle of physical, service, and symbolic attributes designed to satisfy consumer wants. The marketing conception of a product includes the brand, product image, warranty, service attributes, packaging, and labeling, in addition to the physical or functional characteristics of the good or service.

Goods and services can be classified as consumer (B2C) or business (B2B) products. Consumer products are those purchased by ultimate consumers for their own use. They can be convenience products, shopping products, or specialty products, depending on consumer habits in buying them. Business products are those purchased for use either directly or indirectly in the production of other goods and services for resale. They can be classified as installations, accessory equipment, component parts and materials, raw materials, and supplies. This classification is based on how the items are used and product characteristics. Services can be classified as either consumer or business services.

A product mix is the assortment of goods and services a firm offers to individual consumers and B2B users. A product line is a series of related products.

Assessment Check Answers

1.1 How do consumer products differ from business products? Consumer products, such as personal-care items, are sold to end users. Business products, such as copying machines, are sold to firms or organizations.

1.2 Differentiate among convenience, shopping, and specialty products. Convenience products are items the consumer seeks to purchase frequently, immediately, and with little effort. Shopping products are typically purchased after the buyer has compared competing products in competing stores. Specialty products are those a purchaser is willing to make a special effort to obtain.

⌐2⌐ Briefly describe the four stages of the product life cycle.

Every successful new product passes through four stages in its product life cycle: introduction, growth, maturity, and decline. In the introduction stage, the firm attempts to elicit demand for the new product. In the product's growth stage, sales climb, and the company earns its initial profits. In the maturity stage, sales reach a saturation level. In the decline stage, both sales and profits decline. Marketers sometimes employ strategies to extend the product life cycle, including increasing the frequency of use, adding new users, finding new uses for the product, and changing package size, labeling, or product quality.

The new-product development process for most products has six stages: idea generation, screening, concept development and business analysis, product development, test marketing, and commercialization. At each stage, marketers must decide whether to continue to the next stage, modify the new product, or discontinue the development process. Some new products skip the test marketing stage due to the desire to quickly introduce a new product with excellent potential, a desire not to reveal new-product strategies to competitors, and the high costs involved in limited production runs.

Assessment Check Answers

2.1 What are the stages of the product life cycle? In the introduction stage, the firm attempts to promote demand for the new product. In the product's growth stage, sales climb, and the company earns its initial profits. In the maturity stage, sales reach a saturation level. In the decline stage, both sales and profits decline.

2.2 What are the marketing implications of each stage? Marketers sometimes employ strategies to extend the product

life cycle, including increasing frequency of use, adding new users, finding new uses for the product, and changing package size, labeling, or product design.

⌐3⌐ Discuss product identification.

Products are identified by brands, brand names, and trademarks, which are important elements of product images. Effective brand names are easy to pronounce, recognize, and remember, and they project the right images to buyers. Brand names cannot contain generic words. Under certain circumstances, companies lose exclusive rights to their brand names if common use makes them generic terms for product categories. Some brand names belong to retailers or distributors rather than to manufacturers. Brand loyalty is measured in three degrees: brand recognition, brand preference, and brand insistence. Some marketers use family brands to identify several related items in a product line. Others employ individual branding strategies by giving each product within a line a different brand name.

Assessment Check Answers

3.1 Differentiate among a brand, a brand name, and a trademark. A brand is a name, term, sign, symbol, design, or some combination thereof used to identify the products of one firm and differentiate them from competitive offerings. A brand name is that part of the brand consisting of words or letters used to identify and distinguish the firm's offerings from those of competitors. A trademark is a brand that has been given legal protection.

3.2 Define *brand equity*. Brand equity is the added value that a respected and successful name gives to a product.

⌐4⌐ Outline the major components of an effective distribution strategy.

A firm must consider whether to move products through direct or indirect distribution. Once the decision is made, the company needs to identify the types of marketing intermediaries, if any, through which it will distribute its goods and services. The Internet has made direct distribution an attractive option for many retail companies. Another component is distribution intensity. The business must decide on the amount of market coverage—intensive, selective, or exclusive—needed to achieve its marketing strategies. Finally, attention must be paid to managing the distribution channel. It is vital to minimize conflict between channel members.

Assessment Check Answers

4.1 Define *distribution channels*. Distribution channels are the paths that products, and legal ownership of them, follow from producer to consumer or business user.

4.2 What is a marketing intermediary? A marketing intermediary (also called a middleman) is a business firm that moves goods between producers and consumers or business users.

^{**5**} Explain the concept of wholesaling.

Wholesaling is the process of selling goods primarily to retailers, other wholesalers, or business users and is a crucial part of the distribution channel for many products. Wholesaling intermediaries can be classified on the basis of ownership; some are owned by manufacturers, some are owned by retailers, and others are independently owned. Firms operate two main types of manufacturer-owned wholesaling intermediaries: sales branches and sales offices. An independent wholesaling intermediary is a business that represents a number of different manufacturers and makes sales calls on retailers, manufacturers, and other business accounts. Independent wholesalers are classified as either merchant wholesalers or agents and brokers, depending on whether they take title to the products they handle. Retailers sometimes band together to form their own wholesaling organizations. Such organizations can take the form of either a buying group or a cooperative.

Assessment Check Answers

5.1 Define *wholesaling*. Wholesaling is the process of selling goods primarily to retailers, other wholesalers, or business users.

5.2 Differentiate between a merchant wholesaler and an agent or broker in terms of title to the goods. Merchant wholesalers are independently owned wholesaling intermediaries that take title to the goods they handle. Agents and brokers may or may not take possession of the goods they handle, but they never take title, working mainly to bring buyers and sellers together.

^{**6**} Describe how to develop a competitive retail strategy.

Retailers, in contrast to wholesalers, are distribution channel members that sell goods and services to individuals for their own use rather than for resale. Nonstore retailing includes four forms: direct-response retailing, Internet retailing, automatic merchandising, and direct selling. Store retailers range in size from tiny newsstands to multistory department stores and warehouse-like retailers such as Sam's Club.

The first step in developing a competitive retailing strategy is to select a target market. Next, the retailer must develop a product strategy to determine the best mix of merchandise to carry to satisfy that market. A retailer's customer service strategy focuses on attracting and retaining target customers to maximize sales and profits. Retailers base their

pricing decisions on the costs of purchasing products from other channel members and offering services to customers. A good location often marks the difference between success and failure in retailing. A retailer designs advertisements and develops other promotions to stimulate demand and to provide information such as the store's location, merchandise offerings, prices, and hours. A successful retailer closely aligns its merchandising, pricing, and promotion strategies with store atmospherics, the physical characteristics of a store and its amenities, to influence consumers' perceptions of the shopping experience.

Assessment Check Answers

6.1 Define *retailer*. Retailers are distribution channel members that sell goods and services to individuals for their own use rather than for resale.

6.2 What are the elements of a retailer's marketing strategy? After identifying their target markets, retailers must choose merchandising, customer service, pricing, and location strategies that will attract customers in those market segments.

^{**7**} Identify distribution channel decisions and logistics.

Marketers can choose either a direct distribution channel, which moves goods directly from the producer to the consumer, or indirect distribution channels, which involve marketing intermediaries in the paths through which products—and legal ownership of them—flow from producer to the final customer. Ideally, the choice of a distribution channel should support a firm's overall marketing strategy. Before selecting distribution channels, firms must consider their target markets, the types of goods being distributed, their own internal systems and concerns, and competitive factors.

Assessment Check Answers

7.1 What is distribution intensity? Distribution intensity is the number of intermediaries or outlets through which a manufacturer distributes its goods.

7.2 Define *supply chain*. A supply chain is the complete sequence of suppliers that contribute to creating a good or service and delivering it to business users and final consumers.

7.3 What do customer service standards measure? Customer service standards measure the quality of service a firm provides to its customers.

▧ Business Terms You Need to Know

product 336	brand name 343	physical distribution 347
product line 338	trademark 343	wholesaler 350
product mix 338	brand equity 345	retailer 352
product life cycle 338	category advisor 346	supply chain 359
test marketing 342	distribution strategy 347	logistics 359
brand 343	distribution channels 347	vendor-managed inventory 360

Review Questions

1. Classify each of the following business-to-consumer (B2C) and business-to-business (B2B) goods and services. Then choose one and describe how it could be classified as both.

    a. *Runner's World* or *Esquire* magazine

    b. six-pack of apple juice

    c. limousine service

    d. tech support for a communications system

    e. golf course

    f. Thai restaurant

2. What is the relationship between a product line and a product mix? Give an example of each.

3. Identify and briefly describe the six stages of new-product development.

4. What is the difference between a manufacturer's brand and a private brand? What is the difference between a family brand and an individual brand?

5. What are the three stages of brand loyalty? Why is the progression to the last stage so important to marketers?

6. What are the advantages of direct distribution? When is a producer most likely to use direct distribution?

7. What is the wheel of retailing? How has the Internet affected the wheel of retailing?

8. Identify and briefly describe the four different types of nonstore retailers. Give an example of at least one type of good or service that would be suited to each type of nonstore retailer.

9. What are the three intensity levels of distribution? Give an example of two products for each level.

10. Define *logistics*. How does it relate to physical distribution?

Projects and Teamwork Applications

1. On your own or with a classmate, choose one of the following goods or services. Decide whether you want to market it as a consumer product or a business product. Now create a brand name to convey the right image to the buyer, and one that links the product with its positioning strategy.

    a. lawnmower repair service

    b. health foods store

    c. soft drink

    d. English-language class

    e. accounting firm

2. Choose one of the following products that is either in the maturity or decline stage of its life cycle (or select one of your own), and develop a marketing strategy for extending its life cycle.

    a. popcorn

    b. fast-food restaurant chain

    c. newspaper

    d. music CDs

    e. paper stationery or notecards

3. Where do you do most of your shopping—in stores or online? Choose your favorite retailer and analyze why you like it. Outline your reasons for shopping there, then add two or three suggestions for improvement.

4. Choose one of the following products and select a distribution intensity for the product. Describe specifically where and how your product would be sold. Then describe the reasons for your strategy.

    a. line of furniture manufactured from recycled or reclaimed materials

    b. custom-designed jewelry

    c. house-painting service

    d. handicraft supplies

    e. talk radio show

Web Assignments

1. **Product classification.** Visit the website of Kraft Foods Group and click on the "products" link to see the vast variety of items the company produces. Review chapter content about product classification and categorize the company's products.

   www.kraftrecipes.com/home.aspx

2. **Fair Packaging and Labeling Act.** You may not think about what is in your favorite candy bar or bag of chips, but the Fair Packaging and Labeling Act enacted more than 35 years ago regulates how "consumer commodities" are labeled, including ingredients and name and place of the product's manufacturer, packer, or distributor. Compare a product's label to the requirements listed on the government website and discuss some of the regulations used to prevent consumer deception. What are some newer labeling requirements under review by the Federal Trade Commission?

   www.ftc.gov/enforcement/rules
   /rulemaking-regulatory-reform-proceedings
   /fair-packaging-labeling-act

3. **Interbrand and the World's Best Global Brands.** Go to the Interbrand website and research the "Best Global Brands" for the most recent year. Choose three of your favorite brands and evaluate their ranking over the last three years. Discuss and review how the brands were chosen for the list by clicking on the "Methodology and Applications" link.

   www.interbrand.com/en/

Note: Internet web addresses change frequently. If you don't find the exact sites listed, you may need to access the organization's home page and search from there or use a search engine such as Google or Bing.

"Chucks" Brand Appeal from Court to Street

CASE 12.1

Boston-based Converse is one of the most iconic brands in existence today. The plain canvas sneaker, called "Chucks" for short, has remained unchanged for more than 100 years. The shoe is named after a legendary Converse salesman, Chuck Taylor, who went from town to town running basketball clinics and encouraging players to wear the brand, which became a staple among pro basketball players.

In today's race for innovation among shoemakers to produce lighter, stronger, warmer, and even cooler products, Converse has held its own. In fact, its most recent quarterly sales increase was a healthy 16 percent. However, the brand's growth has not always been fast. In the 1970s, the brand lost out to rivals like Adidas and Pro-Keds and fell into a further slump in the 1980s when Nike and Michael Jordan teamed up to dominate the market with its legendary Air Jordan shoes. In bankruptcy by 2001, Converse was rescued by Nike two years later for a purchase price of $305 million and remains the only brand in Nike's lineup where the Nike name or swoosh is nowhere to be found.

What makes the shoe particularly unique is its simple retro look and feel. The company has maintained a countercultural appeal by dropping its all-American image of an on-court shoe in favor of attracting a newer, Millennial audience. Advertising images include rebellious icons of yesteryear, like James Dean and Janis Joplin.

The company's chief marketing officer says the brand's universal appeal explains why the company can sell so many varieties to its culturally diverse audience. Nike's CEO says Converse is a brand that has been bringing energy and style to consumers for many years, and it's all because of one steadfast salesman, Chuck Taylor, who had a hand in creating a global brand.

Questions for Critical Thinking

1. What has Nike's branding strategy been with Converse? Why do you think Nike has chosen to hide any of its own branding on the Converse product?

2. What is it about the Converse brand that has allowed it to maintain its strong staying power in a highly competitive shoe market? Where is Converse in its product life cycle?

Sources: Company website, www.converse.com, accessed March 12, 2014; Laura Lorenzetti, "How Converse Went from Bankruptcy to a $1.4 Billion Business," *Quartz*, accessed March 12, 2014, http://qz.com; "Converse to Unveil Largest Inline Retail Store in San Francisco," *Business Wire*, accessed March 12, 2014, www.businesswire.com; Stephanie Kang, "Nike Takes Chuck Taylors from Antifashion to Fashionista," *The Wall Street Journal*, accessed March 12, 2014, http://online.wsj.com; Leslie Wayne, "For $305 Million, Nike Buys Converse," *The New York Times*, accessed March 12, 2014, www.nytimes.com.

Luxury Brands in China Slow Down

Several years ago, it was projected that about 55 percent of luxury-brand purchases would be made by Chinese consumers by 2020, and that was good news to luxury goods maker, Prada. The company already collects more than 40 percent of its global earnings from China, and Chinese consumers remain the largest nationality of luxury buyers worldwide.

As newly wealthy young Chinese consumers embraced a culture of spending, Prada reaped the benefits, with the country becoming the largest market for high-end watches, leather goods, designer clothing, cosmetics, and perfume. Chinese consumers often bought luxury goods abroad, citing lower prices, better selection, and better service in France, Italy, Great Britain, and Switzerland than they could find at home.

More recently, however, according to a study of the Chinese luxury goods market, the demand for luxury goods has softened, slowing revenue growth for companies in the luxury goods sector. One reason cited for the slowdown has to do with Chinese consumers, whose shopping habits have become increasingly complex and more sophisticated. Some Chinese consumers realize that demonstrating their uniqueness does not necessarily mean buying the luxury accessories that everyone else has. Instead, personalized luxury goods seem to be the driving force in this consumer group.

Questions for Critical Thinking

1. Given current market trends, what advice would you give Western luxury brands such as Prada, Burberry, Ferragamo, and Hugo Boss as they target Chinese luxury shoppers?

2. What does the luxury-buying trend suggest for Western manufacturers of ordinary consumer goods that want to do business in China?

Sources: Company website, "Mainland China Entering New Era of Luxury Cool Down, Finds Bain & Company's 2013 China Luxury Goods Market Study," www.bain.com, accessed March 12, 2014; "Prada Says 2014 Sales May Miss Estimates on China, Italy," *Bloomberg News,* accessed March 12, 2014, www.bloomberg.com; Yang Lina, "Chinese Holidayers Splurge on Luxury Goods Overseas," *Chinese Securities Journal,* accessed March 12, 2014, www.cs.com.cn; Wang Zhuoqiong, "Chinese Snap Up Luxury Products," *China Daily,* accessed March 12, 2014, www.chinadaily.com.

Secret Acres: Getting the Word Out

No matter how powerful they are, comic book heroes can't get themselves into bookstores—and readers' hands—without a little help. Leon Avelino and Barry Matthews, co-founders of Secret Acres, know that one of the greatest challenges of publishing is getting books onto the shelves and into readers' shopping carts. The task is even more difficult for small publishers—in this case, small publishers of comic books and graphic novels—because they don't have the wide distribution network of major publishers. But Avelino and Matthews, whose authors consider them the superheroes of comicbook publishing, are undaunted. They know what they are trying to achieve and work doggedly to make it happen.

"Distribution is a difficult thing right now," admits Matthews. "The publishing industry is changing and comic books themselves have a different distribution methodology and wholesale methodology than traditional books do." Unlike conventional book shops, comic book shops do not operate on a return basis. Conventional bookstores receive a small discount when they purchase books from a publisher, but then have the option to return any unsold books to the publisher. Comic book shops take a deeper discount but make no returns. Matthews also notes that currently there is only one major distributor of comic books—Diamond Distributors—which has the leverage to dictate much of what happens in the business of comic book distribution.

In addition, Matthews observes that Secret Acres' graphic novels could easily be sold to the general book market, but many general book distributors prefer not to deal with smaller publishers because they simply don't produce enough books to be profitable.

All of that said, Matthews explains that they are learning alternative ways to distribute their books. "Amazon is great," he says. "They make it very easy for smaller publishers. They treat your books as if they are Amazon books, giving them the sheen of being part of a larger retail channel." Amazon does take a significant cut of sales, but Matthews says it's worth it to broaden the distribution of

Secret Acres products. Of course, Secret Acres also sells its entire line directly through its website, along with some books from other independent authors and publishers. This sales method is the most profitable for Secret Acres. More importantly, it allows Matthews and Avelino to keep closer tabs on their readers.

Matthews explains that because orders are filled on an individual basis, he can slip promotional materials, notices of upcoming events or new books, and tie-ins right into the package of a customer whose preferences he knows. This one-on-one interaction helps in the management of customer relationships.

Matthews and Avelino also enjoy one other form of distribution—attending comic book conventions around the country, such as the Stumptown Comics Fest in Portland, Oregon. There, they have the opportunity to interact with readers, other publishers, comic book authors and artists, and even some smaller distributors who have begun to attend these events. They note that readers in particular love to meet the authors and artists. "It feeds the interest in what we're doing," says Matthews. While at an event, Matthews and Avelino try to carve out some time to meet with other small publishers. "A lot of small publishers are in the same position" with regard to distribution, Matthews explains. "So we have been talking with them to see if we can band together to share resources."

For the future, Matthews admits that he and Avelino have no idea how some of the new technologies, including e-readers, will ultimately affect distribution, but they plan to research the possibility of digitizing some of Secret Acres' titles for online distribution.

Despite its small size, Secret Acres' authors consider the firm a mighty one. Theo Ellsworth, author of such titles as *Capacity* and *Sleeper Car*, praises Secret Acres for its personal attention and efforts to market and distribute his books. "It feels good to have the distribution part in someone else's hands," says Ellsworth. He explains that having someone else take care of that aspect of publishing frees him up to concentrate on his art, producing more posters and books—which is, after all, the author's job.

Questions for Critical Thinking

1. Visit Secret Acres' website at www.secretacres.com to learn more about the firm's product line. Write a marketing blurb describing the line to a potential distributor.

2. What steps can Secret Acres take to develop brand loyalty and ultimately brand equity for its products?

3. How might Secret Acres expand its Internet retailing presence?

4. Secret Acres is a tiny firm with limited distribution. How can the company use customer service to create a competitive advantage, increase distribution, and help it grow?

Sources: Company website, www.secretacres.com, accessed February 17, 2014; Stumptown Comics Fest, www.stumptowncomics.com, accessed February 17, 2014; organization website, "Great Graphic Novels for Teens," www.ala.org, accessed February 17, 2014; Harry McCracken, "E-Readers May Be Dead, But They're Not Going Away Yet," *PC World*, accessed February 17, 2014, www.pcworld.com.

Learning Objectives

1. Discuss integrated marketing communications (IMC).
2. Summarize the different types of advertising.
3. Outline sales promotion.
4. Describe pushing and pulling strategies.
5. Discuss the pricing objectives in the marketing mix.
6. Outline pricing strategies.
7. Discuss consumer perceptions of prices.

Chapter 13

Promotion and Pricing Strategies

© weareadventurers/iStockphoto

Apple's Pricing Strategies Keep Profits Strong

Take a look at Apple's *Annual Report,* and you will see something pretty amazing. It is not the company's incredible new products or technical developments, nor is it the growth in Apple's retail presence or market penetration. For Apple, the most impressive item in its *Annual Report* is the amount of cash—more than $50 billion—generated from company operations in a recent year.

Part of Apple's financial success is due to its pricing strategy. Apple, under the late Steve Jobs and more recently with Tim Cook at the helm, seeks premium prices for its iconic brand. Take the iPad, for example. As the first major product in a new sector, the iPad was priced at levels that gave Apple significant profits. Apple's competitors, led by electronics giant Samsung, saw the tablet computing market grow rapidly and entered the sector in large numbers. Today there are many companies in the market, and even Android-powered tablets are under $200. As the market leader, it seems logical that Apple might lower its prices to keep market share. However, Apple has done little, if anything, to lower prices in an attempt to protect its position.

Industry analysts believe it was inevitable that Apple's market share would erode because less-expensive tablets entered the market; however, companies making the cheaper tablets operate on razor-thin margins that may not help overall profitability. Analysts also think that consumers recognize the value of Apple's overall brand and are willing to pay a premium for its products. As one analyst said, "Hardware profit plays a big role in Apple's success, enabling the design, durability, and performance innovations that, in turn, support Apple's premium pricing."

To maintain high volume and high margins is the goal of almost all companies. So far, Apple's success seems to be due in large part to being first to market with its tablet. Since the launch of the initial iPad, Apple has sold over 170 million tablets. In contrast, Samsung, with the second largest market share, has shipped about 64 million tablets since it entered the market about six months after Apple. Will Apple be able to sustain its profits? That's a significant challenge, but so far Apple's ability to develop exciting new products has been nothing short of amazing.[1]

Overview

This chapter focuses on the different types of promotional activities and the way prices are established for goods and services. Promotion is the function of informing, persuading, and influencing a purchase decision. This activity is as important to not-for-profit organizations as it is to profit-seeking companies.

Some promotional strategies try to develop *primary demand,* or consumer desire for a general product category. The objective of such a campaign is to stimulate sales for an entire industry so that individual firms benefit from this market growth. For more than a decade, one of the most recognized and well-respected marketing campaigns has been the national "Got Milk?" campaign. Print and television messages about the nutritional benefits of milk show various celebrities sporting milk moustaches. Other promotional campaigns aimed at increasing per-capita consumption have been commissioned by the California Strawberry Commission and the National Cattlemen's Beef Association.

Most promotional strategies, in contrast, seek to stimulate *selective demand*—desire for a specific brand. The San Francisco Giants try to stimulate loyalty with promotions like ballpark tours and their Annual Slumber Party. Country-western star Toby Keith promotes Ford F-150 trucks, which encourages his fans to choose that brand over competitors.

Most promotional strategies seek to stimulate *selective demand*—a desire for a specific brand. Country-western star Toby Keith encourages his fans to buy Ford F-150 trucks.

Marketers choose from among many promotional options to communicate with potential customers. Each marketing message a buyer receives—through a television or radio commercial, newspaper or magazine ad, website, direct-mail flyer, or sales call—reflects the product, place, person, cause, or organization promoted in the content. Through integrated marketing communications (IMC), marketers coordinate all promotional activities—media advertising, direct mail, personal selling, sales promotion, and public relations—to produce a unified, customer-focused promotional strategy. This coordination is designed to avoid confusing the consumer and to focus positive attention on the promotional message.

This chapter begins by explaining the role of IMC and then discusses the objectives of promotion and the importance of promotional planning. Next, it examines the components of the promotional mix: advertising, sales promotion, personal selling, and public relations. Finally, the chapter addresses pricing strategies for goods and services, as described in the chapter opener about Apple's products.

integrated marketing communications (IMC) coordination of all promotional activities— media advertising, direct mail, personal selling, sales promotion, and public relations—to produce a unified, customer-focused promotional strategy.

promotion function of informing, persuading, and influencing a purchase decision.

⌐1⌐ Integrated Marketing Communications

An **integrated marketing communications (IMC)** strategy focuses on customer needs to create a unified promotional message in the firm's ads, in-store displays, product samples, and presentations by company sales representatives. To gain a competitive advantage, marketers that implement IMC need a broad view of **promotion**. Media options continue to multiply, and marketers cannot simply rely on traditional broadcast and print media and direct mail. Plans must include multiple forms of customer contact. Packaging, store displays, sales promotions, sales presentations, and online and interactive media also communicate information about a brand or organization. With IMC, marketers create a unified personality and message for the good, brand, or service they promote. Coordinated activities also enhance the effectiveness of reaching and serving target markets.

370 **Part 4** *Marketing Management*

GoingGreen

Green Seal Certification for the Hotel Industry

What do you look for in a hotel—speedy check-in, free Wi-Fi, good security? What about indoor air quality?

More travelers than ever look for evidence their hotel is "green." In a survey of Expedia customers, 75 percent agreed that sustainability in the hospitality industry should be defined as building, furnishing, and operating hotels in ways that are better for the guest, better for the community, and better for the planet.

Many forms of green certification exist, but perhaps the most respected is Green Seal certification. Green Seal, a nonprofit organization, began in 1989 as the first tool for U.S. shoppers looking for reliably sustainable products. It now certifies 40 categories of goods and services, and since 1995 it has applied its rigorous science-based criteria to assess eco-friendly practices in the hotel industry.

"Green Seal is a trustworthy label guests are much more likely to be familiar with in the products they have in their homes," says its vice president.

Questions for Critical Thinking

1. What advantages can a hotel chain expect from green certification?

2. How might a hotel chain promote its Green Seal certification to prospective guests?

Sources: Scott Parisi and Ray Burger, "Green Hotel Certification Programs Snowball, Sparks Confusion," *Eco Green Hotel*, accessed February 21, 2014, www.ecogreenhotels.com; "Survey of Expedia Consumers Reveals That Hotels Can Drive Growth Through Sustainability But Consumer Benefits Are Critical," *PR Web*, accessed February 21, 2014, www.prweb.com; association website, www.greenseal.org, accessed February 21, 2014, "Green Seal," *Natural Resources Defense Council*, accessed February 21, 2014, www.nrdc.org.

Marketing managers set the goals and objectives for the firm's promotional strategy with overall organizational objectives and marketing goals in mind. Using these objectives, marketers weave the various elements of the strategy—personal selling, advertising, sales promotion, publicity, and public relations—into an integrated communications plan. This document becomes a central part of the firm's total marketing strategy to reach its selected target market. Feedback, including marketing research and sales reports, completes the system by identifying any deviations from the plan and suggesting improvements.

A recent campaign for Oreo cookies had a theme called "wonderfilled," a play on words that combines "wonder" and a reference to the cream filling found between two chocolate cookies. The integrated marketing campaign includes TV commercials that feature original songs, print advertisements, and a strong presence on Facebook, Twitter, and Instagram. The campaign follows a yearlong effort celebrating the iconic brand's 100th birthday with the theme "Celebrate the kid inside."[2] Some hotel chains have added eco-friendly strategies into their integrated marketing plans. See the "Going Green" feature for more.

The Promotional Mix

Just as every organization creates a marketing mix combining product, distribution, promotion, and pricing strategies, each also requires a similar mix to blend the many facets of promotion into a cohesive plan. The **promotional mix** consists of two components—personal and nonpersonal selling—that marketers combine to meet the needs of their firm's target customers and effectively and efficiently communicate its message to them. **Personal selling** is the most basic form of promotion: a direct person-to-person promotional presentation to a potential buyer. The buyer–seller communication can occur during a face-to-face meeting or via telephone, videoconference, or Skype. Salespeople represent their company and should demonstrate high standards of ethical behavior.

Nonpersonal selling consists of advertising, sales promotion, direct marketing, and public relations. Advertising is the best-known form of nonpersonal selling, but sales promotion accounts for about half of these marketing expenditures. Spending for sponsorships, which involves marketing messages delivered in association with another activity such as a golf tournament or a benefit concert, is on the rise as well. Lexus recently sponsored a Justin

promotional mix combination of personal and nonpersonal selling components designed to meet the needs of a firm's target customers and effectively and efficiently communicate its message to them.

personal selling the most basic form of promotion: a direct person-to-person promotional presentation to a potential buyer.

nonpersonal selling consists of advertising, sales promotion, direct marketing, and public relations.

Timberlake concert while using various social media platforms to showcase an all-new sports sedan, engaging the consumer segment the carmaker is trying to reach.[3]

Each component in the promotional mix offers its own advantages and disadvantages, as Table 13.1 demonstrates. By selecting the most effective combination of promotional mix elements, a firm may reach its promotional objectives. Spending within the promotional mix varies by industry. Manufacturers of many business-to-business (B2B) products typically spend more on personal selling than on advertising because those products—such as a new data security and off-site storage system—may require a significant investment. Consumer-goods marketers may focus more on advertising and sponsorships. Later sections of this chapter discuss how the parts of the mix contribute to effective promotion.

Objectives of Promotional Strategy

Promotional strategy objectives vary among organizations. Some use promotion to expand their markets, and others use it to maintain their current positions. As Figure 13.1 illustrates, common objectives include providing information, differentiating a product, increasing sales, stabilizing sales, and accentuating a product's value.

Marketers often pursue multiple promotional objectives at the same time because they may need to convey different messages to different audiences. To promote its customer relationship management (CRM) software services, California–based Salesforce.com has to convince business owners, who buy the software, and their employees, who use the software, that the product is a worthwhile investment. Marketers need to keep their firm's promotional objectives in mind at all times. Sometimes the objectives are obscured by a humorous, fast-paced, creative ad campaign. In this case, the message—or worse, the brand name or image—is lost. While funny ads are good at grabbing viewers' attention and bolstering the product's attributes, they are not necessarily effective in making viewers desire the product featured in the ad. A recent Huggies ad, "Baby Wets the Room," features a baby boy getting his diaper changed as he, in an exaggerated fashion, is shown spraying throughout the room like a fire hose. The unexpected humor of this ad, along with the dad's reaction, distracts the viewer from the product's attributes.[4]

TABLE

13.1 Comparing the Components of the Promotional Mix

COMPONENT	ADVANTAGES	DISADVANTAGES
Advertising	Reaches large consumer audience at low cost per contact Allows strong control of the message Message can be modified to match different audiences	Difficult to measure effectiveness Limited value for closing sales
Personal selling	Message can be tailored for each customer Produces immediate buyer response Effectiveness is easily measured	High cost per contact High expense and difficulty of attracting and retaining effective salespeople
Sales promotion	Attracts attention and creates awareness Effectiveness is easily measured Produces short-term sales increases	Difficult to differentiate from similar programs of competitors Nonpersonal appeal
Public relations	Enhances product or firm credibility Creates a positive attitude about the product or company	Difficult to measure effectiveness Often devoted to nonmarketing activities
Sponsorships	Viewed positively by consumers Enhances brand awareness	Difficult to control message

Providing Information A major portion of U.S. advertising is information oriented. Credit-card ads provide information about benefits and rates. Ads for hair-care products include information about benefits such as shine and volume. Ads for breakfast cereals often contain nutritional information. Television ads for prescription drugs, a nearly $3 billion industry, are sometimes criticized for relying on emotional appeals rather than providing information about the causes, risk factors, and especially the prevention of disease.[5] But print advertisements for drugs often contain an entire page of warnings, side-effects, and usage guidelines.

Differentiating a Product Promotion can also be used to differentiate a firm's offerings from the competition. Applying a concept called **positioning**, marketers attempt to establish their products in the minds of customers. The idea is to communicate to buyers meaningful distinctions about the attributes, price, quality, or use of a good or service.

Marketers of luxury goods position their products as upscale, expensive, high quality, and exclusive. But how do they position goods that are intended for the vast number of "ordinary" consumers? Retailers like Target, Gap, and H&M selling apparel to everyday consumers have had collaborations with a number of high-end brands like Neiman Marcus, Diane von Furstenberg, Missoni, and Valentino.[6]

FIGURE
13.1 Five Major Promotional Objectives

Increasing Sales Increasing sales volume is the most common objective of a promotional strategy. Luxury automakers like Cadillac, Lexus, Infiniti, and Mercedes-Benz are trying to lure younger customers by creating smaller, more performance-oriented car models. In its first year of sales, Mercedes sold more than 14,000 CLA-class cars—with one in five purchasers in their 20s—significantly younger than the majority of the brand's typical customers.[7]

Stabilizing Sales Sales stabilization is another goal of promotional strategy. Firms often use sales contests during slack periods, motivating salespeople by offering prizes such as vacations, TVs, smart phones, and cash to those who meet certain goals. Companies distribute sales promotion materials—such as calendars, pens, and notepads—to customers to stimulate sales during the off-season. Jiffy Lube puts that little sticker on your windshield to remind you when to schedule your car's next oil change—the regular visits help stabilize sales. A stable sales pattern brings several advantages. It evens out the production cycle, reduces some management and production costs, and simplifies financial, purchasing, and marketing planning. An effective promotional strategy can contribute to these goals.

Dorito's recent "Crash the Super Bowl" campaign was a global crowd-sourced ad competition. Consumers worldwide were asked to submit ads, and the ad with the most votes online won its creator a $1 million cash reward and ran during the Super Bowl.[8]

Accentuating the Product's Value Some promotional strategies enhance product values by explaining hidden benefits of ownership. Carmakers offer long-term warranty programs; life insurance companies promote certain policies as investments. The creation of brand awareness and brand loyalty also enhances a product's image and increases its desirability. Advertising with luxurious images supports the reputation of premium brands such as Jaguar, Tiffany, and Rolex.

positioning form of promotion in which marketers attempt to establish their products in the minds of customers by communicating to buyers meaningful distinctions about the attributes, price, quality, or use of a good or service.

Chapter 13 *Promotion and Pricing Strategies*

373

Promotional Planning

Today's marketers can promote their products in many ways, and the lines between the different elements of the promotional mix are blurring. Consider the practice of **product placement**. A growing number of marketers pay placement fees to have their products showcased in various media, ranging from newspapers and magazines to television and movies. The Superman movie, *Man of Steel*, holds the current record for the number of product placements, with more than 100 companies paying $160 million or about 75 percent of the film's total budget. Brands skillfully integrated into the movie include Sears, IHOP, and 7-Eleven. Product placement can be subtle, as shown in the TV series *24*, where the lead character, Jack Bauer, drives a Chevrolet. One of the longest running product placements is Coca-Cola on *American Idol*.[9]

Another type of promotional planning must be considered by firms with small budgets. **Guerrilla marketing** involves innovative, low-cost marketing efforts designed to get consumers' attention in unusual ways. Guerrilla marketing is an increasingly popular tactic for marketers, especially those with limited promotional budgets. Cathay Pacific, a Hong Kong airline, surprised travelers during a recent holiday season by staging a 300-person flash mob at Hong Kong International Airport, which included ground staff, cabin crew, and even pilots. The unannounced dance took place to the tune of "All I Want for Christmas Is You" in the middle of the busy airport.[10]

Marketers for larger companies have caught on and are using guerrilla approaches as well. In addition to online viral campaigns, there is a new breed of guerilla tactics being used by leading brands like Red Bull. Maker of energy drinks, Red Bull made a huge scene during a Formula 1 event when a driver made a pit stop in the London race. In another guerilla marketing move, Red Bull's space stunt, complete with the slogan, "Red Bull Gives You Wings," includes Felix Baumgartner's parachute jump from a capsule at the edge of space—24 miles above Roswell, New Mexico. Baumgartner's spacesuit was branded with Red Bull's logo, and the marketing event was viewed live by millions on YouTube.[11]

From this overview of the promotional mix, we now turn to discussions of each of its elements. The following sections detail the major components of advertising, sales promotion, personal selling, and public relations.

Assessment Check ✓

1. What is the objective of an integrated marketing communications program?
2. Why do firms pursue multiple promotional objectives at the same time?
3. What are product placement and guerrilla marketing?

Red Bull Stratos/AP Photos

Energy drink maker Red Bull used a space stunt as a guerilla marketing tactic to launch Felix Baumgartner from a capsule approximately 24 miles above New Mexico. Baumgartner's space suit was covered with Red Bull logos.

According to one survey, consumers receive from 3,000 to 20,000 marketing messages each day, many of them in the form of advertising.[12] Advertising is the most visible form of nonpersonal promotion—and the most effective for many firms. **Advertising** is paid nonpersonal communication usually targeted at large numbers of potential buyers. Although U.S. citizens often think of advertising as a typically American function, it is a global activity. In a recent year, global ad spending was expected to reach $500 billion—an all-time high. The surge is primarily a result of the growth of mobile technologies and the use of social media. Global ad spending is expected to reach levels experienced prior to the global recession. In addition, consumer electronics and technology is the fastest-growing ad category among the top 100 global firms.[13] The largest U.S. advertisers in a recent year include AT&T at $1.59 billion, Verizon at $1.43 billion, Chevrolet at $958 million, McDonald's at $957 million, and Geico at $921 million.[14]

Advertising expenditures vary among industries, companies, and media. The top five categories for global advertisers are consumer goods, health care, industry and services (business services, property, institutions, power, and water), media, and telecommunications. Personal care marketers make up 25 percent of global ad spending in a recent year, and the three biggest global advertisers are consumer product companies, Procter & Gamble, Unilever, and L'Oréal. Because advertising expenditures are so great, and because consumers around the world are bombarded with messages, advertisers need to be increasingly creative and efficient at attracting consumers' attention.[15]

Types of Advertising

The two basic types of ads are product and institutional advertisements. **Product advertising** consists of messages designed to sell a particular good or service. Advertisements for Chobani Greek yogurt, Apple iPads, and Capital One credit cards are examples of product advertising. **Institutional advertising** involves messages that promote concepts, ideas, philosophies, or goodwill for industries, companies, organizations, or government entities. Each year, the Juvenile Diabetes Research Foundation promotes its Walk for the Cure fund-raising event, and your college may place advertisements in local papers or news shows to promote its activities.

A form of institutional advertising that is growing in importance, **cause advertising**, promotes a specific viewpoint on a public issue as a way to influence public opinion and the legislative process about issues such as literacy, hunger and poverty, and alternative energy sources. Both not-for-profit organizations and businesses use cause advertising, sometimes called *advocacy advertising*. Singer-songwriter Alicia Keys is a global ambassador for Keep a Child Alive, a program that brings treatment, care, and support to families and children affected by HIV in sub-Saharan Africa.[16]

The Bill & Melinda Gates Foundation is a not-for-profit organization dedicated to raising public awareness and generating legislation and other efforts in the fight against poverty, lack of education, and disease. Funded through grants from the Gates family and investment guru Warren Buffett, the foundation operates in all 50 states, the District of Columbia, and more than 100 countries. Through well-publicized grants of $1.6 billion to the United Negro College Fund for its

advertising paid nonpersonal communication, usually targeted at large numbers of potential buyers.

product advertising consists of messages designed to sell a particular good or service.

institutional advertising involves messages that promote concepts, ideas, philosophies, or goodwill for industries, companies, organizations, or government entities.

cause advertising form of institutional advertising that promotes a specific viewpoint on a public issue as a way to influence public opinion and the legislative process.

© digitallife/Alamy Inc.

▤ Product advertising consists of messages designed to sell a particular good or service.

Millennium Scholars Program, 5,000 students are given the chance to graduate from more than 800 colleges throughout the United States.[17]

Advertising and the Product Life Cycle

Both product and institutional advertising fall into one of three categories based on whether the ads are intended to inform, persuade, or remind. A firm uses *informative advertising* to build initial demand for a product in the introductory phase of the product life cycle. Highly publicized new-product entries attract the interest of potential buyers who seek information about the advantages of the new products over existing ones, warranties provided, prices, and places that offer the new products. Ads for new smart phones boast of new features, colors, designs, and pricing options to attract new customers.

Persuasive advertising attempts to improve the competitive status of a product, institution, or concept, usually in the growth and maturity stages of the product life cycle. One of the most popular types of persuasive product advertising, *comparative advertising*, compares products directly with their competitors—either by name or by inference. Tylenol advertisements mention the possible stomach problems that the generic drug aspirin could cause, stating that its own pain reliever does not irritate the stomach. But advertisers need to be careful when they name competing brands in comparison ads because they might leave themselves open to controversy or even legal action by competitors. Notice that Tylenol does not mention a specific aspirin brand in its promotions.

Reminder-oriented advertising often appears in the late maturity or decline stages of the product life cycle to maintain awareness of the importance and usefulness of a product, concept, or institution. Triscuits have been around for a long time, but Nabisco attempts to enhance sales with up-to-date advertising that appeals to health and fitness-conscious consumers. The advertising mentions its no trans-fat formulations.

Advertising Media

Marketers must choose how to allocate their advertising budgets among various media. All media offer advantages and disadvantages. Cost is an important consideration in media selection, but marketers must also choose the media best suited for communicating their message. As Figure 13.2 indicates, the three leading media outlets for advertising are television, the Internet, and newspapers.

Advertising executives have observed that firms are rethinking traditional ad campaigns and incorporating new media, as well as updated uses of traditional media. Less than a decade ago, the Internet ranked sixth in global ad media behind TV, newspapers, magazines, radio, and outdoor advertising. Today, it is second behind television and ahead of newspapers. Global Internet ad spending has surpassed the 20 percent mark, and over the next several years, analysts expect the Internet to account for more than 27 percent of global ad spending.[18]

Television Television is still one of America's leading national advertising media. Television advertising can be classified as network, national, local, and cable ads. The four major national networks—ABC, CBS, NBC, and Fox—broadcast almost one-fifth of all television ads. Despite a decline in audience share and growing competition from cable, network television remains the easiest way for advertisers to reach large numbers of viewers—10 million to 20 million with a single commercial. Automakers, fast-food restaurants, and food manufacturers are heavy users of network TV advertising.

About 32 percent of U.S. households with TVs now subscribe to cable and broadband Internet connections. Cable viewers are drawn to

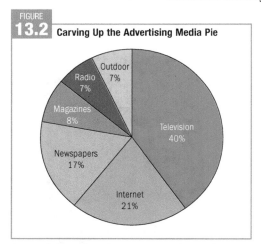

FIGURE 13.2 Carving Up the Advertising Media Pie

- Television 40%
- Internet 21%
- Newspapers 17%
- Magazines 8%
- Radio 7%
- Outdoor 7%

Source: "Advertising Expenditure Forecasts, December 2013," *ZenithOptimedia*, accessed February 20, 2014, www.zenithoptimedia.com; "TV Remains the Reigning Champ, But Display Internet Ads Are the MVPs of 3Q," *Nielsen Newswire*, accessed February 20, 2014, www.nielsen.com.

the more than 800 premium channels available through cable or satellite services. However, according to CitiResearch, broadcast and cable TV have recently experienced negative ratings growth. Nearly 5 million cable TV subscribers have gone elsewhere in the last five years. Says CitiResearch: "We're at the beginning of a major historical shift from watching TV to watching video—including TV shows and movies—on the Internet or on mobile devices. This is going to hurt cable TV providers."[19]

Cable TV, once a threat to broadcast TV, continues to experience competition from the pay-TV industry, like Showtime, AMC, and HBO. However, the pay-TV industry recently experienced its worst 12 months ever. The more recent trend, according to media specialists at ISI Group, is that people are giving up on cable TV as a standalone product, and the market is shifting in favor of companies like AT&T and Verizon, who offer TV as a package with high-speed Internet access. A growing number of viewers are drawn to online services and streaming sites like Netflix, Amazon Prime Instant Video, HuluPlus, YouTube, and iTunes. Cable companies and online services alike are spending millions for quality original shows like *Breaking Bad* and *Orange Is the New Black* and working directly with Hollywood on deals to deliver original programming.[20]

Although—or perhaps because—television reaches the greatest number of consumers at once, it is the most expensive advertising medium. The Super Bowl is widely known for its hefty advertising price tag—and its ability to reach over 100 million people in a three-hour period. Firms such as Budweiser, Frito-Lay, GoDaddy, T-Mobile, and The Coca-Cola Company paid as much as $4 million for a 30-second spot during a recent game, although some of the advertisers posted their ads online in the days leading up to the game. Intuit, a software developer for small businesses, recently sponsored a contest called "Small Business Big Game." The winner was awarded a 30-second commercial spot on the Super Bowl broadcast. Oakland, California–based GoldieBlox, maker of toys intended to get girls interested in science and engineering, has experienced phenomenal success as the winning entry, with more than 100 million viewers exposed to its unique products.[21]

Internet Advertising The digital ad market is growing faster than the rest of the advertising sector due mainly to the rising number of smart phones and tablets in use and increased social media usage. Total digital advertising, including mobile, rose to $27.3 billion in a recent year, making up almost 25 percent of all advertising revenues. Ad types include search and banner, the largest category, along with classified, rich media, video, lead generation, sponsorship, and e-mail.

Second to TV ads in terms of overall dollars, digital ad revenues are expected to reach $42 billion in a few years. Spending on ads delivered to desktops and laptops has slowed in comparison to U.S. mobile advertising, which has doubled over the last few years and is expected to top $10 billion in the not too distant future. The five companies that dominate digital advertising—Google, Yahoo, Facebook, Microsoft, and AOL—accounted for more than 64 percent of all digital ad expenditures in a recent year.[22]

Online advertising can take other forms as well. The Century Council, a nonprofit organization that combats drunk driving and underage drinking, recently launched a public-service campaign called "Ask, Listen, Learn." The organization has teamed up with two-time national champion figure skater Ashley Wagner, who emphatically tells teens to "Just say yes to a healthy lifestyle and no to underage drinking."[23]

Another example is *viral advertising*, which creates a message that is novel or entertaining enough for consumers to forward it to others, spreading it like a virus. The great advantage is that spreading the word online, which often relies on social networking sites such as Facebook, YouTube, and Twitter, costs the advertiser nothing. Although viral marketing can be risky, the best campaigns are edgy or funny. Dove soap's Beauty Sketches campaign, one of the biggest online viral sensations ever, sent the following message to women: "You are more beautiful than you think." The campaign compares a woman's description of herself to a description made by strangers through a series of sketches created by an FBI-trained artist. The stranger's description was typically more attractive than what the women themselves described—with the point being that women tend to be overly critical about the way they look. The viral campaign generated close to 30 million views and 660,000 Facebook shares during its first 10 days online.[24]

Newspapers As companies shift advertising dollars to other platforms, newspaper print advertising revenues continue to fall. Although one advantage of newspaper advertising is the ease with which marketers can tailor ads to local tastes and preferences, the downside is the relatively short lifespan of daily newspapers—people usually discard them soon after reading. Most newspapers now have websites and digital pay plans for viewing content, which have offset some of the declines in advertising dollars.[25]

Radio Despite the proliferation of other media, the average U.S. household owns a number of radios—including those in cars—a market penetration that makes radio, which relies on commercial sponsorship, an important advertising medium. Advertisers like the captive audience of listeners at work or as they commute to and from work. As a result, morning and evening drive-time shows command higher ad rates for airtime. In major markets, many stations, depending on their format, serve different demographic groups with targeted programming. Internet radio programming also offers opportunities for more focused targeting.

A recent study of several music-sharing sites reveals that more than half of people 12 years and older listen to online radio through a computer or smart phone. The top reasons cited for listening to online radio include better variety of music and the ability to skip songs.

Projected ad spending estimates for Internet radio, which includes news, sports, talk, and various music genres, will reach $1.31 billion over the next few years with the number of monthly listeners projected to be over 175 million. Recent marketing research shows that the percentage of people listening to Internet radio will soon surpass traditional platforms like AM and FM stations.[26]

Magazines Magazines include consumer publications and business trade journals. *Time*, *Reader's Digest*, and *Sports Illustrated* are consumer magazines, whereas *Advertising Age* and *Oil & Gas Journal* fall into the trade category.

Magazines can customize their publications and target advertising messages to different regions of the country. One method places local advertising in regional editions of the magazines. Other magazines attach wraparounds—half-size covers on top of full-size covers—to highlight articles or offers inside that relate to particular regions; different wraparounds appear in different parts of the country.

Magazines are a natural choice for targeted advertising. Media buyers study the demographics of subscribers and select magazines that attract the desired readers. American Express advertises in *Fortune* and *Bloomberg Businessweek* to reach businesspeople, while PacSun clothes and Proactiv skin medications are advertised in *Teen Vogue*. Magazine print ads have been driven by a recent shift from print editions to tablet editions.

Direct Mail About 90 percent of consumers receive catalogs through the mail. Approximately 12.5 billion catalogs were mailed last year, and the median annual expenditure per consumer was $347. Retailer J.Crew mailed 40 million catalogs in a recent year, and 30 percent of its revenues come from catalog and online sales. The huge growth in the variety of direct-mail offerings combined with the convenience they offer today's busy, time-pressed shoppers has made direct-mail advertising a multi-billion-dollar business. Even consumers who like to shop online often page through a catalog before placing an online order. Although direct mail is costly per person, a small business can afford a limited direct-mail campaign but not a television or radio ad. For businesses with a small advertising budget, a carefully targeted direct-mail effort can be highly effective. E-mail is a low-cost form of direct marketing. Companies like Amazon can target the most interested Internet users by offering website visitors an option to register to receive e-mail.[27]

Address lists are at the heart of direct-mail advertising. Using data-mining techniques to segment markets, direct-mail marketers create profiles that show the traits of consumers who

Hit&Miss

NBA Says Yes to Floor Ads

Instead of putting corporate logos on its jerseys, the NBA has allowed floor advertising on the courts of its 30 teams. The floor ad space is the idea of NBA commissioner Adam Silver, and it will be evaluated over time to determine if there will be a permanent location to sell ad space in the future. While corporate logos on NBA jerseys would generate about $100 million annually, the NBA management projects the "real estate" on the court floor to be worth far more money from television advertising and exposure.

NBA teams received approval to sell space on part of the basketball court known as the apron—space that covers the out-of-bounds area on the sidelines between the baselines, in front of team benches, and the coaches' box where teams already advertise their websites or Twitter handles. There is a catch, however. Company logos must be removable decals and can only be affixed during games televised locally.

So far, three teams have signed up. The Indiana Pacers signed a deal with the state's Economic Development Corporation; JP Morgan Chase will be on the floor at Madison Square Garden during New York Knicks games, and the Miami Heat has signed a deal with Samsung. Samsung is also one of the NBA's newest league partners, recently signing a reported three-year, $100 million deal.

While pricing varies among the 30 teams, it is rumored that one top franchise has an asking price of $3 million for the ad space on the court. Front Row Marketing Services, a company that tracks what appears on-screen in sports broadcasts, estimates that the prime floor space might fetch anywhere between $450,000 and $2.5 million per year, depending on the franchise.

Questions for Critical Thinking

1. Although ad space sales have been slow initially, observers believe that some teams are holding out for blue chip companies that appear to be a good fit for the team. What types of sponsors would be the best fit with top NBA franchises?

2. While this is a unique marketing opportunity for a corporate sponsor, some argue that the cost is on par with national advertising fees for games that will only be televised locally. So far, nationally televised regular season games, NBA All-Star weekend, and playoff games are not included. How would you evaluate the cost versus the marketing exposure?

Sources: Ira Boudway, "Slow Sales at the Outset for NBA Floor Space," *Bloomberg Businessweek,* accessed February 16, 2014, www.businessweek.com; Darren Rovell, "Limited Use of Ads on Court OK'd," *ESPN.com,* accessed February 16, 2014, http://espn.go.com; Philip Johnson, "The NBA Expects To Make $100 Million with On-Court Ads Next Season," *Business Insider,* accessed February 16, 2014, www.businessinsider.com.

---

are likely to buy their products or donate to their organizations. Catalog retailers sometimes experiment by sending direct-mail pieces randomly to people who subscribe to particular magazines. Next, they analyze the orders received from the mailings and develop profiles of purchasers. Finally, they rent lists of additional subscriber names that match the profiles they have developed.

Studies have shown that most U.S. consumers are annoyed by the amount of so-called junk mail they receive every day, including catalogs, advertising postcards, and flyers. Among Internet users, a major pet peeve is *spam,* or junk e-mail. Many states have outlawed such practices as sending e-mail promotions without legitimate return addresses, although it is difficult to track down and catch offenders.

The Direct Marketing Association (DMA; www.the-dma.org) helps marketers combat negative attitudes by offering its members guidelines on ethical business practices. The DMA also provides consumer information on its website, as well as services that enable consumers to opt out of receiving unsolicited offers. In addition, Federal Trade Commission regulations have taken effect for direct mail in certain industries. With the passage of the Credit CARD Act of 2009, credit-card issuers must follow stricter regulations in their direct mail practices. Unsolicited, preapproved applications sent to consumers must be accompanied by a prominent notice explaining how to get off the issuer's mailing list. Credit card offers are down about 33 percent from previous years.[28]

Outdoor Advertising In one recent year, outdoor advertising accounted for almost $6.7 billion in advertising revenues.[29] The majority of spending on outdoor advertising is for billboards, but spending for other types of outdoor advertising, such as signs in transit stations, stores, airports, and sports stadiums, is growing fast. To see how some NBA teams are using advertising on their courts, see the "Hit & Miss" feature. Advertisers are exploring new forms

Technology plays an important role in advertising, especially for outdoor media. This electronic billboard promotes the recent Super Bowl game held in New Jersey.

of outdoor media, many of which involve technology: computerized paintings; digital billboards; "trivision," which displays three revolving images on a single billboard; and moving billboards mounted on trucks. Other innovations include ads displayed on the Goodyear blimp, using an electronic system that offers animation and video.

Digital, electronic, or LED billboards, introduced less than two decades ago, provide an effective medium for advertisers who want to reach their segment with timely and relevant messages. Digital billboards are dynamic, with content updating every 4 to 10 seconds, with multiple advertisers and messages. Of the approximately 450,000 billboards in the United States, less than 1 percent have been converted to digital. Outdoor advertisers must comply with brightness, flashing, video, and scrolling industry practices based upon geographic location. Law enforcement and community groups have benefited from this medium, where announcements about public safety, community events, and even Amber Alerts can be made in real time.[30] Advertisers such as The Coca-Cola Company, StubHub, Jack in the Box, Chipotle, 7-Eleven, Apple Stores, Netflix, Tiffany, and Chanel had the greatest spending increases in outdoor advertising in the most recent year. Coca-Cola ads appear on an extensive digital network of billboards through CBS Outdoor Americas, a large outdoor advertiser.[31] Digital advertising is also available on taxi tops. With more than 15,000 yellow medallion taxis in New York City, the potential visibility is enormous. Clear Channel Outdoor Advertising offers its Digital Outdoor Networks, a complete line of electronic advertising.[32]

Sponsorship One trend in promotion offers marketers the ability to integrate several elements of the promotional mix. **Sponsorship** involves providing funds for a sporting or cultural event in exchange for a direct association with the event. Sports sponsorships dominate spending in this category at 70 percent, followed by entertainment at 10 percent, causes at 9 percent, and the arts at 4 percent. Spending on sponsorships is expected to soon increase to $20.6 billion.[33]

NASCAR, the biggest spectator sport in the United States, thrives on sponsorships. Sponsorships can run in the tens of millions of dollars. Hendricks Motorsports, based in North Carolina, is the wealthiest and most successful NASCAR team to date, with more than $125 million in sponsorships from firms such as PepsiCo, DuPont, Lowes, and Farmers Insurance Group.[34] Firms may also sponsor charitable or other not-for-profit awards or events. In conjunction with sports network ESPN, Gatorade sponsors its Player of the Year award, presented to the top male and female high school athletes who "strive for their best on and off the field."

Sponsors benefit in two major ways: exposure to the event's audience and association with the image of the activity. If a celebrity is involved, sponsors usually earn the right to use his or her name along with the name of the event in advertisements. They can set up signs at the event, offer sales promotions, and the like. Sponsorships play an important role in relationship marketing, bringing together the event, its participants, and the sponsoring firms.

Other Media Options As consumers filter out familiar advertising messages, marketers look for novel ways to catch their attention. In addition to the major media, firms promote through many other vehicles such as infomercials and specialized media.

Infomercials are a form of broadcast direct marketing, also called *direct-response television* (*DRTV*). These 30-minute programs resemble regular television programs but are devoted to selling goods or services such as exercise equipment, skin-care products, or kitchenware. The lengthy format allows an advertiser to thoroughly present product benefits, increase awareness,

sponsorship involves providing funds for a sporting or cultural event in exchange for a direct association with the event.

infomercials form of broadcast direct marketing; 30-minute programs that resemble regular TV programs, but are devoted to selling goods or services.

380   **Part 4** *Marketing Management*

and make an impact on consumers. Advertisers also receive immediate responses in the form of sales or inquiries because most infomercials feature toll-free phone numbers. Infomercial stars may become celebrities in their own right, attracting more customers wherever they go. The most effective infomercials tend to be for auto-care products, beauty and personal-care items, investing and business opportunities, collectibles, fitness and self-improvement products, and housewares and electronics.[35]

Advertisers use just about any medium they can find. They place messages on New York City MetroCard transit cards and toll receipts on the Massachusetts Turnpike. A more recent development is the use of ATMs for advertising. Some ATMs can play 15-second commercials on their screens, and many can print advertising messages on receipts. An ATM screen has a captive audience because the user must watch the screen to complete a transaction. Commonly found in supermarkets, floor graphics include brand and product advertisements on printed sheets of thin plastic adhered to the floor. Grocery ad sticks, which separate customers' groceries at the checkout, also contain advertisements, as do most supermarket shopping carts.[36]

3

Sales Promotion

Traditionally viewed as a supplement to a firm's sales or advertising efforts, sales promotion has emerged as an integral part of the promotional mix. Promotion now accounts for more than half as many marketing dollars as are spent on advertising, and promotion spending is rising faster than ad spending. **Sales promotion** consists of forms of promotion such as coupons, product samples, and rebates that support advertising and personal selling. Figure 13.3 highlights the most common forms of sales promotions.

Both retailers and manufacturers use sales promotions to offer consumers extra incentives to buy. Beyond the short-term advantage of increased sales, sales promotions can also help marketers build brand equity and enhance customer relationships. Examples include samples, coupons, contests, displays, trade shows, and dealer incentives. In a recent year, Samsung's advertising spending dropped, but the electronics giant spent 40 percent more on sales promotion than in a previous year.[37]

Consumer-Oriented Promotions

The goal of a consumer-oriented sales promotion is to get new and existing customers to try or buy products. In addition, marketers want to encourage repeat purchases by rewarding current users, increase sales of complimentary products, and boost impulse purchases. Total promotions spending in the United States reached $584 billion in a recent year, more than double the amount spent in a previous year.[38]

Premiums, Coupons, Rebates, and Samples

Nearly six of every ten sales promotion dollars are spent on *premiums*—items given free or at a reduced price with the purchase of another product. Cosmetics companies such as Clinique offer sample kits with purchases of their products. Fast-food restaurants are also big users of premiums. McDonald's and Burger King include a toy with every children's meal—the toys often tie in with new movies or popular cartoon shows. In general, marketers choose premiums that are likely to get consumers thinking about and caring about the brand and the product. People who purchase

Assessment Check ✓

1. What are the two basic types of advertising? Into what three categories do they fall?
2. What is the leading advertising medium in the United States?
3. In what two major ways do firms benefit from sponsorship?

sales promotion consists of forms of promotion such as coupons, product samples, and rebates that support advertising and personal selling.

FIGURE
13.3 **The Most Common Forms of Sales Promotions**

Discounts	Coupons
Promotional products	Event marketing
Licensing	Point-of-purchase displays
Samples	Sponsorships
Loyalty programs	Specialty printing
Games/Contests	White paper marketing

health foods at a grocery store may find an offer for a free personal training session at a local health club printed on the back of their sales receipt.

Customers redeem *coupons* for small price discounts when they purchase the promoted products. Such offers may persuade a customer to try a new or different product. Some large supermarket chains double the face value of manufacturers' coupons. Coupons have the disadvantage of focusing customers on price rather than brand loyalty. While some consumers complain that clipping or printing out coupons is too time consuming, others relish the savings, particularly when money is tight and prices seem to be high.

Industrywide coupon redemption remained steady in a recent year at 2.9 billion coupons redeemed, while distribution grew more than 3 percent over the previous year. Of the coupons distributed, approximately 40 percent were for food products. As marketers continue to leverage technology when offering coupons, digital coupon redemption increased more than 140 percent in a recent year. Overall, the use of digital coupons continues to grow faster than traditional coupons. Approximately 87 percent of traditional coupons are distributed through free-standing inserts in the newspaper—and represent 41 percent of the coupons redeemed.

Some people predict that the growing use of paperless mobile coupons, which consumers access on their smart phones while shopping and pioneered by retailers such as Target, could make clippable or printed-out coupons obsolete.[39]

Rebates offer cash back to consumers who previously would mail in required proofs of purchase. Today, firms have simplified the rebate mail-in requirement by offering consumers the opportunity to submit rebates online. Rebates help packaged-goods manufacturers increase purchase rates, promote multiple purchases, and reward product users. Other types of companies also offer rebates, especially for electronics, computers and their accessories, and automobiles. Processing rebates gives marketers a way to collect data about their customers, but many shoppers find it inconvenient to collect the required receipts, forms, and UPC codes and then wait several weeks for their refund. In the past, many manufacturers counted on the fact that consumers would not follow through on rebates.[40]

A *sample* is a gift of a product distributed by mail, door to door, in a demonstration, or inside packages of another product. On any given day you might receive a sample moisturizer, a bar of soap, or a packet of laundry detergent. Three of every four consumers who receive samples will try them.

Games, Contests, and Sweepstakes Games, contests, and sweepstakes offer cash, merchandise, or travel as prizes to participating winners. Firms often sponsor these activities to introduce new goods and services and to attract additional customers. Games and contests require entrants to solve problems or write essays and sometimes provide proof of purchase. Sweepstakes choose winners by chance and require no product purchase. Consumers typically prefer them because games and contests require more effort. Companies like sweepstakes, too, because they are inexpensive to run, and the number of winners is determined from the beginning. With games and contests, the company cannot predict the number of people who will correctly complete a puzzle or gather the right number of symbols from scratch-off cards. Sweepstakes, games, contests, and sweepstakes can reinforce a company's image and advertising message, but consumer attention may focus on the promotion rather than the product.

In recent years, court rulings and legal restrictions have limited the use of games and contests. Companies must proceed carefully in advertising their contests and games and the prizes they award. Marketers must indicate the chances of winning and avoid false promises such as implying that a person has already won.

Specialty Advertising Do you have any pens, t-shirts, or refrigerator magnets imprinted with a business name that you received for free? These offers are examples of **specialty advertising** or *advertising specialties*. This type of sales promotion involves the gift of useful merchandise carrying the name, logo, or slogan of a profit-seeking business or a not-for-profit organization. Because those products are useful and sometimes personalized with recipients' names, people tend to keep and use them, giving advertisers repeated exposure. Originally designed to identify and create goodwill for advertisers, advertising specialties now generate

specialty advertising promotional items that prominently display a firm's name, logo, or business slogan.

sales leads and develop traffic for stores and trade show exhibitors. Like premiums, these promotions should reinforce the brand's image and its relationship with the recipient.

Trade-Oriented Promotions

Sales promotion techniques can also contribute to campaigns directed to retailers and wholesalers. **Trade promotion** is sales promotion geared to marketing intermediaries rather than to consumers. Marketers use trade promotion to encourage retailers to stock new products, continue carrying existing ones, and promote both new and existing products effectively to consumers. Successful trade promotions offer financial incentives. They require careful timing, attention to costs, and easy implementation for intermediaries. These promotions should bring quick results and improve retail sales. Major trade promotions include point-of-purchase advertising and trade shows.

Point-of-purchase (POP) advertising consists of displays or demonstrations that promote products at checkout areas or in the location where consumers buy the item, such as in retail stores. Displays are in various forms, including shelf-mounted signs and hanging posters. Sunscreen, painting supplies, and snacks are typically displayed this way. POP displays can have a significant impact on sales, as an estimated 70 percent of purchase decisions are made within the retail store itself. Recently, electronic, dynamically updated POP displays have been used to present targeted product information and instant coupons. Marketing research has shown that consumers are more likely to purchase certain products when such displays are present. About 78 percent of Facebook's daily users visit the site via mobile and tablet devices, and 41 percent of ad revenue comes from small screens over laptops and desktops. Location-based advertising will be directed primarily to smart phones.[41] See Case 13.2 at the end of the chapter about how jewelry retailer Alex and Ani uses location-based mobile marketing.

Manufacturers and other sellers often exhibit at *trade shows* to promote goods or services to members of their distribution channels. These shows are often organized by industry trade associations. Each year, thousands of trade shows attract millions of exhibitors and hundreds of millions of attendees. Such shows are particularly important in fast-changing industries like those for computers, toys, furniture, and fashions. The International Consumer Electronics Show, which is held annually in Las Vegas and attracts more than 3,200 exhibitors and 150,000 attendees, is the largest. Other trade shows are in the construction, consumer goods, energy, entertainment, manufacturing, and sports and outdoors industries. Trade shows are especially effective for introducing new products and generating sales leads.[42]

Personal Selling

Many companies consider personal selling—a person-to-person promotional presentation to a potential buyer—the key to marketing effectiveness. Unless a seller matches a firm's goods or services to the needs of a particular client or customer, none of the firm's other activities produces any benefits. Today, sales and sales-related jobs employ about 15 million U.S. workers, and that number is expected to increase to 22 million within the next eight years.[43] Businesses often spend 5 to 10 times as much on personal selling as on advertising. Given the significant cost of hiring, training, benefits, and salaries, companies are very concerned with the effectiveness of their sales personnel and their communication skills with customers.

How do marketers decide whether to make personal selling the primary component of their firm's marketing mix? In general, firms are likely to emphasize personal selling rather than advertising or sales promotion under four conditions:

1. Customers are relatively few in number and geographically concentrated.

2. The product is technically complex, involves trade-ins, or requires special handling.

3. The product carries a relatively high price.

4. The product moves through direct-distribution channels.

trade promotion sales promotion geared to marketing intermediaries rather than to final consumers.

point-of-purchase (POP) advertising displays or demonstrations that promote products when and where consumers buy them, such as in retail stores.

All sales activities involve helping customers in some manner. At the cosmetics counter, salepeople provide a free makeup demonstration to reinforce the message of how their products enhance a person's looks.

Selling luxury items such as the carbon fiber constructed Porsche 918 Spyder ($1 million) or a Kuhn Bösendorfer piano ($1.2 million) would require a personal touch. Then there's the $35,000 home theater device offered by California-based Prima Cinema, which automatically sends Hollywood films to customers' home systems the same day they open in theaters. Installation, including instructions on how to use the system, would require personal selling.[44]

The sales functions of most companies are experiencing rapid change. Today's salespeople are more concerned with establishing long-term buyer–seller relationships and acting as consultants to their customers than in the past. In the aftermath of the recession, salespeople continue to face a new challenge—consumers who haggle over prices, even on retail items. Today's consumers have advantages that would astound their predecessors. Anyone with a smart phone or price comparison app can search for competing prices of merchandise while standing in a retail store. Called *showrooming*, these apps have saved consumers the trouble of shopping for deals online or the time of driving and calling around to local stores. Product reviews are helpful with price comparisons as well. Many consumers have become savvy online shoppers, searching for bargains on websites like Overstock, eBay, Expedia, Orbitz, and Priceline. Recently, dynamic pricing has been implemented by online retailers in search of gaining margin advantage. The practice of changing prices, particularly during peak shopping seasons and based on market conditions, consumer behavior, and competitive intelligence, has become more commonplace.[45]

Personal selling can occur in several environments, each of which can involve business-to-business or business-to-consumer selling. Sales representatives who make sales calls on prospective customers at their businesses are involved in *field selling*. Companies that sell major industrial equipment typically rely heavily on field selling. *Over-the-counter selling* describes sales activities in retailing and some wholesale locations, where customers visit the seller's facility to purchase items. *Telemarketing* sales representatives make their presentations over the phone. A later section reviews telemarketing in more detail.

Sales Tasks All sales activities involve assisting customers in some manner. Although a salesperson's work can vary significantly from one company or situation to another, it usually includes a mix of three basic tasks: order processing, creative selling, and missionary selling.

Order Processing Although both field selling and telemarketing involve this activity, order processing is most often related to retail and wholesale firms. The salesperson identifies customer needs, points out merchandise to meet them, and processes the order. Route sales personnel process orders for such consumer goods as bread, milk, soft drinks, and snack foods. They check each store's stock, report inventory needs to the store manager, and complete the sale. Most of these jobs include at least minor order-processing functions.

Creative Selling Sales representatives for most business products and some consumer items perform creative selling, a persuasive type of promotional presentation. Creative selling promotes a good or service whose benefits are not readily apparent or whose purchase decision requires a close analysis of alternatives. Sales of intangible products such as insurance rely heavily on creative selling, but sales of tangible goods benefit as well.

Many retail salespeople just process orders, but many consumers are looking for more in the form of customer service, which is where creative selling comes in. Personal shoppers at Topshop—located in London and New York City and now in Nordstrom stores—help customers create entire looks from three floors of clothing. They also offer customers refreshments and the option to ring up purchases at a special cash register without waiting in line.

order processing
form of selling, mostly at the wholesale and retail levels, that involves identifying customer needs, pointing them out to customers, and completing orders.

creative selling
persuasive type of promotional presentation.

384 **Part 4** *Marketing Management*

Missionary Selling Sales work also includes an indirect form of selling in which the representative promotes goodwill for a company or provides technical or operational assistance to the customer; this practice is called **missionary selling**. Many businesses that sell technical equipment, such as Oracle and Fujitsu, provide systems specialists who act as consultants to customers. These salespeople work to solve problems and sometimes help their clients with questions not directly related to their employers' products. Other industries also use missionary selling techniques. Pharmaceutical company representatives—called *detailers*—visit physicians to introduce the firm's latest offerings, although some firms are finding success with more subtle methods, including web-based sales calls outside office hours. Drug companies are turning to e-detailing, including websites, iPad apps, and other digital devices that are increasingly replacing office visits by human sales reps. The pharmaceutical giant Astra Zeneca recently inaugurated a digital marketing group whose target audience is health care providers. This marketing group set up a website called AZ Touchpoints, where doctors can post questions, request free samples of drugs, and inquire about health insurance coverage. They can also download and print brochures and other literature. If a doctor wants to speak with a sales rep, the site lists a phone number. A company official says that Touchpoints has helped the company "redirect our sales force to new products that need more of a scientific discussion."[46]

Telemarketing **Telemarketing**, personal selling conducted by telephone, provides a firm's marketers with a high return on their expenditures, an immediate response, and an opportunity for personalized two-way conversation. Many firms use telemarketing because expense or other obstacles prevent salespeople from meeting many potential customers in person. Telemarketers can use databases to target prospects based on demographic data. Telemarketing takes two forms. A sales representative who calls you is practicing *outbound telemarketing*. On the other hand, *inbound telemarketing* occurs when you call a toll-free phone number to get product information or place an order.

Outbound telemarketers must abide by the Federal Trade Commission's 1996 Telemarketing Sales Rule. Telemarketers must disclose that they are selling something and on whose behalf they are calling before they make their presentations. The rule also limits calls to between 8 a.m. and 9 p.m., requires sellers to disclose details on exchange policies, and requires them to keep lists of people who do not want to receive calls. In some states, it is also against the law for telemarketers to leave messages for consumers. Congress enacted another law in 2003 that created the National Do Not Call registry, intended to help consumers block unwanted telemarketing calls. Consumers who want to be on the list must call a special number or visit a website to register. Telemarketers must stop calling registered numbers within 31 days or face stiff fines of up to $16,000 for each violation.[47] Charities, surveys, and political campaign calls are exempt from these restrictions. Businesses with which consumers already have a relationship, such as the bank where they have accounts or the dealership where they buy their cars, may conduct telemarketing calls under the guidelines of the Telemarketing Sales Rule.

The Sales Process The sales process typically follows the seven-step sequence shown in Figure 13.4:

missionary selling indirect form of selling in which the representative promotes goodwill for a company or provides technical or operational assistance to the customer.

telemarketing personal selling conducted entirely by telephone, which provides a firm's marketers with a high return on their expenditures, an immediate response, and an opportunity for personalized two-way conversation.

FIGURE 13.4 Seven Steps in the Sales Process

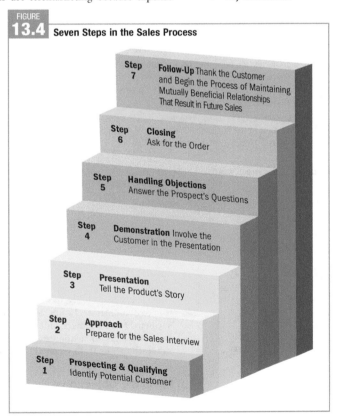

Step 7 **Follow-Up** Thank the Customer and Begin the Process of Maintaining Mutually Beneficial Relationships That Result in Future Sales

Step 6 **Closing** Ask for the Order

Step 5 **Handling Objections** Answer the Prospect's Questions

Step 4 **Demonstration** Involve the Customer in the Presentation

Step 3 **Presentation** Tell the Product's Story

Step 2 **Approach** Prepare for the Sales Interview

Step 1 **Prospecting & Qualifying** Identify Potential Customer

Tips for Closing the Next Big Sale

If you enjoy competition, the thrill of victory, and rewards commensurate with your performance, a sales career might be for you. There is no better feeling than closing a deal—and the potential rewards that come with a close. However, with victory comes a fair share of rejection. Here are some tips for closing a sale:

- *Know your customer.* Review everything the customer has told you about the business and the challenges or issues that need to be resolved.

- *Listen.* Always be the best listener you can be. Listening allows you to develop an effective solution, and selling a solution helps close the deal.

- *Be patient.* Whether it is for a large, multimillion dollar deal or not, building solid relationships takes time, sometimes even years.

- *Create value.* Positioning your goods or services to meet customer needs is at the heart of selling. Part of the sales process involves identifying a customer's objectives, strategy, decision process, and timing. It also involves showing the customer how your goods or service will help overcome issues or challenges. Ask probing questions and obtain honest feedback.

- *Summarize the benefits.* Have the conviction and confidence that your good or service will help solve the customer's problem. Provide a final summary with the benefits of your good or service. This is also the time for your customer to bring up any objections.

- *How to ask for the business.* There comes a time when it simply makes sense to ask your customer for the sale. If your solution is well thought out, organized, and targeted, asking for the sale should be a time for both parties to agree to move forward.

- *If at first you don't succeed.* Remember that the last impression is almost as important as the first, and if the customer doesn't buy, be gracious and professional. Most importantly, always follow up.

Sources: Thomas Phelps, "Why Choose a Career in Sales," *About.com,* accessed February 16, 2014, http://salescareers.about.com; Geoffrey James "How to Close a Sale," *Inc.,* accessed February 16, 2014, www.inc.com; Sloan Brothers, "5 Tips for Closing a Sales Deal," *Startup Nation,* accessed February 16, 2014, www.startupnation.com.

prospecting and qualifying, the approach, presentation, the demonstration, handling objections, closing, and the follow-up. Remember the importance of flexibility, though; a good salesperson is not afraid to tailor the sales process based on a customer's responses and needs. The process of selling to a potential customer who is unfamiliar with a company's products differs from the process of serving a long-time customer.

Prospecting, Qualifying, and Approaching

At the prospecting stage, salespeople identify potential customers. They may seek leads for prospective sales from such sources as existing customers, friends and family, and business associates. The qualifying process identifies potential customers who have the financial ability and authority to buy.

Companies use different tactics to identify and qualify prospects. Some companies rely on business development teams, passing responses from direct mail along to their sales reps. Others believe in personal visits. Many firms are now using social media, which cost little or nothing, to boost sales. Online newsletters, virtual trade shows, podcasts, webinars, and blogs are good examples. Experts advise developing a clear strategy in order to be successful with social media.[48]

Successful salespeople make careful preparations, analyzing available data about a prospective customer's product lines and other pertinent information before making the initial contact. They realize the importance of a first impression in influencing a customer's future attitudes toward the seller and its products.

Presentation and Demonstration At the

presentation stage, salespeople communicate promotional messages. They may describe the major features of their products, highlight the advantages, and cite examples of satisfied consumers. A demonstration helps reinforce the message that the salesperson has been communicating—a critical step in the sales process. Department-store shoppers can get a free makeover at the cosmetics counter. Anyone looking to buy a car will take it for a test drive before deciding whether to purchase it.

Some products are too large to transport to prospective buyers or require special installation to demonstrate. Using laptop computers, multimedia presentations, graphic programs such as SmartDraw, webinars, online videos, and even podcasts, sales representatives can demonstrate these products for customers.[49] Others, such as services, are intangible. So a presentation including testimonials from satisfied customers or graphs illustrating results may be helpful.

Handling Objections Some salespeople fear potential customers' objections because they

view the questions as criticism. But a good salesperson can use objections as an opportunity to answer questions and explain how the product will benefit the customer. As a general rule, the key is to sell benefits, not features: How will this product help the customer?

Closing The critical point in the sales process—the time at which the salesperson actually asks the prospect to buy—is the closing. If the presentation effectively matches product benefits to customer needs, the closing should be a natural conclusion. If there are more bumps in the process, the salesperson can try some different techniques, such as offering alternative products, offering a special incentive for purchase, or restating the product benefits. Closing the sale—and beginning a relationship in which the customer builds loyalty to the brand or product—is the ideal outcome of this interaction. But even if the sale is not made at this time, the salesperson should regard the interaction as the beginning of a potential relationship anyway. The prospect might very well become a customer in the future. See the "Career Kickstart" feature for tips on how to close the big sale.

Follow-Up A salesperson's actions after the sale may determine whether the customer will make another purchase. Follow-up is an important part of building a long-lasting relationship. After closing, the salesperson should process the order efficiently. By making contact soon after a purchase, the salesperson provides reassurance about the customer's decision to buy and creates an opportunity to correct any problems.

Public Relations

A final element of the promotional mix, public relations (PR)—including publicity—supports advertising, personal selling, and sales promotion, usually by pursuing broader objectives. Through PR, companies attempt to improve their prestige and image with the public by distributing specific messages or ideas to target audiences. Cause-related promotional activities are often supported by public relations and publicity campaigns. In addition, PR helps a firm establish awareness of goods and services and then builds a positive image of them.

    Public relations refers to an organization's communications and relationships with its various public audiences, such as customers, vendors, news media, employees, stockholders, the government, and the general public. Many of these communication efforts serve marketing purposes. Public relations is an efficient, indirect communications channel for promoting products. It can publicize products and help create and maintain a positive image of the company.

    The public relations department links a firm with the media. It provides the media with news releases and video and audio clips and holds news conferences to announce new products, the formation of strategic alliances, management changes, financial results, and similar developments. Publications issued by the department include newsletters, brochures, and reports.

Publicity The type of public relations that is tied most closely to promoting a company's products is publicity—nonpersonal stimulation of demand for a good, service, place, idea, event, person, or organization by unpaid placement of information in print or broadcast media. Press releases generate publicity, as does news coverage. Publicity can even help save a struggling business. Fred Daley, owner of Fresh Fish Daley, faced the fact that he might have to close his New Hampshire business when state regulations governing the transportation of fish changed; he could not afford the upgrades to his van. When local news reported Daley's plight, his loyal customers came forward with donations; one man found an affordable van on eBay and helped Daley complete the purchase. "It's a story of goodwill," said Daley with gratitude.[50]

    Not-for-profit organizations benefit from publicity when they receive coverage of events such as the Komen Race for the Cure, which raises money for breast cancer research.[51] When a for-profit firm teams up with a not-for-profit firm in a fund-raising effort, the move usually generates good publicity for both organizations.

public relations organization's communications and relationships with its various public audiences.

publicity nonpersonal stimulation of demand for a good, service, place, idea, event, person, or organization by unpaid placement of information in print or broadcast media.

Assessment Check ☑

1. Why do retailers and manufacturers use sales promotions?

2. When does a firm use personal selling instead of nonpersonal selling?

3. How does public relations serve a marketing purpose?

Assessment Check ☑

1. Give an example of a pushing strategy.

2. Give an example of a pulling strategy.

[4] Pushing and Pulling Strategies

Marketers can choose between two general promotional strategies: a pushing strategy or a pulling strategy. A **pushing strategy** relies on personal selling to market an item to wholesalers and retailers in a company's distribution channels. So companies promote the product to members of the marketing channel, not to end users. Sales personnel explain to marketing intermediaries why they should carry particular merchandise, usually supported by offers of special discounts and promotional materials. Drug manufacturers use a pushing strategy to market to physicians and hospitals. Marketers also provide **cooperative advertising** allowances, in which they share the cost of local advertising of their firm's product or line with channel partners. All of these strategies are designed to motivate wholesalers and retailers to push the good or service to their own customers.

A **pulling strategy** attempts to promote a product by generating consumer demand for it, primarily through advertising and sales promotion appeals. Potential buyers will then request that their suppliers carry the product, thereby pulling it through the distribution channel. Retailers and consumer goods manufacturers typically use a pulling strategy. Nestlé recently launched a new product with a 30-second TV commercial during the Super Bowl, one of the most viewed broadcasts worldwide. A competitor to Reese's Peanut Butter Cups, the new Butterfinger Peanut Butter Cups "combine a smooth and crunchy peanut butter center with a milk chocolate shell."[52] Most marketing situations require combinations of pushing and pulling strategies, although the primary emphasis can vary.

[5] Pricing Objectives in the Marketing Mix

Products offer utility, or want-satisfying power. However, we as consumers determine how much value we associate with each one. In the aftermath of a major storm, we may value electricity and food and water above everything else. If we commute a long distance or are planning a driving vacation, fuel may be of greater concern. But all consumers have limited amounts of money and a variety of possible uses for it. So the **price**—the exchange value of a good or service—becomes a major factor in consumer buying decisions.

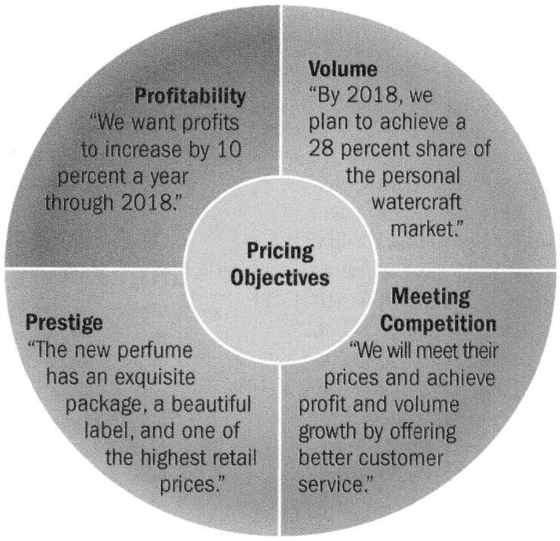

Businesspeople attempt to accomplish certain objectives through their pricing decisions. Pricing objectives vary from firm to firm, and many companies pursue multiple pricing objectives. Some try to improve profits by setting high prices; others set low prices to attract new business. As Figure 13.5 shows, the four basic categories of pricing objectives are (1) profitability, (2) volume, (3) meeting competition, and (4) prestige.

Profitability Objectives

Profitability objectives are the most common objectives included in the strategic plans of most firms. Marketers know that profits are the revenue the company brings in, minus its expenses. Usually a big difference exists between revenue and profit. Automakers try to produce at least one luxury vehicle for which they can charge $50,000 or more instead of relying entirely on the sale of $15,000 to $25,000 models.

FIGURE 13.5 Pricing Objectives

Profitability
"We want profits to increase by 10 percent a year through 2018."

Volume
"By 2018, we plan to achieve a 28 percent share of the personal watercraft market."

Pricing Objectives

Prestige
"The new perfume has an exquisite package, a beautiful label, and one of the highest retail prices."

Meeting Competition
"We will meet their prices and achieve profit and volume growth by offering better customer service."

Some firms maximize profits by reducing costs rather than through higher prices. Companies can maintain prices and increase profitability by operating more efficiently or by modifying the product to make it less costly to produce. One strategy is to maintain a steady price while reducing the size or amount of the product in the package—something that manufacturers of candy, coffee, and cereal have done over the years.

Volume Objectives

A second approach to pricing strategy—**volume objectives**—bases pricing decisions on market share, the percentage of a market controlled by a certain company or product. One firm may seek to achieve a 25 percent market share in a certain product category, and another may want to maintain or expand its market share for particular products. Family Dollar Stores relies on volume sales to make a profit. The nationwide chain of stores, which sells everything from ice cube trays to holiday decorations—for a dollar each—must find ways to attract as much traffic and sell as many products as possible on given day. Recently the North Carolina–based firm announced a strategy to increase the number of consumables, such as grocery, health, and beauty products offered in its stores. Family Dollar recently renovated many of its 8,000 stores and has begun to sell tobacco products. Its largest revenue producer, consumable products, rose almost 5 percent in a recent year, as a result of frozen food, health aids, and tobacco sales.[53]

Pricing to Meet Competition

A third set of pricing objectives seeks simply to meet competitors' prices so that price essentially becomes a nonissue. In many lines of business, firms set their own prices to match those of established industry leaders. However, companies may not legally work together to agree on prices.

Because price is such a highly visible component of a firm's marketing mix, businesses may be tempted to use it to obtain an advantage over competitors. But sometimes the race to match competitors' prices results in a *price war*, which has happened periodically in the airline and fast-food industries. The ability of competitors to match a price cut leads many marketers to try to avoid price wars by favoring other strategies, such as adding value, improving quality, educating consumers, and establishing relationships.

Although price is a major component of the marketing mix, it is not the only one. Electronic readers such as the Kindle and the iPad are in a fierce pricing competition for digital books, as the "Solving an Ethical Controversy" feature explains.

Prestige Objectives

The final category of objectives encompasses the effect of prices on prestige. **Prestige pricing** establishes a relatively high price to develop and maintain an image of quality and exclusiveness. Marketers set such objectives because they recognize the role of price in communicating an overall image of quality, status, and exclusiveness for the firm and its products. People expect to pay more for a Mercedes, Christian Louboutin shoes, or a vacation on St. Barts in the Caribbean.

Scarcity can create prestige. Products that are limited in distribution or so popular that they become scarce generate their own prestige—allowing businesses to charge more for them. Unfortunately, scarcity can also invite crime. Recently, federal prosecutors charged four men with hacking into the computer systems of Ticketmaster, Major League Baseball, Telecharge, and Live Nation Entertainment to highjack 1.5 million tickets to concerts by Bruce Springsteen and Miley Cyrus, baseball playoff games at Yankee Stadium, and other events.

volume objectives objects based on pricing decisions on market share, the percentage of a market controlled by a certain company or product.

prestige pricing strategies that establish relatively high prices to develop and maintain an image of quality and exclusiveness.

Prestige pricing sets a relatively high price to develop and maintain an image of quality and exclusiveness. People expect to pay more for cars adorned with the Mercedes hood ornament known as "the star."

Thomas Kienzle/AFP/Getty Images, Inc.

Chapter 13 *Promotion and Pricing Strategies*   **389**

Solving an Ethical Controversy

Free E-Books: Good or Bad for Business?

When Amazon's Kindle electronic reader first became available, Amazon charged consumers $9.99 for each e-book they purchased. Publishers insisted that that price was too low to keep their business profitable. But Amazon actually gave some e-books away for free, including those of living authors who earn an income from their writing.

Amazon explained that the free e-books were a way to get consumers to check out unfamiliar writers. The hope was that they would then buy other works by those writers. But some publishers delay publication of electronic editions for several months after the hardcover books were issued, much as they delay paperback editions.

Should e-books be given away for free?

PRO

1. Some publishers regard free e-books as promotion to generate buzz about new or unknown authors.

2. Some publishers that give away e-books on a regular basis have noticed an increase in sales that's "all found money," as one executive says.

CON

1. "It is illogical to give books away for free," said David Young of Hachette Book Group, which publishes Stephanie Meyer's Twilight series.

2. The relatively low price of e-books may discourage consumers from buying actual books with suggested retail prices of $25 or more.

Summary

Both Amazon's Kindle and Barnes & Noble's Nook continue to offer free e-books. In addition, both offer the capability for customers to lend e-books to friends and family for 14 days by simply inputting a name and e-mail address. Although some publishers might cringe at these practices, it is likely that the trend will continue.

Sources: Hillel Italie, "Amazon Escalates Standoff with Hachette," *USA Today*, accessed June 17, 2014, www.usatoday.com; Alec Liu, "Kindle, Nook, Whatever: Here's How to Get Free E-Books," *Fox News*, accessed February 21, 2014, www.foxnews.com; Stan Schroeder, "The E-Book Price War Isn't Over Yet," *Mashable Business*, accessed February 21, 2014, http://mashable.com; Motoko Rich, "Apple's Prices for E-Books May Be Lower Than Expected," *The New York Times*, accessed February 21, 2014, www.nytimes.com; Motoko Rich, "With Kindle, the Best Sellers Don't Need to Sell," *The New York Times*, accessed February 21, 2014, www.nytimes.com; "The Kindle Pricing Strategy & the Kindle Pricing History," *Ask Deb*, accessed February 21, 2014, www.askdeb.com.

Assessment Check ☑

1. Define *price*.
2. In addition to profitability, what is another approach to pricing strategy?

The men or their agents posed as individual online buyers, electronically bypassed the vendors' security systems, and bought blocks of tickets that they resold at hugely inflated prices. The scam had been in operation for more than a decade and had generated almost $29 million in illegal profits.[54]

[6] Pricing Strategies

People from different areas of a company contribute their expertise to set the most strategic price for a product. Accountants, financial managers, and marketers provide relevant sales and cost data, along with customer feedback. Designers, engineers, and systems analysts all contribute important data as well.

Prices are determined in two basic ways: by applying the concepts of supply and demand discussed in Chapter 3 and by completing cost-oriented analyses. Economic theory assumes that a market price will be set at the point at which the amount of a product desired at a given price equals the amount that suppliers will offer for sale at that price. In other words, this price

390   **Part 4** *Marketing Management*

occurs at the point at which the amount demanded and the amount supplied are equal. Online auctions, such as those conducted on eBay, are a popular application of the demand-and-supply approach.

Price Determination in Practice

Economic theory might lead to the best pricing decisions, but most businesses do not have all the information they need to make those decisions, so they adopt **cost-based pricing** formulas. These formulas calculate total costs per unit and then add markups to cover overhead costs and generate profits.

Cost-based pricing totals all costs associated with offering a product in the market, including research and development, production, transportation, and marketing expenses. An added amount, the markup, then covers any unexpected or overlooked expenses and provides a profit. The total becomes the price. Although the actual markup used varies by such factors as brand image and type of store, the typical markup for clothing is determined by doubling the wholesale price (the cost to the merchant) to arrive at the retail price for the item.

cost-based pricing formulas that calculate total costs per unit and then add markups to cover overhead costs and generate profits.

Breakeven Analysis

Businesses often conduct a **breakeven analysis** to determine the minimum sales volume a product must generate at a certain price level to cover all costs. This method involves a consideration of various costs and total revenues. *Total cost* is the sum of total variable costs and total fixed costs. *Variable costs* change with the level of production, as labor and raw materials do, while *fixed costs* such as insurance premiums and utility rates charged by water, natural gas, and electric power suppliers are constants regardless of the production level. *Total revenue* is determined by multiplying price by the number of units sold.

breakeven analysis pricing-related technique used to determine the minimum sales volume a product must generate at a certain price level to cover all costs.

Finding the Breakeven Point The level of sales that will generate enough revenue to cover all of the company's fixed and variable costs is called the *breakeven point*. It is the point at which total revenue just equals total costs. Sales beyond the breakeven point will generate profits; sales volume below the breakeven point will result in losses. The following formulas give the breakeven point in units and dollars:

$$\text{Breakeven Point (in units)} = \frac{\text{Total fixed costs}}{\text{Contribution to fixed costs per unit}}$$

$$\text{Breakeven Point (in dollars)} = \frac{\text{Total fixed costs}}{1 - \text{Variable cost per unit/Price}}$$

A product selling for $20 with a variable cost of $14 per unit produces a $6 per-unit contribution to fixed costs. If the firm has total fixed costs of $42,000, then it must sell 7,000 units to break even on the product as shown in Figure 13.6. The calculation of the breakeven point in units and dollars is as follows:

$$\text{Breakeven Point (in units)} = \frac{\$42,000}{\$20 - \$14} = \frac{\$42,000}{\$6} = 7,000 \text{ units}$$

$$\text{Breakeven Point (in dollars)} = \frac{\$42,000}{1 - \$14/\$20} = \frac{\$42,000}{1 - 0.7} = \frac{\$42,000}{0.3} = \$140,000$$

Marketers use breakeven analysis to determine the profits or losses that would result from several different proposed prices. Because different prices produce different breakeven points, marketers could compare their calculations of required sales to break even with sales estimates from marketing research studies. This comparison can identify the best price—one that would attract enough customers to exceed the breakeven point and earn profits for the firm.

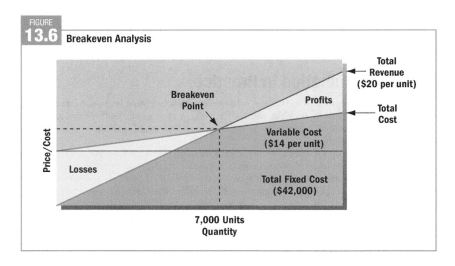

FIGURE 13.6 Breakeven Analysis

Most firms add consumer demand—determining whether enough customers will buy the number of units the firm must sell at a particular price to break even—by developing estimates through surveys of likely customers, interviews with retailers that would be handling the product, and assessments of prices charged by competitors. Then the breakeven points for several possible prices are calculated and compared with sales estimates for each price. This practice is referred to as *modified breakeven analysis.*

Alternative Pricing Strategies

The strategy a company uses to set its prices should grow out of the firm's overall marketing strategy. In general, firms can choose from four alternative pricing strategies: skimming, penetration, discount or everyday low pricing, and competitive pricing.

Skimming Pricing A skimming pricing strategy sets an intentionally high price relative to the prices of competing products. The term comes from the expression "skimming the cream." This pricing strategy often works for the introduction of a distinctive good or service with little or no competition, although it can be used at other stages of the product life cycle as well. A skimming strategy can help marketers set a price that distinguishes a firm's high-end product from those of competitors. It can also help a firm recover its product development costs before competitors enter the field. This is often the case with prescription drugs.

Penetration Pricing By contrast, a penetration pricing strategy sets a low price as a major marketing weapon. Businesses may price new products noticeably lower than competing offerings when they enter new industries characterized by dozens of competing brands. Once the new product achieves some market recognition through consumer trial purchases stimulated by its low price, marketers may increase the price to the level of competing products. However, stiff competition might prevent the price increase.

Everyday Low Pricing and Discount Pricing Everyday low pricing (EDLP) is a strategy devoted to maintaining continuous low prices rather than relying on short-term price-cutting tactics such as cents-off coupons, rebates, and special sales. This strategy has been used successfully by retailers such as Walmart and Lowe's to consistently offer low prices to consumers; manufacturers also use EDLP to set stable prices for retailers.

With *discount pricing*, businesses hope to attract customers by dropping prices for a set period of time. Automakers usually offer consumers special discounts on most or all of their

---

skimming pricing strategy that sets an intentionally high price relative to the prices of competing products.

penetration pricing strategy that sets a low price as a major marketing weapon.

everyday low pricing (EDLP) is a strategy devoted to maintaining continuous low prices rather than relying on short-term price-cutting tactics such as cents-off coupons, rebates, and special sales.

Part 4 *Marketing Management*

vehicles during the holiday shopping season. After the holidays, prices usually rebound. But experts warn that discounting must be done carefully, or profits can disappear. Businesses should offer discounts only for a specified period of time and with a clear understanding of what they are trying to accomplish with the strategy. They should advertise the discount, so customers know it is a special deal. When the time period has elapsed, so should the discount. JC Penney has struggled with its pricing and sales strategy over the past few years. See the "Hit & Miss" feature for more details.

Competitive Pricing Although many organizations rely heavily on price as a competitive weapon, even more implement **competitive pricing** strategies. They try to reduce the

competitive pricing strategy that tries to reduce the emphasis on price competition by matching other firms' prices and concentrating their own marketing efforts on the product, distribution, and promotional elements of the marketing mix.

Some retailers such as Lowe's use an everyday low pricing strategy that maintains continuous low prices rather than relying on short-term price-cutting tactics such as coupons, rebates, and special sales.

Michael Fein/Bloomberg/Getty Images, Inc.

Chapter 13 *Promotion and Pricing Strategies*

393

**Assessment
Check** ☑

1. What is a cost-based
   pricing formula?
2. Why do companies
   implement competitive
   pricing strategies?

emphasis on price competition by matching other firms' prices and concentrating their own marketing efforts on the product, distribution, and promotional elements of the marketing mix. In fact, in industries with relatively homogeneous products, competitors must match one another's price reductions to maintain market share and remain competitive. By pricing their products at the levels of competing offerings, marketers largely negate the price variable in their marketing strategies.

[7] Consumer Perceptions of Prices

How do you perceive prices for certain products? Marketers must consider this. If large numbers of potential buyers consider a price too high or too low, businesses must correct the situation. Price–quality relationships and the use of odd pricing are important considerations in setting prices.

Price–Quality Relationships

Research shows that a consumer's perception of product quality is closely related to an item's price. Most marketers believe that this perceived price–quality relationship remains steady over a relatively wide range of prices, although extremely high or low prices have less credibility. The price–quality relationship can critically affect a firm's pricing strategy.

Many consumers associate prestige, quality, and high price together—believing that paying a high price for an item such as a BMW or a Chanel bag not only conveys prestige but also ensures quality. Others believe that eating at an expensive restaurant automatically means the food will be better than food served at a modestly priced eating establishment. Conversely, consumers may view an extremely low price as an indication that corners have been cut and quality has been compromised. But what about the perception associated with a sale? If a line of designer boots goes on sale for 50 percent off the original price, a bargain hunter will snap them up with a sense of victory—high quality at a rock bottom price.

Marketing researchers also know that the verbal sound of a price influences consumers' perceptions of price, quality, and resulting value. The vowel sound "oo" (as in "two") makes people think of larger sizes and prices, while the vowel sound "ee" (as in "three") evokes a smaller size and price. These perceptions can influence consumers' perception of the quality of the products they are considering buying.[55]

odd pricing pricing method using uneven amounts, which sometimes appear smaller than they really are to consumers.

**Assessment
Check** ☑

1. How does the price–
   quality relationship
   affect a firm's pricing
   strategy?
2. Why is odd pricing used?

Odd Pricing

Have you ever wondered why retailers set prices at $1.99 instead of $2 or $9.95 instead of $10? Before the age of cash registers and sales taxes, retailers reportedly followed this practice of odd pricing—pricing method using uneven amounts, which appear less than they really are to consumers—to force clerks to make correct change as part of their cash control efforts. But now odd pricing is commonly used because many retailers believe that consumers favor uneven amounts or amounts that sound less than they really are. However, some retailers also use this method to identify items that have been marked down. The odd price suggests the item is on sale.

What's Ahead

The chapters in Part 4 have explained the main principles underlying marketing management and described how each fits a firm's overall business strategy. The next few chapters will help you understand how companies manage the technology and information that are available to businesses to create value for their customers and enhance their competitiveness in the marketplace. You'll also learn how firms manage their financial resources.

Chapter in Review

■ Summary of Learning Objectives

⌐1⌐ Discuss integrated marketing communications (IMC).

In practicing IMC, a firm coordinates promotional activities to produce a unified, customer-focused message. IMC identifies consumer needs and shows how a company's products meet them. Marketers select the promotional media that best target and reach customers. Teamwork and careful promotional planning to coordinate IMC strategy components are important elements of these programs.

A company's promotional mix integrates two components: personal selling and nonpersonal selling, which includes advertising, sales promotion, and public relations. By selecting the appropriate combination of promotional mix elements, marketers attempt to achieve the firm's five major promotional objectives: provide information, differentiate a product, increase demand, stabilize sales, and accentuate the product's value.

Assessment Check Answers ☑

1.1 What is the objective of an integrated marketing communications program? An IMC strategy focuses on customer needs to create a unified promotional message about a firm's goods or services.

1.2 Why do firms pursue multiple promotional objectives at the same time? Firms pursue multiple promotional objectives because they may need to convey different messages to different audiences.

1.3 What are product placement and guerrilla marketing? Product placement involves paying a fee to have a product showcased in certain media. Guerrilla marketing consists of innovative, low-cost marketing efforts designed to get consumers' attention in unusual ways.

⌐2⌐ Summarize the different types of advertising.

Advertising, the most visible form of nonpersonal promotion, is designed to inform, persuade, or remind. Product advertising promotes a good or service, while institutional advertising promotes a concept, idea, organization, or philosophy. Television, Internet, and newspapers are the largest advertising media categories. Others include magazines, radio, and outdoor advertising.

Assessment Check Answers ☑

2.1 What are the two basic types of advertising? Into what three categories do they fall? The two basic types of advertising are product and institutional. They fall into the categories of informative, persuasive, and reminder-oriented advertising.

2.2 What is the leading advertising medium in the United States? According to the most recent statistics listed in Figure 13.2, television is the leading advertising medium in the United States.

2.3 In what two major ways do firms benefit from sponsorship? Firms benefit from sponsorship in two ways: they gain exposure to the event's audience, and they become associated with the activity's image.

⌐3⌐ Outline sales promotion.

Sales promotion accounts for greater expenditures than advertising. Consumer-oriented sales promotions such as coupons, games, samples, contests, sweepstakes, loyalty programs, and promotional products offer an extra incentive to buy a product. Point-of-purchase advertising displays and trade shows are sales promotions directed to the trade markets. Personal selling involves face-to-face interactions between seller and buyer. The primary sales tasks are order processing, creative selling, and missionary selling. Public relations is nonpaid promotion that seeks to enhance a company's public image.

Assessment Check Answers ☑

3.1 Why do retailers and manufacturers use sales promotions? Retailers and manufacturers use sales promotions to offer consumers extra incentives to buy their products.

3.2 When does a firm use personal selling instead of nonpersonal selling? Firms generally use personal selling when customers are few and geographically concentrated, the product is technically complex, involves trade-ins, or requires special handling, the price is high, or the product moves through direct-distribution channels.

3.3 How does public relations serve a marketing purpose? Public relations can be an efficient, indirect communications channel for promoting products. It can publicize products and help create and maintain a positive image of the company.

⌐4⌐ Describe pushing and pulling strategies.

A pushing strategy relies on personal selling to market a product to wholesalers and retailers in a company's distribution channels. A pulling strategy promotes the product by generating consumer demand for it, through advertising and sales promotion.

Assessment Check Answers ☑

4.1 Give an example of a pushing strategy. An example of a pushing strategy is one used by drug manufacturers, which is used to market solely to physicians and hospitals.

4.2 Give an example of a pulling strategy. Pulling strategies are used by retailers and by manufacturers of consumer goods such as cosmetics, automobiles, and clothing.

⌐5⌐ Discuss the pricing objectives in the marketing mix.

Pricing objectives can be classified as profitability, volume, meeting competition, and prestige. Profitability objectives are the most common. Volume objectives base pricing decisions on market share. Meeting competitors' prices makes price a nonissue in competition. Prestige pricing establishes a high price to develop and maintain an image of quality or exclusiveness.

Assessment Check Answers ✅

5.1 Define *price.* Price is the exchange value of a good or service.

5.2 In addition to profitability, what is another approach to pricing strategy? A second approach to pricing strategy is *volume objectives*, which bases pricing decisions on market share.

⌐6⌐ Outline pricing strategies.

Although economic theory determines prices by the law of supply and demand, most firms use cost-based pricing, which adds a markup after costs. They usually conduct a breakeven analysis to determine the minimum sales volume a product must generate at a certain price to cover costs. The four alternative pricing strategies are skimming, penetration, everyday low pricing and discounting, and competitive pricing. A skimming strategy sets a high price initially to recover costs and then lowers it; a penetration strategy sets a lower price and then raises it later. Everyday low pricing and discounting offers a lower price for a period of time. Competitive pricing matches other firms' prices and emphasizes nonprice benefits of an item.

Assessment Check Answers ✅

6.1 What is a cost-based pricing formula? A cost-based pricing formula calculates the total costs per unit and then adds markups to cover overhead costs and generate profits.

6.2 Why do companies implement competitive pricing strategies? Companies use competitive pricing strategies to reduce the emphasis on price competition by matching other firms' prices and concentrating their own marketing efforts on the product, distribution, and promotional elements of the marketing mix.

⌐7⌐ Discuss consumer perceptions of prices.

Marketers must consider how consumers perceive the price–quality relationship of their products. Consumers may be willing to pay a higher price if they perceive a product to be of superior quality. Marketers often use odd pricing to convey a message to consumers.

Assessment Check Answers ✅

7.1 How does the price–quality relationship affect a firm's pricing strategy? Consumers must believe that the price of an item reflects its quality, except in extreme cases. So a firm must try to set its prices accordingly.

7.2 Why is odd pricing used? Retailers believe that consumers favor uneven amounts or amounts that sound like less than they really are. Odd pricing may also be used to suggest an item is on sale.

▨ Business Terms You Need to Know

integrated marketing communications (IMC) 370
promotion 370
promotional mix 371
personal selling 371
nonpersonal selling 371
positioning 373
product placement 374
guerrilla marketing 374
advertising 375
product advertising 375
institutional advertising 375
cause advertising 375

sponsorship 380
infomercials 380
sales promotion 381
specialty advertising 382
trade promotion 383
point-of-purchase (POP) advertising 383
order processing 384
creative selling 384
missionary selling 385
telemarketing 385
public relations 387
publicity 387
pushing strategy 388

cooperative advertising 388
pulling strategy 388
price 388
profitability objectives 388
volume objectives 389
prestige pricing 389
cost-based pricing 391
breakeven analysis 391
skimming pricing 392
penetration pricing 392
everyday low pricing (EDLP) 392
competitive pricing 393
odd pricing 394

Review Questions

1. What is the purpose of integrated marketing communications?

2. What are the five major objectives of a promotional strategy?

3. Identify and define each of the three categories of advertising based on their purpose. Which type of advertising might marketers use for the following products?

    a. cars

    b. e-reader

    c. organic produce

    d. renter's insurance

4. What are the benefits of online and interactive advertising? What might be some drawbacks?

5. For each of the following, describe potential benefits and drawbacks of a sponsorship relationship:

    a. BMW and the Snowboard FIS World Cup

    b. Bank of America and the Chicago Marathon

    c. Mattel Corporation and the Special Olympics

6. If you were a marketer for Rolex, what kind of sales promotion might you use for your watches?

7. Under what circumstances are firms likely to emphasize personal selling?

8. Describe the seven-step sales process.

9. Define the four basic categories of pricing objectives.

10. What are the four alternative pricing strategies that marketers use? Give an example of the circumstances under which each might be selected.

Projects and Teamwork Applications

1. Choose a product that you purchased recently. Identify the various media that were used to promote the product and analyze the promotional mix. Do you agree with the company's marketing strategy? Or would you recommend changes to the mix? Why? Create your own print ad for the product you chose, using any business strategies or knowledge you have learned in this course so far.

2. Evaluate the price of the product you selected in the preceding exercise. What appears to be the pricing strategy that its manufacturer used? Do you think the price is fair? Why or why not? Choose a different strategy and develop a new price for the product based on your strategy. Poll your classmates to learn whether they would purchase the product at the new price—and why.

3. Some schools have received financial benefits by allowing companies to promote their goods and services to students. Others have decided against this practice, and some states have laws banning this type of promotion. Find some examples of corporate sponsors in public elementary and high schools and on college campuses. With your class, discuss the pros and cons of promotion in public schools and on college

campuses. In your view, is there a distinction between a public elementary or high school and a college campus? Why or why not?

4. A "freemium" pricing model like Pandora, Dropbox, or LinkedIn offers a basic service free of charge with the option to upgrade at a cost. It's a common pricing strategy among web start-up companies to get users on to the site and then later to convince them to subscribe to a premium or enhanced version of the service. What are some of the benefits of a freemium pricing model to a company? To consumers? Can you think of a situation when freemium pricing wouldn't work?

5. Product placement is also called embedded marketing, and you've probably seen it in TV programming, movies, and even video games. Skipping ads has never been easier due to advances in technology, so marketers have come up with alternative ways of placing their products in various media. One way is to use technology that allows them to digitally place products in TV shows or films after they have been made. What are your thoughts on this practice? What are the benefits to the brand? To the TV show or video game with the virtual product placement?

Web Assignments

1. **Evaluating a social media campaign.** Choose an airline, an automobile company, or a fast-food company (or product). On Facebook, Twitter, YouTube, and Instagram, compare and contrast social media campaigns. How does the company engage its customers? What is its most recent campaign, and what is unique about it? How does the company use each of the social media outlets in different ways to market its products?

2. **Online coupon fraud.** Do some research to learn about online coupon fraud and its estimated annual costs to businesses. Prepare a brief report that includes answers to the following: How big of a problem is online coupon fraud? What are some of the risks, and how can marketers minimize that risk?

    http://multichannelmerchant.com/news/ten-tips-for-curtailing-online-coupon-fraud-08032010/

3. **Outdoor advertising.** Go to the website for Clear Channel Outdoor, one of the world's largest outdoor advertising companies, and click on "Products and Brands" to view the amazing array of outdoor advertising options available. Under the "Insight" link, read three of the case studies and discuss the outcome for each of the companies profiled. What are some of your own observations about the effectiveness of outdoor advertising where you live or near your college campus?

http://clearchanneloutdoor.com/

Note: Internet web addresses change frequently. If you don't find the exact sites listed, you may need to access the organization's home page and search from there or use a search engine such as Google or Bing.

CASE 13.1 — Brand Names versus Store Brands

Shoppers who buy brand-name products usually cite quality as a reason. Shoppers who buy store-brand products usually cite price. Is it possible to have the best of both worlds?

Retailers such as Target, CVS, and Walgreens have found they had too many of the same products under different brand names. They saw that shoppers were buying less and looking for bigger bargains than usual. Items that weren't selling well were replaced by more popular brands or by in-house generics. This was particularly true of such basic items as household and personal products and food staples. As one observer said, "People don't want to have to choose among 15 or 20 different brands of toilet paper or paper towels or even basic food stuff." The retailers were confident that shoppers would be eager to snap up these bargains.

Target guessed that consumers would buy their in-house brands, and it looks like they were correct. The in-store brands up & up, Simply Balanced, Archer Farms, and Market Pantry account for more than 20 percent of all food products sold at Target.

To a great extent, this overall strategy has worked. One study reveals the store brands of major market leaders in discount retail, supermarket, and drug store industries have grown at a faster pace than competing national brands— private label market share in a recent year was 21 percent.

Questions for Critical Thinking

1. Why do you think chain stores carry brand-name items alongside their own in-house brands? From your own experience, is one brand better than the other? Are the national brands worth the additional cost?

2. What are some of the ways that stores such as Target are able to keep their prices low?

Sources: "Private Label Growth Outpaces National Brands," *Store Brands Decisions*, accessed February 21, 2014, www.storebrandsdecisions.com; Morgan Myrmo, "Targeting Retailers with Store Brands for Dividend Growth," *Seeking Alpha*, accessed February 21, 2014, www.seekingalpha.com; "Target's Comeback Plan on Track," *Store Brands Decisions*, accessed February 21, 2014, www.storebrandsdecisions.com; "Target Elevates Store Brands to Front Page Status," *Store Brands Decisions*, accessed February 21, 2014, www.storebrandsdecisions.com; "Dumped! Brand Names Fight to Stay in Stores," *CNNMoney*, accessed February 21, 2014, http://money.cnn.com; Sara Zucker, "Wal-Mart Reintroduces Brands after Customer Complaints," *Brand Channel*, accessed February 21, 2014, www.brandchannel.com.

CASE 13.2 — Alex & Ani Delivers Deals with Real-Time Mobile Marketing

Alex & Ani, a Rhode Island–based jewelry and gift retailer, is experimenting with Apple's iBeacon location technology to target real-time mobile offers to shoppers. The technology uses a low-energy Bluetooth signal, which senses the location of shoppers in a retail environment who have Bluetooth-enabled smart phones.

The company has placed location sensors in its 40 stores and transmits real-time offers and discounts to smart phone users entering its retail shops. Shoppers who have downloaded the iBeacon app are detected in the store and receive offers based upon specific characteristics like gender and habits, time spent in the store, frequency of visits, and dollar amount of purchases. If a customer returns to Alex & Ani multiple times without making a purchase, a discount can be promptly sent to the user's smart phone to close the sale before a competitor does.

In conjunction with an advertising platform called Swirl, shoppers opt in to receive offers from companies like Alex & Ani, which are part of Swirl's retail partner network. A recent survey by Alex & Ani found that of the shoppers who viewed a 20 percent discount offer for a bracelet on their smart phones while in the store, 50 percent actually redeemed the offer.

Questions for Critical Thinking

1. Mobile marketing is becoming an important component of many retailers' integrated marketing strategies. Would you download an app to be notified of discounts and deals while shopping? What impact, if any, will this have on the retail shopping experience and privacy issues? Discuss.
2. Major League Baseball plans to use an iBeacon program at stadiums to guide fans who have downloaded the app to their seats and offer them discounts on food at concession stands throughout the game. Besides retail, list three other ways you envision the iBeacon technology being used.

Sources: Company website, www.alexandani.com, accessed March 18, 2014; Issie Lapowsky, "How Alex and Ani Is Pioneering the Future of Retail," *Inc.*, accessed March 18, 2014, www.inc.com; Clint Boulton, "Fashion Retailer Tries on Apple's iBeacon for Size," *The Wall Street Journal*, accessed February 19, 2014, http://online.wsj.com; Laura Heller, "Apple's iBeacon and the Future of Mobile Shopping," *Forbes*, accessed February 19, 2014, www.forbes.com; Reuven Gorsht, "How Apple's Understated Technology Can Transform Entire Industries," *Forbes*, accessed February 19, 2014, www.forbes.com.

Zipcar Informs, Persuades, and Reminds

CASE 13.3

A Zipster is one of 850,000 members of the world's largest car-sharing service, Cambridge, MA–based Zipcar. The company was founded more than a decade ago by two moms, Antje Danielson and Robin Chase, who met when their children were in the same kindergarten class. Today, Zipcar is owned by Avis Budget and offers self-serve, on-demand automobile reservations by the hour or day to three distinct customer segments: city dwellers, business people, and college students. Using various marketing channels and promotional activities, Zipcar targets each segment using a slightly different approach.

Zipcar employs several forms of advertising to inform, persuade, and remind, but the most effective approach is direct and personalized. Based on demographic information, the company uses technology to find the right target audiences to deliver the most timely and relevant messages. For example, Zipcar uses social media to market to college and university students with a message about the benefits of picking up and driving a Zipcar on or nearby campus and reserving a car using a mobile device or the web. The message to college students centers on the convenience and ultimate benefit of being a Zipster, when considering the expense of owning and maintaining a car while still in school. For city dwellers, Zipcar's marketing focus is on running errands or getting out of the city for a daylong excursion.

Not everyone understands how Zipcar's service works. From an advertising perspective, the company has discovered the effectiveness of direct response TV, which is TV advertising purchased on a national basis that appears in local markets. This approach has proved valuable to Zipcar's marketing mix. TV commercials are used to build awareness and inform users about how the service works. Unlike a traditional car rental service, Zipcar is based on the use of technology. Zipcar members have automated access to rentals using a "Zipcard," which works with the car's technology to unlock the door so customers can locate the keys inside the car. While there are annual membership fees and hourly rental rates, gas, parking, insurance, and maintenance are included.

Outdoor and Internet advertising strategies are effective for marketing Zipcar's services. For those looking online for car rentals, Zipcar's search engine optimization is leveraged on Twitter, YouTube, Facebook, and other social channels. In the early days of the company, promotional events included brand ambassadors from its field marketing organization (on college or university campuses, for example) to educate and inform students about Zipcar's benefits. In mature markets like New York and Boston, the marketing message focuses more on reminding users about Zipcar's value and less about educating and informing. In markets where car sharing is a new concept for most consumers, the promotional strategy centers on informing and differentiating Zipcar from competitors, mainly rental car companies and other modes of transportation.

Zipcar pursues multiple promotional objectives simultaneously. Recently the company collaborated with JetBlue to provide services for the airline's customers traveling to specific destinations. Oftentimes, Zipcar partners with retailers such as Ikea and Target where Zipcar members are known to shop frequently. A promotional program is created to encourage consumers to sign up for Zipcar, so that the next time they shop at the retailer they can get there using a Zipcar.

Zipcar's Chief Marketing Officer oversees membership, which is an integral part of the company's marketing efforts. Zipcar's field marketing representatives show up at farmer's markets, public transportation stations, and companies located in the city to educate and promote its value proposition and the benefits of its brand. Marketing strategies are developed around the seasonality of Zipcar's business, which varies between summer and winter months in each of its market segments.

To remain competitive with other modes of transportation, Zipcar carefully analyzes how it prices the cost of its services. Determining the pricing strategy for Zipcars located in a local city is actually a fairly complex process. With more than 10,000 vehicles across the globe, at 30 airports, and over 30 cities around North America, pricing varies by market. For example, in Boston where the company is headquartered, pricing ranges from $7.50 to $15 per hour. There is a onetime application fee to become a member, and various pricing plans are available depending on customers' needs and the type of vehicles available in each of its markets.

Zipcar remains a lifestyle brand, and the customer experience remains the company's most valuable marketing tool. So whether it's a car to run errands or to enjoy a night on the town, pricing will vary, but the customer experience remains the same. Using Zipcar allows you to avoid paying for gas or visiting the auto repair shop. That's clearly something worth advertising.

Questions for Critical Thinking

1. Discuss and provide examples of the different types of marketing channels and promotional activities Zipcar uses to target each of its three user segments. As marketing manager at Zipcar, discuss additional promotional strategies you would employ for each of the market segments.

2. Discuss how Zipcar is more a lifestyle brand than a travel brand, and what this means. How does this impact the company's promotional efforts? What solutions does Zipcar provide, and how does this make it a lifestyle brand?

3. Who are Zipcar's competitors and how do their promotional and advertising efforts compare? Do competitors vary for each of Zipcar's distinct market segments? What transportation options are there for each of the three segments?

4. Go online and perform additional research to learn more about Zipcar's pricing structure in your local market. Using pricing objectives discussed in the chapter (profitability, volume, meeting competition, and prestige), what do you believe are Zipcar's pricing objectives? Provide examples.

Sources: Company website, "Compare Plans," www.zipcar.com, accessed July 1, 2014; company website, "Zipcar Explained," www .zipcar.com, accessed July 1, 2014; company website, "Zipcar Overview," accessed July 1, 2014; Chris Ready, "Zipcar Rolls Out One-Way Service with Guaranteed Parking," *Boston Globe*, accessed June 27, 2014, www .bostonglobe.com; Mark Rogowsky, "Zipcar, Uber, and the Beginning of Trouble for the Auto Industry," *Forbes*, accessed June 26, 2014, www.forbes .com; Carol Hymowitz, "Zipcar Founder Robin Chase on Starting Buzzcar and a Portugal Venture," *Bloomberg Businessweek*, accessed June 26, 2014, www.businessweek.com; Natalie Zmuda, "Marketers Hitting Campus Harder than Ever," *AdAge*, accessed June 26, 2014, http://adage.com.

GREENSBURG, KS

Think Green, Go Green, Save Green

Not long ago, the phrase "hybrid SUV" would have seemed an oxymoron. But in just a few short years, fuel-efficient hybrids of all shapes and sizes have appeared in showrooms. This new generation of vehicles combines fuel-efficient gas engines, natural gas engines, and hydrogen fuel cells. As gas prices soar and concern over the environment grows, consumers will become more and more interested in them.

Enter Lee Lindquist, alternative fuels specialist at Scholfield Honda in Wichita, Kansas. A passionate environmentalist, Lee was researching alternative-fuel vehicles when he learned that Honda had been selling a natural gas Civic GX in New York and California since 1998. Originally marketed to municipalities and corporations as a way of addressing air quality issues, the Civic GX seemed the perfect way for cost-conscious Kansans to combat rising fuel prices. It was also a way to promote local resources, since Kansas is a major producer of natural gas.

Lee took the idea of the Civic GX to his boss, owner Roger Scholfield, who was skeptical of it at first. Scholfield had long promoted the Honda as a fuel-efficient vehicle and didn't want to muddy the waters with this new vehicle. But eventually he warmed to the idea and began offering the car to his corporate customers.

When the tornado hit Greensburg, the idea of going green took on a whole new life at Scholfield Honda. One of the problems with offering the Civic GX had been the lack of natural gas fueling stations, as well as the high cost of constructing one. Well aware of the media attention surrounding Greensburg, Scholfield decided to donate a natural gas Civic to the town, along with a fueling station.

Scholfield was up-front about the decision to donate the car. The investment was a costly one, and there were many less expensive ways of reaching his customers in Wichita. Scholfield admits he questioned his decision even as he drove into Greensburg for the presentation. But the bottom line was that it was the right thing to do. Today, when customers come into Scholfield's dealership, they are more interested in alternative-fuel and high-efficiency vehicles.

If you want to buy a Civic GX from Scholfield Honda today, get in line, because the staff can't keep them in stock. While you wait, enjoy a nice cup of coffee served in a compostable, corn-based disposable cup. Toss those old soda cans rattling around in your back seat into Scholfield's recycling bins. And on your way out, don't forget to take your complimentary Scholfield Honda reusable green shopping bag and water bottle.

Questions

After viewing the video, answer the following questions:

1. Do you think Scholfield's green marketing campaign will change consumers' opinions of hybrid and alternative-fuel cars?

2. Do you think Scholfield's donation of a natural gas Civic to the town of Greensburg will drive business to his dealership in Wichita? Why or why not?

LAUNCHING YOUR
[Marketing Career]

4

In Part 4, "Marketing Management," you learned about the goals and functions of marketing. The chapters in this part emphasized the central role of customer satisfaction in defining value and developing a marketing strategy in traditional and nontraditional marketing settings. You learned about the part played by marketing research and the need for relationship marketing in today's competitive environment. You discovered how new products are developed and how they evolve through the four stages of the product life cycle, from introduction through growth and maturity to decline. You also learned about the role of different channels in creating effective distribution strategies. Finally, you saw the impact of integrated marketing communications on the firm's promotional strategy, the role of advertising, and the way pricing influences consumer behavior. Perhaps you came across some marketing tasks and functions that sounded especially appealing to you. Here are a few ideas about careers in marketing that you may want to pursue.

The first thing to remember is that, as the chapters in this part made clear, marketing is about a great deal more than personal selling and advertising. For instance, are you curious about why people behave the way they do? Are you good at spotting trends? *Marketing research analysts* seek answers to a wide range of questions about business competition, customer preferences, market trends, and past and future sales. They often design and conduct their own consumer surveys, using the telephone, mail, the

Internet, or personal interviews and focus groups. After they analyze the data they've collected, their recommendations form input for managerial decisions about whether to introduce new products, revamp current ones, enter new markets, or abandon products or markets where profitability is low. As members of a new-product development team, marketing researchers often work directly with members of other business departments such as scientists, production and manufacturing personnel, and finance employees. Also, marketing researchers are increasingly asked to help clients implement their recommendations. With today's highly competitive economy, jobs in this area are expected to grow. Annual earnings for marketing research analysts average about $60,3000.[1]

Another career path in marketing is sales. Do you work well with others and read their feelings accurately? Are you a self-starter? Being a *sales representative* might be for you. Selling jobs exist in every industry, and because many use a combination of salary and performance-based commissions, they can pay handsomely. Sales jobs are often a first step on the ladder to upper-management positions as well. Sales representatives work for wholesalers and manufacturing companies (and even for publishers such as the one that produces this book). They sell automobiles, computer systems and technology, pharmaceuticals, advertising, insurance, real estate, commodities and financial services, and all kinds of consumer goods and services.

If you're interested in mass communications, note that print and online magazines, newspapers, and broadcast companies such as ESPN and MTV generate most of their revenue from advertising, so sales representatives who sell space and time slots in the media contribute a great deal to the success of these firms.[2] And if you like to travel, consider that many sales jobs involve travel.

Advertising, marketing management, and *public relations* are other categories of marketing. In large companies, marketing managers, product managers, promotion managers, and public relations managers often work long hours under pressure; they may travel frequently or transfer between jobs at headquarters and positions in regional offices. Their responsibilities include directing promotional programs, overseeing advertising campaigns and budgets, and creating communications such as press releases for the firm's customers. Thousands of new positions for public relations managers and specialists are expected to open up in the next several years; the field is expected to grow 13 percent over the next decade. Growth of the Internet and new media has especially increased demand for advertising and public relations specialists.[3]

Advertising and public relations firms together employed about 445,000 people in a recent year.[4] About 25 percent of U.S. advertising employees work in California, and another 20 percent work in New York. Most advertising firms develop specialties; many of the largest are international in scope and earn a major proportion of their revenue abroad. Online advertising is just one area in which new jobs will be opening in the future, as more and more client firms expand their online sales operations.

Career Assessment Exercises in Marketing

1. Select a field that interests you. Use the Internet to research types of sales positions available in that field. Locate a few entry-level job openings and see the career steps that the positions can lead to. (You might start with a popular job-posting site such as Monster.com.) Note the job requirements, the starting salary, and the form of compensation—straight salary? salary plus commission?—and write a one-page summary of your findings.

2. Use the Internet to identify and investigate two or three of the leading advertising agencies in the United States, such as Weiden + Kennedy, BBDO, Grey, Ogilvy, or Young & Rubicam. What are some of their recent ad campaigns, or who are their best-known clients? Where do the agencies have offices? What job openings do they currently list, and what qualifications should applicants for these positions have? Write a brief report comparing the agencies you selected, decide which one you would prefer to work for, and give your reasons.

3. Test your research skills. Choose an ordinary product, such as toothpaste or soft drinks, and conduct a survey to find out why people chose the brand they most recently purchased. For instance, suppose you wanted to find out how people choose their shampoo. List as many decision criteria as you can think of, such as availability, scent, price, packaging, benefits from use (conditioning, dandruff-reducing, and so on), brand name, and ad campaign. Ask eight to ten friends to rank these decision factors, and note some simple demographics about your research subjects such as their age, gender, and occupation. Tabulate your results. What did you find out about how your subjects made their purchase decision? Did any of your findings surprise you? Can you think of any ways in which you might have improved your survey?

Chapter 14

Learning Objectives

[1] Distinguish between data and information and discuss information systems.

[2] List the components and types of information systems.

[3] Discuss computer hardware and software.

[4] Describe computer networks.

[5] Outline the security and ethical issues affecting information systems.

[6] Explain disaster recovery and backup.

[7] Review information technology trends.

Using Technology to Manage Information

© violetkaipa/iStockphoto

Big Data Equals Big Profits with the Right Focus

Every time you use a computer or mobile device to send an e-mail, upload a picture, or check a bank balance, you are generating information that is encoded and transmitted to a network of computer servers. While the size of these transactions may generate anywhere from a kilobyte to a few megabytes of data, when these actions are summed together among the billions of computer users worldwide, the amount of information collected is mind boggling. In fact, worldwide data transmitted or stored on computer servers is now estimated to be in the multiple zetta-byte range—with a zettabyte equaling one number followed by *21* zeros.

While technical issues like data storage and data search are being addressed by the likes of Amazon, Cisco, EMC, Google, and Facebook, there are a number of new companies being formed specifically to look through all of this information, which is now called big data. Much of the work done by these firms relies on advanced statistical methods, sifting through huge volumes of data looking for trends, patterns, and new insights. The companies sell this data to other firms, which use it as part of their overall business strategy.

Given the exceedingly large amounts of data available, it is hard to know how to analyze all of this information. Big data startup companies face the same challenge. Kaggle is a business that started several years ago as a platform for hosting public data science challenges, in which companies paid a fee, posted their problems to the Kaggle website, and data scientists from all over the world competed to create the best solution. Recently, however, the San Francisco–based company has shifted its big data business model to focus on creating models and software for the energy industry.

For Kaggle, this meant zeroing in on the oil and gas drilling sector. While the data used in traditional oil drilling is understood, fracking—discussed in Chapter 1's opening story—is a somewhat different process. Variables like how long have deep rock formations existed in the Earth and which operator to partner with may matter when it comes to conducting successful fracking operations. And these types of new and seemingly unrelated variables make big data an important tool for many businesses.

And if Kaggle needs an incentive to stay focused, it might want to consider the case of Climate Corporation. This firm tried to sell predictive data about weather to farmers, house painters, and even golf courses. After it decided to concentrate on data analytics in the agriculture industry, Climate Corporation was bought by chemical giant Monsanto for $930 million. Perhaps the most important trend for big data firms to focus on is how to provide a continuing stream of value to their clients.[1]

Overview

This chapter explores how businesses manage information as a resource, particularly how they use technology to do so. Today, virtually all business functions—from human resources to production to supply chain management—rely on information systems. The chapter begins by differentiating between information and data and then defines an information system. The components of information systems are presented, and two major types of information systems are described. Because of their importance to organizations, the chapter discusses databases, the heart of all information systems. Then the chapter looks at the computer hardware and software that drive information systems. Today, specialized networks make information access and transmission function smoothly, so the chapter examines different types of telecommunications and computer networks to see how companies are applying them for competitive advantage. The chapter then turns to a discussion of the ethical and security issues affecting information systems, followed by a description of how organizations plan for, and recover from, information system disasters. A review of the current trends in information systems concludes the chapter.

[1] Data, Information, and Information Systems

Every day, businesspeople ask themselves questions such as the following:

- How well is our product selling in Boston compared to Phoenix? Have sales among consumers aged 25 to 45 increased or decreased within the past year?

- How will fluctuating energy prices affect production and distribution costs?

- If employees can access the benefits system through our network, will this increase or decrease benefit costs?

- How can we communicate more efficiently and effectively with our increasingly diverse and global workforce?

data raw facts and figures that may or may not be relevant to a business decision.

information knowledge gained from processing data.

information system organized method for collecting, storing, and communicating past, present, and projected information on internal operations and external intelligence.

chief information officer (CIO) executive responsible for managing a firm's information system and related computer technologies.

An effective information system can help answer these and many other questions. **Data** consist of raw facts and figures that may or may not be relevant to a business decision. **Information** is knowledge gained from processing those facts and figures. So although businesspeople need to gather data about the demographics of a target market or the specifications of a certain product, the data are useless unless they are transformed into relevant information that can be used to make a competitive decision. For instance, data might be the sizes of various demographic groups. Information drawn from those data could be how many of those individuals are potential customers for a firm's products. Technology has advanced so quickly that all businesses, regardless of size or location, now have access to data and information that can make them competitive in a global arena.

An **information system** is an organized method for collecting, storing, and communicating past, present, and projected information on internal operations and external intelligence. Most information systems today use computer and telecommunications technology. A large organization typically assigns responsibility for directing its information systems and related operations to an executive called the **chief information officer (CIO)**. Often, the CIO reports directly to the firm's chief executive officer (CEO). An effective CIO will understand and harness technology so that the company can communicate internally and externally in one seamless operation. But small companies rely just as much on information systems as large ones do, even if they do not employ a manager assigned to this area on a full-time basis.

Today's CIO, closely connected to the company's overall business strategies and marketing efforts, is concerned with how cloud-delivered business services of software and data are transmitted to enterprises, with a focus on sales, customer interfaces, and "consumerization," the reorientation of goods and service designs around the individual end user. Yesterday's CIO, focused on installation and design of software, has become increasingly aware of the need for data security, systems availability, and responsiveness. Their expertise makes CIOs and former CIOs good candidates for corporate boards.[2]

Information systems can be tailored to assist many business functions and departments—from marketing and manufacturing to finance and accounting. They can manage the overwhelming information overload by organizing data in a logical and accessible manner. Through the system, a company can not only plan better but also manage all components of its operations and business strategy, identifying challenges and opportunities. Information systems gather data from inside and outside the organization; they then process the data to produce information that is relevant to all aspects of the organization. Processing steps could involve storing data for later use, classifying and analyzing it, and retrieving it easily when needed.

Many companies and nations combine various solutions to manage the flow of information. E-mail, online meetings, intranets, and wireless communications have not totally replaced face-to-face meetings, written correspondence, and phone conversations, but they have become increasingly common. Information can make the difference between a company being profitable or filing for bankruptcy. Keeping on top of changing consumer demands, competitors' actions, and the latest government regulations will help a firm fine-tune existing products, develop new ones, and maintain effective marketing. Today's companies face technological megatrends that include cloud computing, mobile computing, social media, video platforms, and big data.[3]

Assessment Check ☑

1. Distinguish between data and information.

2. What is an information system?

2 Components and Types of Information Systems

The definition of *information system* in the previous section does not specifically mention the use of computers or technology. In fact, information systems have been around since the beginning of civilization but were, by today's standards, very low tech. Think about your college or university's library. At one time the library probably had card catalog files to help users find information. Those files were information systems because they stored data about books and periodicals on 3-by-5-inch index cards.

Today, however, when businesspeople think about information systems, they are most likely thinking about **computer-based information systems**. These systems rely on computer and related technologies to store information electronically in an organized, accessible manner. So, instead of card catalogs, your college library probably uses a computerized information system that allows users to search through periodicals, journals, and books and even digital collections of historic photographs, manuscripts, and maps.

computer-based information systems information systems that rely on computer and related technologies to store information electronically in an organized, accessible manner.

Computer-based information systems consist of four components and technologies:

- computer hardware
- computer software
- telecommunications and computer networks
- data resource management

Computer hardware consists of machines that range from supercomputers to smart phones. It also includes the input, output, and storage devices needed to support computing machines. Software includes operating systems, such as Microsoft's Windows 8 or Linux, and applications programs, such as Adobe Acrobat and Customer Relationship Management, or CRM. Consumer software includes Dropbox and Evernote, while enterprise software includes Salesforce.com and Workday. In addition, mobile software consists primarily of iOS and Android operating systems.

Telecommunications and computer networks encompass the hardware and software needed to provide wired or wireless voice and data communications. This includes support for external networks such as the Internet and private internal networks. Data resource management involves developing and maintaining an organization's databases so that decision makers are able to access the information they need in a timely manner.

In the case of your institution's library, the computer-based information system is generally made up of computer hardware, such as monitors and keyboards, which are linked to the library's network and a database containing information on the library's holdings. Specialized software allows users to access the database. In addition, the library's network is likely also

Libraries typically use a computer-based information system, made up of computer hardware linked to the library's network and a database containing information on the books in the library. Specialized software allows users to access the database.

Purestock/Getty Images, Inc.

Hit&Miss

Target's Customer Data Gets Hacked

At the height of a recent holiday season, a retailer's worst nightmare became a reality for Minneapolis-based Target. In less than three weeks, cyber thieves hacked more than 110 million customer debit and credit card account names and numbers, stealing encrypted PIN data and security codes on the back of the cards used at the 1,797 U.S. Target stores. The hack occurred through Target's point-of-sale-system, where every number was copied as shoppers swiped or entered data at store checkouts.

Target set up a telephone hotline to answer all questions and offered one year of free credit monitoring to all customers, regardless of whether or not they were impacted by the breach. In addition, storewide discounts of 10 percent were offered the weekend after the breach was discovered.

While customers are not responsible for any fraudulent charges on their cards, many are angry, and a number of shoppers have pursued class action lawsuits against the retailer, claiming it was negligent at protecting their data. Then CEO Gregg Steinhafel apologized to customers about the breach and announced that Target would work with banks and other retailers to adopt a more secure technology that uses credit and debit cards with embedded chips, which are more difficult to counterfeit. Both Steinhafel and the company's chief technology officer have since resigned from the company over the data breach.

Questions for Critical Thinking

1. Critics say that what happened to Target is not the retailer's fault, but is more the blame of U.S. data security and how much we lag behind the rest of the world in securing personal financial information. Do you agree or disagree?

2. How much do you think a breach of this nature actually hurts Target in the long run?

Sources: Russell Brandom, "Target CEO Resigns in the Wake of Data Breach," *The Verge*, accessed May 18, 2014, www.theverge.com; Tiffany Hsu, "Target Technology Chief Beth Jacob Resigns after Breach," *Los Angeles Times*, accessed May 18, 2014, http://articles.latimes.com; Michael Riley, Ben Elgin, Dune Lawrence, and Carol Matlack, "Missed Alarms and 40 Million Stolen Credit Card Numbers: How Target Blew It," *Bloomberg Businessweek*, accessed March 20, 2014, www.businessweek.com; Kevin Johnson, "Feds Investigating Target Data Breach," *USA Today*, accessed March 20, 2014, www.usatoday.com; Gregory Wallace, "Target Credit Card Hack: What You Need to Know," *CNN*, accessed March 20, 2014, http://money.cnn.com; Joshua Brustein "Is Target to Blame for Its Data Breach? Let the Lawsuits Begin," *Bloomberg Businessweek*, accessed March 20, 2014, www.businessweek.com.

---

connected to a larger private network and the Internet. This connection gives users remote access to the library's database, as well as access to other computerized databases such as LexisNexis.

Databases

database centralized integrated collection of data resources.

The heart of any information system is its **database**, a centralized integrated collection of data resources. A company designs its databases to meet particular information processing and retrieval needs of its workforce. Businesses obtain databases in many ways. They can hire a staff person to build them on site, hire an outside source to do so, or buy cloud-based services from specialized vendors, such as Oracle, SAP, or Salesforce.com. A database serves as an electronic filing cabinet, capable of storing massive amounts of data and retrieving it within seconds. A database should be continually updated; otherwise, a firm may find itself with information that is obsolete, outdated, and possibly useless. One problem with databases is that they can contribute to information overload—too much data for people to absorb or data that are not relevant to decision making. Because both computer processing speed and storage capacity have increased so dramatically, and because data have become so abundant, businesspeople need to be careful that their databases contain only the facts they need. If they don't, they can waste time wading through unnecessary data. Another challenge with databases is security, as the "Hit & Miss" feature describes.

operational support systems information systems designed to produce a variety of information on an organization's activities for both internal and external users.

transaction processing systems operational support system to record and process data from business transactions.

Decision makers can also look up online data. Online systems give access to enormous amounts of government data, such as economic data from the Bureau of Labor Statistics and the Department of Commerce. One of the largest online databases is that of the U.S. Census Bureau. The census of population, conducted every ten years, collects data on more than 120 million households across the United States. After attempting to count everyone in the country, the Census Bureau has selected participants fill out forms containing questions about marital status, place of birth, ethnic background, citizenship, workplaces, commuting time, income, occupation, type of housing, number of telephones and vehicles, even grandparents as caregivers.[4] Households receiving the most recent questionnaire can respond in English as well as a variety of other languages including Spanish, Chinese, Vietnamese, and Korean. Not surprisingly, sifting through all the collected data takes time. Although certain restrictions limit how businesspeople can access and use specific census data, the general public may access the data via the American FactFinder on the Census Bureau's website (http://factfinder2.census.gov), as well as at state data centers and public libraries.

Another source of free information is company websites. Interested parties can visit a company's site to research customers, suppliers, and competitors. Trade associations and academic institutions also maintain websites with relevant information.

Types of Information Systems

Many different types of information systems exist. In general, however, information systems fall into two broad categories: operational support systems or management support systems.

Operational Support Systems Operational support systems are designed to produce a variety of information on an organization's activities for both internal and external users. Examples of operational support systems include transaction processing systems, process control systems, and enterprise collaboration systems, which facilitate efficient sharing of documents and knowledge between teams and individuals within an organization. Transaction processing systems record and process data from business transactions. For example, major retailers use point-of-sale systems, which link electronic cash registers to the retailer's computer centers. Sales data are transmitted from cash registers to the computer center either immediately or at regular intervals. Process control systems monitor and control physical processes. A steel mill, for instance, may have electronic sensors linked to a computer system monitoring the entire production process. The system makes necessary changes and alerts operators to potential problems.

Management Support Systems Information systems that are designed to provide support for effective decision making are classified as management support systems. Several different types of management support systems are available. A management information system (MIS) is designed to produce reports for managers and other personnel.

A decision support system (DSS) gives direct support to businesspeople during the decision-making process. For instance, a marketing manager might use a decision support system to analyze the impact on sales and profits of a product price change.

An executive support system (ESS) lets senior executives access the firm's primary databases, often by touching the computer screen, pointing and clicking a mouse, or using voice recognition. The typical ESS allows users to choose from many types of data, such as the firm's financial statements and sales figures, as well as stock market trends for the company and for the industry as a whole. Managers can start by looking at summaries and then access more detailed information as needed.

Finally, an expert system is a computer program that imitates human thinking through complicated sets of if-then rules. The system applies human knowledge in a specific subject area to solve a problem. Expert systems

process control systems operational support system to monitor and control physical processes.

management support systems information systems that are designed to provide support for effective decision making.

management information system (MIS) information system that is designed to produce reports for managers and others within the organization.

decision support system (DSS) gives direct support to businesspeople during the decision-making process.

executive support system (ESS) lets senior executives access the firm's primary databases, often by touching the computer screen, pointing and clicking a mouse, or using voice recognition.

expert system computer program that imitates human thinking through complicated sets of if-then rules.

The complex process of airline maintenance is critical to passenger safety. To track parts, schedule inspections, and manage inventory levels, many airlines, including American, use an operational support system.

Chapter 14 *Using Technology to Manage Information* **409**

Assessment Check ✅

1. List the four components of a computer-based information system.
2. What is a database?
3. What are the two general types of information systems? Give examples of each.

are used for a variety of business purposes: determining credit limits for credit card applicants, monitoring machinery in a plant to predict potential problems or breakdowns, making mortgage loans, and determining optimal plant layouts. They are typically developed by capturing the knowledge of recognized experts in a field whether within a business itself or outside it.

⌐3⌐ Computer Hardware and Software

The first commercial computer, UNIVAC I, was sold to the U.S. Census Bureau in the early 1950s. It cost $1 million, took up most of a room, and could perform about 2,000 calculations per second.[5] The invention of transistors and then integrated circuits (microchips) quickly led to smaller and more powerful devices. By the 1980s, computers could routinely perform several million calculations per second. Now, computers perform billions of calculations per second, and many fit in the palm of your hand.

When the first personal computers were introduced in the late 1970s and early 1980s, the idea of a computer on every desk, or in every home, seemed far-fetched. Today they have become indispensable to both businesses and households. Not only have computers become much more powerful and faster over the past 25 years, but they are less expensive as well. IBM's first personal computer (PC), introduced in 1981, cost well over $5,000 fully configured. Today, due to decreased demand and lower production costs, a typical PC sells for between $400 and $700; products in Apple's Mac lineup average $1,300. Average performance laptops sell for between $275 and $500.[6]

Types of Computer Hardware

hardware all tangible elements of a computer system.

Hardware consists of all tangible elements of a computer system—the input devices, the components that store and process data and perform required calculations, and the output devices that present the results to information users. Input devices allow users to enter data and commands for processing, storage, and output. The most common input devices are the keyboard and mouse. Storage and processing components consist of the hard drive found on older computers. Although more expensive, solid-state drives are faster and more power efficient today, and some computers use a disk array controller for greater performance. Backing up important documents with external hardware is less prevalent today, as the Internet has provided storage solutions like Box, a service that allows you to save local files to the cloud. Flash memory devices, also called thumb drives, are small and can hold large amounts of data and are easily accessed by plugging the drive into a USB (universal serial bus) port. Output devices, such as monitors and printers, are the hardware elements that transmit or display documents and other results of a computer system's work.

Different types of computers incorporate widely varying memory capacities and processing speeds. These differences define four broad classifications: mainframe computers, midrange systems, personal computers, and hand-held devices. A mainframe computer is the largest type of computer system with the most extensive storage capacity and the fastest processing speeds. Especially powerful mainframes called *supercomputers* can handle extremely rapid, complex calculations involving thousands of variables, such as weather modeling and forecasting. One of the fastest supercomputers today is the Tianhe-2 in China, with 33,860 trillion calculations per second.[7]

Midrange systems consist of high-end network servers and other types of computers that can handle large-scale processing

Because of their ever-increasing capabilities, smart phones have rapidly replaced cell phones on a worldwide basis.

needs. They are less powerful than mainframe computers but more powerful than most personal computers. A **server** is the heart of a midrange computer network, supporting applications and allowing the sharing of output devices, software, and databases among networked users. Many Internet-related functions at organizations are handled by midrange systems. Midrange systems are also commonly employed in process control systems, computer-aided manufacturing (CAM), and computer-aided design (CAD).

Once the center of the digital universe, a full-scale Windows or Mac OS personal desktop computer was the way most people accessed the Internet, wrote papers, played games, organized music and photos, and more. While some believe the PC is on its way to extinction and ownership rates have declined, PCs are still popular in homes, businesses, schools, and government agencies. Tablet sales recently surpassed PC sales.[8]

Desktop computers used to be the standard PC seen in offices and homes. While millions of desktop computers remain on the job, laptops—including notebooks and netbooks—have surpassed desktop units in sales. The increasing popularity of these computers can be explained by smaller, lighter, more powerful computing, and by their improved displays, faster processing speeds, ability to handle more intense graphics, larger storage capacities, and more durable designs. Business owners, managers, salespeople, and students all benefit from their portability and instantaneous access to information. In the next few years, analysts predict that more than half of the smart connected devices sold will be tablets, followed by laptops and desktops. In a recent quarter, tablet sales surpassed desktop and laptop sales combined.[9]

Prices for full-size laptops, notebooks, and net-books vary greatly—but you can purchase a netbook for an average of $250 to $350 or a MacBook Pro laptop for between $1,200 and $2,600. A netbook does not have the computing capacity of a larger, more expensive notebook, but it can perform basic tasks such as search, e-mail, word processing, and spreadsheet calculations.

Hand-held devices such as smart phones are even smaller. The most popular smart phones today are powered by Google's Android and Apple's iOS mobile operating systems. Smart phones like the iPhone and Samsung's Galaxy essentially combine a mobile phone with more advanced computing capabilities than their predecessor, the basic cell phone.

Two other devices—tablets and e-readers—are taking major market share from laptops. According to Pew Research Center's Internet and American Life Project, more than a third of U.S. adults now own a tablet.[10] In addition to the Apple iPad, the top selling tablet, there are a proliferation of tablet models on the market, including those from Google, Samsung, Amazon, and Sony. E-readers such as Amazon's Kindle continue to expand their market share. Currently, about 32 percent of U.S. adults own an e-reader. A hybrid device, called a phablet, is a cross between a smart phone and a tablet, with a screen larger than a smart phone but smaller than a tablet.

While smart phones can be terrific tools that boost productivity, some people overuse or even misuse them. The "Career Kickstart" feature describes some of the do's and don'ts of smart phone use in the business environment.

Courteous Communications via Mobile Devices

The number of smart phone users worldwide is expected to reach 4.5 billion over the next few years. It is estimated that at least 25 percent of the world's population use a smart phone at least monthly. With so much mobile phone use, it's more important than ever to communicate courteously. Consider these tips:

1 *Be aware of your surroundings and your neighbors.* If you're someplace where a phone conversation would be disruptive, turn off your ringtone. If the call or e-mail simply can't wait, excuse yourself and leave the room to respond.

2 *Lower your voice.* If you're in a room that's quieter than your speaking voice, go somewhere else.

3 *When e-mailing or texting, don't overabbreviate.* Business messages can be concise without being cute or unintelligible. For example, say "See you at 3," not "cu@3."

4 *Before sending a text message or e-mail, reread it carefully.* Typos and grammatical errors have no place in a business message.

5 *Be careful with Facebook photos.* Now that smart phones let users link all their contact information, your photo will appear on the other person's phone when you call. And people beyond those on your Facebook friends list will see it. Be sure your photo is appropriate for both friends and business callers.

Sources: "Smartphone Users Worldwide Will Total 1.75 Billion in 2014," *eMarketer,* accessed February 27, 2014, www.emarketer.com; Christopher Elliott, "E-Mail Etiquette for Wireless Devices," *Microsoft Small Business Center,* accessed February 25, 2014, www.microsoft.com; Taya Flores, "Cell Phone Etiquette Is Important," *JC Online,* accessed February 25, 2014, www.jconline.com; Mike Elgan, "Here Comes the New Cell Phone Etiquette," *IT World,* accessed February 25, 2014, www.itworld.com.

server the heart of a mid-range computer network.

In addition to smart phones, specialized hand-held devices are used in a variety of businesses for different applications. Some restaurants, for example, have small wireless devices that allow servers to swipe a credit card and print out a receipt right at the customer's table. Drivers for UPS and FedEx use special hand-held scanning devices to track package deliveries and accept delivery signatures. The driver scans each package as it is delivered, and the information is transmitted to the delivery firm's network. Within a few seconds, the sender, using an Internet connection, can obtain the delivery information and even see a facsimile of the recipient's signature.

Computer Software

software all the programs, routines, and computer languages that control a computer and tell it how to operate.

Software includes all of the programs, routines, and computer languages that control a computer and tell it how to operate. The software that controls the basic workings of a computer system is its *operating system*. More than 80 percent of personal computers use a version of Microsoft's popular Windows operating system. Personal computers made by Apple use the Mac operating system. The Android and iPhone models have their own operating systems. Other operating systems include Unix, which runs on many midrange computer systems, and Linux, which runs on both PCs and midrange systems.

A program that performs the specific tasks that the user wants to carry out—such as writing a letter or looking up data—is called *application software*. Examples of application software include Adobe Acrobat, Microsoft PowerPoint, and Quicken. Table 14.1 lists the major categories of application software. Most application programs are currently stored on individual computers. However, most application software has become web based, with the programs themselves stored on Internet-connected, cloud-based servers.

TABLE

⌐14.1⌐ Common Types of Application Software

TYPE	DESCRIPTION	EXAMPLES
Word processing	Programs that input, store, retrieve, edit, and print various types of documents.	Microsoft Word, Google Docs
Spreadsheets	Programs that prepare and analyze financial statements, sales forecasts, budgets, and similar numerical and statistical data.	Microsoft Excel, Google Docs
Presentation software	Programs that create presentations. Users can create bulleted lists, charts, graphs, pictures, audio, and even short video clips.	Microsoft PowerPoint, Google Docs, Prezi
Desktop publishing	Software that combines high-quality type, graphics, and layout tools to create output that can look as attractive as documents produced by professional publishers and printers.	Adobe InDesign, Microsoft Publisher
Financial software	Programs that compile accounting and financial data to create financial statements, reports, and budgets; they perform basic financial management tasks such as balancing a checkbook.	Quicken, Intuit QuickBooks
Database programs	Software that searches and retrieves data from a database; it can sort data based on various criteria.	Microsoft Access, Intuit QuickBase
Personal information managers	Specialized database programs that allow people to track communications with personal and business contacts; some combine e-mail capability.	Microsoft Outlook
Enterprise resource planning	Integrated cross-functional software that controls many business activities, including distribution, finance, and human resources.	SAP Enterprise Resource Planning, Salesforce.com

Assessment Check ☑

1. List two input and output devices.
2. What accounts for the increased popularity of laptop and notebook computers?
3. What is software? List the two categories of software.

412

An app is a software program, and most are designed to run on a smart phone or a tablet. Originally intended for e-mail, calendar, and contact databases, apps continue to be in high demand for other areas like games, GPS, factory automation, banking, order tracking, ticket purchases, and travel. In a recent year, more than 102 billion apps were downloaded, most of them free, but they still generated $26 billion in revenue.[11]

4 Computer Networks

As mentioned earlier, virtually all computers today are linked to networks. In fact, if your PC has Internet access, you're linked to a network. Local area networks and wide area networks allow businesses to communicate, transmit and print documents, and share data. These networks, however, require businesses to install special equipment and connections between office sites. But Internet technology has also been applied to internal company communications and business tasks, tapping a ready-made network. Among these Internet-based applications are intranets, virtual private networks (VPNs), and voice over Internet protocol (VoIP). Each has contributed to the effectiveness and speed of business processes, so we discuss them next.

Local Area Networks and Wide Area Networks

Most organizations connect their offices and buildings by creating local area networks (LANs), computer networks that connect machines within limited areas, such as a building or several nearby buildings. LANs are useful because they link computers and allow them to share printers, documents, and information, as well as provide access to the Internet. Figure 14.1 shows what a small business computer network might look like.

Wide area networks (WANs) tie larger geographical regions together by using telephone lines and microwave and satellite transmission. One familiar WAN is long-distance telephone service. Companies such as AT&T and Verizon provide WAN services to businesses and consumers. Firms also use WANs to conduct their own operations. Typically, companies link their own network systems to outside communications equipment and services for transmission across long distances.

Wireless Local Networks

A wireless network allows computers, printers, and other devices to be connected without the hassle of stringing cables in traditional office settings. The current standard for wireless networks is called Wi-Fi. Wi-Fi —short for *wireless fidelity*—is a wireless network that connects various devices and allows them to communicate with one another through radio waves. Any device with a Wi-Fi receptor can connect with the Internet at so-called hot spots— locations with a wireless router and a high-speed Internet modem. There are hundreds of thousands of hot spots worldwide today. Wi-Fi can be found in a variety of places, including restaurants, hotels, airports, libraries, and cafés. Some locations, like

local area networks (LANs) computer networks that connect machines within limited areas, such as a building or several nearby buildings.

wide area networks (WANs) tie larger geographical regions together by using telephone lines and microwave and satellite transmission.

Wi-Fi wireless network that connects various devices and allows them to communicate with one another through radio waves.

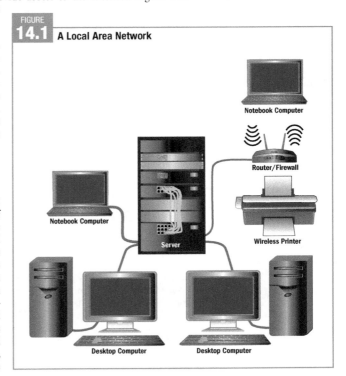

FIGURE 14.1 A Local Area Network

Floresco Productions/Getty Images, Inc.

Wi-Fi connections are often called hot spots—locations with a wireless router and a high-speed Internet modem. There are hundreds of thousands of hot spots worldwide today found in a variety of places, including airports, libraries, and coffee shops.

McDonald's, Starbucks, Panera, Whole Foods, Staples, and Apple Stores, offer free access, while others charge a fee.[12]

Many believe that the successor to Wi-Fi will be *Wi-Max*. Unlike Wi-Fi's relatively limited geographic coverage area—generally around 300 feet—a single Wi-Max access point can provide coverage over many miles. Due to its higher cost, however, the adoption of Wi-Max has been limited.[13] In addition, cell phone service providers, such as Sprint Nextel and AT&T, offer broadband network cards for notebook PCs. These devices allow users to access the provider's mobile broadband network from virtually any location where cell phone reception is available.

Intranets

A broad approach to sharing information in an organization is to establish a company network patterned after the Internet. Such a network is called an **intranet**. Intranets are similar to the Internet, but they limit access to employees or other authorized users. An intranet blocks outsiders without valid passwords from entering its network by incorporating both software and hardware known as a **firewall**. Firewalls limit data transfers to certain locations and log system use so that managers can identify attempts to log on with invalid passwords and other threats to a system's security. Highly sophisticated real-time threat defense alert systems let administrators know about suspicious activities and permit authorized personnel to use smart cards to connect from remote terminals.

Intranets solve the problem of linking different types of computers. Like the Internet, intranets can integrate computers running all kinds of operating systems. In addition, intranets are relatively easy and inexpensive to set up because most businesses already have some of the required hardware and software. All the business's computers will be linked with each other and with the Internet. Microsoft's SharePoint is the dominant software used for creating intranets.

Intranets enable collaboration among employees who are traveling or telecommuting. They can nurture innovation and the development of creative ideas. They can be used to share marketing and brand information worldwide. Mobile intranets—with access from smart phones—are becoming increasingly popular for companies with employees who are often on the go.

Virtual Private Networks

To gain increased security for Internet communications, companies often turn to **virtual private networks (VPNs)**, secure connections between two points on the Internet. These VPNs use firewalls and programs that encapsulate data to make them more secure during transit. Loosely defined, a VPN can include a range of networking technologies, from secure Internet connections to private networks from service providers such as IBM. A VPN is less expensive for a company to use than leasing several of its own lines. It can also take months to install a leased line in some parts of the world, but a new user can be added to a VPN in a day. Because a VPN uses the Internet, it can be wired, wireless, or a combination of the two.

Colorado-based Advanced Systems Group (ASG) provides data storage and management services to other companies. As the company expanded and opened branch offices, its own security became a concern. ASG turned to Check Point, which created a secure VPN

intranet computer network that is similar to the Internet but limits access to authorized users.

firewall limits data transfers to certain locations and log system use so that managers can identify attempts to log on with invalid passwords and other threats to a system's security.

virtual private networks (VPNs) secure connections between two points on the Internet.

Part 5 *Managing Technology and Information*

connecting ASG's home office and its branch offices. The VPN allows ASG to add new sites and new remote users automatically.[14]

VoIP

VoIP—which stands for *voice over Internet Protocol*—is an alternative to traditional telecommunication services provided by companies such as Verizon and Sprint. The VoIP telephone is connected to a personal computer with any type of broadband connection instead of a traditional phone jack. Special software transmits phone conversations over the Internet, rather than through telephone lines. A VoIP user dials the phone as usual. The person can make and receive calls to and from those with traditional telephone connections (landline or wireless).

A growing number of consumers and businesses have embraced VoIP, mainly due to its cost savings and extra features. As technology continues to advance, demand for the service has increased. Several wireless companies, including AT&T and Verizon, permit VoIP on smart phones. Google integrates its Google Voice over VoIP. The various VoIP providers are working together with the goal of creating a single VoIP standard that would permit seamless roaming worldwide.[15]

In spite of VoIP's apparent advantages, there are several potential drawbacks to replacing traditional telephony with Internet telephony. For one thing, your Internet phone service will be only as reliable as your broadband connection. If your broadband connection goes out, so will your phone service. Also, without extensive safeguards, VoIP can expose a phone system to the havoc that can affect the rest of the Internet, such as worms and viruses.

VoIP alternative to traditional telecommunication services provided by companies such as Verizon and Sprint.

Assessment Check ☑

1. What is a LAN?

2. What are the differences between an intranet and a VPN?

3. Briefly explain how VoIP works.

⌐5⌐ Security and Ethical Issues Affecting Information Systems

Numerous security and ethical issues affect information systems. As information systems become increasingly important business assets, they also become progressively harder and more expensive to replace. Damage to information systems or theft of data can have disastrous consequences. When computers are connected to a network, a problem at any individual computer can affect the entire network. Two of the major security threats are cybercrime and so-called malware.

Cybercrime

Computers provide efficient ways for employees to share information. But they may also allow people with more malicious intentions to access information. Or they may allow pranksters—who have no motive other than to see whether they can hack into a system—to gain access to private information. Common cybercrimes involve stealing or altering data in several ways:

- Employees or outsiders may change or invent data to produce inaccurate or misleading information.

- Employees or outsiders may modify computer programs to create false information or illegal transactions or to insert viruses.

- Unauthorized people can access computer systems for their own benefit or knowledge or just to see if they can get in.

Individuals, businesses, and government agencies are all vulnerable to computer crime. Computer hackers—unauthorized users—sometimes work alone and sometimes work in groups. Hackers can break into computer systems just to show that they can do it; other times they have more sinister motives. A recent survey reported that although computer crime decreased slightly recently, the majority of such attacks may go undetected because many firms have concentrated on foiling hackers and blocking pornography while leaving themselves open to cybercriminals who are developing increasingly sophisticated weapons. Even Apple computers, usually immune to cybercrime, are becoming vulnerable as more and more Mac users store data in the cloud—that is, on the Internet itself—rather than on hard drives. Until now there has been no single uniform system for reporting cybercrime, but the Internet Engineering Task Force (IETF) is proposing a common format able to analyze massive amounts of data much faster than human analysts can.[16]

Information system administrators implement two basic protections against computer crime: They try to prevent access to their systems by unauthorized users and the viewing of data by unauthorized system users. The simplest method of preventing access requires authorized users to enter passwords. The company may also install firewalls, described earlier. To prevent system users from reading sensitive information, the company may use encryption software, which encodes, or scrambles, messages. To read encrypted messages, users must use an electronic key to convert them to regular text. But as fast as software developers invent new and more elaborate protective measures, hackers seem to break through their defenses. Thus, security is an ongoing battle.

Consumers with credit cards are particularly at risk from hackers. Recently, luxury retailer Neiman Marcus discovered that hackers had breached its cyber-security system, which compromised customer credit card data. It is important for payment-processing companies used by major credit card companies to put protections in place so that consumer credit and debit card information remain safe.[17]

As the size of computer hardware diminishes, it becomes increasingly vulnerable to theft. Hand-held devices, for instance, are particularly susceptible to theft. At an estimated cost of $30 billion annually, one in three robberies now involves smart phones.[18] Many notebook computers and hand-held devices contain special security software or passwords that make it difficult for a thief or any unauthorized person to access the data stored in the computer's memory. Find My iPhone was introduced for iOS users to locate their device and remotely delete data in the event it was lost or stolen. Apple recently updated its operating system to include software with an activation lock to prevent access to confidential information in the event of theft, similar to a kill switch feature.[19] Lawmakers in several states have proposed legislation requiring manufacturers to install a kill switch or mechanism to disable stolen phones in an effort to protect data and diminish resale value of the stolen device.[20]

Computer Viruses, Worms, Trojan Horses, and Spyware

malware any malicious software program designed to infect computer systems.

Viruses, worms, Trojan horses, and spyware, collectively referred to as malware, are malicious software programs designed to infect computer systems. These programs can destroy data, steal sensitive information, and even render information systems inoperable. Recently, malware has been discovered in advertisements on major sites such as Yahoo, Fox, and Google as well as *The New York Times* and WhitePages.com. Malware attacks cost consumers and businesses billions of dollars annually. And malware is proliferating: according to a recent estimate, companies are spending more than $100 billion annually to deal with malware-related cyber attacks.[21]

viruses programs that secretly attach themselves to other programs (called hosts) and change them or destroy data.

Computer viruses are programs that secretly attach themselves to other programs (called *hosts*) and change them or destroy data. Viruses can be programmed to become active immediately or to remain dormant for a period of time, after which the infections suddenly activate themselves and cause problems. A virus can reproduce by copying itself onto other programs stored in the same drive. It spreads as users install infected software on their systems or exchange files with others, usually by exchanging e-mail, accessing electronic bulletin boards, trading disks, or downloading programs or data from unknown sources on the Internet.

worm small piece of software that exploits a security hole in a network to replicate itself.

A worm is a small piece of software that exploits a security hole in a network to replicate itself. A copy of the worm scans the network for another machine that has a specific security hole. It copies itself to the new machine using the security hole and then starts replicating from there as well. Unlike viruses, worms don't need host programs to damage computer systems.

416

A **botnet** is a network of PCs that have been infected with one or more data-stealing viruses. Computer criminals tie the infected computers into a network, often without the owners being aware of it, and sell the botnet on the black market. They or others use the botnet to commit identity theft, sell fake pharmaceuticals, buy blocks of concert tickets for scalping, and attack the Internet itself. U.S. security company Symantec recently seized part of the 1.9 million computer-strong ZeroAccess, one of the largest botnets worldwide. ZeroAccess worked by targeting and infecting search results from Google, Bing, and Yahoo and generating revenue from artificial clicks associated with display ads from infected computers.[22]

A **Trojan horse** is a program that claims to do one thing but in reality does something else, usually something malicious. For example, a Trojan horse might claim, and even appear, to be a game. When an unsuspecting user clicks on the Trojan horse to launch it, the program might erase the hard drive or steal any personal data stored on the computer.

Spyware is software that secretly gathers user information through the user's Internet connection without his or her knowledge, usually for advertising purposes. Spyware applications are typically bundled with other programs downloaded from the Internet. Once installed, the spyware monitors user activity on the Internet and transmits that information in the background to someone else.

Attacks by malware are not limited to computers and computer networks. Users of smart phones have reported a sharp increase in viruses, worms, and other forms of malware. A recent malware scare known as Backdoor AndroidOS.Obad.a is a Trojan horse that infects the handsets of unsuspecting users. It duplicates itself, installs additional malware, distributes malicious software to other phones via Bluetooth, and performs remote commands in the Android handset, while racking up enormous charges to premium-rate phone numbers.[23]

As viruses, worms, botnets, and Trojan horses become more complex, the technology to fight them must become more sophisticated as well. The simplest way to protect against computer viruses is to install one of the many available antivirus software programs, such as Norton AntiVirus and McAfee VirusScan. These programs, which also protect against worms and some Trojan horses, continuously monitor systems for viruses and automatically eliminate any they spot. Users should regularly update them by downloading the latest virus definitions. In addition, computer users should also install and regularly update antispyware programs because many Trojan horses are forms of spyware.

But management must begin to emphasize security at a deeper level: during software design, in corporate servers, at web gateways, and through Internet service providers. Because the vast majority of the world's computers run on Microsoft operating systems, a single virus, worm, or Trojan horse can spread among them quickly. Individual computer users should carefully choose the files they load onto their systems, scan their systems regularly, make sure their antivirus software is up to date, and install software only from known sources. They should also be very careful when opening attachments to e-mails because many viruses, worms, and Trojan horses are spread that way.

Information Systems and Ethics

The scope and power of today's information systems not surprisingly raise a number of ethical issues and concerns. These affect both employees and organizations. For instance, it is not uncommon for organizations to have specific ethical standards and policies regarding the use of information systems by employees and vendors. These standards include obligations to protect system security and the privacy and confidentiality of data. Policies also may cover the personal use of computers and related technologies, both hardware and software, by employees.

Ethical issues also involve organizational use of information systems. Organizations have an obligation to protect the privacy and confidentiality of data about employees and customers. Employment records contain sensitive personal information, such as bank account numbers, which, if not protected, could lead to identity theft. Another ethical issue is the use of computer technology to monitor employees while they are working. The "Solving an Ethical Controversy" feature debates the issue of employee monitoring in further detail.

botnet a network of PCs that have been infected with one or more data-stealing viruses.

Trojan horse program that claims to do one thing but in reality does something else, usually something malicious.

spyware software that secretly gathers user information through the user's Internet connection without his or her knowledge, usually for advertising purposes.

Assessment Check ✓

1. Explain computer hacking.
2. What is malware?
3. How does a computer virus work?

Solving an Ethical Controversy

Should Employers Monitor Employees' Internet Use?

Nearly three-quarters of employers monitor their employees' Internet use. Internet and desktop surveillance technology allow companies to check the sites employees visit, the amount of time spent online—and even keystrokes on individual computers. Most employees are unable to resist the temptation of searching the Internet at work, and most admit to using the Internet for nonwork purposes. Personal Internet usage includes social media sites, shopping, banking, playing games, and instant messaging. While a company's Facebook can be a powerful marketing tool, it can also be grounds for termination if employees use the social media site to express concerns about the company.

Should employers monitor employees' web use?

PRO

1. Employees spend an estimated one to two hours daily online for personal use. Regardless of the purpose, this is lost time for employers.

2. Employees' inappropriate use of office technology could leave a company vulnerable to security breaches.

CON

1. Some employers say monitoring erodes employees' trust and commitment.

2. Without notification of monitoring, employees have a legitimate privacy concern.

Summary

Federal law permits employers' monitoring of computer activity. However, to avoid privacy issues, employers should establish clear policies on personal use of the organization's technology.

Sources: Pamela S. Stevens, "Employee Monitoring Software Review 2014," *Top Ten Reviews,* accessed March 20, 2014, http://employee-monitoring-software-review.toptenreviews.com; "How Do Employers Monitor Internet Usage at Work," *wiseGeek,* accessed March 20, 2014, www.wisegeek.com; Susan M. Heathfield, "Electronic Surveillance of Employees," *About.com,* accessed March 20, 2014, http://humanresources.about.com; Karen Codere, "Managing Social Media in the Workplace," *The Business Ledger,* accessed March 20, 2014, www.businessledger.com; Laura Petrecca, "More Employers Use Tech to Track Workers," *USA Today,* accessed March 20, 2014, www.usatoday.com.

[6] Disaster Recovery and Backup

Natural disasters, power failures, equipment malfunctions, software glitches, human error, and terrorist attacks can disrupt even the most sophisticated computer information systems. These problems can cost businesses and other organizations billions of dollars. Even more serious consequences can occur. One study found that 60 percent of companies that lose their data will shut down within six months of the disaster.[24]

FalconStor, a global firm headquartered in Melville, New York, provides data back-up applications and sophisticated disaster recovery solutions for businesses. The firm's services go way beyond simply replicating data because organizations that have suffered a major loss have needs well beyond replicating their data. FalconStor's software solutions permit them to access their applications, restart operations, and return to serving customers.[25]

Disaster recovery planning—deciding how to prevent system failures and continue operations if computer systems fail—is a critical function of all organizations. Disaster prevention programs can avoid some of these costly problems. The most basic precaution is routinely backing up software and data—at the organizational and individual levels. However, the organization's data center cannot be the sole repository of critical data because a single location is vulnerable to threats from both natural and human-caused disasters. Consequently, off-site data backup is a necessity, whether in a separate physical location or online. Companies that perform online backups store the encrypted data in secure facilities that in turn have their own backups. The initial backup may take a day or more, but subsequent ones take far less

GoingGreen

Box Inc. Serving in the Cloud

Procter & Gamble, Pandora, and Six Flags are among the more than 25 million customers of Box Inc., a cloud storage company whose 20-something founder, Aaron Levie, started developing the service while still in college. Now the company has 750 employees in its Los Altos, California, offices and is worth about $2 billion.

Box Inc. serves three customer segments: enterprise, business, and personal. The business version of its cloud-based storage system, used by close to 225,000 firms (including 97 percent of the Fortune 500), offers applications for PCs, Macs, and mobile platforms and can provide highly secure shared access for groups of multiple users. Security for the personal version is a bit more limited and works for only one user at a time. But both versions receive high marks for ease of use and simplicity, even for users who are not tech savvy.

Competing services include Dropbox and Microsoft's OneDrive. Box recently doubled its free storage space, announced plans to expand to Europe, and recently announced plans to go public.

Questions for Critical Thinking

1. Do you think business users of cloud services such as Box will ever set up cloud storage as part of their IT departments? Explain.

2. Should Box provide the same degree of security for individual users as for business customers? Why or why not?

Sources: Company website, http://box.com, accessed June 20, 2014; Eric Markowitz, "Don't Bet Against Aaron Levie," *Entrepreneur,* accessed June 20, 2014, www.entrepreneur.com; Donna Tam, "Box Doubles Free Storage to 10GB, Hits 20 Million Users," *CNET,* accessed February 27, 2014, http://news.cnet.com; Douglas MacMillan and Telis Demos, "Web Storage Firm Box Files for IPO," *The Wall Street Journal,* accessed February 27, 2014, http://online.wsj.com.

---

time because they involve only new or modified files. Cloud computing services can greatly simplify off-site backup; see the accompanying "Going Green" feature for a profile of Box, a market leader.

According to security experts, there are five important considerations for off-site data storage. First is planning. The organization needs to decide what data need to be protected. Priority should be given to data having severe legal or business consequences should they be lost. Second, a backup schedule must be established and closely adhered to. Third, when data are transmitted off site, they must be protected by the highest level of security possible. Fourth, care should be taken in selecting the right security vendor. There are dozens of vendors offering different services and having different areas of expertise. Finally, the backup system should be continually tested and evaluated.

[7] Information Technology Trends

Computer information systems are constantly—and rapidly—evolving. To keep their information systems up-to-date, firms must continually keep abreast of changes in technology. A recent report by Accenture of the trends driving the future of technology includes data mining and analytics; data security; social platforms as a new source of business intelligence; cloud computing as a driver of business growth; data privacy, and mobile device diversity and management.[26]

Another topic that has received considerable press is the Internet of Everything or the Internet of Things for short. This refers to a move beyond standalone devices and greater connectivity between items. It consists of an entire Internet-connected eco-system, including TVs, cars, and wearable tech devices. Cisco's CEO says "The Internet of Everything will have five to ten times the impact on society as the Internet itself."[27]

The Distributed Workforce

As discussed in earlier chapters, many companies rely more and more on a *distributed workforce*—employees who no longer work in traditional offices but rather in what are called *virtual*

Assessment Check ✓

1. What are the types of disasters to which information systems are vulnerable?

2. List the five considerations for off-site data storage.

Continued technological advances in data storage and cloud computing allow business-people to work on their laptops, tablets, or smart phones from anywhere in the world.

offices, including at home. Information technology makes a distributed workforce possible. Computers, networks, and other components of information systems allow workers to do their jobs effectively almost anywhere. For instance, none of JetBlue's reservations agents work in offices; they all work at home, connected to the airline's information system. JetBlue is hardly alone in its use of home-based workers. Boeing, Starbucks, Agilent Technologies, Sun Microsystems, and most other companies have policies and options that permit at least some employees to work outside the organization's offices exclusively in a virtual setting. Virtual offices can range from a mailing address, mail forwarding, and voice mail to a physical office, usually leased by the month. The increasing demands of the distributed workforce will likely lead to more innovative and increasingly powerful information systems. Today, co-shared offices are increasingly popular.

Application Service Providers

application service provider (ASP) outside supplier that provides both the computers and the application support for managing an information system.

As with other business functions, many firms find that outsourcing at least some of their information technology function makes sense. Because of the increasing cost and complexity of obtaining and maintaining information systems, many firms hire an **application service provider (ASP)**, an outside supplier that provides both the computers and the application support for managing an information system. An ASP can simplify complex software for its customers so that it is easier for them to manage and use. When an ASP relationship is successful, the buyer can then devote more time and resources to its core businesses instead of struggling to manage its information systems. Other benefits include stretching the firm's technology dollar farther and giving smaller companies more competitive information power. Even large companies turn to ASPs to manage some or all of their information systems. Microsoft outsourced much of its internal information technology services to Infosys Technology to save money and streamline, simplify, and support its services.[28]

Companies that decide to use ASPs should check the backgrounds and references of these firms before hiring them to manage critical systems. In addition, customers should try to ensure that the service provider has strong security measures to block computer hackers or other unauthorized access to the data, that its data centers are running reliably, and that adequate data and applications backups are maintained.

On-Demand, Cloud, and Grid Computing

on-demand computing firms essentially rent the software time from application providers and pay only for their usage of the software.

Another trend that continues with great momentum is **on-demand computing**, also called *utility computing*. Instead of purchasing and maintaining expensive software, firms essentially rent the software time from application providers and pay only for their usage of the software, similar to purchasing electricity from a utility. On-demand computing is particularly useful for firms that experience annual peaks in demand or seasonal spikes in customer usage of their applications. By renting the service they need only when they need it, they can avoid buying the software that is not routinely required. On-demand computing can also help companies remain current with the most efficient software on the market without purchasing huge upgrades.

Hit&Miss

Cloud computing uses powerful servers to store applications software and databases. Users access the software and databases via the web using anything from a PC to a smart phone. The software as a service (SaaS) movement is an example of cloud computing. The "Hit & Miss" feature describes how Facebook's latest acquisition provides the company with the potential to reach a billion more users worldwide.

Small and medium-sized companies occasionally find themselves with jobs that require more computing power than their current systems offer. A cost-effective solution for these firms may be something called **grid computing**, which consists of a network of smaller computers running special software. The software breaks down a large, complex job into smaller tasks and then distributes them to the networked computers. The software then reassembles the individual task results into the finished job. By combining multiple small computers, grid computing creates a virtual mainframe or even a supercomputer.

What's Ahead

This is the first of two chapters devoted to managing technology and information. The next chapter, "Understanding Accounting and Financial Statements," focuses on accounting, financial information, and financing reporting. Accounting is the process of measuring, interpreting, and communicating financial information to enable people inside and outside the firm to make informed decisions. The chapter describes the functions of accounting and role of accountants; the steps in the accounting cycle; the types, functions, and components of financial statements; and the role of budgets in an organization.

cloud computing powerful servers store applications software and databases for users to access the software and databases via the web using anything from a PC to a smart phone.

grid computing consists of a network of smaller computers running special software.

Assessment Check ☑

1. What is an application service provider?

2. Explain on-demand computing.

Chapter in Review

Summary of Learning Objectives

⌐1¬ Distinguish between data and information and discuss information systems.

It is important for businesspeople to know the difference between data and information. Data are raw facts and figures that may or may not be relevant to a business decision. Information is knowledge gained from processing those facts and figures. An information system is an organized method for collecting, storing, and communicating past, present, and projected information on internal operations and external intelligence. Most information systems today use computer and telecommunications technology.

Assessment Check Answers

1.1 Distinguish between data and information. Data consist of raw facts and figures that may or may not be relevant to a decision. Information is the knowledge gained from those facts and figures.

1.2 What is an information system? An information system is an organized method for collecting, storing, and communicating past, present, and projected information on internal operations and external intelligence.

⌐2¬ List the components and types of information systems.

When people think about information systems today, they're generally thinking about computer-based systems, those that rely on computers and related technologies. Computer-based information systems rely on four components: computer hardware, computer software, telecommunications and computer networks, and data resource management. The heart of an information system is its database, a centralized integrated collection of data resources. Information systems fall into two broad categories: operational support systems and management support systems. Operational support systems are designed to produce a variety of information for users. Examples include transaction processing systems and process control systems. Management support systems are those designed to support effective decision making. They include management information systems, decision support systems, executive support systems, and expert systems.

Assessment Check Answers

2.1 List the four components of a computer-based information system. The four components of a computer-based information system are computer hardware, computer software, telecommunications and computer networks, and data resource management.

2.2 What is a database? A database is a centralized, integrated collection of data resources.

2.3 What are the two general types of information systems? Give examples of each. The two categories of information systems are operational support systems (such as transactions processing and process control systems) and management support systems (such as management information, decision support, executive support, and expert systems).

⌐3¬ Discuss computer hardware and software.

Hardware consists of all tangible elements of a computer system, including input and output devices. Major categories of computers include mainframes, supercomputers, midrange systems, personal computers (PCs), and hand-held devices. Computer software provides the instructions that tell the hardware what to do. The software that controls the basic workings of the computer is its operating system. Other programs, called application software, perform specific tasks that users want to complete.

Assessment Check Answers

3.1 List two input and output devices. Input devices include the keyboard and mouse. Output devices include the monitor and printer.

3.2 What accounts for the increasing popularity of laptop and notebook computers? The increased popularity of these devices can be explained by smaller, lighter, more powerful computing, and by the improved displays, faster processing speeds, ability to handle more intense graphics, larger storage capacities, and more durable designs.

3.3 What is software? List the two categories of software. Computer software provides the instructions that tell the hardware what to do. The software that controls the basic workings of the computer is its operating system. Other programs, called application software, perform specific tasks that users want to complete.

⌐4¬ Describe computer networks.

Local area networks connect computers within a limited area. Wide area networks tie together larger geographical regions by using telephone lines, microwave, or satellite transmission. A wireless network allows computers to communicate through radio waves. Intranets allow employees to share information on a ready-made company network. Access to an intranet is restricted to authorized users and is protected by a firewall. Virtual private networks (VPNs) provide a secure Internet connection between two or more points. VoIP—voice over Internet protocol—uses a personal computer running special software and a broadband Internet connection to make and receive telephone calls over the Internet rather than over traditional telephone networks.

Assessment Check Answers ✅

4.1 What is a LAN? A local area network (LAN) is a computer network that connects machines within a limited area, such as a building or several nearby buildings.

4.2 What are the differences between an intranet and a VPN? An intranet is a company network patterned after the Internet. Unlike the Internet, access to an intranet is limited to employees and other authorized users. Virtual private networks (VPNs) are secure connections between two points on the Internet.

4.3 Briefly explain how VoIP works. Special software transmits phone conversations over the Internet. A VoIP user can make and receive calls to and from those with traditional telephone connections (either landline or wireless).

⌐5⌐ Outline the security and ethical issues affecting information systems.

Numerous security and ethical issues affect information systems. Two of the main security threats are cybercrime and malware. Cybercrimes range from hacking—unauthorized penetration of an information system—to the theft of hardware. Malware is any malicious software program designed to infect computer systems. Examples include viruses, worms, botnets, Trojan horses, and spyware. Ethical issues affecting information systems include the proper use of the systems by authorized users. Organizations also have an obligation to employees, vendors, and customers to protect the security and confidentiality of the data stored in information systems.

Assessment Check Answers ✅

5.1 Explain computer hacking. Computer hacking is a breach of a computer system by unauthorized users. Sometimes the hackers' motive is just to see if they can get in. Other times, hackers have more sinister motives, including stealing or altering data.

5.2 What is malware? Malware is any malicious software program designed to infect computer systems.

5.3 How does a computer virus work? A virus is a computer program that secretly attaches itself to another program (called a host). The virus then changes the host, destroys data, or even makes the computer system inoperable.

⌐6⌐ Explain disaster recovery and backup.

Information system disasters, whether human caused or due to natural causes, can cost businesses billions of dollars. The consequences of a disaster can be minimized by routinely backing up software and data, both at an organizational level and at an individual level. Organizations should back up critical data at an off-site location. Some firms may also want to invest in extra hardware and software sites, which can be accessed during emergencies.

Assessment Check Answers ✅

6.1 What are the types of disasters to which information systems are vulnerable? Natural disasters, power failures, equipment malfunctions, software glitches, human error, and even terrorist attacks can disrupt even the most powerful, sophisticated computer information systems.

6.2 List the five considerations for off-site data storage. The five considerations are planning and deciding which data to back up, establishing and following a backup schedule, protecting data when they are transmitted off site, selecting the right security vendor, and continually testing and evaluating the backup system.

⌐7⌐ Review information technology trends.

Information systems are continually and rapidly evolving. Some of the most significant trends are data mining and analytics, data security, social platforms as a new source of business intelligence, cloud computing as a driver of business growth, data privacy, and mobile device diversity and management. Many people now work in virtual offices, including at home. Information technology makes this possible. Application service providers allow organizations to outsource most of their IT functions. Rather than buying and maintaining expensive software, on-demand computing offers users the option of renting software time from outside vendors and paying only for their usage. Grid computing consists of a network of smaller computers running special software creating a virtual mainframe or even supercomputer.

Assessment Check Answers ✅

7.1 What is an application service provider? An application service provider (ASP) is an outside vendor that provides both the computers and application support for managing an information system.

7.2 Explain on-demand computing. Instead of purchasing and maintaining expensive software, some organizations rent software from application providers and pay only for their actual usage.

Business Terms You Need to Know

data 406
information 406
information system 406
chief information
   officer (CIO) 406
computer-based information
   systems 407
database 408
operational support systems 408
transaction processing
   systems 408
process control systems 409
management support systems 409

management information
   system (MIS) 409
decision support system (DSS) 409
executive support system (ESS) 409
expert system 409
hardware 410
server 411
software 412
local area networks (LANs) 413
wide area networks (WAN) 413
Wi-Fi 413
intranet 414
firewall 414

virtual private networks (VPNs) 414
VoIP 415
malware 416
viruses 416
worm 416
botnet 417
Trojan horse 417
spyware 417
application service provider
   (ASP) 420
on-demand computing 420
cloud computing 421
grid computing 421

Review Questions

1. Distinguish between data and information. Why is the distinction important to businesspeople in their management of information?

2. What are the four components of an information system?

3. Describe the two different types of information systems, and give an example of how each might help a particular business.

4. Explain decision support systems, executive support systems, and expert systems.

5. What are the major categories of computers? What is a smart phone?

6. What is an intranet? Give specific examples of benefits for firms that set up their own intranets.

7. What steps can organizations and individuals take to prevent computer crime?

8. How does a computer virus work? What can individuals and organizational computer users do to reduce the likelihood of acquiring a computer virus?

9. Why is disaster recovery important for businesses? Relate your answer to a natural disaster such as a hurricane, tornado, or fire.

10. Describe four information system trends.

Projects and Teamwork Applications

1. Suppose you've been hired to design an information system for a midsized retailer. Describe what that information system might look like, including the necessary components. Would the system be an operational support system, a management support system, or both?

2. Select a local company and contact the person in charge of its information system for a brief interview. Ask that individual to outline his or her company's information system. Also, ask the person what he or she likes most about the job. Did this interview make you more or less interested in a career in information systems?

3. Some individuals choose piracy—a form of unauthorized duplication and/or distribution of music, software, art, or other copyrighted material, which includes downloading and file sharing. Some argue that piracy does not affect a product maker's revenues because pirates might actually help promote

the product they steal by the buzz they generate. Furthermore copying or downloading a product does not present a financial loss to the product maker because the pirate would probably not buy the product in the first place. Working with a partner, discuss both sides of the piracy issue.

4. There are a number of tools available to combat spam, which is unsolicited commercial e-mail in the form of advertising. Some people view these spam-blocking tools as a threat to free expression and idea exchange. What are your thoughts about this point of view in light of the time and money by companies and consumers spent to avoid spam? Discuss with a partner or in groups.

5. Has your computer ever been hacked or attacked by a virus? What steps did you take to recover lost files and data? What steps have you taken to prevent something similar from happening again?

Web Assignments

1. **Enterprise resource planning (ERP).** SAP is one of the world's largest enterprise resource planning software companies. Go to the firm's website (http://www.sap.com) and click on "Customer Testimonials." Choose one of the customers listed and read its testimonial. Prepare a brief summary and explain how this exercise improved your understanding of the business applications of ERP software.

2. **Computer security.** Visit the website listed below for McAfee. Review the items that are listed for security awareness under the link, "Threat Center" and discuss them in terms of how companies and consumers can prevent cybercrimes.

   http://www.mcafee.com/us/business-home.aspx

3. **Cloud computing.** IBM is one of the largest providers of so-called cloud computing. Visit the IBM website (http://www.ibm.com) and click on "solutions" and then "cloud computing." Print out the material and bring it to class to participate in a class discussion on the subject.

Note: Internet web addresses change frequently. If you don't find the exact sites listed, you may need to access the organization's home page and search from there or use a search engine such as Google or Bing.

Khan Academy Distributes Knowledge

CASE 14.1

While attempting to help his cousin Nadia with math, Salman "Sal" Khan stumbled upon the idea to upload a few tutorials onto YouTube for a more interactive learning experience. This was the beginning of Khan's free online education delivery system. Known globally as Khan Academy, this nonprofit organization's mission is to provide a world-class education for anyone, anywhere. Khan Academy has more than 10 million users per month, including students, teachers, and parents, and 300 million views on its YouTube channel.

With over 4,000 ten-minute "micro-lectures" to date, subjects include math, finance, physics, history, biology, astronomy, economics, and computer science. Khan controls the online instruction as well as creates the videos and their content. With no venture capital investment, more than $20 million in funding has been provided by technology philanthropists and their foundations—Bill and Melinda Gates, Ann and John Doerr, Netflix's Reed Hastings, Carlos Slim Foundation, and Google.

Khan's goal of access to secondary education for everyone has been accomplished globally and locally. In remote rural areas, learning opportunities have been made available through the distribution of tablet devices. Offline versions of Khan's lectures have been distributed to rural areas in Asia, Latin America, and Africa.

On a domestic level, in an effort to close the digital divide and help low-income families, Khan Academy has signed a multiyear, multi-million dollar partnership with Comcast. The company provides low-cost broadband service, called Internet Essentials, for $9.95 a month with the option to purchase an Internet-ready computer for under $150. In addition, Comcast is making available multiple options to access free digital literacy training in print, online, and in person. Khan's initial intention to help his cousin with math has sparked a worldwide learning revolution. As Sal Khan continues to produce more homemade videos, he is, according to Bill Gates, "my favorite teacher and 'educator to the world.'"

Questions for Critical Thinking

1. Sal Khan's free lectures demonstrate technology's ability to eliminate economic barriers that can prevent educational opportunities. Discuss additional ways Khan Academy creates a more level playing field for access to education for everyone.

2. Some teachers using Khan Academy have changed the way their class works. Lectures have been replaced with Khan's videos, which students can watch at home. In class, the focus is on problem solving and discussion. Compare and contrast the merits of a traditional approach to teaching with teaching methods using Khan Academy materials. What are the benefits of each?

Sources: Company website, "About," http://khanacademy.org, accessed February 24, 2014; Peter High, "Salman Khan, the Most Influential Person in Education Technology," *Forbes*, accessed February 24, 2014, www.forbes.com; "Comcast and Khan Academy Announce Multi-Year, Multi-Million Dollar Partnership to Help Close the Digital and Educational Divide," *The Wall Street Journal*, accessed February 24, 2014, http://online.wsj.org; "Khan Academy: The Future of Education?" *CBS News*, accessed February 24, 2014, www.cbsnews.com.

Skype Continues to Thrive

On any given Sunday morning, about 60 million people log onto Skype and begin using its free VoIP (voice over Internet protocol) service. More than half a million of those users are making video phone calls with family and friends despite being in different cities around the world.

Skype, now a Microsoft company, popularized the use of the computer as a phone and still offers its basic service and software for free. About 145 million users sign on to the system at least monthly, and more than 9 million pay for premium services that allow them to call mobile phones and landlines and also to do videoconferencing, an option business customers find attractive.

Microsoft, headquartered in Redmond, Washington, allows the Silicon Valley company to operate independently and has begun to integrate Skype's services with its popular online gaming system, Xbox, allowing its 48 million members to communicate while gaming.

Questions for Critical Thinking

1. Microsoft is considering charging business users for some Skype services. Do you think this is a good strategy? Why or why not?
2. What might be motivating Microsoft to let Skype operate independently?

Sources: Company website, www.skype.com, accessed March 20, 2014; Jean Mercier, "Where Are the 70 Million?" *Skype Numerology,* accessed March 20, 2014, http://skypenumerology.blogspot.com; Carly Page, "Skype for Xbox One Gets Updated with Push Notifications, Synced Chats," *The Inquirer,* accessed March 20, 2014, www.theinquirer.net; "Steam Users Eclipse Xbox Live, PSN Still Far and Away Tops," *Slash Gear,* accessed March 20, 2014, www.slashgear.com; Julie Scelfo, "Video Chat Reshapes Domestic Rituals," *The New York Times,* accessed March 20, 2014, www.nytimes.com.

  ## Technology Drives Zipcar's Success

As a member of Zipcar, the world's largest car-sharing service, consumers avoid the costs associated with car ownership: gasoline, insurance, maintenance, and parking. Based in Cambridge, Massachusetts, Zipcar was founded by two moms who met when their children were in the same kindergarten class. Prior to its launch, Zipcar raised $75,000, most of which was spent to develop technology. Today, Zipcar is owned by Avis Budget and offers self-service, on-demand cars by the hour or day. The company provides automobile reservations to its 850,000 members and offers more than 10,000 cars in urban areas, on college campuses, and at airports worldwide.

With a seamless user experience, it may be difficult for Zipsters (the company's name for its members), to realize the complex technology that goes into making the car-sharing service so user friendly. Zipcar relies on a number of different technologies, including mobile, web, telematics, radio-frequency identification (RFID), operational information administration systems, and phone and interactive voice response systems for support and customer service. In addition, there are teams responsible for the company's security infrastructure, mobile app development, and auto maintenance to make sure its fleet of vehicles is ready for members.

At the heart of Zipcar's technologies is an operational administration system. As a data-driven company, Zipcar relies heavily on information to make company decisions and manage assets. The system enables the company to manage its physical assets—its vehicles—in many locations worldwide. The system provides data about car utilization, when and how people are driving, specific locations, hours used, and miles driven. Using the data, analytics are performed that allow the company to optimize utilization levels. This type of information is valuable for making strategic decisions about supply and demand, including when and where to place cars, the models and types to use, and when to change them.

The technology in the cars provides information that allows the company to understand how its cars are being used. Zipcar has created a telematics board for each vehicle with GPS and RFID, which supplies geographic, customer, and utilization information. Using transponders, the RFID technology works with a card reader physically placed on the car's windshield. After the customer makes a reservation either on the web or via mobile device, the RFID card is used to enter and exit any Zipcar. This technology identifies the user and his or her car reservation. Once the car is unlocked, the key is in the car attached to a tether on the steering column. The user will also find a toll pass (members pay for tolls) and a gas card (price of gas is included in the rental fee).

Because of Zipcar's technology, the keys can be left in the car without concern of theft. When a user enters or exits a car, hours, usage, and mileage are uploaded to a central computer via a wireless data link. However, for privacy purposes, the location of the vehicle is not tracked. In addition, all cars are equipped with a "kill" function, which allows the company to prevent theft. For security purposes, the car opens only to the designated user. With a mobile device, a user is able to unlock and lock the car and honk its horn, which helps determine a car's location.

Because 98 percent of Zipcar users have smart phones, mobile and web applications are integral to interfacing with customers. At the heart of the Zipcar's car sharing is a self-serve transaction that allows a user to find, reserve, and access a specific car at a specific location at a specific time. The information is then sent wirelessly to the car, and Zipcar members use their Zipcard to open the car door. Once the car is returned and locked, billing is finalized and information is made available to the member.

Although it is rare that Zipsters interact directly with someone from the company because reservations happen via mobile device or online, providing superior service when something goes wrong requires technology. Dedicated phone systems and customer support systems are crucial for things like on-the-road issues. The Zipcar phone system identifies users who are calling, their reservations, and the cars they are driving, so that timely support and problem solving can happen quickly. Technology also supplies information about the vehicle's service history, which helps with troubleshooting and service.

As transportation needs continue to change, Zipcar is working to improve its technology base. The company remains committed to assessing consumer transportation and parking needs for business and personal use. Zipcar is focused on understanding and assessing trip-type needs, whether it is an errand for a few hours, an afternoon at the beach, or a business meeting. Using various technologies, the company has created a seamless experience for consumers who desire alternatives to car ownership. So, the next time you decide to reserve a Zipcar and drive to the beach for the day, you will have a strong support system at the ready thanks to the company's focus on technology.

Questions for Critical Thinking

1. What type of data does Zipcar use to make decisions on behalf of its customers? Its operations? How does the data used to make customer decisions differ from the data used to make decisions related to operations? Discuss.

2. Discuss how Zipcar manages and deals with information security. What are some of the issues the company faces with regard to security?

3. What information does Zipcar use to manage its fleet? What information is utilized to decide which types of cars to purchase, how they will be used, and where they will be located? How might weather patterns or seasonality impact the types and number of cars the company purchases?

4. Discuss how Zipcar leverages technology to acquire new members. Based upon its segmentation of consumers, businesses, and college students, discuss the various technologies utilized to identify the relevant target audiences and the types of messages conveyed to each of them.

Sources: Company website, "Zipcar Overview," www.zipcar.com, accessed July 1, 2014; company website, "How to Zip," www.zipcar.com, accessed July 1, 2014; Chris Ready, "Zipcar Rolls Out One-Way Service with Guaranteed Parking," *Boston Globe*, accessed June 27, 2014, www.bostonglobe.com; Mark Rogowsky, "Zipcar, Uber, and the Beginning of Trouble for the Auto Industry," *Forbes*, accessed June 26, 2014, www.forbes.com; Carol Hymowitz, "Zipcar Founder Robin Chase on Starting Buzzcar and a Portugal Venture," *Bloomberg Businessweek*, accessed June 26, 2014, www.businessweek.com.

GREENSBURG, KS

The Dog Ate My Laptop

The night of the tornado, Superintendent of Schools Darin Headrick heard the storm sirens go off on his way home from work. He stopped at the home of High School Principal Randy Fulton and the two men headed for the basement, just in case. The next thing they knew, the entire school system was gone. Textbooks were scattered everywhere, computers destroyed.

For the first three months after the storm, no one could live in town. People stayed in shelters or with friends and family outside of town. No one had a home phone anymore, but people were eager to connect with each other and find out what was happening. Although the Federal Emergency Management Agency (FEMA) was distributing information at checkpoints on the edges of town, people had to go to town to get it.

Like 95 percent of the town's 1,500 residents, Headrick himself was homeless. With just four months to rebuild an entire school system, all he had were his laptop and cell phone, so he got into his truck and began searching for a wireless signal. Taking a lesson from his students, he used text messaging to distribute information. Although very few people still had computers, almost everyone had a cell phone. Residents who subscribed to the text service could receive updates and instant messages over the phone, wherever they were.

Rebuilding the schools was a bigger task. Headrick secured temporary trailers for grades K–12 and received generous donations of desks and school supplies. By August 15, he had the basics needed to start the school year, but he still lacked textbooks. Technology would have to fill in the gaps so the students wouldn't fall behind.

One of the school system's existing programs was ITV, for Interactive Distance Learning Network. ITV allowed Greensburg's rural schools to log in to classrooms around the state via web cam. This type of real-time distance learning is referred to as *synchronous learning*, as opposed to the asynchronous online courses given on college campuses. After the tornado, all that was needed to get the program up and running again were a computer, an Internet connection, and a web cam.

Early in the winter each of Greensburg High's students got an unexpected gift: a laptop computer containing e-books, handwriting recognition software, and a tablet screen for note taking. The new laptops replaced their tattered textbooks. Students would hand in their assignments via e-mail and receive feedback from their teachers via instant messaging.

Questions

After viewing the video, answer the following questions:

1. Was Greensburg Public Schools' investment in technology a smart move?

2. Would you consider enrolling in an asynchronous online course? What might be the benefits and drawbacks?

3. Do you think hand-held devices and text messaging improve productivity and communication or distract their users?

448

LAUNCHING YOUR
[Information
Technology Career]

Part 5, "Managing Technology and Information," includes Chapter 14, which discusses using computers and related technology to manage information. In Chapter 14, we discussed well-known technology companies such as Google as well as smaller organizations that use computer technology to manage information. These examples illustrate that all organizations need to manage technology and information. And with the complexity and scope of technology and information likely to increase in the years ahead, the demand for information systems professionals is expected to grow.

According to the U.S. Department of Labor, employment in such information technology occupations as computer systems design, the manufacture of computers, electronic components and peripheral equipment, and information services is expected to grow faster than the average for all occupations in the next decade.[1] In a recent *U.S. News & World Report's* study of "Best Jobs," information technology surpassed health care with software development as the most attractive profession. Employment is expected to increase by more than 20 percent in the next decade due mainly to our increased dependence on mobile software. Software developer, computer systems analyst, web developer, and information security analyst all made the magazine's "11 Best Technology Jobs" list based on salary, projected growth, and job satisfaction.[2]

What types of jobs are available in information systems? What are the working conditions like? What are the career paths? Information technology is a fairly broad occupation and encompasses a wide variety of jobs. In some cases you'll work in the IT department of a business such as Procter & Gamble or Shell. In other cases, you'll work for a specialized information systems firm, such as IBM, which provides the services to governments, not-for-profit organizations, and businesses.

Information technology and information systems are popular business majors, and many entry-level positions are available each year. Many IT graduates spend their entire careers in the field, while others move into other areas. People who began their careers in information systems are well represented in the ranks of senior management today. Let's look briefly at some of the specific jobs you might find after earning an IT degree.

Computer systems analysts are goal focused and process oriented. Computer systems analysts must understand computer hardware, software, and networks and how they work together so they can make recommendations to organizations for the best operations systems to use.

Information security analysts plan and monitor security of computer networks. This occupation will grow by more than 30 percent in the next decade.

Database administrators set up databases to fit a company's need and then maintain those systems as part of the company's day-to-day operations.

IT managers are the go-to personnel when your e-mail won't send or your word processor won't work. As the head of the IT department, they triage the operations of an organization's technical network, and they are part of a growing profession.

Computer systems administrators keep your e-mails moving and your web pages loading, plus they lend their tech-savvy skills to managing various telecommunication networks.

Career Assessment Exercises in Information Systems

1. Assume you're interested in a career as a systems administrator. Go to http://www.usenix.org and click on the "Jobs" tab. Prepare a brief report outlining the responsibilities of a systems administrator, who hires for these positions, and what kind of educational background you need to become one.

2. Identify a person working in your local area in information technology and arrange an interview with that person (your college career center may be able to help you). Ask that person about his or her job responsibilities, educational background, and the best and worst aspects of his or her job.

Part 6 | Managing Financial Resources

Learning Objectives

1. Discuss the users of accounting information.
2. Describe accounting professionals.
3. Identify the foundation of the accounting system.
4. Outline the steps in the accounting cycle.
5. Explain financial statements.
6. Discuss financial ratio analysis.
7. Describe the role of budgeting.
8. Outline international accounting practices.

Chapter 15

Understanding Accounting and Financial Statements

©Elenathewise/iStockphoto

Intuit Asks the Right Questions

Intuit, maker of accounting and financial software, has learned that asking the right question makes a difference when it comes to developing business and consumer products. Creator of products like TurboTax, Quicken, and QuickBooks, the Silicon Valley firm has made its software simple, fast, and easy to use for businesses and consumers alike.

The company's current CEO believes in asking questions that challenge employees to step back and think differently. For years, Intuit's founder dreamed of creating accounting software that would allow consumers to complete their tax forms in 10 minutes or less. The company estimates that 7 billion hours a year are spent inputting information into software to prepare taxes, and that a tax refund is probably the biggest check received by more than half of U.S. consumers each year.

Instead of focusing on mobile technology and its impact on Intuit's business, the CEO asked the TurboTax team how they could create a program consumers could use to make the tax-filing process a quick one. After being asked the question, the team figured out how to photograph tax documents using a smart phone and to create software that allows the device to read the captured data and fill out tax forms—helping some consumers complete their filings in less than 10 minutes. The result is TurboTax's SnapTax app, which is used by millions of individuals each year.

Asking the right question also helped Intuit grow its global business. Rather than set a goal to have a certain percentage of company revenues come from outside the United States, management changed the question to ask how the company could keep its current business customers happy before seeking additional global business. By changing the question and making sure current business customers were happy with its software products, Intuit went from QuickBooks Online customers in five countries to QuickBooks Online now being used by more than 37,000 businesses in more than 160 countries. On average, the company estimates a new QuickBooks Online subscriber signs up every minute.

With more than $4 billion in annual revenues, Intuit continues to find ways to help customers by developing products that make their personal and business lives better when it comes to paying taxes, running a business, or planning a sound financial future.[1]

Overview

Accounting professionals prepare the financial information that organizations present in their annual reports. Whether you begin your career by working for a company or by starting your own firm, you need to understand what accountants do and why their work is so important in contemporary business.

Accounting is the process of measuring, interpreting, and communicating financial information to enable people inside and outside the firm to make informed decisions. In many ways, accounting is the language of business. Accountants gather, record, report, and interpret financial information in a way that describes the status and operation of an organization and aids in decision making.

Millions of men and women throughout the world describe their occupation as an accountant. In the United States alone, more than 1.1 million people work as accountants. According to the Bureau of Labor Statistics, the number of accounting-related jobs is expected to increase by around 13 percent between now and 2022.[2] The availability of jobs and relatively high starting salaries for talented graduates have made accounting one of the most in-demand majors on college campuses. After the recent recession, hiring levels fell, but the most recent report estimates that firms will hire more accounting graduates in the near future.[3]

This chapter begins by describing who uses accounting information. It discusses business activities involving accounting statements: financing, investing, and operations. It explains the accounting process, defines double-entry bookkeeping, and presents the accounting equation. We then discuss the development of financial statements from information about financial transactions, the methods of interpreting these statements, and the roles of budgeting in planning and controlling a business. The chapter concludes with a discussion of the development and implementation schedule of a uniform set of accounting rules for global business.

accounting
process of measuring, interpreting, and communicating financial information to enable people inside and outside the firm to make informed decisions.

Users of Accounting Information

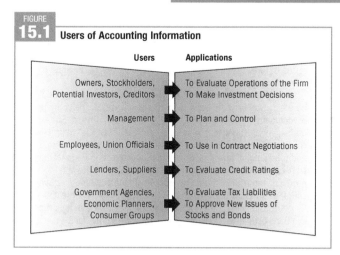

FIGURE 15.1 Users of Accounting Information

Users	Applications
Owners, Stockholders, Potential Investors, Creditors	To Evaluate Operations of the Firm — To Make Investment Decisions
Management	To Plan and Control
Employees, Union Officials	To Use in Contract Negotiations
Lenders, Suppliers	To Evaluate Credit Ratings
Government Agencies, Economic Planners, Consumer Groups	To Evaluate Tax Liabilities — To Approve New Issues of Stocks and Bonds

People both inside and outside an organization rely on accounting information to help them make business decisions. Figure 15.1 lists the users of accounting information and the applications they find for that information. Firms such as Deloitte provide such information and help their customers make the best use of it.

Managers with a business, government agency, or not-for-profit organization are the major users of accounting information because it helps them plan and control daily and long-range operations. Business owners and boards of directors of not-for-profit groups also rely on accounting data to determine how well managers are operating the organizations. Union officials use accounting data in contract negotiations, and employees refer to it as they monitor their firms' productivity and profitability performance.

To help employees understand how their work affects the bottom line, many companies share sensitive financial information with their employees and teach them how to understand and use financial statements. Proponents of what is often referred to as *open book management* believe that allowing employees to view financial information helps them better understand how their work contributes to the company's success, which, in turn, benefits them.

Outside a firm, potential investors evaluate accounting information to help them decide whether to buy a firm's stock. As we'll discuss in more detail later in the chapter, any company whose stock is traded publicly is required to report its financial results on a regular basis. So anyone, for example, can find out what Costco's sales were last year or how much money Intel made during the last quarter. Bankers and other lenders use accounting information to evaluate a potential borrower's creditworthiness. The Internal Revenue Service (IRS) and state tax officials use it to determine a company's tax liability. Citizens' groups and government agencies use such information in assessing the efficiency of operations such as Massachusetts General Hospital; the Topeka, Kansas, school system; Community College of Denver; and the Art Institute of Chicago.

Accountants play fundamental roles not only in business but also in other aspects of society. Their work influences each of the business environments discussed earlier in this book. They clearly contribute important information to help managers deal with changing economic environments.

Less obvious contributions help others understand, predict, and react to the technological, regulatory, and social and cultural environments. For instance, thousands of people volunteer each year to help people with their taxes. One of the largest organized programs is Tax-Aide, sponsored by AARP (formally known as the American Association of Retired Persons). For more than 40 years this volunteer program has assisted about 50 million low- and middle-income Americans—especially people 60 and older—with their income tax preparation at more than 5,000 locations nationwide.[4]

Accountants play a key role in organizations by providing services to businesses, individuals, government agencies, and not-for-profit organizations.

Business Activities Involving Accounting

The natural progression of a business begins with financing. Subsequent steps, including investing, lead to operating the business. All organizations, profit oriented and not-for-profit, perform these three basic activities, and accounting plays a key role in each one:

1. Financing activities provide necessary funds to start a business and expand it after it begins operating.

2. Investing activities provide valuable assets required to run a business.

3. Operating activities focus on selling goods and services, but they also consider expenses as important elements of sound financial management.

Assessment Check ☑

1. Define *accounting.*

2. Who uses accounting information?

3. What are the three business activities that involve accounting?

[2] Accounting Professionals

Accounting professionals work in a variety of areas in and for business firms, government agencies, and not-for-profit organizations. They can be classified as public, management, government, and not-for-profit accountants.

Public Accountants

A **public accountant** provides accounting services to individuals or business firms for a fee. Most public accounting firms provide three basic services to clients: (1) auditing, or examining, financial records; (2) tax preparation, planning, and related services; and (3) management consulting. Because public accountants are not employees of a client firm, they can provide unbiased advice about the firm's financial condition.

Although there are hundreds of public accounting firms in the United States, a handful of firms dominate the industry. The four largest public accounting firms—Deloitte, PwC (PricewaterhouseCoopers), Ernst & Young, and KPMG, referred to as the Big Four—earned nearly $114 billion annually in a recent fiscal year. In contrast, Chicago-based Grant Thornton, the nation's fifth-largest accounting firm, has annual revenues of approximately $1.3 billion. Recently, Deloitte overtook PwC as the largest accounting firm in the world based on total annual revenues.[5]

One challenge these firms face is attracting and hiring the best talent. Ernst & Young recently adopted a new approach to reaching accounting students as well as new grads: inviting them to meet on Facebook. "We want to find the best and brightest, for internships and for full-time jobs," says Dan Black, a licensed CPA who began as an auditor and now holds the title of the Americas Director of Campus Recruiting at the firm. E&Y also reaches out to students via LinkedIn and Twitter. "This is just another way for people to meet us and learn about us and what we do," explains Black.[6]

Some years ago, public accounting firms came under sharp criticism for providing management consulting services to many of the same firms they audited. Critics argued that when a public accounting firm does both—auditing and management consulting—an inherent conflict of interest is created. In addition, this conflict of interest may undermine confidence in the quality of the financial statements that accounting firms audit. The bankruptcies of some high-profile firms increased pressure on public accounting firms to end this practice. Legislation also established strict limits on the types of consulting services auditors can provide. For example, an accounting firm that audits a company's books cannot provide any other services to that company, including tax services. As a result, three of the four largest public accounting firms either sold large portions of their consulting practices or spun them off into separate companies, and they now concentrate on providing auditing and tax services. PwC, for instance, sold much of its consulting business to IBM.

public accountant accountant who provides accounting services to individuals or business firms for a fee.

Hit&Miss

Forensic Accountants Look for Fraud

When most people think of accountants, they usually don't think of crime fighters. But the rapidly growing field of forensic accounting involves investigating such white-collar crimes as business fraud, improper financial reporting, and illegal investment schemes.

Forensic accounting is accounting performed in preparation for legal review. Forensic accountants investigate below the surface of an organization's accounting system to find out what actually happened. They also testify as expert witnesses if a case goes to trial. The job requires a bachelor's degree in accounting and CPA certification, with further training in investigative techniques for certification as a certified fraud examiner (CFE) or a certified forensic accountant (CrFA).

When the energy giant Enron Corporation collapsed, forensic accounting investigations revealed that for several years the firm had issued false financial statements that exaggerated the company's earnings and thereby increased the firm's stock prices. The statements painted a rosy picture of steady profits that met earnings expectations. In reality, Enron's own investments were doing poorly. As for profits, the company was actually losing money. Even after the truth leaked out and the company's stock prices tumbled, top management kept issuing false financial statements, hoping to slow the fall. In a federal trial, two former executives were convicted of conspiracy, wire fraud, and securities fraud.

Annual national conferences focus on issues faced by forensic accountants. RGL Forensics is the largest U.S. forensics accounting company, with 23 offices worldwide. Clients include insurance, legal, corporate, and public sector firms. Increased regulations have helped the forensic accounting services industry grow, particularly over the past decade.

Questions for Critical Thinking

1. Describe how shifts in the economy create new career paths and opportunities for accounting students.
2. How might forensic accounting change the world of business?

Sources: Company website, http://rglforensics.com, accessed March 21, 2014; Jesse Chiang, "Accountants Uncover Opportunities in Forensics," *Ibis World*, accessed March 21, 2014, www.ibisworld.com; Caleb Newquist, "What Are Your Questions for a Forensic Accounting Partner?" *Going Concern*, accessed March 21, 2014, http://goingconcern. com; company website, "Risk Management," http://www.pwc.com/nz, accessed March 21, 2014, Tracy Coenen, "Enron: The Good, the Bad, and the Ugly," *Wisconsin Law Journal*, accessed March 21, 2014, http://wislawjournal.com; James A. DiGabriele, "Applying Forensic Skepticism to Lost Profits Valuations," *Journal of Accountancy*, accessed March 21, 2014, www.journalofaccountancy.com; Rick Romell, "Accountants Who Focus on Fraud," *Milwaukee Journal Sentinel*, accessed March 21, 2014, www.jsonline.com.

Over the past several years, the Big Four have ramped up their consulting practices, which have surpassed traditional tax and audit growth. The Public Company Accounting Oversight Board has met with the firms to discuss their expansion into consulting and to hear their plans to prevent any conflicts of interest between consulting and auditing that might occur.[7]

As the "Hit & Miss" feature describes, a growing number of public accountants are also certified as *forensic accountants*, and some smaller public accounting firms actually specialize in forensic accounting. These professionals, and the firms that employ them, focus on uncovering potential fraud in a variety of organizations.

Certified public accountants (CPAs) demonstrate their accounting knowledge by meeting state requirements for education and experience and successfully completing a number of rigorous tests in accounting theory and practice, auditing, law, and taxes. Other accountants who meet specified educational and experience requirements and pass certification exams carry the title *certified management accountant, certified fraud examiner,* or *certified internal auditor*.

Management Accountants

An accountant employed by a business other than a public accounting firm is called a *management accountant*. Such a person collects and records financial transactions and prepares financial statements used by the firm's managers in decision making. Management accountants provide timely, relevant, accurate, and concise information that executives can use to operate their firms more effectively and more profitably than they could without this input. In addition to preparing financial statements, a management accountant plays a major role in interpreting them. A management accountant should provide answers to many important questions:

- Where is the company going?
- What opportunities await it?

- Do certain situations expose the company to excessive risk?

- Does the firm's technology provide detailed and timely information to all levels of management?

Management accountants frequently specialize in different aspects of accounting. A cost accountant, for example, determines the cost of goods and services and helps set their prices. An internal auditor examines the firm's financial practices to ensure that its records include accurate data and that its operations comply with federal, state, and local laws and regulations. A tax accountant works to minimize a firm's tax bill and assumes responsibility for its federal, state, county, and city tax returns. Some management accountants achieve a *certified management accountant (CMA)* designation through experience and passing a comprehensive examination.

Management accountants are usually involved in the development and enforcement of organizational policies on such items as employee travel. As part of their job, many employees travel and accumulate airline frequent flyer miles and hotel reward points. Although some organizations have strict policies over the personal use of travel perks, many do not.

Changing federal regulations affecting accounting and public reporting have increased the demand for management accountants in recent years. As a result, salaries for these professionals are rising.

Government and Not-for-Profit Accountants

Federal, state, and local governments also require accounting services. Government accountants and those who work for not-for-profit organizations perform professional services similar to those of management accountants. Accountants in these sectors concern themselves primarily with determining how efficiently the organizations accomplish their objectives. Among the many government agencies that employ accountants are the Department of Agriculture, the Federal Bureau of Investigation, the United States Mint, the Commonwealth of Pennsylvania, and the City of Fresno, California. The federal government alone employs thousands of accountants.

Not-for-profit organizations, such as churches, labor unions, charities, schools, hospitals, and universities, also hire accountants. In fact, the not-for-profit sector is one of the fastest growing segments of accounting practice. An increasing number of not-for-profits publish financial information because contributors want more accountability from these organizations and are interested in knowing how the groups spend the money that they raise.

Assessment Check ☑

1. List the three services offered by public accounting firms.

2. What tasks do management accountants perform?

[3] ## The Foundation of the Accounting System

To provide reliable, consistent, and unbiased information to decision makers, accountants follow guidelines, or standards, known as <u>generally accepted accounting principles (GAAP)</u>. These principles encompass the conventions, rules, and procedures for determining acceptable accounting and financial reporting practices at a particular time.

All GAAP standards are based on four basic principles: consistency, relevance, reliability, and comparability. Consistency means that all data should be collected and presented in the same manner across all periods. Any change in the way in which specific data are collected or presented must be noted and explained. Relevance states that all information being reported should be appropriate and assist users in evaluating that information. Reliability implies that the accounting data presented in financial statements are reliable and can be verified by an independent party such as an outside auditor. Finally, comparability ensures that one firm's financial statements can be compared with those of similar businesses.

generally accepted accounting principles (GAAP) principles that encompass the conventions, rules, and procedures for determining acceptable accounting and financial reporting practices at a particular time.

In the United States, the **Financial Accounting Standards Board (FASB)** is primarily responsible for evaluating, setting, or modifying GAAP. The U.S. Securities and Exchange Commission (SEC), the chief federal regulator of the financial markets and accounting industry, actually has the statutory authority to establish financial accounting and reporting standards for publicly held companies. (A publicly held company is one whose stock is publicly traded in a market such as the New York Stock Exchange.) However, the SEC's policy has been to rely on the accounting industry for this function, as long as the SEC believes the private sector is operating in the public interest. Consequently, the Financial Accounting Foundation—an organization made up of members of many different professional groups—actually appoints the members (currently seven) of the FASB, although the SEC does have some input. Board members are all experienced accounting professionals and serve five-year terms. They may be reappointed for a second five-year term. Board members must sever all connections with the firms they served prior to joining the board. The board is supported by a professional staff of more than 60 individuals.[8]

The FASB carefully monitors changing business conditions, enacting new rules and modifying existing rules when necessary. It also considers input and requests from all segments of its diverse constituency, including corporations and the SEC. One major change in accounting rules recently dealt with executive and employee stock options. Stock options give the holder the right to buy stock at a fixed price. The FASB now requires firms that give employees stock options to calculate the cost of the options and treat the cost as an expense, similar to salaries. A recent FASB update provides new accounting standards on goodwill, which permit private companies to amortize goodwill over a period of 10 years or less.[9]

In response to well-known cases of accounting fraud, and questions about the independence of auditors, the Sarbanes-Oxley Act—commonly known as SOX—created the Public Accounting Oversight Board mentioned earlier. The five-member board has the power to set audit standards and to investigate and sanction accounting firms that certify the books of publicly traded firms. Members of the Public Accounting Oversight Board are appointed by the SEC. No more than two of the five members of the board can be certified public accountants.

In addition to creating the Public Accounting Oversight Board, SOX also increased the reporting requirements for publicly traded companies. Senior executives including the CEO and chief financial officer (CFO), for example, must personally certify that the financial information reported by the company is correct. More than a decade after its enactment, the message behind the Sarbanes-Oxley law is that behavior in the boardroom and corporate governance in general were in need of a fundamental overhaul in the form of increased corporate compliance, fiduciary duty to shareholders, and ethical behavior.

It is expensive for firms to adhere to GAAP standards and SOX requirements. Audits, for instance, can cost millions of dollars each year. These expenses can be especially burdensome for small businesses. Consequently, some have proposed modifications to GAAP and SOX for smaller firms, arguing that some accounting rules were really designed for larger companies. Others disagree.

The **Foreign Corrupt Practices Act** is a federal law that prohibits U.S. citizens and companies from bribing foreign officials in order to win or continue business. This law was later extended to make foreign officials subject to penalties if they in any way cause similar corrupt practices to occur within the United States or its territories.

Assessment Check ☑

1. Define *GAAP*.
2. What are the four basic requirements to which all accounting rules must adhere?
3. What is the role played by the FASB?

[4] The Accounting Cycle

Accounting deals with financial transactions between a firm and its employees, customers, suppliers, and owners; bankers; and various government agencies. For example, payroll checks result in a cash outflow to compensate employees. A payment to a vendor results in receipt of needed materials for the production process. Cash, check, and credit purchases by customers generate funds to cover the costs of operations and to earn a profit. Prompt payment of bills preserves the firm's credit rating and its future ability to earn a profit. The procedure by which

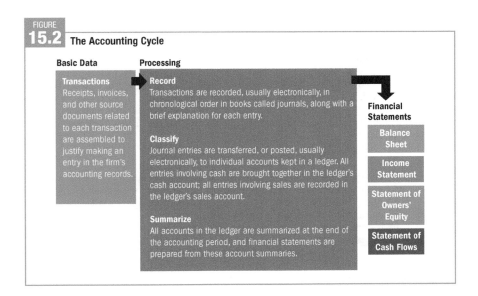

FIGURE
15.2 **The Accounting Cycle**

Basic Data

Processing

Transactions
Receipts, invoices, and other source documents related to each transaction are assembled to justify making an entry in the firm's accounting records.

Record
Transactions are recorded, usually electronically, in chronological order in books called journals, along with a brief explanation for each entry.

Classify
Journal entries are transferred, or posted, usually electronically, to individual accounts kept in a ledger. All entries involving cash are brought together in the ledger's cash account; all entries involving sales are recorded in the ledger's sales account.

Summarize
All accounts in the ledger are summarized at the end of the accounting period, and financial statements are prepared from these account summaries.

Financial Statements

Balance Sheet

Income Statement

Statement of Owners' Equity

Statement of Cash Flows

accountants convert data about individual transactions to financial statements is called the **accounting cycle**.

Figure 15.2 illustrates the activities involved in the accounting cycle: recording, classifying, and summarizing transactions. Initially, any transaction that has a financial impact on the business, such as wages or payments to suppliers, should be documented. All these transactions are recorded in journals, which list transactions in chronological order. Journal listings are then posted to ledgers. A ledger shows increases or decreases in specific accounts such as cash or wages. Ledgers are used to prepare the financial statements, which summarize financial transactions.

The Accounting Equation

Three fundamental terms appear in the accounting equation: assets, liabilities, and owners' equity. An **asset** is anything of value owned or leased by a business. Assets include land, buildings, supplies, cash, accounts receivable (amounts owed to the business as payment for credit sales), and marketable securities.

Although most assets are tangible assets, such as equipment, buildings, and inventories, intangible possessions such as patents and trademarks are often some of a firm's most important assets. This kind of asset is especially essential for many companies, including computer software firms, biotechnology companies, and pharmaceutical companies. For instance, Johnson & Johnson—which has both biotechnology and pharmaceutical operations—reported more than $28 billion in intangible assets (including goodwill) in one recent year, out of a total of almost $121 billion in assets.[10]

Two groups have claims against the assets of a firm: creditors and owners. A **liability** of a business is anything

accounting cycle set of activities involved in converting information and individual transactions into financial statements.

asset anything of value owned or leased by a business.

liability anything owed to creditors—the claims of a firm's creditors.

Although tangible assets such as buildings, equipment, and inventories may look impressive, they are sometimes less important to a company than intangible assets, such as patents and trademarks.

Nikada/iStockphoto

owed to creditors—that is, the claims of a firm's creditors. When a firm borrows money to purchase inventory, land, or machinery, the claims of creditors are shown as accounts payable, notes payable, or long-term debt. Wages and salaries owed to employees also are liabilities (known as *wages payable* or *accrued wages*).

Owners' equity is the owner's initial investment in the business plus profits that were not paid out to owners over time in the form of cash dividends. A strong owners' equity position often is used as evidence of a firm's financial strength and stability.

The **accounting equation** (also referred to as the *accounting identity*) states that assets must equal liabilities plus owners' equity. This equation reflects the financial position of a firm at any point in time:

$$\text{Assets} = \text{Liabilities} + \text{Owners' equity}$$

Because financing comes from either creditors or owners, the right side of the accounting equation also represents the business's financial structure.

The accounting equation also illustrates **double-entry bookkeeping**—the process by which accounting transactions are recorded. Because assets must always equal liabilities plus equity, each transaction must have an offsetting transaction. For example, if a company increases an asset, either another asset must decrease, a liability must increase, or owners' equity must increase. So if a company uses cash to purchase inventory, one asset (inventory) is increased while another (cash) is decreased by the same amount. Similarly, a decrease in an asset must be offset by either an increase in another asset, a decrease in a liability, or a decrease in owners' equity. If a company uses cash to repay a bank loan, both an asset (cash) and a liability (bank loans) decrease, and by the same amount.

Two simple numerical examples will help illustrate the accounting equation and double-entry bookkeeping. First, assume the owner of a photo studio purchases a new camera system for $5,000 using her personal funds. The accounting transaction would look as follows:

Increase plant, property, and equipment (an asset) by $5,000

Increase owners' equity by $5,000

So, the left side of the accounting equation would increase by $5,000 and be offset by a $5,000 increase on the right side.

Second, assume a firm has a $100,000 loan from a bank and decides to pay it off using some of its cash. The transaction would be recorded as:

Decrease bank loan (liability) by $100,000

Decrease cash (asset) by $100,000

In this second example, the left side and right side of the accounting equation would both decrease by $100,000.

The relationship expressed by the accounting equation underlies development of the firm's financial statements. Three financial statements form the foundation: the balance sheet, the income statement, and the statement of owners' equity. The information found in these statements is calculated using the double-entry bookkeeping system and reflects the basic accounting equation. A fourth statement, the statement of cash flows, is also prepared to focus specifically on the sources and uses of cash for a firm from its operating, investing, and financing activities.

The Impact of Computers and the Internet on the Accounting Process

For hundreds of years, bookkeepers recorded, or posted, accounting transactions as manual entries in journals. They then transferred the information, or posted it, to individual accounts listed in ledgers. Computers have dramatically changed the process, increasing speed, accuracy,

GoingGreen

Form 10-K Requires Sustainability Details

Established several years ago, the Sustainability Accounting Standards Board (SASB) was created to develop and disseminate accounting standards that relate to social and environmental measures, which have become increasingly relevant in today's business environment.

The sustainability standards will now be included in Form 10-K, a document all public companies are required to file with the Securities and Exchange Commission. The 10-K includes audited financial statements and management's discussion of company results. Sustainability reporting standards will be specific and standard by industry, and key performance indicators will be updated annually. Sustainability issues include sourcing practices, product impact on health, labor rights and compensation, materials and waste, climate change management, product environmental impact, impact on communities, and pollutants and emissions, among others.

The first set of standards created by SASB is for the health care industry. Provisional standards have been developed for six sectors within the health care industry, and issues include resource management, pharmaceutical water contamination, drug safety and side effects, ethical marketing, affordability and fair pricing, and safety of clinical trial participants.

Questions for Critical Thinking

1. What other industries are in need of the social and environmental measures developed by the SASB?

2. What are some of the challenges faced by the SASB in its efforts to develop and disseminate sustainability accounting standards or integrated reporting?

Sources: Company website, www.sasb.org, accessed March 21, 2014; "State of SASB One Year Later," *GreenBiz.com*, accessed March 21, 2014, www.greenbiz.com; "Accounting Standards for Health Care Industry a Key Milestone in Improving Disclosure of Material Non-Financial Information," *CSR Wire*, accessed March 21, 2014, www.csrwire.com; Ed Crooks, "Calls for Corporate Disclosure of Social Impact," *Financial Times*, accessed March 21, 2014, www.ft.com.

---

and ease. For instance, point-of-sale terminals in retail stores perform a number of functions each time they record sales. These terminals not only recall prices from computer system memory and maintain constant inventory counts of individual items in stock but also automatically perform accounting data entry functions.

Accounting software programs are used widely in both large and small businesses today. They allow a do-it-once approach, in which a single input leads to automatic conversion of a sale into a journal entry, which then is stored until needed. Decision makers can then access up-to-date financial statements and financial ratios instantly. Improvements in technology, access to data, and accounting software continue to make the process even faster and easier. In addition, accounting firms have begun to use mobile computing to better serve their clients. Smart phones provide connections between employees and their company's network, which means they can access current, vital information from anywhere. Accounting firms may also provide mobile computing to clients with branded applications allowing clients to access their financial information and services via their phones. As they increase their Internet capabilities, tablet computers and even smart phones have become important business tools for accounting firms.[11]

Because the accounting needs of entrepreneurs and small businesses differ from those of larger firms, companies like Intuit have designed programs that meet specific user needs. Some examples of accounting software programs designed for entrepreneurs and small businesses, and designed to run on personal computers, include QuickBooks, and Sage50 (formerly Peachtree). Software programs designed for larger firms, often requiring more sophisticated computer systems, include products from NetSuite, Oracle, and SAP.

For firms that conduct business worldwide, software producers have introduced new accounting programs that handle all of a company's accounting information for every country in which it operates. The software handles different languages and currencies, as well as the financial, legal, and tax requirements of each nation in which the firm conducts business.

The Internet also influences the accounting process. Several software producers offer web-based accounting products designed for small and medium-sized businesses. Among other benefits, these products allow users to access their complete accounting systems from anywhere using a standard web browser. The "Going Green" feature explains how a new Sustainability Accounting Standards Board is working to measure companies' impact on the environment.

Assessment Check

1. List the steps in the accounting cycle.

2. What is the accounting equation?

3. Briefly explain double-entry bookkeeping.

Financial Statements

Financial statements provide managers with essential information they need to evaluate the liquidity position of an organization—its ability to meet current obligations and needs by converting assets into cash; the firm's profitability; and its overall financial health. The balance sheet, income statement, statement of owners' equity, and statement of cash flows provide a foundation on which managers can base their decisions. By interpreting the data provided in these statements, managers can communicate the appropriate information to internal decision makers and to interested parties outside the organization.

Of the four financial statements, only the balance sheet is considered to be a permanent statement; its amounts are carried over from year to year. The income statement, statement of owners' equity, and statement of cash flows are considered temporary because they are closed out at the end of each fiscal year.

Public companies are required to report their financial statements at the end of each three-month period, or quarter, as well as at the end of each fiscal year. Annual statements must be examined and verified by the firm's outside auditors. These financial statements are public information available to anyone. The "Solving an Ethical Controversy" feature discusses the problem of financial fraud.

A fiscal year does not have to coincide with the calendar year, and companies set different fiscal years. For instance, Starbucks's fiscal year runs from October 1 to September 30 of the following year. Nike's fiscal year consists of the 12 months between June 1 and May 31. By contrast, GE's fiscal year is the same as the calendar year, running from January 1 to December 31.

The Balance Sheet

balance sheet statement of a firm's financial position on a particular date.

A firm's **balance sheet** shows its financial position on a particular date. It is similar to a photograph of the firm's assets together with its liabilities and owners' equity at a specific moment in time. Balance sheets must be prepared at regular intervals, because a firm's managers and other internal parties often request this information daily, weekly, or at least monthly. On the other hand, external users, such as stockholders or industry analysts, may use this information less frequently, perhaps every quarter or once a year.

The balance sheet follows the accounting equation. On the left side of the balance sheet are the firm's assets—what it owns. These assets, shown in descending order of liquidity (in other words, convertibility to cash), represent the uses that management has made of available funds. Cash is always listed first on the asset side of the balance sheet.

On the right side of the equation are the claims against the firm's assets. Liabilities and owners' equity indicate the sources of the firm's assets and are listed in the order in which they are due. Liabilities reflect the claims of creditors—financial institutions or bondholders that have loaned the firm money; suppliers that have provided goods and services on credit; and others to be paid, such as federal, state, and local tax authorities. Owners' equity represents the owners' claims (those of stockholders, in the case of a corporation) against the firm's assets. It also amounts to the excess of all assets over liabilities.

The balance sheet, the only permanent statement of the four financial statements, shows the firm's financial position on a particular date.

Mateusz Zagorski/iStockphoto

Part 6 *Managing Financial Resources*

Solving an Ethical Controversy

Should Whistle-Blowers Be Rewarded?

The Sarbanes-Oxley Act of 2002 (SOX) was intended to reduce fraud, partly by requiring CEOs and CFOs to sign off on the accuracy of their companies' financial statements. However, the largest percentage of reported fraud is revealed by anonymous whistle-blowers or by journalists or others.

The U.S. False Claims Act allows citizens to file lawsuits alleging fraud against the federal government. In a recent year, $3.8 billion in settlements was recovered involving fraud against the government. The biggest settlements involved health care fraud and procurement fraud related to defense contracts. Provisions of the Foreign Corrupt Practices Act (FCPA) can also potentially result in huge rewards. The Dodd-Frank Wall Street Reform and Consumer Protection Act requires the Securities and Exchange Commission (SEC) to award whistle-blowers between 10 percent and 30 percent of fines the government collects on the basis of "high-quality original information." However, in some cases, some whistle-blowers have been fired, forced to quit, or demoted.

Should whistle-blowers be rewarded for reporting financial fraud?

PRO

1. A recent survey found that "a strong monetary incentive to blow the whistle does motivate people with information to come forward."

2. Despite the strict penalties for fraud under SOX and the FCPA, one survey reported that 83 percent of fraud examiners believe that internal corporate controls over fraud will actually decline.

CON

1. Some observers feel that certain whistle-blower-friendly provisions of the FCPA may discourage accused firms from simply settling with the federal government and paying a fine to avoid costly legal procedures.

2. Not all whistle-blowers are innocent. A former UBS banker exposed tax evasion at the firm but was sentenced to prison because he did not reveal at first that he had participated in the fraud himself.

Summary

Over a decade after co-writing SOX, former Congressman Michael Oxley registered as a lobbyist for the Financial Industry Regulatory Authority (FINRA), which promotes self-regulation of investment advisors. Currently, more than 1,000 whistle-blower cases are pending.

Sources: Government website, "Justice Department Recovers $3.8 Billion in False Claims Act Cases in Fiscal Year 2013," www.justice.gov, accessed March 21, 2014; government website, "Welcome to the Office of the Whistleblower," www.sec.gov, accessed March 21, 2014; "Oxley of Sarbanes-Oxley to Lobby for Financial Self-Regulator," *Bloomberg News,* accessed March 21, 2014, www.bloomberg.com; company website, "Sarbanes-Oxley Can Help Curb Company Fraud," www.mcgladrey.com, accessed March 21, 2014; James Hyatt, "Who Detects Corporate Fraud? (Tip: It's Not Usually the SEC . . .)," *Business Ethics,* accessed March 21, 2014, http://business-ethics.com; Michael Rubinkam, "UBS Tax Evasion Whistle-Blower Reports to Federal Prison," *USA Today,* accessed March 21, 2014, www.usatoday.com; Ben Kerschberg, "The Dodd-Frank Act's Robust Whistleblowing Incentives," *Forbes,* accessed March 21, 2014, www.forbes.com.

Figure 15.3 shows the balance sheet for Belle's Fine Coffees, a small Texas-based coffee wholesaler. The accounting equation is illustrated by the three classifications of assets, liabilities, and owners' equity on the company's balance sheet. Remember, total assets must always equal the sum of liabilities and owners' equity. In other words, the balance sheet must always balance.

The Income Statement

Whereas the balance sheet reflects a firm's financial situation at a specific point in time, the income statement indicates the flow of resources that reveals the performance of the organization over a specific time period. Resembling a video rather than a photograph, the income statement is a financial record summarizing a firm's financial performance in terms of revenues, expenses, and profits over a given time period, say, a quarter or a year.

income statement
financial record summarizing a firm's financial performance in terms of revenues, expenses, and profits over a given time period, say, a quarter or a year.

1 Current Assets:
Cash and other liquid assets that can or will be converted to cash within one year.

2 Plant, Property, and Equipment (net):
Physical assets expected to last for more than one year; shown net of accumulated depreciation—the cumulative value that plant, property, and equipment have been expensed (depreciated).

3 Value of assets such as patents and trademarks.

4 Current Liabilities:
Claims of creditors that are to be repaid within one year; accruals are expenses, such as wages, that have been incurred but not yet paid.

5 Long-Term Debt:
Debts that come due one year or longer after the date on the balance sheet.

6 Owners' (or shareholders') Equity:
Claims of the owners against the assets of the firm; the difference between total assets and total liabilities.

Belle's Fine Coffees

Balance Sheet

($ thousands)	2017	2016
Assets		
1 Current Assets		
Cash	$ 800	$ 600
Short-term investments	1,250	940
Accounts receivable	990	775
Inventory	2,200	1,850
Total current assets	5,240	4,165
2 Plant, property, and equipment (net)	3,300	2,890
3 Goodwill and other intangible assets	250	250
Total Assets	8,790	7,305
Liabilities and Shareholders' Equity		
4 Current Liabilities		
Accruals	$ 350	$ 450
Accounts payable	980	900
Notes payable	700	500
Total current liabilities	2,030	1,850
5 Long-term debt	1,100	1,000
Total liabilities	3,130	2,850
6 Shareholders' equity	5,660	4,455
Total Liabilities and Equity	8,790	7,305

In addition to reporting the firm's profit or loss results, the income statement helps decision makers focus on overall revenues and the costs involved in generating these revenues. Managers of a not-for-profit organization use this statement to determine whether its revenues from contributions, grants, and investments will cover its operating costs. Finally, the income statement provides much of the basic data needed to calculate the financial ratios managers use in planning and controlling activities. Figure 15.4 shows the income statement for Belle's Fine Coffees.

An income statement (some times called *a profit-and-loss*, or *P&L, statement*) begins with total sales or revenues generated during a year, quarter, or month. Subsequent lines then deduct all of the costs related to producing the revenues. Typical categories of costs include those involved in producing the firm's goods or services, operating expenses, interest, and taxes. After all of them have been subtracted, the remaining net income may be distributed to the firm's owners (stockholders, proprietors, or partners) or reinvested in the company as retained earnings. The final figure on the income statement—net income after taxes—is literally the *bottom line*.

Keeping costs under control is an important part of running a business. Too often, however, companies concentrate more on increasing revenue than on controlling costs. Regardless

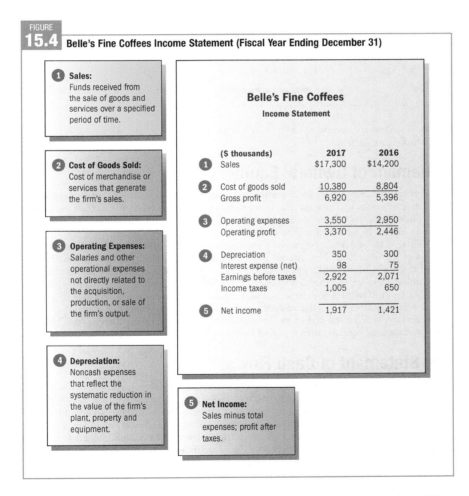

FIGURE 15.4 Belle's Fine Coffees Income Statement (Fiscal Year Ending December 31)

1 Sales: Funds received from the sale of goods and services over a specified period of time.

2 Cost of Goods Sold: Cost of merchandise or services that generate the firm's sales.

3 Operating Expenses: Salaries and other operational expenses not directly related to the acquisition, production, or sale of the firm's output.

4 Depreciation: Noncash expenses that reflect the systematic reduction in the value of the firm's plant, property and equipment.

5 Net Income: Sales minus total expenses; profit after taxes.

Belle's Fine Coffees
Income Statement

($ thousands)	2017	2016
1 Sales	$17,300	$14,200
2 Cost of goods sold	10,380	8,804
Gross profit	6,920	5,396
3 Operating expenses	3,550	2,950
Operating profit	3,370	2,446
4 Depreciation	350	300
Interest expense (net)	98	75
Earnings before taxes	2,922	2,071
Income taxes	1,005	650
5 Net income	1,917	1,421

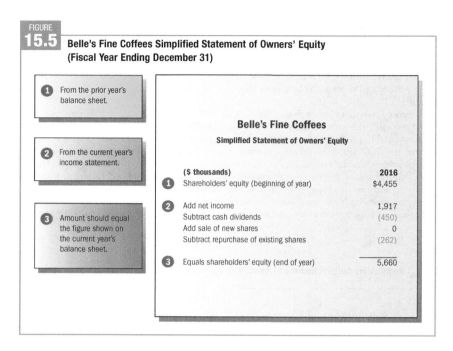

FIGURE 15.5 Belle's Fine Coffees Simplified Statement of Owners' Equity (Fiscal Year Ending December 31)

1. From the prior year's balance sheet.

2. From the current year's income statement.

3. Amount should equal the figure shown on the current year's balance sheet.

Belle's Fine Coffees

Simplified Statement of Owners' Equity

($ thousands)	2016
1 Shareholders' equity (beginning of year)	$4,455
2 Add net income	1,917
Subtract cash dividends	(450)
Add sale of new shares	0
Subtract repurchase of existing shares	(262)
3 Equals shareholders' equity (end of year)	5,660

of how much money a company collects in revenues, it won't stay in business for long unless it eventually earns a profit.

Statement of Owners' Equity

The **statement of owners', or shareholders', equity** is designed to show the components of the change in equity from the end of one fiscal year to the end of the next. It uses information from both the balance sheet and income statement. A somewhat simplified example is shown in Figure 15.5 for Belle's Fine Coffees.

Note that the statement begins with the amount of equity shown on the balance sheet at the end of the prior year. Net income is added, and cash dividends paid to owners are subtracted (both are found on the income statement for the current year). If owners contributed any additional capital, say, through the sale of new shares, this amount is added to equity. On the other hand, if owners withdrew capital, for example, through the repurchase of existing shares, equity declines. All of the additions and subtractions, taken together, equal the change in owners' equity from the end of the last fiscal year to the end of the current one. The new amount of owners' equity is then reported on the balance sheet for the current year.

The Statement of Cash Flows

In addition to the statement of owners' equity, the income statement, and the balance sheet, most firms prepare a fourth accounting statement—the **statement of cash flows**. Public companies are required to prepare and publish a statement of cash flows. In addition, commercial lenders often require a borrower to submit a statement of cash flows. The statement of cash flows provides investors and creditors with relevant information about a firm's cash receipts and cash payments for its operations, investments, and financing during an accounting period. Figure 15.6 shows the statement of cash flows for Belle's Fine Coffees.

statement of owners' equity record of the change in owners' equity from the end of one fiscal period to the end of the next.

statement of cash flows statement showing the sources and uses of cash during a period of time.

1 Operating Activities: The nuts and bolts of day-to-day activities of a company carrying out its regular business; increases in accounts receivable and inventory are uses of cash, while increases in accruals and accounts payables are sources of cash; in financially healthy firms, net cash flow from operating activities should be positive.

2 Investing Activities: Transactions to accumulate or use cash in ways that affect operating activities in the future; often a use of cash.

3 Financing Activities: Ways to transfer cash to or from creditors and to or from owners; can be either positive or negative.

4 Net Cash Flow: The sum of cash flow from operating, investing, and financing activities, a reconcilement of cash from the beginning to the end of the accounting period (one year in this example).

Belle's Fine Coffees
Statement of Cash Flows

($ thousands)	2016
Cash Flow from Operating Activities	
➊ Net income	$1,917
Depreciation	350
Change in accounts receivable	(215)
Change in inventory	(350)
Change in accruals	(100)
Change in accounts payable	80
Total cash flow from operating activities	1,682
➋ Cash Flow from Investing Activities	
Capital expenditures	(760)
Change in short-term investments	(310)
Total cash flow from investing activities	(1,070)
➌ Cash Flow from Financing Activities	
Cash dividends	(450)
Sale/repurchase of shares	(262)
Change in notes payable	200
Change in long-term debt	100
Total cash flow from financing activities	(412)
➍ Net Cash Flow	200
Cash (beginning of year)	600
Cash (end of year)	800

accrual accounting
accounting method that
records revenues and
expenses when they occur,
not necessarily when cash
actually changes hands.

Companies prepare a statement of cash flows due to the widespread use of accrual accounting. **Accrual accounting** recognizes revenues and costs when they occur, not when actual cash changes hands. As a result, there can be differences between what is reported as sales, expenses, and profits, and the amount of cash that actually flows into and out of the business during a period of time. An example is depreciation. Companies depreciate fixed assets—such as machinery and buildings—over a specified period of time, meaning that they systematically reduce the value of the asset. Depreciation is reported as an expense on the firm's income statement (see Figure 15.4) but does not involve any actual cash. The fact that depreciation is a noncash expense means that what a firm reports as net income (profits after tax) for a particular period actually understates the amount of cash the firm took in, less expenses, during that period of time. Consequently, depreciation is added back to net income when calculating cash flow.

The fact that *cash flow* is the lifeblood of every organization is evidenced by the business failure rate. Many former owners of failed firms blame inadequate cash flow for their companies' demise. Those who value the statement of cash flow maintain that its preparation and scrutiny by various parties can prevent financial distress for otherwise profitable firms, too many of which are forced into bankruptcy due to a lack of cash needed to continue day-to-day operations.

Even for firms for which bankruptcy is not an issue, the statement of cash flows can provide investors and other interested parties with vital information. For instance, assume that a firm's income statement reports rising earnings. At the same time, however, the statement of cash flows shows that the firm's inventory is rising faster than sales—often a signal that demand for the firm's products is softening, which may in turn be a sign of impending financial trouble.

Assessment Check ✅

1. List the four financial statements.
2. How is the balance sheet organized?
3. Define *accrual accounting*.

6 Financial Ratio Analysis

Accounting professionals fulfill important responsibilities beyond preparing financial statements. In a more critical role, they help managers interpret the statements by comparing data about the firm's current activities to those for previous periods and to results posted by other companies in the industry. *Ratio analysis* is one of the most commonly used tools for measuring a firm's liquidity, profitability, and reliance on debt financing, as well as the effectiveness of management's resource utilization. This analysis also allows comparisons with other firms and with the firm's own past performance.

Ratios assist managers in interpreting actual performance and making comparisons to the company's previous projections. Comparisons with ratios of similar companies help managers understand their firm's performance relative to competitors' results. These industry standards are important metrics and help pinpoint problem areas, as well as areas of excellence. Ratios for the current accounting period also may be compared with similar calculations for previous periods to spot developing trends. Ratios can be classified according to their specific purposes.

Liquidity Ratios

A firm's ability to meet its short-term obligations when they must be paid is measured by *liquidity ratios*. Increasing liquidity reduces the likelihood that a firm will face emergencies caused by the need to raise funds to repay loans. On the other hand, firms with low liquidity may be forced to choose between default or borrowing from high-cost lending sources to meet their maturing obligations.

Two commonly used liquidity ratios are the current ratio and the acid-test or quick ratio. The current ratio compares current assets to current liabilities, giving executives information about the firm's ability to pay its current debts as they mature. The current ratio of Belle's Fine

Coffees can be computed as follows (unless indicated, all amounts from the balance sheet or income statement are in thousands of dollars):

$$\text{Liquidity ratio} = \frac{\text{Current assests}}{\text{Current liabilities}} = \frac{5,240}{2,030} = 2.58$$

In other words, Belle's Fine Coffees has $2.58 of current assets for every $1.00 of current liabilities. In general, a current ratio of 2:1 is considered satisfactory liquidity. This rule of thumb must be considered along with other factors, such as the nature of the business, its seasonality, and the quality of the company's management team. Belle's Fine Coffees' management and other interested parties are likely to evaluate this ratio of 2.58:1 by comparing it with ratios for previous operating periods and with industry averages.

The acid-test (or quick) ratio measures the ability of a firm to meet its debt payments on short notice. This ratio compares quick assets—the most liquid current assets—against current liabilities. Quick assets generally consist of cash and equivalents, short-term investments, and accounts receivable. So, generally quick assets equal total current assets minus inventory.

Belle's Fine Coffees' current balance sheet lists total current assets of $5.24 million and inventory of $2.2 million. Therefore, its quick ratio is as follows:

$$\text{Acid-test ratio} = \frac{\text{Current assets} - \text{Inventory}}{\text{Current liabilities}} = \frac{(5,240 - 2,200)}{2,030} = 1.50$$

Because the traditional rule of thumb for an adequate acid-test ratio is around 1:1, Belle's Fine Coffees appears to have a strong level of liquidity. However, the same cautions apply here as for the current ratio. The ratio should be compared with industry averages and data from previous operating periods to determine whether it is adequate for the firm.

Activity Ratios

Activity ratios measure the effectiveness of management's use of the firm's resources. One of the most frequently used activity ratios, the inventory turnover ratio, indicates the number of times merchandise moves through a business:

$$\text{Inventory turnover} = \frac{\text{Cost of goods sold}}{\text{Average inventory}} = \frac{10,380}{[(2,200 + 1,850)/2]} = 5.13$$

Average inventory for Belle's Fine Coffees is determined by adding the inventory as of December 31, 2017 ($2.2 million) with the inventory as of December 31, 2016 ($1.85 million) and dividing it by 2. Comparing the 5.13 inventory turnover ratio with industry standards gives a measure of efficiency. It is important to note, however, that inventory turnover can vary substantially, depending on the products a company sells and the industry in which it operates.

If a company makes a substantial portion of its sales on credit, measuring receivables turnover can provide useful information. Receivables turnover can be calculated as follows:

$$\text{Receivables turnover} = \frac{\text{Credit sales}}{\text{Average accounts receivable}}$$

Because Belle's Fine Coffees is a wholesaler, let's assume that all of its sales are credit sales. Average receivables equals the simple average of 2017's receivables and 2016's receivables. The ratio for the company is:

$$\text{Receivables turnover} = \frac{17,300}{[(990 + 775)/2]} = 19.60$$

Dividing 365 by the figure for receivables turnover, 19.6, equals the average age of receivables, 18.62 days. Assume Belle's Fine Coffees expects its retail customers to pay outstanding bills within 30 days of the date of purchase. Given that the average age of its receivables is less than 30 days, Belle's Fine Coffees appears to be doing a good job collecting its credit sales.

Another measure of efficiency is total asset turnover. It measures how much in sales each dollar invested in assets generates:

$$\text{Total asset turnover} = \frac{\text{Sales}}{\text{Average total assets}}$$

$$= \frac{17,300}{[(8,790 + 7,305)/2]} = 2.15$$

Average total assets for Belle's Fine Coffees equals total assets as of December 31, 2017 ($8.79 million) plus total assets as of December 31, 2016 ($7.305 million) divided by 2.

Belle's Fine Coffees generates about $2.15 in sales for each dollar invested in assets. Although a higher ratio generally indicates that a firm is operating more efficiently, care must be taken when comparing firms that operate in different industries. Some industries simply require higher investment in assets than do other industries.

Profitability Ratios

Some ratios measure the organization's overall financial performance by evaluating its ability to generate revenues in excess of operating costs and other expenses. These measures are called *profitability ratios*. To compute these ratios, accountants compare the firm's earnings with total sales or investments. Over a period of time, profitability ratios may reveal the effectiveness of management in operating the business. Three important profitability ratios are gross profit margin, net profit margin, and return on equity:

$$\text{Gross profit margin} = \frac{\text{Gross profit}}{\text{Sales}} = \frac{6,920}{17,300} = 40.0\%$$

$$\text{Net profit margin} = \frac{\text{Net income}}{\text{Sales}} = \frac{1,917}{17,300} = 11.1\%$$

$$\text{Return on equity} = \frac{\text{Net income}}{\text{Average equity}} = \frac{1,917}{[(5,660 + 4,455)/2]} = 37.9\%$$

Rick Wilking/Reuters/Newscom

Walmart Inc. President and CEO Doug McMillon addresses shareholders at a recent meeting and discusses various topics, including the company's return on equity. Return on equity is one measure of a company's profitability.

All of these ratios indicate positive results of the current operations of Belle's Fine Coffees. For example, the net profit margin indicates that the firm realizes a profit of slightly more than 11 cents on each dollar of merchandise it sells. Although this ratio varies widely among business firms, Belle's Fine Coffees compares favorably with wholesalers in general, which have an average net profit margin of around 5 percent. However, this ratio, like the other profitability ratios, should be evaluated in relation to profit forecasts, past performance, or more specific industry averages to enhance the interpretation of results. Similarly, although the firm's return on equity of almost 38 percent appears outstanding, the degree of risk in the industry also must be considered.

Leverage Ratios

Leverage ratios measure the extent to which a firm relies on debt financing. They provide particularly interesting information to potential investors and lenders. If management has assumed too much debt in financing the firm's operations, problems may arise in meeting future interest payments and repaying outstanding loans. As we discuss in Chapter 17, borrowing money does have advantages. However, relying too heavily on debt financing may lead to bankruptcy. More generally, both investors and lenders may prefer to deal with firms whose owners have invested enough of their own money to avoid overreliance on borrowing. The debt ratio and long-term debt to equity ratio help interested parties evaluate a firm's leverage:

$$\text{Debt ratio} = \frac{\text{Total liabilities}}{\text{Total assets}} = \frac{3,130}{8,790} = 35.6\%$$

$$\text{Long-term debt to equity} = \frac{\text{Long-term debt}}{\text{Owners' equity}} = \frac{1,100}{5,660} = 19.43\%$$

A total liabilities to total assets ratio greater than 50 percent indicates that a firm is relying more on borrowed money than owners' equity. Because Belle's Fine Coffees' total liabilities to total assets ratio is 35.6 percent, the firm's owners have invested considerably more than the total amount of liabilities shown on the firm's balance sheet. Moreover, the firm's long-term debt to equity ratio is only 19.43 percent, indicating that Belle's Fine Coffees has only about 19.4 cents in long-term debt to every dollar in equity. The long-term debt to equity ratio also indicates that Belle's Fine Coffees hasn't relied very heavily on borrowed money.

The four categories of financial ratios relate balance sheet and income statement data to one another, help management pinpoint a firm's strengths and weaknesses, and indicate areas in need of further investigation. Large, multiproduct firms that operate in diverse markets use their information systems to update their financial ratios every day or even every hour. Each company's management must decide on an appropriate review schedule to avoid the costly and time-consuming mistake of over-monitoring.

In addition to calculating financial ratios, managers, investors, and lenders should pay close attention to how accountants apply a number of accounting rules when preparing financial statements. GAAP gives accountants leeway in reporting certain revenues and expenses. Public companies are required to disclose, in footnotes to the financial statements, how the various accounting rules were applied.

[7] Budgeting

Although the financial statements discussed in this chapter focus on past business activities, they also provide the basis for planning in the future. A **budget** is a planning and controlling tool that reflects the firm's expected sales revenues, operating expenses, and cash receipts and outlays. It quantifies the firm's plans for a specified future period. Because it reflects

Assessment Check ☑

1. List the four categories of financial ratios.

2. Define the following ratios: *current ratio, inventory turnover, net profit margin,* and *debt ratio.*

budget a planning and controlling tool that reflects the firm's expected sales revenues, operating expenses, and cash receipts and outlays.

Managing Travel Expenses

Business travel is an exciting aspect of many jobs. It also carries a higher level of responsibility, because you must carefully manage and track legitimate travel expenses your company will reimburse. Here are some tips for managing the task.

1 Whenever possible, book travel in advance for the best prices. Avoid deals that include penalties for changing your plans.

2 Save receipts for all expenditures in a single safe place, like a folder or envelope, or on your smartphone.

3 Use credit cards as much as possible, yours or the company's. This guarantees you a receipt of your expenses, or at least a record on your monthly statement.

4 When paying in cash, always ask for a receipt.

5 For small purchases like coffee that don't always generate a receipt, make a note of the amount, the date, and the purpose of the expenditure. Write it down or use your smart phone.

6 Avoid expensive options such as room service, the minibar in your hotel room, and pricey restaurants (unless you are entertaining clients, and it is part of your company's culture).

7 For prompt reimbursement and to avoid memory lapses, complete your expense report within a few days of your return.

Sources: Company website, "6 Tips for Tracking Expenses When Traveling," www.smead.com, accessed March 21, 2014; "5 Tips for Tracking Expenses While Traveling," *Mind Your Decisions*, accessed March 21, 2014, http://mindyour owndecisions.com; Michael Valkevich, "Twenty Tips for Managing Travel Expenses," *Fast Company*, accessed March 21, 2014, www.fastcompany.com; "How to Track Expenses When Traveling," *Traveling Mom*, accessed 21, 2014, http://travelingmom.com.

management estimates of expected sales, cash inflows and outflows, and costs, the budget is a financial blueprint and can be thought of as a short-term financial plan. It becomes the standard for comparison against actual performance.

Budget preparation is frequently a time-consuming task that involves many people from various departments within the organization. The complexity of the budgeting process varies with the size and complexity of the organization. Large corporations such as United Technologies, Paramount Pictures, and Verizon maintain complex and sophisticated budgeting systems. Besides being planning and controlling tools, their budgets help managers integrate their numerous divisions. But budgeting in both large and small firms is similar to household budgeting in its purpose: to match income and expenses in a way that accomplishes objectives and correctly times cash inflows and outflows.

Because the accounting department is an organization's financial nerve center, it provides many of the data for budget development. The overall master, or operating, budget is actually a composite of many individual budgets for separate units of the firm. These individual budgets typically include the production budget, cash budget, capital expenditures budget, advertising budget, sales budget, and travel budget. When you travel for business, you are responsible for keeping track of and recording your own financial transactions for the purpose of compiling your expense report, as the "Career Kickstart" feature describes.

Technology has improved the efficiency of the budgeting process. The accounting software products discussed earlier—such as QuickBooks—all include budgeting features. Many banks now offer their customers personal financial management tools (PFMs). Mint.com is a PFM leader and online tool for managing personal finances. Developed by Aaron Patzer, who was frustrated with available online tools for managing his finances, Mint.com was later sold to Intuit. What makes Mint.com unique is a patent-pending categorization technology that automatically identifies and organizes transactions made in most bank, credit, investment, brokerage, or retirement accounts.[12]

One of the most important budgets prepared by firms is the *cash budget*. The cash budget, usually prepared monthly, tracks the firm's cash inflows and outflows. Figure 15.7 illustrates a sample cash budget for Birchwood Paper, a small Maine-based paper products company. The company has set a $150,000 target cash balance. The cash budget indicates months in which the firm will need temporary loans—May, June, and July—and how much it will need (close to $3 million). The document also indicates that Birchwood will generate a cash surplus in August and can begin repaying the short-term loan. Finally, the cash budget produces a tangible standard against which to compare actual cash inflows and outflows.

Assessment Check ☑

1. What is a budget?
2. How is a cash budget organized?

FIGURE
15.7 Four-Month Cash Budget for Birchwood Paper Company

Birchwood Paper Company
Four-Month Cash Budget

($ thousands)	May	June	July	August
Gross sales	$1,200.0	$3,200.0	$5,500.0	$4,500.0
Cash sales	300.0	800.0	1,375.0	1,125.0
One month prior	600.0	600.0	1,600.0	2,750.0
Two months prior	300.0	300.0	300.0	800.0
Total cash inflows	1,200.0	1,700.0	3,275.0	4,675.0
Purchases				
Cash purchases	1,040.0	1,787.5	1,462.5	390.0
One month prior	390.0	1,040.0	1,787.5	1,462.5
Wages and salaries	250.0	250.0	250.0	250.0
Office rent	75.0	75.0	75.0	75.0
Marketing and other expenses	150.0	150.0	150.0	150.0
Taxes		300.0		
Total cash outflows	1,905.0	3,602.5	3,725.0	2,327.5
Net cash flow				
(Inflows − Outflows)	(705.0)	(1,902.5)	(450.0)	2,347.5
Beginnning cash balance	250.0	150.0	150.0	150.0
Net cash flow	(705.0)	(1,902.5)	(450.0)	2,347.5
Ending cash balance	(455.0)	(1,752.5)	(300.0)	2,497.5
Target cash balance	150.0	150.0	150.0	150.0
Surplus (deficit)	(605.0)	(1,902.5)	(450.0)	2,347.5
Cumulative surplus (deficit)	(605.0)	(2,507.5)	(2,957.5)	610.0

[8] International Accounting

Today, accounting procedures and practices must be adapted to accommodate an international business environment. The Coca-Cola Company and McDonald's both generate more than half their annual revenues from sales outside the United States. Nestlé, the giant chocolate and food products firm, operates throughout the world. It derives the majority of its revenues from outside Switzerland, its home country. International accounting practices for global firms must reliably translate the financial statements of the firm's international affiliates, branches, and subsidiaries and convert data about foreign currency transactions to dollars. Also, foreign currencies and exchange rates influence the accounting and financial reporting processes of firms operating internationally.

The "Hit & Miss" feature describes the role PwC has played over the last 80 years as the accountant for the Academy of Motion Pictures Arts and Sciences and the Oscar® awards.

Hit&Miss

Accountants to the Stars

Once a year, two CPAs dressed in formal wear walk the red carpet among Hollywood's most iconic stars at the annual Academy Awards event. PwC (PricewaterhouseCoopers) is the firm in charge of overseeing ballots for the world-famous Oscar® Awards for the Academy of Motion Picture Arts and Sciences. They are the only two persons in the world who know the identity of the award winners before the envelopes are opened during a live telecast, which airs to an estimated 1 billion people worldwide. For the last 80 years, two PwC accountants have stood at opposite ends of the stage putting envelopes in the hands of celebrity presenters. PwC is also the Academy's auditor and tax preparer.

On the day of event, the two accountants, picked up in separate cars with security escorts in tow, arrive at the venue with a set of ballots in their briefcases, which they carry down the red carpet while posing for pictures and interviews. In the event of a lost envelope or an unexpected error, each CPA has the winners memorized. As would be expected for any client, the two are experts at keeping information confidential—and over the last 80 years, the firm has not experienced any security breaches.

Questions for Critical Thinking

1. Contrast the role the firm plays as the auditor and tax preparer for the not-for-profit Academy, and the role the accountants play as part of the Academy Awards.

2. From a marketing standpoint, how might PwC use its association with the Academy Awards?

Sources: Company website, "PwC Upholds 80-Year Tradition Overseeing Oscars® Balloting and Preserving Secrets for Hollywood's Biggest Night," www.pwc.com, accessed March 21, 2014; Lily Rothman, "Oscars 2014: Who Will Win? These Accountants Already Know," *Time*, accessed March 21, 2014, http://entertainment.time.com; Francine McKenna, "Academy Still Counting on PwC to Pick Oscar Winners," *Forbes*, accessed March 21, 2014, www.forbes.com.

Exchange Rates

As defined in Chapter 4, an exchange rate is the ratio at which a country's currency can be exchanged for other currencies. Currencies can be treated as goods to be bought and sold. Like the price of any product, currency prices change daily according to supply and demand. So exchange rate fluctuations complicate accounting entries and accounting practices.

Accountants who deal with international transactions must appropriately record their firms' foreign sales and purchases. Accounting software helps firms handle all of their international transactions within a single program. An international firm's consolidated financial statements must reflect any gains or losses due to changes in exchange rates during specific periods of time. Financial statements that cover operations in two or more countries also need to treat fluctuations consistently to allow for comparison.

In the United States, GAAP requires firms to make adjustments to their earnings that reflect changes in exchange rates. In general, a weakening dollar increases the earnings of a U.S. firm that has international operations because the same units of a foreign currency will translate into more U.S. dollars. By the same token, a strengthening dollar will have the opposite effect on earnings—the same number of units of a foreign currency will translate into fewer dollars. Recently the Mexican peso increased in value as the United States started to climb out of its recession. The U.S. recovery actually helped boost Mexican exports to nearly $400 billion in a recent year.[13]

International Accounting Standards

International Accounting Standards Board (IASB) organization established in 1973 to promote worldwide consistency in financial reporting practices.

International Financial Reporting Standards (IFRS) standards and interpretations adopted by the IASB.

The International Accounting Standards Committee (IASC) was established in 1973 to promote worldwide consistency in financial reporting practices and soon developed its first set of accounting standards and interpretations. In 2001, the IASC became the **International Accounting Standards Board (IASB)**. **International Financial Reporting Standards (IFRS)** are the standards and interpretations adopted by the IASB. The IASB operates in much the same manner as the FASB does in the United States, interpreting and modifying IFRS.

452

Because of increased global trade, there is a real need for comparability of and uniformity in international accounting rules. Trade agreements such as NAFTA and the expansion of the European Union have only heightened interest in creating a uniform set of global accounting rules. In addition, an increasing number of investors are buying shares in foreign multinational corporations, and they need a practical way to evaluate firms in other countries. To assist global investors, more and more firms are beginning to report their financial information according to international accounting standards. This practice helps investors make informed decisions.

Nearly 100 other countries currently require, permit the use of, or have a policy of convergence with IFRS. These nations and other entities include members of the European Union, India, Australia, Canada, and Hong Kong. At first, the United States was skeptical of IFRS, even though major American accounting organizations have been involved with the IASB since its inception. In fact, the SEC used to require all firms whose shares were publicly traded in the United States to report financial results using GAAP. This rule applied regardless of where firms were located.

Nestlé's Nescafe coffee is packaged for shipment at a Chinese production plant. Because this Swiss corporation operates around the world, its profits and its financial statements are affected by foreign exchange rates.

This requirement started to change some years back, when the FASB and the IASB met and committed to the eventual convergence of IFRS with GAAP. This agreement was further clarified in 2005. Around the same time, the SEC began to loosen its rules on the use of IFRS by foreign firms whose shares trade in the United States. Today, many foreign companies can report results using IFRS as long as they reconcile these results to GAAP in a footnote. Some large U.S. companies were allowed to use international accounting standards beginning in 2009. By 2016, all U.S. firms will be required to do so. Meanwhile, the IASB and the FASB continue to develop convergence standards.[14]

How does IFRS differ from GAAP? Although many similarities between IFRS and GAAP exist, there are some important differences. For example, under GAAP, plant, property, and equipment is reported on the balance sheet at the historical cost minus depreciation. Under IFRS, on the other hand, plant, property, and equipment is shown on the balance sheet at current market value. This gives a better picture of the real value of a firm's assets. Many accounting experts believe that IFRS is overall less complicated than GAAP and more transparent.[15]

Assessment Check ☑

1. How are financial statements adjusted for exchange rates?

2. What is the purpose of the IASB?

What's Ahead

This chapter describes the role of accounting in an organization. Accounting is the process of measuring, interpreting, and communicating financial information to interested parties both inside and outside the firm. The next two chapters discuss the finance function of an organization. Finance deals with planning, obtaining, and managing the organization's funds to accomplish its objectives in the most efficient and effective manner possible. Chapter 16 outlines the financial system, the system by which funds are transferred from savers to borrowers. Organizations rely on the financial system to raise funds for expansion or operations. The chapter includes a description of financial institutions, such as banks; financial markets, such as the New York Stock Exchange; financial instruments, such as stocks and bonds; and the role of the Federal Reserve System. Chapter 17 discusses the role of finance and the financial manager in an organization.

Chapter 15 *Understanding Accounting and Financial Statements* 453

Chapter in Review

■ Summary of Learning Objectives

[1] Discuss the users of accounting information.

Accountants measure, interpret, and communicate financial information to parties inside and outside the firm to support improved decision making. Accountants gather, record, and interpret financial information for management. They also provide financial information on the status and operations of the firm for evaluation by outside parties, such as government agencies, stockholders, potential investors, and lenders. Accounting plays key roles in financing activities, which help start and expand an organization; investing activities, which provide the assets it needs to continue operating; and operating activities, which focus on selling goods and services and paying expenses incurred in regular operations.

Assessment Check Answers ✔

1.1 Define *accounting*. Accounting is the process of measuring, interpreting, and communicating financial information to enable people inside and outside the firm to make informed decisions.

1.2 Who uses accounting information? Managers of all types of organizations use accounting information to help them plan, assess performance, and control daily and long-term operations. Outside users of accounting information include government officials, investors, creditors, and donors.

1.3 What are the three business activities that involve accounting? The three activities involving accounting are financing, investing, and operating activities.

[2] Describe accounting professionals.

Public accountants provide accounting services to other firms or individuals for a fee. They are involved in such activities as auditing, tax return preparation, management consulting, and accounting system design. Management accountants collect and record financial transactions, prepare financial statements, and interpret them for managers in their own firms. Government and not-for-profit accountants perform many of the same functions as management accountants, but they analyze how effectively the organization or agency is operating, rather than its profits and losses.

Assessment Check Answers ✔

2.1 List the three services offered by public accounting firms. The three services offered by public accounting firms are auditing, tax services, and management consulting.

2.2 What tasks do management accountants perform? Management accountants work for the organization and are responsible for collecting and recording financial transactions, and preparing and interpreting financial statements.

[3] Identify the foundation of the accounting system.

The foundation of the accounting system in the United States is GAAP (generally accepted accounting principles), a set of guidelines or standards that accountants follow. There are four basic requirements to which all accounting rules should adhere: consistency, relevance, reliability, and comparability. The Financial Accounting Standards Board (FASB), an independent body made up of accounting professionals, is primarily responsible for evaluating, setting, and modifying GAAP. The U.S. Securities and Exchange Commission (SEC) also plays a role in establishing and modifying accounting standards for public companies, firms whose shares are traded in the financial markets.

Assessment Check Answers ✔

3.1 Define *GAAP*. GAAP stands for generally accepted accounting principles and is a set of standards or guidelines that accountants follow in recording and reporting financial transactions.

3.2 What are the four basic requirements to which all accounting rules must adhere? The four basic requirements to which all accounting rules must adhere are consistency, relevance, reliability, and comparability.

3.3 What is the role played by the FASB? The Financial Accounting Standards Board (FASB) is an independent body made up of accounting professionals and is primarily responsible for evaluating, setting, and modifying GAAP.

[4] Outline the steps in the accounting cycle.

The accounting process involves recording, classifying, and summarizing data about transactions and then using this information to produce financial statements for the firm's managers and other interested parties. Transactions are recorded chronologically in journals, posted in ledgers, and then summarized in accounting statements. Today, much of this activity takes place electronically. The basic accounting equation states that assets (what a firm owns) must always equal liabilities (what a firm owes creditors) plus owners' equity. This equation also illustrates double-entry bookkeeping, the process by which accounting transactions are recorded. Under double-entry bookkeeping, each individual transaction must have an offsetting transaction.

Assessment Check Answers ✔

4.1 List the steps in the accounting cycle. The accounting cycle involves the following steps: recording transactions, classifying the transactions, summarizing transactions, and using the summaries to produce financial statements.

4.2 What is the accounting equation? The accounting equation states that assets (what a firm owns) must always equal liabilities (what a firm owes) plus owners' equity. Therefore, if assets increase or decrease, there must be an offsetting increase or decrease in liabilities, owners' equity, or both.

4.3 Briefly explain double-entry bookkeeping. Double-entry bookkeeping is a process by which accounting transactions are recorded. Each transaction must have an offsetting transaction.

⌐5⌐ Explain financial statements.

The balance sheet shows the financial position of a company on a particular date. The three major classifications of balance sheet data are the components of the accounting equation: assets, liabilities, and owners' equity. The income statement shows the results of a firm's operations over a specific period. It focuses on the firm's activities—its revenues and expenditures—and the resulting profit or loss during the period. The major components of the income statement are revenues, cost of goods sold, expenses, and profit or loss. The statement of owners' equity shows the components of the change in owners' equity from the end of the prior year to the end of the current year. Finally, the statement of cash flows records a firm's cash receipts and cash payments during an accounting period. It outlines the sources and uses of cash in the basic business activities of operating, investing, and financing.

Assessment Check Answers ✅

5.1 List the four financial statements. The four financial statements are the balance sheet, the income statement, the statement of owners' equity, and the statement of cash flows.

5.2 How is the balance sheet organized? Assets (what a firm owns) are shown on one side of the balance sheet and are listed in order of convertibility into cash. On the other side of the balance sheet are claims to assets, liabilities (what a firm owes), and owners' equity. Claims are listed in the order in which they are due, so liabilities are listed before owners' equity. Assets always equal liabilities plus owners' equity.

5.3 Define _accrual accounting_. Accrual accounting recognizes revenues and expenses when they occur, not when cash actually changes hands. Most companies use accrual accounting to prepare their financial statements.

⌐6⌐ Discuss financial ratio analysis.

Liquidity ratios measure a firm's ability to meet short-term obligations. Examples are the current ratio and the quick, or acid-test, ratio. Activity ratios—such as the inventory turnover ratio, accounts receivable turnover ratio, and the total asset turnover ratio—measure how effectively a firm uses its resources. Profitability ratios assess the overall financial performance of the business. The gross profit margin, net profit margin, and return on owners' equity are examples of profitability ratios. Leverage ratios, such as the total liabilities to total assets ratio and the long-term debt to equity ratio, measure the extent to which the firm relies on debt to finance its operations. Financial ratios help managers and outside evaluators compare a firm's current financial information with that of previous years and with results for other firms in the same industry.

Assessment Check Answers ✅

6.1 List the four categories of financial ratios. The four categories of ratios are liquidity, activity, profitability, and leverage.

6.2 Define the following ratios: _current ratio, inventory turnover, net profit margin_, and _debt ratio_. The current ratio equals current assets divided by current liabilities. Inventory turnover equals cost of goods sold divided by average inventory. Net profit margin equals net income divided by sales. The debt ratio equals total liabilities divided by total assets.

⌐7⌐ Describe the role of budgeting.

Budgets are financial guidelines for future periods and reflect expected sales revenues, operating expenses, and cash receipts and outlays. They reflect management expectations for future occurrences and are based on plans that have been made. Budgets are important planning and controlling tools because they provide standards against which actual performance can be measured. One important type of budget is the cash budget, which estimates cash inflows and outflows over a period of time.

Assessment Check Answers ✅

7.1 What is a budget? A budget is a planning and control tool that reflects the firm's expected sales revenues, operating expenses, cash receipts, and cash outlays.

7.2 How is a cash budget organized? Cash budgets are generally prepared monthly. Cash receipts are listed first. They include cash sales as well as the collection of past credit sales. Cash outlays are listed next. These include cash purchases, payment of past credit purchases, and operating expenses. The difference between cash receipts and cash outlays is net cash flow.

⌐8⌐ Outline international accounting practices.

One accounting issue that affects global business is exchange rates. An exchange rate is the ratio at which a country's currency can be exchanged for other currencies. Daily changes in exchange rates affect the accounting entries for sales and purchases of firms involved in international markets. These fluctuations create either losses or gains for particular companies. The International Accounting Standards Board (IASB) was established to provide worldwide consistency in financial reporting practices and comparability of and uniformity in international accounting standards. It has developed International Financial Reporting Standards (IFRS). Many countries have already adopted IFRS, and the United States is in the process of making the transition to it.

Assessment Check Answers ✔

8.1 How are financial statements adjusted for exchange rates? An exchange rate is the ratio at which a country's currency can be exchanged for other currencies. Fluctuations of exchange rates create either gains or losses for particular companies because data about international financial transactions must be translated into the currency of the country in which the parent company is based.

8.2 What is the purpose of the IASB? The International Accounting Standards Board (IASB) was established to provide worldwide consistency in financial reporting practices and comparability and uniformity of international accounting rules. The IASB has developed the International Financial Reporting Standards (IFRS).

■ Business Terms You Need to Know

accounting 431
public accountant 433
generally accepted accounting
  principles (GAAP) 435
Financial Accounting Standards Board
  (FASB) 436
Foreign Corrupt Practices Act 436
accounting cycle 437

asset 437
liability 437
owners' equity 438
accounting equation 438
double-entry bookkeeping 438
balance sheet 440
income statement 441
statement of owners' equity 444

statement of cash flows 444
accrual accounting 446
budget 449
International Accounting Standards
  Board (IASB) 452
International Financial Reporting
  Standards (IFRS) 452

■ Review Questions

1. Define *accounting*. Who are the major users of accounting information?

2. What are the three major business activities in which accountants play a major role? Give an example of each.

3. What does the term *GAAP* mean? Briefly explain the roles of the Financial Accounting Standards Board and the Securities and Exchange Commission.

4. What is double-entry bookkeeping? Give a brief example.

5. List the four major financial statements. Which financial statements are permanent and which are temporary?

6. What is the difference between a current asset and a long-term asset? Why is cash typically listed first on a balance sheet?

7. List and explain the major items found on an income statement.

8. What is accrual accounting? Give an example of how accrual accounting affects a firm's financial statement.

9. List the four categories of financial ratios and give an example of each. What is the purpose of ratio analysis?

10. What is a cash budget? Briefly outline what a simple cash budget might look like.

■ Projects and Teamwork Applications

1. Using LinkedIn or your personal or professional network, make contact with someone who works as an accountant at a public accounting firm to set up an interview. Ask the individual what his or her educational background is, what attracted the individual to the accounting profession, and what he or she does during a typical day. Prepare a brief report on your interview. Do you now want to learn more about the accounting profession? Are you more interested in possibly pursuing a career in accounting?

2. Suppose you work for a U.S. firm that has extensive European operations. You need to restate data from the various European currencies in U.S. dollars in order to prepare your firm's financial statements. Which financial statements and which components of these statements will be affected?

3. Identify two public companies operating in different industries. Collect at least three years' worth of financial statements for the firms. Calculate the financial ratios discussed in the chapter. Prepare an oral report summarizing your findings.

4. Human asset accounting, also referred to as human resource accounting, considers the value and role of people within an organization. This includes their replacement cost. How would you apply the concept of human asset accounting to

Amazon and the role founder Jeff Bezos plays in the organization? You may choose another company with an individual who plays a defining role. Discuss your findings.

5. Adapting the format of Figure 15.7, prepare on a sheet of paper your personal cash budget for next month. Keep in mind the following suggestions as you prepare your budget:

   a. *Cash inflows*. Your sources of cash would include your payroll earnings, if any; gifts; scholarship monies; tax refunds; dividends and interest; and income from self-employment.

   b. *Cash outflows*. When estimating next month's cash outflows, include any of the following that may apply to your situation:

      i. Household expenses (rent or mortgage, utilities, maintenance, home furnishings, telephone/cell phone, cable TV, household supplies, groceries)

      ii. Education (tuition, fees, textbooks, supplies)

      iii. Work (lunches, clothing)

      iv. Clothing (purchases, cleaning, laundry)

      v. Automobile (auto payments, repairs) or other transportation (bus, train)

      vi. Gasoline expenses

      vii. Insurance premiums
         • Renters (or homeowners)
         • Auto
         • Health
         • Life

      viii. Taxes (income, Social Security, Medicare, real estate)

      ix. Savings and investments

      x. Entertainment/recreation (dining, movies, health club, vacation/travel)

      xi. Debt (credit cards, installment loans)

      xii. Miscellaneous (charitable contributions, child care, gifts, medical expenses)

   c. *Beginning cash balance*. This amount could be based on a minimum cash balance you keep in your checking account and should include only the cash available for your use; therefore, money such as that invested in retirement plans should not be included.

Web Assignments

1. **International Accounting Standards Board (IASB).** The IASB is responsible for setting and modifying international accounting rules. Go to the IASB's website at http://www.iasb .org and click on "about us." Print out the material and bring it to class to participate in a class discussion on the IASB.

2. **Apple's balance sheet.** Go to Apple's website to review the company's most recent annual report. Find the balance sheet and the corresponding discussion. Using concepts from the chapter, review and calculate some of the company's key ratios. Based upon this information, what unique and unusual things have you found, and how would you evaluate Apple's current financial situation? Discuss your findings.

www.apple.com

3. **Preparing a personal balance sheet.** Go online to find a template for a personal balance sheet. Fill in as many items as you can, and create your own asset categories if needed. Upon evaluating your results, how would you assess your liquidity, debt, and debt-to-equity ratios? What sort of change would you recommend to modify your current situation?

Note: Internet web addresses change frequently. If you don't find the exact sites listed, you may need to access the organization's home page and search from there or use a search engine such as Google or Bing.

Walnut Scandal Costs Investors Plenty

CASE 15.1

In a recent accounting case, the Securities and Exchange Commission reached a $5 million settlement with California-based snack company Diamond Foods. Maker of Kettle Brand chips, Pop Secret popcorn, and Diamond of California nuts, Diamond neither admitted nor denied guilt in the case. However, the scandal cost the company the opportunity to buy potato chip maker Pringles, a deal seller Procter & Gamble canceled after the story broke.

The case centers around misreported prices paid to purchase walnuts, which caused the company to restate its earnings for the two prior years. The SEC says that Diamond's former CFO instructed the company's finance team to disguise portions of the fees as advances on future crop deliveries. Approximately $80 million paid to walnut growers was underreported by delaying the payments and reporting them in later fiscal periods, which helped inflate company earnings.

The former CEO was found to have misled investors, and he ultimately returned more than $4 million in bonuses and benefits during the period in which the fraud occurred. In addition, he paid a $125,000 negligence fee. The CEO failed to report the true cost of walnuts at the time he certified that the company's financial statements were truthful and correct. SEC litigation against the company's former CFO continues.

Diamond Foods has some work to do to settle the scandal, which involves restating its financial information and rebuilding its reputation along with its share price, which plummeted to a low of $17 from a high of $70. One of the goals of the company's new CFO includes not only creating an internal global audit function but also restoring confidence among its shareholders, banks, and creditors.

Questions for Critical Thinking

1. What steps should the company put in place to ensure financial statements are accurate?
2. How would you react as a shareholder of Diamond Foods? Discuss.

Sources: Mark Calvey, "Diamond Foods, Ex-CEO Pay to Settle with SEC over Accounting Scandal," *San Francisco Business Journal,* accessed March 21, 2014, www.bizjournals.com. Emily Chasan, "Diamond Foods CFO on Recovering from a Crisis," *The Wall Street Journal,* accessed March 21, 2014, http://blogs.wsj.com; James O'Toole, "SEC Charges Diamond Foods over Nutty Accounting," *CNN Money,* accessed March 21, 2014, http://money.cnn.com; Andrew S. Ross, "SEC Charges Diamond Foods with Accounting Fraud," *San Francisco Chronicle,* accessed March 21, 2014, www.sfgate.com.

CASE 15.2 — BDO Seidman: An Accounting Approach for the 21st Century

In 1910, Maximillian Leonard Seidman (1888–1963), the son of Russian immigrants, founded the accounting firm of Seidman & Seidman in New York City. The profession of accounting was also brand new.

When the income tax on individuals was established in 1913 by the Sixteenth Amendment to the U.S. Constitution, Seidman recognized the potential for growth as accountants took on a new role in tax planning for individuals. And when Congress enacted legislation in 1917, instituting corporate income taxes, Seidman—now joined by two brothers—expanded the business to include corporations. The firm opened a second office in Michigan, just when the federal government converted furniture and woodworking factories to airplane manufacturing for World War I. Seidman & Seidman quickly became known for serving this industry when it developed a successful system for keeping track of furniture-plant costs.

Maximillian Seidman ran the firm for 45 years. He wrote many articles and served in many industry organizations. He advocated "Total Involvement" of his firm's employees in the business of their clients. In 1944 he declared, "It is the manner in which we serve our clients today that will determine whether we shall have them to serve as clients in the future."

Seidman & Seidman became a truly national firm by the 1960s. In 1963, it joined other accounting companies from Canada, Britain, the Netherlands and (then West) Germany in an international organization. In 1973, these firms formed a new group called BDO (Binder Dijker Otte & Co.). This group, now called BDO International, is the sixth largest accounting firm in the world, with 1,204 branches in 138 countries. The U.S. member, BDO Seidman LLP, has 42 branches.

BDO has received a number of industry honors. The company recently announced that 34 of its U.S. offices had won the Alfred P. Sloan Award for Business Excellence in Workplace Flexibility. This award acknowledges the personal and workplace advantages of flexibility programs when a firm uses them to improve its effectiveness and to benefit its employees. *Accounting Today* magazine and Best Companies Group named BDO one of the "best accounting firms." The Best Accounting Firms program identifies the best employers in the accounting industry and their benefits to the U.S. economy, workforce, and businesses. And the American Society of Women Accountants (ASWA) and the American Woman's Society of CPAs (AWSCPA) both named BDO one of the best CPA firms for women.

Questions for Critical Thinking

1. What historic and economic factors do you think might have contributed to the growth and expansion of the accounting industry, and Seidman's firm, from the early 20th century to today?
2. What advantages does BDO Seidman LLP enjoy in belonging to a large, international group?

Sources: Company website, www.bdo.com, accessed March 21, 2014; association website, "The Top Accounting Firms in the World," www.big4accountingfirms.org, accessed March 21, 2014; Michael Rapoport, "BDO USA Chief Looks to Grow Through Deals," *The Wall Street Journal,* accessed March 21, 2014, http://online.wsj.com; "BDO USA, LLP Recognized for Exemplary Workplace Practices with the Alfred P. Sloan Award," press release, www.bdo.com, accessed March 21, 2014.

The success of the Mei Mei Group, which includes its Street Kitchen food truck and its new restaurant, can be credited to three siblings from the Boston area. Andy, Irene, and Margaret Li's award-winning food truck serves up creative Chinese American cuisine made with sustainably raised meats and locally sourced produce from small family farms. "Mei Mei" is Mandarin for "little sister," and the secret to Mei Mei's staying power can be partly attributed to one of the "little sisters" in the group, Margaret, or Mei for short. She uses accounting information to make important strategic decisions about labor and food.

A key component of the company's success is its proactive approach and keen attention to recording, summarizing, and analyzing financial data. The food truck has been a great way to test and experiment with different dishes, while spending less money than running a full-service restaurant. After evaluating the results of its operation on a daily basis, the owners decided to expand operations by adding a restaurant to its business.

The Li siblings balance choices that make good financial sense with their business values and practices. The siblings believe cooking and serving food that reflects the humane treatment of animals can make a difference in the local food system, and balancing these values against costs is integral to their budgeting, financial planning, and overall operations. Keeping track of costs on a daily basis actually allows Mei to make decisions to maintain and grow the businesses profitably. Mei uses accounting information to make decisions about food costs, which are maintained at a targeted percentage of sales. For all new product development including new menu items, decisions are made with a focus on the numbers and metrics, or food costs as a percentage of the selling price.

While costs to source locally can be considerably higher, creativity and experience certainly help. For example, Mei purchases whole pigs from suppliers, which lowers the price per pound for pork. In addition, Mei keeps a watchful eye on fixed costs like rent and labor to be sure they remain at a targeted percentage of sales. With 40 employees, tracking labor costs and allocating staff has become increasingly important for the company.

Two business activities, financing and investing, involve accounting, and for the Mei Mei Group and most small businesses, both can be a challenge. For the funds required to get its Street Kitchen rolling, the Li siblings used a lot of their own personal finances, along with loans from other family members. For the Mei Mei restaurant, partial financing of $35,000 came through Kickstarter, an online crowdfunding

site. A wall in the restaurant will be dedicated to Kickstarter donors who believed that adding a restaurant to the Mei Mei business portfolio made good financial sense. The siblings agree that making the right investment decisions early on can make or break any small business.

Because employees and suppliers need to be paid on time, Mei makes it a point to check the books every day to be sure there is sufficient money coming in against the money being paid out. With regularly scheduled owner meetings the siblings communicate business results with one another on an ongoing basis. Information is also shared with managers and employees so accurate decisions can be made regarding food purchases, labor, and other business components. When Mei Mei managers understand the impact of a decision and its effects on company's finances, it proves to be an appetizing combination of continued growth and profitability.

Questions for Critical Thinking

1. In Mei Mei Street Kitchen's accounting equation, what are some of the firm's assets and liabilities? Based upon this data, what assumptions would you make about its owners' equity?

2. Identify the types of expenses that Mei Mei Street Kitchen might list on its income statement. How might these expenses vary?

3. Why is it important for a small company like the Mei Mei Group to prepare a regular budget? Discuss what you believe the budgeting process might look like at Mei Mei Street Kitchen as compared to the company's restaurant.

4. Discuss some of the financial challenges the Li siblings face balancing local sourcing and doing business for a sustainable future. If the siblings did not have this value system, how might company financial statements differ, and what tradeoffs might exist?

Sources: Company website, http://meimeiboston.com, accessed June 3, 2014; Mei Mei Street Kitchen Facebook page, https://www.facebook.com/meimeibostoon, accessed June 3, 2014; "Meet Young Guns Semi-Finalists Irene Li and Max Hull of Boston's Mei Mei," Eater.com, accessed June 3, 2014, www.eater.com; Rachel Leah Blumenthal, "Mei Mei Could Get a Beer & Wine License After All," *Boston Eater*, accessed June 3, 2014, http://boston.eater.com; Christopher Hughes, "Five Reasons You Should Be Eating at Mei Mei Street Kitchen," *Boston Magazine*, accessed June 3, 2014, www.bostonmagazine.com; Morgan Rousseau, "Cray Cray for Mei Mei: Boston Food Truck to Open Green Eatery," *Metro US Magazine*, accessed June 3, 2014, www.metro.us; Rachel Travers, "Rolling with the Mei Mei Street Kitchen," Boston.com, accessed June 3, 2014, www.boston.com.

Learning Objectives

1. Understand the financial system.
2. List the various types of securities.
3. Discuss financial markets.
4. Understand the stock markets.
5. Evaluate financial institutions.
6. Explain the role of the Federal Reserve System.
7. Describe the regulation of the financial system.
8. Discuss the global perspective of the financial system.

Chapter 16

The Financial System

Joshua Putman/Alamy Limited

Bitcoins and Virtual Currency

During the recent global financial crisis, an enterprising and somewhat mysterious individual who went by the name of Satoshi Nakamoto proposed an entirely new type of currency—the Bitcoin. So, what exactly is a Bitcoin? Before answering this question, it is best to start with a description of how existing currencies work.

Whether they are British pounds, Japanese yen, European euros, or U.S. dollars, currencies are known as *fiat* currencies, which means there is no underlying asset such as gold or silver to back the currency. Without an underlying asset, the value of the currency comes from the pledge of the issuing government to accept the currency for all debts owed to it. The issuing government also asserts that the currency can be used for all personal and public transactions within the country. If citizens believe that their government is acting responsibly, they will have faith in the long-term value of the currency and be willing to use it for transactions. However, if the government is acting irresponsibly, their citizens will seek some other means (usually currencies from more stable countries or gold) to hold their wealth.

The Bitcoin is seen as a way to decouple currencies from individual countries. Using Bitcoins, people do not have to worry about a government acting responsibly, as the digital currency exists entirely in the virtual world. While initially just an interesting idea, Bitcoins are gaining acceptance. Businesses and individuals can use them for transactions. For example, you can go to Bitcoin-specific websites and buy books, software, games, and even electronic devices. You can even go to some websites and trade your Bitcoins for more traditional currencies.

Of course with any new technology there are challenges, including maintaining the security of the Bitcoin system. Additional concerns include its use by the global underground economy as a way to avoid taxes and even transfer funds outside of government channels. Bitcoin proponents claim these issues are manageable, and the benefits of a digital currency far outweigh the risks of a country's fiat currency. Time will tell, but Bitcoins have gotten quite a bit of media coverage worldwide. In fact, the IRS announced that Bitcoins will be taxed like a stock investment.[1]

Overview

Businesses, governments, and individuals often need to raise capital. Assume the owner of a small business either forecasts a sharp increase or drop in sales; one might require more inventory and the other reduced production in order to survive. The owner might turn to a major bank or a nontraditional lender for a loan that would provide the needed cash for either situation. On the other hand, some individuals and businesses have incomes that are greater than their current expenditures and wish to earn a rate of return on the excess funds. For instance, say your income this month is $3,000 but your expenditures are only $2,500. You can take the extra $500 and deposit it in your bank savings account, which pays you a minimal rate of interest.

The two transactions just described are small parts of what is known as the financial system, the process by which money flows from savers to users. Virtually all businesses, governments, and individuals participate in the financial system, and a well-functioning one is vital to a nation's economic well-being. The financial system is the topic of this chapter.

We begin by describing the financial system and its components in more detail. Then, the major types of financial instruments, such as stocks and bonds, are outlined. Next we discuss financial markets, where financial instruments are bought and sold. We then describe the world's major stock markets, such as the New York Stock Exchange.

Next, banks and other financial institutions are described in depth. The structure and responsibilities of the U.S. Federal Reserve System (the Fed), along with the tools it uses to control the supply of money and credit, are detailed. The chapter concludes with an overview of the major laws and regulations affecting the financial system and a discussion of today's global financial system.

Understanding the Financial System

Households, businesses, government, financial institutions, and financial markets together form what is known as the **financial system**. A simple diagram of the financial system is shown in Figure 16.1.

On the left are savers—those with excess funds. For a variety of reasons, savers choose not to spend all of their current income, so they have a surplus of funds. Users are the opposite of savers; their spending needs exceed their current income, so they have a deficit. They need to obtain additional funds to make up the difference. Savings are provided by some households, businesses, and the government; but other households, businesses, and the government are borrowers. Households may need money to buy automobiles or homes. Businesses may need money to purchase inventory or build new production facilities. Governments may need money to build highways and courthouses.

Generally, in the United States, households are net savers—meaning that as a whole they save more funds than they use—whereas businesses and governments are net users—meaning that they use more funds than they save. The fact that most of the net savings in the U.S. financial system are provided by households may be a bit of a surprise initially, because Americans do not have a reputation for being savers. Yet even though the savings rate of American households is low compared with those of other countries, American households still save hundreds of billions of dollars each year.

How much an individual saves is a function of many variables. One of the most important is the person's age. People often transition from net borrowers to net savers as they get older. When you graduate from college and begin a career, you likely have little in the way of savings. In fact, you may be deeply in debt. In the early years of your career, you may spend more than you make as you acquire major assets, such as a home. So in these early years your *net worth*—the difference between what you own and what you owe—is very low and may even be negative. However, as your career progresses and your income rises, you will begin to build a financial nest egg to fund retirement and other needs. Your net worth is also likely to increase. It will continue to increase until you retire and begin drawing on your retirement savings.

Funds can be transferred between savers and users in two ways: directly and indirectly. A direct transfer means that the user raises the needed funds directly from savers. While direct transfers occur, the vast majority of funds flow through either financial markets or financial institutions. For example, assume a local school district needs to build a new high school. The district doesn't have enough cash on hand to pay for the school construction costs, so it sells bonds to investors (savers) in the financial market. The district uses the proceeds from the sale to pay for the new school and in return pays bond investors interest each year for the use of their money.

The other way in which funds can be transferred indirectly is through financial institutions—for example, a commercial bank such as Cincinnati-based Fifth Third Bank or Alabama-based Regions Bank. The bank pools customer deposits and uses the funds to make loans to businesses and households. These borrowers pay the bank interest, and it, in turn, pays depositors interest for the use of their money.

The accompanying "Going Green" feature describes the growing appeal of "green" banking.

Assessment Check ✓

1. What is the financial system?

2. In the financial system, who are the borrowers and who are the savers?

3. List the two most common ways in which funds are transferred between borrowers and savers.

FIGURE 16.1 Overview of the Financial Systems and Its Components

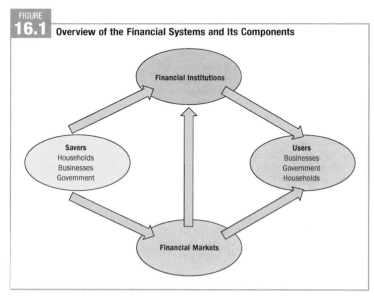

GoingGreen

Green Banking at New Resource Bank

The trend toward small banks with personalized service and environmentally friendly practices has gained steam over the past few years in the wake of financial scandals in which banks and other lenders have paid billions in fines for foreclosure improprieties.

New Resource Bank is a popular green-bank alternative, designed to encourage sustainability among its many San Francisco customers. The bank's growth is in part the result of its philosophy of serving mission-oriented customers, nonprofits, and traditional businesses wanting to incorporate sustainability practices.

New Resource earns part of its appeal from its sustainability focus. It is a Certified B Corporation and a San Francisco–certified Green Business; its headquarters are LEED Gold certified; and it won a regional Outstanding Achievement award from the U.S. Environmental Protection Agency. The bank's approach is lending to businesses and nonprofits with green goods and services. Customers include organic food purveyors, green builders, and solar energy providers.

The bank reuses and recycles to keep 95 percent of its waste from entering local landfills. It also purchases Green e-certified wind power certificates to offset electricity use. And its offices use remanufactured toner cartridges and recycled paper in an effort to reinforce its commitment to sustainability.

Questions for Critical Thinking

1. One bank's COO calls the popularity of green banks "a broader cultural shift in what people expect from their bank." Do you agree? Why or why not?

2. How important to bank customers is community and nonprofit involvement? Discuss the additional types of consumer banking and business customers New Resource might target.

Sources: Company website, www.newresourcebank.com, accessed March 21, 2014; Constance Gustke, "5 Green Banking Tips to Save the Planet," *www.Bankrate.com*, accessed March 21, 2014; Kevin Roose, "Amid Wall Street Protests, Smaller Banks Gain Favor," *The New York Times*, accessed March 21, 2014, www.nytimes.com.

---

[2] Types of Securities

For the funds they borrow from savers, businesses and governments provide different types of guarantees for repayment. **Securities**, also called financial instruments, represent obligations on the part of the issuers—businesses and governments—to provide the purchasers with expected or stated returns on the funds invested or loaned. Securities can be grouped into three categories: money market instruments, bonds, and stock. Money market instruments and bonds are both debt securities. Stocks are units of ownership in corporations like General Electric, McDonald's, Apple, and PepsiCo.

> **securities** financial instruments that represent obligations on the part of the issuers to provide the purchasers with expected stated returns on the funds invested or loaned.

Money Market Instruments

Money market instruments are short-term debt securities issued by governments, financial institutions, and corporations. All money market instruments mature within one year from the date of issue. The issuer pays interest to the investors for the use of their funds. Money market instruments are generally low-risk securities and are purchased by investors when they have surplus cash. Examples of money market instruments include U.S. Treasury bills, commercial paper, and bank certificates of deposit.

Treasury bills are short-term securities issued by the U.S. Treasury and backed by the full faith and credit of the U.S. government. Treasury bills are sold with a maturity of 30, 90, 180, or 360 days and have a minimum denomination of $1,000. They are considered virtually risk free and easy to resell. Commercial paper is securities sold by corporations, such as Raytheon, that mature in from 1 to 270 days from the date of issue. Although slightly riskier than Treasury bills, commercial paper is still generally considered a very low-risk security.

A certificate of deposit (CD) is a time deposit at a financial institution, such as a commercial bank, savings bank, or credit union. The sizes and maturity dates of CDs vary considerably and can often be tailored to meet the needs of purchasers. CDs in denominations of $250,000 or less per depositor are federally insured. CDs in larger denominations are not federally insured but can be sold more easily before they mature.

Bonds

Bondholders are creditors of a corporation or government body. By selling bonds, a firm obtains long-term debt capital. Federal, state, and local governments also acquire funds through bonds. Bonds are issued in various denominations, or face values, usually between $1,000 and $25,000. Each issue indicates a rate of interest to be paid to the bondholder—stated as a percentage of the bond's face value—as well as a maturity date on which the bondholder is paid the bond's full face value. Because bondholders are creditors, they have a claim on the firm's assets that must be satisfied before any claims of stockholders in the event of the firm's bankruptcy, reorganization, or liquidation.

Types of Bonds A prospective bond investor can choose among a variety of bonds. The major types of bonds are summarized in Table 16.1. *Government bonds* are bonds sold by the U.S. Department of the Treasury. Because government bonds are backed by the full faith and credit of the U.S. government, they are considered the least risky of all bonds. The Treasury sells bonds that mature in 2, 3, 5, 7, or 10 years from the date of issue.

TABLE

16.1 Types of Bonds

ISSUER	TYPES OF SECURITIES	RISK	SPECIAL FEATURES
U.S. Treasury (government bonds)	Notes: Mature in 2, 3, 5, 7, or 10 years from date of issue.	Treasury bonds and notes carry virtually no risk.	Interest is exempt from state income taxes.
	Bonds: Mature in 30 years from date of issue.		
State and local governments (municipal bonds)	General obligation: Issued by state or local governmental units with taxing authority; backed by the full faith and credit of the state where issued.	Risk varies, depending on the financial health of the issuer.	Interest is exempt from federal income taxes and may be exempt from state income taxes.
	Revenue: Issued to pay for projects that generate revenue, such as water systems or toll roads; revenue from project used to pay principal and interest.	Most large municipal bond issues are rated in terms of credit risk (AAA or Aaa is the highest rating).	
Corporations	Secured bonds: Bonds are backed by specific assets.	Risk varies depending on the financial health of the issuer.	A few corporate bonds are convertible into shares of common stock of the issuing company.
	Unsecured bonds (debentures): Backed by the financial health and reputation of the issuer.	Most corporate bond issues are rated in terms of credit risk (AAA or Aaa is the highest rating).	
Financial institutions	Mortgage pass-through securities.	Generally very low risk.	They pay monthly income consisting of both interest and principal.

Municipal bonds are bonds issued by state or local governments. Two types of municipal bonds are available. A *revenue bond* is a bond issue whose proceeds will be used to pay for a project that will produce revenue, such as a toll road or bridge. The Niagara Falls Bridge Commission, for example, has issued such bonds. A *general obligation bond* is a bond whose proceeds are to be used to pay for a project that will not produce any revenue, such as a new Indiana State Police post. General obligation bonds can be sold only by states or local governmental units—such as Grand Rapids, Michigan, or Bergen County, New Jersey—that have the power to levy taxes. An important feature of municipal bonds is that their interest payments are exempt from federal income tax. Because of this attractive feature, municipal bonds generally carry lower interest rates than either corporate or government bonds.

Corporate bonds are a diverse group and often vary based on the collateral—the property pledged by the borrower—that backs the bond. For example, a *secured bond* is backed by a specific pledge of company assets. These assets are collateral, just like a home is collateral for a mortgage. However, many firms also issue unsecured bonds, called *debentures*. These bonds are backed only by the financial reputation of the issuing corporation.

Another popular type of bond is the *mortgage pass-through security*. These securities are backed by a pool of mortgage loans purchased from lenders, such as savings banks. As borrowers make their monthly mortgage payments, these payments are "passed through" to the holders of the securities. Most mortgage pass-through securities are relatively safe because all mortgages in the pool are insured. However, in recent years, mortgage pass-through securities consisting of pools of so-called *subprime mortgages*, loans made to borrowers with poor credit ratings, were issued. Many of these securities turned out to be quite risky and, in part, triggered what became known as the *credit crisis*. The extent of the crisis forced the federal government to undertake a massive bailout of the financial system. The Office of Financial Stability—part of the U.S. Treasury department—was created to purchase poor-quality mortgage-backed and other securities from financial institutions.

Quality Ratings for Bonds Two factors determine the price of a bond: its risk and its interest rate. Bonds vary considerably in terms of risk. One tool bond investors use to assess the risk of a bond is its *bond rating*. Several investment firms rate corporate and municipal bonds, the best known of which are Standard & Poor's (S&P), Moody's, and Fitch. Table 16.2 lists the

TABLE

16.2 Standard & Poor's Bond Ratings

Highest	AAA	Investment grade
	AA	
	A	
	BBB	
	BB	Speculative grade
	B	
	CCC	
	CC	
Lowest	C	

Note: Standard & Poor's occasionally assigns a plus or minus following the letter rating. For instance, AA+ means that the bond is higher quality than most AA bonds but hasn't quite met AAA standards. Ratings below C indicate that the bond is currently not paying interest.

S&P bond ratings. Moody's and Fitch use similar rating systems. Bonds with the lowest level of risk are rated AAA. As ratings drop, risk increases. Bonds with ratings of BBB and above are classified as *investment-grade bonds*. By contrast, bonds with ratings of BB and below are classified as *speculative* or *junk bonds*. Junk bonds attract investors by offering high interest rates in exchange for greater risk. Historically, average yields on junk bonds have been 4 to 6 percent higher than those for comparable U.S. Treasuries.

The second factor affecting the price of a bond is its interest rate. Other things being equal, the higher the interest rate, the higher the price of a bond. However, the bonds may not be equally risky, or one may have a longer maturity. Investors must evaluate the trade-offs involved.

Another important influence on bond prices is the *market interest rate*. Because bonds pay fixed rates of interest, as market interest rates rise, bond prices fall, and vice versa. For instance, the price of a ten-year bond, paying 5 percent per year, would fall by about 8 percent if market interest rates rose from 5 percent to 6 percent.

Most corporate and municipal bonds, and some government bonds, are callable. A *call provision* allows the issuer to redeem the bond before its maturity at a specified price. Not surprisingly, issuers tend to call bonds when market interest rates are declining. For example, if York County, Pennsylvania, had $50 million in bonds outstanding with a 3 percent annual interest rate, it would pay $1.5 million annually in interest. If interest rates decline to 1 percent, the county may decide to call the 3 percent bonds, repaying the principal from the proceeds of newly issued 1 percent bonds. Calling the 3 percent bonds and issuing 1 percent bonds will save the county $1 million a year in interest payments. The savings in annual interest expense should more than offset the cost of retiring the old bonds and issuing new ones.

Stock

common stock basic form of corporate ownership.

The basic form of corporate ownership is embodied in **common stock**. Purchasers of common stock represent the owners of a corporation. Holders of common stock vote on major company decisions, such as purchasing another company or electing a board of directors. In return for the money they invest, they expect to receive some sort of return. This return can come in the form of cash dividend payments, expected price appreciation, or both. Dividends vary widely from firm to firm. As a general rule, faster-growing companies pay less in dividends because they need to preserve funds to finance their growth. Consequently, investors expect stocks paying little or no cash dividends to show greater price appreciation compared with stocks paying more generous cash dividends. Dell was the number three computer maker behind Hewlett Packard and Lenovo before the meteoric rise in popularity of smart phones and tablet computers. Only a few short years ago, Dell held the number two position in the PC industry behind Apple.

Dell's profits came to a screeching halt when the company suffered its first holiday decline several years ago. Adding a further setback to Dell, the introduction of Apple's iPad tablet caused consumers to switch to the mobility of these new devices over desktop and laptop PCs.

The story of Dell's decline revealed its struggle to compete with Asian PC manufacturers like Lenovo, Asus, and Acer, who were able to keep their production costs low. As the quality and design of the competing Asian-produced products continued to improve, consumer loyalty to Dell continued to fade. In the throes of a sluggish economy, Dell was also hurt when some of its business customers postponed upgrades of their existing computer systems. In an attempt to offset its declining PC business, which accounted for over half of its revenue, Dell recently expanded into the enterprise market with servers, networking, software, and services.

During the height of the technology bubble in 2000, Dell's all-time high price per share stood at $65. Five years later, its price per share was at $40. As Dell has continued to lose market share and the PC industry continued to shrink, the company was recently taken private in a $24.4 billion leveraged buyout at a small premium over its price per market share. A stock price of $13.65 per share was paid for Dell—far below its prior 52-week high of $18.36 per share and 76 percent less than its all-time high.[2]

Common stockholders benefit from company success, and they risk the loss of their investment if the company declines, as seen in the case of Dell and its major stockholders. If a firm dissolves, claims of creditors must be satisfied before stockholders receive anything. Because creditors have the first (or senior) claim to assets, holders of common stock are said to have a residual claim on company assets.

The market value of a stock is the price at which the stock is currently selling. For example, eBay's stock price fluctuated between $48 and $59 per share during a recent year. What determines this market value is complicated; many variables cause stock prices to move up or down. However, in the long run stock prices tend to follow a company's profits.

Preferred Stock In addition to common stock, a few companies also issue preferred stock—stock whose holders receive preference in the payment of dividends. General Electric and Ford are examples of firms with preferred stock outstanding. Also, if a company is dissolved, holders of preferred stock have claims on the firm's assets that are ahead of the claims of common stockholders. On the other hand, preferred stockholders rarely have any voting rights, and the dividend they are paid is fixed, regardless of how profitable the firm becomes. Therefore, although preferred stock is legally classified as equity, many investors consider it to be more like a bond than common stock.

Convertible Securities Companies may issue bonds or preferred stock that contains a conversion feature. Such bonds or stock are called *convertible securities*. This feature gives the bondholder or preferred stockholder the right to exchange the bond or preferred stock for a fixed number of shares of common stock. Convertible bonds pay lower interest rates than those lacking conversion features, helping to reduce the interest expense of the issuing firms. Investors are willing to accept these lower interest rates because they value the potential for additional gains if the price of the firm's stock increases. For instance, at a price of $61 per share, Valero Energy's convertible bond would have a common stock value of at least $1,043 ($61 × 17.1). Should the price of Valero's common stock increase by $10 per share, the value of the convertible will increase by at least $171.

3 Financial Markets

Securities are issued and traded in <u>financial markets</u>. While there are many different types of financial markets, one of the most important distinctions is between primary and secondary markets. In the <u>primary markets</u>, firms and governments issue securities and sell them initially to the general public. When a company needs capital to purchase inventory, expand a plant, make major investments, acquire another firm, or pursue other business goals, it may sell a bond or stock issue to the investing public. For example, China's Hunan province recently issued special bonds to help address the heavy metal pollution that covers the local area, according to the country's Ministry of Environmental Protection.[3]

A stock offering gives investors the opportunity to purchase ownership shares in a firm and to participate in its future growth, in exchange for providing current capital. When a company offers stock for sale to the general public for the first time, it is called an *initial public offering (IPO)*. Analysts predicted IPOs from a number of American companies during one recent year, including Airbnb, Box, Lending Club, Pinterest, and SurveyMonkey.[4] The "Hit & Miss" feature describes the details of Berkshire Hathaway's astronomical price-per-share of its Class A stock.

Both profit-seeking corporations and government agencies also rely on primary markets to raise funds by issuing bonds. For example, the federal government sells Treasury bonds to finance part of federal outlays such as interest on outstanding federal debt. State and local governments sell bonds to finance capital projects such as the construction of sewer systems, streets, and fire stations.

Assessment Check ☑

1. What are the major types of securities?
2. What is a government bond? A municipal bond?
3. Why do investors purchase common stock?

financial markets market in which securities are issued and traded.

primary markets financial market in which firms and governments issue securities and sell them initially to the general public.

Chapter 16 *The Financial System*

467

Hit&Miss

A Sky-High Stock Price

Billionaire investor and Berkshire Hathaway CEO Warren Buffet has a way of doing things in an extraordinary, yet unassuming fashion. From the annual weekend shareholder meetings attended by over 20,000 in Omaha, Nebraska, to his modest $100,000 annual salary, Buffet is in a league of his own. And there is one more interesting fact worth noting: the sky-high price per share of Berkshire Hathaway's Class A stock.

Berkshire Hathaway Class A (BRK.A) shares represent the highest per-share price ever for a stock traded on the New York Stock Exchange. Over a recent 52-week range, the *per-share* price ranged from $163,000 to $194,000. Berkshire Hathaway has never split its Class A shares or paid a dividend to shareholders, which has contributed to its high per-share price. It's also Buffet's way of letting shareholders know that their investment is long term, and that speculators looking to make a quick buck should go elsewhere.

Berkshire Hathaway created a more reasonably priced Class B stock, with a per-share value of about 1/1,500 the price of its Class A counterpart. Buffet created the Class B shares to prevent the creation of "copycat" unit trusts, a mutual fund structure that would have marketed themselves as Berkshire look-alikes.

Questions for Critical Thinking

1. As an investor, discuss where you would draw the line when it comes to price per share. Would it be a factor in your decision when purchasing a company's stock?

2. Perform some additional research to find out how the Berkshire Hathaway Class B stock has performed, and whether the lower price per share has attracted a different type of investor.

Sources: Company website, http://berkshirehathaway.com, accessed March 29, 2014; Kerry A. Dolan and Luisa Kroll, "The World's Billionaires," *Forbes*, accessed March 29, 2014, www.forbes.com; "Buffett's Berkshire Hathaway Will Stop Small-Caps," *Market Watch*, accessed March 29, 2014, www.marketwatch.com; Robert Lenzer, "The Intrinsic Value of Berkshire Hathaway Shares Exceeds 120% of Book Value 'By a Meaningful Amount,'" *Forbes*, accessed March 29, 2014, www.forbes.com; Google Finance, "Berkshire Hathaway, Inc.," accessed March 29, 2014, www.google.com; Associated Press, "Billionaire Warren Buffet's Salary Remains Unchanged," *Omaha.com*, accessed March 29, 2014, www.omaha.com.

Announcements of new stock and bond offerings appear daily in business publications such as *The Wall Street Journal*. These announcements are often in the form of a simple black-and-white ad called a *tombstone*.

Securities are sold to the investing public in two ways: in open auctions and through investment bankers. Virtually all securities sold through open auctions consist of U.S. Treasury securities. A week before an upcoming auction, the Department of the Treasury announces the type and number of securities it will be auctioning. Treasury bills are auctioned weekly, but longer-term Treasury securities are auctioned once a month or once a quarter. Sales of most corporate and municipal securities are made via financial institutions such as Morgan Stanley. These institutions purchase the issue from the firm or government and then resell the issue to investors. This process is known as *underwriting*.

Financial institutions underwrite stock and bond issues at a discount, meaning that they pay the issuing firm or government less than the price the financial institutions charge investors. This discount is compensation for services rendered, including the risk financial institutions incur whenever they underwrite a new security issue. Although the size of the discount is often negotiable, it usually averages around 5 percent for all types of securities. The size of the underwriting discount, however, is generally higher for stock issues than it is for bond issues. For instance, underwriting discounts for IPOs are generally between 7 and 10 percent.

Corporations and governments are willing to pay for the services provided by financial institutions because they are financial market experts. In addition to locating buyers for the issue, the underwriter typically advises the issuer on such details as the general characteristics of the issue, its pricing, and the timing of the offering. Several financial institutions commonly participate in the underwriting process. The issuer selects a lead, or primary, financial institution, which in turn forms a syndicate consisting of other financial institutions. Each member of the syndicate purchases a portion of the security issue, which it resells to investors.

Media reports of stock and bond trading are most likely to refer to trading in the **secondary market**, a collection of financial markets in which previously issued securities are

secondary market
collection of financial markets in which previously issued securities are traded among investors.

468

traded among investors. The corporations or governments that originally issued the securities being traded are not directly involved in the secondary market. They make no payments when securities are sold nor receive any of the proceeds when securities are purchased. The New York Stock Exchange (NYSE), for example, is a secondary market. In terms of the dollar value of securities bought and sold, the secondary market is four to five times as large as the primary market. Each day, more than 1.5 billion shares worth about $169 billion are traded on the NYSE.[5] The characteristics of the world's major stock exchanges are discussed in the next section.

4 Understanding Stock Markets

Stock markets, or **exchanges**, are probably the best-known of the world's financial markets. In these markets, shares of stock are bought and sold by investors. The two largest stock markets in the world, the New York Stock Exchange (NYSE) and the NASDAQ stock market, are located in the United States. The Dow Jones Industrial Average (often referred to as the Dow) is a price-weighted average of the 30 most significant stocks traded on the NYSE and the NASDAQ.

The New York Stock Exchange

The New York Stock Exchange—sometimes referred to as the Big Board—is the most famous and one of the oldest stock markets in the world, having been founded in 1792. Today, the stocks of about 2,800 companies are listed on the NYSE. These stocks represent most of the largest, best-known companies in the United States and have a total market value exceeding $16 trillion. In terms of the total value of stock traded, the NYSE is the world's largest stock market.

For a company's stock to be traded on the NYSE, the firm must apply to the exchange for listing and meet certain listing requirements. In addition, the firm must continue to meet requirements each year to remain listed on the NYSE. Corporate bonds are also traded on the NYSE, but bond trading makes up less than 1 percent of the total value of securities traded there during a typical year.

Trading on the NYSE takes place face-to-face on a trading floor. Buy and sell orders are transmitted to a specific post on the floor of the exchange. Buyers and sellers then bid against one another in an open auction. Only investment firms that are designated members of the NYSE and that own at least one trading license are allowed to trade on the floor of the exchange. The NYSE issues up to 1,366 one-year trading licenses at a cost of about $40,000 each.[6]

Each NYSE stock is assigned to a specialist broker. Specialists are unique investment firms that maintain an orderly and liquid market in the stocks assigned to them. Specialists must be willing to buy when there are no other buyers and sell when there are no other sellers. Specialists also act as auctioneers and catalysts, bringing buyers and sellers together.

Some observers portray the NYSE and its trading practices as somewhat old fashioned, especially in this technological age. Most markets, they note, have abandoned their trading floors in favor of electronic trading. However, even though the NYSE still retains a trading floor, the exchange has become highly automated in recent years. Its computer systems automatically match and route most orders through wireless handheld computers, and they are typically filled within a few seconds.

The NASDAQ Stock Market

The world's second-largest stock market, NASDAQ, is very different from the NYSE. NASDAQ—which stands for National Association of Securities Dealers Automated Quotation—is actually a computerized communications network that links member investment firms. It is the world's largest intranet. All trading on NASDAQ takes place through

Assessment Check ☑

1. What is a financial market?
2. Distinguish between a primary and a secondary financial market.
3. Briefly explain the role of financial institutions in the sale of securities.

stock markets (exchanges) market in which shares of stock are bought and sold by investors.

its intranet, rather than on a trading floor. Buy and sell orders are entered into the network and executed electronically. All NASDAQ-listed stocks have two or more market makers—investment firms that perform essentially the same functions as NYSE specialists.

More than 3,600 companies have their stocks listed on NASDAQ. Generally, NASDAQ-listed corporations tend to be smaller firms and less well-known than NYSE-listed ones. Some are relatively new businesses and cannot meet NYSE listing requirements. Many NASDAQ firms eventually transfer the trading of their stocks to the NYSE. However, NASDAQ is also home to some of the largest U.S. companies and iconic brands—for example, Amgen, Cisco Systems, Intel, and Microsoft. These firms would easily meet NYSE listing requirements but, for a variety of reasons, decided to remain listed on NASDAQ.

Other U.S. Stock Markets

In addition to the NYSE and NASDAQ, several other stock markets operate in the United States. The American Stock Exchange, or AMEX, focuses on the stocks of smaller firms, as well as other financial instruments such as options. In comparison with the NYSE and NASDAQ, the AMEX is tiny. Daily trading volume is generally less than 100 million shares compared with the more than 1 billion shares on each of the larger two exchanges.

Several regional stock exchanges also operate throughout the United States. They include the Chicago, Boston, and Philadelphia stock exchanges. Originally established to trade the shares of small, regional companies, the regional exchanges now list securities of many large corporations as well. In fact, more than half of the companies listed on the NYSE are also listed on one or more regional exchanges.

Foreign Stock Markets

Stock markets exist throughout the world. Virtually all developed countries and many developing countries have stock exchanges. Examples include Mumbai, Helsinki, Hong Kong, Mexico City, Paris, and Toronto. One of the largest stock exchanges outside the United States

John Angelillo/UPI/Newscom

Often referred to as the Dow, the Dow Jones Industrial Average is a price-weighted average of the 30 most significant stocks traded on the NYSE and the NASDAQ.

is the London Stock Exchange. Founded in the early 17th century, the London Stock Exchange lists approximately 3,000 stock and bond issues by companies from more than 70 countries around the world. Trading on the London Stock Exchange takes place using a NASDAQ-type computerized communications network.

The London Stock Exchange is the most international of all stock markets. Approximately two-thirds of all cross-border trading in the world—for example, the trading of stocks of American companies outside the United States—takes place in London. It is not uncommon for institutional investors in the United States to trade NYSE- or NASDAQ-listed stocks in London.

ECNs and the Future of Stock Markets

For years a so-called *fourth market* has existed—the direct trading of exchange-listed stocks off the floor of the exchange (in the case of NYSE-listed stocks) or outside the network (in the case of NASDAQ-listed stocks). Originally, trading in the fourth market was limited to institutional investors buying or selling large blocks of stock.

Now, however, the fourth market is open to smaller, individual investors through markets called *electronic communications networks* (ECNs). In ECNs, buyers and sellers meet in a virtual stock market and trade directly with one another. No specialist or market maker is involved. ECNs are a significant force in the stock market—around half of all trades involving NASDAQ-listed stocks take place on INET or Archipelago—the two largest ECNs—rather than directly through the NASDAQ system. Some suggest that ECNs represent the future for stock markets, given that INET is owned by NASDAQ and Archipelago, by the NYSE.

Established in the 1700s, the London Stock Exchange is one of the largest stock markets outside of the United States. More than half of all cross-border trading takes place at the London Exchange.

Investor Participation in the Stock Markets

Because most investors aren't members of the NYSE or any other stock market, they need to use the services of a brokerage firm to buy or sell stocks. Examples of brokerage firms include Edward Jones and TD Ameritrade. Investors establish an account with the brokerage firm and then enter orders to trade stocks. The brokerage firm executes the trade on behalf of the investor, charging the investor a fee for the service. While some investors still prefer to phone in orders or visit the brokerage firm in person, many today use their PCs or mobile devices to trade stocks online. The requirements for setting up an account vary from broker to broker. Selecting the right brokerage firm is one of the most important decisions investors make.

The most common type of order is called a *market order*. It instructs the broker to obtain the best possible price—the highest price when selling and the lowest price when buying. If the stock market is open, market orders are filled within seconds. Another popular type of order is called a *limit order*. It sets a price ceiling when buying or a price floor when selling. If the order cannot be executed when it is placed, the order is left with the exchange's market maker. It may be filed later if the price limits are met.

Assessment Check ✓

1. What are the world's two largest stock markets?

2. Why is the London Stock Exchange unique?

3. Explain the difference between a market order and a limit order.

[5] **Financial Institutions**

financial institutions
intermediary between savers and borrowers, collecting funds from savers and then lending the funds to individuals, businesses, and governments.

One of the most important components of the financial system is <u>**financial institutions**</u>. They are an intermediary between savers and borrowers, collecting funds from savers and then lending the funds to individuals, businesses, and governments. Financial institutions greatly increase the efficiency and effectiveness of the transfer of funds from savers to users. Because of financial institutions, savers earn more, and users pay less, than they would without them. In fact, it is difficult to imagine how any modern economy could function without well-developed financial institutions. Think about how difficult it would be for a businessperson to obtain inventory financing or an individual to purchase a new car or home without financial institutions. Prospective borrowers would have to identify and negotiate terms with each saver individually.

Traditionally, financial institutions have been classified into depository institutions—institutions that accept deposits that customers can withdraw on demand—and nondepository institutions. Examples of depository institutions include commercial banks, such as US Bancorp and Sun Trust; savings banks, such as Acacia Federal Savings Bank and Ohio Savings Bank; and credit unions, such as the State Employees' Credit Union of North Carolina. Nondepository institutions include life insurance companies, such as Northwestern Mutual; pension funds, such as the Florida state employee pension fund; and mutual funds. In total, financial institutions have trillions of dollars in assets. Figure 16.2 illustrates the size of the most prominent financial institutions.

FIGURE
16.2 **Assets of Major Financial Institutions**

Sources: Organization website, "U.S. Retirement Assets, 2008 and 2012," and "Investments, Life/Health Insurers, 2010–2012," Insurance Information Institute, www.iii.org, accessed March 28, 2014; Federal Deposit Insurance Corporation, "Statistics at a Glance: Year-End, December 2013," www2.fdic.gov, accessed March 28, 2014; Board of Governors of the Federal Reserve System, "Federal Reserve Statistical Release, Z.1, Flow of Funds Accounts of the United States," www.federalreserve.gov, accessed March 28, 2014; "NCUA: Third-Quarter State Data Show Loan, Membership Growth Trends Continue," National Credit Union Administration, press release, accessed March 28, 2014, www.ncua.gov; Investment Company Institute, "Trends in Mutual Fund Investing February 2014," press release, March 26, 2014, www.ici.org.

Commercial Banks

Commercial banks are the largest and probably most important financial institution in the United States, and in most other countries as well. In the United States, the approximately 6,800 commercial banks hold total assets of more than $14 trillion. Commercial banks offer the most services of any financial institution. These services include a wide range of checking and savings deposit accounts, consumer loans, credit cards, home mortgage loans, business loans, and trust services. Commercial banks also sell other financial products, including securities and insurance.[7]

Although 6,800 may sound like a lot of banks, the number of banks has actually declined dramatically in recent years; just 20 years ago there were 12,000 commercial banks. At the same time, banks have grown larger: today, the typical commercial bank is about five times as large as it was ten years ago. Both changes can be explained by the fact that bank mergers have become increasingly common.

Community banks typically serve a single city or county and have millions, rather than billions, of dollars in assets and deposits. Many consumers and small-business owners prefer smaller banks because they believe they offer a higher level of personal service and often charge lower fees. Recently, however, some community banks have found it difficult to compete with larger banks like Wells Fargo and Bank of America, both of which posted record profits in a recent year. Over the last three decades, the number of banks with assets of less than $100 million fell by 80 percent.[8]

How Banks Operate Banks raise funds by offering a variety of checking and savings deposits to customers. The banks then pool these deposits and lend most of them out in the form of consumer and business loans. Recently, banks held over $10.3 trillion in deposits and had about $7.1 trillion in outstanding loans.[9] The distribution of outstanding loans is shown in Figure 16.3. As the figure shows, banks lend a great deal of money to both households and businesses for a variety of purposes. Commercial banks are an especially important source of funds for small businesses. When evaluating loan applications, banks consider the borrower's ability and willingness to repay the loan.

Banks make money based on the interest rate spread, or the difference between the interest rate charged to borrowers and the rate of interest paid to depositors. Banks also make money from other sources, such as fees they charge customers for checking accounts, using ATMs, or for overdrawing an account.

In the aftermath of the recent credit crisis, many small business owners have suffered because banks have begun pulling their lines of credit. The "Career Kickstart" feature offers some suggestions if this happens to you.

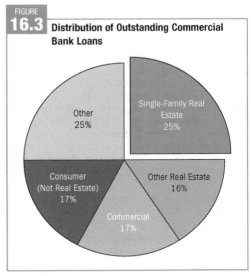

FIGURE 16.3 Distribution of Outstanding Commercial Bank Loans

Source: Federal Deposit Insurance Corporation (FDIC), "Statistics on Depository Institutions Report," http://www2.fdic.gov, accessed March 26, 2014.

Electronic Banking More and more funds each year move through electronic funds transfer systems (EFTSs), computerized systems for conducting financial transactions over electronic links. Millions of businesses and consumers now pay bills and receive payments electronically. Most employers, for example, directly deposit employee paychecks in their bank accounts, rather than issuing employees paper checks. Today nearly all Social Security checks and other federal payments made each year arrive as electronic data rather than paper documents.

One of the original forms of electronic banking, the automated teller machine (ATM) continues to grow in popularity. ATMs allow customers to make banking transactions at any time by inserting an electronic card into the machine and entering a personal identification number (PIN). Networked systems enable ATM users worldwide access to their bank accounts. Most banks offer customers debit cards—also called *check cards*—that allow customers to pay for purchases directly from their checking or savings account. A debit card looks like a credit card but acts like a check and replaces the customer's ATM card. At most large retailers, customers can use their ATM or debit cards for purchases and can often get cash back. Consumers enjoy the convenience of this feature; at the same time, it eliminates the problem of bad checks for retailers. The number of annual ATM and debit card transactions surpassed 53 billion in a recent year.[10]

Online Banking Today, online banking accounts for more than half of all banking transactions, compared with 14 percent for in-branch visits. Two types of online banks exist: Internet-only banks, such as ING Direct, and traditional brick-and-mortar banks with online banking sites, such as Chase and PNC. A major reason people are attracted to online banking is convenience. Customers can transfer money, check account balances, pay bills—and even deposit checks via their smart phones. As a result, as many as a third of the nation's bank branches may be losing money, as a typical bank branch needs at least $30 million in deposits to stay profitable.[11]

Federal Deposit Insurance Most commercial bank deposits are insured by the Federal Deposit Insurance Corporation (FDIC), a federal agency. Deposit insurance means that, in the event the bank fails, insured depositors are paid in full by the FDIC, up

Federal Deposit Insurance Corporation (FDIC) federal agency that insures deposits at commercial and savings banks.

What to Do When Your Borrowing Power Gets Pulled

For years, banks have issued business credit cards to small business owners. The cards include a line of credit—usually several thousand dollars or more—that provides a safety net. After the credit crisis hit, millions of small business owners found themselves working without a net as banks began to call in loans or cap credit lines at the amount outstanding. Thousands of small business owners reported that their credit lines had been decreased or loan extensions rejected. Whereas losing a line of credit was once considered a crisis, today it occurs frequently. Here are some tips if it happens to you.

1 Avoid maxing out your remaining credit or it may impact your credit score.

2 Make monthly payments as quickly as possible, either online or by phone.

3 Apply for a new credit card immediately. By acting quickly, you may receive a new card before your credit score is lowered.

4 If possible, pay down existing credit card debt—but weigh any short-term money need against your credit score before writing the check.

5 Track your credit score. AnnualCreditReport.com is the only government-authorized source for free annual credit reports.

Sources: Federal Trade Commission, "Credit and Your Consumer Rights," www.ftc.com, accessed March 28, 2014; Sam Thacker, "Steps to Take When Your Credit Line Is Pulled," *All Business*, accessed March 28, 2014, www.allbusiness.com; Jeffrey Weber, "What to Do When Your Credit Line Is Decreased," accessed March 28, 2014, www.smartbalancetransfers.com; Julie Bennett, "What to Do When the Bank Pulls Your Line of Credit," *Entrepreneur*, accessed March 28, 2014, www.entrepreneur.com.

to $250,000. Federal deposit insurance was enacted by the Banking Act of 1933 as one of the measures designed to restore public confidence in the banking system. Before deposit insurance, so-called *runs* were common as people rushed to withdraw their money from a bank, often just on a rumor that the bank was in precarious financial condition. With more and more withdrawals in a short period, the bank was eventually unable to meet customer demands and closed its doors. Remaining depositors often lost most of the money they had in the bank. Deposit insurance shifts the risk of bank failures from individual depositors to the FDIC. Although banks still fail today, no insured depositor has ever lost any money.

Savings Banks and Credit Unions

Commercial banks are by far the largest depository financial institution in the United States, but savings banks and credit unions also serve a significant segment of the financial community. Today savings banks and credit unions offer many of the same services as commercial banks.

Savings banks used to be called *savings and loan associations* or *thrift institutions*. They were originally established in the early 1800s to make home mortgage loans. Savings and loans originally raised funds by accepting only savings deposits and then lent these funds to consumers to buy homes. Savings banks still exist today, offering many of the same services as commercial banks, including checking accounts, yet they are not major lenders to businesses. As Internet banking, also called direct banking, has increased in popularity, savings banks commonly provide higher levels of interest in return for clients doing banking solely over the Internet.[12] Deposits in savings banks are FDIC insured.

Credit unions are cooperative financial institutions that are owned by their depositors, all of whom are members. Around 96 million Americans belong to one of the nation's approximately 6,620 federally insured credit unions, which have seen their share of consolidations. Combined, credit unions have more than $1.1 trillion in assets and grew by more than 6 percent in the past few years. By law, credit union members must share similar occupations, employers, or membership in certain organizations. This law effectively caps the size of credit unions. In fact, the nation's largest bank—JP Morgan Chase—holds more deposits than all the country's credit unions combined.[13]

Credit unions are designed to serve consumers, not businesses. Credit unions raise funds by offering members a number of demand and saving deposits—checking accounts at credit unions are referred to as share draft accounts—and then, in turn, lend these funds to members. Because credit unions are not-for-profit institutions, they often pay savers higher rates of interest, charge lower rates of interest on loans, and have fewer fees than other financial institutions. Credit unions can have either state or federal charters, and deposits are insured by a federal agency, the National Credit Union Administration (NCUA), which functions essentially the same way that the FDIC does.

Nondepository Financial Institutions

Nondepository financial institutions accept funds from businesses and households, much of which they then invest. Generally, these institutions do not offer checking accounts (demand deposits). Three examples of nondepository financial institutions are insurance companies, pension funds, and finance companies.

Insurance Companies Households and businesses buy insurance to transfer risk from themselves to the insurance company. The insurance company accepts the risk in return for a series of payments, called *premiums*. Underwriting is the process insurance companies use to determine whom to insure and what to charge. During a typical year, insurance companies collect more in premiums than they pay in claims. After they pay operating expenses, they invest this difference. Insurance companies are a major source of short- and long-term financing for businesses. Life insurance companies alone have total assets of more than $6 trillion invested in everything from bonds and stocks to real estate.[14] Examples of life insurers include Prudential and New York Life.

Pension Funds Pension funds provide retirement benefits to workers and their families. They are set up by employers and are funded by regular contributions made by employers and employees. Because pension funds have predictable long-term cash inflows and very predictable cash outflows, they invest heavily in assets, such as common stocks and real estate. The financial value of private and public pension funds totals more than $16 trillion. Over the last several years, U.S. pension funds have moved out of equities and into long-term bonds at a fast clip. The 100 biggest corporate pension plans are now 95 percent funded, compared to only 77 percent a few years ago. Because pension funds have enjoyed considerable gains in the debt and equity markets over the last few years, they are now selling equities and switching to fixed income investments. In the coming year, pensions will liquidate $150 billion in equities to buy bonds with maturities of 10 years or longer.[15]

Finance Companies Consumer and commercial finance companies, such as Ford Credit, John Deere Capital Corporation, and the Pennsylvania-based Dollar Financial, offer short-term loans to borrowers. A commercial finance company supplies short-term funds to businesses that pledge tangible assets such as inventory, accounts receivable, machinery, or property as collateral for the loan. A consumer finance company plays a similar role for consumers. Finance companies raise funds by selling securities or borrowing funds from commercial banks. Many finance companies, such as GE Capital, are actually subsidiaries of a manufacturer.

Mutual Funds

One of the most significant types of financial institutions today is the mutual fund. *Mutual funds* are financial intermediaries that raise money from investors by selling shares. They then use the money to invest in securities that are consistent with the mutual fund's

John Crowe/Alamy Limited

Life insurance companies such as New York Life are a major source of financing for businesses. Considered a *nondepository financial institution*, insurance companies obtain funds from consumers and businesses and invest most of the money.

Chapter 16 *The Financial System*　　**475**

1. What are the two
   main types of financial
   institutions?
2. What are the primary
   differences between
   commercial banks and
   savings banks?
3. What is a mutual fund?

objectives. For example, a stock mutual fund invests mainly in shares of common stocks. Mutual funds have become extremely popular over the last few decades. The United States' nearly 7,600 mutual funds have about $13 trillion in assets and more than 264 million shareholder accounts. Just 20 years ago, only about 3,400 funds were in existence, with nearly 69 million shareholder accounts and about $1.4 trillion in assets. One reason for this growth is the increased popularity of 401(k) and similar types of retirement plans.[16]

Mutual fund investors are indirect owners of a portfolio of securities. As the value of the securities owned by the mutual fund changes, so too will the value of the mutual fund's shares. Moreover, investment income, such as bond interest and stock dividends, is passed through to fund shareholders.

Slightly less than half of mutual fund assets, around $5.9 trillion, are invested in stock funds. Taxable bond mutual funds—funds that invest in bonds issued by governments or corporations—are also popular. These funds have total assets of nearly $3.4 trillion.[17]

[6] The Role of the Federal Reserve System

Federal Reserve System (Fed) central bank of the United States.

Created in 1913, the **Federal Reserve System, or Fed**, or is the central bank of the United States and is an important part of the nation's financial system. The Fed has four basic responsibilities: regulating commercial banks, performing banking-related activities for the U.S. Department of the Treasury, providing services for banks, and setting monetary policy. Not all banks belong to the Fed. Banks with federal charters are required to belong to the Fed, but membership is optional for state-chartered banks. Because the largest banks in the country are all federally chartered, the bulk of banking assets is controlled by Fed members. The Fed acts as the bankers' bank for members. It provides wire transfer facilities, clears checks, replaces worn-out currency, and lends banks money.

Organization of the Federal Reserve System

The nation is divided into 12 federal reserve districts, each with its own federal reserve bank. Each district bank supplies banks within its district with currency and facilitates the clearing of checks. District banks are run by a nine-member board of directors, headed by a president.

The governing body of the Fed is the board of governors. The board consists of seven members, including a chair and vice chair, appointed by the president and confirmed by the Senate. A full term for a Fed governor is 14 years. If a governor serves a full term, he or she cannot be reappointed. A governor can be reappointed if he or she was initially appointed to an unexpired term. The chair and vice chair serve in those capacities for four years and can be reappointed. The chair of the board of governors is a very important position. Some have commented, only half jokingly, that the Fed chair is the second most powerful person in the nation. See the "Hit & Miss" feature that discusses new Fed chair Janet Yellen and her approach to monetary policy.

The Fed is designed to be politically independent. Terms for Fed governors are staggered in such a way that a president cannot appoint a majority of members, assuming that all members serve their entire terms. The Fed also has its own sources of revenue and does not depend on congressional appropriations.

An important part of the Fed is the *Federal Open Markets Committee (FOMC)*. The FOMC sets most policies concerning monetary policy and interest rates. It consists of 12 members— the seven Fed board governors plus five representatives of the district banks, who serve on a rotating basis. The Fed chair is also chair of the FOMC.

Janet Yellen's Approach to Monetary Policy

Janet Yellen was tapped to become the 15th chair of the Board of Governors of the Federal Reserve System, taking the helm from Ben Bernanke who served two four-year terms. She is the first woman to lead the nation's central bank. The balancing act of the Federal Reserve calls for holding prices low while ensuring the highest level of sustainable U.S. employment. Of course, there remain various schools of thought on how to reach this objective.

Some tend to view higher interest rates, slower growth, and lower levels of unemployment as a price worth paying to keep inflation levels in check. Others take a more relaxed view of inflation if it translates to stronger employment growth, which seems to be Yellen's approach so far. A self-described "sensible central banker," Yellen seems willing to move ahead with the plans put in place by Bernanke. For three years as the Fed's number two in command alongside Bernanke, Yellen pushed for the Fed to adopt easy-money policies, which refer to lower interest rates to make it easier for banks and lenders to loan and for businesses and consumers to borrow. Going forward, Yellen's plan, similar to her predecessor's strategy, is to "tiptoe away" from those monetary policies gradually as the economy shows signs of improvement.

Questions for Critical Thinking

1. Yellen's critics are concerned about her easy-money policies and the possibility that inflation will accelerate as the economic recovery gains strength. Discuss.

2. The balancing act of the Federal Reserve calls for holding prices low while ensuring the highest level of sustainable U.S. employment. How is Janet Yellen's policy doing?

Sources: Gail Marks Jarvis, "Yellen Affirms Fed's 'Extraordinary' Effort," *Chicago Tribune,* April 1, 2014, www.chicagotribune.com; Jon Hilsenrath and Victoria McGrane, "Fed's Yellen Sets Course for Steady Bond-Buy Cuts," *The Wall Street Journal,* accessed March 29, 2014, http://online.wsj.com; Samantha Sharf, "Yellen Echoes Bernanke in First Congressional Testimony as Fed Chair," *Forbes,* accessed March 29, 2014, www.forbes.com; Binyamin Applebaum, "Possible Fed Successor Has Admirers and Foes," *The New York Times,* accessed March 29, 2014, www.nytimes.com; "Definition of 'Easy Money,'" *Investopedia,* accessed March 11, 2014, http://investopedia.com.

Check Clearing and the Fed

As mentioned earlier, one of the Fed's responsibilities is to help facilitate the clearing of checks. Even in this age of electronic and online banking, Americans still wrote more than 18 billion checks in a recent year.[18] The clearing of a check is the process by which funds are transferred from the check writer to the recipient.

Assume the owner of Gulf View Townhouses of Tampa buys a $600 carpet cleaner from the local Home Depot and writes a check. If Home Depot has an account at the same bank as Gulf View, the bank will clear the check in house. It will decrease the balance in the owner's account by $600 and increase the balance in Home Depot's account by $600. If Home Depot has an account at another bank in Tampa, the two banks may still clear the check directly with one another. This process is cumbersome, however, so it is more likely that the banks will use the services of a local check clearinghouse.

But if Home Depot has its account with a bank in another state—perhaps in Atlanta, where Home Depot is based—the check will likely be cleared through the Federal Reserve System. Home Depot will deposit the check in its Atlanta bank account. That bank, in turn, will deposit the check in the Federal Reserve Bank of Atlanta. The Atlanta Federal Reserve bank will present the check to Gulf View's bank for payment, which pays the check by deducting $600 from Gulf View's account. Regardless of the method used, the Check Clearing for the 21st Century Act allows banks and the Fed to use electronic images of checks—rather than the paper documents themselves—during the clearing process. Because these images are transferred electronically, the time it takes to clear a check has been reduced substantially, often to less than 48 hours.

Monetary Policy

The Fed's most important function is controlling the supply of money and credit, or monetary policy. The Fed's job is to make sure that the money supply grows at an appropriate rate, allowing the economy to expand and inflation to remain in check. If the money supply grows too slowly, economic growth will slow, unemployment will increase, and the risk of a recession will increase. If the money supply grows too rapidly, inflationary pressures will build. The Fed uses its policy tools to push interest rates up or down. If the Fed pushes interest rates up, the growth rate in the money supply will slow, economic growth will slow, and inflationary pressures will ease. If the Fed pushes interest rates down, the growth rate in the money supply will increase, economic growth will pick up, and unemployment will fall.

The two common measures of the money supply are called M1 and M2. M1 consists of currency in circulation and balances in bank checking accounts. M2 equals M1 plus balances in some savings accounts and money market mutual funds. Figure 16.4 shows the approximate breakdowns of M1 and M2. The Fed has three major policy tools for controlling the growth in the supply of money and credit: reserve requirements, the discount rate, and open market operations.

The Fed requires banks to maintain reserves—defined as cash in their vaults plus deposits at district Federal Reserve banks or other banks—equal to a certain percentage of what the banks hold in deposits. For example, if the Fed sets the reserve requirement at 5 percent, a bank that receives a $500 deposit must reserve $25, so it has only $475 to invest or lend to individuals or businesses. By changing the reserve requirement, the Fed can affect the amount of money available for making loans. The higher the reserve requirement, the less banks can lend out to consumers and businesses. The lower the reserve requirement, the more banks can lend out. Because any change in the reserve requirement can have a sudden and dramatic impact on the money supply, the Fed rarely uses this tool. Reserve requirements range from 0 to 10 percent, depending on the type of account.

Another policy tool is the so-called *discount rate*, the interest rate at which Federal Reserve banks make short-term loans to member banks. A bank might need a short-term loan if transactions leave it short of reserves. If the Fed wants to slow the growth rate in the money supply, it increases the discount rate. This increase makes it more expensive for banks to borrow funds. Banks, in turn, raise the interest rates they charge on loans to consumers and businesses. The end result is a slowdown in economic activity. Lowering the discount rate has the opposite effect.

The third policy tool, and the one used most often, is *open market operations*, the technique of controlling the money supply growth rate by buying or selling U.S. Treasury securities. If

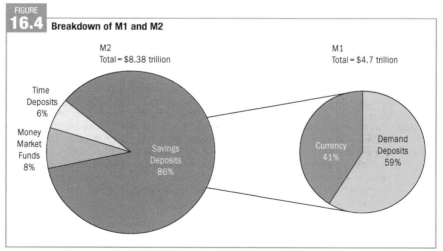

FIGURE 16.4 Breakdown of M1 and M2

Source: Board of Governors of the Federal Reserve System, "Money Stock Measures: H.6," February 28, 2014, http://www.federalreserve.gov, accessed March 31, 2014.

Part 6 *Managing Financial Resources*

16.3 Tools Used by the Federal Reserve to Regulate the Growth in the Money Supply

TOOL	BRIEF DESCRIPTION	IMPACT ON THE GROWTH RATE OF THE MONEY SUPPLY	IMPACT ON INTEREST RATES AND THE ECONOMY	FREQUENCY OF USE
1. Reserve requirements	Change in the percentage of deposits held as reserves.	Increases in reserve requirements slow the growth rate in the money supply.	Increases in reserve requirements push interest rates up and slow economic growth.	Rarely used.
2. Discount rate	Change in the rate the Fed charges banks for loans.	An increase in the discount rate slows the growth rate in the money supply.	An increase in the discount rate pushes interest rates up and slows economic growth.	Used only in conjunction with open market operations.
3. Open market operations	Buying and selling government securities to increase or decrease bank reserves.	Selling government securities reduces bank reserves and slows the growth rate in the money supply.	Selling government securities pushes interest rates up and slows economic growth.	Used frequently.

the Fed buys Treasury securities, the money it pays enters circulation, increasing the money supply and lowering interest rates. When the Fed sells Treasury securities, money is taken out of circulation and interest rates rise. When the Fed uses open market operations it employs the so-called *federal funds rate*—the rate at which banks lend money to each other overnight—as its benchmark.

Table 16.3 illustrates how the tools used by the Federal Reserve can stimulate or slow the economy.

The Federal Reserve has the authority to exercise selective credit controls when it thinks the economy is growing too rapidly or too slowly. These credit controls include the power to set margin requirements—the percentage of the purchase price of a security that an investor must pay in cash on credit purchases of stocks or bonds. The Fed can also inject capital into the financial system in response to a financial crisis. During the recent credit crisis, the Fed pumped hundreds of billions of dollars into the financial system.

Transactions in the foreign exchange markets also affect the U.S. money supply and interest rates. The Fed can lower the exchange value of the dollar by selling dollars and buying foreign currencies, and it can raise the dollar's exchange value by doing the opposite— buying dollars and selling foreign currencies. When the Fed buys foreign currencies, the effect is the same as buying securities because it increases the U.S. banking system's reserves. Selling foreign currencies, on the other hand, is like selling securities, in that it reduces bank reserves.

7 Regulation of the Financial System

Given the importance of the financial system, it is probably not surprising that many components are subject to government regulation and oversight. In addition, industry self-regulation is commonplace.

Assessment Check ✓

1. What is the Federal Reserve System?
2. How is the Fed organized?
3. List the three tools the Fed uses to control the supply of money and credit.

Bank Regulation

Banks are among the nation's most heavily regulated businesses. The main purpose of bank regulation is to ensure public confidence in the safety and security of the banking system. Banks are critical to the overall functioning of the economy, and a collapse of the banking system can have disastrous results. Many believe that one of the major causes of the Great Depression was the collapse of the banking system that started in the late 1920s.

All banks, whether commercial or savings, and credit unions have either state or federal charters. Most commercial banks are state chartered; however, federally chartered banks control more than half of all banking assets. State-chartered banks are regulated by the appropriate state banking authorities; federally chartered commercial banks are regulated by the Federal Reserve, the Federal Deposit Insurance Corporation, and the Comptroller of the Currency. Furthermore, state-chartered commercial banks that are federally insured—and virtually all are—are also subject to FDIC regulation.

At the federal level, savings banks are regulated by the Office of Thrift Supervision and the FDIC. Federal credit unions are subject to NCUA regulation. State-chartered savings banks and credit unions are also regulated by state authorities.

Banks and credit unions are subject to periodic examination by state or federal regulators. Examinations ensure that the institution is following sound banking practices and is complying with all applicable regulations. These examinations include the review of detailed reports on the bank's operating and financial condition, as well as on-site inspections. Regulators can impose various penalties on institutions deemed not in compliance with sound banking practices, including forcing the delinquent financial institution into a merger with a healthier one.

Government Regulation of the Financial Markets

Regulation of U.S. financial markets is primarily a function of the federal government, although states also regulate them. Federal regulation grew out of various trading abuses during the 1920s. To restore confidence and stability in the financial markets after the 1929 stock market crash, Congress passed a series of landmark legislative acts that have formed the basis of federal securities regulation ever since. Many other regulations have followed. One of the most recent, the Dodd-Frank Wall Street Reform and Consumer Protection Act, is having some effects on the banking business and its customers, as the "Solving an Ethical Controversy" feature explains.

As noted in Chapter 15, the U.S. Securities and Exchange Commission, created in 1934, is the principal federal regulatory overseer of the securities markets. The SEC's mission is to administer securities laws and protect investors in public securities transactions. The SEC has broad enforcement power. It can pursue civil actions against individuals and corporations, but actions requiring criminal proceedings are referred to the U.S. Justice Department.

The SEC requires virtually all new public issues of corporate securities to be registered. As part of the registration process for a new security issue, the issuer must prepare a prospectus. The typical prospectus gives a detailed description of the company issuing the securities, including financial data, products, research and development projects, and pending litigation. It also describes the stock or bond issue and underwriting agreement in detail. The registration process seeks to guarantee full and fair disclosure. The SEC does not rule on the investment merits of a registered security. It is concerned only that an issuer gives investors enough information to make their own informed decisions.

Besides primary market registration requirements, SEC regulation extends to the secondary markets as well, keeping tabs on trading activity to make sure it is fair to all participants. Every securities exchange must by law follow a set of trading rules that have been approved by the SEC. In addition, the Market Reform Act of 1990 gave the SEC emergency authority to halt trading and restrict practices such as program trading—whereby computer systems are programmed to buy or sell securities if certain conditions arise—during periods of extreme volatility.

Solving an Ethical Controversy

Are Debit Card Fees Too High?

Recent financial reform legislation capped the fees that banks are allowed to charge retailers when customers make purchases with debit cards. Down from an average of 44 cents per transaction, the top "swipe" fee is now 21 cents. Retailers, who either pass the fee on to consumers or absorb it, think the cap is still too high. Banks, claiming the reduction is costing them billions, tried making up the difference with new charges to customers.

Should debit card swipe fees be capped?

PRO

1. Debit card fees should be capped, says a credit union executive, because "paying a fee to access your own money is . . . unacceptable."

2. High fees impose a burden on retailers, who must pass it on to consumers in higher prices.

CON

1. Banks need swipe fees to fund anti-fraud activities. Consumers, who directly benefit, should help bear the cost.

2. If banks lose money on low fees, they must compensate with more aggressive marketing and new charges for other services.

Summary

Expect bank fees to continue rising. Whatever happens, says one financial analyst, "the consumer is getting stuck with the costs."

Sources: Tara Siegel Bernard, "Appeals Court Upholds Current Fees on Debit Card Purchases," *The New York Times,* accessed March 28, 2014, www.nytimes.com; Alan Zibel, Brent Kendall, and Michael R. Crittenden, "Merchants Notch Win in Feud over Debit Card Fees," *The Wall Street Journal,* accessed March 19, 2014, http://online.wsj.com; Hadley Malcolm, "Retailers Sue Fed, Say Debit Card Fees Are Still Too High," *USA Today,* accessed March 19, 2014, www.usatoday.com; Jennifer Waters, "High Fees? Here's How to Fire Your Bank," *Market Watch,* accessed March 19, 2014, www.marketwatch.com; "The Durbin Amendment Explained," *Nerd Wallet,* accessed March 19, 2014, www.nerdwallet.com.

One area to which the SEC pays particular attention is insider trading. **Insider trading** is defined as the use of material nonpublic information about a company to make investment profits. Examples of material nonpublic information include a pending merger or a major oil discovery, which could affect the firm's stock price. The SEC's definition of insider trading goes beyond corporate insiders—people such as the company's officers and directors. It includes lawyers, accountants, investment bankers, and even reporters—anyone who uses nonpublic information to profit in the stock market at the expense of ordinary investors. Although some actions or communications are clearly insider trading, others are more ambiguous. Consequently, all employees of public companies have to be mindful of what is and isn't permitted.

Securities laws also require every public corporation to file several reports each year with the SEC; the contents of these reports become public information. The best known, of course, is the annual report. Public corporations prepare annual reports for their shareholders, and they file another report containing essentially the same information, Form 10-K, with the SEC. The SEC requires additional reports each time certain company officers and directors buy or sell a company's stock for their own accounts (Form 4) or anytime an investor accumulates more than 5 percent of a company's outstanding stock (Form 13-d). All of these reports are available for viewing and download at the EDGAR Online website (http://www.freeedgar.com).

insider trading use of material nonpublic information about a company to make investment profits.

Industry Self-Regulation

The securities markets are also heavily self-regulated by professional associations and the major financial markets. The securities industry recognizes that rules and regulations designed

The Securities and Exchange Commission is charged with regulating financial markets. Its website, featured here, is a good source of information for would-be investors.

Courtesy SEC

to ensure fair and orderly markets promote investor confidence and benefit all participants. Two examples of self-regulation are the rules of conduct established by the various professional organizations and the market surveillance techniques used by the major securities markets.

Professional Rules of Conduct Prodded initially by federal legislation, the National Association of Securities Dealers (NASD) established and periodically updates rules of conduct for members—both individuals and firms. These rules are intended to ensure that brokers perform their basic functions honestly and fairly, under constant supervision. Failure to adhere to rules of conduct can result in disciplinary action. The NASD also established a formal arbitration procedure through which investors can attempt to resolve disputes with brokers without litigation.

Market Surveillance All securities markets use a variety of methods to spot possible violations of trading rules or securities laws. For example, the NYSE continuously monitors trading activity throughout the trading day. A key technical tool used by the NYSE is called Stock Watch, an electronic monitoring system that flags unusual price and volume activity. The NYSE then seeks explanations for unusual activity from the member firms and companies involved. In addition, all market participants must keep detailed records of every aspect of every trade (called an *audit trail*). The NYSE's enforcement division may impose a variety of penalties on members for rule violations. In addition, the exchange turns over evidence to the SEC for further action if it believes that violations of federal securities laws may have occurred.

Although self-regulation by the financial industry has been an important component of securities market regulation, some contend that the industry can never truly regulate itself effectively in today's market environment.

Assessment Check ✅

1. Who regulates banks?
2. Define *insider trading*.
3. List two ways in which the securities markets are self-regulated.

[8] The Financial System: A Global Perspective

Not surprisingly, the global financial system is becoming more and more integrated each year. As we've noted, financial markets exist throughout the world. Shares of U.S. firms trade in other countries, and shares of international companies trade in the United States. In fact, investors in China and Japan own more U.S. Treasury securities than do domestic investors.

Financial institutions have also become a global industry. Major U.S. banks—such as JPMorgan Chase and Bank of America—have extensive international operations. They have offices, lend money, and accept deposits from customers throughout the world.

482 **Part 6** *Managing Financial Resources*

Although most Americans recognize large U.S. banks such as Citibank among the global financial giants, only 3 of the world's 20 largest banks (measured by total assets) are U.S. institutions—JP Morgan Chase (ranked 12th), Bank of America (ranked 18th), and Wells Fargo (ranked 20th). The other 17 are based in continental Europe, Great Britain, and Asia. The world's largest bank is Industrial & Commercial Bank of China Limited, with $2.8 trillion in assets. These international banks operate worldwide, including locations in the United States.[19]

Virtually all nations have some sort of a central bank, similar to the U.S. Federal Reserve. Examples include the Banks of Canada, England, and Japan and the European Central Bank. These central banks play roles much like that of the Fed, such as controlling the money supply and regulating banks. Policymakers at other nations' central banks often respond to changes in the U.S. financial system by making similar changes in their own systems. For example, if the Fed pushes U.S. interest rates lower, central banks in Japan and Europe may also push their interest rates lower. These changes can influence events in countries around the world. Lower U.S. and European interest rates not only decrease the cost of borrowing for U.S. and European firms but also increase the amount of money available for loans to borrowers in other countries such as Chile and India.

In Frankfurt, Germany, a sculpture of the euro—the symbol for the European Union's currency—stands outside the headquarters of Europe's central bank. The 12 gold stars represent all the peoples of Europe.

Alex Grimm/Reuters/Landov

What's Ahead

This chapter explored the financial system, a key component of the U.S. economy and something that affects many aspects of contemporary business. The financial system is the process by which funds are transferred between savers and borrowers and includes securities, financial markets, and financial institutions. The chapter also described the role of the Federal Reserve and discussed the global financial system. In the next chapter, we discuss the finance function of a business including the role of the financial managers, financial planning, asset management, and sources of short- and long-term funds.

Assessment Check ✓

1. Where do U.S. banks rank compared with international banks?

2. Do other countries have organizations that play roles similar to those played by the Federal Reserve?

Chapter in Review

■ Summary of Learning Objectives

⌐1⌐ Understand the financial system.

The financial system is the process by which funds are transferred between those having excess funds (savers) and those needing additional funds (users). Savers and users are individuals, businesses, and governments. Savers expect to earn a rate of return in exchange for the use of their funds. Financial markets, financial institutions, and financial instruments (securities) make up the financial system. Although direct transfers are possible, most funds flow from savers to

users through the financial markets or financial institutions, such as commercial banks. A well-functioning financial system is critical to the overall health of a nation's economy.

Assessment Check Answers ✓

1.1 What is the financial system? The financial system is the process by which funds are transferred between those having excess funds (savers) and those needing additional funds (users).

Chapter 16 *The Financial System*   **483**

1.2 In the financial system, who are the borrowers and who are the savers? Savers and borrowers are individuals, businesses, and governments. Generally, individuals are net savers, meaning they spend less than they make, whereas businesses and governments are net borrowers.

1.3 List the two most common ways in which funds are transferred between borrowers and savers. The two most common ways funds are transferred are through the financial markets and through financial institutions.

⌐2⌐ List the various types of securities.

Securities, also called *financial instruments*, represent obligations on the part of issuers—businesses and governments—to provide purchasers with expected or stated returns on the funds invested or loaned. Securities can be classified into three categories: money market instruments, bonds, and stock. Money market instruments and bonds are debt instruments. Money market instruments are short-term debt securities and tend to be low-risk securities. Bonds are longer-term debt securities and pay a fixed amount of interest each year. Bonds are sold by the U.S. Department of the Treasury (government bonds), state and local governments (municipal bonds), and corporations. Mortgage pass-through securities are bonds backed by a pool of mortgage loans. Most municipal and corporate bonds have risk ratings. Common stock represents ownership in corporations. Common stockholders have voting rights and a residual claim on the firm's assets.

Assessment Check Answers ✅

2.1 What are the major types of securities? The major types of securities are money market instruments, bonds, and stock.

2.2 What is a government bond? A municipal bond? A government bond is one issued by the U.S. Treasury. Municipal bonds are issued by state and local governments.

2.3 Why do investors purchase common stock? There are two primary motives for purchasing common stock. One is to receive dividends, cash payments to shareholders by the firm. The other is potential price appreciation of the shares.

⌐3⌐ Discuss financial markets.

A financial market is a market where securities are bought and sold. The primary market for securities serves businesses and governments that want to sell new security issues to raise funds. Securities are sold in the primary market either through an open auction or via a process called *underwriting*. The secondary market handles transactions of previously issued securities between investors. The New York Stock Exchange is a secondary market. The business or government that issued the security is not directly involved in secondary market transactions. In terms of the dollar value of trading volume, the secondary market is about four to five times larger than the primary market.

Assessment Check Answers ✅

3.1 What is a financial market? A financial market is a market in which securities are issued and traded.

3.2 Distinguish between a primary and a secondary financial market. The primary market for securities serves businesses and governments that want to sell new security issues to raise funds. The secondary market handles transactions of previously issued securities between investors.

3.3 Briefly explain the role of financial institutions in the sale of securities. Financial institutions purchase new securities issues from corporations or state and local governments and then resell the securities to investors. The institutions charge a fee for their services.

⌐4⌐ Understand the stock markets.

The best-known financial markets are the stock exchanges. They exist throughout the world. The two largest—the New York Stock Exchange and NASDAQ—are located in the United States. The NYSE is bigger, measured in terms of the total value of stock traded. Larger and better-known companies dominate the NYSE. Buy and sell orders are transmitted to the trading floor for execution. The NASDAQ stock market is an electronic market in which buy and sell orders are entered into a computerized communication system for execution. Most of the world's major stock markets today use similar electronic trading systems.

Assessment Check Answers ✅

4.1 What are the world's two largest stock markets? The world's two largest stock markets are the New York Stock Exchange (NYSE) and the NASDAQ.

4.2 Why is the London Stock Exchange unique? The London Stock Exchange is probably the most international of the world's stock markets because a large percentage of the shares traded are not those of British firms.

4.3 Explain the difference between a market order and a limit order. A market order instructs the investor's broker to obtain the best possible price when buying or selling securities. A limit order sets a maximum price (if the investor wants to buy) or a minimum price (if the investor wants to sell).

⌐5⌐ Evaluate financial institutions.

Financial institutions act as intermediaries between savers and users of funds. Depository institutions—commercial banks, savings banks, and credit unions—accept deposits from customers that can be redeemed on demand. Commercial banks are the largest and most important of the depository institutions and offer the widest range of services. Savings banks are a major source of home mortgage loans. Credit unions are not-for-profit institutions offering financial services to consumers. Government agencies, most notably the Federal Deposit Insurance Corporation, insure deposits at these institutions. Nondepository institutions include pension funds and insurance companies. Nondepository institutions invest a large portion of their funds in stocks, bonds, and real estate. Mutual funds are another important financial institution. These companies sell shares to investors and, in turn, invest the proceeds in securities. Many individuals today invest a large portion of their retirement savings in mutual fund shares.

Assessment Check Answers ✅

5.1 What are the two main types of financial institutions? The two major types of financial institutions are depository institutions (those that accept deposits that customers can draw on demand) and nondepository institutions.

5.2 What are the primary differences between commercial banks and savings banks? Today commercial and savings banks offer many of the same services. However, commercial banks lend money to businesses as well as to individuals. Savings banks lend money primarily to individuals, principally in the form of home mortgage loans.

5.3 What is a mutual fund? A mutual fund is an intermediary that raises money by selling shares to investors. It then pools investor funds and purchases securities that are consistent with the fund's objectives.

⌐6⌐ Explain the role of the Federal Reserve System.

The Federal Reserve System is the central bank of the United States. The Federal Reserve regulates banks, performs banking functions for the U.S. Department of the Treasury, and acts as the bankers' bank (clearing checks, lending money to banks, and replacing worn-out currency). It controls the supply of credit and money in the economy to promote growth and control inflation. The Federal Reserve's tools include reserve requirements, the discount rate, and open market operations. Selective credit controls and purchases and sales of foreign currencies also help the Federal Reserve manage the economy.

Assessment Check Answers ✅

6.1 What is the Federal Reserve System? The Federal Reserve System is the U.S. central bank. It is responsible for regulating commercial banks, providing banking-related services for the federal government, providing services for banks, and setting monetary policy.

6.2 How is the Fed organized? The country is divided into 12 districts, each of which has a Federal Reserve Bank. The Fed is run by a seven-member board of governors headed by a chair and vice chair. An important part of the Fed is the Federal Open Markets Committee, which sets monetary and interest rate policy. The Fed is designed to be politically independent.

6.3 List the three tools the Fed uses to control the supply of money and credit. The three tools are reserve requirements, the discount rate, and open market operations.

⌐7⌐ Describe the regulation of the financial system.

Commercial banks, savings banks, and credit unions in the United States are heavily regulated by federal or state banking authorities. Banking regulators require institutions to follow sound banking practices and have the power to close noncompliant ones. In the United States, financial markets are regulated at both the federal and state levels. Markets are also heavily self-regulated by the financial markets and professional organizations. The chief regulatory body is the Securities and Exchange Commission. It sets the requirements for both primary and secondary market activity, prohibiting a number of practices, including insider trading. The SEC also requires public companies to disclose financial information regularly. Professional organizations and the securities markets also have rules and procedures that all members must follow.

Assessment Check Answers ✅

7.1 Who regulates banks? All banks have either state or federal charters. Federally chartered banks are regulated by the Federal Reserve, the FDIC, and the Comptroller of the Currency. State-chartered banks are regulated by state banking authorities and the FDIC.

7.2 Define *insider trading*. Insider trading is defined as the use of material nonpublic information to make an investment profit.

7.3 List two ways in which the securities markets are self-regulated. Professional organizations such as the National Association of Securities Dealers have codes of conduct that members are expected to follow. Major financial markets have trading rules and procedures to identify suspicious trading activity.

⌐8⌐ Discuss the global perspective of the financial system.

Financial markets exist throughout the world and are increasingly interconnected. Investors in other countries purchase U.S. securities, and U.S. investors purchase foreign securities. Large U.S. banks and other financial institutions have a global presence. They accept deposits, make loans, and have branches throughout the world. Foreign banks also operate worldwide. The average European or Japanese bank is much larger than the average American bank. Virtually all nations have central banks that perform the same roles as the U.S. Federal Reserve System. Central bankers often act together, raising and lowering interest rates as economic conditions warrant.

Assessment Check Answers ✅

8.1 Where do U.S. banks rank compared with international banks? Banks in Asia and Europe are generally much larger than U.S. banks. In fact, only 3 out of the world's 20 largest banks are based in the United States.

8.2 Do other countries have organizations that play roles similar to those played by the Federal Reserve? Yes, virtually all nations have central banks that perform many of the same functions that the U.S. Federal Reserve System does.

Business Terms You Need to Know

financial system 462	primary markets 467	Federal Deposit Insurance Corporation
securities 463	secondary market 468	(FDIC) 473
common stock 466	stock markets (exchanges) 469	Federal Reserve System (Fed) 476
financial markets 467	financial institutions 472	insider trading 481

Review Questions

1. What is the financial system? Why is the direct transfer of funds from savers to users rare?

2. What is a security? Give several examples.

3. List the major types of bonds. Explain a mortgage pass-through.

4. What are the differences between common stock and preferred stock?

5. Explain the difference between a primary financial market and a secondary financial market.

6. Why are commercial banks, savings banks, and credit unions classified as depository financial institutions? How do the three differ?

7. Why are life insurance companies, pension funds, and mutual funds considered financial institutions?

8. Briefly explain the role of the Federal Reserve and list the tools it uses to control the supply of money and credit.

9. What methods are used to regulate banks? Why are state-chartered banks also regulated by the FDIC?

10. Explain how the Federal Reserve, acting in conjunction with other central banks, could affect exchange rates.

Projects and Teamwork Applications

1. Collect current interest rates on the following types of bonds: U.S. Treasury bonds, AAA-rated municipal bonds, AAA-rated corporate bonds, and BBB-rated corporate bonds. Arrange the interest rates from lowest to highest. Explain the reasons for the ranking.

2. You've probably heard of U.S. savings bonds—you may even have received some bonds as a gift. What you may not know is that two different types of savings bonds exist. Do some research and compare and contrast the two types of savings bonds. What are their features? Their pros and cons? Assuming you were interested in buying savings bonds, which of the two do you find more attractive?

3. Working with a partner, assume you are considering buying shares of Lowe's or Home Depot. Describe how you would go about analyzing the two companies' stocks and deciding which, if either, you would buy.

4. Discuss investment strategies and asset allocation for someone in their 20s versus someone in their 40s. How does risk tolerance change with age? Discuss in pairs or small groups.

5. Explain the concept of compounding and discuss why it makes sense to invest at an early age using examples.

Web Assignments

1. **Virtual stock trading.** The website listed below is a virtual stock contest and training grounds of sorts for students and investors alike. Go to the site, read "Getting Started" as well as the frequently asked questions, and create a stock portfolio. With $10,000 in virtual dollars, pick three to five stocks and track the results. What did you learn? If you had invested in those same stocks six months earlier, what would your portfolio's gain or loss have been? Are you ready to invest with real money? Discuss.

www.howthemarketworks.com

2. **Researching and managing investments.** Go to the website listed below, which is sponsored by the U.S. Securities and Exchange Commission. Under "Researching & Managing Investments," read more about "Investing on Your Own."

Make a brief presentation to the class or a small group about the different ways to invest on your own and the steps involved. Take the quiz to test your money smarts and discuss your results about what you have learned.

www.investor.gov

3. **Federal Reserve System.** Go to the web site of the Board of Governors of the Federal Reserve System (www.federalreserve .gov). Prepare a short report on the seven-member board. Who are the current members? What are their backgrounds? When were they appointed? When do their terms expire?

Note: Internet web addresses change frequently. If you don't find the exact sites listed, you may need to access the organization's home page and search from there or use a search engine such as Google or Bing.

Silicon Valley's Banker

In his previous job at Credit Suisse First Boston (CSFB), Frank Quattrone brokered some of the biggest tech sales and mergers in Silicon Valley's early days, including taking Cisco and Amazon public. Once he sent a beleaguered prospect a live mule bearing a note: "Stop feeling like a mule and pick CSFB." Quattrone won the business.

After being sidelined for several years, overturning an obstruction-of-justice conviction from that period, he returned to banking and to Silicon Valley in a less flamboyant mode with Qatalyst Partners, an advisory firm he founded with just 32 employees. Several years after its launch, Qatalyst Partners has worked with some of Quattrone's old clients and some new ones to achieve an impressive track record. The company has advised several companies on $70 billion in tech industry transactions, mostly deals in which Qatalyst represented sellers of companies or assets.

Some observers credit Quattrone's successful comeback and continued ability to negotiate high-priced deals to a combination of luck, financial savvy, and strong industry relationships. He says that he and his Qatalyst colleagues are passionate about the tech industry and spend a lot of time thinking about the industry's structure and the strategies of its major participants, which provides clients with an advantage when it comes to understanding the tech business. One prominent client says Quattrone's appeal is simple: "Frank's a very likeable guy who knows what he's talking about."

Questions for Critical Thinking

1. Do you agree with observers' explanations for Quattrone's success? Why or why not?
2. Why are banker–client relationships important in billion-dollar deals?

Sources: Company website, www.qatalyst.com, accessed March 19, 2014; Patrick Hoge, "Financial Dealmaker of the Year: Frank Quattrone," *San Francisco Business Times*, accessed March 19, 2014, www.bizjournals .com; Robert Cyran and John Foley, "Frank Quattrone's Golden Touch," *The New York Times*, accessed March 19, 2014, www.nytimes.com; Serena Saitto, "Frank Quattrone: A Tech Dealmaker's Comeback," *Bloomberg Businessweek*, accessed March 19, 2014, www.businessweek.com.

PayNearMe Serves "Unbanked" Consumers

If you have ever had a love–hate relationship with your bank and have contemplated leaving, you are not alone. There are three groups of consumers to consider: those who have left a bank, those who have been asked to leave, and those who have yet to establish a relationship with a mainstream financial institution. All three groups fall into what is called the "unbanked," and according to a recent study by the Federal Deposit Insurance Corporation, one-third of the U.S. population fits this description.

Being without a checking account, credit cards, or access to consumer loans makes this population invisible to the U.S. financial system. For many different reasons, unbanked individuals have chosen to conduct business and payments primarily with cash. A California-based startup, PayNearMe, targets these consumers in hopes of allowing everyone to pay in a digital economy.

Most unbanked consumers use alternative financial services like payday lenders, money transfer firms like Western Union, and check cashing stores, all of which charge exorbitant fees. PayNearMe has leveled the playing field by developing a technology platform that allows payments to be made with cash.

Unbanked consumers can now pay for online purchases, utility bills, rent, and more using the extensive PayNearMe network. With more than 17,000 locations, which include 7-Eleven stores, ACE Cash Express, and Family Dollar stores, members of the PayNearMe network accept cash for payment seven days a week. The process is simple. Once customers select PayNearMe as a payment option, they bring a preprinted slip or electronic smart phone barcode to any of the PayNearMe locations. The cashier scans the barcode, and using cash to pay a bill, an electronic receipt is generated. Once the transaction is complete, the bill recipient is notified that you've paid, and funds are immediately posted to the biller's account.

Recent research suggests that the potential for mobile banking to reach unbanked consumers is quickly growing. Technology is helping unbanked consumers to move away from high-priced check cashing and alternative financial services.

Chapter 16 *The Financial System* **487**

1. Supporters of PayNearMe argue that the technology gives businesses options to service a broad economic range of consumers—not just those who can swipe a credit or debit card. What might critics say about PayNearMe services?

2. With a market of more than 100 million unbanked consumers, how might other businesses implement strategies to reach this potential group of customers?

Sources: Company website, www.paynearme.com, accessed March 11, 2014; Anisha, "PayNearMe: Bringing Convenience to the Financially Underserved," *Nerd Wallet*, accessed March 11, 2014, http://nerdwallet .com; Meredith Whitney, "America's Unbanked Masses," *The Wall Street Journal*, accessed March 11, 2014, http://online.wsj.com; Andrew Ross, "PayNearMe Attracts Serious Money, Big Partner for Unbanked," *San Francisco Chronicle*, accessed March 11, 2014, www.sfgate.com; Richard Todd, "Rise in Smartphones Puts More Financial Tools in the Hands of the Unbanked," Federal Reserve website, www.minneapolisfed.org, accessed March 11, 2014; "Banking the Unbanked: A How-To," *Forbes*, accessed March 11, 2014, www.forbes.com.

CASE 16.3 New Harvest Coffee Goes Beyond Fair Trade

"Fair Trade has always been part of my legacy in coffee," says Rik Kleinfeldt, president and co-founder of Rhode Island-based New Harvest Coffee Roasters. "That's where I started with New Harvest." But in less than a decade, New Harvest's business model has evolved beyond Fair Trade to something different.

New Harvest is a small-batch coffee roaster specializing in certified organic coffee that is grown and harvested by farms with sustainable practices. Rik Kleinfeldt notes that he built his company on two pillars: 1) the highest quality coffee, and 2) sustainable sourcing practices. "But these two weren't really gelling at first," he admits. At the beginning, Kleinfeldt tried to source from Fair Trade cooperatives, but this wasn't really fulfilling his objective. "Fair Trade is based on the commodity system," Kleinfeldt explains, "which creates a floor price at which coffee can't drop below. But it doesn't really address the issue of quality." The groups that work with Fair Trade are large cooperatives, sometimes encompassing several thousand small farms. All the coffee is blended together as a commodity, so it is impossible for a roaster like New Harvest to deal directly with each farm, selecting the specific harvest that it wants to buy.

Kleinfeldt is quick to point out that when Fair Trade began around a decade ago, it was a lifeline to small farmers because coffee prices were at an all-time low—these growers were selling their crops for less than it cost to produce them. Without Fair Trade, many of these farms would have gone out of business. With the coffee market somewhat stabilized though, commodity pricing brings its own set of problems. "The commodity pricing usually has nothing to do with the coffee itself," says Kleinfeldt. Prices are set at the New York Stock Exchange, not in the growing fields of Costa Rica or Colombia. He notes that roasters, retailers, and consumers may end up paying way too much or way too little for a particular year's crop.

So Kleinfeldt has become part of what he calls the Artisan Coffee movement—growers, roasters, and retailers who prefer to deal directly with each other as individual businesses. "We connect directly with our growers and determine price based on quality," he explains. Kleinfeldt and his staff, along with some of his retailers such as the owner of Blue State Coffee and the owner of Pejamajo Café, travel to the farms in Costa Rica and Colombia where they actually taste the coffee before purchasing a crop. Kleinfeldt believes this is the only way to get the best coffee on the market. These visits help develop strong relationships, find solutions to problems, and develop strategies for surviving and thriving as businesses. Through visiting, he says, "we can understand their challenges." One farm in particular is located in Colombia. The farmer decided he didn't want to participate in a large Fair Trade cooperative—instead, he wanted to develop a market for his own coffee. So he approached New Harvest with the idea, and the match was ideal. He is now one of New Harvest's premier growers.

Sourcing the coffee beans directly from individual farms also helps New Harvest keep close track of organic and sustainability practices. Gerra Harrigan, director of business development for New Harvest Coffee Roasters, notes that this is an important part of the firm's business. The owners of local coffee shops—and their customers—like the reassurance that New Harvest stands behind all of its claims. Harrigan takes the hands-on approach. "When we deal direct-trade coffee, the coffee has to be cared for a little more," she explains. Harrigan grades the coffee on several factors before pricing it for New Harvest.

Kleinfeldt wants consumers to know they are getting a great deal when they ask for New Harvest at their local shop. He points out that the price differentiation isn't as much as people might think. A visit to the supermarket reveals that Starbucks and Green Mountain sell for about

$9 to $11 per pound, whereas most New Harvest coffee sells for about $11 to $13 a pound. Because of the richness of New Harvest, most customers actually get more cups of coffee from a pound of New Harvest than they do from the other premium brands.

Kleinfeldt hopes that the Artisan Coffee movement, as he refers to his company's practices, will flourish and grow. He believes that if you're going to drink a cup of coffee, it should be really fresh and of the highest quality—with beans preferably roasted by New Harvest.

Questions for Critical Thinking

1. What are the benefits and drawbacks of treating coffee as a commodity in the marketplace? What do you predict will be the future of Fair Trade?

2. Should the entire coffee market be regulated in any way? Why or why not? If so, how?

3. How would New Harvest change as a business if it made an initial public offering (IPO)?

4. What is your opinion of the so-called Artisan Coffee movement as a business model? Do you think it will be successful in the long run? Why or why not?

Sources: Company website, www.newharvestcoffee.com, accessed March 29, 2014; "New Harvest Coffee Roasters," *Green People*, accessed March 29, 2014, www.greenpeople.org; Richard Garcia, "Pejamajo Café & New Harvest Coffee Roasters," *Chefs Daily Food Bank*, accessed March 29, 2014, www.chefsdailyfoodbank.com.

Learning Objectives

[1] Define the role of the financial manager.

[2] Describe financial planning.

[3] Outline how organizations manage their assets.

[4] Discuss the sources of funds and capital structure.

[5] Identify short-term funding options.

[6] Discuss sources of long-term financing.

[7] Describe mergers, acquisitions, buyouts, and divestitures.

Chapter 17

Financial Management

NuStock/iStockphoto

Peer Lending Changes Capital Markets

For more than three decades, there has been a quiet revolution going on in world capital markets. In the 1980s, there was the introduction of "micro finance," where individuals in the developing world turned to new sources to borrow money. These new sources were not traditional banks or lenders but were groups, often not-for-profits such as World Vision, set up specifically to make small loans. These groups allowed would-be entrepreneurs in places like Asia, Africa, and South America to create new businesses.

More recently in the developed world there have been bold experiments with a different kind of consumer banking on websites like Prosper and Lending Club. These websites conduct what is known as "peer-to-peer" lending, where individuals with money to invest meet individuals who are seeking loans. The website acts as a financial intermediary, not a gatekeeper, as individuals determine the creditworthiness of the borrower—and assume the risk of the loan. There have also been a wide variety of crowd-funding sites such as Indiegogo and Kickstarter, which provide an Internet-based platform for would-be entrepreneurs to raise funds for commercial or personal projects. So are traditional financial and capital markets at risk of becoming obsolete?

There seems to be a shift in the concept of financial lending. Introducing individuals who have money to invest to those who need money without an intermediary opens up the world of banking and finance to everyone. Basically, individuals can select the projects and individuals they are willing to support financially.

Companies like Facebook and Tesla, because of their inherent market potential or entrepreneurial expertise, will still garner attention from existing investment banks and venture capitalists. Likewise, individuals seeking home mortgages, car loans, or other type of funds that require collateral will continue to go through existing banks and savings and loans. But for individuals who have a product idea that doesn't meet a bank's requirements, or the deal that doesn't have a formalized exit strategy that venture capitalists demand, or even the loan that is too small or risky for bank shareholders, these new financial models provide the means and opportunity for entrepreneurs around the world to fulfill their dreams.[1]

Overview

Previous chapters discuss two essential functions that a business must perform. First, the company must produce a good or service or contract with suppliers to produce it. Second, the firm must market its good or service to prospective customers. This chapter introduces a third, equally important, function: a company's managers must ensure that it has enough money to operate successfully, in both the present and the future, and that these funds are invested properly. Adequate funds must be available to purchase materials, equipment, and other assets; pay bills; and compensate employees. This third business function is finance—planning, obtaining, and managing the company's funds in order to accomplish its objectives as effectively and efficiently as possible.

An organization's financial objectives include not only meeting expenses and investing in assets but also maximizing its overall worth, often determined by the value of the firm's common stock. Financial managers are responsible for meeting expenses, investing in assets, and increasing profits to shareholders. Solid financial management is critical to the success of a business. The successful acquisition of Nest by Google could take place with only carefully planned financial management.

This chapter focuses on the finance function of organizations. It begins by describing the role of financial managers, their place in the organizational hierarchy, and the increasing importance of finance. Next, the financial planning process and the components of a financial plan are outlined. Then the discussion focuses on how organizations manage assets as efficiently and effectively as possible. The two major sources of funds—debt and equity—are then compared, and the concept of leverage is introduced. The major sources of short-term and long-term funding are described in the following sections. A description of mergers, acquisitions, buyouts, and divestitures concludes the chapter.

The Role of the Financial Manager

finance planning, obtaining, and managing a company's funds to accomplish its objectives as effectively and efficiently as possible.

financial managers executives who develop and implement the firm's financial plan and determine the most appropriate sources and uses of funds.

Because of the intense pressures they face today, organizations are increasingly measuring and reducing the costs of business operations, in an effort to maximize revenues and profits. This business function is called <u>finance</u>. As a result, <u>financial managers</u>—executives who develop and implement their firm's financial plan and determine the most appropriate sources and uses of funds—are among the most vital people within an organization.

Figure 17.1 shows what the finance function of a typical company might look like. At the top is the chief financial officer (CFO). The CFO usually reports directly to the company's chief executive officer (CEO) or chief operating officer (COO). In some companies, the CFO is also a member of the board of directors. In the case of the software maker Oracle, both the current CFO and the former CFO serve on that company's board, the latter as its chairman. Moreover, it's not uncommon for CFOs to serve as independent directors on other firms' boards, such as HP, Microsoft, and Target. As noted in Chapter 15, the CFO, along with the firm's CEO, must certify the accuracy of the firm's financial statements.

Reporting directly to the CFO are often three senior managers. Although titles can vary, these three executives are commonly called the *vice president for financial management* (or *planning*), the *treasurer*, and the *controller*. The vice president for financial management or planning is responsible for preparing financial forecasts and analyzing major investment decisions, such as new products, new production facilities, and acquisitions. The treasurer is responsible for all of the company's financing activities, including cash management, tax planning and preparation, and shareholder relations. The treasurer also works on the sale of new security issues to investors. The controller is the chief accounting manager. The controller's functions include keeping the company's books, preparing financial statements, and conducting internal audits. The "Hit & Miss" feature explains the importance of sound financial management and how a merger helped American Airlines and US Airways stay in business.

The growing importance of financial professionals is reflected in the growing number of CEOs who have been promoted from financial positions. Indra Nooyi, CEO of PepsiCo, and John Watson, CEO of Chevron, both served as their firm's CFO prior to assuming the top job. The importance of finance professionals is also reflected in how much CFOs earn today. According to a survey by the executive compensation consulting firm Equilar, the median annual salary for CFOs depends largely on the size of the company. For an S&P 500 firm, CFO median total compensation in a recent year was $3.1 million, up 5 percent from the previous year. For mid-cap and small-cap companies, the median CFO total compensation was $1.67 million and $987,219, respectively.[2]

In performing their jobs, financial professionals continually seek to balance risks with expected financial returns. Risk is the uncertainty of gain or loss; return is the gain or loss

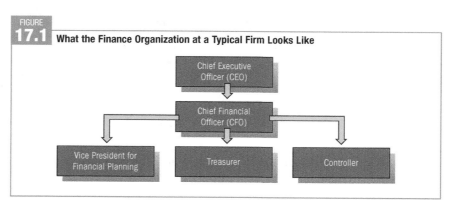

FIGURE 17.1 **What the Finance Organization at a Typical Firm Looks Like**

Hit&Miss

American Airlines and US Airways Merge

In an $11 billion transaction, US Airway's wish for a merger partner recently became a reality. As American Airlines emerged from bankruptcy, the two companies completed a deal to merge, becoming the world's largest airline.

Management at American knew it would be difficult to go it alone in this era of airline consolidation, especially after declaring bankruptcy. The merger involved a stock swap. Bondholders of the parent company of American Airlines now own 72 percent of the new company, and US Airways shareholders own the remaining 28 percent. Typically in airline restructurings, creditors receive pennies on the dollar and common shareholders are wiped out.

In less than a decade, mergers have taken place between Delta and Northwest, Continental and United, and Southwest and AirTran. Today, over 80 percent of the domestic capacity in the airline industry is held by the four airlines. As a result of anti-trust concerns about the merger, American had to give up 60 takeoff and landing gate slots at major U.S. airports. These highly coveted gates are now being eyed by competitors.

Questions for Critical Thinking

1. Typically, consumers view airline mergers in a negative way. Discuss some of the reasons why this might be the case.

2. The departing CEO of American Airlines had hoped to leave with a $20 million exit payment until a judge ruled the payment inappropriate. In a merger, how would you calculate a departing CEO's exit package?

Sources: Susan Carey and Jack Nicas, "American Airlines, US Airways Complete Merger," *The Wall Street Journal*, accessed March 22, 2014, http://online.wsj.com; Dan Burrows, "Mergers and Acquisitions—The 10 Biggest Deals of 2013," *Investorplace.com*, accessed March 22, 2014, http://investorplace.com; Christopher Elliot, "The American–US Airways Merger Promised Improvement. But Is It Delivering? *The Washington Post*, accessed March 22, 2014, www.washingtonpost.com.

---

that results from an investment over a specified period of time. Financial managers strive to maximize the wealth of their firm's shareholders by striking the optimal balance between risk and return. This balance is called the **risk-return trade-off**. For example, relying heavily on borrowed funds may increase the return (in the form of cash) to shareholders, but the more money a firm borrows, the greater the risks to shareholders. An increase in a firm's cash on hand reduces the risk of being unable to meet unexpected cash needs. However, because cash in and of itself does not earn much, if any, return, failure to invest surplus funds in an

risk-return trade-off
process of maximizing the wealth of a firm's shareholders by striking the optimal balance between risk and return.

Charly Diaz Azcue/LatinContent/Getty Images

Before committing to building the A380 jetliner, financial managers at Airbus had to weigh the potential profits for the company against the risk that the financial investment would not be a success. The plane entered commercial service a few years ago, and the company currently has more than 320 confirmed orders.

Chapter 17 *Financial Management*

493

income-earning asset—such as in securities—reduces a firm's potential return or profitability. Many illustrations of the risk-return trade-off are provided throughout this chapter.

Every financial manager must perform this risk-return balancing act. For example, in the late 1990s, Airbus wrestled with a major decision: whether to begin development and production of the giant A380 jetliner. The development costs for the aircraft—the world's largest jetliner—were initially estimated at more than $10 billion. Before committing to such a huge investment, financial managers had to analyze the potential profits of the A380 against the risk that the profits might not materialize. With its future on the line, Airbus decided to go ahead with the development of the A380, spending more than $15 billion on research and development. The A380 entered commercial service more than eight years ago. Airbus currently has more than 320 confirmed orders for the A380, and so far there are 135 aircraft in service with 10 operators, including Emirates, China Southern Airlines, Singapore Airlines, and British Airways.[3]

Financial managers must also learn to adapt to changes in the financial system. The recent credit crisis has made it more difficult for some companies to borrow money from traditional lenders such as banks. This, in turn, has forced firms to scale back expansion plans or seek funding from other sources such as commercial financing companies. In addition, financial managers must adapt to internal changes as well.

Assessment Check ☑

1. What is the structure of the finance function at a typical firm?
2. Explain the risk-return trade-off.

[2] Financial Planning

financial plan document that specifies the funds needed by a firm for a period of time, the timing of inflows and outflows, and the most appropriate sources and uses of funds.

Financial managers develop their organization's **financial plan**, a document that specifies the funds needed by a firm for a given period of time, the timing of inflows and outflows, and the most appropriate sources and uses of funds. Some financial plans, often called *operating plans*, are short-term in nature, focusing on projections no more than a year or two in the future. Other financial plans, sometimes referred to as *strategic plans*, have a much longer time horizon, perhaps up to five or ten years. For colleges selling so-called century bonds, the time period is unusually long, as the "Hit & Miss" feature describes.

Regardless of the time period, a financial plan is based on forecasts of production costs, purchasing needs, plant and equipment expenditures, and expected sales activities for the period covered. Financial managers use forecasts to determine the specific amounts and timing of expenditures and receipts. They build a financial plan based on the answers to three questions:

1. What funds will the firm require during the planning period?
2. When will it need additional funds?
3. Where will it obtain the necessary funds?

Some funds flow into the firm when it sells its goods or services, but funding needs vary. The financial plan must reflect both the amounts and timing of inflows and outflows of funds. Even a profitable firm may face a financial squeeze as a result of its need for funds when sales lag, when the volume of its credit sales increases, or when customers are slow in making payments.

In general, preparing a financial plan consists of three steps. The first is a forecast of sales or revenue over some future time period. This projection is, in fact, the key variable in any financial plan because without an accurate sales forecast, the firm will have difficulty accurately estimating other variables, such as production costs and purchasing needs. The best method of forecasting sales depends on the nature of the business. For instance, a retailer's CFO might begin with the current sales-per-store figure. Then he or she would look toward the near future, factoring in expected same-store sales growth, along with any planned store openings or closings, to come up with a forecast of sales for the next period. If the company sells merchandise through other channels, such as online, the forecast is adjusted to reflect those additional channels.

Hit&Miss

Colleges Sell Century Bonds

Would you lend your money out for 100 years? That's what pension funds, hedge funds, and life insurance companies are doing when they participate in the University of California's $860 million taxable "century bond" offering. In fact, demand for these bonds was so high that the university increased the size of the AA-rated issue, which was originally set for $500 million.

What makes these bonds so attractive? It's partly their higher-than-average return, substantially higher than 30-year Treasury bonds. Adding to the appeal is the stability of the university compared to other bond issuers. "Universities are among the longest-living institutions in the world," said a managing director from Moody's. "The top universities can be expected to be around 100 years from now, whereas many corporations and forms of government may not be."

The University of California is not alone. Massachusetts Institute of Technology, the University Southern California, Tufts University, and the California Institute of Technology have all issued multimillion-dollar bond offerings and plan to apply the proceeds to various projects at their campuses.

Of the bonds' popularity California's state treasurer said, "This deal was extremely well received by the market. We like the outcome."

Questions for Critical Thinking

1. One analyst called century bonds debt "that won't mature until well after everyone involved in the sale is dead." Why are they popular?

2. Do you agree that universities will outlive today's corporations? Why or why not?

Sources: Laura Mandaro, "California's 22nd Century Bond Sale," *Market Watch*, accessed April 2, 2014, http://blogs.marketwatch.com; Kelly Nolan and Patrick McGee, "2012: A Rush for Bonds from University of California System," *The Wall Street Journal*, accessed April 2, 2014, http://online.wsj.com; Michael Aneiro, "California Sells 100-Year 'Century' Bonds," *Barron's*, accessed April 2, 2014, http://blogs.barrons.com; university website, Taylor McNeil, "Tufts Sells Century Bonds for $250 Million," http://now.tufts.edu, accessed March 22, 2014.

Next, the CFO uses the sales forecast to determine the expected level of profits for future periods. This longer-term projection involves estimating expenses such as purchases, employee compensation, and taxes. Many expenses vary with a company's sales. For instance, the more a firm sells, generally the greater its purchases and its expenses. Along with estimating future profits, the CFO should also determine what portion of these profits will likely be paid to shareholders in the form of cash dividends.

After coming up with the sales and profit forecast, the CFO needs to estimate how many additional assets the firm will need to support projected sales. Increased sales, for example, might mean the company needs additional inventory, stepped-up collections for accounts receivable, or even new plant and equipment. Depending on the nature of the industry, some businesses need more assets than do other companies to support the same amount of sales. The technical term for this requirement is *asset intensity*. For instance, the chemical manufacturer DuPont has approximately $1.44 in assets for every dollar in sales. So for every $100 increase in sales, the firm would need about $144 of additional assets. The warehouse retailer Costco, by contrast, has only roughly $0.29 in assets for every dollar in sales. It would require an additional $29 of assets for every $100 of additional sales. This difference is not surprising; manufacturing is a more asset-intensive business than retailing.

A simplified financial plan illustrates these steps. Assume a growing company is forecasting that sales next year will increase by $40 million to $140 million. After estimating expenses, the CFO believes that after-tax profits next year will be $12 million and the firm will not pay dividends. The projected increase in sales next year will require the firm to invest another $20 million in assets, and because increases in assets are uses of funds, the company will need an additional $20 million in funds. The company's after-tax earnings will contribute $12 million, meaning that the other $8 million must come from outside sources. So the financial plan tells the CFO how much money will be needed and when it will be needed. Armed with this knowledge, and given that the firm has decided to borrow the needed funds, the CFO can then begin negotiations with banks and other lenders.

The cash inflows and outflows of a business are similar to those of a household. The members of a household depend on weekly or monthly paychecks for funds, but their expenditures vary greatly from one pay period to the next. The financial plan should indicate when the flows

Chapter 17 *Financial Management*

495

Justin Sullivan/Getty Images, Inc.

■ Costco has a lower *asset intensity* than a typical manufacturing business might have.

Assessment Check ☑

1. What three questions does a financial plan address?

2. Explain the steps involved in preparing a financial plan.

of funds entering and leaving the organization will occur and in what amounts. One of the most significant business expenses is employee compensation.

A good financial plan also includes financial control, a process of comparing actual revenues, costs, and expenses with forecasts. This comparison may reveal significant differences between projected and actual figures, so it is important to discover them early to take quick action.

Bill Morrison is the CFO of Pittsburgh-based Genco Marketplace, which liquidates, or sells off, other companies' excess inventory. Genco buys inventory that is not selling well, then resells it to wholesalers. In turn, the wholesalers sell the inventory to discount retailers. Always vigilant about the cost of freight, including fuel, Genco pays the transportation costs of taking the goods from their current location to where they will be liquidated. Some excess inventory is seasonal. When a retailer has winter coats left over in June, Genco will buy those coats, hold them in inventory, and sell them to a wholesaler in the fall, when demand rises again. But the longer a product remains unsold, the harder it will be to liquidate, even at a deep discount. In all cases, Morrison or members of his team have to prepare a financial plan that takes into account not only the benefits of buying the merchandise but the risks as well.[4]

⌐3⌐ Managing Assets

As we noted in Chapter 15, assets consist of what a firm owns. But assets also represent uses of funds. To grow and prosper, companies need to obtain additional assets. Sound financial management requires assets to be acquired and managed as effectively and efficiently as possible. The "Career Kickstart" feature offers tips for managing assets.

Short-Term Assets

Short-term, or current, assets consist of cash and assets that can be, or are expected to be, converted into cash within a year. The major current assets are cash, marketable securities, accounts receivable, and inventory.

Cash and Marketable Securities The major purpose of cash is to pay day-to-day expenses, much as when individuals maintain balances in checking accounts to pay bills or buy food and clothing. In addition, most organizations strive to maintain a minimum cash balance in order to have funds available in the event of unexpected expenses. As noted earlier, because cash earns little, if any, return, most firms invest excess cash in so-called *marketable securities*— low-risk securities that either have short maturities or can be easily sold in secondary markets. Money market instruments—described in Chapter 16— are popular choices for firms with excess cash. The cash budget, which we discussed in Chapter 15, is one tool for managing cash and marketable securities because it shows expected cash inflows and outflows for a period of time. The cash budget indicates months when the firm will have surplus cash and can invest in marketable securities and months when it will need additional cash.

Critics of some companies' budgeting practices contend that cash on hand has been rising for companies since the recent recession. Interestingly, four of the top five companies holding large amounts of cash are technology companies, including Apple, Microsoft, Google, and Cisco. These firms collectively possess more than $345 billion in cash reserves.[5] Some firms have reasons for holding large amounts of cash and marketable securities. For instance, some might plan on using these funds soon to make a large acquisition or pay dividends to shareholders.

Accounts Receivable Accounts receivable are uncollected credit sales and can represent a significant percentage of assets. The financial manager's job is to collect the funds owed the firm as quickly as possible while still offering sufficient credit to customers to generate increased sales. In general, a more liberal credit policy means higher sales but also increased collection expenses, higher levels of bad debt, and a higher investment in accounts receivable.

Management of accounts receivable is composed of two functions: determining an overall credit policy and deciding which customers will be offered credit. Formulating a credit policy involves deciding whether the firm will offer credit and, if so, on what terms. Will a discount be offered to customers who pay in cash? Often, the overall credit policy is dictated by competitive pressures or general industry practices. If all your competitors offer customers credit, your firm will likely have to as well. The other aspect of a credit policy is deciding which customers will be offered credit. Managers must consider the importance of the customer as well as its financial health and repayment history.

One simple tool for assessing how well receivables are being managed is calculating accounts receivable turnover over successive time periods. We showed how this ratio is calculated in Chapter 15. If receivables turnover shows signs of slowing, it means that the average credit customer is paying later. This trend warrants further investigation.

Inventory Management For many firms, such as retailers, inventory represents the largest single asset. At the home furnishings retailer Bed Bath & Beyond, inventory makes up about 39 percent of total assets. Even for nonretailers, inventory is an important asset. At the heavy-equipment manufacturer Caterpillar, inventory is almost 15 percent of total assets. On

At Bed Bath & Beyond, inventory is the most valuable asset. Managing inventory can be a costly and highly complex undertaking, particularly for retailers that carry thousands of unique products.

the other hand, some types of firms, such as electric utilities and transportation companies, have no inventory. For the majority of firms, which do carry inventory, proper management of it is vital.

Managing inventory can be complex. The cost of inventory includes more than just the acquisition cost. It also includes the cost of ordering, storing, insuring, and financing inventory, as well as the cost of stockouts, lost sales due to insufficient inventory. Financial managers try to minimize the cost of inventory. But production, marketing, and logistics also play important roles in determining proper inventory levels. Because of its close-knit relationship with suppliers, Nordstrom's inventory management is superior to competitors. The company provides data to suppliers to ensure minimum sales levels that allows the best pricing. As a result, Nordstrom can obtain merchandise that is in strong demand before competitors do.

Trends in the inventory turnover ratio—described in Chapter 15—can be early warning signs of impending trouble. For instance, if inventory turnover has been slowing for several consecutive quarters, it indicates that inventory is increasing faster than sales. In turn, this may suggest that customer demand is softening and the firm needs to take action, such as reducing production or increasing promotional efforts.

Capital Investment Analysis

In addition to current assets, firms also invest in long-lived assets. Unlike current assets, long-lived assets are expected to produce economic benefits for more than one year. These investments often involve substantial amounts of money. For example, as noted earlier in the chapter, Airbus invested more than $15 billion in development of the A380. In another example, auto manufacturer BMW recently announced it would spend an additional $1 billion over the next several years to expand its production facility in Spartanburg, South Carolina, to produce a new, large sport utility vehicle with three rows of seats, the X7. This brings the company's total investment in the state to over $7 billion.[6]

The process by which decisions are made regarding investments in long-lived assets is called *capital investment analysis*. Firms make two basic types of capital investment decisions: expansion and replacement. The A380 and the BMW South Carolina plant investments are examples of expansion decisions. Replacement decisions involve upgrading assets by acquiring new ones. A retailer might decide to replace an old store with a new Supercenter, as Walmart did in Oxford, Ohio.

Financial managers must estimate all of the costs and benefits of a proposed investment, which can be quite difficult, especially for very long-lived investments. Only those investments that offer an acceptable return—measured by the difference between benefits and costs—should be undertaken. BMW's financial managers believe that the benefits of continuing to expand the South Carolina production facility outweigh the significant cost. Through a series of expansions, BMW has outpaced its rivals, Audi and Mercedes, as the world's top-selling brand. Built more than 20 years ago, BMW's Spartanburg facility produces the X3, X4, and X5 SUVs and exports over half of the vehicles from its Spartanburg assembly lines. The expected profit from the sales of these models has certainly been considered in the company's expansion decision. Some other expansion benefits cited by BMW include lower production costs due to favorable exchange rates, improved logistics, and expanded use of renewable energy. The Spartanburg facility to date has produced over 2.5 million vehicles and continues to emphasize its commitment to the U.S. market.[7]

Managing International Assets

Today, firms often have assets worldwide. Both McDonald's and The Coca-Cola Company generate more than half of their annual sales outside the United States. The vast majority of sales for Unilever and Nestlé occur outside their home countries (the Netherlands and Switzerland, respectively). Managing international assets creates several challenges for the financial manager, one of the most important of which is the issue of exchange rates.

As we discussed in several other chapters, an exchange rate is the rate at which one currency can be exchanged for another. Exchange rates can vary substantially from year to year, creating a problem for any company with international assets. As an example, assume a U.S. firm has a major subsidiary in the United Kingdom. Assume that the U.K. subsidiary earns an annual profit of £750 million (stated in British pounds). Over the past five years, the exchange rate between the U.S. dollar and the British pound has remained steady between 1.56 (dollars per pound) and 1.60.[8] This means the dollar value of the U.K. profits ranged from $705 million to $720 million.

Consequently, many global firms engage in activities that reduce the risks associated with exchange rate fluctuations. Some are quite complicated. However, one of the simplest and most widely used is called a *balance sheet hedge*. Essentially, a balance sheet hedge creates an offsetting liability to the non-dollar-denominated asset, one that is denominated in the same currency as the asset. In our example, the U.K. subsidiary is a pound-denominated asset. To create an offsetting liability, the firm could take out a loan, denominated in British pounds, creating a pound-denominated liability. If done correctly, this hedge will reduce or even eliminate the risk associated with changes in the value of the dollar relative to the pound. This will improve the financial performance of the firm, which can have a positive impact on its stock price.

Assessment Check ✅

1. Why do firms often choose to invest excess cash in marketable securities?

2. What are the two aspects of accounts receivable management?

3. Explain the difference between an expansion decision and a replacement decision.

[4] Sources of Funds and Capital Structure

The use of debt for financing can increase the potential for return as well as increase loss potential. Recall the accounting equation introduced in Chapter 15:

$$\text{Assets} = \text{Liabilities} + \text{Owners' equity}$$

If you view this equation from a financial management perspective, it reveals that there are only two types of funding: debt and equity. *Debt capital* consists of funds obtained through borrowing. *Equity capital* consists of funds provided by the firm's owners when they reinvest earnings, make additional contributions, liquidate assets, issue stock to the general public, or raise capital from outside investors. The mix of a firm's debt and equity capital is known as its capital structure.

Companies often take very different approaches to choosing a capital structure. As more debt is used, the risk to the company increases since the firm is now obligated to make the interest payments on the money borrowed, regardless of the cash flows coming into or going out of the company. Choosing more debt increases the fixed costs a company must pay, which in turn makes a company more sensitive to changing sales revenues. Debt is frequently the least costly method of raising additional financing dollars, one of the reasons it is so frequently used.

Differing industries choose varying amounts of debt and equity to use when financing. Using the information provided by Datamonitor, we find that the automotive industry has debt ratios (the ratio of liabilities to assets) of over 60 percent for both Toyota and Honda and over 85 percent for Ford. These companies are primarily using debt to finance their asset expenditures. Food-service companies such as McDonald's and Chipotle use only 56 percent debt and 29 percent debt, respectively. The combination of debt and equity a company chooses is a major management decision.

capital structure mix of a firm's debt and equity capital.

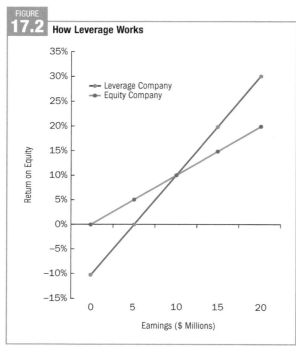

FIGURE 17.2 How Leverage Works

Note: The example assumes that both companies have $100 million in capital. Leverage Company consists of $50 million in equity and $50 million in bonds (with an interest rate of 10 percent). Equity Company consists of $100 million in equity and no bonds. This example also assumes no corporate taxes.

leverage increasing the rate of return on funds invested by borrowing funds.

Leverage and Capital Structure Decisions

Raising needed cash by borrowing allows a firm to benefit from the principle of **leverage**, increasing the rate of return on funds invested by borrowing funds. The key to managing leverage is to ensure that a company's earnings remain larger than its interest payments, which increases the leverage on the rate of return on shareholders' investment. Of course, if the company earns less than its interest payments, shareholders lose money on their original investments.

Figure 17.2 shows the relationship between earnings and shareholder returns for two identical hypothetical firms that choose to raise funds in different ways. Leverage Company obtains 50 percent of its funds from lenders who purchase company bonds. Leverage Company pays 10 percent interest on its bonds. Equity Company raises all of its funds through sales of company stock.

Notice that if earnings double, from, say, $10 million to $20 million, returns to shareholders of Equity Company also double—from 10 percent to 20 percent. But returns to shareholders of Leverage Company more than double—from 10 percent to 30 percent. However, leverage works in the opposite direction as well. If earnings fall from $10 million to $5 million, a decline of 50 percent, returns to shareholders of Equity Company also fall by 50 percent—from 10 percent to 5 percent. By contrast, returns to shareholders of Leverage Company fall from 10 percent to zero. Thus, leverage increases potential returns to shareholders but also increases risk.

Another concern with borrowing money is that an over-reliance on borrowed funds may reduce management's flexibility in future financing decisions. If a company raises equity capital this year and needs to raise funds next year, it will probably be able to raise either debt or equity capital. But if it raises debt capital this year, it may be forced to raise equity capital next year.

Equity capital has drawbacks as well. Because shareholders are owners of the company, they usually have the right to vote on major company issues and elect the board of directors. Whenever new equity is sold, the control of existing shareholders is diluted, and the outcome of these votes could potentially change. One contentious subject today between companies and shareholders is whether shareholders should be able to vote on executive pay packages.

Another disadvantage of equity capital is that it is more expensive than debt capital. First, creditors have a senior claim to the assets of a firm relative to shareholders. Because of this advantage, creditors are willing to accept a lower rate of return than shareholders are. Second, the firm can deduct interest payments on debt, reducing its taxable income and tax bill. Dividends paid to shareholders, on the other hand, are not tax deductible. A key component of the financial manager's job is to weigh the advantages and disadvantages of debt capital and equity capital, creating the most appropriate capital structure for his or her firm.

Mixing Short-Term and Long-Term Funds

Another decision financial managers face is determining the appropriate mix of short-and long-term funds. Short-term funds consist of current liabilities, and long-term funds consist of long-term debt and equity. Short-term funds are generally less expensive than long-term funds,

500   **Part 6** *Managing Financial Resources*

but they also expose the firm to more risk. This is because short-term funds have to be renewed, or rolled over, frequently. Short-term interest rates can be volatile. During a recent 12-month period, for example, rates on commercial paper, a popular short-term financing option, ranged from a high of 11 percent (for 90-day loans) to a low of 6 percent (for 1-day loans).[9]

Because short-term rates move up and down frequently, interest expense on short-term funds can change substantially from year to year. For instance, if a firm borrows $50 million for ten years at 5 percent interest, its annual interest expense is fixed at $2.5 million for the entire ten years. On the other hand, if it borrows $50 million for one year at a rate of 4 percent, its annual interest expense of $2 million is only fixed for that year. If interest rates increase the following year to 6 percent, $1 million will be added to the interest expense bill. Another potential risk of relying on short-term funds is availability. Even financially healthy firms can occasionally find it difficult to borrow money.

Because of the added risk of short-term funding, most firms choose to finance all of their long-term assets, and even a portion of their short-term assets, with long-term funds. Johnson & Johnson is typical of this choice. Figure 17.3 shows a recent balance sheet broken down between short- and long-term assets, and short- and long-term funds.

Dividend Policy

Along with decisions regarding capital structure and the mix of short- and long-term funds, financial managers also make decisions regarding a firm's dividend policy. *Dividends* are periodic cash payments to shareholders. The most common type of dividend is paid quarterly and is often labeled as a *regular dividend*. Occasionally, firms make one-time special or extra dividend payments, as Microsoft did some years ago. Earnings that are paid in dividends are not reinvested in the firm and don't contribute additional equity capital.

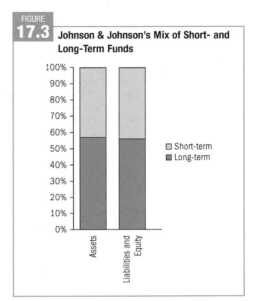

FIGURE 17.3 Johnson & Johnson's Mix of Short- and Long-Term Funds

Source: Johnson & Johnson balance sheet, Yahoo! Finance, http://finance.yahoo.com, accessed March 23, 2014.

Companies are under no legal obligation to pay dividends to their shareholders. However, some companies pay dividends every year, while others pay dividends on a not-so-regular basis. Apple started paying dividends to shareholders several years ago.

Solving an Ethical Controversy

Are Dividends Necessary?

Google, Amazon, Gilead Sciences, eBay, and Salesforce.com all have corporate policies of *not* paying dividends to shareholders. When the S&P tumbled during the recent recession, some companies tightened their purse strings to prepare for possible difficult times ahead by suspending dividends previously in place for years. These companies, in an effort to be competitive in a fierce technology sector through growth initiatives, remain intent on keeping cash on hand. Many argue that companies should share their profits—and more generously than the current S&P aggregate payout ratio of 31.8 percent.

Should successful corporations pay or increase dividends to shareholders?

PRO

1. Shareholders expect a return on their investments, making dividends only fair to the company's real owners.

2. Nearly 84 percent of Standard & Poor's 500 companies pay dividends. The remaining 16 percent should do likewise.

CON

1. Companies should hold their cash in reserve for contingencies so they can respond quickly and flexibly.

2. Earnings reinvested in R&D, for instance, make the company stronger and increase the value of its shares.

Summary

Dividend payouts today are increasing at a growing rate, and more companies are paying investors dividends, even tech companies that have historically held on to their cash. Recently, Apple announced that it would pay dividends to shareholders in the near future—at a cost of more than $10 billion a year for the next three years.

Sources: "Factset Dividend Quarterly," *Factset*, accessed March 22, 2014, www.factset.com; David Sterman, "The Biggest Companies That Don't Pay Dividends—But May Be About To," *Yahoo Finance*, accessed March 22, 2014, http://finance.yahoo.com; Ron DeLegge, "Dividend Payout Ratios Reach 15-Year High," *Yahoo Finance*, accessed March 22, 2014, http://finance.yahoo.com; "How and Why Do Companies Pay Dividends?" *Investopedia*, accessed March 22, 2014, www.investopedia.com.

Assessment Check ☑

1. Explain the concept of leverage.

2. Why do firms generally rely more on long-term funds than short-term funds?

3. What is an important determinant of a firm's dividend policy?

Firms are under no legal obligation to pay dividends to shareholders. Although some companies pay generous dividends, others pay nothing. Until 2010, Starbucks never paid a dividend to its shareholders, and Apple recently announced it would pay its first dividend in nearly 20 years. See the "Solving an Ethical Controversy" feature for some pros and cons of such decisions for investors. In contrast, 3M has paid dividends for over 30 consecutive years, during which time the amount has more than quadrupled. Companies that pay dividends try to increase them or at the very least hold them steady from year to year. However, in rare cases firms must cut or eliminate dividends. For the first time in nearly 20 years, phone maker Nokia announced that it would eliminate its dividend in an effort to strengthen its cash position.[10]

Many factors determine a company's dividend policy, one of which is its investment opportunities. If a firm has numerous investment opportunities and wishes to finance some or all of them with equity funding, it will likely pay little, if any, of its earnings in dividends. Shareholders may actually want the company to retain earnings, because if they are reinvested, the firm's future profits, and the value of its shares, will increase faster. By contrast, a firm with more limited investment opportunities generally pays more of its earnings in dividends.

In addition to dividends, some firms buy back a portion of their outstanding stock. Apple recently repurchased shares of its own stock and increased its current dividend in an effort to appeal to investors.[11] Generally, shares are purchased on the secondary markets. The main purpose of share buy-backs is to raise the market value of the remaining shares, thus benefiting shareholders.

502

Short-Term Funding Options

Many times throughout a year, an organization may discover that its cash needs exceed its available funds. Retailers generate surplus cash for most of the year, but they need to build up inventory during the late summer and fall to get ready for the holiday shopping season. Consequently, they often need funds to pay for merchandise until holiday sales generate revenue. Then they use the incoming funds to repay the amount they borrowed. In these instances, financial managers evaluate short-term sources of funds. By definition, short-term sources of funds are repaid within one year. Three major sources of short-term funds exist: trade credit, short-term loans, and commercial paper. Large firms often rely on a combination of all three sources of short-term financing.

Trade Credit

Trade credit is extended by suppliers when a firm receives goods or services, agreeing to pay for them at a later date. Trade credit is common in many industries such as retailing and manufacturing. Suppliers routinely ship billions of dollars of merchandise to retailers each day and are paid at a later date. Without trade credit, the retailing sector would probably look much different—with fewer selections. Under this system, the supplier records the transactions as an account receivable, and the retailer records it as an account payable. Target alone currently has more than $6.7 billion of accounts payable on its books. The main advantage of trade credit is its easy availability because credit sales are common in many industries. The main drawback to trade credit is that the amount a company can borrow is limited to the amount it purchases.

What is the cost of trade credit? If suppliers do not offer a cash discount, trade credit is effectively free. For example, assume a supplier offers trade credit under the terms net 30—meaning that the buyer has 30 days to pay. This is similar to borrowing $100 and repaying $100 in 30 days. The effective rate of interest is zero. However, some suppliers offer a discount if they are paid in cash. If a discount is offered, trade credit can get quite expensive. Now assume that a 2 percent discount is offered to cash buyers. If they do not take the discount, they have 30 days to pay. Essentially, then, if the buyer doesn't pay cash, it is borrowing $98 today and repaying $100 30 days from today. The annual interest rate on such a loan exceeds 24 percent.

Short-Term Loans

Loans from commercial banks are a significant source of short-term financing for businesses. Often businesses whose sales fluctuate on a seasonal basis use these loans to finance inventory and accounts receivable. For example, late fall and early winter is the period of highest sales for a small manufacturer of ski equipment. To meet this demand, it has to begin building inventory during the summer. The manufacturer also has to finance accounts receivable (credit sales to customers) during the fall and winter. So it takes out a bank loan during the summer. As the inventory is sold and accounts receivable collected, the firm repays the loan.

There are two types of short-term bank loans: lines of credit and revolving credit agreements. A line of credit specifies the maximum amount the firm can borrow over a period of time, usually a year. The bank is under no obligation actually to lend the money, however. It does so only if funds are available. Most lines of credit require the borrower to repay the original amount, plus interest, within one year. By contrast, a revolving credit agreement is essentially a guaranteed line of credit—the bank guarantees that the funds will be available when needed. Banks typically charge a fee, on top of interest, for revolving credit agreements.

The cash budget is an important tool for determining the size of a line of credit because it shows the months when additional financing will be needed or when borrowed funds can

Chapter 17 *Financial Management*   **503**

be repaid. For instance, assume the ski manufacturer's cash budget indicates that it will need $2.5 million for the June through November period. The financial manager might set up a line of credit with the bank for $2.8 million. The extra $300,000 is a cushion for any unexpected cash outflows.

In addition to commercial banks, commercial finance companies also make short-term loans to businesses. Although most bank loans are unsecured, meaning that no specific assets are pledged as collateral, loans from commercial finance companies are often secured with accounts receivable or inventory.

Another form of short-term financing backed by accounts receivable is called *factoring*. The business sells its accounts receivable to either a bank or finance company—called a *factor*—at a discount. The size of the discount determines the cost of the transaction. Factoring allows the firm to convert its receivables into cash quickly without worrying about collections.

The cost of short-term loans depends not only on the interest rate but also on the fees charged by the lender. In addition to fees, some lenders require the borrower to keep so-called *compensating balances*—5 to 20 percent of the outstanding loan amount—in a checking account. Compensating balances increase the effective cost of a loan, because the borrower doesn't have full use of the amount borrowed.

Say, for example, that a firm borrows $100,000 for one year at 5 percent interest. The borrower will pay $5,000 in interest (5 percent × $100,000). If the lender requires that 10 percent of the loan amount be kept as a compensating balance, the firm has use of only $90,000. However, because it still will pay $5,000 in interest, the effective rate on the loan is actually 5.56 percent ($5,000 divided by $90,000).

Commercial Paper

Commercial paper is a short-term IOU sold by a company; this concept was briefly described in Chapter 16. Commercial paper is typically sold in multiples of $100,000 to $1 million and has a maturity that ranges from 1 to 270 days. Most commercial paper is unsecured. It is an attractive source of financing because large amounts of money can be raised at rates that are typically 1 to 2 percent less that those charged by banks. At the end of a recent year, almost $1.05 trillion in commercial paper was outstanding.[12] Although commercial paper is an attractive short-term financing alternative, only a small percentage of businesses can issue it. That is because access to the commercial paper market has traditionally been restricted to large, financially strong corporations.

[6]
Sources of Long-Term Financing

Funds from short-term sources can help a firm meet current needs for cash or inventory. A larger project or plan, however, such as acquiring another company or making a major investment in real estate or equipment, usually requires funds for a much longer period of time. Unlike short-term sources, long-term sources are repaid over many years.

Organizations acquire long-term funds from three sources. One is long-term loans obtained from financial institutions such as commercial banks, life insurance companies, and pension funds. A second source is bonds—certificates of indebtedness—sold to investors. A third source is equity financing that is acquired by selling stock in the firm or reinvesting company profits.

Public Sale of Stocks and Bonds

Public sales of securities such as stocks and bonds are a major source of funds for corporations. Such sales provide cash inflows for the issuing firm and either a share in its ownership (for a stock purchaser) or a specified rate of interest and repayment at a stated time (for a bond purchaser). Because stock and bond issues of many corporations are traded in the secondary markets, stockholders and bondholders can easily sell these securities. Financial healing seems to be under way for Greece. Once a threat to the breakup of the euro, the European Union's bailout of Greece sent ripples through world markets. In the first public bond sale by a Greek lender since the crisis, A Piraeus Bank SA (TPEIR) recently sold $697 million of bonds (U.S. value).[13] Public sales of securities, however, can vary substantially from year to year depending on conditions in the financial markets. Bond sales, for instance, tend to be higher when interest rates are lower.

In Chapter 16, we discussed the process by which most companies sell securities publicly—through investment bankers via a process called *underwriting*. Investment bankers purchase the securities from the issuer and then resell them to investors. The issuer pays a fee to the investment banker, called an *underwriting discount*.

Private Placements

Some new stock or bond issues are not sold publicly but instead to a small group of major investors such as pension funds and insurance companies. These sales are referred to as *private placements*. Most private placements involve corporate debt securities. More than $1.4 trillion in corporate bonds were sold privately in a recent year in the United States.[14]

It is often less expensive for a company to sell a security privately than publicly, and there is less government regulation with which to contend because SEC registration is not required. Institutional investors such as insurance companies and pension funds buy private placements because they typically carry slightly higher interest rates than publicly issued bonds. In addition, the terms of the issue can be tailored to meet the specific needs of both the issuer and the institutional investors. Of course, the institutional investor gives up liquidity because privately placed securities do not trade in secondary markets.

Venture Capitalists

Venture capitalists are an important source of long-term financing, especially to new companies. **Venture capitalists** raise money from wealthy individuals and institutional investors and invest these funds in promising firms. Venture capitalists also provide management consulting advice as well as funds. In exchange for their investment, venture capitalists become part owners of the business. If the business succeeds, venture capitalists can earn substantial profits.

One of the largest venture capital firms is Draper Fisher Jurvetson, based in Menlo Park, California. During the past 20 years, DFJ has invested in hundreds of small start-ups including Hotmail (acquired by Microsoft) and Twitter. Other firms in its $7 billion portfolio are Tesla, Box, Meetup, Bright Source Energy, SpaceX, and Tumbleweed.[15]

venture capitalists person or entity that raises money from wealthy individuals and institutional investors and invests the funds in promising firms.

Private Equity Funds

Similar to venture capitalists, *private equity funds* are investment companies that raise funds from wealthy individuals and institutional investors and use those funds to make large investments in both public and privately held companies. Unlike venture capital funds, which tend to focus on small, start-up companies, private equity funds invest in all types of businesses, including mature ones. For example, 3G Capital, a Brazilian private equity firm, is best known for its acquisition of consumer and retail brands like Burger King. Recently, in conjunction with Berkshire Hathaway, 3G paid $28 billion to

Draper Fisher Jurvetson, one of the largest venture capital firms in the country, has invested in many small start-up companies, including Twitter.

GoingGreen

College Students Invest Responsibly

Colleges and universities control billions of dollars in endowment funds—money or other assets donated to them. Some schools, including Yale University, are giving students hands-on investment experience with money from these endowments.

Almost a decade ago, the Dwight Hall organization at Yale University launched the first socially responsible investment fund run by undergraduates. Initially started with $50,000 of the organization's endowment, the Dwight Hall Socially Responsible Investment Fund (DHSRI) is managed by a team of 20 college students.

DHSRI uses traditional methods of investing but avoids investing in companies that sell or produce tobacco and alcohol or businesses associated with gambling. Instead, the fund seeks out companies engaged in environmental sustainability and clean energy efforts. It invests in mutual funds, exchange-traded funds, real estate investment trusts, and local community development banks.

Providing students with this experience gives them an opportunity to experience hands-on investing and to understand the connections between business and society. Students are given the chance to apply financial theory to hands-on decision making and invest in companies that are responsible corporate citizens.

Questions for Critical Thinking

1. What are the costs and benefits of a socially responsible approach to investing?

2. As a socially responsible investor, what type of investments would you choose? What type would you avoid?

Sources: Organization website, http://dwighthall.org, accessed April 9, 2014; organization website, "About Us," www.dwighthallsri.org, accessed April 9, 2014; university website, Cara Masset, "Socially Responsible Investment Club at University of Pittsburgh to Begin Managing $100,000 Portfolio," www.news.pitt.edu, accessed April 9, 2014; Janet Brown, "Sustainable, Responsible Investing Can Be Profitable, Here's How," *Forbes*, accessed April 9, 2014, www.forbes.com.

---

purchase ketchup maker H.J. Heinz.[16] A variety of different funds, including money market funds and exchange-traded funds, have become increasingly important for socially responsible investors. See the "Going Green" feature to learn more. Often private equity funds invest in transactions to take public companies private or conduct leveraged buyouts (LBOs). In these transactions, discussed in more detail in the next section, a public company reverts to private status.

A variation of the private equity fund is the so-called *sovereign wealth fund*. These companies are owned by governments and invest in a variety of financial and real assets, such as real estate. Although sovereign wealth funds generally make investments based on the best risk-return trade-off, political, social, and strategic considerations also play roles in their investment decisions.

Norway's Government Pension Fund—Global—is the world's largest sovereign wealth fund, valued in excess of $878 billion. Because of the fund's most recent growth of $115 billion in U.S. dollars, it was required to reduce its equity holdings to comply with risk mandates of portfolio limits of 64 percent in equities. In a recent year, the return for the fund was close to 16 percent.[17] The assets of the 10 largest sovereign wealth funds are shown in Figure 17.4. Together, these 10 funds have almost $5 trillion in assets.

Hedge Funds

Hedge funds are private investment companies open only to qualified large investors. In recent years, hedge funds have become a significant presence in U.S. financial markets. Before the recent recession, some analysts estimated that hedge funds accounted for about 60 percent of all secondary bond market trading and around one-third of all activity on stock exchanges. For the last several years, hedge funds have fallen behind the S&P 500 Index by 23 percentage points. The average return in a recent year was 7.4 percent.[18] Hedge funds are estimated to have total assets that exceed $2.6 trillion.[19] Unlike mutual funds, hedge funds are not regulated by the SEC. Traditionally, hedge funds, unlike venture capitalists and private equity funds, did not make direct investments in companies, preferring instead to purchase existing stock and bond issues.

Assessment Check ☑

1. What is the most common type of security sold privately?

2. Describe venture capitalists.

3. What is a sovereign wealth fund?

506   Part 6 *Managing Financial Resources*

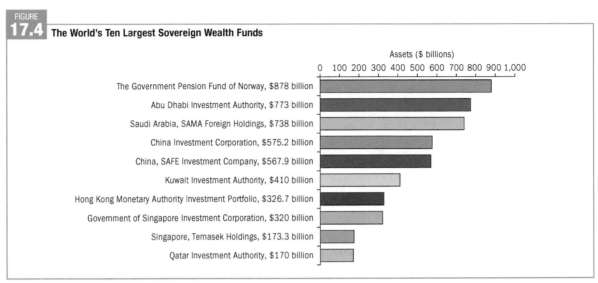

FIGURE 17.4 The World's Ten Largest Sovereign Wealth Funds

Assets ($ billions)

The Government Pension Fund of Norway, $878 billion

Abu Dhabi Investment Authority, $773 billion

Saudi Arabia, SAMA Foreign Holdings, $738 billion

China Investment Corporation, $575.2 billion

China, SAFE Investment Company, $567.9 billion

Kuwait Investment Authority, $410 billion

Hong Kong Monetary Authority Investment Portfolio, $326.7 billion

Government of Singapore Investment Corporation, $320 billion

Singapore, Temasek Holdings, $173.3 billion

Qatar Investment Authority, $170 billion

Source: Sovereign Wealth Fund Institute, "Sovereign Wealth Fund Rankings," http://www.swfinstitute.org, accessed July 6, 2014.

7 Mergers, Acquisitions, Buyouts, and Divestitures

Chapter 5 briefly described mergers and acquisitions. A merger is a transaction in which two or more firms combine into one company. In an acquisition, one firm buys the assets and assumes the obligations of another firm. Chapter 5 also listed the classifications of mergers and acquisitions—vertical, horizontal, and conglomerate—and noted that many of these transactions involve large sums of money. An example is Facebook's acquisition of WhatsApp, a mobile messaging app for $19 billion, and Oculus VR, a maker of virtual reality goggles, for $2 billion.[20] In this section, we focus on the financial implications of not only mergers and acquisitions but also buyouts and divestitures.

Note that even in a merger, there is a buyer and seller. The seller is often referred to as the *target*. Financial managers evaluate a proposed merger or acquisition in much the same way they would evaluate any large investment—by comparing the costs and benefits. To acquire a company, a firm typically offers a higher price than the current market price for the target's shares. The action usually triggers a fluctuation in the stock prices of both firms. When the Walt Disney Company purchased Marvel Entertainment for $4.6 billion, the deal was priced to include a mix of cash and stock. Marvel shareholders received a 29 percent per-share premium that included $30 per share in cash plus approximately three-quarters of a Disney share for each share of Marvel. The value of the deal was affected by the fluctuating closing price of Disney stock on the day of the acquisition.[21]

When the buyer makes what is known as a **tender offer** for the target's shares, it specifies a price and the form of payment. The buyer can offer cash, securities, or a combination of the two, as Disney did when it purchased Marvel. The tender offer can be friendly, meaning it is endorsed by the target firm's board of directors, or unfriendly. Shareholders of both the buyer and target must vote to approve a merger.

Justifying such a premium requires the financial manager also to estimate the benefits of a proposed merger. These benefits could take the form of cost savings from economies

tender offer offer made by a firm to the target firm's shareholders specifying a price and the form of payment.

of scale or reduced workforces or the buyer getting a bargain price for the target's assets. Sometimes, a buyer finds that the most cost-effective method of entering a new market is simply to buy an existing company that serves the market. Johnson & Johnson has a long history of making such acquisitions. When it decided to enter the contact lens market, Johnson & Johnson bought Vistakon, the firm that invented disposable contact lenses under the brand name Acuvue. The term used to describe the benefits produced by a merger or acquisition is *synergy*—the notion that the combined firm is worth more than the buyer and the target are individually.

Leveraged buyouts, or LBOs, were briefly introduced in the preceding section. In an LBO, public shareholders are bought out, and the firm reverts to private status. The term *leverage* comes from the fact that many of these transactions are financed with high degrees of debt—often in excess of 75 percent. Private equity companies and hedge funds provide equity and debt financing for many LBOs. The firm's incumbent senior management is often part of the buyout group. LBO activity decreased sharply with the recent economic downturn. As the economy began to recover, LBO activity increased again. But with the European debt crisis and the weak U.S. economy, LBO financing costs rose once more. According to Standard & Poor's, LBO activity has surged once again, mainly due to jumbo deals like Dell ($25 billion) and Heinz ($28 billion). Several other LBO transactions have taken place recently, each worth more than $4 billion, and LBO volume has doubled over the last several years.[22]

Why do so many LBOs occur? One reason is that private companies enjoy benefits that public companies do not. Private companies are not required to publish financial results, are subject to less SEC oversight, and are not pressured to produce the short-term profits often demanded by Wall Street. Some argue that LBOs, because of the high degree of debt, enforce more discipline on management to control costs. Although LBOs do have advantages, history has shown that many companies that go private reemerge as public companies several years later.

In a sense, a **divestiture** is the reverse of a merger. That is, a company sells assets such as subsidiaries, product lines, or production facilities. Two types of divestitures exist: sell-offs and spin-offs. In a *sell-off*, assets are sold by one firm to another. Google recently sold off its Motorola business to China's Lenovo Group for almost $3 billion, taking the search giant out of the business of manufacturing smart phones.[23]

The other type of divestiture is a *spin-off*. In this transaction, the assets sold form a new firm. Shareholders of the divesting firm become shareholders of the new firm as well. More than a decade ago, Sara Lee Corporation, known mostly for its frozen baked goods, spun off leather handbag manufacturer Coach Inc. In what seemed like an unlikely coupling at the time, Sara Lee justified the $140 million stock sale by saying it wanted to focus more on brands that were market leaders that could be sold globally. Today, as a separate entity, Coach is one of the world's most valuable brands, with recent annual sales topping $5 billion. Several years ago, Sara Lee split into two companies: Hillshire Brands and a European-based coffee and tea company called D.E. Master Blenders 1753.[24]

Firms divest assets for several reasons. Sometimes divestitures result from prior acquisitions that didn't work out as well as expected. In early 2001, America Online and Time Warner merged to create AOL Time Warner, Inc. Nine years later, Time Warner announced it would spin off AOL. The merger—now considered one of the worst mistakes in corporate history—failed to generate the much-heralded synergies between the two companies. Shortly after the merger, AOL had 27 million subscribers; more recently, that number had shrunk to about 2.5 million.

In other cases, a firm makes a strategic decision to concentrate on its core businesses and decides to divest anything that falls outside this core. Newmont Mining Corporation, a Colorado–based producer of gold and copper, announced it would divest its 5.4 percent equity stake in Paladin Energy for $24 million in cash. A company official said the firm evaluates its various holdings on a regular basis and from time to time divests some of its equity positions when financial conditions are favorable.[25]

leveraged buyouts (LBO) transaction in which public shareholders are bought out and the firm reverts to private status.

divestiture sale of assets by a firm.

Assessment Check ☑

1. Define *synergy*.
2. What is an LBO?
3. What are the two types of divestitures?

508

What's Ahead

Contemporary Business concludes with five appendixes. Appendix A, "Business Law," outlines the main legal issues concerning business. It reviews the types of laws, the regulatory environment of business, and the core of business law, including discussions of contract law and property law. Appendix B examines risk management and insurance. It describes the concept of risk, alternative ways of dealing with risk, and the various kinds of insurance available to business and individuals. Appendix C discusses some of the important components of personal financial planning, such as budgeting, credit, and retirement planning. Appendix D describes how to write an effective business plan, and Appendix E discusses career searches and options to help you prepare for your future in business.

Chapter in Review

▮ Summary of Learning Objectives

⌐1⌐ Define the role of the financial manager.

Finance deals with planning, obtaining, and managing a company's funds to accomplish its objectives efficiently and effectively. The major responsibilities of financial managers are to develop and implement financial plans and determine the most appropriate sources and uses of funds. The chief financial officer (CFO) heads a firm's finance organization. Three senior executives reporting to the CFO are the vice president for financial management, the treasurer, and the controller. When making decisions, financial professionals continually seek to balance risks with expected financial returns.

Assessment Check Answers ✔

1.1 What is the structure of the finance function at a typical firm? The person in charge of the finance function of a firm has the title of chief financial officer (CFO) and generally reports directly to the firm's chief executive officer. Reporting to the CFO are the treasurer, the controller, and the vice president for financial management.

1.2 Explain the risk-return trade-off. Financial managers strive to maximize the wealth of their firm's shareholders by striking the optimal balance between risk and return.

⌐2⌐ Describe financial planning.

A financial plan is a document that specifies the funds needed by a firm for a given period of time, the timing of inflows and outflows, and the most appropriate sources and uses of funds. The financial plan addresses three questions: What funds will be required during the planning period? When will funds be needed? Where will funds be obtained? Three steps are involved in the financial planning process: forecasting sales

over a future period of time, estimating the expected level of profits over the planning period, and determining the additional assets needed to support additional sales.

Assessment Check Answers ✔

2.1 What three questions does a financial plan address? The financial plan addresses three questions: What funds will be required during the planning period? When will funds be needed? Where will the necessary funds be obtained?

2.2 Explain the steps involved in preparing a financial plan. The first step is to forecast sales over a future period of time. Second, the financial manager must estimate the expected level of profits over the planning period. The final step is to determine the additional assets needed to support additional sales.

⌐3⌐ Outline how organizations manage their assets.

Assets consist of what a firm owns and also comprise the uses of its funds. Sound financial management requires assets to be acquired and managed as effectively and efficiently as possible. The major current assets are cash, marketable securities, accounts receivable, and inventory. The goal of cash management is to have sufficient funds on hand to meet day-to-day transactions and pay any unexpected expenses. Excess cash should be invested in marketable securities, which are low-risk securities with short maturities. Managing accounts receivable, which are uncollected credit sales, involves securing funds owed the firm as quickly as possible while offering sufficient credit to customers to generate increased sales. The main goal of inventory management is to minimize the overall cost of inventory. Production, marketing, and logistics also play roles in determining proper inventory levels. Capital investment analysis is the process by which financial managers make decisions on long-lived assets. This involves comparing the benefits and costs of a proposed investment. Managing international assets poses additional challenges for the financial manager, including the problem of fluctuating exchange rates.

Assessment Check Answers ✔️

3.1 Why do firms often choose to invest excess cash in marketable securities? Cash earns no rate of return, which is why excess cash should be invested in marketable securities. These are low-risk securities that have short maturities and can be sold easily in the secondary markets. As a result, they are easily converted back into cash, when needed.

3.2 What are the two aspects of accounts receivable management? The two aspects of accounts receivable management are determining an overall credit policy (whether to offer credit and, if so, on what terms) and deciding which customers will be offered credit.

3.3 Explain the difference between an expansion decision and a replacement decision. An expansion decision involves choosing between offering new products or building or acquiring new production facilities. A replacement decision is one that considers whether to replace an existing asset with a new one.

⌜4⌟ Discuss the sources of funds and capital structure.
Businesses have two sources of funds: debt capital and equity capital. Debt capital consists of funds obtained through borrowing, and equity capital consists of funds provided by the firm's owners. The mix of debt and equity capital is known as the firm's capital structure, and the financial manager's job is to find the proper mix. Leverage is a technique of increasing the rate of return on funds invested by borrowing. However, leverage increases risk. Also, overreliance on borrowed funds may reduce management's flexibility in future financing decisions. Equity capital also has drawbacks. When additional equity capital is sold, the control of existing shareholders is diluted. In addition, equity capital is more expensive than debt capital. Financial managers are also faced with decisions concerning the appropriate mix of short- and long-term funds. Short-term funds are generally less expensive than long-term funds but expose firms to more risk. Another decision involving financial managers is determining the firm's dividend policy.

Assessment Check Answers ✔️

4.1 Explain the concept of leverage. Leverage is a technique of increasing the rate of return on funds invested by borrowing funds. However, leverage also increases risk.

4.2 Why do firms generally rely more on long-term funds rather than short-term funds? Although short-term funds are generally less expensive than long-term funds, short-term funds expose the firm to more risk. Thus, most firms choose to finance their long-term assets with long-term funds.

4.3 What is an important determinant of a firm's dividend policy? An important determinant of a firm's dividend policy is its investment opportunities. Firms with more profitable investment opportunities often pay less in dividends than do firms with fewer such opportunities.

⌜5⌟ Identify short-term funding options.
The three major short-term funding options are trade credit, short-term loans from banks and other financial institutions, and commercial paper. Trade credit is extended by suppliers when a firm receives goods or services, agreeing to pay for them at a later date. Trade credit is relatively easy to obtain and costs nothing unless a supplier offers a cash discount. Loans from commercial banks are a significant source of short-term financing and are often used to finance accounts receivable and inventory. Loans can be either unsecured or secured, with accounts receivable or inventory pledged as collateral. Commercial paper is a short-term IOU sold by a company. Although large amounts of money can be raised through the sale of commercial paper, usually at rates below those charged by banks, access to the commercial-paper market is limited to large, financially strong corporations.

Assessment Check Answers ✔️

5.1 What are the three sources of short-term funding? The three sources of short-term funding are trade credit, short-term loans, and commercial paper.

5.2 Explain trade credit. Trade credit is extended by suppliers when a buyer agrees to pay for goods and services at a later date. Trade credit is relatively easy to obtain and costs nothing unless a cash discount is offered.

5.3 Why is commercial paper an attractive short-term financing option? Commercial paper is an attractive financing option because companies can raise large amounts of money by selling commercial paper at rates that are generally lower than those charged by banks.

⌜6⌟ Discuss sources of long-term financing.
Long-term funds are repaid over many years. There are three sources: long-term loans obtained from financial institutions, bonds sold to investors, and equity financing. Public sales of securities represent a major source of funds for corporations. These securities can generally be traded in secondary markets. Public sales can vary substantially from year to year depending on the conditions in the financial markets. Private placements are securities sold to a small number of institutional investors. Most private placements involve debt securities. Venture capitalists are an important source of financing for new companies. If the business succeeds, venture capitalists

stand to earn large profits. Private equity funds are investment companies that raise funds from wealthy individuals and institutional investors and use the funds to make investments in both public and private companies. Unlike venture capitalists, private equity funds invest in all types of businesses. Sovereign wealth funds are investment companies owned by governments.

Assessment Check Answers ✅

6.1 What is the most common type of security sold privately? Corporate debt securities are the most common type of security sold privately.

6.2 Describe venture capitalists. Venture capitalists raise money from wealthy individuals and institutional investors and invest the funds in promising firms. If the business succeeds, venture capitalists can earn substantial profits.

6.3 What is a sovereign wealth fund? A sovereign wealth fund is a government-owned investment company. These companies make investments in a variety of financial and real assets, such as real estate. Although most investments are based on the best risk-return trade-off, political, social, and strategic considerations play roles as well.

⌐7⌐ Describe mergers, acquisitions, buyouts, and divestitures.
A merger is a combination of two or more firms into one company. An acquisition is a transaction in which one company buys another. Even in a merger, there is a buyer and a seller (called the *target*). The buyer offers cash, securities, or a combination of the two in return for the target's shares. Mergers

and acquisitions should be evaluated as any large investment is, by comparing the costs with the benefits. Synergy is the term used to describe the benefits a merger or acquisition is expected to produce. A leveraged buyout (LBO) is a transaction in which shares are purchased from public shareholders, and the company reverts to private status. Usually LBOs are financed with substantial amounts of borrowed funds. Private equity companies are often major financers of LBOs. Divestitures are the opposite of mergers, in which companies sell assets such as subsidiaries, product lines, or production facilities. A sell-off is a divestiture in which assets are sold to another firm. In a spin-off, a new firm is created from the assets divested. Shareholders of the divesting firm become shareholders of the new firm as well.

Assessment Check Answers ✅

7.1 Define *synergy*. Synergy is the term used to describe the benefits produced by a merger or acquisition. It is the notion that the combined firm is worth more than the buyer and the target are individually.

7.2 What is an LBO? An LBO—a leveraged buyout—is a transaction in which public shareholders are bought out, and the firm reverts to private status. LBOs are usually financed with large amounts of borrowed money.

7.3 What are the two types of divestitures? A sell-off is a divestiture in which assets are sold to another firm. In a spin-off, a new firm is created from the assets divested. Shareholders of the divesting firm become shareholders of the new firm as well.

▣ Business Terms You Need to Know

finance 492	capital structure 499	leveraged buyout (LBO) 508
financial managers 492	leverage 500	divestiture 508
risk-return trade-off 493	venture capitalist 505	
financial plan 494	tender offer 507	

▣ Review Questions

1. Explain the risk-return trade-off and give two examples.

2. Describe the financial planning process. How does asset intensity affect a financial plan?

3. What are the principal considerations in determining an overall credit policy? How do the actions of competitors affect a firm's credit policy?

4. Why do exchange rates pose a challenge for financial managers of companies with international operations?

5. Discuss the concept of leverage. Use a numerical example to illustrate the effect of leverage.

6. What are the advantages and disadvantages of both debt and equity financing?

7. Compare and contrast the three sources of short-term financing.

8. Define *venture capitalist, private equity fund, sovereign wealth fund,* and *hedge fund*. Which of these four sources of funds invests the most money in start-up companies?

9. Briefly describe the mechanics of a merger or acquisition.

10. Why do firms divest assets?

■ Projects and Teamwork Applications

1. Using qualitative and quantitative measures, lenders utilize a review process called the "five C's of credit" to evaluate a borrower. They include an evaluation of the borrower's **character** (trustworthiness or reputation); **capacity** (borrowing history and repayment track record); **capital** (the level of capitalization and how much money is invested); **collateral** (while cash flow is very important, a lender will evaluate a secondary source of repayment or the value of an individual's or company's assets); and **conditions** (what are current economic conditions, and how is the company or individual doing?). In small teams or in pairs, compare and contrast each of the five C's, and discuss whether you believe each is an accurate assessment of a borrower's ability to pay. What additional criteria, if any, would you include?

2. Working with a partner, assume that a firm needs $10 million in additional long-term capital. It currently has no debt and $40 million in equity. The options are issuing a ten-year bond (with an interest rate of 7 percent) or selling $10 million in new equity. You expect next year's earnings before interest and taxes to be $5 million. (The firm's tax rate is 35 percent.) Prepare a memo outlining the advantages and disadvantages of debt and equity financing. Using the numbers provided, prepare a numerical illustration of leverage similar to the one shown in Figure 17.2.

3. Your new small business has really grown, but now it needs a substantial infusion of capital. A venture capital firm has agreed to invest the money you need. In return, the venture capital firm will own 75 percent of the business, and you will be replaced as CEO by someone whom the venture capitalist chooses. You will retain the titles of founder and chairman of the board. Would you be willing to take the money but lose control over your business? Why or why not?

4. Working in a small team, select three publicly traded companies. Visit each firm's website. Most have a section devoted to information for investors. Review each firm's dividend policy. Does the company pay dividends? If so, when did it begin paying dividends? Have dividends increased each year? Or have they fluctuated from year to year? Is the company currently repurchasing shares? Has it done so in the past? Prepare a report summarizing your findings.

5. As noted in the chapter, one of the most unfortunate mergers in corporate history involved Time Warner and America Online. Research this merger. Why did analysts expect it to be successful? Why did it fail? What has happened to AOL since then?

■ Web Assignments

1. **Peer-to-peer lending.** Technology has played an integral role in helping entrepreneurs or anyone with a cause to raise funds. The concept of peer-to-peer lending took off during the recent economic downturn, when traditional banks and other institutions tightened the money they were willing to lend. Peer-to-peer lending is an intermediary of sorts between friends and associates to assist with a loan. Go to any of the peer-to-peer lending sites (two links are listed below) and discuss the pros and cons of this type of financing. Is this something you might participate in as a lender or borrower? Explain your reasoning.

   www.prosper.com
   www.lendingclub.com

2. **CFOs and business concerns.** During the recent economic slowdown, many CFOs, for the sake of their companies' survival, initiated a variety of fiscal strategies to better manage credit, cash flow, and overall finances. Conduct research on what are the top concerns for today's CFOs. You may want to go to *CFO* magazine or other business sources like *The Wall Street Journal*, *Forbes*, or *Fortune*. Either individually or in pairs, rank the top five concerns of CFOs in today's economic environment. Which issues have to do with economic recovery? Employment? Consumer spending patterns?

3. **Mergers and acquisitions.** Using a news source, such as Google News (http://news.google.com) or Yahoo! News (http://news.yahoo.com), search for a recent merger or acquisition announcement. An example would be Google's acquisition of Nest. (A link is shown below.) Print out the articles and bring them to class.

   www.forbes.com/sites/aarontilley/2014/01/13/
   google-acquires-nest-for-3-2-billion

Note: Internet web addresses change frequently. If you don't find the exact sites listed, you may need to access the organization's home page and search from there or use a search engine such as Google or Bing.

Macy's CFO Guides Retail Giant with a Steady Hand

During her tenure as Macy's chief financial officer, Karen Hoguet has presided over many complex financial strategies and hurdles. A 30-year veteran of the company, Hoguet served in a number of executive roles before becoming CFO.

As CFO, Hoguet has helped increase Macy's net income fourfold, and same-store sales growth has topped 4 percent despite competitive pressure from other retailers. Customer spending patterns, disposable income levels, consumer confidence, and the cost of basic goods and necessities continue to keep retail finance professionals like Hoguet on their toes.

A highlight of Hoguet's CFO career has been presiding over the $17 billion acquisition of May Department Stores, which also included a string of divestures and a $3 billion debt repayment. More recently, Hoguet has been involved in corporate brand restructuring, which includes unifying brands under the Macy's umbrella. After the recent economic slowdown, Macy's credit ratings have returned to investment grade, a stock buyback program has been executed successfully, and company stock has outperformed that of its retail peers.

Year after year, despite an industry highly dependent on the holiday season and general economic conditions, Hoguet and her Macy's team have developed and implemented successful strategies to keep the retailer financially strong.

Questions for Critical Thinking

1. Numerous factors beyond the company's control impact sales. These include, among others, the competitive environment, economic conditions, strategic actions, retail trends, and consumer spending. Provide examples of each factor's influence on Macy's sales, and any others you can think of.

2. Macy's revenues and cash requirements are affected by the seasonal nature of its business, as a disproportionate amount of the company's revenues occur in the last quarter of the calendar year. Discuss the impact of seasonality on financing decisions, including funding options, sources of funds, and financing requirements.

Sources: Company website, "2014 Store Count and Square Footage," www.macysinc.com, accessed July 5, 2014; company website, "Five Year Performance," www.macysinc.com, accessed July 5, 2014; company website, "Executive Management Team Bios," www.macysinc.com; "Form 10K for Macy's Inc.," *Yahoo Finance*, accessed July 5, 2014, http://biz.yahoo.com; "Macy's Star of Retail," *Day Capital Research*, accessed July 5, 2014, http://daycapitalresearch.com; Matthew Quinn and Alix Stuart, "Not Just Bean Counters," *The Wall Street Journal*, accessed July 5, 2014, http://online.wsj.com; "Best CFOs of 2012," *The Wall Street Journal*, accessed July 5, 2014, http://online.wsj.com.

Hewlett-Packard Continues Its Focus on Hardware

CEO Meg Whitman predicts a multiyear turnaround for Hewlett-Packard (HP), whose product mix ranges from PCs and printers to servers, networking equipment, and software used by large companies. Currently the world's largest seller of servers, HP's strategy includes investing in software that allows connectivity of large clusters of servers.

Sales from HP's enterprise group, which offers computer servers and other hardware, grew slightly, along with an unpredicted increase in personal computer sales to businesses. Printing group sales dipped while sales in enterprise services and software also declined. One opportunity for HP may come from IBM's recent exit from the server market as a result of selling its low-end server division and Dell's recent purchase by a private equity firm.

While some companies like IBM are moving away from hardware, HP has made an even stronger commitment to this business sector. Whitman says that hardware is HP's heritage and that the company is going to commit to that part of the business. In the future, HP plans to invest in new servers, a bright spot for the company; storage technology;

software for servers; and networking equipment. Converged systems, which allow server, storage, and networking technology to be combined into a single machine, also remain a focus that HP hopes will gain sales momentum.

Questions for Critical Thinking

1. What are your thoughts about Hewlett-Packard's continued investment and commitment to hardware?

2. With the meteoric rise in mobile computing and consumers migrating to smart phones and tablets made by competitors, do you believe HP's strategy to invest in servers will return the company to previous levels of profitability? Why or why not?

Sources: Ian King, "Hewlett-Packard Sales, Profit Top Estimates on Server Demand," *Bloomberg Businessweek*, accessed March 22, 2014, www.businessweek.com; Spencer Ante, "For H-P, Hopeful Signs in Its Hardware Push," *The Wall Street Journal*, accessed March 22, 2014, http://online.wsj.com; Patrick Moorhead, "How Hewlett-Packard Proved Me Right," *Forbes*, accessed March 22, 2014, www.forbes.com.

Jason Salfi, co-founder and president of Comet Skateboards, is the first to admit he can let the wheels get away from him. Since the inception of Comet Skateboards, he estimates that he has personally "tanked the company four times. I started the company with a friend and we would sacrifice everything for quality," Salfi admits. It's easy to see how this could happen. Salfi loves skateboarding and he's a fanatic about building the best skateboards on the market with the most sustainable materials available.

During the first years of production—when Comet moved from California to Ithaca, New York in order to source bio-composite materials—Salfi and his partner paid top dollar for all the materials they used in building the boards. "We weren't really watching how much money we were making," Salfi says sheepishly. They were so wrapped up in the excitement of developing and manufacturing an entirely new class of skateboard, they forgot to watch the bank account balance. Salfi recalls that they did all the stereotypical things that small start-ups do to obtain financing—maxed out their credit cards, got friends and family to co-sign for loans, found angel investors. But Comet Skateboards just seemed to roll through the money without enough return to ensure its survival.

Then the firm hired a manager to specialize in financial details. With a professional in place, Salfi began to understand the real and potential impacts certain buying decisions would have on the bottom line, and the way cash flow would affect getting products to the marketplace. Now, Comet can forecast better how a product release will affect cash flow, and how that in turn will affect the way they as a business can reach customers. "Ultimately we're trying to create a sustainable business platform to get our sustainable business vision out there in the marketplace," explains Salfi. But they couldn't do this without managing the company's financial resources.

Comet Skateboards is considered a triple bottom line company, carrying the B Corporation logo. This means that Comet strives to create benefit for the company owners (profit), the community (people), and the environment (planet). Currently there are more than two hundred B Corporations in thirty industries around the nation. Each company has submitted to rigorous evaluation and has put written standards in place addressing social and environmental responsibility. Everything that Comet does, from its closed-loop manufacturing process to its community involvement, refers to its triple bottom line commitment.

Jason Salfi insists that managing the finances for a triple bottom line company is pretty much the same as managing the finances for a traditional company. But there are some differences, particularly in the procurement of raw materials, energy use, and waste disposal. Also, triple bottom line companies are held accountable for the way they treat employees and how they are involved in the community. "The 'magic' is making sure we can afford all that," observes Salfi. "It's just a matter of prioritization. We're not going on $50,000 golf retreats. We're reinvesting the capital we have in the materials we use and the way we interact with people."

Despite the fact that he says he didn't pay attention to finances in the company's early days, Salfi has a good grasp on Comet's role in the larger economic picture. He likes the idea of projecting the impact Comet has on consumers' buying decisions, particularly young people. Teenagers who choose Comet skateboards are choosing products that are made by a triple bottom line firm. "If you look at the way a 14-year-old decides to buy things for the rest of his or her life, and you look at the number of decisions that young person is going to make over the span of 50 or 60 years, you could extrapolate that we have impacted 1,000 people in a certain way that could eventually transfer billions of dollars toward socially responsible businesses," explains Salfi. "We're influencing the buying decisions of youth."

Salfi believes that, decades ago, "commerce used to be about improving the quality of life, but somewhere along the line, profits skewed motivations." He likes the idea of the triple bottom line rebalancing the priorities of business. "We like to think that as a B Corporation, we are part of a group that wants to bring back the original motivation for business, which was all about creating an improved quality of life for everyone, not just a select few." It might actually be possible for a few well-engineered skateboards to change the world.

Questions for Critical Thinking

1. Hiring a financial manager was a major step for Comet Skateboards. Identify some of the factors the manager would have to consider when creating a plan for risk-return trade-off.

2. What might be some short-term funding options for Comet? Some long-term options? Which would be best for this company, and why?

3. Suppose a larger firm approached Comet with an offer of acquisition. Create a chart outlining the major pros and cons of such an offer.

4. How might Comet's designation as a B Corporation affect the way it answers the three essential questions for building a financial plan?

Sources: Company website, www.cometskateboards.com, accessed April 3, 2014; "GOOD Product: Comet Skateboards," *Video Wired*, accessed April 3, 2014, www.videowired.com; "Comet's New Retail Store," *Heelside*, accessed April 3, 2014, www.heelsidemag.com.

GREENSBURG, KS

So Much to Do, So Little Cash

When Dan Wallach started Greensburg GreenTown, he knew it wouldn't be easy. A self-proclaimed idea guy, he admits that the details of high finance elude him. What he is good at is rallying people around a cause and getting them to write a few big checks. This time, though, Wallach decided to involve the largest number of people possible. Greensburg GreenTown's One Million $5.00 Donations campaign was the result.

The money that is raised will be used to cover Green Town's operating expenses, as well as to fund gaps in municipal projects, build model green homes, and educate residents about green building practices. Another aspect of GreenTown's work is to provide information and access to media organizations. Shortly after the tornado, the Planet Green cable channel began production on a television series that would chronicle the town's rebuilding. Wallach thought the exposure created by that show and others like it would be valuable in his fund-raising efforts.

As a not-for-profit organization, Greensburg GreenTown is heavily regulated by the IRS, because the donations it receives are fully tax deductible. It falls into the same category as religious organizations and educational institutions, which are exempt from federal income taxes but must pay other federal taxes, such as employment taxes. Because working through the red tape required to obtain this IRS status can take time, many organizations, GreenTown included, work through an approved intermediary while their applications are processed.

Although Greensburg GreenTown supports and educates Greensburg's residents, the town itself must rely on other sources of funding. All towns have budgets for repairs and improvements, but no one expected to have to rebuild the entire town. After the tornado, Greensburg had no roads, no hospital, no school system, no utilities, or any of the other services one might expect to find in a town. Money was tight even before the tornado, so rebuilding seemed an impossible task.

Luckily, various government and corporate organizations chipped in. The Federal Emergency Management Agency (FEMA) and the U.S. Department of Agriculture (USDA) provided aid in the form of grants. Corporations like Frito-Lay donated significant amounts of money to support the town's innovative business incubator. With millions of dollars at stake and hundreds of projects under way at once, Assistant Town Administrator and Recovery Coordinator Kim Alderfer says the hardest part is keeping track of it all.

Questions

After viewing the video, answer the following questions:

1. What are the key legal and financial distinctions of Greensburg GreenTown?
2. If you were in Kim Alderfer's shoes, what kind of financial contingency plan would you put in place for Greensburg's future?
3. Should not-for-profit organizations be required to open their books to donors? Why or why not?

Chapter 17 *Financial Management* **515**

LAUNCHING YOUR
[Finance Career]

Part 6, "Managing Financial Resources," describes the finance function in organizations. Finance deals with planning, obtaining, and managing an organization's funds to accomplish its objectives in the most effective way possible. In Chapter 15, we covered accounting principles and various financial statements. In Chapter 16, we discussed the financial system, including the various types of securities, financial markets and institutions, the Federal Reserve System, financial regulators, and global financial markets. In Chapter 17, we examined the role financial managers play in an organization; financial planning; short- and long-term financing options; and mergers, acquisitions, buyouts, and divestitures. Throughout these chapters, we described the finance functions of a variety of businesses, governments, and not-for-profit organizations. As Part 6 illustrates, finance is a very diverse profession and encompasses many different occupations. According to the U.S. Department of Labor, over the next decade most finance-related occupations are expected to experience 9 percent employment growth. Employment in the financial investment industry should be strong because of the number of Baby Boomers in their peak earning years with funds to invest and the globalization of securities markets.[1]

In most business schools, finance is one of the most popular majors among undergraduates. Combining finance with accounting is a common double major. Those with degrees in finance also enjoy relatively high starting salaries. A recent survey found that the average starting salary for a person with an undergraduate degree in finance was nearly $77,000 per year.[2]

All organizations need to obtain and manage funds, so they employ finance professionals. Financial institutions and other financial services firms employ a large percentage of finance graduates. These businesses provide important finance-related services to businesses, governments, and not-for-profit organizations. Some graduates with finance degrees take jobs with financial services firms such as Bank of America and JP Morgan Chase, while others begin their careers working in the finance departments of businesses in other industries such as Caterpillar and Boeing, governments, or not-for-profit organizations. You may begin your career evaluating commercial loan applications for a bank, analyzing capital investments for a business, or helping a not-for-profit organization decide how to invest its endowment. Often finance professionals work as members of a team, advising top management. Some individuals spend their entire careers working in finance-related occupations; others use their finance experience to move into other areas of the firm. Today, the chief financial officer—the senior finance executive—holds one of the most critical jobs in any organization. In addition, the number of CEOs who began their careers in finance is growing.

Finance is a diverse, exciting profession. Here are a few of the specific occupations you might find after earning a degree in finance.

Financial managers prepare financial reports, direct investment activities, raise funds, and implement cash management strategies. Computer technology has significantly reduced the time needed to produce financial reports. Many financial managers spend less time preparing reports and more time analyzing financial data. All organizations employ financial managers, although roughly 30 percent of all financial managers work for financial services firms such as commercial banks and insurance companies.[3] Specific responsibilities vary with titles. For instance, credit managers oversee the firm's issuance of credit, establish standards, and monitor the collection of accounts. Cash managers control the flow of cash receipts and disbursements to meet the needs of the organization.

Most *loan officers* work for commercial banks and other financial institutions. They find potential clients and help them apply for loans. Loan officers typically specialize in commercial, consumer, or mortgage loans. In many cases, loan officers act in a sales capacity, contacting individuals and organizations about their need for funds and trying to persuade them to borrow the funds from the loan officer's institution. Thus, loan officers often need marketing as well as finance skills.

Security analysts generally work for financial services firms such as Fidelity or Raymond James & Associates. Security analysts review economic data, financial statements, and other information to determine the outlook for securities such as common stocks and bonds. They make investment recommendations to individual and institutional investors. Many senior security analysts hold a chartered financial analyst (CFA) designation. Obtaining a CFA requires a specific educational background, several years of related experience, and a passing grade on a comprehensive, three-stage examination.

Portfolio managers manage money for an individual or institutional client. Many portfolio managers work for pension funds or mutual funds for which they make investment decisions to benefit the funds' beneficiaries. Portfolio managers generally have extensive experience as financial managers or security analysts, and many are CFAs.

Personal financial planners help individuals make decisions in areas such as insurance, investments, and retirement planning. Personal financial planners meet with their clients, assess their needs and goals, and make recommendations. Approximately 30 percent of personal financial planners are self-employed, and many hold certified financial planner (CFP) designations. Like the CFA, obtaining a CFP requires a specific educational background, related experience, and passing a comprehensive examination.

Career Assessment Exercises in Finance

1. Assume you're interested in pursuing a career as a security analyst. You've heard that the CFA is an important designation and can help enhance your career. Visit the CFA's website (http://www.cfainstitute.org) to learn more about the CFA. Specifically, what are the requirements to obtain a CFA, and what are the professional benefits of having a CFA?

2. Arrange for an interview with a commercial loan officer at a local bank. Ask the loan officer about his or her educational background, what a typical day is like, and what the loan officer likes and doesn't like about his or her job.

3. Ameriprise Financial offers financial planning services to individuals and organizations. Visit the firm's careers website (http:///www.ameriprise.com/careers). Review the material and write a brief summary of what you learned about being a personal financial planner. Does such a career interest you? Why or why not?

Business Law

Shipments Put FedEx in Legal Hot Water

A $235 million lawsuit was recently filed against FedEx by the New York Attorney General's Office for approximately 33,000 shipments of more than 400,000 cartons of untaxed or contraband cigarettes to individuals in New York.

The case against FedEx illustrates the legal vulnerability of a company serving as an intermediary. The attorney general is charging FedEx with violating state and federal laws. In 2006, FedEx signed an agreement with the state that included a promise to no longer make illegal cigarette deliveries. The lawsuit claims that FedEx assisted cigarette smugglers in avoiding millions of dollars in tax payments. FedEx has responded by saying that the case "lacks legal foundation." A FedEx spokesperson also says it is not the company's role to monitor the contents of the packages it ships, and that it "must protect the privacy of our customers and cannot open packages to determine their contents without reason." FedEx officials say they will continue to work with all regulatory agencies while "vigorously defending" the case.[1] The lawsuit is still in the courts.

Appendix A Overview

As the opening story points out, legal issues affect every aspect of business. Despite the best efforts of most businesspeople, legal cases do arise. A dispute may arise over a contract, an employee may protest being passed over for a promotion, or a town may challenge the environmental impact of a new gas station. Unfortunately, the United States has the dubious distinction of being the world's most litigious society. Lawsuits are as common as business deals. Consider Walmart, which is involved in as many as 7,000 legal cases at any one time.

Even if you are never involved in a lawsuit, the cost still affects you. The average U.S. family pays a hidden "litigation tax" of 5 percent each year because of the costs of lawsuits that force businesses to increase their prices. Small businesses, such as dentists' offices, doctors' offices, and daycare providers are often the hardest hit and may cut back on their services or close. The total cost of frivolous lawsuits—those brought for petty reasons—runs about $865 billion a year. Rule 11 of the Federal Rules of Civil Procedure was designed in 1993 to prevent frivolous lawsuits, but has been weakened by loopholes. A bill pending in Congress would tighten the regulations again.[2]

On the lighter side, every day brings news reports of proposed laws intended to protect businesses, consumers, and the general public—but somehow fall short. In addition, laws that no longer serve a purpose are still on the books. For instance, in Alaska, it's illegal to wake a bear to take its picture, but it is perfectly legal to shoot a bear while it is sleeping. In Hawaii, it is against the law to insert pennies in your ear. In Louisiana, it is illegal to gargle in public. In Montana, it is against the law to operate a vehicle with ice picks attached to the wheels. In North Carolina, it is illegal to use elephants to plow cotton fields. And in Arizona, it's illegal to hunt camels.[3] The origins of these laws raise about as many questions as the laws themselves.

Legislation that specifically affects how business functions is analyzed in each chapter of this book. Chapter 2 presents an overview of the legal environment, and legislation affecting international operations is covered in Chapter 4. Chapter 5 discusses laws related to small businesses. Laws regarding human resource management and labor unions are examined in Chapter 8. Laws affecting other business operations, such as environmental regulations and product safety, are one of the topics in Chapter 12, and marketing-related

Appendix A

A-1

legislation is examined in Chapter 13. Finally, legislation pertaining to banking and the securities markets is discussed in Chapters 16 and 17.

In this appendix, we provide a general perspective of legislation at the federal, state, and local levels, and point out that, although business executives may not be legal experts, they do need to be knowledgeable in their specific area of responsibility. A good amount of common sense also helps avoid potential legal problems. This appendix looks at the general nature of business law, the court system, basic legal concepts, and the changing regulatory environment for U.S. business. Let's start with some initial definitions and related examples.

Legal System and Administrative Agencies

judiciary court system, or branch of government that is responsible for settling disputes by applying laws.

The **judiciary**, or court system, is the branch of government responsible for settling disputes among parties by applying laws. This branch consists of several types and levels of courts, each with a specific jurisdiction. Court systems are organized at the federal, state, and local levels. Administrative agencies also perform some limited judicial functions, but these agencies are more properly regarded as belonging to the executive or legislative branches of government.

At both the federal and state levels, *trial courts*—courts of general jurisdiction—hear a wide range of cases. Unless a case is assigned by law to another court or to an administrative agency, a court of general jurisdiction will hear it. The majority of cases, both criminal and civil, pass through these courts. Within the federal system, trial courts are known as U.S. district courts, and at least one such court operates in each state. In state court systems, the general jurisdiction courts are often called circuit courts, and states typically provide one for each county. Other names for general jurisdiction courts are superior courts, common pleas courts, or district courts.

State judiciary systems also include many courts with lower, or more specific, jurisdictions. In most states, parties can appeal the decisions of the lower courts to the general jurisdiction courts. Examples of lower courts are probate courts—which settle the estates of people who have died—and small-claims courts—where people can represent themselves in suits involving limited amounts of money. For example, a landlord might go to small-claims court to settle a dispute with a tenant over a security deposit.

Decisions made at the general trial court level may be appealed in *appellate courts*. Both the federal and state systems have appellate courts. For instance, the U.S. Court of Appeals for the Fourth Circuit, which is based in Richmond, Virginia, covers the states of Maryland, Virginia, West Virginia, North Carolina, and South Carolina.[4] The appeals process allows a higher court to review the case and correct any lower court error indicated by the appellant, the party making the appeal.

Appeals from decisions of the U.S. circuit courts of appeals can go all the way to the nation's highest court, the U.S. Supreme Court. Appeals from state courts of appeal are heard by the highest court in each state, usually called the state supreme court. In a state without intermediate appellate courts, the state supreme court hears appeals directly from the trial courts. Parties who are not satisfied by the verdict of a state supreme court can appeal to the U.S. Supreme Court and may be granted a hearing if they can cite grounds for such an appeal, and if the Supreme Court considers the case significant enough to be heard. The Supreme Court typically has more than 10,000 cases on the docket per year. However, only about 100 are granted review with oral arguments by attorneys. Formal written decisions are delivered for 80 to 90 of those cases.[5]

While most cases are resolved by the system of courts described here, certain highly specialized cases require particular expertise. Examples of specialized federal courts are the U.S. Tax Court for tax cases and the U.S. Court of Claims, which hears claims against the U.S. government itself. Similar specialized courts operate at the state level.

Administrative agencies, also known as bureaus, commissions, or boards, decide a variety of cases at all levels of government. These agencies usually derive their powers and responsibilities from state or federal statutes. Technically, they conduct hearings or inquiries rather than trials. Examples of federal administrative agencies are the Federal Trade Commission (FTC), the National Labor Relations Board (NLRB), and the Federal Energy Regulatory Commission (FERC). The FTC has the broadest power of any of the federal regulatory agencies. It enforces laws regulating unfair business practices, and it can stop false and deceptive advertising practices. Examples at the state level include public utility commissions and boards that govern the licensing of various trades and professions. Zoning boards, planning commissions, and boards of appeal operate at the city or county level.

Types of Law

Law consists of the standards set by government and society in the form of either legislation or custom. This broad body of principles, regulations, rules, and customs that govern the actions of all members of society, including businesspeople, is derived from several sources. **Common law** refers to the body of law arising out of judicial decisions, some of which can be traced back to early England.

Statutory law, or written law, includes state and federal constitutions, legislative enactments, treaties of the federal government, and ordinances of local governments. Statutes must be drawn precisely and reasonably to be constitutional, and thus enforceable. Still, courts frequently must interpret their intentions and meanings.

With the growth of the global economy, knowledge of international law has become crucial. **International law** refers to the numerous regulations that govern companies conducting global business. Companies must be aware of the domestic laws of trading partners, trade agreements such as NAFTA, and the rulings of such organizations as the World Trade Organization. International law affects trade in all kinds of industries. When a range of defective or tainted products manufactured in China—but sold in the United States—was recalled, companies discovered that although the goods came from China, the liability for their defects lay squarely

law standards set by government and society in the form of either legislation or custom.

common law body of law arising out of judicial decisions, some of which can be traced back to early England.

statutory law written law, including state and federal constitutions, legislative enactments, treaties of the federal government, and ordinances of local governments.

international law the numerous regulations that govern international commerce.

Keith Bedford/Bloomberg/Getty Images, Inc.

Expertise in international law has become very important as the global economy continues to expand. In a recent case, the United States, Japan, and the WTO joined forces to bring a case against China for its restrictions on exports of rare metals used to make various electronic goods. The WTO ruled against China's export restrictions.

within the United States. Tainted or defective toothpaste, pet food, toys, tires, and shrimp all fell under the scrutiny of the Food and Drug Administration (FDA), the Consumer Product Safety Commission (CPSC), and other agencies, which hold U.S. manufacturers responsible for the quality of their foreign-made products. Recently, the United States, the World Trade Organization (WTO), and Japan joined forces to bring a lawsuit against China for its restrictions on exports of rare-earth metals, which are used in making electronic goods such as smart phones, flat-screen TVs, compact fluorescent light bulbs, and electric cars. Currently, China mines 95 to 97 percent of these metals, which include scandium, lanthanum, and fifteen other elements. The WTO recently ruled against China's export restrictions on the rare minerals.[6]

In a broad sense, all law is business law because all firms are subject to the entire body of law, just as individuals are. In a narrower sense, however, **business law** consists of those aspects of law that most directly influence and regulate the management of various types of business activity. Specific laws vary widely in their intent from business to business and from industry to industry. The legal interests of airlines, for example, differ from those of oil companies.

State and local statutes also have varying applications. Some state laws affect all businesses that operate in a particular state. Workers' compensation laws, which govern payments to workers for injuries incurred on the job, are an example. Other state laws apply only to certain firms or business activities. States have specific licensing requirements for businesses, such as law firms, funeral homes, and hair salons. Many local ordinances also deal with specific business activities. Local regulations on the sizes and types of business signs are commonplace. Some communities even restrict the sizes of stores, including height and square footage.

> **business law** aspects of law that most directly influence and regulate the management of business activity.

Regulatory Environment for Business

Government regulation of business has changed over time. Depending on public sentiment, the economy, and the political climate, we see the pendulum swing back and forth between increased regulation and deregulation. But the goal of both types of legislation is protection of healthy competition. One industry that has experienced some deregulation in the past is still subject to relatively tight regulations: banking. Despite the relaxation of banking regulations across state lines and the advent of online banking, laws governing everything from stock trading to retirement investing remain strict. In response to a crisis in which lending institutions granted mortgages to home buyers who were then unable to meet payments that later increased—precipitating record numbers of foreclosures—a new bill was introduced in Congress. The Mortgage Reform and Anti-Predatory Lending Act of 2007 modifies the Truth in Lending Act. The intent of this legislation is to protect consumers by establishing fair lending practices. In addition, after the near-collapse of Wall Street, the Dodd-Frank Act was signed into law in 2010. This law created the Bureau of Consumer Financial Protection and tightened regulations on all firms involved in the financial industry. Under the Dodd-Frank Act, taxpayers can no longer be asked to bail out failing financial firms. The Securities and Exchange Commission, along with the FBI, recently announced it would investigate high-frequency stock traders to determine whether they have an unfair speed advantage, sometimes less than a fraction of a second, when executing trades.[7]

Let's look at the issues surrounding regulation and deregulation and the legislation that has characterized them.

Antitrust and Business Regulation

John D. Rockefeller's Standard Oil monopoly launched antitrust legislation. Breaking up monopolies and restraints of trade was a popular issue in the late 1800s and early 1900s. In fact, President Theodore Roosevelt always promoted himself as a "trust-buster." The highly publicized Microsoft case of the 1990s is another example of antitrust litigation.

During the 1930s, several laws designed to regulate business were passed. The basis for many of these laws was protecting employment. The world was in the midst of the Great

Depression, so the government focused on keeping its citizens employed. Recently, government officials became concerned with the security aspects of international business transactions, Internet usage, the sources of funds, and their effects on U.S. business practices. New regulatory legislation in the form of the USA Patriot Act was enacted in 2001. Congress has voted to reauthorize this law several times. The law includes a provision that allows the federal government, with approval from a federal judge, to seize business records in investigations involving national security.[8]

The major federal antitrust and business regulation legislation includes the following:

LAW	WHAT IT DID
Sherman Act (1890)	Set a competitive business system as a national policy goal. The act specifically banned monopolies and restraints of trade.
Clayton Act (1914)	Put restrictions on price discrimination, exclusive dealing, tying contracts, and interlocking boards of directors that lessened competition or might lead to a monopoly.
Federal Trade Commission Act (1914)	Established the FTC with the authority to investigate business practices. The act also prohibited unfair methods of competition.
Robinson-Patman Act (1936)	Outlawed price discrimination in sales to wholesalers, retailers, or other producers. The act also banned pricing designed to eliminate competition.
Wheeler-Lea Act (1938)	Banned deceptive advertising. The act gave the FTC jurisdiction in such cases.
USA Patriot Act (2001)	Limited interactions between U.S. and foreign banks to those with "know your customer" policies; allowed the U.S. Treasury Department to freeze assets and bar a country, government, or institution from doing business in the United States; gave federal authorities broad powers to monitor Internet usage and expanded the way data is shared among different agencies. Reauthorization (2005) created a new Assistant Attorney General for Security, enhanced penalties for terrorism financing, and provided clear standards and penalties for attacks on mass transit systems.

The protection of fair competition remains an issue in industries today. The Federal Communications Commission (FCC) recently announced plans to enact a new net-neutrality regulation, whose goal would be to advocate for a neutral Internet and open platform in which all websites would be treated equally and not subject to additional fees to use Internet "fast lanes."[9]

Business Deregulation

Deregulation was a concept started in the 1970s whose influence continues today. Many formerly regulated industries were freed to pick the markets they wanted to serve. The deregulated industries, such as utilities and airlines, were also allowed to price their products without the guidance of federal regulations. For the most part, deregulation led to lower consumer prices. In some cases, it also led to a loss of service. Many smaller cities and airports lost airline service because of deregulation.

Following are several major laws related to deregulation:

LAW	WHAT IT DID
Airline Deregulation Act (1978)	Allowed airlines to set fares and pick their routes.
Motor Carrier Act and Staggers Rail Act (1980)	Permitted the trucking and railroad industries to negotiate rates and services.

(continued)

LAW	WHAT IT DID
Telecommunications Act (1996)	Cut barriers to competition in local and long-distance phone, cable, and television markets.
Gramm-Leach-Bliley Act (1999)	Permitted banks, securities firms, and insurance companies to affiliate within a new financial organizational structure; required them to disclose to customers their policies and practices for protecting the privacy of personal information.

Consumer Protection

Numerous laws designed to protect consumers have been passed in the last 100 years. In many ways, business itself has evolved to reflect this focus on consumer safety and satisfaction. Recently, Congress passed the broadest changes in the country's consumer protection system in decades, including stricter regulations governing toy manufacturing, public access to complaints about products, and a major overhaul of the Consumer Product Safety Commission (CPSC) designed to improve communication and efficiency. One provision includes stricter limits on the amount of lead in children's toys, and another requires mandatory safety standards for nursery items such as cribs and playpens. The Dodd-Frank Act covers consumer financial protection.[10] The Food and Drug Administration Amendments Act (FDAA) of 2007 reauthorizes existing laws and includes new provisions designed to enhance drug safety, encourage the development of pediatric medical devices, and enhance food safety.[11] The FDA recently announced proposed rulemaking to seek additional information for regulatory options related to monitoring the amount of menthol in cigarettes.[12]

The major federal laws related to consumer protection include the following:

LAW	WHAT IT DID
Federal Food and Drug Act (1906)	Banned adulteration and misbranding of foods and drugs involved in interstate commerce.
Consumer Credit Protection Act (1968)	Required disclosure of annual interest rates on loans and credit purchases.
National Environmental Policy Act (1970)	Established the Environmental Protection Agency to deal with various types of pollution and organizations that create pollution.
Public Health Cigarette Smoking Act (1970)	Prohibited tobacco advertising on radio and television.
Consumer Product Safety Act (1972)	Established the Consumer Product Safety Commission with authority to specify safety standards for most products.
Nutrition Labeling and Education Act (1990)	Stipulated detailed information on the labeling of most foods.
Dietary Supplement Health and Education Act (1994)	Established standards with respect to dietary supplements including vitamins, minerals, herbs, amino acids, and the like.
Food and Drug Administration Amendments Act of 2007	Reauthorized several laws dealing with prescription drugs and added new ones enhancing food safety, drug safety, development of pediatric medical devices, and clinical trial registries.

Employee Protection

Chapters 2 and 8 cover many of the issues employers face in protecting their employees from injury and harm while on the job. But employees must also be protected from unfair practices by employers. Recently, Congress passed the Lilly Ledbetter Fair Pay Act. This law helps protect workers from wage discrimination.[13]

Some of the relevant laws related to employee protection include the following:

LAW	WHAT IT DID
Fair Labor Standards Act (1938)	For hourly workers, provided payment of the minimum wage, overtime pay for time worked over 40 hours in a workweek, restricted the employment of children, and required employers to keep records of wages and hours.
OSHA Act (1970)	Required employers to provide workers with workplaces free of recognized hazards that could cause serious injury or death and required employees to abide by all safety and health standards that apply to their jobs.
Americans with Disabilities Act (1991)	Banned discrimination against the disabled in public accommodations, transportation, and telecommunications.
Family and Medical Leave Act (1993)	Required covered employers to grant eligible employees up to 12 workweeks of unpaid leave during any 12-month period for the birth and care of a newborn child of the employee, placement with the employee of a son or daughter for adoption or foster care, care of an immediate family member with a serious health condition, or medical leave for the employee if unable to work because of a serious health condition.
Uniformed Services Employment and Reemployment Rights Act (1994)	Protects the job rights of individuals who voluntarily or involuntarily leave their jobs to perform military service. Also prohibits employment discrimination in such cases.
American Jobs Creation Act (2004)	Reduced taxes for manufacturing in the United States, provided temporary tax breaks for income repatriated to the United States, and encouraged domestic job growth.
Pension Protection Act (2006)	Required companies with underfunded pension plans to pay extra premiums; made it easier for companies to automatically enroll employees in defined contribution plans; provided greater access to professional advice about investing.
Lilly Ledbetter Fair Pay Act (2009)	Reinstated protection against pay discrimination; made it clear that pay discrimination claims based on sex, race, national origin, age, religion, and disability "accrue" whenever an employee receives a discriminatory paycheck, as well as when a discriminatory pay decision or practice is adopted.
Patient Protection and Affordable Care Act (2010) and the Health Care and Education Reconciliation Act (2010)	Health-related provisions to expand Medicaid eligibility, subsidize insurance premiums, provide businesses with incentives to provide health care benefits, prohibit claims denied for preexisting conditions.

Investor Protection

Chapters 15, 16, and 17 describe the institutions subject to investor protection laws and some of the events that brought the Sarbanes-Oxley law into being. (See the entry in the following table for specific provisions of Sarbanes-Oxley.) Following is a summary of legislation to protect investors:

LAW	WHAT IT DID
Securities Exchange Act (1934)	Created the Securities and Exchange Commission with the authority to register, regulate, and oversee brokerage firms, transfer agents, clearing agencies, and stock exchanges; the SEC also has the power to enforce securities laws and protect investors in public transactions.
Bank Secrecy Act (1970)	Deterred laundering and use of secret foreign bank accounts; created an investigative paper trail for large currency transactions; imposed civil and criminal penalties for noncompliance with reporting requirements; improved detection and investigation of criminal, tax, and regulatory violations.
Sarbanes-Oxley Act (2002)	Required top corporate executives to attest to the validity of the company's financial statements; increased the documentation and monitoring of internal controls; prohibited CPA firms from providing certain types of consulting services for their clients; established a five-member accounting oversight board.
Dodd-Frank Wall Street Reform and Consumer Protection Act (2010)	Established the Bureau of Consumer Financial Protection and the Financial Stability Oversight Council; instituted stringent new regulations for transparency and accountability, designed to protect investors.

Cyberspace and Telecommunications Protection

Computers and widespread use of the Internet and telecommunications have dramatically expanded the reach of businesses. They have also raised some thorny issues such as computer fraud and abuse, online privacy, cyberbullying, and cyberterrorism. Under a Supreme Court ruling, Internet file-sharing services are now held accountable if their intention is for consumers to use software to exchange songs and videos illegally. This ruling helps protect copyrights, which are covered later in this appendix. In a famous case, Viacom—the parent company of MTV and Comedy Central—sued YouTube and its parent company, Google, for $1 billion in federal court, claiming "massive intentional copyright infringement." Viacom argued that YouTube's success was partly built on the unlicensed use of video taken from Viacom cable channels. Google and YouTube denied the claim, but later Google unveiled a copyright filter designed to catch unauthorized use of copyrighted videos and other materials. The judge dismissed the case, finding that YouTube was protected by the Digital Millennium Copyright Act's safe harbor clause. This states that companies can be protected if their services host content without review as long as infringing content is removed quickly.[14]

Following are some of the major laws enacted to regulate cyberspace and telecommunications:

LAW	WHAT IT DID
Computer Fraud and Abuse Act (1986)	Clarified definitions of criminal fraud and abuse for federal computer crimes and removed legal ambiguities and obstacles to prosecuting these crimes; established felony offenses for unauthorized access of "federal interest" computers and made it a misdemeanor to engage in unauthorized trafficking in computer passwords.
Children's Online Privacy Protection Act (1998)	Authorized the FTC to set rules regarding how and when firms must obtain parental permission before asking children marketing research questions.
Identity Theft and Assumption Deterrence Act (1998)	Made it a federal crime to knowingly transfer or use, without lawful authority, a means of identification of another person with intent to commit, aid, or abet any violation of federal, state, or local law.
Anticybersquatting Consumer Protection Act (1999)	Prohibited people from registering Internet domain names similar to company or celebrity names and then offering them for sale to these same parties.
Homeland Security Act (2002)	Established the Department of Homeland Security; gave government wide new powers to collect and mine data on individuals and groups, including databases that combine personal, governmental, and corporate records including e-mails and websites viewed; limited information citizens can obtain under the Freedom of Information Act; gave government committees more latitude for meeting in secret.
Amendments to the Telemarketing Sales Rule (2003), extended by the Do-Not-Call Improvement Act of 2007 and the Do-Not-Call Fee Extension Act of 2007	Created a national do-not-call registry, which prohibits telemarketing calls to registered telephone numbers; restricted the number and duration of telemarketing calls generating dead air space with use of automatic dialers; cracked down on unauthorized billing; and required telemarketers to transmit their caller ID information. Telemarketers must check the do-not-call list quarterly, and violators could be fined for each occurrence. Excluded from the registry's restrictions are charities, opinion pollsters, and political candidates. The 2007 DNC Improvement Act allowed registered numbers to remain on the list permanently, unless consumers call to remove them themselves; the FTC will remove disconnected and reassigned numbers from the list. The Fee Extension Act of 2007 set annual fees telemarketers must pay to access the registry.
Check Clearing for the 21st Century Act (2003)	Created the substitute check, allowing banks to process check information electronically and to deliver substitute checks to banks that want to continue receiving paper checks. A substitute check is the legal equivalent of the original check.

The Core of Business Law

Contract law and the law of agency; the Uniform Commercial Code, sales law, and negotiable instruments law; property law and the law of bailment; trademark, patent, and copyright law; tort law; bankruptcy law; and tax law are the cornerstones of U.S. business law. The sections that follow set out the key provisions of each of these legal concepts.

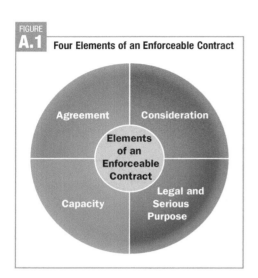

Four Elements of an Enforceable Contract

Contract Law and Law of Agency

Contract law is important because it is the legal foundation on which business dealings are conducted. A <u>contract</u> is a legally enforceable agreement between two or more parties regarding a specified act or thing.

Contract Requirements As Figure A.1 points out, the four elements of an enforceable contract are agreement, consideration, legal and serious purpose, and capacity. The parties must reach agreement about the act or thing specified. For such an agreement, or contract, to be valid and legally enforceable, each party must furnish consideration—the value or benefit that a party provides to the others with whom the contract is made. Assume that a builder hires an electrician to install wiring in a new house. The wiring job and the resulting payment are the considerations in this instance. In addition to consideration, an enforceable contract must involve a legal and serious purpose. Agreements made as a joke or involving the commission of crimes are not enforceable as legal contracts. An agreement between two competitors to fix the prices for their products is not enforceable as a contract because the subject matter is illegal.

The last element of a legally enforceable contract is capacity, the legal ability of a party to enter into agreements. The law does not permit certain people, such as those determined to lack mental capacity, to enter into legally enforceable contracts. Contracts govern almost all types of business activities. You might sign a contract to purchase a car or cell phone service, or to lease an apartment.

contract legally enforceable agreement between two or more parties regarding a specified act or thing.

Breach of Contract A violation of a valid contract is called a *breach of contract*. The injured party can go to court to enforce the contract provisions and, in some cases, collect *damages*—financial payments to compensate for a loss and related suffering.

Law of Agency All types of firms conduct business affairs through a variety of agents, such as partners, directors, corporate officers, and sales personnel. An agency relationship exists when one party, called the principal, appoints another party, called the agent, to enter into contracts with third parties on the principal's behalf.

The law of agency is based on common-law principles and case law decisions of state and federal courts. Relatively little agency law has been enacted into statute. The law of agency is important because the principal is generally bound by the actions of the agent.

The legal basis for holding the principal liable for acts of the agent is the Latin maxim *respondeat superior* ("let the master answer"). In a case involving agency law, the court must decide the rights and obligations of the various parties. Generally, the principal is held liable if an agency relationship exists and the agent has some type of authority to do the wrongful act. The agent in such cases is liable to the principal for any damages.

Uniform Commercial Code

Most U.S. business law is based on the *Uniform Commercial Code*—usually referred to simply as the UCC. The UCC covers topics such as sales law, warranties, and negotiable instruments. All 50 states have adopted the UCC, although Louisiana also relies on elements of civil law based on French, German, and Spanish codes, in addition to Roman law. While the other U.S. states rely on the tenets of English common law, which is also known as judge-based law, Louisiana's civil law system is found in most European nations. The UCC is actually a "model law" first written by the National Conference of Commissioners on Uniform State Laws, which states can then review and adopt, adopt with amendments, or replace with their own laws. The idea of the UCC is to create at least some degree of uniformity among the states.[15]

<u>Sales law</u> governs sales of goods or services for money or on credit. Article 2 of the UCC specifies the circumstances under which a buyer and a seller enter into a sales contract. Such agreements are based on the express conduct of the parties. The UCC generally requires written agreements for enforceable sales contracts for products worth more than $500. The formation of a sales contract is quite flexible because certain missing terms in a written contract or other ambiguities do not prevent the contract from being legally enforceable. A court will look to past dealings, commercial customs, and other standards of reasonableness to evaluate whether a legal contract exists.

Courts also consider these variables when either the buyer or the seller seeks to enforce his or her rights in cases in which the other party fails to perform as specified in the contract, performs only partially, or performs in a defective or unsatisfactory way. The UCC's remedies in such cases usually involve the award of monetary damages to injured parties. The UCC defines the rights of the parties to have the contract performed, to have it terminated, and to reclaim the goods or place a lien—a legal claim—against them.

sales law law governing the sale of goods or services for money or on credit.

Warranties Article 2 of the UCC also sets forth the law of warranties for sales transactions. Products carry two basic types of warranties: an express warranty is a specific representation made by the seller regarding the product, and an implied warranty is only legally imposed on the seller. Generally, unless implied warranties are disclaimed by the seller in writing, they are automatically in effect. Other provisions govern the rights of acceptance, rejection, and inspection of products by the buyer; the rights of the parties during manufacture, shipment, delivery, and passing of title to products; the legal significance of sales documents; and the placement of the risk of loss in the event of destruction or damage to the products during manufacture, shipment, or delivery.

Negotiable Instruments A *negotiable instrument* is commercial paper that is transferable among individuals and businesses. The most common example of a negotiable instrument is a check. Drafts, certificates of deposit (CDs), and notes are also sometimes considered negotiable instruments.

Article 3 of the UCC specifies that a negotiable instrument must be written and must meet the following conditions:

1. It must be signed by the maker or drawer.

2. It must contain an unconditional promise or order to pay a certain sum of money.

3. It must be payable on demand or at a definite time.

4. It must be payable to order or to bearer.

Checks and other forms of commercial paper are transferred when the payee signs the back of the instrument, a procedure known as endorsement.

Property Law and Law of Bailment

Property law is a key feature of the private enterprise system. *Property* is something for which a person or firm has the unrestricted right of possession or use. Property rights are guaranteed and protected by the U.S. Constitution. However, under certain circumstances property may be legally seized under the law of eminent domain. In a U.S. Supreme Court ruling, the city of New London, Connecticut, was granted permission to seize a distressed area of real estate—owned by individual citizens—for future economic development by private business.

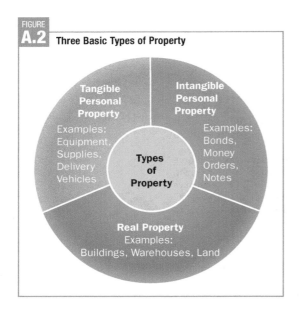

FIGURE A.2 Three Basic Types of Property

Tangible Personal Property
Examples: Equipment, Supplies, Delivery Vehicles

Intangible Personal Property
Examples: Bonds, Money Orders, Notes

Types of Property

Real Property
Examples: Buildings, Warehouses, Land

In fact, this development was never completed. In response, 44 states have since passed legislation limiting the use of eminent domain. Although an appellate court in New York ruled that the state could not seize a tract of land by eminent domain in order for Columbia University to expand its campus, the higher court of appeals overturned the ruling, paving the way for the university's $6.3 billion expansion.[16] And in an unusual twist of the law, Utah passed two bills allowing the state to take some of the U.S. government's vast federal land holdings by eminent domain.[17]

As Figure A.2 shows, property can be divided into three basic categories. Tangible personal property consists of physical items such as equipment, supplies, and delivery vehicles. Intangible personal property is nonphysical property such as mortgages, stocks, and checks that are most often represented by a document or other written instrument, although it may be as vague and remote as a computer entry. You are probably familiar with certain types of intangible personal property such as checks or money orders. But other examples include bonds, notes, letters of credit, and receipts.

A third category of property is real property, or real estate. Most firms have some interaction with real estate law because of the need to buy or lease the space in which they operate. Some companies are created to serve these real estate needs. Real estate developers, builders, contractors, brokers, appraisers, mortgage companies, escrow companies, title companies, and architects all deal with various aspects of real property law.

The law of bailment deals with the surrender of personal property by one person to another when the property is to be returned at a later date. The person delivering the property is known as the bailor, and the person receiving the property is the bailee. Some bailments benefit bailees, others benefit bailors, and still others provide mutual benefits. Most courts now require that all parties practice reasonable care in all bailment situations. The degree of benefit received from the bailment is a factor in court decisions about whether parties have met the reasonable-care standards.

Bailment disputes are most likely to arise in business settings such as hotels, restaurants, banks, and parking lots. A series of rules have been established to govern settlement of these disagreements. The law focuses on actual delivery of an item. For instance, a restaurant owner is not liable if a customer's coat or purse is stolen from the back of his or her chair. This is because the customer has not given the item to the restaurant for safekeeping. However, if the customer delivers the coat or purse to the restaurant checkroom, receives a claim check, and the item is stolen, then the restaurant is liable.

Trademarks, Patents, and Copyrights

Trademarks, patents, and copyrights provide legal protection for key business assets by giving a firm the exclusive right to use these assets. A **trademark** consists of words, symbols, or other designations used by firms to identify their offerings. The Lanham Act (1946) provides for federal registration of trademarks. Trademarks are a valuable commercial property. Coca-Cola and McDonald's are two of the world's most widely recognized trademarks, so they are very valuable to the companies that own them.

If a product becomes too well known, its fame can create issues. Once a trademark becomes a part of everyday usage, it loses its protection as a legal trademark. Consider the words *aspirin, cola, nylon, kerosene,* and *linoleum.* All these product names were once the exclusive property of their manufacturers, but they have passed into common language, and now anyone

trademark words, symbols, or other designations used by firms to identify their offerings.

can use them. More recent examples are *Xerox*, *Kleenex*, and *Velcro*. Although legally these are trademarked names, people often use them in everyday language instead of the correct generic terms *photocopy, facial tissue, and hook-and-loop*.

Companies understand the value of their trademarks and fight hard to protect them. Fashion company Kate Spade recently won a trademark infringement lawsuit against retailer Surf for its SATURDAY brand. Kate Spade filed an action claiming that its new SATURDAY brand does not infringe on the name of a popular men's clothes company, Saturdays SURF, who said Spade's new brand would create "reverse confusion" between Kate Spade brand and its clothing line.[18]

By law, a **patent** guarantees an inventor exclusive rights to an invention for 17 years. Copyrights and patents have a constitutional basis; the U.S. Constitution specifies that the federal government has the power "to promote the progress of science and useful arts, by securing for limited times to authors and inventors the exclusive rights to their respective writings or discoveries." Recently, the patent process and laws have been under scrutiny, and the Patent Reform Act was introduced in 2011. Under the act, which is supported by the information technology industry, it is now more difficult for firms to sue for patent infringement. Instead of filing for a patent on a first-to-invent basis, firms will receive patents on a first-to-file basis, which is more common around the world.[19]

A **copyright** protects written or printed material such as books, designs, cartoon illustrations, photos, computer software, music, and videos. This class of business property is referred to as *intellectual property*. Copyrights are filed with the Library of Congress. Congress recently extended copyright protection for creative material by an additional 20 years, covering artistic works for the lifetime of the creator plus 70 years; for companies, the time is 95 years. Not surprisingly, the Internet has opened up a whole new realm of copyright infringement, ranging from downloading music files to illegally sharing video footage.

In a lawsuit filed recently in federal district court in Illinois, a dozen different individuals are being sued over the use of a song called "Different Strokes," originally recorded more than 45 years ago. In the lawsuit, it is alleged that the song was "sampled" by artists without authorization, including Kanye West, Jay Z, Usher, and Mark Wahlberg.[20]

Despite publicity about Internet copyright infringement, many people engage in this practice unintentionally. Some schools are now making an effort to educate students about the practice so they can make better and more informed choices about downloading material from the Internet.

Law of Torts

A **tort** (French for "wrong") refers to a civil wrong inflicted on another person or the person's property. The law of torts is closely related to the law of agency because a business entity, or principal, can be held liable for torts committed by its agents in the course of business dealings. Tort law differs from both criminal and contract law. While criminal law is concerned with crimes against the state or society, tort law deals with compensation for injured people who are the victims of noncriminal wrongs.

Tort cases are often extremely complex and may result in large monetary awards. Because these awards have skyrocketed, some states have taken steps to limit them. Wisconsin recently limited the amount of any compensatory damages recovered by a plaintiff in a tort litigation dealing with injury or health problems resulting from exposure to toxins to $200,000.[21]

Types of Torts A tort may be intentional, or it may be caused by negligence. Assault, slander, libel, and fraud are all examples of intentional torts. Businesses can become involved in such cases through the actions of both owners and employees. A security guard who uses excessive force to apprehend an alleged shoplifter may have committed a tort. Under agency law, the guard's employers, such as a shopping mall or retailer, can be also held liable for any damages or injury caused by the security guard.

The other major group of torts results from negligence. This type of tort is based on carelessness rather than intentional behavior that causes injury to another person. Under agency law, businesses can also be held liable for the negligence of their employees or agents. A delivery truck driver who injures a pedestrian while transporting goods creates a tort liability for his or her employer if the accident results from negligence.

Product Liability An area of tort law known as *product liability* has been developed by both statutory and case law to hold businesses liable for negligence in the design, manufacture, sale, or use of products. Some states have extended the theory of tort law to cover injuries caused by products, regardless of whether the manufacturer is proven negligent. This legal concept is known as strict product liability.

The business response to product liability has been mixed. To avoid lawsuits and fines, some recall defective products voluntarily; others decide to fight recall mandates if they believe the recall is not justified. Recalls are common among automobile manufacturers. Recently General Motors recalled over 17 million cars on the basis of a faulty ignition switch, which has caused more than 13 deaths to date.[22] In addition, toymakers typically issue voluntary recalls, as do drug manufacturers.

Class-Action Fairness

A *class-action suit* groups a number of individual plaintiffs, such as consumers with adverse reactions to medications, to allow for efficient processing under one lawsuit. Congress passed the Class-Action Fairness Act of 2005, which imposes certain restrictions on class-action lawsuits. First, it automatically moves most large, multistate class actions—those with potential damages exceeding $5 million and in which more than two-thirds of the plaintiffs are geographically dispersed—from state courts into federal courts. This restriction prevents "shopping around" for sympathetic locations but lets cases that belong within a particular state remain there. Second, judges must consider the actual monetary value of any damage done so that plaintiffs receive true compensation for injury instead of large, arbitrary awards. Third, attorneys now receive payment differently. Under the old system, attorneys would receive a percentage of the gross settlement amount, regardless of whether all plaintiffs collected. Now judges can require uncollected awards to go to charity or government agencies, instead of into the pockets of lawyers. If the attorneys' fees are not based on a percentage, then they must charge based on the time they spent on the case.

Effects of the act are already being felt. In many states, the tide has already begun to turn away from huge, long, expensive lawsuits. Some states have passed their own laws restricting the types of suits that can be filed. Michigan has virtually eliminated class-action suits against drug manufacturers, and New York threw out a case accusing investment firms of manipulating the price of certain initial stock offerings. Twenty-three states have instituted statutes prohibiting suits against fast-food restaurants for causing obesity. And damage limits in many states have restricted medical malpractice suits.

Bankruptcy Law

bankruptcy legal nonpayment of financial obligations.

Bankruptcy, legal nonpayment of financial obligations, is a common occurrence in today's economic environment. Federal legislation passed in 1918 and revised several times since then provides a system for handling bankruptcies. Bankruptcy has two purposes. One is to protect creditors by providing a way to obtain compensation through debtors' assets. The second goal, which is almost unique to the United States, is to also protect debtors, allowing them to get a fresh financial start.

Federal law recognizes two types of bankruptcy. Under voluntary bankruptcy, a person or firm asks to be judged bankrupt because of inability to repay creditors. Under involuntary bankruptcy, creditors may request that a party be judged bankrupt.

Personal Bankruptcies

With a growing number of individuals amassing large personal debt—often through credit cards—Congress recently revised personal bankruptcy law to make it more difficult for people to erase their debt instead of being held accountable for it. Under the Bankruptcy Abuse Prevention and Consumer Protection Act of 2005, it is more difficult for individuals to file Chapter 7 bankruptcy, which traditionally has wiped out most debt. If their earnings exceed their state's median income, they will instead be required to file Chapter 13 bankruptcy, which sets up a repayment plan as designed by the court. A few years after the law's passage, personal bankruptcies still hovered at the high mark, likely because of a slow economy. Reports revealed that more homeowners were walking away from large mortgages that they were unable to pay instead of reorganizing their debt and trying to hang onto their homes. As the economy began to recover, the rate of personal bankruptcies declined.[23]

Business Bankruptcies

Businesses can also go bankrupt for a variety of reasons—mismanagement, plunging sales, an inability to keep up with competitors, or changes in the marketplace. Under Chapter 11 of the U.S. Bankruptcy Code, a firm may reorganize and develop a plan to repay its debts. Chapter 11 also permits prepackaged bankruptcies, in which companies enter bankruptcy proceedings after obtaining approval of most—but not necessarily all—of their creditors. Often companies can emerge from prepackaged bankruptcies sooner than those that opt for conventional Chapter 11 filings. Airlines have managed to accomplish this, as well as some large retailers.

Tax Law

A branch of law that affects every business, employee, and consumer in the United States is tax law. A **tax** is an assessment by a governmental unit. Federal, state, and local governments and special taxing authorities all levy taxes. Appendix C, "Personal Financial Planning," also covers tax law.

tax assessment by a governmental unit.

Some taxes are paid by individuals and some by businesses. Both have a decided impact on contemporary business. Business taxes reduce profits, and personal taxes cut the disposable incomes that individuals can spend on the products of industry. Governments spend the revenue from taxes to buy goods and services produced by businesses. Governments also act as transfer agents, moving tax revenue to other consumers and transferring Social Security taxes from the working population to retired or disabled people.

Governments can levy taxes on several different bases: income, sales, business receipts, property, and assets. The type of tax varies from one taxing authority to the other. The individual income tax is the biggest source of revenue for the federal government. Many states also rely heavily on income taxes as well as sales taxes, which vary widely. Cities and towns may collect property taxes in order to operate schools and improve roads. So-called luxury taxes are levied on items such as yachts and expensive sports cars, while so-called sin taxes are levied on items such as cigarettes and alcohol. In addition, the issue of whether to tax different types of Internet services and use has been hotly debated.

Business Terms You Need to Know

judiciary A-2	business law A-4	copyright A-13
law A-3	contract A-10	tort A-13
common law A-3	sales law A-11	bankruptcy A-14
statutory law A-3	trademark A-12	tax A-15
international law A-3	patent A-13	

Appendix A   **A-15**

Projects and Teamwork Applications

1. Considering the pervasiveness of technology in everyday life, why not consider resolving a dispute online using a technology platform like Modria? Cyber-mediation or online dispute resolution (ODR) is gaining traction as a low-cost and efficient way to mediate and resolve disputes. With increasing online purchases, transactions, and exchanges of many kinds, the number of disputes is on the rise. Settling such disputes can be time consuming and costly. Explore www.modria.com and discuss how ODR works and the specifics of how users benefit. What are its drawbacks?

2. Ever wonder about what life as a consumer was like before the creation of the Federal Trade Commission (FTC) in 1914? The FTC has the power to define unfair competition and to issue cease and desist orders so that companies halt unfair business practices. Go to the FTC website at www.ftc.gov and explore the "Tips & Advice" link and then "consumers," to gain additional insight as to how consumers are protected. Present your findings in class. What did you find particularly useful?

3. The business world is filled with tort cases, particularly those involving product liability. One of the most famous cases is probably the one in which a customer sued McDonald's because a cup of hot McDonald's coffee spilled in her lap, causing burns and scalding. A jury awarded her $2.7 million in punitive damages, an amount that was later reduced by a judge to less than $500,000. On your own or with a classmate, go online to research other famous product liability cases. Choose a case and learn as much as you can about it, including the effect the outcome had on the firm or firms involved. Present your findings in class.

4. Go online and research more about the Bankruptcy Abuse Prevention and Consumer Protection Act of 2005, and the implications it has in today's economy. Do you think the law is fair? Why or why not? How does filing for personal bankruptcy affect a person's standing in the marketplace? Present your thoughts to the class.

| Appendix B |

Insurance and Risk Management

Pay-as-You-Drive Insurance Plans

What would you do to save up to 30 percent on your auto insurance? Would you allow your insurance company to track your driving habits, including how far you drive, how fast, and how aggressively?

Several U.S. insurance companies, including Allstate, State Farm, Travelers, and Progressive, are offering pay-as-you-drive auto insurance policies in many states. The programs differ in details, but they generally rely on telematic tracking devices that plug into onboard diagnostic computers and measure statistics about usage that help create a unique driver risk profile. For the first time, those whose profiles put them in lower-risk categories can qualify for individualized lower rates based on their actual driving habits.

For instance, says a Progressive executive, "If you drive a lot compared to average, you are a higher risk. And if you drive aggressively, odds are you're higher risk as well . . . you're probably in closer proximity to other vehicles and trying to get around them, and so you have more braking events." Your rates would likely not go down.

But if you're a particularly safe and cautious driver, you might pay less for insurance even if you fit into a normally higher-risk group, such as teenage males. "This capability has really redefined the way we think about pricing auto," said an executive of Hartford Financial Services Group, which is launching a pilot program.

Some critics say less costly rates are available through other means, like combining discounts. But the biggest obstacle many drivers see isn't price but the potential loss of privacy. Insurers insist they don't need to and won't track *where* the car is driven, or even who is driving it, but GPS devices can already do that, and insurers use them to offer roadside assistance. Some fear insurance companies won't be able to resist drawing on location data to further identify individual drivers and adjust coverage based on destination.[1]

Overview

Appendix B

Risk is a daily fact of life for both individuals and businesses. Sometimes it arrives in the form of a serious illness or injury. In other instances, it takes the form of property loss, such as the extensive damage to homes and businesses due to the tornadoes that swept across midwestern and southern states. Risk can also occur as the result of the actions of others—such as a driver who is texting while driving and runs a stop sign. In still other cases, risk may occur as a result of our own actions—we might venture out in a boat during a thunderstorm or fail to heed warnings about high blood pressure.

Businesspeople must understand the types of risk they face and develop methods for dealing with them. One approach to risk is to shift it to the specialized expertise of insurance companies. This appendix discusses the concept of insurance in a business setting. It begins with a definition of risk. We then describe the various ways in which risk can be managed. Next, we list some of the major insurance concepts, such as what constitutes an insurable risk. The appendix concludes with an overview of the major types of insurance.

The Concept of Risk

risk uncertainty about loss or injury.

Risk is uncertainty about loss or injury. Consider the risks faced by a typical business. A factory or warehouse faces the risk of fire and smoke, burglary, and storm damage. Data loss, injuries to workers, and loss of facilities are some of the risks faced by businesses. Risks can be divided into two major categories: speculative risk and pure risk.

Speculative risk gives the firm or individual the chance of either a profit or a loss. A firm that expands operations into a new market may experience higher profits or the loss of invested funds. A contractor who builds a house without a specific buyer may sell the house at a profit or lose money if the house sits unsold for months.

Pure risk, on the other hand, involves only the chance of loss. Motorists, for example, always face the risk of accidents. If they occur, both financial and physical losses may result. If they do not occur, however, drivers do not profit. Insurance often helps individuals and businesses protect against financial loss resulting from some types of pure risk.

Risk Management

risk management calculations and actions a firm takes to recognize and deal with real or potential risks to its survival.

Because risk is an unavoidable part of business, managers must find ways to deal with it. The first step in any **risk management** plan is to recognize what's at risk and why it's at risk. After that, the manager must decide how to handle the risk. In general, businesses have four alternatives in handling risk: avoid it, minimize it, assume it, or transfer it.

Executives must consider many factors when evaluating risks, both at home and abroad. These factors include a nation's economic stability; social and cultural factors, such as language; available technologies; distribution systems; and government regulations. International businesses are typically exposed to less risk in countries with stable economic, social and cultural, and political and legal environments.

Avoiding Risk

Some of the pure risks facing people can be avoided by leading a healthy lifestyle. Not smoking and not swimming alone are two ways of avoiding personal risk. By the same token, businesses can also avoid some of the pure risks they face. A manufacturer can locate a new production facility away from an area that is prone to floods tornadoes, hurricanes, or earthquakes.

Reducing Risk

Managers can reduce or even eliminate many types of risk by removing hazards or taking preventive measures. Many companies develop safety programs to educate employees about potential hazards and the proper methods of performing certain dangerous tasks. Any employee who works at a hazardous waste site is required to have training and medical monitoring that meet the federal Occupational Safety and Health Administration (OSHA) standards. The training and monitoring not only reduce risk but pay off on the bottom line. Aside from the human tragedy, accidents cost companies time and money.

Businesses can reduce some of the pure risks they encounter. For example, a company could locate a new production facility away from areas that are prone to tornadoes.

A-18   **Appendix B**

Although many preventative measures can reduce the risk involved in business operations, they cannot eliminate risk entirely. Most major insurers help their clients avoid or minimize risk by offering the services of loss-prevention experts to conduct thorough reviews of their operations. These health and safety professionals evaluate customers' work environments and recommend procedures and equipment to help firms minimize worker injuries and property losses.

By the same token, people can take actions to reduce risk. For instance, obeying the rules of the road and doing regular maintenance on a car can reduce the risks associated with driving. Boarding up windows in preparation for a hurricane can reduce the risk of wind damage. However, such actions cannot entirely eliminate risk.

Self-Insuring Against Risk

Instead of purchasing insurance against certain types of pure risk, some companies accumulate funds to cover potential losses. These self-insurance funds are special funds created by periodically setting aside cash reserves that the firm can draw on in the event of a financial loss resulting from a pure risk. A firm makes regular payments to the fund, and it charges losses to the fund. Such a fund typically accompanies a risk-reduction program aimed at minimizing losses.

One of the most common forms of self-insurance is employee health insurance. Most employers provide health insurance coverage to employees as a component of their benefit programs. Some, especially larger ones, find it more economical to create a self-insurance fund covering projected employee health care expenses, as opposed to purchasing a health insurance policy from a health insurance company. Self-insured employers, however, almost always contract with a health insurer to administer their employee health plans.

Shifting Risk to an Insurance Company

Although organizations and individuals can take steps to avoid or reduce risk, the most common method of dealing with it is to shift it to others in the form of insurance—a contract by which an insurer, for a fee, agrees to reimburse another firm or individual a sum of money if a loss occurs. The insured party's fee to the insurance company for coverage against losses is called a *premium*. Insurance substitutes a small, known loss—the insurance premium—for a larger, unknown loss that may or may not occur. In the case of life insurance, the loss—death—is a certainty; the main uncertainty is the date when it will occur.

It is important for the insurer to understand the customer's business, risk exposure, and insurance needs. Firms that operate worldwide usually do business with insurance companies that maintain global networks of offices.

insurance contract by which the insurer, for a fee, agrees to reimburse the insured a sum of money if a loss occurs.

Basic Insurance Concepts

Figure B.1 illustrates how an insurance company operates. The insurer collects premiums from policyholders in exchange for insurance coverage. The insurance company uses some of these funds to pay current claims and operating expenses. What's left over is held in the form of reserves, which are in turn invested. Reserves can be used to pay for unexpected losses. The returns from insurance company reserves may allow the insurer to reduce premiums, generate profits, or both. By investing reserves, the insurance industry represents a major source of long-term financing for other businesses, as discussed in Chapter 16.

An insurance company is a professional risk taker. For a fee, it accepts risks of loss or damage to businesses and individuals. Four basic principles underlie insurance: the concept of insurable interest, the concept of insurable risk, the rule of indemnity, and the law of large numbers.

How an Insurance Company Operates

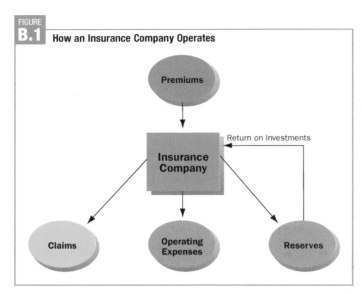

Insurable Interest

To purchase insurance, an applicant must demonstrate an *insurable interest* in the property or life of the insured. In other words, the policyholder must stand to suffer a loss, financial or otherwise, due to fire, storm damage, accident, theft, illness, death, or lawsuit. A homeowner has an insurable interest in his or her home and its contents. In the case of life insurance coverage purchased for the main income provider in a household, the policyholder's spouse and children have a clear insurable interest.

A firm can purchase property and liability insurance on physical assets—such as an office or warehouse—to cover losses due to such hazards as fire and theft because the company can demonstrate an obvious insurable interest. Because top executives are important assets to a company, a business often purchases key-person life insurance, which compensates the business should an important individual die.

Insurable Risk

Insurable risk refers to the requirements that a risk must meet in order for the insurer to provide protection. Only some pure risks, and no speculative ones, are insurable. There are four basic requirements for a pure risk to be considered an insurable risk:

1. The likelihood of loss should be reasonably predictable. If an insurance company cannot reasonably predict losses, it has no basis for setting affordable premiums.

2. The loss should be financially measurable.

3. The loss should be accidental, or fortuitous.

4. The risk should be spread over a certain geographic area.

The insurance company has the right to set standards for accepting risk. This process of setting these standards, and deciding what to charge, is known as *underwriting*.

Rule of Indemnity

rule of indemnity
requirement that the insured cannot collect more than the amount of the loss and cannot collect for the same loss more than once.

The **rule of indemnity** states that the insured cannot collect more than the amount of the loss. Nor can the insured collect for that loss more than once. Assume that a florist's delivery van is damaged in an accident. If the total damage amounts to $2,500, then that is the maximum amount the business can collect from the insurance company.

Occasionally a loss may be covered by more than one policy. For instance, assume that a $5,000 loss is covered by two different policies. The rule of indemnity means that the insured individual or business can only collect a total of $5,000 from both insurance companies. It is up to the insurers to decide which pays how much based on policy specifics.

The Law of Large Numbers

Insurance is based on the law of averages, or statistical probability. Insurance companies simply cannot afford to sell insurance policies unless they can reasonably predict losses. As a result, insurance companies have studied the chances of occurrences of deaths, injuries, property damage, lawsuits, and other types of hazards. From their investigations, insurance companies have developed *actuarial tables*, which predict the number of fires, automobile accidents, or deaths that will occur in a given year. Premiums charged for insurance coverage are based on these tables. Actuarial tables are based on the law of large numbers. In essence, the **law of large numbers** states that seemingly random events will follow a predictable pattern if enough events are observed. An actuary is a professional who uses math, statistics, and financial theory to study the impact of risk and uncertainty, primarily related to insurance and pension programs.

An example can demonstrate how insurers use the law of large numbers to calculate premiums. Previously collected statistical data on a city with 50,000 homes indicates that the city will experience an average of 500 fires a year, with damages averaging $30,000 per occurrence. What is the minimum annual premium an insurance company would charge to insure one residence?

To simplify the calculations, assume that the premiums would not produce profits or cover any of the insurance company's operating expenses—they would just produce enough income to pay policyholders for their losses. In total, fires in the city would generate claims of $15 million (500 homes damaged × $30,000). If these losses were spread over all 50,000 homes, each home-owner would be charged an annual premium of $300 ($15 million × 50,000 homes). In reality, though, the insurer would set the premium at a higher figure to cover operating expenses, build reserves, and earn a reasonable profit. For instance, during a recent year, the purchase of individual life insurance policies totaled over $28.5 trillion in premiums, but the payout of claims was less.[2]

Some losses are easier for insurance companies to predict than others. Life insurance companies can predict with high accuracy the number of policyholders who will die within a specified period of time. But losses from such hazards as automobile accidents and weather events are much more difficult to predict. In a recent year, catastrophes like tornadoes, tropical storms, hail and high winds, wildfires, and other natural disasters totaled $35 billion, the fourth worst year on record.[3]

> **law of large numbers**
> concept that seemingly random events will follow predictable patterns if enough events are observed.

Sources of Insurance Coverage

The insurance industry includes both for-profit companies—such as Prudential, State Farm, and Liberty Mutual—and a number of public agencies that provide insurance coverage for business firms, not-for-profit organizations, and individuals.

Public Insurance Agencies

A *public insurance agency* is a state or federal government unit established to provide specialized insurance protection for individuals and organizations. It provides protection in such areas as job loss (unemployment insurance) and work-related injuries (workers' compensation). Public insurance agencies also sponsor specialized programs, such as deposit, flood, and crop insurance.

Unemployment Insurance Every state in the United States has an unemployment insurance program that assists unemployed workers by providing financial benefits, job counseling, and placement services. Compensation amounts vary depending on workers' previous earnings and the states in which they file claims. These insurance programs are funded by payroll taxes paid by employers.

Workers' Compensation Under state laws, employers must provide workers' compensation insurance to guarantee payment of wages and salaries, medical care costs, and such rehabilitation services as retraining, job placement, and vocational rehabilitation to employees who are injured on the job. In addition, workers' compensation provides benefits in the form of weekly payments or single, lump-sum payments to survivors of workers whose work-related injuries result in death. Premiums are based on the company's payroll, the on-the-job hazards to which it exposes workers, and its safety record.

Social Security The federal government is the nation's largest insurer. The Social Security program, established in 1935, provides retirement, survivor, and disability benefits to millions of Americans. *Medicare* was added to the Social Security program in 1965 to provide health insurance for people age 65 and older and certain other Social Security recipients. More than nine out of ten workers in the United States and their dependents are eligible for Social Security program benefits. The program is funded through a payroll tax, half of which is paid by employers and half by workers. Self-employed people pay the full tax.

Private Insurance Companies

Much of the insurance in effect is provided by private firms. These companies provide protection in exchange for the payment of premiums. Some private insurers are stockholder owned, and therefore are run like any other business, and others are so-called mutual associations. Most, though not all, mutual insurance companies specialize in life insurance. Technically, mutual insurance companies are owned by their policyholders, who may receive premium rebates in the form of dividends. In spite of this, however, there is no evidence that an insurance policy from a mutual company costs any less than a comparable policy from a stockholder-owned insurer. In recent years some mutual insurance companies have reorganized as stockholder-owned companies, including Prudential, one of the nation's largest insurers.

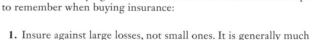

Types of Insurance

Individuals and businesses spend hundreds of billions of dollars each year on insurance coverage. Figure B.2 shows how much insurance companies collected in premiums in a recent year. Unfortunately, both business firms and consumers make poor decisions when buying insurance. Here are four common sense tips to remember when buying insurance:

1. Insure against large losses, not small ones. It is generally much more cost effective to self-insure against small losses.

2. Buy insurance with broad coverage, not narrow coverage. For example, it is much less expensive generally to buy a homeowners policy that protects you from multiple events (perils such as fire and theft) than to buy several policies that cover individual events.

3. Shop around. Premiums for similar policies can vary widely from company to company.

4. Buy insurance only from financially strong companies. Insurance companies occasionally go bankrupt. If that happens, the insured is left with no coverage and little hope of getting premiums back.

Although insurers offer hundreds of different policies, they all fall into three broad categories: property and liability insurance, health and disability insurance, and life insurance.

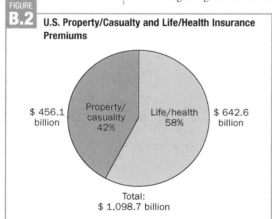

FIGURE B.2 U.S. Property/Casualty and Life/Health Insurance Premiums

$ 456.1 billion — Property/casualty 42%

Life/health 58% — $ 642.6 billion

Total: $ 1,098.7 billion

Note: Property/casualty is defined as net premiums written, excluding state funds. Life/health includes premiums, annuity considerations (fees for annuity contracts), and deposit-type funds.

Source: Insurance Information Institute, "Insurance Industry at a Glance," www.iii.org, accessed April 6, 2014.

A-22   Appendix B

Property and Liability Insurance

Insurance that protects against fire, accident, theft, or other destructive events or perils, is called **property and liability insurance**. Examples of this insurance category include homeowners' insurance, auto insurance, business or commercial insurance, and liability insurance. Most property and liability policies are subject to deductibles. A deductible is the amount of the loss the insured pays out of pocket.

Homeowners' Insurance Homeowners' insurance protects homeowners from damage to their residences due to various perils. If a home is destroyed by fire, for example, the homeowners' policy will pay to replace the home and its contents. Virtually all homeowners carry coverage of this nature.

Homeowners' insurance premiums have risen sharply in recent years. Moreover, homeowners in coastal areas are finding it increasingly difficult to obtain insurance because of the rising number of claims related to erosion, hurricanes, and floods. If homeowners can obtain private coverage, those plans may be very expensive. In some cases they may be able to purchase insurance through a state-run program instead.[4]

Although standard policies cover a wide range of perils, most do not cover damage from widespread catastrophes such as floods and earthquakes. Homeowners must purchase separate policies to protect against damage caused by these perils. Flood insurance is available through the National Flood Insurance Program. Earthquake coverage is offered in several earthquake-prone states such as California and Washington but is very expensive.

Auto Insurance With more than $150 billion in annual premiums, automobile insurance is the country's largest category of property and liability insurance. Automobile insurance policies cover losses due to automobile accidents or theft, including personal and property claims. Almost all states require drivers to have a minimum amount of auto insurance coverage.

Commercial and Business Insurance Commercial and business insurance protects firms from financial losses resulting from the suspension of business operations (*business interruption insurance*) or physical damage to property as a result of destructive events. These policies may also protect employers from employee dishonesty or losses resulting from nonperformance of contracts.

Liability Insurance *Liability insurance* protects an individual or business against financial losses to others for which the individual or business was responsible. If a business sells a defective product, the firm's liability insurance would pay for financial losses sustained by customers. A standard amount of liability coverage is usually attached to auto, homeowners', and commercial insurance policies. Additional amounts of liability insurance can be purchased if needed. Adequate liability insurance is critically important today for both businesses and individuals. Walmart, for example, requires its suppliers to have at least $2 million in liability coverage for their products; some products considered to be high risk can require a minimum of $10 million.[5]

Health and Disability Insurance

Each of us faces the risk of getting sick or being injured in some way. Even a relatively minor illness can result in substantial health care bills. To guard against this risk, most Americans have some form of **health insurance**—insurance that provides coverage for expenses due to sickness or accidents. With soaring costs in health care, this type of insurance has become an important consideration for both businesses and individuals.

Sources of health insurance include private individual policies, private group policies, and the federal government, through Medicare and Medicaid (health insurance for lower-income

property and liability insurance general category of insurance that protects against losses due to a number of perils.

health insurance category of insurance that pays for losses due to illness or injury.

Some providers offer low-cost health plans to companies. The goal for all health insurance is to provide coverage for expenses due to sickness or accidents that require medical care.

people). More than 60 percent of Americans are covered by private group health insurance provided by their employer as an employee benefit. Four of every five U.S. employees work for businesses and not-for-profits that offer some form of group health insurance. Group policies resemble individual health insurance policies but are offered at lower premiums. Health insurance costs have soared in recent years, and employers have responded by cutting back on benefits, requiring employees to pay more of the premium, charging higher deductibles, or even dropping coverage altogether. In response to the growing cost and increasing numbers of individuals without adequate coverage, Congress passed a pair of health care reform bills entitled the Patient Protection and Affordable Care Act and the Health Care and Education Reconciliation Act. Although the bills were the subject of heated debate among legislators, businesspeople, and consumers, they were signed into law.[6]

Private health insurance plans fall into one of two general categories: fee-for-service plans and managed care plans. In a *fee-for-service plan*, the insured picks his or her doctor and has almost unlimited access to specialists. Fee-for-service plans charge an annual deductible and copayments. By contrast, a *managed care plan* pays most of the insured's health care bills. In return, the program has a great deal of say over the conditions of health care provided for the insured. Most managed care plans, for example, restrict the use of specialists and may specify which hospitals and pharmacies can be used. Some employers offer employees a choice between a fee-for-service and a managed care plan. Multiple managed care plans are sometimes available.

Managed care plans have become extremely popular in recent years. More than 150 million Americans are enrolled in some form of managed care plan, and many fee-for-service plans have adopted some elements of managed care. A primary reason for the popularity of managed care is simply cost: managed care plans generally cost employers and employees less than fee-for-service plans. Managed care, however, is not without its critics. The effort to control costs has caused a backlash because of restrictions placed on doctors and patients. Legislation at both the federal and state levels has forced managed care plans to give patients and physicians more control over medical decisions.

Types of Managed Care Plans Two types of managed care plans can be found in the United States: health maintenance organizations and preferred provider organizations. Although both manage health care, important differences exist between the two.

Health maintenance organizations (HMOs) do not provide health insurance; they provide health care. An HMO supplies all of the individual's health care needs, including prescription drugs and hospitalization. The individual must use the HMO's own doctors and approved treatment facilities in order to receive benefits. Doctors and other health care professionals are actually employees of the HMO. Individuals pick a primary care physician and cannot see a specialist without a referral. An HMO charges no deductibles and only a low, fixed-dollar copayment.

The second type of managed care plan is the preferred provider organization (PPO). In the United States, more individuals are covered by PPOs than by HMOs. In a PPO, an employer negotiates a contract between local health care providers (physicians, hospitals, and pharmacies) to provide medical care to its employees at a discount. These plans have low fixed-dollar copayments. They are generally much more flexible than HMOs. Members can choose their primary care physician from a list of doctors. If a referral is given or hospitalization is required, the member again chooses from a list of approved health care providers. A member who obtains treatment from a health care provider outside the PPO network may be reimbursed for only part of the cost.

Disability Income Insurance Not only is *disability income insurance* one of the most overlooked forms of insurance, but many workers also don't have enough coverage. The odds that a person will develop a disability are considerably higher than most people realize. Take a group of five randomly selected 45-year-olds. There is approximately a 95 percent chance that one of the five will develop some form of disability during the next 20 years. Disability income insurance is designed to replace lost income when a wage earner cannot work due to an accident or illness.

Two sources of disability income insurance exist: Social Security and private disability insurance policies. Social Security disability benefits are available to virtually all workers, but they have very strict requirements. Private disability insurance is available on either an individual or group basis. As with health insurance, a group policy is less expensive than an individual policy. Many employers provide at least some disability coverage as an employee benefit. Employees often have the option of obtaining additional coverage by paying more.

Life Insurance

<u>Life insurance</u> protects people against the financial losses that occur with premature death. Three of every four Americans have some form of life insurance. The main reason people buy life insurance is to provide financial security for their families in the event of their death. With assets totaling $5.8 trillion, the life insurance industry is one of the nation's largest businesses.[7]

life insurance protects people against the financial losses that occur with premature death.

Types of Life Insurance As with health and disability insurance, both individual and group life insurance policies are available. Many employers offer life insurance to employees as a component of the firm's benefit program. However, unlike health and disability insurance, an individual life insurance policy is usually cheaper than a group policy for younger people.

The different types of life insurance fall neatly into two categories: term policies and cash value policies. Term policies provide a death benefit if the policyholder dies within a specified period of time. It has no value at the end of that period. Cash value policies—sometimes called whole life and universal life—combine life insurance protection with a savings or investment feature. The cash value represents the amount of the savings or investment portion of the policy. Although there are arguments in favor of cash value policies, many experts believe that term life insurance is a better choice for most consumers. For one thing, a term policy is less expensive than a cash value policy.

How Much Life Insurance Should You Have?

People can purchase life insurance policies for almost any amount. Life insurance purchases are limited only by the amount of premiums people can afford and their ability to meet medical qualifications. The amount of life insurance a person needs, however, is a very personal decision. The general rule of thumb is that a person needs life insurance if he or she has family members who financially depend on that individual. A young parent with three small children could easily need $500,000 or more of life insurance. A single person with no dependents would reasonably see little or no need for a life insurance policy.

Do you need life insurance? The general rule is that a person should have life insurance if he or she has family members who depend financially on that individual. For example, a young parent could easily need $500,000 or more of life insurance. A single person with no dependents may see little or no need for life insurance coverage.

Businesses, as well as individual consumers, buy life insurance. The death of a partner or a key executive is likely to result in a financial loss to an organization. Key person insurance reimburses the organization for the loss of the services of an essential senior executive and to cover the executive search expenses needed to find a replacement. In addition, life insurance policies may be purchased for each member of a partnership to be able to repay the deceased partner's survivors for his or her share of the firm and permit the business to continue.

■ Business Terms You Need to Know

risk A-18
risk management A-18
insurance A-19

rule of indemnity A-20
law of large numbers A-21
property and liability insurance A-23

health insurance A-23
life insurance A-25

■ Projects and Teamwork Applications

1. Choose one of the following companies, or select another one that interests you. Research the company online, learning what you can about the firm's goods and services, work processes, and facilities. Then create a chart identifying risks you believe the company faces—and ways the firm can avoid those risks or reduce the risks. Suggested firms:

   a. Carnival Cruises

   b. Tampa Bay Rays

   c. Whole Food Markets

   d. The Hershey Company

2. Assess your own personal insurance needs. What types of coverage do you currently have? How do you see your insurance needs changing in the next five to ten years? Go to www.life-happens.org to assess your insurance needs by using some of the online calculators.

3. Sometimes an insured consumer, knowing that risk is transferred to the insurer, has a tendency to act carelessly or with a false sense of security. This behavior is sometimes termed a "moral hazard." Research how companies deal with the obligation to provide coverage when the insured consumer behaves in such a way as to increase the company's risk or liability. What impact does this phenomenon have on the insurance company?

4. Insurance fraud is pervasive and occurs when an insured individual receives money from an insurance company through deception over an insurance matter. Go to the website for the Coalition Against Insurance Fraud at www.insurancefraud.org. Click on "Info," and research common forms of insurance fraud. Discuss your findings with the class.

Personal Financial Planning

Personal Saving Strategies for Millennials

Do you know how to have $90,000 in the bank in just 30 years? By saving only $250 a month, beginning now. That's about what most workers today spend on coffee and lunch each month.

Unfortunately, saving isn't as easy for the Millennial generation as it sounds. Burdened with student loan and credit-card debt, many young people view saving for retirement as a job for someone else, despite their declining faith in Social Security. And in the wake of the recent economic slowdown, many U.S. consumers are focusing on paying down personal debt rather than on saving for the long term.

At the same time, however, many financial advisors believe younger workers need to save for retirement even more carefully than earlier generations, because they'll need much more money in reserve than today's retirees to see them through their later years. Most advisors agree that because nothing is certain, including the future of the Social Security system, today's younger workers should be aiming to set aside between $2 and $3 million for themselves and their families for retirement.

That's a daunting number for most people when viewed as a lump sum. The only way to approach it realistically is to save as much as possible on a regular basis, beginning as early as you can. For instance, back to that $250 a month: some advisors suggest simple strategies such as eating breakfast at home and packing a lunch, including a container of home-brewed coffee, instead of stopping at Starbucks on the way to work.

Other advice includes acknowledging that you'll have competing financial priorities, and that their relative importance will change as you get older. Also try thinking of your financial health as being just as important as your physical health. You exercise, so why not save too? If you find it easier to stick with an exercise program when you have a buddy, include your spouse or a friend in your savings plan. A little reinforcement can go a long way.

Finally, even if you start small, be sure you start. As one financial advisor says, "It's the pennies that add up."[1]

Overview

You are studying business, but much of what you learn in this course will also apply to your personal life. For instance, you learn about each of the important functions of a business—from accounting to marketing, from finance to management. Learning about each business function will help you choose a career, and a career choice may be one of the most important personal financial decisions you will make. You will learn why firms prepare budgets and financial statements. But budgets and financial statements are also important tools for individuals and households.

Everyone, regardless of age or income, can probably do a better job of managing his or her finances. As a group, Americans are much better at making money than they are at managing money. This appendix introduces you to personal financial management. **Personal financial management** deals with a variety of issues and decisions that affect a person's financial well-being. It includes basic money management, credit, tax planning, major consumer purchases, insurance, investing, and retirement planning.

The appendix will draw from many of the topics you will learn while studying business, but it introduces you to some new concepts as well. It is hoped that after completing the appendix, you will be a better informed financial

personal financial management study of the economic factors and personal decisions that affect a person's financial well-being.

consumer and personal money manager and that you will be motivated to learn more about personal finance. The rewards, in both monetary and nonmonetary terms, can be tremendous.

The Meaning and Importance of Personal Finance

Personal finance affects, and is affected by, many things we do and many decisions we make throughout our lives.

On one level, personal finance involves money know-how. It is essential to know how to earn money, as well as how to save, spend, invest, and control it in order to achieve goals. The reward of sound money management is an improvement in a person's standard of living. **Standard of living** consists of the necessities, comforts, or luxuries a person seeks to attain or maintain.

On another level, personal finance is intertwined with each person's lifestyle—the way we live our daily lives. Our choice of careers, friends, hobbies, communities, and possessions is determined by personal finances, and yet our personal finances can also be determined by our lifestyles. If you're a college student living on a shoestring budget, you may have to make serious financial sacrifices to achieve your educational goals. Where you live is determined by the school you attend and how much you can afford to pay for room and board; your vacation is set by your academic schedule and your savings account; your clothing depends on the climate and your budget. All these lifestyle decisions are largely determined by your personal finances.

standard of living necessities, comforts, and luxuries one seeks to obtain or to maintain.

The Importance of Personal Finance Today

Good money management has always been important, but major changes in the economic environment over the past few years have made personal finance even more important today. And this is true whether you're a 20-year-old college student with hefty tuition bills, a 40-year-old parent with a mortgage to pay, or a 60-year-old thinking about retirement. Let's look at three reasons personal financial planning is so important in today's environment.

Sluggish Growth in Personal Income Personal income in the United States has grown very slowly in recent years. For example, median household income actually dropped 2.6 percent in a recent year.[2] During this time, financial institutions faltered and unemployment soared. While the U.S. economy is now moving forward slowly, most predict that annual increases in wages and salaries will barely keep pace with the rate of inflation in the coming years.

The sluggish growth in personal income makes sound money management very important. You cannot count on rising personal income by itself to improve your standard of living. Rather, you need to save and invest more money, stick to a budget, and make major purchases wisely.

Changes in the Labor Market Job security and the notion of work have changed in recent years. People rarely work for the same company throughout an entire career; in fact, most people change jobs every five years. One poll revealed that nearly half of Americans age 50 and older say they plan to postpone retirement due to the sluggish

If you're on a budget, skiing at expensive resorts won't leave much money in your savings account.

Ryan McVay/The Image Bank/Getty Images

economy, the current value of their 401(k) retirement plans and other investments, and insufficient savings.[3]

The fact is that you and your classmates will likely change jobs and even employers several times during your careers. Some will end up working part-time or on a contract basis, with little job security and fewer benefits. Others will take time off to care for small children or elderly parents. And a goal many people have today is to start their own business and work for themselves.

Furthermore, it is estimated that one in four workers today will be unemployed at some point during their working lives. You never know when your employer will downsize, taking your job with it, or outsource your job elsewhere. Just review today's headlines and you will see that announcements of well-known companies downsizing and outsourcing are still common.

These changes make sound personal financial management even more important. You must keep your career skills up-to-date and accumulate sufficient financial resources to weather an unexpected crisis.

More Options The number of choices today in such areas as banking, credit, investments, and retirement planning can be bewildering. Today you can do most of your banking with a brokerage firm and then buy mutual fund shares at a bank. Even the simple checking account has become more complicated. The typical bank offers several different types of checking accounts, each with its own features and fees. Choosing the wrong account could easily cost you hundreds of dollars in unnecessary fees each year.

Twenty years ago, few college students carried credit cards, and those who did typically had cards tied to their parents' accounts. Banks and other credit card issuers didn't consider college students to be reasonable risks. Then the situation changed, resulting in a credit card debt crisis among students. The Credit Card Accountability Responsibility and Disclosure Act of 2009 (the CARD Act), however, contains reforms aimed at reversing this trend so that students will become more educated about their use of money.

One of the first things you'll do when you start a full-time job is make decisions about employee benefits. The typical employer may offer lots of choices in such areas as health insurance, disability insurance, group life insurance, and retirement plans. Selecting the right health insurance plan can save you thousands of dollars each year; by the same token, choosing the right retirement plan will enhance your economic security many years from now.

Personal Financial Planning—A Lifelong Activity

Personal financial planning is as important an activity whether you're 20, 40, or 60; whether you're single or married with children; and whether your annual income is $40,000 or $200,000. Many experts say that if you can't stick to a budget and control your spending when you're making $40,000 a year, you'll find it difficult to live within your means even if your income doubles or triples.

The fact that sound planning is a lifelong activity, of course, doesn't mean your financial goals and plans remain the same throughout your life—they won't. The major goal when you're young may be to buy your first car or pay off your college loans. For older people, the major goal is to pay off their home mortgage and have enough funds as possible for retirement.

A Personal Financial Management Model

A **financial plan** is a guide to help you reach targeted goals in the future, closing the gap between your current situation and where you'd like to be in the future. Goals might include buying a home, starting your own business, traveling extensively, sending children to college, or retiring early. Developing a personal financial plan consists of several steps, as illustrated in Figure C.1.

financial plan guide to help a person reach desired financial goals.

FIGURE
C.1 A Model of Personal Financial Management

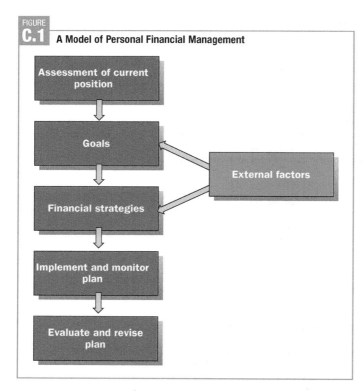

The first step in the process is to establish a clear picture of where you currently stand financially. Next, develop a series of short- and long-term goals. These goals should be influenced by your values, as well as an assessment of your current financial situation. The next step is to establish a set of financial strategies—in each of the personal planning areas—designed to help close the gap between where you are now and where you want to be in the future. Next, put your plan into action and closely monitor its performance. Periodically evaluate the effectiveness of your financial plan and make adjustments when necessary.

Financial plans cannot be developed in a vacuum. They should reflect your available resources—especially salary and fringe benefits, such as health insurance and retirement plans. For example, your goals and financial strategies should be based on a realistic estimate of your future income. If you cannot reach your financial goals through your current career path, you will have to scale back your goals or consider switching careers.

In addition, external factors—such as economic conditions and employment prospects—will influence your financial plan and decisions. For instance, assume you currently rent an apartment but have a goal of buying a duplex. While you can afford to buy right now, you believe there is a good chance you'll be offered a much better job in a new city within the next year. Depending on the real estate market, a wise financial move might be to postpone buying until your employment future becomes clearer.

General Themes Common to All Financial Plans

Regardless of the specifics, all financial plans revolve around three general themes: (1) maximizing income and wealth, (2) using money more effectively, and (3) monitoring expenditures.

Maximizing Income and Wealth Maximizing your income and wealth means getting more money. Work smarter; seek retraining or additional education for a better, higher-paying job; take career risks that may pay off in the long run; make sound investment decisions—all these are examples of the implementation of the first step. The amount of money you earn is a vital part of any financial plan, and it is up to you to make the most of your opportunities.

Using Money More Effectively Money has two basic uses: consumption and savings. Even if you are a regular saver, you'll still spend most of your income, probably more than 90 percent. You must try to spend every dollar wisely and make every major buying decision part of your overall financial plan. Avoid impulsive spending or giving in to a hard sell. Learn to assess the difference between a "want" and a "need."

And it's not just big expenditures you need to watch. Cutting back your spending on small items can make a difference. Little purchases do add up. Packing your own lunch a few times a week rather than buying your sandwiches at the local deli could save at least $20 a week. Invest that savings at 3 percent interest (per year) and you'll have almost $38,000 in 30 years.

Monitoring Expenditures Budgeting is the key to controlling expenditures. A budget provides a view of where the money is going and whether a person's goals are being met. It also suggests appropriate times for reevaluating priorities. If your budget doesn't reflect what you want from life both now and in the future, change it.

Information and knowledge also help you keep your expenditures under control. The more you know about real estate, consumer loans, credit-card rates and laws, insurance, taxes, and major purchases, the more likely you are to spend your money wisely.

The Pitfalls of Poor Financial Planning

Unfortunately, too many people fail to plan effectively for their financial future. Not only do many find it difficult to improve their standard of living, but quite a few also find themselves with mounting debts and a general inability to make ends meet. According to the American Bankruptcy Institute, the number of personal bankruptcy filings hit a record number of more than 1.5 million in a recent year, but has since begun to recede by almost 30 percent.[4] Related to these bankruptcies is foreclosure, which results when homeowners are unable to pay their mortgage loans.

Although there are laws in effect that generally favor consumers who run into difficulty, and although there are credit consolidation and counseling bureaus that help people organize and pay their debt, foreclosure and bankruptcy are generally actions of last resort and it's best to avoid taking these steps.

Small expenses really add up. Bringing your own lunch to the office instead of eating out can really beef up your bank account.

Setting Personal Goals

Whatever your personal financial goals, they are more easily accomplished if they reflect your personal values. Values are a set of fundamental beliefs of what is important, desirable, and worthwhile in your life. Your values will influence how you spend your money and, therefore, should be the foundation of your financial plan. Each person's financial goals will be determined by the individual's values because every individual considers some things more desirable or important than others. Start by asking yourself some questions about your values, the things that are most important to you, and what you would like to accomplish in your life.

Your goals are also influenced by your current financial situation. Prepare a set of current financial statements for yourself and update them at least once a year. Just like a business, a personal income statement reflects income and expenditures during a year. A balance sheet is a statement of what you own (assets) and what you owe (liabilities) at a specific point in time. For an individual or household, the difference between assets and liabilities is called **net worth**. As shown in Figure C.2, as you accumulate assets over your life, your net worth increases.

After reviewing your current financial statements, you should prepare a budget. It is an excellent tool for monitoring your expenditures and cash flow and permits you to track past and current expenditures and plan future ones. Budgets are usually prepared on a monthly basis, but you can make a weekly budget if that works better for you. Most budgets divide expenditures into fixed expenses (those that don't change much from month to month) and variable expenses (those that vary). Your monthly apartment rent or your meal plan at school is probably a fixed expense, but the amount you spend on transportation, gas for your car, or entertainment is a variable expense. One key to effective budgeting is to make sure that the budgeted amounts are realistic.

net worth difference between an individual or household's assets and liabilities.

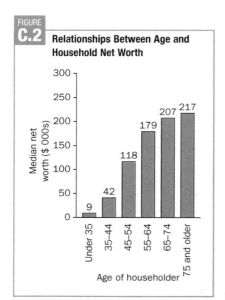

FIGURE C.2

Relationships Between Age and Household Net Worth

Median net worth ($ 000s) by Age of householder:
- Under 35: 9
- 35–44: 42
- 45–54: 118
- 55–64: 179
- 65–74: 207
- 75 and older: 217

Source: "Changes in U.S. Family Finances: Table 4. Family Net Worth, by Selected Characteristics of Families," *Federal Reserve Bulletin*, www.federalreserve.gov, accessed April 4, 2014.

Next, establish a series of financial goals based on your values and current financial situation. Separate your goals into short-term goals (those you want to achieve within the next six months or year) and long-term goals (those you plan to achieve over the next five or ten years). A short-term goal might be to pay off your credit-card balances by the end of this year, or to save enough money to take a vacation next summer. A long-term goal might be to buy a house by age 30. Your goals are reinforced if they support each other—if you pay off your credit cards, you'll likely have enough money saved to take that vacation or eventually buy your house. Some goals are monetary—such as paying off your credit cards. Others are nonmonetary, such as planning to retire by age 55. Whether short-term or long-term, monetary or nonmonetary, the best financial goals are defined specifically and focused on results. Goals also need to be realistic. You might not be able to pay off all of your credit cards by the end of this year, but you might pay off one. You might not buy the house by age 30, but maybe by 35. So be sure to set goals that you can actually attain. Keep in mind also that your financial goals will change over your lifetime. It's a good idea to review them periodically and adjust them when necessary, such as when you lose or get a job, relocate to another area of the country, or have children.

Your Personal Financial Decisions

You can use financial strategies in such areas as career choice, credit management, and tax planning to help you chart your economic future. These strategies should reflect your goals and be designed to close the gap between where you are and where you want to be.

Career Choice

No factor exerts as strong an influence on your personal finances as your career choice. Virtually all of your income, especially when you're just starting out, will come from wages and salaries. It is through work that all of us acquire the income needed to build a lifestyle; to buy goods and services, including insurance protection; to save and invest; and to plan for retirement. Your job is also the source of many important fringe benefits, such as health insurance and retirement savings plans, that are important components of your financial future. Throughout *Contemporary Business*, we've discussed ways to select a career that fits your skills and interests, find a job, and perform in that job.

Basic Money Management

Basic money management involves managing checking and savings accounts. Properly managing these relatively simple financial assets is an important first step toward managing more complicated financial assets such as investment and retirement accounts. You must choose a bank or other financial institution and then select the right checking account. Banks today offer several different types of checking accounts, each with its own set of features and fees.

Table C.1 lists several common sense tips for selecting and managing a checking/debit account. Managing a savings account involves understanding the importance of savings, setting savings goals, and picking the best savings option.

TABLE C.1	Some Common Sense Tips for Choosing and Managing a Checking Account

- Shop around. There are lots of financial institutions that offer checking accounts. Fees and services vary considerably.

- Learn about the various ways to get a free checking account. Some banks require a minimum deposit, while others require a minimum balance, companion savings account, or certificate of deposit.

- Choose the best account for the way you bank. Consider how often you write checks, if at all; how often you use ATMs; when and where you use your debit card; and your average monthly balance.

- Keep good records and balance your account regularly. If there is no fee, sign up for online banking to monitor your account and pay bills electronically.

- Watch how you use your ATM card. Know which ATMs are owned by your bank and how much you're charged to use another bank's ATM.

- Notify your bank immediately if your ATM card is lost or stolen.

- Sign up for overdraft protection.

- Understand how your bank calculates minimum monthly balance.

- Read the fine print in your monthly statement.

Credit Management

Credit is the area of personal finance that gets more people into financial difficulties than any other area. And Americans love credit. According to recent data from the Federal Reserve, Americans now owe in excess of $3.1 trillion, excluding home mortgage loans. This amount has almost doubled over the past 15 years.[5]

Credit allows a person to purchase goods and services by borrowing the necessary funds from a lender, such as a bank. The borrower agrees to repay the loan over a specified period of time, paying a specified rate of interest. The **finance charge** is the difference between the amount borrowed and the amount repaid. Credit is available from many sources today, but rates vary, so it pays to shop around.

There are two broad types of consumer credit: revolving (or open-end) credit and installment credit. Revolving credit is a type of credit arrangement that enables consumers to make a number of different purchases up to a credit limit, specified by the lender. The consumer has the option of repaying some or all of the outstanding balance each month. If the consumer carries a balance from month to month, finance charges (interest) are levied. An example of revolving credit is a credit card, such as Visa or MasterCard.

An installment loan is a credit arrangement in which the borrower takes out a loan for a specified amount, agreeing to repay the loan in regular installments over a specified period of time. Part of each payment is interest and part goes to repay principal (the amount borrowed). Generally, installment loan payments are made monthly and are for the same amount. Most student loans, auto loans, and home mortgage loans are examples of installment loans.

People have good reasons for borrowing money. They include purchasing large, important goods and services (cars, homes, or a college education), dealing with financial emergencies, taking advantage of opportunities, and establishing or improving your credit rating. All of these reasons are appropriate uses of credit if you can repay the loans in a timely manner.

However, a wrong reason for borrowing money is using credit to live beyond your means. For instance, you may want to go to Cancun for vacation but really cannot afford to, so you

credit receiving money, goods, or services on the basis of an agreement between the lender and the borrower that the loan is for a specified period of time with a specified rate of interest.

finance charge difference between the amount borrowed and the amount repaid on a loan.

charge the trip. Using credit to live beyond your means often leads to credit problems. Watch for these warning signs of potential credit problems:

- You use credit to meet basic living expenses.
- You use credit to make impulse purchases.
- You take a cash advance on one credit card to repay another.
- The unpaid balance on your credit cards increases month after month.

Consumers who think of credit purchases as a series of small monthly payments are fooling themselves. As we noted earlier, most college students today have at least one credit card, and more than half carry balances from month to month. The average student has $3,000 in credit-card debt for college expenses, including books, meals, and activities fees (and separate from student loans). Although the CARD Act is aimed at curbing this debt, college students—and consumers in general—must also curb their credit spending.[6] How long would it take you to become debt-free if you had $3,000 on your credit card, if you paid only $50 each month? The answer is more than 18 years—and you would have paid more than $7,600 in interest.

If you feel as though you have a problem with credit, or may be developing one, you should seek help as soon as possible. Your college or university may offer credit counseling services. If not, contact a local not-for-profit credit counseling service or the National Foundation for Credit Counseling (http://www.nfcc.org). According to the experts, one of the keys to the wise use of credit is education. Learning about the pros and cons of borrowing money, as well as learning about responsible spending, can help people avoid problems with credit.

Tax Planning

Everyone pays a variety of taxes to federal, state, and local governments. The major taxes paid by individuals include federal and state income taxes, Social Security and Medicare taxes, real estate taxes, and sales taxes. The median-income family paid almost 27 percent of its income in taxes during a recent year.[7] Think about your own situation and the taxes you pay. You have federal income taxes withheld from each paycheck. In addition, if you live in one of the 41 states with a state income tax, you have state income tax withheld also. Social Security and Medicare taxes amount to a percentage of your wages split between you and your employer (you pay the entire amount if you're self-employed). If you rent an apartment, part of your monthly rent goes to pay the landlord's real estate tax bill. In most states, every time you buy something, you pay sales tax to your state or local government.

By law, you must pay your taxes. You can use some of the popular software such as TurboTax to calculate your federal and state income taxes, or have a professional handle them—these two options are likely to find you any legal deductions you can take. If you do the tax return yourself—even with the aid of software—you will learn more about your personal finances. The Internal Revenue Service (IRS) has several excellent publications to help you prepare a federal income tax return. One of the best is IRS Publication #17 (*Your Federal Income Tax*). This and all other IRS publications are available free of charge from local IRS offices or the IRS website (http://www.irs.gov).

Major Purchases

Even if you follow a strict budget and manage to save money regularly, you may still spend most of your income each year. Effective buying is an important part of your financial plan. Within personal budget limits, an individual exercises his or her rights as a consumer to select or reject the wide range of goods and services that are available. As you purchase an automobile, a home, or any other major item, you need to carefully evaluate alternatives, separate needs from wants, and determine how you are going to finance the purchase. Your goal is to make every dollar you spend count.

Americans spend more than $900 billion annually on transportation, most of which goes to purchasing and maintaining automobiles. Given that new vehicles average more than $30,000 today, and even good used cars can cost in excess of $14,000, buying an automobile is a substantial purchase.[8] On top of that, most car purchases are financed. Buying a car involves weighing many factors, including whether you want a new or used car, what makes and models appeal to you, and how much you can afford to pay. Many consumers today choose not to buy a new car but rather to lease one. While leasing has advantages, it also has drawbacks and, overall, is often more expensive than buying. Some consumers in urban areas choose not to purchase a car, and instead, take advantage of car-sharing services such as Zipcar.

In the long run, leasing a car may cost more than buying one.

For most people, housing consumes a large share of their monthly budgets, whether in rent or mortgage payments. Home ownership is a goal of most people. Owning a home has a number of advantages, both financial and nonfinancial. Some of the financial benefits include tax savings (home mortgage interest and property taxes are both tax deductible) and the potential increase in the home's value called appreciation. Nonfinancial benefits include pride of ownership and the freedom to improve or change the home however you want. The major barrier to home ownership is the money required for a down payment, along with the income required to obtain a mortgage loan.

The other major housing option is renting. Renting also offers a number of advantages, including cost savings (the landlord takes care of maintenance and repairs) and mobility. It is much easier to move if you rent than if you own a home. People who plan on staying in an area for a short period of time are usually better off renting even if they can afford to buy a home. The choice between buying and renting is obviously a major financial decision that needs to be approached rationally, not emotionally.[9]

Insurance

Another important personal planning area is insurance. Insurance is an admittedly expensive but necessary purchase. From age 16 to 78, the average person spends a total of $94,000 on insurance.[10] Some of the basic principles and the various types of insurance are described in Appendix B. Although the focus of that appendix is business insurance, much of what is discussed applies to your personal insurance needs as well.

Your goal is to have adequate and appropriate coverage in each of the major insurance types—life, health, disability, and property and liability. Insurance needs can vary substantially from individual to individual. As noted earlier in *Contemporary Business*, some types of insurance are provided to employees as fringe benefits. They typically include health insurance, disability insurance, and life insurance. In the standard arrangement, employers pay a portion of the premium. A few employers contract with insurance companies to offer employees auto and homeowners' insurance at discounts.

Investment Planning

Investing is a process by which money acquired through work, inheritance, or other sources is preserved and increased. Sound investment management is an important component of the financial plan and can make it easier to attain other personal goals, such as buying a home, sending children to college, starting a business, or retiring comfortably. Furthermore, it is very difficult today to substantially increase wealth without investing. And, given the changes to

Appendix C

A-35

the external environment—such as the economy, health care costs, and employer-sponsored retirement plans—it is likely that you will have to make investment decisions at some point during your life.

The investment process consists of four steps. The first step is to complete some preliminary tasks, including setting overall personal goals, having a regular savings program, and managing credit properly. The second step is to establish a set of investment goals—why you want to invest, what you want to accomplish, and what kind of time frame you have. Obviously, your investment goals should be closely related to your overall personal goals and values. Next, you need to assess risk and return. You invest because you expect to earn some future rate of return. At the same time, however, all investing exposes you to a variety of risks. You need to find the proper balance between risk and return because investments offering the highest potential returns also expose you to more risk. Your age, income, and short- and long-term investment time frames all have an impact on the risk–return trade-off.

The final step is to select the appropriate investments. As discussed in Chapter 16 of *Contemporary Business*, there are three general types of investments: money market instruments, bonds, and common stock. The proper mix of these three investments depends on such factors as your investment goals and investment time horizon. For instance, a 25-year-old investing for retirement should have close to 100 percent of his or her funds invested in common stocks because growth in capital is the overriding investment objective. Stocks have generally outperformed all other investment alternatives over longer periods of time. On the other hand, if the 25-year-old is investing to have sufficient funds for a down payment on a house within the next couple of years, the investor should have a proportion of his or her funds invested in money market instruments or bonds, given the short time horizon. Even after selecting the appropriate investments, the investor must monitor their performance and be prepared to make changes when necessary.

Financial Planning for Tomorrow

The last major personal planning area deals with future financial needs, such as sending children to college and retirement and estate planning. As you know, college is expensive and college costs are rising at a rate that exceeds the overall rate of inflation. By beginning a college savings program early, parents will have a better chance of offering their children a choice of colleges when the time comes. While they may not have enough to cover tuition entirely, they (and their children) will likely have to borrow less and accrue less debt for a college education. A variety of college savings programs exist, some of which provide parents with tax benefits.

Most people want to retire with sufficient funds to ensure a degree of financial security. Social Security will provide only a fraction of what you will need; you will be responsible for the rest. Depending on the standard of living you hope to maintain, you will probably need a savings nest egg of at least $2 million by the time you retire. Four important principles apply when it comes to saving for retirement: start early, save as much as you can each month, take advantage of all tax-deferred retirement savings plans to which you are entitled, and invest your retirement savings appropriately.

Two major sources of retirement income exist: employer-sponsored retirement plans and individual retirement plans. Most employers offer their workers a retirement plan; some offer more than one plan. For most people, employer-sponsored retirement plans will likely provide the bulk of their retirement income. Essentially, two types of employer-sponsored retirement plans exist. A defined benefit plan guarantees a worker a certain retirement benefit each year. The size depends on a number of factors, including the worker's income and the length of time he or she worked for the employer. Pension plans are classified as defined benefit plans.

The other type of employer-sponsored retirement plan is the defined contribution plan. In this type of retirement plan, you contribute to your retirement account and so does your employer. You are given some choice of where your retirement funds can be invested. Often you are given a list of mutual funds in which to invest your money. A so-called 401(k) is an example of a defined contribution plan. Defined contribution plans are widely used and are in many cases replacing defined benefit plans.

Millions of Americans have some sort of individual retirement plan not tied to any employer. These workers may be self-employed or may merely want to supplement their employer-sponsored retirement savings. Examples of individual retirement plans include regular IRAs (individual retirement accounts), Roth IRAs, and simplified employee pension (SEP) plans. To set up one of these retirement plans, you must meet certain eligibility requirements.

Another element of financial planning for the future is estate planning. Of all the personal planning areas, estate planning is probably the least relevant for young people, although your parents and grandparents probably face some estate-planning issues. However, all adults, regardless of age, need to have two documents: a valid will (naming a guardian if you have any minor children) and a durable power of attorney (the name varies from state to state, but it is a document that gives someone else the power to make financial and medical decisions if you are incapacitated).

This appendix has just scratched the surface of personal financial planning. We hope it has encouraged you to learn more. Consider taking a class in personal financial planning if your institution offers one. It may be one of the most helpful classes you take while you're in college.

Business Terms You Need to Know

personal financial management A-27
standard of living A-28
financial plan A-29

net worth A-31
credit A-33
finance charge A-33

Projects and Teamwork Applications

1. Prepare a chart outlining your current standard of living, the standard of living you had while growing up, and the standard of living you expect or hope to achieve once you have completed your education.

2. The "comparison complex" is a phenomenon that makes it difficult for people to feel content with what they have. "Keeping up with the Joneses" is an expression that refers to the comparison to one's friends, co-workers, relatives, or neighbors with regard to accumulating goods as a means of social identification and social standing. Research and discuss the social and financial impact of this phenomenon.

3. Create a weekly budget and a monthly budget. Keep a daily journal of your expenses for the next month to see how well you stick to the budget. Compare your results in class. In what areas did you do well? In what areas do you need improvement? For additional help, you can go to the website http://www .nelliemae.com/calculators to fill out the budget worksheet.

4. Even though you are still in school, you face a number of important financial issues, everything from paying college expenses to dealing with credit cards. Visit the website: http://getcollegefunds.org and click on "10 Steps to Financial Fitness" for more suggestions on managing your money while in college.

5. Evaluate your current credit situation. What are your existing debts? How much are you paying each month? Assess the reason you used credit. Did you borrow for the right reasons? List some steps you think you should take to improve your management of credit. Go to the websites, www.feedthepig.org or http://creditkarma.com, to learn more.

Appendix D

Developing a Business Plan

Business Plan Competitions: More Than Just Prizes

If you have ever considered entering a business plan competition, there are many different types, including local competitions, university and college competitions, and corporate and social entrepreneurship contests, and each has unique benefits.

Aside from the honor of winning the competition, the obvious benefit is the cash prize, which varies in dollar amounts. At one of the largest and best-known annual business plan competitions in the world, the Massachusetts Institute of Technology (MIT) Entrepreneurship Competition, the contest winner comes away with a generous prize of $100,000, which can easily be used as seed money to fund a business. Many schools grant prize money that typically ranges from $5,000 to $10,000. A few of the big-money contests require winners to agree to sign over a percentage of equity in the new business, which might be a difficult decision for a would-be entrepreneur.

Entering a competition focused on a particular industry provides targeted feedback from investors and seasoned professionals in your specific field. This may help prepare you for the rigors of talking to venture capitalists and angel investors and generally becoming comfortable with pitching your business idea to others.

Regardless of whether you make the short list or not, entering a business plan competition can offer entrants invaluable advice, mentoring, exposure, and support. In addition, entrants learn to articulate ideas and strategies, hone financial projections, and talk to potential investors. And there's no limit to the number of competitions a group can enter.

Even the entrants who do not walk away with the prize money agree that the competition provides a sounding board and unparalleled networking—all well worth the pressure and competitive environment of such a competition. With or without a win, introductions are made to a network of judges, some of whom may be willing to finance a business startup or introduce you to other industry experts. While there can only be one winner of the competition, the networking possibilities and connections can be a winning combination.[1]

Appendix

D Overview

Many entrepreneurs and small-business owners have written business plans to help them organize their businesses, get them up and running, and raise money for expansion. In this appendix, we cover the basics of business planning: what business plans are, why they're important, and who needs them. We also explain the steps involved in writing a good plan and the major elements it should contain. Finally, we cover additional resources to get you started with your own business plan—to help you bring your unique ideas to reality with a business of your own.

What Is a Business Plan?

You may wonder how the millions of different businesses operating in the United States and throughout the world today got their start. Often it involves a formal business plan. A *business plan* is a written document that defines what a company's objectives are, how those objectives will be achieved, how the business will be financed, and how much money the company expects to bring in. In short, it describes where a company is, where it wants to go, and how it intends to get there.

Why a Business Plan Is So Important

A well-written business plan serves two key functions:

1. It organizes the business and validates its central idea.

2. It summarizes the business and its strategy to obtain funding from lenders and investors.

First, a business plan gives a business formal direction, whether it is just starting, going through a phase of growth, or struggling. The business plan forces the principals—the owners—through rigorous planning, to think through the realities of running and financing a business. In their planning, they consider many details. How will inventory be stored, shipped, and stocked? Where should the business be located? How will the business use the Internet as part of its overall strategy? And most important, how will the business make enough money to make it all worthwhile?

A business plan also gives the owners a well-reasoned blueprint to refer to when daily challenges arise, and it acts as a benchmark by which successes and disappointments can be measured. Additionally, a solid business plan will sell the potential owner on the validity of the idea. In some cases, the by-product of developing the plan is demonstrating to a starry-eyed person that he or she is trying to start a bad business. In other words, the process of writing a plan benefits a would-be businessperson as much as the final plan benefits potential investors.

Finally, a business plan articulates the business's strategy to financiers who may fund the business, and it is usually required to obtain a bank loan. Lenders and venture capitalists need to see that the business owner has thought through the critical issues and presented a promising idea before they will consider investing in it. They are, after all, interested in whether it will bring them significant returns.

Who Needs a Business Plan?

Every business owner who expects to be successful needs a business plan. Some people mistakenly believe that they need a business plan only if it will land in the hands of a venture capitalist or the loan committee of a bank. Others think that writing a plan is unnecessary if their bank or lending institution doesn't require it. Such assumptions miss the point of planning, because a business plan acts as a map to guide the way through the often tangled roads of running a business. Every small-business owner should develop a business plan because it empowers that person to take control.

How Do I Write a Business Plan?

Developing a business plan should mean something different to everyone. Think of a business plan as a clear statement of a business's identity. A construction company has a different identity from a newly launched magazine, which has yet a different identity from a restaurant hoping to expand its share of the market. Each business has unique objectives and processes, and each faces different obstacles.

At the same time, good business plans contain some similar elements no matter who the business owner or entrepreneur is, what he or she sells, or how far the owner is into the venture. A savvy business owner molds the elements of a business plan into a professional and personal representation of the firm's needs and goals. The plan should also realistically assess the risks and obstacles specific to the business and present solutions for overcoming them.

Because the document is important, it takes time to collect needed information and organize it. Don't be misled into believing that you will simply sit down and begin writing. Before any writing begins, the business owner or entrepreneur must become an expert in his or her field. Readying important information about the company and the market will make the writing easier and faster. Some critical pieces of information to have on hand are the following items:

- The company's name, legal form of organization, location, financial highlights, and owners or shareholders (if any).

- Organization charts, list of top managers, consultants or directors, and employee agreements.

- Marketing research, customer surveys, and information about the company's major competitors.

- Product information, including goods and services offered; brochures; patents, licenses, and trademarks; and research and development plans.

- Marketing plans and materials.

- Financial statements (both current and forecasted).

The business owner also must do a lot of soul searching and brainstorming to answer important questions necessary to build the backbone of a healthy business. Figure D.1 lists some critical questions worth asking.

Once these questions have been answered, you can begin writing the document, which can be anywhere between 10 and 50 pages long. The length of the plan depends on the complexity of the company, whether the company is a start-up (established companies have longer histories to detail), and how the plan will be used. Regardless of size, the business plan should be well organized and easy to use, especially if the business plan is intended for external uses, such as to secure financing. Number all pages, include a table of contents, and make sure the format is attractive and professional. Include two or three illustrative charts or graphs and highlight the sections and important points with headings and bulleted lists. Figure D.2 outlines the major sections of a business plan.

The following paragraphs discuss the most common elements of an effective business plan. When you need additional instruction or information as you write, refer to the "Resources" section at the end of the appendix.

Executive Summary

The primary purpose of an executive summary is to entice readers to read more about the business. An *executive summary* is a one- to two-page snapshot of what the overall business plan explains in detail. Consider it a business plan within a business plan. Through its enthusiasm and quick description, the summary should capture the reader's imagination. Describe your strategy for succeeding in a positive, intriguing, and realistic way and briefly yet thoroughly answer the first questions anyone would have about your business: who, what, why, when, where, and how. Lenders and investors always read the executive summary first. If it isn't presented professionally, or lacks the proper information, they will quickly move on to the next business plan in the stack. The executive summary is just as important to people funding the business with personal resources, however, because it channels their motivations into an articulate mission statement. It is a good idea to write the summary last, because it will inevitably be revised once the business plan is finalized.

FIGURE D.1 Questions to Ask When Starting a Business

**Take a few minutes to read and answer these questions.
Don't worry about answering in too much detail at this point.
The questions are preliminary and
intended to help you think through your venture.**

1. In general terms, how would you explain your idea to a friend?

2. What is the purpose or objective of your venture?

3. What service are you going to provide, or what goods are you going to manufacture?

4. Is there any significant difference between what you are planning and what already exists?

5. How will the quality of your product compare with competitive offerings?

6. What is the overview of the industry or service sector you are going to enter? Write it out.

7. What is the history, current status, and future of the industry?

8. Who is your customer or client base?

9. Where and by whom will your good or service be marketed?

10. How much will you charge for the product you are planning?

11. Where is the financing going to come from to initiate your venture?

12. What training and experience do you have that qualifies you for this venture?

13. Does such training or experience give you a significant edge?

14. If you lack specific experience, how do you plan to gain it?

To write an effective executive summary, focus on the issues that are most important to your business's success and save the supporting matters for the text. The executive summary should describe the firm's mission, vision, strategy, and goals, the good or service it is selling, and the advantages it has over the competition. It should also give a snapshot of how much money will be required to launch the business, how it will be used, and how the lenders or investors will recoup their funds.

Introduction

The introduction follows the executive summary. After the executive summary has offered an attractive synopsis, the introduction should begin to discuss the fine details of the business. It should include any material the upcoming marketing and financing sections do not cover. The

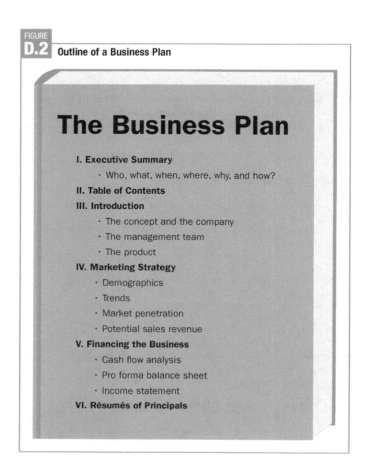

The Business Plan

I. Executive Summary
  · Who, what, when, where, why, and how?

II. Table of Contents

III. Introduction
  · The concept and the company
  · The management team
  · The product

IV. Marketing Strategy
  · Demographics
  · Trends
  · Market penetration
  · Potential sales revenue

V. Financing the Business
  · Cash flow analysis
  · Pro forma balance sheet
  · Income statement

VI. Résumés of Principals

introduction should describe the company, the management team, and the product or service in detail. If one of these topics is particularly noteworthy for your business, you may want to present that topic as its own section. Listen to what you write and respond as the plan takes shape.

Include basic information about the company—its past, present, and future. What are the company's roots, what is its current status, and what actions need to be taken to achieve its goals? If you are starting a company, include a description of the evolution of the concept. Be sure to tie all of the business's goals and plans to the industry in which it will operate, and describe the industry and its recent and historic trends.

A business doesn't run itself, of course. People are the heart of a business, so write an appealing picture of the business's management team. Who are the key players and how does their experience resonate with the company's goals? Describe their—or your, if you are a sole proprietor—education, training, and experience, and highlight and refer to résumés included later in the plan. Be honest, however—not all businesses are started by experts. If you lack demonstrated experience in a certain area, explain how you plan to get it.

Also describe the product, the driving force behind the venture. What are you offering, and why is it special? What are the costs of the service or price tag on the good? Analyze the features of the offering and the effect these features have on the overall cost.

Marketing Strategy

Next comes the marketing strategy section. The *marketing strategy* describes the market's need for the good or service and the way the business will fulfill it. Marketing strategies are not based on informal projections or observations. They are the result of a careful market analysis. So formulating a marketing strategy allows the business owner to become familiar with every aspect of the particular market. If done properly, it will allow you to define your target market and position your business within that sector to get its share of sales.

The marketing strategy includes a discussion of the size of the customer base or market that will want to purchase your good or service and the projected rate of growth for the product or category. Highlight information on the demographics of your customers. *Demographics* are statistical characteristics of the segment of the market, such as income, gender, and age. What types of people will purchase your product? How old are they, and where do they live? What is their lifestyle like? For example, someone starting an interior design business will want to report how many homeowners live within a certain radius of the firm, as well as their median income. Of course, this section of the marketing analysis will be quite different for a company that conducts all of its business online. In that case, you will want to know the types of people who will shop at your website, but your discussion won't be limited to one geographic area. It is also a good idea to describe the trends in your product category. Trends are consumer and business tendencies or patterns that business owners can exploit to gain market share in an industry.

The marketing strategy should also detail your distribution, pricing, and promotional goals. Discuss the average price of your offering and the reasons behind the price you have chosen. How do you intend to let your potential customers know that you have a product to sell? How will you sell it—through a catalog, in a retail location, online, or perhaps a combination of all three? The effectiveness of your distribution, pricing, and promotional goals determines the extent to which you will be able to gain market share.

Competitors are another important part of your marketing strategy. What companies are already selling products similar to yours? Include and thoroughly research your competitors to show that you know exactly who they are and what you are up against. Describe what you think are their major strengths, weaknesses, opportunities, and threats, and how successful they have been within your market.

Also include the *market penetration*, which is the percentage of total customers who have purchased a company's product. If there are 10,000 people in your market, and 5,000 have purchased your product, your market penetration is 50 percent. The *potential sales revenue*, also an important figure to include, is the total revenue of a company if it captured 100 percent market penetration. In other words, this figure represents the total dollar value of sales you would bring in if everyone who is a potential customer purchased your product.

Financing the Business

The goal of a business is to make money. The business plan provides the foundation for the *financing section*. Business owners should not skip this section even if they are not seeking outside money. While it is crucial to have an accurate financial analysis to get financing, it also is a necessary exercise for business owners funding the venture themselves. The financing section provides information related to the cost of the product, operating expenses, expected sales revenue and profit, and the amount of the business owner's personal funds or startup expenses that will be invested to get the business up and running. The financial projections should be compelling but accurate and based on realistic assumptions. The owner should be able to defend them.

Any assumptions made in the body of the business plan should be tied into the financial section. For instance, if you think you will need a staff of five, your cash flow analysis should reveal salary information and how the employees will be paid. A cash flow analysis, a mandatory component of a financial analysis, shows how much money will flow in and out of your business throughout the year. It helps you plan for staggered purchasing, high-volume months, and slow periods. Your business may be cyclical or seasonal, so the cash flow projection lets you know if you need to arrange a line of credit to cover periodic shortfalls. In addition, an income statement is a critical component. The income statement is a statement of income and expenses your company has accrued over a period of time.

Remember that leaving out important details can undercut your credibility, so be thorough. The plan must include your assumptions about the conditions under which your business will operate. It should cover details such as market strength; date of start-up; sales buildup; gross profit margin; equipment, furniture, and fixtures required; and payroll and other key expenses that will affect the financial plan. In addition, a banker will want a pro forma balance sheet, which provides an estimate of what the business owns (assets), what it owes (liabilities), and what it is worth (owner's equity). Refer to Chapters 15, 16, and 17 of *Contemporary Business* for additional details on accounting, financial statements, and financial management.

Résumés of Principals

The final element of the business plan is the inclusion of the résumés of the principals behind the business: the management team. Each résumé should include detailed employment information and accomplishments. If applicable to your business, consider expanding on the traditional résumé by including business affiliations, professional memberships, hobbies, and leisure activities.

However you choose to develop a business plan, make sure that *you* develop the plan. It should sound as though it was written by the entrepreneur, not by some outside "expert."

Resources

A tremendous amount of material is available to help business owners—whether existing or prospective—write effective business plans. The biggest task is narrowing down which resources are right for you. The Internet delivers an abundance of sound business-planning tools and advice, much of which are free. It allows you to seek diverse examples and opinions, which is important because no one source will match your situation exactly. Your library and career center also have a wealth of resources. Following are some helpful resources for business planning.

Books

Dozens of books exist on how to write a business plan. Examples include the following:

- Edward Blackwell, *How to Prepare a Business Plan*, 5th ed. (London: Kogan Page Ltd., 2011).

- Michael Gerber, *The E-Myth Enterprise: How to Turn a Great Idea into a Thriving Business* (New York: Harper Collins, 2010).

- Mike McKeever, *How to Write a Business Plan*, 11th ed. (Berkeley, CA: Nolo Press, 2012).

- John W. Mullins, *The New Business Road Test: What Entrepreneurs and Executives Should Do Before Writing a Business Plan*, 3rd ed. (Financial Times/Prentice Hall, 2012).

- Steven D. Peterson, Peter E. Jaret, and Barbara Findlay Schenck, *Business Plans Kit for Dummies*, 4th ed. (Wiley Publishing, 2013).

- Hal Shelton, *The Secrets to Writing a Successful Business Plan: A Pro Shares a Step-by-Step Guide to Creating a Plan That Gets Results* (Rockville, MD: Summit Valley Press, 2014).

Websites

Useful websites include the following:

- *Entrepreneur, Inc.*, and *Bloomberg Businessweek* magazines offer knowledgeable guides to writing a business plan. *Entrepreneur*'s website also contains sample business plans.

  http://www.entrepreneur.com
  http://www.inc.com
  http://www.businessweek.com

- If you are hoping to obtain funding with your business plan, you should familiarize yourself with what investors are looking for. Two professional associations for the venture capital industry are the following:

  http://www.nvca.org (National Venture Capital Association)
  http://www.nasbic.org (Small Business Investor Alliance—formerly the National Association of Small Business Investment Companies)

Software

Business-planning software can give an initial shape to your business plan. The most widely used business plan software is Business Plan Pro from Palo Alto software. However, a word of caution is in order if you write a business plan using a template from software. Bankers and potential investors, such as venture capitalists, read so many business plans that those based on templates may seem less compelling. Also, if you are not seeking financing, using software can eliminate the main purpose of writing a plan—learning about, through research and analysis, your unique idea and its viability. Remember, software is a tool. It can help you get started, stay organized, and build a professional-looking business plan, but it won't actually write the plan for you.

Associations and Organizations

Many government and professional organizations provide assistance to would-be business owners. Here is a partial list:

- The U.S. Small Business Administration offers planning materials, along with other resources.

  http://www.sba.gov

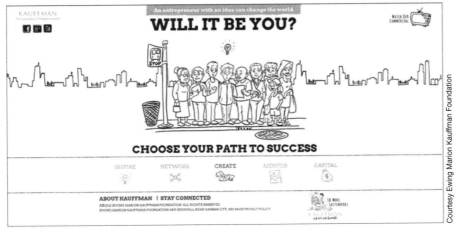

The Ewing Marion Kauffman Foundation's website, www.kauffman.org, offers a wealth of information about starting, managing, and expanding small businesses.

- Women's Business Centers represent a national network, sponsored by the SBA, that helps female entrepreneurs.

  http://www.sba.gov/tools/local-assistance/wbc

- One of the missions of the Ewing Marion Kauffman Foundation is to encourage entrepreneurship across the United States. The foundation's websites offer online resources for new and growing businesses.

  http://www.kauffman.org

Projects and Teamwork Applications

1. Visit the website below and review the various types of business plan competitions, along with the requirements of each. Discuss which would be the most appropriate for you.

   www.businessplancompetition.com

2. Do you dream of starting your own business? Take your idea and answer as many of the self-evaluation questions in Figure D.1 as you can. Share your answers with the class. Then file your answers away to read at a future date—either when you have graduated from college or when you think you are ready to pursue your own business.

3. Write the executive summary portion of the business plan for your potential business. You may use the answers to the questions in Figure D.1 as a springboard.

A-46   Appendix D

| Appendix E |

Careers in Contemporary Business

You'll be hitting the job market soon—if you haven't already. Regardless of what industry you want to work in—financial services, advertising, travel, construction, hospitality, manufacturing, wireless communications—you need an education. Attending college and taking a business course like this one gives you an edge because business skills and knowledge are needed in many different fields. But education comes in many forms. In addition to taking classes, you should try to gain related real-life experience. A summer job, an internship, or even a volunteer opportunity can give you excellent experience that you can build on once you graduate. Cooperative education programs and work-study programs can also give you hands-on experience while you pursue your education. While many students across the country will be doing the same thing, you can set yourself apart through your work ethic and initiative.

You will be responsible for earning a living once you leave school—if you aren't already doing so. Your level of education will probably influence your earnings. As reported by the U.S. Census Bureau, not only is there a wide discrepancy between earnings for high-school graduates and college graduates, but there is still a wage gap between earnings for men and women.[1]

Keep in mind that while a degree may help you get in the door for certain job interviews and may put you on a path for advancement, it doesn't guarantee success; you have to achieve that yourself.

Companies plan their hiring strategies carefully in order to attract and keep the most productive, creative employees and avoid the cost of rehiring. So, soon-to-be graduates still need to be proactive and prepared. But creativity has never been in short supply among business students, and by the time you finish this class—and college—you will be well equipped to take on the challenge. You'll be able to think of your search for employment as a course in itself, at the end of which you will have a job. And you will be on your way toward a rewarding business career.

During this course, you are exposed to all the functional areas of business. You learn how firms are organized and operated. You find out who does what in a company. Gradually, you identify industries and disciplines—such as sales, finance, or product design—that interest you. And you learn about many organizations, large and small—who founded them, what products they offer, how they serve their customers, and what types of decisions they make. In short, you gain knowledge about business that you can apply to your career search and life.

Choosing a career is an important life decision. It sets you on a path that will influence where you live, how much money you earn, what type of people you meet, and what you do every day. And whether your goal is to operate an organic farm or to rise high in the ranks of a major corporation, you'll need to understand the principles of business. Even if you think you're headed down a different path, business skills may prove to be important. In addition, many fields are beginning to recognize the importance of a broader base of knowledge than specialized technical skills, and business knowledge is part of that base.

For example, some careers, like engineering, used to rely almost solely on a foundation of technical skill and expertise. But experts in the industry now report a trend toward a more well-rounded education. While engineers still need a strong technical foundation, they need additional skills as well. Engineers who survived the economic downturn without being laid off claim that having capabilities across several areas made them more valuable to their employer than, say, a colleague whose knowledge was concentrated in one or two areas. That's why this appendix discusses the best way to approach career decisions and to prepare for an *entry-level job*—your first permanent employment after leaving school. We then look at a range of business careers and discuss employment opportunities in a variety of fields.

It's important to remember that you'll be looking for a job regardless of the state of the overall economy. You'll read about job cuts and unemployment rates, hiring freezes and wage increases. But if you stay flexible and are ready to work—just about anytime and anywhere—you'll succeed.

Internships—A Great Way to Acquire Real-World Experience

Many business students complete one or more *internships* prior to completing their academic careers. Some arrange internships during the summer, while others work at them during a semester away from college. An internship gives you hands-on experience in a real business environment, whether it's in banking, the hotel industry, or retailing. Not only does an internship teach you how a business runs, but it can also help you decide whether you want to pursue a career in a particular industry. You might spend a summer interning in the admissions department of a hospital and then graduate with your job search focused on hospital administration. Or you might decide you'd much rather work for a magazine publisher or a retailer.

When you apply for an internship, don't expect to be paid much, if at all. The true value of an internship lies in its hands-on experience. An internship bridges the theory–practice educational gap. It will help carry you from your academic experience to your professional future. Also keep in mind that, as an intern, you will not be running a department. People may not ask for your input or ideas. You may work in the warehouse or copy center. You might be answering phones or entering data. But it is important to make the most of your internship. Because many companies make permanent job offers—or offers to enter paid training programs—to the best interns, you'll want to stand out.

Internships can serve as critical networking and job-hunting tools. In many instances, they lead to future employment opportunities, allowing students to demonstrate technical proficiency while providing cost-effective employee training for the company. Even if you don't end up being hired by the company for which you interned, the experience is extremely valuable to your job hunt because you include it on your résumé. During one recent year, accounting firm Deloitte made job offers to 75 percent of its interns.[2]

With this information in mind, start thinking the way a professional does now. Here are some tips for a successful internship experience. These guidelines are also helpful for your first job.

Internships provide college students with critical hands-on business experience. It is important for students to make the most of the opportunities that internships provide both in terms of experience and a future job hunt once they have completed their schooling.

- **Dress like a professional.** Dress appropriately for your future career. During an interview visit, look around to see what the dress code is like. If you have any questions, ask your supervisor.

- **Act like a professional.** Arrive on time to work. Be punctual for any meetings or assignments. Ask questions and listen to the answers carefully. Complete your work thoroughly and meet deadlines. Maintain good etiquette on the phone, in meetings, in e-mails, and in all interactions with other people.

- **Stand out.** Work hard and take initiative, but behave appropriately. Don't try to use authority that you do not have. Show that you are willing to learn.

- **Be evaluated.** Even if your internship does not include a formal evaluation, ask your employer for feedback to learn how you can improve.

- **Keep in touch.** Once you complete your internship, stay in touch periodically with the firm so that people know what you are currently doing.

An excellent source of information about the nation's outstanding internships can be found at your local bookstore—*The Best 109 Internships*, 9th edition, published by The Princeton Review. The same organization also publishes *The Internship Bible*, 10th edition, which is also helpful.

TheGift777/iStockphoto

In addition to an internship, you can build your résumé with work and life experience through volunteer opportunities, extracurricular activities, and summer or off-campus study programs. *Cooperative education* also provides valuable experience. Cooperative education programs are similar to internships, but the jobs themselves usually pay more. These programs may take place during the summer or during the school year—typically, students might take classes one semester and hold jobs the next semester. Most cooperative programs are specific to a major field of study, such as retailing or information technology. At your cooperative job, you'll be treated like a real full-time employee, meaning you'll work long hours and probably have more responsibility that you would as an intern. And depending on how these programs are scheduled, you might add a semester or two to your college education. But in the long run, you will gain knowledge and work experience that will serve you well as you build your career.[3]

Self-Assessment for Career Development

You are going to spend a lot of time during your life working, so why not find a job—or at least an industry—that interests you? To choose the line of work that suits you best, you must first understand yourself. Self-assessment involves looking in the mirror and seeing the real you—with all your strengths and weaknesses. It means answering some tough questions. But being honest with yourself pays off because it will help you find a career that is challenging, rewarding, and meaningful to you. You may realize that to feel secure, you need to earn enough to put away substantial savings. Or you might learn that you are drawn to risks and the unknown, characteristics that might point you toward owning your own business someday. Each of these discoveries provides you with valuable information in choosing a career.

Many resources are available to help you in selecting a career. They include school libraries, career guidance and placement offices, counseling centers, and online career and job search services. They include alumni from your college, as well as friends, family, and neighbors. Don't forget the contacts you make during an internship—they can help you in many ways. Ask questions of anyone you know—a local accountant, banker, or restaurant owner. Most people will be happy to speak with you or arrange a time to do so.

If you are interested in a particular industry or company, you might be able to arrange an informational interview—an appointment with someone who can provide you with more knowledge about an industry or career path. This type of interview is different from one that follows your application for a specific job, although it may ultimately lead to that. The informational interview can help you decide whether you want to pursue a particular avenue of employment. It also gives you some added experience in the interview process—without the pressure. To arrange an interview, tap anyone you know—friends of your parents, local businesspeople, or coordinators of not-for-profit organizations. Colleges often have databases of graduates who are working in various fields who are willing to talk with students on an informational basis, so be sure to start your search right at your own school.

To help you get started asking and answering the questions that will help you begin looking in the right direction, you can visit a number of websites that offer online career assessment tests. Career Explorer, at http://www.careerexplorer.net is one such site; LiveCareer at http://www.livecareer.com is another. These and other sites, such as Monster.com, help you identify your interests, strengths, and weaknesses—including some that may surprise you.[4] In addition, follow the self-assessment process outlined in the next section to learn more about yourself.

The Self-Assessment Process

For a thorough assessment of your goals and interests, follow these steps:

1. **Outline your career interests.** What field or work activities interest you? What rewards do you want to gain from work?

2. **Outline your career goals.** What do you want to achieve through your career? What type of job can you see yourself doing? Where do you see yourself in a year? In five years? Do you have an ultimate dream job? How long are you willing to work to reach it? Write your goals down so that you can refer to them later.

3. **Make plans to reach your goal.** Do you need more education? Does the career require work experience or a certain number of years on the job? Outline the requirements you'll need to meet in order to reach your goal.

4. **List your skills and specific talents.** Write down your strengths—job skills you already have, as well as skills you have developed in life. For instance, you might know how to use financial software, and you might have strong interpersonal skills. In addition, your school's career development office probably has resources that can help determine your aptitude for specific careers. However, take these only as a guideline. If you really want to pursue a certain career, go for it.

5. **List your weaknesses.** This can be tough, but it can also be fun. If you are shy about meeting new people, put shyness on your list. If you are quick to argue, admit it. If you aren't the best business-letter writer or think you're terrible at math, confess to yourself. This list gives you an opportunity to see where you need improvement—and take steps to turn weaknesses into strengths.

6. **Briefly sketch out your educational background.** Write down the schools, colleges, and special training programs you have attended, along with any courses you plan to complete before starting full-time employment. Make a candid assessment of how your background matches up with the current job market. Then make plans to complete any further education you may need.

7. **List the jobs you have held.** Include paid jobs, internships, and volunteer opportunities. They all gave you valuable experience. As you make your list, think about what you liked and disliked about each. Maybe you liked working with the general public as a supermarket cashier. Perhaps you enjoyed caring for animals at a local shelter.

8. **Consider your hobbies and personal interests.** Many people have turned hobbies and personal pursuits into rewarding careers. Mick Jagger, lead singer of the Rolling Stones, has a master's degree from the London School of Economics. This fact probably helped him manage his rock group's vast business dealings. Jake Burton Carpenter earned a bachelor's degree in economics, but he loved winter sports. So he started a snowboard manufacturing company—and revolutionized the way people get from the top of a snowy mountain to the bottom. Over 25 years ago, Michele Hoskins capitalized on a recipe handed down by her great-great grandmother. With a fond memory of pancakes smothered in butter crème syrup on Sundays with her grandmother, Hoskins took the secret syrup recipe and made it a national success. Today Hoskins sells her products in over 10,000 retail grocery stores.[5] Turning a hobby into a career doesn't happen overnight, though, nor is it easy. It requires the same amount of research and hard work as any other business. But for many people, it is a labor of love—and ultimately it succeeds because they refuse to give up.

Job Search Guidelines

Once you have narrowed your choice of career possibilities to two or three that seem right for you, you are ready to begin your exploration and search. The characteristics that made these career choices attractive to you are also likely to catch the attention of other job seekers, so you must prepare for competition. Locate available positions that interest you; then be resourceful! Your success depends on being as creative as possible, and gathering as much information as possible.

Use Your Career Center

Visit your school's career center. If necessary, either online or in person, establish an applicant file, including letters of recommendation and supporting personal information. Most placement offices list new jobs online, so check frequently. Find out how the career center arranges interviews with company representatives who visit campus. If your school holds career events or sponsors industry speakers, be sure to attend. The career centers of most schools assist students and alumni with a full range of services, ranging from internships to employment opportunities, and even guidance for long-term and lifelong career success. In fact, as an alumnus, your school's career center and job listings can be an invaluable resource.

Creating an Online Profile Using Social Media

Creating a comprehensive online profile using a site like LinkedIn should include the following:

- A comprehensive profile that includes your educational background and detailed descriptions of all of your work experiences and skills

- Examples of your work in the form of videos, slideshows, or other multimedia files worth having prospective employers view

- An updated and professional profile picture.

Studies show that sharing or commenting in an insightful way on various topics at least weekly will increase the chances of your online profile being viewed by the hiring manager. Pay close attention to shared acquaintances and mutual connections on the profiles of those you wish to meet.[6]

Letters of recommendation are very important, because they give prospective employers both personal and professional insights about you. They can influence a hiring decision. So, make a careful list of people who might be willing to write letters of reference. Your references should not be family members or close friends. Instead, choose a coach, an instructor, a former employer, or someone else whose knowledge could contribute to your job application. A soccer coach could vouch for your hard work and determination. A instructor might be able to detail how well you accept instruction. A former employer might describe your solid work ethic and ability to get along with others. If possible, include one or more references from your school's business faculty.

Always ask people personally for letters of reference. Be prepared to give them brief outlines of your academic preparation, along with information about your job interests and career goals. This information will help them prepare their letters quickly and efficiently. It also shows that you are serious about the task and respect their time. Remember, however, that these people are very busy. Allow them at least a couple of weeks to prepare their reference letters; then follow up politely on missing ones. Always call or write to thank them for writing the letters and keep them updated on your progress, especially if you land a great job.

Finding Employment Online

The Internet plays a crucial role in connecting employers and job seekers. Companies of all sizes post their job opportunities on the web, on their own sites, on LinkedIn, and on job sites such as Indeed.com, Vault.com, Craigslist.org, Glassdoor.com, SimplyHired.com, and Monster.com. Specialized or niche sites such as Dice.com and Techcareers.com are also gaining popularity among tech workers, and USAjobs.gov among those interested in government jobs. Some sites are free to applicants, while others charge a subscription fee. Figure E.1 provides a sampling of general and more-focused career sites.

Career websites typically offer job postings, tips on creating an effective résumé, a place to post your résumé, and advice on interviews and careers. If this sounds easy, keep in mind that

General Sites
Craigslist.org
Glassdoor.com
Indeed.com
LinkedIn.com
Monster.com
SimplyHired.com
Snagajob.com
Vault.com

Government Sites
USAJobs.com

Industry and Specialized Sites

Business and Finance
Accounting.com
Careerfinance.com
Efinancialcareers.com

Communication
iABC.com

Healthcare
jobs.cdc.gov
jobs.nih.gov
Medicalworkers.com

Marketing
Marketingjobs.com
Marketingpower.com

Nonprofits/Social Entrepreneurship
Idealist.org
Socialedge.org

Sales
Salescareersonline.com
Salesjobs.com

Technology
Dice.com
Techcareers.com

Women/Minorities
Hirediversity.com
iHispano.com
Womensjoblist.com

---

these sites may receive hundreds of thousands of hits each day from job hunters, which means you have plenty of competition. This doesn't mean you shouldn't use one of these sites as part of your job search; just don't make it your sole source. Savvy job seekers often find that their time is better spent zeroing in on niche boards offering more focused listings. Naturally, if a particular company interests you, go to that firm's website, where available positions will be posted. For example, if you are interested in working at the accounting firm Ernst & Young, visit the Ernst & Young website, http://www.ey.com. If you are looking for a job with Whole Foods Market, visit http://www.wholefoodsmarket.com. And if you fancy yourself working for an outdoor retailer, go to Bass Pro Shops at http://www.basspro.com.

Newspapers, the source for traditional classified want ads, also post their ads on the web. Job seekers can even visit sites that merge ads from many different newspapers into one searchable database, such as CareerBuilder (http://www.careerbuilder.com). Some sites go a step farther and create separate sections for each career area. For example, entire sections may be devoted to accounting, marketing, and other business professions. Searches can then be narrowed according to geographic location, entry level, company name, job title, job description, and other categories.

As mentioned earlier, you can connect with potential employers by creating a profile on a social media site like LinkedIn or even, with 140 characters, on Twitter, or by posting your résumé on job sites. Employers search LinkedIn's site or other job sites for prospects with the right qualifications. One commonly used approach is for an employer to list one or more *keywords* to select candidates for personal interviews—for example, "retail sales experience," "network architecture," or "spa management"—and then browse the résumés that contain all the required keywords. Employers also scan résumés into their human resource database, and then when a manager requests, say, 10 candidates, the database is searched by keywords that have been specified as part of the request. Job seekers are responding to this computer screening of applicants by making sure that relevant keywords appear on their résumés.

The *Contemporary Business* website hosts a comprehensive job and career assistance section. The site is updated frequently to include the best job and career sites for identifying and landing the career you want, as well as current strategies for getting the best results from your web-based career-search activities.

Finding Employment through Other Sources

The importance of utilizing the resources and job leads at your college's career planning or placement office was noted earlier. If you have completed formal academic coursework at more than one institution, you may be able to utilize each. In addition, you may want to contact private and public employment services available in your location or in the area where you would like to live.

Private Employment Agencies These firms often specialize in certain types of jobs—such as marketing, finance, sales, or engineering—offering services for both employers and job candidates that are not available elsewhere. Many private agencies interview, test, and screen job applicants so that potential employers do not have to do so. Job candidates benefit from the service by being accepted by the agency and because the agency makes the first contact with the potential employer.

A private employment agency usually charges the prospective employer a fee for finding a suitable employee. Other firms charge job seekers a fee for helping find them a job. Be sure that you understand the terms of any agreement you sign with a private employment agency.

A-52   Appendix E

State Employment Offices Don't forget to check the employment office of your state government. Remember that in many states, these public agencies process unemployment compensation applications along with other related work. Because of the mix of duties, some people view state employment agencies as providing services for semiskilled or unskilled workers. However, these agencies *do* list jobs in many professional categories and are often intimately involved with identifying job finalists for major new facilities moving to your state. In addition, many of the jobs listed at state employment offices may be with state or federal agencies and may include professionals such as accountants, attorneys, health care professionals, and scientists.

Learning More About Job Opportunities

Carefully study the various employment opportunities you have identified. Obviously, you will like some more than others, but you can examine a variety of factors when assessing each job possibility:

- actual job responsibilities
- industry characteristics
- nature of the company
- geographic location
- salary and opportunities for advancement
- contribution of the job to your long-range career objectives.

Too many job applicants consider only the most striking features of a job, perhaps its location, industry or title, or the salary offer. However, a comprehensive review of job openings should provide a balanced perspective of the overall employment opportunity, including both long-run and short-run factors.

Building a Résumé

Regardless of how you locate job openings, you must learn how to prepare and submit a *résumé*, a written summary of your personal, educational, and professional achievements. The résumé is a personal document covering your educational background, work experience, career preferences and goals, and major interests that may be relevant. It also includes such basic contact information as your home and e-mail addresses, as well as your telephone number. It should *not* include information on your age, marital status, race, or ethnic background.

Your résumé is usually your formal introduction to an employer, so it should present you in the best light, accentuating your strengths and potential to contribute to a firm as an employee. However, it should *never* contain embellishments or inaccuracies. You don't want to begin your career with unethical behavior, and an employer is bound to discover any discrepancies in fact—either immediately or during the months following your employment. Either event is very risky, and typically results in short-circuiting your career path.

Organizing Your Résumé

The primary purpose of a résumé is to highlight your qualifications for a job, usually on a single page. An attractive layout facilitates the employer's review of your qualifications. You can prepare your résumé in several ways. You may use narrative sentences to explain job duties and career goals, or you may present information in outline form. A résumé included as part of your credentials file at the career center on campus should be quite short. Remember to design it around your specific career objectives.

Figures E.2, E.3, and E.4 illustrate different ways to organize your résumé—by *reverse chronology*, or time; by *function*; and by *results*. Regardless of which format you select, you will want to include the following: a career "snapshot" highlighting some of your key skills; your work or professional experience; your education; your personal interests such as sports or music; and your volunteer work. While all three formats are acceptable, recruiters and prospective employers generally prefer the reverse chronological format—with the most recent experience listed first—because it is easiest to follow.[7]

FIGURE E.2 **Chronological Résumé**

FELICIA SMITH-WHITEHEAD
4265 Popular Lane
Cleveland, Ohio 44120
216-555-3296
FeliciaSW@gmail.com

Experienced office manager with excellent organizational and interpersonal skills. Conscientious team player; creative problem solver.

WORK EXPERIENCE
ADM Distribution Enterprises, Cleveland, Ohio   2015–Present
Office Manager of leading regional soft-drink bottler. Coordinate all bookkeeping, correspondence, scheduling of 12-truck fleet to serve 300 customers, promotional mailings, and personnel records, including payroll. Install computerized systems.

Merriweather, Hicks & Bradshaw Attorneys, Columbus, Ohio   2013–2015
Office Supervisor and Executive Assistant for Douglas H. Bradshaw, Managing Partner. Supervised four clerical workers and two paraprofessionals, automated legal research and correspondence functions, and assisted in coordinating outside services and relations with other firms and agencies. Promoted three times from Secretary to Office Supervisor.

Conner & Sons Custom Coverings, Cleveland, Ohio   2009–2013
Secretary in father's upholstery and awning company. Performed all office functions over the years, running the office when the owner was on vacation.

EDUCATION
McBundy Community College, Associate's Degree in Business   2013
Mill Valley High School, Honors   2009

COMPUTER SKILLS
Familiar with Microsoft Office and Adobe Acrobat

LANGUAGE SKILLS
Fluent in Spanish (speaking and writing)
Adequate speaking and writing skills in Portuguese

PERSONAL
Member of various community associations; avid reader; enjoy sports such as camping and cycling; enjoy volunteering in community projects.

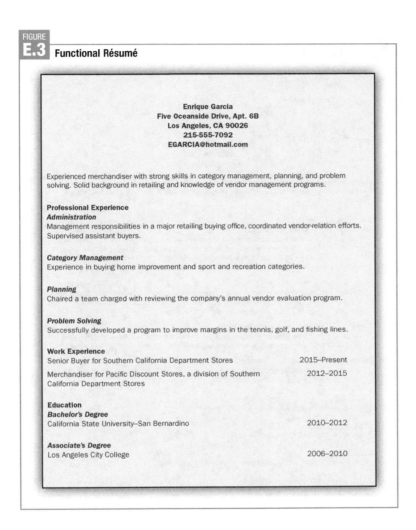

FIGURE E.3 Functional Résumé

Enrique Garcia
Five Oceanside Drive, Apt. 6B
Los Angeles, CA 90026
215-555-7092
EGARCIA@hotmail.com

Experienced merchandiser with strong skills in category management, planning, and problem solving. Solid background in retailing and knowledge of vendor management programs.

Professional Experience
Administration
Management responsibilities in a major retailing buying office, coordinated vendor-relation efforts. Supervised assistant buyers.

Category Management
Experience in buying home improvement and sport and recreation categories.

Planning
Chaired a team charged with reviewing the company's annual vendor evaluation program.

Problem Solving
Successfully developed a program to improve margins in the tennis, golf, and fishing lines.

Work Experience
Senior Buyer for Southern California Department Stores	2015–Present
Merchandiser for Pacific Discount Stores, a division of Southern California Department Stores	2012–2015

Education
Bachelor's Degree
California State University–San Bernardino	2010–2012

Associate's Degree
Los Angeles City College	2006–2010

Tips for Creating a Strong Résumé

Your résumé should help you stand out from the crowd, just as your college admissions application did. A company may receive hundreds or even thousands of résumés, so you want yours to be on the top of the stack. Here are some do's and don'ts:

Do:

- Begin the résumé with a few descriptive phrases that give the reader an immediate "snapshot" of who you are and help set the tone for the reader to review your document.

- Use terms related to your field, so that a human resource manager can locate them quickly. If you are submitting your résumé online, use words that will create an automatic "match" with a job description or field. If you are applying for an entry-level job in marketing, the phrase "communication skills" is likely to generate a match. You can identify such words and phrases by reading job descriptions online.

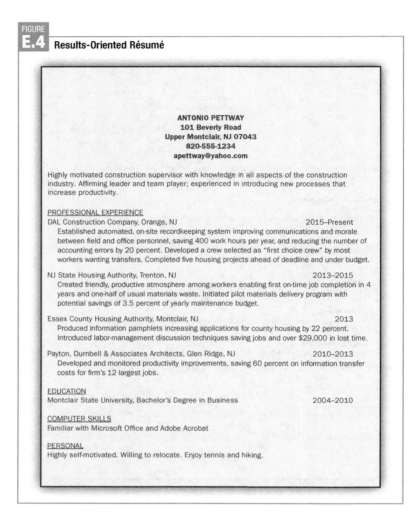

FIGURE E.4 Results-Oriented Résumé

ANTONIO PETTWAY
101 Beverly Road
Upper Montclair, NJ 07043
820-555-1234
apettway@yahoo.com

Highly motivated construction supervisor with knowledge in all aspects of the construction industry. Affirming leader and team player; experienced in introducing new processes that increase productivity.

PROFESSIONAL EXPERIENCE
DAL Construction Company, Orange, NJ   2015–Present
    Established automated, on-site recordkeeping system improving communications and morale between field and office personnel, saving 400 work hours per year, and reducing the number of accounting errors by 20 percent. Developed a crew selected as "first choice crew" by most workers wanting transfers. Completed five housing projects ahead of deadline and under budget.

NJ State Housing Authority, Trenton, NJ   2013–2015
    Created friendly, productive atmosphere among workers enabling first on-time job completion in 4 years and one-half of usual materials waste. Initiated pilot materials delivery program with potential savings of 3.5 percent of yearly maintenance budget.

Essex County Housing Authority, Montclair, NJ   2013
    Produced information pamphlets increasing applications for county housing by 22 percent. Introduced labor-management discussion techniques saving jobs and over $29,000 in lost time.

Payton, Durnbell & Associates Architects, Glen Ridge, NJ   2010–2013
    Developed and monitored productivity improvements, saving 60 percent on information transfer costs for firm's 12 largest jobs.

EDUCATION
Montclair State University, Bachelor's Degree in Business   2004–2010

COMPUTER SKILLS
Familiar with Microsoft Office and Adobe Acrobat

PERSONAL
Highly self-motivated. Willing to relocate. Enjoy tennis and hiking.

- Provide facts about previous jobs, internships, cooperative education programs, or volunteer work, including results or specific achievements. Include any projects or tasks you undertook through your own initiative.

- Emphasize your education if you are a recent graduate. Place it closer to the top of your résumé instead of the bottom.

- Highlight your strengths and skills, such as research, writing, or organizing.

- Write clearly and concisely.

- Proofread your résumé carefully for grammar, usage, and typographical errors. Refer to a dictionary or style manual.

- Keep your résumé to a single page.

- Avoid including personal information unless it is directly related to the job for which you're applying (for example, playing intramural basketball and volleyball during school might be relevant details if you were applying for a job as a recreation director at a community center).

Don't:

- Offer any misleading or inaccurate information.

- Make broad-based statements, such as "I work well with others," or "I want a position in business."

- State your objective as, "to run this company," "to find a job that matches my skill set," or "to advance as quickly as possible."

- Include a salary request.

- Make demands about vacation time, work hours, or excessive benefits.

- Highlight your weaknesses.

- Submit a résumé with typos or grammatical errors.

- Use slang or other inappropriate phrases or comments.

- Include pictures or graphics, or use fancy type fonts.[8]

Take your time creating your résumé; it is one of the most important tools you will use during your career. If you need help, go to your school's career center. If you are dealing with an employment agency, a counselor there should be able to help as well.

Keep in mind that you will probably have to modify your résumé at times to tailor it to a particular company or job. Again, take the time to do this; it may mean the difference between standing out and being lost in a sea of other applicants.

Preparing Your Cover Letter

In most cases, your résumé will be accompanied by a *cover letter*. This letter should introduce you, explain why you are submitting a résumé (cite the specific job opening if possible), call out some specific point in your résumé that qualifies you for the position, and ask for an interview. An effective cover letter will make the recipient want to take the next step and read your résumé. Here are a few tips for preparing an outstanding letter:

- Write the letter to a specific person, if possible. A letter addressed to "To whom it may concern" may never reach the right person. Check the company's website for the name of the person to whom you should send your letter. It might be someone in human resources or a person in the department where you'd actually be working. Be sure to obtain the person's title if possible (such as general manager or director), and spell the person's name correctly.

- Introduce yourself and explain the purpose of your letter—to apply for a job.

- Describe briefly an example of your best work or most ambitious project.

- Keep it short—a page is acceptable, half a page even better.

- Request an interview.

- Thank the person for his or her time and consideration.

- Make sure all your contact information is in the letter—name, address, home phone number, cell phone number, and e-mail address.

- Proofread your letter carefully.[9]

Submitting Your Online Résumé

You may write a sparkling cover letter and stellar résumé, but if your online submission is blocked or tossed aside by an automated processing system, it won't have a chance to impress the person for whom it was intended. Here are a few tips for making certain your letter and résumé reach their mark.

- Review the formatting of your résumé to make sure it will appear the same to the recipient as it does to you. Delete any unusual symbols or fonts.

- Use keywords that create a match and allow your résumé through the company's filter. This applies to the subject line of your e-mail as well, which should be specific and contain keywords such as "application for sales trainee job."

- Include your cover letter in the e-mail.

- Send your résumé in the body of the e-mail—not as an attachment. This is more convenient for the recipient, and it also avoids the disaster of having your attachment automatically deleted by an antivirus system.

- Do not send graphics, because they may be blocked or deleted as well.

- If you are answering an ad, read the instructions for application and follow them exactly.[10]

The Job Interview

Congratulations! You've prepared an effective résumé, and you've been contacted for an interview. An interview is more than a casual conversation, and an initial, prescreening interview can take place over the phone or via Skype. During an interview, at least one manager will learn about you, and you'll learn more about the company and the job. Although you may feel nervous about the interview, you can control some of its outcome by doing your homework: planning and preparing for this important encounter with your potential employer. Before you meet with an interviewer, learn everything you can about the firm. The simplest way to do this is to visit the company's website. You can also check with your school's career center. If you know anyone who works for the company, you may ask the person about the firm. Try to do as much research about a company as possible to learn the answers to the following questions:

- What does the firm do—manufacture clothing, market snack foods, produce films, sell cars? If you are applying for a job at a large corporation, zero in on the division for which you would be working.

- What is the company's mission? Many firms include a statement about their purpose in the business world—to supply affordable energy to communities, to serve fresh food, to make communication easier. Understanding why the company exists will help you grasp where it is headed and why.

- Where, when, and by whom was the company founded? Learn a little about the history of the firm.

- What is its position in the marketplace? Is it a leader or is it trying to gain a competitive advantage? Who are its main competitors?

- Where is the firm based? Does it have facilities located around the country and the world, or is it purely local?

- How is the company organized? Are there multiple divisions and products?

- Learning about the firm indicates to the interviewer that you have initiative and motivation, as well as an interest in the firm's culture and history. You have taken the time and effort to find out more about the organization, and your enthusiasm shows.

Tips for Successful Interviewing

An interview is your personal introduction to the company. You want to make a good impression, but you also want to find out whether you and the firm are a good fit. Although the interviewer will be asking most of the questions, you will want to ask some, as well. People who conduct interviews say that the most important qualities candidates can exhibit are self-confidence, preparedness, and an ability to communicate clearly.

When you are contacted for an interview, find out the name(s) of the person or people who will be interviewing you. It's also appropriate to ask whether the initial interview will be with a human resource manager or with the person to whom you would be reporting on the job, or both. Many people who conduct initial job interviews work in their firms' human resource divisions. These interviewers act as gatekeepers and can make recommendations to managers and supervisors about which individuals to interview further or hire. Managers who head the units in which an applicant will be employed may get involved later in the hiring process. Some hiring decisions come from human resource personnel together with the immediate supervisor of the prospective employee. In other cases, immediate supervisors make the decision alone. If your interview is face to face, keep in mind the following tips.

Do:

- **Dress appropriately.** Dress as if it is your first day of work at the firm. Conceal any tattoos or body piercings and, if you wear jewelry, keep it simple.

- **Arrive a few minutes early.** This gives you time to relax and take in the surroundings. It also shows that you are punctual and care about other people's time.

- **Introduce yourself with a smile and a handshake.** Be friendly, but not overly familiar.

- **Be yourself—at your best.** Don't suddenly adopt a new personality. But try to be confident, polite, respectful, and interested in the people who are spending time with you. Be sure to thank each person who interviews you.

- **Listen.** Pay attention to what the interviewer is saying. If something is unclear to you, ask for clarification. Turn off your cell phone and put it away. Your full attention should be on the conversation you are having in the interview.

- **Use appropriate language.** As in your résumé and cover letter, be sure to use correct English. You don't need to be stiff or formal, but avoid slang or phrases that you know are inappropriate for the situation.

- **Be positive in your outlook.** Be enthusiastic about the firm and the job, but don't go overboard.

Don't:

- **Talk too much.** Avoid telling the interviewer a lot about your personal life, or why you left a particular job. Answer questions honestly and thoroughly, but don't dip into irrelevant details.

- **Be arrogant or aggressive.** Self-confidence is a good trait, but don't miss the mark by behaving in an arrogant or condescending manner. Certainly don't become aggressive, demanding that the interviewer offer you the job or even another interview.

- **Act indifferent or bored.** This may not be the job you ultimately want, but treat the interview and the interviewer with respect and attention. If you make a good impression, the interviewer is likely to keep you in mind should another job come up.

- **Don't get ahead of yourself.** This is not the time to discuss salary, vacation, or benefits.[11]

Answering and Asking Questions

In a typical format, the interviewer gives you ample opportunity to talk about yourself and your goals. Prepare in advance for this opportunity. You want to present your thoughts clearly and concisely, in an organized fashion, without rambling or bringing up unrelated topics. The interviewer may wait until you are finished or prompt you to talk about certain subjects by asking questions. Be as specific as possible when answering questions. The questions that interviewers ask often include the following:

- "Why do you want this job?"
- "Why do you want to work in this field?"
- "What are your short-term goals? Long-term objectives?"
- "Where do you see yourself in five years? In ten years?"
- "What are your strengths? What are your weaknesses?"
- "What motivates you?"
- "Describe a situation in which you made a tough decision or solved a problem."
- "What did you like best about your last job? What did you like least?"
- "Why did you leave your last job?"
- "Why should my firm hire you?"
- "Are you considering other jobs or companies?"

Some of these questions may seem tougher than others, but you can reduce your anxiety by preparing for them. First, figure out which questions you fear the most. Then think about possible answers that are both truthful and positive. Rehearse your delivery in front of a mirror or with a friend.[12]

At some point, the interviewer will probably ask you whether you have any questions of your own. It's a good idea to come prepared with some questions, but others may arise during the interview. Try to keep your list concise, say, three or four of your most important questions. The questions you ask reflect just as much about you as the answers you give to the interviewer's questions. Here is a sample of appropriate questions for the initial interview:

- "Could you clarify a certain aspect of the job responsibilities for me?"
- "Do people who start in entry-level jobs at this company tend to develop their careers here?"
- "In what ways could I perform above and beyond the job requirements?"

At some point during your conversation, the interviewer may give you an idea of the salary range for the job. If not, he or she will do so during a subsequent interview. You may ask about the range, but do not ask exactly how much you will be paid if you get the job. Keep in mind that usually there is little or no negotiation of an entry-level salary. However, you may ask if there is a probationary period with a review at the end of the period. Here are a few other questions *not* to ask:

- "When will I be promoted?"
- "How much time off do I get?"
- "When will I get my first raise?"
- "How many people are applying for this job?"
- "What are my chances of getting this job?"

At the end of the interview, be sure to thank the interviewer with a smile and a handshake, and leave on a positive, upbeat note. Even if you know the job isn't the best fit, another opportunity may come along in the future and you want to leave the door open. Be sure to ask for a business card or contact information from each person who interviewed you. Within 24 hours, write a note or e-mail to each person separately, thanking him or her for the opportunity to speak further about the job opportunity. Thank-you notes really do make a lasting impression on a person, and it gives you another chance to differentiate yourself and reinforce your interest.

A successful first interview often leads to a second. The purpose of a second interview is to better determine your specific qualifications and fit with the company. You may be introduced to more people—potential co-workers, people in other divisions, or sales staff. You may have another meeting with human resource staff members in which you'll learn more about salary, employee benefits, the firm's code of ethics, and the like. Depending on the type of job, you might be asked to take some skills tests. If you are interviewing for an accounting position, you might be required to take some accounting-type tests. If you are going to work for a publisher, you might be asked to take an editing test or do some proofreading. If you are applying for a job as a sales representative, you may be given a test that assesses your personality traits. Don't be intimidated by these tests; you are not expected to know everything or be perfect. They are really just a trial run to give the employer a sense of whether you can think fast on your feet and perform under pressure.

Making the Employment Decision

After receiving your résumé, conducting one or two interviews, and administering a skills test, a potential employer knows a bit more about you. You should also know a lot about the company. If the experience has been positive on both sides, you may be offered a job. If you have interviewed at several companies and are offered more than one job, congratulations! Often, an employer will phone you to make the job offer, saying that the formal offer will follow via e-mail or through the mail. Whether you receive one offer or several, thank the person making the offer. If you choose to accept immediately, feel free to do so. However, employers commonly expect that candidate will want to review the offer letter before formally accepting. If you have doubts about the job or need to decide between two, it is appropriate to ask for 24 hours to respond. If you must decline an offer, do so promptly and politely. After all, you may end up working for that firm sometime in the future. If you get a few rejections before you receive an offer, don't give up. Every application and interview adds to your experience.

As you think about an offer, consider the aspects that are most important. You'll want to choose a job that comes closest to your career interests and objectives. But don't rule out the element of surprise—you might wind up

Congratulations! You've accepted an offer for your first job. You are now a member of the workforce.

Goodluz/iStockphoto

with a job you like in an industry you'd never considered before. Don't worry too much about the salary. The point of an entry-level job is to set you on a forward path, commonly known as a "stepping stone." And keep in mind that your first job won't be your last. Once you have accepted an offer, you'll be given a start date as well as the name of the person to whom you should report on arrival.

Nontraditional Students

Take a quick glance around your class. You'll likely see classmates of all ages. Some will fall into the traditional college age group of 18 to 24, but many don't. Perhaps you are a veteran returning from military duty overseas. Maybe you have been engaged in a full-time career but want to broaden your education. Students who fall outside the 18- to 24-year-old age group are often referred to as *nontraditional students*, but these students have become the norm on many campuses. Stay-at-home parents returning to school to retool and add skills to their résumés before returning to the workforce and workers who have been laid off due to an economic downturn are other examples of nontraditional students. As diverse as this group is, they share one thing in common: they are older than traditional students, typically between 25–34 and 35 and older. This means that they face different challenges—but also enjoy some advantages over their younger classmates.

One major challenge faced by nontraditional students is scheduling. Often they are juggling the responsibilities of work, school, and family. They may have to study at odd times—during meals, while commuting, or after putting the kids to bed. If they are switching careers, they may be learning an entirely new set of skills, as well. But nontraditional students have an important advantage: experience. Even experience in an unrelated field is a plus. Older students know how organizations operate. Often, they have developed useful skills in human relations, management, budgeting, and communications. Even a former stay-at-home parent has skills in all of these areas. Through observing other people's successes and failures—as well as living through their own—they have developed an inventory of what to do and what not to do. So, in some ways, these students have a head start on their younger counterparts. But they also face the reality that they have fewer years in which to develop a career.

The Job Market: Where Do You Fit In?

The industry you choose, and the career you follow within it, are part of a bigger picture. They reflect the needs of society, changing populations, developing technology, and the overall economy. For instance, the U.S. population is expected to increase at a slower rate of growth for the foreseeable future than during the previous two decades. The U.S. workforce will continue to become more diverse, with Hispanics accounting for both the largest share of jobs among minorities by the year 2020 as well as the fastest-growing. The size of the Hispanic workforce is expected to increase more than 3 percent per year to nearly 19 percent of the U.S. workforce. White, non-Hispanic workers will make up a declining share of the workforce, falling from approximately 68 percent to about 62 percent.[13]

The number of women in the workforce is growing at a slightly faster rate than that of men. The male labor force is expected to grow by 6.3 percent by the year 2020, compared with 7.4 percent for women. So the men's share of the labor force will likely continue to decrease, while the women's share will increase.[14]

All of these facts combine to shape a picture of the needs of U.S. society and the workforce available to serve it. As the Baby Boom generation ages, the age group between 55 and 64 will increase by more than one third. Thus, the United States will need more health care services as well as other services for an aging population, such as assisted living facilities and leisure and hospitality. The group between the ages 25 and 54 will rise a mere 1.6 percent, while the youth population between 16 and 24 will decline by more than 12 percent. But today's younger workers are receiving more education and training to fill the need for professional and business service workers. These projections affect both the workforce and the types of goods and services needed to satisfy consumers. So jobs in health care are estimated to increase by more than 5.6 million and in professional and business services by 3.8 million.[15]

Careers in service-providing industries continue a long-term rise. Service jobs in educational services will increase by about 23 percent by the year 2020, while manufacturing jobs will continue to shrink. But industries that produce certain types of goods, such as those related to the needs of an aging population and those related to green technologies or products, will probably increase.[16]

The good news is that even in a weaker job market, employers are looking to hire recent college graduates. Continuing to hire entry-level employees makes good business sense. The National Associate of Colleges and Employers (NACE) reports that college hiring is actually on the rise.[17] Some of the hot jobs can be found in accounting, sales, management training, engineering, and business services. So celebrate your graduation, and keep your résumé current and your outlook positive: a job is out there for you.

A Long-Range View of Your Career

Choosing a career is an important life decision. A career is a professional journey—regardless of whether you want to run a small restaurant or a branch bank, whether you are fascinated by language or math, whether you prefer to work with animals or people. In the end, you hope to contribute something good to society while enjoying what you do—and make a reasonable living at it.

Throughout your career, it is important to stay flexible and continue learning. Challenging new skills will be required of managers and other businesspeople during these first decades of the 21st century. Remain open to unexpected changes and opportunities that can help you learn and develop new skills. Keep in mind that your first job will not be your last. But tackle that first job with the same enthusiasm you'd have if someone asked you to run the company itself, because everything you learn on that job will be valuable at some point during your career—and someday you may actually run the company.

Finally, if you haven't already started your career search, begin now. Do this by utilizing your contacts and network, lining up an internship, looking for a part-time job on or off campus, or volunteering for an organization. Register with the campus career center long before you graduate. Then, when you reach your final semester, you'll be well on your way to finding the job you want.

This textbook presents a panorama of career options for you. Whatever you decide, be sure it is right for you—not your friends, your instructors, or your parents. As the old saying goes, "You pass this way just once." Enjoy the journey!

More Career Information on the *Contemporary Business* Website

More career information is available to students using *Contemporary Business* at the book's website.

The "Management Careers" section on the website enables you to learn more about business careers and to locate currently posted job opportunities. The site provides a vast number of career resources such as links to job sites, career guidance sites, and the like. Also, many links include extensive career information and guidance, such as interviewing techniques and tips for résumé writing.

Projects and Teamwork Applications

1. Visit one of the job websites such as Indeed or Glassdoor and research an industry in which you think you might be interested. Prepare a report on what you learned about the field. Was the site helpful? What types of jobs were available in the field? Based on your report, do you plan to pursue this industry or select another field?

2. Prepare your résumé following the procedures outlined earlier in this section. Exchange your résumé with a classmate so you can critique each other's work. Then revise and proofread your résumé.

3. Go online to the website for a specific company for which you might be interested in working. Click on the "Careers" or "Job Opportunities" section of the site, and read carefully the job descriptions for any entry-level positions and the procedure for applying for them. Also review any general information about career development at the firm. Write a cover letter as if you were actually applying for one of the jobs.

4. With a classmate, practice interviewing for the job you selected in the previous question. Prepare commonly asked questions for each other and take turns interviewing and being interviewed. What parts of the interview did you handle well? What could you improve?

5. Think about where you would like to be in your career in five years and write about your plans. Share your plans with the class, then seal them in an envelope. Keep the envelope and open it in five years to see how close you came to your predictions.

| Glossary |

360-degree performance review employee performance review that gathers feedback from co-workers, supervisors, managers, and sometimes customers.

401(k) plan retirement savings plan to which employees can make pretax contributions; employers often make additional contributions to the plan.

accounting process of measuring, interpreting, and communicating financial information to support internal and external business decision making.

accounting cycle set of activities involved in converting information and individual transactions into financial statements.

accounting equation formula that states that assets must always equal the sum of liabilities and owners' equity.

accrual accounting accounting method that records revenues and expenses when they occur, not necessarily when cash actually changes hands.

acquisition agreement in which one firm purchases another.

activity ratios measures of how efficiently a firm utilizes its assets.

actuarial table probability of the number of events that are expected to occur within a given year.

advertising paid nonpersonal communication usually targeted at large numbers of potential buyers.

affective conflict disagreement that focuses on individuals or personal issues.

affinity program marketing effort sponsored by an organization that solicits involvement by individuals who share common interests and activities.

affirmative action programs programs designed by employers to increase job opportunities for women, minorities, disabled people, and other protected groups.

agency legal relationship whereby one party, called a *principal*, appoints another party, called an *agent*, to enter into contracts with third parties on the principal's behalf.

alien corporation firm incorporated in one nation and operating in another nation.

angel investors wealthy individuals who invest directly in a new venture in exchange for an equity stake.

appellate courts courts that hear appeals of decisions made at the general trial court level; both the federal and state systems have appellate courts.

application service provider (ASP) outside supplier that provides both the computers and the application support for managing an information system.

arbitration bringing in an impartial third party called an arbitrator to render a binding decision in a dispute.

assembly line manufacturing technique that carries the product on a conveyor system past several workstations where workers perform specialized tasks.

asset anything of value owned by a firm.

asset intensity amount of assets needed to generate a given level of sales.

autocratic leadership management approach whereby leaders make decisions on their own without consulting employees.

balance of payments overall money flows into and out of a country.

balance of trade difference between a nation's exports and imports.

balance sheet statement of a firm's financial position—what it owns and claims against its assets—at a particular point in time.

balanced budget situation in which total revenues raised by taxes and fees equal total proposed government spending for the year.

bankruptcy legal nonpayment of financial obligations.

banner ad advertisement placed by an organization on another organization's website; interested parties click on the ad for more information.

benchmarking process of determining how well other companies perform business functions or tasks.

big data information collected in massive amounts and at unprecedented speed from both traditional and digital sources that is used in business decision making.

blog online journal written by a blogger.

board of directors governing body of a corporation.

bot short for *robot*—a program that allows online shoppers to compare prices for a specific product at several e-tailers.

botnet a network of PCs that have been infected with one or more data-stealing viruses.

boycott effort to prevent people from purchasing a firm's goods or services.

brand name, term, sign, symbol, design, or some combination that identifies the products of one firm and differentiates them from competitors' offerings.

brand equity added value that a respected and successful name gives to a product.

brand name part of a brand consisting of words or letters that form a name that identifies and distinguishes an offering from those of competitors.

branding process of creating an identity in consumers' minds for a good, service, or company; a major marketing tool in contemporary business.

breach of contract violation of a valid contract.

breakeven analysis pricing-related technique used to determine the minimum sales volume a product must generate at a certain price level to cover all costs.

budget organization's plan for how it will raise and spend money during a given period of time.

budget deficit situation in which the government spends more than the amount of money it raises through taxes.

budget surplus excess funding that occurs when government spends less than the amount of funds raised through taxes and fees.

business all profit-seeking activities and enterprises that provide goods and services necessary to an economic system.

business (B2B) product good or service purchased to be used, either directly or indirectly, in the production of other goods for resale.

business ethics standards of conduct and moral values regarding right and wrong actions in the work environment.

business incubator local programs designed to provide low-cost shared business facilities to small start-up ventures.

business intelligence activities and technologies for gathering, storing, and analyzing data to make better competitive decisions.

business interruption insurance type of insurance that protects firms from financial losses resulting from the suspension of business operations.

business law aspects of law that most directly influence and regulate the management of business activity.

business plan written document that provides an orderly statement of a company's goals, methods, and standards.

business-to-business (B2B) e-business electronic business transactions between organizations using the Internet.

business-to-consumer (B2C) e-business selling directly to consumers over the Internet.

call provision right of the issuer to buy a bond back from the investor before maturity at a specified price.

capital production inputs consisting of technology, tools, information, and physical facilities.

capital investment analysis process of comparing the costs and benefits of a long-term asset investment.

capital structure mix of a firm's debt and equity capital.

capitalism economic system that rewards firms for their ability to perceive and serve the needs and demands of consumers; also called the private enterprise system.

cash budget budget that shows cash inflows and outflows during a period of time.

cash flow sources of cash minus uses of cash during a specified period of time.

cash value policy type of life insurance that combines insurance protection with a savings feature.

category advisor vendor that is designated by the business customer as the major supplier to assume responsibility for dealing with all the other vendors for a project and presenting the entire package to the business buyer.

category manager person who oversees an entire group of products and assumes profit responsibility for the product group.

cause advertising form of institutional advertising that promotes a specific viewpoint on a public issue as a way to influence public opinion and the legislative process.

cause marketing marketing that promotes a cause or social issue, such as preventing child abuse, anti-littering efforts, and stop-smoking campaigns.

Central America–Dominican Republic Free Trade Agreement (CAFTA-DR) agreement among the United States, Costa Rica, El Salvador, Guatemala, Honduras, Nicaragua, and the Dominican Republic to reduce tariffs and trade restrictions.

centralization decision making based at the top of the management hierarchy.

certified management accountant (CMA) management accountant who meets specified educational and experience requirements and has passed an examination covering management accounting topics.

certified public accountant (CPA) public accountant who meets specified educational and experiential requirements and has passed a comprehensive examination on accounting theory and practice.

chain of command set of relationships that indicates who directs which activities and who reports to whom.

channel conflict conflict between two or more members of a supply chain, such as a manufacturer, wholesaler, or retailer.

chief information officer (CIO) executive responsible for managing a firm's information system and related computer technologies.

Class-Action Fairness Act of 2005 law that moves most large, multistate class-action lawsuits to federal courts, ensures judicial oversight of plaintiffs' compensation, bases lawyers' compensation on awards actually distributed or actual time spent, and ensures plaintiffs' interests are protected equally with those of their lawyers.

classic entrepreneur person who identifies a business opportunity and allocates available resources to tap that market.

click-through rate number of visitors who click on a web banner ad.

cloud computing powerful servers store applications software and databases for users to access the software and databases via the web using anything from a PC to a smart phone.

cobranding cooperative arrangement in which two or more businesses team up to closely link their names on a single product.

code of conduct formal statement that defines how an organization expects its employees to resolve ethical issues.

cognitive ability tests tests that measure job candidates' abilities in perceptual speed, verbal comprehension, numerical aptitude, general reasoning, and spatial aptitude.

cognitive conflict disagreement that focuses on problem- and issue-related differences of opinion.

collective bargaining process of negotiation between management and union representatives.

comarketing cooperative arrangement in which two businesses jointly market each other's products.

committee organization organizational structure that places authority and responsibility jointly in the hands of a group of individuals rather than a single manager.

common law body of law arising out of judicial decisions, some of which can be traced back to early England.

common stock shares that give owners voting rights but only residual claims to the firm's assets and income distributions.

communication meaningful exchange of information through messages.

communism economic system in which all property would be shared equally by the people of a community under the direction of a strong central government.

compensation amount employees are paid in money and benefits.

competition battle among businesses for consumer acceptance.

competitive differentiation unique combination of organizational abilities, products, and approaches that sets a company apart from competitors in the minds of customers.

competitive pricing strategy that tries to reduce the emphasis on price competition by matching other firms' prices and concentrating their own marketing efforts on the product, distribution, and promotional elements of the marketing mix.

compressed workweek scheduling option that allows employees to work the regular number of hours per week in fewer than the typical five days.

computer-aided design (CAD) process that allows engineers to design components as well as entire products on computer screens faster and with fewer mistakes than they could achieve working with traditional drafting systems.

computer-aided manufacturing (CAM) computer tools to analyze CAD output and enable a manufacturer to analyze the steps that a machine must take to produce a needed product or part.

computer-based information systems information systems that rely on computer and related technologies to store information electronically in an organized, accessible manner.

computer-integrated manufacturing (CIM) production system in which computers help workers design products, control machines, handle materials, and control the production function in an integrated fashion.

conceptual skills ability to see the organization as a unified whole and to understand how each part interacts with others.

conflict situation in which one person or group's needs do not match those of another, and attempts may be made to block the opposing side's intentions or goals.

conflict of interest situation in which an employee must choose between a business's welfare and personal gain.

conglomerate merger merger that combines unrelated firms, usually with the goal of diversification, spurring sales growth, or spending a cash surplus in order to avoid a takeover attempt.

consumer (B2C) product good or service that is purchased by end users.

consumer behavior actions of ultimate consumers directly involved in obtaining, consuming, and disposing of products and the decision processes that precede and follow these actions.

consumer orientation business philosophy that focuses first on determining unmet consumer wants and needs and then designing products to satisfy those needs.

Consumer Price Index (CPI) measurement of the monthly average change in prices of goods and services.

consumerism public demand that a business consider the wants and needs of its customers in making decisions.

contingency planning plans that allow a firm to resume operations as quickly and as smoothly as possible after a crisis while openly communicating with the public about what happened.

contract legally enforceable agreement between two or more parties regarding a specified act or thing.

controlling function of evaluating an organization's performance against its objectives.

convenience product item the consumer seeks to purchase frequently, immediately, and with little effort.

conversion rate percentage of visitors to a website who actually make a purchase.

convertible securities bonds or preferred stock issues that are convertible into a set number of shares of the issuing company's common stock.

cooperative organization whose owners join forces to collectively operate all or part of the functions in their business.

cooperative advertising allowances provided by marketers in which they share the cost of local advertising of their firm's product or product line with channel partners.

copyright protection of written material such as textbooks, designs, cartoon illustrations, photos, and computer software.

core inflation rate inflation rate of an economy after energy and food prices are removed.

corporate charter legal document that formally establishes a corporation.

corporate culture organization's system of principles, beliefs, and values.

corporate philanthropy effort of an organization to make a contribution to the communities in which it earns profits.

corporate website website designed to increase a firm's visibility, promote its offerings, and provide information to interested parties.

corporation legal organization with assets and liabilities separate from those of its owner(s).

cost-based pricing formulas that calculate total costs per unit and then add markups to cover overhead costs and generate profits.

countertrade barter agreement whereby trade between two or more nations involves payment made in the form of local products instead of currency.

creative selling persuasive type of promotional presentation.

creativity capacity to develop novel solutions to perceived organizational problems.

credit receiving money, goods, or services on the basis of an agreement between the lender and the borrower that the loan is for a specified period of time with a specified rate of interest.

critical path sequence of operations that requires the longest time for completion.

critical thinking ability to analyze and assess information to pinpoint problems or opportunities.

cross-functional team a team made up of members from different functions, such as production, marketing, and finance.

cyclical unemployment people who are out of work because of a cyclical contraction in the economy.

damages financial payments to compensate for a loss and related suffering.

data raw facts and figures that may or may not be relevant to a business decision.

data mining computer searches of customer data to detect patterns and relationships.

data warehouse customer database that allows managers to combine data from several different organizational functions.

database centralized integrated collection of data resources.

debenture unsecured corporate bond.

debt capital funds obtained from borrowing.

debt financing borrowed funds that entrepreneurs must repay.

decentralization decision makeup based at lower levels of the organization.

decision making process of recognizing a problem or opportunity, evaluating alternative solutions, selecting and implementing an alternative, and assessing the results.

decision support system (DSS) gives direct support to businesspeople during the decision-making process.

deflation opposite of inflation, occurs when prices continue to fall.

delegation managerial process of assigning work to employees.

demand willingness and ability of buyers to purchase goods and services.

demand curve graph of the amount of a product that buyers will purchase at different prices.

democratic leadership management approach whereby leaders delegate assignments, ask employees for suggestions, and encourage their participation.

demographic segmentation dividing markets on the basis of various demographic or socioeconomic characteristics such as gender, age, income, occupation, household size, stage in family life cycle, education, or ethnic group.

demographics statistical characteristics of the segment of the market that might purchase a product.

departmentalization process of dividing work activities into units within the organization.

deregulation regulatory trend toward elimination of legal restraints on competition in industries previously served by a single firm in an attempt to improve customer service and lower prices through increased competition.

devaluation reduction in a currency's value relative to other currencies or to a fixed standard.

direct distribution channel marketing channel that moves goods directly from producer to ultimate user.

directing guiding and motivating employees to accomplish organizational objectives.

disability income insurance type of insurance that pays benefits to those who cannot work due to some sort of disability.

discrimination biased treatment of a job candidate or employee.

dispatching phase of production control in which the manager instructs each department on what work to do and the time allowed for its completion.

display ad glossy-looking online ad often targeted at a specific user.

distribution channel path through which products—and legal ownership of them—flow from producer to consumers or business users.

diversity blending individuals of different genders, ethnic backgrounds, cultures, religions, and ages to enhance a firm's chances of success.

divestiture sale of assets by a firm.

domestic corporation firm that operates in the state where it is incorporated.

double-entry bookkeeping process by which accounting transactions are entered; each individual transaction always has an offsetting transaction.

downsizing process of reducing the number of employees within a firm by eliminating jobs.

dumping selling products abroad at prices below production costs or below typical prices in the home market to capture market share from domestic competitors.

e-business (or e-commerce) conducting business via the Internet.

e-procurement use of the Internet by business and government agencies to solicit bids and purchase goods and services from suppliers.

economics social science that analyzes the choices people and governments make in allocating scarce resources.

electronic data interchange (EDI) computer-to-computer exchanges of invoices, purchase orders, price quotations, and other information between buyers and sellers.

electronic exchange online marketplace that caters to an industry's specific needs.

electronic shopping cart file that holds items that the online shopper has chosen to buy.

electronic storefront company website that sells products to customers.

electronic wallet secure computer data file set up by an online shopper at an e-business site that contains credit card and personal identification information.

embargo total ban on importing specific products or a total halt to trading with a particular country.

employee benefits additional compensation such as vacation, retirement plans, profit-sharing, health insurance, gym membership, child and elder care, and tuition reimbursement, paid entirely or in part by the company.

employee ownership business ownership in which workers own shares of stock in the company that employs them.

employee separation broad term covering the loss of an employee for any reason, voluntary or involuntary.

employee stock-ownership plan (ESOP) plan that benefits employees by giving them ownership stakes in the companies for which they work.

empowerment giving employees shared authority, responsibility, and decision making with their managers.

encryption process of encoding data for security purposes, using software that encodes and scrambles messages.

end-use segmentation marketing strategy that focuses on the precise way a B2B purchaser will use a product.

enterprise zones specific geographic areas designated for economic revitalization.

entrepreneur risk taker in the private enterprise system, a person who seeks a profitable opportunity and takes the necessary risks to set up and operate a business.

entrepreneurship willingness to take risks to create and operate a business.

environmental impact study analyzes how a proposed plant would affect the quality of life in the surrounding area.

Equal Employment Opportunity Commission (EEOC) commission created to increase job opportunities for women and minorities and to help end discrimination based on race, color, religion, disability, gender, or national origin in any personnel action.

equilibrium price prevailing market price at which you can buy an item.

equity capital funds obtained from owners.

equity financing funds invested in new ventures in exchange for part ownership.

equity theory an individual's perception of fair and equitable treatment.

European Union (EU) 28-nation European economic alliance.

event marketing marketing or sponsoring short-term events such as athletic competitions and cultural and charitable performances.

everyday low pricing (EDLP) is a strategy devoted to maintaining continuous low prices rather than relying on short-term price cuts such as cents-off coupons, rebates, and special sales.

exchange control restriction on importation of certain products or against certain companies to reduce trade and expenditures of foreign currency.

exchange process activity in which two or more parties give something of value to each other to satisfy perceived needs.

exchange rate value of one nation's currency relative to the currencies of other countries.

exclusive distribution distribution strategy involving limited market coverage by a single retailer or wholesaler in a specific geographical territory.

executive summary one- to two-page snapshot of what the overall business plan explains in detail.

executive support system (ESS) lets senior executives access the firm's primary databases, often by touching the computer screen, pointing and clicking a mouse, or using voice recognition.

expansionary monetary policy government actions to increase the money supply in an effort to cut the cost of borrowing, which encourages business decision makers to make new investments, in turn stimulating employment and economic growth.

expectancy theory the process people use to evaluate the likelihood that their efforts will yield the results they want, along with the degree to which they want those results.

expert system computer program that imitates human thinking through complicated sets of "if-then" rules.

exports domestically produced goods and services sold in other countries.

external communication meaningful exchange of information through messages transmitted between an organization and its major audiences.

extranet secure network used for e-business and accessible through an organization's website; available to external customers, suppliers, and other authorized users.

factoring selling receivables to another party, called a factor, for cash.

factors of production four basic inputs for effective operation: natural resources, capital, human resources, and entrepreneurship.

fair trade a market-based approach to pay higher prices to producers on exports from developing countries to developed countries in order for the

developing countries to obtain better trading conditions and promote sustainability.

family brand brand name used to identify several different, but related, products.

family leave the Family and Medical Leave Act of 1993 states that employers with 50 or more employees must provide unpaid leave up to 12 weeks annually for any employee who wants time off for the birth or adoption of a child, to become a foster parent, or to care for a seriously ill relative, spouse, or self.

Federal Deposit Insurance Corporation (FDIC) federal agency that insures deposits at commercial and savings banks.

Federal Open Markets Committee Fed body that has primary responsibility for money policy.

Federal Reserve System (Fed) central bank of the United States.

fee-for-service plan traditional form of health insurance in which the insured chooses his or her health care provider, pays for treatment, and is reimbursed by the insurance company; also called an indemnity plan.

finance planning, obtaining, and managing a company's funds to accomplish its objectives as effectively and efficiently as possible.

finance charge the difference between the amount borrowed and the amount repaid on a loan.

Financial Accounting Standards Board (FASB) organization that interprets and modifies GAAP in the United States.

financial institutions intermediary between savers and borrowers, collecting funds from savers and then lending the funds to individuals, businesses, and governments.

financial managers executives who develop and implement the firm's financial plan and determine the most appropriate sources and uses of funds.

financial markets market in which securities are bought and sold.

financial plan document that specifies the funds needed by a firm for a period of time, the timing of inflows and outflows, and the most appropriate sources and uses of funds.

financial system process by which money flows from savers to users.

financing section section of a business plan that demonstrates the cost of the product, operating expenses, expected sales revenue and profit, and the amount of the business owner's own funds that will be invested to get the business up and running.

firewall limits data transfers to certain locations and log system use so that managers can identify attempts to log on with invalid passwords and other threats to a system's security.

fiscal policy government spending and taxation decisions designed to control inflation, reduce

unemployment, improve the general welfare of citizens, and encourage economic growth.

flexible benefit plan benefit system that offers employees a range of options from which they may choose the types of benefits they receive.

flexible manufacturing system (FMS) production facility that workers can quickly modify to manufacture different products.

flexible work plan employment that allows personnel to adjust their working hours and places of work to accommodate their personal needs.

flextime scheduling system that allows employees to set their own work hours within constraints specified by the firm.

follow-up phase of production control in which employees and their supervisors spot problems in the production process and determine needed adjustments.

foreign corporation firm that operates in states where it is not incorporated.

Foreign Corrupt Practices Act federal law that prohibits U.S. citizens and companies from bribing foreign officials to win or continue business.

foreign licensing agreement international agreement in which one firm allows another to produce or sell its product, or use its trademark, patent, or manufacturing processes, in a specific geographical area in return for royalties or other compensation.

formal communication channel messages that flow within the chain of command defined by an organization.

franchise contractual agreement in which a franchisee gains the right to produce and/or sell the franchisor's products under that company's brand name if they agree to certain operating requirements.

franchisee individual or business firm purchasing a franchise.

franchising contractual business arrangement between a manufacturer or other supplier, and a dealer such as a restaurant operator or retailer.

franchisor firm whose products are sold to customers by the franchisee.

free-rein leadership management style of leaders who believe in minimal supervision and leave most decisions to their subordinates.

frequency marketing marketing initiative that rewards frequent purchases with cash, rebates, merchandise, or other premiums.

frictional unemployment applies to members of the workforce who are temporarily not working but are looking for jobs.

General Agreement on Tariffs and Trade (GATT) international trade accord that substantially reduced worldwide tariffs and other trade barriers.

generally accepted accounting principles (GAAP) principles that encompass the conventions, rules, and procedures for determining acceptable accounting practices at a particular time.

geographical segmentation dividing an overall market into homogeneous groups on the basis of their locations.

global business strategy offering a standardized, worldwide product and selling it in essentially the same manner throughout a firm's domestic and foreign markets.

goal target, objective, or result that someone tries to accomplish.

goal-setting theory says that people will be motivated to the extent to which they accept specific, challenging goals and receive feedback that indicates their progress toward goal achievement.

government bonds bonds issued by the U.S. Department of the Treasury.

grapevine internal information channel that transmits information from unofficial sources.

green marketing a marketing strategy that promotes environmentally safe products and production methods.

grid computing consists of a network of smaller computers running special software.

grievance formal complaint filed by an employee or a union that management is violating some provision of a union contract.

gross domestic product (GDP) sum of all goods and services produced within a country's boundaries during a specific time period, such as a year.

guerrilla marketing innovative, low-cost marketing effort designed to get consumers' attention in unusual ways.

hardware all tangible elements of a computer system.

health insurance category of insurance that pays for losses due to illness or injury.

high-context culture society in which communication depends not only on the message itself but also on nonverbal cues, past and present experiences, and personal relationships between the parties.

home-based businesses firm operated from the residence of the business owner.

horizontal merger merger that joins firms in the same industry for the purpose of diversification, increasing customer bases, cutting costs, or expanding product lines.

human resource management function of attracting, developing, and retaining employees who can perform the activities necessary to accomplish organizational objectives.

human resources production inputs consisting of anyone who works, including both the physical labor and the intellectual inputs contributed by workers.

human skills interpersonal skills that enable a manager to work effectively with and through people; the ability to communicate with, motivate, and lead employees to accomplish assigned activities.

hygiene factors factors that if present are essential to job satisfaction, although they cannot motivate an employee.

hyperinflation economic situation characterized by soaring prices.

imports foreign goods and services purchased by domestic customers.

income statement financial record of a company's revenues, expenses, and profits over a period of time.

individual brand different brand names given to each product within a line.

inflation economic situation characterized by rising prices caused by a combination of excess consumer demand and increases in the costs of raw materials, component parts, human resources, and other factors of production.

infomercial form of broadcast direct marketing; 30-minute programs that resemble regular TV programs but are devoted to selling goods or services.

informal communication channel messages outside formally authorized channels within an organization's hierarchy.

information knowledge gained from processing data.

information system organized method for collecting, storing, and communicating past, present, and projected information on internal operations and external intelligence.

infrastructure basic systems of communication, transportation, and energy facilities in a country.

initial public offering (IPO) sale of stock to the public for the first time.

insider trading use of material nonpublic information about a company to make investment profits.

institutional advertising involves messages that promote concepts, ideas, philosophies, or goodwill for industries, companies, organizations, or government entities.

insurable interest demonstration that a direct financial loss will result if some event occurs.

insurable risk requirement that a pure risk must meet for an insurer to agree to provide coverage.

insurance contract by which the insurer for a fee agrees to reimburse the insured a sum of money if a loss occurs.

integrated marketing communications (IMC) coordination of all promotional activities—media advertising, direct mail, personal selling, sales promotion, and public relations—to produce a unified customer-focused message.

integrity adhering to deeply felt ethical principles in business situations.

intensive distribution distribution strategy that involves placing a firm's products in nearly every available outlet.

International Accounting Standards Board (IASB) organization established in 1973 to promote worldwide consistency in financial reporting practices. International Financial Reporting Standards (IFRS) standards and interpretations adopted by the IASB.

international law regulations that govern international commerce.

International Monetary Fund (IMF) organization created to promote trade, eliminate barriers, and make short-term loans to member nations that are unable to meet their budgets.

International Organization for Standardization (ISO) organization whose mission is to develop and promote International Standards for business, government, and society to facilitate global trade and cooperation.

intranet computer network that is similar to the Internet but limits access to authorized users.

intrapreneurship process of promoting innovation within the structure of an existing organization.

introduction section of a business plan that describes the company, the management team, and the product in detail.

inventory control function requiring production and operations managers to balance the need to keep stock on hand to meet demand against the costs of carrying inventory.

investment-grade bond bond with a rating of BBB or above.

job enlargement job design that expands an employee's responsibilities by increasing the number and variety of tasks assigned to the worker.

job enrichment change in job duties to increase employees' authority in planning their work, deciding how it should be done, and learning new skills.

job rotation systematically moving employees from one job to another.

job sharing program management decision that allows two or more employees to divide the tasks of one job.

joint venture partnership between companies formed for a specific undertaking.

judiciary court system, or branch of government that is responsible for settling disputes by applying laws.

just-in-time (JIT) system broad management philosophy that reaches beyond the narrow activity of inventory control to influence the entire system of production and operations management.

labor union group of workers who have banded together to achieve common goals in the areas of wages, hours, and working conditions.

law standards set by government and society in the form of either legislation or custom.

law of large numbers concept that seemingly random events will follow predictable patterns if enough events are observed.

leadership ability to direct or inspire people to attain certain goals.

LEED (Leadership in Energy and Environmental Design) voluntary certification program administered by the U.S. Green Building Council, aimed at promoting the most sustainable construction processes available.

leverage increasing the rate of return on funds invested by borrowing funds.

leverage ratios measures of the extent to which a company relies on borrowed funds.

leveraged buyout (LBO) transaction in which public shareholders are bought out and the firm reverts to private status.

liability claims against assets by creditors.

liability insurance a type of insurance that protects people against financial losses to others for acts for which the insured was responsible.

life insurance a type of insurance that protects people against the financial losses that occur with premature death.

lifestyle entrepreneur person who starts a business to reduce work hours and create a more relaxed lifestyle.

lifetime value of a customer revenues and intangible benefits (referrals and customer feedback) from a customer over the life of the relationship, minus the amount the company must spend to acquire and serve that customer.

limit order order that puts a ceiling or floor on a security purchase or sale.

limited-liability corporation (LLC) company that secures the corporate advantage of limited liability while avoiding the double taxation characteristic of corporations.

line manager executive involved with the functions of production, financing, or marketing.

line organization organizational structure that establishes a direct flow of authority from the chief executive to subordinates.

line-and-staff organization structure that combines the direct flow of authority of a line organization with staff departments that support the line departments.

liquidity ratios measures of a firm's ability to meet its short-term obligations.

listening receiving a message and interpreting its intended meaning by grasping the facts and feelings it conveys.

local area networks (LANs) computer networks that connect machines within limited areas, such as a building or several nearby buildings.

lockout management decision to put pressure on union members by closing the firm.

logistics process of coordinating flow of goods, services, and information among members of the supply chain.

low-context culture society in which communication tends to rely on explicit written and verbal messages.

macroeconomics study of a nation's overall economic issues, such as how an economy maintains and allocates resources and how a government's policies affect the standards of living of its citizens.

make, buy, or lease decision choosing whether to manufacture a needed product or component in-house, purchase it from an outside supplier, or lease it.

malware any malicious software program designed to infect computer systems.

managed care plan health care plan in which most, if not all, of the insured's health care bills are paid by the insurance company; in exchange, the insured has much less say over his or her treatment.

management process of achieving organizational objectives through people and other resources.

management accountant accountant who works for a firm and provides accounting services to that firm.

management by objectives (MBO) systematic approach that allows managers to focus on attainable goals and to achieve the best results based on the organization's resources.

management development program training designed to improve the skills and broaden the knowledge of current and potential executives.

management information system (MIS) information system designed to produce reports for managers and others within the organization.

management support systems information systems that are designed to provide support for effective decision making.

manufacturer's (national) brand brand offered and promoted by a manufacturer or producer.

market order order that instructs the investor's broker to obtain the best possible price.

market penetration percentage of the market that has purchased your product.

market segmentation process of dividing a total market into several relatively homogeneous groups.

marketable securities low-risk securities with short maturities.

marketing activity, set of institutions, and processes for creating, communicating, delivering, and exchanging offerings that have value for customers, clients, partners, and society at large.

marketing concept companywide consumer orientation to promote long-run success.

marketing mix blending the four elements of marketing strategy—product, distribution, promotion, and pricing—to satisfy chosen customer segments.

marketing research collecting and evaluating information to support marketing decision making.

marketing strategy section of a business plan that presents information describing the market's need for a product and how the business will satisfy it.

marketing website website whose main purpose is to increase purchases by visitors.

Maslow's hierarchy of needs theory of motivation proposed by Abraham Maslow. According to the theory, people have five levels of needs that they seek to satisfy: physiological, safety, social, esteem, and self-actualization.

mass production system for manufacturing products in large quantities through effective combinations of employees with specialized skills, mechanization, and standardization.

materials requirement planning (MRP) computer-based production planning system that lets a firm ensure that it has all the parts and materials it needs to produce its output at the right time and place and in the right amounts.

matrix structure project management structure that links employees from different parts of the organization to work together on specific projects.

mediation dispute resolution process that uses a third party, called a mediator, to make recommendations for settling labor–management differences.

Medicare public health insurance program for those age 65 or older.

merger agreement in which two or more firms combine to form one company.

microeconomics study of small economic units, such as individual consumers, families, and businesses.

microloans small-business loans often used to buy equipment or operate a business.

middle management second tier in the management pyramid that focuses on specific operations within the organizations.

mission statement written explanation of an organization's business intentions and aims.

missionary selling indirect form of selling in which the representative promotes goodwill for a company or provides technical or operational assistance to the customer.

mixed market economies systems that draw from both types of economies, to different degrees.

monetary policy government actions to increase or decrease the money supply and change banking requirements and interest rates to influence bankers' willingness to make loans.

money market instruments short-term debt securities issued by financial institutions, companies, and governments.

monopolistic competition market structure in which large numbers of buyers and sellers exchange heterogeneous products so each participant has some control over price.

monopoly market situation in which a single seller dominates trade in a good or service for which buyers can find no close substitutes.

morale mental attitude of employees toward their employer and jobs.

motivator factors factors that can produce high levels of motivation when they are present.

multidomestic business strategy developing and marketing products to serve different needs and tastes of separate national markets.

multinational corporation (MNC) firm with significant operations and marketing activities outside its home country.

municipal bonds bonds issued by state and local governments.

mutual fund financial intermediary that pools funds from investors by selling shares of itself and uses the funds to purchase securities.

national debt money owed by government to individuals, businesses, and government agencies who purchase Treasury bills, Treasury notes, and Treasury bonds sold to cover expenditures.

natural resources all production inputs that are useful in their natural states, including agricultural land, building sites, forests, and mineral deposits.

nearshoring outsourcing production or services to locations near a firm's home base.

negotiable instrument commercial paper that is transferable among individuals and businesses.

net worth the difference between an individual or household's assets and liabilities.

newsgroup noncommercial online forum.

nonpersonal selling consists of advertising, sales promotion, direct marketing, and public relations.

nonprogrammed decision complex and unique problem or opportunity with important consequences for the organization.

nonverbal communication transmission of messages through actions and behaviors.

North American Free Trade Agreement (NAFTA) agreement among the United States, Canada, and Mexico to break down tariffs and trade restrictions.

not-for-profit corporations organizations whose goals do not include pursuing a profit.

not-for-profit organizations organizations that have primary objectives such as public service rather than returning a profit to its owners.

objectives guideposts by which managers define the organization's desired performance in such areas as new-product development, sales, customer service, growth, environmental and social responsibility, and employee satisfaction.

odd pricing pricing method using uneven amounts, which sometimes appear smaller than they really are to consumers.

offshoring relocation of business processes to lower-cost locations overseas.

oligopoly market structure in which relatively few sellers compete and high start-up costs form barriers to keep out new competitors.

on-demand computing firms essentially rent the software time from application providers and pay only for their usage of the software.

on-the-job training training method that teaches an employee to complete new tasks by performing them under the guidance of an experienced employee.

open book management practice of sharing financial information with employees and teaching them how to understand and use financial statements.

open market operations technique in which the Fed buys or sells government bonds to affect the supply of money and credit.

operational planning detailed standards that guide implementation of tactical plans.

operational support systems information systems designed to produce a variety of information on an organization's activities for both internal and external users.

order processing form of selling, mostly at the wholesale and retail levels, that involves identifying customer needs, pointing them out to customers, and completing orders.

organization structured group of people working together to achieve common goals.

organization chart visual representation of a firm's structure that illustrates job positions and functions.

organization marketing marketing strategy that influences consumers to accept the goals of, receive the services of, or contribute in some way to an organization.

organizing process of blending human and material resources through a formal structure of tasks and authority; arranging work, dividing tasks among employees, and coordinating them to ensure implementation of plans and accomplishment of objectives.

outsourcing using outside vendors to produce goods or fulfill services and functions that were previously handled in-house or in-country.

owners' equity funds contributed by owners plus profits not distributed to owners in the form of cash dividends.

ownership utility orderly transfer of goods and services from the seller to the buyer; also called possession utility.

pacing program company-initiated and financed program to develop new products.

paid time off (PTO) bank of time that employees can use for holidays, vacation, and sick days.

partnership association of two or more persons who operate a business as co-owners by voluntary legal agreement.

patent guarantee to an inventor exclusive rights to an invention for 17 years.

penetration pricing strategy that sets a low price as a major marketing tactic.

performance appraisal evaluation of and feedback on an employee's job performance.

perpetual inventory system that continuously monitors the amount and location of a company's stocks.

person marketing use of efforts designed to attract the attention, interest, and preference of a target market toward a person.

personal financial management study of the economic factors and personal decisions that affect a person's financial well-being.

personal selling the most basic form of promotion: a direct person-to-person promotional presentation to a potential buyer.

PERT (Program Evaluation and Review Technique) chart that seeks to minimize delays by coordinating all aspects of the production process.

phishing high-tech scam that uses authentic looking e-mail or pop-up ads to get unsuspecting victims to reveal personal information.

physical distribution actual movement of products from producer to consumers or business users.

picketing workers marching at a plant entrance to protest some management practice.

place marketing attempt to attract people to a particular area, such as a city, state, or nation.

place utility availability of a product in a location convenient for customers.

planned economy economic system in which government controls determine business ownership, profits, and resource allocation to accomplish government goals rather than those set by individual firms.

planning process of anticipating future events and conditions and determining courses of action for achieving organizational objectives.

podcast audio or video blog.

point-of-purchase (POP) advertising displays or demonstrations that promote products when and where consumers buy them, such as in retail stores.

pollution environmental damage caused by a company's products or operating processes.

pop-up ad Internet ad that pops-up in a new window; interested parties can click on the ad for more information.

positioning form of promotion in which marketers attempt to establish their products in the minds of customers by communicating to buyers meaningful distinctions about the attributes, price, quality, or use of a good or service.

potential sales revenue amount of revenue the business would collect if its market penetration were 100 percent.

preferred stock shares that give owners limited voting rights, and the right to receive dividends or assets before owners of common stock.

premium amount paid by the insured to the insurer to exchange for insurance coverage.

pre-roll video ad a short advertising video clip that begins automatically whenever a user visits a particular website.

prestige pricing strategies that establish relatively high prices to develop and maintain an image of quality and exclusiveness.

price exchange value of a good or service.

primary market financial market in which firms and governments issue securities and sell them initially to the general public.

private enterprise system economic system that rewards firms for their ability to identify and serve the needs and demands of customers.

private equity funds investment companies that raise funds from individuals and institutional investors and use the funds to take large stakes in a wide range of public and private companies.

private exchange secure website at which a company and its suppliers share all types of data related to e-business, from product design through order delivery.

private placements sale of securities to a small number of investors.

private property most basic freedom under the private enterprise system; the right to own, use, buy, sell, and bequeath land, buildings, machinery, equipment, patents, individual possessions, and various intangible kinds of property.

private (store) brand product that is not linked to the manufacturer, but instead carries the label of a retailer or wholesaler.

privatization conversion of government-owned and -operated companies into privately held businesses.

problem-solving team temporary or permanent combination of workers who gather to solve a specific problem.

process control systems operational support system to monitor and control physical processes.

product bundle of physical, service, and symbolic attributes designed to satisfy buyers' wants.

product advertising consists of messages designed to sell a particular good or service.

product liability the responsibility of manufacturers for injuries and damages caused by their products.

product life cycle four basic stages—introduction, growth, maturity, and decline—through which a successful product progresses.

product line group of related products marked by physical similarities or intended for the same market.

product mix the assortment of product lines and individual goods and services that a firm offers to consumers and business users.

product placement form of promotion in which marketers pay fees to have their products showcased in various media, ranging from newspapers and magazines to television and movies.

production use of resources, such as people and machinery, to convert materials into finished goods and services.

production and operations management oversee the production process by managing people and machinery in converting materials and resources into finished goods and services.

production control creates a well-defined set of procedures for coordinating people, materials, and machinery to provide maximum production efficiency.

production planning phase of production control that determines the amount of resources (including raw materials and other components) a firm needs in order to produce a certain output.

productivity relationship between the number of units produced and the number of human and other production inputs necessary to produce them.

product-related segmentation dividing consumer markets into groups based on benefits sought by buyers, usage rates, and loyalty levels.

profitability objectives common objectives included in the strategic plans of most firms.

profitability ratios measures of a company's overall financial performance by evaluating its ability to generate revenues in excess of expenses.

profits rewards earned by businesspeople who take the risks involved to offer goods and services to customers.

programmed decision simple, common, and frequently occurring problem for which a solution has already been determined.

promotion function of informing, persuading, and influencing a purchase decision.

promotional mix combination of personal and nonpersonal selling components designed to meet the needs of a firm's target customers and effectively and efficiently communicate its message to them.

property and liability insurance general category of insurance that protects against losses due to a number of perils.

psychographic segmentation dividing consumer markets into groups with similar attitudes, values, and lifestyles.

public accountant accountant who provides accounting services to other organizations.

public insurance agency public agency that provides certain types of insurance coverage.

public ownership organization owned and operated by a unit or agency of government.

public relations organization's communications and relationships with its various public audiences.

publicity nonpersonal stimulation of demand for a good, service, place, idea, event, person, or organization by unpaid placement of information in print or broadcast media.

pulling strategy promoting a product by generating consumer demand for it, primarily through advertising and sales promotion appeals.

pure competition market structure, in which large numbers of buyers and sellers exchange homogeneous products and no single participant has a significant influence on price.

pure risk type of risk where there is only the possibility of loss.

pushing strategy personal selling to market an item to wholesalers and retailers in a company's distribution channels.

quality control measuring output against established quality standards.

quality good or service that is free of deficiencies.

quota limit set on the amounts of particular products that can be imported.

ratio analysis commonly used tool for measuring the financial strength of a firm.

recession cyclical economic contraction that lasts for six months or longer.

recycling reprocessing of used materials for reuse.

regulated monopolies market situations in which local, state, or federal government grants exclusive rights in a certain market to a single firm.

relationship era business era in which firms seek ways to actively nurture customer loyalty by carefully managing every interaction.

relationship management collection of activities that build and maintain ongoing, mutually beneficial ties with customers and other parties.

relationship marketing developing and maintaining long-term, cost-effective exchange relationships with partners.

restrictive monetary policy government actions to reduce the money supply to curb rising prices, overexpansion, and concerns about overly rapid economic growth.

retailer distribution channel members that sell goods and services to individuals for their own use rather than for resale.

risk uncertainty about loss or injury.

risk-return trade-off process of maximizing the wealth of a firm's shareholders by striking the optimal balance between risk and return.

robot reprogrammable machine capable of performing numerous tasks that require manipulation of materials and tools.

routing phase of production control that determines the sequence of work throughout the facility and specifies who will perform each aspect of production at what location.

rule of indemnity requirement that the insured cannot collect more than the amount of the loss and cannot collect for the same loss more than once.

S corporation corporations that do not pay corporate taxes on profits; instead, profits are distributed to shareholders, who pay individual income taxes.

salary pay calculated on a periodic basis, such as weekly or monthly.

sales law law governing the sale of goods or services for money or on credit.

sales promotion consists of forms of promotion such as coupons, product samples, and rebates that support advertising and personal selling.

Sarbanes-Oxley Act federal legislation designed to deter and punish corporate and accounting fraud and corruption and to protect the interests of workers and shareholders through enhanced financial disclosures, criminal penalties on CEOs and CFOs who defraud investors, safeguards for whistle-blowers, and establishment of a new regulatory body for public accounting firms.

scheduling development of timetables that specify how long each operation in the production process takes and when workers should perform it.

search marketing paying search engines, such as Google, a fee to make sure that the company's listing appears toward the top of the search results.

seasonal unemployment joblessness of workers in a seasonal industry.

secondary market collection of financial markets in which previously issued securities are traded among investors.

Secure Sockets Layer (SSL) technology that secures a website by encrypting information and providing authentication.

securities financial instruments that represent obligations on the part of the issuers to provide the purchasers with expected stated returns in the funds invested or loaned.

seed capital initial funding needed to launch a new venture.

selective distribution distribution strategy in which a manufacturer selects only a limited number of retailers to distribute its product lines.

self-managed team work team that has the authority to decide how its members complete their daily tasks.

sell-off transaction in which assets are sold by one firm to another.

serial entrepreneur person who starts one business, runs it, and then starts and runs additional businesses in succession.

server the heart of a midrange computer network

set-aside program component of a government contract specifying that certain government contracts (or portions of those contracts) are restricted to small businesses and/or to women- or minority-owned companies.

sexism discrimination against members of either sex, but primarily affecting women.

sexual harassment unwelcome and inappropriate actions of a sexual nature in the workplace.

shopping product item typically purchased only after the buyer has compared competing products in competing stores.

skimming pricing strategy that sets an intentionally high price relative to the prices of competing products.

skunkworks project initiated by a company employee who conceives the idea, convinces top management of its potential, and then recruits human and other resources from within the firm to turn it into a commercial project.

small business independent business with fewer than 500 employees, not dominant in its market.

Small Business Administration (SBA) principal government agency concerned with helping small U.S. firms.

Small Business Investment Company (SBIC) business licensed by the Small Business Administration to provide loans to small businesses.

social audits formal procedures that identify and evaluate all company activities that relate to social issues such as conservation, employment practices, environmental protection, and philanthropy.

social entrepreneur person who recognizes societal problems and uses business principles to develop innovative solutions.

social responsibility business's consideration of society's well-being and consumer satisfaction, in addition to profits.

socialism economic system characterized by government ownership and operation of major industries, such as communications.

software all the programs, routines, and computer languages that control a computer and tell it how to operate.

sole proprietorship business ownership in which there is no legal distinction between the sole proprietor's status as an individual and his or her status as a business owner.

sovereign wealth funds government-owned investment companies.

spam popular name for junk e-mail.

span of management number of subordinates a manager can supervise effectively.

specialty advertising promotional items that prominently display a firm's name, logo, or business slogan.

specialty product item that a purchaser is willing to make a special effort to obtain.

speculative (junk) bond a bond with a rating below BB.

speculative risk type of risk where the possibility of gain and loss both exist.

spin-off transaction in which divested assets form a new company.

sponsorship involves providing funds for a sporting or cultural event in exchange for a direct association with the event.

spyware software that secretly gathers user information through the user's Internet connections without his or her knowledge, usually for advertising purposes.

staff manager executive who provides information, advice, or technical assistance to aid line managers; does not have the authority to give orders outside his or her own department or to compel line managers to take action.

stakeholders customers, investors, employees, and public affected by or with an interest in a company.

standard of living necessities, comforts, and luxuries one seeks to obtain or to maintain.

statement of cash flows statement showing the sources and uses of cash during a period of time.

statement of owners' equity record of the change in owners' equity from the end of one fiscal period to the end of the next.

statutory law written law, including state and federal constitutions, legislative enactments, treaties of the federal government, and ordinances of local governments.

stock market (exchanges) market in which shares of stock are bought and sold by investors.

stock options rights to buy a specified amount of company stock at a given price within a given time period.

stockholders owners of a corporation due to their purchase of stock in the corporation.

strategic alliance partnership formed to create a competitive advantage for the businesses involved; in international business, a business strategy in which a company finds a partner in the country where it wants to do business.

strategic planning process of determining the primary objectives of an organization and then acting and allocating resources to achieve those objectives.

strike temporary work stoppage by employees until a dispute is settled or a contract signed.

structural unemployment people who remain unemployed for long periods of time, often with little hope of finding new jobs like their old ones.

subcontracting international agreement that involves hiring local companies to produce, distribute, or sell goods or services in a specific country or geographical region.

subprime mortgage loan made to a borrower with a poor credit rating.

supervisory management first-line management; includes positions such as supervisor, line manager, and group leader; responsible for assigning nonmanagerial employees to specific jobs and evaluating their performance every day.

supply willingness and ability of sellers to provide goods and services.

supply chain complete sequence of suppliers that contribute to creating a good or service and delivering it to business users and final consumers.

supply curve graph that shows the relationship between different prices and the quantities that sellers will offer for sale, regardless of demand.

sustainable the capacity to endure in ecology.

SWOT analysis SWOT is an acronym for *strengths, weaknesses, opportunities*, and *threats*. By systematically evaluating all four of these factors, a firm can then develop the best strategies for gaining a competitive advantage.

synergy notion that a combined firm is worth more than the two firms are individually.

tactical planning implementing the activities specified by strategic plans.

target market group of people toward whom an organization markets its goods, services, or ideas with a strategy designed to satisfy their specific needs and preferences.

tariff tax imposed on imported goods.

tax assessment by a governmental unit.

team group of people with certain skills who are committed to a common purpose, approach, and set of performance goals.

team cohesiveness extent to which team members feel attracted to the team and motivated to remain part of it.

team diversity variances or differences in ability, experience, personality, or any other factor on a team.

team level average level of ability, experience, personality, or any other factor on a team.

team norm standard of conduct shared by team members that guides their behavior.

technical skills manager's ability to understand and use techniques, knowledge, and tools and equipment of a specific discipline or department.

technology business application of knowledge based on scientific discoveries, inventions, and innovations.

telecommuter home-based employee.

telemarketing personal selling conducted entirely by telephone, which provides a firm's marketers with a high return on their expenditures, an immediate response, and an opportunity for personalized two-way conversation.

tender offer offer made by a firm to the target firm's shareholders specifying a price and the form of payment.

term policy pure type of life insurance policy providing only a death benefit.

test marketing introduction of a new product supported by a complete marketing campaign to a selected city or TV coverage area.

Theory X assumption that employees dislike work and will try to avoid it.

Theory Y assumption that employees enjoy work and seek social, esteem, and self-actualization fulfillment.

Theory Z assumption that employee involvement is key to productivity and quality of work life.

time utility availability of a good or service when customers want to purchase it.

top management managers at the highest level of the management pyramid who devote most of their time to developing long-range plans for their organizations.

tort civil wrong inflicted on another person or the person's property.

trade credit credit extended by suppliers in which the buyer agrees to pay for goods and services received now at a later date.

trade promotion sales promotion geared to marketing intermediaries rather than to final consumers.

trademark brand a legal protection that has been given.

transaction management building and promoting products in the hope that enough customers will buy them to cover costs and earn profits.

transaction processing systems operational support system to record and process data from business transactions.

trends consumer and business tendencies or patterns that firms can exploit to gain market share in an industry.

trial courts federal and state courts of general jurisdiction.

Trojan horse program that claims to do one thing but in reality does something else, usually something malicious.

underwriting process used by an insurance company to determine who, or what, to insure and how much to charge.

unemployment rate percentage of the total workforce actively seeking work but are currently unemployed.

Uniform Commercial Code The basis of U.S. business law; referred to as UCC.

utility power of a good or service to satisfy a want or need.

vendor-managed inventory process in which the producer and the retailer agree that the producer (or the wholesaler) will determine how much of a product a buyer needs and automatically ship new supplies when needed.

venture capital money invested in a business by another business firm or group of individuals in exchange for an ownership share.

venture capitalists business firms or groups of individuals that invest in new and growing firms in exchange for an ownership share.

vertical merger merger that combines firms operating at different levels in the production and marketing process.

virtual private networks (VPNs) secure connections between two points on the Internet.

virtual team group of geographically or organizationally dispersed coworkers who use a combination of telecommunications and information technologies to accomplish an organizational task.

viruses programs that secretly attach themselves to other programs (called *hosts*) and change them or destroy data.

vishing variation on phishing that involves a voice system in which the intended victim receives a voice message directing him or her to reveal personal financial information.

VoIP alternative to traditional telecommunication services provided by companies such as Verizon and Sprint.

volume objectives objects based on pricing decisions on market share, the percentage of a market controlled by a certain company or product.

wage pay based on an hourly rate or the amount of work accomplished.

web-to-store use of the web to aid shoppers at brick-and-mortar retailers.

wheel of retailing theory of retailing in which new retailers gain a competitive foothold by offering low prices and limited services and then add

services and raise prices, creating opportunities for new low-price competitors.

whistle-blowing employee's disclosure to company officials, government authorities, or the media of illegal, immoral, or unethical practices committed by an organization.

wholesaler distribution channel member that sells primarily to retailers, other wholesalers, or business users.

wide area networks (WANs) tie larger geographical regions together by using telephone lines and microwave and satellite transmission.

Wi-Fi wireless network that connects various devices and allows them to communicate with one another through radio waves.

wiki web page that can be edited by users.

work team relatively permanent group of employees with complementary skills who perform the day-to-day work of organizations.

World Bank organization established by industrialized nations to lend money to less-developed countries.

World Trade Organization (WTO) 159-member international institution that monitors GATT agreements and mediates international trade disputes.

worm small piece of software that exploits a security hole in a network to replicate itself.

| Notes |

Chapter 1

1. Sara Murphy, "Leading Fracking Companies Secure Their Futures," *The Motley Fool*, accessed January 27, 2014, www.fool.com; Wendy Koch, "Big Milestone: US Producing More Oil Than It Imports," *USA Today*, accessed January 10, 2014, www.usatoday.com; Bryant Urstadt, "Here's the Good News about Fracking," *Bloomberg Businessweek*, accessed January 10, 2014, www.businessweek.com; Anthony Watts, "USA Meets Kyoto Protocol Goal—Without Ever Embracing It," *Watts Up with That*, accessed January 10, 2014, http://wattsupwiththat.com; organization website, "Kyoto Protocol," www.kyotoprotocol.com, accessed January 10, 2014.

2. Mark Hrywna, "Nonprofits Down, Filing with IRS Up," *Nonprofit Times*, accessed January 12, 2014, www.thenonprofittimes.com.

3. "Quick Facts About Nonprofits," National Center for Charitable Statistics, http://nccs.urban.org/statistics, accessed January 10, 2014.

4. Organization website, "Quick Facts about St. Jude," http://www.stjude.org, accessed January 10, 2014.

5. Organization website, "Red Cross and Hurricane Sandy NJ Relief Fund Give $15.2 Million," www.redcross.org, accessed January 10, 2014.

6. Issie Lapowsky, "The Social Entrepreneurship Spectrum: Nonprofits," *Inc.*, accessed January 10, 2014, www.inc.com.

7. Company website, "Company Profile," www.netflix.com, accessed January 10, 2014.

8. Company website, "Humanitarian Relief," www.ups.com, accessed January 10, 2014.

9. Company website, "History of Mars," www.mars.com, accessed January 10, 2014; David A. Kaplan, "Mars Incorporated: A Pretty Sweet Place to Work," *Fortune*, accessed January 10, 2014, http://management.fortune.cnn.com.

10. Company website, "About inDinero," www.indinero.com, accessed January 9, 2014.

11. Joshua Brustein, "With CES Antics, Mobile Carriers Make an Eloquent Antitrust Case," *Bloomberg Businessweek*, January 8, 2014, www.businessweek.com.

12. Government website, "Small Business Administration: FAQs," www.sba.gov, accessed January 10, 2014; U.S. Census Bureau, "Statistics about Business Size, Employment Size of Firms, Table 2a," www.census.gov, accessed January 12, 2014.

13. Company website, http://stockboxgrocers, accessed January 10, 2014; "StockBox Grocers," *Echoing Green*, accessed January 10, 2014, www.echoinggreen.org.

14. "eBay President Dials Profits with Mobile Devices," *The Wall Street Journal*, accessed January 10, 2014, http://blogs.wsj.com.

15. Company website, "History," www.steinway.com, accessed January 10, 2014.

16. "Best Global Brands: 2013," *Interbrand*, accessed January 10, 2014, www.interbrand.com.

17. Andreas Kaplan and Michael Haenlein, "Users of the World, Unite! The Challenges and Opportunities of Social Media," *Business Horizons* 53:59-68, 2010.

18. Jennifer Van Grove, "Why Facebook Is Giving Out Free Wi-Fi for Check In," *CNET*, accessed January 10, 2014, http://news.cnet.com.

19. Karen Aho, "2012 Customer Service Hall of Fame," *Money*, accessed January 10, 2014, http://money.msn.com; company website, "Working in the Amazon Fulfillment Network," www.amazon.com, accessed January 10, 2014.

20. "King & King Architects LLP Receives High-Performance Energy Efficiency Award from NYSERDA," press release, www.nyserda.ny.gov, accessed January 9, 2014.

21. Company website, http://greensulate.com, accessed January 10, 2014.

22. Company website, www.solarcity.com, accessed January 10, 2014.

23. "Census: More Diversity, Slower Growth in U.S.A. 2050," press release, *IM Diversity*, accessed January 10, 2014, www.imdiversity.com.

24. Organization website, "Top 50 Companies for Diversity," http://diversityinc.com, accessed January 10, 2014.

25. "2013 Top 100 Outsourcing Destinations," *Tholon.com*, accessed January 10, 2014.

26. Julie Bort, "Mark Benioff: I'm Trying to Fill Steve Jobs Shoes as a Visionary," *Business Insider*, accessed January 10, 2014, www.businessinsider.com; "Mark Benioff," Crunchbase Profile, *Tech Crunch*, accessed January 10, 2014, http://techcrunch.com.

27. "General Motors—How the Brand Turned Around Its Fortunes to Post Record Profits So Quickly," *Medium.com*, accessed January 10, 2014, http://www.medium.com; Associated Press, "Mary Barra, a Child of GM, Prepares to Lead It," *CBS News*, accessed January 10, 2014, www.cbsnews.com; "Mary Barra to Replace Dan Akerson as CEO of GM," *Crains Detroit Business*, accessed January 10, 2014, www.crainsdetroit.com.

28. "World's Most Admired Companies 2014," *Fortune*, accessed April 11, 2014, http://money.cnn.com.

Chapter 2

1. Company website, "What We Do," http://paneracares.org, accessed January 20, 2014; Stephanie Steinberg, "Around the Water Cooler with Panera's CEO," *U.S. News*, accessed January 20, 2014, http://money.usnews.com; Amy Sullivan, "The Panera Model: How to Do Good and Make Money at the Same Time," *The National Journal*, accessed January 20, 2014, www.nationaljournal.com; Stuart Elliott, "Selling Products by Selling Shared Values," *The New York Times*, accessed January 20, 2014, www.nytimes.com; Venessa Wong, "Panera Doesn't Offer a Free Lunch—It Offers Caring," *Bloomberg Businessweek*, accessed January 20, 2014, www.businessweek.com; Larry Bingham, "Panera Cares Pay-What-You-Can Café Learns About Entitlement, Feeding Hungry," *The Oregonian*, accessed January 20, 2014, www.oregonlive.com.

2. Jacquelyn Smith, "The Companies with the Best CSR Reputations," *Forbes*, accessed January 17, 2014, www.forbes.com.

3. Company website, "L'Oreal Announces Its New Sustainability Commitment for 2020 'Sharing Beauty with All,'" http://www.loreal.com/, accessed January 17, 2014.

4. "Fortune Best Companies to Work for 2013," *Fortune*, accessed January 17, 2014, http://money.cnn.com; company website, "Our Credo Values," http://www.jnj.com, accessed January 17, 2014; Matthew Perrone, "J&J Recalls Motrin Due to Plastic Specks," *Associated Press*, accessed January 17, 2014, http://bigstory.ap.org.

5. Company website, "The Coca-Cola Company Releases 2012–2013 Global Sustainability Report," www.coca-colacompany.com, accessed January 17, 2014.

6. Samuel Rubenfeld, "Survey Sees Less Misconduct But More Reporting and Retaliation," *The Wall Street Journal*, accessed January 17, 2014, http://blogs.wsj.com; "2011 Breach List," *Identity Theft Resource Center*, accessed January 17, 2014, http://www.idtheftcenter.org.

7. Daniel Franklin, "Just Good Business," *The Economist*, accessed January 17, 2014, http://www.economist.com.

8. Rubenfeld, "Survey Sees Less Misconduct But More Reporting and Retaliation"; "2011 Breach List," *Identity Theft Resource Center*.

9. Chris Isidore, "Target: Hacking Hit Up to 110 Million Customers," *CNNMoney*, accessed January 17, 2014, http://money.cnn.com; Robin Sidel, Danny Yadron, and Sarah Germano, "Target Hit by Credit Card Breach," *The Wall Street Journal*, accessed January 15, 2014, http://online.wsj.com.

10. Company website, "Garment Collecting," http://about.hm.com, accessed January 15, 2014; Oliver Balch, "H&M: Can Fast Fashion and Sustainability Ever Really Mix?" *The Guardian*, accessed January 15, 2014, www.theguardian.com.

11. Government website, "Executive Order—Prohibiting Certain Imports of Burmese Jadeite and Rubies," http://www.whitehouse.gov, accessed January 15, 2014; "Burmese Ruby, Jade Ban Extended," *JCK Magazine*, accessed January 15, 2014, http://www.jckonline.com, Sophie Song, "Myanmar Gems Emporium Earned Record $2.4 Billion, US-Maintained Ban on Imports of Gems May Not Be Effective," *International Business Times*, accessed January 15, 2014, www.ibtimes.com.

12. Lindsay Olson, "The Top 10 Lies People Put on Their Resumes," *US News and World Report*, accessed January 17, 2014, http://money.usnews.com; Marielle Segarra, "How to Avoid Résumé Fraud," *CFO.com*, accessed January 17, 2014, ww2.cfo.com.

13. "Internet Abuse at Work," *Memory Spy*, accessed January 17, 2014, http://memoryspy.com.

14. "Virgin America Is Investigated by FAA & OSHA for 'Cooking Maintenance Log Books,'" *PR Log*, accessed January 13, 2014, http://www.prlog.org.

15. Company website, "Code of Business Conduct and Ethics," http://investors.linkedin.com, accessed January 15, 2014.

16. Company website, http://www.lockheedmartin.com, accessed January 13, 2014.

17. Company website, http://www.saiglobal.com, accessed January 15, 2014.

18. Natalie Peace, "How Kindness and Generosity Made by Businesses More Profitable," *Forbes*, accessed January 15, 2014, www.forbes.com.

19. Company website, "Cisco Corporate Social Responsibility Report," www.cisco.com, accessed January 15, 2014.

20. Organization website, "Forget Bake Sales: Schools Turn to Luxe Auctions," www.npr.org, accessed January 15, 2014; organization website, "Our Story," www.biddingforgood.com, accessed January 15, 2014.

21. Rachel Abrams, "American Express Ordered to Pay $75 Million over Credit Card Practices," *The New York Times*, accessed January 15, 2014, http://dealbook.nytimes.com.

22. "Many U.S. Kids Still Exposed to Smoke in Cars: Study," *Reuters*, accessed January 15, 2014, www.reuters.com.

23. Company website, "Childhood Obesity Facts," Center for Disease Control and Prevention, www.cdc.gov, accessed January 15, 2014; company website, www.subway.com, accessed January 15, 2014; organization website, Jared Foundation, www.jaredfoundation.org, accessed January 15, 2014.

24. Ray Sanchez, "Alex Rodriguez Drops Lawsuit, Accepts 162-Game Suspension," *CNN*, accessed May 17, 2014, www.cnn.com; Bob Nightengale, "Alex Rodriguez Suspended for 2014 Season," *USA Today*, accessed January 17, 2014, www.usatoday.com.

25. Akhila Vijayaraghavan, "Kaiser Permanente Greens Its Supply Chain by Switching to Safer IV Equipment," *Triple Pundit*, accessed January 15, 2014, www.triplepundit.com; Simon Pitman, "P&G Declares Its Suppliers Sustainability Supplier Assessment Program a Success," *Cosmetics Design*, accessed January 15, 2014, www.cosmeticsdesign.com.

26. Company website, "Tesla Motors, Inc.—Second Quarter 2013 Shareholder Letter," www.tesla.com, accessed January 15, 2014; Jonathan Welsh, "Tesla Model S Might Be the Easiest Car to Drive," *The Wall Street Journal*, accessed January 15, 2014, http://blogs.wsj.com.

27. Dana Capiello and Matthew Daly, "Spill Report Rekindles Democratic Push for Reform," *Associated Press*, accessed January 15 2014, http://news.yahoo.com; "Gulf Oil Spill Findings: Prison Time Unlikely," *CBS News*, accessed January 15, 2014, www.cbsnews.com.

28. Company website, "The Scrap Recycling Industry: Electronics," www.isri.org, accessed January 15, 2014.

29. Company website, "Walmart Launches Smartphone Trade-In Program in the U.S.," www.walmart.com, accessed January 15, 2014.

30. Randall Smith, "Despite Setbacks, Investor Is Bullish on Clean Technology," *The New York Times*, accessed January 19, 2014, http://dealbook.nytimes.com.

31. Company website, "Dove Brand Chocolate Is First Mainstream U.S. Chocolate Brand to Bear Rainforest Alliance™ Certified Seal," press release, www.mars.com, accessed January 19, 2014.

32. U.S. Bureau of Labor Statistics, "Table 5. Quartiles and Selected Deciles of Usual Weekly Earnings of Full-Time Wage and Salary Workers by Selected Characteristics, Third Quarter 2013 Averages, Not Seasonally Adjusted," www.bls.gov, accessed January 19, 2014.

33. Jason Del Rey, "Amazon Boosts Financial Support for Employee Education Program," *All Things Digital*, accessed January 19, 2014, http://allthingsdigital; Tricia Duryee, "Amazon's Homepage Splashes Big News (for a Small Audience)," *All Things Digital*, accessed January 19, 2014, http://allthingsdigital.com.

34. Organization website, "The DiversityInc Top 10 Companies for Supplier Diversity," *DiversityInc*, www.diversityinc.com, accessed January 19, 2014.

35. Organization website, "General Mills and Yoplait USA," http://ww5komen.org, accessed January 19, 2014.

36. Organization website, "Philanthropy's Response to Super Typhoon Haiyan in the Philippines," Grantmakers in Health, www.gih.org, accessed January 19, 2014.

37. Company website, "P&G Voluntarily Recalls Limited Quantity of Dry Pet Food Due to Possible Health Risk," press release, http://news.pg.com, accessed January 19, 2014.

38. Michael Sauter, "America's Most Misleading Product Claims," *24/7 Wall Street*, accessed January 19, 2014, http://247wallst.com; "Changes to

General Mills Packaging in 2014," *Grocery Store Rules,* accessed January 19, 2014, http://grocerystorerules.wordpress.com.

39. Company website, "Rules and Policies," http://pages.ebay.com, accessed January 13, 2014.

40. "Thousands of Teen Worker Injuries Each Year, Including Youth Job Deaths," *PRWeb.com,* accessed January 19, 2014, www.prweb.com; government website, "Young Workers," www.osha.gov, accessed January 19, 2014; organization website, "Youth Rules!" http://youthrules.dol.gov, accessed January 19, 2014.

41. "2013 Working Mother 100 Best Companies," *Working Mother Magazine,* accessed January 20, 2014, www.workingmother.com.

42. Shelley DuBois, "Flexible Vacation Policies Are Here to Stay," *CNNMoney,* accessed January 20, 2014, http://money.cnn.com.

43. "LGBT Equality at the Fortune 500," *Human Rights Campaign,* accessed January 20, 2014, https://www.hrc.org.

44. Government website, www.eeoc.gov, accessed January 20, 2014; Russell Cawyer, "Bill to Add Lilly Ledbetter Act Provisions to Texas Labor Code Enrolled," *Texas Employment Law Update,* accessed January 20, 2014, www.texasemploymentlawupdate.com.

45. "Recent Case Law Threatens Older Workers' Rights Against Age Discrimination," accessed January 20, 2014, www.wrongfultermination-laws.com; Warren Richey, "Supreme Court Sets High Bar for Age-Bias Suits," *Christian Science Monitor,* accessed January 20, 2014, www.csmonitor.com.

46. "Conference Board Job Satisfaction Survey Finds Older Workers as Dissatisfied as Others," *Aging Workforce News,* accessed January 20, 2014, www.agingworkforcenews.com.

47. "Civilian Noninstitutional Population, by Age, Gender, Race, and Ethnicity, 1990, 2000, 2010, and Projected 2020," *Monthly Labor Review,* accessed January 20, 2014, www.bls.gov.

48. Government website, "Sexual Harassment Charges, FY 2010–2012," www.eeoc.gov, accessed January 20, 2014.

49. David Dayen, "Lilly Ledbetter Did Not Alter Pay Equity Gap Whatsoever," http://news.firedoglake.com, accessed January 20, 2014; Russell Cawyer, "Bill to Add Lilly Ledbetter Act Provisions to Texas Labor Code Enrolled," *Texas Employment Law Update,* accessed January 20, 2014, www.texasemploymentlawupdate.com.

50. Susan Adams, "Are Women Catching Up in Pay?" *Forbes,* accessed January 20, 2014, www.forbes.com.

Chapter 3

1. Christopher Mims, "Advice to Microsoft's Satya Nadella: Be More Brave," *The Wall Street Journal,* accessed June 9, 2014, http://online.wsj.com; Dina Bass, "Microsoft, Salesforce Unveil Cloud-Computing Partnership," *Bloomberg News,* accessed June 9, 2014, www.bloomberg.com; Jay Yarow, "In a Six-Day Period, Microsoft's New CEO Satya Nadella Completely Changed the Company," *Business Insider,* accessed June 9, 2014, www.businessinsider.com; Julie Bort, "How Satya Nadella Has Completely Changed Microsoft in Just 3 Months," *Business Insider,* accessed June 9, 2014, www.businessinsider.com; Bill Rigby, "New Microsoft CEO Faces Challenges in Mobile, Investor Relations," *Reuters,* accessed June 9, 2014, www.reuters.com; Dina Bass, "Microsoft's Nadella Named CEO to Transform PC Pioneer," *Bloomberg News,* accessed June 9, 2014, www.bloomberg.com.

2. Jonathan Maze, "The Recession Really Hurt Dinner Visits," *Restaurant Finance Monitor,* accessed January 18, 2014, www.restfinance.com.

3. Mike Isaac, "With Private Messaging, Instagram and Twitter Continue Their Arms Race," *All Things Digital,* accessed January 18, 2014, http://allthingsd.com.

4. Alex Lawler, "OPEC Outages Cut Its Oil Output to Below 2014 Demand," *Reuters,* accessed January 18, 2014, http://uk.reuters.com.

5. Mike Patton, "The U.S. Housing Market: Home Improvement Is Real," *Forbes,* accessed January 14, 2014, www.forbes.com.

6. Anna Prior, "Retailers Have Blue Christmas, But Costco Stands Out," *The Wall Street Journal,* January 18, 2014, http://online.wsj.com.

7. Logan Layden, "Improving Drought Conditions Come Too Late for Oklahoma's 2013 Pecan Crop," *State Impact,* accessed January 14, 2014, www.stateimpact.npr.org.

8. Dina Fine Maron, "FDA Moves to Avert Drug Shortages," *Scientific American,* accessed January 18, 2014, www.scientificamerican.com; Thomas M. Burton, "FDA Sets Rules to Better Address Drug Shortages," *The Wall Street Journal,* accessed January 18, 2014, http://online.wsj.com.

9. Charles Abbott, "Ethanol Cut May Cut Down U.S. Corn Prices, Drive Up Subsidies," *Reuters,* accessed January 18, 2014, www.reuters.com.

10. Rick Munarriz, "5 Things You Don't Know about Chipotle," *Daily Finance,* accessed January 18, 2014, www.dailyfinance.com.

11. Larissa MacFarquhar, "When Giants Fail," *The New Yorker,* accessed January 18, 2014, www.newyorker.com.

12. Tom Gara, "Beginning of the End for Last Century's Phone System," *The Wall Street Journal,* accessed January 18, 2014, http://blogs.wsj.com.

13. Company website, "Sallie Mae History," https://www.salliemae.com, accessed January 18, 2014.

14. Christopher Matthews, "Will Dollar Stores Rule the Retail World?" *Time,* accessed January 18, 2014, http://business.time.com.

15. Central Intelligence Agency, *World Factbook,* accessed January 18, 2014, www.cia.gov.

16. "Beyond GDP: Get Ready for a New Way to Measure the Economy," *Forbes,* accessed January 18, 2014, www.forbes.com.

17. Paul Toscano, "The Worst Hyperinflation Situations of All Time," *CNBC,* accessed January 18, 2014, www.cnbc.com.

18. Robert Frank, "Millionaire Population Grows by 200,000," *The Wall Street Journal,* accessed January 18, 2014, http://blogs.wsj.com.

19. U.S. Bureau of Labor Statistics, *Occupational Outlook Handbook* 2012–2013 Edition, accessed January 18, 2014, http://bls.gov.

20. Organization website, "World Bank Group Increases Package to Nearly $1 Billion in Recovery and Reconstruction Support to the Philippines," www.worldbank.org, accessed January 18, 2014.

21. Organization website, "U.S. National Debt Clock," http://www.brillig.com, accessed January 18, 2014.

22. Organization website, "World Economic Forum 2013 Global Risks Report," http://www3.weforum.org, accessed January 18, 2014.

23. Ibid.

24. U.S. Census Bureau, "U.S. and World Population Clocks," www.census.gov, accessed January 18, 2014.

25. U.S. Consumer Product Safety Commission, "CPSC Regional Product Safety Office, Beijing," accessed January 18, 2014, http://cpsc.gov; Jonathan Carr, "CPSC Opens Office in China," Weil, Gotshal & Manges LLP, accessed January 18, 2014, http://product-liability.weil.com.

26. "Asian Soft Drinks Consumption Continues to Drive Future Closure Demand," *Market Publishers,* accessed January 18, 2014, http://marketpublishers.com.

Chapter 4

1. John Goreman, "As EV Sales Hit the Wall Toyota's Green Hybrids Dominate the Global Market," *Torque News*, accessed January 31, 2014, www.torquenews.com; Alex Taylor III, "Toyota Just Keeps Roaring Back," *CNNMoney*, accessed January 31, 2014, http://money.cnn.com; Chester Dawson, "Toyota Again World's Largest Auto Maker," *The Wall Street Journal*, accessed January 31, 2014, http://online.wsj.com.

2. Government website, "United States," *World Factbook*, www.cia.gov, accessed January 6, 2014.

3. Company website, "Our Locations," http://corporate.walmart.com, accessed January 7, 2014; Kamelia Angelova, "Why Six of the 20 English Elite Soccer Clubs Are Now Owned by Americans," *Business Insider*, accessed January 7, 2014, www.businessinsider.com.

4. Joe Ryan "Companies Look Abroad to Boost Sales," *Newsday*, accessed January 6, 2014, www.newsday.com.

5. U.S. Census Bureau, "International Data Base," accessed January 6, 2014, www.census.gov; "You Think! But Do You Know?" *World Bank*, accessed January 6, 2014, http://youthink.worldbank.org.

6. Organization website, http://data.worldbank.org, accessed January 6, 2014.

7. Company website, "International," http://corporate.walmart.com, accessed January 6, 2014.

8. U.S. Census, "Top Ten Countries with Which the U.S. Trades for the Month of November 2013," accessed January 6, 2014, www.census.gov; U.S. Census, "State Exports for Texas," accessed January 6, 2014, www.census.gov; U.S. Census, "State Exports for California," accessed January 6, 2014, www.census.gov; U.S. Census, "Table 852. Selected Farm Products—U.S. and World Production and Exports: 2000 to 2010," accessed January 6, 2014, www.census.gov.

9. Sammy Said, "The Top 10 Most Expensive Foods in the World," Richest.com, accessed January 6, 2014, www.therichest.com.

10. Peter Loftus and Jonathan D. Rockoff, "Merck Plans Radical Overhaul of Drug R&D Unit," *The Wall Street Journal*, accessed January 6, 2014, http://online.wsj.com.

11. U.S. Census Bureau, "Annual Trade in Goods and Services, 1960–2012," accessed January 30, 2014, www.census.gov; U.S. Bureau of Economic Analysis, "U.S. International Trade in Goods and Services," press release, accessed January 30, 2014, www.bea.gov.

12. Company website, "About the Resort," http://en.shanghaidisneyresort.com.cn, accessed January 6, 2014.

13. Organization website, "Triennial Central Bank Survey of Foreign Exchange Turnover in April 2013," www.bis.org, accessed, January 6, 2014.

14. Nat Rudarakanchana, "McDonald's Going Mobile, Expanding in China and Three Other Takeaways from Last Scheduled Consumer Presentation of Uninspiring 2013," *International Business Times*, accessed January 6, 2014, www.ibtimes.com.

15. "Chinese Taboo," *About.com*, accessed January 6, 2014, http://chineseculture.about.com.

16. Sophia Yan, "Thailand Political Unrest Unleashes Market Turmoil," *CNNMoney*, accessed January 6, 2014, http://money.cnn.com.

17. Eric Blattberg, "Chinese Jails World of Warcraft Cybercrime Ring," *Venture Beat*, accessed January 6, 2014, http://venturebeat.com.

18. Joe Ayling, "'Made in Italy' Thrives Without EU Label Law," *Just Style*, accessed January 6, 2014, www.just-style.com.

19. Ida Torres, "Japan Eyeing Removal of Wine Tariffs to Increase Sake Exports," *Japan Daily Press*, accessed January 8, 2014, http://japandailypress.com.

20. Leslie Josephs, "U.S. Unlikely to Raise Sugar-Import Quota," *The Wall Street Journal*, accessed January 6, 2014, http://online.wsj.com.

21. Agustino Fontevecchia, "Tariffs on Chinese Solar Panels Are Killing American Jobs," *Forbes*, accessed January 6, 2014, www.forbes.com.

22. Mahesh Kulkarni, "WTO Aims to Conclude Doha Round of Talks by End of 2014," *Business Standard*, January 28, 2014, www.business-standard.com.

23. Government website, "North America," *World Factbook*, accessed February 8, 2014, www.cia.gov; Office of the United States Trade Representative, "North American Free Trade Agreement," accessed January 6, 2014, www.ustr.gov.

24. Ibid.

25. Ibid.

26. U.S. Census Bureau, "2013: Trade in Good with CAFTA-DR," accessed January 6, 2014, www.census.gov.

27. Organization website, "Countries," http://europa.eu, accessed January 6, 2014; government website, *World Factbook*, www.cia.gov, accessed January 6, 2014.

28. Company website, www.dlush.com, accessed January 6, 2014.

29. Company website, www.zazzle.com, accessed January 6, 2014.

30. Company website, "Domino's Pizza Bahamas, www.amlfoods.com, accessed January 6, 2014.

31. Company website, www.morinagamilk.co.jp, accessed January 6, 2014.

32. Matt Phillips, "China's Labor Costs Are Now as High as Mexico's," *Quartz*, accessed January 6, 2014, http://qz.com; "2013 Top 100 Outsourcing Destinations Rankings," *Tholons*, accessed January 6, 2014, www.tholons.com.

33. Shayndi Race and Spencer E. Ante, "Insta-Rich: $1 Billion for Instagram," *The Wall Street Journal*, accessed January 6, 2014, http://online.wsj.com.

34. Chris Tutor, "BMW, Toyota Outline New Tech Joint Venture, New Sports Car," *Auto Blog*, accessed January 6, 2014, www.autoblog.com.

35. Company website, "Alcoa Best in Class in Covalence Ethical Reputation Ranking," press release, www.alcoa.com, accessed January 6, 2014.

End of Part 1: Launching Your Global Business and Economics Career

1. C. Brett Lockard and Michael Wolf, "Occupational Employment Projections to 2020," *Monthly Labor Review Online*, accessed January 15, 2014, www.bls.gov.

2. U.S. Bureau of Labor Statistics, "Economists," *Occupational Outlook Handbook, 2014–2015*, accessed February 1, 2014, www.bls.gov.

3. "Character Traits of an Excellent Expat," *Defining Moves*, accessed February 1, 2014, http://definingmoves.com.

Chapter 5

1. Company website, "Franchise Information," www.anytimefitness.com, accessed February 13, 2014; Jason Daley, "Meet the Top Franchise of 2014," *Entrepreneur*, accessed February 11, 2014, www.entrepreneur.com; Kevin Harrington, "The Biggest Trends in Franchising," *Forbes*, accessed February 11, 2014, www.forbes.com; David Tao, "The Netflix of Gyms?

Why Anytime Fitness Thinks the Future of Gyms Is Online," *Forbes*, accessed February 10, 2014, www.forbes.com; Brandon Southward, "Meet the World's Fastest-Growing Fitness Chain," *CNNMoney*, accessed February 10, 2014, http://management.fortune.cnn.com.

2. U.S. Small Business Administration, "Advocacy Small Business Statistics and Research," http://web.sba.gov/faqs, accessed January 11, 2014.

3. Ibid.

4. U.S. Small Business Administration, "Guide to SBA's Definitions of Small Business," http://archive.sba.gov; "Table of Small Business Size Standards Matched to North American Industry Classification System Codes," http://www.sba.gov, accessed January 11, 2014.

5. Keith Liles, "From Jobless to Impact 100 Entrepreneur in 20 Months—Interview with Kitchen Cabinet Kings Founder Anthony Saladino," *Killer Start Ups*, accessed January 14, 2014, www.killerstartups.com; Jun Loayza, "Drop-Shipping Interview: Anthony Saladino from Kitchen Cabinet Kings," *Ecommerce Rules*, accessed January 14, 2014, http://ecommercerules.com.

6. Cristina Rouvalis, "ModCloth's Customers Are Always Right," *United Hemispheres* magazine, May 2014; company website, www.modcloth.com, accessed January 11, 2014.

7. U.S. Department of Agriculture, *Agricultural Fact Book*, pp. 12–23, http://www.usda.gov/factbook, accessed January 11, 2014; "Fast Facts about Agriculture," *The Voice of Agriculture Website*, accessed January 11, 2014, www.fb.org.

8. Company website, www.ciderhill.com, accessed January 11, 2014.

9. Anita Campbell, "69 Percent of U.S. Entrepreneurs Start Their Businesses Start at Home," accessed January 11, 2014, http://smallbiztrends.com; Bureau of Labor Statistics "Home-Based Businesses," www.bls.gov, accessed January 11, 2014.

10. Company website, www.ebeanstalk.com, accessed January 11, 2014; "Toy Testers to the Rescue," *ABC News*, accessed January 14, 2014, www.abcnews.com.

11. Ned Smith, "Small Business Exports Receive Boon from Jobs Act," *Business News Daily*, accessed January 12, 2014, www.businessnewsdaily.com.

12. Rhea Gaur, "Small Businesses Readying Themselves to Compete in Global Markets," *Small Biz Technology*, accessed January 12, 2014, www.smallbiztechnology.com.

13. U.S. Small Business Administration, "Frequently Asked Questions," http://archive.sba.gov/advo/stats/sbfaq.pdf, accessed January 11, 2014.

14. U.S. Small Business Administration, "SBA Lending Activity in FY 2013 Shows SBA Continuing to Help Small Businesses Grow and Create Jobs," press release, www.sba.gov, accessed January 12, 2014.

15. "10 Fortune 500 Companies That Started with Next to Nothing," *Business Pundit*, accessed January 11, 2014, www.businesspundit.com.

16. Rhiannon Lucy Cosslett, "Makeup, Manicures, and Manscaping: How Male Grooming Products Went Mainstream," *The Guardian*, accessed January 11, 2014, www.guardian.com.

17. Nina Boccia, "Generation Green," AzureMagazine.com, accessed May 22, 2014, www.azmagazine.com; Katie Fehrenbacher, "ClearEdge Power Lands World's Largest Utility Fuel Cell Deal," *GigaOM*, accessed January 11, 2014, http://gigaom.com.

18. U.S. Small Business Administration, "Frequently Asked Questions"; "BOC Network Facts," http://www.bocnet.org, accessed January 11, 2014.

19. U.S. Small Business Administration, "Frequently Asked Questions."

20. Jeff Macke, "2013: The Year of the Doughnut, and Krispy Kreme Is Leading the Way," accessed January 11, 2014, http://finance.yahoo.com; John Kell, "Krispy Creme Reports Higher Profits," *The Wall Street Journal*, accessed January 11, 2014, http://online.wsj.com.

21. Patricia Schaefer, "The Seven Pitfalls of Business Failure and How to Avoid Them," *Business Know-How*, accessed January 14, 2014, www.businessknowhow.com.

22. Ibid.

23. U.S. Small Business Administration, "Advocacy Small Business Statistics and Research," http://web.sba.gov/faqs, accessed January 11, 2014.

24. Company website, www.tnmoonshinecakes.com, accessed January 14, 2014; "Local Love: Chattanooga Moonshine Cakes," *News Channel 9*, accessed January 14, 2014, www.newschannel9.com.

25. W. Mark Crain, "The Impact of Regulatory Costs on Small Firms," Office of Advocacy, U.S. Small Business Administration, accessed January 11, 2014, http://archive.sba.gov/advo/research/rs264tot.pdf.

26. U.S. Department of Labor, "elaws: Family and Medical Leave Act Advisor," www.dol.gov, accessed January 17, 2014; "The Affordable Care Act Increases Choice and Saving Money for Small Businesses," *The White House*, accessed January 14, 2014, www.whitehouse.gov.

27. Government website, "Business Tax Credits," www.irs.gov, accessed January 11, 2014; "HUBZone Programs," www.sba.gov, accessed January 11, 2014.

28. Company website, www.warbyparker.com, accessed January 11, 2014.

29. "Top 10 Tips for Writing Your Business Plan," *AllBusiness*, www.allbusiness.com, accessed January 11, 2014.

30. U.S. Small Business Administration, "What We Do," and "Mission Statement," www.sba.gov, accessed January 11, 2014.

31. U.S. Small Business Administration, "Loans and Grants," and "SBA Loan Programs," www.sba.gov, accessed January 11, 2014.

32. U.S. Small Business Administration, "Microloan Program," www.sba.gov, accessed January 11, 2014.

33. U.S. Small Business Administration, "Local Resources," www.sba.gov, accessed January 11, 2014.

34. Thurston County Economic Development Council, "Mission," www.thurstonedc.com, accessed January 11, 2014.

35. National Business Incubator Association, www.nbia.org, accessed January 14, 2014; "Rice Tops Worldwide List of Business Incubators," *Texas Medical Center News*, accessed January 13, 2014, www.tmcnews.org.

36. National Venture Capital Association, www.nvca.org, accessed January 11, 2014; Natalie Jarvey, "Report: Venture Capital on Road to Recovery," *Los Angeles Business Journal*, accessed January 11, 2014, http://labusinessjournal.com; Josh Lipkin and Mark Berniker, "Venture Capitalist's Best Investments for 2013," *CNBC*, accessed January 11, 2014, www.cnbc.com.

37. National Association of Women Business Owners, "Women-Owned Key Business Facts," accessed January 11, 2014, www.nawboindy.org; "Women Owned Businesses in the United States in 2013, *American Express Open*, accessed January 11, 2014, www.womenable.com; Richard Florida, "America's Leading High Tech Venture Capital Centers," *The Atlantic*, accessed January 11, 2014, www.theatlanticcities.com.

38. Company website, www.lexiconinc.com, accessed January 11, 2014; "The 2010 Inc. 5000: The Top 10 Women Entrepreneurs," accessed January 11, 2014, www.inc.com; PR Newswire, "CEO Jamie Arundell-Latshaw, Lexicon,

Inc. Recognized as One of 2013's '100 Most Intriguing Entrepreneurs,'" *The Street*, accessed January 13, 2014, www.thestreet.com.

39. U.S. Small Business Administration, "Mentor-Protégé Program," accessed January 12, 2014, www.sba.gov; U.S. Small Business Administration, "Minority Owned Businesses," accessed January 12, 2014, www.sba.gov.

40. International Franchise Association, "The Economic Impact of Franchised Businesses," accessed February 10, 2014, www.franchise.org; The Franchise Business Economic Outlook 2014, *IHS Global Insight*, February 10, 2014, http://emarket.franchise.org.

41. "2013 Top Global Franchises," *Entrepreneur*, accessed January 14, 2014, www.entrepreneur.com; company website, www.baskinrobbins.com, accessed January 11, 2014; John Schoen, "The Fastest-Growing Global Food Franchises," *Entrepreneur*, accessed January 14, 2014, www.entrepreneur.com.

42. Company website, www.subway.com, accessed January 14, 2014.

43. Edward N. Levitt, "What's So Great About Franchising?" *Franchise Know How*, accessed January 11, 2014, www.franchiseknowhow.com.

44. Ibid.

45. Organization website, "Franchise 101: Why People Are Drawn to Franchising," www.businessfranchiseworld.com, accessed January 15, 2014.

46. Edward N. Levitt, "What's So Great About Franchising?"

47. "How Much Does a Franchise Cost?" *All Business*, accessed January 14, 2014, www.allbusiness.com.

48. Company website, "Heaven's Best Franchises Are Very Affordable," http://heavensbest.com, accessed January 15, 2014.

49. Janean Chun, "Burger King Franchisees Dismiss Lawsuit over $1 Cheeseburger," accessed January 12, 2014, www.smallbusiness.aol.com; Chris Morran, "Judge Dismisses Burger King Franchisee Suit Over Pricing Limits," *The Consumerist*, accessed January 12, 2014, http://theconsumerist.com.

50. Randy Maniloff, "Class Action Lawyers Hope Target Is a Bulls-Eye," *The Wall Street Journal*, accessed January 12, 2014, http://online.wsj.com.

51. Internal Revenue Service, "IRS Launches Study of S Corporation Reporting Compliance," accessed January 11, 2014, www.irs.gov.

52. Benefit Corporation Information Center, http://benefitcorp.net, accessed January 11, 2014.

53. National Center for Employee Ownership, "The World of Employee Ownership," www.nceo.org, accessed January 13, 2014; organization website, "The Employee Ownership Foundation Economic Performance Survey Summary 2000–2013," www.esopassociation.org, accessed January 13, 2014.

54. Michael J. Conway and Stephen J. Baumgartner, "The Family-Owned Business," *Graziado Business Report*, Pepperdine University, http://gbr.pepperdine.edu, accessed January 11, 2014.

55. Company website, www.nhsoda.com, accessed January 14, 2014; Lara Bricker, "Soda Sparkles on West Coast," *Seacoast Sunday*, accessed January 14, 2014, www.seacoastonline.com.

56. Organization website, "About City Year," www.cityyear.org, accessed January 14, 2014.

57. "Company Directory by Business Classification," Hoover's, accessed January 14, 2014, www.hoovers.com.

58. Federal Railroad Administration, "Amtrak," www.fra.dot.gov, accessed January 14, 2014.

59. Organization website, "Cooperatives Around the World," http://usa2012.coop, accessed February 3, 2014.

60. Organization website, "We're Cabot," www.cabotcheese.coop, accessed February 3, 2014.

61. Susan Carey and Jack Nicas, "American Airlines and US Airways Complete Merger," *The Wall Street Journal*, accessed January 11, 2014, http://online.wsj.com.

62. Elizabeth Woyke, "With Deal Dead, Attention Turns to A&T/T-Mobile Roaming Agreement," *Forbes*, accessed January 14, 2014, www.forbes.com; Tom Schoenberg, Sara Forden, and Jeff Bliss, "T-Mobile Antitrust Challenge Leaves AT&T with Little Recourse on Takeover," *Bloomberg News*, accessed January 11, 2014, www.bloomberg.com.

63. "Renault Agrees to Build China Plant with Dongfeng Motor," *Bloomberg News*, accessed January 17, 2014, www.bloomberg.com.

64. Organization website, "About City Year" and "City Year Tumblr," www.cityyear.org, accessed January 11, 2014; "Volunteers Repair War Veteran's West Kendall Home in Appreciation for His Service," http://rebuildingtogethermiami.org, accessed January 11, 2014; "Starbucks Service Day: Operation Rebuild for Heroes at Home," http://cityyearmiami.wordpress.com, accessed January 11, 2014.

Chapter 6

1. N.R. Kleinfield, "Airbnb Host Welcomes Travelers from All Over," *The New York Times*, accessed April 28, 2014, www.nytimes; company website, "About Us," www.airbnb.com, accessed April 28, 2014; company website, "How FlightCar Works," https://flightcar.com, accessed April 28, 2014; Ryan Lawler, "Airport Car Rental Startup FlightCar Launches at LAX, Unveils Mobile App," *Tech Crunch*, accessed February 4, 2014, http://techcrunch.com; Tamara Warren, "Peer-to-Peer Car Sharing at the Airport," *The New York Times*, accessed February 4, 2014, www.nytimes.com; Tomio Geron, "Airbnb and the Unstoppable Rise of the Share Economy," *Forbes*, accessed February 4, 2014, www.forbes.com; Alan Farnham, "Rental Car Co. Run by Teenagers Undercuts Hertz, Avis," *ABC News*, accessed February 4, 2014, http://abcnews.go.com.

2. Company website, http://investors.walmartstores.com, accessed January 19, 2014.

3. Company website, www.bobbieweiner.com, accessed January 19, 2014; Michele Meyer, "The Other Makeup Mogul," *More*, accessed January 19, 2014, www.more.com.

4. Company website, www.dearbloodymary.com, accessed January 19, 2014; Kate Taylor, "How 'Nightmare' Producer Tim Haskell Turned NYC's First Haunted House Into a Year-Round Business," *Entrepreneur*, accessed January 19, 2014, www.entrepreneur.com.

5. Company website, http://stelladot.com, accessed January 19, 2014; Jefferson Graham, "Stella & Dot Brings Tech to At-home Jewelry Parties," *USA TODAY*, accessed January 19, 2014, www.usatoday.com; Vikram Alexei Kansara, "Jessica Herrin of Stella & Dot on Remaking Direct Sales for the Digital Age," *Business of Fashion*, accessed January 19, 2014, www.businessoffashion.com.

6. Company website, http://consciousco.co, accessed January 19, 2014; Caroline Howard, "30-under-30 Who Are Changing the World," *Forbes*, accessed January 19, 2014, www.forbes.com.

7. Organization website, "Kauffman Index of Entrepreneurial Activity," www.kauffman.org, accessed January 19, 2014.

8. Company website, www.craigtechinc.com, accessed January 19, 2014; "Craig Technologies Names Chief Operating Officer," *Space Coast*

Business, accessed January 19, 2014, www.spacecoastbusiness.com; Janet Steele Holloway, "Disabled Vet Designs the Perfect Tech Job," *Women Entrepreneur*, accessed January 19, 2014, www.womenentrepreneur.com.

9. Company website, www.planetfitness.com, accessed January 19, 2014; Maxwell Murphy, "Former Radio Shack CFO Fills Planet Fitness Hole," *The Wall Street Journal*, accessed January 19, 2014, http://blogs.wsj.com.

10. Company website, http://zappos.com, accessed January 19, 2014; John Letzing, "Amazon Buys Retailer Zappos in $807 Million Deal," *Market Watch*, accessed January 19, 2014; "Zappos Culture Survives Acquisition by Amazon," (video), *WSJ Live*, accessed January 19, 2014, http://live.wsj.com.

11. Office of Advocacy, U.S. Small Business Administration, "The Facts About Small Businesses," www.sba.gov, accessed January 19, 2014.

12. "Special Report: The World's Youngest Populations," *Euromonitor*, accessed January 19, 2014, http://blog.euromonitor.com; Hannah Seligson, "Nine Young Chinese Entrepreneurs to Watch," *Forbes*, accessed January 19, 2014, www.forbes.com.

13. Tom Foster, "Tim Ferris' 4-Hour Reality Check," *Inc.*, accessed February 5, 2014, www.inc.com; Joseph Yi, "Examples of Three Successful Lifestyle Entrepreneurs," *Ecommerce Rules*, accessed February 5, 2014, http://ecommercerules.com.

14. Organization website, "2013 Kauffman Index of Entrepreneurial Activity," www.kauffman.org, accessed January 19, 2014; Catherine Rampell, "America's Biggest Entrepreneurs: High School Dropouts," *The New York Times*, accessed January 19, 2014, http://economix.blogs.nytimes.com.

15. Company website, http://anisa.com, accessed January 19, 2014; Max Nisen, "15 Entrepreneurs on What They Wish They'd Known When They First Started Up," *Entrepreneur*, January 18, 2014, www.entrepreneur.com; Trevor Williams, "Brush with Success: China Key to Atlanta Fashion Firm's Corporate Makeup," *Global Atlanta*, accessed January 19, 2014, www.globalatlanta.com.

16. Jose Ernesto Amoros and Niels Bosma, "Global Entrepreneurship Monitor 2013 Global Report," accessed January 21, 2014, www.gemconsortium.org.

17. Organization website, "Global Entrepreneurship Week," http://www.gew.co, accessed January 19, 2014.

18. "Entrepreneurship and Innovation Group," Northeastern University, www.cba.neu.edu, accessed January 19, 2014.

19. "Leadership and Career Connections," Students in Free Enterprise, www.sife.org, accessed January 19, 2014.

20. Mark Henricks, "Honor Roll," *Entrepreneur*, accessed January 19, 2014, www.entrepreneur.com.

21. Tekla S. Perry, "Ge Wang: The iPhone's Music Man," *Spectrum*, accessed January 19, 2014, http://spectrum.ieee.org; Max Chafkin, "Ge Wang: For Turning the App into an Art Form," in "Entrepreneurs We Love," *Inc.*, accessed January 19, 2014, www.inc.com; Oscar Raymundo, "New Singing App Creates Karaoke Party with Lady Antebellum," *Rolling Stone*, accessed January 19, 2014, www.rollingstone.com.

22. Company website, http://4food.com, accessed January 20, 2014.

23. "Kauffman Index of Entrepreneurial Activity," accessed January 20, 2014.

24. Company website, www.paytango.com, accessed January 20, 2014; Carnegie Mellon University, "Fingertip Convenience," accessed January 20, 2014, www.cmu.edu; "America's Coolest College Startups 2013," *Inc.*, accessed January 20, 2014, www.inc.com.

25. Leigh Buchanan, "Bobby Flam Stands Strong," *Inc.*, accessed February 4, 2014, www.inc.com.

26. Company website, "Russell Simmons," www.rushcommunications.com, accessed January 19, 2014.

27. "Whoops! The 10 Greatest (Accidental) Inventions of All Time," *Popular Science*, accessed January 19, 2014, www.popsci.com.

28. "A Day in the Life of an Entrepreneur," *Princeton Review*, accessed January 20, 2014, www.princetonreview.com.

29. Aimee Groth, "Richard Branson: 'Steve Jobs Is the Entrepreneur I Most Admired,'" *Business Insider*, accessed January 20, 2014, www.businessinsider.com.

30. Company website, http://icehouse.com, accessed January 20, 2014; company website, www.trumpetgroup.com, accessed January 20, 2014; company website, http://nakedpizza.biz, accessed January 20, 2014; Christine Champagne, "The Little Shop That Could," *OMMA*, accessed January 20, 2014, www.mediapost.com.

31. Company website, www.bobbibrown.co.uk, accessed January 20, 2014; "How Bobbi Brown Put a New Face on the Makeup Industry," *CBS News*, accessed January 20, 2014, www.cbsnews.com; Bobbi Brown and Athena Schindelheim, "How I Did It," *Inc.*, accessed January 20, 2014, www.inc.com.

32. Company website, www.gogoair.com, accessed January 20, 2014; Jill Krasny, "Gogo Wi-Fi has Big Plans to Keep You Connected," *Inc.*, accessed January 20, 2014, www.inc.com.

33. Company website, www.funeralrecording.com, accessed January 20, 2014; "Cool College Start-ups 2010," *Inc.*, accessed January 20, 2014, www.inc.com.

34. Janko Roettgers, "The Slow, but Inevitable Decline of Netflix's DVD Business," *Gigacom*, accessed January 20, 2014, http://gigaom.com; Logan Hill, "The Business of Being Netflix," *The Wall Street Journal*, accessed January 20, 2014, http://online.wsj.com.

35. Company website, www.braunability.com, accessed January 20, 2014; "Braun Corporation," *Inside View*, accessed January 20, 2014, www.insideview.com

36. Company website, http://shopdeen.com, accessed January 20, 2014; Robert Tuchman, "The Passion's Only as Good as the Plan," *Entrepreneur*, accessed January 20, 2014, www.entrepreneur.com.

37. "What Nibbol Means for Your Pet's Healthcare," *Medium*, accessed February 5, 2014, https://medium.com; "Great Expectations: How We Killed a Startup and Revived It in 72 Hours," *Medium*, accessed February 5, 2014.

38. Company website, www.ableplanet.com, accessed January 20, 2014; "10 of the Most Innovative Small Businesses of 2013," *CNBC News*, accessed January 20, 2014, www.cnbc.com.

39. Ibid.

40. Company website, www.offshoreodysseys.com, accessed January 20, 2014.

41. Darren Dahl, "How to Read a Term Sheet," *Inc.*, accessed January 20, 2014, www.inc.com.

42. Organization website, "Enterprise Florida," www.eflorida.com, accessed January 20, 2014; organization website, "Zone Territory Map," www.advancecolorado.com, accessed January 20, 2014; Jim Siegel, "Tax Breaks for Enterprise Zones Endures Despite Criticism," *Columbus Dispatch*, accessed January 20, 2014, www.dispatch.com.

43. Government website, "Immigration Act of 1990 (IMMACT 90)," www.justice.gov, accessed January 20, 2014.

44. Company website, www.michaelgoldman.com, accessed January 20, 2014.

45. Steve Strauss, "Intrapreneurship: 5 Ways to Get Employees to Be More Entrepreneurial," *Open Forum*, accessed January 20, 2014, www.openforum.com.

46. Company website, www.3m.com, accessed January 20, 2014; Ryan Tate, "Google Couldn't Kill 20 Percent Time Even if It Wanted To," *Wired*, accessed January 20, 2014, www.wired.com; Catherine Clifford, "Keep Your Employees Loyal By Encouraging Them to Pursue Their Own Projects and Passions," *Entrepreneur*, accessed January 20, 2014, www.entrepreneur.com.

End of Part 2: Launching Your Entrepreneurial Career

1. Small Business Association website, www.sba.gov, accessed January 21, 2014.

2. U.S. Bureau of Labor Statistics, "Employment Projections: 2010–2020 Summary," press release, www.bls.gov, accessed January 21, 2014.

3. Alex Salkever, "The Furniture Company Wanted to Sell Him Its Buildings—and Close Down. Should He Buy the Company, Too?" *Inc.*, accessed January 21, 2014, www.inc.com.

4. U.S. Bureau of Labor Statistics, "Industries with the Fastest Growing and Most Rapidly Declining Wage and Salary Employment," http://data.bls.gov, accessed January 21, 2014.

Chapter 7

1. Company website, "Fortune Magazine Names Quicken Loans a Top 5 Best Place to Work in America," press release, www.quickenloans.com, accessed February 11, 2014; "100 Best Companies to Work For," *CNNMoney*, accessed February 11, 2014, http://money.cnn.com; Michael Martinez, "Quicken Loans, Three Other Michigan Companies on 100 Best Workplaces List," *Detroit Business News*, accessed February 11, 2014, www.detroitnews.com; David Segal, "A Missionary's Quest to Remake Motor City," *The New York Times*, accessed February 11, 2014, www.nytimes.com.

2. "The Stop and Shop Supermarket Company," *Hoovers.com*, accessed January 22, 2014, www.hoovers.com.

3. Arnold J. Karr, "Jeff Bezos, John Idol Make First 'Best CEO's' List," *Women's Wear Daily*, accessed January 27, 2014, www.wwd.com.

4. Organization website, "Top 10 in 2013 Temkin Customer Service Rankings," accessed February 11, 2014, http://temkinratings.com.

5. Company website, www.coldstonecreamery.com, accessed January 22, 2014.

6. "Pressure from Generic Drugs Shrinks Profit at Pfizer," *The New York Times*, accessed January 23, 2014, www.nytimes.com.

7. George Stalk and Henry Foley, "Next In Line: The Advantage of Business Succession Planning," *Forbes*, accessed January 23, 2014, www.forbes.com.

8. Associated Press, "Buffett: Succession at Berkshire Will Be Smooth," *USA Today*, accessed January 23, 2014, www.usatoday.com; Anupreeta Das, "Buffett Lieutenants Score Big Payday," *The Wall Street Journal*, accessed January 23, 2014, http://online.wsj.com.

9. Catherine Carlock, "How to Lower Workplace Energy Costs," *The Business Journals*, accessed January 25, 2014, www.bizjournals.com.

10. "10 Leadership Tips from Eileen Fisher," *Inc.*, accessed January 27, 2014, www.inc.com.

11. Laurie Segall, "Lithium Technologies to Buy Klout," *CNNMoney*, February 11, 2014, http://money.cnn.com; company website, http://klout.com, accessed January 23, 2014; Liz Welch, "The Klout Mystique: Staying True to Vision," *Inc.*, January 14, 2014, www.inc.com.

12. Rick Lyman, Illinois Legislature Approves Retiree Benefit Cuts in Troubled Pension System," *The New York Times*, accessed February 11, 2014, www.nytimes.com; Eileen Norcross, "A Reality Check on the Pension Crisis," *The New York Times*, accessed January 23, 2014, www.nytimes.com; Jonathan Weil, "Pension Accounting Rules Led to Overvalued Stock," *The Wall Street Journal*, accessed January 23, 2014, http://online.wsj.com.

13. "World's Most Ethical Companies—Honorees," *Ethnisphere*, accessed January 22, 2014, http://ethnisphere.com; Barbara Farfan, "Most Ethical Retail Companies in the World 2013—Starbucks, Target, Gap," *About.com*, accessed January 23, 2014, http://retailindustry.about.com.

14. "Nintendo's Woes Don't Mean Game Over for Its Consoles," *The Wall Street Journal*, January 20, 2014, http://online.wsj.com; Mayumi Negishi, Hiroyuki Kachi, and Ian Sherr, "Wii's Woes Weigh on Nintendo," *The Wall Street Journal*, January 19, 2014, http://online.wsj.com.

15. Geoff Colvin, "Housing Is Back and So Is Home Depot," *CNNMoney*, accessed January 22 2014, http://money.cnn.com.

16. Brent Robinson, "Omnichannel Retailing and the Mobile Solution to Showroom Shoppers," *Bazaar Voice*, accessed January 23, 2014, http://blog.bazaarvoice.com.

17. Bill Vlasic and Jaclyn Trop, "After 3 Fires, Safety Agency Opens Inquiry into Tesla Model S," *The New York Times*, accessed January 23, 2014, www.nytimes.com.

18. Company website, www.starbucks.com, accessed January 25, 2014; Candice Choi, "Starbucks Hit by Migration to Online Shopping," *Yahoo Finance*, accessed January 25, 2014, http://finance.yahoo.com; Annie Gasparo, "Green Mountain to Change Name to Include Keurig Brand," *The Wall Street Journal*, accessed January 20, 2014, http://online.wsj.com; Stephanie Strom, "Starbucks Aims to Move Beyond Beans," *The New York Times*, accessed January 20, 2014, www.nytimes.com.

19. Ibid.

20. Brooks Barnes, "But It Doesn't Look Like a Marriott," *The New York Times*, accessed January 25, 2014, www.nytimes.com.

21. Issie Lapowsky, "Balbus Speech: Speech Therapy in Your Pocket: 2013 America's Coolest College Start-ups," *Inc.*, accessed February 11, 2014, www.inc.com.

22. Timothy Bednarz, "Seven Key Benefits of an Empowered Workplace," *Examiner.com*, accessed January 25, 2014, www.examiner.com.

23. Retail Institute, "Key to Success in Retail—Developing the Skills of Frontline Managers," *Pharmacy Today*, accessed January 27, 2014, www.pharmacy-today.co.nz.

24. Monica Bauer, "PepsiCo Announces Plans for $5 Billion Investment in Mexico," *The Wall Street Journal*, accessed January 25, 2014, http://online.wsj.com.

25. "CR's 100 Best Corporate Citizens 2013," *Corporate Responsibility Magazine*, accessed January 25, 2014, www.thecro.org.

26. Kathy Gordon, Ian Sherr, and Joann S. Lublin, "Apple Taps Fashion CEO as Retail Magic Fades," *The Wall Street Journal*, accessed January 25, 2014, http://online.wsj.com.

27. Scott D. Anthony, "Google's Management Style Grows Up," *Bloomberg Businessweek*, accessed January 22, 2014, www.businessweek.com.

28. Dylan Stableford, "Sully: 5 Years after the Miracle on the Hudson," *Yahoo News*, accessed February 11, 2014, http://news.yahoo.com; Dean Foust, "US Airways: After the Miracle on the Hudson," *Bloomberg Businessweek*, accessed February 11, 2014, www.businessweek.com.

29. Company website, "Corporate Information," www.google.com, accessed January 25, 2014.

30. Bruce I. Jones, "People Management Lessons from Disney," *Training Industry*, accessed January 24, 2014, www.trainingindustry.com.

31. Company website, http://investors.activision.com, accessed January 25, 2014.

32. Company website, www.petswelcome.com, accessed January 26, 2014.

33. Company website, www.pg.com, accessed February 11, 2014.

34. Brandon Gutman, "Zappos' Marketing Chief: 'Customer Service Is the New Marketing!'" *Fast Company*, accessed January 26, 2014, www.fastcompany.com.

35. Mike Gordon, Chris Musso, Eric Rebentisch, and Nisheeth Gupta, "The Path to Successful New Products," *McKinsey Quarterly*, accessed January 25, 2014, www.mckinseyquarterly.com.

36. Jason Del Rey, "How I Did It: Omniture's Josh James," *Inc.*, accessed January 27, 2014, www.inc.com.

Chapter 8

1. Company website, "About Glassdoor," www.glassdoor.com, accessed February 16, 2014; Matt Charney, "How Job Seekers Use Glassdoor Reviews," *Recruiting Blogs*, accessed February 16, 2014, www.recruitingblogs.com; Charles Coy, "What Job Seekers Look for When Scouting Employer Reviews on Glassdoor," *Cornerstone On Demand*, accessed February 16, 2014, www.cornerstoneondemand.com; Vivian Giang, "Companies Can Now Use Glassdoor to Track Job Seekers," *Business Insider*, accessed February 16, 2014, www.businessinsider.com.

2. "Predicting the Top 5 In Demand Skills for 2014," *Brandresume.com*, accessed January 25, 2014, http://brandresume.com.

3. Mark Kolakowski, "Find a Job Online," *About.com*, accessed January 25, 2014, http://financecareers.about.com; Susan Adams, "How to Make Them Respond When You Apply for a Job Online," *Forbes*, accessed January 25, 2014, www.forbes.com; Lauren Weber, "Your Resume vs. Oblivion," *The Wall Street Journal*, accessed January 24, 2014, http://online.wsj.com.

4. Company website, www.jobsinpods.com, accessed January 25, 2014.

5. Government website, "Fact Sheet on Employment Tests and Selection Procedures," http://eeoc.gov, accessed January 25, 2014.

6. Jacob Bunge and Melanie Trottman, "Cargill to Pay $2.2M in Discrimination Settlement," *TwinCities.com*, accessed January 25, 2014, www.twincities.com.

7. Faith Alejandro, "Only English in the Workplace?" *Virginia Workplace Law*, accessed January 25, 2014, http://virginiaworkplacelaw.com; Chasity Goddard, "Tennessee Passes English Only Bill," *Knoxville Examiner*, accessed January 25, 2014, www.examiner.com.

8. Catherine Dunn, "2014 Best Companies All Stars: Cisco," *Fortune*, accessed February 16, 2014, http://money.cnn.com.

9. "Big Business Bets on Education, Turning Factories and Corporate Campuses into Schools," *Forbes*, accessed January 29, 2014, www.forbes.com; organization website, "BMW Scholars Program," www.sccsc.edu, accessed January 29, 2014.

10. Company website, "Welcome to EYU," www.ey.com, accessed January 25, 2014.

11. Company website, www.glimmerglassgroup.com, accessed January 25, 2014.

12. Company website, www.rothschild.com, accessed January 25, 2014; Julia Werdigier, "Rothschilds Bring in an Outsider to Run the Show," *The New York Times*, accessed January 25, 2014, www.nytimes.com.

13. "Turn Your Performance Review System into One That Works," *Quality Digest Magazine*, accessed January 29, 2014, www.qualitydigest.com.

14. Company website, www.halogensoftware.com, accessed January 25, 2014.

15. Colleen Leahey, "Ten Top Perks from *Fortune's* Best Companies to Work For 2014," *Fortune*, accessed February 16, 2014, http://money.cnn.com.

16. "S.181 Lilly Ledbetter Fair Pay Act of 2009," *Open Congress*, accessed January 25, 2014, www.opencongress.org.

17. Bureau of Labor Statistics, "Employer Costs for Employee Compensation, September 2013" press release, accessed January 25, 2014, www.bls.gov.

18. Company website, www.qualcomm.com, accessed January 25, 2014; "100 Best Companies to Work For 2013: Best Benefits," *Fortune*, accessed January 26, 2014, http://money.cnn.com.

19. Company website, "Careers," www.solipsys.com, accessed January 26, 2014.

20. Steven Greenhouse, "Flex Time Flourishes in Accounting Industry," *The New York Times*, accessed January 26, 2014, www.nytimes.com.

21. Company website, www.shiftboard.com, accessed January 26, 2014.

22. Dan Schawbel, "Why a Flexible Workplace Makes Sense," *ehotelier.com*, accessed January 26, 2014, http://ehotelier.com; Richard Eisenberg, "It's High Time for a Four-Day Workweek," *Next Avenue*, accessed January 26, 2014, www.nextavenue.org.

23. Curt Finch, "The Rise of Telecommuting and What It Means for Your Business," *Small Business Trends*, accessed January 26, 2014, http://smallbiztrends.com.

24. Millennial Branding, "The Gen Y Workplace Expectations Study," *Millennial Branding*, accessed January 28, 2014, http://millennialbranding.com.

25. Laura Hemphill, "Amid Layoffs—A Financial Analyst's Survivor Guilt," *Bloomberg Businessweek*, accessed January 27, 2014, www.businessweek.com; Ken Eisold, "The American Way of Unemployment," *Psychology Today*, accessed January 28, 2014, www.psychologytoday.com.

26. Mark Reilly, "Imation Sells Memorex—Has a Buyer for Xtreme Mac," *Minneapolis/St. Paul Business Journal*, accessed January 28, 2014, www.bizjournals.com.

27. Jackie Northam, "As Overseas Costs Rise, More Companies Are 'Reshoring,'" *National Public Radio*, January 27, 2014, www.npr.org.

28. "Maslow's Hierarchy of Needs," *Accel-Team.com*, accessed January 28, 2014, www.accel-team.com.

29. Brett Stephens, "About Those Income Inequality Statistics," *The Wall Street Journal*, accessed January 28, 2014, http://online.wsj.com; Jennifer Liberto, "CEOs Earn 354 Times More than the Average Worker," *CNNMoney*, accessed January 28, 2014, http://money.cnn.com.

30. Company website, "Our Company," www.pamperedchef.com, accessed January 28, 2014.

31. Company website, www.emc.com, accessed January 28, 2014.

32. Melanie Trotman, "Labor Union Membership Rate Stays Steady in 2013," *The Wall Street Journal*, accessed January 29, 2014, http://online.wsj.com; Bureau of Labor Statistics, "Union Membership (Annual) News Release," January 24, 2014, www.bls.gov.

33. Organization websites: www.nea.org; www.afscme.org; www.seiu.org; www.teamster.org; www.ufcw.org; www.uaw.org, accessed February 15, 2014.

34. Kathleen Madigan, "Vital Signs: Work Stoppages Fall in 2013," *The Wall Street Journal*, February 12, 2014, http://blogs.wsj.com.

35. Howard Stutz, "Culinary's Futile Push Against Cosmo," *Las Vegas Review-Journal*, accessed February 16, 2014, www.reviewjournal.com.

36. "Bureau of Labor Statistics, "Union Members Summary—2013," Bureau of Labor Statistics, accessed January 29, 2014, www.bls.gov.

Chapter 9

1. Greg Lindsay, "Yahoo Says That Killing Working from Home Is Turning Out Perfectly," *Fast Company*, accessed February 20, 2014, www.fastcompany.com; Christopher Tkaczyk, "Marissa Mayer Breaks Her Silence on Yahoo's Telecommuting Policy," *CNNMoney*, accessed February 20, 2014, http://tech.fortune.cnn.com; Claire Cain Miller and Catherine Rampell, "Yahoo Orders Home Workers Back to the Office," *The New York Times*, accessed February 20, 2014, www.nytimes.com; Douglas MacMillan, "Yahoo CEO's Next Task: Woo Madison Avenue," *The Wall Street Journal*, accessed February 20, 2014, http://online.wsj.com; company website, "Give People the Freedom of Where to Work," www.virgin.com, accessed February 20, 2014.

2. Company website, "About KIND," www.kindsnacks.com, accessed February 1, 2014; Jacquelyn Smith, "How to Create an Authentic and Transparent Work Environment," *Forbes*, accessed February 1, 2014, www.forbes.com.

3. Company website, "Toyota Production System," www.setpointusa.com, accessed February 1, 2014.

4. Company website, Lebanon Valley Brethren Home, www.lvbh.org, accessed February 1, 2014; Becka Livesay, "The Culture Change Way: Empowering Direct Care Workers to Improve Care," *Direct Care Alliance*, accessed February 1, 2014, http://blog.directcarealliance.org.

5. National Center for Employee Ownership, "A Brief Overview of Employee Ownership in the U.S.," updated January 2014, www.nceo.org, accessed February 1, 2014.

6. ESOP Association, "Corporate Performance," www.esopassociation.org, accessed February 1, 2014.

7. National Center for Employee Ownership, "A Statistical Profile of Employee Ownership," updated January 2014, http://www.nceo.org, accessed February 1, 2014.

8. National Center for Employee Ownership, "Employee Ownership as a Retirement Plan," www.nceo.org, accessed February 1, 2014.

9. National Center for Employee Ownership, "Employee Stock Options Fact Sheet," www.nceo.org, accessed February 1, 2014.

10. Ibid.

11. Kaite Hafner, "Google Options Make Masseuse a Multi-Millionaire," *The New York Times*, accessed February 1, 2014, www.nytimes.com.

12. "Goldman CEO Blankfein Receives $14.5 Million Restricted Stock Bonus," *Reuters*, accessed February 1, 2014, www.reuters.com; Emily Chasan, "Last Gasp for Stock Options," *The Wall Street Journal*, accessed February 1, 2014, http://blogs.wsj.com.

13. Katie Thomas, "New Recalls by Johnson & Johnson Raise Concern About Quality Control Improvements," *The New York Times*, accessed February 1, 2014, www.nytimes.com; Natasha Singer and Reed Abelson, "Will Johnson & Johnson Get Its Act Together?" *The New York Times*, accessed February 1, 2014, www.nytimes.com.

14. Company website, "Whole Foods Market's Core Values," www.wholefoodsmarket.com, accessed February 1, 2014.

15. Company website, www.salesforce.com, accessed February 2, 2014; Victoria Barret, "Salesforce.com's Marc Benioff on Why Chatter Matters," *Forbes*, accessed February 2, 2014, www.forbes.com.

16. "Global Diversity and Inclusion Fostering Innovation Through a Diverse Workforce," *Forbes Insights*, accessed February 3, 2014, www.forbes.com.

17. Company website, "Hi-Tech Scavenger Hunts," www.teambonding.com, accessed February 1, 2014; Matt Hickman, "6 Unusual Team Building Activities," *Mother Nature Network*, accessed February 1, 2014, www.mnn.com.

18. Company website, "A Career at The Container Store," and "Employee-First Culture," www.containerstore.com, accessed February 3, 2014.

19. Michiel Kruyt, Judy Malan, and Rachel Tuffield, "Three Steps to Building a Better Top Team," *Forbes*, accessed February 3, 2014, www.forbes.com; Tara Duggan, "Leadership vs. Conflict Resolution," *Chron*, accessed February 3, 2014, http://smallbusiness.chron.com.

20. Stephanie Clifford, "U.S. Textile Plants Return, with Floors Largely Empty of People," *The New York Times*, accessed February 19, 2014, www.nytimes.com.

21. Anne D'Innocenzio, "Starbucks to Pay $2.76B in Coffee Spat with Kraft," *Associated Press*, accessed February 19, 2014, http://bigstory.ap.org.

22. Carmine Gallo, "Communicating More Effectively with Employees," *Bloomberg Businessweek*, accessed February 3, 2014, www.businessweek.com; "Managing Mystique: How Ritz-Carlton Delivers Amazing Customer Service," http://ryanestis.com, accessed February 3, 2014.

23. Glenn Llopis, "6 Ways Effective Listening Can Make You a Better Leader," *Forbes*, accessed February 3, 2014, www.forbes.com; Norma Chew, "Are You a Good Listener?," *Yahoo! Voices*, accessed February 3, 2014, http://voices.yahoo.com.

24. Company website, www.sanebox.com, accessed February 3, 2014.

25. "Expand Trust in Your Organization," *Peter Stark.com*, accessed February 3, 2014, www.peterstark.com.

26. Jitendra Mishra, "Managing the Grapevine," *Analytic Tech*, accessed February 2, 2014, www.analytictech.com.

27. John Boe, "How to Read Your Prospect Like a Book!," John Boe International, http://johnboe.com, accessed February 3, 2014.

28. Drew Griffin and Scott Bronstein, "Documents Show Carnival Knew of Fire Danger Before Ill-Fated Cruise," *CNN*, accessed February 3, 2014, www.cnn.com.

29. Jonathan Bernstein, "The Ten Steps of Crisis Communications," *Bernstein Crisis Management*, accessed February 3, 2014, www.bernsteincrisismanagement.com.

30. Hugo Martin, "To Boost Business, Carnival Cruise Lines Offers a 110% Guarantee," *Los Angeles Times*, accessed February 2, 2014, www.latimes.com.

Chapter 10

1. Company website, "Additive Manufacturing Is Reinventing the Way We Work," https://www.ge.com, accessed February 22, 2014; Tim Catts, "GE Printing Engine Fuel Nozzles Propels $6 Billion Market," *Bloomberg News*, accessed February 22, 2014, www.bloomberg.com; Chelsey Levingston, "3-D Manufacturing Next Industrial Revolution?," *Dayton Daily News*, accessed February 22, 2014, www.daytondailynews.com; Rich Benvin, "3D Printing—The Future of Manufacturing," *Association of 3D Printing*, accessed February 22, 2014, http://associationof3dprinting.com.

2. "William Levitt," *Answers.com*, accessed February 19, 2014, www.answers.com.

3. Company website, "Operations Facilities," http://corporate.honda.com, accessed February 5, 2014.

4. Company website, www.custommade.com, accessed February 5, 2014.

5. Company website, "Lego Group Partners with WWF and Focuses on Suppliers to Reduce Climate Impact," http://aboutus.lego.com, accessed February 5, 2014.

6. Organization website, www.usgbc.org, accessed February 5, 2014.

7. Bob Trebilcock, "Gilt Groupe: No Flash in the Distribution Pan," *Modern Materials Handling*," accessed February 5, 2014, www.mmh.com; Adam Ryan, "Robots in Disguise," *Supply Chain Digital*, accessed February 5, 2014, www.supplychaindigital.com; company website, "Baxter: A Unique Robot with Unique Features," www.rethinkrobotics.com, accessed February 5, 2014.

8. "Different Types of Robots," *Ask.com*, accessed February 5, 2014, www.ask.com; company website, www.ni.com, accessed February 5, 2014.

9. "Shaping Dentistry with CAD/CAM Technology," *Your Dentistry Guide*, accessed February 4, 2014, www.yourdentistryguide.com.

10. "Is It Time to Rethink Your Manufacturing Strategy?," *MIT Sloan Management Review*, accessed February 4, 2014, http://sloanreview.mit.edu; event website, "World Drug Manufacturing Summit 2014," www.wdmsummit.com, accessed February 4, 2014.

11. "On the Open Road to CIM with JDF: An EFI White Paper on Computer Integrated Manufacturing," *Office Product News*, accessed February 7, 2014, www.officeproductnews.net.

12. Company website, "Mondelez International to Invest $190 Million in Largest Plant in Asia Pacific," http://ir.mondelezinternational.com, accessed February 6, 2014.

13. Company website, www.holland-car.com, accessed February 4, 2014.

14. Company website, www.americanapparel.com, accessed February 4, 2014.

15. "Ariba Network Gets Bigger, More Global," *Yahoo Finance*, accessed February 5, 2014, http://finance.yahoo.com; company website, www.ariba.com, accessed February 4, 2014.

16. Company website, www.premiumretail.com, accessed February 5, 2014; Ann Zimmerman, "The New Logistics of Christmas," *The Wall Street Journal*, accessed February 5, 2014, http://online.wsj.com.

17. Company website, "Vendor Managed Inventory," www.dow.com, accessed February 5, 2014.

18. Corporate website, "Continuous Performance Improvement," www.seattlechildrens.org, accessed February 4, 2014; "Seattle Children's Hospital Saves $2.5 Million in First Year with Streamlined Inventory Distribution," *Healthcare Financial Management Association*, accessed February 4, 2014, www.hfma.org.

19. Company website, "Turtle Wax Ltd.," www.solarsoft.com, accessed February 4, 2014.

20. Company website, "Wilson Football in the NFL," www.wilson.com, accessed February 5, 2014.

21. Company website, www.jetcam.com, accessed February 4, 2014.

22. Company website, www.swansongroupinc.com, accessed February 5, 2014.

23. Carolyn King and Suzanne Kapner, "Lululemon Founder Puts Quality Issues on Customers," *The Wall Street Journal*, accessed February 8, 2014, http://online.wsj.com.

24. Organization website, "What Is Six Sigma?," www.isixsigma.com, accessed February 4, 2014.

25. Organization website, www.iso.org, accessed February 4, 2014.

End of Part 3: Launching Your Management Career

1. U.S. Bureau of Labor Statistics, "Projected Rate of Employment Changes by Major Occupational Group 2012–2022," press release, accessed February 5, 2014, www.bls.gov.

2. Salary data in this section is taken from U.S. Bureau of Labor Statistics, "Occupational Employment Statistics—Management Occupations," *Occupational Outlook Handbook, 2013–2014 edition*, accessed February 5, 2014, www.bls.gov.

Chapter 11

1. Rick Rothacker, "NASCAR Aiming for Younger, More Diverse Fans, Quicker Finishes," *Charlotte Observer*, accessed February 25, 2014, www.charlotteobserver.com; Steve Olenski, "How NASCAR Uses Relationship Marketing," *Forbes*, accessed February 25, 2014, www.forbes.com; Andrew Dunn and David Scott, "Changing Fan Habits a Challenge for NASCAR," *That's Racing*, accessed February 25, 2014, www.thatsracin.com.

2. American Marketing Association, "Definition of Marketing," www.marketingpower.com, accessed February 25, 2014.

3. American Heart Association, "2013 Prevention Guideline Tools," http://my.americanheart.org, accessed February 10, 2014.

4. Company website, http://airbnb.com, accessed February 10, 2014; Lindsay Harrison, "50 Most Innovative Companies—Airbnb," *Fast Company*, February 10, 2014, www.fastcompany.com.

5. Company website, www.target.com, accessed February 10, 2014; Brad Gilligan, "Target Starts Mobile Coupon Program," *All Tech Considered*, accessed February 10, 2014, www.npr.org; "Target Launches First-Ever Scannable Mobile Coupon Program," *Business Wire*, accessed February 10, 2014, www.businesswire.com; Marguerite Reardon, "Attention Shoppers: Target Offers Mobile Coupons," *CNET News*, accessed February 10, 2014, http://news.cnet.com.

6. Elise Moreau, "What Is Vine?," *Web Trends*, accessed February 10, 2014, http://webtrends.about.com; Althea Chang, "Facebook and Twitter's Growing Competitors," *CNBC*, accessed February 10, 2014, www.cnbc.com; "Another Try by Google to Take on Facebook, *The New York Times*, accessed February 10, 2014, www.nytimes.com.

7. "Scope of the Sector," *Independent Sector*, accessed February 10, 2014, http://independentsector.org.

8. Bureau of Labor Statistics, "Volunteering in the United States, 2013," www.bls.gov, accessed February 25, 2014.

9. Organization website, "Hometown Huddle," www.unitedway.org, accessed February 10, 2014.

10. Company website, "About Us," www.one.org, accessed February 11, 2014; Elaine Pofeldt, "With or Without Aid, Bono Is One with African Capitalism," *CNBC*, accessed February 11, 2014, www.cnbc.com; Debbie McGoldrick, "Bill Gates and Bono Bonded over AIDS Crisis in Africa," *Irish Central*, accessed February 11, 2014, www.irishcentral.com; Randall Lane, "Bill Gates and Bono on Their Alliance of Fortune, Fame and Giving," *Forbes*, accessed February 11, 2014, www.forbes.com.

11. Kurt Badenhausen, "LeBron James Is the NBA's Leading Shoe Salesman," *Forbes*, accessed February 11, 2014, www.forbes.com.

12. Organization website, "Superbowl," www.nfl.com, accessed February 11, 2014.

13. Organization website, "American Diabetes Association Tour de Cure," http://tour.diabetes.org, accessed February 11, 2014.

14. Company website, "Nordstrom Cares," http://shop.nordstrom.com, accessed February 11, 2014.

15. Abigail Tracy, "WaterDrop Shop: Selling Products with a Purpose, *Inc.*, accessed February 11, 2014, www.inc.com.

16. David Broughton, "Fan Social Media Use Passes a Threshold," *Sports Business Daily*, accessed February 11, 2014, www.sportsbusinessdaily.com.

17. Company website, www.takecarehealth.com, accessed February 11, 2014; Jay Green, "In Era of Health Reform, Retail Clinics Become Part of the Health Care Delivery System," *Detroit Business*, accessed February 11, 2014, www.crainsdetroit.com; Bruce Jaspen, "CVS Drives Retail Clinic Growth as Obamacare Launches," *Forbes*, accessed February 11, 2014, www.forbes.com; company website, "Take Care Clinics at Select Walgreens Offer Families Convenient and Affordable Option for Camp and Sports Physicals," press release, http://news.walgreens.com, accessed February 11, 2014; Pamela Lewis Dolan, "Retail Clinics: Struggling to Find Their Place," *American Medical News*, accessed February 11, 2014, www.ama-assn.org; Sarah Kliff, "Retail Clinics Make Their Pitch," *Washington Post*, accessed February 11, 2014, www.washingtonpost.com; Donna Fuscaldo, "Health Care in the Express Lane: Retail Clinics Popping Up All Over the Place," *Fox Business*, accessed February 11, 2014, www.foxbusiness.com.

18. Company website, "Our Story," www.mcdonalds.com, accessed February 11, 2014; company website, "Restaurant Locator," accessed February 11, 2014, http://world.subway.com; Subway Restaurants International website, http://world.subway.com, accessed February 11, 2014; Marco Lui, "Subway Plans to Open 500 Stores across China in Next Five Years," *Bloomberg News*, accessed February 11, 2014, www.bloomberg.com; Farah Master, "Subway Eyes Matching McDonalds in China in 10 Years," *Reuters*, accessed February 11, 2014, www.reuters.com; Ben Yue, "Subway Eyes Further China Expansion," *China Daily USA*, accessed February 11, 2014, http://usa.chinadaily.com.cn.

19. Company website, www.blanklabel.com, accessed February 11, 2014; company website, www.spreadshirt.com, accessed February 11, 2014.

20. Company website, "What Is Big Data? www-01.ibm.com, accessed February 25, 2014; Lisa Arthur, "What Is Big Data?" *Forbes*, accessed February 25, 2014, www.forbes.com.

21. "Smartphones and Tablets Drive Nearly 7 Percent of Total U.S. Digital Traffic," press release, comScore, accessed February 11, 2014, www.comscore.com; "2013 Mobile Future in Focus," *comScore*, accessed February 11, 2014, www.comscore.com; "Mobile Marketing Statistics 2014," *Smart Insights*, accessed February 11, 2014, www.smartinsights.com.

22. "Procter & Gamble Readies Online Market-Research Push," *InformationWeek*, accessed February 10, 2014, www.informationweek.com; Hal Gregerson, "A.G. Lafley's Innovation Skills Will Weather P&G's Storm," *Knowledge.com*, accessed February 10, 2014, http://knowledge.insead.edu.

23. Stephanie Rosenbloom, "In Bid to Sway Sales, Cameras Track Shoppers," *The New York Times*, accessed February 10, 2014, www.nytimes.com; Miles O'Brien and Ann Kellen, "Science of Shopping: Cameras and Software That Track Our Buying Behavior," *Mother Nature Network*, accessed February 11, 2014, www.mnn.com.

24. Company website, "New Campbell's Select Harvest Soup Makes a 'Clean Sweep' over Progresso," http://investor.campbellsoupcompany.com, accessed February 10, 2014.

25. Andrew McMains, "CEO Pushes Soup Giant to Move Faster, 'Think Outside the Can,'" *AdWeek*, accessed February 11, 2014, www.adweek.com.

26. Company website, "Challenges and Wants," www.unilever.com, accessed February 10, 2014; "5 Examples of Companies Innovating with Crowdsourcing," *Innocentive.com*, accessed February 10, 2014, www.innocentive.com.

27. Joseph Walker, "Data Mining to Recruit Sick People," *The Wall Street Journal*, accessed February 13, 2014, http://online.wsj.com.

28. Leah Betancourt, "How Companies Are Using Your Social Media Data," *Mashable*, accessed February 12, 2014, http://mashable.com; Jim Cooper, "Yahoo's Carol Bartz Touts Data," *Mediaweek*, accessed February 12, 2014, www.mediaweek.com; Jared Newman, "Google Buzz Bites the Dust," *PCWorld*, accessed February 12, 2014, www.pcworld.com; Declan McCullagh, "Why No One Cares about Privacy Anymore," *CNET News*, accessed February 12, 2014, http://news.cnet.com.

29. Company website, www.playnomics.com, accessed February 12, 2014; "Playnomics Releases a Free Player Scoring Dashboard for Game Platforms and Publishers," press release, *MarketWatch*, accessed February 12, 2014, www.marketwatch.com.

30. Company website, "Social Media User Demographics," www.pewinternet.org, accessed February 12, 2014.

31. Craig Smith, "21 Interesting Pandora Statistics," *Expanded Ramblings*, accessed July 13, 2014, http://expandedramblings.com; company website, www.pandora.com, accessed February 12, 2014; Marcello Ballve, "Silicon Valley and Detroit Are Battling Over the Future of the Internet-Connected Car," *Business Insider*, accessed February 12, 2014, www.businessinsider.com; Peter High, "Gartner: Top 10 Strategic Technology Trends for 2014," *Forbes*, accessed February 12, 2014, www.forbes.com; Farhad Manjoo, "Smart Cars: Fill 'Er with Apps," *Fast Company*, accessed February 12, 2014, www.fastcompany.com.

32. Company website, "Now on Duty," www.ford.com, accessed February 12, 2014; "Ford e-News—July 24, 2013," *The Wall Street Journal*, accessed February 12, 2014, http://online.wsj.com; Brandon Turkus, "Ford's Explorer-based Police Interceptor to Get 365-hp EcoBoost Option," *Auto Blog*, accessed February 12, 2014, www.autoblog.com; Brent Snavely, "Ford to Unveil Police Interceptor," *Detroit Free Press*, accessed February 12, 2014, www.managemylife.com; Chris Woodyard, "Ford Unveils Next-Generation, V-6-Only Taurus Police Car," *USA Today*, accessed February 12, 2014, www.usatoday.com; Fran Spielman, "Chicago Police Department to Buy 500 Police Cars from

South Side Ford Plant," *Chicago Sun Times*, accessed February 12, 2014, www.suntimes.com; Owen Ray, "San Francisco Police: Ford Police Interceptor to Replace Crown Victoria," *Examiner*, accessed February 12, 2014, www.examiner.com.

33. Joseph Yi, "Male Shopping Habits vs. Female Shopping Habits," *E-Commerce Rules*, accessed February 12, 2014, http://ecommercerules.com.

34. Company website, "Women Control the Purse Strings," www.nielsen.com, accessed February 12, 2014.

35. Company website, "Join Amazon Mom and Enjoy," www.amazon.com, accessed February 12, 2014.

36. U.S. Census Bureau, "*2012 Statistical Abstract*, Resident Population Projections by Sex and Age: 2010 to 2050," accessed February 10, 2014, www.census.gov.

37. Emily Brandon, "The Recession's Impact on Baby Boomer Retirement," *US News Money*, accessed February 13, 2014, http://money.usnews.com.

38. Jeanine Poggi, "Nickelodeon Targets 'Post-Millennials' in Upfront," *Advertising Age*, accessed February 13, 2014, www.adage.com.

39. "Telemundo Novelas for iPhone," *CNET*, accessed February 13, 2014, http://download.cnet.com; Leila Cobo, "Univision Launches Radio App for iPhone," *Billboard Business*, accessed February 10, 2014, www.billboardbiz.com.

40. Emily Maltby, "Immigrant Entrepreneurs Top List," *The Wall Street Journal*, accessed February 14, 2014, http://blogs.wsj.com; government website, Robert W. Fairlie, "Estimating the Contribution of Immigrant Business Owners to the U.S. Economy," http://archive.sba.gov, accessed February 14, 2014.

41. Company website, "GM Social Hub," www.gm.com, accessed February 13, 2014.

42. "Research Shows $15.39 Billion Spent on Video Game Content in US in 2013, a One Percent Increase over 2012," *NPD Group*, accessed February 25, 2014, https://www.npd.com; association website, "Annual Sales Data for Traditional Toy Categories," www.toyassociation.org, accessed February 25, 2014.

43. Company website, "People and the Environment," www.ikea.com, accessed February 13, 2014.

44. Company website, www.sodexousa.com, accessed February 10, 2014; "Sodexo Introduces Food Truck at Assumption College," *Food Service Director*, January 30, 2014, www.foodservicedirector.com.

45. Company website, http://fitbit.com, accessed February 10, 2014; Jennifer Zegler and Stacy Glasgow, "Mintel Releases U.S. 2014 Consumer Trends," *Mintel.com*, accessed February 10, 2014, www.mintel.com

46. Resources for Entrepreneurs staff, "Consumer Habits Could Be Permanently Changed by Recession," *Resources for Entrepreneurs*, accessed February 13, 2014, www.gaebler.com; Joshua Brustein, "Walgreen's Beth Stiller on Customer Behavior and the Recession," *Bloomberg Businessweek*, accessed February 13, 2014, www.businessweek.com.

47. Company website, www.timberland.com, accessed February 13, 2014.

48. Company website, "Atlantis Resort," www.priceline.com, accessed February 13, 2014.

49. Deena Crawley and Steve McKee, "Twenty Co-branding Examples," *Bloomberg Businessweek*, accessed February 13, 2014, www.businessweek.com; company website, "New Treats from Betty

Crocker and Hershey's," http://www.blog.generalmills.com, accessed February 13, 2014.

50. Company website, http://queuebuster.com, accessed February 13, 2014.

51. Company website, "About VALS," www.strategicbusinessinsights.com, accessed February 25, 2014.

Chapter 12

1. Marc Graser, "Mattel's Bold Plan to Take Control Back from Hollywood," *Variety*, accessed March 12, 2014, www.variety.com; company website, www.mattel.com, accessed March 12, 2014; "Mattel Launches Playground Productions, a Creative Storytelling Division Focused on Multiplatform Entertainment," *Market Watch*, accessed March 12, 2014, www.marketwatch.com.

2. "Research and Markets: Global Retail Touch Screen Display Market 2014–2018: One of the Main Drivers Contributing to Market's Growth Is the Use of Hi-Tech Touchscreen Display," *BusinessWire*, accessed February 16, 2014, www.businesswire.com.

3. "Pepsi to Sign Rock Star to Distribution Deal," *AdWeek*, accessed February 15, 2014, www.adweek.com.

4. Natalie Jarvey, "Tablet Company Fuhu Launches Original Animated Series on BabyFirst TV," *The Hollywood Reporter*, March 10, 2014, www.hollywoodreporter.com; company website, http://nabitablet.com, accessed February 15, 2014; Burt Helm, "Kid You Not: The Very Serious Business of Building the Fastest Growing Company in America," *Fast Company*, accessed February 15, 2014, www.fastcompany.com.

5. "A Strong Holiday Quarter for the Worldwide Tablet Market, But Signs of Slower Growth Are Clear," *IDC*, accessed February 16, 2014, www.idc.com; Michael Endler, "iPad Dominates Enterprise Tablet Market," *InformationWeek*, accessed February 15, 2014, http://informationweek.com; "Kindle vs. Nook vs. iPad2 Video Comparison," *Deaf Tech News*, accessed February 15, 2014, www.deaftechnews.com.

6. Raymond Soneira, "From Tablets to TVs: What's Next for Display Tech in 2014," *Gizmodo.com*, accessed February 15, 2014, http://gizmodo.com; Pete Putnam, "HDTV Expert—What Do You Do After You Realize LCD's Glory Days Are Gone?" *HDTV Magazine*, accessed February 15, 2014, www.hdtvmagazine.com; Alfred Poor, "HDTV Almanac—LED Backlight Prices Falling," *HDTV Magazine*, accessed February 15, 2014, www.hdtvmagazine.com.

7. "A Gadget's Life: From Gee-Whiz to Junk," *Washington Post*, accessed February 15, 2014, www.washingtonpost.com; "Retail After Disruption: DVD Rental," *Adam Griff*, accessed February 15, 2014, www.adamgriff.com.

8. Company website, www.burgerking.com, accessed February 16, 2014; Alexandra Sifferlin "Have It the Healthier Way: Burger King Reveals Low Fat Fries," *Time*, accessed February 15, 2014, http://healthland.time.com.

9. "Twenty-Eight Uses for Everyday Items," *Real Simple*, accessed February 15, 2014, www.realsimple.com.

10. Company website, http://rideonewheel.com, accessed February 16, 2014; John Biggs, "The Best of CES," *TechCrunch*, accessed February 16, 2014, http://techcrunch.com; company website, "One Wheel: The Self-Balancing Electric Skateboard by Future Motion," www.kickstarter.com, accessed February 16, 2014.

11. James K. Sanborn, "Tropical Uniform Prototypes Fail to Deliver," *Marine Times*, accessed February 15, 2014, www.marinecorpstimes.com.

12. Erik Derr, "Mercedes Launches Biggest Product Offensive," *Wards Auto*, accessed February 15, 2014, http://wardsauto.com; Jeremy Korzeniewski, "Mercedes S600 Takes Its Place As Brand's Halo Sedan," *Auto Blog*, accessed February 16, 2014, www.autoblog.com.

13. Karen Tumbokon, "Worst Products Seen at CES 2013," *Heavy.com*, accessed February 15, 2014, www.heavy.com; company website, www.brookstone.com, accessed February 15, 2014.

14. Company website, www.ikea.com, accessed February 15, 2014.

15. Brett Casella, "21 Recognizable Brand Logos with Strong Brand Identities," *Impact Bound*, accessed February 16, 2014, www.impactbnd.com; company website, http://interbrand.com, accessed February 15, 2014.

16. Company website, "Green Mission," www.wholefoodsmarket.com, accessed February 16, 2014; Bruce Watson, Fast Food's Green Trend: Making Big Macs and Lattes More Earth-Friendly," *Daily Finance*, accessed February 15, 2014, www.dailyfinance.com.

17. Government website, "Nutrition Labeling Information," www.fsis.usda.gov, accessed February 16, 2014; Alexandra Sifferlin "FDA Revising Food Nutrition Labels," *Time*, accessed February 15, 2014, http://healthland.time.com.

18. James O'Toole, "Google to Sell Motorola Mobility Unit to Lenovo," *CNN Money*, accessed February 15, 2014, http://money.cnn.com; Phil Goldstein, "Google's Nexus One Promises New Distribution Channel for Smartphones," *Fierce Wireless*, accessed February 15, 2014, www.fiercewireless.com; Tom Krazit, "Google's Mobile Hopes Go Beyond Nexus One," *CNET News*, accessed February 15, 2014, http://news.cnet.com; "What Are Unlocked Cell Phones?," *wiseGEEK*, accessed February 15, 2014, www.wisegeek.com.

19. Ian Mount, "Clothing Companies Trying to Find More Direct Paths to Consumers," *The New York Times*, accessed February 15, 2014, www.nytimes.com.

20. Bureau of Labor Statistics, "Occupational Outlook Handbook, 2013–2014 Edition," accessed February 15, 2014, www.bls.gov; U.S. Census Bureau, "County Business Patterns," accessed February 15, 2014, www.census.gov.

21. Company website, www.acehardware.com, accessed February 15, 2014.

22. U.S. Census Bureau, "Quarterly Retail E-Commerce Sales, 3rd Quarter 2013," accessed February 16, 2014, www.census.gov.

23. Herb Weisbaum, "Banks Putting Human Tellers in ATMs," *NBC News*, accessed February 15, 2014, www.nbcnews.com.

24. Company website, http://saksfifthavenue.com, accessed February 15, 2014.

25. Company website, http://soundhawk.com, accessed February 16, 2014; Brad Stone, "Silicon Valley's Hearing Aid," *Bloomberg Businessweek*, accessed February 16, 2014, www.businessweek.com.

26. Company website, www.underarmour.com, accessed February 16, 2014.

27. Company website, www.traderjoes.com, accessed February 16, 2014.

28. Judy Keane, "As Enclosed Malls Decline, 'Lifestyle Centers' Proliferate," *MinnPost*, accessed February 16, 2014, www.minnpost.com; Eric Schwartzberg, "Lifestyle Centers Draw Retailers, Shoppers," *Middletown Journal*, accessed February 16, 2014, www.middletownjournal.com.

29. Twitter website, http://twitter.com/starbucks, accessed June 16, 2014; Facebook website, http://facebook.com/starbucks, accessed June 16, 2014; company website, http://mystarbucksideas.com, accessed February 16, 2014; Robert Gembarski, "How Starbucks Built an Engaging Brand on Social Media," *Branding Personality*, accessed February 16, 2014, www.brandingpersonality.com; "Happy Third Anniversary My Starbucks Idea," *Ideas in Action*, accessed February 16, 2014, http://blogs.starbucks.com.

30. James Kanter, "Luxury Goods May Pick and Choose Venues for Sales," *The New York Times*, accessed February 16, 2014, www.nytimes.com.

31. "Broadway's Serino Coyne and Art Meets Commerce Join Forces," *Broadway World*, accessed February 16, 2014, http://broadwayworld.com.

32. Company website, http://topshop.com, accessed February 16, 2014; company website, http://nordstrom.com, accessed February 16, 2014; "Nordstrom to Expand Topshop and Topman Partnership to 28 Additional Stores This Fall," *PR Newswire*, accessed February 16, 2014, www.prnewswire.com.

33. Company website, www.premiumoutlets.com, accessed February 16, 2014.

34. Company website, www.verayo.com, accessed February 16, 2014; company website, "Metro Group Future Store Initiative," press release, www.metrogroup.com, accessed February 16, 2014.

35. Organization website, "Reports, Trends & Statistics," www.truckline.com, accessed March 12, 2014.

36. Organization website, "Class I Railroad Statistics," www.aar.org, accessed March 12, 2014.

Chapter 13

1. Company website, "Form 10-K," www.apple.com, accessed March 18, 2014; Chris Smith, "Over 40 Million Samsung Tablets Sold This Year, Report Says," *Android Authority*, accessed March 18, 2014, www.androidauthority.com; Sean Patterson, "Tablet Market to Overtake PC's and Notebooks Combined," *WebProNews*, accessed March 18, 2014, www.webpronews.com; Lance Whitney, "Apple Still Tops in Tablets Despite Dwindling Market Share," *CNET News*, accessed March 18, 2014, http://news.cnet.com; Ewan Spence, "Apple's Big Decision on Margin or Market Share Drives Strategy," *Forbes*, accessed March 18, 2014, www.forbes.com.

2. Stuart Elliot, "Creating an Ad Campaign for Oreo as They Turn 100," *The New York Times*, accessed February 19, 2014, www.nytimes.com.

3. John Coyle, "Lexus Sponsors Justin Timberlake Hollywood Concert," *Club Lexus*, accessed February 19, 2014, www.clublexus.com.

4. "In Its Uniquely Objective Analysis of the Impact of Humor in Advertising, Ace Metrix Applies Science to Identify Funniest Ads and Brands for the Last Five Quarters—Doritos, Target and Huggies Found to Be Funniest Brands," *Bull Dog Reporter*, accessed February 20, 2014, www.bulldogreporter.com; Brad Tuttle, "Ha! Ads That Make You Laugh Don't Really Make You Buy," *Time*, accessed February 20, 2014, http://business.time.com.

5. Alexandra Sifferlin "Why We're Spending $1 Trillion on Health Medications," *Time*, accessed February 21, 2014, http://business.time.com; "Persuading the Prescribers: Pharmaceutical Industry Marketing and Its Influence on Physicians and Patients," *Pew Health Research*, accessed February 19, 2014, www.pewhealth.org.

6. Rachel Lamb, "High-End, Mass-Market Brand Collaborations Create Unusual Opportunities for Luxe Marketers: Luxury Institute," *Evins*, accessed February 19, 2014, http://evins.com.

7. Chris Woodyard, "Hot, Small Luxury Cars Target Younger Buyers," *USA Today*, accessed February 19, 2014, www.usatoday.com.

8. Katie Kindelan, "Doritos 'Crash the Super Bowl' Champ Wins $1 Million," *ABC News,* accessed March 17, 2014, http://abcnews.go.com; Dale Buss, "Doritos 'Crash the Super Bowl' Campaign Goes Global with $1 Million Prize," *Brand Channel,* accessed February 20, 2014, www.brandchannel.com.

9. Edward Owen, "10 Incredibly Shameless Product Placements in Well-Loved TV Shows," *WhatCulture.com,* accessed February 20, 2014, http://whatculture.com; Anthony Crupi, "Ford, Coca-Cola Return for Season 13 of American Idol," *AdWeek,* accessed February 20, 2014, www.adweek.com; Brad Tuttle, "Superman the Sellout? Man of Steel Has over 100 Promotional Partners," *Time,* accessed February 20, 2014, http://business.time.com.

10. "Cathay Pacific Staff Surprise Travelers with Festive Flash Mob," *HR Grapevine,* accessed February 20, 2014, http://hrgrapevine.com.

11. Lorraine Carter, "Guerrilla Marketing: Targeting One to Reach Many with Your Brand," accessed February 20, 2014, www.personadesign.ie; Calum McGuigan, "Red Bull: Masterminds of New Age Marketing," *Creative Guerilla Marketing,* accessed February 20, 2014, www.creativeguerillamarketing.com.

12. David Lamoureux, "How Many Marketing Messages Do We See in a Day?" *Fluid Drive Media,* accessed February 20, 2014, www.fluiddrivemedia.com.

13. Bradley Johnson, "10 Things You Should Know About the Global Ad Market," *AdAge,* accessed February 22, 2014, http://adage.com.

14. Jim Edwards, "The 10 Biggest Advertisers In America, Ranked By Dollars Spent Annually," *Business Insider,* accessed February 22, 2014, www.businessinsider.com.

15. Company website, "Kantar Media Reports U.S. Advertising Expenditures Increased 3.5% in the Second Quarter of 2013," *Kantar Media,* accessed February 21, 2014, www.kantarmedia.com; company website, "Top 10 Advertisers January–September 2013," *Kantar Media,* accessed February 21, 2014, http://content.kantarmedia.com.

16. Organization website, http://keepachildalive.org, accessed February 20, 2014.

17. Organization website, "Foundation Fact Sheet," www.gatesfoundation.org, accessed February 20, 2014.

18. Bradley Johnson, "10 Things You Should Know About the Global Ad Market."

19. Jim Edwards, "TV Is Dying and Here Are the Stats That Prove It," *Business Insider,* accessed February 23, 2014, www.businessinsider.com.

20. Todd Spangler, "As Netflix Rises, Subscriptions to HBO, Showtime and Other Premium Nets Shrink as Percentage of U.S. Households: Report," *Variety,* accessed February 23, 2014, http://variety.com; Dustin Rowles, "The 25 Best Streaming Series on Netflix Instant Streaming, Ranked," *Uproxx,* accessed February 23, 2014, www.uproxx.com; Drew Prindle, "Best Media Streaming Services," *Digital Trends,* accessed February 21, 2014; Dorothy Pomerantz, "How Netflix and AMC Are Spurring a New Arms Race," *Forbes,* accessed February 21, 2014, www.forbes.com.

21. Company website, https://www.smallbusinessbiggame.com, accessed February 20, 2014.

22. Jane Sasseen, Kenny Olmstead, and Amy Mitchell, "The State of the News Media 2013," *State of the Media,* accessed February 23, 2014, http://stateofthemedia.org; "Most Digital Ad Growth Now Goes Mobile, Desktop Growth Falters," *eMarketer,* accessed February 23, 2014, www.emarketer.com; Jane Sasseen, Kenny Olmstead, and Amy Mitchell, "Digital: As Mobile Grows Rapidly, the Pressure on

News Intensifies," *State of the Media,* accessed February 23, 2014, http://stateofthemedia.org.

23. Association website, "Ashley Wagner," www.asklistenlearn.org, accessed February 20, 2014; Tessa, "How Advertising Has Changed in the Digital Age," *Damsels in Success,* accessed February 20, 2014, www.damselsinsuccess.com.

24. Laura Stampler, "How Dove's 'Real Beauty Sketches' Became the Most Viral Video Ad of All Time," *BusinessInsider,* accessed February 20, 2014, www.businessinsider.com; "Dove's Sketches of Real Women Hit 30 Million Views, Tops Viral Chart," *AdAge,* accessed February 20, 2014, http://adage.com.

25. "Newspapers by the Numbers," *State of the Media,* accessed February 23, 2014, http://stateofthemedia.org; Amy Mitchell, Mark Jurkowitz, and Emily Guskin, "The Newspaper Industry Overall," *Pew Research Journalism Project,* accessed February 23, 2014, www.journalism.org.

26. Levi Shapiro, "State of the Digital Music Industry 2014: An Insider's View," *Geektime.com,* accessed February 21, 2014, www.geektime.com; "Online Radio Consumption," *Marketing Charts,* accessed February 19, 2014, www.marketingcharts.com; "Despite Small Audience, Internet Radio Ads Have a Special Appeal to Marketers," *eMarketer,* accessed February 19, 2014, www.emarketer.com.

27. Kara Davis, Dino Fire, and Hamilton Davison, "Catalogs: The Consumer's Point of View," *FGI Research,* accessed February 19, 2014, http://www.memberize.net; Michelle Fox, "Why Retail Catalogs Survive, Even Thrive, in the Internet Age," *CNBC,* accessed February 19, 2014, www.cnbc.com.

28. Tanya Irwin, "Credit Card Direct Mail Hits 25-Month Low," *Marketing Daily,* accessed February 19, 2014, www.mediapost.com.

29. Association website, "Out of Home Advertising Second Quarter Revenue up 5%," www.ooaa.org, accessed February 19, 2014.

30. Ibid.

31. Company website, www.cbsoutdoor.com, accessed February 23, 2014; company website, "What Is Digital Outdoor?" accessed February 21, 2014, www.watchfiredigitaloutdoor.com; company website, "Electronic Advertising," www.cbsoutdoor.com, accessed February 21, 2014.

32. "Taxi Cab Statistics," *Statistic Brain,* accessed February 20, 2014, www.statisticbrain.com; Matt Flegenheimer, "$1 Million Medallions Stifling the Dreams of Cab Drivers," *The New York Times,* accessed February 20, 2014, www.nytimes.com.

33. E.J. Schultz, "Forecast: Sponsorship Spending Will Slow in 2014," *AdAge,* accessed February 20, 2014, http://adage.com.

34. Company website, www.hendrickmotorsports.com, accessed February 20, 2014; Kurt Badenhausen, "The Most Valuable Nascar Teams," *Forbes,* accessed February 20, 2014, www.forbes.com; Kurt Badenhausen, "Hendrick Motorsports Tops List of Nascar's Most Valuable Teams," *Forbes,* accessed February 20, 2014, www.forbes.com.

35. Jennifer Wood, "10 Best Selling Infomercial Products," *Mental Floss,* accessed February 21, 2014, http://mentalfloss.com.

36. Company website, www.adsticks.com, accessed February 21, 2014; company website, http://cartvertising.com, accessed February 20, 2014.

37. Yohap News Agency, "Samsung's Sales Promotion Costs Top Ad Spending through September," *Global Post,* accessed February 21, 2014, www.globalpost.com.

38. "Local Biz Spending on Promotion Easily Trumps Ad Dollars," *Marketing Charts,* accessed February 21, 2014, www.marketingcharts.com.

39. Company website, "Motorola Trade Up," www.motorolatradeup.com, accessed February 21, 2014; "Inmar Releases Coupon Trends for 2013," *PR Web*, accessed February 21, 2014, www.prweb.com.

40. Herb Weisbaum, "Fewer Rebates Offered, but Deals Are Getting Better," *Today*, accessed February 21, 2014, www.today.com.

41. Company website, www.wirespring.com, accessed February 21, 2014; Josh Constine, "Facebook Reveals 78% of Its Users Are Mobile," *TechCrunch*, accessed February 21, 2014, http://techcrunch.com.

42. Steve Crowe, "CES 2014 Attendance Tops 150,000," *CEPro*, accessed February 21, 2014, www.cepro.com; "U.S. Trade Shows Certified by U.S. Department of Commerce," *International Trade Administration*, accessed February 21, 2014, http://export.gov.

43. U.S. Department of Labor, Economic News Release, Table 5. Employment by Major Occupational Group, 2010 and Projected 2022, *Bureau of Labor Statistics*, accessed February 21, 2014, www.bls.gov.

44. Richard Lawler, "$35,000 Prima Cinema Player Brings Movies Home As Soon As They Hit Theaters," *Engadget*, accessed February 23, 2014, www.engadget.com; Nick Jaynes, "Porsche 918 Spyder Looks Like a Million Bucks—Because It Is," *Digital Trends*, accessed February 23, 2014, www.digitaltrends.com; "$1,200,000 Piano: The Kuhn Bösendorfer," *YouTube*, accessed February 23, 2014, www.youtube.com.

45. "Dynamic Pricing: What Retailers Need to Know About Competing in Real Time," *eMarketer*, accessed February 21, 2014, www.emarketer.com.

46. Company website, www.astrazeneca.com, accessed February 21, 2014; company website, www.aztouchpoints.com, accessed February 21, 2014; Jeanne Whalen, "Drug Makers Replace Reps with Digital Tools," *The Wall Street Journal*, accessed February 21, 2014, http://online.wsj.com.

47. Government website, "Q&A for Telemarketers and Sellers About the Do Not Call Provisions of the FTC's Telemarketing Sales Rule," www.business.ftc.gov, accessed February 21, 2014.

48. Barbara Weaver Smith, "Ten Tactics to Drive B2B Sales with Social Media," *Blog World*, accessed February 21, 2014, www.blogworld.com.

49. Nat Robinson, "SlideRocket Presentation Tip—4 Ways for Using Multimedia Strategically," *SlideRocket*, accessed February 21, 2014, www.sliderocket.com.

50. Marisa Novello, "Outpouring of Support for Local Merchant," *Seacoastonline.com*, accessed February 21, 2014, www.seacoastonline.com.

51. Association website, www.komen.org, accessed February 21, 2014.

52. Company website, "Nestlé Launches First Ever Super Bowl Commercial," www.nestleusa.com, accessed February 21, 2014.

53. Dhanya Skariachan, "Family Dollar Hurt by Internal Problems COO Resigns," *Reuters*, accessed February 21, 2014, www.reuters.com; Paul Ziobro, "Family Dollar Cuts Outlook on Weaker Same-Store Sales," *The Wall Street Journal*, accessed February 21, 2014, http://online.wsj.com.

54. Richard Esposito, "'Wise Guys' Accused of Scalping $29 Million in Springsteen, Yankees, Miley Cyrus Tickets," *ABC News*, accessed February 21, 2014, http://abcnews.go.com.

55. Alex Mindlin, "$2.22? Gosh, That Sounds Expensive," *The New York Times*, accessed February 21, 2014, www.nytimes.com.

End of Part 4: Launching Your Marketing Career

1. U.S. Department of Labor, "Market and Survey Researchers," *Occupational Outlook Handbook, 2014–2015*, Bureau of Labor Statistics, accessed February 23, 2014, www.bls.gov.

2. U.S. Department of Labor, "Advertising Sales Agents," *Occupational Outlook Handbook, 2014–2015*, Bureau of Labor Statistics, accessed February 23, 2014, www.bls.gov.

3. U.S. Department of Labor, "Public Relations Managers and Specialists and Advertising Managers," *Occupational Outlook Handbook, 2014–2015*, Bureau of Labor Statistics, accessed February 23, 2014, www.bls.gov.

4. Ibid.

Chapter 14

1. Company website, "Our Business," https://www.kaggle.com; Joshua Brustein, "Kaggle's William Cukierski on Data Sharing, Competitions," *Bloomberg Businessweek*, accessed March 20, 2014, www.businessweek.com; Darren Dahl, "How Kaggle Uses the Crowd to Solve Your Big Data Problems," *Inc.*, accessed March 20, 2014, www.inc.com; Quentin Hardy, "Big Data Shrinks to Grow," *The New York Times*, accessed March 20, 2014, http://bits.blogs.nytimes.com; company website, "The Zettabyte Era—Trends and Analysis," www.cisco.com, accessed March 20, 2014.

2. Ernest Von Simpson, "The New Role of the CIO," *Bloomberg Businessweek*, accessed February 24, 2014, www.businessweek.com; David Moschella, Doug Neal, John Taylor, and Piet Opperman, "*Consumerization of Information Technology*," *Leading Edge Forum*, accessed February 24, 2014, http://lef.csc.com.

3. Chunka Mui, "These 6 Technologies Will Make or Break Every Information-Intensive Company—Including Yours," *Forbes*, accessed February 24, 2014, www.forbes.com.

4. Government website, "Questions Planned for the 2010 Census and American Community Survey (March 2008)," http://2010census.gov, accessed February 27, 2014.

5. Museum website, "Timeline of Computer History," www.computerhistory.org, accessed February 24, 2014.

6. "Apple Mac's Average Selling Price Holds Steady at $1300 as iPad Erodes PC Sales," *Mac Daily News*, accessed February 25, 2014, http://macdailynews.com; "Average Cost of PCs Today," *Noble PCs*, accessed February 25, 2014, http://noblepcs.com.

7. "Chinese Supercomputer Is the World's Fastest at 33,860 Trillion Calculations per Second," *Telegraph UK*, accessed February 26, 2014, www.telegraph.co.uk.

8. Nicole Kobie, "Tablet Sales to Overtake PCs This Quarter," *PC Pro*, accessed February 21, 2014, www.pcpro.co.uk.

9. Ibid.

10. Stephen Vaughan-Nickels, "A Third of American Adults Now Own Tablet Computers," *ZDNet*, accessed February 25, 2014, http://zdnet.com.

11. Stuart Dredge, "Mobile Apps Revenues Tipped to Reach $26 Billion in 2013," *The Guardian*, accessed February 27, 2014, www.theguardian.com.

12. David Pierce, "5 Wi-Fi Hotspot Finders to Find Free Wi-Fi Spots Near You," *Make Use of*, accessed February 21, 2014, www.makeuseof.com.

13. Bradley Mitchell, "WiMAX", *About.com*, accessed February 25, 2014, http://compnetworking.about.com.

14. Company website, www.virtual.com, accessed February 25, 2014.

15. Leena Rao, "Google Voice Founder Sets His Sights on VoIP Once Again," *Tech Crunch*, accessed February 25, 2014, http://techcrunch.com; Charles Schelle, "Update: Verizon VoIP Phone Outage Resolved." *Sarasota Patch*, accessed February 25, 2014, http://sarasota.patch.com; Bryan M. Wolfe,

"AT&T Offering VoIP International Calls for Anyone with a Smartphone," *App Advice*, accessed February 25, 2014, http://appadvice.com.

16. Organization website, "Recommendations for the Remediation of Bots in ISP Networks," http://tools.ietf.org, accessed February 25, 2014.

17. Gillian Mahoney, "Hackers Steal Credit Card Data from Neiman Marcus Customers," *ABC News*, accessed February 25, 2014, http://abcnews.go.com.

18. Abby Simmons, "Lawmakers Take on Smart Phone Theft," *Star Tribune*, accessed February 26, 2014, www.startribune.com.

19. "Protect Your iPhone Against Theft with Activation Lock in iOS 7," *iPhone Hacks*, accessed February 26 2014, www.iphonehacks.com.

20. Abby Simmons, "Lawmakers Take on Smart Phone Theft."

21. Dan Steiner, "Staggering Cost of Malware Is Now over $100 billion a Year," *Yahoo Small Business*, accessed February 26, 2014, http://smallbusiness.yahoo.com.

22. Charlie Osbourne, "Symantec Takes on One of Largest Botnets in History," *CNET*, accessed February 27, 2014, http://news.cnet.com; James Vincent, "Microsoft Disrupts Zero Access, One of the Largest Botnets," accessed February 27, 2014, www.independent.co.uk.

23. Joshua Levinson, "Watchout—There's a New Android Trojan Horse About," *Cult of Android*, accessed February 26, 2014, http://cultofandroid.com.

24. Company website, "Data Loss Statistics," www.bostoncomputing.net, accessed February 27, 2014.

25. Company website, www.falconstor.com, accessed February 27, 2014; company website, "FalconStor Provides Data Migration Technology for Dell Services Offering," press release, www.falconstor.com, accessed February 27, 2014.

26. "Eight Trends Driving the Future of Information Technology," *IT Business Edge*, accessed February 27, 2014, www.itbusinessedge.com; "Top 10 Strategic Technology Trends for 2014," *Information Management*, accessed February 26, 2014, www.information-management.com; Timiko De Freytas-Tamura, "Box, a Data Storage Company Prepares to Compete Overseas," *The New York Times*, accessed February 27, 2014, www.nytimes.com.

27. Roger Cheng, "How Much Is the Internet of Everything Worth? Cisco Says $19 Trillion, *CNET*, February 26, 2014, http://reviews.cnet.com.

28. Company website, http://Infosys.com, accessed February 27, 2014.

End of Part 5: Launching Your Information Technology Career

1. Government website, "Computer and Information Technology Occupations," *Occupational Outlook Handbook: 2014–2015*," www.bls.gov, accessed February 27, 2014; "Computer and Information Systems Managers," *Occupational Outlook Handbook: 2014–2015*," www.bls.gov, accessed February 27, 2014.

2. Jada Graves, "The Best Jobs of 2014," *US News and World Report*, accessed February 27, 2014, http://money.usnews.com; Jada Graves, "11 Best Technology Jobs of 2014," *US News and World Report*, accessed February 27, 2014, http://money.usnews.com.

Chapter 15

1. Company website, www.intuit.com, accessed March 24, 2014; Jeffery Battersby, "Tax Apps for iOS Review: File Your Taxes on Your iPad or iPhone," *Mac World*, accessed March 24, 2014, www.macworld.com; Hal Gregersen, "How Intuit Innovates by Challenging Itself," *HBR Blog Network*, accessed March 22, 2014, http://blogs.hbr.org; Ysa Perez, "Intuit: How Design Drove Its Turnaround," *Bloomberg Businessweek*, accessed March 20, 2014, www.businessweek.com; Dan Schwabel, "Intuit's Brad Smith: How to Succeed in a Bad Economy," *Forbes*, accessed March 20, 2014, www.forbes.com; Max Nisen, "Intuit Founder: Success Makes Companies Stupid," *Business Insider*, accessed March 20, 2014, www.businessinsider.com.

2. Bureau of Labor Statistics, *Occupational Outlook Handbook, 2014–2015*, http://data.bls.gov, accessed March 1, 2014; "Occupational Employment Statistics, Accountants and Auditors," www.bls.gov, accessed March 1, 2014.

3. Company website, "2014 Accounting Entry Level Jobs," http://internmatch.com, accessed March 2, 2014; NACE Research, *Job Outlook 2012*, Fig. 8, National Association of Colleges and Employers, www.unco.edu, accessed March 2, 2014.

4. Association website, "AARP Foundation Tax-Aide Locator," accessed March 1, 2014, www.aarp.org.

5. Company website, "Grant Thornton LLP Revenue Up for Fiscal Year 2013," http://news.grantthornton.com, accessed March 4, 2014; "The 2013 *Accounting Today* Top 100 Firms," *Accounting Today*, accessed March 1, 2014, www.accountant.adp.com; "Deloitte Replaces PwC as Biggest Global Firm," *Economia*, accessed March 1, 2014, http://economia.icaew.com.

6. "A New Way to Attract Accounting Talent? E&Y Might Be onto Something Big," *Accounting WEB*, accessed March 1, 2014, www.accountingweb.com; Matt Berndt, "Getting Your Foot in the Door at Ernst & Young," *The Campus Career Coach*, accessed March 1, 2014, http://thecampuscareercoach.com.

7. Michael Rapoport, "Big Four Firms to Be Questioned on Push into Consulting," *The Wall Street Journal*, accessed March 1, 2014, http://online.wsj.com.

8. Association website, www.fasb.org, accessed March 1, 2014.

9. Association website, "Updates for Private Companies for Accounting for Goodwill, Interest Rate Swaps," www.fasb.org, accessed March 2, 2014.

10. Company website, "Johnson & Johnson Annual Report 2013: Consolidated Balance Sheets," http://files.shareholder.com/downloads/JNJ, accessed March 3, 2014.

11. Matt Jagst, "Mobile Computing Takes Accountants to a New Level of Productivity," *Accounting WEB*, accessed March 3, 2014, www.accountingweb.com.

12. Company website, "Back in the Day," http://mint.com, accessed March 3, 2014; Willy Staley, "Which Are the Best Personal Financial Management (PFM) Tools?" *MyBankTracker.com*, accessed March 2, 2014, www.mybanktracker.com.

13. Nacha Cattan and Eric Martin, "Mexico Central Bank Cuts 2013 Growth Forecast as Exports Stall," *Bloomberg News*, accessed March 3, 2014, www.bloomberg.com.

14. IFRS website, "Comprehensive Review 2012–2014," www.ifrs.org, accessed March 3, 2014; company website, "IFRS and US GAAP: Similarities and Differences," www.pwc.com, accessed March 3, 2014.

15. Company website, "SEC Reaffirms Its Commitment to IFRS," www.ey.com, accessed March 2, 2014; company website, "IFRS vs. GAAP—What Does This Have to Do with the Financial Crisis?" www.meirc.com, accessed March 2, 2014.

Chapter 16

1. Kelly Phillips Erb, "IRS Says Bitcoin, Other Convertible Virtual Currency to Be Taxed Like Stock," *Forbes,* accessed March 30, 2014, www.forbes.com; Kashmir Hill, "Bitcoin Battle: Warren Buffet vs. Marc Andreessen," *Forbes,* accessed March 30, 2014, www.forbes.com; Jim Edwards, "If Bitcoin Is So Secure, Why Have There Been Dozens of Bitcoin Bank Robberies and Millions in Losses?," *Business Insider,* accessed March 30, 2014, www.businessinsider.com; Robert McMillan, "Bitcoin Boomtown: Digital Currency Tops $400, Mining Rigs Sell for $3M," *Wired,* accessed March 30, 2014, www.wired.com; Maria Bustillos, "The Bitcoin Boom," *The New Yorker,* accessed March 30, 2014, www.newyorker.com.

2. Shira Ovide, "Dell Offers Employee Buyouts to Cut Costs," *The Wall Street Journal,* accessed March 26, 2014, http://blogs.wsj.com; Scott Cendrowski and Stephen Gandel, "20 Biggest Stock Losers—Dell," *CNN,* accessed March 26, 2014, http://money.cnn.com; David Gelles, "Daring $24 Billion Deal to Make Dell Relevant," *Financial Times,* accessed March 25, 2014, www.ft.com; "Dell's Buy-Out: Heading for the Exit," *The Economist,* accessed March 25, 2014, www.economist.com; Loren Steffy, "HP, Dell Fight to Stay Relevant," *Houston Chronicle,* accessed March 25, 2014, www.chron.com; Charles Arthur, "Dell Revenues Slump as Tablets and Smartphones Eat into Market," *The Guardian,* accessed March 25, 2014, www.guardian.com; Jeffrey Burt, "Dell Finances Continue to Be Hit by Struggling PC Market," *eWeek.com,* accessed March 25, 2014, www.eweek.com; Andrew Cunningham, "Lenovo and Asus Are Up, Dell and HP Are Down, and PC Sales Are Slowing," *Ars Technica,* accessed March 25, 2014, http://arstechnica.com; Ben Worthen, "H-P, Dell Struggle as Buyers Shun PCs," *The Wall Street Journal,* accessed March 25, 2014, http://online.wsj.com; Ben Berkowitz and Edwin Chan, "Dell to Go Private in Landmark $24.4 Billion Deal," *Reuters,* accessed March 25, 2014, www.reuters.com.

3. "China's Hunan Issues Special Bonds to Tackle Heavy Metal Pollution," *Metal.com,* accessed March 4, 2014, www.metal.com.

4. Patrick Hoge, "Tech IPO Pipeline Very Strong," *San Francisco Business Times,* accessed March 24, 2014, www.bizjournals.com; Kevin Kelleher, "2014's Tech IPO Pipeline Is Clogged. Here's What Could Clear It," *Time,* accessed March 24, 2014, http://business.time.com.

5. Organization website, "NYSE Statistics Archive," www.nyse.com, accessed March 24, 2014.

6. Organization website, "Rule 300. Trading Licenses," http://rules.nyse.com, accessed March 24, 2014; "Fee Changes Effective January 1, 2012," *Trader Update,* accessed March 20, 2014, www.nyse.com.

7. Ryan Tracy, "Tally of U.S. Banks Sink to Record Low," *The Wall Street Journal,* accessed March 24, 2014, http://online.wsj.com; government website, "Total Assets of U.S. Commercial Banks," accessed March 24, 2014, http://research.stlouisfed.org.

8. Joseph Rizzi, "Community Banks Can Survive and Prosper—If They Adapt," *American Banker,* accessed March 24, 2014, www.americanbanker.com.

9. Government website, "FDIC—Statistics on Depository Institutions Report," accessed March 24, 2014, www.fdic.gov.

10. Jim Romeo, "The Debit Card Two-Step: Fees and Fraud," *Transaction World,* accessed March 28, 2014, www.transactionworld.net.

11. Robin Sidel, "After Years of Growth, Banks Are Pruning Their Branches," *The Wall Street Journal,* accessed March 4, 2014, http://online.wsj.com.

12. Government website, "Safe Internet Banking," accessed March 9, 2014, www.fdic.gov.

13. Association website, "NCUA Quarterly U.S. Map Review," www.ncua.gov, accessed March 28, 2014; Halah Touryaiai, "America's Biggest Banks, JPMorgan Takes a Bigger Lead over Bank of America," *Forbes,* accessed March 28, 2014, www.forbes.com.

14. Government website, "Financial Accounts of the United States," www.federalreserve.gov, accessed March 17, 2014.

15. Organization website, "Assets of Private Pension Funds by Type of Asset, 2008–2010," www.iii.org, accessed March 18, 2014; Robin Farzad, "Pensions Sell Stocks to Buy Bonds," *Bloomberg Businessweek,* accessed March 17, 2014, www.businessweek.com; government website, "Financial Accounts of the United States, F.117 Private Pension Funds," and "Financial Accounts of the United States, L.116 Private and Public Pension Funds," www.federalreserve.gov, accessed March 17, 2014.

16. "Table 1 Total Net Assets, Number of Funds, Number of Share Classes, and Number of Shareholder Accounts of the U.S. Mutual Fund Industry," *2013 Investment Company Fact Book,* accessed March 17, 2014, www.icifactbook.org.

17. "Table 1 Total Net Assets, Number of Funds, Number of Share Classes, and Number of Shareholder Accounts of the U.S. Mutual Fund Industry," *2013 Investment Company Fact Book,* accessed March 17, 2014, www.icifactbook.org.

18. Government website, "The 2013 Federal Reserve Payments Study," http://fedpaymentsimprovement.org, accessed March 19, 2014.

19. "Bank Rankings—Top Banks in the World," *Acuity.com,* accessed March 19, 2014, www.acuity.com.

Chapter 17

1. Organization website, www.worldvisionmicro.org, accessed April 3, 2014; company website, www.prosper.com, accessed April 3, 2014; company website, www.lendingclub.com; Andrew Blackman, "Borrow or Lend Online—But Be Careful," *The Wall Street Journal,* accessed April 3, 2014, http://online.wsj.com; Dave Michaels, "Crowdfunding for Internet Stock Sales Approved by SEC," *Bloomberg News,* accessed April 3, 2014, www.bloomberg.com.

2. Russ Banham, "Earning Their Keep," *CFO Magazine,* accessed March 23, 2014, www.cfo.com.

3. Company website, "Orders and Deliveries," www.airbus.com, accessed July 6, 2014.

4. Company website, www.gencomarketplace.com, accessed March 22, 2014.

5. Richard Smith, "Why Are U.S. Corporations Still Hoarding $1.5 Trillion in Cash?" *Daily Finance,* accessed March 24, 2014, www.dailyfinance.com.

6. Neal E. Boudette and William Boston, "BMW Readies U.S. Factory Expansion," *The Wall Street Journal,* accessed March 24, 2014, http://online.wsj.com.

7. Company website, "Production Overview Stats and Information," www.bmwusfactory.com, accessed April 2, 2014; Neal E. Boudette, "BMW to Invest $1 Billion to Expand Plant in South Carolina," *The Wall Street Journal,* accessed April 2, 2014, http://online.wsj.com; Neal E. Boudette and William Boston, "BMW Readies U.S. Factory Expansion," *The Wall Street Journal,* accessed March 24, 2014, http://online.wsj.com.

8. Government website, "Federal Reserve Bank of St. Louis, Series: AEXUSUK, U.S./U.K. Foreign Exchange Rate," http://research.stlouisfed.org, accessed March 23, 2014.

9. "Federal Reserve Board, Commercial Paper Outstanding, Federal Reserve Release," www.federalreserve.gov, accessed March 24, 2014.

10. Sven Grundberg, "Nokia, Back in Black, Scraps Dividend," *The Wall Street Journal*, accessed March 25, 2014, http://online.wsj.com.

11. Daniel Eran Dilger, "Shares of Apple Inc. near Ex-Dividend as It Gears Up to Distribute $2.7 Billion to Shareholders," *Apple Insider*, accessed July 6, 2014, http://appleinsider.com.

12. "Commercial Paper Outstanding," www.federalreserve.gov, accessed March 25, 2014.

13. Katie Linsell and Jessica Summers, "Greece Recovery Gains Momentum in First Bank Bond Sale Since '09," *Bloomberg News*, accessed March 25, 2014, www.bloomberg.com.

14. Sarika Gangar, "U.S. Company Bond Sales of $1.48 Trillion Set Annual Record," *Bloomberg News*, accessed March 25, 2014, www.bloomberg.com.

15. Company website, www.dfj.com, accessed March 25, 2014.

16. "Company Overview of 3G Capital," *Bloomberg Businessweek*, accessed March 26, 2014, http://investing.businessweek.com.

17. Company website, www.swfinstitute.org, accessed March 26, 2014; Mikael Holter, "Biggest Wealth Fund Forced to Sell Stocks as Limit Breached," *Bloomberg News*, accessed March 26, 2014, www.bloomberg.com.

18. Kelly Bit, "Hedge Funds Trail Stocks for 5th Year with a 7.4% Return," *Bloomberg News*, accessed March 25, 2014, www.bloomberg.com.

19. "Hedge Fund Industry Reports," *Hedge Fund Research*, www.hedgeresearch.com, accessed March 25, 2014.

20. Reed Albergotti and Ian Sherr, "Facebook to Buy Virtual Reality Firm, Oculus, for $2 Billion," *The Wall Street Journal*, accessed March 25, 2014, http://online.wsj.com.

21. Rory Maher, "Disney to Acquire Marvel in $4 Billion Deal," *Business Insider*, accessed March 25, 2014, www.businessinsider.com.

22. Steven Miller, "Leveraged Loans: LBO Volume Surges in 2013 Thanks to Jumbo Deals," accessed March 24, 2014, www.forbes.com; Hamid Mehran and Stavros Peristiani, "U.S. Leveraged Buyouts: The Importance of Financial Visibility," *Liberty Street Economics*, accessed March 24, 2014, http://libertystreeteconomics.newyorkfed.org.

23. Alistair Barr, "Google Agrees to Sell Motorola to Lenovo for $2.9 Billion," *USA Today*, accessed April 2, 2014, www.usatoday.com.

24. "6 Spinoff Successes," *Forbes*, accessed March 24, 2014, www.forbes.com; Coach, Inc. (COH New York), *Bloomberg Businessweek*, http://investing.businessweek.com, accessed March 24, 2014; Emily Morris, "Sara Lee Spinoff Hillshire Brands to Debut Amid Acquisition Speculation," *Chicago Sun Times*, www.suntimes.com, accessed March 24, 2014, www.suntimes.com; "Sara Lee Plans Coach Spin Off," *The New York Times*, accessed March 24, 2014, www.nytimes.com.

25. Newmont Mining Corporation, "Newmont Continues to Divest Non-Core Assets with Sale of 5.4% Equity Interest in Paladin Energy," *Yahoo Finance*, accessed March 25, 2014, http://finance.yahoo.com.

End of Part 6: Launching Your Finance Career

1. Bureau of Labor Statistics, "Projections Overview," *Occupational Outlook Handbook, 2014–2015*, www.bls.gov, accessed March 24, 2014.

2. Bureau of Labor Statistics, "Business and Finance: Financial Analysts," *Occupational Outlook Handbook 2014–2015*, www.bls.gov, accessed April 7, 2014.

3. Bureau of Labor Statistics, "Financial Managers," *Occupational Outlook Handbook, 2014–2015*, www.bls.gov, accessed March 24, 2014.

Appendix A

1. Joel Schectman, "The Morning Risk Report: FedEx Caught in New York Tobacco Tax Fight," *The Wall Street Journal*, accessed April 1, 2014, http://online.wsj.com,; Larry Neumeister, "NY Attorney General Sues FedEx over Cigarettes," *Bloomberg Businessweek*, accessed April 1, 2014, www.businessweek.com; Dareh Gregorian, "FedEx Faces $235 Million Lawsuit over Untaxed Cigarettes," *New York Daily News*, accessed April 1, 2014, www.nydailynews.com.

2. Joanna C. Schwartz, "Learning from Litigation," *The New York Times*, accessed April 1, 2014, www.nytimes.com; National Federation of Independent Business, "Frivolous Lawsuits," accessed April 1, 2014, www.nfib.com.

3. "All States Have Silly Laws," http://foodstamp.aphsa.org/01wkshps/AllStatesHaveSillyLaws.pdf, accessed April 2, 2014.

4. United States Court of Appeals for the Fourth Circuit, www.ca4.uscourts.gov, accessed April 2, 2014.

5. U.S. Supreme Court government website, "The Justices' Caseload," Supreme Court of the United States, www.supremecourt.gov, accessed April 2, 2014.

6. Matthew Dalton and William Mauldin, "WTO Confirms China Loses Rare-Earths Case," *The Wall Street Journal*, accessed April 1, 2014, http://online.wsj.com; Shawn Donnan, "WTO Rules Against China on 'Rare Earths' Export Restrictions," *Financial Times*, accessed April 1, 2014, www.ft.com; Keith Bradsher, "Trade Issues with China Flare Anew," *The New York Times*, accessed April 1, 2014, www.nytimes.com; Stephanie Ginter, "WTO Lawsuit over China's Rare Earth," *Energy & Capital*, accessed April 1, 2014, www.energyandcapital.com.

7. Peter J. Henning, "High-Frequency Trading Falls in the Cracks of Criminal Law," *The New York Times*, accessed April 9, 2014, www.nytimes.com; "FBI to Probe High-Frequency Stock Trading," *CBS News*, accessed April 1, 2014, www.cbsnews.com.

8. Charlie Savage, "Deal Reached on Extension of Patriot Act," *The New York Times*, accessed April 1, 2014, www.nytimes.com; Gail Russell Chaddock, "Patriot Act: Three Controversial Provisions That Congress Voted to Keep," *Christian Science Monitor*, accessed April 1, 2014, www.csmonitor.com.

9. Brendan Sasso, "FCC Moves to Revive Net-Neutrality Rules," *National Journal*, accessed April 1, 2014, www.nationaljournal.com; Rob Pegoraro, "Court Cuts FCC's Net-Neutrality Power; Now What?" *The Washington Post*, accessed April 1, 2014, http://voices.washingtonpost.com.

10. U.S. Senate Committee on Banking, House, and Urban Affairs, "Brief Summary of the Dodd-Frank Wall Street Reform and Consumer Protection Act." Consumer Product Safety Commission website, accessed April 1, 2014, www.cpsc.gov.

11. "Food and Drug Administration Amendments Act (FDAAA) of 2007," U.S. Food and Drug Administration, www.fda.gov, accessed April 1, 2014.

12. Government website, "FDA Invites Public Input on Menthol in Cigarettes," www.fda.gov, accessed April 1, 2014; Lydia Zuraw, "FDA Seeks Input on Reportable Food Registry Amendments," *Food Safety News*, accessed April 1, 2014, www.foodsafetynews.com.

13. U.S. Equal Employment Opportunity Commission, "Notice Concerning the Lilly Ledbetter Fair Pay Act of 2009," www.eeoc.gov, accessed April 2, 2014.

14. Miguel Helft, "Judge Sides with Google in Viacom Video Suit," *The New York Times*, accessed April 2, 2014, www.nytimes.com.

15. Kelly Kunsch, "Commercial Law and the Uniform Code," Seattle University School of Law, accessed April 2, 2014, http://lawlibguides.seattleu.edu.

16. Jeff Jacoby, "Eminent Disaster," *Boston Globe*, accessed April 1, 2014, www.bostonglobe.com; Scott Streater and Charles V. Bagli, "Court Upholds Columbia Campus Expansion Plan," *The New York Times*, accessed April 2, 2014, www.nytimes.com.

17. Nick Sabilia, "It's Time for Congress to Actively Condemn Eminent Domain Abuses," *Forbes*, www.forbes.com, accessed April 1, 2014; "Utah Eminent Domain Law More Than a 'Message Bill,'" *The New York Times*, accessed April 2, 2014, www.nytimes.com.

18. Company website, www.saturdaysnyc.com, accessed April 1, 2014; "This Is Trademark: Kate Spade Had to Go to Court to Use the Word 'Saturday' in a Clothing Line," *Tech Dirt*, accessed April 1, 2014, www.techdirt.com; Stefanie Mosca, "Kate Spade Wins Trademark Infringement Case Against Surf for Saturday Brand," *InsideCounsel.com*, accessed April 1, 2014, www.insidecounsel.com.

19. "Patent Reform Act of 2011: An Overview," *Patently-O*, www.patentlyo.com, accessed April 2, 2014.

20. Kim Kenneally, "Usher, Mark Wahlberg, Run-D.M.C. and More Slapped with Copyright Infringement Lawsuit," *The Wrap*, accessed April 1, 2014, www.thewrap.com.

21. Melissa J. Lauritch, "New Wisconsin Law in Toxic Tort Litigation," *Martindale.com*, accessed April 2, 2014, www.martindale.com.

22. Associated Press, "Numbers on GM Recall for Faulty Ignition Switches," *ABC News*, accessed July 3, 2014, http://go.abcnews.com.

23. "U.S. Personal Bankruptcies Set to Drop Again," *Reuters*, accessed April 6, 2014, www.reuters.com.

Appendix B

1. Company website, "Snapshot," www.progressive.com, accessed April 6, 2014; Nick DiUlio, "Pay-as-You-Drive Auto Insurance Picks Up Speed," *Insurance Quotes*, accessed April 6, 2014, www.insurancequotes.com; Geoff Williams, "Should You Try Pay-As-You-Drive Insurance?," *US News*, accessed April 6, 2014, http://money.usnews.com.

2. *ACLI Life Insurers Fact Book 2013*, Table 10.3, "Life Insurance in Force, by State," www.acli.com, accessed April 3, 2014.

3. Robert P. Hartwig, "2012—Year End Results," *Insurance Information Institute*, accessed April 3, 2014, www.iii.org.

4. "Home Buyers Insurance Checklist," *Insurance Information Institute*, accessed April 3, 2014, www.iii.org.

5. Company website, "Insurance Requirements," http://cdn.corporate.walmart.com, accessed April 3, 2014.

6. Amy Goldstein and Juliet Eilperin, "Affordable Care Act," www.dol.gov, accessed April 2, 2014; "More than 7 Million Have Enrolled in Affordable Care Act," *The Washington Post*, accessed April 2, 2014, www.washingtonpost.com.

7. *ACLI Life Insurers Fact Book 2013*, "Assets," www.acli.com, accessed April 2, 2014.

Appendix C

1. Erin Lowry, "Millennials: It's Not Too Late to Plan for an Early Retirement," *Daily Finance*, accessed April 7, 2014, www.dailyfinance.com; "Millennials, Younger Americans Continue to Show More Anxiety about Common Financial Planning Issues Than Older Generations," *PRNewswire*, accessed April 7, 2014, www.prnewswire.com; John Wasik, "The One Retirement Savings Strategy That Always Works," *Forbes*, accessed April 7, 2014, www.forbes.com; Jinnie Regli, "Retirement Planning: 12 Practical Tips for Millennials," *Milliman Insights*, accessed April 7, 2014, www.milliman.com.

2. Government website, "State Personal Income 2013," www.bea.gov, accessed April 4, 2014.

3. Emily Brandon, "Poll: More Americans Postpone Retirement," *Second Act*, accessed April 4, 2014, www.secondact.com; Sandra De Carlavho, "Boomers Risk Straining Finances to Support Boomerang Kids," *The Wall Street Journal*, accessed April 4, 2014, http://online.wsj.com.

4. American Bankruptcy Institute, "Quarterly Non-Business Filings By Chapter," http://news.abi.org, accessed April 4, 2014.

5. "Consumer Credit," *Federal Reserve Statistical Release G.19*, December 2013, http://federalreserve.gov, accessed April 4, 2014.

6. Blake Ellis, "Class of 2013 Grads Average $35,200 in Total Debt," *CNN Money*, accessed April 4, 2014, http://money.cnn.com.

7. Citizens for Tax Justice website, "Who Pays Taxes in America in 2013?" http://ctj.org, accessed April 4, 2014.

8. Bureau of Labor Statistics, "Consumer Expenditures 2012," www.bls.gov, accessed April 4, 2014; James Healy, "Report: Average Price of New Car Hits Record in August," *USA Today*, accessed April 4, 2014, www.usatoday.com; Jim Gorzelany, "Used Car Prices Stay High: Here's Where to Find the Best Deals," *Forbes*, accessed April 4, 2014, www.forbes.com.

9. "Buying A Home Is Now 38% Cheaper Than Renting," *Forbes*, accessed April 4, 2014, www.forbes.com.

10. "Your Lifetime Insurance Bill: $94,000," *USA Today*, accessed April 4, 2014, www.usatoday.com.

Appendix D

1. Organization website, "5 Reasons to Enter a Business Plan Competition," www.bizplancompetitions.com, accessed April 5, 2014; Michelle Goodman, "Crash Course in Business Plan Competitions," *Inc.*, accessed April 5, 2014, www.inc.com; organization website, "MIT $100K Entrepreneurship Competition," www.mit100k.org, accessed April 5, 2014.

Appendix E

1. U.S. Census Bureau, "Table P-32. Educational Attainment—Full-Time, Year-Round Workers 18 Years Old and Over by Mean Earnings, Age, and Sex: 1991 to 2012," *Current Population Reports*, www.census.gov, accessed April 5, 2014.

2. "College Internships," *College View*, www.collegeview.com, accessed April 6, 2014; Susan Adams, "The Best Internships for 2011," *Forbes*, accessed April 6, 2014, www.forbes.com.

3. "The Cooperative Education Model," National Commission for Cooperative Education, www.co-op.edu, accessed April 6, 2014.

4. "Take Our Career Aptitude Test!," *Career Explorer,* www.careerexplorer.net, accessed April 15, 2014; "Free Career Test!" *Live Career,* www.livecareer.com, accessed April 15, 2014; "Assessing Your Skills," *Monster,* http://career-advice.monster.com, accessed April 15, 2014.

5. Company website, www.michelefoods.com, accessed April 6, 2014.

6. Sarah Halzack, "Tips for Using LinkedIn to Find a Job," *The Washington Post,* accessed April 6, 2014, www.washingtonpost.com.

7. "Chronological Resume: The Preferred Resume Layout," *Top Sales Jobs,* accessed April 6, 2014, www.topsalesjobs.com.

8. Kim Isaacs, "Five Resume Tips for College Students," *Monster.com,* accessed April 6, 2014, www.monster.com; Michael Murray, "Five Resume Tips for College Students," *The Student Development Company,* www.thestudentdevelopment.com, accessed April 6, 2014.

9. Eugene Volokh, "How to Write a Great Cover Letter: Top 7 Tips," *Opposing Views,* accessed April 6, 2014, www.opposingviews.com; "Here's an Example of a Great Cover Letter," *Ask a Manager,* accessed April 6, 2014, www.askamanager.com.

10. Debra Wheatman, "5 Tricks to Get Noticed When Submitting a Resume Online," *GlassDoor.com,* accessed April 6, 2014, www.glassdoor.com; Pattie Hunt Sinacole, "Tips on Sending a Resume via Email," *Boston.com,* accessed April 6, 2014, www.boston.com.

11. Carole Martin, "Ten Tips to Boost Your Interview Skills," *Monster.com,* accessed April 9, 2014, http://career-advice.monster.com.

12. Rob Taub, "How to Answer Tough Interview Questions Correctly," *Career Realism,* accessed April 6, 2014, www.careerrealism.com.

13. U.S. Bureau of Labor Statistics, "Overview of Projections to 2020," *Monthly Labor Review,* www.bls.gov, accessed April 6, 2014.

14. Ibid.

15. Ibid.

16. Ibid.

17. Organization website, "Job Outlook 2014," www.nace.org, accessed April 6, 2014.

Name Index

Entries in **bold** refer to the "Business Terms You Need to Know," which are listed at the end of each chapter.

AARP (American Association of Retired Persons), 432
ABB, 75
Abbott, 46
ABC, 376
Abington Shoe Company, 60
Able Planet, 177
Acacia Federal Savings Bank, 472
Academy of Motion Pictures Arts and Sciences, 451
Accenture, 46, 222, 419
ACCION USA, 79
Ace Cash Express, 487
Ace Hardware, 352
Acer, 465–466
Activision Blizzard Inc., 207
Adidas, 365
Adler, Jeffery, 111
Adobe Acrobat, 407, 412
Advanced Systems Group (ASG), 414
Advertising Age and Oil & Gas Journal, 378
AFLAC, 228
African-American Women Business Owners Association, 161
Agilent Technologies, 420
Agriculture, Department of, 435, 515
Agriculture Bank of China, 115
Ahrendts, Angela, 203
Airbnb, 161, 467
Airbus, 493–494
Alaskan Railroad Corp., 148
Alcoa, 115–116
Aldana, Hector, 38
Alderfer, Kim, 301, 515
ALDI, 355
Alex & Ani, 398–399
Alghanim Sons Group, 111
Alibaba Group, 17
AllBusiness.com, 176
Allen, Paul, 164
Allstate Insurance, 97
Almond Joy, 327
ALS Association, 311
Amazon, 15, 23, 46, 90, 116, 129, 132, 322, 339, 348, 352, 357, 366–367, 390, 405, 411, 502
America Online, 508
American Academy of Orthopaedic Surgeons, 309
American Airlines, 151, 492, 493

American Association of Retired Persons (AARP), 432
American Cancer Society, 306
American Diabetes Association, 310
American Express, 224, 256, 343
American FactFinder, 410
American Federation of State, County & Municipal Employees, 236
American Giant, 257, 348–349
American Heart Association, 306
American Idol, 374
American Library Association, 90
American Red Cross, 5, 6, 47
American Society for Prevention of Cruelty to Animals (ASPCA), 206
American Stock Exchange (AMEX), 469
Amtrak (National Railroad Passenger Corporation), 148
Android, 342, 407, 411, 412
Anisa International, 166
Annual Credit Report Request Service, 313
Anytime Fitness, 127
AOL, 377
AOL Time Warner, Inc, 508
Apex Hotel, 328
Appalachian Mountain Club, 5
Apple, 4, 23, 45, 71, 113–114, 130, 137, 170, 179, 203, 256, 309, 318, 344, 370, 375, 398, 411, 412, 416, 462, 465–466, 497, 502
Apple Stores, 380, 414
Arbor Day Foundation, 104
Archer Farms, 398
Ariba, 286
Arm & Hammer, 344
Armani Exchange, 359
Armorós, José Ernesto, 167
Art Institute of Chicago, 432
Art Meets Commerce, 358
Arthritis Foundation, 332
Arundell-Latshaw, Jamie, 139
ASG (Advanced Systems Group), 414
ASPCA (American Society for Prevention of Cruelty to Animals), 206
Association of Collegiate Entrepreneurs, 168

Association of South East Asian Nations (ASEAN), 107
Aston Martin, 215
Astra Zeneca, 385
Asus, 465–466
AT&T, 45, 46, 51, 152, 202, 221, 375, 377, 413, 414
Atlanta Federal Reserve, 479
ATM, 293
Ava Anderson Non-Toxic, 340, 341
Aveda, 163
Avelino, Leon, 90, 366–367
Avengers, 335
Avis Budget, 399–400, 426
Axe, 317
AZ Touchpoints, 385

BabyFirst cable network, 339
Backdoor AndroidOS. Obad.a, 417
Bainbridge Graduate Institute, 10
Balbus Speech, 200
Baldwin, Kelly, 116
Ballmer, Steve, 63
BambooHR, 216
Bank of America, 47, 50, 270, 473, 482, 483, 516
Bank of Canada, 483
Bank of England, 483
Bank of Japan, 483
Barnes, Julian E., 51
Barnes & Noble, 90, 339, 354, 390
Barra, Mary, 21, 203, 204
Baskin-Robbins, 141
Bauer, Jack, 374
Baumgartner, Felix, 374
BEA (Bureau of Economic Analysis), 76
Bed Bath & Beyond, 497
Belle's Fine Coffees, 441–449
Ben and Jerry's, 317
Ben Franklin variety stores, 162
Benefit Corporations, 146
Benioff, Marc, 19–20, 252
Benjamin Moore Paints, 192
Bentley, Craig E., 84
Berkshire Hathaway, 23, 115, 192, 202, 467, 468, 505
Bernanke, Ben, 477
Best Buy, 45, 157
Betty Crocker, 327
Beyoncé, 307
Bezos, Jeff, 182
Bidding for Good, 43

Big Brothers/Big Sisters, 224
Bill & Melinda Gates
    Foundation, 375
Bing, 416
Birchwood Paper, 450
Bitcoin, 461
BJ's, 354
Black, Dan, 433
Black Enterprise magazine, 161
Blank Label, 315
Block, H&R, 276
Bloomberg Businessweek, 378
BLS (Bureau of Labor Statistics),
    51, 77, 408
Blue Chip Marketing
    Worldwide, 317
Blue State Coffee, 28, 488
Bluhm-Sauriol, Paulette, 217
BMW, 114, 223, 282, 358,
    394, 498
Bobbie Weiner Enterprises, 162
Boeing, 94, 215, 230,
    420, 516
Bon Appétit, 313
Bono, 309
Bonobos, 348
Booth, Ted, 122
Borro, 89
Bosma, Niels, 167
Boston Consulting Group, 230
Boston Scientific, 278
Boston University, 158
Box Inc, 419, 467, 505
Boys & Girls Clubs of
    America, 309
BP, 44
Brandresume.com,
    220–221
Branson, Richard, 170
Braun, Ralph, 172
Braun Corporation, 172
Brigham, Alex, 194
Bright Source Energy, 505
Brin, Sergey, 164, 205
Bristol-Myers Squibb, 202
British Airways, 494
Broderick, Mike, 138
Bronner, Michael, 183
Bronner, Nicky, 183
Brooks, Chad, 40
Brown, Bobbi, 171
Brown, Bonnie, 250
Buckley, George, 179
Buffet, Howard, 192
Buffett, Warren, 192, 202,
    375, 468
Burberry, 203, 357
Burch, Tory, 79
Bureau of Economic Analysis
    (BEA), 76
Bureau of Labor Statistics (BLS),
    51, 77, 408
Burger King, 143, 381, 505

Butterfinger Peanut Butter
    Cups, 387
Buy.com, 354

Cabot Creamery, 149
Cadillac, 373
California Institute of Technology,
    495
California Strawberry
    Commission, 369
Campbell Soup Company, 202,
    316–317, 349
Canon, 104
Capital One credit cards, 375
Career Explorer, A-49
CareerBuilder, A-52
Cargill, 221
Carlos Slim Foundation, 425
Carnegie, Andrew, 12
Carnegie Mellon University,
    168–169
Carnival Cruise Lines, 264–265
Carpenter, Jake Burton, A-50
Case, Brendan, 102
Caterpillar, 497, 516
Cathay Pacific, 374
CBS, 376
CBS Outdoor Americas, 380
Census Bureau, 94, 319–320,
    408–409, 410
Centers for Disease Control and
    Prevention, 44
Century Council, 377
CFPB (Consumer Financial
    Protection Bureau), 43
Chanel, 380, 394
Charles Schwab, 351
Chase, 473
Chase, Oliver, 299–300
Chase, Robin, 399–400
Check Point, 414
Cheer, 344
Cheerios, 344
Cheesecake Factory, 244
Chevrolet, 374, 375
Chevron, 492
Chicago Bulls, 311
China Construction Bank, 115
China Southern Airlines, 494
Chinese Ministry of Commerce,
    290, 293
Chipotle, 68–69, 380
Chobani Greek yogurt, 375
Choice Books, 351
Christian Louboutin, 389
Chrysler, 108, 282
"Chucks," 365
Cider Hill Farm, 129–130
Cisco Systems, 42, 148,
    223, 249, 344, 405, 419,
    487, 497
Citibank, 97, 483
City Year, 148, 153, 322, 326

City Year Miami, 152, 153
Civic GX, 401
Clarkson, Kelly, 150
Clear Channel Outdoor
    Advertising, 380
ClearEdge Power, 132
Climate Corporation, 405
Clinique, 381
Coach, 508
Coca-Cola Company, 23, 33,
    72, 202, 337, 343, 374,
    377, 380, 450, 499, A-12
Coinstar, 322
Coke Classic, 338
Cold Stone Creamery, 190
Coleman, Susan, 134
Colgate Kitchen Entrees, 343
Combs, Todd, 192
Comcast, 153, 425
Comet Skateboards,
    183–184, 514
Commerce, Department of, 76,
    107, 110, 408
Commonwealth of
    Pennsylvania, 435
Community College of
    Denver, 432
Comptroller of the Currency, 480
Conner, Alfred, 147
Conner, Alfred, Jr., 147
Conner, Dan, 147
Conner, Tom, 147
Conner, William H., 147
Conscious Commerce, 163
Consumer Financial Protection
    Bureau (CFPB), 43
Consumer Products Safety
    Commission (CPSC), 83, A-4,
    A-6
Consumer Protection Act,
    441, 480
Consumer Reports, 204
The Container Store, 256
Converse, 365
Cool, Tracy, 202
Cooley, 225
Copyright Office, 174
Cornell University, 158
Costco, 66–67, 177, 190, 199,
    200, 354, 432, 496
Coyle, Emily, 142
Craftsman tools, 344
Craig, Carol, 164
Craig Technologies, 164
Craigslist.org, A-51
Credit CARD Act of 2009, 379
Credit Suisse First Boston
    (CSFB), 487
Crest, 344
CRM (Customer Relationship
    Management), 407
CRO Magazine, 202
Crystal Pepsi, 343

CSFB (Credit Suisse First Boston), 487
Custom Made, 276
Customer Relationship Management (CRM), 407
CVS, 183
CVS Caremark, 152, 306, 314, 398
Cyger, Michael, 42
Cyrus, Miley, 389

Dai, Shasha, 51
Dairy Queen, 192
Daley, Fred, 387
Danielson, Antje, 399–400
Days Inn, 142
D.E. Master Blenders, 508
Dean, James, 365
Defense, Department of, 139, 360
Dell, 465–466, 513
Deloitte, 431, 433
Delta Airlines, 292, 493
Desert Hills Premium Outlets, 359
Detkowski, Rick, 186
DHSRI (Dwight Hall Socially Responsible Investment Fund), 506
Diamond Foods, 457
Diane von Furstenberg, 373
Dice.com, A-51
Dick's Sporting Goods, 357
Dickerson, Ann, 134–135
Diesel, 359
Diet Pepsi, 338
Digital Outdoor Networks, 380
Digitas, 183
Direct Marketing Association (DMA), 379
Disney, 339
Dlush Beverage Joints, 111
DMA (Direct Marketing Association), 379
Dodd-Frank Wall Street Reform, 441, 480
Dodge, 320
Doerr, Ann, 425
Doerr, John, 425
Dole, 224
Dollar Financial, 475
Dollar General, 74, 354
Dollar Tree, 74, 190
Domino's Pizza, 112–113
Dongfeng Motor Group, 153
Dorito's, 373
Dorsey, Jack, 20, 168
Dove, 317, 377
Dow Chemical, 210, 287
Dow Jones Industrial Average, 468
DPR Construction, 230
Draper Fisher Jurvetson, 505

Dropbox, 407, 419
Drucker, Peter, 234
Dunkin' Brands, 141
Dunkin' Donuts, 112, 344
DuPont, 50, 380
Dwight Hall organization, 506
Dwight Hall Socially Responsible Investment Fund (DHSRI), 506

E&Y, 433
e2e Materials, 184
East Alabama Medical Center, 148
Eaton, 75, 202
eBay, 10, 49, 278, 344, 352, 357, 384, 467, 502
eBeanstalk.com, 130
EDGAR Online, 481
Edward Jones, 230, 471
EEOC (Equal Employment Opportunity Commission), 52–54, 221, 222, 229
Egg PLC, 116
Elements Therapeutic Massage and Day Spa, 185
Ells, Steve, 69
Ellsworth, Theo, 367
EMC, 405
Emerson, Bill, 189
Enron Corporation, 434
Enterprise UK, 167
Entrepreneur Magazine, 127, 161
Entrepreneur.com, 162
Entrepreneurs' Organization, 161
Entrepreneurship and Innovation Group, 167
Environmental Protection Agency, 45, 265, 462
Equal Employment Opportunity Commission (EEOC), 52–54, 221, 222, 229
Equifax, 313
Equilar, 492
Ernst & Young, 223, 228, 433, A-52
ESPN, 216, 380
Estée Lauder, 171
Estes, Kelly, 123
Estes, Mike, 123
Etherington, Darrell, 84
Ethics Resource Center, 33, 40
Ethisphere Institute, 193
Etsy, 146
European Alliance, 357
European Central Bank, 483
European Commission, 357
Evernote, 243, 407
Evolution Fresh, 199
Expedia, 384

Experian, 313
Exxon Mobil, 115
Eyring, Pamela, 36
E-Z washing machines, 344

Facebook, 14, 28, 71, 114, 129, 179, 193, 219, 221, 254, 255, 258, 307–308, 317, 358, 369, 377, 383, 399–400, 405, 421, 491, 507
Fair Trade USA (FTUSA), 22
Fairtrade Labeling Organization (FLO), 22
FalconStor, 418
Family Dollar Stores, 389, 487
Farmers Insurance Group, 380
Fast Company, 129, 161
FastLane, 322
FCPA (Foreign Corrupt Practices Act), 436, 441
FDA (Food and Drug Administration), 48, 67
Federal Bureau of Investigation, 435
Federal Communication Commission (FCC), 71
Federal Deposit Insurance Corporation (FDIC), 473–474, 480
Federal Emergency Management Agency (FEMA), 428, 515
Federal Energy Regulatory Commission (FERC), A-3
Federal Express, 97
Federal Open Market Committee (FOMC), 80
Federal Reserve System (Fed), 80, 452, 461, 476–480, 480
Federal Trade Commission (FTC), 45, 143, 379, A-3
FedEx, 23, 137, 412, A-1
Fernandez, Joe, 193, 194
Ferrence, Carrie, 10
Ferriss, Tim, 166
Fidelity, 516
Field, Marshall, 306
Fields, Mark, 215
Fifth Third Bank, 462
Financial Accounting Foundation, 436
Financial Accounting Standards Board (FASB), 426
Financial Times, 17
Find My iPhone, 416
Fisher, Eileen, 193
Fitch, 465
Flam, Bobby, 169
FlightCar, 161
FLO (Fairtrade Labeling Organization), 22

Fogle, Jared, 44
FOMC (Federal Open Market
  Committee), 80
Food, Drug, and Cosmetic
  Act, 347
Food and Drug Administration
  (FDA), 48, 67, 347,
  A-4, A-6
Forbes magazine, 161
Ford, Henry, 12, 275–276
Ford Credit, 475
Ford Crown Victoria, 320
Ford F-150 trucks, 369
Ford Motor Company, 93, 102,
  108, 145, 147, 215, 216,
  282, 318, 467
Foreign Corrupt Practices Act
  (FCPA), 436, 441
Forest Stewardship Council
  (FSC), 323
Formosa, Dan, 216–217
Fortune, 22, 27, 32, 189, 199,
  223, 225, 230, 378
4food, 168
Fox, 376
Foxconn, 157
France, 73
FREEDM Center (for Future
  Renewable Electric
  Energy, Delivery, and
  Management), 75
Fresh Fish Daley, 387
Fresno, California, 435
Frisk, Patrik, 61
Frito-Lay, 515
FSC (Forest Stewardship
  Council), 323
FTC (Federal Trade Commission),
  45, 143, 379
FTUSA (Fair Trade USA), 22
Fuhu, 339
Fujitsu, 385
Fulton, Randy, 428
FuneralRecording.com, 172
Funk, Curtis, 172
Future Motion, 341

Gain, 344
Ganeshram, Shri, 161
Gap, 193, 202
Gara, Tom, 69
Gates, Bill, 63, 121, 164, 165,
  425
Gates, Melinda, 425
Gatorade, 343, 380
GE (General Electric), 23,
  115, 152, 273, 294, 439,
  462, 467
GE Capital, 476
GE Energy Ventures, 175
Geico Insurance, 192, 375
Genco Marketplace, 496
Genentech, 230

General Electric (GE), 23,
  115, 152, 273, 294, 439,
  462, 467
General Mills, 47, 48, 50, 345
General Motors (GM), 20–21,
  49, 93, 108, 203, 204, 282,
  320, 322
Generation Y, 321
Gilbert, Dan, 189
Gilead Sciences, 502
Gilt Groupe, 278
Girard, Lisa, 42
Girl Scouts of the USA, 5
Gjurgevic, Jacqueline, 10
Glassdoor, 219, 220, 269,
  A-51
Glassybaby, 182
Glimmerglass Consulting Group,
  223–224
Global (Norway), 506
Global Soap Project, 58
GM (General Motors), 20–21,
  49, 93, 108, 203, 204, 282,
  320, 322
Gogo, 172
GoldieBlox, 377
Goldman Sachs, 139
Goldsberry, Clare, 114
Goodman, Jodi, 8
Goodman, Michelle, 146
Goodwill Industries, 275
Goodwill Industries
  International, 190
Goodyear blimp, 380
Google, 3, 4, 23, 71, 132,
  164, 179, 194, 203, 204,
  205, 220, 230, 250, 343,
  377, 405, 411, 416, 425,
  497, 502, A-8
Google Buzz, 317
Google Play, 348
Google+, 307–308
GoPro, 157
Gorbachev, Mikhail, 72
Gorsky, Alex, 199
Government Accountability
  Office, 321
Grant Thornton, 433
Great Clips, 142
Green, Alison, 84
Green Building Council, 15
Green Mountain Coffee, 22
Green Mountain Roasters, 199
Green Resource Hub, 184
Greensulate, 16
Grondahl, Michael, 164
Groupon, 157
Gucci, 357
Gulf View Townhouses of
  Tampa, 479

H&M, 35–36, 373
Häagen-Dazs, 309, 311

Habitat for Humanity,
  47, 309
Hachette Book Group, 390
Hain Celestial Group, 94
Halogen Software, 224
Haney, Janice, 301
Haney, John, 301
Harley-Davidson, 285–286
Harley-Davidson Perfume, 343
Harrigan, Gerra, 488
Harris, Parker, 19
Hasbro, 202, 335
Haskell, Tim, 163
Hastings, Reed, 172, 425
Hay Group, 22
HBO, 377
Headrick, Darin, 428
Health Care Service
  Corporation, 46
Heaven's Best, 143
Heinz, 294
He-Man, 335
Hendricks Motorsports, 380
Herrin, Jessica, 163
Hershey's Milk Chocolate
  Bars, 327
Herzberg, Frederick, 233
Hewitt, Steve, 123, 301
Hewlett-Packard, 344,
  465–466, 492, 513
Heyman, Marshall, 79
Higgins, Nigel, 224
Hillshire Brands, 508
Hilton Worldwide, 46, 58
Hispanic magazine, 161
H.J. Heinz, 506
Hoguet, Karen, 513
Holland Car PLC, 285
Home Depot, 66, 195–196,
  298, 479
Honda, 108, 282
Hong Kong International
  Airport, 374
Hoskins, Michele, A-50
Hotmail, 505
HSBC Holdings, 115
Hsieh, Tony, 165, 200
Huang, Alex, 75
Hudson, Jennifer, 150
Huggies, 372
Hull, Chuck, 179
Hulu, 322
HuluPlus, 377
Humane Society, 47
Hurley, Paul, 157

IAEA (International Atomic
  Energy Agency), 89
IASB (International Accounting
  Standards Board), 452
IASC (International Accounting
  Standards Committee), 452
iBeacon, 398

IBM, 50, 221, 344, 414, 433, 513
ICBC, 115
Icehouse, 171
Ideeli, 157
Idol, John, 190
IFRS (International Financial
    Reporting Standards), 452
IHOP, 374
IKEA, 322, 323, 344
IMF (International Monetary
    Fund), 107
Inc. magazine, 161, 169,
    172, 176
Indeed.com, A-51
Indiegogo, 491
inDinero, 7
Industrial & Commercial Bank of
    China Limited, 483
Infiniti, 373
Infosys Technology, 420
ING Direct, 473
Instagram, 65, 114, 369
Instagram Direct, 65
Institute of Scrap Recycling
    Industries, 45
Intel, 75, 202, 221, 344
Interactive Distance Learning
    Network, 428
Internal Revenue Service (IRS), 5,
    432, A-34
**International Accounting
    Standards Board
    (IASB)**, 452
International Accounting
    Standards Committee
    (IASC), 452
International Atomic Energy
    Agency (IAEA), 89
International Brotherhood of
    Teamsters, 236
International Consumer
    Electronics Show, 383
**International Financial
    Reporting Standards
    (IFRS)**, 452
International Franchise
    Association, 141
**International Monetary
    Fund (IMF)**, 107
**International Organization
    for Standardization
    (ISO)**, 294
Intuit, 230, 431
iOS, 407, 411, 416
iPad, 339, 375, 385, 389,
    465–466
iPawn, 89
iPhone, 342, 412
IRS (Internal Revenue Service), 5,
    432, A-34
ISI Group, 377
ISO (International Organization
    for Standardization), 294

Jack in the Box, 380
Jackman, Hugh, 150
Jagger, Mick, A-50
Jaguar, 215, 373
James, LeBron, 310
Jargon, Julie, 142
Jay Z, A-13
JC Penney, 306, 393
J.Crew, 378
Jelly Belly, 224
JetBlue, 420
JETCAM, 290
Jiffy Lube, 277, 373
Jimmy John's, 306
Jobs, Steve, 20, 130, 170
JobsinPods.com, 221
John Deere Capital
    Corporation, 475
John Watson, 492
Johnson, Fisk, 265
Johnson & Johnson, 32–33,
    39, 122, 198, 199, 251,
    264–265, 344, 437, 508
Joplin, Janis, 365
Jordan, Michael, 310, 365
JP Morgan Chase, 115, 482,
    483, 516
Jumbo's Restaurant, 169
Just Salad, 346
Juvenile Diabetes Research
    Foundation, 309, 375

Kaggle, 405
Kaiser Permanente, 44
Karns, Michael, 111
Kate Spade, A-13
Kauffman Center for
    Entrepreneurial
    Leadership, 168
Kauffman Foundation,
    162, 167
Kayongo, Derreck, 58
Keith, Toby, 369
Kelly Services, 337
Kennedy, John F., 47
Kettle Brand chips, 457
Keurig, 199
KeyCorp, 46
Keys, Alicia, 375
KFC, 112, 141
Khan, Salman "Sal," 425
Khan Academy, 425–426
Khosla, Vinod, 45
Kickstarter, 10, 159
Kidron, Adam, 168
Kiehl's, 163
Kind Healthy Snacks, 248
Kindle, 339, 389, 390, 411
King & King Architects, 15
Kitchen Cabinet Kings, 128
KitchenAid, 344
Kiva, 278
Kleinfeldt, Rik, 28–29, 488–489

Klout, 193, 194
The Knot, 163
Koger, Eric, 128
Koger, Susan, 128
Kohler, Mark, 146
Komen Race for the Cure, 387
Korn, Melissa, 101
KPMG, 433
Kraft, 257
Krispy Kreme, 133, 143
Kroger, 183
Kuhn Bösendorfer, 384

La Boulange Café and
    Bakery, 199
LA Fitness, 142
Labor, Department of, 50, 78,
    186, 429, 516
Lafley, A. G., 316
Land Rover, 215
Las Vegas Premium
    Outlets, 359
**Leadership in Energy and
    Environmental Design
    (LEED)**, 277–278
Learning Express, 169
Lebanon Valley Brethren Home,
    248–249
Ledbetter, Lilly, 54
**LEED (Leadership in Energy
    and Environmental
    Design)**, 277–278
Legend, John, 150
LEGO Group, 277
Lending Club, 467, 491
Lenova Group (China), 508
Lenovo, 465–466
Levi Strauss & Company, 3
Levie, Aaron, 419
Levitt, William, 275
Lexicon Consulting, 139
Lexus, 371, 373
Li, Andy, 158, 333, 459
Li, Irene, 158, 333, 459
Li, Margaret, 158, 333, 459
Libin, Phil, 243
Library of Congress, A-13
Lifefyre, 305
Lin, Alfred, 165
Lindquist, Lee, 401
LinkedIn, 39, 179, 221,
    307–308, 433, A-51, A-52
Linux, 407, 412
Lithium Technologies, 193
Live Nation Entertainment,
    8, 389
LiveCareer, A-49
Lockheed Martin, 39, 298
London Stock Exchange, 471
Lonza, 293
L'Oréal, 32, 254, 344, 375
Louis Vuitton, 332
Lowe's, 66, 129, 354, 392

Lucas, Suzanne, 132
Lululemon, 292
LVMH (Louis Vuitton Moët Hennessey), 357

M&S (Marks & Spencer), 45
Ma, Jack, 17
Mac OS, 411
MacBook Pro, 411
Macy's, 129, 352, 513
Mah, Jessica, 7
Make-A-Wish Foundation, 306
Mall of America, 355
Man of Steel, 374
Market Pantry, 398
Market Reform Act, 480
Marks & Spencer (M&S), 45
Marriott, J. W., 200
Marriott International, 46, 190, 200
Mars, Frank C., 27
Mars, Inc., 7, 27, 45
Marshalls, 354
Martinez, Andres, 102
Marvel Entertainment, 507
Marx, Karl, 72
Mary Kay Cosmetics, 348
Maslow, Abraham H., 232, 236
Massachusetts General Hospital, 432
Massachusetts Institute of Technology, 495
Mattel, 202
Matthews, Barry, 90, 366–367
Mattle, 335
Max Steel, 335
Mayer, Marissa, 247
Mazda, 282
McAfee VirusScan, 417
McClurg, Gavin, 177–178
McCollum, Lonnie, 123, 301
McCormick, Cyrus, 12
McCormick, Robert, 12
McDermott, Jack, 200
McDonald's, 68, 72, 97, 100, 112, 120, 141, 143, 276, 314, 343, 344, 375, 381, 450, 462, 499, A-12
McGregor, Douglas, 235
MCI, 39–40
Mei Mei Group, 158–159, 333, 459
Mei Mei Street Kitchen, 158
Meister, Jeanne, 40
Memorex, 230
Mercedes Benz, 342, 373
Merck & Co., 71, 97, 202
Merrill Lynch, 270
Method Soap, 146, 163
Metro, Marty, 42
Metro Group, 360
Meyer, Stephanie, 390

MF Global Holdings, 195
Miami Heat, 311
Michael Kors, 190, 359
Michael's Crafts, 169
Microsoft, 63, 71, 148, 164, 217, 322, 377, 407, 412, 414, 419, 426, 492, 497, 501, 505, A-4
Millennium Scholars Program, 375–376
Ministry of Environmental Protection (China), 467
Mint.com, 450
"MinuteClinic," 306
Missoni, 373
Mobile World Congress Trade Show, 421
ModCloth, 128–129
Mondelez International, 257, 282
Monsanto, 405
Monster High, 335
Monster.com, A-49, A-51
Moody's, 465–466
Moon Valley Rustic Furniture, 186
MoreBusiness.com, 176
Morgan, J. P., 12
Morinaga, 113
Morphie, 163
Morrison, Bill, 496
Mortensen, Dave, 127
Motor Trend, 204
Motorola, 508
Motorola Solutions, 294
Mulally, Alan R., 215
Musk, Elon, 163, 164
Mycoskie, Blake, 121

Nabi, 339
Nabisco, 376
Nadella, Satya, 63
NAICS (North American Industry Classification System), 323–324
Nakamoto, Satoshi, 461
Naked Pizza, 171
NASCAR, 305, 380
NASDAQ (National Association of Securities Dealers Automated Quotation), 469–470
National Association of Securities Dealers (NASD), 482
National Cattlemen's Beef Association, 369
National Credit Union Administration (NCUA), 474
National Do Not Call registry, 385
National Education Association (NEA), 236
National Football League (NFL), 309

National Foundation for Credit Counseling, A-34
National Franchise Association, 143
National Highway Traffic Safety Administration, 196
National Instruments, 279
National Labor Relations Board (NLRB), 237, A-3
National Railroad Passenger Corporation (Amtrak), 148
National Science Foundation, 75
Nation's Restaurant News, 244
NBA, 311, 379–380
NBC, 376
NCR Corporation, 353
NCUA (National Credit Union Administration), 474
NEA (National Education Association), 236
Necco (New England Confectionary Company), 270–271, 299–300
Neiman Marcus, 373, 416
Nest, 492
Nestlé, 450, 499
Netflix, 6, 172, 322, 377
NetSuite, 439
New Coke, 343
New England Clean Energy Council, 61
New England Confectionary Company (Necco), 270–271, 299–300
New England GreenStart, 29
New Harvest Coffee Roasters, 28–29, 488–489
New Light India, 163
New Resource Bank, 462
New York City MetroCard transit cards, 381
New York Life, 474
New York State Energy Research and Development Authority (NYSERDA), 15–16
New York Stock Exchange (NYSE), 452, 468, 469, 488
New York Times, 36, 416
Newman's Own, 47
Newmont Mining Corporation, 508
NFL (National Football League), 309
Ng, Cheong-Choon, 169
Niagara Falls Bridge Commission, 465
Nibbol, 176
Nickelodeon, 339
Nightmare, 163
Nike, 114, 198, 217, 343, 344, 365, 439
Nintendo, 194

Nixon, David, 131
NLRB (National Labor Relations Board), 237
Noki, 63
Nokia, 502
Nook, 339, 390
Nordstrom, 27–28, 311, 352, 357, 358, 384
Nordstrom, John W., 132
North American Industry Classification System (NAICS), 323–324
North Carolina State University (NCSU), 75
North Face, 344
Northeastern University, 167
Northwest, 493
Northwestern Mutual, 472
Norton AntiVirus, 417
Numi Organic Tea, 146
NYSE (New York Stock Exchange), 452, 468, 469, 488
NYSERDA (New York State Energy Research and Development Authority), 15–16

Ocarina, 168
Occupational Safety and Health Administration (OSHA), 50
Oculus VR, 507
Odeo, 20
Office Depot, 354
Office of Thrift Supervision, 480
Offshore Odysseys, 177–178
Ohio Savings Bank, 472
Okinawa, Japan, 342
ONE, 309
Onewheel, 341
Operative Plasterers and Cement Masons International Association (OPCMIA), 239
Oracle, 385, 408, 439, 492
Orange Is the New Black, 377
Orbitz, 384
Oreo cookies, 369
Oscar®, 450
OSHA (Occupational Safety and Health Administration), 50
Ouchi, William, 236
Outdoor Industry Association, 60
Outerwall, 322
Overstock, 384
Oxfam, 45
OXO, 216

P&G Share, 348
Pacific Bridge Medical, 113
PacSun, 378
Page, Larry, 164, 205

Paladin Energy, 508
Pampered Chef, 235, 353
Pandora, 318
Panera Bread, 31, 414
Panera Cares restaurants, 31
Papa John's, 142
Paramount Pictures, 335, 450
Patagonia, 146
Patent and Trademark Office, 174
Patzer, Aaron, 450
Pavlo, Walter, 39–40
Pawn Stars, 89
Pawngo, 89
PayNearMe, 487
PayPal, 71, 163
Payson, Alex, 28
PayTango, 169
Peapod, 355
Pejamajo Café, 488
Pennsylvania Turnpike Authority, 148
Pepsi Bottling Group, 337
Pepsi Bottling Ventures, 337
PepsiCo, 47, 148, 153, 201, 337, 338, 343, 380, 462, 492
Peterson, Ben, 216
PetroChina, 115
Petrovic, Kevin, 161
PetSmart, 354
Petswelcome.com, 207
Petty, Ashley, 185
Pew Research Center's Internet and American Life Project, 411
Pfizer, 71, 191, 224
Philadelphia Zoo, 309
Pier 1 Imports, 111
Pinterest, 467
Piraeus Bank SA (TPEIR), 505
Pizza Hut, 141
Planet Fitness, 164
Planet Water Foundation, 322, 326
Play-Doh, 170
Playground, 335
Playnomics, 317
Police Interceptor, 320
Ponce, Anthony, 138
Popular Science, 313
Porsche 918 Spyder, 384
PortionPac, 357–358
Post-it Notes, 340
Prada, 366
Priceline, 384
PricewaterhouseCoopers (PwC), 433, 450, 451
Prima Cinema, 384
Prince, Shawna, 138
Princess Cruises, 224
Princeton Review, A-48
Pringles, 457

Proactiv skin medications, 378
Procter & Gamble, 44, 48, 50, 147, 190, 207, 210, 316, 344, 345, 375, 419, 429, 457
Pro-Keds, 365
Prosper, 491
Prudential, 474
Public Accounting Oversight Board, 436
Public Company Accounting Oversight Board, 434
Publix Super Markets, 147
PwC (PricewaterhouseCoopers), 433, 450, 451

Qatalyst Partners, 487
Qualcomm, 227
Quattrone, Frank, 487
QueueBuster, 328
QuickBooks, 431, 439, 450
Quicken, 412, 431
Quicken Loans, 189, 230
Quinton, Sophie, 51

Rainbow Loom, 169
Rainforest Alliance, 29
Ramsey, Lydia, 36
Ray, Jimmy, 172
Raymond James & Associates, 517
Raytheon Solipsys, 227
Read, Ian, 191
Reader's Digest, 378
Rebuilding Together Miami Dade, 152, 153
Recreational Equipment Inc. (REI), 148, 157
Red Bull, 374
Red Cross/Red Crescent, 309
Redbox, 322
Redken, 344
Reese's Peanut Butter Cups, 327, 387
Regions Bank, 462
REI, 148, 157
RE/MAX, 351
Renault, 153
Rexrode, Christina, 151
RGL Forensics, 434
Rhodes, Lee, 182
Rice, Paul, 22
Rice University, 139
Ritz-Carlton, 259
Robert W. Baird & Co., 230
Rockefeller, John D., A-4
Rockstar Energy, 337
Rodriguez, Alex, 44
Rolex, 373
Roosevelt, Theodore, A-4
Roscoe Wind Complex, 6

Rossi, Bob, 184
Rothschild, David de, 224
Roundtable on Sustainable Palm
    Oil, 32
Royal Dutch Shell, 115
Runyon, Chuck, 127
Rush Communications, 170

S&P (Standard & Poor's),
    465–466, 492, 508
S&P 500 Index, 506
Sage50, 439
SAI Global, 39
Saks Fifth Avenue, 354
Saladino, Anthony, 128
Salesforce.com, 19–20, 230,
    252, 372, 407, 408, 502
Salfi, Jason, 183–184, 514
Salvation Army, 206
Sam's Club, 45, 353
Samsung, 217, 411
Samsung Galaxy Nexus, 348
San Diego Zoo, 224
San Francisco Giants, 369
Sandberg, Sheryl, 254, 255
Sanders, Ryan, 216
SaneBox, 261
SAP, 286–287, 408, 439
Sara Lee Corporation, 508
SAS, 230
SASB (Sustainability Accounting
    Standards Board), 439
SBA (Small Business
    Administration), 128,
    136–137, 140, 162, 165,
    176, 178, 186
SBICs (Small Business Investment
    Companies), 137
S.C. Johnson & Son, 150, 264, 265
Scholfield, Roger, 401
Scholfield Honda, 401
Seagate, 292
Sears, 152, 153, 294,
    344, 374
Seattle Children's Hospital,
    287–288
Seattle Premium Outlets, 359
Seattle's Best, 306
Secret Acres, 90, 366–367
Securities and Exchange
    Commission (SEC), 54–55,
    193, 436, 441, 457, A-4
Seidman, Maximillian
    Leonard, 458
Seidman & Seidman, 458,
    458–459
Semcken, Kevin, 177
Service Employees International
    Union (SEIU), 236
ServiceMaster, 338, 344
7-Eleven, 140, 354, 374,
    380, 487

Shaich, Ron, 31
Shaw, Brian, 69
Shell, 429
Shell International, 224
ShiftBoard.com, 228
Showtime, 377
SHRM (Society for Human
    Resource Management),
    222, 230
Siemens, 75
Sierra Club, 5
SIFE (Students in Free
    Enterprise), 168
Silverblatt, Rob, 151
Silverman, Rachel Emma, 132
Simmons, Russell, 170
Simply Balanced, 398
SimplyHired.com, A-51
Singapore Airline, 494
Siri, 318
Skype, 253, 426, A-58
SLMA (Student Loan Marketing
    Association), 73
**Small Business
    Administration (SBA)**,
    128, 136–137, 140, 162,
    165, 176, 178, 186
Small Business Investment
    Companies (SBICs), 137
Smallholder Farmers
    Alliance, 60
Smart Design, 121–122,
    216–217
SmartDraw, 386
Smith, Adam, 8
Smith, Jeff, 168
Society for Human Resource
    Management (SHRM),
    222, 230
Sodexo, 323
Software Advice, 219
SolarCity, 15–16, 163
Sonic Drive-Ins, 190
Sonic Lighter, 168
Sony, 157, 198, 411
Sony Betamax, 343
Sony PlayStation 3, 322
Sorenson, Arne M., 200
Southwest Airlines, 23, 147,
    269, 493
SpaceX, 163, 505
Sponge Bob Square Pants, 335
Springsteen, Bruce, 389
Sprint Nextel, 414
Squamscot Beverages, 147
Square, 20
St. Barts, 389
St. Jude Children's Research
    Hospital, 5, 275
Standard & Poor's (S&P),
    465–466, 492, 508
Standard Oil, A-4

Staples, 137, 414
Starbucks, 23, 28, 97, 142,
    152, 153, 198, 199, 257,
    309, 344, 356, 414,
    420, 502
State Department, 110
State Employees' Credit Union of
    North Carolina, 472
Steinway, Henry Engelhard, 12
Steinway Musical Instruments, 12
Stella & Dot, 163
Stock Watch, 482
Stockbox Grocers, 10
Stonyfield Farm, 322
Stop & Shop Supermarket
    Company, 190
Stouffer's, 324
Street Kitchen, 459
StubHub, 380
Student Loan Marketing
    Association (SLMA), 73
Students in Free Enterprise
    (SIFE), 168
Stumptown Comics Fest, 367
Subway, 44, 141, 314
Success magazine, 161
Sullenberger, Chesley, 204
Sun Microsystems, 45, 420
Sun Trust, 472
Sungevity, 175
Super Bowl, 310, 373,
    377, 387
Supreme Court, 53, 54, A-2,
    A-11
SurveyMonkey, 467
Susan G. Komen Foundation, 47
Sustainability Accounting
    Standards Board (SASB), 439
Sustainable Apparel
    Coalition, 60
Swanson Group, 290
Swart, Gary, 84
Swartz, Nathan, 60–61, 244
Swartz, Sydney, 244
Sweeney, Deborah, 42
Swinmurn, Nick, 165
Swirl, 398
Sysco, 350

Taco Bell, 141
Tantalus Solutions, 75
Target, 34–35, 45, 145, 183,
    199, 314, 339, 340, 344,
    360, 372, 398, 399–400,
    408, 492
Tax-Aide, 432
Taylor, Chuck, 365
Taylor, John W., 131
TD Ameritrade, 471
TeamBonding, 256
Teavana, 199
Techcareers.com, A-51

Technology Review, 75
Teen Vogue, 378
Teenage Research Unlimited, 316
Telecharge, 389
TeleZapper, 353
Telwar, Anisa, 166
Temkin Group, 190
Tennessee Moonshine Cakes, 134
Tesla Motors, 44, 93, 163, 196, 491, 505
Texas Instruments, 40
ThinkEco, 132
3D Systems, 179
3M Corporation, 21, 179, 207, 340, 502
3G Capital, 505–506
Thurston County Economic Development Council, 138
Tianhe-2, 410
Ticketmaster, 389
Ticketmaster Entertainment, 8
Tide, 344
Tiffany, 373, 380
Timberlake, Justin, 371–372
Timberland, 60–61, 153, 244–245, 326
Time, 378
Time Warner, 508
Tindell, Kip, 256
T-Mobile, 152, 377
TOMS Shoes, 121, 163
Topshop, 358, 384
Tory Burch Foundation, 79
Toyota Motor Sales, 93, 108, 114, 248
Toys 'R Us, 287
Trader Joe's, 190, 355
Transparency International, 104
TransUnion, 313
Travelers Insurance, 47
Treasury, Department of the, 464, 468
TreeHouse Island, 228
Triangle Shirtwaist Factory, 49–50
Triscuits, 376
Tropicana, 343
TRU, 316
Trumpet, 170–171
Tufts University, 495
Tumbleweed, 505
Tumblr, 317
TurboTax, 431
Turning Technologies, 138
Turtle Wax Ltd, 288–289, 24, 374
Twitter, 20, 28, 65, 128, 132, 168, 172, 193, 221, 258, 307–308, 358, 369, 377, 399–400, 433, 505

UCB, 217
Under Armour, 355
Unified Grocers, 352
Unilever, 317, 375, 499
Union Bank, 46
United, 493
United Automobile, Aerospace and Agricultural Implement Workers of America, 236
United Food and Commercial Workers, 236
United Negro College Fund, 375–376
United States Olympic Committee, 309
United Technologies, 450
UNIVAC I, 410
University of California, 495
University of Southern California, 495
Univision, 321
Unix, 412
Unreal Brands, 183
UPS, 6, 412
US Airways, 151, 204, 492, 493
US Bancorp, 472
U.S. Chamber of Commerce, 161
U.S. Commercial Service, 110
U.S. Copyright Office, 174
U.S. False Claims Act, 441
U.S. Green Building Council, 277–278
U.S. Hispanic Chamber of Commerce, 178
U.S. International Trade Commission, 110
U.S. News & World Report, 429
U.S. Patent and Trademark Office, 174
U.S. Postal Service, 71, 311
U.S. Sentencing Commission, 31, 33
U.S. Small Business Advisor, 110
USAjobs.gov, A-51
UsedCardboardBoxes.com, 42
Usher, A-13
Utah Business, 216

Valentino, 373
Vanderbilt, Cornelius, 12
Vault.com, A-51
Velcro, 170
Verizon, 45, 49, 322, 375, 377, 414, 450
Viacom, A-8
Virgin America Airlines, 38
Virgin Group, 170
Visa, 344

Vistakon, 508
Viswanatha, Aruna, 116
Vitrano, Robbie, 170–171
Volkswagen, 93, 152
Vroom, Victor, 233

Wagner, Ashley, 377
Wahlberg, Mark, A-13
Walgreens, 183, 398
Walk for the Cure, 375
Wall Street Journal, 468
Wall Street Journal Small Business, 162
Wallach, Dan, 123, 515
Walmart, 45, 66, 70, 94, 95, 114, 147, 150, 162, 177, 219, 220, 251, 314, 322, 339, 340, 344, 352, 360, 392, 498, A-1
Walmart International, 95
Walt Disney Company, 3, 23, 97, 198, 205, 256, 507
Walt Disney World, 281
Walton, Sam, 147, 162
Walton Five and Dime, 162
WAN, 413
Wang, Ge, 168
Warby Parker, 136, 146
Ward, Constance, 84
Washington State Ferries, 148
WaterDrop Shop, 311
Wayfair.com, 15, 348
Weber, Lauren, 132
WeddingChannel.com, 163
Weiner, Bobbie, 162, 164
Weingart, Josh, 311
WellPoint, 46
Wells Fargo, 473, 483
Wendy's, 140
West, Kanye, A-13
WhatsApp, 421, 507
White, Shaun, 157
Whitehall, Richard, 122
WhitePages.com, 416
Whitman, Meg, 513
Whitney, Eli, 12
Whole Foods Market, 132, 251, 346, 414, A-52
WholesaleSarong.com, 351
Wilde, Olivia, 163
Wilson Sporting Goods Company, 289
Windex, 344
Windham Worldwide, 46
Windows, 411, 412
Windows 8, 407
Winthrop, Bayard, 348–349
WNA (World Nuclear Association), 88–89
Women's Venture Capital Fund, 178
Wong, Venessa, 75

Woodman, Nicholas, 157
Woodman Labs, 157–158
Workday, 407
Working Mother, 50
World Bank, 81, 107
World Bank Group, 81
World Economic Forum, 82–83
World Nuclear Association
(WNA), 88–89
**World Trade Organization
(WTO)**, 106–107, 110, A-4

World Wildlife Fund, 277
Wozniak, Steve, 130

Xerox, 344

Yahoo, 247, 377, 416
Yale University, 506
Yankee Stadium, 389
Yellen, Janet, 80, 477
Yoplait, 47
Young, David, 390

YouTube, 358, 377, 399–400, A-8
Yum! Brands, 141

Zack, Bill, 134–135
Zamrudeen, Shez, 175
Zaparde, Rujul, 161
Zappos, 165, 200, 208, 306
Zazzle, 111
ZeroAccess, 416
Zipcar, 399–400, 426
Zuckerberg, Mark, 421

Subject Index

Entries in **bold** refer to the "Business Terms You Need to Know," which are listed at the end of each chapter.

Absolute advantage, 96–97
Academy Awards, 452
Accessory equipment, 337
Accounting. See also Financial statements
  budgeting, 449–451
  business activities involving, 433
  cycle of, 436–439
  financial ratio analysis, 446–449
  foundation of, 435–436
  international, 451–453
  overview, 431
  professionals, 433–435
  users of information, 432–433
Accounting, international exchange rates, 452
  International Accounting Standards Board (IASB), 452–453
  International Financial Reporting Standards (IFRS), 452–453
  overview, 451
Accounting cycle, 437–439
Accounting equation, 437–438
Accounting professionals, 433–435
Accounts receivable, 497
Accrual accounting, 446
Acquisitions, 114, 151–152, 507–508
Active listening, 260
Activity ratios, 447–448
Adaptation, 116, 314, 315
Additive manufacturing, 273
Adjourning stage of team development, 255
Administrative agencies, A-2–A-3
Administrative service managers, 302
Admired companies, 21–23
Advertising
  advertising media, 376–380
  direct mail, 378–379
  infomercials, 380–381
  Internet, 377–378
  magazines, 378
  media, 376–377
  newspapers, 378
  outdoor advertising, 379–380
  product life cycle and, 376
  public relations, 402
  radio, 378
  sponsorship, 380
  types of, 375–376
Advertising specialities, 382–383
Advocacy advertising, 375
Affective conflict, 257
Affinity programs, 327–328
Affirmative action programs, 221
Africa, 308–309, 311, 346, 375
Age discrimination, 53
Age Discrimination in Employment Act, 51, 52, 53
Agents, 351
Aging population, 16–17, 83
Agreement, A-10
Agriculture, and sustainability, 45
AIO statements, 322
Airline Deregulation Act, A-5
Alien corporations, 149
AllBusiness.com, 176
Alternative distribution channels, 349
Alternative energy, 45
Ambiguity, tolerance for, 172
American Jobs Creation Act, A-7
Americans with Disabilities Act, 51, 52, 221, A-7
Analysts (product associates), 345
Analytic production system, 276–277
Angel investors, 178
Angry customer, calming, 327
Anticybersquatting Consumer Protection Act, A-9
Antitrust and business regulation, A-4–A-5
Appellate courts, A-3
Application service provider (ASP), 420
Application software, 412
Apps, 222
Arbitration, 238
Argentina, 107
Articles of incorporation, 149
Asian Americans, 17–18
Assembly line, 12–13, 275
Asset, 437
Asset intensity, 495
Association of South East Asian Nations (ASEAN), 107
Australia, 105, 453
Austria, 258
Auto industry, 93, 102
Auto insurance, A-23
Auto manufacturing, 282
Autocratic leadership, 203
Automatic merchandising, 354

B Corporations, 146
B2B (Business-to-business) products, 313
B2C (Business-to-consumer) products, 313
Baby Boomers, 16, 53, 321, A-49–A-50
Bahamas, 113
Bailment, law of, A-12
Balance of payments, 97
Balance of trade, 97
Balance sheet, 440–441, 442
Balance sheet hedge, 499
Balanced budget, 81
Balance-of-payments deficit, 97
Balance-of-payments surplus, 97
Bank operations, 473
Bank regulation, 479–480
Bank Secrecy Act, A-8
Bankruptcy, A-14–A-15
Bankruptcy Abuse Prevention and Consumer Protection Act of 2005, A-15
Banks, 473–474
Basic money management, A-32–A-33
BDO Seidman LLP, accounting approach, 458
Benchmarking, 292
Benefit corporations, 146
Benefits, 226–228
The Best 109 Internships, A-48
Best companies to work for, 230
BFOQ (Bona fide occupational qualification), 222
Big data, 315, 405
Biodegradability, 46
Birthrate, global, 94
Bitcoins, 461
Board of directors, 150
Bolivia, 107
Bona fide occupational qualification (BFOQ), 222
Bond rating, 465–466
Bonds, 464–466
Botnet, 417
Bottom line, 443
Boycotts, 238, 239
BP oil spill, 44
Brand, 13, 344–347
Brand awareness, 345
Brand control, 335
Brand insistence, 345
Brand loyalty, 323
Brand manager, 345

647

Brand names vs. store brands, 398
Brand preference, 345
Brand recognition, 345
Branding, 13
Brazil, 96, 107, 114
Breach of contract, A-10
Breakeven analysis, 391–392
Breaking Bad, 377
Breast cancer, 47
Bribery, 116. *See also* Corruption
Brokers, 351
Budget, 81, 449
Budget, federal, 81–82
Budget deficit, 81
Budget surplus, 81
Budgeting, 449–450
Business
21st-century managers, 19–21
admirable qualities in, 21–23
definition, 4–5
factors of production, 6–7
history of, 10–16
not-for-profit organizations, 5
overview of, 3–4
private enterprise system, 7–10
workforce, 16–19
Business bankruptcies, A-15
Business cycles, 74–75
Business ethics
bribery, 116
Chinese-made multivitamins, 293
code of ethics, 171
common challenges, 37
concern for ethical and societal issues, 32
conflict of interest, 36–37
contemporary environment, 32–38
credos, 32–33, 39
debit card fees, 481
definition, 32
dividends, necesssity of, 502
electronics recycling, 82
ethical action, 38, 40–41
ethical awareness, 38, 39
ethical development, 35
ethical education, 38, 39–40
ethical environment, 38–41
ethical leadership, 38, 41
ethical standards, 193–194
executive compensation, 151
fair trade, 22
free credit reports, 313
free ebooks, 390
honesty and integrity, 37
importing vitamins, 293
individual ethics, 34–35

on-the-job dilemmas, 35–38
loss of customer money, 195
loyalty vs. truth, 37
monitoring employees' internet use, 418
organizational shaping of, 38–41
overview of, 31–32
quality controls, 293
social media screening, 231
social networking policy, 40
social responsibility, 41–54
teens at malls, 356
and top management, 193
virtual teamwork, 253
whistle blowers, 441
whistle-blowing, 37–38
Business goods, classification of, 335–336
Business idea, selection of, 173–175
Business incubators, 138–139
Business intelligence, 317
Business law
administrative agencies, A-2–A-3
bankruptcy law, A-14–A-15
class-action suits, A-14
consumer protection, A-6
core of, A-9–A-12
cyberspace and telecommunications protection, A-8–A-9
definition, A-4
employee protection, A-7
investor protection, A-8
legal system, A-2–A-3
overview of, A-1–A-2
regulatory environment, A-4–A-6
tax law, A-15
types of, A-3–A-4
Business markets, segmentation of, 323–324
Business ownership
corporations, 145–146
forms of, 143–148
partnerships, 144–145
sole proprietorship, 144
Business plan, 135–136, 175–176
definition, A-39
overview of, A-38
resources, A-44–A-46
writting, A-39–A-44
Business products, 313
Business-to-business (B2B) products, 313
Business-to-consumer (B2C) products, 313
Buyers, number of, 66

Buyers' income, and the demand curve, 66
Buyer's market, 308
Buyouts, 507–508

C Corporations, 146
CAD (Computer-aided design), 273, 279
Cafeteria plans, 227
Call provision, 466
CAM (Computer-aided manufacturing), 279
Canada, 96, 98, 107–108, 453, 470, 483
Capacity, A-10
Capital, 6, 67
Capital investment analysis, 498
Capital items, 337
Capital structure
dividend policy, 501–502
and leverage, 500
long-term financing, 504–507
overview, 499–500
short-term and long-term funds, 500–501
short-term funding options, 503–504
Capitalism, 8, 69–72, 73
Career centers, A-51
Career choice, A-32
Career development, self-assessment for, A-49–A-50
Careers in contemporary business
building a résumé, A-53–A-58
employment decisions, A-61–A-62
internships, A-48–A-49
job interviews, A-58–A-62
job market, A-62–A-63
job searching, A-50–A-53
long-range view, A-63
nontraditional students, A-62
overview of, A-47
self-assessment for career development, A-49–A-50
Cash budget, 450, 451
Cash flow, 446
Cash flow statement, 444–446
Cash value policies, A-25
Catalogs, advertising media, 378–379
Category advisor, 346
Category manager, 345
Cause advertising, 375
Cause marketing, 311
Cause-related marketing, 47
Central America–Dominican Republic Free Trade Agreement (CAFTA-DR), 109

Central Contractor
    Registration, 137
Centralization, 208–209
Century Bonds, 495
CEO (Chief executive officer),
    150–151, 190, 302, 492
Certified forensic accountant
    (CrFA), 434
Certified fraud examiner, 434
Certified internal auditors, 434
Certified management accountant
    (CMA), 434–435
Certified public accountants
    (CPAs), 434
CFO (Chief financial officer),
    150, 151, 190, 302, 492
CFPB (Consumer Financial
    Protection Bureau), 43
Chain of command, 209
Change, and leadership, 21
Channels of communication,
    258, 260–263
"Charitable commerce"
    websites, 43
Check clearing, Fed, 477
Check Clearing for the 21st
    Century Act, A-9
Checking accounts, A-33
Chief executive officer (CEO),
    150–151, 190, 302, 492
Chief financial officer (CFO),
    150, 151, 190, 302, 492
**Chief information officer
    (CIO)**, 150, 302, 406
Chief operating officer (COO),
    150, 302
Childhood obesity, 44
Children's Online Privacy
    Protection Act, A-9
Chile, 107
China, 17
    absolute advantage, 96
    censorship in, 194
    comparative advantage, 96
    flexible manufacturing
        systems, 279
    GDP, 95
    Hong Kong and the IFRS, 453
    human resources in, 94
    Hunan bond for metal clean-
        up, 467
    Industrial & Commercial Bank
        of China Limited, 483
    international law, A-3–A-4
    and legal environment, 104
    Lenova Group, 508
    and luxury brands, 366
    marketing mix for, 314–315
    and multinational
        corporations, 114
    multivitamins made in, 293
    and offshoring, 113
    potential market in, 95

and reshoring, 114
supercomputer Tianhe-2, 410
trade deficit with, 98
as a trading partner, 96
and U.S. Treasury Bonds, 482
vitamins and ethics, 293
Choice, right to, 48–49
Chonological résumé, A-54
Cigarettes, A-1
CIM (Computer-integrated
    manufacturing), 280
CIO (Chief information officer),
    150, 302, 406
Civil Rights Act of 1964, 52, 53,
    221
Civil Rights Act of 1991, 51, 52,
    221
Class-Action Fairness Act,
    A-14
Class-action suits, A-14
Classic entrepreneurs, 163
Classification of goods and
    services
    business goods, 335–336
    classification of services,
        337–338
    consumer goods and
        services, 335
Classroom training, 223
Clayton Act, 71, A-5
Clean tech, 45
Cleaning products, 358
Closed corporations, 150
Closely held corporations, 150
Clothing donations, 35–36
Cloud computing, 421
CMA (Certified management
    accountant), 434–435
Cobranding, 327–328
Code of conduct, 39
Code of ethics, 171. See also
    Business ethics
Cognitive conflict, 256–257
Cohesiveness, team, 256
Collaboration, innovation
    through, 18–19
Collective bargaining, 237
Collective business ownership,
    148–149
Colonial period, in history of
    business, 11
Colony collapse disorder, 311
Comarketing, 327–328
Commercial and business
    insurance, A-23
Commercial paper, 504
Commericial banks, 472–473
Committee organizations,
    209–210
Common law, A-3
Common markets, 105–109
Common stock, 150,
    466–467

Communication
    barriers to, 100–101
    basic forms of, 259–264
    channels of, 258, 260–263
    electronic, 165
    external, 264–265
    formal, 261–262
    importance of, 257–259
    informal, 262–263
    nonverbal, 263–264
    oral, 259–260
    process of, 257–259
    in teams, 257
    written, 260–261
Communism, 72, 73
Community cafes, 31
Company performance,
    employee rewards linked to,
    249–250
Comparative advantage,
    96–97
Comparative advertising, 376
Compensating balances, 504
Compensation, 225–229
    average costs for, 227
    employee benefits,
        226–227
    flexible benefits, 227–228
    flexible work, 228–229
Competition, 8, 69–72, 136,
    354–357. See also World
    markets, competition in
Competitive differentiation,
    8, 200
Competitive position, assessment
    of, 198–200
Competitive pricing,
    393–394
Complementary goods, prices
    of, 66
Component parts and materials,
    337
Compressed workweek, 228
Computer Fraud and Abuse Act,
    A-9
Computer hardware and
    software, 410–413
Computer networks
    Intranets, 414
    LANs and WANs, 413
    virtual private networks
        (VPNs), 414–415
    viruses, worms, Trojan horses,
        spyware,
        416–417
    VoIP, 415
    wireless local networks,
        413–414
Computer systems
    administrators, 429
Computer systems analysts, 429
**Computer-aided design
    (CAD)**, 273, 279

Computer-aided
  manufacturing
  (CAM), 279
Computer-based
  information systems,
  406–407
Computer-based training, 223
Computer-integrated
  manufacturing (CIM), 280
Computers, impact on
  accounting, 438–439
Concept testing, 342
Conceptual skills for managers,
  191–192
Conflict, 256–257
Conflict of interest, 36–37
Conglomerate merger, 152
Consideration, A-10
Construction industry, 239
Construction managers, 302
Consumer behavior, 324–325
Consumer complaints, 49
Consumer Credit Protection
  Act, A-6
Consumer Financial Protection
  Bureau (CFPB), 43
Consumer goods, classification
  of, 335
Consumer interests and
  preferences, 131–132
Consumer markets,
  segmentation of
  demographic segmentation,
  319–321, 323
  geographical segmentation,
  319, 323
  product-related segmentation,
  322–323
  psychological segmentation,
  321–322
Consumer orientation, 13
Consumer perception of
  prices, 394
Consumer Price Index (CPI),
  77, 78
Consumer product classification,
  336–337
Consumer Product Safety
  Act, A-6
Consumer products, 313
Consumer protection, A-6
Consumer rights, 46–49
Consumerism, 47
Consumer-oriented promotions,
  381–383
Context, and
  communication, 258
Contingency planning, 196, 197
Continuous production
  system, 277
Contract, A-10
Contract Assistance for Women
  Business Owners, 140

Contractual agreements, 112
Control, internal locus of, 172
Controller, 492
Controlling, 193
Convenience products, 337
Conventional stage of individual
  ethics, 35
Convertible securities, 467
COO (Chief operating officer),
  150, 302
Cooperative
  advertising, 387
Cooperative education, A-49
Cooperative ownership,
  148–149
Copyright, A-13
Core inflation rate, 76
Corporate charters, 149
Corporate culture,
  204–205
Corporate downsizing, 132
Corporate management,
  150–151
Corporate managers,
  150–151
Corporate officers, 150–151
Corporate philanthropy, 43,
  46–47
Corporate social responsibility.
  See Social responsibility
Corporations
  levels of management in, 150
  management of, 150–151
  organization of, 149–151
  overview of, 145–146
  types of, 149
Corruption, 103–104, 116
Corruption Perceptions
  Index, 104
Costa Rica, 109
Cost-based pricing, 391
Countertrade, 112
Coupons, 382
Court system, A-2
Covalence Ethical Rankings, 116
Cover letter, A-57
CPAs (Certified public
  accountants), 434
CPI (Consumer Price Index),
  77, 78
Creative selling, 384
Creativity, 20–21, 172
Credit, A-33
Credit Card Accountability
  Responsibility and
  Disclosure Act (CARD Act),
  A-29, A-34
Credit CARD Act of 2009, 379
Credit cards, 134
Credit crisis, 465
Credit management,
  A-33–A-34
Credit reports, 313

Credit Unions, 474
Credos, and business ethics,
  32–33, 39
CrFA (Certified forensic
  accountant), 434
Crisis management, 264–265
Critical path, 291
Critical thinking, 20–21
CRM (Customer relationship
  management), 328
CRO Magazine, 202
Cross-functional team, 252
Cruise industry, 264–265
Cuba, 105–106
Cultural differences, and
  international trade, 100–101
Currency conversion, 102
Customer
  departmentalization, 207
Customer preferences, and the
  demand curve, 66
Customer relationship
  management (CRM), 328
Customer relationships, 14
Customer service standards, 361
Customer service strategy, 355
Customer-based segmentation,
  319–321, 323
Customer-driven marketing
  consumer behavior, 324–325
  market segmentation,
  317–324
  marketing concept, evolution
  of, 307–308
  marketing research, 315–317
  marketing strategy
  development, 312–315
  not-for-profit and nontraditional
  marketing, 308–311
  overview, 305–307
  relationship marketing,
  325–328
Customer-driven production, 276
Customer-oriented layout,
  284–285
Customers
  connecting too, 305
  identification of in a business
  plan, 136
  social responsibility and, 47–49
Customs unions, 107
Cybercrime, 415–416
Cyberspace, A-8–A-9
Cyclical unemployment,
  78–79
Cynical listening, 260
Czech Republic, 109

Data, marketing research
  application of, 317
  data mining, 317
  external data, 316
  focus group, 317

internal data, 315–316
primary data, 316
secondary data, 316
Data information, 406
Data mining, 317
Data warehouses, 317
Database administrators, 429
Databases, 408–409
Debt capital, 499–500
Debt financing, 176–177
Decentralization, 208–209
Decision making, 201–202, 248–249
Decision support system (DSS), 409
Decline stage of product life cycle, 340
Defensive listening, 260
Deflation, 77
Delegation, 208–209
Demand
  definition, 64
  factors driving, 64–67
  global increase in, 115
  interactions with supply, 67–69
Demand curve, 65–66
Demand flow, 287–288
Demand-pull inflation, 76
Democratic leadership, 203
Demographic segmentation, 319–321, 323
Departmentalization, 206–208
Deregulation, A-5–A-6
Devaluation, 99, 102
Developing nations, 94–95
Dietary Supplement Health and Education Act, A-6
"Different Strokes," A-13
Digital Millennium Copyright Act, A-8
Direct distribution, 348–349
Direct distribution channel, 347
Direct exporting, 111–112
Direct mail, 378–379
Direct selling, 354
Directing, 192–193
Direct-response retailing, 353
Disability income insurance, A-25
Discount pricing, 392–393
Discount rate, 478
Discrimination
  age, 53
  equal opportunity, 51–53
  in hiring, 221
  in the workplace, 51
Dispatching, 291
Distribution channels
  customer service, 361
  definition of, 347–348
  direct distribution, 348–349
  intensity, selection of, 358–359

international, 357–358
marketing intermediaries, 349–350
physical distribution and logistics, 359–361
selection of, 357–358
Distribution intensity, 358–359
Distribution strategy, 314, 347–350
Diversity, 17–18
Divestitures, 507–508
Dividend policy, 501–502
Dodd-Frank Wall Street Reform and Consumer Protection Act, 441, A-4, A-6, A-8
Doha Round, 107
Domestic corporations, 149
Dominican Republic, 109
Do-Not-Call Fee Extension Act of 2007, A-9
Do-Not-Call Improvement Act of 2007, A-9
Double taxation, 145
Double-entry bookkeeping, 438
Downsizing, 229–230
Downward communication, 261
Drop shipper, 351
Drug testing, 222
DSS (Decision support system), 409
Dumping, 105–106
DVD rentals, 322

ECNs (Electronic communications networks), 471
E-commerce sites, 17, 43, 104
Economic challenges
  evaluation of economic performance, 74–80
  global challenges of the 21st century, 82–84
  macroeconomics, 69–73
  management of economy's performance, 80–82
  microeconomics, 64–69
  overview of, 63–64
Economic Development Administration, 137
Economic differences, and international trade, 101–102
Economic performance
  evaluation of, 74–80
  flattening the business cycle, 74–75
  price-level changes, 76–80
  productivity and gross domestic product, 75–76
Economic trends, and entrepreneurship, 168–169
Economic unions, 107
Economics, 63

Economy, management of performance of, 80–82
EDI (Electronic data interchange), 360, 361
EDLP (Everyday low pricing), 392–393
Education, 46, 167–168
El Salvador, 109
Electric cars, 44
Electronic banking, 473
Electronic communications, 165
Electronic communications networks (ECNs), 471
Electronic data interchange (EDI), 360, 361
Electronics, disposal of, 44–45
E-mail, 261
Embargo, 105–106
Emerging market economies (EMEs), 107
Emirates, 494
Employee benefits, 226–227
Employee motivation
  equity theory, 233–234
  expectancy theory, 233–234
  goal-setting theory, 234–235
  Herzog's two-factor model of motivation, 233
  job design, 235
  linking rewards to company performance, 249–250
  management by objectives, 234–235
  managers' attitudes and, 235–236
  Maslow's hierarchy of needs, 232
  morale, 226
  overview of, 230–232
Employee ownership, 146–147
Employee protection, A-7
Employee separation, 229–230
Employee stock ownership plans (ESOPs), 147, 250
Employee training, 249
Employees. *See also* Employee benefits; Employee motivation
  empowerment of, 248–250
  equal opportunity, 51–53
  recruitment and selection, 220–223
  rights of, 73
  social responsibility and, 49–54
Employment decisions, A-61–A-62
Employment levels, 77–80
Empowerment, 203, 248–250
Encoding messages, 257–258
Endowment funds, 506

End-use segmentation, 324
Energy, and environmental
    concerns, 15–16
Energy level, and
    entrepreneurs, 170
Energy production, 3
England, 11–12, 483
Enterprise software, 19–20
Enterprise zones, 178
Entrepreneur
    categories of, 16
    characteristics of, 169–173
    definition, 9
    funding sources, 176–177
Entrepreneurship, 9–10
    business plans, creation of,
        175–176
    categories of, 163
    characteristics of, 169–173
    definition, 7, 162
    and demographic trends,
        168–169
    and economic trends,
        168–169
    and education, 167–168
    environment for, 166–169
    globalization, 166–167
    and information
        technology, 168
    international levels of, 167
    overview of, 161–162
    and quality-of-life issues,
        165–166
    reasons to choose, 164–166
    starting a new venture,
        173–178
    and the supply curve, 67
Environmental concerns, 15–16,
    17, 42, 199
Environmental impact
    study, 281
Environmental protection,
    44–46
Equal Employement Opportunity
    Act, 51
Equal opportunity, employees
    and, 51–53
Equal Pay Act, 51, 52
Equilibrium price, 68
**Equity, statement of owners'
    or shareholders'**, 444
Equity capital, 499–500
Equity financing, 177–178
Equity theory, 233–234
ESOPs (Employee stock
    ownership plans), 147, 250
ESS (Executive support
    system), 409
Esteem needs, 231
Ethical action, 38, 40–41
Ethical awareness, 38, 39
Ethical development, 35
Ethical education, 38, 39–40

Ethical environment, 38–41
Ethical leadership, 38, 41
Ethical standards, 193–194
Ethics. *See* **Business ethics**
Ethics compliance programs,
    33–34, 39
Ethics hotlines, 39, 41
Ethiopia, 102
EU (European Union), 98,
    101, 109, 453, 505
Euro, 505
Europages, 110
European Alliance, 357
European Commission, 357
European Union (EU), 98,
    101, 109, 453, 505
Event marketing, 310–311
**Everyday low pricing
    (EDLP)**, 392–393
Exchange control, 106
Exchange process, 306
Exchange rates, 98–99, 102,
    452, 499
Exchanges, stock, 469
Exclusive distribution, 359
Executive compensation,
    151, 234
Executive summary, of a business
    plan, 135, A-40–A-41
**Executive support system
    (ESS)**, 409
Existing business, purchase
    of, 174
**Expansionary monetary
    policy**, 80
Expectancy theory, 233–234
Expense items, 337
Expert system, 409–410
Export management
    company, 112
Exporters, 111–112
Exports, 93, 94, 97–98,
    111–112
External communication,
    264–265
External data, 316
Eye contact, 263

Facility layout, 283–285
Factor, 504
Factor payments, 6
Factoring, 504
Factors of production, 6–7,
    67, 94
Failed products, 343
Failure, tolerance for, 171
Fair Credit Reporting Act (FCRA),
    313
Fair Disclosure (Regulation
    FD), 55
Fair Labor Standards Act of
    1938, 237, A-7
Fair trade, 22

Fair Trade exchanges,
    488–489
False Claims Act, 38
Family and Medical Leave Act
    of 1993, 50, 52, 135,
    226, A-7
Family brand, 344
Family leave, 50
Family-owned businesses, 147
Fast-casual dining, 68–69
FCRA (Fair Credit Reporting Act),
    313
FDIC (Federal Deposit Insurance
    Corporation), 473–474
Federal budget, 81–82
**Federal Deposit Insurance
    Corporation (FDIC)**,
    473–474
Federal Food and Drug
    Act, A-6
Federal funds rate, 479
Federal Reserve
    organization, 476
**Federal Reserve System
    (Fed)**, 476–479
Federal Rules of Civil Procedure,
    A-1
Federal Trade Commission Act,
    A-5
Federal Trade Commission (FTC),
    48, 379
Feedback, and
    communcation, 258
Fee-for-service plan, A-24
Field selling, 384
Finance, 491–493
Finance charge, A-33
Finance companies, 475
**Financial Accounting
    Standards Board
    (FASB)**, 436
Financial community,
    responsibilities to, 54–55
Financial institutions
    commercial banks, 472–473
    mutual funds, 475–476
    nondepository financial
        institutions, 475
    saving banks and credit
        unions, 474
Financial management
    asset management,
        496–499
    financial manager, role of,
        492–494
    financial planning, 494–496
    long-term financing sources,
        504–507
    mergers, acquisitions, buyouts,
        divestitures, 507–508
    overview, 491
    short-term funding options,
        503–504

sources of funds and capital structure, 499–502
Financial managers, 488–489, 491–493, 516
Financial markets, 467–469
Financial plan, 494–496, A-29–A-31
Financial ratio analysis
  activity ratios, 447–448
  leverage ratios, 449
  liquidity ratios, 446–447
  profitability ratios, 448–449
Financial section of a business plan, 135, A-43–A-44
Financial statements
  balance sheet, 440–441
  income statement, 441–444
  statement of cash flows, 444–446
  statement of owners,' or shareholders', equity, 444
Financial success, and entrepreneurship, 164–165
Financial system
  Federal Reserve System, 476–479
  financial institutions, 472–476
  financial markets, 467–469
  global perspective, 482–483
  overview, 461
  regulation of, 479–482
  securities, types of, 463–467
  stock markets, 469–471
  understanding, 462
Financing
  for entrepreneurs, 176–178
  inadequacy of in small businesses, 134
  sources of for small businesses, 134
  types of, 176–178
fingerprint-based payment identification system, 168–169
Firewall, 414
First-line management, 190, 191
Fiscal imbalances, 83
Fiscal policy, 80–82
Fishing industry, 70
Fitch, 465–466
Fitness club industry, 127
Fixed-position layout, 284–285
Flexibility, in the workforce, 18
Flexible benefit plans, 227–228
Flexible manufacturing systems (FMS), 279
Flexible production, 276
Flexible work plans, 228–229
Flexible work schedules, 50
Flextime, 228
Floating exchange rates, 98–99
Floor ads, 379
Focus group, 317, 342

Follow-up, production plan, 291
Food and Drug Administration Amendments Act, A-6
Food and Drug Administration Amendments Act of 2007, A-6
Food and Drug Administration (FDA), 48, 347
Food service managers, 302
Foreign corporations, 149
Foreign Corrupt Practices Act, 103
Foreign Corrupt Practices Act, 435–436, 441
Foreign currency, 112. *See also* **Exchange rates**
Foreign licensing agreement, 113
Foreign stock markets, 470–471
Forensic accountants, 434
Form utility, 306
Formal communication, 259, 261–262
Formation stage of team development, 254–255
401(k) plans, 227
Fracking, 3
France, 96, 103, 104, 470
Franchisee, 141, 143
Franchise/franchising, 112–113
  agreements, 141
  Anytime Fitness, 127
  benefits and challenges of, 141–143
  overview of, 140–141
  purchase of, 174–175
  sector overview, 141
Franchisor, 141, 143
"Free" credit reports (marketing strategy), 313
Free trade. *See* Common markets; **North American Free Trade Agreement (NAFTA)**
Free-rein leadership, 203
Free-trade areas, 107
Frequency marketing, 327–328
Frictional unemployment, 78, 79
Friendship, commerce, and navigation (FCN) treaties, 104
FTC (Federal Trade Commission), 48, 379
Full-function merchant wholesalers, 351
Functional departmentalization, 207
Functional résumé, A-55
Funds, sources of, 499–502
Future expectations, 66

GAAP (Generally accepted accounting principles), 435, 453
Games, contests and sweepstakes, 382
Gantt chart, 290
Gasoline, and the demand curve, 65–66
General Agreement on Tariffs and Trade (GATT), 106
General obligation bond, 465
Generally accepted accounting principles (GAAP), 435, 453
Generation X, 16
Generation Y, 16, 229
Genetic Information Nondiscrimination Act, 51, 52
Geographical departmentalization, 207
Geographical segmentation, 319, 323
Germany, 96, 103, 104, 258, 286–287, 360
Gestures, 263
GEW (Global Entrepreneurship Week), 167
Glass ceiling, 139–140
Global (Norway), 506
Global business strategies, 115–116
Global Entrepreneurship Week (GEW), 167
Global Risks Report, 83
Globalization, and entrepreneurship, 166–167
GO (Gross output), 76
Goal acceptance, 234
Goal specificity, 234
Goal-setting theory, 234–235
Gossip, 263
"Got Milk?," 369
Government regulation, and small businesses, 134–135
Government regulation of the financial markets, 480–481
Government support for new ventures, 178
Gramm-Leach-Bliley Act, A-6
Grapevine, 262–263
Great Depression, 13, 74, A-4–A-5
Greece, 505
Green advantage, 15–16
Green banks, 463
Green construction, 239
Green Five, 239
Green manufacturing processes, 277–278, 293
Green marketing, 45, 46
Greenhouse gas emissions, 83

Grid computing, 421
Grievances, 238
Grooming products, 132
Gross domestic product (GDP)
in developing nations, 95
and the European Union, 109
imports and exports, 93
and NAFTA, 108
nations with highest, 76
and productivity, 75–76
and small businesses, 129, 130
Gross output (GO), 76
Growth, sustained, 74
Growth stage of product life cycle, 339–340
Guatemala, 109
Guerrilla marketing, 374

Hard currencies, 99
Hardware, 410–412
Health Care and Education Reconciliation Act, A-7
Health care benefits, 226–227
Health care industry, 248–249
Health insurance, A-23–A-25
Health maintenance organizations (HMOs), A-24
Hedge funds, 506–507
Helsinkski, stock market, 470
Herzog's two-factor model of motivation, 233
High-context cultures, 258
Hispanic Americans, 17, 54
Historically Underutilized Business (HUBZones), 135
History of business, 10
colonial period, 11
green advantage, 15–16
industrial entrepreneurs, 11, 12
Industrial Revolution, 11–12
marketing era, 11, 13, 307, 308
production era, 11, 12–13, 307, 308
relationship era, 11, 13–14, 307, 308
social era, 11, 14
strategic alliances, 15
Home-based businesses, 130
Homeland Security Act, A-9
Homeowners' insurance, A-23
Honduras, 109
Honesty, 37
Honey bee research, 311
Hong Kong, 374, 453, 470
Horizontal drilling, 3
Horizontal merger, 152
Household income, 66
Housing costs, A-34

HUBZones (Historically Underutilized Business), 135
Human resource management
compensation, 225–229
definition, 220
employee motivation, 230–236
employee separation, 229–230
orientation, training, and evaluation, 223–224
overview of, 219–220
recruitment and selection, 220–223
Human resource managers, 302–303
Human resources, 6–7, 67
Human skills for managers, 191
Hungary, 109
Hygiene factors, 233
Hyperinflation, 76

IASB (International Accounting Standards Board), 452–453
IASC (International Accounting Standards Committee), 452–453
Iceland, 109
Identity Theft and Assumption Deterrence Act, A-9
IFRS (International Financial Reporting Standards), 452–453
IMMACT 90 (Immigration Act of 1990), 178
Immigration Act of 1990 (IMMACT 90), 178
Importers, 111–112
Imports, 93, 94, 97–98, 111–112
Inbound telemarketing, 385
Inc. magazine, 176
Income inequality, 234
Income statement, 441–444
Incorporators, 149
Incubators, business, 138–139
India, 94, 95, 113, 258, 279, 319, 453
Indirect exporting, 111
Individual branding, 344
Individual ethics, 34–35
Industrial entrepreneurs, 11, 12
Industrial Revolution, 11–12
Industries, creation of, 131–132
Industries and sectors dominated by small businesses, 129–130
Industries best for starting a new business, 131
Industry conditions, in a business plan, 136

Industry self-regulation, 481–482
Inflation, 76
Infomercials, 380–381
Informal communication, 259, 262–263
Information, right to, 48
Information security analysts, 429
Information sharing, 248–249
Information systems
components of, 407–409
computer networks, 413–415
computer-based information systems, 406–407
databases, 408–409
disaster recovery and backup, 418–419
and ethics, 417–418
hardware and software, 410–413
overview, 406
security and ethical issues, 415–418
technology trends, 419–421
types of, 409–410
Information technology (IT), 168
Information technology trends, 419–420
Informative advertising, 376
Infrastructure, 102
Initial public offering (IPO), 467
Innovation
and small businesses, 132–133
through collaboration, 18–19
and work-at-home policies, 247
Inputs, costs of, 68
Installations, 337
Installment loans, A-33
Institutional advertising, 375
Insurable interest, A-20
Insurable risk, A-20
Insurance
basic concepts, A-19–A-21
concept of risk, A-18
overview of, A-17
in personal financial planning, A-35
shifting risk, A-19
sources of coverage, A-21–A-22
types of, A-22–A-26
Insurance companies, 475
Intangible personal property, A-12
Integrated marketing communications (IMC)
advertising, 375–381
definition of, 370
promotional mix, 371–372

promotional planning, 374
promtional strategy objectives, 372–373
sales promotion, 381–387
Integrity, 37
Intellectual property, A-13
Intensive distribution, 358
Intermittent production process, 277
Internal data, 315–316
Internal locus of control, 172
International Accounting, 451, 452–453
International Accounting Standards Board (IASB), 452–453
International Accounting Standards Committee (IASC), 452–453
International assets, management of, 499
International banks, 482–483
International Consumer Electronics Show, 383
International direct investment, 113–114
International economic communities, 107
International Financial Reporting Standards (IFRS), 452–453
International fiscal policy, 81
International law, A-3
International marketplace, size of, 94–96
International Organization for Standardization (ISO), 294
International regulations, and trade, 104–105
International trade
barriers to, 99–106
and economic differences, 101–102
expansion into, 110–115
international economic communities, 107
involvement, levels of, 111–114
multinational corporations, 114–115
overview of, 99–100
political and legal differences, 102–105
promotion organizations, 106–107
reduction of barriers, 106–109
research resources, 110
social and cultural differences, 100–101
trade restrictions, types of, 105–106

International unions, 236
Internet, 130, 377–378. *See also* Technology
Internet misuse, 37
Internet recruiting, 221
Internet retailing, 353. *See also* E-commerce
The Internship Bible, A-48
Internships, A-48–A-49
Interpersonal skills for managers, 191
Intranet, 414
Intrapreneurship, 178–179
Introduction, to a business plan, 135, A-41–A-42
Introduction stage of product life cycle, 339
Inventory control, 287
Inventory management, 497–498
Investment planning, A-35–A-36
Investment-grade bonds, 466
Investor participation, stock market, 471
Investor protection, A-8
Investors, responsibilities to, 54–55
Invisible hand, 8
Involuntary turnover, 229
IPO (Initial public offering), 467
IT (Information technology), 168
IT managers, 429
Italy, 104–105

Japan, 96, 98, 105, 113, 258, 482, 483, A-4
Job creation, 131, 138
Job design, 235
Job enlargement, 235
Job enrichment, 235
Job interviews, A-58–A-62
Job market, A-62–A-63
Job rotation, 235
Job searching, 219, A-50–A-53
Job security, 165
Job sharing, 18, 228
Jobcasts, 221
JobsinPods.com, 221
Joint venture, 114, 152–153
Judiciary, A-2
Junk bonds, 466
Just-in-time (JIT) system, 287–288

Kindness campaign, 41

Labor disputes, 237–238
Labor legislation, 237
Labor market, A-28–A-29
Labor pool, 16–17
Labor relations, 236–239
Labor union, 286
collective bargaining, 237
competitive tactics, 238–239

development of, 236
future of, 239
and green construction, 239
legislation, 237
settling disputes, 237–238
tactics of, 238–239
Labor-management relations, 236–239
Labor-Management Relations Act, 237
Labor-Management Reporting and Disclosure Act, 237
Landrum-Griffin Act of 1959, 237
Language, and international trade, 100–101
Lanham Act, A-12
LANs (Local area networks), 413
Latin America, 258, 264, 279
Law, A-3. *See also* Business law
Law of agency, A-10
Law of bailment, A-12
Law of large numbers, A-20–A-21
Law of supply and demand, 68. *See also* **Demand; Supply**
LBOs (Leveraged buyouts), 508
Leadership, 21, 203–204
Leadership in Energy and Environmental Design (LEED), 277–278
Leadership styles, 203–204
Leading companies, 115
Lean manufacturing process, 286
LEED (Leadership in Energy and Environmental Design), 277–278
Legal and serious purpose, A-10
Legal differences, and international trade, 102–105
Legal environment, and international trade, 103–104
Legal system, A-2–A-3
Leverage, 500
Leverage ratios, 449
Leveraged buyouts (LBOs), 508
Liability, 437–438
Liability insurance, A-23
Life insurance, A-25–A-26
Lifestyle centers, 356
Lifestyle entrepreneur, 166
Lifetime value of a customer, 326
Lilly Ledbetter Fair Pay Act of 2009, 225, A-7
Limited liability corporations (LLCs), 146
Limited-function merchant wholesaler, 351

Line organizations, 209
Line-and-staff organizations, 209, 210
Liquidity ratios, 446–447
Listening, 260
Listening skills, 261
LLCs (Limited liability corporations), 146
Loan guarantees, 137
Loan officers, 516
Local area networks (LANs), 413
Local unions, 236
Location decision, 280–282, 355–356
Location decisions, 280–282
Lockouts, 239
Lodging managers, 303
Logistics, 359
Long-term financing
  hedge funds, 506–507
  private equity funds, 505–506
  private placements (stocks), 505
  public sale of stocks and bonds, 504–505
  venture capitalists, 505
Low-context cultures, 258
Loyalty vs. truth, 37
Luxury tax, A-15

Macedonia, 109
Macroeconomics
  capitalism, 69–72
  definition, 69
  mixed market economies, 72–73
  planned economies, 72
Magazines, 378
Major purchases, A-34–A-35
Make, buy, or lease decision, 285–286
Malaysia, 104
Malware, 416
Managed care plan, A-24–A-25
Management. *See also* Human resource management
  corporate culture, 204–205
  decision making, 201–202, 248–249
  functions of, 192–193
  hierarchy of, 190–191
  labor relations, 236–239
  leadership, 21, 203–204
  organizational structures, 205–211
  overview of, 189–190
  planning, importance of, 194–197
  shortcomings of in small businesses, 133
  skills required for success, 191–192

  strategic planning process, 197–201
  vision and ethical standards, 193–194
Management accountants, 434–435
Management by objectives (MBO), 234–235
Management career, launching, 302–303
Management development programs, 223–224
Management information system (MIS), 409
Management of enterprises, 73
Management style, 202
Managers, production
  determining layout, 283–285
  planning production process, 283
  production plan, implementation of, 285–288
Managers for the 21st century, 19–21
Managing assets, short-term, 496–498
Mandarin Chinese language, 100
Manufacturers' agents, 351
Manufacturer's brand, 344
Manufacturers' reps, 351
"Market basket," 77, 78
Market conditions, in a business plan, 136
Market interest rate, 466
Market segmentation
  business markets, 323–324
  consumer markets, 319–323
  process of, 318–319
Market survillance, 482
Marketable securities, 497
Marketing
  cause marketing, 311
  connecting to customers, 305–306
  consumer behavior, 324–325
  definition of, 306–307
  event marketing, 310–311
  market segmentation, 318–324
  marketing concept, 307–308
  marketing research, 315–317
  marketing strategy, 312–315
  nontraditional marketing, 309–311
  not-for-profit marketing, 308–309
  organizational marketing, 311
  place marketing, 310
  relationship marketing, 325–326
  utility, 306–307

Marketing concept, 307–308
Marketing era, in the history of business, 13, 307, 308
Marketing intermediaries, 347, 349–350
Marketing management, 402
Marketing mix, 312, 313, 314–315, 388–390
Marketing research, 315–317
Marketing research analysts, 402
Marketing section of a business plan, 135, A-43
Marketing strategy, 312, 313–314, 338
Maslow's hierarchy of needs, 232
Mass customization, 314–315
Mass production, 275
Materials handling, 361
Materials requirement planning (MRP), 288–289
Matrix organizations, 210–211
Maturity stage of product life cycle, 340
MBO (Management by objectives), 234–235
Media, advertising, 376–380
Mediation, 238
Medicaid, A-23–A-24
Medical and health service managers, 303
Medicare, A-23–A-24
Men, 10
Merchant wholesalers, 351
MERCOSUR customs union, 107
Merger, 151–152, 493, 507–508
Mexico
  auto manufacturing, 280–282
  and Domino's Pizza, 112–113
  and Ford Motor Company, 102
  investment in, 201
  and NAFTA, 107–108
  and offshoring, 113
  stock exchange, 470
  as a trading partner, 96
Microeconomics
  demand, factors driving, 64–67
  interactions between demand and supply, 67–69
  supply, factors driving, 67
Microlending, 79
Microloans, 137
Middle management, 190–191, 302
Middleman. *See* Marketing intermediaries
Military veterans, 51

Millenials, 209, A-27
Minorities, small business opportunities for, 139–140
MIS (Management information system), 409
Misleading advertising, 48
Mission statement, 136, 197–198
Missionary selling, 385
Mixed market economies, 72–73
MNC (Multinational corporations), 114–115
Mobile apps, 222
Mobile devices, 14
Mobile recruiting, 222
Mobility, in the workforce, 18
Monetary policy, 80, 477–479
Money management, 497
Money market instruments, 463–464
Monopolistic competition, 70
Monopoly, 70, 71, A-4–A-5
Montenegro, 109
Moody's, 465–466
Morale, 226
MoreBusiness.com, 176
Mortgage pass-through security, 465
Mortgage Reform and Anti-Predatory Lending Act of 2007, A-4
Motivation. *See* Employee motivation
Motivator factors, 233
Motor Carrier Act and Staffers Rail Act, A-5
Moving boxes, 42
MRP (Materials requirement planning), 288–289
Multidomestic business strategies, 116
Multinational corporations (MNC), 114–115
Multivitamins, 293
Mumbai, stock market, 470
Municipal bonds, 465
Music concerts, 8
Mutual funds, 475–476
Myanmar, 36

NAFTA (North American Free Trade Agreement), 107–108, 323–324, 452
NAICS (North American Industry Classification System), 323–324
National brand, 344
National debt, 81
National Environmental Policy Act, A-6

National Labor Relations Act of 1935, 237
National unions, 236
Natural gas, 3
Natural resources, 6, 67
Nearshoring, 18
Negotiable instrument, A-11
Net worth, A-31–A-32
Netherlands, 114
New industries, creation of, 131–132
New Zealand, 105
New-product development, 341–343
Newspapers, 378
Nicaragua, 109
Noise, and communication, 258–259
Nonpersonal selling, 371–372
Nonprogrammed decisions, 201
Nonstore retailers, 352–353
Non-tariff barriers, 105–106
Nontraditional marketing, 309–310
Nontraditional students, A-62
Nonverbal communication, 259, 263–264
Norming stage of team development, 255
North American Free Trade Agreement (NAFTA), 107–108, 323–324, 452
North American Industry Classification System (NAICS), 323–324
Norway, 506
Not-for-profit corporations, 147–148
Not-for-profit marketing, 308–309
Not-for-profit organizations, 5
Nutrition Labeling and Education Act, A-6

Obesity, 44
Objectives, 200
Occupational Safety and Health Administration (OSHA), 50
Odd pricing, 394
Offensive listening, 260
Offset agreement, 112
Offshoring, 18, 113
Oil spills, 44
Oligopoly, 70, 71
On-demand computing, 420–421
One-on-one marketing, 328
Online banking, 473
Online payment systems, 17
Online résumé submission, A-58
On-the-job training, 223

Open market operations, 478–479
Operating systems, 412
Operational planning, 196, 197
Operational support systems, 409
Opportunities. *See* **SWOT analysis**
Optimism, 170–171
Oral communication, 259–260
Order processing, 361, 384
Organization, 205–206
Organization chart, 206
Organization for Economic Cooperation and Development Anti-Bribery Convention, 103
Organizational shaping of ethical conduct
ethical action, 40–41
ethical awareness, 39
ethical education, 39–40
ethical leadership, 41
Organizational structures
delegation, 208–209
departmentalization, 206–208
types of, 209–211
Organizations, promotion of international trade, 106–107
Organizing, 192
OSHA (Occupational Safety and Health Administration), 50
OSHA Act, A-7
Oubound telemarketing, 385
Outdoor advertising, 379–380
Outsourcing, 18, 230
Over-the-counter selling, 384
Owners' equity, 438
Ownership. *See* Business ownership; Collective business ownership; Private business ownership; Public business ownership
Ownership of enterprises, 73
Ownership utility, 307
Ozone safe/friendly, 46

P&L (Profit-and-Loss) statement, 443
Packages and labels (brand identification), 346–347
Paid time off (PTO), 228
Palm oil industry, 32
Paraguay, 107
Partnerships, 144–145
Part-time workers, 18
Patent, A-13
Patient Protection and Affordable Care Act, A-7, A-24
Peer lending, 491
Peer-to-peer sharing, 161
Penetration pricing, 392
Pension funds, 475
Pension Protection Act, A-7

Perferred provider organizations (PPO), A-24–A-25

Performance. *See* Economic performance

Performance appraisals, 224

Performing stage of team development, 255

Perpetual inventory, 287

Person marketing, 309–310

Personal bankruptcies, A-15

Personal financial management
decisions affecting, A-32–A-37
meaning and importance of, A-28–A-29
model of, A-29–A-31
overview of, A-27–A-28
personal goals, A-31–A-32

Personal financial management tools (PFMs), 450

Personal financial planners, 517

Personal income, A-28

Personal Protection and Affordable Care Act, 135

Personal savings, A-27

Personal selling
closing, 387
creative selling, 384
definition, 371–372
follow-up, 387
handling objections, 386–387
missionary selling, 385
order processing, 384
presentation and demonstration, 386
prospecting, qualifying, and approaching, 386
sales process, 385–386
sales promotion, 383–384
telemarketing, 385

Personal space, 263–264

Persuasive advertising, 376

PERT (program evaluation and review technique), 291

Pet food market, 70–71

PFMs (Personal financial management tools), 450

Philippines, 113

Physical distribution, 359–361

Physiological needs, 231

Picketing, 238, 239

Place marketing, 310

Place utility, 307

Planned economies, 72, 73

Planned shopping center, 355–356

Planning, 192
at different organizational levels, 196–197
importance of, 194–197
types of, 194–196

Podcasts, 221

Point-of-purchase (POP) advertising, 383

Poland, 109

Polite listening, 260

Political climate, and international trade, 103

Political differences, and international trade, 102–105

Population, top ten nations based on, 95

Portfolio managers, 517

Positioning, 373

Postconventional stage of individual ethics, 35

Posture, 263

The Practice of Management (Drucker), 234

Preconventional stage of individual ethics, 35

Preferred stock, 467

Preferred stock, 150

Pregnancy Discriminatioin Act, 51, 52

Premiums, 381

Prestige pricing, 389–390

Price, 388

Price-level changes
employment levels, 77–80
measurement of, 77
overview of, 76–77

Price-quality relationships, 394

Pricing objectives, 388–390

Pricing strategies, 314, 369
alternative pricing strategies, 392–394
breakeven analysis, 391–392
competitive pricing, 393–394
overview of, 390–391
price determination, 391
retailing, 355

Primary data, 316

Primary demand, 369

Primary markets, 467

Private brand, 344

Private business ownership, 143–148

Private employment agencies, A-52

Private enterprise system, 7–10, 69–72

Private equity funds, 505–506

Private insurance companies, A-22

Private investment, and small businesses, 139

Private placements (stocks), 505

Private property, 9

Privatization, 73

Problem-solving team, 251

Process control systems, 409

Process departmentalization, 207

Process layout, 283–285

Product, 335

Product advertising, 375

Product departmentalization, 207

Product identification, 343–347

Product layout, 283–285

Product liability, 48, A-14

Product life cycle
advertising, 376
decline stage, 340
growth stage, 339–340
introduction stage, 339
marketing strategy implications, 340–343
maturity stage, 340

Product line, 338

Product manager, 345

Product mix, 338

Product placement, 374

Product strategy, 314
classifying goods and services, 335–337
marketing strategy implications, 338
new-product development, 341–343
product identification, 343–347
product line, 338
product mix, 338
retailing, 355

Product usage rate, 323

Production
customer-driven production, 276
factors of, 6–7, 67, 94
flexible production, 276
location decision, 280–282
managers, 282–288
mass production, 275
overview, 273–274
processes of, 276–277
production control, 289–291
production managers, 282–288
production processes, 276–280
quality, importance of, 292–294
strategic importance of, 275–276
and technology, 277–280
technology and production processes, 277–280
typical production systems, 274

Production and operations management, 275

Production control, 289–291

Production era, in the history of business, 12–13, 307, 308

Production identification brand, 343

brand catagories, 344
brand equity, 344–346
brand loyalty, 344–345
brand name, 343, 344
packages and labels, 346–347
trademark, 343
Production managers, 282
facility layout, 283–285
implementation of production plan, 285–288
planning production process, 283
Production plan
inventory control, 287
just-in-time system, 287–288
make, buy, or lease decision, 285–286
materials requirement planning, 288–289
selection of suppliers, 286–287
Production planning, 289
Production processes, 276–277
Productivity, 75–76
Product-related segmentation, 322–323
Professional rules of conduct, financial systems, 482
Profitability objectives, 388–389
Profitabilty ratios, 448–449
Profit-and-Loss (P&L) statement, 443
Profits, 4
Profits, rights to, 73
Programmed decisions, 201
Promotional mix, 371–372
Promotional planning, 374
Promotional strategy
definition of, 314
differentiating a product, 373
objectives of, 372–373
providing information, 373
retailing, 356
Promotions, 370
Property and liability insurance, A-23
Property law, A-11–A-12
Psychological segmentation, 321–322
PTO (Paid time off), 228
Public accountants, 433–434
Public business ownership, 148–149
Public Health Cigarette Smoking Act, A-6
Public insurance agencies, A-21
Public relations, 387, 402
Public relations crises, 264–265
Public sale of bonds, 504–505
Public-health issues, 43–44
Publicity, 387

Publicly held corporations, 150
Pulling strategy, 387
Pure competition, 69–70
Pushing strategy, 387

Quality, 292–294
Quality control, 293–294
Quality ratings for bonds, 465–466
Quality-of-life issues, 50, 165–166
Quotas, 105

Rack jobber, 351
Radio, 378
Radio-frequency identification (RFID) technology, 346–347, 359–360
Ratio analysis, 446
Raw materials, 337
Real property, A-12
Real-time mobile marketing, 399–400
Rebates, 382
Recession, 74
Recruitment of human resources, 220–223
Recycling, 44–45, 46
Refillable, 46
Reforestation, 104
Regular dividend, 501
Regulated monopolies, 71–72
Regulation FD (Fair Disclosure), 55
Regulation of the financial system, 479–482
Regulatory environment for business, A-4–A-6
Relationship era, 13–14, 307, 308
Relationship management, 14
Relationship marketing, 307
affinity programs, 327–328
benefits of, 326–327
definition of, 325–326
tools for, 327–328
Religious attitudes, and international trade, 101
Reminder-oriented advertising, 376
Rent, A-34
Reshoring, 114
Restricted stock awards, 250
Restrictive monetary policy, 80
Results-oriented résumé, A-56
Résumés, 135, 221, A-44, A-53–A-58,
Retail competition
choosing location, 355–356

creating store atmosphere, 357
customer service strategy, 355
identifying target market, 354–355
pricing strategy, 355
promotional strategy, 356
selecting a product strategy, 355
Retail stores, types of, 353
Retailer
competition, 354–357
distribution channels, 357–361
nonstore retailers, 352–353
store retailers, 353–354
wheel of retailing, 354
Retirement benefits, 227
Revenue bond, 465
Revolving credit, A-33
RFID (Radio-frequency identification) technology, 346–347, 359–360
Rights, in the private enterprise system, 9
Risk, A-18
Risk, assessment of in a business plan, 136
Risk management, A-17, A-19. *See also* **Insurance**
Risk-return trade-off, 493
Robinson-Patman Act, A-5
Robots, 278–279
Routing, 289–290
Rubber band bracelets, 169
Rule 11, A-1
Rule of idemnity, A-20

S corporations, 145–146
Safety, 47–50
Safety needs, 231
Salaries, 225
Sale branches, 351
Sales era, 307, 308
Sales law, A-11
Sales managers, 303
Sales office, 351
Sales process, 385–386
Sales promotion
consumer-oriented promotions, 381–382
personal selling, 383–387
pricing objectives, 388–390
pricing strategy, 390–391
public relations, 387
pushing and pulling strategies, 388
trade-oriented promotions, 383
Sales representative, 402
Sales tasks, 384
Sample, 382
Sandwich generation, 50

Sarbanes-Oxley Act of 2002, 33, 38, 55, 436, 441, A-8
Saudi Arabia, 96, 101
Saving and loan associations, 474
SBICs (Small Business Investment Companies), 137
Scheduling, 290–291
Seasonal unemployment, 78, 79
Secondary data, 316
Secondary market, 468–469
Securities, 463
    bonds, 464–466
    money market instruments, 463–464
    stocks, 466–467
Securities Exchange Act, A-8
Security analysts, 516–517
Seed capital, 176
Segmentation of business markets, 323–324
Segmentation of consumer markets
    demographic segmentation, 319–321, 323
    geographical segmentation, 319, 323
    product-related segmentation, 322–323
    psychological segmentation, 321–322
Selection of human resources, 220–223
Selective demand, 369
Selective distribution, 358–359
Self-actualization needs, 231
Self-assessment for career development, A-49–A-50
Self-confidence, 170–171
Self-insuring, A-19
Self-managed team, 251
Sell off, 508
Seller's market, 308
Sender, 257–258
Serbia, 109
Serial entrepreneurs, 163
Server, 411
Service sector, 97
Sexism, 53–54
Sexual harassment, 53–54
Sharing services, 161
Sherman Act, 71, A-5
Shifts, and international trade, 102
Shopping products, 335, 337
Short-term and long-term funds, mixing, 500–501
Short-term assets, 497–498
Short-term funding options, 503–504
Short-term loans, 503–504

Short-term monopolies, 71
"Shwopping," 45
Silk Road, 96
Simulation games, 249
Singapore, 279
Six Sigma, 294
Skimming pricing, 392
Skunkworks, 179
Small and Disadvantaged Business Utilization, Office of, 137
Small business
    assistance for, 136–140
    best industries for starting a new business, 131
    business plans, 135–136
    contributions to the economy, 130–133
    education level of owners, 10
    and entrepreneurs, 9
    local assistance for, 138–139
    overview of, 127–128, 130–133
    reasons for failure of, 133–135
    sectors dominated by, 129–130
Small Business Investment Companies (SBICs), 137
Small Business Training Network, 137–138
Smart grid technology, 75
Smoking, 43
Social (belongingness) needs, 231
Social audits, 43
Social differences, and international trade, 100–101
Social entrepreneurs, 163
Social era, 11, 14
Social networking
    and demand, 65
    and entrepreneurship, 168
    job candidates, 132
    job searching, A-51
    monitoring employees, 231
    policies for, 40
    tips for, 14
    and Twitter, 20
Social responsibility, 22. See also Business ethics
    corporate philanthropy, 46–47
    to customers, 47–49
    to employees, 49–54
    to the general public, 43–47
    to investors and the financial community, 54–55
    overview of, 41–43
    workforce quality, development of, 46
Social Security, A-22, A-25
Socialism, 72, 73
Soft currencies, 99
Software, 412–413, 439, A-46
Solar power, 175

Sole proprietorships, 144
South Korea, 96
Sovereign wealth funds, 507
Spam, 379
Span of management, 208
Speciality products, 337
Specialty advertising, 382–383
Specialty products, 335
Speculative bonds, 466
Spin off, 508
Sponsorship, 380
Spyware, 416–417
Stable business environment, 74
Stakeholders, 41
Standard of living, A-28
Standardization, 115, 314
State employment agencies, A-53
Statement of cash flows, 444–446
Statement of owners' or shareholders' equity, 444
Statutory law, A-3
Steroids, 44
Stock, 150
Stock exchanges, foreign markets, 470–471
Stock markets
    ECNs and future of stock markets, 471
    foreign stock markets, 470–471
    investor participation, 471
    NASDAQ stock market, 469–470
    New York Stock Exchange, 469
    other U.S. markets, 470
Stock options, 249, 250
Stock ownership, 150, 249
Stockholder rights, 150
Stockholders, 150
Stocks, 466–467
Store atmospherics, 357
Store brands vs. brand names, 398
Store retailers, 353–354
Storming stage of team development, 255
Strategic alliances, 15
Strategic planning, 195, 197–201
Strategic plans, 200–201
Strategies
    distribution, 314
    global business, 115–116
    multidomestic business, 116
    pricing, 314
    product, 314
    promotional, 314
Streaming video, 322
Strengths. See **SWOT analysis**

Strikes, 237, 238–239
Structural unemployment, 79–80
Subcontracting, 113
Subprime mortgages, 465
Substance abuse, 44
Substitute goods, prices of, 66
Succession in fmaily-owned businesses, 147
Super-computers, 410
Supervisory management, 190, 191
Supplier selection, 286–287
Suppliers, number of, 68
Supplies, 337
Supply, 64, 67–69
Supply chain, 359
Supply curve, 67, 68
Sustainability, 45, 439
Sustainability initiatives, 44
Switzerland, 258
SWOT analysis, 198–200
Synthetic production system, 277
Systemic discrimination, 53

Tactical planning, 195–196, 197
Taft-Hartley Act of 1947, 237
Tangible personal property, A-12
Target market, 312, 313, 354–355
Targeted employment area, 178
Tariffs, 105
Tax, 68, 81, 135, 145, A-15
Tax credits, 135
Tax planning, A-34
Team
    characteristics of, 252–255
    cohesiveness and norms, 256
    conflict, 256–257
    overview of, 250–252
    stages of development, 254–255
Team cohesiveness, 256
Team diversity, 254, 255, 256
Team level, 254
Team norm, 256
Team-building retreats, 256
Technical skills for manager, 191
Technologies, costs of, 68
Technology. See also **Information Systems**;
    Social networking
    as capital, 6
    cyberspace and telecommunications protection, A-8–A-9
    and ethical behavior, 34–35
    high-tech jobs, 138
    and home-based businesses, 130

impact on accounting cycle, 438–439
information technology, 168
job searching, 219
mobile apps, 222
online employment searching, A-51–A-52
and outsourcing, 18
and production processes, 277–280
recruiting techniques, 221
and venture capital, 139
Technology in production processes
    computer-aided design (CAD), 279
    computer-integrated manufacturing (CIM), 280
    flexible manufacturing systems, 279
    green manufacturing processes, 277–278
    robots, 278–279
Telecommunications Act, A-6
Telecommunications protection, A-8–A-9
Telecommuting, 18, 228–229, 247
Telemarketing, 384–385
Telemarketing Sales Rule, 385, A-9
Television, advertising media, 377
Temporary workers, 18
Tender offer, 507
Term policies, A-25
Test marketing, 342
Theory X, 236
Theory Y, 236
Theory Z, 236
Threats. See **SWOT analysis**
360-degree performance review, 222
3D printing, 179, 273
Thrift institutions, 474
Time utility, 306–307
Title VII. See Civil Rights Act of 1964
Tobacco products, 43
Tombstone, 468
Tools for customer relationships, 327–328
Top management, 190, 302
Tort, A-13–A-14
Trade credit, 503
Trade deficit, 97
Trade oriented promotions, 383
Trade promotion, 383
Trade restrictions, 105–106
Trade shows, 383
Trade surplus, 97
Trade unions, 107
Trademark, A-12–A-13

Trading partners, 96
Training programs, 223–224, 249
Transaction management, 13
Transaction processing systems, 409
Transportation costs, A-34
Transportation modes, 360
Travel expenses, 450
Treasurer, 492
Treasury bills, 81–82
Treasury bonds, foreign holdings of, 482–483
Treaties, 104
Trial courts, A-3
Triangle Shirtwaist Factory fire, 49–50
Trojan horse, 417
Truth in Lending Act, A-4
Truth vs. loyalty, 37
Turkey, 109
Turnover, 229
Two-factor model of motivation, 233

Unbanked customers, 487–488
Underwriting, 468, 505
Underwriting discount, 505
Unemployment, 78–80
Unemployment insurance, A-21
Unemployment rate, 78
Uniform Commercial Code (UCC), A-10–A-11
Uniformed Services Employment and Reemployment Rights Act, 52, A-7
Union contracts, 237–238
United Kingdom, 96, 103, 104, 114, 142
United States, major exports and imports, 97–98
Universal product code (UPC), 347
Uruguay, 107
U.S. Bankruptcy Code, A-15
U.S. False Claims Act, 441
USA Patriot Act, A-5
Utility, 273, 306–307

Values, and international trade, 101
Vendor-managed inventory, 287, 360
Venezuela, 99
Venture capital, 139
Venture capitalists, 178, 505
Vertical merger, 152
Vice president for financial managment (planning), 492
Vietnam, 113
Vietnam Era Veterans Readjustment Act, 51, 52

Viral advertising, 377–378
Virtual private networks (VPNs), 414–415
Virtual teams, 252, 253
Viruses, 416
Vision, 19–20, 170, 193–194
Vocational Rehabilitation Act, 52
VoIP, 415
Volume objectives, 389
Voluntary turnover, 229
Volunteerism, 47
VPNs (Virtual private networks), 414–415

Wages, 225
Wagner Act, 237
Walkouts, 238
Walnut scandal, 457–458
WANs (Wide area networks), 413
Warehouses, 348
Warehousing, 360–361
Warning labels, 49
Warranties, 361, A-11
Water supply crisis, 83
Weaknesses. *See* **SWOT analysis**
Wealth, top ten nations based on, 95
The Wealth of Nations (Smith), 8
Websites, and recruiting, 221
Wheel of retailing, 354
Wheeler-Lea Act, A-5, 48
Whistle-blowing, 37–38
Wholesaler, 350–352

Wholesaling
  independent intermediaries, 351
  manufacturer-owned intermediaries, 351
  retailer-owned cooperatives and buying offices, 351–352
Wide area networks (WANs), 413
Wi-Fi, 413–414
Wi-Max, 414
Wind energy, 265
Wireless fidelity, 413–414
Wireless local networks, 413–414
Women
  as CEO, 204
  education level of small business owners, 10
  sexual harrassment, 53–54
  small business opportunities for, 139–140
  Tory Burch Foundation and, 79
Women-owned small businesses (WOSBs), 140
Wonderlic Basic Skills Test, 223
Work, changing nature of, 18
Work teams, 251
Work-at-home policies, 247
Worker incentives, 73
Workers' compensation, A-21–A-22
Workforce
  aging population and shrinking labor pool, 16–17

  changes in, 16–19
  demographic trends and, A-49–A-50
  development of, 46
  diversity of, 17–18
  flexibility and mobility, 18
  innovation through collaboration, 18–19
  outsourcing and changing nature of work, 18
Work-life balance, 50
Workplace safety, 49–50
World Factbook (CIA), 110
World markets, competition in
  barriers, reduction of, 106–109
  barriers to international trade, 99–106
  expansion into global trade, 110–115
  factors driving, 94–97
  measurement of trade between nations, 97–99
  overview of, 93–94
  strategy for international business, development of, 115–116
Worm, 416–417
WOSBs (Women-owned small businesses), 140
Written communication, 259, 260–261

YouthRules! initiative, 50

International Index

*Entries in **bold** refer to the "Business Terms You Need to Know," which are listed at the end of each chapter.*

Absolute advantage, 96–97
Accounting, 451–453
Acquisitions, 114
Adaptation, 116
Advertising, 402
Africa, 308–309, 311, 346, 375
Argentina, 107
Association of South East Asian Nations (ASEAN), 107
Australia, 105, 453
Austria, 258
Auto industry, 93, 102
Auto manufacturing, 282

Bahamas, 113
Balance of payments, 97
Balance of trade, 97
Balance sheet hedge, 499
Balance-of-payments deficit, 97
Balance-of-payments surplus, 97
Birthrate, global, 94
Bolivia, 107
Brazil, 96, 107, 114

Canada, 96, 98, 107–108
Central America–Dominican Republic Free Trade Agreement (CAFTA-DR), 109
Chile, 107
China
    absolute advantage, 96
    censorship in, 194
    comparative advantage, 96
    environmental preservation, 17
    flexible manufacturing systems, 279
    GDP, 95
    Hong Kong and the IFRS, 453
    human resources in, 94
    Hunan bond for metal clean-up, 467
    legal environment, 104
    luxury brands, 366
    marketing mix for, 314–315
    multinational corporations, 114
    multivitamins made in, 293
    offshoring, 113
    potential market in, 95
    reshoring, 114
    supercomputer Tianhe-2, 410
    trade deficit with, 98
    as a trading partner, 96
    and U.S. Treasury Bonds, 482
Common markets, 105–109
Communication, 100–101, 258
Communism, 72, 73

Comparative advantage, 96–97
Competition in world markets
    barriers, 99–106
    barriers, reduction of, 106–109
    expansion into global trade, 110–115
    factors driving, 94–97
    measurement of trade between nations, 97–99
    overview of, 93–94
    strategy for international business, development of, 115–116
Context, and communication, 258
Contractual agreements, 112
Corruption, 103–104, 116
Corruption Perceptions Index, 104
Costa Rica, 109
Countertrade, 112
Covalence Ethical Rankings, 116
Cruise industry, 264–265
Cuba, 105–106
Cultural differences, 100–101
Currency conversion, 102
Customs unions, 107
Czech Republic, 109

Demand, 115
Devaluation, 99, 102
Developing nations, 94–95
Direct exporting, 111–112
Distribution channels, 357–358
Doha Round, 107
Dominican Republic, 109
Dumping, 105–106

E-commerce sites, 104
Economic challenges, 82–84
Economic differences, 101–102
Economic performance, 75–76
Economic unions, 107
El Salvador, 109
Embargo, 105–106
Emerging market economies (EMEs), 107
Emirates, 494
England, 11–12, 483. *See also* United Kingdom
Entrepreneurship, 166–167
Ethiopia, 102
Euro, 505
Europages, 110
European Alliance, 357
European Commission, 357
European Union (EU), 98, 101, 109

Exchange control, 106
Exchange rates, 98–99, 102, 452, 499
Export management company, 112
Exporters, 111–112
Exports, 93, 94, 97–98, 111–112

Factors of production, 94
Financial system, 482–483
Fiscal imbalances, 83
Flexible manufacturing systems (FMS), 279
Foreign Corrupt Practices Act, 103
Foreign currency, 112. *See also* **Exchange rates**
Foreign licensing agreement, 113
Foreign stock markets, 470–471
France, 96, 103, 104, 470
Franchise/franchising, 112–113
Free-trade areas, 107
Friendship, commerce, and navigation (FCN) treaties, 104

General Agreement on Tariffs and Trade (GATT), 106
Geographical segmentation, 319, 323
Germany, 96, 103, 104, 258, 286–287, 360
Global (Norway), 506
Global business strategies, 115–116
Greece, 505
Greenhouse gas emissions, 83
Gross domestic product (GDP)
    in developing nations, 95
    and the European Union, 109
    imports and exports, 93
    and NAFTA, 108
    nations with highest, 76
    and productivity, 75–76
Guatemala, 109
Guerrilla marketing, 374

Hard currencies, 99
Helsinkski, stock market, 470
High-context cultures, 258
Honduras, 109
Hong Kong, 374, 453, 470
Hungary, 109

Iceland, 109
IFRS (International Financial Reporting Standards), 452–453
Importers, 111–112
Imports, 93, 94, 97–98, 111–112
India, 94, 95, 113, 258, 279, 319, 453
Indirect exporting, 111
Infrastructure, 102
Institutional advertising, 375
International accounting, 451, 452–453
International Accounting Standards Board (IASB), 452–453
International Accounting Standards Committee (IASC), 452–453
International assets, management of, 499
International banks, 482–483
International Consumer Electronics Show, 383
International direct investment, 113–114
International economic communities, 107
International Financial Reporting Standards (IFRS), 452–453
International fiscal policy, 81
International law, A-3–A-4
International marketplace, size of, 94–96
International Organization for Standardization (ISO), 294
International regulations, and trade, 104–105
International trade
barriers to, 99–106
economic differences, 101–102
expansion into, 110–115
international economic communities, 107
involvement, levels of, 111–114
multidomestic corporations, 114–115
overview of, 99–100
political and legal differences, 102–105
promotion organizations, 106–107
reduction of barriers, 106–109
research resources, 110

social and cultural differences, 100–101
trade restrictions, types of, 105–106
International unions, 236
Intranet, 414
ISO (International Organization for Standardization), 294
Italy, 104–105

Japan, 96, 98, 105, 113, 258, 482, 483
Joint venture, 114

Language, and international trade, 100–101
Latin America, 258, 264, 279
Leading companies, 115
Legal differences, and international trade, 102–105
Legal environment, and international trade, 103–104
Location decision, 280–282, 355–356
Low-context cultures, 258

Macedonia, 109
Macroeconomics, 72–73
Malaysia, 104
Mandarin Chinese language, 100
Marketing mix, 314–315
Mass production, 275
MERCOSUR customs union, 107
Mexico
auto manufacturing, 280–282
Domino's Pizza, 112–113
Ford Motor Company, 102
investment in, 201
NAFTA, 107–108
offshoring, 113
stock exchange, 470
as a trading partner, 96
Mixed market economies, 72–73
Montenegro, 109
Multidomestic business strategies, 116
Multinational corporations (MNC), 114–115
Mumbai, stock market, 470
Myanmar, 36

NAFTA (North American Free Trade Agreement), 107–108, 323–324, 452
Netherlands, 114
New Zealand, 105
Nicaragua, 109
Non-tariff barriers, 105–106

Nonverbal communication, 259, 263–264
North American Free Trade Agreement (NAFTA), 107–108, 323–324, 452
Norway, 506

Offset agreement, 112
Offshoring, 18, 113
Organization for Economic Cooperation and Development Anti-Bribery Convention, 103
Organizations, promotion of international trade, 106–107

Packages and labels (brand identification), 346–347
Paraguay, 107
Philippines, 113
Planned economies, 72, 73
Poland, 109
Political climate, and international trade, 103
Political differences, and international trade, 102–105
Population, top ten nations based on, 95
Private equity funds, 505–506
Productivity, 75–76
Promotional planning, 374
Public relations, 402
Public sale of bonds, 504–505

Quality control, 293–294
Quotas, 105

Reforestation, 104
Regulated monopolies, 71–72
Religious attitudes, and international trade, 101
Reshoring, 114

Saudi Arabia, 96, 101
Segmentation of business markets, 323–324
Serbia, 109
Shifts, and international trade, 102
Silk Road, 96
Singapore, 279
Social differences, and international trade, 100–101
Socialism, 72, 73
Soft currencies, 99
South Korea, 96
Standardization, 115
Stock exchanges, foreign markets, 470–471
Strategies, 115–116
Subcontracting, 113
Super-computers, 410

Tariffs, 105
Trade deficit, 97
**Trade oriented
    promotions**, 383
Trade restrictions, 105–106
Trade surplus, 97
Trade unions, 107
Trading partners, 96
Treasury bonds, foreign holdings
    of, 482–483
Treaties, 104
Turkey, 109

United Kingdom, 96, 103, 104,
    114, 142. *See also* England

United States, major exports and
    imports, 97–98
Uruguay, 107

Values, and international
    trade, 101
Venezuela, 99
Vietnam, 113
VoIP, 415

Water supply crisis, 83
Wealth, top ten nations based
    on, 95
**Wide area networks
    (WANs)**, 413

World Factbook (CIA), 110
World markets, competition in
    barriers, reduction of,
        106–109
    barriers to international trade,
        99–106
    expansion into global trade,
        110–115
    factors driving, 94–97
    measurement of trade between
        nations, 97–99
    overview of, 93–94
    strategy for international
        business, development of,
        115–116